SIXTH EDITION 6

# BANK MANAGEMENT

**TIMOTHY W. KOCH**
*UNIVERSITY OF SOUTH CAROLINA*

**S. SCOTT MACDONALD**
*Southern Methodist University*

**THOMSON**

**SOUTH-WESTERN**

**Bank Management, Sixth Edition**
Timothy W. Koch and S. Scott MacDonald

**VP/Editorial Director:**
Jack W. Calhoun

**VP/Editor-in-Chief:**
Alex von Rosenberg

**Executive Editor:**
Mike Reynolds

**Sr. Developmental Editor:**
Elizabeth R. Thomson

**Marketing Manager:**
Heather MacMaster

**Sr. Production Editor:**
Cliff Kallemeyn

**Technology Project Editor:**
John Barans

**Media Editor:**
Karen Schaffer

**Manufacturing Coordinator:**
Sandee Milewski

**Production House:**
Pre-Press Company, Inc.

**Printer:**
Courier Westford
Westford, MA

**Art Director:**
Bethany Casey

**Internal Designer:**
Anne Marie Rekow

Library of Congress Control Number:
2004115554

For more information about our
products, contact us at:

Thomson Learning Academic Resource
Center

1-800-423-0563

**Thomson Higher Education**
5191 Natorp Boulevard
Mason, OH 45040
USA

**Asia (including India)**
Thomson Learning
5 Shenton Way
#01-01 UIC Building
Singapore 068808

**Australia/New Zealand**
Thomson Learning Australia
102 Dodds Street
Southbank, Victoria 3006
Australia

**Canada**
Thomson Nelson
1120 Birchmount Road
Toronto, Ontario
M1K 5G4
Canada

**Latin America**
Thomson Learning
Seneca, 53
Colonia Polanco
11560 Mexico
D.F.Mexico

**UK/Europe/Middle East/Africa**
Thomson Learning
High Holborn House
50/51 Bedford Row
London WC1R 4LR
United Kingdom

**Spain (including Portugal)**
Thomson Paraninfo
Calle Magallanes, 25
28015 Madrid, Spain

# PREFACE

While competition has increased the number of firms offering financial products and services, the removal of interstate branching restrictions in the U.S. has dramatically reduced the number of independently operated banks but increased the number of banking offices, primarily branches. Consolidation, in turn, has significantly increased the proportion of banking assets controlled by the largest banks. Not surprisingly, the same trends appear globally. The United States currently has several banks that operate in all 50 states and many locales outside the U.S. The largest foreign banks have significant operations in the U.S. and throughout the world. In fact, you might not know if your bank is headquartered outside the U.S.! Different financial institutions seem to announce acquisitions of other financial companies (not always banks) on a regular basis, and frequently these institutions are headquartered in different countries. These factors as well as many others demonstrate that the banking environment is continually changing.

Increased competition also means that geography no longer limits a financial institution's trade area or the markets in which it competes. Individuals can open a checking account at a traditional depository institution, such as a commercial bank, savings bank, or credit union, a brokerage firm, such as Charles Schwab or Merrill Lynch, a nonbank firm, such as GE Capital and State Farm Insurance, or a non-traditional Internet bank such as NetBank. At all of these firms, you don't even have to leave your home as you can open an account via the Internet. You can deposit money electronically, transfer funds from one account to another, purchase stocks, bonds and mutual funds, or even request and receive a loan from any of these firms. Most of them will allow you to conduct this business over the phone, by mail or over the Internet. All firms compete for business with each other, pay and charge market interest rates determined by competitive conditions, and are generally not limited in the scope of products and services they offer or the geographic regions where they offer these products.

This book explains the impacts of such competitive forces on banks and banking services. The reader will better understand the ever changing banking environment.

## AUDIENCE

*Bank Management* is designed for use in upper division undergraduate or master's level banking and financial institutions courses at universities as well as professional banking programs. As prerequisites, students should be familiar with elementary accounting, basic interest rate and bond pricing concepts, and basic macroeconomics. The book is also well suited for broad based instructional purposes in bank training programs. For someone new to banking, the book describes the range of banking activities and demonstrates how bank managers make financial decisions. For practitioners, it explains how decisions in one area affect performance and opportunities in other areas. As such, it provides a comprehensive view of balance sheet management with an emphasis on the trade-offs between profitability and risk.

## ABOUT *BANK MANAGEMENT*

The book focuses on decision making and offers a unique approach to understanding bank management. Key chapters address the specific aspects of an issue or problem, explain how a financial model or decision framework applies, and then demonstrate the application of the model or framework using sample data. The reader not only observes how certain factors influence credit, investment, funding, and pricing decisions, but also develops an appreciation of the trade-offs between return and risk. Several Microsoft Excel templates, which include various models and applications using sample data, are available to users. A wide range of cases related to bank performance evaluation, making new loans, managing the investment portfolio, asset and liability management, and liquidity management are available via the Internet. These cases, end-of-chapter questions, and problems provide an opportunity to test the reader's understanding of important issues and data analysis.

After reading *Bank Management*, the reader should have a solid foundation in the key issues confronting managers today, a familiarization with the basic financial models that are used to formulate decisions, and an understanding of the strengths and weaknesses of data analysis. The text and numerous applications help the reader to recognize the trade-offs involved in making financial decisions and to develop the logical thought processes needed to reach reasonable conclusions.

## NEW FEATURES OF THIS EDITION

The sixth edition of the book builds on the topics and features of earlier editions, with several important changes:
- A complete regulatory update has been applied throughout the book. In particular, the impacts of financial modernization (Gramm-Leach-Bliley), repeal of Glass-Steagall, and the Bank Secrecy Act have reshaped the regulatory and competitive environment coverage.
- A complete discussion of the changing landscape of the financial services industry—including the impact of Sarbanes Oxley and increased competition on the industry.
- An updated and comprehensive evaluation of bank performance—traditional banking, investment banking, and off-balance sheet financing—and the impact this has on the analyst's job in evaluating performance. A direct comparison of PNC Bank's financial performance from 2003–2004 versus peer institutions as well as important contrasts with the performance of community banks.
- An analysis of the most current data from the Uniform Bank Performance Report, the FDIC, and the Federal Reserve Bank, including discussion of key performance ratios, an explanation of alternative performance measures and strengths and weaknesses of the traditional analysis.
- Comprehensive discussion of Federal Home Loan Bank advances as funding instruments and their use in liquidity management; as well as a discussion of Basel II Capital Standards.
- A discussion of the current developments in credit scoring, credit reports, bankruptcy reform, check truncation and Check 21, and applications to consumer lending.
- Extensive use of new tools and examples such as total return analysis and option-adjusted spread analysis are introduced to assist in the evaluation of alternative investment instruments.
- New cases in Bank Performance Analysis, Commercial Lending, Funding, and Managing a Bank's Investment Portfolio incorporate current data and issues; available on our web site http://koch.swcollege.com.
- New data and analysis on international banking and the role and size of U.S. banking abroad as well as the ownership and composition of foreign banking in the U.S. Discussion of foreign exchange risk associated with a bank having assets and liabilities denominated in different currencies.
- The book remains the only text that focuses on cash flow analysis as part of the lending decision. It introduces a comprehensive procedure to generate cash-based income statements, explains how to interpret the results, and provides an approach to forecast a potential borrower's future performance. An Excel template is provided to conduct the comprehensive analysis.

## ORGANIZATION OF THE BOOK

While the unifying theme of the book is risk management, the material is divided into six parts, each consisting of chapters that cover related issues. As a lead-in to each chapter, the text will describe a current issue or provide an example of a key topic discussed in the chapter. This introduction reinforces the risk focus by emphasizing that managers make both good and bad decisions, but consistent application of finance theory and models should lead to a better understanding of the trade-off between risk and return.

*Part I, Overview of the Banking Industry and Regulation,* provides background information related to bank management and current banking trends. It describes the role of competition in forcing change in banking, the move to expanded products, services, and geographic markets served, and the impact on banking industry consolidation. It also examines the organizational structure of small banks and large bank holding companies, describes the regulatory environment, and explains the impact of key banking legislation.

*Part II, Evaluating Bank Performance,* examines the basic risk and return features of commercial banks and how analysts evaluate performance. Chapter 2 introduces bank financial statements and presents the traditional DuPont model for evaluating bank performance using financial ratios from the Uniform Bank Performance Report (UBPR) to analyze the strengths and weaknesses of bank performance over time and versus peer institutions. It provides the foundation and building blocks for understanding how banks make a profit and the trade-offs involved in balancing credit risk, liquidity risk, market risk, operational risk, reputational risk, legal risk, and solvency risk. Chapter 3 documents recent strategies and trends in controlling noninterest expense relative to noninterest income to help meet efficiency objectives.

*Part III, Managing Interest Rate Risk,* demonstrates how banks measure and manage interest rate risk. Chapter 4 provides background information on the pricing of securities, total return analysis to investors, and the determinants of interest rates. Chapter 5 introduces GAP analysis and the use of earnings sensitivity analysis to assess the potential impact of interest rate and balance sheet changes on net interest income. Chapter 6 describes duration gap analysis and the use of sensitivity analysis to assess the potential impact of interest rate and balance sheet changes on the economic value of stockholders' equity. The discussion emphasizes the impact of embedded options and the necessity behind incorporating sensitivity analysis to assess the impact of such options on profits and risk. Chapter 7 describes the basic features of financial futures, forward contracts, interest rate swaps, and interest rate caps and floors and explains how banks use them to both hedge and speculate. Emphasis is directed toward understanding the models, data output, and strategies to improve performance.

*Part IV, Managing the Cost of Funds, Bank Capital, and Liquidity,* describes the features of bank liabilities, regulatory capital requirements and overall liquidity analysis. It presents a procedure for estimating the marginal cost of funds that is used in making investment decisions and pricing assets. It also explains how banks meet legal reserve requirements and manage cash assets, and it develops a model to estimate liquidity needs and plan for temporary cash deficiencies and longer-term liquidity needs. Special attention is focused on the nature of Federal Home Loan Bank advances and their use in liquidity management and the new Basel II Capital requirements.

*Part V, Extending Credit to Businesses and Individuals,* addresses how banks manage credit risk. It initially describes basic credit analysis principles and the characteristics of different types of loans. Subsequent chapters present a procedure for estimating a business borrower's cash flow from operations and the basic credit scoring models applied to individual borrowers.

Considerable emphasis is placed on interpreting financial statements and generating cash flow estimates to determine repayment prospects. A section on profitability analysis describes the basic framework used to assess whether a bank is profiting from a customer's total relationship.

*Part VI, Managing the Investment Portfolio and Special Topics,* describes the role of fixed income securities in helping a bank meet profit and risk objectives. It identifies the basic objectives of a bank's investment portfolio and the nature of investment policy guidelines, and explains the basic features of taxable and tax-exempt securities that banks buy. It then introduces various strategies related to choosing security maturities, the composition between taxable and tax-exempt securities, and purchases or sales timed to take advantage of the business cycle. It explains the impact of embedded options on security pricing and the risk-return trade-off to investors of callable bonds and mortgage-backed securities with significant prepayment risk. The final chapter describes recent trends in global banking activities and the management of foreign exchange risk.

Each chapter of *Bank Management* concludes with a series of discussion questions and problems that require the student to apply the decision models introduced in the chapter. The Excel template can be used to generate and address additional problems as well as provide a useful tool for future analysis.

The sixth edition contains 14 chapters, rather than the 22 in the fifth edition. While some of the material from the omitted chapters is included in the sixth edition, selected parts of the remaining material are available via the Internet. The primary purpose behind omitting some material from the hardbound text is to emphasize the key information that can be reasonably covered during a semester course.

## ANCILLARY PACKAGE

### INSTRUCTOR'S MANUAL AND TEST BANK

A comprehensive Instructor's Manual and Test Bank accompanies *Bank Management.* It provides teaching objectives and outlines for each chapter. It further offers detailed answers to end-of-chapter questions and problems. Finally, multiple choice questions are provided with answers on disk.

### LECTURE PRESENTATION SOFTWARE

Microsoft PowerPoint™ presentations are available to those professors who wish to incorporate multimedia in the classroom. This multimedia presentation allows the student to explore the almost unlimited number of different financial situations that banks face on a daily basis. Furthermore, it provides the instructor a method by which he or she can integrate a financial analysis spreadsheet template directly into the class presentation. Many tables and diagrams are featured in the lecture software package.

### PREFACE SPREADSHEET TEMPLATE

Microsoft Excel templates are available for those who wish to use microcomputers to perform and extend the data analysis presented in the book. The templates provide a generic decision model for applications related to analyzing bank performance and key financial ratios, and cash flow from operations for nonfinancial firms. Each model can be used to conduct "what if" *pro forma* sensitivity analysis beyond the period for which historical data are available. The templates also provide a full range of decision models with data for key problems and cases in the text. Students can use the templates to analyze historical balance sheet and income statement data and conduct the same "what if" analysis. This allows the user to quickly examine a range of outcomes rather than just simple, static solutions. The templates cover topics including bank performance analysis, duration analysis, risk-based capital requirements and planning, credit analysis, and customer profitability analysis.

## CASES

New Cases in Bank Performance Analysis, Commercial Lending, Funding, and Managing a Bank's Investment Portfolio are available on our Web site http://koch.swcollege.com.

## WEB SITE

The product support Web site, located at http://koch.swcollege.com, contains the PowerPoint slide presentation, Instructor's Manual, Spreadsheet Templates, and new Cases for instructors; and the PowerPoint slide presentation and Spreadsheet Templates for students.

## ACKNOWLEDGMENTS

Throughout the writing of the sixth edition, we have relied on the assistance and expertise of many friends in the banking industry and academic community. This revision has benefited from ongoing discussions with the following individuals and former students. We especially thank Linda Allen, John Barrickman, William Chittenden Steve Christensen, Ken Cyree, David Davis, Charles Funk, Scott Hein, Charley Hoffman, Jeff Judy, Ira Kawaller, Randy King, Ed Krei, Charles Moyer, Don Mullineaux, Don Musso, James Pappas, Ramesh Rao, Joshua Robinson, Ron Rogers, J. T. Rose, Robert Schweitzer, Lynda Swenson, Ernie Swift, Randy Woodward, and Buddy Wood.

We would also like to thank the reviewers who contributed invaluable comments and suggestions. These individuals are:

Yea-Mow Chen, San Francisco State University
Steven J. Cross, Troy State University
William F. Ford, Middle Tennessee State University
F. Phillip Ghazanfari, California State Polytechnic University
William F. Kennedy, University of North Carolina – Charlotte
Matthew A. Walker, North Dakota State University

Also, we appreciate the guidance and assistance of the staff at South-Western/Thomson Learning, especially Mike Reynolds, Elizabeth Thomson, and Cliff Kallemeyn. It was a pleasure working with them.

Finally, we want to thank our families—Susan, Michala, and Andy; and Becky, Cassy, and Erin—for their encouragement, support, and insights in seeing this project through to completion.

Timothy W. Koch, Ph.D.
Moore School of Business
University of South Carolina
Columbia, SC 29208

S. Scott MacDonald, Ph.D.
Southwestern Graduate School of Banking
Southern Methodist University
Dallas, TX 75275

# ABOUT THE AUTHORS

## TIMOTHY W. KOCH

Timothy W. Koch is Professor of Finance and holds the South Carolina Bankers Association Chair of Banking at the University of South Carolina. He received a B.A. degree in mathematics from Wartburg College and a Ph.D. in economics from Purdue University. He taught previously at Baylor University and Texas Tech University. In addition to college teaching, Dr. Koch currently serves as President of the Graduate School of Banking at Colorado and teaches at several graduate schools for professional bankers throughout the United States. He also serves as faculty advisor to the Graduate School of Bank Investments and Financial Management offered at the University of South Carolina. He has taught seminars on risk management to bankers in Poland, Hungary, Slovakia, and the Ukraine as part of a U.S. Treasury program to assist private banking in Eastern Europe.

Dr. Koch's research and writing focuses on bank risk management, performance analysis and improvement, the pricing of financial futures and fixed-income securities, and public finance. He has published in a wide range of academic journals, including the *Journal of Finance, Journal of Financial & Quantitative Analysis, Journal of Futures Markets, National Tax Journal, Journal of Banking and Finance, Journal of Fixed Income, Journal of Financial Research, Journal of Macroeconomics, Journal of Portfolio Management, Municipal Finance Journal,* and the *Journal of Money, Credit and Banking.* He has served as Treasurer of the Financial Management Association and President of the Eastern Finance Association and Southern Finance Association. He also authors the *General Banking* curriculum materials used at many state-sponsored banking schools and is a frequent seminar leader for the banking industry.

## S. SCOTT MACDONALD

S. Scott MacDonald is President and CEO, SW Graduate School of Banking (SWGSB) Foundation, Director of the Assemblies for Bank Directors, and Adjunct Professor of Finance, Edwin L. Cox School of Business, Southern Methodist University. He received his B.A. degree in economics from the University of Alabama and his Ph.D. from Texas A&M University. Dr. MacDonald joined the Southern Methodist University faculty as a visiting professor of Finance in 1997. He took over as director of the SWGSB Foundation in 1998. Prior to joining SMU, he was an associate professor of Finance and director of the School of Applied Banking at Texas Tech University. He also served as assistant director of Business and Financial Analysis at RRC Inc., a research consulting firm, before joining the Texas Tech faculty. He is a frequent speaker and seminar leader for the banking industry, professional programs and banking schools. Dr. MacDonald has also served as an expert resource witness before the Texas state Senate.

Dr. MacDonald is the author of articles in academic journals such as the *Journal of Financial Economics, The Journal of Business, The Journal of Futures Markets, The Review of Futures Markets, Quarterly Journal of Business and Economics,* and the *Journal of Money, Credit and Banking.* He is also the author of professional curriculum materials for the Independent Bankers Association, The Assemblies for Bank Directors, and other professional banking programs throughout the nation. Dr. MacDonald, the recipient of numerous teaching and research awards, is past chairman of the board of directors, Texas Tech Federal Credit Union, an advisory board member of the Independent Bankers Association Education Council, and board member of the North Texas Chapter of the Risk Management Association.

# DEDICATION

*To my parents, Lowell and Marilyn Koch, who always encouraged and supported me.*
*Timothy W. Koch*

*To my family, Becky, Cassy and Erin for their never ending support and encouragement.*
*S. Scott MacDonald*

# BRIEF CONTENTS

# CONTENTS

# OVERVIEW OF THE BANKING INDUSTRY AND REGULATION

# The Changing Banking Environment

*In 1999, the U.S. Congress enacted the Financial Services Modernization Act (Gramm-Leach-Bliley Act of 1999), which dramatically altered the competitive environment for financial services firms operating in the United States. The act generally expanded the range of services that banks could offer and lines of business that banks could enter as long as they operated with sufficient capital. Previously, domestic banks were restricted in the types of activities they could engage in within the borders of the United States. For example, banks could underwrite corporate securities outside the United States, but were not allowed to do the same domestically. Banks in other developed countries have generally been allowed to engage in these activities in their home countries as well as in the U.S. The Financial Services Modernization Act of 1999 largely eliminated this differential treatment, allowed U.S. banks to enter new lines of business, and permitted other types of financial services companies to more aggressively engage in traditional banking activities. Consumers who want to open a checking account can go to a local commercial bank, savings and loan, mutual savings bank, credit union, full-service brokerage house or deal with a discount broker like Charles Schwab. Until May 2004, even the U.S. Postal Service offered bill payment services.*

*Consumers simply have more choices now than ever before when purchasing financial services. Not surprisingly, firms compete aggressively for consumers' business. Competition, in turn, puts a premium on innovation and precision in delivering service and personalizing it for individuals. In some cases, however, the opportunities are not the same for all service providers. Even though commercial banks have gained greater flexibility in diversifying their asset base across geographic boundaries and into new product lines in recent years, federal and state regulations often still put them at a competitive disadvantage. Why were such restrictions ever imposed? More importantly, will the new regulatory environment enhance competition and benefit consumers?*

*This chapter describes the recent operational and regulatory environment as well as five fundamental forces of change—market-driven competitive factors, product innovation and deregulation, securitization, globalization, and technological advances—that have changed the banking landscape. It demonstrates the interaction between how regulation affects the competitive environment of the banking industry and how competition affects the regulatory environment. As an example, consider the sharp increase in stock prices during the 1990s which increased the public's awareness of alternative investment vehicles. As insurance companies, investment banks, real estate firms, and other institutions offered traditional bank services, commercial banks found that they were competing directly for funds and investments with all financial services firms, yet were at a competitive disadvantage due to regulatory restrictions. Passage of the Financial Services Modernization Act was a direct result of these and related global competitive pressures on the U.S. financial system.*

In order to understand banks, one must understand bank regulation. Barriers that once separated banking from other activities have rapidly disappeared. This creates opportunities for well-managed banks and related firms, but also puts pressure on management to perform. As regulatory differences among commercial banks, savings and loans, credit unions, investment banks, and insurance companies rapidly disappear, the concepts and decision models presented in this book generally apply to any firms that make loans or accept deposits. Thus, while the term *bank* serves as an abbreviation for commercial bank, the material presented encompasses the behavior of other financial institutions.

## HISTORICAL BANK REGULATION

What makes a bank special? Why do we call Bank of America a bank, J.P. Morgan an investment bank, Merrill Lynch a securities brokerage company, and State Farm an insurance company? The answer lies in our history of regulation. Historically, a commercial bank was defined as a firm that both accepted demand deposits (non-interest bearing checking accounts) and made business loans. More than 70 years ago, the Glass-Steagall Act created three separate industries: commercial banking, investment banking, and insurance in order to separate commerce from banking. Commercial banks made business loans and accepted demand deposits. The Bank Holding Act specifically limited the scope of activities a company could engage in if it owned a bank. The McFadden Act limited the geographic market of banking by allowing individual states to determine the extent to which a bank could branch within or outside its home state. Under these acts, the United States developed a banking system with a large number of small banks, a relatively short list of products and services that banks could offer and narrow geographic areas where individual banks could compete. Each of these limitations was intended to reduce competition and speculation in the banking industry and thereby promote a safe, sound, and stable banking system.

**GEOGRAPHIC SCOPE.** Historical restrictions on branching, both interstate and intrastate, were significant contributors to the structure of the banking system during the twentieth century. Some states prohibited bank branches such that every institution could have only one office (unit bank). In some cases, this meant that automatic teller machines (ATMs) were not allowed because they were viewed as branches. These same branching restrictions did not apply to investment companies like Merrill Lynch or insurance companies like State Farm that could operate branches or offices in communities across the nation. Not surprisingly, historical branching restrictions created a system of independent banks that were significantly greater in number and smaller in size compared with banks in other countries. They further prevented banks from geographically diversifying their credit risk. Thus, a unit banking state like Texas experienced numerous bank failures during the late 1980s as oil prices plunged and local economies crumbled.

Branching restrictions were gradually removed to where the Riegle-Neal Interstate Banking and Branching Efficiency Act of 1994 effectively allowed banks to locate offices and compete anywhere in the country. The result was the creation of the first *nationwide* bank (with branches coast to coast) in the late 1990s by Bank of America. Today, numerous banking firms offer coast-to-coast financial services. In addition to the easing of geographic restrictions, advances in technology have allowed banks to open electronic branches, first by using the ATM network and later by using the Internet. By the end of 2004, the number of independent banks was reduced by almost half, the number of branches increased by almost 50 percent, and the size of the largest U.S. banks increased almost five times. By size rankings, U.S. banks did not reach the largest ten banks in the world until the late 1990s. Today, some of the largest banks in the world are U.S. banks.

**PRODUCTS AND SERVICES.** Legal restrictions on branching and the range of permissible activities and products were designed to promote a safe and sound banking system. Until the late 1970s, banks were the only firms allowed to offer demand deposits (checking accounts). While thrifts and credit unions offered savings accounts along with banks, all were limited to specific maximum interest rates they could pay deposit holders. On the asset side, banks focused on commercial lending, thrifts (savings and loans) focused on mortgage lending, credit unions made consumer loans, investment banks underwrote stocks and bonds and provided brokerage services, and insurance companies underwrote insurance products. Regulations similarly limited the rates that banks, thrifts and credit unions could charge on their primary loans.

New product innovations and technological advances eventually allowed investment banks to circumvent regulations restricting their banking activities. Consider the following:

- In the late 1970s, Merrill Lynch effectively created money market mutual funds as an alternative to demand deposits. Customers had to maintain large balances (typically over $2,000) but customers could write checks against their balances and the accounts paid interest. Money market mutual funds soon grew at a rapid rate—effectively drawing funds from traditional banks.
- Various lending institutions opened loan production offices across state boundaries. They avoided regulation as a bank because they would not accept demand deposits.
- High-quality corporations found that they could issue securities, such as commercial paper and corporate bonds, directly to investors and thereby circumvent bank loans.
- Junk bonds became an alternative financing source for small business and other companies began to encroach upon the banks' primary commercial lending market.
- New technologies and products, including credit cards, debit cards, and Internet bill pay, created new forms of competition for bank payment services, that is, checking accounts.

While these products were direct substitutes for a bank's traditional product line, the bank was generally prohibited from offering them. Exceptional returns from stock market investments during the 1990s increased the average person's awareness of higher promised returns from equity mutual funds and stock transactions. The greater acceptance of non-FDIC insured deposit products (mutual funds and stocks), while banks were generally restricted to offering CDs and savings accounts, further eroded banks' share of the consumer's investment wallet. Investment companies like Merrill Lynch operated with few if any product restrictions and were regulated only by the Securities and Exchange Commission (SEC). This allowed investment companies to avoid the restrictions imposed on banks, while offering bank-like products stemming from the product innovations. Banks, however, were restricted from competing with these new products given Glass-Steagall and the Bank Holding Company Act. So the 1980s and 1990s saw a mass movement of banking customers to competitors like investment companies.

## GOALS AND FUNCTIONS OF BANK REGULATION

Commercial banks are the most heavily regulated financial institutions in the United States. This largely reflects the critically important role banks play in the payments system and in providing credit to individuals and businesses, as well as the fact that banks carry FDIC insurance on their deposits. Prior to the establishment of the Federal Reserve System in 1913, private banks operated free of close government scrutiny. The frequency of abuses and large number of failed banks during the Depression forced the federal government to redesign its regulatory framework encompassing supervision and deposit insurance. Fundamentally, there are five reasons for bank regulation:

- To ensure the safety and soundness of banks and financial instruments
- To provide an efficient and competitive financial system
- To provide monetary stability
- To maintain the integrity of the nation's payments system
- To protect consumers from abuses by credit-granting institutions

These five goals are obviously not independent. The primary purpose behind **safety and soundness** is to maintain domestic and international confidence, protect depositors and, ultimately, taxpayers, and maintain financial stability. With safety and soundness, a financial system provides for the efficient allocation of the nation's scarce resources because the payments system is reliable and institutions willingly extend credit that stimulates economic growth. This goal has traditionally been accomplished by limiting risk taking at individual institutions, by limiting entry and exit, and by the federal government's willingness to act as a lender of last resort.

 Providing an **efficient and competitive financial system** is related to safety and soundness. Regulation is designed to prevent undue concentration of banking resources that would be anticompetitive, yet allow firms to alter their product mix and delivery systems to meet economic and market needs. This goal has generally been accomplished by restricting mergers and acquisitions that reduce the number and market power of competing institutions. There are also limitations on the fraction of deposits that any one institution can control in a single state.

The third objective of bank regulation is that the Federal Reserve System provides **monetary stability**. In particular, the Fed attempts to control the growth in the banking system's liquidity and hence the nation's money supply and influence the general level of interest rates by buying and selling government securities and targeting the federal funds rate. The fourth objective is to **maintain the integrity of the nation's payments system**. Thomas Hoenig, president of the Federal Reserve Bank of Kansas City, argues that the payments system revolves around banks. As long as regulators ensure that banks clear checks and settle noncash payments in a fair and predictable way, participants will have confidence that the payments media can be used to effect transactions. This is especially important given the trend toward electronic commerce and e-cash.

The final objective is to **protect consumers from abuses by credit-granting institutions**. Historically, some individuals have found it difficult to obtain loans for reasons not related to their financial condition. Thus, regulations now stipulate that borrowers should have equal credit opportunities such that banks cannot discriminate on the basis of race, gender, age, geographic location, and so on. Lenders must also report key borrowing and savings rates in a manner that allows meaningful comparisons and disclose why a borrower is denied a loan. The Community Reinvestment Act (CRA), passed in 1977, prevents a bank from acquiring another institution if the parent receives a poor CRA evaluation; that is, the bank is not doing enough to insure that its credit and services are available to all members of the defined community.

Three separate federal agencies, along with each state's banking department, issue and enforce regulations related to a wide variety of commercial bank activities. The federal agencies are the Federal Reserve System (Fed), the Federal Deposit Insurance Corporation (FDIC), and the Office of the Comptroller of the Currency (OCC). The different regulatory groups' responsibilities overlap, but the agencies generally coordinate policies and decisions. The Office of Thrift Supervision (OTS) has similar responsibilities for savings and loan associations while the National Credit Union Administration (NCUA) is the federal agency enforcing regulations for the credit union industry.

# ENSURE SAFETY AND SOUNDNESS AND PROVIDE AN EFFICIENT AND COMPETITIVE SYSTEM

Although the goals of safety and soundness and that of providing an efficient and competitive financial system are related, they are often at odds with each other. Much of the regulation to ensure safety and soundness is designed to accomplish this goal through supervision and examination, deposit insurance, and by the federal government's willingness to act as a lender of last resort. Regulations have similarly controlled when individuals can obtain new banking charters (start a new bank) and prevented banks from offering products and services not closely related to banking. Regulation historically attempted to prevent concentration of banking resources that would be anti-competitive by restricting mergers and acquisitions that reduce the number and market power of competing institutions. In today's competitive environment, these regulators are not binding. There are few restrictions on where banks can compete and what products they can offer. Individuals with sufficient capital and clean records can open new banks almost at will.

## SUPERVISION AND EXAMINATION

Regulators periodically examine individual banks and provide supervisory directives that request changes in operating policies. The purpose is to guarantee the safety and soundness of the banking system by identifying problems before a bank's financial condition deteriorates to the point where it fails and the FDIC has to pay off insured depositors. The OCC and FDIC assess the overall quality of a bank's condition according to a CAMELS system. The letters in CAMELS refer to: **c**apital adequacy, **a**sset quality, **m**anagement quality, **e**arnings quality, **l**iquidity, and **s**ensitivity to market risk, respectively.

Examiners spend most of their efforts appraising asset quality, management, and market risk.[1] The *asset quality* rating generally indicates the relative volume of problem loans and loan losses. Examiners review the terms and documentation on loans, particularly those with past-due payments, to determine the magnitude of likely loan losses. If repayment prospects are poor, regulators may force a bank to recognize the loss and build up loan-loss reserves in support of future losses. *Management quality* is assessed in terms of senior officers' awareness and control of a bank's policies and performance. Examiners carefully review bank policy statements regarding loans, investments, capital, and general budgeting to determine whether the bank is well run. Members of a bank's board of directors are expected to be involved in policy setting and review. *Sensitivity to market risk* considers management's ability to identify, measure, monitor, and control price risk. For most banks, market risk is primarily composed of the sensitivity of their income and equity to changes in interest rates. Larger banks, however, have active trading portfolios and some exposure to equities and off-balance sheet activities, so they are more sensitive to changes in exchange rates, commodity prices, and equity prices. These facets of risk are addressed in detail in subsequent chapters. *Capital adequacy*, *earnings strength*, and *liquidity* are determined primarily by key performance ratios based on the composition and size of various bank balance sheet accounts and components of net income; for example, equity capital to total assets, return on equity or return on assets, and liquid assets to total assets.

When an examination is completed, the regulatory staff makes a series of policy recommendations that address problems discovered. The recommendations may be informal advisories, a memorandum of understanding, or a cease and desist order. A **memorandum of understanding (MOU)** is a formal regulatory document that identifies specific violations and prescribes corrective action by the problem institution. A **cease and desist order (C&D)** is a legal document that orders a firm to stop an unfair practice under full penalty of law. Only the cease and desist order has legal standing, but each type of recommendation notifies a bank if its house is in order.

## NEW CHARTERS

The United States operates using a **dual banking system**. Individual states, as well as the federal government, issue bank, savings banks, and credit union charters. The OCC charters *national* banks while individual state banking departments charter *state* banks and *state* savings institutes. The Office of Thrift Supervision (OTS) charters *federal savings banks* and *savings associations* while individual state savings authorities charter *state savings banks*. Finally, the National Credit Union Administration (NCUA) charters *federal credit unions* while state credit union authorities charter *state credit unions*. Hence, groups interested in starting a *depository institution* have the option of starting a commercial bank, a savings bank, or a credit union and obtaining a charter from the OCC, OTS, NCUA, or the appropriate state authority.

The source of the charter determines how the bank is regulated (see the section below on "National versus State Charter"). Bank, savings institutions, and credit union regulation and supervision is conducted by five federal

---

[1]Cocheo (1986) analyzes the steps in the typical examination process of a community bank and describes the basic questions and problems that arise.

agencies (OCC, OTS, NCUA, FDIC, and the Federal Reserve), as well as many more than fifty state agencies—many states have separate banking, savings, and credit union authorities, hence there are many more than fifty state depository supervising authorities. Although this is a complicated system, it allows for a separation of duties, as well as "competition" among the various regulatory agencies to produce a safe and efficient banking system.

State-chartered banks have the option of joining the Fed and applying for FDIC insurance. It is highly unlikely, however, that a state banking agency would approve a banking charter without the bank obtaining FDIC insurance. All state banks that choose Federal Reserve membership must obtain deposit insurance. Insured state banks that choose not to join the Fed are regulated predominantly by the FDIC, while noninsured nonmembers are supervised by state banking authorities.

**NATIONAL VERSUS STATE CHARTER.** Before issuing a new charter, the chartering agencies ensure that the (de novo) bank will have the necessary capital and management expertise to ensure soundness and allow the bank to meet the public's financial needs. The agency that charters the institution is the institution's primary regulator with primary responsibility to ensure safety and soundness of the banking system. All banks obtain FDIC deposit insurance coverage as part of the chartering process. In addition, while national banks are regulated only by federal regulatory agencies, state-chartered banks also have a *primary federal regulator*. The Federal Reserve is the primary federal regulator of an FDIC-insured state bank which is a member of the Federal Reserve System, while the primary regulator of state non-Fed member banks is the FDIC. Regulatory agencies conduct periodic on-site examinations to assess a bank's condition and monitor compliance with banking laws. They issue regulations, take enforcement actions, and close banks if they fail. In addition to granting charters, state bank agencies and the OCC conduct periodic examinations of their chartered banks, evaluate merger applications when the resulting firm is their chartered bank, and authorize branches where applicable. Exhibit 1.1 outlines the number and type of depository institutions by their charter type.

Exhibit 1.2 summarizes the division of responsibilities for commercial bank regulators. A 1993 study by the Treasury Department estimated that two or more of these federal regulators supervise approximately 58 percent of commercial banks. Three or more regulators supervise 15 percent of the banks and there are even 2 percent of the banks regulated by four regulators. Not surprisingly, many bankers and legislators believe that this duplication is costly and provides little benefit.

With the removal of many regulations, the U.S. financial system has seen increasing competition among the various regulators. Within many states, community banks often believe they can get a better hearing from a state banking department over a federal regulator because the state regulators better understand their local economy and market participants. The costs also differ to where the choice of regulator can affect a bank's total expenses. Thus, it is not unusual to see mid-size and smaller banks converting to where a state banking department is the primary

| EXHIBIT 1.1 | Number of Commercial Banks, Savings Institutions, and Credit Unions by Charter Class and Primary Federal Regulator (Thousands of Dollars), June 2004 | | | |
|---|---|---|---|---|
| **Charter Class** | **# Institutions** | **# Offices** | **Deposits\*** | **Primary Federal Regulator** |
| Commercial Banks | 7,692 | 75,773 | 4,504,174,000 | |
| National Charter | 1,959 | 36,596 | 2,447,320,000 | OCC |
| State Charter | 5,733 | 39,177 | 2,056,854,000 | |
| Federal Reserve Member | 931 | 14,398 | 985,293,000 | Fed |
| Federal Reserve Nonmember | 4,802 | 24,779 | 1,071,561,000 | FDIC |
| Savings Institutions | 1,361 | 14,000 | 955,638,000 | |
| Federal Charter Savings Associations | 773 | 8,816 | 679,263,000 | OTS |
| State Charter Savings Institutions | 588 | 5,184 | 276,375,000 | |
| FDIC-Supervised Savings Banks | 477 | 4,702 | 259,371,000 | FDIC |
| OTS-Supervised Savings Associations | 111 | 482 | 17,005,000 | OTS |
| U.S. Branches of Foreign Banks | 13 | 13 | 4,970,000 | |
| Total Banks and Savings Institutions | 9,066 | 89,786 | 5,464,782,000 | |
| Credit Unions | 9,324 | NA | 558,573,488 | |
| National Charter | 5,686 | NA | 303,294,525 | NCUA |
| State Charter | 3,638 | NA | 255,278,963 | NCUA |

Source: FDIC Quarterly Banking Profiles and NCUA Annual Reports.

\*Includes deposits in domestic offices (50 states and D.C.), Puerto Rico, and U.S. Territories.

| EXHIBIT 1.2 | Commercial Banks and Their Regulators | | | | |
|---|---|---|---|---|---|
| | **Type of Commercial Bank** | | | | |
| **Type of Regulation** | **National** | **State/Member** | **Insured State Nonmember** | **Noninsured State Nonmember** | **Bank Holding Companies** |
| **Safety and Soundness** | | | | | |
| Supervision and examination | Comptroller | Federal Reserve and state authority | FDIC and state authority | State authority | Federal reserve |
| Deposit insurance | FDIC | FDIC | FDIC | State insurance or none | Not applicable |
| Chartering and licensing | OCC | State authority | State authority | State authority | Federal Reserve and state authority |
| **Efficiency and Competitiveness** | | | | | |
| Branching | Comptroller | Federal Reserve and state authority | FDIC and state authority | State authority | Federal Reserve and state authority |
| Mergers and acquisitions | Comptroller | Federal Reserve and state authority | FDIC and state authority | State authority | Federal Reserve and state authority |
| Pricing new products | Federal Reserve and state authority | Federal Reserve and state authority | Federal Reserve and state authority | Federal Reserve and state authority | Not applicable |
| Consumer protection | Federal Reserve | Federal Reserve and state authority | Federal Reserve, FDIC, and state authority | Federal Reserve and state authority | Not applicable |

regulator along with the FDIC. In contrast, JPMorgan Chase announced in 2004 that it was converting to a national charter from a New York State Charter to have its entire operations under the regulatory auspices of the OCC.

**COMMERCIAL BANKS, SAVINGS INSTITUTIONS, AND CREDIT UNIONS CHARTERS.** Because commercial banks were the only firms allowed to issue demand deposits they dominated the payments system throughout the United States. As such, authorities closely regulated bank operations to control deposit growth and ensure the safety of customer deposits. Among other restrictions, government regulators required cash reserves against deposits, specified maximum interest rates banks could pay on deposits, set minimum capital requirements and placed limits on the size of loans to borrowers. Federal banking law further limited bank operations to activities closely related to banking and, in conjunction with state laws, prohibited interstate branching.

Historically, banks, savings associations, and credit unions each served a different purpose and a different market. **Commercial banks** mostly specialize in short-term business credit, but also make consumer loans and mortgages, and have a broad range of financial powers. Commercial banks are stock corporations whose primary purpose is to maximize shareholder wealth. Banks accept deposits in a variety of different accounts and invest these funds into loans and other financial instruments. Their corporate charters and the powers granted to them under state and federal law determine the range of their activities.

**Savings institutions**, savings and loan associations, and savings banks, have historically specialized in real estate lending; for example, loans for single-family homes and other residential properties. Savings institutions are generally referred to as "thrifts" because they originally offered only savings or time deposits to attract funds. They have acquired a wide range of financial powers over the past quarter-century, and now offer checking accounts, make business and consumer loans and mortgages, and offer virtually any other product a bank offers. Most savings institutions are owned by shareholders ("stock" ownership), but some are owned by their depositors and borrowers ("mutual" ownership). Savings institutions must maintain 65 percent of their assets in housing-related or other qualified assets to maintain their savings institution status. This is called the "qualified thrift lender" (QTL) test. Recent liberalization of naming requirements and of the QTL test has allowed thrifts to use some nonhousing assets to meet this requirement and, in fact, many customers do not know today if their financial institution is a bank or savings institution.

The restrictive impact of the QTL test, as well as the savings and loan crisis of the 1980s which forced many institutions to close or merge with others at an extraordinary cost to the federal government, have dramatically reduced the number of savings institutions from 3,677 in 1986 to 1,345 at year-end 2004. Liberalization of the QTL in the 1990s brought a resurgence of interest in the thrift charter. As a result, many insurance companies and securities firms, as well as commercial firms, organized as a **unitary thrift holding company** in order to own a depository institution and bypass prohibitions in the Glass-Steagall and the Bank Holding Company acts.[2] This resurgence of interest stopped with the passage of Gramm-Leach-Bliley, which eliminated the issuance of new unitary thrift charters.

Credit unions represent another type of depository institution. They are nonprofit institutions with an original purpose to encourage savings and provide loans within a community at low cost to their members. A "common bond" defines their members, although this common bond can be very loosely defined today. Hence the differences between credit unions and banks are disappearing. Members of the credit union pool their funds to form the institution's deposit base and these same members own and control the institution. All credit unions offer savings accounts or time deposits, while the larger institutions also offer checking and money market accounts. Credit unions were first chartered at the state level in 1909. By 1934, the federal government began to charter credit unions under the Farm Credit Association, and created the National Credit Union Administration in 1970. A dual credit union system, similar to banks, exists today as both states and the NCUA charter credit unions. Credit unions have similarly expanded the scope of products and activities they offer to include almost anything a bank or savings association offers, including making home loans, issuing credit cards, and even making some commercial loans. Credit unions are exempt from federal taxation and sometimes receive subsidies in the form of free space or supplies, from their sponsoring organizations. This tax-exempt status puts them at a competitive advantage over other financial institutions. Although credit unions tend to be much smaller than banks or savings associations, there are several large credit unions.

Exhibit 1.3 lists the largest commercial banks, savings institutions, and credit unions as of the end of 2004. Clearly, commercial banks are the largest institutions by asset size, followed by savings institution, while credit unions represent the smallest type of financial institutions. Still, there are many very large credit unions and savings institutions.

**NONDEPOSITORY FINANCIAL COMPANIES.** In addition to depository institutions, there are many nondepository financial companies, sometimes called nonbank banks, that compete in broad product markets. Since 1980, all depository institutions have been able to make commercial loans, issue credit cards, establish trust departments, and enter other related lines of business. Large brokerage houses, mortgage companies, insurance companies, finance companies, and retailers offer transactions accounts, credit cards, and other loans that compete directly with products offered by depository institutions. Many of these firms own commercial banks and thrift institutions that either do not offer demand deposit accounts or make commercial loans, or are otherwise exempt by owning exempt-type banks (for example, industrial banks or consumer banks). Many banks, on the other hand, have entered the securities and insurance business by forming a financial holding company (see the section below on Financial Holding Companies) and buying brokerages or insurance companies.

Passage of the Gramm-Leach-Bliley Act eliminated many, but not all, of the fundamental limitations that banks faced. The act specifically allows a bank, technically a financial holding company, to engage in activities other than banking as long as they are financial in nature. These activities include securities underwriting and dealing, insurance underwriting, insurance agency activities, and merchant banking (a form of equity financing). Prior to the passage of the act, bank holding companies could be involved in the securities business but were strictly limited in the type of activities in which they could engage. Some banks also sold insurance products but for the most part, no bank, whether state or federally chartered, could engage in insurance underwriting with the exception of credit-related insurance.

The fundamental inequities that exist today center around a few issues. The first is the fact that some full-line insurance companies and investment banks can own limited-service commercial banks but are not required to form a financial holding company and hence are not restricted in the types of nonbank activities in which they can engage. For example, commerce activities such as retail and manufacturing.[3] Second, the tax-exempt status of credit unions, which can engage in banking activities including commercial lending, allows them to offer lower loan rates and higher deposit rates than banks.

## FEDERAL DEPOSIT INSURANCE

Regulators attempt to maintain public confidence in banks and the financial system through federal deposit insurance. The FDIC currently insures customer deposits up to $100,000 per account in commercial banks and savings institutions. Under a similar arrangement, almost all credit unions are insured by the National Credit Union

---

[2]Savings and loan associations and mutual savings banks are designated as thrift institutions. Nonbanking firms have entered banking by obtaining a unitary thrift charter that allows them to operate a federal savings bank. Included in this group are Merrill Lynch, GE, State Farm, and many insurance companies.

[3]For example, Prudential owns a securities firm (Prudential Investment), a bank (Prudential Bank and Trust Co.), and a property firm (Prudential Real Estate). Merrill Lynch owns a bank (ML Bank and Trust).

**EXHIBIT 1.3** The Largest Commercial Banks, Savings Institutions, and Credit Unions, December 31, 2004 (Thousands of Dollars)

| Rank | Commercial Bank | Total Assets |
|---|---|---|
| 1 | JPMorgan Chase Bank, National Association | $967,365,000 |
| 2 | Bank of America, National Association | 771,618,758 |
| 3 | Citibank, National Association | 694,529,000 |
| 4 | Wachovia Bank, National Association | 389,963,000 |
| 5 | Wells Fargo Bank, National Association | 366,256,000 |
| 6 | Fleet National Bank | 218,740,377 |
| 7 | U.S. Bank National Association | 194,436,638 |
| 8 | HSBC Bank USA, National Association | 138,296,274 |
| 9 | SunTrust Bank | 130,780,100 |
| 10 | The Bank of New York | 92,138,427 |

| Rank | Savings Institutions | Total Assets |
|---|---|---|
| 1 | World Savings Bank, FSB | $106,816,527 |
| 2 | Citibank (West), FSB | 101,916,468 |
| 3 | Sovereign Bank | 54,454,684 |
| 4 | ING Bank, FSB | 36,023,828 |
| 5 | Citicorp Trust Bank, FSB | 32,424,600 |
| 6 | Citizens Bank of Pennsylvania | 29,788,816 |
| 7 | Washington Mutual Bank FSB | 29,028,537 |
| 8 | Citibank, Federal Savings Bank | 27,779,034 |
| 9 | E*TRADE Bank | 25,548,964 |
| 10 | New York Community Bank | 23,963,342 |

| Rank | Credit Union | Total Assets |
|---|---|---|
| 1 | Navy Federal Credit Union, Merrifield, Va. | $22,927,745 |
| 2 | State Employees Credit Union, Raleigh | 12,116,796 |
| 3 | Pentagon Federal Credit Union, Alexandria, Va. | 7,021,387 |
| 4 | Golden 1 Credit Union, Sacramento | 5,436,125 |
| 5 | Orange County Teachers Federal Credit Union, Santa Ana, Calif. | 5,197,078 |
| 6 | Boeing Employees Credit Union, Tukwila, Wash. | 5,151,935 |
| 7 | Suncoast Schools Federal Credit Union, Tampa | 4,491,816 |
| 8 | Alliant Credit Union, Chicago | 4,467,456 |
| 9 | American Airlines Federal Credit Union, Dallas | 3,992,925 |
| 10 | Security Service Federal Credit Union, San Antonio | 3,588,543 |

Share Insurance Fund (NCUSIF), which the NCUA controls. The FDIC was created by the Banking Act of 1933 in response to the large number of bank failures that followed the stock market crash of 1929. Originally the FDIC insured deposits up to $5,000. The OCC and NCUA require all national banks and credit unions to acquire deposit insurance, while all state banking authorities require newly chartered state banks to join the FDIC and credit unions to join NCUSIF before they can accept deposits from the public. Under the 1991 Federal Deposit Insurance Corporation Improvement Act (FDICIA), both state-chartered and national banks must apply to the FDIC for deposit insurance. Previously, national banks had received insurance automatically with their new charters.

Deposit insurance has been especially important during times when the number of problem banks and bank failures increased. Following World War II, bank failures were negligible, given the heavy regulation of banking activities and strict policies regarding who could open and operate a bank. However, the number of bank and thrift failures rose from under 50 in 1982 to 382 in 1990, only to fall to 6 in 1996 and 29 from 2000–2004.

Banks find insured deposits very attractive. With FDIC insurance, depositors with less than $100,000 per qualifying account are assured that the federal government will guarantee the funds in the event that the bank fails. Deposit customers are thus willing to accept interest rates on insured deposits that are below the rates that banks would have to pay without FDIC insurance. Such deposits are generally more stable in that they don't leave the bank as quickly when the economic climate changes or when a bank's financial condition changes.

Banks pay premiums for insured deposits depending on the size of the FDIC's insurance reserve and the perceived quality of the bank. There once were two insurance funds under the FDIC: the Bank Insurance Fund (BIF) for banks and the Savings Association Insurance Fund (SAIF) for savings and loans.[4] The FDIC Improvement Act of 1991 required the FDIC to assign insurance premiums based on the risk assessment of the banks and to maintain the insurance fund to a minimum level of 1.25 percent of insured deposits. By the late 1990s, the FDIC insurance fund was well funded (over 1.25 percent) and as a result, 93.3 percent of all banks pay no insurance premiums today. Chapter 9 directly addresses bank capital and FDIC insurance premiums.

The FDIC acts as the primary federal regulator of state-chartered banks that do not belong to the Federal Reserve System. State banks that are members of the Federal Reserve System have that agency for their primary federal regulator. The FDIC cooperates with state banking departments to supervise and examine these banks, and has considerable authority to intervene and prevent unsafe and unsound banking practices. The FDIC also has backup examination and regulatory authority over national and Fed-member banks.

The FDIC is the receiver of failed institutions. The FDIC declares banks and savings associations insolvent and handles failed institutions by either liquidating them or selling the institutions to redeem insured deposits. When a bank or thrift fails, the government pays insured depositors the full amount of their account balance up to $100,000 per eligible account. Customers with uninsured deposits bear the risk that they will not recover the full value of their account balance. Historically, regulators have not allowed the largest institutions to fail such that uninsured depositors received de facto 100 percent deposit insurance. Regulators implicitly assume that large bank failures would seriously undermine public confidence in financial institutions and markets, so they generally prop up large banks with federal aid or find a merger partner. The OCC and state banking authorities officially designate banks as insolvent, but the Federal Reserve and FDIC assist in closings. Frequently, the Fed extends credit to a problem bank until an ownership transfer occurs. The FDIC's liquidation staff handles the disposition of a failed bank's assets and liabilities. These and other problems with deposit insurance are described in Chapter 9.

## PRODUCT RESTRICTIONS: BANKS VERSUS NONBANKS

The Federal Reserve regulates specific activities of banks, bank holding companies, and financial holding companies. Exhibit 1.4 is a general description of the types of regulation the Federal Reserve imposes on banks. In the area of safety and soundness, regulations take the form of restricting interlocking relationships among directors of banks and between banks and securities firms to ensure independence, and restricting the terms of loans to insiders, such as directors, bank officers, and shareholders. Exhibit 1.5 lists a brief, and somewhat incomplete, summary of permissible activities of national banks. Since most states have provisions that allow state banks to engage in all activities permissible for national banks, the list of permissible activities for national banks is a strong guide for the banking system. One of the provisions of the Gramm-Leach-Bliley Act was that the OCC would compile a list of permissible activities for national banks. This list is available on the OCC Internet Web site.[5]

## SHORTCOMINGS OF RESTRICTIVE BANK REGULATION

Although regulation is designed to ensure the safety and soundness of the financial system, it cannot accomplish all of its goals. For example, regulation does not prevent bank failures. It cannot eliminate risk in the economic environment or in a bank's normal operations. It does not guarantee that bankers will make sound management decisions or act ethically. It simply serves as a guideline for sound operating policies.

Effective bank regulation is a delicate balance between the banking system's competitiveness and general safety and soundness concerns. Imposing barriers to entry and restricting the types of activities banks can engage in clearly enhance safety and soundness, but also hinder competition. Hence, the historical approach of restricting the geographic and product scope of banking activities has three drawbacks:

1.  It assumed that the markets for bank products, largely bank loans and deposits, could be protected and that other firms could not encroach upon these markets. Not surprisingly, investment banks, hybrid financial companies (General Electric and American Express), insurance firms, and others found ways to provide the same products as banks across different geographic markets.

2.  It discriminated against U.S.-based firms versus foreign-based firms. For example, prior regulations prohibited U.S. banks from underwriting (helping businesses issue new stock or bonds) securities for firms in the United States. In contrast, foreign banks are generally not restricted as to their domestic corporate structure and thus have long been able to circumvent U.S. restrictions on underwriting activities. Such restrictions place U.S. banks at a competitive disadvantage.

---

[4]Congress passed the Financial Institutions Reform, Recovery and Enforcement Act of 1989 (FIRREA) largely to address problems in the thrift industry. Specific provisions of the act are discussed later in the chapter. The two insurance funds were established to maintain the appearance that banks were distinguishable from savings and loans. In actuality, both funds were deficient at the time. Congress mandated an increase in premiums, with thrifts paying higher rates over time. Deposit insurance works because the federal government stands behind it with its full faith, credit, and taxing authority.

[5]At the time of this writing, this list could be obtained at http://www.occ.treas.gov/corpapps/BankAct.pdf.

| EXHIBIT 1.4 | Federal Reserve Bank Regulations |

| Reg. | Title |
| --- | --- |
| A | Extensions of Credit by Federal Reserve Banks |
| B | Equal Credit Opportunity |
| C | Home Mortgage Disclosure |
| D | Reserve Requirements of Depository Institutions |
| E | Electronic Fund Transfers |
| F | Limitations on Interbank Liabilities |
| G | Disclosure and Reporting of CRA-Related Agreements |
| H | Membership of State Banking Institutions in the Federal Reserve System |
| I | Issue and Cancellation of Federal Reserve Bank Capital Stock |
| J | Collection of Checks and Other Items by Federal Reserve Banks and Funds Transfers through Fedwire |
| K | International Banking Operations |
| L | Management Official Interlocks |
| M | Consumer Leasing |
| N | Relations with Foreign Banks and Bankers |
| O | Loans to Executive Officers, Directors, and Principal Shareholders of Member Banks |
| P | Privacy of Consumer Financial Information |
| Q | Prohibition against Payment of Interest on Demand Deposits |
| S | Reimbursement to Financial Institutions for Providing Financial Records; Recordkeeping Requirements for Certain Financial Records |
| T | Credit by Brokers and Dealers |
| U | Credit by Banks or Persons other than Brokers or Dealers for the Purpose of Purchasing or Carrying Margin Stocks |
| V | Fair Credit Reporting |
| W | Transactions between Member Banks and Their Affiliates |
| X | Borrowers of Securities Credit |
| Y | Bank Holding Companies and Change in Bank Control |
| Z | Truth in Lending |
| AA | Unfair or Deceptive Acts or Practices |
| BB | Community Reinvestment |
| CC | Availability of Funds and Collection of Checks |
| DD | Truth in Savings |
| EE | Netting Eligibility for Financial Institutions |

SOURCE: Federal Reserve Bank, http://www.federalreserve.gov/regulations/default.htm.

3. Historical regulation has penalized bank customers who do not have convenient access to the range of products they demand. In addition, such restrictions generally raise prices above those obtained in a purely competitive marketplace.

## MAINTAINING MONETARY STABILITY AND THE INTEGRITY OF THE PAYMENTS SYSTEM

The two objectives of bank regulation, *monetary stability* and *to maintain the integrity of the nation's payments system,* are generally the domain of the Federal Reserve System. The Fed attempts to control the growth in the nation's money supply and maintain the efficient operation of the payments system. Monetary stability ensures that the growth in the money supply is kept in check such that the value of the nation's money is strong, predictable, and an effective means of making payment.

### THE ROLE OF THE CENTRAL BANK IN THE ECONOMY: THE FEDERAL RESERVE SYSTEM

Congress created the Federal Reserve System in 1913 to serve as the central bank of the United States and to provide the nation with a safe, flexible, and more stable monetary and financial system. The Fed controls the growth in the nation's money supply, sets reserve requirements, approves proposed mergers and new branches, and examines state member banks. It also makes loans to banks, establishes consumer regulations, authorizes the formation

**EXHIBIT 1.5** Summary of Permissible Activities of National Banks for Their Subsidiaries

### General Authority

*Branching:* loan offices and facilities

*Consulting and financial advice:* financial, investment, or economic

*Corporate governance:* reorganizational activities to streamline operations

*Correspondent service:* hold deposits for other banks and perform services

*Finder activities:* serve as a finder for certain goods

*Leasing:* engage in personal property leasing

*Lending:* make, purchase, sell, service, or warehouse loans or extensions of credit

*Payment services:* cash management and letters of credit

*Other activities and services:* borrow money and support services

### Fiduciary Activities: may be granted at time of charter or subsequently

*General:* trust activities, employee benefit accounts, and real estate brokerage

*Insurance and annuities activities:* insurance underwriting, reinsurance, and title insurance

*Securities activities:* asset securitization, broker-dealer activities, clearing and execution services, closed-end mutual funds, derivatives activities, investment vehicle for bank clients, mutual find activities, online securities trading, options contracts, private placement services, securities brokerage (secondary and primary markets), securities exchanges, securities lending, sweeps, transfer agent, and underwriting and dealing in government and municipal securities

### Technology and Electronic Activities

*Digital certification:* act as a certification authority

*Electronic bill payments:* presentment, EDI services, electronic toll collections, merchant process of credit cards via Internet, and stored-value cards

*Electronic commerce:* commercial Web site hosting, electronic marketplace, electronic storage, facilitation of electronic commerce, hyperlinks between bank and third-party sites, virtual malls, and Web design and development services

Electronic correspondent services

Internet access service

Internet and PC banking

Software development and production

### Investments: a wide range of investments are permissible

Asset-backed securities, bank stock, bankers acceptances, corporate bonds (subject to 10 percent of capital surplus), collateralized mortgage-related investments, commercial paper, foreign government loans, hosing investments, insurance investments, investment in limited liability companies, money market preferred stock, mutual fund shares (limited), small business investments, stock in life insurance underwriter, trust preferred securities, and state and local bonds

SOURCE: Office of Comptroller of the Currency, Activities Permissible for a National Bank, http://www.occ.treas.gov (http://www.occ.treas.gov/corpapps/BankAct.pdf).

of bank holding companies, and approves all holding company activities and acquisitions, regardless of how a bank was chartered. The Fed's role in banking and the economy has expanded over the years, but its primary focus has remained the same. The Fed's three fundamental functions are:

1. Conduct the nation's monetary policy

2. Provide and maintain an effective and efficient payments system

3. Supervise and regulate banking operations

All three roles have a similar purpose, that of maintaining monetary and economic stability and prosperity. The Federal Reserve System is a decentralized central bank, with Reserve Banks and branches in 12 districts across the country. The Fed is coordinated by a Board of Governors in Washington, D.C., whose members are appointed by the President of the United States and confirmed by the Senate for staggered 14-year terms. The seven members of the Board of Governors represent the main governing body of the Fed charged with overseeing the 12 District Reserve Banks and with helping implement national monetary policy.

The Federal Reserve also serves as the federal government's lender of last resort. When a bank loses funding sources, the Fed may make a discount window loan to support operations until a solution appears. When Continental Illinois experienced difficulties in 1984, for example, the Federal Reserve loaned it more than $4 billion until it effectively nationalized the bank. The same occurred with the Bank of New England in late 1990. The Federal Reserve's crisis management, however, is not limited to direct bank assistance. In recent years, it has intervened in disputes related to the collapse of silver prices during the Hunt family's problems, junk bond financing of leveraged buyouts, the failure of securities dealers in repurchase agreements, the failures of privately insured thrift institutions in Ohio and Maryland, and the funding crisis faced by the Farm Credit System and the hedge fund long-term capital management.[6] The Fed also stood ready to provide liquidity to financial firms immediately following the terrorist attack on the World Trade Center of September 11, 2001. In most cases, the injured party requests back-up financing from the Fed if a crisis worsens. In other cases, market participants simply need expert advice. As lender of last resort, the Federal Reserve has the resources and clout to advise management and prevent serious financial problems.

**MONETARY POLICY.** The Fed conducts monetary policy through actions designed to influence the supply of money and credit in order to promote price stability and long-term sustainable economic growth. There are three distinct monetary policy tools:
- Open market operations
- Changes in the discount rate
- Changes in the required reserve ratio

**Open market operations** are conducted by the Federal Reserve Bank of New York under the direction of the Federal Open Market Committee (FOMC). The sale or purchase of U.S. government securities in the "open market", or secondary market, is the Federal Reserve's most flexible means of carrying out its policy objectives. Through these transactions carried out daily, the Fed can adjust the level of reserves in the banking system and thereby influence short-term interest rates and the growth of the money supply. Fed open market purchases of securities increase liquidity, hence reserves in the banking system, by increasing bank deposit balances at the Fed. Fed open market sales of securities decrease bank reserves and liquidity by lowering deposit balances at the Fed.

**Changes in the discount rate** directly affect the cost of reserve borrowing. When the Fed raises the discount rate, it discourages borrowing by making it more expensive. Fed decreases in the discount rate make borrowing less expensive. In October 2002, the Federal Reserve established a new discount rate policy in which the Fed would lend to most financial institutions under their primary and secondary credit programs at 1 percent and 1.5 percent over the current federal funds target rate. Previously, the Fed generally discouraged borrowing directly from the Fed and established the discount rate well below the current federal funds rate. Under the old policy, changes in the discount rate were infrequent and primarily were a signal of future policy toward monetary ease or tightness rather than a move to change bank borrowing activity. Under the new policy, the Fed does not "discourage" borrowing as it did in the previous policy. In its role as lender of last resort, banks can borrow deposit balances, or required reserves, directly from Federal Reserve Banks with the discount rate representing the interest rate that banks pay.

**Changes in reserve requirements** directly affect the amount of legally required reserves that banks are required to hold as an asset and thus change the amount of funds a bank can lend out. For example, a required reserve ratio of 10 percent means that a bank with $100 in demand deposit liabilities outstanding must hold $10 in legally required reserves in support of these deposits. Thus, the bank can lend only 90 percent of its demand deposit liabilities (DDAs). When the Fed increases (decreases) reserve requirements, it formally increases (decreases) the required reserve ratio, which directly reduces (increases) the amount of money a bank can lend per dollar of DDAs. Thus, lower reserve requirements increase bank liquidity and lending capacity while higher reserve requirements decrease bank liquidity and lending capacity.

**THE ROLE OF COMMERCIAL BANKS IN THE ECONOMY.** Commercial banks play an important role in facilitating economic growth. On a macroeconomic level, they represent the primary conduit of Federal Reserve monetary policy. Bank deposits represent the most liquid form of money such that the Federal Reserve System's efforts to control the nation's money supply and level of aggregate economic activity is accomplished by changing the availability of credit at banks. On a microeconomic level, commercial banks represent the primary source of credit to most small businesses and many individuals. A community's vitality typically reflects the strength of its major financial institutions and the innovative character of its business leaders.

While the economic role of commercial banks has varied little over time, the nature of commercial banks and competing financial institutions is constantly changing. In addition to banks, savings and loans, credit unions, brokerage firms, insurance companies, and general retail stores now offer products and services traditionally associated only with commercial banks. Hence, the term *bank* today refers as much to the *range of services* traditionally offered by depository institutions as to a specific type of institution.

Exhibit 1.6 documents changes in the number of institutions and total assets controlled by commercial banks, savings banks, and credit unions from 1970 through 2004. During the 35 years, commercial banks' share of

---

[6]During late 1979 and early 1980 the Hunt family cornered the silver market and the price of silver increased dramatically. By March 1980, however, the price of silver collapsed and the Hunt brothers declared bankruptcy.

**EXHIBIT 1.6**  Number and Total Assets of Various Depository Institutions, 1997–2004

| | Monetary Amounts, Billions of Dollars | | | | | Annual Growth Rate 1970– 1980 | Annual Growth Rate 1980– 1990 | Annual Growth Rate 1990– 2000 | Annual Growth Rate 2000– 2004[b] |
|---|---|---|---|---|---|---|---|---|---|
| | 1970 | 1980 | 1990 | 2000 | 2004 | | | | |
| Commercial Banks | | | | | | | | | |
| Number | 13,500 | 14,163 | 12,343 | 8,315 | 7,630 | 0.4% | −1.4% | −3.9% | −2.1% |
| Total assets | $517.4 | $1,484.6 | $3,389.5 | $6,238.7 | $8,413 | 11.1% | 8.6% | 6.3% | 7.8% |
| (% of Total Assets) | 66.0% | 63.6% | 71.0% | 79.0% | 78.15% | | | | |
| Savings Institutions[a] | | | | | | | | | |
| Number | 5,669 | 4,594 | 2,815 | 1,590 | 1,345 | −2.1% | −4.8% | −5.6% | −4.1% |
| Total assets | $249.5 | $783.6 | $1,259.2 | $1,222.6 | $1,692 | 12.1% | 4.9% | −0.3% | 8.5% |
| (% of Total Assets) | 31.8% | 33.6% | 26.4% | 15.5% | 15.7% | | | | |
| Credit Unions | | | | | | | | | |
| Number | 23,819 | 21,930 | 8,821 | 10,316 | 9,128 | −0.82% | −8.70% | 1.58% | −3.01% |
| Total assets | $17.6 | $67.3 | $126.7 | $438.2 | $660.0 | 14.35% | 6.53% | 13.21% | 10.78% |
| (% of Total Assets) | 2.2% | 2.9% | 2.7% | 5.5% | 6.1% | | | | |

[a]Includes savings and loan associations and mutual savings banks.

SOURCE: Graph Book at www.fdic.gov and NCUA annual reports.

depository institution assets varied from around 64 percent in the early 1980s to 79 percent during the 2000s. This growth came at the expense of thrift institutions whose share dropped from almost 32 percent to 15.7 percent by 2004, while credit unions increased their share from just over 2 percent to 6.1 percent during this period. Note also the sharp drop in the number of all institutions. This consolidation reflects the combined impact of relaxation of restrictions on bank branching, failures, mergers, acquisitions, and consolidations. The banking industry now comprises fewer, but larger, firms that control an increased share of loans and deposits, with the number of competitors shrinking rapidly.

Although revealing, these figures disguise the fact that there has been a fundamental shift in the structure of financial institutions since 1980. In particular, depository institutions' share of U.S. financial assets has systematically declined relative to assets held by other financial intermediaries. Exhibit 1.7 documents the shift from 1970 to 2004. During the 35 years, banks, savings and loans, and credit unions decreased their share from 61 percent to less than 31 percent, with almost all of the decrease occurring since the late 1970s. Insurance, private pension and state and local government retirement funds, mutual funds, mortgage related (mortgage assets and real estate investment trusts), and all other nonbanks (which include securities brokers and dealers, issuers of securitized assets, and government sponsored enterprises) evidenced the greatest growth. This graph is dramatic evidence of the competition that depository institutions face from nonbank institutions that compete in the same general product lines, but are less regulated. The decline in banks' market share is overstated, however, because many banks strategically choose to move business off-balance sheet via securitization. When market share is measured in terms of revenues, banks have done better in maintaining their historical market share.

## EFFICIENT AND COMPETITIVE FINANCIAL SYSTEM

Regulators spend considerable effort analyzing and modifying regulations regarding what prices financial institutions can charge and what products and services they can offer. Product restrictions, barriers to entry, and restricting mergers and the degree of branching can clearly enhance safety and soundness, but they also hinder competition. Effective bank regulation requires a delicate balance between the banking system's competitiveness and general safety and soundness concerns. In general, regulators approve new charters when the ownership group invests sufficient capital and hires strong management to run the bank. Branching restrictions, which previously were the exclusive domain of the states to determine, are no longer relevant with all states permitting interstate branching. Regulators approve virtually all mergers after all interested parties voice their assessments. With the largest institutions, the process entails allowing consumer groups to argue why the big banks aren't serving disadvantaged customers. Normally, the large banks commit to assistance in the form of mortgage loans and other services in certain trade areas where customers frequently underutilize banking services.

**EXHIBIT 1.7** Percentage Distribution of U.S. Financial Assets Held by Various Financial Institutions, 1970–2004

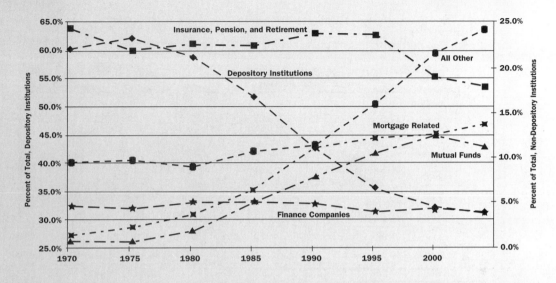

| | Dec-70 | Dec-75 | Dec-80 | Dec-85 | Dec-90 | Dec-95 | Dec-00 | Dec-04 |
|---|---|---|---|---|---|---|---|---|
| ◆ - Depository Institutions | 60.5% | 62.1% | 58.9% | 51.8% | 42.7% | 35.7% | 32.1% | 31.3% |
| ■ - Insurance, Pension, and Retirement | 23.8% | 21.4% | 22.1% | 21.9% | 23.2% | 23.1% | 18.5% | 17.3% |
| ▲ Mutual Funds | 0.6% | 0.6% | 1.7% | 4.9% | 7.6% | 10.2% | 12.0% | 10.9% |
| ★ Finance Companies | 4.5% | 4.2% | 4.9% | 4.9% | 4.6% | 3.8% | 4.1% | 3.8% |
| ✳ Mortgage Related | 1.3% | 2.2% | 3.6% | 6.3% | 10.8% | 11.8% | 12.3% | 13.3% |
| ■ - All Other | 9.3% | 9.5% | 8.8% | 10.3% | 11.1% | 15.5% | 21.0% | 23.4% |

SOURCE: Federal Reserve Statistical Release, Flow of Funds Accounts of the United States: www.federalreserve.gov/releases/zl

## ORGANIZATIONAL FORM OF THE BANKING INDUSTRY

**UNIT BANKING VERSUS BRANCH BANKING.** Commercial banks are classified either as **unit banks** with all operations housed in a single office or **branch banks** with multiple offices. Unit banks have their own board of directors, staff of officers, and separate documents and technology for conducting business. Clearly, operating expenses are higher for the parent company that owns and operates multiple independent banks than they would be if the parent chose to operate these banks as branches of a single "lead" bank. Obviously, economic efficiency is a primary motivating factor for a bank to convert separate unit banks into branches and the relaxation in branching restrictions allowed them to do it. Historically, branch banking was controlled by each individual state.

One of the primary reasons the number of banks has declined almost 50 percent since the mid-1980s is the relaxation of branching restrictions provided by the Riegle-Neal Interstate Banking and Branching Efficiency Act of 1994.[7] Even though the number of banks has fallen, the number of bank branches has almost doubled since the early 1980s.

Until the passage of the Riegle-Neal Act, branch banking was controlled by the states. The states originally limited branches to help retain deposits in local communities and to provide local bank ownership and management. The fear was that large banks in metropolitan areas with branches would take deposits out of rural areas to lend in the bigger cities. Branching restrictions presumably increased credit availability in these rural areas, especially for small businesses and farmers. They also prevented a few large banks from gaining too much market power, in which case they could presumably charge higher interest rates and provide second-rate services. Most experts who have analyzed the arguments against branches have concluded that they were generally unsupported.[8] In addition, risk in the banking industry is considered higher with restrictive branching because individual banks are less diversified and more prone to problems if depositors withdraw their funds en masse. Not surprisingly, states with

---

[7]Even though the act was passed in 1994, it did not go into effect until 1995, and was not fully effective until 1997.

[8]See Evanoff and Fortier, 1986.

## EXHIBIT 1.8

Changes In the Number of Banks and Bank Branches, 1960–2004

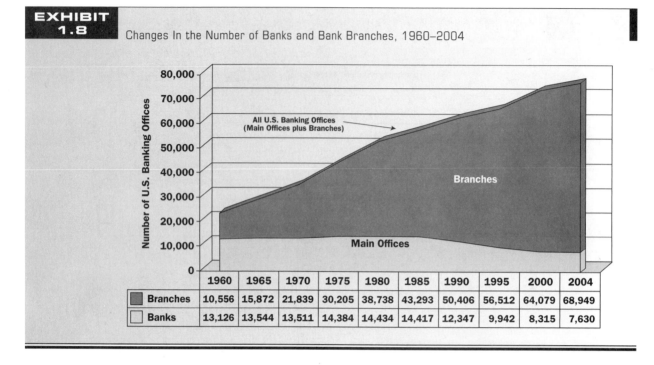

| | 1960 | 1965 | 1970 | 1975 | 1980 | 1985 | 1990 | 1995 | 2000 | 2004 |
|---|---|---|---|---|---|---|---|---|---|---|
| Branches | 10,556 | 15,872 | 21,839 | 30,205 | 38,738 | 43,293 | 50,406 | 56,512 | 64,079 | 68,949 |
| Banks | 13,126 | 13,544 | 13,511 | 14,384 | 14,434 | 14,417 | 12,347 | 9,942 | 8,315 | 7,630 |

the highest bank failure rates historically restricted branching. Branching generally reduces the number of competitors, lowers expenses, allows greater asset diversification, and expands each bank's consumer deposit base, reducing the likelihood of a run on deposits. Each of these factors decreases the chances of failure, everything else being equal.

**BRANCHING AND INTERSTATE EXPANSION.** Through 1993, efforts to extend interstate banking focused on convincing state legislatures to permit reciprocal agreements. Before 1980, no states allowed interstate acquisitions. By the end of 1993, only Hawaii did not allow some form of interstate banking. Most allowed both out-of-state banks and thrifts to acquire in-state firms or open new banks. Some states saw an opportunity to increase capital availability in-state simply by opening their doors. These states included those that are geographically isolated, such as Alaska, as well as those that had severe economic problems, such as Oklahoma and Texas. Other states used interstate compacts as a defense mechanism to allow their in-state banks to grow large enough to compete with national money center banks. These states included those in the Northeast and Southeast that entered regional compacts that prohibited banks in certain states (especially California and New York) from entering.

Historical branching restrictions shaped the U.S. banking system into one in which there were, and still are, many separate smaller banks, as well as substantially more banks than in any other country in the world. Branching restrictions also created a banking system in which there was no bank with a coast-to-coast presence until the NationsBank and Bank of America merger in 1998. For most of the later half of the twentieth century, the vast majority of banks conducted banking business exclusively in the state where the head office was located. A few bank holding companies ventured out of state to buy banks, but these transactions were generally small.[9]

Provision of the Garn-St. Germain Depository Institutions Act of 1982 allowed interstate takeovers of failed or failing institutions, but the number of transactions was small until the late 1980s. Intrastate bidders of the same type, however, generally have the advantage. Once in a state, a firm could expand by buying other sound institutions in that state as permitted by law. It was this provision, allowing a bank to acquire a failing institution, that was the backbone of some of the largest financial institutions today. Specifically, in 1983 Bank of America Corporation in California purchased Seafirst Corporation in Washington; in 1985, Chase Manhattan Bank in New York purchased several privately insured savings and loans in Ohio; New York's Citicorp similarly acquired several failed savings and loans, allowing it to enter the California, Illinois, Florida, Maryland, and Nevada markets. In Texas,

---

[9]Prior to the passage of the Douglas amendment, 16 bank holding companies owned affiliate banks outside their home states. These banks can subsequently continue all interstate operations initiated before interstate restrictions. Seven of the groups are foreign-based, and nine have their main office in the United States. Several of these banking organizations, such as Norwest (now part of Wells Fargo) and NCNB (now Bank of America) have aggressively expanded into other states through normal channels via the purchase of failed and healthy institutions.

*Efficient and Competitive Financial System*

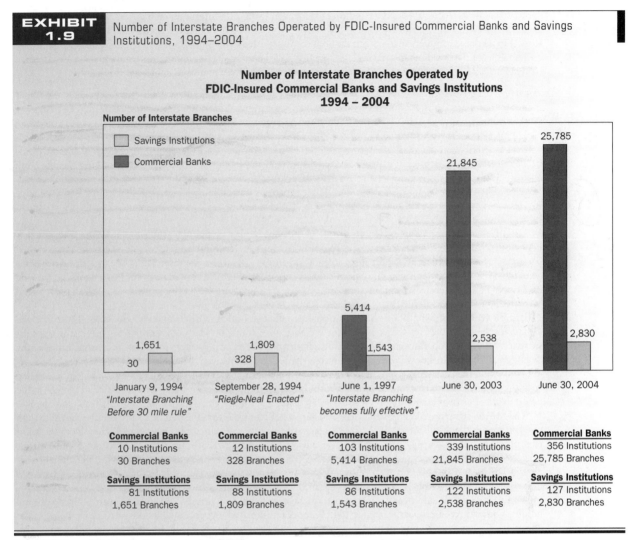

**EXHIBIT 1.9** Number of Interstate Branches Operated by FDIC-Insured Commercial Banks and Savings Institutions, 1994–2004

**Number of Interstate Branches Operated by FDIC-Insured Commercial Banks and Savings Institutions 1994 – 2004**

Number of Interstate Branches

- ☐ Savings Institutions
- ■ Commercial Banks

| | January 9, 1994 *"Interstate Branching Before 30 mile rule"* | September 28, 1994 *"Riegle-Neal Enacted"* | June 1, 1997 *"Interstate Branching becomes fully effective"* | June 30, 2003 | June 30, 2004 |
|---|---|---|---|---|---|
| Savings Institutions branches | 1,651 | 1,809 | 1,543 | 2,538 | 2,830 |
| Commercial Banks branches | 30 | 328 | 5,414 | 21,845 | 25,785 |

| **Commercial Banks** | **Commercial Banks** | **Commercial Banks** | **Commercial Banks** | **Commercial Banks** |
|---|---|---|---|---|
| 10 Institutions | 12 Institutions | 103 Institutions | 339 Institutions | 356 Institutions |
| 30 Branches | 328 Branches | 5,414 Branches | 21,845 Branches | 25,785 Branches |
| **Savings Institutions** | **Savings Institutions** | **Savings Institutions** | **Savings Institutions** | **Savings Institutions** |
| 81 Institutions | 88 Institutions | 86 Institutions | 122 Institutions | 127 Institutions |
| 1,651 Branches | 1,809 Branches | 1,543 Branches | 2,538 Branches | 2,830 Branches |

SOURCE: FDIC Quarterly Banking Profile.

NCNB purchased First Republic Bancorp which later became NationsBank and then Bank of America, and Bank One acquired 20 of MCorp's (Texas) largest banks.

The pace of interstate activity quickened during the mid-1980s when many states authorized some form of interstate banking. The passge of the Riegle-Neal Act permitted adequately capitalized and managed bank holding companies to acquire banks in any state—unless the state legislature opted out. Only two states originally "opted out" of interstate banking: Texas and Montana. Texas chose to delay interstate branching until September 1999 and Montana until October 2001.[10] Exhibit 1.9 demonstrates the impact restrictive branching laws had on the development of interstate branch offices. At the beginning of 1994 there were 10,452 commercial banks and savings insititutions but only 10 had a total of 30 interstate branches. By June 2004, there were 356 commercial banks with over 25,785 interstate branches.

**INTERSTATE EXPANSION OF NONBANKS.** Even before commercial banks had explicit interstate banking authority, they could conduct business nationwide through bank holding company subsidiaries. Most large banking organizations have established Edge Act corporations, loan production offices, and consumer banks outside their home state. **Edge Act corporations** provide a full range of banking services but, by law, deal only in international transactions. There are two types of Edge corporations: banks and investment companies. *Banking Edges* operate as

---

[10]Several restrictions and conditions apply. Good CRA evaluations by the Federal Reserve are required before acquisitions are approved. Mergers are also subject to concentration limits (generally a merger cannot mean that the bank will control more than 20 percent of deposits in the state).

commercial banks, accepting deposits and making loans to firms with international business. *Investment Edges* engage strictly in activities outside the United States that are permitted under federal regulation. **Loan production offices (LPOs)** make commercial loans but do not accept deposits. **Consumer banks** accept deposits but make only consumer loans. Federal Reserve approval of these firms allowed large bank holding companies to form an interstate banking network throughout the nation even prior to the enactment of nationwide interstate branching.

**BANK HOLDING COMPANIES.** A bank holding company is essentially a shell organization that owns and manages subsidiary firms. Any organization that owns controlling interest in one or more commercial banks is a **bank holding company (BHC).**[11] Control is defined as ownership or indirect control via the power to vote more than 25 percent of the voting shares in a bank. Prior to the enactment of interstate branching, the primary motivation behind forming a bank holding company was to circumvent restrictions regarding branching and the products and services that banks could offer. Today, the primary motive is to broaden the scope of products the bank can offer. The holding company obtains financing from stockholders and creditors and uses the proceeds to buy stock in other companies, make loans, and purchase securities. The holding company is labeled the *parent* organization and the operating entities are the *subsidiaries.* If the parent owns at least 80 percent of a subsidiary's stock, it files a consolidated tax return.

One-bank holding companies (OBHCs) control only one bank and typically arise when the owners of an existing bank exchange their shares for stock in the holding company. The holding company then acquires the original bank stock. Multibank holding companies (MBHCs) control at least two commercial banks. Large organizations generally form OBHCs or a small number of banks in an MBHC because they want to control a bank and provide traditional banking services, but more importantly, want to combine the bank's capabilities with their financial activities nonbank subsidiaries in order to better compete nationwide.

Exhibit 1.10 outlines the simple organizational structure of both an OBHC and an MBHC. Consider first the OBHC. At the top is the board of directors for the parent organization that owns controlling interest in the subsidiaries. This board operates much like the board for an independent bank, except that its responsibilities now extend to all lines of business in which the entire organization is involved. In an OBHC the subsidiary bank normally operates like an independent bank. The only difference is that business decisions must now be reconciled with the objectives and decisions associated with the nonbank subsidiaries. Bank officers are represented on the board as are officers of the nonbank subsidiaries. In general, nonbank firms have fewer senior officers than banks.

The MBHC structure differs slightly. The substantive difference is that the parent corporation owns more than one commercial bank subsidiary. Prior to the advent of interstate banking, this enabled the banking organization to compete in different geographic markets. Even within this structure, operating styles may vary. Some MBHCs operate as closely knit units with the management of each subsidiary bank reporting daily to key personnel either at the lead bank or the parent company. In this case the subsidiaries are effectively branches. Important decisions must be approved by authorities outside the local community such that local bank officers have only limited autonomy. Local bank loan officers, for example, might have to get all loans over $100,000 approved by a regional holding company credit officer located in a different community who oversees all lending decisions. This has the advantage of guaranteeing uniformity in loan decisions. It also has disadvantages related to perceptions that local authorities have limited powers. Decisions are too often delayed and subsequently relayed to customers too late. Not surprisingly, well-run community banks play on their local autonomy and "special" community focus.

Other MBHCs allow managers of subsidiary banks to retain key decision-making authority and essentially operate quasi-independently as long as performance is strong. It is more difficult for these firms to realize economies of scale—consider the inability to run a single marketing and advertising program—and thus some of the benefits of size are lost. The advantage, however, is that such banks typically retain close ties to their communities and realize the associated benefits.

The Bank Holding Company Act of 1956 assigned regulatory responsibility to the Federal Reserve for these companies, while leaving the supervision of banks within holding companies in the hands of their traditional regulators. The Gramm-Leach-Bliley Act also gave regulatory responsibility over *financial holding companies* to the Federal Reserve. Like commercial banks, bank holding companies are heavily regulated by states and the federal government. The Bank Holding Company Act stipulates that the Board of Governors of the Federal Reserve System must approve all holding company formations and acquisitions. Approval is normally granted unless there is evidence that the acquisition will substantially lessen competition in the local banking market. The Federal Reserve examines ownership or control of less than 25 percent on a case-by-case basis to determine whether effective control exists.

Many MBHCs have folded their separate banks operating across state lines into a branch of the main bank and thus eliminated the various independent banking operations. NationsBank (now Bank of America), for example, changed NationsBank Texas from being a separate bank into a branch of the North Carolina bank. Typi-

[11]It should be noted that a banking company can be a bank holding company but not a financial holding company as defined by Gramm-Leach-Bliley. See the section below on financial holding companies.

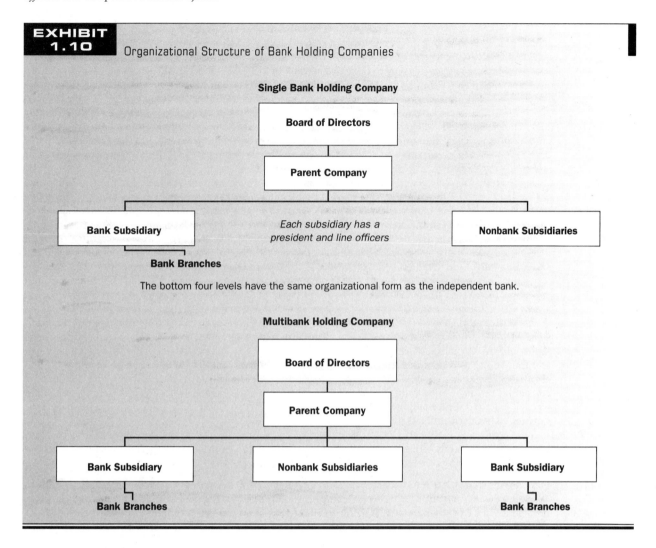

**EXHIBIT 1.10** Organizational Structure of Bank Holding Companies

cally, however, the largest banks do not form an OBHC, but rather operate a small number of banks in an MBHC. Often, large organizations operate MBHCs to get the benefits from having charters in states with more relaxed corporate and usury laws and to control limited purposes banks, such as credit card banks. For example, many large MBHCs have a Delaware bank charter due to that state's corporate and usury law advantages. Small organizations more often form OBHCs because the owners can realize tax benefits and gain better access to funds via the capital markets.

Under current regulation, bank holding companies (BHCs) can acquire nonbank subsidiaries that offer products and services closely related to banking. This presumably limits speculation and thus overall risk. Many insurance companies, finance companies, and general retail firms have formed OBHCs to operate banks as part of their financial services efforts.

**FINANCIAL HOLDING COMPANIES.** The Glass-Steagall Act effectively separated commercial banking from investment banking but left open the possibility of banks engaging in investment banking activities through a Section 20 affiliate so long as the bank was not "principally engaged" in these activities. In 1987, commercial banks received permission from the Federal Reserve to underwrite and deal in securities and five banks quickly set up the necessary Section 20 subsidiaries.[12] The Fed resolved the issue of "principally engaged" initially by allowing banks to earn only 5 percent of the revenue in their securities affiliates. This was raised to 10 percent in 1989 and

---

[12]The first five Section 20s were established by Bankers Trust New York Corp., Chase Manhattan Corp., Citicorp, J.P. Morgan & Co., and PNC Financial Corp.

to 25 percent in March 1997. Pursuant to the Securities Act of 1933 and the Securities Exchange Act of 1934, these so-called Section 20 subsidiaries were required to register with the SEC as broker-dealers and are subject to all the rules applicable to broker-dealers. In addition, transactions between insured depository institutions and their Section 20 affiliates are restricted by sections 23A and 23B of the Federal Reserve Act.

The Gramm-Leach-Bliley Act of 1999 repealed the restrictions on banks affiliating with securities firms under the Glass-Steagall Act and modified portions of the Bank Holding Company Act to allow affiliations between banks and insurance underwriters. While preserving authority of states to regulate insurance, the act prohibited state actions that have the effect of preventing bank-affiliated firms from selling insurance on an equal basis with other insurance agents. The law created a new financial holding company, which was authorized to engage in underwriting and selling insurance and securities, conducting both commercial and merchant banking, investing in and developing real estate, and other "complementary activities."

*Financial holding companies* (FHC) are distinct entities from bank holding companies. A company can form a BHC, an FHC, or both. The primary advantage to forming an FHC is that the entity can engage in a wide range of financial activities not permitted in the bank or in a BHC. Some of these activities include insurance and securities underwriting and agency activities, merchant banking, and insurance company portfolio investment activities. Activities that are "complementary" to financial activities also are authorized. The primary disadvantage to forming an FHC, or converting a BHC to an FHC, is that the Fed may not permit a company to form an FHC if any one of its insured depository institution subsidiaries is not well capitalized or well managed, or did not receive at least a satisfactory rating in its most recent CRA exam. Most importantly, if any one of the insured depository institutions or affiliates of an FHC received less than a satisfactory rating in its most recent CRA exam, the appropriate federal banking agency may not approve any additional new activities or acquisitions under the authorities granted under the act.

An FHC can own a bank or BHC or a thrift or thrift holding company. Each of these companies owns subsidiaries, while the parent financial holding company also owns other subsidiaries directly. The structure is similar to that of a bank holding company's relationship to its subsidiaries but there is one more layer of management and thus control. As commercial banks consolidate with other financial institutions, both domestically and abroad, this type of organization is expected to become more prevalent. Alternatively, we may see nonfinancial companies affiliate with banks in this type of structure. Exhibit 1.11 demonstrates a general form of an FHC in which a BHC and thrift holding company are owned by an FHC. Each of these holding companies owns subsidiaries, while the parent FHC also owns subsidiaries.

The specific organizational form, permissible activities, and stream of cash flows between a holding company and its subsidiaries are described in the following sections. Subsequent sections document regulatory restrictions regarding bank products offered, geographic markets served, and pricing.

**HOLDING COMPANY FINANCIAL STATEMENTS AND CASH FLOWS.** MBHC expansion enables banks to diversify their operations by competing in different geographic and product markets. Diversification reduces the risk of failure by stabilizing earnings. The parent company typically coordinates the operating strategies for the entire organization and provides services for which it charges fees. It assists bank subsidiaries in

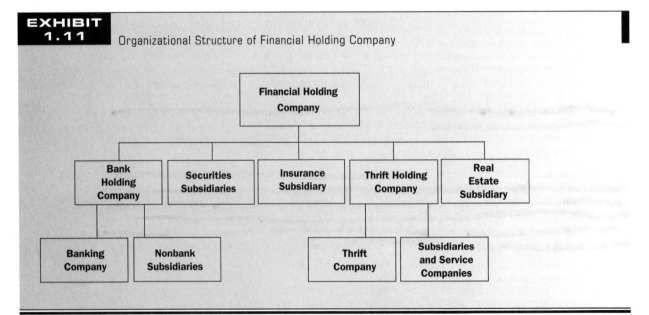

**EXHIBIT 1.11**  Organizational Structure of Financial Holding Company

## EXHIBIT 1.12

### Consolidated Balance Sheet: Citigroup and Subsidiaries

| In millions of dollars | 2004 | 2003 | 2002 |
|---|---|---|---|
| **Assets** | | | |
| Cash and due from banks | $23,556 | $21,149 | $17,326 |
| Deposits at interest with banks | 23,889 | 19,777 | 16,382 |
| Federal funds sold and repurchase agreements | 200,739 | 172,174 | 139,946 |
| Brokerage receivables | 39,273 | 26,476 | 25,358 |
| Trading account assets | 280,167 | 235,319 | 155,208 |
| Investments | 213,243 | 182,892 | 169,513 |
| Loans, net of unearned income | | | |
| Consumer | 435,226 | 379,932 | 337,681 |
| Corporate | 113,603 | 98,074 | 110,124 |
| Loans, net of unearned income | 548,829 | 478,006 | 447,805 |
| Allowance for credit losses | −11,269 | −12,643 | −11,101 |
| Total loans, net | 537,560 | 465,363 | 436,704 |
| Goodwill | 31,992 | 27,581 | 26,961 |
| Intangible assets | 15,271 | 13,881 | 8,509 |
| Reinsurance recoverables | 4,783 | 4,577 | 4,356 |
| Separate and variable accounts | 32,264 | 27,473 | 22,118 |
| Other assets | 81,364 | 67,370 | 75,209 |
| Total assets | $1,484,101 | $1,264,032 | $1,097,590 |
| | | | |
| **Liabilities** | | | |
| Non-interest-bearing deposits in U.S. offices | $31,533 | $30,074 | $29,545 |
| Interest-bearing deposits in U.S. offices | 161,113 | 146,675 | 141,787 |
| Non-interest-bearing deposits in foreign offices | 28,379 | 22,940 | 21,422 |
| Interest-bearing deposits in foreign offices | 341,056 | 274,326 | 238,141 |
| **Total deposits** | 562,081 | 474,015 | 430,895 |
| Federal funds purchased and repurchase agreements | 209,555 | 181,156 | 162,643 |
| Brokerage payables | 50,208 | 37,330 | 22,024 |
| Trading account liabilities | 135,487 | 121,869 | 91,426 |
| Contract holder funds and separate accounts | 68,801 | 58,402 | 49,331 |
| Insurance policy and claims reserves | 19,177 | 17,478 | 16,350 |
| Investment banking and brokerage borrowings | 25,799 | 22,442 | 21,353 |
| Short-term borrowings | 30,968 | 36,187 | 30,629 |
| Long-term debt | 207,910 | 162,702 | 126,927 |
| Other liabilities | 64,824 | 48,380 | 53,142 |
| Citigroup or subsidiary-obligated mandatorily redeemable securities of subsidiary trusts holding solely junior subordinated debt securities of | | | |
| —Parent | — | 5,217 | 4,657 |
| —Subsidiary | — | 840 | 1,495 |
| **Total liabilities** | 1,374,810 | 1,166,018 | 1,010,872 |
| **Stockholders' equity** | | | |
| Preferred stock | 1,125 | 1,125 | 1,400 |
| Common stock | 55 | 55 | 55 |
| Additional paid-in capital | 18,851 | 17,531 | 17,381 |
| Retained earnings | 102,154 | 93,483 | 81,403 |
| Treasury stock | −10,644 | −11,524 | −11,637 |
| Other changes in equity from nonowner sources | −304 | −806 | −193 |
| Unearned compensation | −1,946 | −1,850 | −1,691 |
| **Total stockholders' equity** | 109,291 | 98,014 | 86,718 |
| **Total liabilities and stockholders' equity** | $1,484,101 | $1,264,032 | $1,097,590 |

asset and liability management, loan review, data processing, and business development and may provide debt and equity funding. It also provides strategic planning, project analysis, and financing for nonbank subsidiaries.

The consolidated financial statements of a holding company and its subsidiaries reflect aggregate or consolidate performance. Exhibits 1.12 and 1.13 contain the consolidated balance sheet and income statement for Citigroup and its bank and nonbank subsidiaries. The parent, Citigroup, is a financial holding company that owns a large multitude of bank and nonbank subsidiaries and holding companies. The consolidated balance sheet represents the aggregate

## EXHIBIT 1.13 — Consolidated Income Statement: Citigroup Inc. and Subsidiaries

| In millions of dollars | 2004 | 2003 | 2002 |
|---|---|---|---|
| **Revenues** | | | |
| Loan interest, including fees | $43,981 | $38,110 | $37,903 |
| Other interest and dividends | 22,728 | 18,937 | 21,036 |
| Insurance premiums | 3,993 | 3,749 | 3,410 |
| Commissions and fees | 16,772 | 16,314 | 15,258 |
| Principal transactions | 3,756 | 5,120 | 4,513 |
| Asset management and administration fees | 6,845 | 5,665 | 5,146 |
| Realized gains (losses) from sales of investments | 831 | 510 | −485 |
| Other revenue | 9,370 | 6,308 | 5,775 |
| **Total revenues** | 108,276 | 94,713 | 92,556 |
| **Interest expense** | 22,086 | 17,271 | 21,248 |
| **Total revenues, net of interest expense** | 86,190 | 77,442 | 71,308 |
| **Benefits, claims, and credit losses** | | | |
| Policyholder benefits and claims | 3,801 | 3,895 | 3,478 |
| Provision for credit losses | 6,233 | 8,046 | 9,995 |
| **Total benefits, claims, and credit losses** | 10,034 | 11,941 | 13,473 |
| **Operating expenses** | | | |
| Non-insurance compensation and benefits | 23,707 | 21,288 | 18,650 |
| Net occupancy expense | 4,847 | 4,280 | 4,005 |
| Technology/communications expense | 3,586 | 3,414 | 3,139 |
| Insurance underwriting, acquisition, and operating | 1,234 | 1,063 | 992 |
| Restructuring-related items | −5 | −46 | −15 |
| Other operating expenses | 18,605 | 9,169 | 10,527 |
| **Total operating expenses** | 51,974 | 39,168 | 37,298 |
| **Income from continuing operations before income taxes, minority interest, and cumulative effect of accounting changes** | 24,182 | 26,333 | 20,537 |
| Provision for income taxes | 6,909 | 8,195 | 6,998 |
| Minority interest, net of income taxes | 227 | 285 | 91 |
| **Income from continuing operations before cumulative effect of accounting changes** | 17,046 | 17,853 | 13,448 |
| **Discontinued operations** | — | — | 965 |
| Income from discontinued operations | | | |
| Gain on sale of stock by subsidiary | — | — | 1,270 |
| Provision for income taxes | — | — | 360 |
| **Income from discontinued operations, net** | — | — | 1,875 |
| **Cumulative effect of accounting changes, net** | — | — | −47 |
| **Net income** | $17,046 | $17,853 | $15,276 |

ownership of the individual assets of the subsidiaries while the income statement is a compilation of income and expense sources of Citigroup and its subsidiaries. In practice, the parent company (Citigroup.) acts somewhat as a clearing company and will even purchase loans (investments and advances) from a bank subsidiary (Citibank) when a credit exceeds the maximum legal loan size permitted a single member bank. (With a bank the size of Citibank, this will rarely happen.) These loan participations may be distributed to other banks in the holding company or kept by the parent. Finally, the parent advances funds to subsidiaries through the purchase of notes and receivables or equity. The equity investment represents the value of subsidiary stock at the time of purchase. These assets are financed by short-term debt, long-term debt, and bank holding company stockholders.

While the consolidated financial statements of a holding company and its subsidiaries reflect aggregate performance, it is useful to examine the parent company's statements alone. Exhibit 1.14 contains the *parent company only* income statement. Note that the net income figure is the same as that of Exhibit 1.13 but the information is presented from the parent's ownership view. The parent's (Citigroup) net income is derived from dividends, interest, management fees from equity in bank and nonbank subsidiaries in excess of operating expenses, interest paid on holding company debt, and other revenues. The parent company also reports equity in undistributed income of subsidiaries. Subsidiary accounting requires the parent company to declare, as income, the unrealized gains in the equity of a consolidated subsidiary regardless of whether the income is actually paid (distributed) to the par-

Citigroup Inc.'s Parent Company Only Income Statement (Millions of Dollars)

| Operating income | 2004 | 2003 |
|---|---|---|
| Income from bank subsidiaries | | |
|   Dividends | $ — | $ — |
|   Interest | $ — | $ — |
|   Other | $ 15 | $ 15 |
| Income from nonbank subsidiaries | | |
|   Dividends | $ 2,874 | $ 1,805 |
|   Interest | $ 235 | $ 87 |
|   Other | $ 85 | $ 54 |
| Income from subsidiary bank holding companies | | |
|   Dividends | $ 4,629 | $ 4,210 |
|   Interest | $ 1,988 | $ 1,606 |
|   Other | $ 17 | $ 5,816 |
|  All other operating income | $ 119 | $ 310 |
|  Total operating income | $ 9,962 | $ 8,155 |
| **Total operating expense** | $ 2,847 | $ 2,216 |
| Income (loss) before taxes and undistributed income | $ 7,115 | $ 5,939 |
| Applicable income taxes | $ (290) | $ (33) |
| Extraordinary items, net of tax effect | $ — | $ — |
| Income (loss) before undistributed income of subsidiaries | $ 7,405 | $ 5,972 |
| Equity in undistributed income (losses) of subsidiaries | | |
|  Bank | $ — | $ — |
|  Nonbank | $(2,637) | $ 2,550 |
|  Subsidiary bank holding companies | $12,278 | $ 9,331 |
| Net income | $17,046 | $17,853 |

ent. The bulk of the Citigroup's $17.046 billion in net income in 2004 came from its banking activities, including income from bank subsidiaries and subsidiary bank holding companies.

The parent typically pays very little in income tax (Citigroup actually received a tax benefit) because 80 percent of the dividends from subsidiaries is exempt. Taxable income from the remaining 20 percent and interest income is small (or less than) relative to deductible expenses. Under IRS provisions, each subsidiary actually pays taxes quarterly on its taxable income. With a consolidated tax return, however, the parent company can use taxable income from its subsidiaries to offset its loss. Thus, the parent could report a noncash tax benefit representing the reclamation of tax overpayments by subsidiaries. The final item before net income represents the holding company's claim to $2.6 billion in losses from non-bank subsidiaries and $12.3 billion in subsidiary income subsidiary bank holding companies respectively, that was not paid out as dividends.

Finally, Exhibit 1.15 represents financial data for Citigroup's FDIC-insured bank and thrift subsidiaries, not including nondeposit subsidiaries or parent companies. Citigroup owns several banks, both national and state chartered as well as federal savings banks. At year-end 2004, Citigroup controlled almost $800 billion in total assets through bank and thrift subsidiaries.

**NONBANK ACTIVITIES PERMITTED BANK HOLDING COMPANIES.** The Fed similarly regulates allowable nonbank activities that are "closely related to banking" in which bank holding companies may acquire subsidiaries. Restrictions came about for three reasons. First, it was feared that large financial conglomerates would control the financial system because they would have a competitive advantage. Second, there was concern that banks would require customers to buy nonbank services in order to obtain loans. Third, some critics simply did not believe that bank holding companies should engage in businesses that were not allowed banks because these businesses were less regulated and thus relatively risky.

Under amendments to the Bank Holding Company Act of 1956, the Federal Reserve allows banks to offer a wide range of services "closely related to banking" anywhere in the United States. Most of these activities relate to the extension of specific types of loans, underwriting and brokerage services, consulting services, general management services, and data processing. The largest bank holding companies must report to the Federal Reserve annually regarding the performance of their nonbank subsidiaries. The Gramm-Leach-Bliley Act allows national bank subsidiaries to sell all types of insurance, including title insurance, and affiliates may underwrite or sell all types of insurance including title insurance. The act, however, left the state general authority to regulate insurance activities and hence national banks are restricted in the types of insurance activities in which they may engage. Due to

**EXHIBIT 1.15** Financial Data for All FDIC-Insured Bank and Thrift Subsidiaries of Citigroup Inc.

| Bank Holding Company Name | City | State | Class* | Domestic Deposits† | Total Assets† |
|---|---|---|---|---|---|
| CITIGROUP INC. | New York | NY | HC | 180,752,109 | 795,941,998 |
| **Bank and thrift subsidiaries of the bank holding company:** | | | | | |
| Citibank, National Association | New York City | NY | N | 113,879,000 | 582,123,000 |
| Citibank (West), FSB | San Francisco | CA | SA | 34,508,773 | 82,089,034 |
| Citibank (South Dakota), N.A. | Sioux Falls | SD | N | 1,531,715 | 56,549,931 |
| Citibank, Federal Savings Bank | Reston | VA | SA | 19,204,271 | 24,659,500 |
| Citibank (Nevada), National Association | Las Vegas | NV | N | 5,768,414 | 18,973,997 |
| Citicorp Trust Bank, FSB | Newark | DE | SA | 1,376,926 | 17,022,330 |
| Citibank (Delaware) | New Castle | DE | NM | 1,466,190 | 6,285,165 |
| Citibank USA, National Association | Sioux Falls | SD | N | 1,120,018 | 5,508,389 |
| California Commerce Bank | Century City | CA | NM | 1,382,917 | 1,874,749 |
| Universal Financial Corp. | Salt Lake City | UT | NM | 285,833 | 523,234 |
| Associates Capital Bank, Inc. | Salt Lake City | UT | NM | 228,052 | 332,669 |

*The class or type of organization is represented by:

**HC** = holding company

**N** = commercial bank, national (federal) charter and Fed member

**NM** = commercial bank, state charter and Fed nonmember

**SA** = savings associations, federal charter

†thousands of dollars

the fact that national banks can be owned by a financial holding company, which can engage in all types of insurance activities, this distinction seems one of administrative complication rather than one of restricting activities.

Interestingly, the 1998 merger between Citicorp and Travelers that created Citigroup was not permissible at the time the merger was approved. Prior to the passage of the Gramm-Leach-Bliley Act in 1999, Citigroup would have had between two and five years to divest itself of Travelers' insurance underwriting. Citigroup formed a financial holding company under the provisions of the Gramm-Leach-Bliley Act and created its integrated financial services company engaged in investment services, asset management, life insurance and property casualty insurance, and consumer lending. Its operating companies include Salomon Smith Barney, Salomon Smith Barney Asset Management, Travelers Life & Annuity, Primerica Financial Services, Travelers Property Casualty Corporation, and Commercial Credit. Citigroup, with all its entities, engages in a wide range of businesses throughout the world. In 2002, Citigroup sold Travelers Property Casualty but retained other units of Travelers, which it then announced it would sell in 2005.

## MERGERS, CONSOLIDATIONS, NEW CHARTERS, AND BANK FAILURES

By combining operations, most banks can offer the same or better quality of service, a broader list of products and services, and at lower costs. Research, however, generally shows that economies of scale in banking are reached at a relatively small firm size; for example, for banks with up to $1 billion in assets. Large size is thus not justified strictly on the basis of lower unit production costs. Larger size, however, increases market share and market power, the efficiency of offering a larger product line, visibility, and brand equity.

Too many resources under one firm's control, however, may adversely affect pricing and credit availability. Regulators, therefore, closely monitor bank expansion through mergers and acquisitions, consolidations and new charters. The intent is to protect consumers from undue concentration of banking resources and to provide for the efficient delivery of services. A different regulatory agency must approve each merger, depending on the classification of the surviving bank. National banks are approved by the OCC, state member banks by the Federal Reserve, state nonmember insured banks by the FDIC, and uninsured nonmembers by the appropriate state authority. In terms of banking capacity, there are too many banks.

Historically, regulators applied strict criteria when evaluating potential anticompetitive effects. They would define the geographic market in which the acquired firm operated, determine the number of direct competitors, and calculate concentration measures that indicated the degree of control by the combined firm versus all competitors. Because commercial banks were viewed as the only direct competitors, bank mergers and acquisitions were frequently denied if the acquiring firm already had a presence in the market. In the current environment, however, the criteria are much more flexible. Other depository institutions and nonbank financial institutions are included

*Efficient and Competitive Financial System*

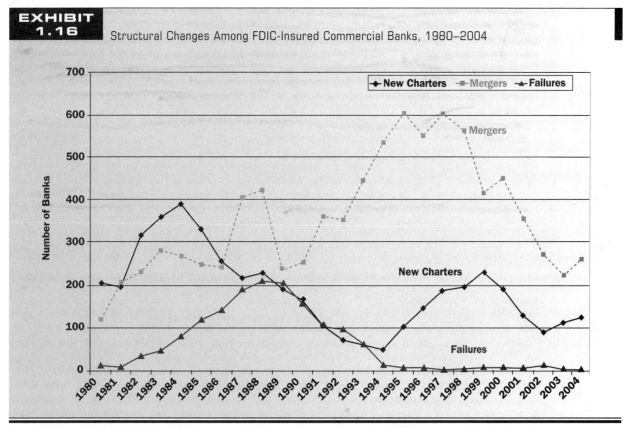

**EXHIBIT 1.16** Structural Changes Among FDIC-Insured Commercial Banks, 1980–2004

SOURCE: FDIC Quaterly Banking Profile: www.fdic.gov

as competitors. The relevant geographic market now includes a much broader area, which lowers the degree of concentration and makes it easier to approve an acquisition.[13] Regulators seem to agree that expansion via merger and acquisition is necessary to improve the safety and soundness of the nation's banking system. It is also easier to regulate a smaller number of distinct firms.

Structural changes within the commercial banking industry are documented in Exhibit 1.16. The major force behind consolidation has been mergers and acquisitions in which existing banks combine operations in order to cut costs, improve profitability, and increase their competitive position. There were at least two significant changes in the regulatory environment during the later part the twentieth century that were primary drivers of the increased merger activity. One was the relaxation of branching restrictions, which allowed banks to consolidate banks into branches, and the other was deregulation of the types of products and services bank could offer, allowing banks to merge outside of traditional banking markets. States began relaxing branching restrictions in the late 1980s and 1990s and mergers peaked in the late 1990s as the Riegle-Neal Interstate Banking and Branching Efficiency Act mandated nationwide interstate branching. During the 1990s, banks also began finding ways around Glass-Steagall, the separation of commercial banking, investment banking and insurance, using a provision of the Glass-Steagall (Section 20 companies) that allow for banks to enter into investment banking activities so long as they were not "principally engaged." They expanded into discount brokerage, mutual funds, derivative securities, and other fields where appropriate to generate fee income and thus diversify from a reliance on interest income.

Today, the pace of mergers and acquisitions largely reflects stock market values. When buyers experience rising stock prices, they make more acquisitions as their 'currency' appears to be more highly regarded. Also, the Basel II change in capital requirements should stimulate mergers, particularly because the largest firms that use internal risk assessment systems will see their required capital fall. Other banks will become targets because they will operate with what the largest banks believe is excess capital.

---

[13] When evaluating anticompetitive effects during the 1980s, the Federal Reserve used the Herfindahl-Hirschmann Index (HHI) to measure market concentration. The HHI is computed by identifying the appropriate market, then summing the squares of each competitor's market share. For example, three competing firms with market shares of 50 percent, 30 percent, and 20 percent would produce an index of 3,800 (2,500+900+400). To be guaranteed approval, the HHI after a merger or acquisition must be no greater than 1,800 and/or cause the HHI to increase by 200. Since 1990, regulators have been much more lenient in approving transactions that violate this standard.

It is also interesting to note that as mergers increased, so did the formation of new banks. New charters representing the start-up of a new bank's operations declined from 1984 to 1994, increased through 1998, and then decreased through 2002, somewhat following merger activity. New charters again picked up in 2003–2004 as economic conditions improved. Almost all of the new charters were community banks that specialized in small business lending. Bankers who either lose their jobs in a merger or choose not to work for a large banking organization often find investors to put up the capital needed to start a new bank. Many larger banks specialize in large company lending and transactions-oriented business, which purportedly leaves a void in the market—lending to small business.

Note also the sharp increase in the number of failed banks from 1980 through 1988 with a gradual decrease to zero failures in 1996. With the exception of ten commercial banks' failures in 2002, total annual failures have been in the low single digits since 1995. Interestingly, data for the 1980s period actually understate the true number of failures because regulators often arranged mergers during this period rather than simply close failed banks and savings institutions. The sharp increase in failures during this period coincides with economic problems throughout various sectors of the U.S. economy ranging from agriculture to energy to real estate. As regional economies faltered, problem loans grew at banks and thrifts that were overextended and subsequent losses forced closings.

## CONSUMER PROTECTION

State legislatures and the Federal Reserve have implemented numerous laws and regulations to protect the rights of individuals who try to borrow. The purposes are wide ranging, varying from restricting deceptive advertising or trade practices to prohibiting discrimination. Exhibit 1.4 lists the broad areas in which the Federal Reserve has established regulations, including those of consumer regulations. Regs. B, C, E, M, S, V, Z, AA, BB, and DD apply specifically to consumer regulation. Equal credit opportunity (Reg. B), for example, makes it illegal for any lender to discriminate against a borrower on the basis of race, sex, marital status, religion, age, or national origin. It establishes guidelines for structuring loan applications and specifies how information can be used in making credit decisions. Community reinvestment prohibits redlining in which lenders as a matter of policy do not lend in certain geographic markets. Chapter 12 summarizes the key federal regulations as they pertain to consumer borrowing. Reg. Z requires disclosure of effective rates of interest, total interest paid, the total of all payments, as well as full disclosure as to why a customer was denied credit.

## TRENDS IN FEDERAL LEGISLATION AND REGULATION[14]

Legislation prior to the 1970s focused on limiting geographic and product expansion while restricting prices (interest rates) banks could charge on loans, and pay on their deposits. The fundamental focus of federal banking legislation and regulation since 1970 has been to better define and expand the product and geographic markets served by depository institutions, and to increase competition. Subsequent problems with failed savings and loans and commercial banks raised concerns that only a few large organizations would survive because all financial institutions would eventually have the same powers and large firms would drive small firms out of business. Today, the banking and financial services industry is evolving into a new and more exciting industry full of challenges and opportunities. Smaller banks appear to have opportunities in providing specialized products and services. Larger banks have expanded their product mix and have all but eliminated the distinction between a bank, securities firm, and insurance company.

Key legislative and regulatory changes have attempted to address these basic issues: What is a bank? Where can banks conduct business? What products can banks offer and what interest rates may they charge or pay? Significant regulatory developments are identified in the following section, with particular attention paid to the Depository Institutions Deregulation and Monetary Control Act (DIDMCA) of 1980, the Garn-St. Germain Depository Institutions Act (GSG) of 1982, the Riegle-Neal Interstate Banking and Branching Efficiency Act of 1994, and the Financial Services Modernization Act (Gramm-Leach-Bliley Act of 1999) which are credited with accelerating changes in the current banking environment, facilitating the thrift and banking crisis, and in stabilizing the deposit insurance funds.

---

[14]See the appendix for details regarding key regulations.

## KEY FEDERAL LEGISLATION: 1970–1993

Legislation of the late 1970s and early 1980s focused on the deregulation of pricing and products within the banking system. The **Depository Institutions Deregulation and Monetary Control Act (DIDMCA) of 1980** removed interest rate ceilings and authorized banks and savings institutions to pay interest on checking accounts through the use of negotiable orders of withdrawal (NOW) Accounts." By the early 1980s, regulation was sidetracked by bills designed to assist the beleaguered S&L industry and to ensure that commercial banks did not succumb to the same fate. The **Depository Institutions Act of 1982** (also know as Garn-St. Germain) expanded FDIC powers to assist troubled banks and established the Net Worth Certificate program for savings and loans to assist these institutions in acquiring needed capital. The act authorized money market deposit accounts to allow banks and thrifts to compete with products offered by brokerage firms, such as Merrill Lynch's Cash Management Account. The act also expanded the powers of thrift institutions in a misguided attempt at allowing these institutions to "earn" their way out of their financial problems. Many have suggested that these additional authorities, such as direct investments into real estate, created more problems and losses during the 1980s for thrift institutions.

Regulation subsequently returned to deregulation of the banking industry, allowing new brokerage, underwriting, and insurance powers on a limited basis. With the rolling recession of the late 1980s and early 1990s, many commercial banks throughout the United States suffered severe asset-quality problems leading to numerous failures. The **Competitive Equality Banking Act of 1987** recapitalized the Federal Savings and Loan Insurance Corporation (FSLIC) and expanded the FDIC's authority for open bank assistance transactions.

Problems in the savings and loan industry persisted and the late 1980s and early 1990s saw legislation designed to solve the leftover problems from the S&L crisis, as well as address commercial bank asset-quality and capital problems. Congress passed the **Financial Institutions Reform, Recovery and Enforcement Act of 1989** with the primary purpose of restoring public confidence in the savings and loan industry. It abolished the FSLIC and placed the FDIC in charge of insurance of the industry and created two insurance funds, the Bank Insurance Fund (BIF) and the Savings Association Insurance Fund (SAIF). The act also abolished the Federal Home Loan Bank Board and created the Office of Thrift Supervision (OTS) and the Resolution Trust Corporation (RTC), which was to manage and dispose of the assets of failed institutions. The act further established severe penalties for bank boards and management for their actions or failure of action. Congress also passed the **Federal Deposit Insurance Corporation Improvement Act of 1991** which greatly increased the powers and authority of the FDIC, recapitalized the Bank Insurance Fund and allowed the FDIC to borrow from the Treasury. The act mandated a least-cost method and *prompt corrective action* for dealing with failing banks, as well as establishing new capital requirements for banks.

Accounting standards during the 1980s meant that the significant increases in interest rates during the 1980s left long-term assets, such as mortgages, significantly overvalued on the books of savings and loans. The Financial Accounting Standards Board issued **FASB 115** in 1993 to addresses the market value accounting of all investments in equity securities that have readily determinable fair values, and all investments in debt securities. Investments subject to the standard are classified in three categories:

1. *Held-to-maturity securities.* Debt securities that the institution has the positive intent and ability to hold to maturity are classified as held-to-maturity securities and reported at historical (amortized) cost.

2. *Trading account securities.* Debt and equity securities that are bought and held primarily for the purpose of selling (or trading) them in the near term. Trading securities are reported at fair value, with unrealized gains and losses including in earnings (net income).

3. *Available-for-sale securities.* Debt and equity securities not classified as either held-to-maturity securities or trading securities. Available-for-sale securities are reported at fair value, with unrealized gains and losses excluded from earnings but reported as a net amount in a separate component of shareholders' equity.

One potential weakness of FASB 115 is that it does not apply to loans, including mortgage loans that have not been securitized (sold in the secondary market).

## KEY FEDERAL LEGISLATION: 1994–2000

By the mid-1990s, legislation again turned to deregulation of the financial services industry (note we did not use the term "banking industry"), both in geographic scope as well as product lines and types of permissible activities. The **Riegle-Neal Interstate Banking and Branching Efficiency Act of 1994** permits adequately capitalized bank holding companies to acquire banks in any state. The **Gramm-Leach-Bliley Act of 1999** repealed the Glass-Steagall Act and modified the Bank Holding Company Act to create a new **financial holding company** authorized to engage in underwriting and selling insurance and securities, conducting both commercial and merchant banking, investing in and developing real estate, and other activities "complementary" to banking. The act also restricts the disclosure of nonpublic customer information, requires disclosure of a *privacy policy,* as well as provides a new funding source for some banks by easing membership and collateral requirements to access funds from the Federal

Home Loan Bank (FHLB). The 1990s ended with unprecedented merger and consolidation activities as holding companies consolidated separate banks into branches and acquired new lines of business, including investment underwriting and insurance.

## KEY FEDERAL LEGISLATION: 2001–2004

The beginning of the twenty-first century started with an economic recession, the terrorist events of September 11, 2001, and widespread corporate scandals. These events have not only had a dramatic impact upon the legislation of the early 2000s but also upon the lives of just about everyone in the world. In 2001, Congress passed the International Money Laundering Abatement and Financial Anti-Terrorism Act, also known as Title III of the **USA Patriot Act**, designed to prevent terrorists and others from using the U.S. financial system to move funds to support illegal activity. The act specifically required financial institutions to keep additional records and establish anti–money laundering programs. Congress passed the **Sarbanes-Oxley Act** in 2002, which established the Public Company Oversight Board to regulate public accounting firms that audit publicly-traded companies. It specifically addresses issues of conflicts among company executives, accounting firms and their affiliates, as well as requires CEOs and CFOs to certify the annual and quarterly reports of publicly-traded companies. The act also established many required policies and procedures in the area of corporate governance for the boards of publicly-traded companies.

## CURRENT UNRESOLVED REGULATORY ISSUES

It is interesting to note that the restrictions of geographic and product scope in the banking industry have only recently been removed. The trend today is toward greater competition and market determination of prices, available services, and allowing institutions to fail. Bank regulation is continuously evolving in response to economic and competitive conditions. During the early 2000s, many issues were under debate regarding the future structure and operating environment of financial services institutions. Key facets of the debate are identified below, with the topics discussed in greater detail throughout the book.

**CAPITAL ADEQUACY.** The adequacy of bank capital levels is constantly debated. During the 1980s, when bank and thrift failures soared, capital levels were generally considered inadequate, especially at larger institutions. Effective in 1992, banks and thrifts were subject to minimum capital requirements designed to reduce the overall risk of the banking industry. These standards, however, were based on the minimum levels of equity on the general default riskiness of bank assets. Today, Basel I and the new proposed Basel II capital standards require equity capital based on the riskiness of financial institutions' assets. In addition, the FDIC now charges insurance premiums based on bank capital levels.

In 1998, a large hedge fund, Long Term Capital Management, effectively failed because it assumed considerable risk. Large foreign and U.S. commercial and investment banks were heavily exposed to the firm because they had loaned substantial amounts of funds to the firm for it to use as it chose. It was clear, after the firm ran into problems, that the banks had not monitored their risk exposure well. This series of events was repeated with Enron's failure in late 2001. Banks, as well as other lenders and investment bankers, entered into a wide array of contracts with Enron including partnerships in questionable special-purpose vehicles (SPVs) designed to move debt off Enron's balance sheet. When Enron failed, firms like JPMorgan Chase and Citigroup recorded losses of approximately $3 billion and $1 billion, respectively. These new types of firms, as well as an increased use of off-balance sheet activities, have prompted bank regulators to want to increase minimum capital requirements, especially when they do not have other means to monitor or control bank risk taking.

Regulators have followed the "capital is king" approach during the late 1990s and 2000s. Well-capitalized banks have been allowed to expand the range of products they offer—including establishing affiliates that can underwrite and deal in securities. Well-capitalized banks' regulatory burdens are lessened as well. Since the amount of capital needed is related to the degree of risk and types of activities in which banks engage, the difficulty is in identifying which firms are truly well capitalized and which firms need additional capital. Hence, the debate regarding how much capital is enough continues today. As banks enter into new product lines and nontraditional business activities, the concern of regulators is that the FDIC may be underwriting additional risks not covered by a bank's capital position. Regulators would like to increase the minimum requirement because it reduces the likelihood of failure. Bankers, in contrast, argue that it is expensive and difficult to obtain additional equity, and high requirements restrict their competitiveness.

The ramifications of greater capital requirements are enormous. First, equity is more expensive than debt because interest payments are deductible to the bank while dividends on stock are not. It is thus costly to issue new stock. Second, the majority of banks do not have ready access to the equity market and most banks subsequently find it extremely difficult to add capital externally. Small banks' stocks are simply not broadly traded. Banks that need capital must rely either on retaining earnings or finding a merger partner. Thus, the final impact is that increased capital requirements restrict growth and make it difficult to compete as a small entity, leading to consolidation. The net effect will be increasingly larger firms. The largest banks, however, have found access to equity

## CONTEMPORARY ISSUES

### MORAL HAZARD AND REDUCED MARKET DISCIPLINE: DEPOSIT INSURANCE

Prior to the Depository Institutions Deregulation and Monetary Control Act (DIDMCA) of 1980, federal deposit insurance amounted to $40,000 per account. Due at least in part to the efforts of the U.S. League of Savings Institutions, the savings and loan association lobbying arm, and the chairman of the

House Banking Committee, Fernand St. Germain, Congress raised coverage to $100,000 with little debate. The effect, however, was monumental and immediate. Brokerage houses quickly negotiated deals with aggressive thrifts and banks to sell certificates of deposit in $100,000 blocks to interested investors anywhere in the world. Because the principal was fully federally insured, an investor did not have to worry about the bank or issuer defaulting—the insurance (the U.S. Treasury) would pay. To attract funds, a bank or thrift needed only to pay a rate that was slightly above the prevailing market rate. Unfortunately, there were no controls on the banks and thrifts by either the regulatory authorities or the market regarding how to invest the funds. As later performance revealed, many of these institutions speculated on real estate or simply frittered the money away. Thrift managers were essentially playing with the government's (taxpayer's) money. Thrift failures alone cost taxpayers an estimated $150 billion.

markets much quicker, easier, and cheaper. Capital-rich firms have market power to purchase capital-deficient firms relatively inexpensively.

**DEPOSIT INSURANCE REFORM.** While FDIC insurance protects consumers from bank failure it simultaneously creates a moral hazard issue and removes some market discipline. The structure of deposit insurance during the 1980s clearly contributed to the high rate of failures and huge cost of the thrift bailout. For example, in the past, regulators have not allowed the largest commercial banks to fail. In 1991 the Bank of New England, with $22 billion in assets, failed and all depositors were fully protected. When large banks have gotten into trouble, regulators have arranged mergers or acquisitions and effectively protected depositors who held balances in excess of $100,000. Thus, federal deposit insurance was extended to all depositors regardless of their balances. This clearly removes market discipline in which investors (depositors) in a company would examine the riskiness of the firm prior to investing. With FDIC insurance, depositors are more concerned with the safety of the FDIC and its policies rather than the underlying risk of the financial company. In contrast, small banks are routinely allowed to fail and uninsured depositors lose a portion of their uninsured balance. Isn't this discriminatory? Why are large banks not allowed to fail? FDICIA altered this, effective in 1995, because regulators are not allowed to protect uninsured depositors of large banks at failure unless this is shown to be the least costly method.

The ongoing debate today concerns the appropriate amount of insurance, as well as its structure, purpose, and cost. FDIC insurance coverage has remained at $100,000 since 1980. With inflation, should the ceiling not be increased? Higher coverage, however, increases moral hazard problems, as fewer depositors are concerned with the true risk of the bank. On the other hand, the original purpose of insurance was to insure the small depositor; hence, should the amount of insurance not be reduced? If it truly is insurance, shouldn't premiums paid reflect the bank's risk and thus probability of failure? FDICIA required the FDIC to assess insurance premiums based on a bank's risk but almost 99 percent of all banks, as of December 2004, were considered well capitalized and hence pay no insurance premiums. If the regulators will not allow the largest banks to fail, shouldn't insurance premiums be based on total deposits, including both foreign and domestic deposits? Finally, as financial institutions enter into new business lines, does this not change their business model as well as appropriate capital requirements? Should banks be able to use insured deposits to fund additional lines of business they have traditionally not had the authority to enter?

**NONBANK FINANCIAL SERVICES COMPANIES.** During 1998, Long-Term Capital Management, a U.S.-based hedge fund managed by well-known bankers, with two Nobel Prize winners as part of the management team, effectively failed and was bailed out by a consortium of financial institutions. The Fed helped arrange the bailout. Similar issues arose when Enron, the world's largest natural gas distributor and pipeline company, filed for bankruptcy in December 2001. Enron had effectively become a financial intermediary by trading oil, gas, and weather futures as well as other financial products, rather than a holder of hard, physical assets. In essence, it was a hedge fund. The ongoing debate is whether these types of financial firms should disclose more information so that investors are aware of a fund's risk exposure as well as whether these firms should be regulated. More importantly, should banks that lend to these funds be forced to operate with additional capital? The debate on whether nonbanks, such as Wal-Mart, should be allowed to own and operate a bank continues to push the envelope of the type of activities banking companies, or their holding companies, can or should engage in. Finally, the debate on the growth of large credit unions with their tax-exempt status and their entry into business lending, brings forth the question of taxation equality, as well as the continuing issue of a level playing field for financial services companies.

**NEW POWERS.** Banks are continually pressing for additional investment powers and the opportunity to enter new lines of business. Many banks, for example, would like to offer full lines of securities and insurance products and be regulated to a lesser degree as securities firms are. But as banks move into new lines of business, the adequacy of their capital and the use of insured deposits funding these activities will be debated. It is ironic that with all the new powers granted to banks at the end of the 1990s, they were still not allowed to offer interest on business checking accounts through 2004. Investment firms, however, could offer "sweep" accounts that effectively allow them to pay interest on business accounts. Although banks can offer sweep accounts, they must sweep business accounts out of FDIC insured deposits. This effectively means that they must sweep them to investment firms, or start their own mutual fund!

## BANKING BUSINESS MODELS

When people think of banks, many think of the largest U.S. institutions, such as Bank of America, JPMorgan Chase, Citibank, Wachovia, and Wells Fargo. When examining the data contained in Exhibit 1.17, one might not realize that of the 7,630 commercial banks operating in the United States at the end of 2004, only 85 have more

---

**EXHIBIT 1.17**  Distribution of the Number of Banks and Total Assets by Total Assets, 1995–2004

| | Number of Banks | Number of Banks, Year-End Assets Size | | | |
|---|---|---|---|---|---|
| | | < $100 M | $100M–$1B | $1B–$10B | > $10B |
| **1995** | 10,242 | 7,123 | 2,741 | 331 | 63 |
| | | (69.55%) | (26.76%) | (3.23%) | (0.62%) |
| **1997** | 9,451 | 6,147 | 2,900 | 331 | 73 |
| | | (65.04%) | (30.68%) | (3.50%) | (0.77%) |
| **1999** | 8,580 | 5,157 | 3,029 | 318 | 76 |
| | | (60.10%) | (35.30%) | (3.71%) | (0.89%) |
| **2001** | 8,080 | 4,486 | 3,194 | 320 | 80 |
| | | (55.52%) | (39.53%) | (3.96%) | (0.99%) |
| **2003** | 7,769 | 3,911 | 3,434 | 341 | 83 |
| | | (50.34%) | (44.20%) | (4.39%) | (1.07%) |
| **2004** | 7,630 | 3,655 | 3,530 | 360 | 85 |
| | | (47.90%) | (46.26%) | (4.72%) | (1.11%) |

| | Total Assets | Total Assets ($billions), Year-End Assets Size | | | |
|---|---|---|---|---|---|
| | | < $100 M | $100M–$1B | $1B–$10B | > $10B |
| **1995** | $4,116 | $310 | $668 | $1,077 | $2,061 |
| | | (7.54%) | (16.22%) | (26.17%) | (50.07%) |
| **1997** | $4,642 | $277 | $711 | $995 | $2,658 |
| | | (5.97%) | (15.32%) | (21.45%) | (57.27%) |
| **1999** | $5,735 | $243 | $755 | $915 | $3,823 |
| | | (4.23%) | (13.16%) | (15.96%) | (66.65%) |
| **2001** | $6,569 | $222 | $819 | $915 | $4,613 |
| | | (3.37%) | (12.47%) | (13.93%) | (70.22%) |
| **2003** | $7,603 | $201 | $910 | $947 | $5,545 |
| | | (2.64%) | (11.97%) | (12.46%) | (72.93%) |
| **2004** | $8,413 | $189 | $953 | $973 | $6,297 |
| | | (2.25%) | (11.33%) | (11.57%) | (74.85%) |

SOURCE: FDIC, Quarterly Banking Profile.

Note: Values in parentheses are percent of total.

than $10 billion in assets. In turn, approximately 94 percent have less than $1 billion in assets with a legal lending limit of less than $10 million. Even more surprising to some is that more than 50 percent of banks are small, with less than $100 million in total assets and a legal lending limit of approximately $1 million or less. Still, the largest banks (over $10 billion) hold almost 75 percent of total bank assets and follow business models far different than those of smaller banks. Banks with less than $1 billion in assets are generally called community banks, while larger banks are labeled large holding company banks, multibank holding companies, or even money center banks. Banks of the same size, however, often pursue substantially different strategies, competing in different geographic markets with different products and services. Today, we separate the business model structure of banks into five categories determined by size and geographic market penetration:

- Global banks: for example, Citibank and JPMorgan Chase
- Nationwide banks: for example, Bank of America, Wells Fargo
- Super regional banks: for example, SunTrust, Wachovia Bank
- Regional banks: for examle, banks operating primarily in a limited number of states
- Specialty banks (community banks): your local bank, "First National *Hometown*"

The business model of *global banks* is to have a large international presence. The United States has few global banks because restrictive banking laws and domestic economic opportunities have constrained many banks from venturing overseas in any significant way. Those that have extensive global activities include Citigroup, JPMorgan Chase, Bank of America, State Street Bank and Trust Company, and Bank of New York, and their activities range far beyond traditional lending and deposit gathering. Obviously, there are many global banks that operate primarily outside the U.S. Among the best known are the Royal Bank of Scotland, HBSC, and Deutsche Bank.

The 1998 merger between NationsBank and Bank of America, now Bank of America, created the first true *nationwide bank* with a coast-to-coast presence. The original Bank of America had operations in almost all 50 states and a dominant position in the key banking states of California, Texas, and Florida where growth is strong and the population includes a high percentage of retirees and wealthy individuals who buy fee-based banking services. Wells Fargo and Washington Mutual are also considered nationwide banks.

*Super regional banks* have extensive operations in a limited geographic region of the United States. They exist today as a direct result of interstate branching restrictions. Prior to the enactment of the Riegle-Neal Interstate Banking and Branching Efficiency Act of 1994, interstate branching was only allowed to the degree that states formed reciprocal pacts. A typical state law allowed out-of-state banks to buy banks in the home state if in-state banks were allowed to buy banks in those states. The intent was to allow in-state banks to grow and prevent large New York City and Chicago banks from entering the state. Super regional banks continue to expand their activities by entering businesses such as investment banking and insurance by acquiring regional firms. These banks include firms such as AmSouth, Wachovia, Fleet Financial, SouthTrust, Regions Bank, and U.S. Trust, among others.

*Regional banks* are similar to super regional banks except that their scope is more limited geographically and in terms of products or services. They typically operate banks in one or a few contiguous states. Finally, *specialty banks* are generally independent or community banks that specialize in a limited region or limited product line. Smaller specialty banks are often part of a one-bank holding company and may operate branches, but are most often linked closely with a single community in which the bank is located or they offer a limited range of products. Many bankers view community banks as synonymous with independent banks. The vast majority of banks in the United States would be considered specialty (community or independent) banks.

## SPECIALTY BANKS (COMMUNITY BANKS)

The term **independent bank** normally refers to a bank that is not controlled by a multibank holding company or any other outside interest. A **community bank** is generally a bank that operates primarily in, or has ties to, one community. Most stock analysts designate community banks as those with less than $1 billion in assets. In the banking industry, the terms independent bank and community bank are often used interchangeably which sometimes leads to confusion. Consider a community bank that is not part of a holding company. Its general organizational form will follow the outline of Exhibit 1.18. The structure can and does vary but generally consists of five levels of responsibilities and reporting.

At the top of the organizational structure is the bank's board of directors, which oversees the entire operation of the bank. There are two types of directors: inside and outside or independent directors.[15] Inside members often consist of the bank's chief executive officer (CEO), president, and sometimes the senior lending officer. Outside members of the board of directors are not bank employees, are generally key business leaders in the community, and often are significant bank customers and even bank stockholders. The primary role of directors is to represent and serve stockholders who are the owners of the bank. A secondary role is to represent customers and employees. Directors use their expertise to oversee the broad direction of the bank, solve problems, and make decisions

[15]Technically speaking, Sarbanes-Oxley defines an "independent" director as one who does not work for the firm, and does not have significant stock ownership or material relationship with the firm.

## EXHIBIT 1.18  Organizational Structure of an Independent Bank

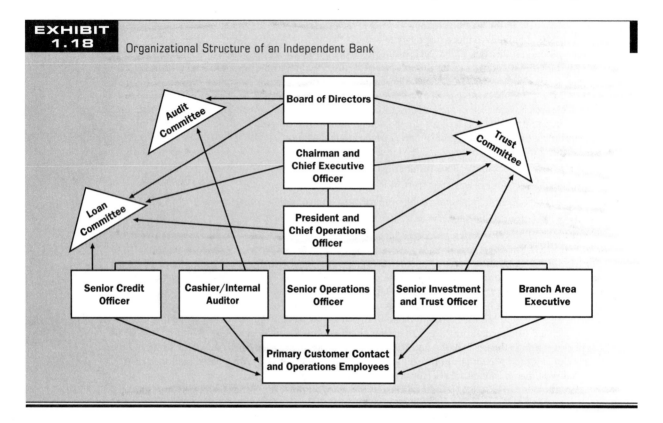

regarding bank policy. The role of the board is not, however, to manage the bank by getting involved in day-to-day operations or the details of each specific pricing, investment, or credit decision.

Because the board is ultimately responsible for the bank's performance, most banks establish directors' committees that set policy guidelines in the major functional areas and regularly monitor performance. Typical directors' committees consist of:

1. Loan committee. Oversees the lending function to ensure loan quality and verify that regulatory guidelines are met. The loan committee typically approves all loans over some base amount and thus serves as a final review board. Because business leaders are familiar with the community and are experts in their own lines of business, they should bring experience and keen judgment to the evaluation process.

2. Trust committee. By law, any bank with a trust department must have a directors' trust committee. Trust departments handle estates, guardianships, and related services under legal trust agreements. A trust committee monitors the legal aspects of the trust business and whether trust business contributes to the bank's overall profitability.

3. Audit committee. Selects the bank's auditors, reviews the audit report, and makes recommendations to management. The audit committee is the only committee that has no inside directors. This reflects the monitoring role inherent in an audit in which all of these activities should be independent of the bank's operating officers.

4. Asset and liability management committee. Manages and evaluates the impact of changes in interest rates, deposit withdrawals, and loan repayments among other factors affect changes in the bank's assets and liabilities. Many banks will have a director representative on the bank's asset and liability management committee.

The next tiers of management, following the board of directors, will vary depending on bank size and organizational structure but typically consist of the positions of chairman of the board, president, CEO, and chief operations officer (COO). Many organizations also designate a chief financial officer (CFO), a chief compliance officer (CCO), and even a chief information officer (CIO) who is charged with managing technology. Often, the bank's COO carries the title of president. Senior officers in each of the functional areas normally report to this individual who then conveys the information to the CEO (who can also be the president). At most independent banks, the CEO is in charge of the bank's entire operation. He or she often makes loans, reviews key loan and investment decisions made by others, and handles much of the bank's marketing and public relations efforts. In this case, the president is the COO only when the CEO is out of town. Although it is not uncommon for one individual to hold the titles of chairman of the board, president, and CEO, today's business demands, as well as new corporate governance expectations of the Sarbanes-Oxley Act, mean these positions are being handled by separate individuals more and more.

The next tier of management consists of senior management and control positions. Most independent banks separate activities into at least the four or five functional areas listed above the line personnel:

1. Senior credit officer. Responsible for implementing a bank's credit policy. Some banks also designate a chief lending officer. Often, the president and CEO also manage the loan portfolio because they deal directly with borrowers.

2. Cashier or chief financial officer. Responsible for financial management responsibilities in the areas of budgeting, accounting, and record keeping. This individual verifies that financial information conforms to regulatory guidelines and is conveyed correctly to stockholders and regulators. Each bank should also have an internal auditor who monitors financial reporting.

3. Senior operations officer. Responsible for backroom operations involving data processing, lock box services, and check processing.

4. Senior investment officer. Buys and sells securities for the investment portfolio, and also handles trust business if the bank has a trust department. At small banks, the president or CEO may handle these responsibilities.

5. Branch area executive. A bank with branches will typically designate an individual who is responsible for all branches; or the branches may be segmented by city, county, or other area such that several individuals serve as branch executives and report directly to the president. If the bank is large enough, it may also separate the human resources function and designate a senior officer who reports to the president.

At the bottom of the chart are the line personnel who have primary responsibility in customer contact and handling backroom operations such as check processing and teller services. Their role is extremely important because most depositors and loan customers deal with these individuals. They largely project the bank's image and serve to market bank services.

## THE FUNDAMENTAL FORCES OF CHANGE

Five fundamental forces have transformed the structure of financial markets and institutions and reflect the intense competition financial firms face today: deregulation/reregulation, financial innovation, securitization, globalization, and advances in technology. The latter factors actually represent responses to deregulation and reregulation. These combined forces have altered corporate balance sheets by inducing firms to compete in new product and geographic markets and use new financial instruments to facilitate transactions and adjust their risk profile. Although consumers have benefited from these changes, the long-term trend for financial institutions entails consolidation, realignment of corporate objectives, and diversification of products offered as firms attempt to develop a market niche. Firms can expect regulators to closely monitor changes in risk and continually increase capital requirements, particularly against new lines of business.

Many analysts attribute much of the change in the financial services industry to deregulation. Actually, deregulation was a natural response to increased competition between depository institutions and nondepository financial firms, and between the same type of competitors across world markets rather than the catalyst of competition. Deregulation sped up the process, but did not necessarily start it. New regulations brought about the development of new products that increased competition with firms not regulated like banks, such as investment banks. Regulation also contributed to the problems of savings and loans in the early 1980s as S&L portfolios were restricted to long-term mortgage securities financed by short-term savings accounts. Today, we consider this to be a very high interest rate risk position, enough to bring about major regulatory sanctions! Yet, in the late 1970s, this was the legally mandated balance sheet profile of S&Ls.

The basic theme is that increased competition, brought about not only by continued deregulation but also as financial firms find ways around regulation, has encouraged banks to assume increased portfolio risks in order to earn acceptable returns. As bank regulators have tried to reduce overall risk by raising capital requirements, banks have moved assets off their balance sheets and tried to replace interest income with fee income. In these efforts, banks attempt to be more like insurance brokers, realtors, and investment bankers—competing with a broader range of firms in more product markets. As capital becomes increasingly costly or impossible to obtain, individual firms are forced to merge to continue operations.

## THE ROLE OF REGULATION

Historically, commercial banks have been one of the most heavily regulated companies in the United States—and thus among the safest and most conservative businesses around. Regulations took many forms, including maximum interest rates that could be paid on deposits or charged on loans, minimum capital-to-asset ratios, minimum legal reserve requirements, limited geographic markets for full-service banking, constraints on the type of investments permitted, and restrictions on the range of activities, products, and services offered. Although regulations limited opportunities and risks, they virtually guaranteed a profit if management did not perpetrate fraud.

Since World War II, banks and other market participants have consistently restructured their operations to circumvent regulation and meet perceived customer needs. In response, regulators or lawmakers imposed new restrictions, which market participants circumvented again. This process of regulation and market response (financial innovation) and imposition of new regulations (reregulation) is the *regulatory dialectic*.[16] One aspect of regulatory response is *financial innovation.* Securitization, globalization, and new technologies are extensions of this response in the development of new products and international competition. The fear is that competitive forces have influenced financial markets and institutions so rapidly that the aggregate risk of the U.S. financial system has increased.

Rose (1993) points out that the changing nature of banking can be examined in two distinct areas: the traditional role of banks as financial intermediaries; and the evolution of banking into nontraditional roles as a result of changing regulation, technology, and financial innovation. Banks' traditional role as an intermediary has declined as new products such as cash management accounts, mutual funds, commercial paper, and junk bonds have become more prevalent. Banks have responded by accepting lower spreads, taking on more risk, and expanding their customer and product base. Banks have also expanded into nontraditional areas and products, especially investment banking activities, off-balance sheet activities, such as standby letters of credit, mortgage servicing, and credit enhancement products, to generate more fee income. They are also actively pursuing the use of technology in the development and delivery of products such as business sweep accounts and Internet banking. Finally, the Gramm-Leach-Bliley Act effectively eliminates most of the remaining restrictions that have separated commercial banking, investment banking, and insurance for more than 70 years. Banking organizations will continue to expand their operations by identifying specific products and services to offer and will subsequently compete against a broader array of firms.

## INCREASED COMPETITION

Following the enactment of the Glass-Steagall Act and through the early 1980s, the commercial banking industry was quite stable. Individuals who wanted to start a new bank found it difficult to get a charter from either federal or state regulators. The Federal Reserve System, in turn, limited interest rates that banks could pay depositors, effectively subsidizing banks by mandating low-cost sources of funds. Depositors had few substitutes for saving unless they held more than $100,000. As a result, bank deposits grew systematically with economic conditions. Regulations also specified maximum rates that banks could charge on certain types of loans. Such usury ceilings were intended to protect customers from price gouging and essentially passed through a portion of the value of low-cost bank deposits to bank borrowers.

During this period, banks could not compete on price because the price of their inputs (deposits) was regulated (Regulation Q) and the price of their outputs (loans) was regulated (usury ceilings). For all practical purposes, all banks had the same price and had to find other ways to compete. Banks would give away toasters, silverware sets, and wine and dine prospective customers as one means of product differentiation. Many senior bank executives spent considerable time out of the office attempting to earn business. They would take customers to lunch, dinner, golf, and so on, trying to win their business. Today, banks are free to set the price for their services as well as the type of services they offer, as are other companies also free to offer banking-type services at competitive prices. Bankers now compete directly on price, product offerings, and service.

**COMPETITION FOR DEPOSITS.** The free ride of a guaranteed spread between asset yields and liability costs abruptly ended during the late 1970s. The primary catalyst was high inflation due in part to foreign control of the oil market and the doubling of oil prices. Although ceiling rates on bank deposits limited interest to 5.25 percent on savings accounts (5.50 percent at S&Ls) and nothing on checking accounts, 8 to 12 percent inflation rates guaranteed that consumers lost purchasing power. Individuals had two choices: save less and spend more or find higher-yielding investments. In 1973, several investment banks created money market mutual funds (MMMFs), which accepted deposits from individuals and invested the proceeds in Treasury bills, large certificates of deposit (CDs), and other securities that paid market yields.[17] Not surprisingly, the attractiveness and growth of

---

[16]A discussion of the regulatory dialectic can be found in Kane (1977 and 1981).

[17]Technically, money market mutual funds sell shares to individuals. The funds buy money market instruments, insured CDs, or Treasury securities for example, and transfer the income to shareholders, minus a management fee. Most funds allow shareholders to write checks against their balance or transfer funds to other investments. The shares exhibit little default risk but are not directly federally insured.

MMMFs tracked the spread between money market interest rates and Regulation Q ceilings. Without competing instruments, MMMFs increased from $10.8 billion in 1978 to $186 billion in 1981 and $2 trillion at the end of 2004. During this interval, three-month Treasury bill rates exceeded the rate on bank savings accounts by as much as 9 percent.

In today's environment, deposit competition takes many forms. First, institutions are virtually unconstrained in the terms they can offer. Thus, customers can negotiate any minimum denomination, market interest rate, and maturity. Firms cannot discriminate, so they make the same deposit available to all qualified customers. As such, the range of deposit products is much broader than what was previously available. Second, a wide variety of firms accept time deposits and offer checking accounts. Almost every investment company that offers mutual funds also offers a cash management account for high-balance customers (some as small as $5,000) to use as part of their investment activity. Individuals can have proceeds from all financial transactions automatically invested at market rates until they make new investment decisions. Until that time, they can write checks against outstanding balances. Customers can transfer money from a core money market account to thousands of mutual funds with many investment companies such as Fidelity Investments. Finally, the combination of advances in technology and elimination of bank branching restrictions means that business and consumers have many more choices than before. Prior to the elimination of branching restrictions, most individuals were limited in choice to the local bank and information about rates and prices at other institutions was difficult to obtain. The vast amount of information available on the Internet means that customers can quickly and easily obtain rate quotes from financial institutions all over the world. The elimination of branching restrictions means that just about any financial institution can open a branch in any community. Not surprisingly, the competition for deposits is fierce.

American Express, GE, State Farm, and others similarly offer their credit card customers the opportunity to invest in small time deposits that pay competitive rates. For high-balance depositors, foreign banks and branches of large U.S. banks offer eurodollar deposits that pay higher rates than domestic certificates of deposits. Finally, deposit services are often priced to encourage customers to conduct the bulk of their banking business with one firm. Thus, as a customer's balances increase, yields increase and service charges decline. The providers often make other services, such as travel discounts and life insurance, available in a package with deposit accounts.

**COMPETITION FOR LOANS.** As bank funding costs increased, competition for loans put downward pressure on loan yields and interest spreads over the cost of bank funds. High quality corporate borrowers have always had the option to issue commercial paper or long-term bonds rather than borrow from banks. **Commercial paper** is an unsecured short-term promissory note issued in bearer form by large corporations, with maturities ranging from 5 to 270 days. The growth in MMMFs accelerated the development and growth of the commercial paper market and improved investment banks' ties with nonfinancial corporations. Investment banks continued to underwrite commercial paper and use money market funds to purchase the paper. Because the Glass-Steagall Act prevented commercial banks from underwriting commercial paper, banks lost corporate borrowers who bypassed them by issuing commercial paper at lower cost. Today, commercial banks can underwrite and deal in securities using a Glass-Steagall Section 20 affiliate or operate a subsidiary of a financial holding company that specializes in underwriting.

The development of the junk bond market extended loan competition to medium-size companies representing lower-quality borrowers. **Junk bonds** are corporate securities that are unrated or rated Ba (BB) and lower and thus are not investment grade. Historically, firms with debt ratings below Baa (BBB) were precluded from issuing significant amounts of new debt and had to rely instead on bank loans. During the early 1980s, several investment banks, particularly Drexel Burnham Lambert, convinced investors that many Ba and lower-rated bonds were sound investments and that the historical default rates were so low that the 3.5 to 5 percent yield premium offered on the bonds more than compensated for default risk. Investment banks were soon able to help companies that could not issue prime-grade commercial paper sell junk bonds in the new issue market. These bonds had several advantages over bank loans, including access to larger amounts of funds, longer-term financing, and fewer restrictive covenants. In many cases, the interest costs were well below loan rates quoted by a bank. New issue junk bonds effectively served as substitutes for commercial loans.

In 1989, the junk bond market started a long decline as the federal government charged Drexel Burnham and its junk bond specialist, Michael Milken, with a series of securities law violations. At that time, Drexel provided much of the secondary market support for junk bonds that investors wanted to trade. With Drexel's bankruptcy filing in 1990, the secondary market shrunk and junk bond prices collapsed. These customers once again gravitated to banks until junk bonds reclaimed their popularity. Today, the junk bond market is again quite active. Fed policymakers actually look at the interest spread between junk bond yields and yields on low-default-risk Treasury securities as an indicator of the appropriate monetary policy. When the spreads are extremely high, lower-quality borrowers have more difficulty obtaining financing and the Federal Reserve System often provides additional liquidity to the market.

These developments permanently altered the commercial banking industry. The growth in junk bonds reduced the pool of good-quality loans and lowered risk-adjusted yield spreads over bank borrowing costs. Banks generally responded either by increasing the riskiness of their loan portfolios or trying to move into investment banking and other service areas that generate fee income. Banks choosing the first path sacrificed long-term profitability and solvency for short-term gains. They maintained yield spreads temporarily, but increased default risk on the loans, which ultimately eroded earnings through higher loan charge-offs. Banks choosing the second path, generating greater fee income, had limited options. They would like to underwrite securities, sell new types of insurance, and offer other products without the inherent credit risk of loans. This would allow them to diversify their asset base and revenue stream and lower the risk of failure. Only recently have commercial banks been able to engage in many of these activities.

Today, different-sized banks pursue different strategies. Small- to medium-size banks continue to concentrate on loans but seek to strengthen customer relationships by offering personal service. They now measure their costs better and price loans and deposits to cover their costs plus meet profit targets. The best evidence is that most banks now calculate their own cost of funds and price loans off this index rather than off a money center bank's prime rate. Many of these same banks have rediscovered the consumer loan. The proportion of consumer loans increased for some banks during the 1980s and early 1990s but has slowed somewhat since 1995, due primarily to the rapid increase in default rates and personal bankruptcy rates. Rates charged on consumer loans generally far exceed their respective default rates and the cost of financing such that net profits have exceeded those on commercial loans. A further advantage with retail customers is that consumer deposits are much less rate sensitive than large certificates of deposit and other borrowed funds. The biggest losers are low-balance depositors who have seen service charges increase to cover the banks' costs of providing transactions services.

**OFF-BALANCE SHEET ACTIVITIES AND ASSETS.** The largest banks move assets off the balance sheet as part of their normal business because commercial and consumer loans are risky relative to the available returns. Regulatory capital requirements raise the cost of holding loans on balance sheets, and pricing pressures on new loans make owning loans too expensive and risky, given the available yield spreads. Thus, some institutions consciously originate loans and securitize them, or issue securities using the loans as collateral, and effectively move the loans off the bank's balance sheet. Off-balance sheet activity of the largest U.S. commercial banks has increased dramatically since the early 1980s. Meanwhile, noninterest income, as a percentage of total operating income, has increased to 46 percent at year-end 2004 from only 20 percent in 1985.

This trend is not without risk. Commitments and guaranties take the form of loan commitments, standby letters of credit, commitments related to interest rate swaps, currency exchange, leases, insurance on securities, and third party guaranties, all of which generate excellent fee income and do not require large capital support. However, because unfunded commitments and guaranties do not appear explicitly on published financial statements, banks continue to assume the risk that they might need to fund the commitments and make good on a defaulted obligation. This was dramatically demonstrated in late 2001 and 2002 with the bankruptcies of Enron and Kmart and the problems of Tyco and other distressed firms. As these nonfinancial companies approached bankruptcy, the money and capital markets closed down to them so they drew down their credit lines at banks. Thus, just before filing for bankruptcy, Enron and Kmart increased their borrowing from banks that quickly charged-off the loans and found themselves to be general creditors for a failed firm. Tyco didn't fail, but substituted bank borrowing for commercial paper issues by its CIT subsidiary when investors refused to buy CIT's commercial paper at traditional rate levels.

**THE IMPACT OF NONBANK COMPETITION.** Competition for the bank's product line comes in many forms. Merrill Lynch began to offer its *Cash Management Account* (CMA) during the late 1970s in which smaller depositors (minimum deposit of $10,000) could earn "market" rates. During this same time, banks were restricted from paying more than 5.25 percent on savings accounts and could not pay interest on checking accounts. It did not take long for Merrill Lynch's CMA to become quite popular, especially during periods of high inflation and high interest rates. At one point, Merrill Lynch's CMA was paying a short-term rate of almost 15 percent as compared with a bank's restricted 5.25 percent. It is no wonder the average investor began to look beyond the bank for a place to put investment dollars. It was not until the early 1980s that banks were allowed to offer interest on checking accounts and money market deposit accounts to compete with Merrill Lynch's CMA.

The 1980s and 1990s represented a period of intense competition where nonbank competitors aggressively entered traditional banking business lines. Commercial banks competed fiercely with nonbank institutions, finance companies, captive automobile finance companies, high-growth thrifts and technology firms for loans and deposits. Once-loyal customers moved their business for better terms. Unfortunately, the increased competition coincided with many regulatory restrictions on the type of products banks could offer, as well as loan problems in energy, real estate, and agriculture, which made it even more difficult to maintain quality assets and market share. Competitors engaged in activities that many banks wanted, but were unable to pursue due to regulation, thereby making the degree of competition even more intense.

Much like other companies, the largest automobile manufacturers have aggressively expanded in the financial services industry as part of their long-term strategic plans. The captive finance companies of General Motors, Ford Motor, DaimlerChrysler, and Toyota Motor Credit have long provided a steady stream of financing for automobile buyers. They also provide dealer financing for inventories, capital improvements, and lease programs. Profitability of these groups also compares favorably with that of commercial banks. Part of the success is due to operations beyond automobile finance. General Motors Acceptance Corporation owns two mortgage-servicing companies and ranks as one of the largest mortgage servicers in the United States. Ford Motor Credit, one of the nation's largest captive auto finance companies, is also one of the largest diversified finance companies alongside General Electric Capital Services (GECS). The financing divisions of these companies often contribute a great deal to the parent companies' bottom line.

General-purpose finance companies cover the spectrum of lending activities. Most specialize in lending to individuals for durable goods purchases. They traditionally emphasize automobile loans, home improvement loans, and second mortgage loans, which are secured by real estate. Others specialize in lending to businesses, either directly or through factoring a firm's accounts receivable, or equipment leasing. GECS, a wholly owned subsidiary of General Electric, is clearly the largest diversified finance company. Besides captive automotive finance companies, the Associates First Capital, Household Finance, American Express Credit Corporation, and Sears Roebuck Acceptance Corporation also finance various types of consumer and business receivables. Financing receivables (loans) for GECS were $280 billion and total assets were $618 billion in 2003, sizes that rival the largest banks in the United States. Most large finance companies are owned by a parent, such as GECS. In 2004, GE's net income was $16.6 billion while GECS's net income was $8.2 billion.

Finance companies fund their investments by issuing commercial paper and long-term bonds and by borrowing directly from banks. Historically, their loans have been to relatively high credit risks. Even though their default experience exceeds that of banks, finance companies have generally earned greater returns because they price their loans at a premium, which compensates for the greater charge-offs. The returns to the largest finance companies have been as good as if not better than those of banks.

**COMPETITION FOR PAYMENT SERVICES.** Once the exclusive domain of banks and other depository institutions, the nation's payment system has become highly competitive. Even the Federal Reserve System's role in processing and clearing checks could be replaced by new technology. This, of course, would not come without risks. Only the Fed can prevent default by one large institution from causing the system to collapse. The real challenge for the Fed and banks in the delivery of payment processing services is emerging electronic payment systems, such as smart and stored-value cards, automatic bill payment, and bill presentment processing. Many private companies offer these products but the Fed still settles the accounts.

With recent electronic innovations, the role of paper checks is diminishing. Finally, plastic is overtaking checks. A recent study concluded that credit cards and debit cards accounted for 52 percent of transactions in 2003, up from just 10 percent in 1995. Checks accounted for 15 percent in 2003—one-half its contribution in 1995—while cash transactions represented 32 percent (down from 60 percent in 1995). Prepaid cards accounted for the other 1 percent in 2003. In October 2004, a new federal law labeled Check 21 went into effect. Check 21 enables banks to process checks faster by allowing electronic (substitute) checks to meet check clearing requirements. A bank simply needs to capture the front and back of a paper check in picture form which it then transfers electronically. If done correctly, the substitute check is legally the same as the original paper check. Gone are the days of customers taking advantage of check-clearing delays (float). Customers must now have sufficient balances on deposit to cover checks written or they will pay substantial overdraft charges.

Although cash remains the dominant form of payment, it has the smallest payment size, averaging about $4 per transaction. Large wholesale transactions, using Fed Wire and the Clearing House Interbank Payment System (CHIPS) are fewer in number but are much larger in average transaction size. The Fed Wire, operated by the Federal Reserve System, is used to settle interbank transactions while CHIPS is a private alternative operated by the New York Clearing House Association and used principally to settle foreign exchange transactions. Generally, wire transfers are "wholesale" payments made between financial institutions with an average transaction size for the Fed Wire and CHIPS of about $3.8 and $5.3 million, respectively.[18]

Checks are the second most active payment method in the United States with just over 10 percent of transaction volume handled by checkwriting. Electronic check presentment (ECP), including point-of-sale (POS) check truncation, has been especially well received and 40 to 50 million paper checks are converted into electronic ACH (Automated Clearing House) debits each year at retail locations.[19] POS check truncation occurs when a paper check does not follow the payment. For example, when someone writes a check at a store, the store electronically transmits the information from the check using an ACH transaction and returns the paper check to the person writing the check. As a result, the growth in ACH payments has been much higher than that of checks.

Credit cards remain the principal retail, or small value, electronic payment method. Ignoring cash, credit cards are used in almost 20 percent of the volume of transactions. Debit cards, on the other hand, are clearly

---

[18]The authors' estimates based on compiled data from a multitude of sources.

[19]The authors' estimates based on compiled data from a multitude of sources.

the fastest growing payment method; more than a quarter of a million debit cards are in circulation and more than 80 percent of banks offer debit cards. Similar to credit cards, debit cards are used for POS transactions but are not linked to credit. Instead, they are directly linked to the user's bank account. When used, the customer's balance is immediately reduced as if a check had cleared the account. Basically, a debit card is a check without the paper. The growth in debit cards is also a result of electronic benefits transfer (EBT) programs. The vast majority of states and various governmental agencies offer EBT programs to deliver entitlement and food assistance benefits to those with or without a bank account. In these programs, EBT cards can be used like debit or ATM cards.

Factors other than changes in electronic payments systems are also eroding banks' traditional markets. The growth and acceptance of electronic payment systems means that there is less of a need for anyone to physically go to a bank or any other financial services company. Anyone with the appropriate account can obtain cash at an ATM machine or make payment at the POS anywhere in the world, eliminating the need to go to the bank to obtain cash. Anyone can open a checking account, apply for a loan, make deposits, or receive a loan electronically. Direct deposit of paychecks, the use of credit cards, electronic bill payment, electronic check presentment, and smart cards all indicate that competition for financial services goes well beyond the traditional mechanisms we think of from the recent past. Many analysts argue that the future delivery of banking services will not take place in the brick and mortar branches of a bank building but rather through smart cards, ATM networks (which the banks control), credit cards, and the Internet (which banks do not control). No individual owns the Internet and any business can offer services over the Internet. Hence, more and more payments and financial services will be conducted over the Internet using smart and stored-value cards as well as private payments. The payments system is highly dynamic and constantly changing.

**COMPETITION FOR OTHER BANK SERVICES.** Banks and their affiliates offer many products and services in addition to deposits and loans. A partial list includes trust services, brokerage, data processing, securities underwriting, real estate appraisal, credit life insurance, and personal financial consulting. Although a bank cannot directly underwrite securities domestically, there are generally two methods by which banks can enter this line of business. One is to form a financial holding company. The financial holding company, owns a bank or bank holding company, as well as an investment subsidiary. The investment subsidiary of a financial holding company is not restricted in the amount or type of investment underwriting engaged in. A second method is to form a subsidiary of a national bank using Glass-Steagall Section 20 subsidiaries. Securities powers are basically unrestricted, however, if underwriting is done through a financial holding company.

Another method of combining nonbanking companies and banking is to use exemptions in the Bank Holding Company Act, which allows a nonbank to own certain types of banks or savings banks. In particular, Merrill Lynch owns a state savings bank, Merrill Lynch Trust Company, an "industrial bank," Merrill Lynch Bank USA, as well as a consumer bank, Merrill Lynch Bank and Trust Company. These exempt "banks" or savings banks do not force Merrill Lynch to become a bank holding company because they are limited-purpose banks, or are a savings bank or do not accept deposits and make commercial loans. This structure allows Merrill Lynch to compete directly with banks by offering insured deposits and other banking services while avoiding regulation as a bank holding company.

## INVESTMENT BANKING

Commercial banks consider investment banking attractive because most investment banks already offer many banking services to prime commercial customers and high net worth individuals and sell a wide range of products not available through banks. They can compete in any geographic market without the heavy regulation of the Federal Reserve, FDIC, and OCC. They earn extraordinarily high fees for certain types of transactions and can put their own capital at risk in selected investments. Of course, some risks are great such that there is the potential for highly volatile profits.

The Securities and Exchange Commission, which regulates investment banks, classifies firms in terms of their primary trading activity and head office location. Two categories of firms dominate the investment banking industry. *National full-line firms,* such as Merrill Lynch and Morgan Stanley, offer a complete set of services, including an extensive network of branch offices located throughout the United States to handle retail business. Large *investment banking firms,* such as Smith Barney and Goldman Sachs, do not have extensive branch networks and instead focus on large-scale trading, underwriting, and mergers and acquisitions. Both types of firms generate earnings from fee-based services, trading, and brokerage services. One attractive source of fees is securities underwriting in which investment banks help firms issue new equity and debt. The top investment banking houses manage the bulk of new issue investment-grade securities and thus are referred to as special bracket firms. Even though fewer than 20 firms qualify as national full-line or large investment banks, they control more than two-thirds of all assets held by investment banks. An **underwriter** typically buys the new securities from the issuer at an agreed-upon price and redistributes them to investors. As temporary owner of the securities, an underwriter acts as *a dealer* in assuming the risk that it can resell the securities at higher prices. The differential between the final sale price and the negotiated purchase price represents its profit. For this reason, an underwriter normally pre-sells the issue by obtaining commitments from investors.[20] Underwriters may also act as agents and help issuers place new securities directly with the final investor. As such, they earn fees without taking ownership of the underlying securities. Because risk increases with issue size, investment banks frequently form **underwriting syndicates**, or groups of investment banks, to diversify the risk and increase the number of selling firms.

Investment banks also serve as brokers or dealers in secondary market transactions. Through trading departments, they make markets in previously issued securities by executing trades for selected customers or for their own account. Many trades, especially those involving retail customers, are simply **brokered**; that is, the trader matches prospective buyers and sellers. The investment bank assumes no inventory risk and earns a straight commission on the exchange. Traders may also act as **dealers**, setting bid and ask prices for every security traded. The bid indicates the price at which the firm agrees to buy securities, and the ask indicates the sales price. Dealers incur inventory risk and adjust the size of the bid-ask spread to vary the size of their inventory. If necessary, a dealer may hedge inventory risk by trading futures, swaps, and options.

Investment banks also generate substantial fees from facilitating corporate mergers and acquisitions and asset management. In the first case, an investment bank helps in the valuation and offers advice and assistance in negotiating deal terms. Corporate takeover specialists and junk bond financing spur this activity. Target companies are often those with stock market values far below the value of corporate assets. Acquiring firms issue large volumes of common stock or junk bond debt and use the proceeds to buy controlling interest in a target company's stock. After purchase, they sell some of the acquired firm's assets to refund the initial debt or to generate cash flow that covers the debt service. Companies pursuing these leveraged buyouts often earn extraordinary profits when the market values of the firms' stocks later increase. In the second case, investment banks serve as agents and manage investment funds for clients earning a management fee. This generally represents a stable, low-risk source of revenue as long as the funds perform adequately.

Securities trading and brokerage represent the other sources of profit. The first involves either making a market in securities or trading for the firm's own account. When making a market, a bank serves as a ready buyer and/or seller of the underlying security or commodity. For example, in foreign exchange trading, a bank may operate as a dealer by posting bid and ask quotes for which it is willing to buy and sell specific currencies. It makes a profit from the difference between the ask and bid prices. Some investment banks allow employees to trade for the bank's own account. In this situation, the trader takes speculative positions in an effort to buy the underlying asset at prices below the sale price. Obviously, speculative trading embodies greater risk. In the brokerage business, investment banks serve as customer representatives helping individuals, pension funds, and businesses buy and sell securities. As agents, the bank makes the bulk of its profit from sales commissions.

The Wall Street investment giants such as Goldman Sachs and Merrill Lynch continue to be the largest players in the merger and acquisition market, but commercial banks' share of the market has increased at a rapid pace. Acquisitions of investment banking companies by banks have reshaped the banking industry since 1995 and blurred the lines of distinction between commercial banking and investment banking. Mellon Bank owns Drexel Corp.; Bank of America owns Montgomery Securities; Citigroup owns Salomon Smith Barney; Credit Suisse owns Donaldson, Lufkin & Jenrette; UBS AG owns Paine Webber; and Regions Bank owns Morgan Keegan. Some investment firms have acquired commercial banks as well: Charles Schwab owns U.S. Trust and MetLife owns Grand Bank Kingston. Due to the restrictions of becoming a financial holding company, however, the acquisitions have generally gone the other way. It is interesting to note that Citigroup is now classified as a securities company rather than a bank.

## DEREGULATION AND REREGULATION

Commercial bank regulatory agencies have always tried to control the individuals and activities associated with financial intermediation. Their fundamental purpose is to protect the public's resources and confidence in the financial system. Banking is a public trust that, if left to industry whims, might assume too much risk, ultimately leading to extensive losses and widespread lack of confidence in the soundness and integrity underlying financial intermediation. **Deregulation** is the process of eliminating existing regulations, such as the elimination of Regulation Q interest rate ceilings imposed on time and demand deposits offered by depository institutions or the repeal of sections of the Glass-Steagall Act removing restrictions on investment banking activities. Deregulation is often confused with **reregulation**, which is the process of implementing new restrictions or modifying existing controls on individuals and activities associated with banking. Reregulation arises in response to market participants' efforts to circumvent existing regulations.

An issue related to Federal Reserve membership arose during the 1970s and serves as an excellent example of the regulator-bank relationship. Banks that are members of the Fed are required to hold reserves in the form of nonearning cash assets equal to a percentage of qualifying liabilities. These reserves represent an implicit tax on

---

[20]Original issuers let investment banks either bid competitively for the right to underwrite a new issue or negotiate directly with a single firm to handle the entire issue. Underwriters contact final investors prior to submitting a bid to assess market demand and determine a market price.

banking operations because banks do not earn explicit interest on the assets. During the 1970s, this tax increased dramatically as short-term market interest rates increased. Banks that were not Fed members were required to hold fewer reserves and could typically hold interest-bearing securities to meet requirements. As such, their lost interest income was much smaller. To circumvent regulation, many member banks gave up Fed membership rather than absorb the loss. The Federal Reserve System (FRS) and Congress, concerned about losing control of the money supply, passed the Depository Institutions Monetary Control Act in 1980, which allowed interest-bearing checking accounts but forced all financial institutions that offered them to hold reserves set by the Fed. This reregulation was an attempt to reimpose regulatory control over all depository institutions.

Efforts at deregulation and reregulation generally address pricing issues, allowable geographic market penetration, or the ability to offer new products and services. Recent pricing regulations have focused on removing price controls, such as the maximum interest rates paid to depositors and the rate charged to borrowers (usury ceilings). Deregulation, addressing geographic markets, has expanded the locations where competing firms can conduct business. Finally, deregulation of the restrictions that separated commercial banking, investment banking, and insurance have allowed banks to form financial holding companies and quickly expand product choices such as insurance, brokerage services, and securities underwriting. These changes, combined with new technology, have expanded opportunities across geographic markets and produced a greater number of competitors offering banking services and intense price competition. Greater competition has, in turn, lowered aggregate returns as firms attempt to establish a permanent market presence.

## FINANCIAL INNOVATION

Financial innovation is the catalyst behind the evolving financial services industry and the restructuring of financial markets. It represents the systematic process of change in instruments, institutions, and operating policies that determine the structure of our financial system. Innovations take the form of new securities and financial markets, new products and services, new organizational forms, and new delivery systems. Financial institutions change the characteristics of financial instruments traded by the public and create new financial markets, which provide liquidity. Bank managers change the composition of their banks' balance sheets by altering the mix of products or services offered and by competing in extended geographic markets. Financial institutions form holding companies and reverse holding companies, acquire subsidiaries, and merge with other entities. Finally, institutions may modify the means by which they offer products and services. Recent trends incorporate technological advances with the development of cash management accounts, including the use of ATMs, home banking via computer and the Internet, and shared national and international electronic funds transfer (EFT) systems.

Innovations have many causes. Firms may need to stop the loss of deposits, enter new geographic or product markets, deliver services with cheaper and better technology, increase their capital base, alter their tax position, reduce their risk profile, or cut operating costs. In virtually every case, the intent is to improve their competitive position. The external environment, evidenced by volatile economic conditions, new regulations, and technological developments, creates the opportunity for innovation.

Financial innovation related to Regulation Q (which restricted banks from offering more than 5.25 percent interest on savings accounts) evolved as depository institutions tried to slow disintermediation, in which depositors withdrew funds from fixed-rate accounts at banks and reinvested the funds in instruments paying market rates of interest. Until 1986, when Regulation Q was voided, many banks developed new vehicles to compete with Treasury bills, money market mutual funds, and cash management accounts offered through brokerage houses. Citibank issued negotiable CDs and variable-rate CDs; eurodollar deposits were developed; and NOW accounts (interest-bearing checking accounts) were permitted in Massachusetts. Federal regulators often responded to these innovations by imposing marginal reserve requirements against the new instrument, raising the interest rate ceiling, then authorizing a new deposit instrument. Some of these restrictions remain such as the prohibition against banks paying interest on commercial demand deposits.[21]

More recent innovations with securities take the form of new futures, swaps, options, and options-on-futures contracts, or the development of markets for a wide range of securitized assets. Banks use financial futures to hedge interest rate and foreign exchange risk in their portfolios as well as offset mismatches in maturities of assets and liabilities or different amounts of assets and liabilities denominated in different currencies, to price fixed-rate loans or to create synthetic deposits. Several large banks also earn fee income and commissions by serving as futures merchants and advisers.

Of course, innovations are not restricted to banks. Major retailers such as J.C. Penney, Kroger, and Sears acquired banks, savings and loans, insurance companies, and real estate companies, enabling them to offer banking

---

[21]Interestingly, banks have found ways around this regulation (Reg. DD) as well. Competitive pressures from investment banks and mutual fund companies have encouraged banks to offer "sweep" accounts. These accounts move a commercial customer's checking account balance to a money market account that is not a bank insured deposit account and hence can be interest bearing. The funds are then moved back as the company needs them. See Chapter 8 for a detailed discussion of sweep accounts.

products. State Farm Insurance and related firms now offer full commercial banking services. These nonbank firms operate offices nationwide without regulatory interference. Investment banks have similarly linked up with consumer banks to provide a vehicle for offering credit card and transactions services nationally.

Innovation in delivery systems normally takes the form of new technological developments to facilitate funds transfers. During the 1980s, banks popularized ATMs and POS terminals in retail outlets. More recent innovations include the development of the smart cards, debit cards, home banking networks, and Internet banking. Although customer acceptance has been slower than expected, these systems are growing at an increasing rate.

## SECURITIZATION

Because loans offer the highest gross yields, many banks try to compensate for declining interest margins (a direct result of increased competition) by increasing loan-to-asset ratios. This fundamentally means that there is an increasing demand for a decreasing pool of quality credits. In many cases, this eventually leads to greater loan losses and long-term earnings problems. High loan growth also increases bank capital requirements. Regulators consider most loans to be risky assets and require banks to add to their loan loss reserves and capital base, the more loans they put on the books. Higher provisions for loan losses reduce reported net income. Because equity capital is more expensive than debt, higher capital requirements, in turn, increase the marginal cost of financing operations.

One competitive response to asset-quality problems and earnings pressure has been to substitute fee income for interest income by offering more fee-based services. Banks also lower their capital requirements and reduce credit risk by selling assets and servicing the payments between borrower and lender, rather than holding the same assets to earn interest.

This process of converting assets into marketable securities is called **securitization**. A bank originates assets, typically loans, combines them in pools with similar features, and sells pass-through certificates, which are secured by the interest and principal payments on the original assets. Residential mortgages and mortgage-backed pass-through certificates served as the prototype. The originating bank charges fees for making the loans. If it services the loans, it collects interest and principal payments on the loans, which it passes through to certificate holders minus a servicing fee. If the bank sells the certificates without recourse, regulators permit it to take the original assets off its books.[22] The bank does not have to allocate loan-loss reserves against the assets, and its capital requirements decline proportionately. Securitization also eliminates interest rate risk associated with financing the underlying assets. In essence, the bank serves as an investment banker generating fee income from servicing the loans without assuming additional credit risk.

## GLOBALIZATION

Financial markets and institutions are becoming increasingly international in scope. U.S. corporations, for example, can borrow from domestic or foreign institutions. They can issue securities denominated in U.S. dollars or foreign currencies of the countries in which they do business. Foreign corporations have the same alternatives. Investors increasingly view securities issued in different countries as substitutes. Large firms thus participate in both domestic and foreign markets such that interest rates on domestic instruments closely track foreign interest rates.

**Globalization** is the gradual evolution of markets and institutions such that geographic boundaries do not restrict financial transactions. One country's economic policies affect the economies of other countries. Funds flow freely between countries because of efficient money and capital markets and currency exchange. The establishment of the European Community (EC) in 1992 represents a prime example. Under the original formal agreement, 12 industrialized nations in Western Europe eliminated most trade restrictions, standardized basic product designs, reduced taxes and fees, and linked monetary control in order to facilitate trade. Today, there are now 16 countries in the EC.[23] The original intent was to have a common currency and fully integrated market that operates as one without borders. Starting in January 1999, the euro (a European unified currency) has been usable in wholesale financial transactions in all European Union countries except for Sweden, Denmark, Greece, and the United Kingdom. Since January 2002, coins and currency euros are the authorized and dominant transaction vehicle in the EC. Monetary policy for the single currency is set by the European Central Bank, located in Frankfurt. One presumed benefit of the euro is that it should sharply lower inflation rates and enhance export opportunities for all member countries.

Businesses, individuals, and governments recognize that events throughout the world influence their domestic performance. They should be aware of foreign competition and foreign opportunities when developing market

---

[22]Banks that issue securities backed by their assets are legally classified as investment companies. If they are not exempted, the SEC, according to the Investment Company Act of 1940, regulates them. The SEC also requires that banks guarantee securities before it grants an exemption. This inconsistency with bank regulatory treatment effectively restricts banks to private rather than public placement for the securities. See Brenner (May 1986).

[23]The 16 countries in the EC are Austria, Belgium, Denmark, Finland, France, Germany, Greece, Ireland, Italy, Luxembourg, the Netherlands, Norway, Portugal, Spain, Sweden, and the United Kingdom.

strategies. Chapter 14 analyzes the nature of international transactions in detail, including both the impacts of U.S. firms abroad and foreign firms in the United States.

Most large money center banks have the capability and expertise to help customers access capital in any currency in the form of either debt or equity. Many firms have offices all over the world and offer services in a wide range of product markets. Several Japanese banks, for example, serve as primary securities dealers in activities with the U.S. Federal Reserve. Some of the best-known U.S. investment banks, Lehman, Goldman Sachs, PaineWebber, Blackstone, and Wasserstein, are at least partially owned by foreign investors. Borrowers look less at where the supplier of a good or service is located and more at the quality and price of the good or service. Clearly, only the largest firms can successfully compete worldwide. Globalization in financial services implies that the top layer of firms will consist of a few, very large consolidated organizations.

Although product innovation and the acquisition of domestic firms by foreign firms has led to a removal of the physical borders that separate firms internationally, technology has clearly had one of the most dramatic impacts on the globalization of markets. Technological innovations, such as the commercialization of the Internet, mean that distance is no longer a limiting factor. One can search for and purchase products and services from anywhere in the world from just about anywhere in the world. Large, as well as small, companies now have global markets for their products and services. Consumers and businesses now search beyond their traditional local market in pursuit of price, quality, and availability.

## ADVANCES IN TECHNOLOGY

It took more than 80 years until 50 percent of U.S. households owned an automobile. It only took about 70 years for the telephone, 50 years for electricity, 35 years for the VCR, 27 years for television, and 15 years for the cell phone. But the Internet reached 50 percent of U.S. households in only seven years. Clearly, the impact of technology on business over the past decade has been unprecedented and technology's impact on the financial services industry has been even greater than in other industries. Technology has had the biggest impact on efficiency and productivity. Technology allows one person to do more or handle more people and transactions, thereby dramatically reducing the cost of delivering products and services. In addition to gains in productivity, advances in technology—especially in the areas of telecommunications—have expanded the banks' marketplace from around the block to around the world. Banks can now offer banking services to anyone with a computer—but so can just about any other firm.

While advances in technology have dramatically increased the efficiency of banks providing services, they have also simultaneously increased competition. As an intermediary, banks add value in the economy by providing and processing "soft" information about those they provide services for. The Internet makes obtaining information on smaller business customers less costly and easier to do, thereby increasing competition for the banks' primary business of lending to small to medium-size businesses. Technology also makes it less costly to offer banking services and expands a company's market geographically with little cost. This all leads to increased competition for banking services. Technological advances allow firms to compete for customers electronically without branch facilities on every street corner.

## SUMMARY

According to historical regulatory definition, a commercial bank is a firm that both accepts demand deposits and makes commercial loans. Although this has been the legal definition, it is not fundamentally useful today. Banks can now own and operate securities businesses, insurance companies, and other financial services firms and such firms can own and operate banks. It is now more appropriate to refer to the banking industry as a combination of traditional banks, represented by community and regional banks and savings associations, and more complex financial services firms. Managers can choose an organizational structure that allows them to offer a wide range of products and services and compete across many different geographic markets. Most of the legal and regulatory differences that have historically separated various types of depository institutions are gone. Banks now compete with savings and loans, credit unions, insurance companies, and other affiliates of nationwide financial conglomerates in providing basic banking services. Most of us would not know if our depository institution was a bank, savings and loan, or credit union by the types of products and services they offer.

Even though some of the same types of regulatory constraints, which separated commercial banking, investment banking, and insurance have been removed, banks do not operate on an equal footing with other nonbank firms. As a result, only the largest banks have embraced the full line of these new product powers. In fact, Citigroup is the only U.S. banking company that is a major player in all three of these areas: commercial banking, investment banking, and insurance. Many other large banking companies have, however, aggressively entered the securities business. Banks, however, are required to form a financial holding company and be regulated by the Federal Reserve System. Firms like General Electric provide all of the same basic services that Citigroup provides and GE's "banking" unit, GE Capital Services, is less than one-half of GE's business. GE is not, however, a financial holding company.

The Office of Comptroller of the Currency and state banking departments approve new bank charters and, along with the Federal Reserve and FDIC, regulate and examine qualifying banks. Many banks operate as unit banks with only one office while others are part of branch banking systems. Both unit and branch banks may be part of a bank holding company, which owns controlling interest in subsidiary banks. Through holding companies, many banking organizations engage in activities closely related to banking, such as leasing, data processing, investment banking, and mortgage banking. Federal legislation now permits interstate banking, which represents a significant catalyst for change.

Commercial banks compete with other banks and depository institutions. Savings and loans, in particular, can offer identical deposit products and invest in the same assets, as well as possess additional real estate, investment, and insurance powers. Banks also compete with limited-service banks, or nonbanks, that operate as part of nationwide financial service companies. Depending on their choice of organizational structure, banks can also compete with securities firms, real estate firms, insurance companies, finance companies, and other providers of financial services.

This chapter describes the organizational structure of the commercial banking industry and the legislation and regulation that guide operating policies. Early restrictions regarding branching encouraged the formation of holding companies and the development of nonbank institutions as a means of circumventing branching restrictions. The impact of interest deregulation and increased deposit insurance was to encourage risk-taking by banks and thrifts, so that many firms failed during the 1980s and early 1990s. Congress approved legislation (the Financial Institutions Reform, Recovery and Enforcement Act, FIRREA) in 1989 that substantially restructured the thrift industry by redefining acceptable business activities. The current regulatory trend is to remove differences in opportunities now available to different types of financial services companies, and thus expand the number of competitors in most product areas. The Financial Modernization Act of 1999 greatly enhanced such opportunities such that all managers must constantly assess what businesses and products their firms should offer and in what form.

Increased competition has arisen from financial innovation, deregulation, securitization, globalization of financial institutions and markets, and technological developments. Deregulation is the removal of regulations that limit financial institutions' activities. Financial innovation is the continual development of new products and change in market structure to circumvent regulation and meet customer needs. Securitization is the process of converting assets to marketable securities. From a bank's perspective, securitization moves assets off the balance sheet and substitutes fee income for interest income. Globalization involves the de facto elimination of geographic barriers to trade and financial market activity. Finally, technology has opened the door to competition from many more areas including the once sacred payments system.

Consumers and businesses benefit from lower interest rates and increased capital availability. Market participants can choose from a larger number of suppliers, which places a premium on customer service. To remain competitive, banks should identify the products with which they have a market advantage and provide personal service that distinguishes them from their competitors.

## QUESTIONS

1. What are the advantages of a bank having many branches in a city or state as opposed to just one main office location? What are the disadvantages? *— Courier Services* ⊕

2. Explain why there are so many different bank regulatory agencies. Devise a regulatory structure that would improve the existing system.

3. What are the basic objectives of banking regulation? How do regulators attempt to achieve these objectives?

4. Is the purpose of bank regulation to prevent bank failures?

5. Federal deposit insurance used to cover a maximum of $40,000 per eligible account. It was later raised to $100,000 per account. What cost and/or risk did this present to the FDIC? What role, if any, did this play in the banking industry's problems during the 1980s?

6. What does the acronym CAMELS refer to in bank examinations? What are the most important facets of an examination?

7. Why were commercial banks prohibited from underwriting corporate securities within the United States but not abroad? How can a bank engage in underwriting corporate securities today?

8. Many experts argue that it was not deregulation that brought about fundamental change in the banking industry, but rather increases in competition from all providers of financial services. These experts argue that deregulation was a response to increased competitive pressures. Outline the fundamental competitive forces of change and how this has pushed regulators and legislators to deregulate the industry.

9. What impact is securitization likely to have on the quality of assets that banks keep in their portfolios?

10. Change is always good for some participants and bad for others. Which types of banks appear best situated to gain from increased competition in the financial services arena? Which banks seem most likely to lose?

11. Outline the major provisions of the Gramm-Leach-Bliley Act of 1999. Many experts considered this bill to favor larger multibank holding companies. What are some of the advantages or disadvantages of this bill to the largest and smallest banks? Do you think this bill will hasten the reduction in the number of smaller banks?

12. Describe the basic services provided by investment banks. Why are large commercial banks eager to offer investment banking services domestically?

13. What are the basic assets and liabilities of a multibank holding company? In what form does a holding company generate income?

14. What are the primary differences between a bank holding company and a financial holding company?

15. Will specialty or small community banks be able to compete successfully with larger commercial banks now that interstate banking is allowed? Will small community banks be able to compete successfully with firms such as Merrill Lynch, Charles Schwab, Bank of America, and HSBC?

16. Exhibit 1.7 documents the sharp drop in financial assets controlled by depository institutions. Explain why banks are losing market share. What must happen for them to reverse this trend? Explain why mutual funds and pension funds are increasing their market shares.

17. What are the duties of outside members of a bank's board of directors? To whom are directors responsible?

18. Suppose that you are the president of a commercial bank in a town of 22,000 residents. There are five other banks, two savings and loans, and a credit union. Your town also has Internet access through which the residents can access services from a number of national banking organizations, and a range of discount brokerage services, insurance products, and real estate brokerage. One of the savings banks constantly pays 0.5 percent more on all deposits. Devise a strategic plan to compete against each type of institution or competitive factor. What issues will enter into the analysis?

19. What problems are likely to arise when a bank tries to securitize the following: mortgages, credit card loans, automobile loans, and small business loans?

20. Explain how the growth in commercial paper and junk bonds has affected commercial lending and yield spreads at banks.

21. Some analysts contend that the federal government plays a game of catch-up in reregulation. Bankers start the game by offering new and creative products that circumvent existing regulations. Regulators try to catch up by eliminating or rewriting old rules to reflect the new situation. Meanwhile, bankers are circumventing regulation in different areas and the process continues. Explain how offering interest on checking accounts supports this view.

22. Globalization results in more efficient financial markets. Why do some bankers fear globalization? Will globalization have a different impact on community banks than on nationwide banking organizations?

23. In what areas do captive finance companies and other finance companies compete with banks? Who has the advantage?

24. What are the basic arguments for increasing capital requirements at banks? In what ways will bank depositors, stockholders, and society in general benefit? How might each group be disadvantaged? As banks enter new lines of business such as brokerage, how much additional capital should be required? Should these new lines of business be insured by the FDIC? Why or why not?

25. Much of the intense competition in the financial services industry comes from products that are the most standardized, such as mortgages, automobile loans, money market accounts, savings accounts, and so on. These products will offer very low profit margins. If you managed a small community bank today, devise a strategy to compete in this environment.

## ACTIVITIES

1. Which banks in your area seem to have best adapted to change? What criteria will you use to decide? Which nonbank financial firms compete aggressively in your area? Do they operate with any advantages or disadvantages versus banks? What about financial services available on the Internet? What portion of your financial business do you do on the Internet? How much of this business do you expect to transact on the Internet in five, seven, ten, and fifteen years?

2. What banks headquartered out of state have a major presence in your state? Are there any foreign banks in your state? List their competitive advantages and disadvantages versus in-state banks. What nonbank firms offer competing products in your market? Make a list of which firms will allow you to open a checking account. Which firms will allow you to borrow money as an individual? Are they all banks? If not, what type of firm are they?

3. Many experts argue that banking has been extremely vertically integrated. Vertical integration is the degree to which a company creates all parts of its product or the degree to which it distributes and sells those products itself. It seems likely that the degree of vertical integration will fall dramatically at many banks in the future. Most banks will have to purchase Internet payment systems, mutual fund products, and investment banking products from third parties. After all, does General Motors make its own tires or purchase them? Although General Motors does produce many of the products used in the automobiles that it sells, it acts as a general contractor to produce and sell the final product. The merger between Citicorp and Travelers—Citigroup—appears to be a move toward a more vertically integrated approach to banking. Sears tried this approach once before by integrating a retail store with an investment banker (Dean Witter), a real estate broker (Coldwell Banker), S&Ls, and insurance sales and underwriting (Allstate). This system did not appear to work as Sears has since completely divested itself of these lines of business and Citigroup has divested Travelers. Do you think vertical integration will work this time? What advantages do you think the new Citigroup has that Sears did not? What about the future of smaller banks that are less vertically integrated? Do they have a future as general contractors of services? Explain.

4. There are many proponents of expanding the types of activities allowed banks in the United States. Do you think the United States should allow banks to provide any service? What are the primary advantages of expanded powers? What are the primary disadvantages? Choose a large multibank holding company you might be familiar with and compare the services offered with those of a smaller community bank that you or someone you know uses. Does the community bank offer all the services you demand? Does the larger multibank? Do you use these services at a bank? Why or why not?

5. Search the Internet to find Web-based (virtual) banks that do not have brick-and-mortar branches. What products and services can a customer obtain from one of these virtual banks?

APPENDIX

## IMPORTANT BANKING LEGISLATION[25]

- **National Bank Act of 1864** (Chapter 106, 13 STAT. 99). Established a national banking system and the chartering of national banks.

- **Federal Reserve Act of 1913** (P.L. 63-43, 38 STAT. 251, 12 USC 221). Established the Federal Reserve System as the central banking system of the United States.

- **To Amend the National Banking Laws and the Federal Reserve Act** (P.L. 69-639, 44 STAT. 1224). Also known as the **McFadden Act** of 1927. Prohibited interstate banking.

- **Banking Act of 1933** (P.L. 73-66, 48 STAT. 162). Also known as the **Glass-Steagall Act**. Established the FDIC as a temporary agency. Separated commercial banking from investment banking, establishing them as separate lines of commerce.

- **Banking Act of 1935** (P.L. 74-305, 49 STAT. 684). Established the FDIC as a permanent agency of the government.

- **Federal Deposit Insurance Act of 1950** (P.L. 81-797, 64 STAT. 873). Revised and consolidated earlier FDIC legislation into one act. Embodied the basic authority for the operation of the FDIC.

- **Bank Holding Company Act of 1956** (P.L. 84-511, 70 STAT. 133). Required Federal Reserve Board approval for the establishment of a bank holding company. Prohibited bank holding companies headquartered in one state from acquiring a bank in another state.

- **International Banking Act of 1978** (P.L. 95-369, 92 STAT. 607). Brought foreign banks within the federal regulatory framework. Required deposit insurance for branches of foreign banks engaged in retail deposit taking in the United States.

- **Financial Institutions Regulatory and Interest Rate Control Act of 1978** (P.L. 95-630, 92 STAT. 3641). Also known as FIRIRCA. Created the Federal Financial Institutions Examination Council. Established limits and reporting requirements for bank insider transactions. Created major statutory provisions regarding electronic fund transfers.

- **Depository Institutions Deregulation and Monetary Control Act of 1980** (P.L. 96-221, 94 STAT. 132). Also known as **DIDMCA**. Established *interest bearing* "NOW Accounts." Began the phase-out of interest-rate ceilings on deposits. Established the Depository Institutions Deregulation Committee. Granted new powers to thrift institutions. Raised the deposit insurance ceiling to $100,000. *Implemented improvements in monetary control by extending reserve requirements, set by the Federal Reserve, to all federally insured depository institutions and imposed new reserve requirements on transaction and nonpersonal time deposits, as well as establishing equal percentage reserve requirements for all firms of equal size. Established new powers for thrift institutions, including allowing limited investments in consumer loans, commercial paper, corporate debt securities, and unsecured construction loans. Finally, the act required the Federal Reserve System to make its services available to member and nonmember institutions and explicitly price these services based on the cost of providing the services.*

- **Depository Institutions Act of 1982** (P.L. 97-320, 96 STAT. 1469). Also known as **Garn-St. Germain**. Expanded FDIC powers to assist troubled banks. Established the Net Worth Certificate program. Expanded the powers of thrift institutions *to include making commercial loans and increased the legal lending limit for an single customer. Authorized depository institutions to issue money market deposit accounts (MMDAs).*

- **Tax Reform Act of 1986** (P.L. 99-514). Allowed banks with less than $400 million in total assets to continue to use the loan-loss reserve system and deduct allocations (provisions) to the reserve from income. Banks over $400 million can only deduct what was actually charged-off. Limited the deductibility of interest expense to 80 percent of the borrowing costs associated with buying municipals for public purposes if the municipality issues less than $10 million in securities per year (no interest expense deductibility for other municipals). Eliminated the investment tax credit, the tax deduction for IRA contributions for high-income individuals, and established the alternative minimum tax (AMT).

- **Competitive Equality Banking Act of 1987** (P.L. 100-86, 101 STAT. 552). Also known as **CEBA**. Established new standards for expedited funds availability. Recapitalized the Federal Savings and Loan Insurance Corporation (FSLIC). Expanded FDIC authority for open bank assistance transactions, including bridge banks.

---

[25]Source: FDIC Library (http://www.fdic.gov/regulations/laws/important) with updates and additions by the authors indicated in italics.

- **Financial Institutions Reform, Recovery and Enforcement Act of 1989** (P.L. 101-73, 103 STAT. 183). Also known as **FIRREA**. FIRREA's purpose was to restore the public's confidence in the savings and loan industry. FIRREA abolished the Federal Savings and Loan Insurance Corporation (FSLIC), and the FDIC was given the responsibility of insuring the deposits of thrift institutions in its place. The FDIC insurance fund created to cover thrifts was named the Savings Association Insurance Fund (SAIF), while the fund covering banks was called the Bank Insurance Fund (BIF). FIRREA also abolished the Federal Home Loan Bank Board. Two new agencies, the Federal Housing Finance Board (FHFB) and the Office of Thrift Supervision (OTS), were created to replace it. Finally, FIRREA created the Resolution Trust Corporation (RTC) as a temporary agency of the government. The RTC was given the responsibility of managing and disposing of the assets of failed institutions. An Oversight Board was created to provide supervisory authority over the policies of the RTC, and the Resolution Funding Corporation (RFC) was created to provide funding for RTC operations. *The act mandated the OTS set minimum capital requirements, similar to national banks, and required thrifts divest themselves of all junk bonds. Required savings and loans meet the qualified thrift lender (QTL) test, no less than 70 percent (65 percent today) of the firms assets must be held in mortgage-related investments.*

- **Crime Control Act of 1990** (P.L. 101-647, 104 STAT. 4789). Title XXV of the Crime Control Act, known as the Comprehensive Thrift and Bank Fraud Prosecution and Taxpayer Recovery Act of 1990, greatly expanded the authority of federal regulators to combat financial fraud. This act prohibited undercapitalized banks from making golden parachute and other indemnification payments to institution-affiliated parties. It also increased penalties and prison time for those convicted of bank crimes, increased the powers and authority of the FDIC to take enforcement actions against institutions operating in an unsafe or unsound manner, and gave regulators new procedural powers to recover assets improperly diverted from financial institutions.

- **Federal Deposit Insurance Corporation Improvement Act of 1991** (P.L. 102-242, 105 STAT. 2236). Also known as **FDICIA**. FDICIA greatly increased the powers and authority of the FDIC. Major provisions recapitalized the Bank Insurance Fund and allowed the FDIC to strengthen the fund by borrowing from the Treasury. The act mandated a least-cost resolution method and prompt resolution approach to problem and failing banks and ordered the creation of a risk-based deposit insurance assessment scheme. Brokered deposits and the solicitation of deposits were restricted, as were the nonbank activities of insured state banks. FDICIA created new supervisory and regulatory examination standards and put forth new capital requirements for banks. It also expanded prohibitions against insider activities and created new Truth in Savings provisions.

- **Housing and Community Development Act of 1992** (P.L. 102-550, 106 STAT. 3672). Established regulatory structure for government-sponsored enterprises (GSEs), combated money laundering, and provided regulatory relief to financial institutions.

- **Riegle Community Development and Regulatory Improvement Act of 1994** (P.L. 103-325, 108 STAT. 2160). Established a Community Development Financial Institutions Fund, a wholly owned government corporation that would provide financial and technical assistance to community development financial institutions (CDFIs). Contains several provisions aimed at curbing the practice of "reverse redlining" in which nonbank lenders target low and moderate income homeowners, minorities, and the elderly for home equity loans on abusive terms. Relaxes capital requirements and other regulations to encourage the private sector secondary market for small business loans. Contains more than 50 provisions to reduce bank regulatory burden and paperwork requirements. Requires the Treasury Deptartment to develop ways to substantially reduce the number of currency transactions filed by financial institutions. Contains provisions aimed at shoring up the National Flood Insurance Program.

- **Riegle-Neal Interstate Banking and Branching Efficiency Act of 1994** (P.L. 103-328, 108 STAT. 2338). Permits adequately capitalized and managed bank holding companies to acquire banks in any state one year after enactment. Concentration limits apply and CRA evaluations by the Federal Reserve are required before acquisitions are approved. Beginning June 1, 1997, allows interstate mergers between adequately capitalized and managed banks, subject to concentration limits, state laws, and CRA evaluations. Extends the statute of limitations to permit the FDIC and RTC to revive lawsuits that had expired under state statutes of limitations.

- **Economic Growth and Regulatory Paperwork Reduction Act of 1996** (P.L. 104-208, 110 STAT. 3009). Modified financial institution regulations, including regulations impeding the flow of credit from lending institutions to businesses and consumers. Amended the Truth in Lending Act and the Real Estate Settlement Procedures Act of 1974 to streamline the mortgage lending process. Amended the FDIA to eliminate or revise various application, notice, and recordkeeping requirements to reduce regulatory burden and the cost of credit. Amended the Fair Credit Reporting Act to strengthen consumer protections relating to credit reporting agency practices. Established consumer protections for potential clients of consumer repair services. Clarified lender liability and federal agency liability issues under the CERCLA. Directed FDIC to impose a special assessment on depository institutions to recapitalize the SAIF, aligned SAIF assessment rates with BIF assessment rates, and merged the SAIF and BIF into a new Deposit Insurance Fund.

- **Credit Union Membership Access Act of 1998** (P.L. 105-219). *Addresses four basic areas: membership limits, business lending limits and other regulations, capital requirements, and studies of the industry required.[26] Federal credit union membership falls into one of three basic categories: single common bond, multiple common bonds, and community. Limits additional members of these groups to the immediate family or household of the member. Grandfathers current members, and existing federal credit unions can enroll new members from the employee groups they currently serve. Also allows for multiple common bond federal credit unions to serve unrelated groups provided they have fewer than 3,000 employees or members—service to larger groups requires approval from the National Credit Union Administration and is subject to needs. Finally, the bill limits community credit unions to accepting members from a "well-defined local community, neighborhood, or rural district."*

- **Gramm-Leach-Bliley Act of 1999** (P.L. 106-102, 113 STAT 1338). Repeals last vestiges of the Glass-Steagall Act of 1933. Modifies portions of the Bank Holding Company Act to allow affiliations between banks and insurance underwriters. While preserving authority of states to regulate insurance, the act prohibits state actions that have the effect of preventing bank-affiliated firms from selling insurance on an equal basis with other insurance agents. Law creates a new financial holding company under section 4 of the BHCA, authorized to engage in: underwriting and selling insurance and securities, conducting both commercial and merchant banking, investing in and developing real estate and other "complementary activities." There are limits on the kinds of nonfinancial activities these new entities may engage in. Allows national banks to underwrite municipal bonds. Restricts the disclosure of nonpublic customer information by financial institutions. All financial institutions must provide customers the opportunity to "opt-out" of the sharing of the customers' nonpublic information with unaffiliated third parties. The act imposes criminal penalties on anyone who obtains customer information from a financial institution under false pretenses. Amends the Community Reinvestment Act to require that financial holding companies cannot be formed before their insured depository institutions receive and maintain a satisfactory CRA rating. Also requires public disclosure of bank-community CRA-related agreements. Grants some regulatory relief to small institutions in the shape of reducing the frequency of their CRA examinations if they have received outstanding or satisfactory ratings. Prohibits affiliations and acquisitions between commercial firms and unitary thrift institutions. Makes significant changes in the operation of the Federal Home Loan Bank System, easing membership requirements and loosening restrictions on the use of FHLB funds.

- **International Money Laundering Abatement and Financial Anti-Terrorism Act of 2001** (P.L. 107-56). *Also known as* **Title III of the USA Patriot Act**. Legislation designed to prevent terrorists and others from using the U.S. financial system anonymously to move funds obtained from or destined for illegal activity. Authorizes and requires additional record keeping and reporting by financial institutions and greater scrutiny of accounts held for foreign banks and of private banking conducted for foreign persons. Requires financial institutions to establish anti–money laundering programs and imposes various standards on money-transmitting businesses. Amends criminal anti–money laundering statutes and procedures for forfeitures in money laundering cases and requires further cooperation between financial institutions and government agencies in fighting money laundering. Requires additional reports and "know-your-customer" standards for private banking and correspondent relationships.

- **Sarbanes-Oxley Act of 2002** (P.L. 107-204). Establishes the Public Company Oversight Board to regulate public accounting firms that audit publicly traded companies. Prohibits such firms from providing other services to such companies along with the audit. Requires that CEOs and CFOs certify the annual and quarterly reports of publicly traded companies. Authorizes, and in some cases requires, that the Securities and Exchange Commission (SEC) issue rules governing audits. Requires that insiders may no longer trade their company's securities during pension fund blackout periods. Mandates various studies including a study of the involvement of investment banks and financial advisors in the scandals preceding the legislation. Also included are whistle blower protections, new federal criminal laws, including a ban on alteration of documents.

---

[26]Anason, Dean, "The Major Provisions of Controversial New Law," *American Banker*, August 10, 1998.

- **Fair and Accurate Credit Transactions Act of 2003** (P.L. 108-159). Also known as FACT. Contains extensive amendments to the Fair Credit Reporting Act and is designed to improve the accuracy and transparency of the national credit reporting system and prevent identity theft and assist victims. Contains provisions enhancing consumer rights in situations involving alleged identity theft, credit scoring, and claims of inaccurate information. Requires use of consumer reports to provide certain information to consumers who are offered credit on terms that are materially less favorable than the offers that the creditor makes to a substantial portion of its consumers. Companies that share consumer information among affiliated companies must provide consumers notice and an opt-out for sharing of such information if the information will be used for marketing purposes.

PART II

# EVALUATING BANK PERFORMANCE

# Analyzing Bank Performance

After more than three years of squabbling over documents, accounting procedures, loan exposure, and multiple earnings restatements, the Office of the Comptroller of the Currency (OCC) closed the $1.3 billion Hamilton Bank on January 11, 2002, and appointed the Federal Deposit Insurance Corporation (FDIC) as receiver. The FDIC immediately started preparing for the possible sale of $1 billion in loans. On January 14, 2002, NASDAQ halted trading in the stock of the bank's parent, Hamilton Bancorp. The closure was the climax of a three-year battle between regulators and Hamilton Bank over accounting practices and the bank's loan portfolio, which was built around loans to nonfinancial firms and banks in Latin America and to importers/exporters in South Florida. In 2001, Hamilton agreed to the OCC's demands to start charging-off some of the Latin American loans. As of September 30, 2001, the bank had about $80 million in equity remaining and $75.1 million in loans that were nonperforming, or about 8 percent of total loans. The bank's charge-offs and losses on sales of Latin American loans resulted in a net loss in excess of $28 million for 2001.

At the time the OCC closed Hamilton Bank, it still reported a 2.25 percent risk-based capital ratio, which made it "undercapitalized" for regulatory purposes. The OCC used its power in conjunction with the FDIC under "prompt corrective action" provided by the Federal Deposit Insurance Corporation Improvement Act of 1991 to close a bank when its capital falls below minimum levels in order to protect the FDIC insurance fund. At the last safety-and-soundness examination of Hamilton, shortly before its failure, the OCC indicated that the bank's condition had deteriorated from its already unsatisfactory condition reported in prior exams. The OCC also stated that management had failed to make progress in resolving the problems and that the board of directors failed to hold management accountable for the needed improvements. The OCC said the bank's capital was rapidly being depleted and that classified loans had increased to more than 150 percent of capital. Hamilton had been operating under a cease-and-desist order that imposed significant operational and financial guidelines upon reserves to cover foreign loans, the purchase and sale of loans, and required capital levels. As an example of its problems, Hamilton sold loans to Ecuadorean banks valued at $38.3 million for $22.3 million in cash during the third quarter of 2001, improving asset quality but depleting capital.

Although banks fail for different reasons, Hamilton is unusual because it successfully battled over accounting principles with regulators for almost three years. Hamilton restated 1999 and 2000 earnings to report a $7.3 million loss and then reported a $24.7 million loss (about one-third of total equity) for the second quarter of 2001. How can a bank's loan losses get this extreme? Did a few large bad loans surprise managers and bring about failure? Did the bank's managers disguise loan problems that were always there? The OCC apparently believed that managers hid the problem loans, the bank's profits were systematically overstated and true profits were below average—hence the requirement to restate earnings.

Many banks experience dramatic changes in profits from one period to the next or relative to what stock analysts expect. In many cases, profits are lower because of unanticipated loan losses. PNC Bank, discussed extensively in this chapter, is a prime example. From 2000–2004, PNC reported a return on equity (ROE) that ranged from 5.65 percent to 21.63 percent due to volatile loan loss provisions and noninterest revenue. In other cases, profits are higher because of extraordinary growth in noninterest income. A key point is that it is becoming increasingly difficult to evaluate *performance by looking at reported balance sheet and income statement data. Bank managers can manage, or manip-ulate, net income to disguise potential problems.*

*This chapter presents a procedure for analyzing bank performance using periodic balance sheet and income statement data. It describes the components of financial statements, provides a framework for comparing the trade-offs between profitability and risk, and compares the performance of a small community bank with that of a large super regional banking organization. It uses data presented in a bank's Uniform Bank Performance Report (UBPR) to demonstrate the analysis.*

---

From 1985 to 1990, 1,016 commercial banks failed throughout the United States, a rate of just over 169 bank failures each year. Many other banks avoided closing only because of arranged mergers and forbearance, or were placed on the regulators' problem bank list—indicating severe operating difficulties. The recent trend, however, has been quite favorable as banks earned record profits and only 55 banks failed from 1995 to 2004, or over 5 per year. Can an objective observer identify problem institutions before they fail? Is it possible to distinguish between strong and weak banks on the basis of reported earnings and balance sheet figures? How can the trade-off between risk and profitability be evaluated; in particular, how should risk be measured? Financial institutions are fundamentally unique in that they assume credit risk, liquidity risk, interest rate risk, operational risk, compliance, regulatory and legal risk, as well as reputational risk every day as part of their normal business. Managers must set a level of risk tolerance consistent with their expected returns.

U.S. commercial banks reported record aggregate profits every year throughout the 1990s and early 2000s. Return on equity (ROE) and return on assets (ROA) set new standards for the banking industry with aggregate bank net income equal to a record $127.2 billion in 2004 (see Exhibit 2.1). The 1990s evidenced improved asset quality with fewer loan defaults, higher interest income on assets relative to interest expense on liabilities, and significantly greater noninterest income relative to noninterest expense. While the events of September 11, 2001, the recession of 2001 and corporate scandals of 2001–2004 reduced returns to shareholders, they have been largely earnings events rather than solvency events. Loan losses increased in 2001 and 2002, particularly at larger banks, but fell through 2004. The primary problem areas have been personal (individual) bankruptcies, relatively high losses on credit card loans,

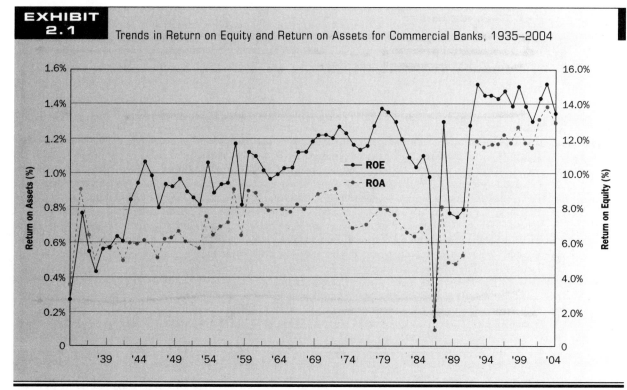

**EXHIBIT 2.1** Trends in Return on Equity and Return on Assets for Commercial Banks, 1935–2004

Source: FDIC Quarterly Banking Profile, http://www.fdic.gov/, http://www2.fdic.gov/qbp.

trading account losses, commercial and industrial loan losses, and restructuring charges as a result of mergers and acquisitions at the largest banks.[1]

This chapter details the essential elements of evaluating financial institution performance. The analysis begins by introducing bank financial statements. A return on equity framework is then used to describe the trade-offs between profitability and risk and provide measures that differentiate between high- and low-performance banks. A high performance bank is one that makes an exceptional return to shareholders while maintaining an acceptable level of risk. This definition makes it clear that high performance is more than high returns. It is the ability to generate high returns for the level of risk assumed by the institution.

The analytical framework is applied to data for **PNC Bank**, a large multibank company owned by PNC Bank Corporation, and **Community National Bank**, a representative specialized community bank.[2] The analysis allows us to compare the financial characteristics of different-sized banks. The chapter also introduces the CAMELS system used by federal supervisors to rate banks. Finally, because banks can disguise adverse changes in their performance from year to year, special attention is paid to sources of financial statement manipulation.

## COMMERCIAL BANK FINANCIAL STATEMENTS

Like other financial intermediaries, commercial banks facilitate the flow of funds from surplus spending units (savers) to deficit spending units (borrowers). Their financial characteristics largely reflect government-imposed operating restrictions and peculiar features of the specific markets served. Three unique characteristics stand out and each presents special problems and risks to the bank manager:

1. Because their function is primarily financial, most banks own few fixed assets and thus exhibit low operating leverage.

2. Most bank liabilities are payable on demand or carry short-term maturities so depositors can renegotiate deposit rates as market interest rates change. As a result, interest expense changes coincidentally with short-run changes in market interest rates creating significant asset allocation and pricing problems.

3. Banks operate with less equity capital than nonfinancial companies, which increases financial leverage and the volatility of earnings.

### THE BALANCE SHEET

A bank's balance sheet presents financial information comparing what a bank owns with what it owes and the ownership interest of stockholders. Assets indicate what the bank owns; liabilities represent what the bank owes; and equity refers to the owners' interest such that:

$$\text{Assets} = \text{Liabilities} + \text{Equity} \qquad (2.1)$$

Balance sheet figures are stock values calculated for a particular day or point in time. As such, values on the balance sheet represent the balance of cash, loans, investments, and premises owned by the bank on a particular day. Regulators require that banks report balance sheet and income statement data quarterly, so figures are available publicly for the three-month periods ending March, June, September, and December each year. Exhibit 2.2 shows balance sheets for two separate banking organizations. The first two blocks of data represent the consolidated statement for PNC Bank. PNC Bank is the principal subsidiary bank of the *financial holding company,* The PNC Financial Services Group, headquartered in Pittsburgh, Pennsylvania (http://www.pncbank.com).[3] At year-end 2004, PNC Bank reported assets of $73.8 billion, representing over 95 percent of the holding company's consolidated assets. PNC increased its total assets by more than $10 billion in 2004 after having shrunk its assets from just under $68 billion in 1999 due to loan problems and accounting issues. The final two blocks of data in Exhibit 2.2 are for Community National Bank (CNB), which represents a typical small independent bank. This bank's main office is located in a metropolitan area with three branches and no nonbank subsidiaries. At year-end 2004, CNB had $210 million in assets, up 9 percent from 2003.

At year-end 2004, PNC Bank held approximately 4 percent of its assets in nonearning cash and due from banks, 26 percent in investments and 58 percent in loans. CNB held 5.6 percent of its assets in nonearning cash and due from banks, 25.5 percent in investments, and 62 percent in net loans. PNC, which owned proportionately fewer

---

[1] A good reference for up-to-date banking statistics on the Internet is the FDIC's Web page at www.fdic.gov.

[2] PNC Bank Corp. is a large and complex banking organization. We will only deal with PNC Bank in this chapter, assuming that PNC Bank can be evaluated independently of PNC Bank Corp.

[3] PNC went through a major restructuring from 2000 to 2001. For more details, see the Contempory Issues Box: "PNC: A Case of Restated Financials" later in the chapter.

**EXHIBIT 2.2**  2003–2004 Balance Sheet Information for PNC Bank and Community National Bank

| Balance Sheet | PNC Bank, National Association | | | | | | Community National Bank | | | | | |
| --- | --- | --- | --- | --- | --- | --- | --- | --- | --- | --- | --- | --- |
| | Dec-03 | | | Dec-04 | | | Dec-03 | | | Dec-04 | | |
| | % Cha | $ 1,000 | % of Total | % Cha | $ 1,000 | % of Total | % Cha | $ 1,000 | % of Total | % Cha | $ 1,000 | % of Total |
| **ASSETS** | | | | | | | | | | | | |
| **Loans:** | | | | | | | | | | | | |
| Real estate loans | 1.2% | 15,639,089 | 25.2% | 32.4% | 20,701,904 | 28.0% | 4.0% | 75,324 | 39.1% | 12.9% | 85,050 | 40.5% |
| Commercial loans | -8.4% | 11,879,285 | 19.2% | 23.8% | 14,707,458 | 19.9% | -5.8% | 34,288 | 17.8% | 12.9% | 38,716 | 18.4% |
| Individual loans | -4.4% | 2,501,847 | 4.0% | 52.6% | 3,816,861 | 5.2% | 26.7% | 8,454 | 4.4% | -5.2% | 8,011 | 3.8% |
| Agricultural loans | 9.2% | 984 | 0.0% | 57.0% | 1,545 | 0.0% | 0.0% | 0 | 0.0% | 0.0% | 0 | 0.0% |
| Other LN&LS in domestic off. | -20.5% | 3,022,795 | 4.9% | -0.8% | 2,999,113 | 4.1% | 13.0% | 26 | 0.0% | 284.6% | 100 | 0.0% |
| LN&LS in foreign off. | 15.6% | 1,190,025 | 1.9% | 2.8% | 1,222,904 | 1.7% | 0.0% | 0 | 0.0% | 0.0% | 0 | 0.0% |
| Gross Loans & Leases | -4.6% | 34,234,025 | 55.2% | 26.9% | 43,449,785 | 58.9% | 2.2% | 118,092 | 61.3% | 11.7% | 131,877 | 62.8% |
| Less: Unearned Income | 8.0% | 44,867 | 0.1% | 0.2% | 44,949 | 0.1% | 0.0% | 0 | 0.0% | 0.0% | 0 | 0.0% |
| Loan & Lease loss Allowance | -5.8% | 606,886 | 1.0% | -3.8% | 583,915 | 0.8% | 6.7% | 1,258 | 0.7% | 28.5% | 1,617 | 0.8% |
| Net Loans & Leases | -4.5% | 33,582,272 | 54.1% | 27.5% | 42,820,921 | 58.0% | 2.2% | 116,834 | 60.6% | 11.5% | 130,260 | 62.0% |
| **Investments:** | | | | | | | | | | | | |
| U.S. Treasury & Agency securities | 90.6% | 5,574,108 | 9.0% | 15.9% | 6,460,936 | 8.8% | 73.9% | 34,937 | 18.1% | 24.8% | 43,591 | 20.7% |
| Municipal securities | -46.9% | 7,719 | 0.0% | 1606.0% | 131,685 | 0.2% | -0.5% | 613 | 0.3% | -0.5% | 610 | 0.3% |
| Foreign debt securities | -100.0% | 0 | 0.0% | 0.0% | 0 | 0.0% | 0.0% | 0 | 0.0% | 0.0% | 0 | 0.0% |
| All other securities | 1.1% | 8,804,028 | 14.2% | 3.0% | 9,064,146 | 12.3% | #N/A | 2,104 | 1.1% | -2.2% | 2,057 | 1.0% |
| Interest bearing bank balances | 16.4% | 259,318 | 0.4% | 51.8% | 393,713 | 0.5% | #N/A | 4,428 | 2.3% | -57.5% | 1,881 | 0.9% |
| Fed funds sold & resales | -54.6% | 1,106,733 | 1.8% | 56.2% | 1,728,372 | 2.3% | 175.0% | 7,000 | 3.6% | -21.4% | 5,500 | 2.6% |
| Trading account assets | -9.1% | 935,042 | 1.5% | 78.3% | 1,667,330 | 2.3% | 0.0% | 0 | 0.0% | 0.0% | 0 | 0.0% |
| Total Investments | 8.7% | 16,686,948 | 26.9% | 16.5% | 19,446,182 | 26.3% | 111.1% | 49,082 | 25.5% | 9.3% | 53,639 | 25.5% |
| Total Earning Assets | -0.5% | 50,269,220 | 81.1% | 23.9% | 62,267,103 | 84.4% | 20.6% | 165,916 | 86.1% | 10.8% | 183,899 | 87.5% |
| Nonint Cash & Due from banks | -6.9% | 2,926,330 | 4.7% | 8.5% | 3,174,493 | 4.3% | -16.6% | 13,083 | 6.8% | -10.7% | 11,682 | 5.6% |
| Premises, fixed assets & capital leases | 24.4% | 1,039,603 | 1.7% | 2.5% | 1,066,028 | 1.4% | -12.2% | 5,642 | 2.9% | 2.2% | 5,768 | 2.7% |
| Other real estate owned | 21.8% | 14,208 | 0.0% | 0.7% | 14,301 | 0.0% | -84.3% | 325 | 0.2% | -100.0% | 0 | 0.0% |
| Investment in unconsolidated subs. | 252.4% | 17,386 | 0.0% | -12.4% | 15,223 | 0.0% | 0.0% | 0 | 0.0% | 0.0% | 0 | 0.0% |
| Acceptances and other assets | 51.8% | 7,754,149 | 12.5% | -6.2% | 7,272,017 | 9.9% | 259.8% | 7,761 | 4.0% | 13.2% | 8,783 | 4.2% |
| **Total Assets** | 4.0% | 62,020,896 | 100.0% | 19.0% | 73,809,165 | 100.0% | 18.6% | 192,727 | 100.0% | 9.0% | 210,132 | 100.0% |
| Average Assets During Quarter | 6.8% | 62,719,462 | 101.1% | 17.0% | 73,391,052 | 99.4% | 17.5% | 191,480 | 99.4% | 9.4% | 209,525 | 99.7% |

*(continues)*

**EXHIBIT 2.2** (continued)

| Balance Sheet | PNC Bank, National Association | | | | | | Community National Bank | | | | | |
|---|---|---|---|---|---|---|---|---|---|---|---|---|
| | % Cha | Dec-03 $1,000 | % of Total | % Cha | Dec-04 $1,000 | % of Total | % Cha | Dec-03 $1,000 | % of Total | % Cha | Dec-04 $1,000 | % of Total |
| *LIABILITIES* | | | | | | | | | | | | |
| Demand deposits | 2.6% | 7,070,434 | 11.4% | 20.1% | 8,488,607 | 11.5% | 12.6% | 72,500 | 37.6% | 12.4% | 81,514 | 38.8% |
| All NOW & ATS accounts | 9.9% | 1,529,861 | 2.5% | 8.9% | 1,666,003 | 2.3% | 15.5% | 12,478 | 6.5% | 39.7% | 17,437 | 8.3% |
| Money market deposit accounts | 6.8% | 24,502,371 | 39.5% | 8.8% | 26,665,024 | 36.1% | 56.7% | 46,458 | 24.1% | 5.3% | 48,908 | 23.3% |
| Other savings deposits | 5.0% | 2,055,659 | 3.3% | 35.4% | 2,782,931 | 3.8% | 7.3% | 7,812 | 4.1% | 26.7% | 9,896 | 4.7% |
| Time deposits under $100M | -15.9% | 6,242,628 | 10.1% | 13.1% | 7,063,499 | 9.6% | 4.0% | 24,469 | 12.7% | -14.4% | 20,949 | 10.0% |
| **Core Deposits** | 2.0% | 41,400,953 | 66.8% | 12.7% | 46,666,064 | 63.2% | 20.7% | 163,717 | 84.9% | 9.2% | 178,704 | 85.0% |
| Time deposits of $100M or more | -17.6% | 1,775,943 | 2.9% | 80.5% | 3,205,331 | 4.3% | 4.9% | 13,572 | 7.0% | 8.4% | 14,714 | 7.0% |
| Deposits held in foreign offices | 71.5% | 2,371,548 | 3.8% | 26.3% | 2,994,623 | 4.1% | 0.0% | 0 | 0.0% | 0.0% | 0 | 0.0% |
| **Total deposits** | 3.2% | 45,548,444 | 73.4% | 16.1% | 52,866,018 | 71.6% | 19.3% | 177,289 | 92.0% | 9.1% | 193,418 | 92.0% |
| Fed funds purchased & resale | 25.2% | 499,232 | 0.8% | 221.8% | 1,606,647 | 2.2% | 0.0% | 1,000 | 0.5% | 0.0% | 1,000 | 0.5% |
| FHLB borrowings < 1 Yr | 898.2% | 1,000,000 | 1.6% | -100.0% | 0 | 0.0% | 0.0% | 0 | 0.0% | 0.0% | 0 | 0.0% |
| Other borrowings inc mat < 1 yr | 99.4% | 2,264,921 | 3.7% | 34.5% | 3,046,632 | 4.1% | 0.0% | 0 | 0.0% | 0.0% | 0 | 0.0% |
| **Memo: S.T. non core funding** | 73.5% | 7,111,124 | 11.5% | 25.7% | 8,936,809 | 12.1% | 0.1% | 7,901 | 4.1% | 28.7% | 10,169 | 4.8% |
| **Memo: S.T. Volatile liabilities** | 36.2% | 6,911,644 | 11.1% | 57.0% | 10,853,233 | 14.7% | 4.5% | 14,572 | 7.6% | 7.8% | 15,714 | 7.5% |
| FHLB borrowings > 1 Yr | -90.0% | 115,406 | 0.2% | -23.3% | 88,508 | 0.1% | 0.0% | 0 | 0.0% | 0.0% | 0 | 0.0% |
| Other borrowings inc mat > 1 yr | -2.9% | 1,765,851 | 2.8% | 105.2% | 3,624,223 | 4.9% | 0.0% | 0 | 0.0% | 0.0% | 0 | 0.0% |
| Acceptances & other liabilities | -0.1% | 3,864,388 | 6.2% | 18.7% | 4,585,994 | 6.2% | -11.0% | 395 | 0.2% | 31.6% | 520 | 0.2% |
| **Total Liabilities before Sub. Notes** | 4.6% | 55,058,242 | 88.8% | 19.5% | 65,818,022 | 89.2% | 19.1% | 178,684 | 92.7% | 9.1% | 194,938 | 92.8% |
| Sub. Notes & Debentures | 16.2% | 1,340,133 | 2.2% | 41.4% | 1,895,482 | 2.6% | 0.0% | 0 | 0.0% | 0.0% | 0 | 0.0% |
| **Total Liabilities** | 4.9% | 56,398,375 | 90.9% | 20.1% | 67,713,504 | 91.7% | 19.1% | 178,684 | 92.7% | 9.1% | 194,938 | 92.8% |
| All common and preferred capital | -4.1% | 5,622,521 | 9.1% | 8.4% | 6,095,661 | 8.3% | 12.0% | 14,043 | 7.3% | 8.2% | 15,194 | 7.2% |
| **Total Liabilities & Capital** | 4.0% | 62,020,896 | 100.0% | 19.0% | 73,809,165 | 100.0% | 18.6% | 192,727 | 100.0% | 9.0% | 210,132 | 100.0% |
| Memoranda: | | | | | | | | | | | | |
| Officer, Shareholder Loans (#) | 0.0% | 2 | 0.0% | 50.0% | 3 | 0.0% | -50.0% | 1 | 0.0% | 0.0% | 1 | 0.0% |
| Officer, Shareholder Loans ($) | -19.4% | 14,211 | 0.0% | 58.0% | 22,449 | 0.0% | 31.7% | 1,852 | 1.0% | 22.2% | 2,263 | 1.1% |
| Non-investment ORE | 21.8% | 14,208 | 0.0% | 0.7% | 14,301 | 0.0% | -84.3% | 325 | 0.2% | -100.0% | 0 | 0.0% |
| Loans held for sale | -10.2% | 1,378,603 | 2.2% | 20.9% | 1,667,154 | 2.3% | 0.0% | 0 | 0.0% | 0.0% | 0 | 0.0% |
| Held-to maturity securities | #N/A | 2,114 | 0.0% | -100.0% | 0 | 0.0% | 36.7% | 4,073 | 2.1% | -56.2% | 1,785 | 0.8% |
| Available-for-sale-securities | 23.4% | 14,383,741 | 23.2% | 8.9% | 15,656,767 | 21.2% | 89.4% | 33,581 | 17.4% | 32.4% | 44,473 | 21.2% |
| Total Securities | 23.4% | 14,385,855 | 23.2% | 8.8% | 15,656,767 | 21.2% | 81.8% | 37,654 | 19.5% | 22.9% | 46,258 | 22.0% |
| All Brokered Deposits | 14.2% | 1,533,123 | 2.5% | 49.3% | 2,289,151 | 3.1% | 0.0% | 0 | 0.0% | 0.0% | 0 | 0.0% |

loans, investments, and noninterest bearing cash and due balances from banks in 2004 as compared with CNB, changed its portfolio rather dramatically during the year. For the first time in five years, PNC increased its loans—in this case by over $9 billion. During 2003 PNC restructured its operations and divested higher-risk loans. PNC's position is somewhat unusual in that most large banks tend to have larger loan portfolios (as a percentage of total assets) and a smaller proportion of investments than do smaller banks. In summary, PNC's accounting problems and loan losses of the early 2000s forced it to reduce its loan portfolio only to finally reverse the trend in 2004.

The PNC Financial Services Group is a *financial holding company* as discussed in Chapter 1. Its corporate legal structure consists of two subsidiary banks (PNC Bank, Delaware, with $2.3 billion in assets and PNC Bank, NA in Pittsburgh, Pennsylvania, with $73.8 billion in assets) and more than 13 active nonbank subsidiaries. PNC Bank, NA, headquartered in Pittsburgh, is the corporation's principal bank subsidiary. The holding company operates five major lines of business engaged in community banking, wholesale banking, wealth management, asset management, and mutual fund services:

- **Regional community banking** provides banking and financial services to 1.8 million consumers and more than 200,000 small businesses.
- **Wholesale banking** provides financial services solutions to middle market and large corporations in PNC's region and specialized real estate finance and asset-based lending nationally.
- **PNC Advisors** covers the spectrum of wealth management and institutional investment management needs through a network of 115 offices in 20 states.
- **BlackRock** is a large publicly traded asset management company with almost $350 billion in assets under management.
- **PFPC** is in the global funds servicing industry and one of the nation's largest providers of mutual fund transfer agency and fund accounting and administration services.

**BANK ASSETS.** Bank assets fall into one of four general categories: loans, investment securities, noninterest cash and due from banks, and other assets:

1. **Loans** are the major asset in most banks' portfolios and generate the greatest amount of income before expenses and taxes. They also exhibit the highest default risk and some are relatively illiquid.

2. **Investment securities** are held to earn interest, help meet liquidity needs, speculate on interest rate movements, meet pledging requirements, and serve as part of a bank's dealer functions.

3. **Noninterest cash and due from banks** consists of vault cash, deposits held at Federal Reserve Banks, deposits held at other financial institutions, and cash items in the process of collection. These assets are held to meet customer withdrawal needs and legal reserve requirements, assist in check clearing and wire transfers, and effect the purchase and sale of Treasury securities.

4. **Other assets** are residual assets of relatively small magnitudes such as bankers' acceptances, premises and equipment, other real estate owned, and other smaller amounts.

## Loans.
A bank negotiates loan terms with each borrower that vary with the use of proceeds, source of repayment and type of collateral. Maturities range from call loans payable on demand to residential mortgages amortized over 30 years. The interest rate may be fixed over the life of the loan or vary with changes in market interest rates. Similarly, the loan principal may be repaid periodically or as a lump sum. Exhibit 2.2 groups loans into six categories according to the use of proceeds: real estate, commercial, individual, agricultural, other loans in domestic offices, and loans in foreign offices:

1. **Real estate loans** are loans secured by real estate and generally consist either of property loans secured by first mortgages or interim construction loans.

2. **Commercial loans** consist of commercial and industrial loans, loans to financial institutions, and obligations (other than securities) to states and political subdivisions. Commercial loans appear in many forms but typically finance a firm's working capital needs, equipment purchases and plant expansions. This category also includes credit extended to other financial institutions, security brokers and dealers.

3. **Individual loans** include those negotiated directly with individuals for household, family, and other personal expenditures, and those obtained indirectly through the purchase of retail paper. Loans made for the purchase of credit card items and durable goods constitute the greatest volume of this consumer credit.

4. **Agricultural loans** appear in many forms but typically finance agricultural production and include other loans to farmers.

5. **Other loans in domestic offices** include all other loans and all lease-financing receivables in domestic offices. The dollar amount of **outstanding leases** is included in gross loans because lease financing is an alternative to direct loans.

6. **International loans**, labeled **loans and leases in foreign offices,** are essentially business loans and lease receivables made to foreign enterprises or loans guaranteed by foreign governments. International loans carry significant risks beyond normal default risk. During the fourth quarter of 2001, for example, Fleet-Boston charged-off more than $700 million in loans to Argentina when local governments and businesses could not pay.

Two adjustments are made to *gross loans and leases* to obtain a *net loan* figure. First, unearned income is deducted from gross interest received. **Unearned income** is income that has been received but not yet earned. Second, gross loans are reduced by the dollar magnitude of a bank's loan and lease loss allowance (loan loss reserve). The **loan and lease loss allowance** is a contra-asset (negative asset) reserve account that exists in recognition that some loans will not be repaid. The reserve's maximum size is determined by tax law but increases with the growth in problem loans and decreases with net loan charge-offs. A bank is permitted a tax deduction for net additions to the loss reserve, denoted as the provision for loan losses on the income statement.[4]

**Investments.** A bank's investments include both short-term and long-term investment securities, interest-bearing bank balances (deposits due from other banks), federal funds sold, securities purchased under agreement to resell (repurchase agreements or RPs), and other trading account assets.[5] The primary attraction to *investment securities* is that they earn interest, and administration and transaction costs are extremely low. Banks also concentrate their purchases on higher-quality instruments so that defaults are rare. When interest rates fall, most investment securities increase in value because they eventually carry above-average interest rates. Banks can either earn very attractive yields relative to their borrowing costs or sell the securities at a gain. Of course, when rates rise, investment securities decrease in value as they carry below-market interest rates.

In terms of liquidity, banks own a large amount of low-risk, **short-term securities**—those with a maturity of one year or less—that can be easily sold to obtain cash. They have maturities ranging from overnight to one year and carry returns that vary quickly with changes in money market conditions. Short-term securities are extremely liquid and can be easily sold at a price close to that initially paid by the bank. Because of their lower risk and short term to mature, the bank earns significantly less interest than what could be earned on longer-term securities. Short-term securities include U.S. Treasury and Agency securities, municipal securities, foreign debt securities, and other securities.

**Long-term investment securities** consist of notes and bonds that have a maturity of more than one year and generate taxable or tax-exempt interest. Treasury securities and obligations of federal agencies represent the bulk of taxable investments but banks also purchase mortgage-backed securities and small amounts of foreign and corporate bonds.[6] Most of these carry fixed interest rates with maturities up to 20 years. Banks own some municipal securities with interest payments that are exempt from federal income taxes. Municipal securities are classified as either **general obligation** or **revenue bonds.** Changes in bank tax rules have made most municipal securities unattractive to banks.[7] Banks are generally restricted from purchasing corporate stock as an investment, but can own it under two conditions: if it is acquired as collateral on a loan, and in order to be members of the Federal Reserve System or Federal Home Loan Bank system, banks must own stock in the Federal Reserve Bank or Federal Home Loan Bank.

**Accounting for Investment Securities.** At purchase, a bank must designate the objective behind buying investment securities as either held-to-maturity, trading, or available-for-sale. Following FASB 115:

- **Held-to-maturity securities** are recorded on the balance sheet at amortized cost. This treatment reflects the objective to hold the securities until they mature so that the expected income is interest income with a return of principal at maturity.

- A bank actively buys and sells **trading account securities** principally to speculate on interest rate movements and profit on price changes. These securities are typically held for brief periods, such as a few days, so the bank marks the securities to market (reports them at current market value) on the balance sheet and reports unrealized gains and losses on the income statement.

---

[4]The reported provision for loan losses is normally less than the actual tax deduction allowed by the Internal Revenue Service and claimed by the bank. Large banks report loan loss provisions determined by average loan loss experience during the previous 5 years.

[5]The Uniform Bank Performance Report differentiates between "Investments" and "Investment Securities." "Investments" includes "Investment Securities."

[6]The asset category "U.S. Treasury & Agency Securities" listed in the Uniform Bank Performance Report is somewhat misleading. This category is actually defined as the total of U.S. Treasury and Agency securities and corporate obligations. This, in practice, would include almost all of the securities in a bank's portfolio except for municipal, foreign, and equity securities. For more information, consult the UBPR User's Guide available from the FFIEC on the Internet at http://www.ffiec.gov.

[7]As noted in Chapter 1, the Tax Reform Act of 1986 eliminated bank deductions for borrowing costs associated with financing the purchase of most municipal bonds. The impact of this tax change is described in Chapter 13.

- All other investment securities are classified as **available-for-sale** because management may choose to sell them prior to final maturity. As such, they are recorded at market value on the balance sheet with a corresponding change to stockholders' equity as unrealized gains and losses on securities holdings. There is no reporting of gains or losses on the income statement with these securities.

Many large banks also operate as security dealers that maintain an inventory of securities for resale and underwrite municipal issues. Banks that form *a financial holding company* can underwrite and deal in bonds and equity securities (see Chapter 1). The inventory, which is listed as *trading account securities* on the balance sheet, comprises mainly Treasury obligations and collateralized mortgage obligations. The bank earns interest on this inventory but also tries to profit on the difference between the purchase and sale price of the securities. It subsequently bears the risk that the market value of its inventory might decrease. Large banks, in addition, earn fee income by underwriting securities.

**Noninterest Cash and Due from Banks.** This asset category consists of vault cash, deposits held at Federal Reserve Banks, deposits held at other financial institutions, and cash items in the process of collection:

1. **Vault cash** is coin and currency that the bank holds to meet customer withdrawals.

2. **Deposits held at the Federal Reserve** are demand balances used to meet legal reserve requirements, assist in check clearing and wire transfers, or effect the purchase and sale of Treasury securities. The amount of required reserve deposits is set by regulation as a fraction of qualifying bank deposit liabilities and currently stands at 10 percent of transactions deposits. Banks hold **balances at other financial institutions**, called correspondent banks, primarily to purchase services. The amount is determined by the volume and cost of services provided such that income from investing the deposits at least covers the cost of the services provided by the correspondent bank.

3. **Cash items in the process of collection (CIPC)** are generally the largest component of cash, representing checks written against other institutions and presented to the bank for payment for which credit has not been given. To verify that actual balances support each check, the bank delays credit until the check clears or a reasonable time elapses. The volume of net deferred credit is commonly called *float*. The recent passage of federal legislation (Check 21) has reduced float by accelerating check clearing time.

**Other Assets.** This category consists of residual assets of relatively small magnitudes, including the depreciated value of bank **premises and equipment, other real estate owned (OREO), investment in unconsolidated subsidiaries, customers' liability to the bank under acceptances** and **other assets**. For many problem banks, other real estate owned is substantial because it normally represents property taken as collateral against a loan that was unpaid. Commercial banks own relatively few fixed assets. They operate with low fixed costs relative to nonfinancial firms and exhibit low operating leverage.

**BANK LIABILITIES AND STOCKHOLDERS' EQUITY.** Bank funding sources are classified according to the type of debt instrument and equity component. The characteristics of various debt instruments differ in terms of check-writing capabilities, interest paid, maturity, whether they carry FDIC insurance, and whether they can be traded in the secondary market. The components of equity (common and preferred capital) also have different characteristics and arise under varied circumstances such as the issuance of stock, net income not paid out as dividends, and Treasury stock or related transactions.

Historically, banks were limited in what interest rates they could pay on different types of deposits. Since 1986, all interest rate restrictions have been eliminated, except for the prohibition of interest on corporate demand deposits. Banks can now compete for deposits by offering unrestricted interest rates on virtually all of their liabilities. Larger banks also issue subordinated notes and debentures, which are long-term uninsured debt. Bank liabilities are composed of transactions accounts, savings and time deposits, and other borrowings:

Transactions Accounts

1. **Demand deposits** are held by individuals, partnerships, corporations, and governments that pay no interest. Prior to the Depository Institutions Act of 1980, they served as the only legal transactions account nationally that could be offered by depository institutions. Businesses now own the bulk of existing demand deposits because they are not allowed to own interest-bearing transactions accounts at banks.

2. **Negotiable orders of withdrawal (NOW)** and **automatic transfers from savings (ATS)** pay interest set by each bank without federal restrictions.[8] These accounts are most commonly referred to as interest checking accounts. Banks often require minimum balances before a depositor earns interest, impose service

---

[8]Prior to 1983, banks and savings and loans could not pay market interest rates on most deposits less than $100,000. Limits were gradually removed so that, by 1986, only demand deposit rates were restricted.

charges, and may limit the number of free checks a customer can write each month, but these terms vary among institutions. These accounts are available only to noncommercial customers.

3. **Money market deposit accounts (MMDAs)** similarly pay market rates, but a customer is limited to no more than six checks and automatic transfers each month. This restriction exempts banks from holding required reserves against MMDAs as they are technically savings accounts, not transactions accounts. With no required reserves, banks can pay higher rates of interest on MMDAs versus NOWs for the same effective cost.

Savings and Time Deposits

1. **Savings and time deposits** contribute a large portion of funding, especially at community banks. Passbook savings deposits are small-denomination accounts that have no set maturity and no check-writing capabilities. Two general time deposit categories exist with a $100,000 denomination separating the groups.

2. **Time deposits less than $100,000** are most often called small certificates of deposits (CDs). The features of small CDs are not as standardized as large CDs although most banks market standardized instruments so that customers are not confused. Banks and customers negotiate the maturity, interest rate and dollar magnitude of each deposit. The only stipulation is that small time deposits carry early withdrawal penalties whereby banks reduce the effective interest paid if a depositor withdraws funds prior to the stated maturity date.

3. **Time deposits of $100,000 or more** are labeled jumbo certificates of deposit (CDs) and are negotiable (can be bought and sold in the secondary market) with a well-established secondary market. Anyone who buys a jumbo CD can easily sell it in the secondary market as long as the issuing bank is not suffering known problems. The most common maturities are one month, three months, and six months, with $1 million the typical size. Most CDs are sold to nonfinancial corporations, local governmental units and other financial institutions.

Other Borrowings

1. **Federal funds and securities sold under agreement to repurchase** (Repos) are liabilities created from the exchange of immediately available funds, or balances that can be cleared immediately. Federal funds purchased generally have maturities of 1–7 days and represent the exchange of clearing balances at the Federal Reserve Bank or correspondent bank. Federal funds are unsecured while repos are collateralizes by securities owned by the borrowing institution.

2. **Brokered deposits** most often refer to jumbo CDs that a bank obtains through a third-party broker or brokerage house that markets the CDs to its customers. These are separated because the bank has virtually no customer contact with the holders of these CDs. The funds are considered *volatile* and will leave the bank quickly when a competitor offers a higher rate. Regulators can designate other bank deposits as brokered deposits depending on the rate paid to customers. Specifically, if a bank pays an above-market rate, such as 3 percent on NOWs, when all other competitors in the same trade area are paying 2 percent, regulators may choose to designate the NOWs as brokered deposits because the bank is viewed as "buying the funds." Banks that fund operations by marketing time deposits on the Internet suffer the same problem, as they generally pay rates substantially above rates paid by local (geographic) competitors.

3. **Deposits held in foreign offices** refer to the same types of dollar-denominated demand and time deposits discussed above except that the balances are issued by a bank subsidiary (owned by the bank holding company) located outside the United States. The average foreign deposit balance is generally quite large. Nonfinancial corporations engaged in international trade and governmental units own most of these deposits.

4. **Subordinated notes and debentures** consist of notes and bonds with maturities in excess of one year. Most meet requirements as bank capital for regulatory purposes. Unlike deposits, the debt is not federally insured and claims of bondholders are subordinated to claims of depositors. Thus, when a bank fails, depositors are paid before subordinated debt holders. Other liabilities include acceptances outstanding, taxes and dividends payable, trade credit, and other miscellaneous claims.

Banks differentiate between core deposits and volatile or noncore borrowings. **Core deposits,** which consist of demand deposits, NOW and ATS accounts, MMDAs, savings, other savings and time deposits less than $100,000, are stable deposits that are typically not withdrawn over short periods of time. The owners are not highly rate-sensitive, such that the interest elasticity is low, and do not quickly move their balances to another institution when it pays a higher rate. Core deposits represent a more permanent funding base than large-denomination, volatile (noncore) liabilities. They are also attractive because they are relatively cheap as compared with the interest cost of noncore liabilities. Most banks closely monitor changes in their core deposits as an indicator of liquidity risk and funding cost.

Large banks also rely on highly rate-sensitive borrowings that can be used to acquire funds quickly. Liabilities that are highly rate-sensitive do not represent a stable source of funding, particularly when a bank gets into trouble. These types of liabilities are subsequently referred to as **volatile (or noncore) liabilities,** purchased liabilities, or hot money, and consist of jumbo CDs, deposits in foreign offices, federal funds purchased, repurchase agreements (Repos or RPs), Federal Home Loan Bank borrowings and other borrowings with maturities of less than one year.[9] They are normally issued in denominations above the amount that is federally insured so the customer bears some risk of default. Thus, if a bank reports problems or a competitor offers a higher rate, customers are quite willing to move their deposits. Federal funds purchased and Repos are the most popular source. Reputable banks need only offer a small premium over the current market rate to acquire funds. Large banks also issue commercial paper through their holding companies. **Commercial paper** represents short-term, unsecured corporate promissory notes.

**All Common and Preferred Capital.** Capital represents stockholders' equity, or ownership interest in the bank. Common and preferred stocks are listed at their par values while the surplus account represents the amount of proceeds received by the bank in excess of par when the stock was issued. Retained earnings represent the bank's cumulative net income since the firm started operation, minus all cash dividends paid to stockholders. Other equity is small and usually reflects capital reserves. The book value of equity equals the difference between the book value of assets and aggregate liabilities. A detailed discussion of each component of stockholders' equity and associated regulatory requirements appears in Chapter 9.

## THE INCOME STATEMENT

A bank's income statement reflects the financial nature of banking, as interest on loans and investments represents the bulk of revenue (see Exhibit 2.3). The income statement format starts with **interest income,** then subtracts **interest expense** to produce **net interest income.** The other major source of bank revenue is **noninterest income.** After adding noninterest income, banks subtract **noninterest expense,** or overhead costs. Although banks constantly try to increase their noninterest income and reduce noninterest expense, the noninterest expense usually exceeds noninterest income such that the difference is labeled the bank's **burden**. The next step is to subtract **provisions for loan and lease losses**. The resulting figure essentially represents operating income before securities transactions and taxes. Next, **realized gains or losses** from the sale of securities are added to produce pretax net operating income. Subtracting applicable income taxes, tax-equivalent adjustments, and any extraordinary items yields **net income**. The components of the bank's income statement are:

1. **Interest income (II)** is the sum of interest and fees earned on all of a bank's assets, including loans, deposits held at other institutions, municipal and taxable securities, and trading account securities. It also includes rental receipts from lease financing. All income is taxable, except for the interest on state and municipal securities and some loan and lease income, which is exempt from federal income taxes.

   - The **estimated tax benefit** for loan and lease financing and tax-exempt securities income is the estimated dollar tax benefit from not paying taxes on these items. For comparative purposes, tax-exempt interest income can be converted to a taxable equivalent (te) amount by dividing tax-exempt interest by 1 minus the bank's marginal income tax rate. The estimated tax benefit on municipal securities can be approximated by:[10]

$$\text{municipal interest income (te)} = \frac{\text{municipal interest income}}{1 - \text{bank marginal tax rate}}$$

$$\text{Estimated tax benefit} = \text{municipal interest income (te)} - \text{municipal interest income}^{[11]}$$

---

[9]Short-term noncore funding, as defined in the UBPR, includes brokered deposits less than $100,000 but does not include FHLB borrowings less than one year. Due to the lack of detail data, calculated volatile liabilities in exhibits 2.7 and 2.8 do not include brokered deposits. The calculated value of volatile liabilities also excludes FHLB borrowings to be consistent with the UBPR.

[10]Actually, the estimated tax benefit is calculated on the UBPR using a tax-equivalent adjustment worksheet. You can find this worksheet on the FFIEC's Web page at http://www.ffiec.gov.

[11]Tax-equivalent municipal interest for PNC equaled $11.702 million in 2004. This was composed of $8.350 million in tax-exempt securities income plus $3.352 million in estimated tax benefit. PNC also had tax benefits from loan and lease financing estimated at $ 5.711 million. Total tax-equivalent income on loans and leases was $2 billion. CNB's tax-equivalent income can be found similarly. The 1986 change in tax laws made municipal securities less attractive to commercial banks, which has substantially lowered the municipal holdings of both PNC and CNB over time.

**EXHIBIT 2.3** 2003–2004 Income Statements of PNC Bank and Community National Bank

| | PNC Bank, National Association | | | | | | Community National Bank | | | | | |
| Income Statement | % Cha | Dec-03 $ 1,000 | % of Total | % Cha | Dec-04 $ 1,000 | % of Total | % Cha | Dec-03 $ 1,000 | % of Total | % Cha | Dec-04 $ 1,000 | % of Total |
|---|---|---|---|---|---|---|---|---|---|---|---|---|
| **Interest Income:** | | | | | | | | | | | | |
| Interest and fees on loans | -17.5% | 1,730,575 | 37.5% | 8.3% | 1,875,058 | 38.4% | 0.0% | 7,923 | 73.6% | 7.5% | 8,521 | 72.1% |
| Income from lease financing | -20.6% | 189,910 | 4.1% | -30.1% | 132,839 | 2.7% | 0.0% | 0 | 0.0% | 0.0% | 0 | 0.0% |
| Memo: Fully taxable | -17.7% | 1,905,782 | 41.3% | 4.6% | 1,993,668 | 40.8% | 0.0% | 7,923 | 73.6% | 7.5% | 8,521 | 72.1% |
| Tax-exempt | -25.7% | 14,703 | 0.3% | -3.2% | 14,229 | 0.3% | 0.0% | 0 | 0.0% | 0.0% | 0 | 0.0% |
| Estimated tax benefit | -27.7% | 7,347 | 0.2% | -22.3% | 5,711 | 0.1% | 0.0% | 0 | 0.0% | 0.0% | 0 | 0.0% |
| Income on Loans & Leases (TE) | -17.8% | 1,927,832 | 41.7% | 4.4% | 2,013,608 | 41.2% | 0.0% | 7,923 | 73.6% | 7.5% | 8,521 | 72.1% |
| U.S. Treasury & Agency securities | 48.2% | 34,418 | 0.7% | 221.4% | 110,614 | 2.3% | -6.2% | 427 | 4.0% | 28.3% | 548 | 4.6% |
| Mortgage backed securities | -0.7% | 366,877 | 7.9% | -8.1% | 337,110 | 6.9% | -12.6% | 368 | 3.4% | 62.8% | 599 | 5.1% |
| Estimated tax benefit | 1.0% | 504 | 0.0% | 565.1% | 3,352 | 0.1% | 23.5% | 21 | 0.2% | 81.0% | 38 | 0.3% |
| All other securities income | -15.4% | 117,866 | 2.6% | -31.2% | 81,129 | 1.7% | 28.1% | 41 | 0.4% | 80.5% | 74 | 0.6% |
| Memo: tax-exempt securities income | 3.7% | 1,008 | 0.0% | 728.4% | 8,350 | 0.2% | 28.1% | 41 | 0.4% | 80.5% | 74 | 0.6% |
| Investment Interest Income (TE) | -2.4% | 519,665 | 11.2% | 2.4% | 532,205 | 10.9% | -7.4% | 857 | 8.0% | 46.9% | 1,259 | 10.7% |
| Interest on due from banks | 43.8% | 4,835 | 0.1% | -24.8% | 3,638 | 0.1% | 164.3% | 37 | 0.3% | 21.6% | 45 | 0.4% |
| Interest on Fed funds sold & resales | -32.4% | 18,682 | 0.4% | 57.9% | 29,503 | 0.6% | -7.0% | 133 | 1.2% | -23.3% | 102 | 0.9% |
| Trading account income | 216.9% | 805 | 0.0% | 2455.9% | 20,575 | 0.4% | 0.0% | 0 | 0.0% | 0.0% | 0 | 0.0% |
| Other interest income | 127.2% | 39,447 | 0.9% | -47.2% | 20,847 | 0.4% | 0.0% | 15 | 0.1% | 13.3% | 17 | 0.1% |
| **Total Interest Income (TE)** | -14.2% | 2,511,266 | 54.4% | 4.3% | 2,620,376 | 53.6% | -0.6% | 8,965 | 83.3% | 10.9% | 9,944 | 84.1% |
| **Interest Expense:** | | | | | | | | | | | | |
| Int. on deposits held in foreign offices | -14.7% | 17,335 | 0.4% | 144.0% | 42,290 | 0.9% | 0.0% | 0 | 0.0% | 0.0% | 0 | 0.0% |
| Interest on CDs over $100M | -29.5% | 67,714 | 1.5% | 6.4% | 72,032 | 1.5% | -19.2% | 375 | 3.5% | 6.4% | 399 | 3.4% |
| Interest on all other deposits: | -30.5% | 369,702 | 8.0% | 1.8% | 376,244 | 7.7% | -20.5% | 1,060 | 9.8% | 3.6% | 1,098 | 9.3% |
| **Total interest exp. on deposits** | -29.8% | 454,751 | 9.8% | 7.9% | 490,566 | 10.0% | -20.2% | 1,435 | 13.3% | 4.3% | 1,497 | 12.7% |
| Interest on Fed Funds purchased & resale | 2.2% | 13,260 | 0.3% | 204.9% | 40,432 | 0.8% | -52.2% | 11 | 0.1% | 90.9% | 21 | 0.2% |
| Interest on trad. liab. & other borrowings | -59.0% | 26,001 | 0.6% | 429.4% | 137,637 | 2.8% | 0.0% | 0 | 0.0% | 0.0% | 0 | 0.0% |
| Interest on mortgages & leases | 0.0% | 0 | 0.0% | 0.0% | 0 | 0.0% | 0.0% | 0 | 0.0% | 0.0% | 0 | 0.0% |
| Interest on sub. notes & debentures | -17.9% | 55,449 | 1.2% | 52.1% | 84,340 | 1.7% | 0.0% | 0 | 0.0% | 0.0% | 0 | 0.0% |
| **Total Interest Expense** | -30.6% | 549,461 | 11.9% | 37.0% | 752,975 | 15.4% | -20.6% | 1,446 | 13.4% | 5.0% | 1,518 | 12.8% |
| **Net Interest Income (TE)** | -8.1% | 1,961,805 | 42.5% | -4.8% | 1,867,401 | 38.2% | 4.5% | 7,519 | 69.8% | 12.1% | 8,426 | 71.3% |

**EXHIBIT 2.3** (continued)

| Income Statement | PNC Bank, National Association | | | | | | Community National Bank | | | | | |
|---|---|---|---|---|---|---|---|---|---|---|---|---|
| | % Cha | Dec-03 $ 1,000 | % of Total | Dec-04 $ 1,000 | % Cha | % of Total | % Cha | Dec-03 $ 1,000 | % of Total | Dec-04 $ 1,000 | % Cha | % of Total |
| **Noninterest Income:** | | | | | | | | | | | | |
| Fiduciary activities | −5.4% | 291,582 | 6.3% | 296,226 | 1.6% | 6.1% | 0.0% | 0 | 0.0% | 0 | 0.0% | 0.0% |
| Deposit service charges | 4.8% | 422,100 | 9.1% | 431,169 | 2.1% | 8.8% | 16.7% | 1,070 | 9.9% | 1,396 | 30.5% | 11.8% |
| Trading rev, venture cap., securitize inc. | 61.8% | 88,985 | 1.9% | 67,267 | −24.4% | 1.4% | 0.0% | 0 | 0.0% | 0 | 0.0% | 0.0% |
| Invesment banking, advisory inc. | 3.5% | 562,482 | 12.2% | 746,475 | 32.7% | 15.3% | 0.0% | 0 | 0.0% | 0 | 0.0% | 0.0% |
| Insurance commissions & fees | −74.8% | (660) | 0.0% | 11,856 | −1,896% | 0.2% | −66.7% | 1 | 0.0% | 0 | 100.0% | 0.0% |
| Net servicing fees | −7.9% | 35,245 | 0.8% | 51,212 | 45.3% | 1.0% | 0.0% | 0 | 0.0% | 2 | 0.0% | 0.0% |
| Loan & lease net gains (losses) | −13.4% | 134,969 | 2.9% | 130,953 | −3.0% | 2.7% | −100.0% | 0 | 0.0% | 0 | 0.0% | 0.0% |
| Other net gains (losses) | −39.1% | 10,036 | 0.2% | 1,124 | −88.8% | 0.0% | −1012.5% | (73) | −0.7% | (18) | −75.3% | −0.2% |
| Other noninterest income | 10.5% | 474,040 | 10.3% | 479,982 | 1.3% | 9.8% | −31.9% | 590 | 5.5% | 497 | −15.8% | 4.2% |
| **Total Noninterest Income** | 3.7% | 2,018,779 | 43.7% | 2,216,264 | 9.8% | 45.4% | −16.6% | 1,588 | 14.7% | 1,877 | 18.2% | 15.9% |
| **Adjusted Operating Income (TE)** | −2.5% | 3,980,584 | 86.2% | 4,083,665 | 2.6% | 83.6% | 0.1% | 9,107 | 84.6% | 10,303 | 13.1% | 87.2% |
| **Non-Interest Expenses:** | | | | | | | | | | | | |
| Personnel expense | 5.7% | 1,112,208 | 24.1% | 1,421,341 | 27.8% | 29.1% | −2.4% | 4,202 | 39.0% | 4,335 | 3.2% | 36.7% |
| Occupancy expense | 11.8% | 352,506 | 7.6% | 350,550 | −0.6% | 7.2% | 4.5% | 1,256 | 11.7% | 1,284 | 2.2% | 10.9% |
| Goodwill impairment | 0.0% | 0 | 0.0% | 0 | 0.0% | 0.0% | 0.0% | 0 | 0.0% | 0 | 0.0% | 0.0% |
| Other intangible amortization | −4.6% | 4,006 | 0.1% | 11,476 | 186.5% | 0.2% | 0.0% | 11 | 0.1% | 11 | 0.0% | 0.1% |
| Other oper. exp. (incl. intangibles) | 10.9% | 956,533 | 20.7% | 994,122 | 3.9% | 20.3% | −2.8% | 2,064 | 19.2% | 2,133 | 3.3% | 18.0% |
| **Total Noninterest Expenses** | 8.6% | 2,425,253 | 52.5% | 2,777,489 | 14.5% | 56.8% | −1.4% | 7,533 | 70.0% | 7,763 | 3.1% | 65.7% |
| **Provision: Loan & Lease Losses** | −39.1% | 176,612 | 3.8% | 51,553 | −70.8% | 1.1% | 42.5% | 684 | 6.4% | 600 | −12.3% | 5.1% |
| **Pretax Operating Income (TE)** | −11.5% | 1,378,719 | 29.8% | 1,254,623 | −9.0% | 25.7% | −8.9% | 890 | 8.3% | 1,940 | 118.0% | 16.4% |
| Realized G/L hld-to-maturity sec. | 0.0% | 0 | 0.0% | 0 | 0.0% | 0.0% | 0.0% | 0 | 0.0% | 0 | 0.0% | 0.0% |
| Realized G/L avail.-for-sale sec. | 12.6% | 89,786 | 1.9% | 49,792 | −44.5% | 1.0% | 110.8% | 215 | 2.0% | 0 | −100.0% | 0.0% |
| **Pretax Net Operating Income (TE)** | −10.4% | 1,468,505 | 31.8% | 1,304,415 | −11.2% | 26.7% | 2.4% | 1,105 | 10.3% | 1,940 | 75.6% | 16.4% |
| Applicable income taxes | −13.4% | 490,376 | 10.6% | 381,926 | −22.1% | 7.8% | −2.2% | 355 | 3.3% | 641 | 80.6% | 5.4% |
| Current tax equivalent adjustment | −26.4% | 7,851 | 0.2% | 9,063 | 15.4% | 0.2% | 23.5% | 21 | 0.2% | 38 | 81.0% | 0.3% |
| Other tax equivalent adjustments | 0.0% | 0 | 0.0% | 0 | 0.0% | 0.0% | 0.0% | 0 | 0.0% | 0 | 0.0% | 0.0% |
| **Applicable Income Taxes (TE)** | −13.6% | 498,227 | 10.8% | 390,989 | −21.5% | 8.0% | −1.1% | 376 | 3.5% | 679 | 80.6% | 5.7% |
| **Net Operating Income** | −8.6% | 970,278 | 21.0% | 913,426 | −5.9% | 18.7% | 4.3% | 729 | 6.8% | 1,261 | 73.0% | 10.7% |
| Net extraordinary items | 0.0% | 0 | 0.0% | 0 | 0.0% | 0.0% | 0.0% | 0 | 0.0% | 0 | 0.0% | 0.0% |
| **Net Income** | −8.6% | 970,278 | 21.0% | 913,426 | −5.9% | 18.7% | 4.3% | 729 | 6.8% | 1,261 | 73.0% | 10.7% |
| Cash dividends declared | 87.5% | 750,000 | 16.2% | 800,000 | 6.7% | 16.4% | −100.0% | 0 | 0.0% | 0 | 0.0% | 0.0% |
| Retained earnings | −66.7% | 220,278 | 4.8% | 113,426 | −48.5% | 2.3% | 58.8% | 729 | 6.8% | 1,261 | 73.0% | 10.7% |
| Memo: net international income | 0.0% | 0 | 0.0% | 0 | 0.0% | 0.0% | 0.0% | 0 | 0.0% | 0 | 0.0% | 0.0% |
| Memo: Total operating income | −6.7% | 4,619,831 | 100.0% | 4,886,432 | 5.8% | 100.0% | −2.3% | 10,768 | 100.0% | 11,821 | 9.8% | 100.0% |
| Memo: Net operating income | −2.5% | 3,980,584 | 86.2% | 4,083,665 | 2.6% | 83.6% | 0.1% | 9,107 | 84.6% | 10,303 | 13.1% | 87.2% |

2. **Interest expense (IE)** is the sum of interest paid on all interest-bearing liabilities, including transactions accounts, time and savings deposits, volatile liabilities and other borrowings, and long-term debt. Gross interest income minus gross interest expense is labeled **net interest income.** This figure is important because its variation over time indicates how well management is controlling interest rate risk.

3. **Noninterest income (OI)** is becoming increasingly important because of pricing pressure on net interest income. Many large banks have determined that the expected returns from lending are not as attractive as they once were given the associated risks. Fortunately, many customers are demanding additional products and services such as brokerage accounts and insurance which generate fee income. As a result, we have seen the importance of net interest income fall from about 80 percent of a bank's net operating revenue in 1980 to only 57.5 percent by the end of 2004 (see Exhibit 2.4). More importantly, if this trend continues, it is expected that noninterest income will represent more than 50 percent of a bank's revenue by 2009. Financial modernization has expanded the types of noninterest sources available to banks including:

   a. **Fiduciary activities** reflect income from the institution's trust department.

   b. **Deposit service charges**, such as checking account fees, generally constitute the bulk of noninterest income.

   c. **Trading revenue, venture capital revenue, and securitization income** reflect gains (losses) from trading securities (making a market in securities) and off-balance sheet derivative; venture capital activities; net securitization income and fees from securitization transactions; and unrealized losses (recovery of losses) on loans and leases held for sale.

   d. **Investment banking, advisory, brokerage, and underwriting fees and commissions** include report fees and commissions from underwriting securities, private placements of securities, investment advisory and management services, or merger and acquisition services.

   e. **Insurance commission fees and income** are reported income from underwriting insurance, from the sale of insurance or from reinsurance; including fees, commissions, and service charges.

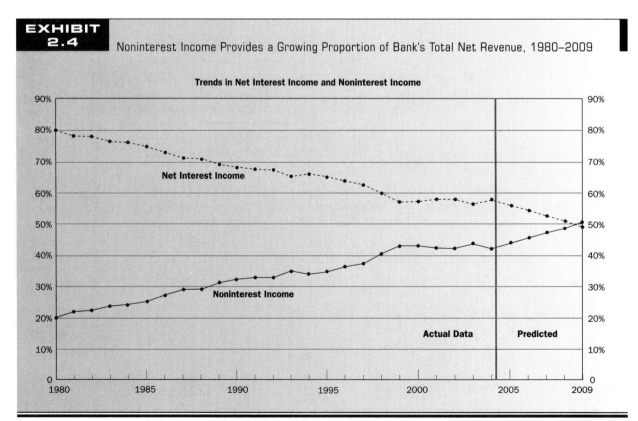

**EXHIBIT 2.4**

Noninterest Income Provides a Growing Proportion of Bank's Total Net Revenue, 1980–2009

**Trends in Net Interest Income and Noninterest Income**

*Net Interest Income*

*Noninterest Income*

*Actual Data*

*Predicted*

SOURCE: FDIC Quarterly Banking Profile and the author's estimates, http://www.fdic.gov/, http://www2.fdic.gov/qbp.

    f. **Net servicing fees** are from servicing real estate mortgages, credit cards, and other financial assets held by others.

    g. **Net gains (losses) on sales of loans** are net gains or (losses) on sales or other disposal of loans and leases.

    h. **Other net gains (losses)** includes net gains (losses) on sales of other real estate owned, on the sales or other disposals of other real estate owned, and sales of other assets (excluding securities) such as premises and fixed assets and personal property acquired for debts previously contracted (such as automobiles, boats, equipment, and appliances).

4. **Noninterest expense (OE)** is composed primarily of **personnel expense,** which includes salaries and fringe benefits paid to bank employees; **occupancy expense** from rent and depreciation on equipment and premises; and **other operating expense,** including technology expenditures, utilities, and deposit insurance premiums. Other noninterest expenses include **goodwill impairment** amortization and **other intangible amortizations.** Noninterest expense far exceeds noninterest income at most banks, hence the label **burden.** Reducing this burden will improve profitability. Because most banks today face great pressure to keep net interest income from shrinking, they have aggressively tried to raise fee income and cut overhead expenses to support profit growth.

5. **Provision for loan and lease losses (PLL)** represents management's estimate of the potential incremental lost revenue from bad loans and is a deduction from income representing a bank's periodic allocation to its loan and lease loss allowance (loan loss reserve) on the balance sheet. Conceptually, management is allocating a portion of income to the loan loss reserve to protect against potential loan losses. It is a non-cash expense, but indicates management's perception of the quality of the bank's loans. It is subtracted from net interest income in recognition that some of the reported interest income overstates what will actually be received when some of the loans go into default. Although management determines the size of the provision and, thus, what is reported to stockholders, Internal Revenue Service (IRS) rules specify the maximum allowable tax deduction. As is discussed later, provisions for loan and lease losses differ from loan charge-offs, which indicate loans and leases that a bank formally recognizes as uncollectible and charges-off against the loss reserve.

6. **Realized securities gains or losses (SG)** arise when a bank sells securities from its investment portfolio prior to final maturity at prices above (or below) the initial or amortized cost to the bank. All such profits are reported and taxed as ordinary income. Securities gains are generally viewed as an unpredictable and unstable source of income because it is difficult to forecast interest rates and whether the bank can sell securities for a profit or loss. Realized securities gains (or losses) are listed separately for *held-to-maturity securities* and *available-for-sale securities.* Generally, securities change in value as interest rates change, but the gains or losses are unrealized—meaning that the bank has not sold the securities to capture the change in value.

7. **Pretax net operating income (te)** equals tax-equivalent net interest income, plus noninterest income, minus noninterest expense, minus provision for loan losses, plus realized securities gains or losses. It represents the bank's operating profit before taxes and extraordinary items.

8. **Applicable income taxes (T)** equals estimated taxes to be paid over time, not actual tax payments. In addition to applicable income taxes, two additional tax items are subtracted from pretax net operating income. The **current tax equivalent adjustment** simply reverses the current part of the tax benefit included in interest income on loan and lease financing, as well as the estimated tax benefit from municipal securities. **Other tax equivalent adjustments** reverse the remainder of the tax equivalent adjustment included in interest income on loans, leases, and municipal securities income. This is an estimate of the tax benefit that is attributable to tax loss carrybacks.

9. **Net income (NI)** is the operating profit less all federal, state, and local income taxes, plus or minus any accounting adjustments and **extraordinary items.**[12] Accounting adjustments generally represent a restatement of earnings resulting from a change in accounting treatment of certain transactions.

---

[12]Extraordinary items include such items as revenue from the sale of real assets, the sale of a subsidiary and other one-time transactions. It is important that analysts distinguish between these one-time gains or losses and normal operating income and expenses. One-time transactions are nonrecurring and affect the income statement only in the period they appear. As such, reported net income may overstate true operating income.

Finally, **total revenue (TR)**, or **total operating income (TOI)**, equals total interest income plus noninterest income and realized securities gains (losses). It is comparable to net sales for a nonfinancial firm. **Total operating expense (EXP)** equals the sum of interest expense, noninterest expense, and provisions for loan losses, and is comparable to cost of goods sold plus other operating expenses at a nonfinancial firm. A bank's net interest income (NII) equals interest income (II) minus interest expense (IE) and burden equals noninterest expense (OE) minus noninterest income (OI). Conceptually, therefore, a bank's net income (NI) can be viewed as having five contributing factors: net interest income (NII), burden, provisions for loan losses (PLL), securities gains or losses (SG) and taxes (T):

$$NI = NII - Burden - PLL + SG - T \qquad (2.2)$$

Income statements for the two banking organizations were presented in Exhibit 2.3. Not surprisingly, the components of net income differ substantially, reflecting their diverse portfolios. Net income for PNC Bank equaled $913 million in 2004, down almost 6 percent from 2003 as a result of a sharp drop in net interest income and increase in noninterest expense. The reduction in realized securities gains was more than offset by a reduction in taxes. PNC has undergone a significant restructuring of its operations and credit activities since 1999. Note the variation in provisions for loan losses over the different years when PLL ranged from $51.5 million in 2004 to almost $900 million in 2001. Community National Bank's net income was up about 73 percent in 2004 to $1,261 million due primarily to higher income on investments and noninterest income. The contribution of each of the five components to PNC's and CNB's profitability in 2004 is summarized below.

| Components of Net Income in 2004 | PNC ($000) | CNB ($000) |
|---|---:|---:|
| Net interest income (NII) (te) | 1,867,401 | 8,426 |
| − Burden | (561,225) | (5,886) |
| − Provisions for loan losses (PLL) | (51,553) | (600) |
| + Securities gains (losses) (SG) | 49,792 | 0 |
| − Taxes (T) | (390,989) | (697) |
| = Net income (NI) | 913,426 | 1,261 |

## THE RELATIONSHIP BETWEEN THE BALANCE SHEET AND INCOME STATEMENT

A bank's balance sheet and income statement are interrelated. The composition of assets and liabilities and the relationships between different interest rates determine net interest income. The mix of deposits between consumer and commercial customers affects the services provided and, thus, the magnitude of noninterest income and noninterest expense. The ownership of nonbank subsidiaries increases fee income, but often raises noninterest expense. The following analysis emphasizes these interrelationships. Let:

$$A_i \quad = \text{dollar magnitude of the } i^{th} \text{ asset}$$
$$L_j \quad = \text{dollar magnitude of the } j^{th} \text{ liability}$$
$$NW = \text{dollar magnitude of stockholders' equity}$$
$$y_i \quad = \text{average pretax yield on the } i^{th} \text{ asset}$$
$$c_j \quad = \text{average interest cost of the } j^{th} \text{ liability,}$$

where n equals the number of assets and m equals the number of liabilities. The balance sheet identity in Equation 2.1 can be restated as:

$$\sum_{i=1}^{n} A_i = \sum_{j=1}^{m} L_j + NW \qquad (2.3)$$

Interest earned on each asset equals the product of the average yield $(y_i)$ and the average dollar investment $(A_i)$. Thus:

$$\text{Interest income} = \sum_{i=1}^{n} y_i A_i \qquad (2.4)$$

Similarly, interest paid on each liability equals the product of the average interest cost ($c_j$) and the average dollar funding ($L_j$) from that source, so that:

$$\text{Interest expense} = \sum_{j=1}^{m} c_j L_j \tag{2.5}$$

Net interest income (NII) equals the difference:

$$\text{NII} = \sum_{i=1}^{n} y_i A_i - \sum_{i=1}^{m} c_j L_j \tag{2.6}$$

This restatement of NII indicates what factors can cause net interest income to change over time or differ between institutions. First, net interest income changes when the ***composition*** or ***volume*** of assets and liabilities changes. In terms of Equation 2.6, as portfolio composition changes, the respective As and Ls change in magnitude. This alters net interest income because each $A_i$ or $L_j$ is multiplied by a different interest rate. Second, even if portfolio composition is unchanged, the average ***rate earned*** on assets (asset yields) and ***rate paid*** on liabilities (interest costs) may rise or fall due to changing interest rates and lengthening or shortening of maturities on the underlying instruments.

Analysts, for example, generally distinguish between retail and wholesale banks based on their target customers. Each type of bank has a fundamentally different balance sheet composition reflecting the preferences of its customers. Retail banks are those that focus on individual consumer banking relationships. Thus, individual demand, savings, and time deposits represent most of the liabilities, while consumer and small business loans linked to key individuals are a higher fraction of the loan portfolio. Wholesale banks deal primarily with commercial customers such that they operate with fewer consumer deposits, more purchased (noncore) liabilities, and they hold proportionately more business loans to large firms. This difference in portfolio composition, in turn, produces different yields on earning assets ($y_i$) and costs of liabilities ($c_j$).

Noninterest income, noninterest expense, and provisions for loan losses indirectly reflect the same balance sheet composition. The greater is a bank's loan portfolio, the greater is its operating overhead and provision for loan losses. Likewise, banks that emphasize consumer loans operate with more noninterest expense (overhead). They often invest in extensive branch systems and equipment to attract consumer deposits and handle small, multiple-payment consumer loans. Bank holding companies with nonbank subsidiaries, on the other hand, generate more fee income.

A bank's net income thus varies with the magnitudes of assets and liabilities and the associated cash flows:

$$\text{NI} = \sum_{i=1}^{n} y_i A_i - \sum_{j=1}^{m} c_j L_j - \text{Burden} - \text{PLL} + \text{SG} - \text{T} \tag{2.7}$$

Net income in excess of dividend payments to shareholders increases retained earnings and, thus, net worth or total equity.

## THE RETURN ON EQUITY MODEL

In 1972, David Cole introduced a procedure for evaluating bank performance via ratio analysis.[13] This procedure, summarized in Exhibit 2.5, enables an analyst to evaluate the source and magnitude of bank profits relative to selected risks taken. This section employs the **return on equity model** to analyze bank profitability and identifies specific measures of credit risk, liquidity risk, interest rate risk, operational risk, and capital risk. The ratios are used to assess the performance of the two banking organizations introduced earlier.

The Uniform Bank Performance Report (UBPR) is a comprehensive analytical tool created by the FDIC from the Federal Financial Institutions Examination Council (FFIEC) quarterly Call Reports for bank supervisory purposes.[14] The UBPR contains a wealth of profitability and risk information presented in a consistent and uniform manner. Although the 22 pages of data and ratio information might appear a bit intimidating, the advantage of

---

[13]The following discussion is based on the Dupont system of financial analysis and adaptations by Cole (1972). A more meaningful definition of return on equity is the ratio of net income minus dividends on preferred stock to common stockholders' equity, because it indicates the potential return to common stockholders.

[14]Complete UBPR reports, including peer group data, can be found at the FDIC's Internet Web page at http://www.fdic.gov (http://www2.fdic.gov/ubpr) in the FDIC Uniform Bank Performance Report section. Anyone can also obtain a UBPR for any bank or FDIC-insured savings bank by calling or writing the FDIC. The UBPR is available for banks since 1986, and for FDIC-insured savings banks since 1990. Public disclosure tapes can also be obtained. Data for thrift institutions are available via a Uniform Thrift Performance Report (UTPR).

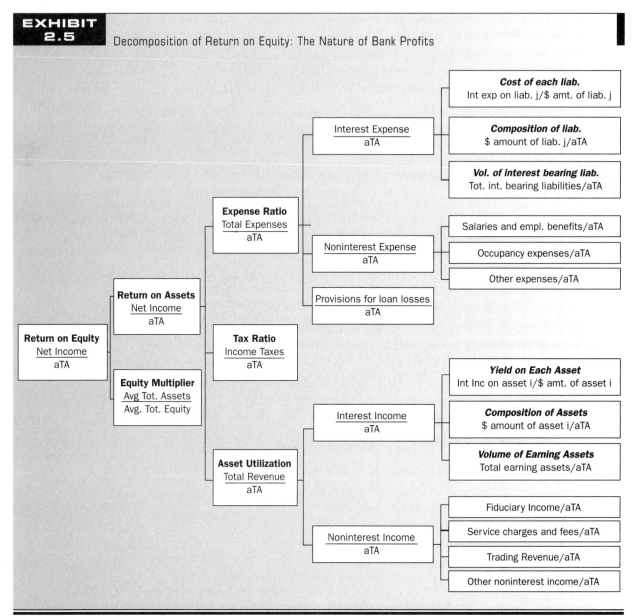

**EXHIBIT 2.5** Decomposition of Return on Equity: The Nature of Bank Profits

NOTE: aTA = average total assets.

this report over "typical" financial statements is the uniformity in the presentation of the data. Once you learn how to use one UBPR, you can evaluate any bank's or savings bank's performance. Most of the UBPR for PNC Bank is contained in the Appendix to this chapter. All data for Community National Bank were obtained from its UBPR as well.

The year-end UBPR consists of information over a consecutive five-year period. Non-year-end reports provide data on the current quarter, one year prior to the current quarter, and the three latest year-end periods. Although the strength of the UBPR is its consistency, there are unfortunately several versions of the report. These versions, however, differ only by the amount of detail provided, with larger banks' UBPRs providing more information. The report format is updated virtually every year.

The data contained in the UBPR consist of three basic types: bank-level ratios and dollar values, peer group averages and bank percentile ranks. Bank-level dollar values consist primarily of detailed income statement and balance sheet data. Ratios provide data on almost all aspects of a specific bank's profitability and risk (BANK). Peer group averages (PG #) are classified into 27 different groups based on the size of banks, their general location, and their number of branches. Percentile ranks (PCT) allow for more comprehensive analysis and rank each bank's

PROFITABILITY ANALYSIS

If you cornered a group of bank presidents and asked them to summarize performance for the past year, most would quote either their bank's return on equity (ROE) or return on assets (ROA). If these measures were higher than peers, they would drop the phrase "high-performance bank" in the conversation. Of course, for a firm to report higher returns, it must either take on more risk, price assets and liabilities better, or realize cost advantages compared with peers. The following analysis starts with these aggregate profit measures, then decomposes return on assets into component ratios to determine why performance varies from peers.

Aggregate bank profitability is measured and compared in terms of return on equity and return on assets. The ROE model simply relates ROE to ROA and financial leverage, then decomposes ROA into its contributing elements. By definition:

$$\text{ROE} = \text{Net income/Average total equity}^{15}$$

ROE equals net income divided by average total equity and, thus, measures the percentage return on each dollar of stockholders' equity.[16] It is the aggregate return to stockholders before dividends. The higher the return the better, as banks can add more to retained earnings and pay more in cash dividends when profits are higher.

ROA equals net income divided by average total assets and, thus, measures net income per dollar of average assets owned during the period. ROE is linked to ROA by the equity multiplier (EM), which equals average total assets divided by total equity, via the following accounting identity:

$$\text{ROE} = \frac{\text{Net income}}{\text{Average total assets}} \times \frac{\text{Average total assets}}{\text{Average total equity}} \qquad (2.8)$$

$$= \text{ROA} \times \text{EM}$$

A bank's equity multiplier compares assets with equity such that large values indicate a large amount of debt financing relative to stockholders' equity. EM thus measures financial leverage and represents both a profit and risk measure. Consider two competing banks, each holding $100 million in assets with the identical composition. Asset quality is the same. One bank is financed with $90 million in debt and $10 million in total equity, while the other bank is financed with $95 million in debt and just $5 million in total equity. In this example, EM equals 10x for the first bank and 20x for the second bank.

$$\text{EM} = 10x = \$100/\$10 \text{ for the bank with } \$10 \text{ million in equity}$$

$$\text{EM} = 20x = \$100/\$5 \text{ for the bank with } \$5 \text{ million in equity}$$

EM affects a bank's profits because it has a multiplier impact on ROA to determine a bank's ROE. In the above example, if both banks earned 1 percent on assets, the first bank would report an ROE of 10 percent, while the second bank's ROE would equal 20 percent. Financial leverage works to the bank's advantage when earnings are positive, as the second bank provides shareholders a return that is twice that of its competitor. But there are two sides to leverage, as it also accentuates the negative impact of losses. If each bank reported an ROA equal to −1 percent, the second bank's ROE would equal −20 percent, or twice the loss of the first bank. Equation 2.8 suggests that higher ROE targets can be obtained either by increasing ROA or increasing financial leverage.

EM represents a risk measure because it reflects how many assets can go into default before a bank becomes insolvent. Consider the ratio of total equity to total assets, or 1/EM. This ratio equals 10 percent for the first bank in the example, and 5 percent for the second bank. Although both banks hold identical assets, the first is in a less risky position because twice as many of its assets can default (and, thus, be reduced in value to zero on the balance sheet) compared with the second bank before it is insolvent. Thus, a high EM raises ROE when net income is positive, but also indicates high capital or solvency risk.

[15]ROE for PNC in 2004 was calculated as: ROE = 913,426 / ((5,622,521+6,095,661) / 2) = 15.59%.

[16]Balance sheet figures should always be averaged for use with income statement figures. This reduces any distortion caused by unusual transactions around reporting dates. All balance sheet values listed in Exhibit 2.2 are for end of period (EOP). Average total assets and average total loans and leases data are included in Exhibit 2.6. and were used in the calculated ratios presented in Exhibits 2.7 and 2.8 when possible. All other ratios, which call for "average" balance sheet figures, calculated in Exhibits 2.7 and 2.8, use averages of annual data. See Contemporary Issues Box: "Interpreting Financial Ratios and the Use of Average Balance Sheet Data"

## CONTEMPORARY ISSUES

### INTERPRETING FINANCIAL RATIOS AND THE USE OF AVERAGE BALANCE SHEET DATA

The interpretation of historical financial data typically begins with ratio analysis. To be meaningful, ratios must be calculated consistently and compared with benchmark figures. Ratios are constructed by dividing one balance sheet or income statement item by another. The value of any ratio depends on the magnitude of both the numerator and denominator and will change when either changes.

Several rules apply when constructing ratios. First, balance sheet items are stock figures, measuring value at a point in time, while income statement items are flow figures, measuring value over time, such as one year. When constructing ratios combining balance sheet and income statement figures, average balance sheet data should be used. For example, suppose that only year-end balance sheet figures for 2003 and 2004 are available along with 2004 income statement figures. Return on equity in 2004 is calculated as the ratio of 2004 net income to one-half the sum of year-end 2003 and 2004 total equity. It would be better to use quarterly average balance sheet figures, with daily averages the best. In fact, the UBPR calculates three different types of average assets and liabilities for use on selected pages.

The first type of average used in the UBPR is a *cumulative* or year-to-date average of the one-quarter averages for assets and liabilities reported in the call report. The resulting year-to-date averages are used as the denominator in earnings ratios, yield and rate calculations found on pages 1 and 3 of the UBPR. As an example, the average assets used for page 1 earnings analysis in the September 30 UBPR would reflect an average of the quarterly average assets reported in March, June, and September of the current year. The second type of average used in the UBPR is a *year-to-date* average of end-of-period balances reported in the call report from the beginning of the year forward. To provide an accurate average, the asset or liability balance at the prior year-end is also included. Averages calculated in this manner are used to determine the percentage composition of assets and liabilities on page 6. For example, the September 30 year-to-date average total loans is composed of the spot balances for total loans from the call report for the prior December, and current March, June, and September divided by 4. The final type of average used in the

UBPR is a *moving* four-quarter average using quarterly average data. These averages are used as the denominator in last-four-quarters income analysis on page 12. A four-quarter window compares four quarters of income/expense to selected assets or liabilities averaged for a similar period of time. Thus, average assets used in the September 30 UBPR analysis of net income on page 12 would include the quarterly average assets for the prior December, and current March, June, and September. That average creates a window stretching from October 1 of the prior year to September 30 of the current year.

All balance sheet values listed in Exhibit 2.2 are for end-of-period (EOP). Average total assets and average total loans and leases data are included in Exhibit 2.6. Average total assets and average total loans reported in Exhibit 2.6 were used in the calculated ratios presented in Exhibits 2.7 and 2.8 when called for and when possible. All other ratios, which call for "average" balance sheet figures, calculated in Exhibits 2.7 and 2.8 use averages of annual data. A special note, however, applies to the composition of asset and liability data that appear on page 6 of the UBPR. The UBPR uses averages in the numerator as well as the denominator. Recall that the UBPR uses averages of quarterly data rather than averages of end-of-year data. To be consistent, end-of-period averages are used in the numerator and denominator when calculating data consistent with page 6 of the UBPR.

The second rule that applies is that a single ratio by itself is generally meaningless. Calculate ratios over different intervals to discern notable changes. Determine whether the changes are due to factors affecting the numerator or denominator. This typically requires comparing trends in two related ratios. Third, compare ratios with similar figures from a control or representative peer group at the same point in time. The peer group represents average performance for a comparable firm. Of course, it is extremely important to identify the correct peer group. Peers should be the same approximate size, operate in the same geographic and product markets, and have the same strategies. The UBPR identifies peers by size, state, and metropolitan or nonmetropolitan area along with the number of branches. This is generally too broad a group to be meaningful. Most banks create their own peer groups to compare performance.

Finally, accounting data may not reflect accepted accounting procedures and may be manipulated. Important data, such as the volume of a bank's outstanding loan commitments and other off-balance sheet activities, may be omitted. This potentially biases traditional ratios. The UBPR now provides a section on "Off-Balance Sheet Items." Footnotes to financial statements generally provide sources and an explanation for many calculations. Additional explanations for balance sheet, income statement, and ratio calculations can be obtained from the UBPR Users Manual available from the FDIC or on the Internet at http://www.FFIEC.gov.

## EXPENSE RATIO AND ASSET UTILIZATION

The Dupont Analysis has been used for many years and can be modified slightly for use in a financial institution. It represents a straightforward decomposition of ROA. The UBPR provides a wealth of data to assist in the analysis of a bank's or thrift institution's performance.[17] The basic return on total assets, ROA, is composed of two principal parts: income generation and expense control (including taxes). Recall that net income (NI) is:

$$\text{NI} = \text{Total revenue (TR)} - \text{Total operating expense (EXP)} - \text{Taxes} \qquad (2.9)$$

Total revenue is analogous to net sales plus other income at a nonfinancial company, and equals the sum of interest income, noninterest income and securities gains (losses).[18] Total operating expense (EXP) equals the sum of interest expense, noninterest expense, and provisions for loan and lease losses. Dividing both sides by **average total assets (aTA)** "decomposes" ROA into its components:[19]

$$\text{ROA} = \left(\frac{\text{NI}}{\text{aTA}}\right) = \frac{\text{TR}}{\text{aTA}} - \frac{\text{EXP}}{\text{aTA}} - \frac{\text{Taxes}}{\text{aTA}} \qquad (2.10)$$

$$\text{ROA} = \text{AU} - \text{ER} - \text{TAX} \qquad (2.11)$$

where:

$$\text{AU} = \text{Total revenue} / \text{aTA}$$
$$\text{ER} = \text{Total operating expenses} / \text{aTA}$$
$$\text{TAX} = \text{Applicable income taxes} / \text{aTA}$$

Hence, a bank's ROA is composed of asset utilization (AU), the expense ratio (ER) and the tax ratio (TAX). The greater is AU and the lower are ER and TAX, the higher is ROA.

**EXPENSE DECOMPOSITION: EXPENSE RATIO COMPONENTS (ER).** Consider first the expense ratio (ER), which has a very intuitive interpretation. For example, an ER of 5 percent indicates that a bank's gross operating expenses equal 5 percent of total investment; that is, total assets. Thus, the lower (greater) is the ER, the more (less) efficient a bank will be in controlling expenses. The decomposition of ER appears at the top of Exhibit 2.5. Three additional ratios isolate the impact of specific types of operating expenses:

Interest expense ratio $=$ Interest expense (IE) / aTA

Noninterest expense ratio $=$ Noninterest expense (OE) / aTA

Provision for loan loss ratio $=$ Provisions for loan losses (PLL) / aTA

The sum of these ratios equals the expense ratio.[20]

$$\text{ER} = \left(\frac{\text{EXP}}{\text{aTA}}\right) = \frac{\text{IE}}{\text{aTA}} + \frac{\text{OE}}{\text{aTA}} + \frac{\text{PLL}}{\text{aTA}} \qquad (2.12)$$

All other factors being equal, the lower is each ratio, the more profitable is the bank. The value of each measure compared with similar ratios of peer banks reveals whether specific types of expenses contribute to significant differences in performance. When the ratios differ, an analyst should examine additional ratios that reflect the underlying reasons and causes of the differences.

---

[17]Similar information can be obtained on credit unions from the National Credit Union Administration at http://www.ncua.gov.

[18]Extraordinary income and expense are included in the definitions of total revenue and total expense. Because they are one-time occurrences, they should be excluded when evaluating operating performance and comparing key ratios over time and versus peers. We assume that extraordinary income and expense are relatively small. If they are substantive, they should be excluded from the analysis. As such, net income would equal net income before extraordinary income.

[19]The standard Dupont Analysis approach decomposes ROA into the product of profit margin (PM) and asset utilization (AU) as ROA = AU × PM, where PM equals NI/TR and AU equals TR/aTA. These ratios are not directly available in the UBPR. AU can be derived in the UBPR by adding (interest income/aTA) plus (noninterest income/aTA) plus (securities gains/aTA). PM can then be obtained indirectly by dividing ROA by AU (PM = ROA/AU).

[20]This relationship is quite useful but ER is not directly reported on the UBPR. ER can be obtained from the UBPR in two ways. First, it can be calculated as the ratio of total operating expenses to average total assets. Using average asset data from Exhibit 2.6 for PNC in 2004 this is:
ER for PNC= 5.15% = [(752,975 + 2,777,489 + 51,553) / 69,596,163].

Second, ER can be calculated using relationship 2.12 from data on page 1 of the UBPR:

ER for PNC= 5.14% = 1.08% + 3.99% + 0.07%

ER for Peer Group = 4.23% = 1.20% + 2.89% + 0.14%

Interest expense and noninterest expense should be further examined by source. Interest expense may vary between banks for three reasons: rate, composition, or volume effects. **Rate effects** suggest that the interest cost per liability, $c_j$ from Equation 2.5, which indicates the average cost of financing assets, may differ between banks. The gross interest cost of each liability can be calculated by dividing interest expense on the particular liability by the average total dollar amount of the liability from the balance sheet.[21]

Cost of liability$_j$ = $c_j$ = Interest expense on liability$_j$ / Average balance of liability$_j$

Differences in interest expense arise for many reasons, including differences in risk premiums, timing of their borrowing, and the initial maturity of the borrowing. Banks pay different ***risk premiums*** indicating how the market perceives their asset quality and overall risk. The greater is the risk, the higher is the cost of liabilities. Banks also ***time their borrowings*** differently relative to the interest rate cycle. If they borrow when rates are low, their interest costs will fall below banks that issue new debt when rates are higher. Finally, banks use different ***maturities*** of deposits and debt that pay different rates depending on the yield curve at the time of issue. Generally, longer-term deposits pay higher rates than do short-term deposits. The $c_j$ will differ among banks for any of these reasons.

**Composition (mix) effects** suggest that the mix of liabilities may differ. Banks with substantial amounts of demand deposits pay less in interest because these deposits are noninterest bearing. A bank that relies on CDs and federal funds purchased will pay higher average rates than a bank with a larger base of lower-cost demand and small time deposits because these noncore liabilities are riskier than core deposits and, therefore, pay higher rates. This example represents a key advantage of core deposits over volatile or noncore liabilities. Composition effects are revealed by common size ratios that measure each liability as a percentage of average total assets:[22]

% of total assets funded by liability$_j$ = $ amount of liability$_j$/ Average total assets

**Volume effects** recognize that a bank may pay more or less in interest expense simply because it operates with different amounts of interest-bearing debt and equity and, thus, pays interest on a different amount of liabilities. The UBPR reports the ratio, average interest-bearing funds divided by average assets, which reveals the fraction of assets financed by debt subject to interest payments. A bank's relative amount of debt to equity is further revealed by its equity multiplier. When EM is high, interest expense may be high, reflecting proportionately high amounts of debt financing. When EM is low, interest expense is normally low. This is true even if the bank pays the same effective interest rates and has the same percentage composition of liabilities.

**Noninterest expense,** or overhead expense, can be similarly decomposed. Measures of personnel expense, which includes salaries and benefit payments, occupancy expense, and other operating expenses as a percentage of total overhead expense indicate where cost efficiencies are being realized or where a bank has a comparative disadvantage. Similar ratios are often constructed comparing these expenses to average assets to allow comparisons across different-sized banks. Noninterest expense may vary between banks depending on the composition of liabilities. Banks with large amounts of transactions deposits, for example, exhibit greater relative overhead costs.

**INCOME DECOMPOSITION: ASSET UTILIZATION COMPONENTS (AU).** The decomposition of AU appears at the bottom of Exhibit 2.5. Asset utilization is a measure of the bank's ability to generate total revenue (interest income, noninterest income, and realized security gains (losses)). The greater is AU, the greater is the bank's ability to generate income from the assets it owns. For example, if a bank's AU equals 7 percent, its gross return (before expenses and taxes) on average total assets equals 7 percent. A higher figure indicates greater profits, everything else held constant. If the same bank's ER is 5 percent, the bank's net return on investment (assets) before taxes is 2 percent. **Total revenue (TR),** or total operating income, can be divided into three components:

TR = Interest income (II) + Noninterest income (OI) + Realized security gains or losses (SG)

Dividing both sides by average total assets produces:[23]

$$AU = \left( \frac{TR}{aTA} \right) = \frac{II}{aTA} + \frac{OI}{aTA} + \frac{SG}{aTA} \qquad (2.13)$$

---

[21]Costs and yields calculated using balance sheet data and costs and yields provided in the UBPR may differ. For example, the average cost of CDs over $100M is calculated to be 2.89% = 72,032 / [(1,775,943 + 3,205,331) / 2]. The value reported for PNC in the UBPR is 2.81%. The costs and yields provided on page 3 of the UBPR use averages of quarterly figures for the individual asset values. Hence, calculating costs or yields using averages of end-of-year data may not be as accurate and will likely differ from those reported in the UBPR.

[22]To be consistent, the percent of total assets funded by liabilities is calculated using averages of end-of-year data for both the numerator and denominator. So, PNC's 2004 CDs > $100M as a percent of average assets = 3.67% = (1,775,943+3,205,331)/(62,020,896 + 73,809,165) and the UBPR reports 3.76%. For consistancy, end-of-year averages are used for both the numerator and denominator.

[23]AU, like ER, cannot be found directly in the UBPR, but can be calculated for the bank by either using balance sheet and income statement data or adding the components in Equation 2.13, which are provided on page 1 of the UBPR. AU for PNC and its Peer Group, using data for 2004 are:

AU (PNC) = 7.02% = 3.77% + 3.18% + 0.07%

AU (peer) = 6.21% = 4.46% + 1.73% + 0.02%

This indicates how much of a bank's gross yield on assets results from interest income, noninterest income and realized securities gains (losses). Interest income may differ between banks for the same three reasons discussed with interest expense: rate, composition, and volume effects. For the **rate effect,** an examination of pretax (gross) yields per asset, $y_i$ from Equation 2.4, allows the bank to compare realized interest yields with those of peer banks. Differences may reflect different *maturities*, the *timing of purchases* relative to the interest rate cycle, or a different *composition* of holdings (hence risk of the assets) within each asset category. For example, a bank that invests heavily in new construction loans should earn higher gross yields on loans than a bank that lends primarily to Fortune 500 companies because construction loans are riskier. Differences in investment security yields, in turn, reflect differences in average maturities with generally higher yields on longer-term securities. Gross yields on assets can be calculated similar to costs of liabilities by dividing interest income on the particular asset by the average dollar amount of the asset from the balance sheet:[24]

$$\text{Yield on asset}_i = y_i = \text{Interest income on asset}_i / \text{Average balance of asset}_i$$

Even if two banks earned the same yields on all assets, interest income would be greater at the one that invested proportionately more in higher gross yielding loans. Thus, the **mix effect** suggests that asset composition also affects AU. Measures of asset composition can be obtained by examining the percentage of total assets contributed by each asset type. Generally, a comparison of loans to assets and securities to assets indicates the overall impact. A high loan-to-asset ratio increases interest income because loans carry higher gross yields than securities, on average.

Finally, a higher **volume** of earning assets will result in great interest income and AU, all else being equal. *Earning assets* include all assets that generate explicit interest income plus lease receipts. It can be measured most easily by subtracting all nonearning assets, such as noninterest cash and due from banks, acceptances, premises, and other assets, from total assets. A review of a bank's **earnings base (EB)** compares the proportionate investment in average earning assets to average total assets and indicates whether one bank has more or less assets earning interest than peers.[25]

$$\text{Earnings base (EB)} = \text{Average earning assets} / \text{aTA}$$

**Noninterest income** can also be decomposed into its contributing sources. Examining the proportion of noninterest income contributed by fees, fiduciary activities, deposit service charges, trading revenue, and other noninterest income relative to average total assets or total noninterest income indicates which component contributes the most to AU and why differences might exist with peers. It also identifies whether other income might be biased by substantial nonrecurring items. When a bank reports extraordinary income, an analyst should subtract the amount from net income before calculating the performance ratios. This purges extraordinary income so that a truer picture of operating performance appears.

The last factor affecting ROA is a bank's tax payments. Generally, applicable income taxes are divided by average assets. Although taxes are important to a bank's bottom line they are often affected by issues unrelated to their long-run operations. Tax treatment of municipal securities, as well as the bank loan loss reserve, can have a significant effect on the bank's level of tax payments.[26]

Several other aggregate profitability measures are commonly cited. These include net interest margin, spread, burden, and efficiency ratios. **Net interest margin (NIM)** is a summary measure of the net interest return on income-producing assets:

$$\text{NIM} = \text{Net interest income} / \text{Average earning assets}$$

**Spread,** which equals the average yield on earning assets minus the average cost of interest-bearing liabilities, is a measure of the rate spread or funding differential on balance sheet items that earn or pay interest:[27]

$$\text{Spread (SPRD)} = \frac{\text{Interest income}}{\text{Average earning assets}} - \frac{\text{Interest expense}}{\text{Average interest-bearing liabilities}}$$

---

[24]This is another area of discrepancy between yields calculated using average asset data from the UBPR and yields provided in the UBPR.

[25]PNC's 2004 earnings base (EB) is calculated as 82.85% = (50,269,220+62,267,103) / (62,020,896+73,809,165) and the UBPR reports 82.92%.

[26]The bank's tax ratio (TAX) cannot be found directly in the UBPR, but can be calculated using balance sheet and income statement data (0.56%) or data from page 1 of the UBPR as:

$$\text{TAX} = 0.57\% = \text{AU} - \text{ER} - \text{ROA} = 7.02\% - 5.14\% - 1.31\%.$$

[27]SPRD is not directly available in the UBPR, but can be calculated for the bank using balance sheet and income statement data or from data on page 1 and 3 of the UBPR. For PNC in 2004:

$$\text{SPRD} = \text{INT INC (TE) TO AVG EARN ASSETS (page 1)} - \text{COST OF ALL INTEREST-BEARING FUNDS (page 3)}$$

$$3.02\% = 4.46\% - 1.44\%$$

Net interest margin and spread are extremely important in evaluating a bank's ability to manage interest rate risk. As interest rates change, so will a bank's interest income and interest expense. For example, if interest rates increase, both interest income and interest expense will increase because some assets and liabilities will reprice at higher rates. Variation in NIM and SPRD indicates whether a bank has positioned its assets and liabilities to take advantage of rate changes—that is, whether it has actually profited or lost when interest rates increased or declined. Also, NIM and spread must be large enough to cover burden, provisions for loan losses, securities losses, and taxes for a bank to be profitable and grow its earnings.

The **burden ratio** measures the amount of noninterest expense covered by fees, service charges, securities gains, and other income as a fraction of average total assets:

$$\text{Burden ratio (BURDEN)} = \frac{\text{Noninterest expense} - \text{Noninterest income}}{\text{aTA}}$$

The greater is this ratio, the more noninterest expense exceeds noninterest income for the bank's balance sheet size. A bank is thus better off with a low burden ratio, ceteris paribus.

The **efficiency ratio** has become quite popular recently and measures a bank's ability to control noninterest expense relative to net (adjusted) operating income:[28]

$$\text{Efficiency ratio (EFF)} = \frac{\text{Noninterest expense}}{\text{NII} + \text{Noninterest income}}$$

Conceptually, it indicates how much a bank pays in noninterest expense for one dollar of operating income. Bank analysts expect larger banks to keep this ratio below 55 percent, or 55 cents per dollar of net operating income. Banks use this ratio to measure the success of recent efforts to control noninterest expense while supplementing earnings from increasing fees. The smaller is the efficiency ratio, the more profitable is the bank, all other factors being equal. Profitability measures for PNC and CNB are presented later in the chapter under the section "Evaluating Bank Performance: An Application."

## MANAGING RISK AND RETURNS

The fundamental objective of bank management is to maximize shareholders' wealth. This goal is interpreted to mean *maximizing* the market value of a firm's common stock. Wealth maximization, in turn, requires that managers evaluate the present value of cash flows under uncertainty with larger, near-term cash flows preferred when evaluated on a risk-adjusted basis. In terms of Equation 2.8, profit maximization appears to suggest that the bank manager simply invest in assets that generate the highest gross yields and keep costs down. But profit maximization differs from wealth maximization. To obtain higher yields, a bank must either take on increased risk or lower operating costs. Greater risk manifests itself in greater volatility of net income and market value of stockholders' equity. Wealth maximization requires the manager to evaluate and balance the trade-offs between the opportunity for higher returns, the probability of not realizing those returns, and the possibility that the bank might fail.

A bank's profitability will generally vary directly with the riskiness of its portfolio and operations. Although some risks can be sought out or avoided, others are inherent in the prevailing economic environment and specific markets served. Banks in agriculture or energy-related areas, for example, lend to businesses involved in cyclical industries. Even though management can control the credit evaluation procedure, returns to the bank vary with returns to its customers, and these returns are heavily dependent on local economic conditions.

**Risk management** is the process by which managers identify, assess, monitor, and control risks associated with a financial institution's activities. The complexity and range of financial products have made risk management more difficult to accomplish and evaluate. In larger financial institutions, risk management is used to identify all risks associated with particular business activities and to aggregate information such that exposures can be evaluated on a common basis. A formal process enables these institutions to manage risks on both a transactions basis and by portfolio in light of the institution's exposures in a global strategic environment. The Federal Reserve Board has identified six types of risk:[29]

1. Credit risk
2. Liquidity risk

---

[28]There can be some confusion in terminology when defining a bank's efficiency ratio. The definition of net operating income is net interest income plus noninterest income. On page 2 of the UBPR, this income number is called "adjusted operating income." "Net operating income" on page 2 of the UBPR is defined as net income before extraordinary items.

[29]The Office of the Comptroller of the Currency (OCC) uses a nine-part matrix of risk. The OCC's definition of risk includes the same general types of risk as the Board of Governors' definition, except that market risk is divided into price risk, interest rate risk, and foreign exchange risk. The OCC also includes strategic risk, which is considered to be included in all of the other categories based on the Board of Governors' model.

3. Market risk

4. Operational risk

5. Reputation risk

6. Legal risk

Although capital or solvency risk is not listed as a separate risk category by either the Federal Reserve Board or the OCC, it represents the summary of all listed risks. Each of these risks is fundamental to the likelihood that current events or potential events will negatively affect an institution's profitability and the market value of its assets, liabilities, and stock holders' equity. The impact of adverse risk events can be absorbed by sufficient bank capital such that the institution will remain solvent. As a result, capital or solvency risk is addressed separately and represents a summary of the six risks listed above.

Using historical accounting data, it is possible to examine potential sources of risk assumed in achieving the returns indicated by the ROE model, with the exception of comprehensive operational risk, reputation risk, and legal risk. Although there may be some financial indicators of these types of risk, they are more difficult to quantify.[30] One must proceed with caution, however, when using historical data as a measure of a firm's risk position, as many potential problems exist. First, historical data only tell the analyst what has happened, not what is going to happen. Risk is about the future, not the past. We use historical data as a measure of the business policies and practices of the company. If events change, such as an economic recession, or management changes its business model, such as moving into subprime lending, historical data may not be representative of the firm's risk profile.

## CREDIT RISK

Credit risk is associated with the quality of individual assets and the likelihood of default. It is extremely difficult to assess individual asset quality because limited published information is available. In fact, many banks that buy banks are surprised at the acquired bank's poor asset quality, even though they conducted a due diligence review of the acquired bank prior to the purchase.

Whenever a bank acquires an earning asset, it assumes the risk that the borrower will default, that is, not repay the principal and interest on a timely basis. **Credit risk** is the potential variation in net income and market value of equity resulting from this nonpayment or delayed payment. Different types of assets and off-balance sheet activities have different default probabilities. Loans typically exhibit the greatest credit risk. Changes in general economic conditions and a firm's operating environment alter the cash flow available for debt service. These conditions are difficult to predict. Similarly, an individual's ability to repay debts varies with changes in employment and personal net worth. For this reason, banks perform a credit analysis on each loan request to assess a borrower's capacity to repay. Unfortunately, loans tend to deteriorate long before accounting information reveals any problems. In addition, many banks enter into off-balance sheet activities, such as loan commitments, guaranty offers, and derivative contracts. The prospective borrowers and counterparties must perform or the bank may take a loss. These risks can be substantial, but are difficult to measure from published data.

Bank investment securities generally exhibit less credit risk because the borrowers are predominantly federal, state, and local governmental units. Banks are also generally restricted to investment-grade securities, those rated Baa (BBB) or higher, which exhibit less default risk. However, even municipal bonds are subject to defaults, such as the 1983 default of the Washington Public Power Supply System on $2.25 billion in bonds to finance nuclear power plants.

Banks evaluate their general credit risk by asking three basic questions and their credit risk measures focus predominantly on these same general areas:

1. What is the historical loss rate on loans and investments?

2. What are expected losses in the future?

3. How is the bank prepared to weather the losses?

**HISTORICAL LOSS RATE.** Managers typically focus their attention initially on a bank's historical loan loss experience because loans exhibit the highest default rates. Ratios (as a percentage of total loans and leases) that examine the historical loss experience are related to gross losses, recoveries, and net losses. The UBPR provides aggregate loss data as well as loss data by type of loans. A summary of aggregate loan quality data is provided in Exhibit 2.6 under the sections Summary of Loan Loss Account and Noncurrent LN&LS. **Gross loan losses (charge-offs)** equal the dollar value of loans actually written off as uncollectible during a period. **Recoveries** refer to the dollar amount of loans that were previously charged-off but now collected. **Net losses (net charge-offs)** equal the difference between gross loan losses and recoveries.

---

[30]Risk is traditionally measured by the standard deviation or coefficient of variation of returns. The following discussion identifies sources of potential variation in returns. Sources of returns risk are evidenced by simple ratios that reflect portfolio allocations or income streams that differ from industry averages. Of course, some variation is beneficial. If returns are systematically greater than norms or what is expected, a bank will be better off.

# EXHIBIT 2.6

Supplemental Operational and Loan Data for PNC Bank and Community National Bank, 2003–2004

| Enter analysts name here | Pg # | PNC Bank, National Association | | | | | | Community National Bank | | | | | |
|---|---|---|---|---|---|---|---|---|---|---|---|---|---|
| | | % Cha | Dec-03 $ 1,000 | % of Total | % Cha | Dec-04 $ 1,000 | % of Total | % Cha | Dec-03 $ 1,000 | % of Total | % Cha | Dec-04 $ 1,000 | % of Total |
| **SUPPLEMENTAL DATA** | | | | | | | | | | | | | |
| Average assets | 1 | 2.36% | 60,890,137 | | 14.30% | 69,596,163 | | 11.59% | 176,531 | | 13.45% | 200,271 | |
| Domestic banking offices | 3 | 0.59% | 684 | | 7.75% | 737 | | 0.00% | 5 | | 20.00% | 6 | |
| Foreign branches | 3 | 0.00% | 8 | | 0.00% | 8 | | 0.00% | 0 | | 0.00% | 0 | |
| Number of equivalent employees | 3 | -1.72% | 15,147 | | 3.49% | 15,675 | | -3.02% | 64 | | 9.85% | 71 | |
| **SUMMARY OF RISK BASED CAPITAL** | | | | | | | | | | | | | |
| Net tier 1 | 11A | -0.49% | 5,134,748 | 9.9% | -0.90% | 5,088,306 | 8.4% | 14.19% | 14,005 | 10.7% | 9.09% | 15,278 | 10.3% |
| Net eligible tier 2 | 11A | -9.20% | 1,566,924 | 3.0% | 28.12% | 2,007,618 | 3.3% | 6.70% | 1,258 | 1.0% | 28.54% | 1,617 | 1.1% |
| Tier 3 | 11A | 36.19% | (12,269) | 0.0% | 408.06% | (62,334) | -0.1% | 0.00% | 0 | 0.0% | 0.00% | 0 | 0.0% |
| Deductions | 11A | -2.73% | 6,689,403 | 12.9% | 5.15% | 7,033,591 | 11.5% | 13.53% | 15,263 | 11.7% | 10.69% | 16,895 | 11.4% |
| Total risk-based capital | 11A | -2.73% | 13,378,806 | 25.8% | 5.15% | 14,067,181 | 23.1% | 13.53% | 30,526 | 23.4% | 10.69% | 33,790 | 22.7% |
| Total risk-weighted assets | 11A | -1.95% | 51,908,044 | 100.0% | 17.32% | 60,897,630 | 100.0% | 12.72% | 130,506 | 100.0% | 14.03% | 148,814 | 100.0% |
| **SUMMARY OF LOAN LOSS ACCOUNT** | | | | | | | | | | | | | |
| Balance at beginning of period | 7 | 6.92% | 644,475 | 1.8% | -5.83% | 606,886 | 1.5% | 38.87% | 1,179 | 1.0% | 6.70% | 1,258 | 1.0% |
| Gross credit losses | 7 | 2.40% | 255,377 | 0.7% | -36.75% | 161,537 | 0.4% | 277.91% | 616 | 0.5% | -57.79% | 260 | 0.2% |
| Memo: loans HFS writedown | 7 | 14.01% | 26,060 | 0.1% | -67.16% | 8,558 | 0.0% | 0.00% | 0 | 0.0% | 0.00% | 0 | 0.0% |
| Recoveries | 7 | 11.29% | 47,453 | 0.1% | 5.05% | 49,849 | 0.1% | -15.38% | 11 | 0.0% | 72.73% | 19 | 0.0% |
| Net credit losses | 7 | 0.56% | 207,924 | 0.6% | -46.28% | 111,688 | 0.3% | 303.33% | 605 | 0.5% | -60.17% | 241 | 0.2% |
| Provisions for credit losses | 7 | -39.11% | 176,612 | 0.5% | -70.81% | 51,553 | 0.1% | 42.50% | 684 | 0.6% | -12.28% | 600 | 0.5% |
| Other adjustments | 7 | -84.91% | (6,277) | 0.0% | -692.07% | 37,164 | 0.1% | 0.00% | 0 | 0.0% | 0.00% | 0 | 0.0% |
| Balance at end of period | 7 | -5.83% | 606,886 | 1.7% | -3.79% | 583,915 | 1.5% | 6.70% | 1,258 | 1.1% | 28.54% | 1,617 | 1.3% |
| Average total loans & leases | 7 | -8.74% | 35,193,158 | 100.0% | 13.55% | 39,960,849 | 100.0% | 5.43% | 114,953 | 100.0% | 7.38% | 123,431 | 100.0% |
| **NON-CURRENT LN&LS** | | | | | | | | | | | | | |
| 90 days and over past due | 8 | -53.71% | 72,963 | 0.2% | -20.54% | 57,979 | 0.1% | -38.05% | 184 | 0.2% | -100.00% | 0 | 0.0% |
| Total nonaccrual LN&LS | 8 | -21.98% | 270,782 | 0.8% | -47.60% | 141,887 | 0.4% | -42.61% | 229 | 0.2% | -9.17% | 208 | 0.2% |
| Total non-current LN&LS | 8 | -31.89% | 343,745 | 1.0% | -41.86% | 199,866 | 0.5% | -40.66% | 413 | 0.4% | -49.64% | 208 | 0.2% |
| LN&LS 30–89 days past due | 8 | -49.74% | 126,455 | 0.4% | -25.05% | 94,779 | 0.2% | -68.98% | 844 | 0.7% | 167.89% | 2,261 | 1.8% |
| Restructured LN&LS 90+ days P/D | 8 | 0.0% | 0 | 0.0% | 0.0% | 0 | 0.0% | 0.0% | 0 | 0.0% | 0.0% | 0 | 0.0% |
| Restructured LN&LS nonaccrual | 8 | -65.1% | 424 | 0.0% | -100.0% | 0 | 0.0% | 0.0% | 0 | 0.0% | 0.0% | 0 | 0.0% |
| Current restructured LN&LS | 8 | 0.0% | 0 | 0.0% | 0.0% | 0 | 0.0% | 0.0% | 0 | 0.0% | 0.0% | 0 | 0.0% |
| All other real estate owned | 8 | 21.8% | 14,208 | 0.0% | 0.7% | 14,301 | 0.0% | -84.3% | 325 | 0.3% | -100.0% | 0 | 0.0% |

Net losses directly reduce loan loss reserves that a bank sets aside for potential losses. Data at the top of page 7 of the UBPR summarize the initial balance and adjustments to the loan loss allowance during each period. It is important to note that net losses are not directly reported on the income statement. Instead, a bank reports provisions for loan losses, which represents a transfer of funds (deferral of income taxes because it is deducted from income before determining taxes) to build the allowance for loan losses (loan loss reserve) up to its desired level. A review of Exhibit 2.2 reveals that a bank's balance sheet lists the allowance for loan and lease losses under gross loans as a contra-asset account. Importantly, this allowance or loan loss reserve is only an accounting entry and does not represent funds in some cookie jar that a bank can go to when it needs cash. The greater is a bank's loss reserves, the more it has provided for loan losses but not charged-off.

**EXPECTED FUTURE LOSSES.** Ratios that examine expected future loss rates are based on past-due loans, nonaccrual loans, total noncurrent loans, and classified loans as a fraction of total loans. **Past-due loans** represent loans for which contracted interest and principal payments have not been made but are still accruing interest. Past-due loans are often separated into 30–89 days past due and 90 days and over past due date. The formal designation of **nonperforming loans** are loans that are more than 90 days past due. **Nonaccrual loans** are those not currently accruing interest. These loans are currently—or have been habitually—past due, or have other problems, which have placed them in nonaccrual status. **Total noncurrent loans** are the sum of these two types of loans. **Restructured loans** are loans for which the lender has modified the required payments on principal or interest. The lender may have lengthened maturity and/or renegotiated the interest rate. **Classified loans** are a general category of loans in which regulators have forced management to set aside reserves for clearly recognized losses. Because some loans, such as speculative construction loans, are riskier than others, an analyst should examine the composition of a bank's loan portfolio and the magnitude of past due, nonaccrual, noncurrent, restructured, and classified loans relative to total loans.

The UBPR presents a series of ratios that examine a bank's ability to handle current and expected future losses. These include the bank's provisions for loan losses to average total assets, the loan and lease loss allowance (loan loss reserve) as a percentage of total loans, earning coverage of net losses, and loan and lease loss allowance to net losses. When management expects to charge-off large amounts of loans, it will build up the allowance for loan losses. It does this by adding to provisions for loan losses. Thus, a large allowance may indicate both good and bad performance. If asset quality is poor, a bank needs a large allowance because it will need to charge-off many loans. The allowance should be large because charge-offs will deplete it. Cash flows from loans will decline along with reported interest income. In this case, a high-loss reserve signals bad performance. With high-quality assets, banks charge-off fewer loans, so the allowance can be proportionately less. A bank with a large allowance for loan losses and few past due, nonaccrual, or nonperforming loans will not need all of the reserve to cover charge-offs, which will be low. Such a bank has reported provisions for loan losses that are higher than needed such that prior period net income is too low. Future profit measures should benefit once provisions are lowered.

**PREPARATION FOR LOSSES.** Ideally, management should relate the size of the loan loss reserve to noncurrent loans, which represent potential charge-offs. With a reserve equal to noncurrent loans (100 percent coverage), a bank should be well protected because it shouldn't expect to charge-off all nonperforming and nonaccrual loans. GAAP (Generally Accepted Accounting Principles) and Call Reporting guidelines require that a bank's loan loss reserve be adequate to cover the known and inherent risk in the loan portfolio. For tax purposes, however, the maximum allowable deduction for losses and the size of the reserve are set by IRS rules. Thus, prudent management could lead to a conflict with the IRS. Banks with less than $500 million in assets can use a reserve for bad debt system for tax purposes. Using this system, the IRS requires the bank to use a five-year historical average charge-off method for calculating provisions for loan losses. Banks with more than $500 million in assets use a direct charge-off method for tax purposes. In either case, when regulators consider the current loan portfolio to be more risky, regulators and GAAP accounting require higher provisions or a greater loan loss reserve than the IRS will allow. This leads to the unpleasant situation in which the bank must expense greater provisions than the IRS will allow it to deduct from taxable income. That is, the excess is not tax-deductible!

Another ratio used to measure a bank's ability to cover current period losses is **earnings coverage of net losses.** This is a measure of net operating income before taxes, securities gains (losses), extraordinary items, and the provision for loan losses divided by net loan and lease losses. It indicates how many times current earnings can cover current net charge-offs. A higher ratio signals greater coverage and, thus, greater protection. However, for the ratio to be useful, a bank must consistently report realistic figures for earnings and net losses. It is widely known that when banks have asset quality problems, management often plays games by deferring the recognition of charge-offs, thereby understating reserves and overstating earnings. Thus, the ratio is less revealing than ratios that directly incorporate the size of the loss reserve.

Three other sources of credit risk should be identified. First, banks that lend in a narrow geographic area or concentrate their loans to a certain industry have risk that is not fully measured by balance sheet or historical charge-off data. This **lack of diversification** could dramatically affect a majority of the bank's portfolio if economic factors negatively affected the geographic or industry concentration. This type of bank could be subject to risks that the rest of the banking industry is not subject to in its operations. Second, banks with **high loan growth** often assume greater risk, as credit analysis and review procedures are less rigorous. In addition, banks with high loan growth rates may be achieving this growth by making loans they have not made in the past. Hence, their historical data may not represent the risk of the current portfolio. In many instances, the loans perform for a while, but losses eventually rise. Thus, high loan growth rates, particularly when the loans are generated externally through acquisitions or entering new trade areas, often lead to future charge-offs. Third, banks that lend funds in foreign countries take country risk. **Country risk** refers to the potential loss of interest and principal on international loans due to borrowers in a country refusing to make timely payments, as per a loan agreement. In essence, foreign governments and corporate borrowers may default on their loans due to government controls over the actions of businesses and individuals, internal politics that may disrupt payments, general market disruptions, and problems that arise when governments reduce or eliminate subsidies used as a source of repayment.

Ideally, it would be useful to examine the credit files (actual loan files) of a bank to assess the quality of specific loans. Although this information is provided to regulators, it is not available to the public. Regulators, in fact, assign each bank a rating for asset quality ("A" for asset quality) as part of the CAMELS rating system. There has been some discussion of publishing these ratings, a policy that analysts desire but bankers fear.

## LIQUIDITY RISK

**Liquidity risk** is the current and potential risk to earnings and the market value of stockholders' equity that results from a bank's inability to meet payment or clearing obligations in a timely and cost-effective manner. Liquidity risk is greatest when a bank cannot anticipate new loan demand or deposit withdrawals, and does not have access to new sources of cash. This risk can be the result of either funding problems or market liquidity risk. **Funding liquidity risk** is the inability to liquidate assets or obtain adequate funding from new borrowing. **Market liquidity risk** is the inability of the bank to easily unwind or offset specific exposures without significant losses from inadequate market depth or market disturbances. This risk is greatest when risky securities are trading at high premiums to low-risk Treasury securities because market participants are avoiding high-risk borrowers.

Generally speaking, a firm can provide for its liquidity needs in one of two ways: 1) by holding liquid assets, and 2) by securing its ability to borrow (issuing new liabilities) at reasonable costs. Thus, when banks need cash, they can either sell liquid assets or increase borrowings. Liquidity risk measures, therefore, focus on the quantity and quality of liquid assets near maturity or available-for-sale at reasonable prices, as well as the bank's ability to cheaply and easily borrow funds to meet cash outflows.

**HOLDING LIQUID ASSETS.** Liquidity is often discussed in terms of assets with reference to an owner's ability to convert the asset to cash with minimal loss from price depreciation. Most banks hold some assets that can be readily sold near par to meet liquidity needs. These liquid assets provide immediate access to cash but are costly for the bank to hold. Liquid assets generally pay very low rates of interest, which could be below a bank's average cost of funds. For example, **cash assets** are held to satisfy customer withdrawal needs, meet legal reserve requirements, or to purchase services from other financial institutions, but do not pay interest. Hence, banks attempt to minimize cash holdings due to the cost of holding them. For this reason, cash assets do not represent a source of long-term liquidity for the bank. Cash balances held at banks for clearing purposes can decline temporarily but must be replenished to meet required reserves or pay for correspondent services.[31] Cash items in the process of collection (CIPC) vary with the volume of checks handled and cannot be manipulated by the bank.  Cash assets as a group are thus illiquid because a bank cannot reduce its holdings for any length of time. **Liquid assets**, therefore, consist of unpledged, marketable short-term securities that are classified as available-for-sale, plus federal funds sold and securities purchased under agreement to resell.

Banks purchase short-term investment securities for yield and to satisfy liquidity needs. Federal funds sold, securities purchased under agreement to resell, and unpledged available-for-sale securities are the most liquid assets. Short-term securities are generally more liquid than longer-term securities because they are less volatile in price and the bank gets its principal back earlier if it holds the securities until maturity. *Held-to-maturity* securities are not considered as liquid as *available-for-sale* securities because they can create regulatory and accounting issues if sold prior to maturity.[32] Banks are, however, generally more willing to sell any security that currently trades at a price above book value because, at worst, they can report a securities gain. **Pledging requirements** often stipulate that banks pledge either Treasury or municipal securities as collateral against deposit liabilities such as Treasury deposits, municipal deposits, and borrowings from Federal Reserve banks. These pledged securities are often held by a third-party trustee and cannot be sold without a release. The greater is the proportion of securities

---

[31]See Chapter 8 for a discussion of cash assets and required reserve planning.

[32]As a result of FASB 115, most banks are reluctant to classify any securities as held-to-maturity. Hence, differentiating between available-for-sale and held-to-maturity might be a moot point!

pledged, the smaller is the proportion that might be available for sale. Analysts, therefore, examine the proportion of, and type of, assets held in available-for-sale securities, short-term investments, and pledged securities as measures of liquidly through holding of liquid assets.

**ABILITY TO BORROW FOR LIQUIDITY.** If two banks hold similar assets, the one with the greater total equity or lower financial leverage can take on more debt with less chance of becoming insolvent. A bank that relies less on large volatile borrowings such as jumbo CDs, federal funds, Repos, euro dollars, and commercial paper, can issue greater amounts of new debt (acquire cash) in this form. In both instances, the cost of borrowing is lower than for a bank with the opposite profile. The equity-to-asset ratio and volatile (net noncore) liability-to-asset ratio, therefore, represent the bank's equity base and borrowing capacity in the money markets. *Volatile liabilities* or **short-term net noncore liabilities**, as they are listed in the UBPR, include large CDs (over $100,000), deposits in foreign offices, federal funds purchased, repurchase agreements, and other borrowings with maturities less than one year.[33] Although the UBPR does not include Federal Home Loan Bank borrowings less than one year, a more accurate definition should include these as they are purchased money. Volatile or purchased liquidity is **asset-quality sensitive**, meaning the lower a bank's equity position or greater are high-risk assets relative to equity, the lower is the bank's borrowing capacity and the higher are its borrowing costs.

**Core deposits** are stable deposits that are not highly interest-rate sensitive. These types of deposits are less sensitive to the interest rate paid but more sensitive to the fees charged, services rendered, and location of the bank. Thus, a bank will retain most of these deposits even when interest rates paid by competitors increase relative to the bank's own rates. As such, the interest elasticity of the demand for core deposits is low. Core deposits include demand deposits, NOW and ATS accounts, MMDAs, and small time deposits that the bank expects to remain on deposit over the business cycle. The greater are the core deposits in the funding mix, the lower are the unexpected deposit withdrawals and potential new funding requirements; hence, the greater is the bank's liquidity.

Although it is difficult to assess loan liquidity from general balance sheet information, loans can provide liquidity in two ways. First, cash inflows from periodic interest and principal payments can be used to meet cash outflows. Second, some loans are highly marketable and can be sold to other institutions. For example, the federal government guaranties a large portion of Small Business Administration (SBA) loans. The guaranteed portion of an SBA loan is highly marketable because default risk is low.

## MARKET RISK

*Market risk* is the current and potential risk to earnings and stockholders' equity resulting from adverse movements in market rates or prices. The three areas of market risk are: interest rate or reinvestment rate risk, equity or security price risk, and foreign exchange risk:

- **Interest rate risk** is the potential variability in a bank's net interest income and market value of equity due to changes in the level of market interest rates.

- **Equity and security price risk** is the potential risk of loss associated with a bank's trading account portfolios.

- **Foreign exchange risk** is the risk to a financial institution's condition resulting from adverse movements in foreign exchange rates.

**INTEREST RATE RISK.** Traditionally, interest rate risk analysis compares the sensitivity of interest income to changes in asset yields with the sensitivity of interest expense to changes in the interest costs of liabilities. This is done using **GAP** and **earnings sensitivity** analysis. The purpose is to determine how much net interest income will vary with movements in market interest rates. A more comprehensive portfolio analysis approach compares the duration of assets with the duration of liabilities using **duration gap** and **economic value of equity sensitivity** analysis to assess the impact of rate changes on net interest income and the market value (or price) of stockholders' equity. Duration is an elasticity measure that indicates the relative price sensitivity of different securities.[34]

Both GAP and duration gap focus on mismatched asset and liability maturities and durations as well as potential changes in interest rates. An asset or liability is **rate sensitive** if management expects it to be repriced (change of rate) within a certain time period. A bank's net interest sensitivity position, or funding GAP between assets and liabilities, is approximated by comparing the dollar amount of assets with liabilities that can be repriced over similar time frames. The dollar difference between rate-sensitive assets and rate-sensitive liabilities for 30 days, 31 to 90 days, and so forth, indicates whether more assets or liabilities will reprice within a given time interval. If this measure is positive, the bank will likely realize a decrease in net interest income if the level of short-term interest

---

[33]Actually, short-term noncore funding, as defined in the UBPR, also includes brokered deposits less than $100,000 and does not include FHLB borrowings less than one year. Due to the lack of detail data, calculated volatile liabilities in exhibits 2.7 and 2.8 do not include brokered deposits. The calculated value of volatile liabilities also excludes FHLB borrowings, to be consistent with the UBPR, but a more accurate measure of volatility should include FHLB borrowings less than one year as these are purchased money as well.

[34]Chapter 5 presents funding GAP and Chapter 6 formally defines duration measures and demonstrates their application to risk analysis and management.

rates falls as assets reprice downward faster than liabilities, and an increase in net interest income if short-term interest rates increase. If the bank's GAP measure is negative, on the other hand, meaning liabilities reprice faster than assets, the bank's net interest income will likely increase with a decline in rates and decrease with an increase in interest rates. The larger is the absolute value of the ratio, the greater is the risk. In practice, most banks conduct earnings sensitivity or market value of equity sensitivity analysis to examine volatility in net interest income and stockholders' equity to best identify interest rate risk exposures. Unfortunately, data contained in the UBPR are insufficient to evaluate a bank's interest rate risk position. More details on interest rate risk are provided in Chapters 5 and 6.

**EQUITY AND SECURITY PRICE RISK.** Changes in market prices, interest rates, and foreign exchange rates affect the market values of any equities, fixed-income securities, foreign currency holdings, and associated derivative and other off-balance sheet contracts. Large banks must conduct value-at-risk analysis to assess the risk of loss with their portfolio of these trading assets and hold specific amounts of capital in support of this market risk. Small banks identify their exposure by conducting sensitivity analysis. Value-at-risk analysis is introduced in Chapters 5, 6, and 9 but is generally beyond the scope of this book.

**FOREIGN EXCHANGE RISK.** Changes in foreign exchange rates affect the values of assets, liabilities, and off-balance sheet activities denominated in currencies different from the bank's domestic (home) currency. This risk exists because some banks hold assets and issue liabilities denominated in different currencies. When the amount of assets differs from the amount of liabilities in a currency, any change in exchange rates produces a gain or loss that affects the market value of the bank's stockholders' equity. This risk is also found in off-balance sheet loan commitments and guaranties denominated in foreign currencies and is also known as *foreign currency translation risk.* Banks that do not conduct business in nondomestic currencies do not directly assume this risk. Most banks measure foreign exchange risk by calculating measures of net exposure by each currency. A bank's net exposure is the amount of assets minus the amount of liabilities denominated in the same currency. Thus, a bank has a net exposure for each currency for which it books assets and liabilities. The potential gain or loss from the exposure is indicated by relating each net exposure to the potential change in the exchange rate for that currency versus the domestic currency.

## OPERATIONAL RISK

**Operational risk** refers to the possibility that operating expenses might vary significantly from what is expected, producing a decline in net income and firm value. The Basel Committee defines operational risk as:

> *The risk of loss resulting from inadequate or failed internal processes, people, and systems, or from external events.*[35]

A new focus of the Basel II Accord is operational risk (see Chapter 9 for more details on capital requirements). Starting in 2006, the proposed Basel capital requirements will require a bank to make capital allocations for operational risk. The focus is on the optimum use of capital in the technology and business process operations of a financial institution. The events of September 11, 2001, tragically demonstrated the need for banks to protect themselves against operational risk to their systems and people. From a capital adequacy point of view, this covers technology risks, management- and people-related operational risks, and legal risks.

There are many causes of earnings variability in a bank's operating policies. Some banks are relatively inefficient in controlling direct costs and employee processing errors. Banks must also absorb losses due to employee and customer theft and fraud. A bank's operating risk is closely related to its operating policies and processes and whether it has adequate controls. Losses from external events, such as an electrical outage, are easy to identify but difficult to forecast because they are not tied to specific tasks or products within the bank. Operational risk is difficult to measure directly but is likely greater the higher are the numbers of divisions or subsidiaries, employees, and loans to insiders.

Historically, measures of operating risk were limited to measures of operational efficiency and expense control or productivity, and included ratios such as total assets per employee and total personnel expense per employee. More recently, banks and other firms have come to realize that operational risk is much greater than this. Operational risk also arises from the more difficult to measure risk of unexpected loss or risk that might occur as the result of: **business interruptions** from loss or damage to assets, facilities, systems, or people; **transaction processing** from failed, late, or incorrect settlements; **inadequate information systems** in which the security of data or systems is compromised; **breaches in internal controls** resulting in fraud, theft, or unauthorized activities; and **client**

---

[35]See "What is Operational Risk?," Economic Letter, Federal Reserve Bank of San Francisco, January 25, 2002, by Jose Lopez.

**liability** resulting in restitution payments or reputation losses. Unfortunately, there is no concrete way to estimate the likelihood of these contingencies from published data. The key is to have strong internal audit procedures with follow-up to reduce exposures and for management to meticulously identify and quantify potential losses by type of event and the line of business where the event has an impact.

## LEGAL AND REPUTATION RISK

Almost by definition, legal and reputation risk are difficult to measure. **Legal risk** is the risk that unenforceable contracts, lawsuits, or adverse judgments could disrupt or negatively affect the operations, profitability, condition, or solvency of the institution. Legal risk not only addresses general liability issues, but also the bank's compliance risk. Banking is a heavily regulated industry and one with extensive regulatory compliance requirements. Lending to consumers, for example, requires very specific and detailed disclosures on the interest rate, maturity, and repayment schedule. Also, a bank must report its data and activities quarterly in a very detailed and specific manner, to name only a few of these extensive compliance issues. Failure to comply with the long list of regulatory mandated operational and reporting requirements can spell disaster for an institution. **Reputation risk** is the risk that negative publicity, either true or untrue, can adversely affect a bank's customer base or bring forth costly litigation, hence negatively affecting profitability. Because these risks are basically unforeseen, they are all but impossible to measure. Although it is difficult to measure and therefore manage reputation risk, firms can mitigate this risk by ensuring their employees receive effective and consistent training, such that they are well informed as to how to communicate with external customers and how to properly handle and deliver customer information. Senior management should also make sure regular and consistent assessments of internal controls are performed to ensure that they are fully effective and still applicable. Finally, transactional documentation should be reviewed and strengthened as necessary and systems should be in place as to how to fully and effectively address and deal with customer complaints.

## CAPITAL OR SOLVENCY RISK

Capital risk is not considered a separate risk because all of the risks mentioned previously will, in one form or another, affect a bank's capital and hence solvency. It does, however, represent the risk that a bank may become insolvent and fail. A firm is technically insolvent when it has negative net worth or stockholders' equity. The economic net worth of a firm is the difference between the market value of its assets and liabilities. Thus, *capital risk* refers to the potential decrease in the market value of assets below the market value of liabilities, indicating economic net worth is zero or less. If such a bank were to liquidate its assets, it would not be able to pay all creditors, and would be bankrupt. A bank with equity capital equal to 10 percent of assets can withstand a greater percentage decline in asset value than a bank with capital equal to only 6 percent of assets. One indicator of capital risk is a comparison of stockholders' equity with the bank's assets. The greater equity is to assets, the greater is the amount of assets that can default without the bank becoming insolvent. Chapter 9 introduces more formal risk-based capital ratios that indicate solvency risk.

Formally, a firm is insolvent when its net worth is negative. In practice, however, a bank that assumes too much risk can become insolvent and fail. Fundamentally, a bank fails when its cash inflows from operations, debt service receipts, new borrowings, and asset sales are insufficient to meet mandatory cash outflows due to operating expenses, deposit withdrawals, and payment of maturing debt obligations. A cash flow deficiency is caused by the market's evaluation that the market value of bank equity is falling and potentially negative. When creditors and shareholders perceive that a bank has high risk, they demand a premium on bank debt and bid share prices lower. This creates liquidity problems by increasing the cost of borrowing and potentially creating a run on the bank. Banks ultimately fail because they cannot independently generate cash to meet deposit withdrawals and operate with insufficient capital to absorb losses if they were forced to liquidate assets. As such, the market value of liabilities exceeds the market value of assets.

Capital risk is closely tied to financial leverage, asset quality, and a bank's overall risk profile; the more risk that is taken, the greater is the amount of capital required. High credit risk manifests itself through significant loan charge-offs. High interest rate risk manifests itself through mismatched maturities and durations between assets and liabilities. High operational risk appears with operational costs being out of control or significant unexpected charges. High amounts of fixed-rate sources of funds increase the expected volatility of a firm's income because interest payments are mandatory. If a bank was funded entirely from common equity, it would pay dividends, but these payments are discretionary. Omitting dividends does not produce default. Banks operating with high risk are expected to have greater capital than banks with low risk. Fundamentally, banks with high capital risk—evidenced by low capital-to-asset ratios—exhibit high levels of financial leverage, has a higher cost of capital, and normally experiences greater periodic fluctuations in earnings.

**OFF-BALANCE SHEET RISK.** Many banks engage in activities off-balance sheet. This means that they enter into agreements that do not have a balance sheet reporting impact until a transaction is affected. An example might be a long-term loan commitment to a potential borrower. Until the customer actually borrows the funds, no loan is booked as part of the bank's assets. **Off-balance sheet risk** refers to the volatility in income and market value of bank equity that may arise from unanticipated losses due to these off-balance sheet liabilities.

Banks earn fees when they engage in off-balance sheet agreements. These agreements, in turn, entail some risk as the bank must perform under the contract. As an example, Enron borrowed billions of dollars against outstanding credit lines right before it declared bankruptcy at year-end 2001. Early in 2002, PNC reclassified its treatment of a presumed asset sale and reduced net income for the prior year (2001) by $155 million due to a disagreement with the Federal Reserve Board on the method used to move some assets off its books. The $155 million was a charge that PNC took to income after adding loans it had moved off-balance sheet in the fourth quarter of 2001 back on its balance sheet. The rules about "qualified special-purpose entities" and FASB 140 are considered vague and have been under heavy scrutiny. See the section on "Financial Statement Manipulation" and the Contemporary Issues Box: "The Fall of Enron and Its Impact on PNC Bank" presented later in the chapter.

To account for the potential risk of off-balance sheet activities, risk-based capital requirements oblige a bank to convert off-balance sheet activities to "on-balance" sheet equivalents and hold capital against these activities. Appropriate capital risk measures include all the risk measures discussed earlier, as well as ratios measuring the ratio of: Tier 1 capital and total risk-based capital to risk-weighted assets, equity capital to total assets, dividend payout, and the growth rate in Tier 1 capital. **Tier 1 capital** or **Tier 1 leverage capital** is total common equity capital plus noncumulative preferred stock, plus minority interest in unconsolidated subsidiaries, less ineligible intangibles. **Risk-weighted assets** are the total of risk-adjusted assets where the risk weights are based on four risk classes of assets. See Chapter 9 for more details on calculation of capital at banks. Importantly, a bank's dividend policy also affects its capital risk by influencing retained earnings.

## EVALUATING BANK PERFORMANCE: AN APPLICATION

A complete analysis of a financial firm is similar to that of any other industry with a few exceptions. The analyst begins by gathering background information on the firm's operations, including specific characteristics of the business and intensity of competition, organizational and business structure, management character and quality, as well as the quality of reported data. Is the bank a holding company or financial holding company with subsidiaries and branches, or a single entity? Does it operate as a C-corporation or an S-corporation?[36] Is the firm privately held or publicly traded? When did the firm begin operations, and in what geographic markets does it now compete? The evaluation should also identify the products or services provided and the bank's competitive position in the marketplace as measured by market share, degree of product differentiation, presence of economies of scale or scope in the cost structure, and the bargaining power of customers with whom the bank deals. Much of this discussion for PNC Bank was presented earlier in the chapter and hence the following discussion focuses on the financial data of PNC introduced in Exhibits 2.2, 2.3, and 2.6. It examines the data for 2004 relative to peer banks and summarizes trends from 2000 to 2004. Profitability is evaluated following the ROE model presented in the chapter using data from PNC Bank's UBPR data. This evaluation is contrasted with the firm's risk position using the risk categories discussed in the "Managing Risk and Returns" section presented previously.

### PROFITABILITY ANALYSIS FOR PNC IN 2004

Profitability ratios are provided in Exhibit 2.7. The first column in 2004, "CALC," contains the ratios calculated using data listed in Exhibits 2.2, 2.3, and 2.6. The second column, "BANK," provides profitability ratios taken directly from the UBPR. The third column, titled "PG 1," represents peer group comparative figures obtained from the UBPR for other U.S. banks with more than $3 billion in assets.[37] The equations provided in the chapter apply to data in the column labeled "CALC." Because the UBPR uses several different methods of averaging balance sheet data, the calculated ratios will not always equal the UBPR ratios. Quarterly average balance sheet data are not published in the UBPR except for average total assets and average total loans. When other average balance sheet data are needed to calculate a ratio, the average value is obtained by using an average of end-of-year data. The calculated values are provided as a reference in applying the formulas and equations presented earlier in the chapter. Because the use of quarterly average balance sheet data will generally provide more accurate ratios, the following analysis will use ratios obtained directly from the UBPR and compare these with the listed peer group figures.[38]

---

[36]It is very important to know if the bank operates as an S-corporation. S-corporations do not pay taxes at the bank level, rather these tax obligations are passed on to shareholders. This means that net income is "overstated" relative to a C-corporation since it does not consider the taxes that must be paid by shareholders on behalf of the bank. The analysts must adjust all after-tax figures for S-corporation banks to compare to C-corporation banks.

[37]There are actually 27 bank peer groups. Peer group 1 is for banks over $3 billion.

[38]Although the following analysis will directly compare PNC's ratio to the peer group, it is important to recognize that the peer group may or may not be the appropriate comparison. To say a bank is doing better than the peer means it is doing better than average and does not always indicate that the bank is "doing well."

**EXHIBIT 2.7** Profitability Measures for PNC Bank and Community National Bank, 2003–2004

| Profitability Ratios | Pg # | PNC Bank, National Association Dec-03 CALC | Dec-03 BANK | Dec-03 PG 1 | Dec-04 CALC | Dec-04 BANK | Dec-04 PG 1 | Community National Bank Dec-03 CALC | Dec-03 BANK | Dec-03 PG 4 | Dec-04 CALC | Dec-04 BANK | Dec-04 PG 4 |
|---|---|---|---|---|---|---|---|---|---|---|---|---|---|
| ROE: Net Income / Average total equity | 11 | 16.90% | 16.56% | 14.41% | 15.59% | 15.26% | 14.55% | 5.48% | 5.56% | 11.56% | 8.63% | 8.67% | 11.72% |
| ROA: Net income / aTA | 1 | 1.59% | 1.59% | 1.28% | 1.31% | 1.31% | 1.31% | 0.41% | 0.41% | 1.07% | 0.63% | 0.63% | 1.09% |
| AU: Total revenue / aTA | 1 calc | 7.59% | 7.59% | 6.45% | 7.02% | 7.02% | 6.21% | 6.10% | 6.10% | 6.50% | 5.90% | 5.91% | 6.23% |
| ER: Total expenses (less taxes) / aTA | 1 calc | 5.18% | 5.17% | 4.51% | 5.15% | 5.14% | 4.23% | 5.47% | 5.48% | 5.01% | 4.93% | 4.94% | 4.73% |
| EM: aTA / Avg, total equity | 6 calc | 10.59x | 10.48x | 11.20x | 11.59x | 11.47x | 10.65x | 13.37x | 13.76x | 10.85x | 13.78x | 13.97x | 10.67x |
| EB: Earning Assets / aTA | 6 | 82.86% | 82.60% | 89.84% | 82.85% | 82.92% | 90.08% | 85.43% | 86.74% | 91.45% | 86.83% | 86.98% | 91.76% |
| NIM: Net interest margin (te) | 1 | 3.89% | 3.82% | 3.51% | 3.32% | 3.18% | 3.52% | 4.95% | 4.80% | 4.33% | 4.82% | 4.74% | 4.36% |
| Spread (te) | 3 calc | 3.74% | 3.62% | 3.36% | 3.15% | 3.02% | 3.37% | 4.39% | 4.25% | 3.97% | 4.30% | 4.25% | 4.04% |
| Efficiency ratio | 3 | 60.93% | 60.86% | 57.73% | 68.01% | 68.01% | 57.01% | 82.72% | 82.75% | 66.06% | 75.35% | 75.34% | 65.99% |
| Burden / aTA | 1 calc | 0.67% | 0.66% | 1.12% | 0.81% | 0.81% | 1.16% | 3.37% | 3.37% | 2.33% | 2.94% | 2.94% | 2.39% |
| Noninterest income / Noninterest exp. | 1 calc | 83.24% | 83.42% | 62.03% | 79.79% | 79.70% | 59.86% | 21.08% | 21.08% | 29.18% | 24.18% | 24.23% | 26.23% |
| **EXPENSES: ER*: Expense Ratio (Expense components)** | | | | | | | | | | | | | |
| Total interest expense / aTA | 1 | 0.90% | 0.90% | 1.29% | 1.08% | 1.08% | 1.20% | 0.82% | 0.82% | 1.50% | 0.76% | 0.76% | 1.31% |
| *Memo: Interest expense / Avg. Earn assets* | 1 | 1.09% | 1.07% | 1.41% | 1.34% | 1.28% | 1.31% | 0.95% | 0.92% | 1.61% | 0.87% | 0.85% | 1.41% |
| Noninterest expenses / aTA | 1 | 3.98% | 3.98% | 2.95% | 3.99% | 3.99% | 2.89% | 4.27% | 4.27% | 3.29% | 3.88% | 3.88% | 3.24% |
| Personnel expense | 3 | 1.83% | 1.83% | 1.37% | 2.04% | 2.04% | 1.38% | 2.38% | 2.38% | 1.79% | 2.16% | 2.16% | 1.78% |
| Occupancy expense | 3 | 0.58% | 0.58% | 0.38% | 0.50% | 0.50% | 0.36% | 0.71% | 0.71% | 0.48% | 0.64% | 0.64% | 0.47% |
| Other oper. exp. (incl. intangibles) | 3 | 1.57% | 1.58% | 1.13% | 1.43% | 1.44% | 1.08% | 1.17% | 1.18% | 1.00% | 1.07% | 1.07% | 0.98% |
| Provision: loan & lease losses / aTA | 1 | 0.29% | 0.29% | 0.27% | 0.07% | 0.07% | 0.14% | 0.39% | 0.39% | 0.22% | 0.30% | 0.30% | 0.18% |
| Income taxes / aTA | 1 calc | 0.82% | 0.83% | 0.66% | 0.56% | 0.57% | 0.67% | 0.21% | 0.21% | 0.42% | 0.34% | 0.34% | 0.41% |
| **INCOME: AU: Asset utilization (Income components):** | | | | | | | | | | | | | |
| Interest income / aTA | 1 | 4.12% | 4.12% | 4.57% | 3.77% | 3.77% | 4.46% | 5.08% | 5.08% | 5.52% | 4.97% | 4.97% | 5.37% |
| *Memo: Avg, yield on earning assets* | 1 | 4.98% | 4.89% | 4.98% | 4.66% | 4.46% | 4.88% | 5.91% | 5.73% | 5.95% | 5.69% | 5.59% | 5.78% |
| Noninterest income / aTA | 1 | 3.32% | 3.32% | 1.83% | 3.18% | 3.18% | 1.73% | 0.90% | 0.90% | 0.96% | 0.94% | 0.94% | 0.85% |
| Realized security gains (losses) / aTA | 1 | 0.15% | 0.15% | 0.05% | 0.07% | 0.07% | 0.02% | 0.12% | 0.12% | 0.02% | 0.00% | 0.00% | 0.01% |
| **Interest expense: composition, rate and volume effects** | | | | | | | | | | | | | |
| Rate: Avg, interest cost of interest bearing liabilities | 3 | 1.24% | 1.27% | 1.62% | 1.50% | 1.44% | 1.51% | 1.51% | 1.48% | 1.98% | 1.39% | 1.34% | 1.74% |
| *Memo: Interest expense / Earning assets* | 1 | 1.09% | 1.07% | 1.41% | 1.34% | 1.28% | 1.31% | 0.95% | 0.92% | 1.61% | 0.87% | 0.85% | 1.41% |
| Volume: All Interest bearing debt (avg.) / aTA | 1 | 72.73% | 70.78% | 80.81% | 73.70% | 74.97% | 80.65% | 53.76% | 55.17% | 75.51% | 54.29% | 56.69% | 74.88% |

*(continues)*

**EXHIBIT 2.7** (continued)

| Profitability Ratios | Pg # | PNC Bank, National Association | | | | | | Community National Bank | | | | | |
|---|---|---|---|---|---|---|---|---|---|---|---|---|---|
| | | Dec-03 | | | Dec-04 | | | Dec-03 | | | Dec-04 | | |
| | | CALC | BANK | PG 1 | CALC | BANK | PG 1 | CALC | BANK | PG 4 | CALC | BANK | PG 4 |
| **Mix and cost of individual liabilities:*** | | | | | | | | | | | | | |
| Total deposits (avg.) / aTA: | 6 | 73.72% | 73.84% | 67.79% | 72.45% | 72.30% | 68.32% | 91.72% | 91.94% | 85.07% | 92.02% | 91.96% | 84.46% |
| Cost (rate): Int bearing total deposits | 3 | 1.20% | 1.22% | 1.39% | 1.18% | 1.14% | 1.25% | 1.52% | 1.49% | 1.90% | 1.38% | 1.33% | 1.66% |
| Core deposits (avg.) / aTA | 6 | 67.41% | 68.16% | 53.90% | 64.84% | 64.29% | 54.64% | 84.26% | 84.50% | 72.07% | 85.00% | 84.90% | 71.52% |
| All other deposits (avg.) / aTA | 6-calc | 55.93% | 55.41% | 42.13% | 53.38% | 53.19% | 43.03% | 45.73% | 45.52% | 54.88% | 46.77% | 47.73% | 53.88% |
| Transaction (NOW & ATS) Accounts (avg.) / aTA | 6 | 2.40% | 2.23% | 1.81% | 2.35% | 2.15% | 1.92% | 6.55% | 6.58% | 10.37% | 7.43% | 7.02% | 10.60% |
| Cost (rate): Transaction (NOW & ATS) Accts* | 3 | #N/A | 0.90% | 0.60% | #N/A | 0.86% | 0.62% | #N/A | 0.29% | 0.63% | #N/A | 0.28% | 0.59% |
| MMDA's and other sav. Accts (avg) / aTA | 6-calc | 42.29% | 42.15% | 30.73% | 41.23% | 41.28% | 32.75% | 25.67% | 25.71% | 22.70% | 28.07% | 29.57% | 22.85% |
| Cost (rate): Other savings deposits* | 3 | #N/A | 0.57% | 0.70% | #N/A | 0.60% | 0.69% | #N/A | 0.90% | 1.08% | #N/A | 0.98% | 1.00% |
| Time deposits under $100M (avg.) / aTA | 6 | 11.24% | 11.03% | 9.59% | 9.80% | 9.76% | 8.36% | 13.51% | 13.23% | 21.81% | 11.27% | 11.14% | 20.43% |
| Cost (rate): All other time dep. (CD < $100M)* | 3 | #N/A | 3.12% | 2.41% | #N/A | 2.78% | 2.03% | #N/A | 2.51% | 2.80% | #N/A | 2.01% | 2.43% |
| Volatile (S.T noncore) liab. (avg.) / aTA | 10 | 9.85% | 11.47% | 23.24% | 13.08% | 12.11% | 23.42% | 8.03% | 4.10% | 11.90% | 7.52% | 4.84% | 12.21% |
| Large CDs (inc. brokered) (avg.) / aTA | 6 | 3.23% | 3.14% | 9.02% | 3.67% | 3.76% | 8.99% | 7.46% | 7.44% | 12.41% | 7.02% | 7.06% | 12.39% |
| Cost (rate): CD's over $100M | 3 | 3.44% | 3.66% | 2.38% | 2.89% | 2.81% | 2.17% | 2.83% | 2.79% | 2.72% | 2.82% | 2.78% | 2.40% |
| Fed funds purchased & resale (avg.)/ aTA | 6 | 0.74% | 0.99% | 8.16% | 1.55% | 3.18% | 8.00% | 0.56% | 0.55% | 1.05% | 0.50% | 0.55% | 1.07% |
| Cost (rate): Fed funds purchased & resale | 3 | 2.95% | 1.10% | 1.15% | 3.84% | 1.37% | 1.41% | 1.10% | 1.10% | 0.82% | 2.10% | 1.75% | 0.98% |
| Memo: All brokered deposits (avg.) / aTA | 6 | 2.36% | 2.19% | 2.29% | 2.81% | 3.00% | 2.81% | 0.00% | 0.00% | 0.51% | 0.00% | 0.11% | 0.84% |
| All common and preferred capital (avg.) / aTA | 6 | 9.44% | 9.54% | 8.93% | 8.63% | 8.72% | 9.39% | 7.48% | 7.27% | 9.22% | 7.26% | 7.16% | 9.37% |
| **Interest income: Composition, rate and volume effects** | | | | | | | | | | | | | |
| Rate: Avg. yield on aTA | | | | | | | | | | | | | |
| Memo: Avg. yield on earn. assets (rate) | 1 | 4.98% | 4.89% | 4.98% | 4.66% | 4.46% | 4.88% | 5.91% | 5.73% | 5.95% | 5.69% | 5.59% | 5.78% |
| Volume: Earn assets (avg.) / aTA | 6 | 82.86% | 82.60% | 89.84% | 82.85% | 82.92% | 90.08% | 85.43% | 86.74% | 91.45% | 86.83% | 86.98% | 91.76% |
| Nonearning assets (avg.) / aTA | 6-calc | 17.14% | 17.39% | 9.75% | 17.15% | 17.07% | 9.64% | 14.57% | 13.27% | 8.25% | 13.17% | 13.03% | 7.93% |
| **Mix and yield on individual assets:*** * | | | | | | | | | | | | | |
| Total loans and leases (avg.) / aTA | 6 calc | 57.55% | 57.17% | 57.69% | 57.13% | 57.25% | 58.22% | 65.76% | 64.10% | 66.45% | 62.05% | 61.33% | 67.80% |
| Yield (rate): Total loans & leases (te) | 3 | 5.48% | 5.48% | 5.66% | 5.04% | 5.04% | 5.47% | 6.89% | 6.89% | 6.91% | 6.90% | 6.90% | 6.58% |
| Total investments (avg.) / aTA: | 6-calc | 26.33% | 26.46% | 26.43% | 26.60% | 26.52% | 26.50% | 20.36% | 23.28% | 21.82% | 25.50% | 26.35% | 20.98% |
| Total investment securities (avg.) / aTA | 6-calc | 21.41% | 21.90% | 22.56% | 22.12% | 22.03% | 23.03% | 16.43% | 14.97% | 17.89% | 20.83% | 20.78% | 17.81% |
| Yield (rate): Total investment securities (TE) | 3 | 3.99% | 3.81% | 4.18% | 3.54% | 3.51% | 3.98% | 2.94% | 3.32% | 4.08% | 3.00% | 2.92% | 3.91% |
| Yield (rate): Total investment securities (Book) | 3 | 3.99% | 3.81% | 4.00% | 3.52% | 3.48% | 3.84% | 2.86% | 3.24% | 3.75% | 2.91% | 2.83% | 3.61% |
| Fed funds sold & resales (avg.) / aTA | 6 | 2.92% | 2.60% | 2.61% | 2.09% | 1.98% | 2.37% | 2.69% | 7.14% | 3.19% | 3.10% | 4.10% | 2.52% |
| Yield (rate): Fed funds sold & resales | 3 | 1.05% | 1.60% | 1.09% | 2.08% | 2.00% | 1.24% | 2.79% | 1.04% | 0.97% | 1.63% | 1.33% | 1.19% |
| Trading account assets (avg.) / aTA | 6 | 1.61% | 1.63% | 0.39% | 1.92% | 2.09% | 0.34% | 0.00% | 0.00% | 0.00% | 0.00% | 0.00% | 0.00% |
| Held-to-maturity securities (avg.) / aTA | 6 | 0.00% | 0.00% | 1.45% | 0.00% | 0.00% | 2.03% | 1.99% | 1.58% | 2.01% | 1.45% | 1.74% | 2.01% |
| Available-for-sale-securities (avg.) / aTA | 6 | 21.41% | 21.90% | 21.11% | 22.12% | 22.03% | 21.00% | 14.44% | 13.39% | 15.88% | 19.38% | 19.04% | 15.80% |

*When income statement numbers are used in the numerator, aTA is average total assets from Exhibit 2.6. For consistency, however, all "Mix" or composition values use averages of current and prior period. For Example, numerator and denominator averages for "Total deposits (avg.) / aTA" are both calculated using end-of-period annual average data.

**Short-term noncore funding is defined in the UBPR as certificates of deposit of $100,000 or more, brokered deposits less than $100,000, other borrowings (less than one year), deposits in foreign offices, securities sold under agreements to repurchase, and federal funds purchased with maturities less than one year. Due to the lack of detail data, *calculated* volatile liabilities does not include brokered deposits.

PNC's profitability fell dramatically in 2004, such that the return on equity (ROE) equaled 15.26 percent, above that of peers for the year but well below returns for 2003.[39] ROE was generated by an ROA of 1.31 percent and an equity multiplier of 11.47. While profitability at the bank was equal to that of peers according to ROA, its financial leverage was greater than peers (EM equals 10.65) which produced the higher ROE. The bank's higher returns, combined with higher risk (greater leverage), is a potential sign it has dealt with its loan problems of 2001. The 2004 performance is in sharp contrast to what appeared to be a bank with significant loan problems in 2001 (see the Contemporary Issues Box: "The Fall of Enron and Its Impact on PNC Bank"). One of the greatest challenges to evaluating a bank, or any company, is that a bank that assumes a higher degree of risk typically also reports higher profits, at first, and only later when those higher-risk loans begin to go bad does the bank report higher charge-offs or additional provisions for loan losses.

PNC's higher ROA is a result of a greater ability to generate income, as evidenced by the bank's asset utilization being 81 basis points above peers, rather than its ability to control expenses. The bank's higher expense ratio of 5.14 percent (versus 4.23 percent for peers) indicates that PNC was less efficient than its peers in controlling total expenses. PNC's tax ratio of 0.57 percent was lower than that for peers at 0.67 percent offsetting some of the higher expense. Thus, PNC's profitability would have been even greater if not for the much higher expenses that offset the higher profitability relative to peers. By breaking down asset utilization into interest income and noninterest income, and the expense ratio into interest and noninterest expense and provisions for loan losses, we can better determine the operational strengths and weaknesses of PNC's profitability.

PNC's higher overall expenses are attributed to significantly greater noninterest expense and not interest expense. PNC actually paid 0.12 percent less in interest expense relative to average assets than peers (1.08 percent versus peers of 1.20 percent). This difference suggests that PNC operates differently than peers in at least one of the areas of *rates* paid, liability *composition,* and *volume* of interest-bearing liabilities. Overall, PNC's average cost of interest-bearing liabilities was 7 basis points lower than peers (1.44 versus 1.51 percent for peers). Of benefit was the 17 basis points lower average cost of total interest bearing deposits (1.14 versus 1.25 percent for peers). Interestingly, the interest cost of some liabilities was higher than peers and some were lower. In terms of mix, PNC's core deposits contributed almost 10 percent more of total funding while short-term noncore funding comprised 11.3 percent less, which indicates that a favorable mix of lower cost liabilities reduced the bank's overall interest expense versus peers. Core deposits include noninterest-bearing checking accounts, interest-bearing checking accounts, and money market funds, all of which pay little or no interest. Lower interest expense was, therefore, the result of PNC's reliance on a less expensive composition of funds offset somewhat by a higher rate paid some of these funds. Finally, we know that the volume effect was positive because PNC's volume of interest-bearing liabilities was a smaller fraction of average assets than that of peers (74.97 percent versus 80.65 percent). In this case, two of the three factors—a less expensive composition of funds and a lower volume of interest-bearing liabilities—produce the lower aggregate interest expense for PNC relative to peers.

Profitability for PNC was lowered by the bank's higher noninterest expense to assets (3.99 versus 2.89 percent for peers). All noninterest expense factors, personnel, occupancy, and other operating expenses were higher at PNC. PNC delivers banking services through an extensive branching network, including some foreign branches, and focuses on funding the bank with core deposits. PNC's lower interest expenses are attributed to a larger volume of core deposits, which require more noninterest costs such as personnel, occupancy (branches), and technology expense (other operating expenses). This trade-off, between noninterest and interest expense, does not appear to be working as well for PNC today since noninterest expenses were 110 basis points higher while interest expense was only 12 basis points lower.[40]

However, interest versus noninterest expense is not the only trade-off. First, a larger retail network of branches and services also produces more noninterest income and PNC's noninterest income is substantially higher than peers, more than making up for the higher noninterest expense! Second, the relationship between interest income and interest expense is expressed in terms of net interest margin (NIM). PNC's lower net interest margin (3.18 percent versus 3.52 percent) indicates that PNC's lower interest expense is more than offset by its lower interest income. PNC's net interest margin is lower than peers, in part, because it has fewer earning assets. With the multitude of trade-offs between interest and noninterest income and interest and noninterest expense, banks use the efficiency ratio to measure their ability to control noninterest expense relative to net operating income. Somewhat surprisingly, PNC's efficiency ratio is sharply higher than peers at 68.01 percent versus 57.01 percent. This indicates that PNC spends almost 11 cents more in noninterest expense than peers to earn a dollar of net operating income. The final factor is that PNC operates with 7.16 percent fewer earning assets than

[39]The following analysis will use ratios reported in the UBPR rather than those calculated. For example, the ROE reported in the UBPR under the column "BANK," and listed in the second column under Dec-04 of Exhibit 2.7, is 15.26. The ROE calculated from 2004 data presented in Exhibits 2.2 and 2.3 is 15.59. Ratios reported in the UBPR use one of three types of averages of quarterly figures from balance sheet data and the use of quarterly averages generally produces more accurate ratios. Hence, some of the ratios calculated using data from Exhibits 2.2 and 2.3 will not equal those reported in the UBPR in the Appendix. See the Contemporary Issues box on "Interpreting Financial Ratios and the Use of Average Balance Sheet Data."

[40]It should be noted that the trade-off between lower retail deposit costs and higher noninterest expenses is generally not as successful when interest rates are low as they were in 2004.

peers.[41] Fundamentally, even though PNC's net interest margin was higher and its noninterest income more than compensated for the higher noninterest expense, the bank's lower earnings base made the final difference. The efficiency ratio is an extremely useful measure for a bank when examining a significant number of trade-offs, as in PNC's case.

Consider the components of asset utilization. Even though PNC's AU was much greater than peers, its interest income was lower (3.77 versus 4.46 percent for peers) and noninterest income was significantly higher (3.18 versus 1.73 percent for peers). Again, lower interest income could be due to lower yields on assets, fewer loans, a smaller volume of earning assets, or a combination of these. Upon examining the yield on earning assets, we find that PNC earned 42 basis points less on earning assets (4.46 percent versus 4.88 percent for peers) and invested 7.16 percent less in earning assets. PNC earned lower yields on both loans and investments and operated with 0.97 percent fewer total loans and leases but approximately the same porportion of investments. PNC clearly invested more of its assets in noninterest bearing cash and due from banks, as well as acceptances and other assets. Other assets include loans available for sale; PNC has been selling some of its loan portfolio over the past few years. The fact that PNC held fewer assets in loans and investments and more assets in noninterest bearing funds, and that its loans and investments earned lower rates, resulted in lower interest income.

Until 2002 PNC operated with substantially more loans than peer banks, but reduced the size of its loan portfolio since then. In addition to the almost $10 billion reduction in loans in 2001, due in large part to loan sales in late 2001, PNC's loan portfolio has fallen from $53 billion in 1999 to just over $43 billion at the end of 2004. The lower yield on loans might suggest lower risk, but PNC's history has shown loan problems in the past. PNC's loan rates were also lower in 2000 and the loan problems of 2001 were not indicative of a lower-risk loan portfolio.[42] As such, the analyst should carefully examine the bank's credit risk. If PNC did indeed "sell" or eliminate its higher-risk loans, this would mean improved profitability and lower risk in the future.

Noninterest income was significantly higher at PNC. PNC and other large banking organizations have generally structured their banking business to rely proportionately more on noninterest income and less on loan income. In fact, one of the primary motives to PNC's loan sales in 2001 was a restructuring of its primary business to reflect asset management and the custody business as core operations. PNC wanted to restructure its core business and operate a bank with a "low-risk" balance sheet. Following this model, management stated the objective to become more selective in the types of loans made. Many large banks generally encourage loans to businesses with more easily verifiable credit qualities, hence lower loan rates. This assists them in keeping overhead cost down and in cross-selling other products, thus producing more noninterest income in the form of product and service fees. Consistent with the sale of more products, PNC's higher noninterest income is generated from investment banking, advisory, brokerage, and underwriting fees and commissions; fiduciary activities; service charges; and net gains on loan sales.[43]

| Composition of Noninterest Income in 2004 as a percent of assets* | PNC | Banks Assets >$10B* | All Commercial Banks |
|---|---|---|---|
| Number of institutions reporting | 1 | 85 | 7630 |
| Total noninterest income | 3.23% | 2.49% | 2.30% |
| Fiduciary activities | 0.43% | 0.30% | 0.28% |
| Service charges on deposit accounts | 0.63% | 0.40% | 0.40% |
| Trading account gains & fees | 0.09% | 0.16% | 0.12% |
| Investment banking, advisory, brokerage, and underwriting fees and commissions | 1.09% | 0.15% | 0.12% |
| Venture capital revenue | 0.00% | 0.00% | 0.00% |
| Net servicing fees | 0.07% | 0.22% | 0.19% |
| Net securitization income | 0.01% | 0.33% | 0.28% |
| Insurance commission fees and income | 0.02% | 0.05% | 0.05% |
| Net gains(losses) on sales of loans | 0.19% | 0.06% | 0.09% |
| Net gains (losses) on sales of other real estate owned | 0.00% | 0.00% | 0.00% |

*Peer data for banks with assets greater than $10 billion are taken from a different source than the UBPR. These data are obtained from the FDIC's SDI system (http://www3.fdic.gov/sdi). The UBPR "trims" the upper 5 percent and lower 5 percent of data to adjust for outliers and PG 1 is now for banks with assets greater than $3 billion rather than $10 billion as reported above. The data presented in the table above represent all banks in the respective asset category. Obviously, as compared with the UBPR peer figure of 1.83 percent for all banks in excess of $3 billion, the largest banks do a better job of producing noninterest income.

[41]The UBPR reports "Average earning assets / Average assets" on page 1 and "Total earning assets" on page 6. The first measure reported on page 1, includes total loans (rather than net loans) and a five period average of interest only strips and equity securities. Hence, we use the measure on page 6 for the analysis.

[42]See the Contemporary Issues Box: "The Fall of Enron and Its Impact on PNC Bank."

[43]Other noninterest income and fee income include: investment banking, advisory, brokerage and underwriting fees and commissions, venture capital revenue, net servicing fees, net securitization income, insurance commissions and fees, net gains (losses) on sales of loans, other real estate owned, other assets, and other noninterest income.

PNC's more aggressive noninterest position is emphasized by the fact that PNC's burden was 35 basis points better than peers as a fraction of assets (0.81 versus 1.16 percent), indicating that the bank performed better than peers in generating noninterest income to cover its noninterest expense.

In summary, PNC appears to be a high-performance bank based on its strong return on equity and lower financial leverage. PNC's return on assets is supported by greater overall income generation and, in particular, much higher noninterest income. PNC produces less interest income due to lower rates on loans and investments, a slightly smaller loan and investment portfolio, but most significantly fewer earning assets. PNC's profitability strength is its lower overall expenses. Although its noninterest expenses are significantly higher than peers, interest expenses are lower due to a low-cost composition of core deposits and fewer volatile liabilities.

## RISK ANALYSIS FOR PNC IN 2004

Higher returns are generally indicative of above-average risk, while lower returns should indicate a lower-risk position. A high-performance bank, however, is a bank that can produce higher returns with similar risk. Could PNC's higher returns relative to shareholders, and seemingly lower-risk portfolio of loans, be an indicator that it is again a high-performance bank? What appeared to be a high return in the past ended with the conclusion that PNC took above-average risk in prior periods and suffered the consequences in 2001, relative to peers. One of the problems in evaluating financial statements is that they are aggregate measures of past "reported" performance and might not be accurate in representing the current or future financial position of the company. As was the case with PNC, losses associated with the loan portfolio were restated several times for fiscal year 2001, casting a shadow on management and lowering the confidence one might have in the reported financials. Events in late 2001 and early 2002 were clear indicators that reported profits from the past were "overstated" and that the true risk of a company cannot always be determined by evaluating aggregate balance sheet and income statement data.

Often, the analyst must dig deeper into the actual credit files, footnotes to the balance sheet, as well as any off-balance sheet activities to discover risk not reported on these financials. With this said, the following section on Financial Statement Manipulation will discuss the analysis of reported financial statements, with the understanding that the analysis is only as accurate as the reported data. Selected risk ratios for PNC and CNB appear in Exhibit 2.8. Additional data used to calculate some of the risk ratios, including loan charge-offs, past due loans, and noncurrent loans are taken from the supplemental data in Exhibit 2.6 and the UBPR for PNC included in the Appendix. Exhibit 2.8 lists selected risk measures categorized under the risk types introduced earlier.

In terms of credit risk in 2004, PNC held a lower fraction of assets in loans but its gross loan loss experience overall was 4 basis points higher than peers at 0.40 percent versus 0.36 percent. Recoveries were comparable for both PNC and peers, hence, net loan losses were also above peers—0.28 percent versus 0.25 percent. At the end of 2004, both PNC's and peers' net losses were well below those of 2001–2003. Banks, in general, reported low loan losses during the late 1990s due to the strong U.S. economy. Unfortunately, loan losses again began to increase in the early 2000s, and PNC's increase was substantial. The economy moved into recession by the end of 2001 and the tragic events of September 11, 2001, exacerbated the economic slowdown. The timing of PNC's charge-offs, however, may have had more to do with how the bank had reported its higher-risk loan sales. PNC's performance in 2002–2004 represents a complete turnaround from 2001, in which it reported net loan losses of well over 2 percent. Prior to 2001, PNC also reported very low net loan losses of about one-quarter of one percent in 2000—about half that of peers. The reported losses of 2001 were most likely present in 2000, just not reported, hence, profits in 2000 were overstated. This clearly demonstrates the need to examine a longer time series of data when assessing overall credit risk, as management can readily manipulate figures in any one year. Many argue that lending is a "last in–first out system." That is, the last loans made during the peak of an economic expansion are most likely to default first.

Returning to year-end 2004 data, PNC's past due and total nonaccrual loans were a higher percentage of total loans as compared with peers, leading to a larger percentage of nonperforming loans (total of 90 days past due and nonaccrual loans) to total loans for PNC. The ratio of noncurrent loans to total loans was 13 basis points below peers (0.46 percent for PNC and 0.59 percent for peers), a reversal of the trend from 2001–2003, and well below levels in 2003. With respect to potential losses, if noncurrent loans are an accurate predictor of future losses, the higher levels of nonperforming loans are an indicator of a "lower" quality loan portfolio, which exhibits greater potential default risk, and will likely result in slightly higher future loan losses.

Finally, although PNC's loan and lease loss allowance (reserves) relative to total loans was slightly above peers, its loan loss allowance to net losses and to total nonaccrual loans was lower. Earnings coverage of net losses was also well below peers—indicating poor coverage of current and potential losses. The low earnings coverage is a result of higher charge-offs relative to earnings. In summary, a higher loan loss reserve to a smaller portfolio of loans does not make up for the higher noncurrent loans and lower loan loss reserve to net losses and lower earnings coverage. Although PNC has reportedly sold its problem loans without recourse, the loan portfolio still exhibits somewhat higher credit risk and the data for 2003 do not fully support PNC's notion of having significantly reduced the risk of its loan portfolio since 2001.

PNC's liquidity risk appears good in 2004, but there are some areas of concern. PNC's much higher level of core deposits, low dependence on volatile liabilities, fewer loans, and roughly comparable total equity provide

**EXHIBIT 2.8** Risk Measures for PNC Bank and Community National Bank, 2003–2004

| Risk Ratios | Pg # | PNC Bank, National Association Dec-03 CALC | BANK | PG 1 | Dec-04 CALC | BANK | PG 1 | Community National Bank Dec-03 CALC | BANK | PG 4 | Dec-04 CALC | BANK | PG 4 |
|---|---|---|---|---|---|---|---|---|---|---|---|---|---|
| **Credit Risk** | | | | | | | | | | | | | |
| Gross loss / Avg. tot. LN&LS | 7 | 0.73% | 0.73% | 0.53% | 0.40% | 0.40% | 0.36% | 0.54% | 0.54% | 0.26% | 0.21% | 0.21% | 0.20% |
| Net loss / Avg. tot. LN&LS | 7 | 0.59% | 0.59% | 0.41% | 0.28% | 0.28% | 0.25% | 0.53% | 0.53% | 0.21% | 0.20% | 0.20% | 0.16% |
| Recoveries / Avg. tot. LN&LS | 7 | 0.13% | 0.13% | 0.12% | 0.12% | 0.12% | 0.11% | 0.01% | 0.01% | 0.06% | 0.02% | 0.02% | 0.05% |
| Recoveries to prior credit loss | 7 | 19.0% | 19.03% | 22.26% | 19.5% | 19.52% | 23.76% | 6.7% | 6.75% | 29.21% | 3.1% | 3.08% | 24.53% |
| 90 days past due / EOP LN&LS | 8A | 0.21% | 0.21% | 0.13% | 0.13% | 0.13% | 0.10% | 0.16% | 0.16% | 0.13% | 0.00% | 0.00% | 0.10% |
| Total nonaccrual LN&LS / EOP LN&LS | 8A | 0.79% | 0.79% | 0.66% | 0.33% | 0.33% | 0.46% | 0.19% | 0.19% | 0.47% | 0.16% | 0.16% | 0.41% |
| Total noncurrent / EOP LN&LS | 8A | 1.00% | 1.00% | 0.83% | 0.46% | 0.46% | 0.59% | 0.35% | 0.35% | 0.66% | 0.16% | 0.16% | 0.55% |
| LN&LS allowance to total LN&LS | 7 | 1.77% | 1.78% | 1.44% | 1.34% | 1.35% | 1.27% | 1.07% | 1.07% | 1.25% | 1.23% | 1.23% | 1.20% |
| LN&LS allowance / Net losses | 7 | 2.9x | 2.92x | 4.18x | 5.2x | 5.23x | 7.51x | 2.1x | 2.08x | 11.89x | 6.7x | 6.71x | 14.52x |
| LN&LS allowance / Total nonaccural LN&LS | 7 | 1.77x | 2.24x | 2.73x | 2.92x | 4.12x | 3.73x | 3.05x | 5.49x | 4.35x | 7.77x | 7.77x | 5.63x |
| Earn coverage of net losses | 7 | 7.44x | 7.44x | 10.92x | 11.61x | 11.61x | 19.94x | 2.57x | 2.57x | 23.89x | 10.38x | 10.38x | 30.80x |
| Net loan and lease growth rate | 1 | -4.55% | -4.55% | 10.14% | 27.51% | 27.51% | 17.96% | 2.16% | 2.16% | 11.61% | 11.49% | 11.49% | 14.24% |
| **Liquidity Risk** | | | | | | | | | | | | | |
| *%Total (EOP) Assets (except where noted)* | | | | | | | | | | | | | |
| Total equity | 11 | 9.07% | 9.07% | 8.95% | 8.26% | 8.26% | 9.74% | 7.29% | 7.29% | 9.28% | 7.23% | 7.23% | 9.42% |
| Core deposits | 10 | 67.41% | 66.75% | 53.75% | 64.84% | 63.23% | 54.19% | 84.26% | 84.95% | 71.85% | 85.00% | 85.04% | 71.10% |
| S.T Noncore funding | 10 | #N/A | 11.47% | 23.24% | #N/A | 12.11% | 23.42% | #N/A | 4.10% | 11.90% | #N/A | 4.84% | 12.21% |
| Net loans & leases / Total deposits | 10 | 73.73% | 73.73% | 87.72% | 81.00% | 81.00% | 88.28% | 65.90% | 65.90% | 78.94% | 67.35% | 67.35% | 81.42% |
| Net loans & leases / Core deposits | 10 | 81.11% | 81.11% | 115.16% | 91.76% | 91.76% | 116.10% | 71.36% | 71.36% | 93.85% | 72.89% | 72.89% | 97.58% |
| Avg. available for sale securities / aTA | 6 | 21.41% | 21.90% | 21.11% | 22.12% | 22.03% | 21.00% | 14.44% | 13.39% | 15.88% | 19.38% | 19.04% | 15.80% |
| Short-term investments | 10 | #N/A | 2.73% | 6.25% | #N/A | 3.02% | 5.23% | #N/A | 5.99% | 5.41% | #N/A | 5.72% | 5.26% |
| Pledged securities | 10 | #N/A | 46.50% | 49.08% | #N/A | 51.76% | 54.78% | #N/A | 29.25% | 40.34% | #N/A | 28.49% | 41.20% |
| **Capital Risk** | | | | | | | | | | | | | |
| Tier 1 leverage capital / Total assets | 11A | 8.28% | 8.37% | 7.67% | 6.89% | 7.14% | 7.71% | 7.27% | 7.31% | 8.97% | 7.27% | 7.29% | 9.11% |
| Tier 1 Capital / Risk-weighted assets | 11A | 9.91% | 9.89% | 11.13% | 8.65% | 8.36% | 11.17% | 10.73% | 10.73% | 12.64% | 10.27% | 10.27% | 12.64% |
| Total RBC / Risk weighted Assets | 11A | 12.91% | 12.89% | 13.08% | 11.95% | 11.55% | 12.98% | 11.70% | 11.70% | 13.80% | 11.35% | 11.35% | 13.76% |
| Equity capital / Total assets | 11 | 9.07% | 9.07% | 8.95% | 8.26% | 8.26% | 9.74% | 7.29% | 7.29% | 9.28% | 7.23% | 7.23% | 9.42% |
| Dividend payout | 11 | 77.30% | 77.30% | 57.26% | 87.58% | 87.58% | 46.73% | 0.00% | 0.00% | 30.77% | 0.00% | 0.00% | 29.34% |
| Growth rate in total equity capital | 11 | -4.09% | -4.09% | 10.34% | 8.42% | 8.42% | 20.28% | 11.99% | 11.99% | 10.99% | 8.20% | 8.20% | 11.32% |
| Equity growth less asset growth | 11 | -8.09% | -8.09% | 0.59% | -10.59% | -10.59% | 4.55% | -6.56% | -6.56% | 0.41% | -0.83% | -0.83% | 0.28% |
| **Operational Risk** | | | | | | | | | | | | | |
| Total assets / Number of employees | 3 | $4.09 | $4.02 | $5.17 | $4.71 | $4.44 | $6.09 | $3.00 | $2.75 | $2.95 | $2.98 | $2.84 | $3.08 |
| Personnel expense / Number of employees | 3 | 73.43x | 72.06x | 60.48x | 90.68x | 85.48x | 65.26x | 65.46x | 60.03x | 48.27x | 61.47x | 58.58x | 50.10x |
| Efficiency ratio | 3 | 60.93% | 60.86% | 57.73% | 68.01% | 67.97% | 57.92% | 82.72% | 82.75% | 66.06% | 75.35% | 75.34% | 65.99% |

excellent borrowing capacity. PNC's significantly great core deposit base and low dependence on volatile (noncore) liabilities indicates that PNC has more stable deposits and greater capacity to issue new volatile liabilities because it relies proportionately less on these high-cost funds. PNC's equity position also strengthens its ability to provide liquidity through borrowing as does it lower net loans to total deposits and net loans to core deposits ratios. The bank's loan-to-deposit ratios provide a direct comparison of the bank's least liquid assets, loans, to its most stable funding source, deposits. Lower loan-to-deposit ratios indicate that PNC's loan portfolio is financed proportionately less by volatile funds.

On the negative side, however, is PNC's low level of short-term investments (3.02 versus 5.23 percent for peers) with almost 52 percent of these securities pledged to secure deposits, repurchase agreements, or other borrowings. Large, or volatile borrowings, are "asset-quality sensitive." Truly liquid assets, like short-term investments, can be sold for liquidity purposes anytime. But the degree to which a bank can borrow to satisfy its liquidity needs is sensitive to the market's perception of the bank's asset quality. A strong core-funding base and higher equity levels are needed to make up for lower perceived asset quality. Because a majority of PNC's liquidity is supported by the bank's ability to borrow liquidity, some of these sources could be more difficult to obtain in the event PNC's asset quality were to deteriorate again.

Higher-risk banks are expected to hold greater levels of capital while lower-risk banks might be able to hold less capital than comparable peer banks. PNC's equity-to-asset ratio indicates that PNC had a lower level of end-of-period total equity to end-of-period total assets relative to peer banks, 8.26 percent versus 9.74 percent (page 11). Tier 1 leverage capital to total assets must be at least 3 percent to meet regulatory minimums and at least 5 percent to be considered "well capitalized." PNC's exceeds both requirements but is below comparable peer ratios. PNC's Tier 1 capital-to-risk weighted assets and total risk-based capital ratio must be at least 4 percent and 8 percent, respectively, to meet regulator minimums and at least 6 percent and 10 percent, respectively, to be considered a "well-capitalized" bank (see Chapter 9 for details on risk-based capital). PNC's total risk-based capital ratio of 11.55 percent clearly exceeded these levels but fell short of peers (12.98 percent). Having a higher Tier 1 leverage capital-to-total-assets ratio but lower capital-to-risk-weight assets means that PNC has more accounting capital but less capital as compared to a risk weighting of their assets. Loans and some off-balance sheet activities carry the highest risk weighting. Because PNC has fewer loans, its off-balance sheet loan commitments and loans held for sale clearly increase its risk-weighted assets and, therefore, reduce the ratio of total risk-based capital to risk-weighted assets.

PNC's capital-to-total-asset ratio fell in 2004 as a result of a high dividend payout (87.58 percent of earnings) and a 19 percent growth in total assets. PNC's higher equity capital but lower risk-based capital and its history of loan problems in 2001 reflect the greater amount of risk assets that PNC holds relative to peers, and this clearly makes PNC's capital risk appear somewhat higher than peers. The bank's interest rate risk position is indicated by the difference between repriceable assets and liabilities. Unfortunately, UBPR data on interest rate risks are very limited. Total interest rate risk cannot be determined without more detailed rate-sensitivity data and measures of duration that will be discussed in Chapters 5 and 6.

Operational risk is also difficult to assess because only limited information is available. From a purely operational efficiency point of view, PNC operates with fewer assets per employee, indicating the bank employs more people relative to its asset base. This could indicate a lower productivity level, but most likely reflects the larger branch network PNC employs to gather its inexpensive core deposit base. It appears, however, that although the cost-benefit trade-offs of PNC's large branch bank system and higher noninterest expenses worked in the past; 2004 data indicate that the bank's lower cost of funds, lower interest income, higher amount of noninterest income, and higher amount of noninterest expense led to a higher efficiency ratio. PNC also exhibits much higher personnel expense per employee. This indicates a higher paid labor force that could be due to the geographic region in which PNC operates.

In summary, PNC's profit performance was above peers in 2004 but lingering risk issues might prevent one from labeling it a "high-performance" bank. PNC's higher returns have come with a somewhat higher-risk loan portfolio, and some liquidity risk as well as higher capital risk. PNC exhibited a dramatic "cleansing" of its loan portfolio in 2001 and has continued to reduce the portion of loans to total assets each year since then. The challenge facing the analyst is to assess the remaining loan portfolio. If PNC has, or will, continue to purge its high-risk loans, the company is positioned to be a high-performance bank in the near future.

## PNC's Profitability versus Risk: 2000–2004

PNC's 2004 performance can be better understood by examining trends in the performance ratios for the five prior years. Page 1 of the UBPR presented in the Appendix to this chapter presents key profitability and risk ratios from 2000–2004. During this period, assets increased by $10.7 billion while net income exhibited a great deal of volatility. Profitability and total assets were clearly negatively affected by loan sales, and the resulting write-offs taken in 2001. With the exception of 2001, the bank's ROA had consistently been above or equivalent to peers and occasionally greater than 1.5 percent. This information, however, indicates that PNC's past profitability, especially the years leading up to 2001, were likely overstated. Prior to 2000, PNC's interest income was slightly below but similar to

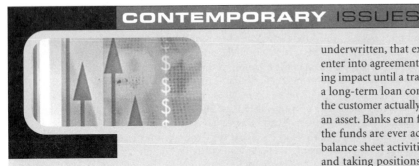

## THE FALL OF ENRON AND ITS IMPACT ON PNC BANK

When Enron announced that it would file a voluntary petition for Chapter 11 reorganization on December 2, 2001, the world was shocked, as it was the largest U.S. bankruptcy in recent history. Just prior to declaring bankruptcy, Enron reported sales growth that put it on track to be the largest company in the U.S. ranked by sales. The figures were biased, however, as Enron would report the full notional value of derivative contracts as revenue rather than the much smaller commissions it received for trades. In addition, Enron would book estimated cost savings over future years in its current fiscal year. Throughout the 1990s and early 2000s, Enron had transformed itself from a pure energy company to an energy broker and giant hedge fund. Prior to its failure, many market participants viewed Enron as a "New Economy" success story with its highly profitable (at least as reported in audited financial statements) move from hard assets (natural gas production and processing) to soft assets (trading activities). As it was eventually discovered, however, Enron engaged in many questionable activities, including not reporting losses from business activities that the firm inappropriately moved off-balance sheet. Enron was thus able to hide losses on some business activities and/or use its off-balance sheet activities to artificially inflate reported earnings and hide debt.

Although most companies do not exploit accounting rules to the degree Enron did, Enron served as a wake-up call to the financial community and made clear the importance of understanding the nature of accrual accounting. Under accrual accounting a company "books" earnings prior to the profits actually being realized. In banking, this often means that when high risk loans are booked, the bank initially reports extraordinary profits. It is only later, if the risk has not been correctly underwritten, that exceptional losses follow. Many banks also enter into agreements that do not have a balance sheet reporting impact until a transaction is effected. An example might be a long-term loan commitment to a potential borrower. Until the customer actually borrows the funds, no loan is reported as an asset. Banks earn fees on loan commitments whether or not the funds are ever actually borrowed. Other examples of off-balance sheet activities at banks include providing guarantees and taking positions in derivative contracts, such as interest rate swaps and financial futures. Obviously, off-balance sheet positions generate noninterest income but also entail some risk as the bank must perform under the contracts.

From 1999 to 2001, PNC had been moving out of certain lending businesses by selling off $20 billion in loans and reducing unfunded loan commitments by $25 billion. In October 2001, PNC reported lower net income due primarily to problems with its venture capital business. On January 3, 2002, PNC announced that it was taking a $615 million after-tax charge for the fourth quarter of 2001 as it wrote down loans (that is, recognized that the real loan values were less than reported) and its venture capital and auto leasing business. It took a specific $424 million charge for moving loans to the "held-for-sale" category and indicated that it would sell about $3.1 billion in loans and $8.2 billion in letters of credit and unfunded commitments. The stock market reacted favorably as PNC's stock price increased from $56 to $58.50 a share. The positive response echoed the market's sentiment on bad loans that the sooner an organization recognizes them and moves them off the balance sheet, the better.

In late January, it was reported that the Federal Reserve and SEC were examining the special third-party structure that PNC used to shift assets off the balance sheet in late 2001. Not surprisingly, PNC's shares immediately dropped almost 10 percent in value as the use of such off-balance sheet accounting was reminiscent of the Enron fiasco. PNC reclassified its treatment of the problematic deals and subsequently lowered its reported net income for 2001 by $155 million. The earnings were restated due to new perceived risks of special-purpose vehicles. Then, just as things were beginning to get better, PNC again lowered its 2001 earnings in February 2002 by another $35 million because it had not properly recorded a loss from a residential mortgage banking business.

*(continues)*

peers. In 2000, interest income fell significantly below peer averages and has remained well below into 2004. Lower interest income would be consistent with PNC's stated goal of a lower-risk loan portfolio. Interest expense, on the other hand, was slightly above peers prior to 2000 but fell well below peers in 2000 and has remained below into 2004. PNC's noninterest expense and noninterest income have remained above peers and noninterest expense, as a percent of assets, has increased every year since 2000. It appears that PNC's smaller asset base, combined with its existing overhead structure, produces higher overhead costs relative to its new smaller loan portfolio. PNC will likely have to continue to improve its new business model in this area. PNC's net interest income to total assets has fallen since 2000 but likely indicates increased competition as its relative position to peers remains similar.

| | 12/31/2002 | | 12/31/2001 | | 12/31/2000 | | 12/31/1999 | |
|---|---|---|---|---|---|---|---|---|
| Average assets ($000) | 59,488,016 | | 63,486,660 | | 66,975,064 | | 69,105,444 | |
| Net income ($000) | 1,061,504 | | 491,731 | | 1,007,226 | | 1,057,038 | |
| Percent of average assets: | **BANK** | **PG 1** | **BANK** | **PG 1** | **BANK** | **PG 1** | **BANK** | **PG 1** |
| Interest income (te) | 4.92 | 5.33 | 6.10 | 6.55 | 6.65 | 7.41 | 6.61 | 6.88 |
| − Interest expense | 1.33 | 1.76 | 2.62 | 3.04 | 3.49 | 3.88 | 3.27 | 3.24 |
| Net interest income (te) | 3.59 | 3.52 | 3.47 | 3.52 | 3.16 | 3.53 | 3.35 | 3.67 |
| + Noninterest income | 3.27 | 1.77 | 2.80 | 1.83 | 2.56 | 1.79 | 2.92 | 1.92 |
| − Noninterest expense | 3.75 | 3.05 | 3.84 | 3.22 | 3.27 | 3.25 | 3.51 | 3.25 |
| − Provision: Loan & lease losses | 0.49 | 0.38 | **1.42** | 0.40 | 0.20 | 0.33 | 0.23 | 0.25 |
| + Realized gains/losses sec | 0.13 | 0.07 | 0.20 | 0.06 | 0.03 | −0.04 | −0.17 | −0.01 |
| **Return on Assets** | **1.78** | **1.29** | **0.77** | **1.19** | **1.50** | **1.11** | **1.53** | **1.32** |
| Net loss to average total LN&LS | 0.54 | 0.56 | **2.11** | 0.56 | 0.26 | 0.39 | 0.29 | 0.39 |
| LN&LS allowance to net losses(X) | 3.12 | 3.60 | **0.64** | 3.66 | 4.90 | 5.14 | 4.16 | 5.47 |
| Noncur LN&LS to gross LN&LS | 1.41 | 1.06 | 1.05 | 1.12 | 0.96 | 0.89 | 0.83 | 0.74 |
| Tier 1 leverage capital | 8.99 | 7.50 | **7.62** | 7.34 | 8.77 | 7.17 | 7.65 | 7.18 |
| Growth rates | | | | | | | | |
| Assets | −4.75 | 11.73 | −0.91 | 15.79 | −7.33 | 18.63 | −4.27 | 14.41 |
| Tier 1 capital | 9.71 | 11.97 | −12.94 | 16.37 | 6.02 | 17.35 | −6.82 | 17.75 |
| Net loans & leases | −11.71 | 9.74 | −19.18 | 11.90 | −5.23 | 19.60 | −8.35 | 14.12 |

SOURCE: PNC's Uniform Bank Performance Report, http://www2.fdic.gov/ubpr/UbprReport/SearchEngine/Default.asp.

Examining PNC's financial performance for the years 1999–2002, we find that prior to 2001, most analysts would have considered PNC to be a high-performance bank generating above-average returns with below-average loan losses. In 2001, we see that PNC's below-average returns were generated almost exclusively by extraordinary charge-offs.

An important lesson is that reported balance sheet and income statement figures may not always be an accurate measure of a firm's profitability and risk profile. As banks engage in more and more off-balance sheet activities and begin to produce more fee income from related products and services, assets become less representative of risks and less a measure of potential profitability. Fee income is often generated from services not identifiable from listed assets. The traditional model based on assets generating income might not be representative of the banking activities that emphasize securitization and fee-generating lines of business.

Net losses to average total loans were extremely low until the dramatic increase in 2001. PNC's net charge-offs increased dramatically in 2001, and remained above peers until 2004. Prior to, and including 2001, PNC's loan loss allowance to total loans was below peers. Obviously knowing what we know today, PNC's provisions for loan losses were understated and the bank's loan loss reserve was insufficient. The good news is that PNC has dramatically increased the level of the reserve for loan losses to total loans, in recognition of its past loan problems.

PNC's liquidity picture has always relied more on a higher level of core deposits, lower volatile liabilities, and fewer liquid assets. Until 2003, PNC also held a large proportion of its assets in less liquid loans. In fact, in 2000, PNC held over 76 percent of its assets in loans. Today, the proportion of assets held in loans is down dramatically to where PNC only invests about 56 percent of its assets in loans. Finally, PNC's Tier 1 capital has remained above peers, even in 2001 with the significant write-off of problem loans.

## MAXIMIZING THE MARKET VALUE OF BANK EQUITY

A bank manager's role is to make and implement decisions that increase the value of shareholders' wealth.[44] Firm value is, in turn, closely tied to the underlying portfolio risk and return profile. The greater is perceived risk relative to expected returns, the lower is perceived value as shareholders discount anticipated cash flows to a

[44]An extensive list of literature suggests that bank managers may pursue goals other than wealth maximization, such as trying to capture the greatest market share or expense preference behavior in which owners and managers extract benefits by having the bank pay expenses for individuals that might normally be paid from personal resources. Heggestad (1979) summarizes key concepts and empirical results related to these alternative objectives.

greater degree. The lower is perceived risk, the lower is the discount rate, but the lower are expected cash flows. Banks with actively traded common stock can look to quoted share prices and cumulative market value as measures of firm value. Share prices are determined by return prospects versus risk characteristics and capture the market's perception of historical and anticipated performance.

Given the objective of maximizing the market value of bank equity, managers pursue strategies in several policy areas including:

1. Asset management (composition and volume)
2. Liability management (composition and volume)
3. Management of off-balance sheet activities
4. Interest rate margin or spread management
5. Credit risk management
6. Liquidity management
7. Management of noninterest expense
8. Tax management

Each area of strategic decisions is closely tied with a bank's profitability, as measured in Equation 2.7. The primary responsibilities are to acquire assets through appropriate financing and to control the burden while maintaining an acceptable risk profile. Bank regulators attempt to help managers keep their firm operating by regulating allowable activities. Bank regulation is largely designed to limit risk taking by commercial banks. Regulators also limit the size of a loan to any single borrower to reduce the concentration of bank resources. To assess bank risk, regulators routinely examine the quality of assets, mismatched maturities of assets and liabilities, and internal operating controls. If they determine that a bank has assumed too much risk, they require additional equity capital. Regulators use a rating system called **CAMELS** to access the quality of banks' earnings and risk management.

## CAMELS RATINGS

Federal and state regulators regularly assess the financial condition of each bank and specific risks faced via on-site examinations and periodic reports. Federal regulators rate banks according to the Uniform Financial Institutions Rating system, which now encompasses six general categories of performance under the label CAMELS. Each letter refers to a specific category, including:

$$\begin{aligned}
\mathbf{C} &= \text{Capital adequacy} \\
\mathbf{A} &= \text{Asset quality} \\
\mathbf{M} &= \text{Management quality} \\
\mathbf{E} &= \text{Earnings} \\
\mathbf{L} &= \text{Liquidity} \\
\mathbf{S} &= \text{Sensitivity to market risk}
\end{aligned}$$

The **capital component (C)** signals the institution's ability to maintain capital commensurate with the nature and extent of all types of risk, and the ability of management to identify, measure, monitor, and control these risks. **Asset quality (A)** reflects the amount of existing credit risk associated with the loan and investment portfolio, as well as off-balance sheet activities. The **management category (M)** reflects the adequacy of the board of directors and senior management systems and procedures to identify, measure, monitor, and control risks. Regulators emphasize the existence and use of policies and processes to manage risks within targets. **Earnings (E)** reflects not only the quantity and trend in earnings, but also the factors that may affect the sustainability or quality or earnings. **Liquidity (L)** reflects the adequacy of the institution's current and prospective sources of liquidity and funds management practices. Finally, the last category, **sensitivity to market risk (S),** reflects the degree to which changes in interest rates, foreign exchange rates, commodity prices, and equity prices can adversely affect earnings or economic capital.

Regulators numerically rate each bank in each of the six categories, ranging from the highest or best rating (1) to the worst or lowest rating (5). Regulators also assign a composite rating for the bank's overall operation. A composite rating of 1 or 2 indicates a fundamentally sound bank. A rating of 3 indicates that the bank shows some underlying weakness that should be corrected. A rating of 4 or 5 indicates a problem bank with some near-term potential for failure. Exhibit 2.9 shows a dramatic increase in the number of commercial banks and savings banks on the FDIC's problem list (those with 4 and 5 ratings), from 1984 through 1987 when 1,575 institutions were on the problem list. It also shows a dramatic reduction beginning in 1992 through 1999, when only 79 banks were given these lowest ratings. The mid- to late 1980s were considered the "worst of times" while the mid- to late 1990s were considered the "best of times" for banking. As economic conditions deteriorated in the early 2000s, the number of problem institutions again increased. The year 2004, however, appears to show improvement as do economic conditions.

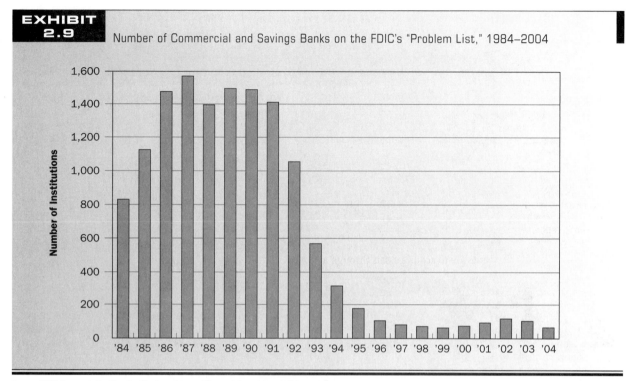

**EXHIBIT 2.9** Number of Commercial and Savings Banks on the FDIC's "Problem List," 1984–2004

SOURCE: FDIC Quarterly Banking Profile, http://www.fdic.gov/, http://www2.fdic.gov/qbp.

## PERFORMANCE CHARACTERISTICS OF BANKS BY BUSINESS CONCENTRATION AND SIZE

Commercial banks of different sizes exhibit sharply different operating characteristics. Some differences reflect government regulation; others are associated with variances in the markets served. Prior to the mid-1980s, small banks generated higher ROAs, on average, and generally assumed less risk. This has changed with increased competition, expansion into new product and geographic markets, and more recent economic events. Today, according to the data in Exhibit 2.10, it appears that the most profitable banks (by ROA) are those in the $1 billion to $10 billion asset size category but the highest return to shareholders is produced by the largest banks. This section examines differences in the risk-return performance of different-sized banks, as well as different business models.

Summary profitability and risk measures for all U.S. banks, as of end-of-year 2004, appear in Exhibit 2.10. The banks are divided into four groups by total assets. The fifth column indicates general trends in each ratio from the smallest banks with less than $100 million in assets to the largest banks with assets greater than $10 billion. The final column provides average performance ratios for all commercial banks. As indicated by the trend with size column, many of the ratios exhibit a consistent relationship with size. ROE, for example, generally increases with size with the largest banks' reporting the highest return to shareholders. ROA increases with size up to the $1 billion to $10 billion in assets category, with the smallest banks having the lowest return on assets and the largest banks having the second highest. The low return to the smallest banks can be attributed to their extremely low noninterest income, while the largest banks' lower return can be attributed to their low average net interest margin and slightly higher noninterest expense. The reduction in net interest margins for the largest banks is the result of much lower yields on earning assets, but only somewhat by a lower cost of funds. The lower cost of funds for the largest banks is a change in their aggregate position. Until 2001, the largest banks typically reported a higher average cost of funds. The largest banks are generally offering very standardized loans and deposit products, hence competition is steep and margins small.

The largest banks generally employ fewer people per dollar of assets than smaller banks. Noninterest expense control generally decreases with size. This seems somewhat contrary to the notion that larger size brings more efficiencies and economies of scale until one examines the efficiency ratio. The largest banks, however, have the lowest efficiency ratios, which indicates that these banks have the best trade-offs between net interest margin, noninterest expense,

**Summary Profitability and Risk Measures for Different-Sized Banks, December 31, 2004**

| Assets Size | < $100M | $100M–$1B | $1B–$10B | > $10B | Trend with Size | All Commercial Banks |
|---|---|---|---|---|---|---|
| Number of institutions reporting | 3,655 | 3,530 | 360 | 85 | ↓ | 7,630 |
| % of unprofitable institutions | 9.80 | 2.00 | 1.90 | 1.20 | ↓ | 5.70 |
| % of institutions with earn gains | 59.30 | 70.70 | 71.90 | 68.20 | ↑ then ↓ | 65.30 |
| Performance ratios (%) | | | | | | |
| Return on equity | 8.46 | 12.88 | 13.48 | 14.24 | generally ↑ | 13.82 |
| Return on assets | 0.99 | 1.28 | 1.46 | 1.30 | ↑ then ↓ | 1.31 |
| *Pretax ROA* | 1.24 | 1.73 | 2.21 | 1.93 | ↑ then ↓ | 1.92 |
| Equity capital ratio | 11.52 | 10.00 | 10.90 | 9.95 | ↓ | 10.10 |
| Net interest margin | 4.18 | 4.22 | 4.00 | 3.43 | ↓ | 3.61 |
| Yield on earning assets | 5.65 | 5.73 | 5.39 | 4.83 | ↓ | 5.02 |
| Cost of funding earn assets | 1.47 | 1.51 | 1.39 | 1.40 | ↓ | 1.41 |
| Earning assets to total assets | 91.86 | 91.93 | 91.01 | 84.39 | ↓ | 86.18 |
| Efficiency ratio | 69.54 | 62.22 | 55.54 | 57.42 | ↓ | 57.96 |
| Burden ratio | 2.60 | 2.07 | 1.21 | 0.82 | ↓ | 1.06 |
| Noninterest inc. to earn assets | 1.03 | 1.54 | 2.46 | 2.93 | ↑ | 2.66 |
| Noninterest exp. to earn assets | 3.63 | 3.61 | 3.67 | 3.75 | ↑ | 3.72 |
| Net charge-offs to LN&LS | 0.27 | 0.31 | 0.43 | 0.73 | ↑ | 0.63 |
| LN&LS loss provision to assets | 0.22 | 0.26 | 0.34 | 0.34 | ↑ | 0.33 |
| **Asset Quality** | | | | | | |
| Net charge-offs to LN&LS | 0.27 | 0.31 | 0.43 | 0.73 | ↑ | 0.63 |
| Loss allow to noncurr. LN&LS | 151.5 | 196.2 | 206.0 | 168.0 | ↑ then ↓ | 174.6 |
| LN&LS provision to net charge-offs | 134.2 | 125.7 | 125.5 | 83.0 | ↓ | 89.9 |
| Loss allowance to LN&LS | 1.44 | 1.39 | 1.47 | 1.53 | ↑ | 1.50 |
| Net LN&LS to deposits | 72.67 | 82.11 | 92.82 | 86.68 | ↑ then ↓ | 86.38 |
| **Capital Ratios** | | | | | | |
| Core capital (leverage) ratio | 11.31 | 9.47 | 9.36 | 7.23 | ↓ | 7.83 |
| Tier 1 risk-based capital ratio | 16.83 | 12.85 | 12.34 | 9.11 | ↓ | 10.04 |
| Total risk-based capital ratio | 17.93 | 14.06 | 13.92 | 12.07 | ↓ | 12.62 |
| **Structural Changes** | | | | | | |
| New charters | 118 | 2 | 1 | 1 | ↓ | 122 |
| Banks absorbed by mergers | 102 | 125 | 30 | 7 | ↓ | 264 |
| Failed banks | 3 | 0 | 0 | 0 | ↓ | 3 |

SOURCE: FDIC Quarterly Banking Profile, http://www.fdic.gov/, http://www2.fdic.gov/qbp.

and noninterest income. The largest banks do generate significantly more noninterest income (service charges and fees) but have the highest noninterest expenses and the lowest net interest margin of all asset classes.

Examining assets quality, we find larger banks invest a larger percentage of their total deposits in loans but a hold a smaller percentage of total assets in earning assets. This reflects two distinct factors. First, smaller banks generally operate with proportionately more core deposits and fewer volatile liabilities as compared with the largest banks. This reflects the larger banks' reputation advantage both nationally and internationally, which means they have far greater access to purchased funds in the money and capital markets. Second, the lower earnings base of the largest banks reflects their de-emphasis of loans and lending and their increased emphasis on products and services and the generation of fee income. Finally, and somewhat surprising, is that the largest banks report much higher net charge-offs than smaller banks. This is somewhat surprising because smaller banks' loan portfolios reflect less geographic and industry diversification than larger banks. Smaller banks, however, use more "soft" information in the lending decision while larger banks use more hard data.[45] This tends to result in great volatility in the charge-off patterns of the largest banks.

Equity-to-asset ratios decrease with size (the equity multiplier increases with size) because larger banks operate with less equity and more debt. Regulation effectively mandates the equity multiplier relationship as regulators

---

[45] Soft information is information that is generally not published, such as the loan officers personal knowledge of the customers and their business.

require more equity at smaller banks to compensate for less asset diversification and more limited borrowing options. Percentage equity requirements were equalized in 1985, and raised effective in 1992, but small banks strategically choose to operate with a greater equity cushion.

Next consider the distinction between different banking models. Wholesale banks focus their credit efforts on the largest commercial customers and purchase substantial funds from large corporate and government depositors. Retail banks, in contrast, obtain considerably more of their deposits from individual and small business deposits and emphasize small to midsize commercial lending, consumer loans, mortgage loans, and agriculture loans. Within each category, there are significant differences in the types of loans and funding sources. Recently the FDIC began publishing summary data on banks and savings banks by their asset concentrations. The data presented in Exhibit 2.11 compare the financial results of nine different asset concentrations. The data in Exhibit 2.11 show a distinct pattern in banking business models and risk and return. Credit card banks are the most profitable with average ROA of just over 22 percent. These banks, however, have the highest charge-offs, at 4.7 percent, and carry more capital (at 16.6 percent) than the other business models. Commercial lenders are clearly the largest single category of institutions and represent about 49 percent of all institutions. Average returns to commercial lending banks are good based on ROE, but very much in the middle of performance. These institutions do, however, average much lower loan losses and lower capital levels. Credit card lending is more specialized as only 34 out of 8,975 institutions specialize in credit card lending. Clearly, banking is about managing risk. If an institution assumes more risk and manages it correctly, its performance will improve. The mistake seen most often in business, however, is assuming above-average risk but receiving average or below-average returns.

## FINANCIAL STATEMENT MANIPULATION

The usefulness of bank financial statements depends on the quality and consistency of the data. Ideally, banks would use the same accounting rules in each period and isolate the effects of nonrecurring events. This would make comparisons over time and between banks simple. Unfortunately, banks have wide discretion in reporting certain items and can use extraordinary transactions to disguise unfavorable events or trends. Analysts should delete the impact of any unusual changes to make valid comparisons. Banks use numerous techniques to manage earnings or, as some would say, to manipulate their financial statements. The primary ones are the use of nonrecurring extraordinary transactions, discretionary interpretation of reporting requirements, discretionary timing of reported loan charge-offs, off-balance sheet special-purpose vehicles (as in the case of Enron and PNC), and accounting changes that mask true operating performance. The net effect is to potentially distort the magnitude of period-ending balance sheet figures, net income, and related ratios, which makes comparisons difficult over time and versus peers. In most cases, banks do not violate federal regulations or generally accepted accounting principles. Often, the reporting techniques are mandated.

**OFF-BALANCE SHEET ACTIVITIES.** The recent failure of Enron is indicative of the problems associated with special-purpose vehicles and off-balance sheet activities, the ambiguous accounting requirements associated with them, and the lack of guidance from the regulatory authorities on what is or is not acceptable. In general, parent companies create a "special-purpose vehicle" (SPV) as an independent company. The SPV acquires funds from lenders and investors. The parent company then sells assets to the SPV, such as loans or shares of stock, and in return gets the proceeds from the lenders and investors. Rather than counting the funds as debt on the books of the parent company, however, it counts them as debt to the SPV, thereby possibly understating the parent's risk. Income, on the other hand, is reported by the parent company, thereby possibly overstating its income. Everything works well unless the SPV fails and the parent is required to "make good" on the loans to the SPV. The real issue is to what degree the parent company has exposure to the debts of the SPV. If the assets of the SPV are backed by government guarantees or insurance, accounting rules (FAS 140) generally allow for these off-balance sheet activities to remain off the balance sheet. Unfortunately, there is vague guidance on when and how the activities of SPVs must be consolidated into the financial statements of the parent.

**WINDOW DRESSING.** Many banks have long engaged in window dressing for size purposes, or increasing period-ending assets or deposits, and SPVs are only one method. Some banks want to be the largest or fastest-growing bank in their market because customers like to associate with "bigness." One technique used to increase total assets is to encourage large business customers to borrow from the bank temporarily rather than issue commercial paper. The bank finances the loans in the federal funds market. Another technique involves inducing institutions to which the bank provides correspondent services to increase their deposit balances at the bank. Some large banks similarly solicit short-term deposits from overseas entities. None of these transactions materially alters earnings, but all give a false impression of true size.

In some instances, banks engage in transactions that substantially improve their perceived operating performance. Some banks eliminate borrowing from Federal Reserve Banks because of the perception that such

## EXHIBIT 2.11 — Summary Profitability and Risk Measures for Different-Asset Concentration Groups, December 31, 2004

| | All Institutions | Asset Concentration Groups | | | | | | | | |
|---|---|---|---|---|---|---|---|---|---|---|
| | | Credit Card | International | Ag. Lending | Commercial Lending | Mortgage | Consumer Lending | Other spec. <$1B | All Other <$1B | All Other >$1B |
| # of institutions reporting | 8,975 | 34 | 5 | 1,730 | 4,424 | 990 | 132 | 465 | 1,120 | 75 |
| Commercial banks | 7,630 | 30 | 5 | 1,725 | 4,019 | 250 | 101 | 414 | 1,026 | 60 |
| Savings institutions | 1,345 | 4 | 0 | 5 | 405 | 740 | 31 | 51 | 94 | 15 |
| **Performance ratios (%)** | | | | | | | | | | |
| Return on equity | 13.28 | 22.16 | 10.35 | 11.45 | 13.48 | 11.61 | 16.81 | 10.03 | 10.18 | 13.69 |
| Return on assets | 1.29 | 4.01 | 0.76 | 1.23 | 1.30 | 1.18 | 1.66 | 1.66 | 1.10 | 1.35 |
| Pretax ROA | 1.90 | 6.21 | 1.09 | 1.51 | 1.89 | 1.81 | 2.56 | 2.43 | 1.41 | 1.98 |
| Equity capital ratio | 10.28 | 20.52 | 8.05 | 10.79 | 10.09 | 10.55 | 11.36 | 16.94 | 10.79 | 10.25 |
| Net interest margin | 3.53 | 9.05 | 2.50 | 4.07 | 3.86 | 3.05 | 4.71 | 3.20 | 3.86 | 3.27 |
| Yield on earning assets | 5.02 | 11.25 | 4.02 | 5.68 | 5.26 | 4.80 | 6.88 | 4.54 | 5.40 | 4.54 |
| Cost of funding earn assets | 1.49 | 2.20 | 1.52 | 1.61 | 1.40 | 1.75 | 2.17 | 1.33 | 1.53 | 1.27 |
| Earning assets to total assets | 87.13 | 82.95 | 81.47 | 91.91 | 90.18 | 92.17 | 90.73 | 88.93 | 92.11 | 84.36 |
| Efficiency ratio | 58.03 | 45.29 | 70.16 | 62.07 | 57.10 | 56.46 | 45.53 | 72.42 | 66.92 | 57.71 |
| Burden | 0.97 | −2.15 | 0.75 | 2.08 | 1.40 | 1.07 | 0.78 | 0.34 | 2.01 | 0.84 |
| Noninterest inc. to earn assets | 2.13 | 11.18 | 2.51 | 0.69 | 1.51 | 1.20 | 2.26 | 6.55 | 1.16 | 1.96 |
| Noninterest exp. to earn assets | 3.10 | 9.03 | 3.26 | 2.77 | 2.91 | 2.27 | 3.04 | 6.89 | 3.17 | 2.80 |
| LN&LS loss provision to assets | 0.30 | 3.96 | 0.25 | 0.16 | 0.22 | 0.08 | 1.05 | 0.11 | 0.17 | 0.07 |
| **Asset Quality** | | | | | | | | | | |
| Net charge-offs to LN&LS | 0.56 | 4.67 | 0.91 | 0.21 | 0.30 | 0.12 | 1.57 | 0.59 | 0.31 | 0.25 |
| Loss allow to noncur. LN&LS | 167.8 | 215.8 | 135.3 | 156.7 | 206.3 | 97.1 | 259.4 | 168.4 | 155.3 | 156.3 |
| LN&LS provision to net charge-offs | 90.6 | 108.8 | 63.1 | 118.3 | 105.2 | 100.2 | 85.5 | 67.3 | 99.4 | 52.0 |
| Loss allowance to LN&LS | 1.34 | 4.27 | 1.74 | 1.43 | 1.30 | 0.53 | 1.66 | 1.66 | 1.34 | 1.16 |
| Net LN&LS to deposits | 91.69 | 239.79 | 69.91 | 76.64 | 93.90 | 120.82 | 135.96 | 33.54 | 67.56 | 80.51 |
| **Capital Ratios** | | | | | | | | | | |
| Core capital (leverage) ratio | 8.12 | 16.64 | 6.05 | 10.37 | 8.29 | 9.10 | 8.82 | 15.17 | 10.38 | 7.20 |
| Tier 1 risk-based capital ratio | 10.76 | 14.59 | 8.38 | 14.71 | 10.14 | 15.36 | 13.07 | 34.70 | 17.32 | 9.45 |
| Total risk-based capital ratio | 13.19 | 17.34 | 12.03 | 15.82 | 12.18 | 16.86 | 14.62 | 35.95 | 18.55 | 12.12 |
| **Structural Changes** | | | | | | | | | | |
| New charters | 128 | 0 | 0 | 5 | 35 | 4 | 1 | 77 | 5 | 1 |
| Banks absorbed by mergers | 322 | 1 | 2 | 24 | 210 | 26 | 13 | 6 | 20 | 20 |
| Failed institutions | 4 | 0 | 0 | 0 | 3 | 0 | 0 | 0 | 1 | 0 |

Source: FDIC Quarterly Banking Profile, http://www.fdic.gov/, http://www2.fdic.gov/qbp.

borrowing indicates weakness, paying off Federal Reserve loans just prior to the reporting date. The biggest reporting problems arise when banks attempt to offset declines in reported net income or improve credit quality measures. Some banks smooth earnings by underreporting provisions for loan losses when profits are otherwise low, and overreporting provisions for loan losses when profits are otherwise high. This reduces the volatility in earnings and helps management meet earnings targets set by the board of directors or stock analysts. They might also sell nonconventional assets for one-time profits or understate problem loans. In many cases, banks have temporarily sold loan participations just before reporting periods to reduce loan exposures. Transactions and reporting requirements involving preferred stock, nonperforming loans, securities transactions, and nonrecurring asset sales complicate the evaluation process.

**PREFERRED STOCK.** Preferred stock can help a bank meet equity capital requirements imposed by regulators but it does not pay interest; rather, it pays dividends out of earnings available for common stockholders. Banks that use preferred stock overstate their NIM, NI, ROE, and ROA, as well as other profitability measures relative to actual fixed charges, as compared with banks that don't use preferred stock. Preferred stock is not FDIC insured, and although dividends do not theoretically have to be paid, it can be almost devastating to a bank to pay preferred stock dividends. Hence, preferred stock more closely resembles debt and operating performance is best compared by netting preferred dividends from income when computing profit measures.

**NONPERFORMING LOANS.** Loans are designated as nonperforming when they are placed on nonaccrual status or when the terms are substantially altered in a restructuring. Nonaccrual means that banks deduct all interest on the loans that was recorded but not actually collected. Banks have traditionally stopped accruing interest when debt payments were more than 90 days past due. However, the interpretation of when loans qualified as past due varies widely. Many banks did not place loans on nonaccrual if they were brought under 90 days past due by the end of the reporting period. This permitted borrowers to make late partial payments and the banks to report all interest as accrued, even when it was not collected. On occasion, banks would lend the borrower the funds that were used to make the late payment.

The impact of this practice on financial statements is twofold. First, nonperforming loans are understated on the balance sheet, so that credit risk is actually higher than it appears. Second, interest accrued but not collected increases net interest income, thus overstating NIM, ROA, and ROE. In response to foreign loan problems at large banks in 1983 and 1984, federal regulators formally tightened the accounting rules for nonperforming loans. On July 1, 1984, loans were put on nonaccrual as soon as any repayment went beyond 90 days past due. Interest could not be recorded until the bank received an actual payment or the loan was made current.

**ALLOWANCE FOR LOAN LOSSES.** A related factor that distorts financial reports is the bank's provisions for loan losses and the allowance (reserve) for loan losses. For tax purposes, the maximum size of the reserve and the allowable deduction for losses is set by IRS regulations. However, management uses discretion in determining how much it should report as provisions for loan losses in financial statements. During some periods, banks have minimized the provision, understating the reported reserve for losses and overstating earnings. Severe loan problems in the early 1980s forced many banks to report large provisions for losses to compensate for prior understatements.

**SECURITIES GAINS AND LOSSES.** FASB 115 requires banks to designate the objective behind buying investment securities as either held-to-maturity, trading, or available-for-sale. Held-to-maturity securities are recorded on the balance sheet at amortized cost. Trading account securities are those securities that the bank actively buys and sells, principally to speculate on interest rate movements and profit on price changes. These securities must be marked to market (reported at current market value) on the balance sheet and unrealized gains (losses) reported on the income statement. All other investment securities are classified as available-for-sale and, as such, recorded at market value on the balance sheet with a corresponding change to stockholders' equity as unrealized gains and losses on securities holdings.

There is no reporting of gains or losses on the income statement with these securities. This accounting standard is designed to make the financial statements more closely match the bank's intended purpose when buying the securities. Unfortunately, regulators have often required a bank to report all securities of a certain type, such as Treasury bills, as available-for-sale if the bank ever sells a security prior to maturity. Hence, most banks report all investment securities as "available-for-sale" today due to restrictions against selling a security prior to maturity if the security is classified as "held-to-maturity."

**NONRECURRING SALES OF ASSETS.** Banks can often bolster earnings with one-time sales of assets. Most sales involve loan sales, real estate, subsidiaries, lease assets, or hidden assets that banks have acquired through debt restructuring and foreclosures. Typically, many foreclosed assets are listed at little value on the bank's books, but may generate large gains if the problem customer's performance improves. The Lockheed Corporation's debt restructuring is a good example. In the early 1970s, Lockheed ran into financial difficulty and restructured its loan commitments from creditors. As part of the agreement, many large banks acquired Lockheed common stock. By the early 1980s, the value of the stock had soared so that banks sold their shares for substantial profits. Manufacturer's Hanover, Bankers Trust, J.P. Morgan, and Irving Bank each reported large gains in 1983 from the sale of these securities. In 1983, Mercantile Texas Corporation reported a similar $7.2 million pretax gain from the sale of $90 million in credit card receivables to Southwest Bancshares. Interestingly, the two bank holding companies had agreed to merge that same year. Although the merger was not formally approved until 1984, Mercantile effectively sold its receivables to itself and reported the profit to shareholders. Shareholders actually lost with the transaction, though, because Mercantile had to pay taxes on the gain. By 1989, the merged bank, renamed MCorp, failed and was sold to Bank One, which used MCorp as its entree into the Texas market.

The essential point is that once a bank sells the asset, it cannot do it again. Thus, the gain or loss will have a one-time impact on earnings. A careful analysis requires that these extraordinary gains or losses be excluded from any comparison of the bank's performance with other banks, and with its own performance over time as the trend behavior will be biased.

## SUMMARY

The chapter introduces financial statements of commercial banks and presents a procedure for analyzing bank profitability and risks using historical data. The procedure involves decomposing aggregate profit ratios into their components to help identify key factors that influence performance with the focus on risk management. It then associates financial ratios for credit risk, liquidity risk, market risk, operational risk, reputational risk, legal risk, and capital or solvency risk to demonstrate the trade-off between risks and returns. Actual bank data are provided for PNC Bank and a smaller Community National Bank. The model developed is applied to the actual data for PNC Bank to interpret performance in 2004 versus peer banks, and over the period from 2000 to 2004. The same performance ratios are then used to compare the profitability and risk profile of two different-sized banking groups. The final sections examine profitability across size and asset concentrations of institutions, introduce the regulatory CAMELS ratings, and describe how banks may manipulate financial data to alter summary profit and risk measures.

The emphasis in the chapter is that of risk management. Financial institutions must assume risk—credit risk, liquidity risk, market risk, and so on—in order to earn optimal returns. High-performing institutions are those that manage and control their risk the best. Hence, the issue is that of the trade-off between risk and return. Clearly, an institution that assumes more risk, and underwrites or manages this risk correctly, will generate greater profits than an institution assuming less risk. Often, however, institutions assume more risk only to receive average or below-average return. A lower-risk position is not always a low-performance position and a high-risk position is not always a high-performance position. A high-performance institution is one that earns a greater return for the risk position it has assumed.

### QUESTIONS

1. What are the major categories of bank assets and their approximate percentage contribution to total resources? What are the major categories of bank liabilities? What are the fundamental differences between them?

2. Banks typically differentiate between interest and noninterest income and expense. What are the primary components of each? Define net interest income (NIM) and burden. What does a bank's efficiency ratio measure?

3. Using PNC in Exhibit 2.2 as a typical large bank, which balance sheet accounts would be affected by the following transactions? Indicate at least two accounts with each transaction.

   a. Arturo Rojas opens a money market deposit account with $5,000. The funds are loaned in the overnight market for one week.

   b. Just as a real estate developer pays off a strip shopping mall loan, a new resident optometrist takes out a mortgage on a home.

   c. The bank hires an investment banker to sell shares of stock to the public. It plans to use the proceeds to finance additional commercial loans.

4. Arrange the following items into an income statement. Label each item, place it in the appropriate category, and determine the bank's bottom-line net income.

   a. Interest paid on time deposit under $ 100,000

   b. Interest paid on jumbo CDs $ 101,000

    c. Interest received on U.S. Treasury and agency securities $ 44,500

    d. Fees received on mortgage originations $ 23,000

    e. Dividends paid to stockholders of $ 0.50 per share for 5,000 shares

    f. Provisions for loan losses $ 18,000

    g. Interest and fees on loans $ 189,700

    h. Interest paid on interest checking accounts $ 33,500

    i. Interest received on municipal bonds $ 60,000

    j. Employee salaries and benefits $ 145,000

    k. Purchase of a new computer system $ 50,000

    l. Service charge receipts from customer accounts $ 41,000

    m. Occupancy expense for bank building $ 22,000

    n. Taxes of 34 percent of taxable income are paid

    o. Trust department income equals $ 15,000

5. What are the primary sources of risk bank managers face? Describe how each potentially affects bank performance. Provide one financial ratio to measure each type of risk and explain how to interpret high versus low values.

6. Bank L operates with an equity-to-asset ratio of 6 percent, while Bank S operates with a similar ratio of 10 percent. Calculate the equity multiplier for each bank and the corresponding return on equity if each bank earns 1.5 percent on assets. Suppose, instead, that both banks report an ROA of 1.2 percent. What does this suggest about financial leverage?

7. Define each of the following components of the return on equity model and discuss their interrelationships:

    a. ROE

    b. ROA

    c. EM

    d. ER

    e. AU

8. Explain why profitability ratios at small banks typically differ from those at the largest money center banks.

9. Regulators use the CAMELS system to analyze bank risk. What does CAMELS stand for and what financial ratios might best capture each factor?

10. Rank the following assets from lowest to highest liquidity risk:

    a. Three-month Treasury bills one-year construction loan

    b. Four-year car loan with monthly payments

    c. Five-year Treasury bond five-year municipal bond

    d. One-year individual loan to speculate in stocks

    e. Three-month Treasury bill pledged as collateral

11. In each pair below, indicate which asset exhibits the greatest credit risk. Describe why.

    a. Commercial loan to a Fortune 500 company or a loan to a corner grocery store

    b. Commercial loans to two businesses in the same industry; one is collateralized by accounts receivable from sales, while the other is collateralized by inventory as work-in-process

    c. Five-year Ba-rated municipal bond or a five-year agency bond from the Federal Home Loan Mortgage Corporation (Freddie Mac)

    d. One-year student loan (college) or a one-year car loan

12. What ratios on common-sized financial statements would indicate a small bank versus a large, multibank holding company? Cite at least five.

13. In some instances, when a bank borrower cannot make the promised principal and interest payment on a loan, the bank will extend another loan for the customer to make the payment.

    a. Is the first loan classified as a nonperforming loan?

    b. What is the rationale for this type of lending?

    c. What are the risks in this type of lending?

14. Suppose that your bank had reported a substantial loss during the past year. You are meeting with the bank's board of directors to discuss whether the bank should make its traditional (25 years straight) dividend payment to common stockholders. Provide several arguments that the bank should authorize and make the dividend payment. Then, provide several arguments that it should not make the payment. What should decide the issue?

15. Explain how each of the following potentially affects a bank's liquidity risk:

    a. Most (95 percent) of the bank's securities holdings are classified as held-to-maturity.

    b. The bank's core deposit base is a low (35 percent) fraction of total assets.

    c. The bank's securities all mature after eight years.

    d. The bank has no pledged securities out of the $10 million in securities it owns.

## PROBLEMS

16. Evaluate the performance of Community National Bank relative to peer banks using the data in Exhibits 2.2, 2.3, 2.6, 2.7, and 2.8. Did the bank perform above or below average in 2004? Did it operate with more or less relative risk?

    a. Conduct a return on equity decomposition analysis for 2004, identifying where the bank's performance compared favorably and unfavorably with peer banks.

    b. Compare the bank's risk measures with those of peer banks. What are the implications of any significant differences?

    c. What recommendations would you make to adjust the bank's risk and return profile to improve its performance?

17. The summary UBPR page for Citibank, NA is shown on the following page. Average total assets for Citibank were quite high as of December 31, 2004. Use the data from December 31, 2004, to explain whether this bank was a high- or low-performance bank. Discuss specifically (1) financial leverage, (2) expense control, and (3) the contribution of interest and noninterest income to overall bank profitability. List three areas that management should focus on to improve performance. Using the limited information provided, evaluate Citibank's credit, liquidity, and capital risk.

*Problems*

**Summary Ratios from Citibank's 2004 UBPR**

CERT # 7213    DIST/RSSD: / 476810
CHARTER # 1461    COUNTY:

CITIBANK, NATIONAL ASSOCIATION
SUMMARY RATIOS
NEW YORK CITY, NY

PAGE 01

|  | 12/31/2004 | | | 12/31/2003 | | | 12/31/2002 | | | 12/31/2001 | | 12/31/2000 | |
|---|---|---|---|---|---|---|---|---|---|---|---|---|---|
| AVERAGE ASSETS ($000) | 632,756,000 | | | 524,098,750 | | | 470,811,000 | | | 404,101,500 | | 349,170,000 | |
| NET INCOME ($000) | 9,413,000 | | | 7,919,000 | | | 6,356,000 | | | 5,270,000 | | 4,923,000 | |
| NUMBER OF BANKS IN PEER GROUP | 170 | | | 163 | | | 166 | | | 158 | | 157 | |
|  | BANK | PG 1 | PCT | BANK | PG 1 | PCT | BANK | PG 1 | PCT | BANK | PG 1 | BANK | PG 1 |
| **EARNINGS AND PROFITABILITY** | | | | | | | | | | | | | |
| **PERCENT OF AVERAGE ASSETS:** | | | | | | | | | | | | | |
| INTEREST INCOME (TE) | 5.25 | 4.46 | 85 | 5.49 | 4.57 | 87 | 6.60 | 5.33 | 95 | 6.78 | 6.55 | 7.51 | 7.41 |
| − INTEREST EXPENSE | 1.67 | 1.20 | 86 | 1.55 | 1.29 | 71 | 2.16 | 1.76 | 75 | 3.32 | 3.04 | 4.35 | 3.88 |
| NET INTEREST INCOME (TE) | 3.58 | 3.23 | 64 | 3.94 | 3.23 | 78 | 4.44 | 3.52 | 89 | 3.46 | 3.52 | 3.15 | 3.53 |
| + NONINTEREST INCOME | 3.07 | 1.73 | 84 | 2.90 | 1.83 | 81 | 3.19 | 1.77 | 86 | 2.90 | 1.83 | 3.51 | 1.79 |
| − NONINTEREST EXPENSE | 4.02 | 2.89 | 84 | 3.72 | 2.95 | 79 | 3.93 | 3.05 | 80 | 3.79 | 3.22 | 4.17 | 3.25 |
| − PROVISION: LOAN&LEASE LOSSES | 0.58 | 0.14 | 95 | 1.02 | 0.27 | 96 | 1.61 | 0.38 | 98 | 0.59 | 0.40 | 0.39 | 0.33 |
| = PRETAX OPERATING INCOME (TE) | 2.05 | 1.97 | 57 | 2.10 | 1.89 | 62 | 2.09 | 1.90 | 58 | 1.98 | 1.75 | 2.11 | 1.80 |
| + REALIZED GAINS/LOSSES SEC | 0.06 | 0.02 | 79 | 0.06 | 0.05 | 68 | 0.01 | 0.07 | 40 | 0.06 | 0.06 | 0.15 | −0.04 |
| = PRETAX NET OPERATING INC (TE) | 2.10 | 2.00 | 57 | 2.16 | 1.95 | 64 | 2.10 | 1.98 | 55 | 2.04 | 1.83 | 2.25 | 1.74 |
| NET OPERATING INCOME | 1.49 | 1.31 | 67 | 1.51 | 1.28 | 71 | 1.35 | 1.29 | 55 | 1.31 | 1.18 | 1.41 | 1.11 |
| ADJUSTED NET OPERATING INCOME | 1.22 | 1.29 | 42 | 1.34 | 1.29 | 55 | 1.58 | 1.34 | 65 | 1.23 | 1.25 | 1.36 | 1.20 |
| NET INCOME ADJUSTED SUB S | N/A | 1.31 | N/A | N/A | 1.28 | N/A | N/A | 1.29 | N/A | | 1.19 | | 1.11 |
| NET INCOME | 1.49 | 1.31 | 67 | 1.51 | 1.28 | 70 | 1.35 | 1.29 | 55 | 1.30 | 1.19 | 1.41 | 1.11 |
| **MARGIN ANALYSIS:** | | | | | | | | | | | | | |
| AVG EARNING ASSETS TO AVG ASSETS | 91.45 | 91.97 | 37 | 90.51 | 92.14 | 29 | 90.80 | 91.97 | 32 | 91.36 | 91.76 | 91.47 | 91.71 |
| AVG INT-BEARING FUNDS TO AVG AST | 75.61 | 80.65 | 22 | 74.49 | 80.81 | 18 | 74.59 | 80.17 | 19 | 77.04 | 80.54 | 76.04 | 80.57 |
| INT INC (TE) TO AVG EARN ASSETS | 5.74 | 4.88 | 90 | 6.06 | 4.98 | 90 | 7.27 | 5.82 | 97 | 7.42 | 7.17 | 8.21 | 8.12 |
| INT EXPENSE TO AVG EARN ASSETS | 1.83 | 1.31 | 87 | 1.71 | 1.41 | 73 | 2.38 | 1.92 | 76 | 3.64 | 3.32 | 4.76 | 4.23 |
| NET INT INC-TE TO AVG EARN ASSET | 3.91 | 3.52 | 64 | 4.36 | 3.51 | 82 | 4.89 | 3.85 | 88 | 3.79 | 3.86 | 3.45 | 3.88 |
| **LOAN & LEASE ANALYSIS** | | | | | | | | | | | | | |
| NET LOSS TO AVERAGE TOTAL LN&LS | 1.53 | 0.25 | 97 | 2.05 | 0.41 | 98 | 2.17 | 0.56 | 96 | 1.05 | 0.56 | 0.69 | 0.39 |
| EARNINGS COVERAGE OF NET LOSS(X) | 3.04 | 19.94 | 15 | 2.60 | 10.92 | 15 | 2.65 | 9.33 | 15 | 3.78 | 8.81 | 5.54 | 12.65 |
| LN&LS ALLOWANCE TO NET LOSSES(X) | 1.46 | 7.51 | 14 | 1.40 | 4.18 | 14 | 1.26 | 3.60 | 10 | 2.02 | 3.66 | 2.95 | 5.14 |
| LN&LS ALLOWANCE TO TOTAL LN&LS | 2.07 | 1.27 | 92 | 2.66 | 1.44 | 95 | 2.62 | 1.52 | 90 | 1.91 | 1.54 | 1.86 | 1.49 |
| NON-CUR LN&LS TO GROSS LN&LS | 1.78 | 0.59 | 94 | 2.75 | 0.83 | 96 | 2.74 | 1.06 | 95 | 2.07 | 1.12 | 1.55 | 0.89 |
| **LIQUIDITY** | | | | | | | | | | | | | |
| NET NON CORE FUND DEPENDENCE | 87.05 | 32.55 | 97 | 83.12 | 33.01 | 95 | 80.39 | 30.57 | 96 | 80.03 | 31.86 | 81.25 | 34.13 |
| NET LOANS & LEASES TO ASSETS | 53.82 | 59.94 | 30 | 54.75 | 58.37 | 37 | 61.04 | 58.77 | 50 | 61.76 | 60.31 | 63.54 | 62.63 |
| **CAPITALIZATION** | | | | | | | | | | | | | |
| TIER ONE LEVERAGE CAPITAL | 6.28 | 7.71 | 18 | 6.57 | 7.67 | 26 | 7.00 | 7.50 | 39 | 7.16 | 7.34 | 6.68 | 7.17 |
| CASH DIVIDENDS TO NET INCOME | 31.80 | 46.73 | 36 | 77.64 | 57.57 | 63 | 126.83 | 56.79 | 91 | 32.50 | 66.20 | 11.98 | 65.35 |
| RETAIN EARNS TO AVG TOTAL EQUITY | 12.84 | 6.53 | 83 | 4.16 | 5.09 | 48 | −4.36 | 5.16 | 7 | 11.80 | 3.75 | 17.62 | 3.21 |
| RESTR+NONAC+RE ACQ TO EQCAP+ALLL | 7.87 | 3.25 | 93 | 11.97 | 4.73 | 93 | 14.10 | 5.87 | 91 | 13.45 | 6.24 | 11.82 | |
| **GROWTH RATES** | | | | | | | | | | | | | |
| ASSETS | 19.31 | 15.00 | 70 | 16.73 | 10.78 | 72 | 10.24 | 11.73 | 59 | 18.38 | 15.79 | 16.53 | 18.63 |
| TIER ONE CAPITAL | 16.25 | 14.11 | 65 | 7.34 | 11.43 | 47 | 5.22 | 11.97 | 38 | 28.70 | 16.37 | 20.36 | 17.35 |
| NET LOANS & LEASES | 17.28 | 17.96 | 65 | 4.71 | 10.14 | 39 | 8.96 | 9.74 | 59 | 15.06 | 11.90 | 18.69 | 19.60 |
| SHORT TERM INVESTMENTS | 15.67 | 39.92 | 57 | 42.19 | 21.85 | 66 | −19.79 | 41.81 | 32 | 35.78 | 71.51 | 12.90 | 71.88 |
| SHORT TERM NON CORE FUNDING | 15.71 | 21.27 | 52 | 3.18 | 13.12 | 42 | 15.99 | 8.86 | 68 | 24.60 | 11.84 | 23.69 | 19.49 |

##ONE OR MORE MERGERS, CONSOLIDATIONS OR PURCHASES HAVE OCCURRED DURING THE PERIOD.
12/31/2001 12/31/2003

Source: Citibank's Uniform Bank Performance Report, http://www2.fdic.gov/ubpr/UbprReport/SearchEngine/Default.asp.

CERT # 6384
CHARTER # 1316
Update Date: 1/28/2005

PNC BANK, NATIONAL ASSOCIATION                          PITTSBURGH, PA
ALLEGHENY
DECEMBER 31, 2004 UNIFORM BANK PERFORMANCE REPORT

## INFORMATION

## TABLE OF CONTENTS

FOR ORDERING ASSISTANCE CONTACT THE FDIC PUBLIC INFORMATION CENTER: 877 275-3342 (IN THE WASHINGTON, DC AREA: (202) 898-7108) QUESTIONS CONCERNING CONTENT OF REPORTS CONTACT: JOHN SMULLEN 703 516-5732 OR email jsmullen@fdic.gov

BANK AND BANK HOLDING COMPANY INFORMATION
CERTIFICATE # 6384      CHARTER # 1316

PNC FINANCIAL SERVICES GROUP, INC., THE
(HOLDING CO. # 1069778 )
PITTSBURGH      PA
(HOLDING COMPANY REFERS TO TOP HOLDER)

## INTRODUCTION

THIS UNIFORM BANK PERFORMANCE REPORT COVERS THE OPERATIONS OF YOUR BANK AND THAT OF A COMPARABLE GROUP OF PEER BANKS. IT IS PROVIDED FOR YOUR USE AS A MANAGEMENT TOOL BY THE FEDERAL FINANCIAL INSTITUTIONS EXAMINATION COUNCIL. DETAILED INFORMATION CONCERNING THIS REPORT IS PROVIDED IN "A USER'S GUIDE FOR THE UNIFORM BANK PERFORMANCE REPORT" FORWARDED TO YOUR BANK UNDER SEPARATE COVER. TO OBTAIN ADDITIONAL USER'S GUIDE OR OTHER UBPR MATERIALS, CALL THE NUMBER INDICATED AT RIGHT FOR ORDERING ASSISTANCE.

AS OF THE DATE OF PREPARATION OF THIS REPORT, YOUR BANK'S FEDERAL REGULATOR WAS THE OFFICE OF THE COMPTROLLER OF THE CURRENCY

YOUR CURRENT PEER GROUP # 1
INCLUDES ALL INSURED COMMERCIAL BANKS HAVING ASSETS IN EXCESS OF $3 BILLION.

PEER GROUPS BY REPORTING PERIOD:
12/31/2004: 1, 12/31/2003: 1, 12/31/2002: 1, 12/31/2001: 1, 12/31/2000: 1.

FOR THE DEFINITION OF OTHER UBPR PEER GROUPS, REFER TO THE UBPR USER'S GUIDE.

ADDRESSEE    CHIEF EXECUTIVE OFFICER
PNC BANK, NATIONAL ASSOCIATION
249 FIFTH AVENUE, 1 PNC PLAZA, 24TH FLOOR
PITTSBURGH, PA 15222-2707

## NOTE

THIS REPORT HAS BEEN PRODUCED FOR THE USE OF THE FEDERAL REGULATORS OF FINANCIAL INSTITUTIONS IN CARRYING OUT THEIR SUPERVISORY RESPONSIBILITIES. ALL INFORMATION CONTAINED HEREIN WAS OBTAINED FROM SOURCES DEEMED RELIABLE. HOWEVER NO GUARANTEE IS GIVEN AS TO THE ACCURACY OF THE DATA OR OF THE CALCULATIONS DERIVED THEREFROM. THE DATA AND CALCULATIONS IN THIS REPORT DO NOT INDICATE APPROVAL OR DISAPPROVAL OF ANY PARTICULAR INSTITUTION'S PERFORMANCE AND ARE NOT TO BE CONSTRUED AS A RATING OF ANY INSTITUTION BY FEDERAL BANK REGULATORS. USERS ARE CAUTIONED THAT ANY CONCLUSIONS DRAWN FROM THIS REPORT ARE THEIR OWN AND ARE NOT TO BE ATTRIBUTED TO THE FEDERAL BANK REGULATORS.

THE REPORTS OF CONDITION AND INCOME FOR THIS BANK CONTAIN ADDITIONAL INFORMATION NOT INCLUDED IN THIS PERFORMANCE REPORT, SUCH AS AN OPTIONAL NARRATIVE STATEMENT BY THE BANK.

CERT # 6384
CHARTER # 1316

PNC BANK, NATIONAL ASSOCIATION
SUMMARY RATIOS

PITTSBURGH, PA

PAGE 01

| | 12/31/2004 BANK | PG 1 | PCT | 12/31/2003 BANK | PG 1 | PCT | 12/31/2002 BANK | PG 1 | PCT | 12/31/2001 BANK | PG 1 | 12/31/2000 BANK | PG 1 |
|---|---|---|---|---|---|---|---|---|---|---|---|---|---|
| AVERAGE ASSETS ($000) | 69,596,163 | | | 60,890,137 | | | 59,488,016 | | | 63,486,660 | | 66,975,064 | |
| NET INCOME ($000) | 913,426 | | | 970,278 | | | 1,061,504 | | | 491,731 | | 1,007,226 | |
| NUMBER OF BANKS IN PEER GROUP | 170 | | | 163 | | | 166 | | | 158 | | 157 | |
| **EARNINGS AND PROFITABILITY** | | | | | | | | | | | | | |
| PERCENT OF AVERAGE ASSETS: | | | | | | | | | | | | | |
| INTEREST INCOME (TE) | 3.77 | 4.46 | 18 | 4.12 | 4.57 | 25 | 4.92 | 5.33 | 28 | 6.10 | 6.55 | 6.65 | 7.41 |
| − INTEREST EXPENSE | 1.08 | 1.20 | 40 | 0.90 | 1.29 | 25 | 1.33 | 1.76 | 25 | 2.62 | 3.04 | 3.49 | 3.88 |
| NET INTEREST INCOME (TE) | 2.68 | 3.23 | 23 | 3.22 | 3.23 | 41 | 3.59 | 3.52 | 46 | 3.47 | 3.52 | 3.16 | 3.53 |
| + NONINTEREST INCOME | 3.18 | 1.73 | 85 | 3.32 | 1.83 | 84 | 3.27 | 1.77 | 87 | 2.80 | 1.83 | 2.56 | 1.79 |
| − NONINTEREST EXPENSE | 3.99 | 2.89 | 84 | 3.98 | 2.95 | 82 | 3.75 | 3.05 | 77 | 3.84 | 3.22 | 3.27 | 3.25 |
| − PROVISION: LOAN&LEASE LOSSES | 0.07 | 0.14 | 34 | 0.29 | 0.27 | 64 | 0.49 | 0.38 | 73 | 1.42 | 0.40 | 0.20 | 0.33 |
| = PRETAX OPERATING INCOME (TE) | 1.80 | 1.97 | 38 | 2.26 | 1.89 | 71 | 2.62 | 1.90 | 83 | 1.02 | 1.75 | 2.26 | 1.80 |
| + REALIZED GAINS/LOSSES SEC | 0.07 | 0.02 | 84 | 0.15 | 0.05 | 84 | 0.13 | 0.07 | 77 | 0.20 | 0.06 | 0.03 | −0.04 |
| = PRETAX NET OPERATING INC (TE) | 1.87 | 2.00 | 41 | 2.41 | 1.95 | 76 | 2.75 | 1.98 | 84 | 1.21 | 1.83 | 2.29 | 1.74 |
| NET OPERATING INCOME | 1.31 | 1.31 | 52 | 1.59 | 1.28 | 77 | 1.78 | 1.29 | 84 | 0.78 | 1.18 | 1.50 | 1.11 |
| ADJUSTED NET OPERATING INCOME | 1.23 | 1.29 | 43 | 1.54 | 1.29 | 71 | 1.92 | 1.34 | 86 | 0.71 | 1.25 | 1.50 | 1.20 |
| NET INCOME ADJUSTED SUB S | | | N/A | | | N/A | | | N/A | | 1.19 | | 1.11 |
| NET INCOME | 1.31 | 1.31 | 52 | 1.59 | 1.28 | 77 | 1.78 | 1.29 | 84 | 0.77 | 1.19 | 1.50 | 1.11 |
| **MARGIN ANALYSIS:** | | | | | | | | | | | | | |
| AVG EARNING ASSETS TO AVG ASSETS | 84.35 | 91.97 | 7 | 84.38 | 92.14 | 6 | 87.27 | 91.97 | 14 | 88.50 | 91.76 | 88.42 | 91.71 |
| AVG INT-BEARING FUNDS TO AVG AST | 74.97 | 80.65 | 18 | 70.78 | 80.81 | 10 | 72.22 | 80.17 | 14 | 75.29 | 80.54 | 79.02 | 80.57 |
| INT INC (TE) TO AVG EARN ASSETS | 4.46 | 4.88 | 23 | 4.89 | 4.98 | 34 | 5.64 | 5.82 | 34 | 6.89 | 7.17 | 7.52 | 8.12 |
| INT EXPENSE TO AVG EARN ASSETS | 1.28 | 1.31 | 48 | 1.07 | 1.41 | 26 | 1.53 | 1.92 | 24 | 2.97 | 3.32 | 3.94 | 4.23 |
| NET INT INC-TE TO AVG EARN ASSET | 3.18 | 3.52 | 30 | 3.82 | 3.51 | 57 | 4.11 | 3.85 | 55 | 3.92 | 3.86 | 3.58 | 3.88 |
| **LOAN & LEASE ANALYSIS** | | | | | | | | | | | | | |
| NET LOSS TO AVERAGE TOTAL LN&LS | 0.28 | 0.25 | 60 | 0.59 | 0.41 | 71 | 0.54 | 0.56 | 62 | 2.11 | 0.56 | 0.26 | 0.39 |
| EARNINGS COVERAGE OF NET LOSS(X) | 11.61 | 19.94 | 50 | 7.44 | 10.92 | 45 | 8.89 | 9.33 | 56 | 1.62 | 8.81 | 12.32 | 12.65 |
| LN&LS ALLOWANCE TO NET LOSSES(X) | 5.23 | 7.51 | 51 | 2.92 | 4.18 | 41 | 3.12 | 3.60 | 47 | 0.64 | 3.66 | 4.90 | 5.14 |
| LN&LS ALLOWANCE TO TOTAL LN&LS | 1.35 | 1.27 | 61 | 1.78 | 1.44 | 75 | 1.80 | 1.52 | 77 | 1.49 | 1.54 | 1.30 | 1.49 |
| NON-CUR LN&LS TO GROSS LN&LS | 0.46 | 0.59 | 40 | 1.00 | 0.83 | 64 | 1.41 | 1.06 | 73 | 1.05 | 1.12 | 0.96 | 0.89 |
| **LIQUIDITY** | | | | | | | | | | | | | |
| NET NON CORE FUND DEPENDENCE | 18.27 | 32.55 | 25 | 15.25 | 33.01 | 18 | 9.49 | 30.57 | 14 | 20.10 | 31.86 | 24.15 | 34.13 |
| NET LOANS & LEASES TO ASSETS | 58.02 | 59.94 | 38 | 54.15 | 58.37 | 34 | 59.00 | 58.77 | 43 | 63.65 | 60.31 | 78.03 | 62.63 |
| **CAPITALIZATION** | | | | | | | | | | | | | |
| TIER ONE LEVERAGE CAPITAL | 7.14 | 7.71 | 40 | 8.37 | 7.67 | 76 | 8.99 | 7.50 | 86 | 7.62 | 7.34 | 8.77 | 7.17 |
| CASH DIVIDENDS TO NET INCOME | 87.58 | 46.73 | 82 | 77.30 | 57.57 | 62 | 37.68 | 56.79 | 35 | 213.53 | 66.20 | 64.53 | 65.35 |
| RETAIN EARNS TO AVG TOTAL EQUITY | 1.90 | 6.53 | 22 | 3.76 | 5.09 | 45 | 12.14 | 5.16 | 82 | −10.64 | 3.75 | 6.72 | 3.21 |
| RESTR+NONAC+RE ACQ TO EQCAP+ALLL | 2.34 | 3.25 | 38 | 4.57 | 4.73 | 56 | 5.51 | 5.87 | 55 | 4.80 | 6.24 | 6.27 | |
| **GROWTH RATES** | | | | | | | | | | | | | |
| ASSETS | 19.01 | 15.00 | 69 | 4.00 | 10.78 | 35 | −4.75 | 11.73 | 6 | −0.91 | 15.79 | −7.33 | 18.63 |
| TIER ONE CAPITAL | −0.90 | 14.11 | 9 | −0.49 | 11.43 | 15 | 9.71 | 11.97 | 55 | −12.94 | 16.37 | 6.02 | 17.35 |
| NET LOANS & LEASES | 27.51 | 17.96 | 77 | −4.55 | 10.14 | 14 | −11.71 | 9.74 | 10 | −19.18 | 11.90 | −5.23 | 19.60 |
| SHORT TERM INVESTMENTS | 31.73 | 39.92 | 63 | −36.62 | 21.85 | 23 | 476.17 | 41.81 | 94 | 11.84 | 71.51 | −41.42 | 71.88 |
| SHORT TERM NON CORE FUNDING | 25.67 | 21.27 | 68 | 73.50 | 13.12 | 91 | −32.80 | 8.86 | 8 | −32.83 | 11.84 | −41.28 | 19.49 |

##ONE OR MORE MERGERS, CONSOLIDATIONS OR PURCHASES HAVE OCCURRED DURING THE PERIOD.
 12/31/2000 12/31/2001

CERT # 6384
CHARTER # 1316

PITTSBURGH, PA

PAGE 02

## PNC BANK, NATIONAL ASSOCIATION
### INCOME STATEMENT – REVENUE AND EXPENSES ($000)

| | 12/31/2004 | 12/31/2003 | 12/31/2002 | 12/31/2001 | 12/31/2000 | PERCENT CHANGE 1 YEAR |
|---|---|---|---|---|---|---|
| INTEREST AND FEES ON LOANS | 1,875,058 | 1,730,575 | 2,097,264 | 2,992,253 | 3,845,374 | 8.35 |
| INCOME FROM LEASE FINANCING | 132,839 | 189,910 | 239,200 | 258,790 | 208,494 | -30.05 |
| TAX-EXEMPT | 14,229 | 14,703 | 19,792 | 26,649 | 31,944 | -3.22 |
| ESTIMATED TAX BENEFIT | 5,711 | 7,347 | 10,166 | 13,394 | 15,701 | 4.45 |
| INCOME ON LOANS & LEASES (TE) | 2,013,608 | 1,927,832 | 2,346,630 | 3,264,437 | 4,069,569 | NA |
| U.S. TREAS & AGENCY (EXCL MBS) | 110,614 | 34,418 | 23,225 | 65,970 | NA | 221.38 |
| MORTGAGE BACKED SECURITIES | 337,110 | 366,877 | 369,396 | 446,662 | NA | -8.11 |
| ESTIMATED TAX BENEFIT | 3,352 | 504 | 499 | 635 | 792 | NA |
| ALL OTHER SECURITIES | 81,129 | 117,866 | 139,281 | 54,082 | NA | -31.17 |
| TAX EXEMPT SECURITIES INCOME | 8,350 | 1,008 | 972 | 1,263 | 1,611 | 728.37 |
| INVESTMT INTEREST INCOME (TE) | 532,205 | 519,665 | 532,401 | 567,349 | 330,813 | 2.41 |
| INT ON DUE FROM BANKS | 3,638 | 4,835 | 3,363 | 5,447 | 8,137 | -24.76 |
| INT ON FED FUNDS SOLD & RESALES | 29,503 | 18,682 | 27,653 | 12,664 | 44,290 | 57.92 |
| TRADING ACCOUNT INCOME | 20,575 | 805 | 254 | 1,467 | 2,374 | 2,455.90 |
| OTHER INTEREST INCOME | 20,847 | 39,447 | 17,361 | 19,998 | NA | -47.15 |
| TOTAL INTEREST INCOME (TE) | 2,620,376 | 2,511,266 | 2,927,663 | 3,871,362 | 4,455,183 | 4.34 |
| INT ON DEPOSITS IN FOREIGN OFF | 42,290 | 17,335 | 20,321 | 53,928 | 111,622 | 143.96 |
| INTEREST ON TIME DEP OVER $100M | 72,032 | 67,714 | 95,996 | 151,082 | 211,127 | 6.38 |
| INTEREST ON ALL OTHER DEPOSITS | 376,244 | 369,702 | 531,721 | 993,952 | 1,286,558 | 1.77 |
| INT ON FED FUNDS PURCH & REPOS | 40,432 | 13,260 | 12,969 | 99,507 | 168,549 | 204.92 |
| INT TRAD LIAB & OTH BORROWINGS | 137,637 | 26,001 | 63,452 | 292,561 | 473,858 | 429.35 |
| INT ON MORTGAGES & LEASES | NA | NA | NA | NA | NA | NA |
| INT ON SUB NOTES & DEBENTURES | 84,340 | 55,449 | 67,521 | 75,145 | 84,270 | 52.10 |
| TOTAL INTEREST EXPENSE | 752,975 | 549,461 | 791,980 | 1,666,175 | 2,335,984 | 37.04 |
| NET INTEREST INCOME (TE) | 1,867,401 | 1,961,805 | 2,135,683 | 2,205,187 | 2,119,199 | -4.81 |
| NONINTEREST INCOME | 2,216,264 | 2,018,779 | 1,946,676 | 1,776,499 | 1,717,828 | 9.78 |
| ADJUSTED OPERATING INCOME (TE) | 4,083,665 | 3,980,584 | 4,082,359 | 3,981,686 | 3,837,027 | 2.59 |
| NON-INTEREST EXPENSE | 2,777,489 | 2,425,253 | 2,233,665 | 2,435,920 | 2,188,675 | 14.52 |
| PROVISION: LOAN & LEASE LOSSES | 51,553 | 176,612 | 290,050 | 898,743 | 133,000 | -70.81 |
| PRETAX OPERATING INCOME (TE) | 1,254,623 | 1,378,719 | 1,558,644 | 647,023 | 1,515,352 | -9.00 |
| REALIZED G/L HLD-TO-MATURITY SEC | 0 | 0 | 0 | 0 | NA | NA |
| REALIZED G/L AVAIL-FOR SALE SEC | 49,792 | 89,786 | 79,766 | 123,985 | 19,561 | -44.54 |
| PRETAX NET OPERATING INC (TE) | 1,304,415 | 1,468,505 | 1,638,410 | 771,008 | 1,534,913 | -11.17 |
| APPLICABLE INCOME TAXES | 381,926 | 490,376 | 566,240 | 260,608 | 511,194 | |
| CURRENT TAX EQUIV ADJUSTMENT | 9,063 | 7,851 | 10,666 | 14,029 | 16,493 | |
| OTHER TAX EQUIV ADJUSTMENTS | 0 | 0 | 0 | 0 | 0 | |
| APPLICABLE INCOME TAXES(TE) | 390,989 | 498,227 | 576,906 | 274,637 | 527,687 | |
| NET OPERATING INCOME | 913,426 | 970,278 | 1,061,504 | 496,371 | 1,007,226 | -5.86 |
| NET EXTRAORDINARY ITEMS | 0 | 0 | 0 | -4,640 | 0 | |
| NET INCOME | 913,426 | 970,278 | 1,061,504 | 491,731 | 1,007,226 | -5.86 |
| CASH DIVIDENDS DECLARED | 800,000 | 750,000 | 400,000 | 1,050,000 | 650,000 | 6.67 |
| RETAINED EARNINGS | 113,426 | 220,278 | 661,504 | -558,269 | 357,226 | -48.51 |
| MEMO: NET INTERNATIONAL INCOME | 0 | 0 | 0 | 0 | 0 | NA |

CERT # 6384
CHARTER # 1316

PNC BANK, NATIONAL ASSOCIATION
NONINTEREST INCOME AND EXPENSES ($000) AND YIELDS

PITTSBURGH, PA

PAGE 03

**NONINTEREST INCOME & EXPENSES**

| | 12/31/2004 | 12/31/2003 | 12/31/2002 | 12/31/2001 | 12/31/2000 |
|---|---|---|---|---|---|
| FIDUCIARY ACTIVITIES | 296,226 | 291,582 | 308,291 | 365,434 | 771,456 |
| DEPOSIT SERVICE CHARGES | 431,169 | 422,100 | 402,750 | 355,931 | 335,720 |
| TRADING,VENT CAP,SECURTZ INC | 67,267 | 88,985 | 54,990 | 82,591 | 34,225 |
| INV BANKING,ADVISORY INC | 746,475 | 562,482 | 543,672 | 510,905 | N/A |
| INSURANCE COMM & FEES | 11,856 | −660 | −2,623 | 7,554 | N/A |
| NET SERVICING FEES | 51,212 | 35,245 | 38,274 | 36,101 | N/A |
| LOAN & LSE NET GAIN/LOSS | 130,953 | 134,969 | 155,768 | 32,248 | N/A |
| OTHER NET GAINS/LOSSES | 1,124 | 10,036 | 16,480 | −3,838 | N/A |
| OTHER NONINTEREST INCOME | 479,982 | 474,040 | 429,074 | 389,573 | 576,427 |
| NONINTEREST INCOME | 2,216,264 | 2,018,779 | 1,946,676 | 1,776,499 | 1,717,828 |
| PERSONNEL EXPENSE | 1,421,341 | 1,112,208 | 1,051,766 | 1,055,515 | 978,446 |
| OCCUPANCY EXPENSE | 350,550 | 352,506 | 315,189 | 303,353 | 279,144 |
| GOODWILLL IMPAIRMENT | 0 | 0 | 0 | N/A | N/A |
| OTHER INTANGIBLE AMORTIZ | 11,476 | 4,006 | 4,197 | N/A | N/A |
| OTHER OPER EXP(INCL INTANGIBLES) | 994,122 | 956,533 | 862,513 | 1,077,052 | 931,085 |
| TOTAL OVERHEAD EXPENSE | 2,777,489 | 2,425,253 | 2,233,665 | 2,435,920 | 2,188,675 |
| DOMESTIC BANKING OFFICES(#) | 737 | 684 | 680 | 680 | 698 |
| FOREIGN BRANCHES (#) | 8 | 8 | 8 | 8 | 8 |
| ASSETS PER DOMESTIC OFFICE | 98,006 | 88,831 | 86,094 | 90,883 | 89,996 |

| | 12/31/2004 | | | 12/31/2003 | | | 12/31/2002 | | | 12/31/2001 | | 12/31/2000 | |
|---|---|---|---|---|---|---|---|---|---|---|---|---|---|
| | BANK | PG 1 | PCT | BANK | PG 1 | PCT | BANK | PG 1 | PCT | BANK | PG 1 | BANK | PG 1 |
| **PERCENT OF AVERAGE ASSETS** | | | | | | | | | | | | | |
| PERSONNEL EXPENSE | 2.04 | 1.38 | 85 | 1.83 | 1.37 | 80 | 1.77 | 1.40 | 76 | 1.66 | 1.36 | 1.46 | 1.37 |
| OCCUPANCY EXPENSE | 0.50 | 0.36 | 81 | 0.58 | 0.38 | 89 | 0.53 | 0.40 | 80 | 0.48 | 0.41 | 0.42 | 0.42 |
| OTHER OPER EXP(INCL INTANGIBLES) | 1.44 | 1.08 | 78 | 1.58 | 1.13 | 83 | 1.46 | 1.23 | 73 | 1.70 | 1.40 | 1.39 | 1.41 |
| TOTAL OVERHEAD EXPENSE | 3.99 | 2.89 | 84 | 3.98 | 2.95 | 82 | 3.75 | 3.05 | 77 | 3.84 | 3.22 | 3.27 | 3.25 |
| OVERHEAD LESS NONINT INC | 0.81 | 1.10 | 25 | 0.67 | 1.06 | 23 | 0.48 | 1.23 | 14 | 1.04 | 1.34 | 0.70 | 1.37 |
| **OTHER INCOME & EXPENSE RATIOS:** | | | | | | | | | | | | | |
| EFFICIENCY RATIO | 68.01 | 57.01 | 81 | 60.93 | 57.24 | 66 | 54.72 | 57.09 | 46 | 61.18 | 59.15 | 57.04 | 59.35 |
| AVG PERSONNEL EXP PER EMPL($000) | 85.48 | 65.26 | 81 | 72.06 | 60.48 | 76 | 68.03 | 57.00 | 76 | 66.14 | 55.37 | 59.40 | 54.12 |
| ASSETS PER EMPLOYEE ($MILLION) | 4.44 | 6.09 | 43 | 4.02 | 5.17 | 38 | 3.86 | 5.00 | 39 | 3.92 | 4.79 | 3.84 | 4.50 |
| **YIELD ON OR COST OF:** | | | | | | | | | | | | | |
| TOTAL LOANS & LEASES (TE) | 5.04 | 5.47 | 25 | 5.48 | 5.66 | 37 | 6.09 | 6.42 | 29 | 7.29 | 7.74 | 7.90 | 8.73 |
| LOANS IN DOMESTIC OFFICES | 5.00 | 5.42 | 24 | 5.41 | 5.62 | 36 | 6.01 | 6.38 | 27 | 7.28 | 7.71 | 7.89 | 8.76 |
| REAL ESTATE | 5.00 | 5.40 | 27 | 5.47 | 5.69 | 32 | 6.37 | 6.56 | 36 | 7.41 | 7.84 | 7.36 | 8.61 |
| COMMERCIAL & INDUSTRIAL | 5.43 | 5.23 | 61 | 6.05 | 5.20 | 76 | 6.20 | 5.79 | 62 | 7.38 | 7.57 | 8.49 | 9.18 |
| INDIVIDUAL | 4.21 | 6.64 | 13 | 4.25 | 6.80 | 13 | 5.34 | 7.68 | 13 | 7.52 | 8.63 | 9.15 | 9.73 |
| CREDIT CARD | 3.10 | 4.86 | 52 | 0.00 | 4.69 | 52 | 0.00 | 5.17 | 53 | 0.00 | 6.09 | N/A | 0.00 |
| AGRICULTURAL | 5.65 | 3.37 | 76 | 5.06 | 3.54 | 54 | 5.74 | 4.21 | 55 | 7.10 | 5.76 | 8.76 | 6.86 |
| LOANS IN FOREIGN OFFICES | 19.35 | 0.53 | 99 | 8.94 | 0.70 | 98 | 10.09 | 0.70 | 98 | 8.69 | 1.11 | 8.70 | 1.49 |
| TOTAL INVESTMENT SECURITES(TE) | 3.51 | 3.98 | 25 | 3.81 | 4.18 | 31 | 5.05 | 5.33 | 32 | 5.55 | 6.27 | 4.98 | 6.70 |
| TOTAL INVESTMENT SECURITES(BOOK) | 3.48 | 3.84 | 28 | 3.81 | 4.00 | 34 | 5.04 | 5.15 | 40 | 5.54 | 6.08 | 4.97 | 6.54 |
| U.S. TREAS & AGENCY (EXCL MBS) | 2.82 | 2.93 | 36 | 2.42 | 3.08 | 25 | 3.59 | 4.18 | 26 | 4.54 | 5.81 | N/A | 0.00 |
| MORTGAGE BACKED SECURITIES | 3.91 | 4.14 | 32 | 4.18 | 4.18 | 51 | 5.48 | 5.49 | 43 | 6.17 | 6.35 | N/A | 0.00 |
| ALL OTHER SECURITIES | 3.08 | 3.88 | 25 | 3.43 | 4.25 | 26 | 4.41 | 4.74 | 39 | 3.54 | 5.54 | N/A | 0.00 |
| INTEREST-BEARING BANK BALANCES | 1.39 | 1.45 | 50 | 2.80 | 1.42 | 87 | 2.43 | 1.93 | 72 | 5.33 | 3.93 | 7.02 | 5.32 |
| FEDERAL FUNDS SOLD & RESALES | 2.00 | 1.24 | 92 | 1.60 | 1.09 | 89 | 1.63 | 1.73 | 32 | 3.86 | 3.88 | 6.30 | 6.30 |
| TOTAL-INT BEARING DEPOSITS | 1.14 | 1.25 | 39 | 1.22 | 1.39 | 40 | 1.77 | 1.97 | 36 | 3.18 | 3.50 | 4.23 | 4.34 |
| TRANSACTION ACCOUNTS | 0.86 | 0.62 | 67 | 0.90 | 0.60 | 76 | 1.13 | 0.96 | 66 | 2.17 | 1.94 | 2.98 | 2.12 |
| OTHER SAVINGS DEPOSITS | 0.60 | 0.69 | 40 | 0.57 | 0.70 | 37 | 0.96 | 1.09 | 41 | 2.08 | 2.09 | 1.62 | 1.92 |
| TIME DEPS OVER $100M | 2.81 | 2.17 | 81 | 3.66 | 2.38 | 91 | 3.91 | 3.13 | 80 | 5.46 | 5.03 | 6.30 | 5.82 |
| ALL OTHER TIME DEPOSITS | 2.78 | 2.03 | 81 | 3.12 | 2.41 | 75 | 3.67 | 3.45 | 62 | 5.21 | 5.21 | 5.82 | 5.61 |
| FOREIGN OFFICE DEPOSITS | 1.36 | 0.43 | 82 | 1.12 | 0.38 | 82 | 1.61 | 0.60 | 75 | 4.13 | 1.46 | 6.31 | 2.77 |
| FEDERAL FUNDS PURCHASED & REPOS | 1.37 | 1.41 | 57 | 1.10 | 1.15 | 47 | 1.49 | 1.83 | 33 | 4.19 | 3.83 | 7.37 | 6.04 |
| OTHER BORROWED MONEY | 2.95 | 2.64 | 55 | 0.72 | 3.00 | 5 | 1.48 | 3.77 | 7 | 4.46 | 5.29 | 4.14 | 5.92 |
| SUBORD NOTES & DEBENTURES | 5.69 | 1.91 | 80 | 5.10 | 2.03 | 76 | 5.85 | 2.10 | 79 | 6.52 | 3.09 | 7.31 | 3.85 |
| ALL INTEREST-BEARING FUNDS | 1.44 | 1.51 | 44 | 1.27 | 1.62 | 28 | 1.84 | 2.22 | 25 | 3.49 | 3.79 | 4.41 | 4.85 |

CERT # 6384
CHARTER # 1316

**PNC BANK, NATIONAL ASSOCIATION**
BALANCE SHEET — ASSETS, LIABILITIES AND CAPITAL ($000)

PITTSBURGH, PA

**PAGE 04**

| | 12/31/2004 | 12/31/2003 | 12/31/2002 | 12/31/2001 | 12/31/2000 | PERCENT CHANGE 1 QTR | PERCENT CHANGE 1 YEAR |
|---|---|---|---|---|---|---|---|
| **ASSETS:** | | | | | | | |
| REAL ESTATE LOANS | 20,701,904 | 15,639,089 | 15,453,881 | 17,136,390 | 23,403,724 | 2.75 | 32.37 |
| COMMERCIAL LOANS | 14,707,458 | 11,879,285 | 12,965,958 | 14,616,251 | 18,180,941 | 2.10 | 23.81 |
| INDIVIDUAL LOANS | 3,816,861 | 2,501,847 | 2,616,335 | 3,261,827 | 3,529,627 | 7.88 | 52.56 |
| AGRICULTURAL LOANS | 1,545 | 984 | 901 | 1,096 | 1,717 | 12.86 | 57.01 |
| OTHER LN&LS IN DOMESTIC OFFICES | 2,999,113 | 3,022,795 | 3,802,413 | 4,710,235 | 4,588,422 | -1.24 | -0.78 |
| LN&LS IN FOREIGN OFFICES | 1,222,904 | 1,190,025 | 1,029,389 | 777,443 | 347,421 | 1.30 | 2.76 |
| GROSS LOANS & LEASES | 43,449,785 | 34,234,025 | 35,868,877 | 40,503,242 | 50,051,852 | 2.63 | 26.92 |
| LESS: UNEARNED INCOME | 44,949 | 44,867 | 41,538 | 51,223 | 96,913 | | |
| LN&LS ALLOWANCE | 583,915 | 606,886 | 644,475 | 602,790 | 648,833 | 4.61 | -3.79 |
| NET LOANS & LEASES | 42,820,921 | 33,582,272 | 35,182,864 | 39,849,229 | 49,306,106 | 2.61 | 27.51 |
| U.S. TREASURY & AGENCY SECURITIES | 6,460,936 | 5,574,108 | 2,924,045 | 3,451,036 | 1,887,310 | -6.53 | 15.91 |
| MUNICIPAL SECURITIES | 131,685 | 7,719 | 14,538 | 18,679 | 45,237 | -1.35 | 1,605.99 |
| FOREIGN DEBT SECURITIES | 0 | 0 | 12,095 | 25,835 | 27,401 | N/A | N/A |
| ALL OTHER SECURITIES | 9,064,146 | 8,804,028 | 8,706,948 | 8,805,746 | 2,971,309 | 3.10 | 2.95 |
| INTEREST-BEARING BANK BALANCES | 393,713 | 259,318 | 222,788 | 157,670 | 167,916 | 17.28 | 51.83 |
| FEDERAL FUNDS SOLD & RESALES | 1,728,372 | 1,106,733 | 2,440,012 | 301,986 | 217,241 | | |
| TRADING ACCOUNT ASSETS | 1,667,330 | 935,042 | 1,028,769 | 487,251 | 168,345 | -4.52 | 78.32 |
| TOTAL INVESTMENTS | 19,446,182 | 16,686,948 | 15,349,195 | 13,248,203 | 5,484,759 | | |
| TOTAL EARNING ASSETS | 62,267,103 | 50,269,220 | 50,532,059 | 53,097,432 | 54,790,865 | | |
| NONINT CASH & DUE FROM BANKS | 3,174,493 | 2,926,330 | 3,142,917 | 4,156,160 | 3,565,214 | 8.59 | 8.48 |
| PREMISES, FIX ASSTS, CAP LEASES | 1,066,028 | 1,039,603 | 835,429 | 800,451 | 800,722 | -0.10 | 2.54 |
| OTHER REAL ESTATE OWNED | 14,301 | 14,208 | 11,663 | 9,325 | 15,047 | -11.74 | 0.65 |
| INV IN UNCONSOLIDATED SUBS | 15,223 | 17,386 | 4,934 | 6,400 | 4,320 | | |
| ACCEPTANCES & OTH ASSETS | 7,272,017 | 7,754,149 | 5,108,659 | 4,540,012 | 4,009,735 | 7.90 | -6.22 |
| TOTAL ASSETS | 73,809,165 | 62,020,896 | 59,635,661 | 62,609,780 | 63,185,903 | 2.87 | 19.01 |
| AVERAGE ASSETS DURING QUARTER | 73,391,052 | 62,719,462 | 58,731,693 | 62,838,680 | 62,706,833 | 4.52 | 17.01 |
| **LIABILITIES** | | | | | | | |
| DEMAND DEPOSITS | 8,488,607 | 7,070,434 | 6,888,749 | 8,024,609 | 6,581,761 | 11.59 | 20.06 |
| ALL NOW & ATS ACCOUNTS | 1,666,003 | 1,529,861 | 1,391,811 | 1,426,841 | 1,228,615 | 15.25 | 8.90 |
| MONEY MARKET DEPOSIT ACCOUNTS | 26,665,024 | 24,502,371 | 22,938,491 | 22,173,721 | 19,973,653 | 1.22 | 8.83 |
| OTHER SAVINGS DEPOSITS | 2,782,931 | 2,055,659 | 1,957,041 | 1,889,720 | 1,856,609 | 3.25 | 35.38 |
| TIME DEP UNDER $100M | 7,063,499 | 6,242,628 | 7,426,968 | 8,243,535 | 10,549,034 | 3.24 | 13.15 |
| CORE DEPOSITS | 46,666,064 | 41,400,953 | 40,603,060 | 41,758,064 | 40,189,672 | 3.86 | 12.72 |
| TIME DEP OF $100M OR MORE | 3,205,331 | 1,775,943 | 2,155,690 | 2,320,116 | 3,412,724 | 5.83 | 80.49 |
| DEPOSITS IN FOREIGN OFFICES | 2,994,623 | 2,371,548 | 1,382,555 | 2,306,590 | 2,397,676 | -4.21 | 26.27 |
| TOTAL DEPOSITS | 52,866,018 | 45,548,444 | 44,141,305 | 46,385,132 | 46,000,072 | 3.48 | 16.07 |
| FEDERAL FUNDS PURCH & RESALE | 1,606,647 | 499,232 | 398,639 | 582,306 | 1,586,709 | N/A | |
| FED HOME LOAN BOR MAT < 1 YR | 0 | 1,000,000 | 100,178 | 251,487 | 0 | N/A | -100.00 |
| FED HOME LOAN BOR MAT > 1 YR | 88,508 | 115,406 | 1,156,185 | 1,795,156 | 0 | -8.20 | -23.31 |
| OTH BORROWING MAT < 1 YR | 3,046,632 | 2,264,921 | 1,136,140 | 1,522,016 | 2,496,693 | 8.62 | 34.51 |
| OTH BORROWING MAT > 1 YR | 3,624,223 | 1,765,851 | 1,819,091 | 2,660,077 | 3,793,924 | 26.71 | 105.24 |
| ACCEPTANCES & OTHER LIABILITIES | 4,585,994 | 3,864,388 | 3,867,803 | 3,372,710 | 2,904,691 | 13.75 | 18.67 |
| TOTAL LIABILITIES (INCL MORTG) | 65,818,022 | 55,058,242 | 52,619,341 | 56,568,884 | 56,782,089 | 2.31 | 19.54 |
| SUBORD NOTES AND DEBENTURES | 1,895,482 | 1,340,133 | 1,153,771 | 1,153,235 | 1,152,698 | 36.31 | 41.44 |
| ALL COMMON & PREFERRED CAPITAL | 6,095,661 | 5,622,521 | 5,862,549 | 4,887,661 | 5,251,116 | | 8.42 |
| TOTAL LIBILITIES & CAPITAL | 73,809,165 | 62,020,896 | 59,635,661 | 62,609,780 | 63,185,903 | 2.87 | 19.01 |
| **MEMORANDA:** | | | | | | | |
| OFFICER, SHAREHOLDER LOANS (#) | 3 | 2 | 2 | 4 | 4 | | |
| OFFICER, SHAREHOLDER LOANS ($) | 22,449 | 14,211 | 17,628 | 20,933 | 19,539 | -0.96 | 57.97 |
| NON-INVESTMENT ORE | 14,301 | 14,208 | 11,663 | 9,325 | 15,047 | -11.74 | 0.65 |
| LOANS HELD FOR SALE | 1,667,154 | 1,378,603 | 1,535,037 | 3,900,766 | 1,655,003 | 5.81 | 20.93 |
| HELD-TO-MATURITY SECURITIES | 0 | 2,114 | 0 | 0 | 0 | N/A | -100.00 |
| AVAILABLE-FOR-SALE-SECURITIES | 15,656,767 | 14,383,741 | 11,657,626 | 12,301,296 | 4,931,257 | -1.14 | 8.85 |
| ALL BROKERED DEPOSITS | 2,289,151 | 1,533,123 | 1,342,871 | 1,175,114 | 586,684 | 10.23 | 49.31 |

CERT # 6384
CHARTER # 1316

PNC BANK, NATIONAL ASSOCIATION
OFF-BALANCE SHEET ITEMS & DERIVATIVES ANALYSIS

PITTSBURGH, PA

PAGE 05

**OUTSTANDING ($000)**

| | 12/31/2004 | 12/31/2003 | 12/31/2002 | 12/31/2001 | 12/31/2000 | PERCENT CHANGE 1 QTR | PERCENT CHANGE 1 YEAR |
|---|---|---|---|---|---|---|---|
| HOME EQUITY (1-4 FAMILY) | 5,741,792 | 4,184,431 | 3,951,448 | 3,578,540 | 3,137,699 | 3.35 | 37.22 |
| CREDIT CARD | 0 | 0 | 0 | 0 | 0 | | |
| COMMERCIAL RE SECURED BY RE | 1,411,906 | 927,004 | 904,057 | 925,314 | 1,302,778 | 18.51 | 52.31 |
| COMMERCIAL RE NOT SECURED BY RE | 2,326,566 | 1,697,883 | 1,626,243 | 1,709,755 | 1,675,731 | 16.26 | 37.03 |
| ALL OTHER | 19,679,421 | 17,239,929 | 19,883,135 | 24,662,036 | 25,628,908 | 2.68 | 14.15 |
| SECURITIES UNDERWRITING | 0 | 0 | 0 | 0 | 0 | | |
| MEMO: UNUSED COMMIT W/MAT GT 1 YR | 15,777,807 | 11,712,882 | 11,406,341 | 12,425,899 | 14,169,017 | 12.12 | 34.7 |
| STANDBY LETTERS OF CREDIT | 5,163,716 | 5,076,720 | 4,503,773 | 4,122,020 | 4,061,186 | 6.46 | 1.71 |
| AMOUNT CONVEYED TO OTHERS | 1,409,679 | 1,115,781 | 723,492 | 290,210 | 244,260 | 3.08 | 26.34 |
| COMMERCIAL LETTERS OF CREDIT | 142,835 | 94,477 | 97,971 | 119,809 | 108,349 | -21.06 | 51.18 |
| ASSETS SECURITIZED OR SOLD W REC | 2,872,742 | 3,203,446 | 3,529,593 | 4,122,870 | 0 | -3.59 | -10.32 |
| AMOUNT OF RECOURSE EXPOSURE | 40,365 | 47,115 | 57,364 | 106,779 | 0 | 2.64 | -14.33 |
| CREDIT DERIVS BANK AS GTR | 0 | 0 | 109,389 | 0 | 0 | | |
| CREDIT DERIVS BANK AS BENEF | 381,710 | 165,625 | 227,448 | 197,550 | 4,390,723 | 18.24 | 130.47 |
| ALL OTH OFF-BALANCE SHEET ITEMS | 2,075,779 | 4,102,836 | 2,906,089 | 9,233,190 | 8,909,432 | -46.27 | -49.41 |
| OFF-BALANCE SHEET ITEMS | 39,796,467 | 36,692,351 | 37,739,146 | 48,671,084 | 49,214,806 | -0.78 | 8.46 |

**OUTSTANDING (% OF TOTAL)**

| | 2004 BANK | 2004 PG 1 | 2004 PCT | 2003 BANK | 2003 PG 1 | 2003 PCT | 2002 BANK | 2002 PG 1 | 2002 PCT | 2001 BANK | 2001 PG 1 |
|---|---|---|---|---|---|---|---|---|---|---|---|
| HOME EQUITY (1-4 FAMILY) | 7.78 | 3.44 | 83 | 6.75 | 3.10 | 81 | 6.63 | 2.83 | 85 | 5.72 | 2.58 |
| CREDIT CARD | 0.00 | 1.59 | 48 | 0.00 | 1.42 | 48 | 0.00 | 1.02 | 51 | 0.00 | 1.15 |
| COMMERCIAL RE SECURED BY RE | 1.91 | 3.11 | 38 | 1.49 | 2.45 | 43 | 1.52 | 2.24 | 43 | 1.48 | 2.42 |
| COMMERCIAL RE NOT SECURED BY RE | 3.15 | 0.11 | 96 | 2.74 | 0.12 | 96 | 2.73 | 0.15 | 96 | 2.73 | 0.26 |
| ALL OTHER | 26.66 | 11.93 | 85 | 27.80 | 11.52 | 88 | 33.34 | 12.20 | 90 | 39.39 | 14.27 |
| TOTAL LN&LS COMMITMENTS | 39.51 | 24.71 | 82 | 38.78 | 22.70 | 84 | 44.21 | 21.41 | 89 | 49.31 | 23.15 |
| SECURITIES UNDERWRITING | 0.00 | 0.00 | 96 | 0.00 | 0.00 | 95 | 0.00 | 0.00 | 97 | 0.00 | 0.00 |
| STANDBY LETTERS OF CREDIT | 7.00 | 2.23 | 89 | 8.19 | 2.29 | 92 | 7.55 | 2.38 | 86 | 6.58 | 2.56 |
| AMOUNT CONVEYED TO OTHERS | 1.91 | 0.16 | 94 | 1.80 | 0.16 | 93 | 1.21 | 0.16 | 92 | 0.46 | 0.16 |
| COMMERCIAL LETTERS OF CREDIT | 0.19 | 0.12 | 77 | 0.15 | 0.12 | 69 | 0.16 | 0.12 | 70 | 0.19 | 0.13 |
| ASSETS SECURITIZED OR SOLD W REC | 3.89 | 1.37 | 84 | 5.17 | 1.91 | 83 | 5.92 | 2.34 | 81 | 6.59 | 3.10 |
| AMOUNT OF RECOURSE EXPOSURE | 0.05 | 0.11 | 72 | 0.08 | 0.14 | 68 | 0.10 | 0.19 | 70 | 0.17 | 0.22 |
| CREDIT DERIVS BANK AS GTR | 0.00 | 0.01 | 90 | 0.00 | 0.01 | 90 | 0.18 | 0.02 | 92 | 0.00 | 0.02 |
| CREDIT DERIVS BANK AS BENEF | 0.52 | 0.11 | 91 | 0.27 | 0.12 | 90 | 0.38 | 0.09 | 91 | 0.32 | 0.04 |
| ALL OTH OFF-BALANCE SHEET ITEMS | 2.81 | 0.59 | 88 | 6.62 | 1.04 | 87 | 4.87 | 1.57 | 84 | 14.75 | 2.41 |
| OFF-BALANCE SHEET ITEMS | 53.92 | 38.41 | 78 | 59.16 | 35.05 | 82 | 63.28 | 33.25 | 85 | 77.74 | 36.47 |

CERT # 6384
CHARTER # 1316

PITTSBURGH, PA

PNC BANK, NATIONAL ASSOCIATION
OFF-BALANCE SHEET ITEMS & DERIVATIVES ANALYSIS

| | 12/31/2004 | 12/31/2003 | 12/31/2002 | 12/31/2001 | 12/31/2000 |
|---|---|---|---|---|---|
| **NOTIONAL AMOUNT ($000)** | | | | | |
| DERIVATIVE CONTRACTS | 109,507,119 | 47,978,882 | 47,551,168 | 50,934,116 | 43,924,533 |
| INTEREST RATE CONTRACTS | 99,676,621 | 43,682,217 | 43,209,041 | 46,904,961 | 38,384,632 |
| FOREIGN EXCHANGE CONTRACTS | 6,804,646 | 2,658,419 | 2,946,797 | 4,022,155 | 5,520,831 |
| EQUITY, COMM & OTH CONTRACTS | 3,025,852 | 1,638,246 | 1,395,330 | 7,000 | 19,070 |
| | | | | | |
| **DERIVATIVES POSITION** | | | | | |
| FUTURES AND FORWARDS | 18,410,745 | 3,205,934 | 3,521,216 | 4,178,370 | 4,614,075 |
| WRITTEN OPTIONS | 28,165,144 | 2,130,957 | 3,390,262 | 5,343,653 | 8,282,539 |
| EXCHANGE TRADED | 20,120,000 | 66,388 | 0 | 0 | 8,070 |
| OVER-THE-COUNTER | 8,045,144 | 2,064,569 | 3,390,262 | 5,343,653 | 8,274,469 |
| PURCHASED OPTIONS | 15,977,320 | 1,676,050 | 3,476,993 | 8,075,266 | 8,989,659 |
| EXCHANGE TRADED | 8,520,000 | 66,147 | 0 | 0 | 0 |
| OVER-THE-COUNTER | 7,457,320 | 1,609,903 | 3,476,993 | 8,075,266 | 8,989,659 |
| SWAPS | 46,953,910 | 40,965,941 | 37,162,697 | 33,336,827 | 22,038,260 |
| | | | | | |
| HELD-FOR-TRADING | 105,054,536 | 43,254,800 | 43,238,184 | 40,968,606 | 31,430,645 |
| INTEREST RATE CONTRACTS | 95,237,420 | 38,958,135 | 38,896,057 | 36,939,451 | 25,905,439 |
| FOREIGN EXCHANGE CONTRACTS | 6,791,264 | 2,658,419 | 2,946,797 | 4,022,155 | 5,506,136 |
| EQUITY, COMM & OTH CONTRACTS | 3,025,852 | 1,638,246 | 1,395,330 | 7,000 | 19,070 |
| NON-TRADED | 4,452,583 | 4,724,082 | 4,312,984 | 9,965,510 | 12,493,888 |
| INTEREST RATE CONTRACTS | 4,439,201 | 4,724,082 | 4,312,984 | 9,965,510 | 12,479,193 |
| FOREIGN EXCHANGE CONTRACTS | 13,382 | 0 | 0 | 0 | 14,695 |
| EQUITY, COMM & OTH CONTRACTS | 0 | 0 | 0 | 0 | 0 |
| MEMO: MARKED-TO-MARKET | 4,452,583 | 4,724,082 | 4,312,984 | 9,965,510 | 0 |
| | | | | | |
| DERIVATIVE CONTRACTS (RBC DEF ) | 59,989,453 | 39,603,563 | 36,879,140 | 37,631,791 | 32,073,546 |
| ONE YEAR OR LESS | 19,353,979 | 13,556,628 | 13,631,800 | 9,525,537 | 9,923,739 |
| OVER 1 YEAR TO 5 YEARS | 24,250,474 | 16,369,026 | 15,744,141 | 22,174,113 | 16,977,069 |
| OVER 5 YEARS | 16,385,000 | 9,677,909 | 7,503,199 | 5,932,141 | 5,172,738 |
| | | | | | |
| GROSS NEGATIVE FAIR VALUE | 915,252 | 898,113 | 1,129,656 | 573,820 | 315,983 |
| GROSS POSTIVE FAIR VALUE | 935,454 | 970,681 | 1,276,234 | 711,223 | 338,182 |
| HELD-FOR-TRADING | 916,506 | 895,956 | 1,103,743 | 425,603 | 214,198 |
| NON-TRADED | 18,948 | 74,725 | 172,491 | 285,620 | 123,984 |
| MEMO MARKED-TO-MARKET | 18,948 | 74,725 | 172,491 | 285,620 | 0 |
| CURR CREDIT EXP ON RBC DERIV CONTR | 935,454 | 970,681 | 1,276,234 | 711,223 | 338,182 |
| CREDIT LOSSES OFF-BS DERIVS | 1,491 | 679 | 5,669 | 0 | 0 |
| | | | | | |
| **PAST DUE DERIV INSTRUMENTS:** | | | | | |
| FAIR VALUE CARRIED AS ASSETS | 0 | 0 | 0 | 122 | 0 |
| | | | | | |
| **IMPACT NONTRADED DERIV CONTRACTS:** | | | | | |
| INCREASE (DECR) IN INTEREST INC | 62,967 | 141,990 | 117,453 | 25,170 | -56,473 |
| INCREASE (DECR) IN INTEREST EXP | 955 | 710 | -369 | -1,696 | -1,687 |
| INCREADE (DECR) IN NONINT ALLOC | -2,220 | -10,258 | -24,420 | -25,193 | 0 |
| INCREASE (DECR) IN NET INCOME | 61,702 | 132,442 | 92,664 | -1,719 | -58,160 |

CERT # 6384
CHARTER # 1316

PNC BANK, NATIONAL ASSOCIATION
OFF BALANCE SHEET ITEMS & DERIVATIVES ANALYSIS

PITTSBURGH, PA

PAGE 05B

| | 12/31/2004 | | | 12/31/2003 | | | 12/31/2002 | | | 12/31/2001 | | 12/31/2000 | |
|---|---|---|---|---|---|---|---|---|---|---|---|---|---|
| | BANK | PG 1 | PCT | BANK | PG 1 | PCT | BANK | PG 1 | PCT | BANK | PG 1 | BANK | PG 1 |
| PERCENT OF NOTIONAL AMOUNT | | | | | | | | | | | | | |
| INTEREST RATE CONTRACTS | 91.02 | 51.85 | 43 | 91.04 | 53.45 | 45 | 90.87 | 49.41 | 46 | 92.09 | 48.07 | 87.39 | 53.10 |
| FOREIGN EXCHANGE CONTRACTS | 6.21 | 5.05 | 75 | 5.54 | 4.17 | 75 | 6.20 | 3.66 | 79 | 7.90 | 5.21 | 12.57 | 7.12 |
| EQUITY, COMM, & OTHER CONTR | 2.76 | 0.37 | 90 | 3.41 | 0.14 | 94 | 2.93 | 0.18 | 93 | 0.01 | 0.14 | 0.04 | 0.23 |
| FUTURES AND FORWARDS | 16.81 | 11.23 | 74 | 6.68 | 11.67 | 56 | 7.41 | 14.69 | 58 | 8.20 | 14.40 | 10.50 | 14.38 |
| WRITTEN OPTIONS | 25.72 | 3.72 | 93 | 4.44 | 3.41 | 70 | 7.13 | 2.97 | 79 | 10.49 | 2.88 | 18.86 | 3.40 |
| EXCHANGE TRADED | 18.37 | 0.02 | 99 | 0.14 | 0.01 | 93 | 0.00 | 0.01 | 92 | 0.00 | 0.02 | 0.02 | 0.03 |
| OVER-THE-COUNTER | 7.35 | 3.25 | 77 | 4.30 | 3.11 | 70 | 7.13 | 2.66 | 79 | 10.49 | 2.44 | 18.84 | 3.03 |
| PURCHASED OPTIONS | 14.59 | 3.27 | 87 | 3.49 | 3.18 | 73 | 7.31 | 3.62 | 76 | 15.85 | 5.62 | 20.47 | 10.11 |
| EXCHANGE TRADED | 7.78 | 0.06 | 97 | 0.14 | 0.06 | 89 | 0.00 | 0.06 | 88 | 0.00 | 0.07 | 0.00 | 0.14 |
| OVER-THE-COUNTER | 6.81 | 2.77 | 81 | 3.36 | 2.65 | 74 | 7.31 | 3.04 | 79 | 15.85 | 4.62 | 20.47 | 8.95 |
| SWAPS | 42.88 | 44.77 | 38 | 85.38 | 44.14 | 67 | 78.15 | 35.63 | 68 | 65.45 | 34.55 | 50.17 | 36.47 |
| HELD-FOR-TRADING | 95.93 | 20.83 | 90 | 90.15 | 22.04 | 86 | 90.93 | 20.32 | 82 | 80.43 | 21.26 | 71.56 | 21.97 |
| INTEREST RATE CONTRACTS | 86.97 | 13.26 | 94 | 81.20 | 15.90 | 89 | 81.80 | 16.88 | 88 | 72.52 | 16.56 | 58.98 | 14.79 |
| FOREIGN EXCHANGE CONTRACTS | 6.20 | 2.10 | 83 | 5.54 | 1.90 | 81 | 6.20 | 1.71 | 82 | 7.90 | 2.97 | 12.54 | 3.49 |
| EQUITY, COMM & OTH CONTRACTS | 2.76 | 0.08 | 94 | 3.41 | 0.07 | 96 | 2.93 | 0.10 | 95 | 0.01 | 0.08 | 0.04 | 0.10 |
| NON-TRADED | 4.07 | 28.13 | 29 | 9.85 | 26.98 | 33 | 9.07 | 25.05 | 42 | 19.57 | 22.86 | 28.44 | 24.95 |
| INTEREST RATE CONTRACTS | 4.05 | 35.03 | 32 | 9.85 | 33.56 | 35 | 9.07 | 29.94 | 44 | 19.57 | 30.15 | 28.41 | 32.87 |
| FOREIGN EXCHANGE CONTRACTS | 0.01 | 0.33 | 77 | 0.00 | 0.00 | 75 | 0.00 | 0.36 | 78 | 0.00 | 0.40 | 0.03 | 1.01 |
| EQUITY, COMM & OTH CONTRACTS | 0.00 | 0.02 | 90 | 0.00 | 0.00 | 92 | 0.00 | 0.00 | 93 | 0.00 | 0.00 | 0.00 | 0.00 |
| MEMO: MARKED-TO-MARKET | 4.07 | 28.13 | 29 | 9.85 | 26.98 | 33 | 9.07 | 25.05 | 42 | 19.57 | 22.86 | 0.00 | 8.76 |
| DERIVATIVE CONTRACTS (RBC DEF ) | 54.78 | 58.89 | 26 | 82.54 | 58.52 | 39 | 77.56 | 49.76 | 40 | 73.88 | 49.82 | 73.02 | 56.26 |
| ONE YEAR OR LESS | 17.67 | 19.20 | 54 | 28.26 | 17.90 | 71 | 28.67 | 20.63 | 65 | 18.70 | 18.30 | 22.59 | 22.17 |
| OVER 1 YEAR TO 5 YEARS | 22.15 | 23.39 | 50 | 34.12 | 24.68 | 60 | 33.11 | 21.79 | 66 | 43.53 | 26.63 | 38.65 | 27.07 |
| OVER 5 YEARS | 14.96 | 15.98 | 59 | 20.17 | 15.03 | 68 | 15.78 | 10.93 | 68 | 11.65 | 8.32 | 11.78 | 8.40 |
| GROSS NEGATIVE FAIR VALUE | 0.84 | 0.71 | 60 | 1.87 | 0.90 | 78 | 2.38 | 1.19 | 79 | 1.13 | 0.74 | 0.72 | 0.66 |
| GROSS POSTIVE FAIR VALUE | 0.85 | 0.68 | 61 | 2.02 | 0.94 | 78 | 2.68 | 1.23 | 79 | 1.40 | 0.83 | 0.77 | 0.68 |
| BY TIER ONE CAPITAL: | | | | | | | | | | | | | |
| GROSS NEGATIVE FAIR VALUE (X) | 0.18 | 0.03 | 91 | 0.17 | 0.05 | 87 | 0.22 | 0.05 | 87 | 0.12 | 0.05 | 0.06 | 0.04 |
| GROSS POSTIVE FAIR VALUE (X) | 0.18 | 0.03 | 91 | 0.19 | 0.04 | 89 | 0.25 | 0.06 | 88 | 0.15 | 0.05 | 0.06 | 0.04 |
| HELD-FOR-TRADING (X) | 20.65 | 1.19 | 94 | 8.42 | 1.36 | 91 | 8.38 | 1.38 | 91 | 8.71 | 1.93 | 5.82 | 1.67 |
| NON-TRADED (X) | 0.88 | 1.25 | 60 | 0.92 | 1.19 | 60 | 0.84 | 1.14 | 59 | 2.12 | 1.23 | 2.31 | 1.32 |
| NON-TRADED MARKED-TO-MKT(X) | 0.88 | 1.25 | 60 | 0.92 | 1.19 | 60 | 0.84 | 1.14 | 59 | 2.12 | 1.23 | 0.00 | 0.21 |
| CURR CREDIT EXPOSURE (X) | 0.18 | 0.02 | 91 | 0.19 | 0.03 | 90 | 0.25 | 0.05 | 89 | 0.15 | 0.04 | 0.06 | 0.03 |
| CREDIT LOSSES ON DERIVATIVES | 0.03 | 0.00 | 95 | 0.01 | 0.00 | 93 | 0.11 | 0.00 | 96 | 0.00 | 0.00 | 0.00 | 0.00 |
| PAST DUE DERIVATIVE INSTRUMENTS : | | | | | | | | | | | | | |
| FAIR VALUE CARRIED AS ASSETS | 0.00 | 0.00 | 98 | 0.00 | 0.00 | 96 | 0.00 | 0.00 | 97 | 0.00 | 0.00 | 0.00 | 0.00 |
| OTHER RATIOS: | | | | | | | | | | | | | |
| CUR CREDIT EXPOSURE/ RISK WT AST | 1.54 | 0.24 | 90 | 1.87 | 0.33 | 89 | 2.41 | 0.43 | 89 | 1.31 | 0.36 | 0.58 | 0.23 |
| CREDIT LOSSES ON DERIVS /CR ALLOW | 0.26 | 0.00 | 95 | 0.11 | 0.00 | 95 | 0.88 | 0.00 | 97 | 0.00 | 0.00 | 0.00 | 0.00 |
| IMPACT OF NONTRADED DERIV CONTRACTS: | | | | | | | | | | | | | |
| INCR(DEC) INTEREST INC/NET INC | 6.89 | 0.67 | 90 | 14.63 | 1.54 | 91 | 11.06 | 1.34 | 89 | 5.12 | 1.06 | -5.61 | 0.18 |
| INCR(DEC) INTEREST EXP/NET INC | 0.10 | 1.39 | 63 | 0.07 | 0.49 | 70 | -0.03 | -0.83 | 26 | -0.34 | -0.24 | -0.17 | 0.20 |
| INCR(DEC) NONINT ALLOC/NET INC | -0.24 | 0.23 | 12 | -1.06 | 0.11 | 9 | -2.30 | 0.29 | 5 | -5.12 | 0.35 | 0.00 | 0.05 |
| INCR(DEC) NET INCOME/NET INC | 6.76 | 2.77 | 74 | 13.65 | 2.48 | 84 | 8.73 | 3.53 | 81 | -0.35 | 1.55 | -5.77 | 0.54 |

CERT # 6384
CHARTER # 1316

PNC BANK, NATIONAL ASSOCIATION  PITTSBURGH, PA  PAGE 06
BALANCE SHEET—PERCENTAGE COMPOSITION OF ASSETS AND LIABILITIES

| ASSETS, PERCENT OF AVG ASSETS | 12/31/2004 BANK | PG 1 | PCT | 12/31/2003 BANK | PG 1 | PCT | 12/31/2002 BANK | PG 1 | PCT | 12/31/2001 BANK | PG 1 | 12/31/2000 BANK | PG 1 |
|---|---|---|---|---|---|---|---|---|---|---|---|---|---|
| TOTAL LOANS | 53.34 | 58.22 | 32 | 51.89 | 57.69 | 29 | 57.50 | 58.58 | 42 | 63.88 | 60.83 | 72.59 | 61.20 |
| LEASE FINANCING RECEIVABLES | 3.91 | 1.03 | 88 | 5.28 | 1.19 | 90 | 6.19 | 1.35 | 92 | 5.81 | 1.55 | 4.28 | 1.78 |
| LESS: LN&LS ALLOWANCE | 0.85 | 0.80 | 51 | 1.03 | 0.86 | 66 | 1.05 | 0.90 | 68 | 1.02 | 0.91 | 0.96 | 0.90 |
| NET LOANS & LEASES | 56.40 | 58.91 | 38 | 56.14 | 58.47 | 40 | 62.64 | 59.53 | 51 | 68.67 | 62.04 | 75.91 | 62.77 |
| INTEREST-BEARING BANK BALANCES | 0.42 | 0.76 | 69 | 0.33 | 0.87 | 65 | 0.27 | 0.91 | 60 | 0.20 | 0.71 | 0.18 | 0.54 |
| FEDERAL FUNDS SOLD & RESALES | 1.98 | 2.37 | 61 | 2.60 | 2.61 | 64 | 2.81 | 3.09 | 59 | 0.58 | 2.95 | 1.01 | 2.63 |
| TRADING ACCOUNT ASSETS | 2.09 | 0.34 | 89 | 1.63 | 0.39 | 86 | 1.23 | 0.38 | 85 | 0.59 | 0.41 | 0.33 | 0.41 |
| HELD-TO-MATURITY SECURITIES | 0.00 | 2.03 | 36 | 0.00 | 1.45 | 43 | 0.00 | 1.44 | 46 | 0.00 | 1.74 | 0.00 | 2.79 |
| AVAILABLE-FOR-SALE SECURITIES | 22.03 | 21.00 | 58 | 21.90 | 21.11 | 56 | 17.98 | 19.39 | 48 | 15.09 | 17.26 | 9.52 | 16.52 |
| TOTAL EARNING ASSETS | 82.92 | 90.08 | 8 | 82.60 | 89.84 | 8 | 84.93 | 89.78 | 14 | 85.13 | 89.27 | 86.95 | 89.76 |
| NONINT CASH & DUE FROM BANKS | 4.24 | 2.68 | 83 | 5.40 | 3.13 | 87 | 5.38 | 3.40 | 83 | 5.50 | 3.87 | 4.16 | 4.02 |
| PREMISES, FIX ASSTS & CAP LEASES | 1.55 | 1.09 | 77 | 1.49 | 1.08 | 75 | 1.34 | 1.12 | 65 | 1.27 | 1.12 | 1.14 | 1.10 |
| OTHER REAL ESTATE OWNED | 0.02 | 0.05 | 43 | 0.02 | 0.05 | 42 | 0.02 | 0.05 | 42 | 0.02 | 0.04 | 0.03 | 0.03 |
| ACCEPTANCES & OTHER ASSETS | 11.26 | 5.82 | 88 | 10.48 | 5.49 | 89 | 8.34 | 5.24 | 82 | 8.09 | 5.28 | 7.72 | 4.70 |
| SUBTOTAL | 17.08 | 9.92 | 91 | 17.39 | 10.16 | 91 | 15.08 | 10.22 | 85 | 14.87 | 10.73 | 13.05 | 10.24 |
| TOTAL ASSETS | 100.00 | 100.00 | | 99.99 | 100.00 | | 100.01 | 100.00 | | 100.00 | 100.00 | 100.00 | 100.00 |
| STANDBY LETTERS OF CREDIT | 7.22 | 2.19 | 89 | 7.68 | 2.25 | 89 | 7.27 | 2.29 | 86 | 6.50 | 2.51 | 6.49 | 2.83 |
| LIABILITIES, PERCENT OF AVG ASST | | | | | | | | | | | | | |
| DEMAND DEPOSITS | 11.09 | 6.61 | 84 | 12.74 | 6.56 | 89 | 11.75 | 7.27 | 82 | 10.95 | 7.82 | 10.01 | 8.57 |
| ALL NOW & ATS ACCOUNTS | 2.15 | 1.92 | 62 | 2.23 | 1.81 | 62 | 2.11 | 1.63 | 69 | 1.96 | 1.62 | 1.77 | 1.55 |
| MONEY MARKET DEPOSIT ACCOUNTS | 37.63 | 24.33 | 83 | 38.84 | 22.00 | 87 | 36.95 | 21.58 | 86 | 33.11 | 19.12 | 28.31 | 17.99 |
| OTHER SAVINGS DEPOSITS | 3.65 | 8.42 | 35 | 3.31 | 8.73 | 34 | 3.25 | 8.73 | 32 | 2.95 | 7.75 | 2.97 | 7.55 |
| TIME DEP LESS THAN $100M | 9.76 | 8.36 | 58 | 11.03 | 9.59 | 59 | 13.06 | 11.14 | 58 | 14.77 | 12.86 | 15.69 | 13.69 |
| CORE DEPOSITS | 64.29 | 54.64 | 67 | 68.16 | 53.90 | 76 | 67.12 | 55.21 | 73 | 63.74 | 54.02 | 58.74 | 53.60 |
| TIME DEP OF $100M OR MORE | 3.76 | 8.99 | 20 | 3.14 | 9.02 | 17 | 3.98 | 9.12 | 22 | 4.37 | 9.70 | 4.85 | 9.80 |
| DEPOSITS IN FOREIGN OFFICES | 4.26 | 1.94 | 77 | 2.53 | 2.04 | 71 | 2.26 | 1.97 | 70 | 2.83 | 2.33 | 3.69 | 3.26 |
| TOTAL DEPOSITS | 72.30 | 68.32 | 56 | 73.84 | 67.79 | 61 | 73.35 | 69.21 | 57 | 70.93 | 68.98 | 67.28 | 69.23 |
| FEDERAL FUNDS PURCH & REPOS | 3.18 | 8.00 | 28 | 0.99 | 8.16 | 10 | 0.83 | 7.82 | 7 | 2.28 | 8.94 | 2.28 | 8.64 |
| TOTAL FED HOME LOAN BORROWINGS | 0.61 | 4.63 | 31 | 1.88 | 4.81 | 37 | 2.53 | 4.45 | 43 | 3.01 | 3.71 | N/A | 0.00 |
| TOTAL OTH BORROWINGS | 7.47 | 2.66 | 82 | 5.10 | 2.87 | 73 | 6.00 | 2.72 | 76 | 7.60 | 4.15 | 17.39 | 9.72 |
| MEMO: SHT TER N CORE FUNDING | 13.34 | 22.87 | 22 | 8.44 | 22.88 | 7 | 8.34 | 22.90 | 7 | 11.02 | 25.17 | 17.48 | 27.13 |
| ACCEPTANCES & OTHER LIABILITIES | 5.55 | 2.11 | 92 | 6.89 | 2.46 | 92 | 6.36 | 2.33 | 91 | 6.11 | 2.32 | 3.41 | 2.01 |
| TOTAL LIABILITIES (INCL MORTG) | 89.12 | 89.83 | 28 | 88.70 | 90.24 | 21 | 89.06 | 90.31 | 23 | 89.94 | 90.55 | 90.36 | 91.02 |
| SUBORDINATED NOTES & DEBENTURES | 2.16 | 0.62 | 86 | 1.77 | 0.71 | 80 | 1.91 | 0.76 | 80 | 1.81 | 0.83 | 1.72 | 0.88 |
| ALL COMMON & PREFERRED CAPITAL | 8.72 | 9.39 | 52 | 9.54 | 8.93 | 70 | 9.02 | 8.81 | 65 | 8.25 | 8.48 | 7.92 | 7.95 |
| TOTAL LIABILITIES & CAPITAL | 99.99 | 100.00 | | 100.01 | 100.00 | | 100.00 | 100.00 | | 99.99 | 100.00 | 100.00 | 100.00 |
| MEMO: ALL BROKERED DEPOSITS | 3.00 | 2.81 | 67 | 2.19 | 2.29 | 67 | 2.12 | 1.87 | 71 | 1.41 | 1.82 | 0.60 | 1.83 |
| INSURED BROKERED DEP | 2.60 | 1.84 | 71 | 1.73 | 1.45 | 73 | 1.55 | 1.29 | 72 | 0.00 | 1.17 | 0.00 | 1.15 |
| DIRECT & INDIRECT INV IN RE | 0.00 | 0.01 | 81 | 0.00 | 0.00 | 85 | 0.00 | 0.00 | 84 | 0.00 | 0.01 | 0.00 | 0.00 |
| LOANS HELD FOR SALE | 3.87 | 1.32 | 85 | 4.27 | 2.11 | 80 | 6.73 | 2.27 | 85 | 4.81 | 2.04 | 8.19 | 1.40 |

CERT # 6384
CHARTER # 1316

**PNC BANK, NATIONAL ASSOCIATION**
**ANALYSIS OF CREDIT ALLOWANCE AND LOAN MIX**

PITTSBURGH, PA

PAGE 07

| CHANGE: CREDIT ALLOWANCE ($000) | 12/31/2004 | 12/31/2003 | 12/31/2002 | 12/31/2001 | 12/31/2000 |
|---|---|---|---|---|---|
| BEGINNING BALANCE | 606,886 | 644,475 | 602,790 | 648,833 | 643,905 |
| GROSS CREDIT LOSSES | 161,537 | 255,377 | 249,396 | 980,672 | 181,385 |
| MEMO: LOANS HFS WRITEDOWN | 8,558 | 26,060 | 22,857 | 661,594 | N/A |
| RECOVERIES | 49,849 | 47,453 | 42,639 | 35,886 | 48,917 |
| NET CREDIT LOSSES | 111,688 | 207,924 | 206,757 | 944,786 | 132,468 |
| PROVISION FOR CREDIT LOSS | 51,553 | 176,612 | 290,050 | 898,743 | 133,000 |
| OTHER ADJUSTMENTS | 37,164 | -6,277 | -41,608 | 0 | 4,396 |
| ENDING BALANCE | 583,915 | 606,886 | 644,475 | 602,790 | 648,833 |
| AVERAGE TOTAL LOANS & LEASES | 39,960,849 | 35,193,158 | 38,562,898 | 44,804,389 | 51,542,871 |

| | 12/31/2004 | | | 12/31/2003 | | | 12/31/2002 | | | 12/31/2001 | | 12/31/2000 | |
|---|---|---|---|---|---|---|---|---|---|---|---|---|---|
| **ANALYSIS RATIOS** | BANK | PG 1 | PCT | BANK | PG 1 | PCT | BANK | PG 1 | PCT | BANK | PG 1 | BANK | PG 1 |
| LOSS PROVISION TO AVERAGE ASSETS | 0.07 | 0.14 | 34 | 0.29 | 0.27 | 64 | 0.49 | 0.38 | 73 | 1.42 | 0.40 | 0.20 | 0.33 |
| RECOVERIES TO PRIOR CREDIT LOSS | 19.52 | 23.76 | 38 | 19.03 | 22.26 | 50 | 4.35 | 23.80 | 6 | 19.78 | 31.22 | 23.51 | 32.01 |
| NET LOSS TO AVERAGE TOTAL LN&LS | 0.28 | 0.25 | 60 | 0.59 | 0.41 | 71 | 0.54 | 0.56 | 62 | 2.11 | 0.56 | 0.26 | 0.39 |
| GROSS LOSS TO AVERAGE TOT LN&LS | 0.40 | 0.36 | 61 | 0.73 | 0.53 | 72 | 0.65 | 0.69 | 59 | 2.19 | 0.69 | 0.35 | 0.52 |
| RECOVERIES TO AVERAGE TOT LN&LS | 0.12 | 0.11 | 61 | 0.13 | 0.12 | 60 | 0.11 | 0.12 | 56 | 0.08 | 0.11 | 0.09 | 0.12 |
| LN&LS ALLOWANCE TO TOTAL LN&LS | 1.35 | 1.27 | 61 | 1.78 | 1.44 | 75 | 1.80 | 1.52 | 77 | 1.49 | 1.54 | 1.30 | 1.49 |
| LN&LS ALLOWANCE TO NET LOSSES (X) | 5.23 | 7.51 | 51 | 2.92 | 4.18 | 41 | 3.12 | 3.60 | 47 | 0.64 | 3.66 | 4.90 | 5.14 |
| LN&LS ALL TO NONACCURAL LN&LS (X) | 4.12 | 3.73 | | 2.24 | 2.73 | | 1.86 | 2.35 | | 2.37 | 2.40 | 1.83 | 2.93 |
| EARN COVER OF NET LN&LS LOSS (X) | 11.61 | 19.94 | 50 | 7.44 | 10.92 | 45 | 8.89 | 9.33 | 56 | 1.62 | 8.81 | 12.32 | 12.65 |
| **NET LOSSES BY TYPE OF LN&LS** | | | | | | | | | | | | | |
| REAL ESTATE LOANS | 0.12 | 0.07 | 74 | 0.11 | 0.11 | 64 | 0.12 | 0.11 | 59 | 0.28 | 0.14 | 0.04 | 0.08 |
| LOANS TO FINANCE COMML REAL EST | -0.01 | 0.00 | 2 | 0.00 | 0.01 | 91 | 0.00 | 0.00 | 92 | 0.00 | 0.01 | -0.01 | 0.00 |
| CONTRUCTION & LAND DEV | 0.01 | 0.03 | 71 | -0.01 | 0.06 | 9 | 0.15 | 0.09 | 77 | -0.01 | 0.07 | 0.08 | 0.03 |
| SECURED BY FARMLAND | 0.00 | 0.01 | 84 | -0.04 | 0.02 | 7 | -0.55 | 0.03 | 2 | 0.00 | 0.09 | 0.26 | 0.00 |
| SINGLE & MULTI FAMILY MORTGAGE | 0.12 | 0.06 | 75 | 0.12 | 0.10 | 67 | 0.11 | 0.09 | 70 | 0.10 | 0.11 | 0.06 | 0.09 |
| HOME EQUITY LOANS | 0.11 | 0.05 | 77 | 0.11 | 0.07 | 72 | 0.11 | 0.08 | 68 | 0.07 | 0.13 | 0.05 | 0.09 |
| 1-4 FAMILY NONREVOLVING | 0.12 | 0.07 | 73 | 0.12 | 0.12 | 68 | 0.12 | 0.08 | 70 | 0.11 | 0.10 | 0.06 | 0.09 |
| MULTIFAMILY LOANS | 0.13 | 0.01 | 91 | 0.03 | 0.00 | 89 | 0.02 | 0.02 | 87 | -0.01 | 0.01 | -0.01 | 0.01 |
| NON-FARM NON-RESIDENTIAL MTG | 0.15 | 0.06 | 81 | 0.12 | 0.08 | 73 | 0.10 | 0.10 | 64 | 1.49 | 0.11 | -0.06 | 0.03 |
| RE LOANS IN FOREIGN OFFICES | N/A | 0.00 | 95 | N/A | 0.00 | 95 | N/A | 0.00 | 95 | N/A | 0.00 | N/A | 0.00 |
| AGRICULTURAL LOANS | 0.00 | 0.07 | 75 | 0.00 | 0.11 | 74 | 0.49 | 0.20 | 83 | 2.72 | 0.15 | 0.16 | 0.10 |
| COMMERCIAL AND INDUSTRIAL LOANS | 0.54 | 0.41 | 67 | 1.11 | 0.78 | 72 | 1.11 | 1.08 | 59 | 5.14 | 0.99 | 0.54 | 0.55 |
| LEASE FINANCING | -0.02 | 0.27 | 9 | 1.32 | 0.43 | 84 | 0.57 | 0.54 | 62 | 0.32 | 0.54 | 0.22 | 0.19 |
| LOANS TO INDIVIDUALS | 0.31 | 0.98 | 28 | 0.34 | 1.14 | 23 | 0.35 | 1.15 | 21 | 0.45 | 1.17 | 0.36 | 1.05 |
| CREDIT CARD PLANS | -0.02 | 1.40 | 5 | 0.00 | 1.54 | 57 | 0.00 | 1.44 | 62 | 0.00 | 1.79 | 3.02 | 2.93 |
| ALL OTHER LOANS & LEASES | 0.47 | 0.12 | 89 | 0.35 | 0.18 | 81 | 0.25 | 0.19 | 76 | 1.29 | 0.23 | 0.19 | 0.20 |
| LOANS TO FOREIGN GOVERNMENTS | N/A | 0.00 | 98 | N/A | 0.00 | 96 | N/A | 0.00 | 97 | N/A | 0.00 | N/A | 0.00 |

CERT # 6384
CHARTER # 1316

PNC BANK, NATIONAL ASSOCIATION
ANALYSIS OF LOAN AND LEASE ALLOWANCE AND LOAN MIX

PITTSBURGH, PA

PAGE 07A

| | 12/31/2004 | | | 12/31/2003 | | | 12/31/2002 | | | 12/31/2001 | | 12/31/2000 | |
|---|---|---|---|---|---|---|---|---|---|---|---|---|---|
| | BANK | PG 1 | PCT | BANK | PG 1 | PCT | BANK | PG 1 | PCT | BANK | PG 1 | BANK | PG 1 |
| LOAN MIX, % AVERAGE GROSS LN&LS | | | | | | | | | | | | | |
| CONTRUCTION & DEVELOPMENT | 2.08 | 6.36 | 27 | 2.45 | 5.55 | 32 | 3.08 | 5.50 | 36 | 2.74 | 5.37 | 2.31 | 4.46 |
| 1-4 FAMILY RESIDENTIAL | 37.89 | 27.10 | 72 | 33.83 | 25.83 | 67 | 31.45 | 25.92 | 68 | 33.57 | 25.63 | 38.70 | 24.20 |
| HOME EQUITY LOANS | 11.31 | 5.38 | 82 | 9.57 | 4.58 | 82 | 7.60 | 3.96 | 82 | 4.93 | 3.38 | 3.61 | 2.98 |
| OTHER REAL ESTATE LOANS | 7.50 | 19.87 | 20 | 7.60 | 17.67 | 22 | 7.28 | 16.91 | 20 | 6.60 | 16.01 | 6.32 | 15.68 |
| FARMLAND | 0.02 | 0.35 | 39 | 0.04 | 0.38 | 43 | 0.05 | 0.38 | 43 | 0.05 | 0.38 | 0.06 | 0.32 |
| MULTIFAMILY | 0.86 | 1.95 | 38 | 0.92 | 1.68 | 41 | 0.94 | 1.45 | 44 | 0.90 | 1.36 | 0.89 | 1.30 |
| NON-FARM NON-RESIDENTIAL | 6.63 | 16.86 | 22 | 6.64 | 15.18 | 23 | 6.28 | 14.64 | 19 | 5.64 | 13.67 | 5.36 | 12.78 |
| TOTAL REAL ESTATE | 47.47 | 59.22 | 27 | 43.88 | 55.79 | 26 | 41.80 | 52.95 | 28 | 42.90 | 50.71 | 47.33 | 47.08 |
| FINANCIAL INSTITUTION LOANS | 0.13 | 0.29 | 74 | 0.67 | 0.75 | 76 | 0.74 | 0.77 | 75 | 0.18 | 0.69 | 0.25 | 0.42 |
| AGRICULTURAL LOANS | 0.00 | 0.30 | 37 | 0.00 | 0.39 | 34 | 0.00 | 0.47 | 30 | 0.00 | 0.51 | 0.01 | 0.48 |
| COMMERCIAL & INDUSTRIAL LOANS | 32.73 | 19.24 | 82 | 33.85 | 19.55 | 84 | 34.99 | 21.17 | 82 | 36.25 | 22.83 | 35.17 | 25.04 |
| LOANS TO INDIVIDUALS | 8.15 | 8.37 | 52 | 7.46 | 10.04 | 46 | 7.76 | 10.72 | 44 | 7.58 | 11.12 | 6.99 | 12.31 |
| CREDIT CARD LOANS | 0.47 | 0.52 | 74 | 0.00 | 0.51 | 52 | 0.00 | 0.41 | 49 | 0.06 | 0.66 | 0.24 | 1.15 |
| MUNICIPAL LOANS | 1.14 | 0.41 | 84 | 1.17 | 0.43 | 82 | 1.25 | 0.50 | 83 | 1.20 | 0.52 | 1.06 | 0.50 |
| ACCEPTANCES OF OTHER BANKS | N/A | 0.00 | 99 | N/A | 0.00 | 99 | N/A | 0.00 | 99 | 0.00 | 0.00 | 0.00 | 0.00 |
| FOREIGN OFFICE LOANS & LEASES | 3.05 | 0.58 | 87 | 3.15 | 0.73 | 84 | 2.35 | 0.73 | 85 | 1.07 | 0.83 | 0.36 | 0.96 |
| ALL OTHER LOANS | 3.55 | 1.43 | 87 | 3.69 | 1.53 | 86 | 3.69 | 1.65 | 83 | 3.45 | 1.75 | 3.46 | 2.09 |
| LEASE FINANCING RECEIVABLES | 3.78 | 1.72 | 81 | 6.13 | 2.00 | 84 | 7.41 | 2.23 | 85 | 7.36 | 2.43 | 5.38 | 2.78 |
| SUPPLEMENTAL: | | | | | | | | | | | | | |
| LOANS TO FOREIGN GOVERNMENTS | 0.00 | 0.01 | 85 | 0.00 | 0.01 | 82 | 0.00 | 0.01 | 82 | 0.00 | 0.02 | 0.00 | 0.03 |
| LOANS TO FINANCE COMML REAL EST | 3.24 | 0.36 | 96 | 3.23 | 0.44 | 95 | 3.05 | 0.62 | 92 | 2.87 | 0.69 | 2.88 | 0.62 |
| MEMORANDUM (% OF AVG TOT LOANS): | | | | | | | | | | | | | |
| LOAN & LEASE COMMITMENTS | 72.18 | 47.58 | 81 | 75.59 | 44.01 | 85 | 80.86 | 41.24 | 88 | 82.32 | 42.11 | 68.34 | 46.47 |
| OFFICER, SHAREHOLDER LOANS | 0.06 | 0.56 | 29 | 0.04 | 0.58 | 30 | 0.05 | 0.59 | 32 | 0.06 | 0.60 | 0.04 | 0.65 |
| OFFICER, SHAREH LOANS TO ASSETS | 0.03 | 0.33 | 29 | 0.02 | 0.33 | 32 | 0.03 | 0.34 | 35 | 0.03 | 0.36 | 0.03 | 0.39 |
| OTHER REAL ESTATE OWNED % ASSETS | | | | | | | | | | | | | |
| CONSTRUCTION & LAND DEVELOPMENT | 0.00 | 0.00 | 77 | 0.00 | 0.00 | 76 | 0.00 | 0.00 | 79 | 0.00 | 0.00 | 0.00 | 0.00 |
| FARMLAND | 0.00 | 0.00 | 97 | 0.00 | 0.00 | 96 | 0.00 | 0.00 | 95 | 0.00 | 0.00 | 0.00 | 0.00 |
| 1-4 FAMILY | 0.01 | 0.01 | 64 | 0.01 | 0.02 | 59 | 0.01 | 0.02 | 59 | 0.01 | 0.02 | 0.02 | 0.01 |
| MULTIFAMILY | 0.00 | 0.00 | 94 | 0.00 | 0.00 | 96 | 0.00 | 0.00 | 96 | 0.00 | 0.00 | 0.00 | 0.00 |
| NON-FARM-NON-RESID | 0.01 | 0.01 | 65 | 0.01 | 0.01 | 64 | 0.01 | 0.02 | 64 | 0.01 | 0.01 | 0.01 | 0.01 |
| FOREIGN OFFICES | 0.00 | 0.00 | 97 | 0.00 | 0.00 | 96 | 0.00 | 0.00 | 97 | 0.00 | 0.01 | 0.00 | 0.00 |
| SUBTOTAL | 0.02 | 0.04 | 48 | 0.02 | 0.04 | 45 | 0.02 | 0.04 | 46 | 0.02 | 0.04 | 0.03 | 0.03 |
| DIRECT AND INDIRECT INV | 0.00 | 0.00 | 88 | 0.00 | 0.00 | 93 | 0.00 | 0.00 | 91 | 0.00 | 0.00 | 0.00 | 0.00 |
| TOTAL | 0.02 | 0.05 | 43 | 0.02 | 0.05 | 42 | 0.02 | 0.05 | 42 | 0.02 | 0.04 | 0.03 | 0.03 |
| ASSET SERVICING % ASSETS | | | | | | | | | | | | | |
| SERV W RECOURSE | 0.00 | 0.08 | 71 | 0.00 | 0.19 | 67 | 0.00 | 0.21 | 66 | 0.00 | 0.22 | N/A | 0.00 |
| MORTG SERV WO RECOURSE | 0.00 | 7.74 | 42 | 0.00 | 8.52 | 38 | 0.00 | 8.88 | 43 | 0.00 | 7.22 | N/A | 0.00 |
| OTHER FINANCIAL ASSETS | 136.69 | 0.89 | 98 | 137.39 | 0.75 | 99 | 127.07 | 0.90 | 99 | 111.86 | 1.09 | N/A | 0.00 |
| TOTAL | 136.69 | 11.66 | 95 | 137.39 | 11.73 | 96 | 127.07 | 11.99 | 96 | 111.86 | 10.89 | N/A | 0.00 |

PAGE 08

PITTSBURGH, PA

CERT # 6384
CHARTER # 1316

## PNC BANK, NATIONAL ASSOCIATION
### ANALYSIS OF PAST DUE, NONACCRUAL & RESTRUCTURED LOANS & LEASES

| | 12/31/2004 | 12/31/2003 | 12/31/2002 | 12/31/2001 | 12/31/2000 |
|---|---|---|---|---|---|
| NONCURRENT LN&LS ($000) | | | | | |
| 90 DAYS AND OVER PAST DUE | 57,979 | 72,963 | 157,622 | 169,798 | 125,264 |
| TOTAL NONACCRUAL LN&LS | 141,887 | 270,782 | 347,078 | 253,945 | 354,651 |
| TOTAL NONCURRENT LN&LS | 199,866 | 343,745 | 504,700 | 423,743 | 479,915 |
| LN&LS 30-89 DAYS PAST DUE | 94,779 | 126,455 | 251,586 | 332,103 | |
| RESTRUCTURED LN&LS 90+ DAYS P/D | 0 | 0 | 0 | 0 | 0 |
| RESTRUCTURED LN&LS NONACCRL | 0 | 424 | 1,215 | 0 | 380 |
| RESTRUCTURE LN&LS 30-89 DAYS PD | 0 | 0 | 0 | 0 | |
| CURRENT RESTRUCTURED LN&LS | 0 | 0 | 0 | 0 | 0 |
| ALL OTHER REAL ESTATE OWNED | 14,301 | 14,208 | 11,663 | 9,325 | 15,047 |

| % OF NONCURR LN&LS BY LN TYPE | 2004 BANK | 2004 PG 1 | 2004 PCT | 2003 BANK | 2003 PG 1 | 2003 PCT | 2002 BANK | 2002 PG 1 | 2002 PCT | 2001 BANK | 2001 PG 1 | 2000 BANK | 2000 PG 1 |
|---|---|---|---|---|---|---|---|---|---|---|---|---|---|
| REAL ESTATE LNS-90+ DAYS P/D | 0.15 | 0.08 | 77 | 0.31 | 0.12 | 83 | 0.52 | 0.13 | 89 | 0.47 | 0.17 | 0.25 | 0.14 |
| -NONACCRUAL | 0.29 | 0.36 | 50 | 0.36 | 0.51 | 44 | 0.23 | 0.62 | 22 | 0.14 | 0.61 | 0.11 | 0.48 |
| -TOTAL | 0.44 | 0.45 | 54 | 0.67 | 0.67 | 56 | 0.75 | 0.85 | 53 | 0.61 | 0.83 | 0.36 | 0.65 |
| -30-89 DAYS P/D | 0.30 | 0.53 | 32 | 0.40 | 0.69 | 31 | 0.61 | 0.85 | 36 | 0.67 | 1.09 | | |
| LNS FIN COML RE-90+ DAYS P/D | 0.07 | 0.00 | 95 | 0.00 | 0.00 | 91 | 0.00 | 0.01 | 87 | 0.00 | 0.02 | 0.00 | 0.00 |
| -NONACCRUAL | 0.00 | 0.02 | 84 | 0.00 | 0.08 | 81 | 0.05 | 0.17 | 77 | 0.00 | 0.11 | 0.01 | 0.10 |
| -TOTAL | 0.07 | 0.03 | 85 | 0.00 | 0.10 | 79 | 0.05 | 0.19 | 76 | 0.00 | 0.16 | 0.01 | 0.14 |
| -30-89 DAYS P/D | 0.00 | 0.10 | 80 | 0.05 | 0.16 | 75 | 0.09 | 0.31 | 74 | 0.01 | 0.26 | | |
| CONST & LAND DEV-90+ DAYS P/D | 0.04 | 0.03 | 79 | 0.00 | 0.03 | 68 | 0.18 | 0.03 | 91 | 0.35 | 0.08 | 0.02 | 0.05 |
| -NONACCRUAL | 0.42 | 0.19 | 80 | 0.05 | 0.34 | 43 | 0.14 | 0.58 | 46 | 0.15 | 0.51 | 0.12 | 0.46 |
| -TOTAL | 0.47 | 0.25 | 75 | 0.05 | 0.41 | 40 | 0.32 | 0.65 | 52 | 0.50 | 0.64 | 0.13 | 0.55 |
| -30-89 DAYS P/D | 0.01 | 0.42 | 35 | 0.01 | 0.55 | 31 | 0.46 | 0.64 | 60 | 0.35 | 0.96 | | |
| SINGLE & MULTI MTG-90+ DAYS P/D | 0.18 | 0.10 | 76 | 0.37 | 0.16 | 80 | 0.49 | 0.18 | 82 | 0.53 | 0.23 | 0.26 | 0.20 |
| -NONACCRUAL | 0.25 | 0.27 | 56 | 0.31 | 0.40 | 50 | 0.17 | 0.45 | 23 | 0.08 | 0.46 | 0.04 | 0.38 |
| -TOTAL | 0.43 | 0.40 | 58 | 0.68 | 0.63 | 62 | 0.66 | 0.70 | 58 | 0.60 | 0.75 | 0.30 | 0.63 |
| -30-89 DAYS P/D | 0.32 | 0.61 | 32 | 0.47 | 0.82 | 32 | 0.70 | 1.03 | 35 | 0.76 | 1.26 | | |
| NON-FARM/RESI MTG-90+ DAYS P/D | 0.03 | 0.03 | 69 | 0.06 | 0.04 | 74 | 0.81 | 0.05 | 98 | 0.22 | 0.07 | 0.30 | 0.06 |
| -NONACCRUAL | 0.50 | 0.48 | 57 | 0.75 | 0.57 | 64 | 0.53 | 0.62 | 47 | 0.51 | 0.64 | 0.62 | 0.50 |
| -TOTAL | 0.53 | 0.53 | 52 | 0.81 | 0.66 | 64 | 1.34 | 0.69 | 82 | 0.74 | 0.74 | 0.92 | 0.59 |
| -30-89 DAYS P/D | 0.26 | 0.31 | 52 | 0.14 | 0.40 | 31 | 0.23 | 0.46 | 28 | 0.36 | 0.72 | | |
| RE LNS FOR OFF-90+ DAYS P/D | N/A | 0.00 | 96 | N/A | 0.00 | 95 | N/A | 0.00 | 95 | N/A | 0.00 | N/A | 0.00 |
| -NONACCRUAL | N/A | 0.00 | 93 | N/A | 0.01 | 92 | N/A | 0.00 | 93 | N/A | 0.00 | N/A | 0.00 |
| -TOTAL | N/A | 0.00 | 93 | N/A | 0.02 | 92 | N/A | 0.00 | 93 | N/A | 0.00 | N/A | 0.00 |
| -30-89 DAYS P/D | N/A | 0.00 | 93 | N/A | 0.03 | 92 | N/A | 0.00 | 94 | N/A | 0.00 | | |
| COML & INDUST LNS-90+ DAYS P/D | 0.10 | 0.07 | 73 | 0.13 | 0.08 | 71 | 0.34 | 0.09 | 89 | 0.36 | 0.12 | 0.20 | 0.11 |
| -NONACCRUAL | 0.54 | 0.74 | 39 | 1.72 | 1.13 | 72 | 2.05 | 1.47 | 68 | 1.53 | 1.44 | 1.68 | 1.14 |
| -TOTAL | 0.63 | 0.83 | 36 | 1.85 | 1.25 | 71 | 2.38 | 1.59 | 70 | 1.88 | 1.62 | 1.89 | 1.32 |
| -30-89 DAYS P/D | 0.10 | 0.51 | 18 | 0.33 | 0.64 | 34 | 0.91 | 0.80 | 61 | 0.99 | 1.00 | | |
| LOANS TO INDIVDLS-90+ DAYS P/D | 0.36 | 0.13 | 83 | 0.36 | 0.16 | 78 | 0.75 | 0.21 | 91 | 0.78 | 0.24 | 0.66 | 0.34 |
| -NONACCRUAL | 0.01 | 0.15 | 31 | 0.09 | 0.18 | 57 | 0.14 | 0.20 | 61 | 0.08 | 0.22 | 0.03 | 0.17 |
| -TOTAL | 0.37 | 0.33 | 66 | 0.45 | 0.39 | 65 | 0.89 | 0.47 | 81 | 0.86 | 0.52 | 0.69 | 0.59 |
| -30-89 DAYS P/D | 0.56 | 1.06 | 27 | 0.76 | 1.31 | 23 | 1.15 | 1.55 | 34 | 1.45 | 1.94 | | |

CERT # 6384
CHARTER # 1316

PNC BANK, NATIONAL ASSOCIATION
ANALYSIS OF PAST DUE, NONACCRUAL & RESTRUCTURED LOANS & LEASES

PITTSBURGH, PA

PAGE 08A

| % OF NONCURR LN&LS BY LN TYPE | 12/31/2004 BANK | PG 1 | PCT | 12/31/2003 BANK | PG 1 | PCT | 12/31/2002 BANK | PG 1 | PCT | 12/31/2001 BANK | PG 1 | 12/31/2000 BANK | PG 1 |
|---|---|---|---|---|---|---|---|---|---|---|---|---|---|
| CREDIT CARD PLANS-90+ DAYS P/D | 0.00 | 0.30 | 63 | 0.00 | 0.36 | 64 | 0.00 | 0.37 | 64 | 0.00 | 0.42 | 0.34 | 0.49 |
| -NONACCRUAL | 0.00 | 0.03 | 87 | 0.00 | 0.04 | 84 | 0.00 | 0.01 | 89 | 0.00 | 0.03 | 0.00 | 0.05 |
| -TOTAL | 0.00 | 0.39 | 59 | 0.00 | 0.51 | 59 | 0.00 | 0.46 | 62 | 0.00 | 0.58 | 0.34 | 0.59 |
| -30-89 DAYS P/D | 0.02 | 0.75 | 57 | 0.00 | 0.75 | 59 | 0.00 | 0.69 | 61 | 0.00 | 0.91 | | |
| FOREIGN GOVT LNS-90+ DAYS P/D | N/A | 0.00 | 98 | N/A | 0.00 | 99 | N/A | 0.00 | 97 | N/A | 0.00 | N/A | 0.00 |
| -NONACCRUAL | N/A | 0.00 | 97 | N/A | 0.00 | 96 | N/A | 0.00 | 95 | N/A | 0.00 | N/A | 0.00 |
| -TOTAL | N/A | 0.00 | 96 | N/A | 0.00 | 96 | N/A | 0.01 | 93 | N/A | 0.00 | N/A | 0.00 |
| -30-89 DAYS P/D | N/A | 0.00 | 96 | N/A | 0.00 | 96 | N/A | 0.00 | 95 | N/A | 0.00 | | |
| LEASE FINANCING-90+ DAYS P/D | 0.00 | 0.02 | 76 | 0.02 | 0.03 | 78 | 0.03 | 0.03 | 74 | 0.03 | 0.04 | 0.03 | 0.04 |
| -NONACCRUAL | 0.12 | 0.20 | 70 | 0.35 | 0.30 | 72 | 1.51 | 0.41 | 85 | 0.24 | 0.39 | 0.04 | 0.27 |
| -TOTAL | 0.00 | 0.28 | 63 | 0.00 | 0.37 | 68 | 1.00 | 0.49 | 82 | 0.00 | 0.50 | 0.00 | 0.38 |
| -30-89 DAYS P/D | 0.01 | 0.35 | 56 | 0.22 | 0.44 | 59 | 0.41 | 0.60 | 63 | 0.48 | 0.54 | | |
| AGRICULTURAL LNS-90+ DAYS P/D | 0.00 | 0.00 | 87 | 0.00 | 0.01 | 82 | 0.00 | 0.01 | 82 | 0.00 | 0.03 | 0.00 | 0.05 |
| -NONACCRUAL | 0.00 | 0.26 | 65 | 0.00 | 0.53 | 57 | 0.00 | 0.75 | 50 | 2.37 | 0.80 | 0.00 | 0.60 |
| -TOTAL | 0.00 | 0.29 | 61 | 0.00 | 0.57 | 56 | 0.00 | 0.82 | 48 | 2.37 | 0.87 | 0.00 | 0.74 |
| -30-89 DAYS P/D | 0.00 | 0.13 | 65 | 0.00 | 0.29 | 60 | 0.00 | 0.43 | 54 | 1.82 | 0.56 | | |
| OTHER LN&LS-90+ DAYS P/D | 0.06 | 0.02 | 85 | 0.07 | 0.02 | 85 | 0.79 | 0.03 | 97 | 0.58 | 0.07 | 0.12 | 0.07 |
| -NONACCRUAL | 0.07 | 0.10 | 70 | 0.24 | 0.16 | 76 | 0.18 | 0.25 | 65 | 0.24 | 0.22 | 0.57 | 0.28 |
| -TOTAL | 0.12 | 0.18 | 64 | 0.31 | 0.21 | 73 | 0.97 | 0.36 | 84 | 0.81 | 0.38 | 0.69 | 0.38 |
| -30-89 DAYS P/D | 0.04 | 0.28 | 46 | 0.04 | 0.32 | 41 | 0.06 | 0.35 | 45 | 0.55 | 0.56 | | |
| GROSS LN&LS-90+ DAYS P/D | 0.13 | 0.10 | 67 | 0.21 | 0.13 | 71 | 0.44 | 0.16 | 86 | 0.42 | 0.20 | 0.25 | 0.18 |
| -NONACCRUAL | 0.33 | 0.46 | 40 | 0.79 | 0.66 | 64 | 0.97 | 0.83 | 65 | 0.63 | 0.84 | 0.71 | 0.67 |
| -TOTAL | 0.46 | 0.59 | 40 | 1.00 | 0.83 | 64 | 1.41 | 1.06 | 73 | 1.05 | 1.12 | 0.96 | 0.89 |
| -30-89 DAYS P/D | 0.22 | 0.64 | 16 | 0.37 | 0.81 | 21 | 0.70 | 1.02 | 33 | 0.82 | 1.27 | | |
| OTHER PERTINENT RATIOS: | | | | | | | | | | | | | |
| NONCUR LN&LS TO-LN&LS ALLOWANCE | 34.23 | 48.60 | 34 | 56.64 | 59.80 | 53 | 78.31 | 70.12 | 66 | 70.30 | 70.77 | | |
| -EQUITY CAPITAL | 3.28 | 3.93 | 44 | 6.11 | 5.89 | 60 | 8.61 | 7.43 | 65 | 8.67 | 8.19 | | |
| %TOTAL P/D LN&LS-INCL NONACCRUAL | 0.68 | 1.29 | 21 | 1.37 | 1.71 | 38 | 2.11 | 2.12 | 55 | 1.87 | 2.45 | | |
| IENC-LOANS TO TOTAL LOANS | N/A | 0.00 | 99 | N/A | 0.00 | 99 | N/A | 0.00 | 99 | N/A | 0.00 | | |
| NONCURR LNS+OREO TO LNS+OREO | 0.49 | 0.65 | 38 | 1.05 | 0.91 | 63 | 1.44 | 1.15 | 70 | 1.07 | 1.20 | 0.80 | 0.75 |
| NONCURR RESTRUCT DEBT/GR LN&LS | 0.00 | 0.00 | 82 | 0.00 | 0.00 | 82 | 0.00 | 0.00 | 85 | 0.00 | 0.00 | | |
| CURR+NONCURR RESTRUCT/GR LN&LS | 0.00 | 0.00 | 82 | 0.00 | 0.00 | 82 | 0.00 | 0.00 | 85 | 0.00 | 0.00 | | |
| CURRENT RESTRUCT LN&LS | 0.00 | 0.01 | 77 | 0.01 | 0.01 | 76 | 0.00 | 0.01 | 78 | 0.00 | 0.01 | | |

CERT # 6384
CHARTER # 1316

PNC BANK, NATIONAL ASSOCIATION
INTEREST RATE RISK ANALYSIS AS A PERCENT OF ASSETS

PITTSBURGH, PA

PAGE 09

| | 12/31/2004 BANK | PG 1 | PCT | 12/31/2003 BANK | PG 1 | PCT | 12/31/2002 BANK | PG 1 | PCT | 12/31/2001 BANK | PG 1 | 12/31/2000 BANK | PG 1 |
|---|---|---|---|---|---|---|---|---|---|---|---|---|---|
| LONG ASSETS INSTS W/ OPTIONS | | | | | | | | | | | | | |
| MORTGAGE LOANS & PASS THRUS | 17.68 | 19.25 | 48 | 11.56 | 19.98 | 31 | 16.77 | 18.58 | 46 | 20.17 | 18.25 | 25.14 | 17.13 |
| LOANS & SECURITIES OVER 15 YRS | 2.44 | 4.31 | 50 | 1.18 | 5.29 | 23 | 1.25 | 5.89 | 27 | 2.23 | 6.6 | 2.49 | 5.61 |
| LOANS & SECURITIES 5-15 YRS | 3.90 | 5.66 | 46 | 3.34 | 6.32 | 37 | 5.42 | 4.50 | 66 | 6.81 | 4.19 | 12.66 | 4.07 |
| OTHER LOANS AND SECURITIES | 56.47 | 57.33 | 43 | 55.09 | 56.33 | 39 | 55.21 | 56.69 | 37 | 57.46 | 57.82 | 57.00 | 60.41 |
| LOANS & SECURITIES OVER 15 YRS | 6.42 | 1.80 | 91 | 6.81 | 1.81 | 92 | 3.63 | 1.55 | 85 | 2.27 | 1.73 | 1.79 | 1.65 |
| LOANS & SECURITIES 5-15 YRS | 8.59 | 6.02 | 74 | 8.12 | 6.51 | 74 | 8.02 | 6.05 | 73 | 8.51 | 6.93 | 9.25 | 7.45 |
| TOTAL LOANS & SECURITIES OVR 15 | 8.87 | 6.59 | 70 | 7.99 | 7.64 | 62 | 4.88 | 7.97 | 41 | 4.50 | 8.73 | 4.27 | 7.46 |
| CMO'S TOTAL | 5.59 | 5.01 | 57 | 10.86 | 4.35 | 83 | 6.57 | 4.17 | 70 | 6.04 | 3.67 | 3.66 | 3.43 |
| AVG LIFE OVER 3 YEARS | 1.92 | 2.77 | 49 | 6.56 | 2.48 | 82 | 4.50 | 1.75 | 81 | 3.88 | 2.09 | 2.77 | 2.22 |
| STRUCTURED NOTES | 2.54 | 0.09 | 96 | 3.71 | 0.02 | 97 | 1.71 | 0.00 | 97 | 3.67 | 0.01 | 0.00 | 0.01 |
| MORTGAGE SERVICING | 0.44 | 0.09 | 89 | 0.40 | 0.09 | 89 | 0.38 | 0.08 | 87 | 0.36 | 0.10 | 0.42 | 0.10 |
| TOTAL | 2.98 | 0.28 | 94 | 4.10 | 0.21 | 96 | 2.09 | 0.12 | 95 | 4.03 | 0.15 | 0.42 | 0.15 |
| OVERALL RISK INDICATORS | | | | | | | | | | | | | |
| AVAILABLE FOR SALE | 21.21 | 19.92 | 57 | 23.19 | 21.08 | 59 | 19.55 | 19.74 | 53 | 19.65 | 18.31 | 7.80 | 16.03 |
| HELD TO MATURITY | 0.00 | 2.21 | 39 | 0.00 | 1.49 | 45 | 0.00 | 1.32 | 47 | 0.00 | 1.27 | 0.00 | 2.55 |
| OFF BALANCE SHEET | 53.92 | 38.41 | 78 | 59.16 | 35.05 | 82 | 63.28 | 33.25 | 85 | 77.74 | 36.47 | 77.89 | 37.65 |
| UNREALIZED APPN/DEPN | 0.00 | 0.01 | 75 | 0.00 | 0.01 | 71 | 0.00 | 0.03 | 62 | 0.00 | 0.01 | 0.00 | 0.00 |
| UNREAL APP/DEP % TIER ONE CAP | 0.00 | 0.09 | 66 | 0.00 | 0.20 | 60 | 0.00 | 0.41 | 53 | 0.00 | 0.18 | 0.00 | -0.04 |
| CONTRACTUAL MAT/REPRICE DATA | | | | | | | | | | | | | |
| LOANS/SECURITIES OVER 3 YEARS | 31.26 | 34.86 | 39 | 33.65 | 36.73 | 42 | 29.34 | 32.81 | 43 | 31.56 | 33.89 | 39.58 | 34.43 |
| LIABILITIES OVER 3 YEARS | 3.94 | 3.69 | 61 | 2.60 | 4.35 | 40 | 2.80 | 4.23 | 46 | 4.80 | 4.14 | 2.91 | 3.15 |
| NET 3 YEAR POSITION | 27.32 | 30.47 | 42 | 31.05 | 31.94 | 49 | 26.54 | 28.15 | 44 | 26.77 | 29.35 | 36.67 | 30.79 |
| LOANS/SECURITIES OVER 1 YEAR | 39.64 | 48.26 | 28 | 44.25 | 49.32 | 37 | 38.03 | 47.26 | 31 | 41.58 | 47.08 | 47.92 | 46.79 |
| LIABILITIES OVER 1 YEAR | 10.12 | 10.15 | 53 | 6.82 | 10.89 | 35 | 11.00 | 10.96 | 54 | 12.45 | 9.84 | 9.55 | 9.33 |
| NET OVER 1 YEAR POSITION | 29.52 | 37.04 | 34 | 37.43 | 37.97 | 48 | 27.03 | 35.29 | 28 | 29.13 | 36.51 | 38.37 | 36.59 |
| NON-MATURITY DEPOSITS | 53.66 | 44.45 | 71 | 56.69 | 43.23 | 79 | 55.63 | 43.48 | 76 | 53.53 | 41.35 | 46.91 | 38.41 |
| NON-MATURITY DEPS % LONG ASSETS | 171.62 | 148.12 | 67 | 168.46 | 137.21 | 74 | 189.59 | 164.25 | 70 | 169.60 | 149.68 | 118.51 | 132.80 |
| NET OVER 3 YEAR POSITION | -22.39 | -9.97 | 31 | -23.04 | -6.76 | 21 | 226.29 | -10.93 | 28 | -21.97 | -7.77 | -7.33 | -4.21 |
| AS % TIER 1 CAPITAL | | | | | | | | | | | | | |
| STRUCTURED NOTES | 36.85 | 1.25 | 97 | 44.79 | 0.26 | 97 | 19.78 | 0.02 | 97 | 48.87 | 0.11 | 0.00 | 0.20 |
| MORTGAGE SERVICING (FV) | 6.32 | 1.28 | 89 | 4.79 | 1.32 | 84 | 4.40 | 1.22 | 83 | 4.82 | 1.41 | 4.94 | 1.52 |
| TOTAL | 43.17 | 3.99 | 95 | 49.58 | 3.04 | 95 | 24.18 | 1.80 | 94 | 53.69 | 2.23 | 4.94 | 2.23 |

CERT # 6384
CHARTER # 1316

**PNC BANK, NATIONAL ASSOCIATION**
**LIQUIDITY AND INVESTMENT PORTFOLIO**
PITTSBURGH, PA

### Dollar Amounts

| | 12/31/2004 | 12/31/2003 | 12/31/2002 | 12/31/2001 | 12/31/2000 |
|---|---|---|---|---|---|
| SHORT-TERM INVESTMENTS | 2,229,243 | 1,692,295 | 2,670,109 | 463,423 | 414,363 |
| SHORT-TERM ASSETS | 9,724,037 | 8,787,184 | 11,005,166 | 9,304,052 | 9,320,772 |
| SHORT-TERM NONCORE FUNDING | 8,936,809 | 7,111,124 | 4,098,514 | 6,099,247 | 9,080,920 |
| NONCORE LIABILITIES | 12,895,115 | 8,961,089 | 7,113,717 | 10,946,665 | 13,508,285 |
| FED HOME LOAN BOR MAT , 1 YR | 0 | 1,000,000 | 100,178 | 251,487 | 0 |
| FED HOME LOAN BOR MAT , 1 YR | 88,508 | 115,406 | 1,156,185 | 1,795,156 | 0 |
| OTH BORROWING MAT , 1 YR | 3,046,632 | 2,264,921 | 1,136,140 | 1,522,016 | 2,496,693 |
| OTH BORROWING MAT , 1 YR | 3,624,223 | 1,765,851 | 1,819,091 | 2,660,077 | 3,793,924 |
| DEBT SECURITIES 901 DAYS P/D | 0 | 0 | 0 | 0 | 0 |
| TOTAL NON-CURRENT DEBT SEC | 0 | 0 | 0 | 0 | 0 |
| FAIR VALUE STRUCTURED NOTES | 1,870,471 | 2,308,446 | 1,091,963 | 2,282,713 | 0 |

### Ratios

| | 2004 BANK | 2004 PG 1 | 2004 PCT | 2003 BANK | 2003 PG 1 | 2003 PCT | 2002 BANK | 2002 PG 1 | 2002 PCT | 2001 BANK | 2001 PG 1 | 2000 BANK | 2000 PG 1 |
|---|---|---|---|---|---|---|---|---|---|---|---|---|---|
| **PERCENT OF TOTAL ASSETS** | | | | | | | | | | | | | |
| SHORT-TERM INVESTMENTS | 3.02 | 5.23 | 52 | 2.73 | 6.25 | 50 | 4.48 | 6.80 | 52 | 0.74 | 6.66 | 0.66 | 6.42 |
| MARKETABLE EQUITY SEC (MES) | 0.14 | 0.13 | 69 | 0.44 | 0.11 | 89 | 0.56 | 0.14 | 88 | 0.27 | 0.19 | 0.06 | 0.14 |
| CORE DEPOSITS | 63.23 | 54.19 | 68 | 66.75 | 53.75 | 75 | 68.00 | 55.49 | 74 | 66.70 | 54.90 | 63.61 | 53.80 |
| S T NONCORE FUNDING | 12.11 | 23.42 | 18 | 11.47 | 23.24 | 18 | 6.87 | 22.36 | 3 | 9.74 | 24.00 | 14.37 | 26.19 |
| **LIQUIDITY RATIOS** | | | | | | | | | | | | | |
| NET S T NONCORE FUND DEPENDENCE | 11.49 | 20.74 | 26 | 11.37 | 19.74 | 26 | 3.05 | 18.12 | 15 | 10.81 | 20.54 | 15.98 | 23.90 |
| NET NONCORE FUND DEPENDENCE | 18.27 | 32.55 | 25 | 15.25 | 33.01 | 18 | 9.49 | 30.57 | 14 | 20.10 | 31.86 | 24.15 | 34.13 |
| BROKERED DEPOSITS TO DEPOSITS | 4.33 | 4.78 | 63 | 3.37 | 4.04 | 67 | 3.04 | 3.37 | 68 | 2.53 | 3.01 | 1.28 | 3.04 |
| BROKER DEP MAT , 1YR TO BKR DEPS | 79.99 | 30.44 | 74 | 82.75 | 23.86 | 76 | 79.98 | 23.74 | 72 | 75.72 | 23.98 | 23.22 | 26.56 |
| SHORT TRM INV TO S T NCORE FUND | 24.94 | 27.31 | 64 | 23.80 | 31.19 | 65 | 65.15 | 36.36 | 81 | 7.60 | 31.52 | 4.56 | 27.78 |
| SHORT TERM ASSET TO S T LIABS | 79.16 | 84.55 | 57 | 80.23 | 86.18 | 56 | 138.34 | 85.20 | 85 | 81.85 | 78.07 | 51.86 | 69.20 |
| NET S T LIAB TO ASSETS | 3.47 | 7.44 | 40 | 3.49 | 6.97 | 37 | 25.11 | 6.47 | 22 | 3.30 | 9.80 | 13.70 | 13.32 |
| NET LOANS & LEASES TO DEPOSITS | 81.00 | 88.28 | 36 | 73.73 | 87.72 | 28 | 79.71 | 85.95 | 37 | 85.91 | 88.91 | 107.19 | 90.79 |
| NET LN&LS TO CORE DEPOSITS | 91.76 | 116.10 | 28 | 81.11 | 115.16 | 17 | 86.65 | 111.58 | 26 | 95.43 | 114.98 | 122.68 | 124.76 |
| NET LN&LS & SBLC TO ASSETS | 65.01 | 62.79 | 44 | 62.33 | 61.43 | 46 | 66.55 | 61.96 | 56 | 70.23 | 63.58 | 84.46 | 65.93 |
| **SECURITIES MIX** | | | | | | | | | | | | | |
| **HELD-TO-MATURITY % TOTAL SECS** | | | | | | | | | | | | | |
| US TREAS & GOVT AGENCIES | 0.00 | 1.24 | 79 | 0.00 | 0.91 | 81 | 0.00 | 0.87 | 82 | 0.00 | 0.55 | 0.00 | 2.19 |
| MUNICIPAL SECURITIES | 0.00 | 1.17 | 56 | 0.00 | 0.74 | 59 | 0.00 | 0.89 | 60 | 0.00 | 0.81 | 0.00 | 1.21 |
| PASS-THROUGH MTG BACKED SECS | 0.00 | 1.07 | 63 | 0.00 | 0.53 | 68 | 0.00 | 0.30 | 69 | 0.00 | 0.42 | 0.00 | 1.28 |
| CMO & REMIC MTG BACKED SECS | 0.00 | 0.53 | 84 | 0.00 | 0.23 | 86 | 0.00 | 0.13 | 86 | 0.00 | 0.21 | 0.00 | 0.55 |
| ASSET BACKED SECURITIES | 0.00 | 0.00 | 95 | 0.01 | 0.00 | 95 | 0.00 | 0.00 | 94 | 0.00 | 0.00 | N/A | 0.00 |
| OTHER DOMESTIC DEBT SECS | 0.00 | 0.48 | 77 | 0.00 | 0.16 | 78 | 0.00 | 0.21 | 75 | 0.00 | 0.53 | 0.00 | 1.00 |
| FOREIGN DEBT SECURITIES | 0.00 | 0.01 | 84 | 0.00 | 0.00 | 83 | 0.00 | 0.00 | 82 | 0.00 | 0.00 | 0.00 | 0.01 |
| TOTAL HELD-TO-MATURITY | 0.00 | 8.01 | 38 | 0.01 | 5.50 | 45 | 0.00 | 5.12 | 47 | 0.00 | 5.44 | 0.00 | 10.20 |
| **AVAILABLE-FOR-SALE % TOTAL SECS** | | | | | | | | | | | | | |
| US TREASURY & GOVT AGENCIES | 27.52 | 18.04 | 70 | 23.19 | 17.03 | 68 | 5.20 | 17.29 | 33 | 5.48 | 17.15 | 3.85 | 19.17 |
| MUNICIPAL SECURITIES | 0.84 | 3.30 | 51 | 0.05 | 4.11 | 24 | 0.12 | 3.93 | 24 | 0.15 | 4.47 | 0.92 | 3.78 |
| PASS-THROUGH MTG BACKED SECS | 6.41 | 25.79 | 22 | 2.71 | 29.20 | 15 | 14.05 | 27.74 | 40 | 20.36 | 28.13 | 26.19 | 23.32 |
| CMO & REMIC MTG BACKED SECS | 7.33 | 12.51 | 49 | 12.84 | 11.44 | 60 | 5.83 | 12.98 | 45 | 2.22 | 12.45 | 8.24 | 10.11 |
| ASSET BACKED SECURITIES | 11.33 | 1.13 | 94 | 17.00 | 1.29 | 93 | 20.98 | 1.72 | 94 | 20.33 | 2.07 | N/A | 0.00 |
| OTHER DOMESTIC DEBT SECS | 45.89 | 8.05 | 95 | 42.28 | 7.10 | 95 | 50.86 | 6.88 | 97 | 49.90 | 6.64 | 51.88 | 8.48 |
| FOREIGN DEBT SECURITIES | 0.00 | 0.26 | 64 | 0.00 | 0.26 | 62 | 0.10 | 0.23 | 81 | 0.21 | 0.34 | 0.56 | 0.53 |
| INV MUT FND & OTH MKTBL | 0.67 | 0.70 | 68 | 1.90 | 0.59 | 85 | 2.85 | 0.91 | 84 | 1.35 | 1.32 | 0.73 | 0.89 |
| OTHER EQUITY SECURITIES | N/A | 0.00 | 99 | N/A | 0.00 | 99 | N/A | 0.00 | 99 | N/A | 0.00 | 7.65 | 3.02 |
| TOTAL AVAILABLE-FOR-SALE | 100.00 | 84.59 | 99 | 99.99 | 87.27 | 59 | 100.00 | 87.79 | 99 | 100.00 | 85.85 | 100.00 | 81.10 |
| **OTHER SECURITIES RATIOS:** | | | | | | | | | | | | | |
| APP (DEP) HI RISK & STRUC/T1CAP | -0.09 | -0.04 | 5 | 0.16 | -0.03 | 98 | 0.00 | 0.00 | 98 | -0.34 | 0.00 | 0.00 | -0.02 |
| APP (DEP) IN HTM SEC TO HTM SEC | N/A | 0.62 | 60 | 0.00 | 1.01 | 57 | N/A | 1.28 | 53 | N/A | 0.53 | N/A | 0.13 |
| APP (DEP) IN HTM SEC TO EQY CAP | 0.00 | 0.08 | 67 | 0.00 | 0.18 | 61 | 0.00 | 0.36 | 53 | 0.00 | 0.16 | 0.00 | 20.04 |
| PLEDGED SECURITIES TO TOT SEC | 51.76 | 54.78 | 38 | 46.50 | 49.08 | 42 | 71.85 | 51.03 | 70 | 45.01 | 49.63 | 74.50 | 53.39 |

CERT # 6384
CHARTER # 1316

PNC BANK, NATIONAL ASSOCIATION
CAPITAL ANALYSIS

PITTSBURGH, PA

PAGE 11

| | 12/31/2004 | | | 12/31/2003 | | | 12/31/2002 | | | 12/31/2001 | | 12/31/2000 | |
|---|---|---|---|---|---|---|---|---|---|---|---|---|---|
| | BANK | PG 1 | PCT | BANK | PG 1 | PCT | BANK | PG 1 | PCT | BANK | PG 1 | BANK | PG 1 |
| **END OF PERIOD CAPITAL ($000)** | | | | | | | | | | | | | |
| PERPETUAL PREFERRED | 0 | | | 0 | | | 0 | | | 0 | | 0 | |
| + COMMON STOCK | 218,918 | | | 218,919 | | | 218,919 | | | 218,918 | | 218,919 | |
| + SURPLUS | 1,569,359 | | | 1,168,354 | | | 1,373,195 | | | 1,344,558 | | 1,255,760 | |
| + UNDIVIDED PROFITS | 4,355,113 | | | 4,179,193 | | | 3,958,844 | | | 3,298,500 | | 3,845,935 | |
| + ACCUM OTHER COMP INCOME | -47,729 | | | 56,055 | | | 311,591 | | | 25,685 | | -69,498 | |
| + OTHER EQUITY CAPITAL COMP | 0 | | | 0 | | | 0 | | | 0 | | 0 | |
| TOTAL EQUITY CAPITAL | 6,095,661 | | | 5,622,521 | | | 5,862,549 | | | 4,887,661 | | 5,251,116 | |
| SUBORD NOTES & DEBENTURES | 1,895,482 | | | 1,340,133 | | | 1,153,771 | | | 1,153,235 | | 1,152,698 | |
| **CHANGES IN TOTAL EQUITY ($000)** | | | | | | | | | | | | | |
| BALANCE AT BEGINNING OF PERIOD | 5,622,521 | | | 5,862,549 | | | 4,887,661 | | | 5,251,116 | | 5,541,015 | |
| + NET INCOME | 913,426 | | | 970,278 | | | 1,061,504 | | | 491,731 | | 1,007,226 | |
| + SALE OR PURCHASE OF CAPITAL | 0 | | | 0 | | | 1,933 | | | 18,960 | | 8,801 | |
| + MERGER & ABSORPTIONS | 754,217 | | | 0 | | | 0 | | | 70,284 | | 142,053 | |
| + RESTATE DUE TO ACCTG ERROR&CHG | 0 | | | 0 | | | 0 | | | 0 | | 0 | |
| – TRANS WITH PARENT | -290,719 | | | -204,770 | | | 25,545 | | | 5,345 | | -969,849 | |
| – DIVIDENDS | 800,000 | | | 750,000 | | | 400,000 | | | 1,050,000 | | 650,000 | |
| + OTHER COMPREHENSIVE INCOME | -103,784 | | | -255,536 | | | 285,906 | | | 100,225 | | 171,870 | |
| BALANCE AT END OF PERIOD | 6,095,661 | | | 5,622,521 | | | 5,862,549 | | | 4,887,661 | | 5,251,116 | |
| **INTANGIBLE ASSETS** | | | | | | | | | | | | | |
| MORTGAGE SERVICING RIGHTS | 242,457 | | | 208,957 | | | 200,658 | | | 199,344 | | 155,229 | |
| + PURCH CRED CARD RELATION | 0 | | | 0 | | | 0 | | | 0 | | 0 | |
| + OTHER INTANGIBLES | 40,840 | | | 25,015 | | | 20,955 | | | 4,220 | | 18,619 | |
| + GOODWILL | 1,942,558 | | | 1,330,947 | | | 1,290,209 | | | 1,016,636 | | 1,051,192 | |
| TOTAL INTANGIBLES | 2,225,855 | | | 1,564,919 | | | 1,511,822 | | | 1,220,200 | | 1,225,040 | |
| MEMO: GRANDFATHERED INTANG | 0 | | | 0 | | | 0 | | | 0 | | 0 | |
| **CAPITAL RATIOS** | | | | | | | | | | | | | |
| **PERCENT OF TOTAL EQUITY:** | | | | | | | | | | | | | |
| NET LOANS & LEASES (X) | 7.02 | 6.44 | 60 | 5.97 | 6.71 | 30 | 6.00 | 6.84 | 30 | 8.15 | 7.29 | 9.39 | 7.81 |
| SUBORD NOTES & DEBENTURES | 31.10 | 6.96 | 91 | 23.84 | 8.04 | 81 | 19.68 | 8.56 | 75 | 23.59 | 10.22 | 21.95 | 11.33 |
| LONG-TERM DEBT | 31.10 | 6.96 | 91 | 23.84 | 8.04 | 81 | 19.68 | 8.56 | 75 | 23.59 | 10.22 | 21.95 | 11.33 |
| COM RE & RELATED VENTURES | 84.04 | 175.40 | 28 | 73.59 | 165.00 | 26 | 78.36 | 160.71 | 29 | 101.51 | 168.29 | 95.98 | 159.49 |
| **PERCENT OF AVERAGE TOTAL EQUITY:** | | | | | | | | | | | | | |
| NET INCOME | 15.26 | 14.55 | 57 | 16.56 | 14.41 | 64 | 19.48 | 14.95 | 74 | 9.37 | 14.35 | 18.94 | 14.14 |
| DIVIDENDS | 13.37 | 6.85 | 81 | 12.80 | 8.27 | 71 | 7.34 | 8.52 | 46 | 20.01 | 9.54 | 12.22 | 9.74 |
| RETAINED EARNINGS | 1.90 | 6.53 | 22 | 3.76 | 5.09 | 45 | 12.14 | 5.16 | 82 | -10.64 | 3.75 | 6.72 | 3.21 |
| **OTHER CAPITAL RATIOS:** | | | | | | | | | | | | | |
| DIVIDENDS TO NET OPER INCOME | 87.58 | 46.73 | 82 | 77.30 | 57.26 | 62 | 37.68 | 55.73 | 35 | 211.54 | 64.32 | 64.53 | 62.27 |
| EQUITY CAPITAL TO ASSETS | 8.26 | 9.74 | 40 | 9.07 | 8.95 | 61 | 9.83 | 8.79 | 76 | 7.81 | 8.48 | 8.31 | 8.03 |
| **GROWTH RATES:** | | | | | | | | | | | | | |
| TOTAL EQUITY CAPITAL | 8.42 | 20.28 | 40 | -4.09 | 10.34 | 10 | 19.95 | 14.57 | 74 | -6.92 | 21.62 | -5.23 | 26.75 |
| EQUITY GROWTH LESS ASST GROWTH | -10.59 | 4.55 | 10 | -8.09 | 0.59 | 23 | 24.70 | 2.62 | 92 | -6.01 | 4.03 | 2.10 | 4.17 |
| **INTANG ASSET'S % TOTAL EQUITY:** | | | | | | | | | | | | | |
| MORTGAGE SERVICING RIGHTS | 3.98 | 0.92 | 84 | 3.72 | 1.04 | 84 | 3.42 | 0.96 | 84 | 4.08 | 1.10 | 2.96 | 1.13 |
| GOODWILL | 31.87 | 13.50 | 81 | 23.67 | 10.19 | 82 | 22.01 | 8.95 | 83 | 20.80 | 9.32 | 20.02 | 8.69 |
| PURCH CREDIT CARD RELATION | 0.00 | 0.02 | 82 | 0.00 | 0.02 | 84 | 0.00 | 0.01 | 85 | 0.00 | 0.01 | 0.00 | 0.02 |
| ALL OTHER INTANGIBLES | 0.67 | 1.54 | 42 | 0.44 | 1.28 | 39 | 0.36 | 1.16 | 40 | 0.09 | 1.10 | 0.35 | 1.04 |
| TOTAL INTANGIBLES | 36.52 | 18.43 | 74 | 27.83 | 14.50 | 78 | 25.79 | 12.41 | 80 | 24.96 | 13.17 | 23.33 | 12.24 |

**CERT # 6384**
**CHARTER # 1316**

**PNC BANK, NATIONAL ASSOCIATION**
**CAPITAL ANALYSIS**
**PITTSBURGH, PA**
**PAGE 11A**

| RISK BASED CAPITAL ($000) | 12/31/2004 | 12/31/2003 | 12/31/2002 | 12/31/2001 | 12/31/2000 |
|---|---|---|---|---|---|
| **TIER ONE CAPITAL** | | | | | |
| TOTAL EQUITY CAPITAL ADJUSTED | 7,071,705 | 6,490,710 | 6,471,249 | 5,724,451 | 6,472,461 |
| − INELIGIBLE DEF TAX ASSETS | 0 | 0 | 0 | 0 | 0 |
| − INELIGIBLE INTANGIBLES | 1,983,398 | 1,355,962 | 1,311,164 | 1,020,856 | 1,069,811 |
| NET TIER ONE | 5,088,306 | 5,134,748 | 5,160,085 | 4,703,595 | 5,402,650 |
| **TIER TWO CAPITAL** | | | | | |
| + QUALIF DEBT AND REDEEM PFD | 1,272,000 | 917,308 | 712,771 | 873,235 | 977,698 |
| + CUMULATIVE PREFERRED STOCK | 0 | 0 | 0 | 0 | 0 |
| + ALLOWABLE LN&LS LOSS ALLOW | 658,214 | 649,616 | 662,994 | 679,876 | 648,833 |
| + UNRL GAIN MKTBL EQY SEC (45%) | 0 | 0 | 0 | 0 | 0 |
| + OTHER TIER 2 CAPITAL COMP | 77,404 | 0 | 350,000 | 350,000 | 0 |
| NET ELIGIBLE TIER TWO | 2,007,618 | 1,566,924 | 1,725,765 | 1,903,111 | 1,626,531 |
| **TOTAL RBC BEFORE DEDUCTIONS** | | | | | |
| TIER ONE & TIER TWO | 7,095,924 | 6,701,672 | 6,885,850 | 6,606,706 | 7,029,181 |
| TIER THREE & FIN SUB ADJ | −62,334 | −12,269 | −9,009 | −25,680 | 0 |
| − RECIPROCAL CAPITAL HOLDINGS | 0 | 0 | 0 | 0 | 0 |
| − DEDUCTIONS FOR TOTAL RBC | 0 | 0 | 0 | 0 | 0 |
| TOTAL RISK-BASED-CAPITAL | 7,033,591 | 6,689,403 | 6,876,841 | 6,581,026 | 7,029,181 |
| **RISK-WEIGHTED ASSETS** | | | | | |
| **ON-BALANCE SHEET** | | | | | |
| CATEGORY TWO - 20% | 4,206,612 | 3,535,137 | 3,381,595 | 3,194,204 | 1,222,745 |
| CATEGORY THREE - 50% | 4,512,269 | 3,112,875 | 3,047,353 | 4,503,881 | 8,176,952 |
| CATEGORY FOUR - 100% | 36,951,584 | 32,782,615 | 33,264,483 | 35,803,526 | 37,763,675 |
| TOTAL ON-BALANCE SHEET | 45,670,466 | 39,430,627 | 39,693,431 | 43,501,612 | 47,163,372 |
| MEMO: CATEGORY ONE - 0% | 3,761,701 | 3,504,114 | 1,347,215 | 1,073,140 | 2,634,074 |
| **OFF-BALANCE SHEET** | | | | | |
| CATEGORY TWO - 20% | 277,012 | 239,996 | 166,520 | 176,825 | 77,001 |
| CATEGORY THREE - 50% | 631,630 | 554,319 | 736,087 | 672,296 | 227,232 |
| CATEGORY FOUR - 100% | 13,287,052 | 11,676,745 | 12,415,158 | 9,943,952 | 10,365,854 |
| TOTAL OFF-BALANCE SHEET | 14,195,694 | 12,471,060 | 13,317,765 | 10,793,073 | 10,670,087 |
| MEMO: CATEGORY ONE - 0% | 1,368,912 | 3,295,906 | 1,442,363 | 9,218,899 | 8,909,432 |
| **ADJUSTMENTS TO RISK-WGT ASSETS** | | | | | |
| RISK-WIEGHTED ASSET BEFORE DED | 59,866,160 | 51,901,687 | 53,011,197 | 54,294,685 | 57,833,459 |
| − INELIGIBLE DEF TAX ASSETS | 0 | 0 | 0 | 0 | 0 |
| − INELIGIBLE INTANGIBLES | 0 | 0 | 0 | 0 | 0 |
| − RECIPROCAL CAPITAL HOLDINGS | 0 | 0 | 0 | 0 | 0 |
| − EXCESS ALLOWABLE LN&LS LOSS AL | 0 | 48,755 | 86,480 | 0 | 0 |
| − ALLOCATED TRANSFER RISK RESERV | 0 | 0 | 0 | 0 | 0 |
| + MKT RISK ASSETS & FIN SUB ADJ | 1,031,469 | 55,111 | 15,583 | 63,771 | 0 |
| TOTAL RISK-WEIGHTED ASSETS (PCT) | 60,897,630 (43) | 51,908,044 (51) | 52,940,301 (55) | 54,358,457 (55) | 57,833,459 |

Ratios (columns shown as BANK / PG 1 / PCT):

| RISK-BASED CAPITAL | 12/31/2004 | 12/31/2003 | 12/31/2002 | 12/31/2001 | 12/31/2000 |
|---|---|---|---|---|---|
| TIER ONE RBC TO RISK-WGT ASSETS | 8.36 / 11.17 / 14 | 9.89 / 11.13 / 45 | 9.75 / 10.83 / 43 | 8.65 / 10.08 | 9.34 / 9.40 |
| TOTAL RBC TO RISK-WEIGHT ASSETS | 11.55 / 12.98 / 45 | 12.89 / 13.08 / 60 | 12.99 / 12.88 / 65 | 12.11 / 12.24 | 12.15 / 11.54 |
| TIER ONE LEVERAGE CAPITAL | 7.14 / 7.71 / 40 | 8.37 / 7.67 / 76 | 8.99 / 7.50 / 86 | 7.62 / 7.34 | 8.77 / 7.17 |
| **OTHER CAPITAL RATIO:** | | | | | |
| DEF TAX ASSET TO T1 CAP | 0.00 / 1.72 | 0.00 / 1.42 | 0.00 / 1.09 | 0.00 / 1.73 | 0.00 / 2.27 |

NOTE: FROM MARCH 31, 2001 FORWARD RISK BASED CAPITAL RATIOS AND DATA DO INCLUDE ADJUSTMENT FOR FINANCIAL SUBSIDIARIES.
FOR BANKS WITH FINANCIAL SUBSIDIARIES PLEASE REFER TO CALL REPORT FOR INFORMATION ON THE ADJUSTMENT.

# MANAGING NONINTEREST INCOME AND NONINTEREST EXPENSE

*A common view among bank managers and analysts is that banks will rely less on net interest income and more on noninterest income to improve profitability. The highest-earning banks will be those that generate an increasing share of operating revenue from noninterest sources. A related assumption is that not all fees are created equal. Some fees are stable and predictable over time, while others are highly volatile because they derive from cyclical activities. The fundamental issue among managers is to determine the appropriate customer mix and business mix to grow profits at high rates, with a strong focus on fee-based revenues.*

*The bank's traditional business of lending and producing net interest income is seen by some large banks as a less-than-optimal approach. Lending requires an almost one-for-one increase in the bank's assets and supporting capital and entails significant risk of loss. Recall that interest income equals the interest rate charged times the dollar amount of earning assets. Hence, increasing income requires either increasing the rate, which is difficult to do in a competitive environment, or increasing the volume of loans. More loans often means more default risk. Noninterest income typically equals the price of the product times the number of products or services sold. Growing income does not always require an increase in assets or risk. Volume is the key to effectively selling products and services, especially those that are based on technology.*

*This chapter examines three basic issues related to managing a bank's noninterest income and noninterest expense. First, it describes the strengths and weaknesses of commonly used financial ratios of expense control and noninterest income growth. Second, it discusses why banks should focus on customer profitability and the mix of fee-based businesses when evaluating performance. Finally, it explains how banks utilize different noninterest expense management strategies to enhance performance.*

———————————————●———————————————

**I** t is widely recognized that the days of record-breaking net interest margins (NIMs) are long gone. Exhibit 3.1, for example, documents the long-term trend in NIM for commercial banks since 1934. Note the sharp increase in NIM from 1945 until its modern-day peak of 4.32 percent in 1992 and the apparent reversal in this trend since 1992. By the end of 2004, average NIM had fallen to 3.61 percent. The natural question is, what factors have led to these long-term trends and will NIM continue to fall? The answer is obviously complex, but can be answered by examining the recent history. Beginning in 1934, the Glass-Steagall Act effectively prohibited banks, securities firms, and insurance companies from venturing into one another's businesses. Obviously, limiting competition for loans and deposits promotes an environment of higher margins. Beyond traditional commercial lending, banks also began moving into other lines of lending such as consumer and subprime lending, both of which pay higher promised yields. During the early part of this period, the stock market still suffered the stigma of the 1929 collapse and most bank customers had few options for investing their funds—either deposits in a bank or the stock market. Regulation Q limited the interest rate that banks could pay for deposits, effectively limiting competition from other banks. This allowed for a long period of relatively stable yet increasing NIMs for the banking community. The sharp, temporary declines in NIM of the early 1960s and early 1970 generally followed economic declines.

NIM =

net int. income
——————————
avg earn. assets

*Managing Noninterest Income and Noninterest Expense*

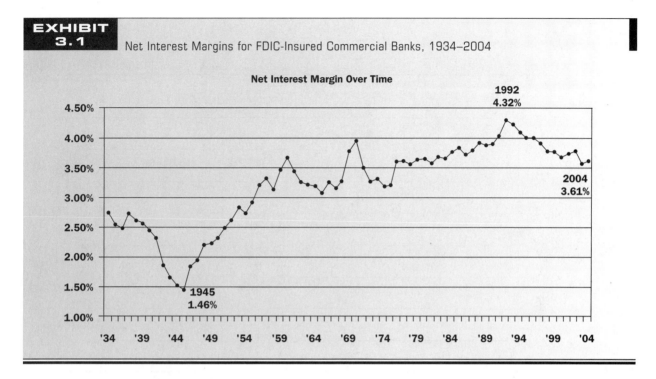

**EXHIBIT 3.1** Net Interest Margins for FDIC-Insured Commercial Banks, 1934–2004

The answer as to why net interest margins have been steadily decreasing since 1992 most likely lies in a reversal of the very factors that led to the sharp increase. First, where there are profits, competition follows. Glass-Steagall and Regulation Q were designed to limit competition and promote a safer banking system. The restrictions were effective for a long period of time, but banks and, nonbanks found innovative ways around Glass-Steagall, slowly and methodically eroding the banks' protected marketplace. Financial innovation, for example, led to the creation of the cash management account and money market mutual fund in the mid 1970s. This was during a time in which banks were restricted from offering competing products due to Regulation Q, which was not completely eliminated until 1986. In addition, during the later half of the twentieth century, the United States experienced a general increase in the popularity of mutual funds and the stock market. Many customers moved funds out of banks (disintermediation) which started to significantly erode banks' market share. Banks were further restricted in the types of products (especially securities products, mutual funds, and insurance products) they could offer while securities firms and insurance companies had significantly greater powers.

The 1990s represented a period of deregulation as well as innovation for nonbanks to enter the banking business. The increased supply of banking, lending, and investment banking products and services put pressure on banks' loan rates and deposit costs. The additional powers and reduced regulatory restrictions of the nonbanks significantly increased competition for the banks' core deposit and lending business, once again eroding NIMs. Finally, bank customers discovered their implicit "option" to refinance. When interest rates fall, loan customers refinance at lower rates thereby lowering the yields that banks charge.

Banks began the later half of the twentieth century with a protected market but ended the period with these same protections preventing them from effectively competing with securities firms and insurance companies. This led to a long-term disintermediation of funds from the bank industry. By the late 1990s, however, many of the restrictions of Glass-Steagall had been eroded by court decisions, regulatory rulings, and marketplace practices that increasingly blurred the distinctions between different segments of the financial industry. For example, it is section 20 of the Glass-Steagall act that forbids banks from affiliating with a company *principally engaged* in the issue, flotation, underwriting, public sale, or distribution at wholesale, or retail or through syndicate participation of stocks, bonds, debentures, notes, or other securities. In 1988, the U.S. Supreme Court upheld the Federal Reserve Board's definition of principally engaged as no more than 5 percent of the affiliate's total revenue. This restriction was increased to 10 percent in 1989 and 25 percent in 1996. Finally, in 1999, Congress passed the Gramm-Leach-Bliley Act, which repealed many sections of Glass-Steagall and allowed banks to enter businesses they were previously forbidden to enter.

The trends and evidence presented above support the fact that net interest margins generally increased until 1992 because of restricted competition and are declining as the distinctions between financial firms is blurred—leading to an increased number of competitors, financial sector combinations, and regulatory change. These data, however, may mask some of the differences among financial institutions. Larger banks and financial institutions have, in general, de-emphasized lending in favor of generating fees from securitizing the loans they make, as well

**EXHIBIT 3.2**

Net Interest Margins by Bank Asset Size, 1992–2004

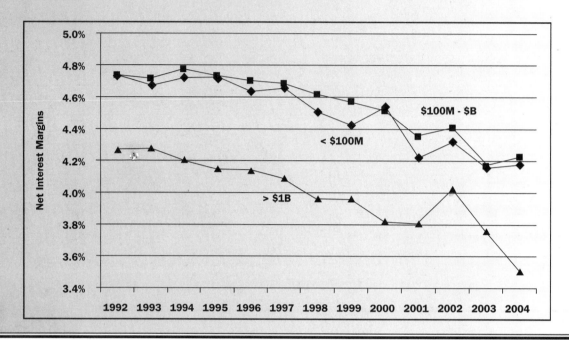

SOURCE: FDIC Statistics on Depository Institutions, http://www2.fdic.gov/sdi/main.asp.

as offering a wide variety of products and services that generate fees. Today, noninterest income comes primarily from fiduciary activities, deposit service charges, trading revenue, venture capital revenue, securitization income, investment banking, advisory, brokerage, underwriting fees and commissions, insurance commission fees, and fees from servicing real estate mortgages, credit cards, and other financial assets. Smaller banks, in contrast, have continued to be much more dependent on lending and their net interest margins. Exhibit 3.2 presents NIMs for different-sized FDIC-insured banks from 1992 to 2004. NIMs are clearly lower for larger banks, those with assets greater than $1 billion, but the decline in margins since 1992 has clearly been greater for the largest banks.

## NONINTEREST INCOME

For years, banks have tried to increase noninterest income. Exhibit 3.3 documents the sustained increase in banks' noninterest income as a fraction of net operating revenue, where net operating revenue equals the sum of net interest income and noninterest income. This ratio equaled just 20.4 percent in 1980 for all FDIC-insured banks but has increased sharply to 42.5 percent in 2004. As discussed in Chapter 2, the Uniform Bank Performance Report (UBPR) lists several sources of noninterest income for financial institutions:

1. **Fiduciary activities** reflect income from an institution's trust department.

2. **Deposit service charges,** such as checking account fees, generally represent the bulk of noninterest income.

3. **Trading revenue, venture capital revenue, and securitization income** reflect gains (losses) from trading securities (making a market in securities) and off-balance sheet derivative contracts recognized during the period; venture capital activities; as well as fees from securitization transactions and unrealized losses (recovery of losses) on loans and leases held for sale.

4. **Investment banking, advisory, brokerage, and underwriting fees and commissions** include fees and commissions from underwriting securities, private placements of securities, investment advisory and management services, or merger and acquisition services.

5. **Insurance commission fees and income** are reported income from underwriting insurance, from the sale of insurance, or from reinsurance including fees, commissions, and service charges.

6. **Net servicing fees** are derived from servicing real estate mortgages, credit cards, and other financial assets held by others.

7. **Net gains (losses) on sales of loans** are net gains (losses) on sales or other disposal of loans and leases.

8. **Other net gains (losses)** include net gains (losses) on sales of other real estate owned, on the sales or other disposals of other real estate owned, and sales of other assets (excluding securities) such as premises, fixed assets, and personal property acquired for debts previously contracted (such as automobiles, boats, equipment, and appliances).

9. **Other noninterest income** includes income from safe deposit boxes, sale of bank drafts, money orders, checks, etc.; execution of acceptances and letters of credit; notarizing; advisory services; rentals and other income from real estate owned; credit card fees; loan commitment fees; foreign currency fees; life insurance proceeds; penalties for early withdrawals; data processing fees to others, as well as a multitude of other miscellaneous income.

The data in Exhibit 3.3 mask some of the significant differences in noninterest income by bank size and type of income. Exhibit 3.4 documents the composition of noninterest income, as a percentage of total assets, for all FDIC-insured banks in 2004 by size. First, the biggest contributors to noninterest income are deposit service charges and other noninterest income. Deposit service charges represent a stable source of revenue for banks, but are difficult to increase sharply over time because they are very visible and the perception is that banks "stick it to customers" when they impose the charges.

While all banks are increasing their noninterest income, the largest banks rely much more on this source of revenue than smaller banks, which still rely more heavily on net interest income. Large banks not only have greater amounts of noninterest income, they also rely on a wider variety of sources of noninterest income.

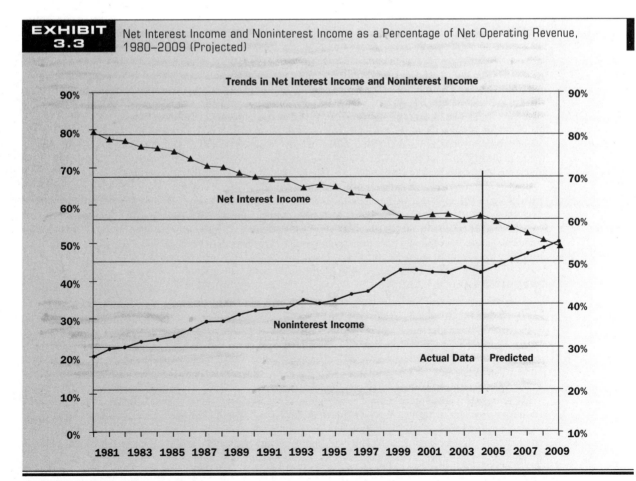

**EXHIBIT 3.3** Net Interest Income and Noninterest Income as a Percentage of Net Operating Revenue, 1980–2009 (Projected)

Trends in Net Interest Income and Noninterest Income

Net Interest Income

Noninterest Income

Actual Data | Predicted

**EXHIBIT 3.4**

Composition of Noninterest Income by Bank Size as a Percentage of Total Assets, 2004

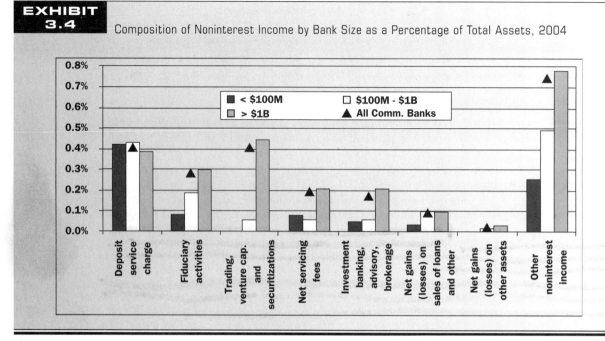

SOURCE: FDIC Statistics on Depository Institutions, http://www2.fdic.gov/sdi/main.asp.

With respect to the largest banks, income from investment banking, advisory, brokerage, and underwriting fees and commissions contributes a far greater portion of noninterest income and has increased the most over the past few years. Mergers of banks and investment companies such as Citibank and Solomon Smith Barney and JPMorgan Chase, as well as the repeal of Glass-Steagall, demonstrate that banks are rapidly entering the securities business. The problem, however, with nondeposit fees and trading revenue is that they are highly cyclical in nature because they depend on capital market activity. When mergers, acquisitions, trading, and brokerage activities are booming, banks (and investment banks) can earn enormous fees that increase with the volume of activity. When these activities decline, fee revenue shrinks accordingly. This was demonstrated late in 1998 when large banking organizations around the world reported sizeable trading losses on activities in Russia and Asia, and again in 2001–2002 with the decline in the stock market. In 2002–2003 large investment banks were laying off employees given the sharp drop in fee revenue. As activity grew in 2004–2005, they reinitiated hiring and lucrative bonus payments.

Large banks generally price services differently than smaller banks. Exhibit 3.5 summarizes the results of the 1999 and 2002 studies of the *Annual Report to the Congress on Retail Fees and Services of Depository Institutions*, which showed that, on average, large banks charged higher fees and had higher minimum balance requirements than did small banks on just about all noninterest income products. The average nonsufficient funds (NSF) charge in 2002 was more than $6 higher per item at large banks at just over $26 versus $20 at the smallest institutions. From 1999 to 2002, most of the fees increased as well.

## DEPOSIT SERVICE FEES

Bank fees change over time for many reasons. First, with deregulation, banks are "unbundling" their products and now charge fees for individual services rather than offering many "free" services. Second, competition has lowered the basic fees for checking accounts while those for NSF and overdraft charges, as well as ATM fees, are increasing. Free checking has been a popular way to attract new business, but bank managers know that customers are largely price insensitive when it comes to some service charges and fees, which means that banks can raise these charges and fees on a regular basis and their total revenues will rise. Not surprisingly, banks systematically raise fees annually but by modest amounts so as not to raise too much criticism.

The terms and types of services bundled with noninterest products and services vary significantly across institutions as do minimum balance requirements to avoid fees and the types of fees charged. Financial institutions can, and do, offer various types of accounts with different fee structures. Each year the Board of Governors of the Federal Reserve System is required to report to Congress on the fees and services of financial institutions in the *Annual Report to the Congress on Retail Fees and Services of Depository Institutions*. The most recent report summarized in Exhibit 3.5 lists fees for many different products including noninterest checking accounts, NOW (interest) checking accounts, ATM services, as well as various other deposit services.

*Noninterest Income*

EXHIBIT 3.5 Various Fee Structures by Bank Size and Type of Services, 1999 and 2002

| Account availability and fee averages | 1999 Institution Size | | | | 2002 Institution Size | | | |
|---|---|---|---|---|---|---|---|---|
| Dollars except as noted | All | Large | Medium | Small | All | Large | Medium | Small |
| **Percent offering noninterest checking** | 93.10 | 96.10 | 92.90 | 93.00 | 96.10 | 96.90 | 97.00 | 95.40 |
| *Single-balance, single-fee account[1]* | | | | | | | | |
| Percent offering | 37.20 | 50.80 | 42.30 | 33.80 | 32.30 | 39.40 | 32.20 | 31.80 |
| Monthly fee (low balance) | 6.17 | 8.20 | 6.77 | 5.58 | 7.35 | 9.75 | 7.77 | 6.78 |
| Minimum balance to avoid fee | 517.72 | 723.01 | 583.42 | 455.61 | 591.46 | 890.43 | 582.00 | 566.28 |
| Minimum balance to open | 109.05 | 102.61 | 108.03 | 110.37 | 159.21 | 122.72 | 136.88 | 179.61 |
| *Fee-only account[2]* | | | | | | | | |
| Percent offering | 37.30 | 64.50 | 42.80 | 32.70 | 39.90 | 64.80 | 44.90 | 34.10 |
| Monthly fee | 4.95 | 5.02 | 5.05 | 4.88 | 5.27 | 6.09 | 5.25 | 5.14 |
| Check charge | | | | | | | | |
| Percent charging | 36.80 | 38.50 | 45.30 | 31.10 | 23.70 | 4.70 | 25.00 | 24.70 |
| Average | 0.39 | 0.63 | 0.45 | 0.30 | 0.22 | NS | 0.26 | 0.19 |
| Minimum balance to open | 60.98 | 56.73 | 65.47 | 58.68 | 78.41 | 98.29 | 70.22 | 82.98 |
| *Free account[3]* | | | | | | | | |
| Percent offering | 13.60 | 21.90 | 16.50 | 11.50 | 30.10 | 38.20 | 31.20 | 28.60 |
| Minimum balance to open | 41.87 | 53.66 | 53.63 | NS | 73.82 | NS | 66.27 | 73.65 |
| **Percent offering NOW (interest checking) accounts** | 93.3 | 90.8 | 96.7 | 91.8 | 95.6 | 96.8 | 96.4 | 95 |
| *Single-fee account[1]* | | | | | | | | |
| Percent offering | 51.9 | 51.8 | 49.6 | 53 | 40.9 | 53.2 | 40.1 | 40.5 |
| Monthly fee (low balance) | 8.24 | 10.37 | 8.5 | 7.97 | 8.71 | 10.05 | 9.13 | 8.26 |
| Minimum balance to avoid fee | 1,014.23 | 1,444.78 | 1,096.75 | 946.6 | 1,090.78 | 1,755.94 | 1,048.41 | 1,049.79 |
| Minimum balance to open | 587.23 | 431.34 | 393.36 | 686.62 | 469.59 | 606.54 | 449.47 | 469.37 |
| *Single-fee, single-check-charge account[2]* | | | | | | | | |
| Percent offering | 12.4 | 12.2 | 9.6 | 13.8 | 12.5 | 17.5 | 12.3 | 12.3 |
| Monthly fee (low balance) | 6.35 | 6.84 | 7.08 | 6.07 | 7.06 | 7.83 | 7.28 | 6.82 |
| Check charge | 0.21 | 0.33 | 0.23 | 0.19 | 0.25 | 0.33 | 0.24 | 0.24 |
| Minimum balance to avoid fee | 1,002.25 | 1,543.02 | 941.09 | 988.84 | 1,034.36 | 1,407.35 | 1,007.07 | 1,010.71 |
| Minimum balance to open | 683.4 | 634.27 | 459.07 | 762.13 | 591.05 | 388.12 | 392.3 | 760.15 |
| *No-fee account* | | | | | | | | |
| Percent offering | 0.9 | 0.3 | 1 | 0.9 | 1.8 | 7.2 | 1.3 | 1.7 |
| Minimum balance to open | 1 | NS | NS | NS | 199.44 | NS | NS | NS |
| **Special account fees** | | | | | | | | |
| Stop-payment orders average fee | 15.26 | 20.46 | 17.61 | 13.70 | 18.93 | 23.54 | 21.06 | 17.00 |
| NSF checks average fee [1] | 17.88 | 22.84 | 20.05 | 16.43 | 21.73 | 26.19 | 23.41 | 20.14 |
| Overdrafts average fee [2] | 17.66 | 22.95 | 20.24 | 15.97 | 21.80 | 26.84 | 23.69 | 20.00 |
| Deposit items returned average fee | 6.33 | 7.47 | 6.37 | 6.16 | 6.88 | 6.13 | 6.82 | 7.03 |
| **Automated teller machines** | | | | | | | | |
| Percent offering ATM card | 83.10 | 96.20 | 97.20 | 75.30 | 93.40 | 98.80 | 98.00 | 89.60 |
| Percent charging annual ATM fee | 16.20 | 13.10 | 10.20 | 20.30 | 10.30 | 5.50 | 7.20 | 13.20 |
| *Average fee $* | 7.97 | 15.47 | 7.35 | 7.83 | 11.65 | NR | 9.77 | 12.25 |
| Percent charging ATM card fee | 7.70 | 2.60 | 4.10 | 10.40 | 4.00 | 1.20 | 1.80 | 6.00 |
| *Average fee $* | 4.16 | NS | 5.18 | 3.92 | 6.39 | NS | NS | 5.73 |
| Percent charging "on others" ATM fee | 72.00 | 87.20 | 75.70 | 68.20 | 69.00 | 76.90 | 78.50 | 60.70 |
| *Average fee $* | 1.17 | 1.27 | 1.23 | 1.12 | 1.14 | 1.31 | 1.21 | 1.04 |
| Percent charging ATM surcharge fee | 81.50 | 85.30 | 86.70 | 77.60 | 89.40 | 93.50 | 92.20 | 86.60 |
| *Average fee $* | 1.25 | 1.36 | 1.28 | 1.21 | 1.36 | 1.42 | 1.38 | 1.33 |

SOURCE: Annual Report to the Congress on Retail Fees and Services of Depository Institutions.

**NONINTEREST CHECKING ACCOUNTS.** The Federal Reserve report on retail fees details three types of fee structures for noninterest checking accounts: (1) single balance, single fee, (2) fee only, and (3) free. In addition to these types of accounts, financial institutions also offer *package* or *club accounts* that offer a variety of services in addition to the checking accounts. Institutions also offer *tiered accounts*, which have more complicated minimum balance requirements, and offer many more services and discounts based upon higher balances. Although these types of accounts are not reported in the Federal Reserve report, the Federal Reserve report does provide data on the following three types of noninterest checking accounts:

- A **single-balance, single-fee noninterest account** incurs no fee if a minimum balance is met; otherwise, there is a single monthly fee. In 2002, about 32 percent of institutions offered accounts with this structure. The average minimum balance was $591.46, the average fee for falling below the minimum balance was $7.35, and the average minimum amount to open the account was $159.21. The minimum balance to avoid fees, the monthly fee charge for low balance, and the minimum amount to open the account have all increased since 1999. Minimum balances and fees also increase with bank size.

- An **account fee-only noninterest checking account** incurs a monthly fee regardless of the account balance, as well as a possible *per-check charge*. About 40 percent of institutions offer this type of account but only 24 percent also charge a per-check charge. The average monthly fee was $5.27 in 2002 and increased with bank size. The average monthly fee has increased significantly since 1999 while the proportion of institutions requiring a per-check charge for this type of account has declined significantly as few of the largest institutions charge a per-check fee.

- A **free noninterest checking account** imposes no fees of any kind. About 30 percent of institutions offered this type of account in 2002. Although these accounts are called "free," there are often restrictions as to the number of free services allowed before a fee will be charged. For example, many times these accounts require automatic deposit and will charge a fee for the use of a live teller or drive-through teller transaction.

**INTEREST-BEARING CHECKING ACCOUNT—NOW ACCOUNTS.** Most banks also offer negotiable order of withdrawal (NOW) accounts, or interest-bearing checking accounts, and these accounts may have different fee structures than noninterest checking accounts. The Federal Reserve's report on fees lists three types of fee structures: (1) single fee, (2) single fee, single-check-charge and (3) no fee:

- **Single-fee NOW accounts** are similar to noninterest accounts in that they charge no fee if the account balance remains above a minimum amount; otherwise, the institution charges a monthly fee with no check charge. About 41 percent of institutions offered this account in 2002, down significantly from those offering this type of account in 1999. The average monthly fee charge for failing to meet the required minimum balance increased significantly, from $8.24 in 1999 to $8.71 in 2002 and this fee is significantly higher for larger institutions. The minimum balance required to avoid the fee increased at the largest and smallest institutions, but declined for medium-size institutions.

- **Single-fee, single-check-charge NOW accounts** are similar to single-fee NOW accounts in that they charge a monthly fee if the account balance falls below a minimum, but this triggers a per-check charge as well. **No-fee NOW accounts** are interest-bearing checking accounts that charge no fees. Both types of account are rare as only 13 percent and 2 percent, respectively, of institutions offered them in 2002.

**SPECIAL FEES.** In addition to monthly fees and per-check fees, almost all institutions offer other transactions account services for which they charge fees, such as: (1) NSF checks, (2) overdrafts, (3) deposit items returned, and (4) stop-payment orders. *NSF checks* and *overdrafts* are checks written against insufficient funds with the distinction being that NSF checks are returned unpaid while overdrafts are honored. Many institutions have introduced overdraft programs in which they make loans to cover overdrafts up to some predetermined amount. It is surprising how many account holders overdraw their accounts considering the high fees charged. *Deposit items returned* are checks deposited by a bank's customer and returned for insufficient funds. All of these fees have increased dramatically since 1999 and are the highest at the largest institutions. In 2002, the average overdraft fee was $21.80 at all institutions, but $26.84 at the largest institutions and only $20.00 at the smallest institutions. A *stop-payment order* arises when a customer requests that the bank not pay a check previously written. Similar to overdraft and NSF charges, stop-payment charges have also increased significantly since 1999.

**ATM SERVICES.** A vast majority of institutions, 93 percent, offered ATM services in 2002. The ATM popularity has grown substantially over the past 20 years, and the average customer would likely not know how to live without the weekly or even daily visits to the ATM machine! The number of banks offering an ATM card, which was already high in 1999, increased significantly in 2002. The Federal Reserve report lists several types of fees that various institutions charge including: yearly fees for issuing the ATM card; surcharges; as well as the two transaction fees, *on us* and *on others* ATM fees:

- **Annual fees** and **ATM card fees** are relatively uncommon as only 10.3 percent charge annual fees and only 4 percent charge an ATM card issue fee. The percentage of institutions charging these fees has dropped significantly since 1999. **Surcharges** are the fees charged by ATM owners on users of their ATMs who are not the institution's direct customers; that is, users who do not maintain an account with the institution that owns the ATM. The percentage of financial institutions charging these fees has increased dramatically since the first Federal Reserve study in 1996 with 89.4 percent of financial institution imposing the surcharge in 2002 and almost 94 percent of the largest banks charging the surcharge in 2002.

- **"On us" withdrawal fees** are the transaction fees for ATM withdrawals levied on the institution's depositor. The proportion of institutions charging their own depositors for withdrawing cash from the institution's machines is quite small as only 3 percent charged a fee in 2002, and the average fee charged has declined significantly. **"On others" withdrawal fees** are the fees charged to the institution's own customers for making withdrawals at other institutions' ATMs. This fee is much more common as 70 percent of institutions charged the fee in 2002. The incidence of the fee and amount of this fee, however, has declined somewhat with the exception of the largest banks.

The critical decision for management is to determine the appropriate fee-based business mix. Many institutions prefer mortgage banking because of the built-in hedge between loan origination and mortgage servicing. When interest rates are low or falling, firms can earn substantial origination fees from making new loans and mortgage refinancings. When interest rates are high or rising, loan origination fees decline but mortgage-servicing revenue increases because existing mortgages prepay slower and, thus, remain outstanding longer.[1] Mortgage origination can also be somewhat countercycle to the bank's net interest margin business. For example, in May 2000, the Federal Reserve was targeting the federal funds rate at 6.5 percent, but two and a half years later, in November 2002, the Federal Reserve was targeting only a 1.25 percent federal funds rate.[2] During this period, the number of households that refinanced their homes was unprecedented. By early 2004, roughly 75 percent of all 1–4 family mortgages had been put on the books in the prior three years! When rates increase, however, the number of new mortgages decreases dramatically. In some cases, firms lay off employees and lose money in the origination side of the business. The reduction in origination of new mortgages, however, generally means that mortgage-servicing revenues increase.

The negative side of the mortgage banking business is that firms benefit from size because there are considerable scale economies with larger portfolios. Unfortunately, it is difficult for many firms to acquire the volume of servicing business needed given the extreme competitive conditions.[3] Hence, many mortgage orginators do not service the loans but instead sell the servicing rights. Without the servicing side of the mortgage business, fee income from mortgage origination is highly cyclical with interest rates. As a result, many large banks prefer the huge potential fee income from nonmortgage businesses such as leasing, subprime lending (to high default risk customers), factoring, and related activities. Not surprisingly, fees from these activities are also highly volatile because the volume and quality of business changes when economic conditions change.

## NONINTEREST EXPENSE

One source of earnings growth is straightforward—cost cutting. This has been a primary motive for most bank mergers in recent years. In fact, analysts and bank stock investors are constantly trying to identify likely in-market merger partners where cost savings can be substantial. With an *in-market merger,* the two firms have significant duplication of banking offices and services such that any merger leads to the elimination of branches and personnel. Cost savings from eliminating this duplication represent an annuity to the extent that the combined firm can continue to service existing customers. Berry and McDermott (1996) reported that cost savings from in-market mergers in 1995 averaged 39 percent of the acquired bank's noninterest expense base, a substantial annuity if sustained. For mergers that were not in-market, the cost savings averaged 23 percent of the acquired bank's expenses. With respect to overhead or operating expenses, the UBPR reports five components of a bank's noninterest expense:

1. Personnel expense, which includes wages, salaries, and benefits
2. Occupancy expense, which includes rent and depreciation on buildings and equipment
3. Goodwill impairment, which includes any amortization from permanently impaired goodwill
4. Other intangible amortization, which includes amortization expense and impairment losses for other intangible assets
5. Other operating expense, which includes all other noninterest expenses

---

[1]A mortgage servicer collects the actual payments from the borrower and transfers the funds, less a servicing fee, to the ultimate holder of the loan. Mortgage-servicing revenue varies directly with the amount of loans serviced. The faster that mortgages prepay, the lower are outstanding mortgage balances such that servicing revenue falls, ceteris paribus.

[2]The Fed subsequently lowers the targeted federal funds rate again to 1 percent in June 2003. However, by March 2005 the Fed had raised the targeted federal funds rate to     .

[3]The term *economies of scale* refers to the situation where a firm's average unit costs decrease as output increases.

The sum of these five components expenses is called **overhead expense**. For most banks, personnel expenses are the greatest, reflecting the heavy dependency on people relative to capital assets.

## KEY RATIOS

Bank managers generally track a variety of financial ratios in an effort to measure and monitor a bank's ability to control expenses and generate noninterest income. The three most common ratios are a bank's burden or net overhead expense, efficiency ratio and productivity ratios. The following discussion should be viewed in the context that any single bank's ratios would reflect the mix of businesses it represents. Some lines of business require substantial capital investments, while others are more labor intensive or may primarily be off-balance sheet in their impact.

**BURDEN/NET OVERHEAD EXPENSE.** As noted in Chapter 2, a bank's burden, or net overhead expense, equals the difference between noninterest expense and noninterest income in dollar terms or as a fraction of total assets:

$$\text{Burden} = \text{Noninterest expense} - \text{Noninterest income} \tag{3.1}$$

$$\text{Net noninterest margin} = \frac{\text{Burden}}{\text{Average total assets}} \tag{3.2}$$

Because noninterest expense is higher than noninterest income for most banks, these measures are generally positive and indicate the extent to which a bank generates noninterest income to help cover its noninterest expense. Noninterest expense is generally higher because considerable 3.6 noninterest expense is incurred as a result of generating interest income and low cost deposits. Consider, for example, that occupancy costs for buildings, computer systems, loan officers' salaries, and branch costs do attract deposits. The smaller are a bank's burden and net overhead, the better a bank has performed on trend and versus peers. When differences appear, managers examine the components of noninterest expense to determine whether personnel, occupancy, or other expense is greater as a fraction of assets. They will also compare service charges on deposits and other fee income as a fraction of noninterest income and assets to assess their relative performance related to asset utilization. Importantly, gains or losses on the sale of securities and other nonrecurring income and/or expenses are netted or ignored when making these comparisons.

**EFFICIENCY RATIO.** The most popular ratio to evaluate performance is a bank's efficiency ratio. Banks frequently report this measure along with ROE, ROA, and NIM as a key driver of profitability and indicator of potential profit growth. Many banks announce their target ratio at the beginning of each year, and some banks tie employee bonuses to whether the bank meets its target. Formally, the **efficiency ratio** equals a bank's noninterest expense as a fraction of net operating revenue, where net operating revenue is the sum of net interest income and noninterest income. The ratio measures the amount of noninterest expense a bank pays to earn one dollar of net operating revenue. Thus, a ratio of 0.60 indicates that a bank pays 60 cents in noninterest expense per dollar of net operating revenue. Banks that are more efficient are presumably those with the lowest efficiency ratios.

$$\text{Efficiency ratio} = \frac{\text{Noninterest expense}}{\text{Net interest income} + \text{Noninterest income}} \tag{3.3}$$

Exhibit 3.6 reports average efficiency ratios from 1992 through 2004 for U.S. commercial banks with total assets of less than $100 million, $100 million to $1 billion, and more than $10 billion. Approximately 83 institutions with large regional, national, or global operations drive the data for the largest banks. Exhibit 3.6 demonstrates some of the key differences between large and small banks' business models. First, there is a remarkable difference in efficiency ratios by bank size. Large banks clearly have lower efficiency ratios on average. This generally reflects their relative advantage in generating noninterest income by entering businesses such as investment banking, trading, and asset management. At year-end 2004, banks with less than $100 million in assets paid just under 70 cents in overhead for each dollar of revenue generated; banks with total assets between $100 million and $1 billion paid 62 cents, while the largest banks with more than $10 billion in assets paid just 57 cents per dollar of revenue. These results clearly reflect the trade-offs between overhead, net interest income and noninterest income.

The second most striking implication of the data presented in Exhibit 3.6 is the systematic decline in efficiency ratios through 1996 for all banks. However, only the largest banks continued to lower efficiency ratios after 1997. Note that the denominator of the efficiency ratios is composed of two parts, net interest income and noninterest income. As shown in Exhibits 3.1 and 3.2, net interest margins systematically declined since 1992, and the rate of decline increased significantly since 1997. Smaller banks are more dependent on net interest margins and the decline in their NIMs has been larger relative to that of the largest banks. In addition, large banks have been more successful in increasing noninterest income relative to smaller banks. The net result is that the largest banks with the ability to generate substantial fee income continue to improve their efficiency ratios, while smaller banks do not.

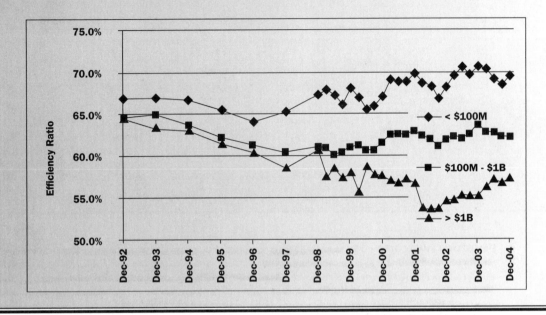

**EXHIBIT 3.6** Efficiency Ratios of U.S. Commercial Banks with Different Asset Size, 1992–2004

SOURCE: FDIC Statistics on Depository Institutions, http://www2.fdic.gov/sdi/main.asp.: $100m is $100 million, $1B is $1 billion.

Once again, the efficiency ratio demonstrates the trade-offs among noninterest expense, net interest margin, and noninterest income. Lower efficiency ratios are derived from a combination of cost control (cost cutting), improvements in noninterest income and growing NIM or slowing its decline. The old phrase, "you must spend money to make money," is truly shown in the efficiency ratio. Smaller banks have seen their net interest income decline relative to their noninterest expense and have not made up the difference in noninterest income.

A crucial issue is whether low efficiency ratios correspond to higher profitability ratios. Osborne (1994) and Holliday (2000) argue that they do not, and banks that focus on lowering their efficiency ratio may make suboptimal decisions. Using data from 1989 to 1993 for the 50 largest U.S. banks, Osborne demonstrates that banks with the highest ROEs reported a wide range of efficiency ratios. These studies point out two essential criticisms of efficiency ratios. First, the efficiency ratio does not take into account a bank's mix of businesses. It is perfectly logical for banks to invest in businesses where they must incur larger noninterest expense if the marginal revenue obtained from the businesses exceeds the marginal expense. Thus, while the efficiency ratio may increase or exceed peers, the investment adds value to shareholders. Second, the efficiency ratio is not directly tied to a bank's target return to shareholders. Holliday similarly argues that banks should focus on growing revenues at the lowest possible cost. If successful, banks will retain customers and increase profitability. Fundamentally, as long as the bank earns more than its marginal cost of capital, the investment is value enhancing. The implication is that managers who evaluate noninterest expense and revenue must carefully measure marginal cost and marginal revenue and compare their bank's performance to similar competitors.

**OPERATING RISK RATIO.** Some analysts (Wilson 2001) focus on a bank's operating risk ratio in order to better differentiate performance attributable to cost controls versus fee generation. The lower is the operating risk ratio, the better is the bank's operating performance because it generates proportionately more of its revenues from noninterest income or fees, which are more stable and thus more valuable. The ratio subtracts noninterest (fee) income from noninterest expense and divides the total by NIM.

$$\text{Operating Risk Ratio} = \frac{\text{Noninterest expense} - \text{Fee income}}{\text{Net interest margin}} \qquad (3.4)$$

Consider the data for Bay Bank and River Bank in Exhibit 3.7. Both banks report identical ROAs, overhead expense as a fraction of assets, operating revenue as a fraction of assets, and efficiency ratios, but Bay Bank reports a lower operating risk ratio. A closer review of the components of the two ratios indicates that Bay Bank generates a higher fraction of its operating revenue from fee income. Hence, it reports a lower operating risk ratio.

**EXHIBIT 3.7**

Operating Risk Ratio Signals the Benefit of Fee Income

| Ratio | Bay Bank | River Bank |
|---|---|---|
| Return on assets (ROA) | 1.40% | 1.40% |
| Net interest margin (NIM) | 4.000% | 4.625% |
| Percent of average total assets: | | |
| Net interest income | 3.20% | 3.70% |
| Noninterest income (fee) | 1.40% | 0.90% |
| Operating revenue | 4.60% | 4.60% |
| Noninterest expense | 3.00% | 3.00% |
| Earning assets | 80.00% | 80.00% |
| Taxes | 0.20% | 0.20% |
| Efficiency Ratio: | 65.22% = 0.03 / (0.032 + 0.014) | 65.22% = 0.03 / (0.037 + 0.009) |
| Operating Risk Ratio: | 40.00% = (0.03 − 0.014) / 0.04 | 45.41% = (0.03 − 0.014) / 0.04625 |

**PRODUCTIVITY RATIOS.** Many managers track a variety of productivity ratios to assess whether they are getting the maximum use of employees and capital. Typical ratios included in the UBPR are assets per employee and average personnel expense per employee. In the first case, a higher ratio indicates that fewer employees handle business associated with a larger volume of assets. In a sense, it is an asset efficiency ratio where a high number is good. Of course, the ratio ignores the amount of off-balance sheet activity that a bank conducts. In the second case, the ratio measures the average cost of an employee when salaries and benefits are recognized.

$$\text{Assets per employee} = \frac{\text{Average assets}}{\text{Number of full-time employees}} \tag{3.5}$$

$$\text{Average personnel expense} = \frac{\text{Personnel expense}}{\text{Number of full-time employees}} \tag{3.6}$$

There is no widely recognized optimal value for either of these ratios. In fact, many high-performing banks have fewer full-time employees, but pay them better than the average employee at comparable banks. Furthermore, the personnel expense ratio may be biased by large compensation packages for just a handful of bank officers. For example, a community bank with a highly paid CEO will often report a higher ratio, which provides meaningless information about how well the average employee is paid versus peers.

For community banks, two related ratios can provide useful information about productivity. Because loans typically represent the largest asset holding, it is meaningful to calculate a loans-per-employee ratio as an indicator of loan productivity. Similarly, a ratio of net income per employee generally indicates the productivity and profitability of a bank's workforce. For both of these latter ratios, a higher value indicates greater productivity.

$$\text{Loans per employee} = \frac{\text{Average loans}}{\text{Number of full-time employees}} \tag{3.7}$$

$$\text{Net income per employee} = \frac{\text{Net income}}{\text{Number of full-time employees}} \tag{3.8}$$

With declining net interest margins, it is essential that bank managers identify the appropriate mix of products and lines of business because future earnings growth will likely come from fee income. Traditionally, banks have relied on deposit service charges and trust fees for those with trust departments. The key point is that not all fees are created equal and not all customers are profitable. Banks must recognize the risk associated with different sources of fee income and be able to measure whether specific customers generate more revenue than the cost of servicing their account.

## WHICH LINES OF BUSINESS AND CUSTOMERS ARE PROFITABLE?

The first step in identifying profitable growth is to determine which lines of business are profitable as well as which of the bank's customers are profitable. Once the returns to these lines of business and customers are identified, banks should allocate resources to the lines of business and customers generating the highest expected returns over time.

### LINE-OF-BUSINESS PROFITABILITY ANALYSIS

In order to analyze precisely the profitability and risk of various business lines, each line of business must have its own balance sheet and income statement. These statements are difficult to construct because many nontraditional activities, such as trust and mortgage servicing, do not explicitly require any direct equity support. Even traditional activities, such as commercial lending and consumer banking, complicate the issue because these business units do not have equal amounts of assets and liabilities generated by customers. Furthermore, the critical issue is to determine how much equity capital to assign each unit. This is not a simple task as Kimball (1997) points out and materials from ERisk demonstrate (www.erisk.com). Alternative capital allocation methods include using regulatory risk-based capital standards; assignment based on the size of assets; benchmarking each unit to "pure-play" peers that are stand-alone, publicly held firms; and measures of each line of business's riskiness. Today, many large banks evaluate line-of-business profitability and risk via RAROC or RORAC systems. **RAROC** refers to risk-adjusted return on capital, while **RORAC** refers to return on risk-adjusted capital. The terms are often used interchangeably, but are formally defined as follows:

$$\text{RAROC} = \frac{\text{Risk} - \text{adjusted income}}{\text{Capital}} \tag{3.9}$$

$$\text{RORAC} = \frac{\text{Income}}{\text{Allocated risk capital}} \tag{3.10}$$

What constitutes risk-adjusted income and allocated-risk capital may vary across institutions, but the concept is to identify some measure of return generated by a line of business and compare that return to the allocated capital. The income or return measure may be adjusted for risk (RAROC), which typically means that expected losses are subtracted from revenues along with other expenses. Alternatively, the capital measure may be adjusted for risk (RORAC), which typically means that it represents a maximum potential loss based on the probability of future returns or an amount necessary to cover loss associated with the volatility of earnings. In addition, some banks subtract a charge for capital from the return measure to estimate "economic returns."

### CUSTOMER PROFITABILITY ANALYSIS

Customer profitability analysis is used to evaluate whether net revenue from an account meets a bank's profit objective. The general customer profitability rule is that 20 percent of a firm's customers contribute about 80 percent of overall profits. The fundamental objective, therefore, of customer profitability analysis is to identify the profitability of individual customers. Banks that are more progressive also use customer profitability analysis to differential between the firm's high-value customers and those customers who are marginally profitable in order to move these latter customers to a more profitable position for the bank.

Exhibit 3.8 graphically demonstrates that with respect to the most profitable 20 percent of the business's customers, or high-value customers, the firm's objective is to identify them and determine their needs in order to protect and promote this important source of revenue. Next are the value and average customers, who contribute much less to profits but represent the second biggest strategic opportunity for the firm. The fundamental objective here is to move these customers into a more profitable position by selling them additional products or encouraging them to move additional business to the bank. The final two categories of customers represent the low-value and loss-type or high-maintenance customers. These customers are usually break-even or negative-value relationships. The primary object with these customers is to determine a way to increase their profitability or encourage them to obtain services from other firms. Management must be extremely careful with these customers, however, in that they tend to be the most vocal and will often do more damage as noncustomers than as customers if they feel they have been treated poorly by the bank. See the Contemporary Issues Box: "Strategies for Increasing Noninterest Income."

Customer profitability analysis is most often performed using monthly or quarterly historical data so that pricing can be modified where appropriate. The procedure involves comparing revenues from all services provided a customer with associated costs and the bank's target profit. Although the analysis applies particularly well to loan customers, it can be easily modified to evaluate noncredit activities. The appropriate comparison is:

$$\text{Account revenues} \gtreqless \text{Account expenses} + \text{Target profit} \tag{3.11}$$

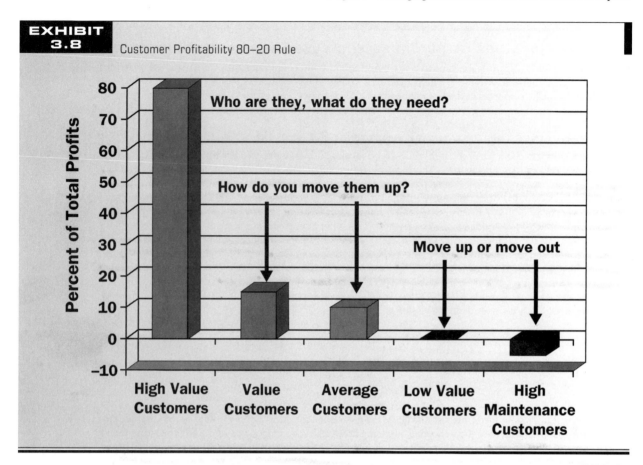

**EXHIBIT 3.8** Customer Profitability 80–20 Rule

If revenues exceed the sum of expenses and the target profit, the account generates a return in excess of the minimum return required by the bank. If revenues equal expenses plus the target profit, the account just meets the required return objective. There are two other possible outcomes: If revenues fall short of expenses, the account is clearly unprofitable. When revenues exceed expenses but are less than the sum of expenses and target profit, the account is profitable but does not generate the minimum acceptable return to the bank.

The first step in evaluating customer profitability is to identify the full list of services used by a customer. The list normally includes transactions account activity, extension of credit, security safekeeping, and related items such as wire transfers, safety deposit boxes, and letters of credit. The next step is to assess the cost of providing each service. Unit costs can be determined from the bank's cost accounting system or approximated from private sources. Often, specific figures vary substantially among banks because they allocate fixed costs and overhead differently. There is no best method for allocating fixed costs, so estimating unit expenses is, at best, an approximation. Banks that do not have formal customer profitability models typically attribute it to the inability to allocate costs due to systems limitations.

**EXPENSE COMPONENTS.** Customer expenses consist of a host of various items but are usually categorized into one of three areas: noncredit services, credit services, and business risk expenses. Aggregate cost estimates for **noncredit services** are obtained by multiplying the unit cost of each service by the corresponding activity level. If, for example, it costs $7 to facilitate a wire transfer and the customer authorized eight such transfers, the total periodic wire transfer expense to the bank is $56 for that account. In general, check-processing expenses are the major noncredit cost item for commercial customers. If priced separately, service charge income should at least equal this aggregate cost. Estimating the cost of noncredit services, such as deposit accounts, is discussed in more detail in Chapter 8.

Cost estimates for **credit services** usually represent the largest expense and are related to the size and type of loan. These costs include the interest cost of financing the loan as well as loan administration expense. The **cost of**

# CONTEMPORARY ISSUES

## STRATEGIES FOR INCREASING NONINTEREST INCOME

Increasing noninterest income is the goal of many bankers today. The question of *how* is central to that mission. Determining the best method to increase noninterest income is critical not only to profitability, but to the overall mission of the bank. It would generally not make sense for a retirement community bank to begin offering the latest in high-technology gadgets to its customer base. Most experts agree that it usually makes more sense to increase the profitability of existing customers first, before going after new customers.

Former Citigroup Co-chair, John S. Reed said the banking industry has failed to fully understand and seize the potential of the consumer banking business. "We have a tendency to practice what I call harassment pricing—stick an extra 50 cents on that ATM because you need the revenue," explains Reed. "Most people want access to their money at no cost, and you can understand why." Today, in addition to ATM surcharges, NSF (not sufficient funds) fees are popular methods of increasing noninterest income. Although these methods do increase income, at least in the short run, they might not create value for the institutions. Therefore, the first step to increasing noninterest income is to *know your customer*. This seems obvious but many businesses do not always have a good handle on who their best customers are and what they need that the bank could provide. By banks not knowing their needs, these best customers often go to another provider and find all of the services they need. They then ask themselves, "Why do we need to do business at the old bank?"

To improve noninterest income, banks should profile their best five or six customers and ask why they do business with them? Managers should then determine what type of financial business these cusotmers do with the bank. Based on this information, banks can then determine how to increase the profitability of these best customers by satisfying their needs. The following list represents the order and priority of a successful strategy to increase noninterest income:

1. Determine if all existing products and services are priced appropriately. If not, adjust pricing.
2. Examine exceptions to existing pricing policies to determine if policy adjustments are needed.
3. Effectively sell *existing* products and services.
4. Ensure that the bank's staff is properly trained on various product lines and create incentives to cross-market and cross-sell existing products.
5. Examine and evaluate the bank's market to determine if the bank is in the right markets and offering the right products for that market and its customers. If not, then consider expanding the bank's geographic market and product and service lines:
   - Expand into new markets with existing products by developing new products and services that:
     –Leverage and retain existing customers
     –Attract new customers

The central theme is that offering the latest trendy products is often not the best business strategy. Determine the appropriateness of existing products. Are they priced correctly and is the bank charging the appropriate fees at the appropriate times? Do the bank's employees know about the bank's existing product line and are they effectively cross-selling the bank's existing products? Experts agree that the first three strategies often bring the best results in the short run. Expanding the product line or the market in which the bank sells these products is expensive and risky. This is often a good strategy for growth but requires extensive market research.

---

**funds** estimate may be a bank's weighted marginal cost of pooled debt or its weighted marginal cost of capital at the time the loan was made. This calculation follows that described in Chapter 8. **Loan administration expense** is the cost of a loan's credit analysis and execution. It includes personnel and overhead costs as well as direct costs for sending interest bills, processing payments, and maintaining collateral. The charge may be imposed on a per-item basis, determined by the unit cost of handling a loan times the number of notes outstanding, or computed as a fixed percentage of the loan amount.

The final expense, **business risk expense,** is difficult to measure directly and represents both actual cash expense (losses) as well as noncash expense, or allocations for potential losses. There are several types of business risk associated with the provision of banking services. With respect to noncredit services, the largest single risk is transaction risk. **Transaction risk** is the current and prospective risk inherent in transactions from fraud; theft; error; integrity of computing systems; internal controls; and delays or disruptions in processing, clearing, and settling payment transactions, which could lead to credit and liquidity problems as well as affect earnings and capital. Each time a customer makes a deposit or withdrawal to his or her account, writes a check, or makes a purchase with a credit card, the bank is at risk. As most of us know, consumers have well-defined limits of liability on their credit cards in the event the card is lost, stolen, or otherwise unauthorized charges appear on the bill. The risk to the bank can be enormous and is determined by the quality of its control systems. The bank must allocate reserve funds for the potential that a customer may lose his or her credit card or checkbook, have an ATM pin number compromised, or that a computer hacker might break into the bank's systems. The majority of transaction risk resides with the bank. More importantly, the extensive use of the Internet and other electronic data sources puts the bank at risk from unauthorized entry into its data systems, illegal transfer of funds, fraud, and embellishment. These expenses are difficult to predict at the individual level but can represent tremendous amounts of money. With effective controls, these transactions risks can be controlled and estimated in the aggregate relatively accurately but the bank is always at risk for that one in a million chance that a serious breach in controls or security could create liquidity or even solvency problems.

With respect to credit services, **default risk** represents the largest single risk. A formal allocation of risk expense represents one method of handling the impact of potential loan losses. Many banks categorize loans according to their risk characteristics at the time of issue. Low-risk loans, which typically have short-term maturities, are those extended to borrowers with strong financial statements, adequate cash flow and collateral, and sound management. High-risk loans, which generally have longer maturities, are extended to borrowers with weaker financial statements, low cash flow, and collateral that potentially fluctuates widely in value. Management first ranks loans by these characteristics and historical default experience, assigning each credit to a particular risk class. This risk rating system allows different charges for potential loss in the event of default for loans with different likelihoods of default and different magnitudes of loss when in default. The actual risk expense measure equals the historical default percentage for loans in that risk class times the outstanding loan balance.

**REVENUE COMPONENTS.** Banks generate three types of revenue from customer accounts: investment income from the customer's deposit balances held at the bank, fee income from services, and interest and fee income on loans. Account profitability analysis provides a pricing framework that compares the sum of these revenues with expenses and the target profit.

Every deposit that customers hold generates **investment income from deposit balances** for the bank. In cases involving transactions accounts, banks must set aside legal reserves as a percentage of deposits, but they can invest remaining balances that exceed customer float on the account. Many customers are net depositors as their balances exceed any loans the bank has extended them. Other customers are net borrowers as their outstanding loans are greater than their total deposits. As such, a customer does not borrow his own deposits, but rather all funding comes from all pooled debt and equity. Implicitly, customer deposits are viewed as part of a bank's total available funds. Thus, the cost of financing a loan equals the weighted cost of debt times the full amount of the loan plus the cost of equity, which is the target return to shareholders. Investment income is allocated using an *earnings credit* as an estimate of the interest a bank can earn on the customer's investable balances.

Banks increasingly rely on noninterest income (**fee income**) to supplement earnings. Competition among savings banks, credit unions, brokerage houses, insurance companies, and other commercial banks has increased borrowing costs relative to yields available on loans. This pressure on net interest margins and growth constraints from capital restrictions make new products and services income the most promising source of earnings growth. Many corporate customers, in turn, are so efficient in minimizing their deposit balances that fees represent a better source of income than interest income from compensating deposit balances. When analyzing a customer's account relationship, fee income from all services rendered is included in total revenue. Fees are frequently charged on a per-item basis, as with Federal Reserve wire transfers, or as a fixed periodic charge for a bundle of services, regardless of usage rates. Fees for servicing mortgage loans supported by pass-through securities and providing letters of credit, financial guarantees, data processing, and cash management have recently risen at banks, which aggressively market these services.

**Loan interest** represents the primary revenue source in a vast majority of banks, as loans are the dominant asset in the portfolios of these institutions. The actual interest earned depends on the contractual loan rate and the outstanding principal. Although banks quote many different loan rates to customers, several general features stand out. Most banks price commercial loans off base rates, which serve as indexes of a bank's cost of funds. Common base rate alternatives include the federal funds rate, CD rate, commercial paper rate, the London Interbank Offer Rate (LIBOR), the LIBOR swap curve, Wall Street prime, and a bank's own weighted cost of funds. The contractual loan rate is set at some mark-up over the base rate, so that interest income varies directly with movements in the level of borrowing costs. Such floating-rate loans are popular at banks because they increase the rate sensitivity of loans in line with the increased rate sensitivity of bank liabilities. In addition, the magnitude of the mark-up reflects differences in perceived default and liquidity risk associated with the borrower. The mark-up increases with loans in higher-risk classes and with maturity as there is more time for the borrower's condition to deteriorate.[4] Finally, a substantial portion of commercial loans and most consumer loans carry fixed rates. In each case, the contractual rates should reflect the estimated cost of bank funds, perceived default risk, and a term liquidity and interest rate risk premium over the life of the agreement.

## AGGREGATE PROFITABILITY RESULTS FROM CUSTOMER PROFITABILITY ANALYSIS

---

[4]When a comprehensive customer profitability analysis is used, the mark-up reflects either default risk or required interest to cover expenses and meet profit targets. Many banks price loans independently from other account activity.

Examining aggregate results from customer profitability analyses across different banks' reveals several interesting points. First, as indicated above, a small fraction of customers contributes the bulk of bank profits. In 1997, for example, First Chicago reported that the most profitable 6 percent of its customers produced $1,600 in revenue and cost $350 to serve annually. The least profitable 14 percent of customers produced $230 in revenue and cost $700 to serve. Canadian Imperial Bank of Commerce (CIBC) similarly reported that just 20 percent of its customers were profitable.[5] The majority of studies show that about 70 percent of Internet banking accounts are unprofitable. This supports the widely held view that approximately 80 percent of a typical bank's customers are unprofitable while 70 percent of the typical bank's Internet customers are unprofitable.

Many customer profitability models show that a significant difference between profitable and unprofitable accounts is that profitable customers maintain multiple relationships with the bank, such as substantial loan and investment business. Unprofitable customers, on the other hand, tend to go where they get the best price or do not use multiple products. This should encourage banks to offer product bundles based on the size of the bank's relationships. For example, Wells Fargo offers multiple types of checking accounts that come bundled with free or reduced costs for a variety of services for various tiers of high combined balance (total of deposit and loan balances) customers.

Finally, banks that want to increase revenues should identify the perceived value of services by customers and price the services accordingly. In 1995, First Chicago imposed a $3 fee each time customers used a live teller in the bank's branches. Not surprisingly, this was a public relations nightmare once the media got word of it. Other Chicago banks aggressively marketed their no-fee teller services in an attempt to draw business from First Chicago. Still, First Chicago lost less than 1 percent of its customers, cut its branch employees by 30 percent, and saw ATM usage and deposits grow by 100 percent in the first three months. In 1997, First Chicago imposed a teller fee on its no-minimum-balance transactions account because customers perceived the value of low minimum balances to be far higher than the negative impact of fees. This account eventually became First Chicago's most popular checking account. Bank One (now JP Morgan Chase) also offers a "free" checking account that imposes a $3 fee for the use of live tellers and drive-in transactions.

Although these types of accounts may be public relations nightmares, they make great business sense. Live teller transactions are the highest cost type of transactions for a bank. Most banks give these services away for free and then charge their customers to use their lower-cost ATM and electronic transactions services. Even though this makes poor business sense, it continues to be done because of the customer backlash of imposing fees on transactions that have traditionally been free. By charging a fee for the higher-cost-type transactions, banks can offer lower-cost products to those who do not use, or need, a substantial number of the higher cost services such as live transactions. Few if any young people actually visit the bank today and these accounts fit their need for low-cost, low-minimum-balance accounts. In the future, successful banks will offer products that meet their customers' needs and price all of their services according to costs, not tradition! See the Contemporary Issues Box: "Online Banking: How Are Bank's Getting Their Customers to 'Change Their Ways?'"

It is important to recognize that just knowing how profitable a customer is does not demonstrate how to use the information. To increase noninterest income, banks should attempt to make unprofitable customers profitable by providing them with incentives to buy more services or buy a package of services that meet their wants and needs. This often involves offering price incentives to use ATMs or other low-cost channels for delivering services. For example, Wachovia has offered a no-minimum balance, no-service-charge checking account for students with the restriction that the student does not enter a branch office. USAA Savings Bank offers to pay for its customers use of other banks' ATMs as well as offers its customers 0.5 percent cash back for using a non-PIN-based debit transaction. The non-PIN based debit transaction is less expensive for the bank! Banks similarly waive fees and offer attractive interest rates to customers who are highly profitable in order to keep their relationship or encourage them to use the services that are best for the bank.

The primary difficulty with profit data is that it is descriptive, but not necessarily predictive of future customer behavior. Carroll and Tadikonda (1997) provide an example of two checking account customers who each generate a $55 profit for a bank. One maintains a high deposit balance, writes a large number of checks, and makes frequent balance inquiries. The other maintains a low balance and writes a large number of insufficient funds checks. The first customer generates investment income from the balances that exceeds the cost of check processing. The second customer generates fee income from overdrafts that covers a loss from processing checks net of any investment income. The point is that these two customers are quite different, even though their account profitability is the same.

A bank should treat these two customers differently in terms of how it markets other services. Specifically, management should examine customer data to assess how customers use existing services and what factors affect usage. It should then forecast likely usage and delinquencies or defaults going forward and calculate the present value of expected cash flows from selling the other services. The two customers described above will exhibit differ-

---

[5]See O'Sullivan (1997) for these and other examples.

## CONTEMPORARY ISSUES

### ONLINE BANKING: HOW ARE BANKS GETTING THEIR CUSTOMERS TO "CHANGE THEIR WAYS"?

Today, many bank customers are set in their way of doing things. They expect to go to the bank and not pay to make a transaction. The questions many bankers are asking is, When was the last time you went into the store to purchase something and did not pay for it? When was the last time you purchased a stock or bond and did not pay a transaction fee?' Banking customers have gotten used to not paying to make live teller transactions and many of these free transactions offered by the bank are the bank's most expensive delivery method. The Gartner Group estimates that only 18.8 million customers used online bill payment at the beginning of 2004 but expect that more than 56 million households will bank online by 2008. About 85 percent of them will pay their bills online.

Banking customers want access to their money as inexpensively as possible and most prefer free. So banks must encourage their customers to stop using the more expensive traditional delivery channels for their banking needs; for example, live teller transactions, paper checks, and paper check deposits. Instead, the banks need their customers to use automatic deposits, debit cards, and Internet bill pay if they are going to reduce the cost, and therefore the price, of banking services. Until recently, most banks charged their customers to use Internet bill pay and allowed them to use live tellers, paper checks, and paper deposits for free.

Today, banks such as Citibank, Bank of America, Wells Fargo, and Sun Trust, to name a few, have some form of free checking and free Internet bill pay. In fact, a recent Tower-Group report indicates that 38 percent of the top 50 U.S. banks presently offer online bill payment free to all customers. The

intent is to "switch" customers from old delivery channels to making electronic payments. Banks are offering monetary incentives and changing their pricing structure to encourage customers to change their ways. Citibank's customers, with their EZ checking account and a balance of $2,500 or more, are eligible for a free iPod if they use online bill pay to pay at least two bills online each month. E*Trade Financial Corporation, which has no retail branches, is offering checking account customers $100 cash back for opening new accounts with at least $1,000. Wells Fargo is offering customers $10 for enrolling and activating their online accounts. On the other end, Chase, JP Morgan, Wells Fargo, US Bank. and many other banks charge a fee, on some accounts, to see a live teller.

Why are banks just now jumping on the electronic bandwagon? Simple: costs and customer needs. Many customers do not understand why a bank charges them $1.50 to use an ATM to access their own money. The answer is cost as well as profit. Fundamentally, the ATM network costs the bank to build and maintain. In addition, one of the costs most often overlooked by banking customers is that of insuring against fraud. If a customer loses his or her credit card or ATM card, that customer expects the bank to cover all unauthorized charges. The bank must charge its customers for this insurance. Otherwise, it would be like an automobile owner not having insurance coverage on the automobile; if the car was stolen, the owner would not have coverage.

Customers want cheap or free access to their money but according to a study by Booz Allen Hamilton, the average transaction at a full-service branch costs a bank $4.07. Still, most banks give this away for free. A phone transaction costs $0.54 and an ATM transaction $0.27, while the cost is only $0.01 for a Web-based transaction. So why charge for Internet bill pay and give live teller transactions away for free? Customers are accustomed to free live teller transactions and do not understand why they should have to pay for them. On the other hand, most bank customers are accustomed to paying to use the ATM and Internet bill pay. Hence, the average bank charges to use the less expensive services to help pay for providing the more expensive delivery channels. Today, the younger generation is more comfortable with electronic payment systems and wants "free" access to their money. More and more banks are changing their pricing structure to reflect this demand.

ent patterns of usage and will likely generate different cash flows from any new service. It is these expected usage patterns that should be consolidated with pricing strategies.

### WHAT IS THE APPROPRIATE BUSINESS MIX?

Some fee income derives from relatively stable services and lines of business, while other fees are highly volatile and reflect changing volumes and pricing. In today's environment, most banks attempt to manage fee income in a portfolio context. Fee income from deposit service charges is quite stable and will likely exhibit modest growth.

| EXHIBIT 3.9 | Percentage of Various Components of Total Noninterest Income, 2004 | | | |
|---|---|---|---|---|
| **Percentage of Total Noninterest Income** | **<$100M** | **$100M–$1B** | **>$1B** | **All Comm. Banks** |
| Deposit service charges | 45.7% | 30.7% | 15.9% | 17.5% |
| Fiduciary activities | 8.7% | 13.6% | 12.2% | 12.2% |
| Trading, venture capital and securitizations | 0.0% | 4.3% | 18.3% | 17.5% |
| Net servicing fees | 8.7% | 4.3% | 8.5% | 8.3% |
| Investment banking, advisory, brokerage, and insurance | 1.1% | 2.1% | 5.7% | 5.2% |
| Insurance commissions and fees | 4.3% | 2.1% | 2.4% | 2.2% |
| Net gains (losses) on sales of loans and other assets | 3.3% | 7.1% | 4.1% | 3.9% |
| Net gains (losses) on other assets | 0.0% | 0.7% | 1.2% | 0.9% |
| Other noninterest income | 28.3% | 35.0% | 31.7% | 32.3% |

SOURCE: FDIC Statistics on Depository Institutions, http://www2.fdic.gov/sdi/main.asp.

Still, banks must be aware that they are at great risk from brokerage firms that continue to eat into banks' share of this business. This is particularly true of Internet brokerage firms.

↩ Deposit charges should be balanced with fees from other lines of business or products with higher growth potential. Exhibit 3.9 shows the composition of various noninterest income components as a percentage of total noninterest income. Furash argues that large banks should generate 30 percent of noninterest income from deposit activities, including ATMs, telephone banking, and home banking.[6] They should obtain another 10 to 15 percent from businesses driven by the capital markets, such as investment banking and trading. Investment banking generally refers to the combination of securities underwriting, creating markets in securities, and fees from investment or merger and acquisitions advice. Trading income derives from operating a trading desk for customers whereby the bank maintains an inventory of securities to buy and sell, and from proprietary trading of securities and derivatives for its own account. Finally, banks should generate the remaining 55 to 60 percent of noninterest income from specialty intermediation and/or fee-based operating businesses. Included in this last group of activities are specialized consumer finance, specialty leasing, factoring, insurance products, mutual fund sales, and investment management. In fact, this is the motivation behind banks acquiring or merging with insurance companies. It will likely lead to a number of financial services holding companies that offer a wide range of products such as credit cards, mortgages, small business loans, consumer loans, leases, insurance, brokerage services, securities underwriting, and so on, via subsidiaries that specialize in each.

Community banks do not have the same opportunities to enter investment banking and specialty intermediation. However, they do have other potential avenues. Many banks work with bankers' banks in the same geographic area to offer services that they could not offer independently. These bankers' banks are effectively correspondent banks that are owned by member institutions, such that community banks own the bankers' banks. Bankers' banks typically make loans to members, trade federal funds, and offer investment trust and data processing services. A relatively new twist finds bankers' banks offering trust services to customers of non-member institutions.

Alternatively, many community banks are entering new product and service areas. Exhibit 3.10 describes the results of the 2004 Community Bank Competitiveness Survey by the American Bankers Association (ABA) regarding the banking services banks offered in 2003. The number of products offered by banks and the percentage of banks offering these products has increased significantly over the past five years. Not surprisingly, most banks relied heavily on residential mortgage originations, debit cards, Automated Clearing House (ACH) origination, credit life insurance, and credit cards. The logic underlying this portfolio view of fee income is that a bank is diversified when it relies on different sources of income. As economic conditions change, some businesses will generate increasing fees while others will see fees drop. This same rationale applies in mortgage banking, where loan origination fees vary inversely with mortgage servicing revenue.

An obvious problem is that some managers view these volatile fees as permanent sources of income. In fact, they are not. This point has been demonstrated by the reduction in mortgage activity and associated fees with the increase in interest rates during 2004–2005. The vast majority of home mortgages were created during the early 2000s and as interest rates increase, the rate of refinancing slows dramatically. In addition, the stock market crash of the early 2000s dramatically reduced retail stock trades and the fees associated with them. A related problem is that banks view these businesses on a transactions basis. They cut interest rates on loans so that they can book the fee income. This creates the perception that they will win the business only when they are the low

---

[6]A summary appears in Kantrow (1998).

**EXHIBIT 3.10**

Product Offerings at Community Banks to Generate Noninterest Income in 2003

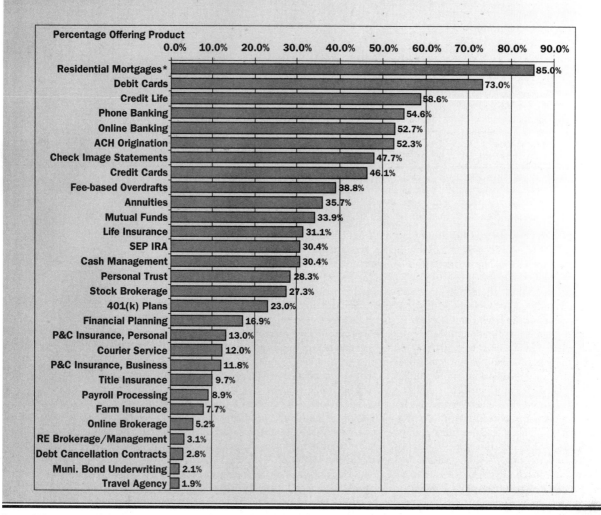

Percentage Offering Product

| Product | Percentage |
|---|---|
| Residential Mortgages* | 85.0% |
| Debit Cards | 73.0% |
| Credit Life | 58.6% |
| Phone Banking | 54.6% |
| Online Banking | 52.7% |
| ACH Origination | 52.3% |
| Check Image Statements | 47.7% |
| Credit Cards | 46.1% |
| Fee-based Overdrafts | 38.8% |
| Annuities | 35.7% |
| Mutual Funds | 33.9% |
| Life Insurance | 31.1% |
| SEP IRA | 30.4% |
| Cash Management | 30.4% |
| Personal Trust | 28.3% |
| Stock Brokerage | 27.3% |
| 401(k) Plans | 23.0% |
| Financial Planning | 16.9% |
| P&C Insurance, Personal | 13.0% |
| Courier Service | 12.0% |
| P&C Insurance, Business | 11.8% |
| Title Insurance | 9.7% |
| Payroll Processing | 8.9% |
| Farm Insurance | 7.7% |
| Online Brokerage | 5.2% |
| RE Brokerage/Management | 3.1% |
| Debt Cancellation Contracts | 2.8% |
| Muni. Bond Underwriting | 2.1% |
| Travel Agency | 1.9% |

SOURCE: 2004 Community Bank Competitiveness Survey, American Bankers Association.

*Not published in the survey. Represents authors' estimate based on prior years data.

price provider. Instead, banks should attempt to build the same type of customer relationships that they have successfully built with many deposit and loan customers. This can be accomplished by focusing on the customers' needs across a broad range of services, rather than on single transactions, and pricing them accordingly.

## STRATEGIES TO MANAGE NONINTEREST EXPENSE

Consider the competitive environment in which commercial banks operate. The basic business of banking has always been accepting deposits and making loans. In today's world, banks are high-cost producers relative to money market funds run by brokerage houses and relative to the commercial paper and bond markets used by corporate borrowers. Comparatively, noninterest expense is too high and earnings are too low. For many bank managers, this mandates austere budgets directed at controlling expenses.

Since 1985, noninterest expense at commercial banks has increased each year at a declining rate. This primarily reflects efforts to cut costs and increase profitability that are driven by a fear of being acquired and/or noncompetitive. Quite simply, senior managers of acquired banks typically find that they are looking for new positions shortly after an acquisition, a fate they most aggressively try to avoid. This begs an obvious question, however: Are there too many banks, credit unions, and other financial institutions in the United States? Do we need three different competing institutions on every downtown street corner? If banks in the same market combined their operations, they could cut payroll and occupancy expenses, eliminate boards of directors, and use computer technology more efficiently. The cost savings would be recurring and fall right to the bottom line. In fact, potential cost savings has motivated much of the recent bank merger and acquisition activity.

When they initially consider noninterest expenses, many managers focus on reducing costs. A more comprehensive strategy, however, is to manage costs in line with strategic objectives. Does it not seem sensible, for example, to invest in new technologies if they will reduce operating costs long-term, even if the investment adds to noninterest expense in the near term? The basic issue is to determine whether the return on the investment exceeds the bank's weighted marginal cost of capital. If it does, the investment adds value to shareholders.

Gregor and Hedges (1990) examine the relationship between the ratio of noninterest expense to assets, the relative growth rate in noninterest expense to assets, and the market-to-book value of stockholders' equity and conclude that there is no systematic link between cost management strategies and the market value of bank equity. Specifically, banks reporting the lowest expense ratios for both ratios reported the lowest market-to-book values of stockholders' equity. Banks with the highest expenses and relative expense growth actually reported the highest relative stock market values. The essential point is that there is no systematic link between reported expenses and the market value of firm equity.

## COST MANAGEMENT STRATEGIES

What then is cost management? In general, it is a philosophy of allocating resources to the most profitable lines of business to achieve improved performance. There are four basic expense management strategies: expense reduction, operating efficiencies, revenue enhancement, and contribution growth.

**EXPENSE REDUCTION.** Many banks begin cost management efforts by identifying excessive expenses and eliminating them. Given that noninterest expenses consist primarily of personnel, occupancy, and data processing costs, these are the areas where cuts are initially made. It is not unusual to hear of banks announcing widespread employee reductions even absent any merger or acquisition. Because of the high cost of employee benefits, many banks use temporary workers who do not receive health insurance coverage and other benefits. Other common areas for cutting include the number of branch offices and employee medical benefits. Many banks have eliminated their data processing department altogether and contracted to buy data processing services from a nonbank vendor, such as IBM or EDS. In industry jargon, this is referred to as **outsourcing.** The Contemporary Issues Box: "Expense Reduction Opportunities" identifies key areas in which a bank's expense structure can be improved.

**OPERATING EFFICIENCIES.** Another strategy is to increase operating efficiency in providing products and services. This can be achieved in one of three ways:

1. By reducing costs but maintaining the existing level of products and services
2. By increasing the level of output but maintaining the level of current expenses
3. By improving workflow

All of these approaches fall under the label of increasing productivity because they involve delivering products at lower unit costs. The first typically involves cutting staff and increasing work requirements to maintain output. Fewer people do the same amount or more work. The second addresses economies of scale and economies of scope in banking. **Economies of scale** are said to exist when a bank's average costs decrease as output increases. Diseconomies exist when average costs increase with greater output. **Economies of scope** focus on how the joint costs of providing several products change as new products are added or existing product output is enhanced. The argument is that joint costs will grow by much less than the costs associated with producing products or providing services independently. For example, if a bank adds a new product line and can provide it and existing products at a lower unit cost than previously, economies of scope exist. Finally, improving workflow involves increasing productivity by accelerating the rate at which a task or function is performed. The intent is to eliminate redundant reviews or tasks and thereby shorten the time to finish a task.

The results of a Booz Allen Hamilton study, summarized by Sanford Rose (1989), identified three myths in bank managers' perceptions about noninterest expense. The first is that banks operate with high fixed costs. Fixed costs create problems because they cannot be reduced (that is, controlled) by managers. If banks eliminate some products or services, existing fixed costs must then be allocated to any remaining products. According to the study, however, only 10 percent of costs are shared among products and thus are truly fixed. The

## CONTEMPORARY ISSUES

### EXPENSE REDUCTION OPPORTUNITIES

Earnings Performance Group has identified several areas in which expense reduction opportunities typically arise. The following list introduces the broad areas and presents key questions that managers should address when evaluating their existing expense structure.

1. Identify ways to more effectively utilize automated systems.
   - Is data being keyed from a computer report into another personal computer system?
2. Eliminate redundant tasks/functions.
3. Complete a review of all reports to determine whether they are actually used.
   - Are multiple copies produced when only one is needed?
   - Would imaging be just as adequate?
   - Are there online screens that provide the same information as reports?
   - Can reports be eliminated or combined?
   - What happens to paper? Is it recycled?
4. Can we decrease the number of statements and/or notices mailed to a customer?
5. Reevaluate telephone expenses, particularly long-distance charges.
6. If outside couriers/messengers are used, when was the last time the routes were rebid? Have the number of stops and/or routes been reviewed in relation to work available?
7. Are ZIP-sorts used to reduce postage expenses?
8. Are PC purchases and related peripherals centrally controlled?
9. What are the opportunities regarding reducing cost of copiers and/or fax machines by handling them centrally?
10. Review all contracts with outside vendors to determine the last time they were put out to bid. How are maintenance contracts handled?

implication is that banks can eliminate products that are unprofitable or marginally profitable and the average costs of remaining products will be largely unchanged. The second myth is that banks produce many products at the point of minimum unit costs. In their study, just three out of 15 large banks were scale producers. The remaining 12 banks would be better off either merging with other banks or outsourcing products. The third myth is that most reductions in expenses are permanent and have a significant impact on overall profitability.

### REVENUE ENHANCEMENT

Revenue enhancement involves changing the pricing of specific products and services but maintaining a sufficiently high volume of business so that total revenues increase. It is closely linked to the concept of price elasticity. Here, management wants to identify products or services that exhibit price inelastic demand. As such, an increase in price will lower the quantity demanded of the underlying product, but the proportionate decrease in demand is less than the proportionate increase in price. Revenues thus increase. Alternatively, management can attempt to expand volume while keeping price constant. This can often be achieved by target marketing to enlarge the base of consumers. It also is a by-product of improving product quality. If customers perceive an improvement in quality, they will consume more and/or willingly pay a higher price.

**CONTRIBUTION GROWTH.** With the strategy of contribution growth, management allocates resources to best improve overall long-term profitability. Increases in expenses are acceptable and expected, but must coincide with greater anticipated increases in associated revenues. An example might be investing in new computer systems and technology to provide better customer service at reduced unit costs once volume is sufficiently large. In essence, expenses are cut in the long run but not in the near future.

Obviously, different banks follow different cost management strategies. This follows from differences in individual bank operating environments as determined by business mix, overall corporate strategic objectives, the geographic markets served, and history of cost management behavior. Each strategy can be successfully implemented if pursued with long-term objectives. Rather than use traditional measures of expense control to monitor performance, managers should examine noninterest expense relative to operating revenue compared with peers that offer the same business mix. Remember that cost management does not necessarily mean that expenses decline in absolute terms.

The net result of cost management is that banks will operate as leaner competitors. This should enhance long-term profitability and survival prospects in the consolidating banking industry. The negative aspects include the painful effects of replacing people with machines, requiring greater on-the-job work effort that potentially increases employee stress, and in many cases reduced support of community activities.

## SUMMARY

This chapter examines three issues related to managing a bank's noninterest income and noninterest expense. First, it describes the strengths and weaknesses of commonly used financial ratios that presumably measure a bank's ability to control noninterest expense and grow noninterest income. Second, it discusses why banks should focus on customer profitability and the mix of fee-based businesses to improve operating performance. Third, it describes different cost management strategies intended to enhance performance.

The most commonly cited ratio today is the efficiency ratio, which is equal to noninterest expense divided by the sum of net interest income and noninterest income. The lower the ratio, the better a bank's performance—ceteris paribus—because it indicates how much a bank must pay in noninterest expense to generate one dollar of operating revenue. Many banks cite this ratio along with return on equity, return on assets, and net interest margin when describing performance for the whole bank. Stock analysts, in turn, cite this ratio when recommending bank stocks. Other key ratios describe a bank's productivity in terms of assets, expense, and net income relative to the number of full-time employees.

A crucial facet of managing noninterest income and expense is knowledge about the profitability of different customer relationships. This information allows management to target products and services and alter pricing strategies to ensure that customers get what they want and that the packages of services or products are profitable. Finally, it is appropriate for banks to follow many different cost management strategies as long as the objective is to enhance shareholder value.

## QUESTIONS

1. When confronted with runaway noninterest expense, management's first impulse is to cut costs. What are the advantages and disadvantages of this approach? What other approaches are possible?

2. What are the primary sources of noninterest income for both a small community bank and a large bank with many subsidiaries and global operations?

3. What are the components of noninterest expense?

4. Describe why the efficiency ratio is a meaningful measure of cost control. Describe why it may not accurately measure cost control.

5. Which of the following banks evidences better productivity? Both banks have $700 million in assets and conduct the same volume and type of business off-balance sheet.

|  | Tri-Cities Bank | Pacific Rail Bank |
| --- | --- | --- |
| Assets per employee | $1,530,000 | $1,880,000 |
| Personnel expense per employee | 33,750 | 42,600 |

6. Pacific Coast Bank reports that just 20 percent of its customers were profitable. Assuming that this applies to individuals' account relationships, make three recommendations to increase the profitability of these accounts.

7. Suppose that your bank imposes the following fees and/or service charges. Explain the bank's rationale and describe how you would respond as a customer.

   a. $1.50 per item for use of an ATM run by an entity other than your own bank

   b. $4 per transaction for using a live teller rather than an ATM or telephone transaction

   c. Increase in the charge for insufficient funds (where a customer writes a check for an amount greater than the balance available in the account) from $25 per item to $30 per item

   d. A 1 percent origination fee for refinancing a mortgage

8. List the three primary sources of revenue from a commercial customer's account. In today's economic environment, indicate whether each is growing or declining in use and explain why.

9. In each of the following situations, evaluate the profitability of the customer's account relationship with the bank. Did profits meet expectations? The expense figure includes the cost of debt but not the cost of equity. Figures are in millions of dollars.

| | Expenses | Revenue | Target Profit |
|---|---|---|---|
| Class Action Corp. | $ 11.45 | $ 12.98 | $ 1.50 |
| Zisk Drive | 131.81 | 130.27 | 4.66 |
| Gonzo Ltd. | 88.35 | 93.77 | 6.58 |

10. What impact will online brokerages have on traditional commercial banks? Why?

11. Describe the strengths and weaknesses of expense reduction, revenue enhancement, and contribution growth strategies.

12. Your bank has just calculated the profitability of two small business customers. In both instances, the bank earned a monthly profit of $375 from both Detail Labs and The Right Stuff. Detail Labs had a large loan with the bank and small balances. Its principals bought no other services from the bank. The Right Stuff had only a small loan, but used the bank for payroll processing and the firm's checking account transactions. The principals also had checking and CD accounts with the bank.

13. What additional services or products would you suggest that the bank market to each of these customers?

14. Discuss how the source of profitability will influence the choice of services and products that you recommend.

## PROBLEM

Suppose that you operate a large bank, the performance of which is closely followed by a large number of stock analysts. You have just received a summary of five different analysts' reviews of your bank's performance. The essence of each report is that the bank must lower its efficiency ratio from the current 59 percent to less than 52 percent before the analysts will put a strong buy recommendation on the stock. Otherwise, the bank is viewed as a takeover target.

   a. Describe several strategies that you might pursue in response to these reports.
   b. Discuss the strengths and weaknesses of each. Generally, do stock analysts have a reasonable influence on bank managers, or is their influence too great?
   c. Discuss whether management should focus on the operating risk ratio and what the likely impact of efforts to reduce this ratio will be.

# PART III

# MANAGING INTEREST RATE RISK

# CHAPTER

# 4

# Pricing Fixed-Income Securities

*Suppose that you have $1 million to invest for one year. The interest rate quoted on every 1-year fixed-income security you consider is 8 percent. If the security pays simple interest, interest income for the year will equal $80,000. If the security pays interest compounded continuously, interest income will total $83,287, or $3,287 more. If the rate is quoted on a money market basis assuming a 360-day year, interest income will equal $81,111. The point is, interest rates are not necessarily equal. The same percentage quote may produce a different return depending on the frequency of compounding and whether the quote assumes a 360-day or 365-day year.*

*Of course, interest rates are important to both borrowers and investors. Regulations assist consumer borrowers by requiring banks to quote financing charges as an annual percentage rate that adjusts for these computational differences, thus enabling a direct comparison of alternative borrowing costs. Truth in Savings regulations similarly enable depositors to compare rates across various deposits. However, security investors must fend for themselves and decipher how alternative rate quotes affect the true yield.*

*This chapter examines four basic issues. First, it introduces the mathematics of interest rates for fixed-income securities and demonstrates the impact of compounding. Second, it describes the relationship between the interest rate on a security and the security's market price. The concepts of duration and convexity are used to measure relative price sensitivity to interest rate changes, which can then be compared among securities. Third, it explains how specific interest rates on different money market and capital market instruments are quoted. Particular attention is paid to differences between money market, bond equivalent, and effective interest rate calculations. Finally, it describes recent innovations in how securities are valued when related to viewing any fixed-income security as a package of zero coupon cash flows and introduces the concept of total return, used by investors to compare expected realized yields over some predetermined holding period. Subsequent chapters will refer to these concepts and calculations and incorporate them in various applications.*

## THE MATHEMATICS OF INTEREST RATES

Just as there are many different types of securities, interest rates are calculated and reported differently. Depending on the characteristics of the security and pricing conventions of securities traders, interest may be simple or compounded, interest rates may be quoted on a discount basis or interest-bearing basis, and the assumed number of days in a year for reporting purposes may be 360 or 365. Hence, it is virtually impossible to compare quoted rates without a precise understanding of the differences in calculations.

## FUTURE VALUE AND PRESENT VALUE: SINGLE PAYMENT

The mathematics of interest rates is based on the simple recognition that cash in your possession today is worth more than the same amount of cash to be received at some time in the future. For example, are you better off with $50,000 today or a contract to receive $50,000 in six months? Obviously, if you had the cash today, you could invest it for six months and it would grow in value. The difference in value depends on the relevant interest rate that characterizes your opportunity cost or investment opportunities. This concept, or more precisely that of future value and present value, provides the framework for interest rate calculations.

Suppose that at the beginning of a year, an individual purchases a security for $1,000. The seller of the security, in turn, promises to pay the individual $1,080 exactly one year later. In this scenario, $1,000 represents the present value (PV) of the security, $1,080 represents the future value after one year (FV1), and $80 is interest. Expressing the $80 relative to the initial investment as a rate of interest (i),

$$i = \$80/\$1,000 = 0.08$$

Alternatively,

$$\$1,000(1 + i) = \$1,080$$

or

$$i = \$1,080/\$1,000 - 1$$
$$= 0.08 = 8\%$$

In general, with a single payment after one year (FV1) that includes interest and the initial investment, the following relationship applies:

$$PV(1 + i) = FV1 \tag{4.1}$$

Suppose that the same individual decides to buy another one-year security at the end of the first year and that the seller agrees to pay 8 percent on the entire $1,080 invested. Note that the individual is effectively earning interest on the initial $1,000 plus the first year's $80 in interest, so $1,080 represents the present value at the beginning of the second year. Substituting $1,080 for PV and .08 for i in Equation 4.1 reveals that the future value after the second year (FV2) equals $1,166.40.[1]

$$\$1,080(1 + 0.08) = \$1,166.40 = FV2$$

Combining this with Equation 4.1 produces

$$\$1,000(1 + .08)(1 + 0.08) = \$1,166.40 = FV2$$

or

$$PV(1 + i)^2 = FV2 \tag{4.2}$$

Alternatively, if the future value and present value are known, we can calculate the fixed annual interest rate from Equation 4.2 as:

$$i = [FV2/PV]^{1/2} - 1 \tag{4.3}$$

Using data from the previous example,

$$i = [\$1,166.40/\$1,000]^{1/2} - 1 = 0.08$$

When an amount is invested for several periods and interest is earned on both the initial investment plus periodic interest (compound interest), the following general relationship holds:

$$PV(1 + i)^n = FVn \tag{4.4}$$

where n represents the number of periods until the future value is determined. Equation 4.4 can be viewed from several vantage points. Since there are four variables, as long as three are known, we can solve for the fourth. Thus,

---

[1]The number in the notation FV1 and FV2 refers to the number of periods from the present until the cash flow arises. This example assumes that interest is earned on interest (compounding) and that interest is compounded annually.

if we know the initial present value, the periodic interest rate, and the number of years that interest applies, we can solve for the future value as in Equation 4.4. If we know everything except the interest rate, we can use Equation 4.5 to solve for i.

$$i = [FVn/PV]^{1/n} - 1 \qquad (4.5)$$

For example, the future value of $1,000 invested for six years at 8 percent per year with annual compounding (FV6) is $1,586.87

$$\$1,000(1.08)^6 = \$1,586.87$$

Suppose, instead, that we know that with $1,000 invested today for six years, the initial investment plus accumulated interest will be worth $1,700 in six years. What is the annual interest rate? Clearly, the rate must exceed 8 percent because the future value is greater than the $1,586.87 realized above. Using Equation 4.5, we know that

$$i = [\$1,700/\$1,000]^{1/6} - 1$$
$$= 0.0925$$

Note that in both examples, the interest rate used (annual rate) is matched with the frequency of compounding (annual).

In many instances, investors and borrowers want to determine the present value of some future cash payment or receipt. Investors often forecast future cash flows from an asset and want to know the value in today's dollars; that is, how much to pay. Equation 4.4 provides the calculation for the present value of a single future cash flow when we solve for PV and is restated as Equation 4.6.

$$PV = \frac{FVn}{(1 + i)^n} \qquad (4.6)$$

In this case, the future value is said to be discounted back to a present-value equivalent. Suppose that you have a choice between receiving an immediate $30,000 cash payment, or $37,500 in two years. Which would you choose? Assuming you aren't in desperate need of cash today, compare the present value of $37,500 to $30,000. If your opportunity cost of money is 8 percent annually—that is, your investment alternatives yield 8 percent per year—the present value of the $37,500 future cash flow is $32,150.

$$PV = \frac{\$37,500}{(1.08)^2} = \$32,150$$

Intuitively, you would need to invest $32,150 today at 8 percent to accumulate $37,500 in two years. Alternatively, the future cash flow is worth $2,150 more today than the immediate cash payment, so you would prefer the $37,500.

## FUTURE VALUE AND PRESENT VALUE: MULTIPLE PAYMENTS

Future value and present value analysis are only slightly more complicated when more than one cash flow is involved. The only difference is that the future or present value of each cash flow is computed separately, with the cumulative value determined as the sum of the computations for each cash flow (CF).

Suppose that an individual makes a $1,000 deposit in a bank earning 8 percent annually at the beginning of each of the next two years. What is the cumulative future value of both deposits after the second year? The first deposit earns two years of interest, while the second deposit earns just one year of interest. The future value of both deposits after two years is:

$$\text{FV of first deposit} = \$1,000(1.08)^2 = \$1,166.40$$
$$\text{FV of second deposit} = \$1,000(1.08) = \underline{\$1,080.00}$$
$$\text{Cumulative future value} = \$2,246.40$$

In general, setting CFn equal to the periodic cash flow in period n and assuming that all cash flows are invested at the beginning of each year at the fixed rate i, the cumulative future value of a series of cash flows (CFVn) after n periods can be expressed as:

$$CFVn = CF1(1 + i)^n + CF2(1 + i)^{n-1} + CF3(1 + i)^{n-2} + \ldots + CFn(1 + i) \tag{4.7}$$

This type of calculation is often used when trying to determine how much needs to be invested periodically to fund a future expenditure, such as payments for a child's college education.

The present value concept is more typically applied to a series of future cash flows. Investors may know the promised payments on a bond, or they may forecast the expected cash flows from buying a business. The present value of a series of cash flows equals the sum of the present values of the individual cash flows. Assuming the cash flows (CFCN) are received at the end of each period, n, the present value of a series of n cash flows received at the end of each period can be expressed as:

$$PV = \frac{CF(1)}{(1 + i)} + \frac{CF(2)}{(1 + i)^2} + \frac{CF(3)}{(1 + i)^3} + \ldots + \frac{CF(n)}{(1 + i)^n} \tag{4.8}$$

or, using summation notation

$$PV = \sum_{t=1}^{n} \frac{CF(t)}{(1 + i)^t}$$

Each future cash flow is discounted back to its present-value equivalent and the respective present values are added. Note that Equation 4.8 assumes that the same discount rate (i) applies to each cash flow. We will modify this later when we discuss the valuation of fixed-income securities.

In this context, determine how much you would pay for a security that pays $90 at the end of each of the next three years plus another $1,000 at the end of the third year if the relevant interest rate is 10 percent. Using Equation 4.8,

$$PV = \frac{\$90}{(1.1)} + \frac{\$90}{(1.1)^2} + \frac{\$1,090}{(1.1)^3} = \$975.13$$

Again, if the present value, future values, and number of periods are known, we can solve Equation 4.8 for i to determine the relevant discount rate. For fixed-income securities, this discount rate is the market rate of interest typically labeled the yield to maturity.[2]

## SIMPLE VERSUS COMPOUND INTEREST

In practice, the amount of interest paid on a security is determined in many different ways. One difference is that interest may be computed as **simple interest** or **compound interest.** Simple interest is interest that is paid only on the initial principal invested. Bank commercial loans, for example, normally quote simple interest payments. In contrast, compound interest is interest paid on outstanding principal plus any interest that has been earned but not paid out. Most bank deposits pay compound interest.

Simple interest equals the outstanding principal amount times the periodic interest rate times the number of periods. With the previous notation, simple interest equals

$$\text{Simple interest} = PV(i)n \tag{4.9}$$

In this case, the interest rate i is the periodic rate while n refers to the number of periods. Thus, if n equals one year and i equals 12 percent per year, simple interest on $1,000 equals

$$\text{Simple interest} = \$1,000(0.12)1 = \$120$$

Suppose that interest on the above contract is paid monthly. What is the monthly simple interest payment?

$$\text{Monthly simple interest} = \$1,000(0.12)(1/12) = \$10$$

The example following Equation 4.5 showed that $1,000 invested for six years at 8 percent with annual interest compounding produced a future value of $1,586.87. This assumed that interest was earned annually on the

---

[2]Another way to view the above calculation is to note that if you deposited $975.13 in an account that earns 10 percent interest per year, you could withdraw $90 at the end of each of the next two years and $1,090 at the end of the third year, which would leave a zero balance.

previous years' cumulative interest. Suppose, instead, that interest is 8 percent simple interest. What will the future value of principal plus interest equal?

$$\text{simple interest} = \$1,000(0.08)6 = \$480$$
$$\text{original principal} = \$1,000$$
$$\text{future value} = \$1,480$$

Obviously, the actual interest varies dramatically depending on whether simple or compound interest applies. As indicated, compound interest assumes that interest is paid on principal and interest. Each of the Equations 4.1 through 4.8 uses annual interest rates and assumes annual compounding. Equation 4.9, however, assumes no compounding.

## COMPOUNDING FREQUENCY

Interest may be compounded over a variety of intervals. In many cases, it is compounded over periods much less than one year, such as daily or monthly. Fortunately, the same formulas apply, with a small adjustment that consists of converting the annual interest rate to a periodic interest rate that coincides with the compounding interval, and letting the number of periods equal n times the number of compounding periods in a year (m):

$$PV(1 + i/m)^{nm} = FV_n \tag{4.10}$$

and

$$PV = \frac{FV_n}{(1 + i/m)^{nm}} \tag{4.11}$$

If compounding occurs daily, m equals 365 and the periodic rate equals the annual rate divided by 365. If compounding occurs monthly, m equals 12 and the periodic rate equals i divided by 12. The product of n times m (nm) is the total number of compounding periods. Exhibit 4.1 demonstrates the impact of different intra-year compounding intervals on future value and present value in line with Equations 4.10 and 4.11. As indicated, the

---

| **EXHIBIT 4.1** | The Effect of Compounding on Future Value and Present Value |
|---|---|

**A. What is the future value after 1 year of $1,000 invested at an 8% annual nominal rate?**

| Compounding Interval | Number of Compounding Intervals in 1 Year (m) | Future Value (FV1)* | Effective Interest Rate* |
|---|---|---|---|
| Year | 1 | $1,080.00 | 8.00% |
| Semiannual | 2 | 1,081.60 | 8.16 |
| Quarter | 4 | 1,082.43 | 8.24 |
| Month | 12 | 1,083.00 | 8.30 |
| Day | 365 | 1,083.28 | 8.33 |
| Continuous | † | 1,083.29 | 8.33 |

**B. What is the present value of $1,000 received at the end of 1 year with compounding at 8%?**

| Compounding Interval | Number of Compounding Intervals in 1 Year (m) | Present Value (PV)* | Effective Interest Rate* |
|---|---|---|---|
| Year | 1 | $925.93 | 8.00% |
| Semiannual | 2 | 924.56 | 8.16 |
| Quarter | 4 | 923.85 | 8.24 |
| Month | 12 | 923.36 | 8.30 |
| Day | 365 | 923.12 | 8.33 |
| Continuous | † | 923.12 | 8.33 |

*Most financial calculators can easily generate the required calculations.

†Continuous compounding assumes that compounding occurs over such short intervals that it is instantaneous, or that m in Equations 4.10 and 4.11 approaches infinity. Mathematically, continuous compounding is based on Euler's e such that $\lim_{m \to \infty}\left(1 + \frac{i}{m}\right)^m = e^i$, where e = 2.71828. Thus, equations 4.10 and 4.11 produce $FV_n = PVe^{in}$, and $PV = \frac{FV_n}{e^{in}}$.

future value after one year is greatest when compounding frequency is the highest because more frequent compounding means that interest is applied to previous interest more frequently. In a similar vein, the present value of a fixed amount is lowest when compounding frequency is highest as the more interest that can be earned, the lower is the initial value required to invest and return the same future value.

Exhibit 4.1 also demonstrates the impact of different effective interest rates. An effective interest rate, in contrast to a nominal or contract rate, incorporates the effect of compounding and thus allows a comparison of yields. Assuming compounding frequency of at least once a year, the effective annual interest rate, i*, can be calculated from Equation 4.12.[3]

$$i^* = (1 + i/m)^m - 1 \qquad (4.12)$$

## THE RELATIONSHIP BETWEEN INTEREST RATES AND OPTION-FREE BOND PRICES

As indicated earlier, present value and future value are linked via precise mathematical relationships in Equations 4.4 and 4.8. This suggests that there are systematic relationships between PV, future cash flows, i, and n. In fact, much research has attempted to characterize the exact influence of each variable on the pricing relationships. The following analysis focuses on the relationship between bond prices and their associated market interest rates, and how this relationship changes as the magnitude and timing of future cash flows vary. This discussion can be characterized as the traditional analysis of bond pricing for bonds that do not have options. Exhibit 4.2 summarizes the features of four systematic price relationships. These apply to option-free securities in the traditional framework.

### BOND PRICES AND INTEREST RATES VARY INVERSELY

The typical option free fixed-rate coupon bond has the following features: a par or face value that represents the return of principal at maturity, a final maturity in years, and a coupon payment that is fixed (hence fixed income) over the life of the bond. The other two components are the market price (PV in Equation 4.8) and the market interest rate (i in Equation 4.8). Most fixed-coupon bonds are initially sold in the primary market at prices close to par or face value. The fixed coupon rate, defined as the coupon payment divided by the face value, determines the amount of coupon interest that is paid periodically (typically semiannually) until final maturity. After issue, bonds trade in the secondary market, at which time their prices reflect current market conditions. Thus, current market prices reflect the size of the fixed coupon payment (coupon rate) versus the coupon interest paid (determined by the market rate) on a newly issued bond with otherwise similar features.

---

**EXHIBIT 4.2** Price and Yield Relationships for Option-Free Bonds That Are Equivalent Except for the Feature Analyzed

| Relationship | Impact |
|---|---|
| 1. Market interest rates and bond prices vary inversely. | 1. Bond prices fall as interest rates rise and rise as interest rates fall. |
| 2. For a specific absolute change in interest rates, the proportionate increase in bond prices when rates fall exceeds the proportionate decrease in bond prices when rates rise. The proportionate difference increases with maturity and is larger the lower a bond's periodic interest payment. | 2. For the identical absolute change in interest rates, a bondholder will realize a greater capital gain when rates decline than capital loss when rates increase. |
| 3. Long-term bonds change proportionately more in price than short-term bonds for a given change in interest rates from the same base level. | 3. Investors will realize greater capital gains and capital losses on long-term securities than on short-term securities when interest rates change by the same amount. |
| 4. Low-coupon bonds change proportionately more in price than high-coupon bonds for a given change in interest rates from the same base level. | 4. Low-coupon bonds exhibit greater relative price volatility than do high-coupon bonds. |

---

[3]With continuous compounding $i^* = e^i - 1$.

Market interest rates and prices on fixed-income securities vary coincidentally and are inversely related.[4] As such, prices decline when interest rates rise and prices rise when interest rates decline. The sensitivity of the price move relative to the change in interest rates is determined by the size and timing of the cash flows on the underlying security. For coupon bonds, the periodic cash flows consist of interest payments and par value at maturity. The appropriate pricing relationship is characterized by Equation 4.8 where i represents the market yield to maturity.

Consider a bond with a $10,000 face value that makes fixed semiannual interest payments of $470 and matures in exactly three years, at which time the investor receives $10,000 in principal. Note that the semiannual coupon rate is 4.7 percent ($470/$10,000). If the current market interest rate equals 4.7 percent semiannually (9.4 percent per annum), the prevailing price of the bond equals $10,000 as determined below. There are six semiannual compounding periods.

$$Price = \sum_{t=1}^{6} \frac{\$470}{(1.047)^t} + \frac{10,000}{(1.047)^6} = \$10,000$$

At 9.4 percent, this bond sells at a price equal to par or face value.

Now suppose that the corporate issuer of the bonds announces unexpectedly poor earnings and forecasts a declining capacity to service its debt in the future. Owners of the bonds subsequently rush to sell their holdings. What should happen to the market interest rate and price of the bond? If the announcement was truly unexpected, then the perceived riskiness of the security has increased. Holders recognize that there is a greater probability that the promised cash flows may not materialize, so they discount the expected cash flows at a higher rate. This essentially means that investors now need a larger default risk premium, reflected by a higher market interest rate, to entice them to buy the bond. If the annual yield to maturity immediately increased to 10 percent (5 percent semiannually), the price of the bond would fall to $9,847.73. With a price below par, this bond becomes a discount bond.

$$Price = \sum_{t=1}^{6} \frac{\$470}{(1.05)^t} + \frac{\$10,000}{(1.05)^6} = \$9,847.73$$

Thus, a bond's price and market interest rate vary inversely when market rates rise. If, instead, the annual market interest rate immediately fell to 8.8 percent (4.4 percent semiannually), the bond's price would rise to $10,155.24. In this scenario, the bond becomes a premium bond because its price exceeds par.

$$Price = \sum_{t=1}^{} \frac{\$470}{(1.044)^t} + \frac{\$10,000}{(1.044)^6} = \$10,155.24$$

Exhibit 4.3 plots the relationship between the price and market interest rate on this bond. As indicated, higher bond prices are associated with lower market interest rates, and vice versa.

Again, the ratio of the annualized periodic interest payment to a bond's par value is labeled the coupon rate. In the previous example, the coupon rate equaled 9.4 percent (2 × $470 / $10,000). In bond trading circles, if this bond was issued in 2005, it would be labeled the 9.4s of 2008. The following schedule describes the general relationship among yield to maturity, coupon rate and bond price.

| Type of Bond | Yield to Maturity vs. Coupon Rate |
| --- | --- |
| Par bond | Yield to maturity = coupon rate |
| Discount bond | Yield to maturity > coupon rate |
| Premium bond | Yield to maturity < coupon rate |

## BOND PRICES CHANGE ASYMMETRICALLY TO RISING AND FALLING RATES

For a given absolute change in interest rates, the percentage increase in an option free bond's price will exceed the percentage decrease. Consider the price-to-yield relationship in Exhibit 4.3. When the bond is priced at par, the market rate equals 9.4 percent. If the market yield suddenly increases by 60 basis points to 10 percent, the price falls by $152.27 or 1.52 percent. If the market yield suddenly decreases by the same 60 basis points to 8.8 percent, the price rises by $155.24, or 1.55 percent. While the proportionate difference may seem small, it increases with maturity and is larger for bonds with lower periodic interest payments. The dollar difference will also increase with greater par value.

---

[4]Securities that carry floating rates or variable rates pay interest that changes as market rates change. Such instruments subsequently trade close to par. The price/yield relationships in Exhibit 4.2 apply only to fixed-coupon securities.

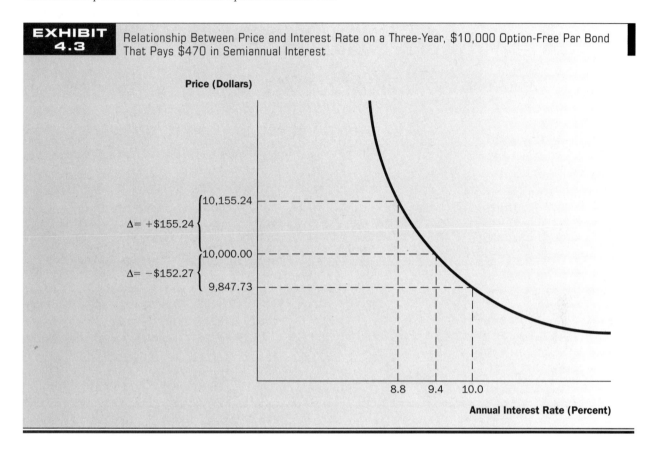

**EXHIBIT 4.3** Relationship Between Price and Interest Rate on a Three-Year, $10,000 Option-Free Par Bond That Pays $470 in Semiannual Interest

This asymmetric price relationship is due to the convex shape of the curve in Exhibit 4.3, which reflects a difference in bond duration at different interest rate levels. The duration concept and applications are discussed later in this chapter. The primary implication is that for the same change in interest rates, bondholders will realize a greater capital gain when rates fall than capital loss when rates rise for all option-free bonds.

## MATURITY INFLUENCES BOND PRICE SENSITIVITY

Short-term and long-term bonds exhibit different price volatility. For bonds that pay the same coupon interest rate, long-term bonds change proportionately more in price than do short-term bonds for a given rate change. Exhibit 4.4 contrasts the price-yield relationship for a 9.4 percent coupon bond with six years to maturity to that of the three-year bond with the same 9.4 percent coupon discussed earlier. Note that the only difference between the two bonds is final maturity and thus the number of interim cash flows. When both market rates equal 9.4 percent, both bonds are priced at par. The following calculations indicate the price of the six-year bond when the market rate rises to 10 percent and falls to 8.8 percent, respectively.

$$\text{Price} = \sum_{t=1}^{12} \frac{\$470}{(1.05)^t} + \frac{\$10,000}{(1.05)^{12}} = \$9,734.10$$

$$\text{Price} = \sum_{t=1}^{12} \frac{\$470}{(1.044)^t} + \frac{\$10,000}{(1.044)^{12}} = \$10,275.13$$

As indicated in Exhibit 4.4, when rates on both bonds increase by 60 basis points, the price of the six-year bond falls more than the price of the three-year bond. The proportionate price declines are 2.66 percent and 1.52 percent, respectively. When rates decline by 60 basis points, the six-year bond's price increases 2.75 percent while the three-year bond's price increases by 1.55 percent.

The rationale for the different price sensitivity has to do with the basic present value in Equation 4.8. The buyer of a six-year bond contracts to receive fixed-interest payments for twice as many periods as the buyer of a three-year bond. When priced at par, the coupon and market rate are 9.4 percent. If market rates increase, buyers of newly issued par bonds will receive periodic interest at a higher market (and coupon) rate. Holders of "old"

| EXHIBIT 4.4 | The Effect of Maturity on the Relationship Between Price and Interest Rate on Fixed-Income, Option-Free Bonds with 3-Year and 6-Year Maturities |
|---|---|

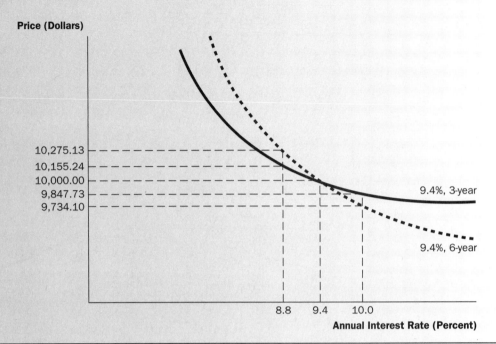

discount bonds now receive below-market interest payments. With the six-year bond, these below-market payments will persist for twice as long as with the three-year bond. Thus, the price of the six-year bond declines more than does the price of the three-year bond. The opposite holds when interest rates fall. The holder of a six-year bond receives above-market interest payments, which are locked in for twice as long as for the three-year bond. Thus, the price of a six-year bond will rise above the price of a three-year bond.

Suppose that an investor owns a 9.4 percent coupon bond with nine years to maturity. If the market rate changes from 9.4 percent to 10 percent, its price drops from $10,000 to $9,649.31.

$$\text{Price} = \sum_{t=1}^{18} \frac{\$470}{(1.05)^t} + \frac{\$10,000}{(1.05)^{18}} = \$9,649.31$$

Not surprisingly, this is well below the price of the six-year bond at 10 percent.

The following schedule compares the percentage price changes for the three-, six-, and nine-year bonds when interest rates rise from 9.4 percent to 10 percent.

|  | Price Change | | |
|---|---|---|---|
|  | **3-Year** | **6-Year** | **9-Year** |
| Percentage Change | −1.52% | −2.66% | −3.51% |
| Difference |  | −1.14% | −0.85% |

Note that the rate of change in the percentage price decline falls from 1.14 percent to 0.85 percent as maturity lengthens. This general relationship holds: As maturity lengthens, the rate of change in the percentage price change declines. You should verify this for the nine-year bond in the case where its rate falls to 8.8 percent.

### THE SIZE OF COUPON INFLUENCES BOND PRICE SENSITIVITY

High-coupon and low-coupon bonds exhibit different price volatility. Suppose that two bonds are priced to yield the same yield to maturity. For a given change in market rate, the bond with the lower coupon will change more in price than the bond with the higher coupon. This is demonstrated in Exhibit 4.5, which plots the price and yield relationship for two otherwise identical three-year maturity instruments: a zero coupon bond with three years to maturity,

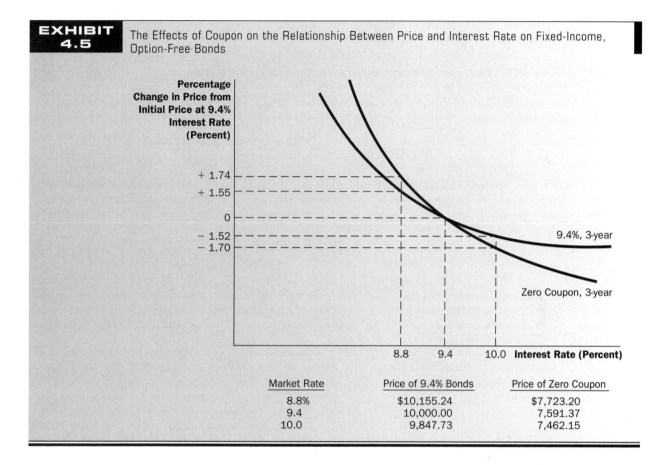

**EXHIBIT 4.5** The Effects of Coupon on the Relationship Between Price and Interest Rate on Fixed-Income, Option-Free Bonds

| Market Rate | Price of 9.4% Bonds | Price of Zero Coupon |
|---|---|---|
| 8.8% | $10,155.24 | $7,723.20 |
| 9.4 | 10,000.00 | 7,591.37 |
| 10.0 | 9,847.73 | 7,462.15 |

and one cash flow of $10,000 paid at maturity, and the 9.4 percent coupon bond introduced earlier. As the market rate falls below 9.4 percent, the price of the zero coupon bond rises by proportionately more than the price of the coupon bond. At 8.8 percent, the price of the zero rises by 1.74 percent while the price of the 9.4 percent coupon bond rises by just 1.55 percent. The same relationship appears when the market rate rises to 10 percent. Again, this difference increases with maturity and may be quite substantial with large-denomination securities.

# DURATION AND PRICE VOLATILITY

The previous discussion of bond price volatility focuses on the relationship between a security's market rate of interest, periodic interest payment, and maturity. In fact, the price rules indicate that volatility changes systematically as each of these factors changes. Most financial economists look to **duration** as a comprehensive measure of these relationships. Simply focusing on interest rate changes ignores the size of interest payment and length of time until each payment is received. Because maturity simply identifies how much time elapses until final payment, it ignores all information about the timing and magnitude of interim payments. The size of coupon, in turn, provides no information about the rate at which interim cash flows can be reinvested or even how many cash flows are promised.

## DURATION AS AN ELASTICITY MEASURE

Duration is a measure of effective maturity that incorporates the timing and size of a security's cash flows. It captures the combined impact of market rate, the size of interim payments and maturity on a security's price volatility. Conceptually, duration is most easily understood as a measure of interest elasticity in determining a security's market value. Thus, if a security's duration is known, an investor can readily estimate the size of a change in value (or price) for different interest rate changes.[5]

---

[5]The following discussion uses Macaulay's measure of duration, which is introduced formally later in the chapter.

There are two important interpretations of duration analysis that apply to valuing most option-free securities and portfolios without embedded options.

1.  Duration is a measure of how price sensitive a security (or portfolio) is to a change in interest rates.

2.  The greater (shorter) is duration, the greater (lesser) is price sensitivity.

Remember when you were first introduced to the concept of price elasticity? If you knew the price elasticity of demand for a good or service, you could estimate how much quantity demanded would change when the price changed. In general,

$$\text{price elasticity of demand} = -\frac{\% \text{ change in quantity demanded}}{\% \text{ change in price}}$$

Because quantity demanded varies inversely with price changes, the minus sign converts the relative percentage changes to a positive measure. Thus, if a bank raises its charge for usage of an automatic teller machine (ATM) from 50 cents to 75 cents per transaction, and the number of monthly ATM transactions drops from 100,000 to 70,000, the price elasticity of demand is estimated at 0.6.

$$\text{price elasticity of demand} = -\frac{-30,000/100,000}{\$0.25/\$0.50} = \frac{0.3}{0.5} = 0.6$$

This elasticity measure indicates that a proportionate change in price coincides with a smaller proportionate change in quantity demanded. If the elasticity remained constant at higher prices, the bank could estimate that a further price increase to \$1 per item (+33 percent) would lower usage to approximately 56,000 (−20 percent = −0.33 × 0.6) items monthly.

A security's duration can similarly be interpreted as an elasticity measure. But instead of the relationship between quantity demanded and price, duration provides information about the change in market value as a result of interest rate changes. Letting P equal the price of a security and i equal the security's prevailing market interest rate, duration can be approximated by the following expression:

$$\text{Duration} \cong -\frac{\dfrac{\Delta P}{P}}{\dfrac{\Delta i}{(1 + i)}} \tag{4.13}$$

The numerator represents the percentage change in price, while the denominator represents the approximate percentage change in interest rates.

Consider the three-year zero coupon bond from Exhibit 4.5 that pays \$10,000 at maturity. At an annual market rate of 9.4 percent, this bond's price equals \$7,591.37 assuming semiannual compounding. As demonstrated later, this bond has a duration of exactly three years, or six semiannual periods. An analyst can use Equation 4.13 to estimate the change in price of this bond when its market rate changes. Restating the expression,

$$\Delta P \cong -\text{Duration} \, [\Delta i/(1 + i)]P \tag{4.14}$$

Suppose the market rate rises immediately from 4.7 percent to 5 percent semiannually. Using semiannual data, the estimated change in price equals −\$130.51, or 1.72 percent of the price.

$$\Delta P \cong -6 \, [.003/1.047]\$7,591.37$$
$$\cong -\$130.51$$

This overstates the true price decline as Exhibit 4.5 demonstrates that the actual price change equals −\$129.21.

## MEASURING DURATION

Duration is measured in units of time and represents a security's effective maturity. More precisely, it is a weighted average of the time until expected cash flows from a security will be received, relative to the current price of the security. The weights are the present values of each cash flow divided by the current price. Early cash flows thus carry a greater weight than later cash flows, and the greater the size of the cash flow the greater is the weight and contribution to the duration estimate.

The following examples use Macaulay's duration, which was first introduced in 1938. While this duration measure has been modified to improve its applicability, it serves as a useful first approximation.

Using general notation, Macaulay's duration (D) appears as:

$$D = \frac{\sum_{t=1}^{k} \frac{CFt(t)}{(1+i)^t}}{\sum_{t=1}^{k} \frac{CFt}{(1+i)^t}} \tag{4.15}$$

where

$CFt$ = dollar value of the cash flow at time t,
$t$ = the number of periods of time until the cash flow payment,
$i$ = the periodic yield to maturity of the security generating the cash flow, and
$k$ = the number of cash flows.

Duration is thus a weighted average of the time until the cash flows arise. As described earlier, the numerator equals the present value of each cash flow times the number of periods until the cash flow arises. The denominator is simply the price of the instrument. The weight for each cash flow equals the present value from the numerator divided by the current price (the entire denominator). The weighted average is therefore measured in some unit of time, such as days, months, and so on, but is usually discussed in terms of years.

Consider the 9.4 percent, three-year coupon bond with a face value of $10,000. The duration of this security—assuming that it is currently priced at par, is noncallable and nonputable prior to maturity, and all interest and principal payments are made as scheduled—is 5.37 semiannual periods. The calculation is demonstrated in Exhibit 4.6. Note that each cash flow is converted to its present value by discounting at the prevailing market rate of 4.7 percent. Each present value is then divided by the prevailing price ($10,000) and multiplied by the units of time until the cash flow rises. Because the largest cash flow is the principal payment received at maturity, its weight in the duration calculation is greatest at 79 percent, and the duration of 5.37 semiannual periods is close to final maturity.

Contrast duration of the coupon bond with duration of the zero coupon bond described in Exhibit 4.5. With the zero coupon security there are no interim cash flows. The only payment is $10,000 after three years. Using Equation 4.15, its estimated duration is six semiannual periods. There is only one cash flow such that an investor receives 100 percent (weight is one) of the expected cash flows back at maturity.

$$\text{Duration of 3-year zero} = \frac{[\$10,000/(1.047)^6](6)}{\$10,000/(1.047)^6} = 6$$

The three-year coupon bond's duration is shorter at 5.37 semiannual periods because there are interim cash flows and an investor receives some of the cash payments prior to final maturity. In general, Macaulay's duration of a zero coupon security equals its final maturity. The duration of any security with interim cash flows will be less than maturity.

---

**EXHIBIT 4.6**  A Sample Duration Calculation

**A. Time Line Characterizing Cash Flows**

| 0 | 1 | 2 | 3 | 4 | 5 | 6 |
|---|---|---|---|---|---|---|
| | 470 | 470 | 470 | 470 | 470 | 470 |
| | | | | | | 10,000 |

**B. Estimated Macaulay's Duration**

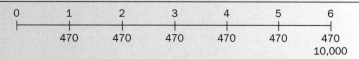

$$\text{Duration} = \frac{\frac{470[1]}{(1.047)^1} + \frac{470[2]}{(1.047)^2} + \frac{470[3]}{(1.047)^3} + \frac{470[4]}{(1.047)^4} + \frac{470[5]}{(1.047)^5} + \frac{10,470[6]}{(1.047)^6}}{10,000}$$

$$= \frac{448.9[1] + 428.8[2] + 409.5[3] + 391.1[4] + 373.6[5] + 7,948.2[6]}{10,000}$$

$$= .0449[1] + .0429[2] + .0409[3] + .0391[4] + .0374[5] + .7948[6]$$

$$= 5.37 \text{ semiannual periods (or 2.68 years)}$$

A basic contribution of duration is that it accounts for differences in time until interim cash flows are received between securities. Large, near-term cash flows receive the greatest weight and thus shorten estimated duration. Large cash flows arising near maturity lengthen duration. In both of these examples, the bulk of cash flows was received near maturity, so duration was relatively long.

## COMPARATIVE PRICE SENSITIVITY

The duration concept is useful because it enables market participants to estimate the relative price volatility of different securities. Remember the second rule for interpreting duration: the greater is duration, the greater is price sensitivity. This is reflected in Equation 4.14 and the following extension.

$$\frac{\Delta P}{P} \cong - \left[ \frac{\text{Duration}}{(1 + i)} \right] \Delta i \tag{4.16}$$

Equation 4.16 characterizes the formal elasticity relationship between interest rates and bond prices and is the same as Equation 4.14 except that the percentage change in price is on the left-hand side of the equality and Macaulay's duration is divided by one plus the market interest rate. This latter ratio *(in brackets)* is labeled **modified duration** and is widely used by bond market participants,

$$\text{modified duration} = \frac{\text{Macaulay's duration}}{(1 + i)}$$

such that the percentage price change of a security or portfolio approximately equals modified duration times the change in market rate.

These relationships are quite intuitive because they demonstrate that the greater is duration or modified duration, the greater is the percentage change and/or actual change in price for a given change in interest rates. For example, consider the two par bonds from Exhibit 4.4 that are priced at par when market rates equal 9.4 percent. According to the above formulas, the bond with the longest duration will exhibit the greatest price volatility.

This relationship is demonstrated in Exhibit 4.7 for these two coupon bonds and two zero coupon bonds. All of the bonds are assumed to carry an annual yield of 9.4 percent, but they have different prices and durations, depending on maturity and whether interim interest payments are made. Thus, the two zero coupon bonds have Macaulay durations of six and 12 semiannual periods equal to maturity and trade at discount prices well below their $10,000 face value. As implied above, the Macaulay durations of the coupon bonds are slightly less than maturity and the modified durations for all bonds are slightly less than the corresponding Macaulay durations.

| EXHIBIT 4.7 | Comparative Price Sensitivity Indicated by Duration |

| | Type of Bond | | | |
|---|---|---|---|---|
| | **3-Yr. Zero** | **6-Yr. Zero** | **3-Yr. Coupon** | **6-Yr. Coupon** |
| Initial market rate (annual) | 9.40% | 9.40% | 9.40% | 9.40% |
| Initial market rate (semiannual) | 4.70% | 4.70% | 4.70% | 4.70% |
| Maturity value | $10,000 | $10,000 | $10,000 | $10,000 |
| Initial price | $7,591.37 | $5,762.88 | $10,000 | $10,000 |
| Duration: semiannual periods | 6.00 | 12.00 | 5.37 | 9.44 |
| Modified duration | 5.73 | 11.46 | 5.12 | 9.02 |
| **Rate Increases to 10% (5% Semiannually)** | | | | |
| Estimated $\Delta P$ | −$130.51 | −$198.15 | −$153.74 | −$270.45 |
| Estimated $\dfrac{\Delta P}{P}$ | −1.72% | −3.44% | −1.54% | −2.70% |
| Initial elasticity | 0.2693 | 0.5387 | 0.2406 | 0.4242 |

**Formulas**

$\Delta P \cong -\text{Duration} \left[ \Delta i / 1 + i \right] P$

$\dfrac{\Delta P}{P} \cong -\left[ \text{Duration} / (1 + i) \right] \Delta i$

where Duration equals Macaulay's duration.

The bottom part of the exhibit demonstrates how to interpret duration data. Suppose that market yields on all four bonds suddenly increase to 10 percent, or 5 percent semiannually. The comparative absolute change in price, percentage change in price, and initial elasticities are provided at the bottom of the exhibit. Consider the three-year and six-year zero coupon bonds. Using Equation 4.14, the estimated change in price is −$131 and −$198, respectively. Using Equation 4.16, the estimated percentage change in price is −1.72 percent and −3.44 percent, respectively. Thus, with the same absolute and percentage change in market rates, the longer-duration six-year bond exhibits the greater price decline both in absolute and percentage terms. This is consistent with its greater duration and interest rate elasticity of 0.5387 versus 0.2693. Consider now the two coupon bonds. Not surprisingly, the same relative price sensitivity appears. With the rate increase, the price of the bond with a duration of 9.44 semiannual periods falls by almost $271 from the same $10,000 base compared with the $154 price decline with the shorter-duration bond. This is again consistent with its higher duration and interest rate elasticity.

The key implication of Exhibit 4.7 is the direct relationship between duration and relative price sensitivity. The greater is duration, the greater are a security's percentage change in price and interest rate elasticity when securities carry the same initial yields. When securities carry different yields, they can similarly be ranked by relative interest rate elasticities.

## RECENT INNOVATIONS IN THE VALUATION OF FIXED-INCOME SECURITIES AND TOTAL RETURN ANALYSIS

The traditional way of valuing fixed-income securities and analyzing yields is too simplistic given the complexities of today's marketplace. There are many reasons for this. First, many investors do not hold securities until maturity so that yield to maturity is of limited interest. Second, the present value calculation in Equation 4.8 that applies to bonds assumes that all coupon payments are reinvested at the calculated yield to maturity, which is generally not the case. Many investors want to know how changes in reinvestment rates affect the actual realized yield. Third, many securities carry embedded options, such as a call or put option, which complicates valuation because it is difficult to know whether the option will be exercised and thus what cash flows an investor will actually receive. As an example, consider a bond that has a three-year maturity and carries a fixed coupon rate but can be called anytime after one year. This means that the issuer of the security (the borrower) can repay the outstanding principal on the bond at its discretion after one year. How long will an investor receive interest payments before the bond is repaid? It may be called after one year—or not at all. To know how to value a security with options, the investor must estimate when the options will be exercised and what value they will have. Finally, it is relatively easy for anyone who owns a security to separate, or strip, the coupon payments from each other and from the principal payment on a traditional bond. The holder can buy a security, strip the promised cash flows and sell them as distinct zero coupon securities. Alternatively, someone can buy zero coupon securities and construct a traditional coupon bond. The implication is that any fixed-income security should be priced as a package of cash flows with each cash flow discounted at the appropriate zero coupon rate.

### TOTAL RETURN ANALYSIS

Many market participants attempt to estimate the actual realized yield on a bond by calculating an estimated total return.[6] This yield measure allows the investor to vary assumptions about how long he or she will hold the bond (the holding period), the rate at which interim cash flows will be reinvested (the reinvestment rate), and the value of the bond at the end of the holding period (sale value, or maturity value). The calculated total return can then be compared across securities to assess whether the return sufficiently compensates for the risks assumed.

Total return analysis applied to option-free bonds recognizes that there are three different sources of return from owning a bond: coupon interest, reinvestment income—labeled interest-on-interest—and any capital gain or loss realized at maturity or sale if the bond is sold before maturity.[7] The mathematics require that one specify a holding period, reinvestment rate or rates, and the market price of the bond at maturity or sale. Having done this, the analysis involves estimating the total future value of coupon interest, interest-on-interest, and sale/maturity value, comparing this to the initial purchase price and calculating a zero coupon yield.

Consider the three-year, 9.4 percent coupon bond trading at par of $10,000 from Exhibit 4.3. You buy the bond expecting to hold it until it matures. Coupon interest of $470 is paid every six months so that total interest will be $2,820 (6 × $470). You believe that you can invest each of the coupon payments at a 3 percent semiannual rate through maturity. Equation 4.17 provides the formula for calculating the future value of coupon interest plus interest-on-interest with a constant reinvestment rate (r).

---

[6]This discussion follows that from *Fixed Income Mathematics* by Frank Fabozzi.

[7]This analysis assumes that bonds have no options. Total return analysis for securities with options is discussed in Chapter 13.

$$\text{future value of coupon interest} + \text{interest-on-interest} = \left[ C\frac{(1 + r)^n - 1}{r} \right] \qquad (4.17)$$

where C is the periodic coupon interest payment and n is the number of periods until the end of the holding period. In this case, the total future value is

$$\$470[(1.03)^6 - 1]/0.03 = \$3,040.15$$

With $2,820 in coupon interest (C × n), interest-on-interest equals $220.15. Finally, if held to maturity, you will receive $10,000 return of principal after three years. The total future value of the three components of return is thus:

$$\begin{aligned}
\text{Coupon interest} &= \quad \$2,820.00 \\
\text{Interest-on-interest} &= \quad \$220.15 \\
\text{Principal at maturity} &= \$10,000.00 \\
\text{Total future value} &= \$13,040.15
\end{aligned}$$

The total return as a yield measure is obtained by comparing this total future value with the initial investment of $10,000 and calculating the equivalent zero coupon yield. In general,

$$\text{Total return} = [\text{Total future value/Purchase price}]^{1/n} - 1 \qquad (4.18)$$

For this investment, the total return is

$$[\$13,040.15/\$10,000]^{1/6} - 1 = 1.04523 - 1 = 0.04523$$

or 9.05 annually.

Note that this is less than the 9.4 percent yield to maturity of the bond because you assumed a 3 percent semiannual reinvestment rate. Remember that the yield to maturity calculation assumes that all interim cash flows can be reinvested at the yield to maturity. If we use a 4.7 percent reinvestment rate assumption in this example, the interest-on-interest component increases to $352.86. As expected, the total return increases to 4.7 percent semiannually:

$$[(\$13,172.86/\$10,000)^{1/6} - 1] = 0.047$$

Exhibit 4.8 provides a similar application for a nine-year bond that pays a 7.3 percent coupon and currently sells for $99.62 per $100 par value. In this example, the holding period is exactly five years and the investor assumes a reinvestment rate of 6 percent annually. After five years, it is believed that a comparable bond with four years remaining until maturity will be priced to yield 7 percent to maturity. Thus, the calculation assumes a holding period far shorter than maturity and requires an estimate of the bond's sale price. Note that in this example, the bond is assumed to sell at a premium after five years, which raises the total return to 7.34 percent.

Total return is especially applicable when securities have embedded options, such as a call option or put option, or with mortgages and mortgage-backed securities where the principal can be prepaid. It allows an investor

---

**EXHIBIT 4.8**  Calculation of Total Return for a Nine-Year Bond Purchased at $99.62 per $100 Par Value That Pays a 7.3 Percent (3.65 Percent Semiannual) Coupon and Is Held for Five Years

Assume: semiannual reinvestment rate = 3% after five years; a comparable 4-year maturity bond will be priced to yield 7% (3.5% semiannually) to maturity

| | |
|---|---|
| Coupon interest: | $10 \times \$3.65 = \$36.50$ |
| Interest-on-interest: | $\$3.65 [(1.03)^{10} - 1] / 0.03 - \$36.50 = \$5.34$ |
| Sale price after five years: | $\displaystyle\sum_{t=1}^{8} \frac{\$3.65}{(1.035)^t} + \frac{\$100}{(1.350)^8} = \$101.03$ |
| Total future value: | $\$36.50 + \$5.34 + \$101.03 = \$142.87$ |
| Total return: | $[\$142.87/\$99.62]^{1/10} - 1 = 0.0367$ semiannually |
| | or 7.34% annually |

*Money Market Yields*

to identify how much of the yield can be attributed to reinvestment income and potential capital gains and losses. It also is important when the investor's holding period differs from maturity.

## VALUING BONDS AS A PACKAGE OF CASH FLOWS

Consider the same three-year maturity, 9.4 percent coupon bond from Exhibit 4.3, which has six remaining coupon payments of $470 and one remaining principal payment of $10,000 at maturity. This bond should be viewed as a package of seven separate cash flows. Formally, if stripped and sold separately, each of the coupon payments is labeled an interest-only security while the principal payment is a principal-only security. Because the payments can be stripped, an arbitrageur who believes the bond is currently undervalued can buy the entire bond, strip the coupons and principal payment, and sell each as a distinct zero coupon (single cash flow) bond for a profit.[8]

The implication is that the bond will be priced as a package of zero coupon instruments. Thus, a different discount rate will apply to each periodic interest payment and the principal payment. The first coupon will be discounted at the six-month zero coupon rate, the second coupon at the one-year zero coupon rate, and so forth.

Suppose that at the time you are considering buying this bond, the following zero coupon rates apply to comparable risk securities.

| Maturity | Zero Coupon (semiannual) |
|---|---|
| 6 months | 3.90% |
| 1 year | 4.00% |
| 18 months | 4.20% |
| 2 years | 4.40% |
| 30 months | 4.60% |
| 3 years | 4.70% |

The bond could be bought, stripped, and sold for $10,021.48.

Value of package of cash flows:

$$\frac{\$470}{(1.039)^1} + \frac{\$470}{(1.04)^2} + \frac{\$470}{(1.042)^3} + \frac{\$470}{(1.044)^4} + \frac{\$470}{(1.046)^5} + \frac{\$470}{(1.047)^6} + \frac{\$10,000}{(1.047)^6} = \$10,021.48$$

Thus, an arbitrageur could make a riskless profit of $21.48 per $10,000 of par bonds if the whole bond could be bought for $10,000.

The implication is that bond valuation is more complex than that described under the traditional analysis. It requires the use of zero coupon rates as discount rates and different discount rates at each maturity.

## MONEY MARKET YIELDS

Unfortunately, while the general pricing relationships introduced above are straightforward, practical applications are complicated by the fact that interest rates on different securities are measured and quoted in different terms. This is particularly true of yields on money market instruments such as Treasury bills, federal funds, CDs, repurchase agreements, euro dollars, bankers acceptances, and commercial paper, which have initial maturities under one year. Some of these instruments trade on a discount basis, while others bear interest. Some yields are quoted assuming a 360-day year, while others assume a 365-day year. The following discussion extends the analysis of interest rate mathematics to money market instruments and provides procedures that allow a comparison of effective annual yields.

### INTEREST-BEARING LOANS WITH MATURITIES OF ONE YEAR OR LESS

Many short-term consumer and commercial loans have maturities less than one year. The borrower makes periodic interest payments and repays the principal at maturity. The effective annual rate of interest depends on the

---

[8]If the bond is overpriced, an arbitrageur will short sell the bond and buy each of the coupons and principal payment as zero coupon instruments to reconstruct the bond and profit on the difference.

term of the loan and the compounding frequency. If the loan has exactly one year to maturity, Equation 4.12 characterizes the effective annual yield. Thus, a one-year loan that requires monthly interest payments at 12 percent annually (1 percent monthly) carries an effective yield to the investor of 12.68 percent.

$$i^* = (1.01)^{12} - 1 = 0.1268$$

Suppose that the same loan was made for just 90 days at an annualized stated rate of 12 percent. There is now more than one compounding period in one year. The modified form of Equation 4.12 assumes a 365-day year and calculates the number of compounding periods as 365 divided by the number of days in the contract holding period (h), which is 90 in this example. In general,

$$i^* = \left[ 1 + \frac{i}{(365/h)} \right]^{(365/h)} - 1 \tag{4.19}$$

This 90-day loan thus has 365/90 compounding periods in a year, and the effective annual yield is 12.55 percent.

$$i^* = \left[ 1 + \frac{0.12}{(365/90)} \right]^{(365/90)} - 1 = 0.1255$$

## 360-DAY VERSUS 365-DAY YIELDS

A security's effective annual yield must reflect the true yield to an investor who holds the underlying instrument for a full year (365 days in all but leap years). Some money market rates are, in fact, reported on the basis of an assumed 360-day year. While interest is actually earned for all 365 days in a year, the full amount of interest implied by the reported rate is earned in just 360 days. Thus, $1,000 invested for one year at 8 percent under the 360-day method pays $80 in interest after 360 days, not $80 after 365 days. Because the investor gets the same interest five days earlier, the principal and interest can be invested for five additional days, and the investor earns a higher effective rate of interest.

It is easy to convert a 360-day rate to a 365-day rate, and vice versa. This is done according to the following formula:

$$i_{365} = i_{360} \, (365/360)$$

where $i_{365}$ = 365-day rate, and
$i_{360}$ = 360-day rate

The 360-day rate is simply multiplied by a factor of 365/360. In turn, the effective annual yields must reflect both 365 days of interest and compounding frequency. Converting a 360-day yield to an effective annual yield involves two steps. First, the yield is converted to a 365-day yield. Second, the 365-day yield is used for i in Equations 4.12 and 4.19.

For example, a one-year investment that carries an 8 percent nominal rate quoted on a 360-day basis generates a 365-day yield of 8.11 percent.

$$i_{365} = 0.08(365/360)$$
$$= 0.0811$$

This rate would be used in all formulas to compute effective yields.

## DISCOUNT YIELDS

Some money market instruments, such as Treasury bills, repurchase agreements, commercial paper, and bankers acceptances, are pure discount instruments. This means that the purchase price is always less than the par value at maturity. The difference between the purchase price and par value equals the periodic interest. Yields on discount instruments are calculated and quoted on a discount basis assuming a 360-day year and thus are not directly comparable to yields on interest-bearing instruments.

The pricing equation for discount instruments used by professional traders is:

$$i_{dr} = \left[ \frac{Pf - Po}{Pf} \right] \left[ \frac{(360)}{h} \right] \tag{4.20}$$

where

$i_{dr}$ = discount rate,

Po = initial price of the instrument,

Pf = final price of the instrument at maturity or sale, and

h = number of days in holding period

The discount rate has several peculiar features. First, the amount of interest earned is divided by the final price or maturity value, not by the initial amount invested, to obtain a percentage return. Second, as noted above, it assumes a 360-day year. The discount rate thus understates the effective annual rate. In order to obtain an effective yield, the formula must be modified to reflect a 365-day year and to account for the fact that returns are normally computed by dividing interest received by the amount invested. These problems can be addressed by calculating a **bond equivalent rate** ($i_{be}$) according to Equation 4.21.

$$i_{be} = \left[\frac{Pf - Po}{Po}\right]\left[\frac{(365)}{h}\right] \qquad (4.21)$$

Consider, for example, a $1 million par value Treasury bill with exactly 182 days to maturity, priced at $964,500. The discount rate on the bill is 7.02 percent.

$$i_{dr} = \frac{\$1,000,000 - \$964,500}{\$1,000,000}\left(\frac{360}{182}\right) = 0.0702$$

The bond equivalent rate equals 7.38 percent.

$$i_{be} = \frac{\$1,000,000 - \$964,500}{\$964,500}\left(\frac{365}{182}\right) = 0.0738$$

To obtain an effective annual rate, incorporate compounding by applying Equation 4.19. Implicitly, an investor is assumed to reinvest the proceeds at the same periodic rate for the remainder of the 365 days in a year. Here the effective annual rate equals 7.52 percent.

$$i^* = \left[1 + \frac{0.0738}{(365/182)}\right]^{365/182} - 1 = 0.0752$$

Yields on repurchase agreements, commercial paper, and bankers acceptances are also quoted on a discount basis. For comparative purposes with nondiscount instruments, their yields must be converted in the same manner as Treasury bills, in a two-step process. The 360-day yield is converted to a 365-day bond equivalent yield; then compounding is taken into account via Equation 4.19.

## YIELDS ON SINGLE-PAYMENT, INTEREST-BEARING SECURITIES

Some money market instruments, such as large, negotiable certificates of deposit (CDs), eurodollars, and federal funds, pay interest calculated against the par value of the security and make a single payment of both interest and principal at maturity. The nominal interest rate is quoted as a percent of par and assumes a 360-day year. The nominal rate again understates the effective annual rate.

Consider a 182-day CD with a par value of $1,000,000 and quoted yield of 7.02 percent, the same quote as the Treasury bill. The actual amount of interest paid after 182 days equals

$$(0.0702)(182/360)\$1,000,000 \text{ or } \$35,490$$

The 365-day yield is

$$i_{365} = 0.0702(365/360) = 0.0712$$

Finally, the effective annual rate is

$$i^* = \left[1 + \frac{0.0712}{(365/182)}\right]^{365/182} - 1 = 0.0724$$

**EXHIBIT 4.9**

Summary of Money Market Yield Quotations and Calculations

**A. Simple interest rate $i_s$ :**

$$i_s = \frac{Pf - Po}{Po}$$

**B. Discount rate $i_{dr}$ :**

$$i_{dr} = \left[\frac{Pf - Po}{Pf}\right]\left[\frac{360}{h}\right]$$

**C. Money market 360-day rate $i_{360}$ :**

$$i_{360} = \left[\frac{Pf - Po}{Pf}\right]\left[\frac{360}{h}\right]$$

**D. Bond equivalent 365-day rate $i_{365}$ or $i_{be}$ :**

$$i_{365} = \left[\frac{Pf - Po}{Pf}\right]\left[\frac{365}{h}\right]$$

**E. Effective annual interest rate $i^*$:**

$$i^* = \left[1 + \frac{i}{365/h}\right]^{365/h} - 1$$

A careful reader will note that both the 365-day yield and effective annual rate on the CD are below the corresponding bond equivalent yield and effective annual rate on the aforementioned Treasury bill. This demonstrates the difference between discount and interest-bearing instruments. In particular, the discount rate is calculated as a return on par value, not initial investment, as with interest-bearing instruments. Thus, a discount rate understates both the 365-day rate and effective rate by a greater percentage.

Exhibit 4.9 summarizes the conventions for interest rate quotations in the money market and identifies specific instruments priced under each convention. Market participants must be aware of how yields are quoted and calculated before they compare percentages.

## SUMMARY

Interest rates play an important role in facilitating the flow of funds between lenders and borrowers. Borrowers prefer low rates that lower interest expense while lenders prefer high rates that increase interest income. This chapter provides an overview of the mathematics of interest rates to assist in comparing quoted rates between securities, and presents concepts that are useful in valuing fixed-income securities and evaluating their price sensitivity.

There are several key conclusions. First, fixed-income securities are priced according to the mathematics of present value and future value. The effective price and yield depend on the frequency of compounding. The greater is the compounding frequency, the greater is the amount of interest. Second, prices and yields on fixed-income securities without options exhibit well-defined relationships. When interest rates change, prices move inversely. The proportionate price move is relatively greater when rates fall compared to when rates rise. Similarly, the proportionate magnitude of the price move increases with maturity and decreases with the size of the coupon payment. This is largely revealed by a security's duration because the greater is duration, the greater is the proportionate price change for a given change in interest rates. Thus, longer-duration securities exhibit greater price volatility. Third, many investors use total return analysis when deciding which securities to buy. Total return analysis allows an investor to vary the assumed holding period, select different reinvestment rates and incorporate the expected impact of selling the security prior to final maturity. All of these considerations are not permitted by the yield to maturity calculation. Finally, rates on specific money market securities differ because some are quoted on a 360-day versus 365-day basis and some are discount rates versus bond-equivalent rates. The primary point is that borrowers and lenders must carefully examine the contract terms of specific securities to understand the effective cost or yield.

## QUESTIONS

1. If you invest $1,000 today in a security paying 8 percent compounded quarterly, how much will the investment be worth seven years from today?

2. If you invest $20,000 in a security today, how much will it be worth in six years? The security pays 6 percent compounded monthly.

3. What is the effective interest rate of 10 percent compounded quarterly, versus 10 percent compounded monthly?

4. Consider a $15,000 loan with interest at 12 percent compounded monthly and 24 monthly payments. How much will the loan payment be? Set up an amortization schedule for the first four months, indicating the amount and timing of principal and interest payments.

5. How much would you be willing to pay today for an investment that will return $6,800 to you eight years from today if your required rate of return is 12 percent?

6. Six years ago you placed $250 in a savings account which is now worth $1,040.28. When you put the funds into the account, you were told it would pay 24 percent interest. You expected to find the account worth $908.80. What compounding did you think this account used, and what did it actually use?

7. If you invest $9,000 today at 8 percent compounded annually, but after three years the interest rate increases to 10 percent compounded semiannually, what is the investment worth seven years from today?

8. Suppose a customer's house increased in value over five years from $150,000 to $250,000. What was the annual growth rate of the property value during this five-year interval? Three local banks pay different interest rates on time deposits with one-year maturities. Rank the three banks from highest to lowest in terms of the depositor's return.

   Bank 1—4.5 percent per year compounded annually

   Bank 2—4.3 percent per year compounded quarterly

   Bank 3—4.1 percent per year compounded daily

9. You want to buy a new car, but you know that the most you can afford for payments is $375 per month. You want 48-month financing, and you can arrange such a loan at 12 percent compounded monthly. You have nothing to trade and no down payment. The most expensive car you can purchase is: (1) an old junker for $4,000, (2) a Honda Civic for $6,000, (3) a Ford Escort for $10,000, (4) a Toyota Camry for $12,000, or (5) an Infiniti G35 for $16,000.

10. Consider a 7 percent coupon U.S. Treasury note that has a $10,000 face value and matures ten years from today. This note pays interest semiannually. The current market interest rate on this bond is 6 percent. Would you expect the bond to be a discount, premium, or par bond? Calculate the actual price of the bond using the present value formula.

11. A Treasury security carries a fixed 6 percent annual coupon rate and matures in exactly two years. The Treasury is currently priced at $10,000 par value to yield 6 percent to maturity. Assume that you can buy the bond and strip the coupons and final principal payment and sell each of them as a zero coupon security. Given the following zero coupon rates, what price would you get for this purchase and subsequent sales?

| Maturity | 6-month | 1-year | 18-month | 2-year |
|---|---|---|---|---|
| Zero coupon yield | 5.4% | 5.8% | 6.2% | 6.8% |

12. Lamar Briggs purchased a 7 percent coupon corporate bond that matured in ten years and paid interest semiannually. He paid $2,800 and six months later, immediately following an interest payment, he sold the bond. At the time of sale, the market interest rate on bonds of this type was 6 percent. What was Briggs's selling price? What was Briggs's rate of return for the six months? What is this return on an annual basis?

13. What is the duration of a bond with a par value of $10,000 that has a coupon rate of 6.5 percent annually and a final maturity of two years? Assume that the required rate of return is 6 percent compounded semi-annually. What is the duration of a two-year zero coupon bond that pays $10,000 at maturity and is priced to yield 6 percent with semiannual compounding? Why do the durations differ?

14. Guess the duration of the following investment. Is it less than two years, two to three years, three to four years, or greater than four years? After your guess, use a discount rate of 6 percent and calculate the present value of the cash flows and then duration.

| Years from now | 1 | 2 | 3 | 4 |
|---|---|---|---|---|
| Cash flow | $0 | $1,000 | $5,000 | $2,000 |

15. In each of the following financial situations, fill in the blank with the terms *high duration, low duration,* or *zero duration,* as appropriate.

    a. If you were considering buying a bond and you expected interest rates to increase, you would prefer a bond with a _____.

    b. Relative to a bond with a high coupon rate, a bond with a low coupon rate would have a _____.

    c. A bond with a short maturity generally has a _____ compared to a bond with a long maturity.

    d. A 1-year corporate bond with a 5 percent coupon rate has a _____ relative to a one-year T-bill.

16. One author says that duration is the weighted average life of a financial instrument. A different one says that duration is a measure of elasticity. Which of the authors is correct? Or, are they both correct?

17. Suppose that a zero coupon bond selling at $1,000 par has a duration of four years. If interest rates increase from 6 percent to 7 percent annually, the value of the bond will fall by what amount using Equation 4.14? Use semiannual compounding. Then, use the present value formula to determine the actual price of the bond at 7 percent. What is the difference? Why is there a difference?

18. If interest rates fall from 6 percent to 5 percent, the price of the bond in the above problem will increase. Will the change in price (regardless of sign) be smaller or larger than in the above problem? Show how much by using the present value formula, Equation 4.8, and Equation 4.14. How does this conclusion relate to the interpretation of duration as an approximate elasticity measure?

19. Which money market instruments are typically quoted on a discount basis?

20. What is the bond equivalent yield of a 180-day, $1 million face value Treasury bill with a discount rate of 4.5 percent?

21. For which money market instruments are rates calculated based on par value rather than purchase price?

22. You would like to purchase a T-bill that has a $10,000 face value and 270 days to maturity. The current price of the T-bill is $9,620. What is the discount rate on this security? What is its bond equivalent yield?

23. You have just purchased a five-year maturity bond for $10,000 par value that pays $610 in coupon interest annually ($305 every six months). You expect to hold the bond until maturity. Calculate your expected total return if you can reinvest all coupon payments at 5 percent (2.5 percent semiannually). Suppose, instead, that you plan to sell the bond after two years when you expect that a similar risk three-year bond will be priced to yield 5.2 percent to maturity. Calculate the expected sale price of the bond and your expected total return using the same reinvestment rates. Explain why the two calculated total returns differ.

24. You are planning to buy a corporate bond with a seven-year maturity that pays 7 percent coupon interest. The bond is priced at $108,500 per $100,000 par value. You expect to sell the bond in two years when a similar risk five-year bond is priced to yield 7.2 percent annually to maturity. Assuming that you can reinvest all cash flows at an 8 percent annual rate (4 percent semiannually), calculate your expected total return over the two-year holding period.

25. You buy 100 shares in Bondex Corporation for $25 a share. Each share pays $1 in dividends every three months. You have a five-year holding period and expect to invest all dividends received in the first two years at 6 percent, and all dividends received the next three years at 9 percent. Calculate your expected total return (as a percentage yield) if you can sell the shares at $30 each after five years.

## ACTIVITY PROJECTS

1. Rates for the most popular financial instruments can be found in the *Wall Street Journal*. Collect the rates for the following securities. This information can be found on the front of the "Money and Investing" section as well as in the "Credit Markets" column.

   | | |
   |---|---|
   | 3-month T-bill | 3-month eurodollar deposit (LIBOR) |
   | federal funds | 3-month CD |
   | DJ 20 Bond Index | 10-year municipal |
   | 10-year Treasury | 10+ year Treasury |

   Rank the rates from highest to lowest. Why do the rates differ?

2. Locate the first General Electric (GE) corporate bond maturing after the year 2008 as reported in the *Wall Street Journal*. What is its coupon rate, maturity, and stream of coupon and principal payments? At the rate of return earned most recently on the DJ 20 Bond Index, what price would you be willing to pay for this bond? Comparing this price with its closing price, is the bond earning more or less in coupon interest than the DJ Bond Index? If you were going to buy a bond, would you choose this one? What factors would you consider in selecting a bond for your portfolio?

# Managing Interest Rate Risk: GAP and Earnings Sensitivity

*Sensitivity to market risk (S) is one of the basic components of a bank's CAMELS rating. For most banks, interest rate risk is the primary contributor to market risk because they don't have trading accounts. Given the recent volatility of interest rates and related potential swings in profitability, banks and regulators have paid increased attention to measuring and monitoring how rate changes affect performance. Senior managers and analysts continuously monitor what interest rate "bet" the bank is making.*

*Interest rate risk arises largely from traditional banking activities associated with accepting deposits and making loans. When liabilities and assets do not reprice coincidentally, the interest yield and market value of the loans can vary over time much differently than the interest cost and market value of liabilities. The result is a change in net interest income and value of stockholders' equity. When the repricing is dramatically different, the swings in earnings can potentially produce a net loss to the bank.*

*At year-end 2004, PNC conducted a simulation analysis that produced the following summary of outcomes regarding the bank's interest rate risk:*

Effect on net interest income in the first year from a gradual interest rate change:
   100 basis point increase in rates        0.60%
   100 basis point decrease in rates        −1.20%

Effect on net interest income in the second year from a gradual interest rate change:
   100 basis point increase in rates        3.60%
   100 basis point decrease in rates        −6.60%

*What does this mean? Does a rate increase help or hurt the bank? What about a rate decrease? How much does PNC have at risk? After reading the material in this chapter, you will be able to assess PNC's aggregate interest rate risk according to these figures.*

---

**T**his chapter examines the management of a bank's interest rate risk position in terms of GAP and earnings sensitivity analysis. In this context, interest rate risk refers to the volatility in net interest income and, ultimately, net income attributable to changes in the level of interest rates and shifts in the composition and volume of bank assets and liabilities. A bank that takes substantial risk will see its net interest margin vary widely from that expected when rates increase or decrease. A bank that assumes little interest rate risk will observe little change in its performance due to rate changes. Chapter 6 extends the analysis by relating interest rate risk to the volatility in a bank's market value of stockholders' equity and risk measures associated with the difference in average durations of a bank's assets and liabilities.

The analysis initially introduces traditional measures of interest rate risk associated with static GAP models. These models focus on GAP as a static measure of risk and net interest income as the target measure of bank performance. Sensitivity analysis extends GAP analysis to focus on the variation in bank earnings across different interest rate environments. This net interest income simulation, or "What if?" forecasting, provides information regarding how much net interest income changes when rates are alternatively assumed to rise and fall by various amounts. It takes into account shifts in asset and liability composition and embedded options in a bank's assets and liabilities and off-balance sheet activities. It provides a better understanding of potential changes in earnings than simple static models. As such, it is labeled **earnings sensitivity analysis.** Throughout, we provide numerous examples that clarify how changes in interest rates and other factors affect potential earnings.

Prior to the deregulation of interest rates in the mid-1980s, banks and savings and loans were effectively guaranteed a positive spread between what they earned in interest on loans and securities and what they paid in interest on liabilities. Virtually all institutions charged the maximum rates allowed on assets and paid the maximum rates allowed on liabilities. They were not allowed by regulation to compete on the basis of interest rates. Thus, charging 6 percent on loans and paying 2 percent on deposits ensured a 4 percent spread if loans didn't default. Since interest rate deregulation, banks are no longer guaranteed a profitable spread between asset yields and funding costs. Interest rate fluctuations alter bank earnings and the value of stockholders' claims unless management implements strategies to reduce their impact. Interest rate risk management is extremely important because no one can consistently forecast interest rates accurately. A bank's asset and liability management committee (ALCO), or alternatively its risk management committee, is responsible for measuring and monitoring interest rate risk. It also recommends pricing, investment, funding, and marketing strategies to achieve the desired trade-off between risk and expected return.

Bank managers generally have greater expertise in managing credit risk than interest rate risk, especially at smaller institutions. This reflects the perception that earnings problems and possible bank failure are more closely tied to bad loans than mismatched pricing of assets and liabilities. They often rely on brokers to recommend specific investment securities for purchase and sale and outsource interest rate risk analytics to consulting companies. During the late 1990s through 2004, many banks invested heavily in callable federal agency securities and mortgage-backed securities with little or no default risk, but with extensive call and prepayment risk. With the decline in interest rates, they saw their interest income drop as borrowers refinanced high-rate mortgages so that mortgage-backed securities were paid off early and issuers called high-rate agency bonds and refinanced them at lower rates.

The fundamental issue is whether bank managers understand the magnitude of interest rate risk that they assume and whether earnings will fall sharply when interest rates change adversely. The basic questions are: "Do banks understand the nature of their interest rate bet?" and "Do banks understand how big the bet is?"

Banks use two basic models to assess interest rate risk. The first, GAP and earnings sensitivity analysis, emphasizes income statement effects by focusing on how changes in interest rates and the bank's balance sheet affect net interest income and net income. The second, duration gap and economic value of equity analysis, emphasizes the market value of stockholders' equity by focusing on how these same types of changes affect the market value of assets versus the market value of liabilities. This chapter examines the first model.

## MEASURING INTEREST RATE RISK WITH GAP

Unexpected changes in interest rates can significantly alter a bank's profitability. GAP and earnings sensitivity analysis targets the volatility in net interest income associated with changing interest rates and balance sheet composition. Depending on the cash flow characteristics of a bank's assets and liabilities and the existence of embedded options, interest rate changes may raise or lower net interest income.

Consider a bank that makes 30-year, fixed-rate mortgage loans financed primarily with 3-month to 1-year deposits. Why would management choose this portfolio? The bank receives interest and principal payments on the mortgages monthly and pays monthly interest on deposits. With an upward sloping yield curve, the mortgage rate will exceed the short-term deposit rates by a large spread. For example, if the mortgage rate is 7 percent and deposit rates are 2 percent, the initial spread is 5 percent. This initial spread should be large enough to cover the cost of doing business, cover the expected change in rates over the investment horizon, and provide for a reasonable profit.

What happens if interest rates change? Because the mortgages have a 30-year maturity, these rates are fixed as long as the mortgages are outstanding. Rate changes will, therefore, affect the deposit rates and not the mortgage rates directly. If the deposit rates rise, the spread will fall below 5 percent. Similarly, if deposit rates fall, the spread will rise above 5 percent. The bank's choice of long-term, fixed-rate assets financed by short-term deposits evidences a specific interest rate bet. Rising rates lower net interest income while falling rates increase net interest income.

Of course, it's not quite that simple. For one, the balance sheet is dynamic and thus changing constantly over time. Rate changes are only one factor that affects earnings. Similarly, an upward sloping yield curve indicates a consensus view that short-term rates are going to increase over time. For a bank to take the position described, management is essentially betting that rates will not rise above expectations. Finally, there are embedded options in the mortgages that will likely alter the cash flows and eventual interest payments and receipts if rates change. In the case of falling rates, some mortgage borrowers will refinance and the bank will lose some interest income because it must reinvest the proceeds at lower rates.

**EXHIBIT 5.1** Important Interest Rate Risk Terminology

**ALCO:** Acronym for asset and liability management committee.

**ALM:** Acronym for asset and liability management.

**Base rate:** Any interest rate used as an index to price loans or deposits; quoted interest rates are typically set at some markup, such as 0.25 percent or 1 percent, over the base rate and thus change whenever the base rate changes.

**Cost of funds:** Interest expense divided by the dollar volume of interest-bearing liabilities.

**Duration:** A measure of the approximate price sensitivity of an asset or portfolio to a change in interest rates.

**Earnings change ratio:** A percentage measure that indicates how much of each type of a bank's assets or liabilities will reprice when some index rate changes. An earnings change ratio of 1 indicates that the underlying asset or liability changes in yield or cost 1-to-1 with changes in the index rate.

**Earning ratio:** The dollar volume of a bank's earning assets divided by the dollar volume of total assets.

**Earnings sensitivity analysis:** Conducting "what if" analysis by varying factors that affect interest income and expense to determine how changes in key factors affect a bank's net interest income and net interest margin. The output indicates how much net interest income will change in dollars and in percentage terms under different interest rate scenarios.

**Effective GAP:** The "true" measure of GAP that takes into account a specific interest rate forecast and when embedded options will either be exercised or will affect the actual repricing of an asset or liability.

**Embedded option:** A specific feature of a bank's asset, liability, or off-balance sheet contract that potentially changes the cash flows of the item when interest rates vary. Examples include early prepayment of principal on loans, issuers calling outstanding bonds, and depositors withdrawing funds prior to maturity.

**Floating rate:** Assets or liabilities that carry rates tied to the prime rate or other base rates. The instrument is repriced whenever the base rate changes.

**GAP:** The dollar volume of rate-sensitive assets minus the dollar volume of rate-sensitive liabilities.

**GAP ratio:** The dollar volume of rate-sensitive assets divided by the dollar volume of rate-sensitive liabilities.

**Gradual rate shock:** An assumed change in interest rates that occurs over time; a 1 percent annual increase in rates may translate into a monthly increase of 8.3 basis points.

**Hedging:** Taking a position or implementing a transaction to reduce overall risk associated with an existing position.

**Instantaneous rate shock:** An immediate increase or decrease in all interest rates by the same amount; a parallel shift in the yield curve.

**Net interest margin (NIM):** Tax-equivalent net interest income divided by earning assets.

**Net overhead:** Noninterest income minus noninterest expense.

**Nonrate GAP:** Noninterest-bearing liabilities plus equity minus nonearning assets as a ratio of earning assets.

**Rate-sensitive assets (RSAs):** The dollar value of assets that either mature or can be repriced within a selected time period, such as 90 days.

**Rate-sensitive liabilities (RSLs):** The dollar value of liabilities that either mature or can be repriced within a selected time period, such as 90 days.

**Risk management committee:** Central committee charged with enterprise-wide risk management, measurement, monitoring and policies. Members typically set strategy regarding market risk within the organization.

**Simulation:** An analysis of possible outcomes for net interest margin resulting from selecting hypothetical values for key variables that influence the repricing of assets, liabilities, and off-balance sheet items, and conducting forecasts to determine the effects of changes in these variables on a bank's net interest income.

**Speculation:** Taking a position or implementing a transaction that increases risk in hopes of earning above average returns.

**Spread:** The interest yield on earning assets minus the interest cost of interest-bearing funds.

**Variable rate:** Assets or liabilities that are automatically repriced at regular intervals.

---

Efforts at managing interest rate risk force a bank's ALCO to establish specific targets for net interest income, measure overall risk exposure, and formulate strategies to attain the targets. Specific targets and strategies presumably reflect management's view of actions that will lead to maximizing the value of the bank.

The following sections describe the traditional static GAP model and explain its shortcomings, then describe how earnings sensitivity analysis provides a meaningful extension. Exhibit 5.1 summarizes important terminology.

## TRADITIONAL STATIC GAP ANALYSIS

Traditional static GAP models attempt to measure how much interest rate risk a bank evidences at a fixed point in time by comparing the rate sensitivity of assets with the rate sensitivity of liabilities. Static GAP focuses on managing net interest income in the short run. The objective is typically to measure expected net interest income and then identify strategies to stabilize or improve it. Interest rate risk is measured by calculating GAPs over different time intervals based on aggregate balance sheet data at a fixed point in time—hence, the term static GAP. These GAP values are then examined to infer how much net interest income will change if rates change.

There are several basic steps to static GAP analysis.

1. Develop an interest rate forecast.

2. Select a series of sequential time intervals for determining what amount of assets and liabilities are rate sensitive within each time interval.

3. Group assets and liabilities into these time intervals, or "buckets," according to the time until the first repricing. The principal portion of the asset or liability that management expects to reprice is classified as rate sensitive. The effects of any off-balance sheet positions, such as those associated with interest rate swaps, futures, and so on, are also added to the balance sheet position according to whether the item effectively represents a rate-sensitive asset or rate-sensitive liability.

4. Calculate GAP. A bank's static GAP equals the dollar amount of rate-sensitive assets (RSAs) minus the dollar amount of rate-sensitive liabilities (RSLs) for each time interval.

5. Forecast net interest income given the assumed interest rate environment and assumed repricing characteristics of the underlying instruments.

Note that GAP measures balance sheet values. It represents the principal amounts of cash flows that are reflected in the measures. Expected interest income and interest expense components of cash flows are ignored in the GAP measure. Formally,

$$GAP = RSAs - RSLs$$

where rate-sensitive assets and liabilities are those identified within each time bucket. As such, there is a periodic GAP and a cumulative GAP for each time bucket. The periodic GAP compares RSAs with RSLs across each single time bucket. The cumulative GAP compares RSAs with RSLs over all time buckets from the present through the last day in each successive time bucket. For example, the cumulative GAP through 90 days (0–90 days) equals the sum of the periodic GAPs for the two time buckets, 0–30 days and 31–90 days.

This information is used to identify the bank's interest rate risk and to develop strategies to manage this risk. Management can alter the size of the GAP to either hedge net interest income against changing interest rates or speculatively try to increase net interest income. Hedging involves reducing the volatility of net interest income either by directly adjusting the dollar amounts of rate-sensitive assets and liabilities, or by taking an off-balance sheet position such as with forwards, futures, option contracts, and interest rate swaps.[1] Changing the size of GAP to take advantage of perceived rate changes is speculative because it assumes that management can forecast interest rates better than the market.

## WHAT DETERMINES RATE SENSITIVITY?

The first three steps in GAP analysis require the classification of the principal portions of specific assets and liabilities that are rate sensitive within specific time intervals. Other balance sheet items either carry fixed rates or do not earn or pay interest. Interest payments are not included directly because GAP is a balance sheet (plus off-balance sheet) measure of risk. Management typically selects a variety of time buckets that provide useful information, as outlined later. The initial issue is to determine what features make an asset or liability rate sensitive.

**CONSIDER A 0–90 DAY TIME INTERVAL.** The key issue is to identify what assets and liabilities listed on a bank's balance sheet will be repriced within 90 days given the specific interest forecast. Note that the GAP definition and steps in the analysis require that the person determining rate sensitivity forecast when something will be repriced. The question typically arises as to whether the contractual date or expected date of repricing is the correct one. The answer depends on the purpose of the analysis. If the purpose is to simply inform the interpreter, knowing when items contractually reprice is helpful. For example, knowing how many loans are priced off of the bank's prime rate is good information. However, it is generally more valuable to assess the impact of repricing variations on earnings. Thus, the impact of having loans priced off of prime will vary if prime changes in three months versus nine months. The model can help estimate the different impacts only if prime loans are categorized according to when prime is expected to change. In practice, analysts use expected repricing dates under the relevant interest rate scenario to assess risk.

In general, an asset or liability is normally classified as rate sensitive within a time interval if:

1. It matures.

2. It represents an interim or partial principal payment.

---

3. The interest rate applied to the outstanding principal balance changes contractually during the interval.

4. The interest rate applied to the outstanding principal balance changes when some base rate or index changes and management expects the base rate/index to change during the time interval.

**MATURITY.** If any asset or liability matures within a time interval, the principal amount will be repriced. If an asset matures, the bank must reinvest the proceeds. If a liability matures, the bank must replace the liability with new funding. Both hold true regardless of whether interest rates change or not. The question is what principal amount is *expected to* reprice. Step *two* in GAP analysis determines the *time frame* for which proceeds will be reinvested or liabilities refinanced.[2] In the case of a 0–90 day time interval, any investment security, loan, deposit, or purchased liability that matures within 90 days is rate sensitive.

**INTERIM OR PARTIAL PRINCIPAL PAYMENT.** More generally, any principal payment on a loan is rate sensitive if management expects to receive it within the time interval. This includes final principal payments as well as interim principal payments. Consider a bank that makes a 1-year $100,000 loan with principal payments of $25,000 due every three months (every 90 days). When making the initial assessment of rate sensitivity, $25,000 would be classified as a rate-sensitive asset within 90 days because the bank expects to receive and reinvest this portion of the total principal on the loan. Thus, banks that make car loans and residential mortgages, which typically include set fixed-dollar payments that include both principal and interest, record the principal component of each regular monthly payment on the loans as rate-sensitive assets.

**CONTRACTUAL CHANGE IN RATE.** Some assets and deposit liabilities earn or pay rates that vary contractually with some index. These instruments are repriced whenever the index changes. If management knows that the index will contractually change within 90 days, the underlying asset or liability is rate sensitive.

Consider an adjustable rate mortgage with a 15-year maturity and principal balance of $250,000. The rate equals the prevailing 10-year Treasury rate plus 1 pecent and adjusts annually on the anniversary date of when the loan was originated according to changes in the 10-year Treasury rate. When the loan is first booked, the principal (ignoring monthly payments) is not rate sensitive within 90 days because the principal will not reprice until the Treasury rate changes. After nine months, the rate automatically adjusts within the 90 day window according to what the 10-year Treasury rate equals at the end the first year. The full outstanding principal balance is classified as rate sensitive once the known repricing (reset date for the ten-year Treasury rate) is within 90 days.

**CHANGE IN BASE RATE OR INDEX.** Some loans and deposits carry rates tied to indexes where the bank has no control or definite knowledge of when the index will change. For example, a commercial loan priced at 1 percent over some other bank's prime rate carries a floating rate, but may or may not be repriced with any known frequency. Such prime rate loans typically state that the bank can change prime daily. The loan is rate sensitive in the sense that its yield can change at any time but its effective rate sensitivity depends on how frequently the prime rate actually changes. For the GAP figures to be most meaningful, management must forecast when the prime rate or other index will change. The full amount of principal should be allocated to the time interval that coincides with when the index or base rate is expected to change. The GAP and effect on net interest income will vary accordingly. This is why the first step, having an interest rate forecast, is important. The classification will differ across different economic environments.

Many asset and liability management models used by banks classify prime-based loans and other floating-rate instruments as immediately repriceable. Although this is true, assuming that the indexes and base rates can contractually change at any time, the resulting GAP figure is not very meaningful because such rates do not change simultaneously or in many cases all that frequently. For example, although Wall Street prime changed more than 50 times in 1980, there are years when it never changed. In 2004, prime increased by 25 basis points at four different times and the pattern continued in 2005. How a bank classifies these base rate loans and other accounts, such as NOWs and MMDAs, can dramatically alter the GAP measures reported and the effective (or actual) GAP measures if the underlying indexes do not change as assumed.

## FACTORS AFFECTING NET INTEREST INCOME

Although GAP presumably provides information about a bank's interest rate risk exposure, many factors affect net interest income. In addition to changes in the *level* of interest rates, changes in the *composition* of assets and liabilities, changes in the *volume* of assets and liabilities outstanding, and changes in the *relationship* between the yields on earning assets and rates paid on interest-bearing liabilities will alter net interest income from that expected. Some factors are at least partially controllable, while others are not. Asset and liability management examines the impact of all factors on net interest income. The following analysis documents circumstances when net interest income increases and decreases by comparing it at a hypothetical bank before and after each influence.

---

[2]In this context, an instrument will still be repriced if rates do not change because new contract terms will be determined. As discussed later, this is important because not all rates change by the same amount at the same time.

| EXHIBIT 5.2 | Expected Balance Sheet Composition and Average Interest Rates for a Hypothetical Bank |

|  | Assets | Yield Rates | Liabilities | Interest Costs |
|---|---|---|---|---|
| Rate-sensitive | $ 500 | 6% | $ 600 | 2% |
| Fixed-rate | 350 | 9 | 220 | 4 |
| Nonearning/Nonpaying | 150 | | 100 | |
| Total | | | $ 920 | |
| | | | **Equity** | |
| | | | $ 80 | |
| Total | $1,000 | | $1,000 | |

$$\text{Net interest income} = 0.06(\$500) + 0.09(\$350) - 0.02(\$600) - 0.04(\$220)$$
$$= \$61.50 - \$20.80$$
$$= \$40.70$$
$$\text{Net interest margin} = \$40.70/\$850 = 4.79\%$$
$$\text{GAP} = \text{RSAs} - \text{RSLs} = \$500 - \$600 = -\$100$$

NOTE: RSAs are rate-sensitive assets; RSLs are rate-sensitive liabilities. The assumed time frame for classifying RSAs and RSLs is 1 year. Yield rates are computed on a tax-equivalent basis. All rates are expected to remain constant at current levels.

Consider a bank with the general balance sheet accounts listed in Exhibit 5.2. For ease of example, the RSAs and RSLs represent principal amounts that are expected to be repriced within a 1-year time interval when interest rates are assumed to remain constant at current levels. Thus, the RSAs and RSLs either mature within one year, represent partial principal payments made during the next year, are variable-rate contracts that are automatically repriced within one year, or carry floating-rate yields that management forecasts will change during the year. The RSAs include short-term securities, federal funds sold, expected principal payments on loans, and the outstanding principal on all repriced variable-rate and floating-rate loans. The RSLs include small time deposits and jumbo CDs maturing within one year, federal funds purchased, some interest-bearing transactions accounts, and money market deposit accounts. The crucial feature is that cash flows associated with rate-sensitive contracts vary with changes in interest rates. Fixed-rate assets and liabilities carry rates that are constant throughout the one-year time interval. Cash flows do not change unless there is a default, early withdrawal, or prepayment that is not forecasted accurately. Nonearning assets generate no explicit income and nonpaying liabilities pay no interest. Both of these are classified as fixed-rate (at zero) in this static analysis. Note that all embedded options are ignored.

Expected average earning asset yield rates and interest costs for the year appear beside each account and represent expected values. If these balance sheet and interest rate figures reflect average performance during the year, the bank's tax-equivalent net interest income is expected to equal $40.70 per $850 in earning assets for a net interest margin (NIM) of 4.79 percent. These figures represent benchmark estimates. During the year, the level of interest rates normally changes from that initially projected, as do the composition and volume of assets and liabilities. This bank's one-year cumulative GAP equals −$100. The sign and magnitude of GAP presumably provide information regarding interest-rate risk.

## CHANGES IN THE LEVEL OF INTEREST RATES

The sign of GAP (positive or negative) indicates the nature of the bank's interest rate bet. The GAP measure compares the dollar value of a bank's assets that reprice within an interval to the dollar value of liabilities that reprice within the same time frame. A negative GAP, such as that shown in Exhibit 5.2, indicates that the bank has more RSLs than RSAs. When interest rates rise during the time interval, the bank pays higher rates on all repriceable liabilities and earns higher yields on all repriceable assets. If all rates rise by equal amounts at the same time, both interest income and interest expense rise, but interest expense rises more because more liabilities are repriced. Net interest income thus declines, as does the bank's net interest margin. When interest rates fall during the interval, more liabilities than assets are repriced at the lower rates such that interest expense falls more than interest income falls. In this case, both net interest income and net interest margin increase. The sign of a bank's GAP thus indicates whether interest income or interest expense will likely change more when interest rates change. A bank with a negative GAP is said to be *liability sensitive* because more liabilities are expected to reprice versus assets and interest expense is expected to change more than interest income.

A positive GAP indicates that a bank has more RSAs than RSLs across some time interval. When rates rise, interest income increases more than interest expense because more assets are repriced such that net interest income similarly increases. Rate decreases have the opposite effect. Because interest income falls more than interest expense, net interest income falls. Such a bank is said to be *asset sensitive*. More assets than liabilities are expected to reprice and interest income changes more than interest expense.

If a bank has a zero GAP, RSAs equal RSLs and equal interest rate changes do not alter net interest income because changes in interest income equal changes in interest expense. It is virtually impossible for a bank to have a zero GAP given the complexity and size of bank balance sheets. These relationships are summarized as follows:

**GAP Summary**

| GAP | Change in Interest Rates | Change in Interest Income | | Change in Interest Expense | Change in Net Interest Income |
|---|---|---|---|---|---|
| Positive | Increase | Increase | > | Increase | Increase |
| Positive | Decrease | Decrease | > | Decrease | Decrease |
| Negative | Increase | Increase | < | Increase | Decrease |
| Negative | Decrease | Decrease | < | Decrease | Increase |
| Zero | Increase | Increase | = | Increase | None |
| Zero | Decrease | Decrease | = | Decrease | None |

Section A of Exhibit 5.3 shows the relationship between an increase in the level of rates and a negative GAP for the hypothetical bank in Exhibit 5.2. All rates are assumed to increase by an average of 1 percent during the year, with the bank's portfolio composition and size unchanged.[3] This is characterized as assuming a parallel shift in the yield curve by +1 percent. With these assumptions, the only items that change are the yield rates and interest costs on rate-sensitive assets and liabilities. Interest income increases by $5 to $66.50, but interest expense increases by $6 to $26.80, such that net interest income declines by $1 relative to that initially projected in Exhibit 5.2. NIM subsequently falls by 12 basis points to 4.67 percent.

Suppose instead that rates decrease by 1 percent relative to the base case. The average yield earned on rate-sensitive assets declines to 5 percent while the interest cost of rate-sensitive liabilities declines to 1 percent. By assumption, fixed rates do not change. Interest income falls by $5 while interest expense falls by $6 such that net interest income increases by $1. This occurs because the bank now pays lower rates on a greater amount of liabilities ($600) than assets ($500) that are now earning lower yields. NIM subsequently widens.

The change in net interest income arises because the amount of rate-sensitive assets differs from the amount of rate-sensitive liabilities and all rates are assumed to change by the same amount in the same direction. The larger the GAP difference, the greater the impact. If RSAs equaled RSLs, the change in interest income would be matched by the change in interest expense regardless of whether rates rise or fall, so that net interest income would be unchanged. In this framework, whether NIM rises or falls depends on whether the GAP is positive or negative and how much the level of interest rates changes. The following relationship summarizes this framework.

$$\Delta NII_{exp} = GAP \times \Delta i_{exp} \tag{5.1}$$

where

$\Delta NII_{exp}$ = the expected change in net interest income over a period of time from some base amount,

GAP = cumulative GAP over the interval through the end of the period of time, and

$\Delta i_{exp}$ = the expected permanent change in the level of interest rates.

Again, this applies only in the case of a parallel shift in the yield curve, which rarely occurs. Specifically, if the 1-year GAP is any positive value, net interest income increases when rates are assumed to rise and decreases when rates fall. Suppose, for example, that the above bank's initial position consists of $650 in rate-sensitive assets and $200 in fixed-rate assets with all other factors the same. The 1-year GAP equals $50. At the rates listed, interest income is expected to equal $58 while interest expense is still $20.80, producing $38.80 in net interest income. If rates rise by 1 percent, interest income rises by $6.50 while interest expense rises by just $6. With this positive GAP, net interest income now increases by $0.50. It declines when rates fall.[4]

In this context, the sign and size of GAP provide information regarding a bank's interest rate risk position. The sign indicates the bank's interest rate bet. If GAP is positive, the bank wins (net interest income should rise) when rates rise and loses when rates fall. If GAP is negative, the bank wins when rates fall and loses when rates rise. The size of GAP indicates how much risk a bank assumes. Specifically, a zero GAP indicates the lowest risk. The farther GAP is from zero (lowest risk), the greater is the potential variation in net interest income and thus, the greater the assumed risk.

---

[3]Earnings-sensitivity analysis recognizes that the amount of rate-sensitive assets and rate-sensitive liabilities changes when interest rates change, and that various rates change by different amounts at different times. The discussion ignores this possibility, which is why static GAP is not very meaningful as a risk measure.

[4]The reader should verify that interest income changes by the same amount as interest expense in these examples when the GAP equals zero.

| **EXHIBIT 5.3** | Expected Changes in Net Interest Income from Changes in the Level of Rates, Spread Volume and Balance Sheet Mix |
|---|---|

### A. 1% Increase in Level of All Short-Term Rates

|  | Assets | Yield Rates | Liabilities | Interest Costs |
|---|---|---|---|---|
| Rate-sensitive | $ 500 | 7% | $ 600 | 3% |
| Fixed-rate | 350 | 9% | 220 | 4 |
| Nonearning/Nonpaying | 150 |  | 100 |  |
|  |  |  | **Equity** |  |
|  |  |  | 80 |  |
| Total | $1,000 |  | $1,000 |  |

Net interest income = 0.07($500) + 0.09($350) − 0.03($600) − 0.04($220)
$$= \$66.50 - \$26.80$$
$$= \$39.70$$
Net interest margin = $39.70/$850 = 4.67%
GAP        = $500 − $600 = −$100

### B. 1% Decrease in Spread between Asset Yields and Interest Costs

|  | Assets | Yield Rates | Liabilities | Interest Costs |
|---|---|---|---|---|
| Rate-sensitive | $ 500 | 6.5% | $ 600 | 3.5% |
| Fixed-rate | 350 | 9.0 | 220 | 4.0 |
| Nonearning/Nonpaying | 150 |  | 100 |  |
|  |  |  | **Equity** |  |
|  |  |  | 80 |  |
| Total | $1,000 |  | $1,000 |  |

Net interest income = 0.065($500) + 0.09($350) − 0.035($600) − 0.04($220)
$$= \$64.00 - \$29.80$$
$$= \$34.20$$
Net interest margin = $34.20/$850 = 4.02%
GAP        = $500 − $600 = −$100

### C. Proportionate Doubling in Size

|  | Assets | Yield Rates | Liabilities | Interest Costs |
|---|---|---|---|---|
| Rate-sensitive | $1,000 | 6% | $1,200 | 2% |
| Fixed-rate | 700 | 9 | 440 | 4 |
| Nonearning/Nonpaying | 300 |  | 200 |  |
|  |  |  | **Equity** |  |
|  |  |  | 160 |  |
| Total | $2,000 |  | $2,000 |  |

Net interest income = 0.06($1,000) + 0091($700) − 0.02($1,200) − 0.04($440) = $81.40
Net interest margin = $81.40/$1,700 = 4.79%
GAP        = $1,000 − $1,200 = −$200

### D. Increase in RSAs and Decrease in RSLs

|  | Assets | Yield Rates | Liabilities | Interest Costs |
|---|---|---|---|---|
| Rate-sensitive | $ 540 | 6% | $ 560 | 2% |
| Fixed-rate | 310 | 9 | 260 | 4 |
| Nonearning/Nonpaying | 150 |  | 100 |  |
|  |  |  | **Equity** |  |
|  |  |  | 80 |  |
| Total | $1,000 |  | $1,000 |  |

Net interest income = 0.06($540) + 0.09($310) − 0.02($560) − 0.04($260)
$$= \$60.30 - \$21.60$$
$$= \$38.70$$
Net interest margin = $38.70/$850 = 4.55%
GAP        = $540 − $560 = −$20

NOTE: RSAs are rate-sensitive assets; RSLs are rate-sensitive liabilities.

## CHANGES IN THE RELATIONSHIP BETWEEN SHORT-TERM ASSET YIELDS AND LIABILITY COSTS

Net interest income may similarly differ from that expected if the spread between earning asset yields and the interest cost of interest-bearing liabilities changes. There is no reason that all rates should change by the same amount over time. Asset yields may vary relative to interest costs because of an unexpected shift in the yield curve (unequal changes in the level of different maturity interest rates are labeled a nonparallel shift in the yield curve), an increase or decrease in risk premiums, and nonsynchronous changes in indexes on floating-rate assets or liabilities. If, for instance, liabilities are short-term and assets are long-term, the spread will narrow when the yield curve inverts and will widen when the yield curve increases in slope. Similarly, asset yields may be tied to base rates that change monthly while liability costs change weekly with money market rates.

Section B of Exhibit 5.3 examines the impact of a 1 percent decrease in the spread (from 4 percent to 3 percent) on rate-sensitive assets and liabilities for the year. With the portfolio composition unchanged, net interest income declines to $34.20. Of course, net interest income increases whenever the spread increases. Changes in net interest income associated with changes in the difference between different interest rates, say prime minus 3-month LIBOR, are a reflection of *basis risk.*

## CHANGES IN VOLUME

Net interest income varies directly with changes in the volume of earning assets and interest-bearing liabilities, regardless of the level of interest rates. Consider Section C in Exhibit 5.3 where the bank doubles in size. The portfolio composition and interest rates are unchanged. Net interest income doubles because the bank earns the same interest spread on twice the volume of earning assets such that NIM is unchanged. GAP now doubles to −$200 but is the same fraction of total assets. The net effect is that growth, by itself, leads to an increase in the dollar amount of earnings but does not alter profitability measures or the relative size of GAP to assets. A bank that alternatively contracts in size experiences a decrease in net interest income with no change in profitability measures or the relative size of GAP to assets.

## CHANGES IN PORTFOLIO COMPOSITION

Any variation in portfolio mix potentially alters net interest income. A manager who wants to reduce risk for the sample bank in Exhibit 5.3 might attempt to increase asset rate sensitivity by pricing more loans on a floating-rate basis or shortening maturities of investment securities. Alternatively, the manager might decrease liability rate sensitivity by substituting longer-term CDs for overnight federal funds purchased. These transactions change both the GAP and the bank's interest rate risk position. They also change net interest income from that initially expected. Section D of Exhibit 5.3 summarizes the impact of a $40 shift of fixed-rate assets to RSAs and a corresponding $40 shift from RSLs to fixed-rate liabilities. In this case, the level of rates is unchanged and net interest income falls by $2 from the initial estimate of $40.70. This decline is caused by a decline in the average yield on earning assets which produces a $1.20 drop in interest income, and an increase in the average interest cost of liabilities that produces a $0.80 increase in interest expense. In addition to changing expected net interest income, this change in composition alters the GAP to −$20 and thus reduces the bank's interest rate risk profile.

There is no fixed relationship between changes in portfolio mix and net interest income. The impact varies with the relationships between interest rates on rate-sensitive and fixed-rate instruments and with the magnitude of funds shifts. If, for example, the change in mix was reversed in the above case, net interest income would increase. Net interest income would drop if the $40 shift in liabilities was the only change in portfolio composition. In many cases, banks change mix as part of initiatives to offset anticipated adverse changes in net interest margin. Generally, any shift to loans from securities will increase net interest income near-term because loan yields exceed most security yields on a pretax and prerisk (default loss) basis. Similarly, any shift from core deposits to noncore liabilities reduces net interest income because noncore liabilities generally carry higher interest rates.

Changes in the magnitudes of nonearning assets and nonpaying liabilities also influence net interest income and NIM. If a bank can reduce its nonearning assets, net interest income increases automatically, with the magnitude determined by how the funds are invested. For example, net interest income rises by $3 [.06($50) − 0] with a $50 shift to RSAs. A $50 shift to fixed-rate assets increases net interest income by $4.50 [.09($50) − 0]. In both cases, NIM rises because the bank's funding costs are unchanged with higher interest income.

## RATE, VOLUME, AND MIX ANALYSIS

Many banks publish a summary in their annual report of how net interest income has changed over time. They separate changes attributable to shifts in asset and liability composition and volume from changes associated with movements in interest rates. Exhibit 5.4 represents such a report for Synovus, headquartered in Columbus, Georgia, for 2004 versus 2003, and 2003 versus 2002.

Consider the data for 2004 compared with 2003. The figures refer to the change in either interest income, interest expense, or net interest income attributable to changes in the volume of earning assets and interest-bearing liabilities—under the "Volume" heading—or that attributable to changes in earning asset yields or rates

**EXHIBIT
5.4**    Rate/Volume Analysis for Synovus

| | 2004 Compared to 2003 Change Due to (a) | | | 2003 Compared to 2002 Change Due to (a) | | |
|---|---|---|---|---|---|---|
| | **Volume** | **Yield/ Rate** | **Net Change** | **Volume** | **Yield/ Rate** | **Net Change** |
| **Interest earned on:** | | | | | | |
| Taxable loans, net .......................... | $141,842 | (41,856) | 99,986 | 155,237 | (127,481) | 27,756 |
| Tax-exempt loans, net [b] ................... | 104 | (797) | (693) | 147 | 194 | 341 |
| Taxable investment securities ................ | 12,179 | (7,346) | 4,833 | 13,417 | (33,378) | (19,961) |
| Tax-exempt investment securities[b] ........... | (330) | (322) | (652) | 137 | (384) | (247) |
| Interest earning deposits with banks ........... | (2) | 9 | 7 | 9 | (35) | (26) |
| Federal funds sold and securities | | | | | | |
|    purchased under resale agreements ......... | 508 | (109) | 399 | 859 | (851) | 8 |
| Mortgage loans held for sale ................ | (7,194) | 414 | (6,780) | 1,611 | (2,907) | (1,296) |
|      Total interest income .................... | 147,107 | (50,007) | 97,100 | 171,417 | (164,842) | 6,575 |
| | | | | | | |
| **Interest paid on:** | | | | | | |
| Interest bearing demand deposits ............. | 1,753 | (2,768) | (1,015) | 4,601 | (6,354) | (1,753) |
| Money market accounts .................... | 8,718 | 4,583 | 13,301 | 10,518 | (20,026) | (9,508) |
| Savings deposits ......................... | 116 | (357) | (241) | 303 | (1,491) | (1,188) |
| Time deposits ........................... | 9,808 | (23,130) | (13,322) | 17,666 | (48,312) | (30,646) |
| Federal funds purchased and securities | | | | | | |
|    sold under repurchase agreements .......... | 4,051 | (3,406) | 7,457 | (499) | (6,311) | (6,810) |
| Other borrowed funds ..................... | 3,329 | (9,596) | (6,267) | 21,354 | (10,557) | 10,797 |
|      Total interest expense ................... | 27,775 | (27,862) | (87) | 53,943 | (93,051) | (39,108) |
|      Net interest income ..................... | $119,332 | (22,145) | 97,187 | 117,474 | (71,791) | 45,683 |

NOTE: Figures are in thousands of dollars.

(a) The change in interest due to both rate and volume has been allocated to the rate component.

(b) Reflects taxable-equivalent adjustments using the statutory federal income tax rate of 35% in adjusting interest on tax-exempt loans and investment securities to a taxable-equivalent basis.

SOURCE: Synovus 2004 Annual Report.

paid on liabilities—under the "Yield/Rate" heading. The "Net Change" column represents the sum of these two figures.

The purpose is to assess what factors influence shifts in net interest income over time. Data in the column headed Volume indicate how much interest income and interest expense would have changed if rates were held constant at the prior year's levels and the only impact was balance sheet changes in the amounts of earning assets and interest-bearing liabilities. In 2004, volume effects for Synovus exceeded interest rate effects for interest income, with yield/rate effects greater than volume for interest expense. From 2003 to 2004, net interest income increased by $97,187,000, of which $119,332,000 was attributed to the growth in earning assets versus interest-bearing liabilities with all interest rates held constant at 2003 levels. As such, Synovus grew its loans and securities holdings relative to its funding, which added significantly to earnings given the prior year's spread. Data in the column headed Yield/Rate assumes that volumes of the balance sheet items are held constant at 2003 levels and the effects reflect primarily changes in earning asset yields and liability costs (rates). From 2003 to 2004, Synovus saw its interest income fall by $50,007,000 associated with declines on earning assets while its interest expense fell by just $27,862,000. The net was a loss of $22,145,000, which reduced net interest income. While interest rates decreased modestly in 2004, those on earning assets fell more than those on interest-bearing liabilities.

This view of GAP and net interest income is simplistic. Obviously, asset yields and interest costs do not change coincidentally or by equal amounts. Even within distinct time intervals, assets and liabilities are repriced at varied intervals, producing cash flows that may differ substantially from those implied by the GAP. For example, if all RSAs from Exhibit 5.2 matured in one month while all RSLs matured in six months, projected cash flows would reflect interest rate and portfolio changes occurring five months apart such that the forecast change in net interest income could be substantially wrong.

For more meaningful comparisons, managers should calculate the GAP over relatively short periods and allow for a wide range of interest rates and repricings. The next section introduces a rate-sensitivity report, a framework that is commonly used to evaluate a bank's interest rate risk position. It essentially calculates GAPs across different time buckets. Data for Security Bank, a $100 million organization, are used to demonstrate the framework.

## RATE-SENSITIVITY REPORTS

Many managers monitor their bank's risk position and potential changes in net interest income using a framework like that in Exhibit 5.5. This report classifies Security Bank's assets and liabilities as rate sensitive in selected time buckets through one year. Underlying each report should be an assumed interest rate environment. The last column lists the totals for all balance sheet items as of year-end. Note that Security Bank reports $85.3 million in earning assets and $14.7 million in nonearning assets, $78.5 million in interest-bearing liabilities and $21.5 million in liabilities and equity not subject to interest payments. Each earlier column of data reflects the dollar volume of repriceable items within a distinct but sequential time period. For example, of the $9.5 million in Treasury and agency securities owned, $700,000 will be repriced in 8 to 30 days, $3.6 million is repriceable in 31 to 90 days, and so forth. All floating-rate commercial loans tied to a base rate are designated as rate sensitive from 8 to 30 days out. This classification reflects Security Bank's experience in changing base rates monthly on average during the past year. The column labeled "Non-Rate-Sensitive" indicates amounts that do not earn or pay interest.

Figures for rate-sensitive liabilities similarly indicate when the items are expected to be repriced. Thus, NOW accounts will presumably be repriced within 91 to 180 days while a portion of money market deposit accounts will be repriced in 8 to 30 days and the bulk in 31 to 90 days. Note that savings accounts are assumed not to reprice for at least one year even though the rates can be changed more frequently. This classification differentiates

---

## EXHIBIT 5.5

### Rate-Sensitivity Analysis for Security Bank, December 31, 2004

| | 1–7 Days | 8–30 Days | 31–90 Days | 91–180 Days | 181–365 Days | Over 1 Year | Non Rate-Sensitive | Total |
|---|---|---|---|---|---|---|---|---|
| **Assets** | | | | | | | | |
| U.S. Treasury and agency securities | | $ 0.7 | $ 3.6 | $ 1.2 | $ 0.3 | $ 3.7 | | $ 9.5 |
| Money market investments | | | 1.2 | 1.8 | | | | 3.0 |
| Municipal securities | | | 0.7 | 1.0 | 2.2 | 7.6 | | 11.5 |
| Federal funds sold and repurchase agreements | $ 5.0 | | | | | | | 5.0 |
| Commercial loans* | 1.0 | 13.8 | 2.9 | 4.7 | 4.6 | 15.5 | | 42.5 |
| Installment loans | 0.3 | 0.5 | 1.6 | 1.3 | 1.9 | 8.2 | | 13.8 |
| Earning assets | | | | | | | | $ 85.3 |
| Cash and due from banks | | | | | | | $ 9.0 | 9.0 |
| Other assets | | | | | | | 5.7 | 5.7 |
| Nonearning assets | | | | | | | | $ 14.7 |
| **Total assets** | $ 6.3 | $15.0 | $10.0 | $10.0 | $ 9.0 | $35.0 | $14.7 | $100.0 |
| **Liabilities and Equity** | | | | | | | | |
| Money market deposit accounts | | $ 5.0 | $12.3 | | | | | $ 17.3 |
| Time deposits < $100,000 | $ 0.9 | 2.0 | 5.1 | $ 6.9 | $ 1.8 | $ 2.9 | | 19.6 |
| CDs ≥ $100,000 | 4.1 | 4.0 | 12.9 | 7.9 | 1.2 | | | 30.1 |
| Federal funds purchased and repurchase agreements | | | | | | | | |
| NOW accounts | | | | 9.6 | | | | 9.6 |
| Savings accounts | | | | | | 1.9 | | 1.9 |
| Market-rate liabilities | | | | | | | | $ 78.5 |
| Demand deposits | | | | | | | $13.5 | 13.5 |
| Other liabilities | | | | | | | 1.0 | 1.0 |
| Equity | | | | | | | 7.0 | 7.0 |
| Nonpaying liabilities and equity | | | | | | | 21.5 | $ 21.5 |
| **Total liabilities and equity** | $ 5.0 | $11.0 | $30.3 | $24.4 | $3.0 | $ 4.8 | $21.5 | $100.0 |
| **Periodic GAP** | $ 1.3 | $ 4.0 | −$20.3 | −$14.4 | $6.0 | $30.2 | | |
| **Cumulative GAP** | $ 1.3 | $ 5.3 | −$15.0 | −$29.4 | −$23.4 | $ 6.8 | | |

NOTE: Figures are in millions of dollars.

*Floating-rate loans total $10 million and are classified as repriceable in 8 to 30 days. There is no guarantee that base rates will change in this time period.

between when an asset or liability can be repriced and when management believes it will be repriced. Prime-based loans can reprice daily if prime changes daily. The prime rate typically changes much less frequently. Banks can change MMDA rates daily, but unless they actually do, these deposits will only be as rate sensitive as their actual repricing schedule. A comparison of RSAs and RSLs that can change immediately would indicate differences in **contractual** repricing, but is likely not meaningful unless rates are highly volatile and these items are actually repriced as frequently as contracts allow.

Two types of GAP measures are reported at the bottom of the report. The **periodic GAP** compares RSAs with RSLs across each of the different time buckets and in a measure of the timing of changes in interest rates on net interest income. RSAs exceed RSLs in each interval through 30 days and for 181 days through one year, while RSLs exceed RSAs in the 31–90 day and 91–180 day intervals. The **cumulative GAP,** in contrast, measures the sum of the periodic GAPs through the longest time frame considered and measures aggregate interest rate risk exposure. Thus, the cumulative GAP at 31–90 days of −$15 million equals the sum of the periodic GAPs for 1–7 days ($1.3 million), 8–30 days ($4 million), and 31–90 days (−$20.3 million).

Each periodic GAP figure simply indicates whether more assets or liabilities can be repriced within a specific time interval. Because it ignores whether assets and liabilities in other periods can be repriced, it is not all that meaningful. Cumulative GAP figures are more important because they directly measure a bank's net interest sensitivity through the last day of the time bucket by comparing how many assets and liabilities reprice through that last day. Thus, the cumulative GAP of −$15 million indicates that Security Bank can reprice $15 million more of rate-sensitive liabilities than rate-sensitive assets during the next 90 days. The 1-year cumulative GAP indicates that $23.4 million more in liabilities than assets are expected to be repriced over this longer period. It is important to note that GAP figures for the interval over one year provide no new information about a bank's interest rate risk position. The periodic GAP of $30.2 simply reflects the fact that the bank has $35 million in earning assets that reprice beyond one year, while it pays interest on $4.8 million in similar long-term liabilities. The subsequent $6.8 million cumulative GAP simply measures the difference between $85.3 million in earning assets and $78.5 million in interest-bearing liabilities.

Note that the cumulative GAPs are positive for the first two periods with the remainder negative through one year. According to the previous discussion, Security Bank has positioned itself to gain if rates fall over the next year. Specifically, if rates decrease uniformly during the year, the bank's net interest income would increase unless offset by changes in portfolio mix or bank size because interest income should fall less than interest expense. If rates increase, net interest income should decline. Furthermore, the size of the GAP indicates that the bank's performance may vary substantially as the cumulative GAP through one year is almost 25 percent of total assets. Many community banks have policy statements that presumably limit interest rate risk by specifying that selected GAPs, as a fraction of earning assets, cannot fall outside of ±15 percent.

The rate-sensitivity report provides a view of a bank's interest rate risk profile at a single point in time. It reflects a point estimate of risk implied by the basic concept of a static GAP. Most banks employ earnings sensitivity analysis to address weaknesses in the static GAP concept. They also evaluate interest rate risk using duration-based measures of relative asset and liability price sensitivity.

## STRENGTHS AND WEAKNESSES: STATIC GAP ANALYSIS

The principal attraction of static GAP analysis is that it is easy to understand. Periodic GAPs indicate the relevant amount and timing of interest rate risk over distinct maturities and clearly suggest magnitudes of portfolio changes to alter risk. They indicate the specific balance sheet items that are responsible for the risk. GAP measures can also be easily calculated once the cash flow characteristics of each instrument are identified.

Unfortunately, the static GAP procedure also contains numerous weaknesses. First, there are serious *ex post* measurement errors. Consider, for example, loans whose rates are tied to base rates or indexes. The frequency of changes in base rates or indexes cannot be accurately forecast because management does not know when market interest rates will change. In 1980, the prime rate listed in the *Wall Street Journal,* a popular base rate for commercial loans, changed 52 times. In 1983, it changed only three times and, in 2000, it changed twice. Prime-based loans were considerably more rate sensitive in 1980, and in 2001 when it changed 11 times. Between mid-2004 and mid-2005, the prime rate increased 7 times from 4 percent to 5.75% at 25 basis point increments as the Federal Reserve increased the targeted federal funds rate 7 times. GAP figures do not directly reflect this historical frequency of base rate changes. When there is uncertainty over the frequency of base rate changes, GAP measures reflect any errors in allocating loans differently than actual rate changes would require. To overcome this problem, a bank should evaluate the statistical rate sensitivity of all base rates to selected market indexes. To avoid mismeasuring risk, funds should be allocated to time buckets according to their effective (expected) rate sensitivity, which is often linked to the historical frequency of rate changes. With GAP analysis, rate sensitivity for these loans is not known.

Second, GAP analysis ignores the time value of money. The construction of maturity buckets does not differentiate between cash flows that arise at the beginning of the period versus those at the end. If a bank buys a one-month T-bill financed by overnight borrowing in the federal funds market, the one-month GAP is zero. This suggests no interest rate risk when, in fact, this transaction exposes the bank to losses when the federal funds rate rises. Whether a bank gains with rising or falling interest rates depends on the actual timing of repricings within each interval. Thus, a bank with a zero GAP will still see net interest income change when rates change. Similarly, GAP ignores interest flows. One attraction of duration-based measures of interest rate risk is that they incorporate the present value of all cash flows.

Third, the procedure essentially ignores the cumulative impact of interest rate changes on a bank's risk position. GAP measures should be calculated over the entire range of repricings, yet they often focus only on near-term changes in net interest income. As such, many banks evaluate GAP measures and variation in net interest income only through the upcoming year. Interest rate changes also affect the value of fixed-rate assets and liabilities and total risk beyond one year. These changes are ignored.

Fourth, liabilities that pay no interest are often ignored in rate-sensitivity comparisons because many banks allocate demand deposits as non-rate-sensitive liabilities. As such, GAP analysis does not recognize any rate risk associated with demand deposit flows, even though a bank typically loses deposits when interest rates rise. This occurs because the opportunity cost of demand deposits increases for the owners and the benefits of better cash management rise. Many compensating balance agreements, in turn, allow the owners of demand deposits to reduce the dollar amount of compensating balances when rates rise because the bank can earn a higher yield from investing these funds. To be useful, GAP analysis must allocate the rate-sensitive portion of demand deposits to the appropriate time buckets depending on their actual rate sensitivity. When rates are expected to increase, more demand deposits will be rate sensitive. It is extremely difficult, however, to know the exact rate sensitivity of these deposits.

Finally, static GAP does not capture risk associated with options embedded in the loans, securities, and deposits that banks deal with. Examples include the prepayment option that mortgage borrowers have and often exercise when interest rates fall, and the early withdrawal option that depositors have and often exercise when interest rates rise. These options have different values and a different probability of being exercised when interest rates are at different levels and rate volatility changes. The impact of these options is to alter the effective size of GAP over different time intervals when interest rates are rising versus falling and when rates are at high levels versus low levels. Earnings-sensitivity analysis addresses these concerns.

**GAP RATIO.** Some asset and liability management (ALM) programs focus on the GAP ratio when evaluating interest rate risk. The GAP ratio equals RSAs divided by RSLs with the typical focus on a one-year cumulative GAP ratio.

$$\text{GAP Ratio} = \text{RSAs/RSLs}$$

When GAP is positive, the GAP ratio is greater than one. A negative GAP, in turn, is consistent with a GAP ratio less than one.

Neither the GAP nor GAP ratio provides direct information on the potential variability in earnings when rates change. The GAP ratio is further deficient because it ignores size. Consider two banks that have $500 million in total assets. The first bank has $3 million in RSAs and $2 million in RSLs so that its GAP equals $1 million and its GAP ratio equals 1.5. The second bank has $300 million in RSAs and $200 million in RSLs. Its GAP equals $100 million, yet it reports the same 1.5 GAP ratio. Clearly, the second bank assumes greater interest rate risk because its net interest income will change more when interest rates change.

## LINK BETWEEN GAP AND NET INTEREST MARGIN

A better risk measure relates the absolute value of a bank's GAP to earning assets. The greater is this ratio, the greater is the interest rate risk.[5] Many banks actually specify a target GAP to earning asset ratio in their ALCO policy statements. Consider a bank with the policy target that the one-year cumulative GAP as a fraction of earning assets should be greater than $-15$ percent and not more than $+15$ percent. This target allows management to position the bank to be either asset sensitive or liability sensitive, depending on the outlook for interest rates. Yet, the policy limits the size of the GAP and implicitly how much risk management can take.

The ratio of GAP to earning assets has the additional advantage in that it can be directly linked to variations in NIM. In particular, management can determine a target value for GAP in light of specific risk objectives stated in terms of a bank's target NIM.[6] Consider a bank with $50 million in earning assets that expects to generate a 5 percent NIM. As part of its management strategy, the bank has decided it will risk changes in NIM equal $\pm 20$ percent during the year. Thus, NIM should fall between 4 and 6 percent. This risk assessment, in conjunction with expected interest rates, imposes policy limits on an acceptable GAP. The general relationship is:

$$\frac{\text{Target GAP}}{\text{Earning assets}} = \frac{(\text{Allowable \% change in NIM})(\text{Expected NIM})}{\text{Expected \% change in interest rates}} \tag{5.2}$$

---

[5] Remember that risk in this context is associated with the volatility in net interest income. The use of absolute value demonstrates that the sign of GAP does not influence the volatility of net interest income, only whether net interest income rises or falls when rates change in a specific direction.

[6] Binder and Lindquist (1982) elaborate on this and provide a matrix that outlines potential GAP variances for different levels of NIM risk.

For example, suppose that management expects interest rates to vary up to 4 percent during the upcoming year. According to Equation 5.2, the bank's ratio of its one-year cumulative GAP (absolute value) to earning assets should not exceed 25 percent.

$$\text{Target GAP/Earning assets} = (.20)(.05)/.04 = .25$$

Equation 5.2 and management's willingness to allow only a 20 percent variation in NIM sets limits on the GAP which would be allowed to vary from −$12.5 million to $12.5 million, based on $50 million in earning assets.

Using the data from Exhibit 5.5, suppose that Security Bank's management establishes the same 20 percent variance in NIM as a risk objective but expects its NIM to equal 4.5 percent over the next year. If it expects interest rates to rise by 2 percent, it would target the GAP to earning asset ratio at no more than 45 percent. Exhibit 5.5 indicates that the bank's one-year cumulative GAP is −$23.4 million, or 27.5 percent of earning assets. Thus, management could increase its negative GAP to as much as −$38 million and remain within its target risk profile.

The important point is that a bank's effective GAP and net interest margin are closely linked. Ideally, banks should identify the amount of net interest income at risk if interest rates change. Rather than do this directly via earnings-sensitivity analysis, many banks limit the size of GAP as a fraction of assets, which indirectly limits the variation in net interest income.

## EARNINGS SENSITIVITY ANALYSIS

In recent years, many bank managers have used an earnings sensitivity framework to measure and monitor interest rate risk. This framework extends static GAP analysis by making it dynamic. It does this by model simulation or "what if" analysis of all the factors that affect net interest income across a wide range of potential interest rate environments. The analysis essentially repeats static GAP analysis assuming different interest rate environments and compares expected net interest income between the different environments. The steps include:

1. Forecast interest rates.

2. Forecast balance sheet size and composition given the assumed interest rate environment.

3. Forecast when embedded options in assets and liabilities will be in the money and, hence, exercised such that prepayments change, securities are called or put, deposits are withdrawn early, or rate caps and rate floors are exceeded under the assumed interest rate environment.

4. Identify which assets and liabilities will reprice over different time horizons, and by how much, under the assumed interest rate environment. Identify off-balance sheet items that have cash flow implications under the assumed rate environment.

5. Calculate (estimated) net interest income and net income under the assumed rate environment.

6. Select a new interest rate environment and compare the forecasts of net interest income and net income across different rate environments versus the base case.

The primary value of this framework is that it allows managers to assess how much net interest income might vary across a wide range of interest rates. The typical comparison looks at seven different interest rate environments beginning with a base case, or most likely, scenario. This may be based on current rates, forward rates implied by the yield curve, or management's specific forecast of rates. Each of the other scenarios then assumes that rates move systematically higher by +1 percent, +2 percent, and +3 percent or systematically lower by −1 percent, −2 percent, and −3 percent. An important part of these forecast environments is the recognition that different customer options may go "in the money" such that they are exercised at different times. In addition, management can specify different interest rate changes for different instruments such that the spread between asset yields and liability costs varies. For example, if a bank's prime rate is assumed to increase by 1 percent, retail time deposit rates might be assumed to increase by just 0.5 percent. The difference in rate changes will have the impact of increasing a bank's net interest income.

In each environment, management determines different amounts of assets, liabilities, and off-balance sheet positions that are effectively rate sensitive, and implicitly calculates a different effective GAP for each scenario. The output then is the change in net interest income or change in NIM from the base case. Policy or risk limits are commonly set relative to allowable changes in net interest income and NIM from the base case. A more extensive framework has managers forecast the change in noninterest income and noninterest expense across different rate environments with the final output being the change in net income versus the base case. Finally, the assumed rate changes may reflect instantaneous, or immediate shocks, or gradual rate changes over time.

### EXERCISE OF EMBEDDED OPTIONS IN ASSETS AND LIABILITIES

To fully understand the risk inherent in a bank's operations, it is necessary to understand the different types of options that bank customers have. The most obvious include a customer's option to refinance a loan. Although the option is not generally explicit in a loan contract, any borrower can repay a loan early. A more obvious option is the call option on a federal agency bond that a bank might own. For example, the Federal Home Loan Bank (FHLB) might issue a bond with a three-year maturity that is callable at face value after 30 days. This means that the FHLB, at its option, can pay the bank the principal any time after 30 days. Thus, the bank might expect to own the bond for three years, but end up owning it just 30 days or a fraction of the time until maturity. An option embedded in bank liabilities is a depositor's option to withdraw funds prior to final maturity. Such an early withdrawal might also surprise a bank by forcing it to pay the depositor back far in advance of final maturity.

Whenever options are embedded in bank assets and liabilities, managers should address three issues. The first is whether the bank is the buyer or seller of the option. This is the same as asking "Does the bank or its customer determine when the option is exercised?" The buyer is the party that controls when the option is exercised while the seller presumably receives some compensation for selling (or writing) the option. In each of the above examples, the bank is the seller of the option and the customer is the buyer. Borrowers decide when to refinance, the FHLB decides when to call (repay) the bond, and the depositor decides when to withdraw the deposit. The second issue is how, and by what amount, is the bank being compensated for selling the option, or how much must it pay if it buys the option. In the three previous cases, there may be explicit prepayment penalties on a loan and deposit (for early withdrawal) that represent fees (if they are not waived), and the bank receives a higher promised yield on a callable bond compared with the yield on an otherwise similar noncallable bond. Finally, the bank should forecast when the option will be exercised. In the above examples, this involves forecasting when a loan will be prepaid, when the agency bond will be called, and when the depositor will withdraw funds early. These forecasts, in turn, will depend on the assumed rate environment. Loan refinancing (prepayments) typically rise sharply when interest rates fall. Bonds are called when interest rates fall. Deposits are withdrawn early when deposit rates rise sufficiently.

Market participants cannot generally forecast interest rates accurately for long periods of time. The focus on embedded options is important, however, because it forces management to recognize the risks inherent in their portfolios. These risks exist even if rates do not change because there is always the possibility that rates might change. It also allows management to identify a worst-case scenario and have a better sense of maximum loss potential.

When doing earnings-sensitivity analysis, it is important to recognize that banks often enter into off-balance sheet contracts with futures, forward rate agreements, swaps and options that also affect aggregate interest flows. Chapter 7 introduces these derivatives including caps and floors on interest rates that are used to manage interest rate risk. Each type of contract may have different cash flow effects in different rate environments that potentially alter a bank's interest income and/or interest expense. The effects of these must also be included in any forecast of net interest income and net income volatility.

## DIFFERENT INTEREST RATES CHANGE BY DIFFERENT AMOUNTS AT DIFFERENT TIMES

Earnings sensitivity analysis allows management to incorporate the impact of different competitive markets for various balance sheet accounts with alternative pricing strategies. This enables managers to forecast different spreads between asset yields and liability interest costs when rates change by different amounts. It is widely recognized, for example, that banks are quick to increase base loan rates, such as their prime rate, when interest rates increase in general, but are slow to lower base loan rates when interest rates fall. The implication is that floating rate loans are more rate sensitive in rising rate environments versus falling rate environments. In like manner, banks typically increase loan rates more than they increase deposit rates in a rising rate environment such that the spread widens. During a falling rate environment, the opposite often occurs as deposit rates lag in being lowered relative to other money market rates and certain loan rates such that the spread narrows. The implication is that although the rate sensitivity of different instruments might be nominally the same, the impact is different due to different timing of rate changes and different magnitudes of rate changes.

This impact is even more apparent when examining callable bonds that banks own as part of their investment portfolios. Consider the three-year FHLB bond that is callable after 30 days, described earlier. If rates fall enough, the entire bond will likely be called because the FHLB can refinance at lower rates and save on interest expense. In a falling rate environment, this bond is very rate sensitive and might be classified as such in the 31- to 90-day time interval. In a rising rate environment, the bank might end up owning the bond for three years because it will not be called. As such, it is not rate sensitive because it will not be repriced for three years. It is clear that the bank's effective (actual) GAP will be different in a rising versus falling rate environment because the bond is only rate sensitive when rates fall.

The net effect is that when conducting the "what if" analysis, managers can examine the impact of these nonparallel shifts in interest rates and the differing degrees or effective rate sensitivity. Not surprisingly, the impact of interest rate changes is not as straightforward as that suggested by Equation 5.1 or simple GAP.

## EARNINGS SENSITIVITY ANALYSIS: AN EXAMPLE

Consider the Rate-Sensitivity Report for First Savings Bank (FSB) as of year-end 2004 presented in Exhibit 5.6. This report is based on the most likely interest rate scenario summarized in Charts A and B of Exhibit 5.7. FSB is a $1 billion bank that bases its analysis on forecasts of the federal funds rate (Chart A) and ties other rates to this

**EXHIBIT 5.6**

First Savings Bank Rate-Sensitivity Report for Most Likely (Base Case) Interest Rate Scenario: December 31, 2004

| | Total | 3 Months or Less | >3–6 Months | >6–12 Months | >1–3 Years | >3–5 Years | >5–10 Years | >10–20 Years | >20 Years |
|---|---|---|---|---|---|---|---|---|---|
| **Loans** | | | | | | | | | |
| Prime Based | 100,000 | 100,000 | | | | | | | |
| Equity Credit Lines | 25,000 | 25,000 | | | | | | | |
| Fixed Rate >1 Yr. | | 170,000 | 18,000 | 18,000 | 36,000 | 96,000 | 2,000 | | |
| Var. Rate Mtg 1 Yr. | 55,000 | 13,750 | 13,750 | 27,500 | | | | | |
| 30-Yr. Fix Mortgage | 250,000 | 5,127 | 5,129 | 9,329 | 32,792 | 28,916 | 116,789 | 51,918 | |
| Consumer | 100,000 | 6,000 | 6,000 | 12,000 | 48,000 | 28,000 | | | |
| Credit Card | 25,000 | 3,000 | 3,000 | 6,000 | 13,000 | | | | |
| **Investments** | | | | | | | | | |
| Eurodollars | 80,000 | 80,000 | | | | | | | |
| CMOs FixRate | 35,000 | 2,871 | 2,872 | 5,224 | 13,790 | 5,284 | 4,959 | | |
| U.S. Treasury | 75,000 | | 5,000 | 5,000 | 25,000 | 40,000 | | | |
| Fed Funds Sold | 25,000 | 25,000 | | | | | | | |
| Cash & Due From Banks | 15,000 | | | | | | | | 15,000 |
| Loan Loss Reserve | (15,000) | | | | | | | | (15,000) |
| Non-Earning Assets | 60,000 | | | | | | | | 60,000 |
| Total Assets | 1,000,000 | 278,748 | 53,751 | 101,053 | 228,582 | 104,200 | 121,748 | 51,918 | 60,000 |
| **Deposits** | | | | | | | | | |
| MMDAs | 240,000 | 240,000 | | | | | | | |
| Retail CDs | 400,000 | 60,000 | 60,000 | 90,000 | 160,000 | 30,000 | | | |
| Savings | 35,000 | | | | | | | | 35,000 |
| NOW | 40,000 | | | | | | | | 40,000 |
| DDA Personal | 55,000 | | | | | | | | 55,000 |
| Comm'l DDA | 60,000 | 24,000 | | | | | | | 36,000 |
| **Borrowings** | | | | | | | | | |
| Treasury Tax & Loan | 25,000 | 25,000 | | | | | | | |
| L-T Notes Fixed Rate | 50,000 | | | | | | 50,000 | | |
| Fed Funds Purchased | | | | | | | | | |
| Non-Int. Bearing Liabilities | 30,000 | | | | | | | | 30,000 |
| Capital | 65,000 | | | | | | | | 65,000 |
| Tot Liab & Equity | 1,000,000 | 349,000 | 60,000 | 90,000 | 160,000 | 30,000 | 50,000 | | 261,000 |
| Swap: Pay Fixed/ Receive Float | | 50,000 | | | (25,000) | (25,000) | | | |
| Periodic GAP | | (20,252) | (6,249) | 11,053 | 43,582 | 49,200 | 71,748 | 51,918 | (201,000) |
| Cumulative GAP | | (20,252) | (26,501) | (15,448) | 28,134 | 77,334 | 149,082 | 201,000 | 0 |

overnight rate. As such, the federal funds rate serves as the bank's benchmark interest rate. Chart A also presents implied forward rates from the market for federal funds futures contracts (market implied rates), which provide a consensus forecast of expected rates. FSB conducts earnings sensitivity analysis across seven different rate environments (rate shocks) with the specific forecasts for federal funds in three rising (+1 percent, +2 percent, +3 percent) and three falling (−1 percent, −2 percent, −3 percent) rate environments, as noted in Chart B. Rates are assumed to change gradually in each case. A 200 basis point (2 percent) rate change is calculated by cumulatively adding or subtracting approximately 17 basis points per month for one year from the most likely scenario and maintaining these levels during a second year of forecasts.

Importantly, FSB uses a base case interest rate forecast that is drawn from market-implied forecast rates. Examine Chart A in Exhibit 5.7. Note the dashed line that represents federal funds futures rates. Because the futures rate increase continuously the farther from the present, the market is expecting an increase in the federal funds rate. FSB uses the data appearing as the solid line as its base case interest rate environment. As such, it is a most likely scenario if rates track those expected in the marketplace. After 12 months the federal funds rate is expected to level off around 4 percent for most of the second year. Importantly, this framework is quite different from using constant (rates remain at current levels) rates as the base case.

Ignore for now the explanation of the data for interest rate swaps (third row of data from the bottom of Exhibit 5.6) except that the swaps effectively represent a rate-sensitive asset in the three months or less time bucket.[7]

---

[7]Note that the $50,000 reported for swaps in under three months effectively increases the periodic GAP without swaps of −$70,252 to a periodic GAP after swaps of −$20,252.

**EXHIBIT 5.7**

Base Case Interest Rate Scenario and Rate Ramps

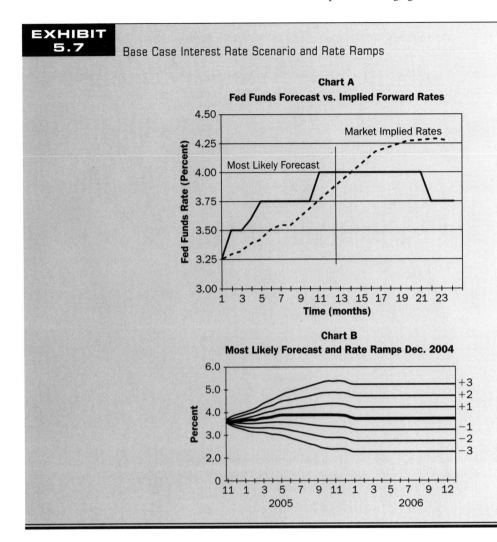

**Chart A**
**Fed Funds Forecast vs. Implied Forward Rates**

**Chart B**
**Most Likely Forecast and Rate Ramps Dec. 2004**

Exhibit 5.6 reports data for eight different time buckets from three months or less to more than 20 years. The majority of assets are in 30-year fixed-rate mortgages, fixed-rate loans with maturities over one year, prime-based loans, and consumer loans. In fact, the assets have a very long average contractual maturity as 25 percent are 30-year mortgages. The majority of deposits are retail CDs and MMDAs representing 64 percent of the total funding. According to this static GAP report, FSB's one-year cumulative GAP equals −$15,448,000, or −1.64 percent of the $940 million in earning assets. Under static GAP analysis, the bank has little rate risk, but is positioned to lose modestly if interest rates increase through one year. Of course, this ignores the significant embedded options in the bank's mortgage holdings as well as other factors.

Exhibit 5.8 presents the results of earnings sensitivity analysis. The top figure is for the year 2005—one year out, while the bottom figure is for the year 2006—two years out. The seven different interest rate environments are noted on the horizontal axis with the base case scenario in the middle.

The +100, +200, and +300 listings refer to the environments where the federal funds rate is assumed to be 1 percent, 2 percent, and 3 percent higher, respectively, than the base case (most likely) scenario. The three assumed lower-rate environments are identified to the left of the most likely case. The vertical axis lists the change in net interest income (NII) from the most likely scenario under each interest rate scenario. Note the zero value for the base case because it is the reference point for comparing forecasts from the other rate environments. Each forecast of net interest income incorporates assumed shifts in volume and composition of assets and liabilities, changes in spreads recognizing that asset yields and liability interest costs do not change coincidentally by the same amount, and different exercises of embedded customer options.

As indicated in Exhibit 5.8, net interest income will fall slightly if rates increase by 1 to 2 percent during the first year relative to the most likely scenario. However, if rates increase by 3 percent, NII will actually increase, contrary to that suggested by a negative GAP. If rates fall by 1 percent relative to the most likely case, net interest income increases

*Earnings-Sensitivity Analysis*

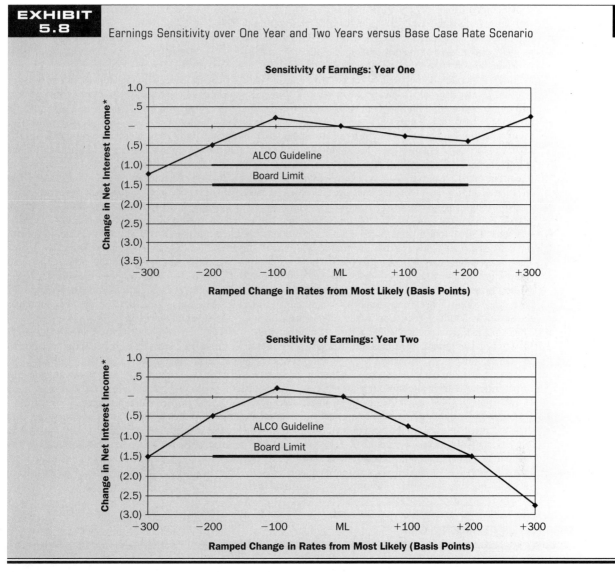

**EXHIBIT 5.8**  Earnings Sensitivity over One Year and Two Years versus Base Case Rate Scenario

*Millions of dollars.

slightly, but if rates fall 2 or 3 percent, NII also falls. This again contradicts the implications of the negative GAP from Exhibit 5.6. This is possible because the data in Exhibit 5.6 apply only to the most likely case. In each of the other rate scenarios, different amounts of assets and liabilities are rate sensitive based on the exercise of embedded options. Similarly, rates on each balance sheet item are assumed to change by different amounts when rates change.

**EXPLANATION OF SENSITIVITY RESULTS.** FSB's earnings sensitivity results reflect two typical impacts of rate changes. The first is that embedded options potentially alter cash flows when the options go in the money. The second is that rates change by different amounts at different times. When rates increase in the analysis, asset yields are assumed to increase more than liability costs and sooner such that spreads widen. The opposite occurs when rates fall. Such differences are common because banks have some pricing power over loans tied to base rates and with their core deposits. Consider the times when the Federal Reserve increases the target federal funds rate. Banks typically increase their quoted prime rates immediately by the same amount as the increase in the federal funds rate. In turn, they lag any increases in their deposit rates. Spreads thus initially widen.

Regarding embedded options, FSB owns many fixed-rate mortgages subject to prepayment risk. As rates decline, borrowers will refinance these mortgages so that they are effectively called away from FSB. Generally, fixed-rate loans are refinanced and callable bonds are called such that more assets become rate sensitive. When rates rise, these loans and securities are not nearly as rate sensitive to where mortgage prepayments and other loan refinancings drop sharply and there are fewer rate-sensitive assets. Deposits are more rate sensitive when rates rise with more early withdrawals (RSLs increase). This shift may at least partially offset the impact of spreads widening. These same deposits are less rate sensitive (RSLs decrease) when rates fall, but the spread between earning asset yields and the cost of interest-bearing liabilities falls.

Under this structure, there is a different effective GAP for each rate scenario. If rates fall sharply by 2 or 3 percent, net interest income will fall because the effective GAP is positive as many assets with embedded options must be repriced. If rates rise sharply, loan prepayment options are not exercised but early withdrawal options are. For FSB, an assumed reduction in rates of 1 percent is actually consistent with rates being virtually constant as the federal funds rate would change from 3.25 percent initially to 3 percent, or 1 percent below that forecast at the end of 12 months. Net interest income is thus forecast to remain fairly stable. Still, if rates fall by 2 or 3 percent, FSB sees NII decline as the long-term mortgages prepay and the funds are invested at lower rates. Net interest income falls in the +1 percent and +2 percent cases because more liabilities reprice than assets as loan refinancings drop sharply. Net interest income rises in the +3 percent case because the spread widens and offsets the impact of a small GAP. These factors explain why net interest income might fall when rates fall and not change significantly when rates rise.

The bottom part of Exhibit 5.8 reveals the comparative forecasts under each scenario in the year 2006, or two years from the date of the report. Over this time frame, the bank loses in both sharply rising and falling rate environments. FSB no longer gains with a +3 percent rate move because the interest cost of liabilities catches up with the increased asset yields as banks cannot lag rate increases forever. Thus, the spread is no longer as large. This again reflects the fact that FSB's effective GAP becomes more negative in an increasing rate environment and positive in a declining rate environment. The key point is that this analysis clearly reveals potential volatility in net interest income over sharply different rate environments. Also, FSB sets ALCO guidelines and risk policy limits according to allowable earnings sensitivity as noted in Exhibit 5.8. The bank has a board of directors' limit of a maximum $1.5 million reduction in net interest income for any 2 percent rate move up or down over two years. The bank violates its risk guidelines according to forecasts of year two in a +3 percent environment. Steps would have to be taken to reduce the bank's risk exposure to meet these limits. In general, the greater is the variation in forecast net interest income across rate environments, the greater is interest rate risk.

Some banks and bank analysts refer to the summary results of a bank's earnings sensitivity as **earnings-at-risk** or **net interest margin simulation.** Most banks measure interest rate risk using this framework because it is easy to understand and because it focuses on earnings, which drive bank performance in the near term. Review the introduction to the chapter, which presents sensitivity data for PNC. As indicated, PNC's simulation at year-end 2004 produced an expected 0.6 percent increase in net interest income if rates gradually increased by 1 percent in 2005. Net interest income would fall by 1.2 percent with a 1 percent gradual decrease in rates during 2005. The following year, net interest income would increase by 3.6 percent in a + 1 percent rate environment and decrease by 6.6 percent in a −1 percent rate environment. PNC loses the most in a falling rate environment (asset sensitive) two years out. The bank's rate risk appears to be small for 2005.

## INCOME STATEMENT GAP

Many managers of community banks interpret their bank's interest rate risk using a simplified framework compared with comprehensive earnings-sensitivity analysis. They feel comfortable with this because the complexity and size of assets and liabilities does not change dramatically over short periods of time. They similarly do not have significant risk exposure with off-balance sheet transactions that significantly affects the bank's net interest income. The models do, however, recognize the existence of embedded options and the different speeds and amounts of repricing specific assets and liabilities when rates change.

One common practice is to calculate an **income statement GAP,** or **Beta GAP,** that takes some of these factors into account. Consider the rate-sensitivity report presented in Exhibit 5.9 for a bank with just under $30 million in total assets. This particular report uses the prime rate as the benchmark rate and contains two forecasts of the change in net interest income: one for an environment where the bank's prime rate is assumed to fall by 100 basis points and another when prime is assumed to increase by 100 basis points over the next year. The first three columns of data relate to the case where the prime rate falls. The **balance sheet GAP** is a 1-year cumulative GAP that reflects contractual repricing and indicates that the bank is liability sensitive in the amount of −$7,466,000, or almost 25 percent of assets. The second column of data provides information about each asset's or liability's **earnings change ratio (ECR).** As the footnote suggests, this figure indicates how the yield on each asset, and rate paid on each liability, is assumed to change relative to a 1 percent drop in the prime rate. Thus, the effective yield on federal agency securities is assumed to fall by 71 basis points (0.71 percent), while the effective yield on federal funds sold will fall by 96 basis points (0.96 percent) if prime falls by 1 percent. Not surprisingly, deposit rates lag such that they generally fall by smaller amounts relative to the 1 percent drop in prime. Note that MMDA rates are assumed to fall by 60 basis points. The third column of data reports the amount of each balance sheet item that

## EXHIBIT 5.9

Income Statement GAP and Earnings Variability

| Amounts in Thousands | Prime Down 100bp | | | Prime Up 100bp | | |
|---|---|---|---|---|---|---|
| Report Data as of December 31, 2004 | Balance Sheet GAP[a] | ECR[b] | Income Statement GAP | Balance Sheet GAP* | ECR[b] | Income Statement GAP |
| Rate-Sensitive Assets | A | B | A × B | C | D | C × D |
| Loans | | | | | | |
| Fixed Rate | $ 5,661 | 100% | $5,661 | $5,661 | 100% | $5,661 |
| Floating Rate | 3,678 | 100% | 3,678 | 3,678 | 100% | 3,678 |
| Securities | | | | | | |
| Principal Cash Flows | | | | | | |
| Agencies | 200 | 71% | 142 | 200 | 71% | 142 |
| Agency Callables | 2,940 | 71% | 2,087 | 300 | 60% | 180 |
| CMO Fixed | 315 | 58% | 183 | 41 | 51% | 21 |
| Fed Funds Sold | 2,700 | 96% | 2,592 | 2,700 | 96% | 2,592 |
| Floating Rate | | | | | | |
| Total Rate-Sensitive Assets | $15,494 | | $14,343 | $12,580 | | $12,274 |
| Rate-Sensitive Liabilities | | | | | | |
| Savings | $ 1,925 | 75% | $1,444 | $ 1,925 | 5% | $   96 |
| Money Mkt. accounts | 11,001 | 60% | 6,600 | 11,001 | 40% | 4,400 |
| NOW | 2,196 | 80% | 1,757 | 2,196 | 20% | 439 |
| Fed Funds Purch./Repo. | 0 | 96% | 0 | 0 | 96% | 0 |
| CDs $ 100M | 3,468 | 85% | 2,948 | 3,468 | 85% | 2,948 |
| CDs , 100M | 4,370 | 84% | 3,671 | 4,370 | 84% | 3,671 |
| Total Rate-Sensitive Liabilities | $22,960 | | $16,420 | $22,960 | | $11,554 |
| Rate Sensitivity Gap (Assets-Liab) | ($7,466) | | ($2,077) | ($10,380) | | $719 |
| Total Assets | $29,909 | | $29,909 | $29,909 | | $29,909 |
| GAP as a Percent of Total Assets | −24.96% | | −6.94% | −34.71% | | 2.41% |
| Change in Net Interest Income | | | $20.8 | | | $7.2 |
| Change in Net Interest Margin | | | 0.07% | | | 0.02% |
| Net Interest Margin | | | 5.20% | | | 5.20% |
| Percentage Change in Net Interest Margin | | | 1.34% | | | 0.46% |

[a]One year balance sheet GAP includes all balances that may change in rate in the next 12 months.

[b]The Earnings Change Ratio (ECR) is an estimate of the change in rate of a rate-sensitive instrument per 100 basis point (100 bp) move in prime.

will effectively be repriced at a 1 percent lower rate and equals the ECR times the balance sheet amount. These figures represent how much of the balance sheet amount will be effectively repriced by 1 percent less if the prime rate falls by 1 percent. The objective is to obtain an income statement GAP figure that indicates the net amount of assets or liabilities that effectively reprices 1 percent lower.

The bank's income statement GAP is listed at −$2,077,000, as the difference between $14,343,000 in effective RSAs that will reprice 1 percent lower and $16,420,000 in effective RSLs that will reprice 1 percent lower. This is an effective GAP estimate. As such, we can apply Equation 5.1 to interpret the impact on net interest income. Here, a 1 percent reduction in the prime rate will lead to an estimated $20,770 increase in net interest income and a corresponding 7 basis point increase in net interest margin.

$$\Delta \text{Net interest income} = -\$2,077,000(-0.01) = +\$20,770$$

The three columns of data at the right of Exhibit 5.9 refer to the estimated impact of a 1 percent increase in the prime rate over the next year. Note that in a rising rate environment, a smaller amount of callable agency securities is assumed to be rate sensitive because fewer securities will likely be called. Also, the ECRs for some of the assets and core deposit liabilities are different, reflecting the fact that effective reinvestment rates on agency callables and CMOs will not rise as much with slower prepayments, and the bank will not increase its deposit rates in line with increases in prime or by the same amount as they would be lowered in a falling rate environment. The net impact is that the bank's effective income statement GAP is positive at $719,000. A 1 percent increase in prime will increase net interest income by an estimated $7,190. Importantly, different assumed changes in prime will produce different estimated changes in net interest income depending on the same factors that alter a bank's effective rate sensitivity of assets and liabilities.

## MANAGING THE GAP AND EARNINGS SENSITIVITY RISK

Effective GAP measures and the potential variation in net interest income indicate the general interest rate risk a bank faces. Equation 5.1 applies in the income statement GAP framework but not the general earnings-sensitivity framework. It generally suggests that if interest rates are expected to increase during the GAP period, a positive cumulative GAP will lead to an increase in net interest income. If rates are expected to fall, a negative GAP will lead to an increase in net interest income. The actual change in net interest income will meet expectations only if interest rates change in the direction and amount anticipated and if RSAs and RSLs are accurately forecast. Importantly, the size of the effective GAP, or the range of variation in net interest income, signifies how much risk a bank is taking. The larger is the absolute value of GAP, the greater is the change in net interest income for a given change in rates. The greater is the potential variation in net interest income from the base case, the greater is the risk.

The GAP model suggests that a bank that chooses not to speculate on future interest rates can reduce interest rate risk by obtaining a zero effective GAP or no variability in net interest income. The bank is fully hedged because its interest rate risk is negligible. Of course, this zero-risk position is rarely achieved and is rarely desired. Alternatively, a bank may choose to speculate on future interest rates and actively manage the GAP. Equation 5.1 suggests that a bank can systematically increase net interest income if it can accurately forecast rates and vary its effective GAP accordingly. If management expects rates to increase, it should become more asset sensitive. If it expects rates to decrease, it should become more liability sensitive.

Listed below are steps that banks can take to reduce risk in the context of effective GAP management.

1. Calculate periodic GAPs over short time intervals.
2. Match fund repriceable assets with similar repriceable liabilities so that periodic GAPs approach zero.
3. Match fund long-term assets with non-interest-bearing liabilities.
4. Use off-balance sheet transactions, such as interest rate swaps and financial futures, to hedge.

Management may alternatively choose to alter the rate sensitivity of assets and liabilities to take greater risk. Chapter 6 discusses the specific bets that management makes when it speculatively adjusts its effective GAP or earnings-sensitivity profile. Listed below are various ways to adjust the effective rate sensitivity of a bank's assets and liabilities on-balance sheet.

| Objective | Approach |
| --- | --- |
| Reduce asset sensitivity | Buy longer-term securities. Lengthen the maturities of loans. Move from floating-rate loans to term loans. |
| Increase asset sensitivity | Buy short-term securities. Shorten loan maturities. Make more loans on a floating-rate basis. |
| Reduce liability sensitivity | Pay premiums to attract longer-term deposit instruments. Issue long-term subordinated debt. |
| Increase liability sensitivity | Pay premiums to attract short-term deposit instruments. Borrow more via non-core purchased liabilities. |

The benefits and costs of these approaches are discussed at the end of Chapter 6.

## SUMMARY

A bank's asset and liability management committee is responsible for monitoring and managing a bank's interest rate risk profile. This chapter initially introduces the traditional static GAP model as a means of measuring interest rate risk. It then extends the discussion to focus on earnings sensitivity analysis, which essentially represents net income simulation under different assumed interest rate environments. It allows management to assess the sensitivity of net interest income to changes in balance sheet volume and composition, shifts in the relationship between asset yields and the costs of interest-bearing liabilities, and general shifts in the level of interest rates.

The earnings sensitivity framework is helpful in measuring the earnings impact when options embedded in bank loans, securities, and deposits are exercised. The analysis is critical in today's environment in which many banks have sold options on both sides of the balance sheet. Borrowers have the option to refinance loans and depositors have the option to withdraw funds prior to deposit maturity. As such, interest income and interest expense may vary sharply from that expected when interest rates change. Earnings sensitivity analysis provides a methodology for analyzing the range of potential outcomes from interest rate changes, shifts in balance sheet composition and the exercise of embedded options. The net result is an understanding of the relationship between how much net interest income might rise or fall over the next one to two years relative to potential interest rate changes and, thus, how much risk is assumed. It provides information regarding how management might position itself to gain if it wants to take on additional risk or how it might hedge if it wants to reduce overall risk.

## QUESTIONS

1. List the basic steps in static GAP analysis. What is the objective of each?

2. Are the following assets rate sensitive within a 6-month time frame? Explain.

   a. Three-month T-bill

   b. Federal funds sold (daily repricing)

   c. Two-year Treasury bond with semiannual coupon payments

   d. Four-year fully amortized car loan with $450 monthly payments including both principal and interest (for the first six months, principal payments total $578)

   e. Commercial loan priced at the bank's prime rate plus 2 percent

3. Consider the following bank balance sheet and associated average interest rates. The time frame for rate sensitivity is one year.

| Assets | Amount | Rate | Liabilities & Equity | Amount | Rate |
|---|---|---|---|---|---|
| Rate sensitive | $3,300 | 7.3% | Rate sensitive | $2,900 | 3.8% |
| Fixed-rate | 1,400 | 8.7% | Fixed-rate | 1,650 | 6.1% |
| Nonearning | 500 | | Nonpaying liabilities | 650 | |
| Total | $5,200 | | Total | $5,200 | |

   a. Calculate the bank's GAP, expected net interest income, and net interest margin if interest rates and portfolio composition remain constant during the year. This bank is positioned to profit if interest rates move in which direction?

   b. Calculate the change in expected net interest income and NIM if the entire yield curve shifts 2 percent higher during the year. Is this consistent with the bank's static GAP?

   c. Suppose that, instead of the parallel shift in the yield curve in part b, interest rates increase unevenly. Specifically, suppose that asset yields rise by 1 percent while liability rates rise by 1.75 percent. Calculate the change in net interest income and NIM. Is this uneven shift in rates more or less likely than a parallel shift?

   d. Suppose the bank converts $300 of rate-sensitive liabilities to fixed-rate liabilities during the year and interest rates remain constant. What would the bank's net interest income equal compared with the amount initially expected? Explain why there is a difference.

4. Suppose that your bank buys a T-bill yielding 4% that matures in six months and finances the purchase with a three-month time deposit paying 3%. The purchase price of the T-bill is $3 million financed with a $3 million deposit.

   a. Calculate the six-month GAP associated with this transaction. What does this GAP measure indicate about interest rate risk in this transaction?

   b. Calculate the three-month GAP associated with this transaction. Is this a better GAP measure of the bank's risk? Why or why not?

5. What is the fundamental weakness of the GAP ratio compared with GAP as a measure of interest rate risk?

6. Discuss the problems that loans tied to a bank's base rate present in measuring interest rate risk where the base rate is not tied directly to a specific market interest rate that changes on a systematic basis.

7. Consider the following asset and liability structures:

> ### County Bank
> ---
> Asset: $10 million in a one-year, fixed-rate commercial loan
> Liability: $10 million in a three-month CD
>
> ### City Bank
> ---
> Asset: $10 million in a three-year, fixed-rate commercial loan
> Liability: $10 million in a six-month CD

a. Calculate each bank's three-month, six-month, and one-year cumulative GAP.

b. Which bank has the greatest interest rate risk exposure as suggested by each GAP measure? Consider the risk position over the different intervals.

8. Consider the Rate-Sensitivity Report in Exhibit 5.6.

a. Is First Savings Bank (FSB) positioned to profit or lose if interest rates rise over the next 90 days?

b. Suppose that management has misstated the rate sensitivity of the bank's money market deposit accounts because the bank has not changed the rate it pays on these liabilities for six months and doesn't plan to change them in the near future. Will the bank profit if rates rise over the next 90 days?

9. Assume that you manage the interest rate risk position for your bank. Your bank currently has a positive cumulative GAP for all time intervals through one year. You expect that interest rates will fall sharply during the year and want to reduce your bank's risk position. The current yield curve is inverted with long-term rates below short-term rates.

a. To reduce risk, would you recommend issuing a three-month time deposit and investing the proceeds in one-year T-bills? Will you profit if rates fall during the year?

b. To reduce risk, would you recommend issuing a three-month time deposit and making a two-year commercial loan priced at prime plus 1 percent? Why?

10. Management at Bay Bank expects its net interest margin to equal 4.8 percent during the next year. It will allow variation in NIM of just 10 percent during the year and expects interest rates to either rise or fall by 2 percent. If management expects the bank to have $400 million in earning assets, determine how large its one-year cumulative GAP can be to not exceed the allowable variation in NIM.

11. Each of the following potentially alters the rate sensitivity of the underlying instrument. Presumably there is an embedded option associated with each. Indicate when the option is typically exercised and how it affects rate sensitivity.

a. Fixed-rate mortgage loan with a yield of 8 percent and 30-year final maturity.

b. Time deposit with five years remaining to maturity; carries a fixed rate of 5 percent.

c. Commercial loan with a two-year maturity and a floating rate set at prime plus 2.5 percent. There is a cap of 8 percent representing the maximum rate that the bank can charge on the loan.

12. What information is available from earnings sensitivity analysis that is not provided by static GAP analysis?

13. Exhibit 5.8 demonstrates that FSB loses in year two if rates either rise or fall sharply from the most likely scenario. Explain why in terms of when embedded options are expected to be exercised and what happens to spreads.

14. Interpret the following earnings-at-risk data. What does it suggest regarding the bank's risk exposure?

| | Earnings-at-Risk | |
| --- | --- | --- |
| Interest Rate Change (%) | 1 Year | 2 Years |
| +1% shock | +2.4% | +4.9% |
| −1% shock | −1.7% | −5.5% |
| −1% yield curve inversion | +1.1% | −2.6% |

*Problem*

15. Given the following information for E-Bank, calculate its income statement (effective) GAP. How much will net interest income change if the one-year Treasury rate falls 1 percent?

| *Rate-Sensitive Assets* | 1-Year Balance Sheet GAP | ECR |
|---|---|---|
| Loans | $55,120,000 | 82% |
| Securities | $28,615,000 | 67% |
| *Rate-Sensitive Liabilities* | | |
| MMDAs | $41,640,000 | 34% |
| NOWs | $37,260,000 | 90% |
| CDs $\geq$ 100,000 | $20,975,000 | 85% |

## PROBLEM

The data on the next page are taken from the 2004 annual report for Synovus, which reported $860.7 million in net interest income before provisions and just over $25 billion in assets at year-end. Review the information and determine the bank's risk exposure at the end of 2004. The information for interest rate swaps represents the effect of off-balance sheet transactions used to hedge interest rate risk.

1. Interpret the periodic and cumulative interest-sensitivity gap information. Was the bank positioned to profit or lose if interest rates fell in 2005? Explain.

2. Interpret the GAP impact of interest rate swaps. Was the bank's net interest rate risk exposure greater or lower as a result of swap activity through 1 year? Explain. Did the bank use swaps to hedge or speculate when viewed in this context?

3. Examine GAP as a fraction of earning assets. Did the bank assume much risk at each year-end? Explain.

**Table 18   Interest Rate Sensitivity**

*(Dollars in millions)*                                        **December 31, 2004**

| | 0–3 Months | 4–12 Months | 1–5 Years | Over 5 Years |
|---|---|---|---|---|
| Investment securities available for sale (*) ............ | $ 287.7 | 249.6 | 1,659.8 | 498.7 |
| Loans, net of unearned income .................... | 13,800.4 | 1,965.9 | 3,337.3 | 376.9 |
| Mortgage loans held for sale ..................... | 120.2 | — | — | — |
| Other ........................................ | 139.6 | — | — | — |
| Interest sensitive assets ...................... | 14,347.8 | 2,215.5 | 4,997.1 | 875.0 |
| Deposits...................................... | 7,826.8 | 2,698.3 | 4,640.7 | 578.8 |
| Other borrowings............................... | 1,870.0 | 329.6 | 390.8 | 497.3 |
| Interest sensitive liabilities..................... | 9,196.8 | 3,022.9 | 5,031.5 | 1,076.1 |
| Interest rate swaps .......................... | (977.5) | 300.0 | 330.0 | 347.5 |
| Interest sensitivity gap ...................... | $4,173.5 | (507.4) | 296.6 | 147.0 |
| Cumulative interest sensitivity gap.............. | $4,173.5 | 3,666.1 | 8,961.7 | 4,108.7 |
| Cumulative interest sensitivity gap as a percentage of total interest sensitive assets .............. | 18.6% | 16.3 | 17.7 | 18.3 |

**December 31, 2003**

| | 0–3 Months | 4–12 Months | 1–5 Years | Over 5 Years |
|---|---|---|---|---|
| Investment securities available for sale (*) ............ | $ 465.5 | 708.1 | 970.0 | 352.8 |
| Loans, net of unearned income ................... | 9,460.3 | 2,320.3 | 4,066.5 | 617.8 |
| Mortgage loans held for sale ..................... | 133.3 | — | — | — |
| Other ........................................ | 177.3 | — | — | — |
| Interest sensitive assets ...................... | 10,236.4 | 3,028.4 | 5,036.5 | 970.6 |
| Deposits...................................... | 4,509.8 | 3,144.3 | 4,850.1 | 597.9 |
| Other borrowings............................... | 1,686.1 | 31.9 | 667.2 | 504.0 |
| Interest sensitive liabilities..................... | 6,195.9 | 3,176.2 | 5,523.3 | 1,101.9 |
| Interest rate swaps .......................... | (337.5) | 45.0 | 570.0 | 272.5 |
| Interest sensitivity gap ...................... | $3,153.0 | (102.8) | 83.2 | 141.2 |
| Cumulative interest sensitivity gap.............. | $3,153.0 | 3,050.2 | 3,133.4 | 3,274.6 |
| Cumulative interest sensitivity gap as a percentage of total interest sensitive assets...... | 16.4% | 15.8 | 16.3 | 17.0 |

(*) Excludes net unrealized losses of $224 thousand and net unrealized gains of $32.8 million at December 31, 2004 and 2003, respectively.

# Managing Interest Rate Risk: Duration GAP and Economic Value of Equity

*A fundamental criticism of GAP and earnings-sensitivity analysis is that they emphasize a bank's risk profile over the short run and largely ignore cash flows beyond one or two years. Yet, a bank's assets and liabilities may be substantially mismatched beyond two years and thus exhibit considerable risk, which goes undetected. Duration gap and economic value of equity sensitivity analysis represent alternative methods of analyzing interest rate risk. They emphasize the price sensitivity of assets and liabilities to changes in interest rates and the corresponding impact on stockholders' equity. As the labels suggest, they incorporate estimates of the duration of assets and duration of liabilities, which reflect the value of promised cash flows through final maturity. As such, they provide a comprehensive measure of the interest rate risk embodied in the entire balance sheet of a bank. In most cases, the implications concerning when banks win and lose are comparable to those of GAP and earnings-sensitivity analysis, but the magnitude of the estimated effects may differ sharply.*

*At year-end 2004, PNC conducted a simulation analysis that produced the following summary of outcomes regarding the bank's interest rate risk:*

*Effect on value of on- and off-balance sheet positions as a percentage of economic value of equity from instantaneous change in interest rates of:*

| | |
|---|---|
| *200 basis point increase* | *−7.00%* |
| *200 basis point decrease* | *−0.20%* |

*The model used to generate these results differs from earnings sensitivity, but has similar implications. What do the figures mean? Does a rate increase help or hurt PNC? What about a rate decrease? How much does PNC have at risk? After reading the material in this chapter, you will be able to assess PNC's aggregate interest rate risk according to these figures and explain why it is useful to assess interest rate risk under both earnings-sensitivity and economic value of equity-sensitivity analysis.*

***T***his chapter examines the management of a bank's interest rate risk position in terms of duration gap and the sensitivity of the market value of stockholders' equity to changes in interest rates. In this framework, interest rate risk refers to the volatility in the market value of stockholders' equity attributable to changes in the level of interest rates and associated changes in balance sheet and off-balance sheet mix and volume. A bank that assumes substantial risk will see its value of equity rise or fall sharply when interest rates change unexpectedly.

Duration gap analysis represents an application of duration concepts to a bank's entire balance sheet. As such, the model builds on the discussion of Macaulay's duration applied to single securities that was introduced in Chapter 4. It parallels static GAP and earnings-sensitivity analysis in the sense that both duration gap and the potential variation in market value of stockholders' equity are viewed as measures of risk, with more sophisticated users focusing on the latter. Some banks set targets for allowable risk in terms of how much equity values are allowed to change for specific 2 or 3 percent rate shocks. The analysis is dynamic in the sense that it incorporates the impact of potential rate increases and decreases and it recognizes that customers' exercise of embedded options will affect a bank's true risk exposure depending on how interest rates change. As such, the analytical procedure is similar to that for earnings-sensitivity analysis. This analysis appears under such labels as market value of equity (MVE), economic value of equity (EVE) and net portfolio value (NPV) analysis.

## MEASURING INTEREST RATE RISK WITH DURATION GAP

Economic value of equity analysis differs from earnings-sensitivity analysis in its focus on stockholders' equity rather than net interest income and its emphasis on all cash flows, not just those arising one or two years after the analysis. It takes a longer-term perspective of risk. The analysis is based on the use of duration estimates of each class of assets and liabilities. Changes in the economic value of equity reflect differences in the durations of assets and liabilities and thus differences in the market value sensitivity of assets and liabilities.

As Chapter 4 demonstrates, duration is most easily understood as an elasticity measure. As such, it provides information regarding how much a security's price will change when market interest rates change. Recall that the longer is duration, the greater is price sensitivity. Thus, the price of a 5-year duration bond will change more than the price of a 1-year duration bond for a similar change in interest rates. **Duration gap analysis** compares the price sensitivity of a bank's total assets with the price sensitivity of its total liabilities to assess whether the economic value of assets or liabilities changes more when rates change. Any differential impact will indicate how the bank's economic value of equity will change. Before introducing the model, we provide a brief review of duration concepts.

### DURATION, MODIFIED DURATION, AND EFFECTIVE DURATION

Market participants often use three different duration measures—Macaulay's duration, modified duration, and effective duration—as if they were the same. In fact, while the interpretations are similar, they differ in terms of how they are calculated and how they should be used.[1]

**Macaulay's duration** (D) is computed as a weighted average of the time until cash flows are received. The weights equal the present value of each cash flow as a fraction of the security's current price, and time refers to the length of time in the future until payment or receipt. It is measured and quoted in units of time. Conceptually, duration measures the average life of an instrument. In the context of immunization, an investor knows that by matching duration with the preferred holding period, interest rate risk can be minimized because price risk is balanced with reinvestment risk. For example, a bond with four years until final maturity with a duration of 3.5 years indicates that an investor with a 3.5-year holding period could lock in a rate of return by buying a 3.5-year duration instrument. If interest rates increase, the decrease in market value of the bond will be just offset by higher reinvestment income from the periodic coupon interest payments, so that the promised return is realized after 3.5 years. If interest rates decrease, the price appreciation will offset the lost reinvestment income. Thus, value and total return are fixed.[2]

Following is Macaulay's duration (D) formula for a security with n cash flows discounted at the market interest rate i, with an initial price P*, and t equal to the time until the cash payment is made.

$$C = \sum_{t}^{n} \frac{[\text{cash flow}_t/(1 + i)^t] \times t}{P*} \tag{6.1}$$

We use this measure of price sensitivity in the approximate price elasticity relationship:

$$\frac{\Delta P}{P} \cong - \frac{D}{(1 + i)} \times \Delta i \tag{6.2}$$

with

$$\text{modified duration} = D/(1 + i) \tag{6.3}$$

**Modified duration** equals Macaulay's duration divided by $(1 + i)$. It has the useful feature of indicating how much the price of a security will change in percentage terms for a given change in interest rates. A 5-year zero coupon bond will have a Macaulay's duration of 10 semiannual periods or five years. Assume that its current

---

[1]There are many other definitions of duration, using different discount rates and cash flow assumptions, that are ignored here. For a useful discussion, see Bierwag (1987), Ho (1992), and Phoa (1997).

[2]This ignores the fact that duration will change as time passes and immunization would require a rebalancing of the security or portfolio's duration. To be useful, the user must specify *ex ante* (beforehand) what rebalancing is appropriate.

price is $7,441 and market rate of interest is 6 percent (3 percent semiannual compounding). The bond's modified duration equals 9.71 semiannual periods (10/1.03) or 4.85 years. If the market interest rate rises to 7 percent ($\Delta i = 0.01$), the bond's price will fall by 4.85 percent, or by $361 (0.01 × 4.85 × $7,441). Securities can be easily ranked by modified duration to determine which ones are most price volatile.

Both of these measures calculate duration assuming that all promised cash flows will be realized. While this is true for option-free securities, it does not hold for securities with options. When a loan is prepaid or a bond is called, the exercise of the underlying option changes the instrument's duration. For example, a 3-year bond may be callable in one year. If market rates fall and the bond is called, its duration changes compared to when rates are higher and the bond is not called. The concept of **effective duration** is used to estimate how price sensitive a security is when the security contains embedded options. It compares a security's estimated price in a falling rate environment with an estimated price in a rising rate environment relative to the initial price times the assumed rate differential. Formally, effective duration (Eff Dur) equals:

$$\text{Eff Dur} = \frac{P_{i-} - P_{i+}}{P_0(i+ - i-)} \qquad (6.4)$$

where

$P_{i-}$ = price if rates fall,
$P_{i+}$ = price if rates rise,
$P_0$ = initial (current) price,
$i+$ = initial market rate plus the increase in rate, and
$i-$ = initial market rate minus the decrease in rate.

Consider a 3-year, 9.4 percent coupon bond selling for $10,000 par to yield 9.4 percent to maturity. This bond is callable at par and will presumably be called if rates fall 50 basis points or more. The Macaulay's duration for the option-free version of this bond with semiannual coupons and compounding was calculated in Chapter 4 to be 5.36 semiannual periods, or 2.68 years at the market rate of 4.7 percent semiannually. The modified duration was 5.12 semiannual periods or 2.56 years. If this bond is immediately callable at par, its price will never increase much more than $10,000. When the call option is in the money—that is, when market rates fall by 0.5 percent (25 basis points semiannually) or more and the bond will likely be called—the bond's price will equal its call price of $10,000. If rates rise, the bond will not be called and its price will fall as it would without any embedded option. As noted in Chapter 4, a 30 basis point increase in rate to 5 percent semiannually will lower the price to $9,847.72. Thus, the callable bond's effective duration for a 30 basis point (0.3 percent) semiannual movement in rates either up or down is 2.54.

$$\text{Eff Dur} = \frac{\$10,000 - \$9,847.72}{\$10,000(0.05 - 0.044)} = 2.54$$

As expected, the chance that the bond will be called shortens duration from what it would be if all cash flows materialized as originally scheduled.

The use of effective duration allows the cash flows of the underlying instrument to change when interest rates change. An analyst must have rate forecasts and a model to explain the pricing of the security in different interest rate environments to calculate effective duration. It is just an approximation, but is useful because it recognizes that an embedded option may be exercised and thus dramatically alter the expected cash flows and value of a security. Effective duration also demonstrates how some securities can exhibit negative duration. Negative duration actually refers to an effective duration calculation that is negative. For this to happen, the price of a security in a declining rate environment must fall below the price in a rising rate environment, such that the numerator of Equation 6.4 is negative. This can occur when some types of mortgage-backed securities prepay so rapidly that the promised cash flow stream collapses.[3]

**DURATION GAP MODEL.** Duration gap (DGAP) models focus on managing net interest income or the market value of stockholders' equity, recognizing the timing of all cash flows for every security on a bank's balance sheet.[4] The following analysis emphasizes duration's use as an elasticity measure. Unlike static GAP analysis, which

---

[3]The standard example is a high coupon, interest-only (IO) mortgage-backed security that currently prepays at a high speed. The holder of this IO receives only the interest payments on the principal outstanding for a pool of mortgages. If rates fall, the pool prepays even faster so that expected interest payments fall—perhaps to zero. With fewer payments made, the price drops. If rates increase, the pool prepays slower so that expected interest payments increase and will appear over a longer period of time. Thus, the IO's price might increase. This security will have a negative effective duration.

[4]The following discussion focuses on the market (economic) value of stockholders' equity as a target variable and follows the discussion in Kaufman (1984). Toevs (1983) addresses the use of net interest income as a target measure of performance.

## CONTEMPORARY ISSUES

### RATE SENSITIVITY VERSUS PRICE SENSITIVITY

GAP and duration gap represent two ways of viewing interest rate risk. To best understand the differences, you should understand how rate sensitivity differs from price sensitivity. Rate sensitivity refers to the ability to reprice the principal on an asset or liability. Price sensitivity refers to how much the price of an asset or liability will change when interest rates change. If an instrument is very rate sensitive, it is typically not very price sensitive, and vice versa.

GAP and earnings-sensitivity analysis focus on how frequently the principal amount of an asset or liability will reprice. For example, if a bank's federal funds sold mature daily, this asset is extremely rate sensitive because the bank can reinvest the principal amount at the prevailing rate every 24 hours. The same federal funds sold loan is not price sensitive. Because the rate changes daily when the principal matures, the loan will be priced at par or face value daily. The changing interest will reflect the change in rates. In contrast, a 10-year zero coupon bond is not very rate sensitive because the owner cannot reinvest the principal for 10 years without selling the bond. This same bond is very price sensitive, however, because its value will rise or fall sharply in percentage terms as rates either fall or rise. Thus, rate sensitivity and price sensitivity are two alternate, but consistent, ways of interpreting a security's features.

---

focuses on rate sensitivity or the frequency of repricing, duration gap analysis focuses on price sensitivity. The Contemporary Issues box, "Rate Sensitivity versus Price Sensitivity,"clarifies the difference. Duration is an attractive measure because it is additive across securities in a portfolio. A bank's interest rate risk is indicated by comparing the weighted average duration of assets with the weighted average duration of liabilities. As with GAP analysis, the sign and magnitude of DGAP provide information about when a bank potentially wins and loses, and the magnitude of the interest rate bet. Management can adjust DGAP to hedge or accept interest rate risk by speculating on future interest rate changes.

Duration gap analysis compares the duration of bank assets with the duration of bank liabilities and examines how the economic value of stockholders' equity will change when interest rates change. As with GAP and earnings-sensitivity analysis, the analysis produces different outcomes in different interest rate environments. After introducing the framework of the analysis and defining duration gap, the following discussion extends this to incorporate embedded options and sensitivity analysis for potential variation in the economic value of stockholders' equity.

There are four steps in duration gap analysis:

1. Forecast interest rates.

2. Estimate the market value of bank assets, liabilities, and stockholders' equity. The economic (market) value of equity (EVE) equals the amount that makes the market value of assets equal to the market value of liabilities plus EVE.

3. Estimate the weighted average duration of assets and weighted average duration of liabilities. The effects of both on- and off-balance sheet items and embedded options are incorporated. These estimates are used to calculate duration gap.

4. Management forecasts changes in the economic value of stockholders' equity across different interest rate environments.

The weighted average duration of bank assets (DA) is calculated as:

$$DA = \sum_{i}^{n} w_i Da_i \qquad (6.5)$$

where

$A_i$ = market value of asset i (i equals 1, 2, . . . n),
$w_i$ = $A_i$ divided by the market value of all bank assets (MVA); (MVA = $A_1$ + $A_2$ + . . .+ $A_n$),
$Da_i$ = Macaulay's duration of asset i, and
$n$ = number of different bank assets.

The weighted duration of bank liabilities (DL) is calculated similarly as:

$$DL = \sum_{j}^{m} z_j Dl_j \qquad (6.6)$$

where

$L_j$ = market value of liability j (j equals 1, 2, ... m),
$z_j$ = $L_j$ divided by the market value of all bank liabilities (MVL); (MVL = $L_1$ + $L_2$ + ... + L),
$Dl_j$ = Macaulay's duration of liability j, and
m = number of different bank liabilities.

With the focus on the economic value of stockholders' equity (EVE) and the general level of interest rates (characterized by y):

$$\Delta EVE = \Delta MVA - \Delta MVL \qquad (6.7)$$

Using Equation 6.2 we know that $\Delta A_i = -Da_i[\Delta y/(1 + y)]A_i$; and $\Delta Lj = -Dl_j[\Delta y/(1 + y)]$, such that:

$$\Delta EVE = -[DA - (MVL/MVA) DL] [\Delta y/(1 + y)] MVA \qquad (6.8)$$

If we define a bank's duration gap (DGAP) as

$$(DGAP) = DA - (MVL/MVA)DL.$$

then

$$\Delta EVE = -DGAP[\Delta y/(1 + y)]MVA \qquad (6.9)$$

Note that both DA and DL take into account the present value of all promised or expected cash flows. There is no need for time buckets or classifying assets and liabilities. Thus, duration gap indicates the difference between the weighted average duration of assets and the leverage-adjusted weighted average duration of liabilities. Hence it is an approximate estimate of the sensitivity of EVE to changes in the level of interest rates. The leverage adjustment takes into account the existence of equity as a means of financing assets. The interest factor (y) is typically measured as some weighted average of earning asset yields across all interest-earning assets. According to Equation 6.9, the greater is DGAP, the greater is the potential variation in EVE for a given change in interest rates. As such, DGAP provides information about when a bank wins and loses and the amount of risk assumed. If DGAP is positive, an increase in rates will lower EVE, while a decrease in rates will increase EVE. If DGAP is negative, an increase in rates will increase EVE, while a decrease in rates will lower EVE. The closer DGAP is to zero, the smaller is the potential change in EVE for any change in rates.

## A DURATION APPLICATION FOR BANKS

Most bank managers are concerned with the bank's total risk exposure from all assets and liabilities. When it receives cash inflows from assets prior to making its obligated payments on liabilities, it bears the risk that it may have to reinvest the proceeds at reduced rates. When it makes debt payments before it receives cash inflows, it bears the risk that borrowing costs will increase. Any differential in the timing of asset and liability cash flows is reflected in average durations.

Duration gap analysis requires that a bank specify a performance target, such as the economic value of equity, and strategically manage the difference between the average duration of total assets and the average duration of total liabilities. Consider the balance sheet of the hypothetical bank in Exhibit 6.1. The bank just opened for business and all dollar amounts are market values. It owns $1,000 worth of three assets: cash, a 3-year final maturity commercial loan earning 12 percent, and a 6-year Treasury bond earning 8 percent. It pays interest on 1-year time deposits (TDs) at 5 percent and on 3-year CDs at 7 percent. The economic value of equity represents the residual (plug figure) between asset and liability values and equals $80, or 8 percent of assets. The analysis assumes that there will be no defaults, prepayments, or early withdrawals. All securities make equal annual interest payments with annual compounding. Macaulay's duration for each item is listed beside the current market rate. The duration of cash is zero because cash doesn't change in value when interest rates change. Duration measures for the commercial loan, the 3-year CD, and the weighted average total asset and liability durations are computed at the bottom of the exhibit. Initially, the average duration of assets equals 2.88 years and exceeds the 1.61 year average duration of liabilities by over one year. Expected net interest income, assuming no change in interest rates, is $48 per $1,000 of assets.[5]

---

[5]This analysis uses economic income instead of accounting income. Economic interest is calculated as the product of the market value of each asset or liability and its market interest rate. Economic income varies directly with accounting income in these examples, although the relationship is not linear. Note that the use of Macaulay's duration ignores the impact of embedded options.

**EXHIBIT
6.1** — EVE Analysis: Hypothetical Bank Balance Sheet

| Assets | Market Value | Rate | Duration | Liabilities and Equity | Market Value | Rate | Duration |
|---|---|---|---|---|---|---|---|
| Cash | $ 100 | | | 1-yr. Time deposit | $ 620 | 5% | 1.00 yr. |
| 3-yr. Commercial loan | 700 | 12% | 2.69 yrs. | 3-yr. Certificate of deposit | 300 | 7% | 2.81 |
| 6-yr. Treasury bond | 200 | 8 | 4.99 | Total liabilities | 920 | | 1.59 yrs. |
| | | | 2.88 yrs. | Equity (EVE) | $ 80 | | |
| Total | $1,000 | | | | $1,000 | | |

Weighted avg. duration of assets (DA) = ($700/$1,000)(2.69) + ($200/$1,000)(4.99) = 2.88 yrs.
Weighted avg. duration of liabilities (DL) = ($620/$920)(1.0) + ($300/$920)(2.81) = 1.59 yrs.
Expected economic net interest income = 0.12($700) + 0.08($200) − 0.05($620) − 0.07($300) = $48.00
DGAP = 2.88 − ($920/$1,000)(1.59) = 1.42 yrs.

**Sample Duration Calculations Using Equation 9.1**

$$\text{Commercial loan} = \frac{\dfrac{84}{(1.12)^1} + \dfrac{84(2)}{(1.12)^2} + \dfrac{784(3)}{(1.12)^3}}{\$700} = .107(1) + .096(2) + .797(3) = 2.69 \text{ years}$$

$$\text{Certificate of deposit} = \frac{\dfrac{21}{(1.07)^1} + \dfrac{21(2)}{(1.07)^2} + \dfrac{321(3)}{(1.07)^3}}{\$300} = .065(1) + .061(2) + .874(3) = 2.81 \text{ yrs.}$$

Interest rate risk is evidenced by the mismatch in average durations of assets and liabilities and the DGAP of 1.42 years. When interest rates change, the market values of assets and liabilities will change by different amounts, and future interest income will change relative to future interest expense. The fact that the average duration of assets exceeds the average duration of liabilities (adjusted for leverage) indicates that the market value of assets will change more than the market value of liabilities if all rates change by comparable amounts. For example, suppose that all interest rates increase by 1 percent immediately after the bank contracts for its assets and liabilities. An adjusted balance sheet at market values appears in Exhibit 6.2. It shows that with the increase in rates, the market value of assets declines by $26, the market value of liabilities decreases by $14, and the economic value of equity falls by $12 to $68.

This result reflects the positive duration gap. The new value of each instrument can be obtained using Equation 6.2. The value of assets falls more than the value of liabilities because the weighted duration of assets (2.86 years) exceeds the weighted duration of liabilities (1.58 years) by a substantial amount. The equity-to-asset ratio declines from 8 percent to 7.1 percent. Expected net interest income similarly decreases because the bank will pay higher rates on liabilities relative to the higher yields it receives on reinvested cash inflows over the combined lifetime of the securities. Clearly, this bank's operating position has worsened with the increase in rates.

A decrease in rates produces the opposite result. Because of the duration mismatch, the market value of assets will increase more than the market value of liabilities so that the economic value of equity will increase. Net interest income also rises, and the bank is better off. The general relationship between the sign of a bank's duration gap and the impact of changing rates on EVE is summarized below:

**DGAP Summary**

| DGAP | Change in Interest Rates | Change in Economic (Market) Value | | | | | |
|---|---|---|---|---|---|---|---|
| | | Assets | | Liabilities | | Equity | |
| Positive | Increase | Decrease | > | Decrease | → | Decrease | |
| Positive | Decrease | Increase | > | Increase | → | Increase | |
| Negative | Increase | Decrease | < | Decrease | → | Increase | |
| Negative | Decrease | Increase | < | Increase | → | Decrease | |
| Zero | Increase | Decrease | = | Decrease | → | None | |
| Zero | Decrease | Increase | = | Increase | → | None | |

Bank management can use duration measures to evaluate interest rate risk. It is, however, a static measure. The greater is the absolute value of DGAP, the greater is interest rate risk. A bank that is perfectly hedged will have a DGAP of zero and thus operate with its average asset duration slightly below its average liability duration.

DGAP measures can be used to approximate the expected change in economic value of equity for a given change in interest rates. In particular, Equation 6.9 can be used to estimate the change in economic value of equity.

| **EXHIBIT 6.2** | EVE Analysis: Hypothetical Bank Balance Sheet after an Immediate 1 Percent Increase in All Interest Rates |
|---|---|

| Assets | Market Value | Rate | Duration | Liabilities and Equity | Market Value | Rate | Duration |
|---|---|---|---|---|---|---|---|
| Cash | $100 | | | 1-yr. Time deposit | $614 | 6% | 1.00 yr. |
| 3-yr. Commercial loan | 683 | 13% | 2.68 yrs. | 3-yr. Certificate of deposit | 292 | 8 | 2.80 |
| 6-yr. Treasury bond | 191 | 9 | 4.97 | Total liabilities | $906 | | 1.58 yrs. |
| Total | $974 | | 2.86 yrs. | Equity (EVE) | $68 | | |
| | | | | | $974 | | |

Duration of assets = .702(2.68) + .196(4.97) = 2.86 yrs.
Duration of liabilities = .68(1) + .32(2.80) = 1.58 yrs.
Expected economic net interest income = $45.81
DGAP = 2.86 − ($906/$974)(1.58) = 1.36
Change in market value of:   assets = −$26
                                        liabilities = −$14
                                        equity = −$12

*Sample Duration Calculations of Market Value Using Equation 9.2*
Commercial loan: $\Delta P$ = (.01/1.12)(−2.69)($700) = −$16.8
Certificate of deposit: $\Delta P$ = (.01/1.07)(−2.81)($300) = −$7.9

Applying this to the hypothetical bank in Exhibit 6.1, the 1 percent increase in interest rates lowered the economic value of equity by approximately 1.27 percent of assets, or $12.70.[6]

$$\Delta EVE = -DGAP[\Delta y/(1 + y)]MVA$$
$$\Delta EVE = -1.42[.01/1.10]\$1,000$$
$$= -.0127[\$1,000]$$
$$= -\$12.70$$

The actual decrease was $12. This bank's assets will change in value by approximately 90 percent more than the value of its liabilities for any interest rate change, as measured by the leverage-adjusted relative average durations, and EVE will vary accordingly.

## AN IMMUNIZED PORTFOLIO

To insulate, or immunize, the economic value of equity from rate changes, the hypothetical bank would need to either shorten its asset duration by 1.42 years, increase its liability duration by 1.54 years (.92 × 1.54 = 1.42), or use some combination of these adjustments. For example, immunization as measured by obtaining a DGAP equal to zero, could be accomplished by reducing time deposits to $340 and issuing $280 in new 6-year zero coupon CDs (see Exhibit 6.3). With this profile, DGAP approximately equals zero and any immediate rate change leaves EVE unchanged. This is demonstrated in the bottom part of the exhibit, where all interest rates are assumed to increase by 1 percent. The market value of every price-sensitive account declines. Equity value remains constant at $80 because the $26 decrease in market value of assets just equals the $26 decrease in market value of liabilities. There are, of course, many other alternatives to adjust the size of DGAP to zero, but each would produce the desired hedge.

Banks may choose to target variables other than the market value of equity in managing interest rate risk. Many banks, for example, are interested in stabilizing the book value of net interest income. This can be done for a 1-year time horizon, with the appropriate duration gap measure shown below:[7]

$$DGAP^* = MVRSA(1 - DRSA) - MVRSL(1 - DRSL) \tag{6.10}$$

---

[6]As an approximation, it is acceptable to use the average yield on total assets as the market interest rate, y. In the case of the hypothetical bank of Exhibit 6.1, y equals 10 percent [(700/1,000) .12 + (200/1,000) .08 = 0.10].

[7]Toevs (1983) introduces this formula and discusses its implications in detail. Alternatives include targeting the market value of net interest income by setting the duration of a bank's equity equal to the length of the time horizon that the bank wishes to use in hedging net interest income. Duration of equity (DUR EQ) can be approximated as follows, where MV refers to market value:

$$DUR\ EQ = \frac{MV\ of\ assets \times duration\ of\ assets - MV\ of\ liabilities \times duration\ of\ liabilities}{Economic\ value\ of\ equity}$$

## EXHIBIT 6.3 Immunized Portfolio

**Bank Balance Sheet: DGAP = 0**

| Assets | Market Value | Rate | Duration | Liabilities and Equity | Market Value | Rate | Duration |
|---|---|---|---|---|---|---|---|
| Cash | $ 100 | | | 1-yr. Time deposit | $ 340 | 5% | 1.00 yr. |
| 3-yr. Commercial loan | 700 | 12% | 2.69 yrs. | 3-yr. certificate of deposit | 300 | 7 | 2.81 |
| 6-yr. Treasury bond | 200 | 8 | 4.99 | 6-yr. zero-coupon CD* | 280 | 8 | 6.00 |
| | | | 2.88 yrs. | Total liabilities | $ 920 | | 3.11 yrs. |
| | | | | Equity | $ 80 | | |
| Total | $1,000 | | | | $1,000 | | |

DGAP = 2.88 − .92(3.11) ≅ 0

**1% Increase in All Rates**

| | Market Value | Rate | Duration | | Market Value | Rate | Duration |
|---|---|---|---|---|---|---|---|
| Cash | $ 100 | | | 1-yr. Time deposits | $ 337 | 6% | 1.00 yr. |
| 3-yr. Commercial loan | 683 | 13% | 2.68 yrs. | 3-yr. certificate of deposit | 292 | 8 | 2.80 |
| 6-yr. Treasury bond | 191 | 9 | 4.97 | 6-yr. certificate of deposit | 265 | 9 | 6.00 |
| | | | 2.86 yrs. | Total liabilities | $ 894 | | 3.07 yrs. |
| | | | | Equity | $ 80 | | |
| Total | $ 974 | | | | $ 974 | | |

*Par (maturity) value = $444.33

where

> MVRSA = cumulative market value of rate-sensitive assets (RSAs),
> MVRSL = cumulative market value of rate-sensitive liabilities (RSLs),
> DRSA = composite duration of RSAs for the given time horizon; equal to the sum of the products of each asset's duration with the relative share of its total asset market value, and
> DRSL = composite duration of RSLs for the given time horizon; equal to the sum of the products of each liability's duration with the relative share of its total liability market value.

If DGAP* is positive, the bank's net interest income will decrease when interest rates decrease, and increase when rates increase. If DGAP* is negative, the relationship is reversed. Only when DGAP* equals zero is interest rate risk eliminated. The important point is that banks can use duration analysis to stabilize a number of different variables reflecting bank performance.

## ECONOMIC VALUE OF EQUITY—SENSITIVITY ANALYSIS

Many bank managers use an EVE-sensitivity analysis framework like that for earnings sensitivity to better assess interest rate risk. The framework extends the static duration gap analysis by making it dynamic. This can be accomplished by model simulation. As with earnings-sensitivity analysis, the procedure consists of conducting "what if" analysis of all the factors that affect EVE across a wide range of interest rate environments. The analysis repeats static DGAP analysis under different assumed interest rates. It is often labeled net portfolio value (NPV) or market value of equity (MVE) analysis.

The basic output of this analysis is a comparison of changes in EVE across different interest rate environments. It signals how volatile EVE might be compared with some base case or most likely rate scenario. Again, the typical comparison looks at seven rate environments beginning with the base case, and other scenarios that alternatively consider rates 1 percent, 2 percent, and 3 percent higher and lower, respectively. An important component of this sensitivity analysis is the projection of when embedded customer options will be exercised and what their values will be. Management also varies assumptions about rate spreads and shifts or twists in the yield curve. The same embedded options that affect earnings sensitivity, such as loan prepayments, callable and putable bonds, and early deposit withdrawals, sharply influence the estimated volatility in EVE. The greater is the potential volatility in EVE, the greater is risk.

Generally,

1. Prepayments that exceed (fall short of) that expected will shorten (lengthen) duration.

2. A bond being called will shorten duration.

3. A deposit that is withdrawn early will shorten duration. A deposit that is not withdrawn as expected will lengthen duration.

Unanticipated changes in interest rates typically cause durations to vary over time. The effective duration calculation supposedly accounts for some of this variation, and should be used in EVE analysis. Alternatively, an analyst may use an estimated price consistent with call price, expected prepayment impact, and so on, for each asset or liability with an embedded option.

## EVE-SENSITIVITY ANALYSIS: AN EXAMPLE

Consider First Savings Bank (FSB) with the rate sensitivity report introduced in Exhibit 5.6 of Chapter 5. This bank had a portfolio of relatively long-term, fixed-rate mortgages and other loans financed largely by liabilities that were more rate sensitive. Charts A and B of Exhibit 5.7 summarize the most likely rate environment and six alternative rate environments. Exhibit 6.4 provides a summary of the same balance sheet data in

**EXHIBIT 6.4**

First Savings Bank's Economic Value of Stockholders' Equity

**Market Value/Duration Report as of 12/31/2004**
**Most Likely Rate Scenario—Base Strategy**

| | Book Value | Market Value | Book Yield | Duration* | |
|---|---|---|---|---|---|
| **Loans** | | | | | |
| Prime Based Ln. | $ 100,000 | $ 102,000 | 9.00% | — | |
| Equity Credit Lines | 25,000 | 25,500 | 8.75% | — | |
| Fixed Rate > 1 yr. | 170,000 | 170,850 | 7.50% | 1.1 | |
| Var. Rate Mtg. 1 Yr. | 55,000 | 54,725 | 6.90% | 0.5 | |
| 30-Year Mortgage | 250,000 | 245,000 | 7.60% | 6.0 | |
| Consumer Ln. | 100,000 | 100,500 | 8.00% | 1.9 | |
| Credit Card | 25,000 | 25,000 | 14.00% | 1.0 | |
| Total Loans | 725,000 | 723,575 | 8.03% | 2.6 | |
| Loan Loss Reserve | (15,000) | (11,250) | 0.00% | 8.0 | |
| Net Loans | 710,000 | 712,325 | 8.03% | 2.5 | |
| **Investments** | | | | | |
| Eurodollars | 80,000 | 80,000 | 5.50% | 0.1 | |
| CMO Fix Rate | 35,000 | 34,825 | 6.25% | 2.0 | |
| U.S. Treasury | 75,000 | 74,813 | 5.80% | 1.8 | |
| Total Investments | 190,000 | 189,638 | 5.76% | 1.1 | |
| Fed Funds Sold | 25,000 | 25,000 | 5.25% | — | |
| Cash & Due From | 15,000 | 15,000 | 0.00% | 6.5 | |
| Non-Int. Rel. Assets | 60,000 | 60,000 | 0.00% | 8.0 | |
| Total Assets | 1,000,000 | 1,001,963 | 6.93% | 2.6 | |
| **Deposits** | | | | | |
| MMDA | 240,000 | 232,800 | 2.25% | — | |
| Retail CDs | 400,000 | 400,000 | 5.40% | 1.1 | |
| Savings | 35,000 | 33,600 | 4.00% | 1.9 | |
| NOW | 40,000 | 38,800 | 2.00% | 1.9 | |
| DDA Personal | 55,000 | 52,250 | | 8.0 | |
| Comm'l DDA | 60,000 | 58,200 | | 4.8 | |
| Total Deposits | 830,000 | 815,650 | | 1.6 | |
| TT&L | 25,000 | 25,000 | 5.00% | — | |
| L-T Notes Fixed | 50,000 | 50,250 | 8.00% | 5.9 | |
| Fed Funds Purch | — | — | 5.25% | — | |
| NIR Liabilities | 30,000 | 28,500 | | 8.0 | |
| Total Liabilities | 935,000 | 919,400 | | 2.0 | |
| Equity | 65,000 | 82,563 | | 9.9 | |
| Total Liab. & Equity | 1,000,000 | 1,001,963 | | 2.6 | |
| Off-Balance Sheet | | | | | Notional |
| Int Rate Swaps | — | 1,250 | 6.00% | 2.8 | $ 50,000 |
| Adjusted Equity | 65,000 | 83,813 | | 7.9 | |

NOTE: Values are in thousands of dollars.

*Duration is reported in years.

**EXHIBIT 6.5** Sensitivity of Economic Value of Equity (EVE) versus Most Likely (Zero Shock) Interest Rate Scenario

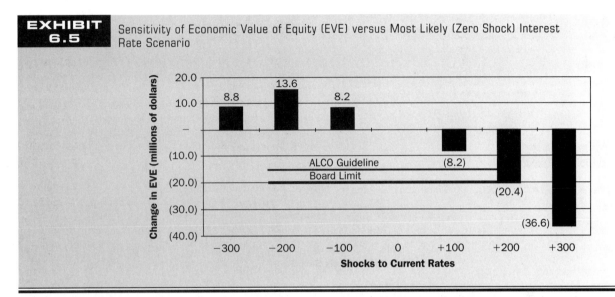

NOTE: *Sensitivity of Economic Value of Equity* measures the change in the economic value of the corporation's equity under various changes in interest rates. Rate changes are instantaneous changes from current rates. The change in economic value of equity is derived from the difference between changes in the market value of assets and changes in the market value of liabilities.

both book value and market value terms. The final two columns of data list the book yield and estimated duration under the most likely rate scenario. Under the most likely scenario, the market value of assets exceeds the book value by $1,963,000 and the economic value of equity equals $82,563,000 or $17,563,000 more than book value. Note that the average duration of assets equals 2.6 years while the average duration of liabilities equals 2 years. For this discussion, ignore how the duration estimates for demand deposit accounts (DDAs) are obtained.[8]

Using these duration estimates and the market values listed, FSB's duration gap is 0.765 years [2.6 − (919,400/1,001,963) 2.0]. In light of the previous DGAP discussion and assuming no change in duration when rates change, a 1 percent increase in rates would be expected to reduce FSB's economic value of equity by approximately $7.2 million (0.765)(0.01/1.0693) (1,001,963,000).

This estimate ignores the impact of interest rates on embedded options and the effective duration of assets and liabilities. It also ignores the impact of swaps that are noted at the bottom of the exhibit.[9] EVE sensitivity analysis incorporates these influences. Exhibit 6.5 presents a summary of the changes in EVE for six interest rate environments compared with the most likely (zero shock) rate scenario. Three of the scenarios are for higher rates (+100, +200, and +300 basis points) and three are for lower rates (−100, −200, and −300 basis points). The vertical axis lists the estimated change in EVE from the most likely case for each scenario. In contrast with earnings-sensitivity analysis, which projected earnings one year forward and two years forward, there is only one comparative exhibit because duration analysis incorporates the present value of all cash flows.

Note that higher rates are associated with a decline in EVE while lower rates are associated with an increase in EVE. This is consistent with FSB having a positive duration gap in all rate environments. It is also expected given FSB's huge portfolio of long-term, fixed-rate mortgages. If rates rise unexpectedly, market values will drop substantially. If rates fall sharply, prepayments will temper the potential gains in market value because borrowers will refinance such that the bank will replace high-rate loans with lower-rate ones. Thus, the benefit of selling the prepayment option to borrowers effectively places a cap on potential portfolio gains. According to Exhibit 6.5, FSB's EVE will change by $8.2 million either up or down if rates are 1 percent lower or higher than the base case. By definition, duration measures the percentage change in market value for a given change in interest rates, hence a bank's *duration of equity* measures the *percent* change in EVE that will occur with a 1 percent change in rates. Thus, FSB's duration of equity is 9.9 ($8,200/$82,563).

---

[8]Remember that demand deposits do not pay interest. A crucial part of duration analysis involves determining the effective duration of these liabilities, which typically make up a substantial portion of most banks' liabilities.

[9]The nature and influence of interest rate swaps are described in Chapter 7.

## CONTEMPORARY ISSUES

### INTEREST RATE RISK AT FREDDIE MAC AND FANNIE MAE

The Federal Home Loan Mortgage Corporation (Freddie Mac) and the Federal National Mortgage Association (FNMA, or Fannie Mae) have long been the dominant government sponsored enterprises (GSEs). These entities were formed to assist the housing market and for years generated large profits and grew at very high rates. During the early 2000s, several economists and members of the U.S. Congress argued that their growth was excessive and not supported by

adequate capital. While both Fannie and Freddie claimed to hedge interest rate risk, they provided little evidence to support the claims.

Both Fannie and Freddie report duration gap information to analysts. Fannie Mae reported the data in the following chart in April 2004. At that time, the duration gap was equal to a positive three months. Over the previous year, it had ranged from −5 months to +6 months—all of which suggested that there was little interest rate risk in its operations given its asset size of almost $900 billion.

Unfortunately, both Freddie and Fannie may have been consistently minimizing reported interest rate risk. In 2003, Freddie's management admitted that the bank had understated profits by more than $1 billion. In 2004, Fannie's auditors claimed that Fannie's management had used unacceptable hedge accounting to smooth earnings over the prior years. In one instance, management had presumably deferred expenses so that senior management could be paid incentive bonuses in a year when the bonus payments totaled more than $70 million for the top 21 managers.

**Spring Swing**
Fannie Mae's duration gap, in months

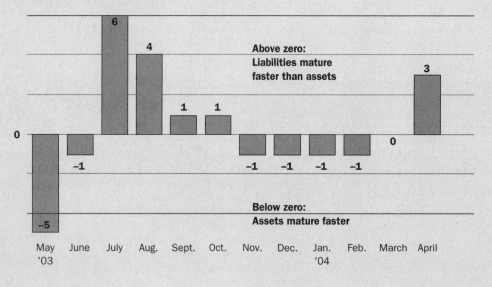

EVE-sensitivity analysis clearly provides a different type of information to FSB's management. In contrast to the earnings-sensitivity results, the bank is exposed to substantive losses in market value of equity if rates increase sharply above that expected. This is further evidenced by the fact that FSB will see its EVE decline more than the asset and liability management committee (ALCO) guideline if rates increase 2 percent or more from the base case. The EVE decline will exceed the limit set by the bank's board of directors in a +3 percent rate environment. FSB's management must address these violations of policy.

## EARNINGS-SENSITIVITY ANALYSIS VERSUS EVE-SENSITIVITY ANALYSIS: WHICH MODEL IS BETTER?

Bankers use both static GAP and duration gap models, as well as earnings-sensitivity and EVE-sensitivity analysis when assessing interest rate risk. Each has slightly different objectives and implications. GAP and earnings-sensitivity analysis focus on the potential volatility of net interest income over distinct time intervals. Net interest income is calculated in book value terms, not market values. A bank manages the effects of volatile interest rates within each time period separately. In contrast, the duration and EVE-sensitivity approach focuses on the potential variability of a bank's economic value of equity. Duration gap is a single measure that summarizes the cumulative impact of interest rate changes on a bank's total portfolio. Thus, the bank continuously manages total firm rate risk according to this one number. Because the models have different objectives, they address different issues.

### STRENGTHS AND WEAKNESSES: DGAP AND EVE-SENSITIVITY ANALYSIS

The principal attraction of duration analysis is that it provides a comprehensive measure of interest rate risk for the total portfolio. The smaller the absolute value of DGAP, the less sensitive the market value of equity is to interest rate changes. Unlike GAP, DGAP recognizes the time value of each cash flow, avoiding the difficulty with time buckets. Cash flows that arise after one year are included in duration calculations, but often ignored in GAP calculations. Duration measures are also additive so the bank can match total assets with total liabilities rather than match individual accounts. Finally, duration analysis takes a longer-term viewpoint and provides managers with greater flexibility in adjusting rate sensitivity because they can use a wide range of instruments to balance value sensitivity.

Duration and EVE sensitivity analysis have weaknesses as well. First, it is difficult to compute duration accurately. Duration measurement requires numerous subjective assumptions. Data needs are complex, requiring information on each account's interest rate, repricing schedule, possibility of principal prepayment, call and put options, early withdrawal potential, and default probability. A bank must routinely assess the probability that contracted cash flows will be received on a timely basis, forecast the timing of base rate changes and the level of rates at the time of future cash flows, and constantly monitor whether actual cash flows conform to expectations. To be meaningful, DGAP and sensitivity analysis further require accurate forecasts of when embedded options will be exercised and what their value is. Of course, this is the same information necessary to conduct earnings-sensitivity analysis.

Second, to be correct duration analysis requires that each future cash flow be discounted by a distinct discount rate reflecting the expected future rate at the time the cash flow arises. Most analysts use forward rates from the Treasury spot yield curve for this purpose. To eliminate coupon bias, they first estimate a zero coupon–equivalent yield curve, then compute forward rates. It is well known, however, that these forward rates do not accurately predict future interest rates. The complexity of calculating duration then, increases further when nonparallel shifts in the yield curve are considered.

Third, a bank must continuously monitor and adjust the duration of its portfolio. As Macaulay's duration measure indicates, duration changes with changes in interest rates. Thus, a bank should recalculate duration and EVE sensitivity and potentially restructure its balance sheet whenever rates change substantially, which could be daily or weekly. As discussed in Chapter 4, the duration calculation is only accurate for small changes in interest rates. Furthermore, even when rates are constant, duration changes with the passage of time as the time factor decreases over time. The duration of assets and liabilities may "drift" at different rates and require constant rebalancing. These problems are compounded by difficulties in estimating price effects and effective durations when there are embedded options.

Finally, it is difficult to estimate the duration on assets and liabilities that do not earn or pay interest. To get an accurate assessment of cash flows and market value changes, a bank must estimate the true rate sensitivity of demand deposits and estimate their duration. There is little agreement as to how this should be done. As noted in Exhibit 6.4, the management of FSB estimated the duration of personal DDAs at 8 years and the duration of commercial DDAs at 4.8 years. The difference presumably reflects the greater propensity of businesses to move DDAs in rising rate environments. Still, what are the estimated cash flows when DDAs have no stated fixed maturity or periodic cash payments? Many models attempt to estimate a core amount of DDAs that remain on deposit and classify these funds as having a long duration. Other, noncore DDAs are more volatile and have a shorter duration. The key point is that these are imprecise estimates. Given the size of most banks' DDA balances, any misestimate, in turn, can produce wide swings in a bank's DGAP value and wide variations in EVE sensitivity.

In summary, duration measures are highly subjective. Active management requires constant tinkering with the bank portfolio to adjust the duration gap. For many firms with simple balance sheets without significant amounts of customer options that are commonly exercised, the costs may exceed the benefits.

## A CRITIQUE OF STRATEGIES TO MANAGE EARNINGS AND ECONOMIC VALUE OF EQUITY SENSITIVITY

The business of banking involves taking risks. Most bankers feel comfortable making loans to individuals and businesses because they spend a considerable amount of time nurturing customer relationships and measuring and monitoring credit risk. In general, bankers are less comfortable taking interest rate risk. This may reflect a lack of familiarity with the relationship between risk and return or a belief that the returns have not historically warranted the risks taken. Because most banks depend on net interest margin to generate earnings growth, it is imperative that managers develop strategies to maintain or grow their net interest income over time and to maintain and grow the market value of stockholders' equity. The following discussion emphasizes the type of risks assumed in managing GAP, DGAP, and the sensitivity of net interest income and EVE to changes in interest rates. The important implication can be summarized as "know your bets."

### GAP AND DGAP MANAGEMENT STRATEGIES: WHAT ARE YOUR BETS?

Chapter 5 introduced a variety of objectives and strategic approaches to manage a bank's GAP and earnings sensitivity. The discussion was incomplete because it did not address how to implement the approaches to changing asset and liability sensitivity and did not identify their risk and return trade-offs. Generally, it is widely accepted that banks do and should assume some interest rate risk. The issue is to determine how much risk is acceptable and how to best achieve the desired risk profile.

Unfortunately, it is difficult to actively vary GAP or DGAP and consistently win. First, interest rate forecasts are frequently wrong. To change an asset or liability's rate or price sensitivity accurately and increase earnings and EVE, management must predict future interest rates better than consensus market forecasts embedded in current rates and act accordingly. Second, even when rate changes are predicted correctly, banks have limited flexibility in varying GAP and DGAP and must often sacrifice yield to do so. Loan customers and depositors select terms from a range of alternatives provided by the bank such that banks have only partial control over pricing and maturities. To entice a customer to select the bank's preferred alternative, management must often offer favorable yields or prices as an inducement. This has a cost because profits are below what they otherwise would be without the inducement.

These difficulties can be demonstrated by an example. Suppose a bank is liability sensitive and operates with a negative GAP through one year and a positive DGAP. Management believes that interest rates will rise and decides to hedge by taking steps that move the GAP closer to zero through one year. At this time, the yield curve is upsloping because the consensus forecast is that interest rates will increase over time. Active GAP management strategies typically focus on increasing RSAs and lowering RSLs. If a stable EVE were desired, DGAP strategies would emphasize shortening average asset durations and lengthening average liability durations.

Consider the effect of the following strategies: the bank (1) shortens the maturities of its bond portfolio, and (2) reprices its CDs to attract long-term deposits relative to short-term deposits. With an upsloping yield curve, long-term interest rates exceed short-term interest rates. The bank will accept a lower yield initially when it buys short-term securities, and can only attract long-term deposits by paying a premium rate over short-term deposit rates. The first strategy lowers interest income near-term while the second increases interest expense. Both tend to reduce a bank's initial net interest margin, which is a cost of hedging. More importantly, management should know the explicit bets that it has made regarding future interest rates by implementing these strategies. Specifically, the bank gains in terms of an increase in net interest income and EVE only when interest rates move and remain above current forward rates. The investment in short-term rather than long-term securities is advantageous only if interest rates rise above forward rates; that is, only if rates increase above the "break-even" yield contained in the yield curve. Long-term deposits are better than short-term deposits only in the same instance when market rates ultimately rise above forward rates. The bank loses if rates remain below forward rates because it would earn less interest income on the short-term securities versus long-term securities and could have borrowed at lower cost by issuing a series of short-term deposits rather than a long-term deposit. By adjusting GAP or DGAP, management is speculating that its interest rate forecast is better than the consensus.

## AN EXAMPLE

Consider the case where a liability-sensitive bank loses when rates rise and management decides to reduce risk by marketing two-year time deposits paying 6 percent to retail customers rather than one-year time deposits paying 5.5 percent. As described in Chapter 4, these two spot rates embody a one-year forward rate, one year from the present. The following time line and analysis indicate that this forward rate equals 6.5 percent ignoring compounding and assuming annual interest payments. This represents the deposit holder's break-even rate when comparing the two alternatives.

**Cash flows from investing \$1,000 either in a two-year security yielding 6 percent or two consecutive one-year securities, with the current one-year yield equal to 5.5 percent.**

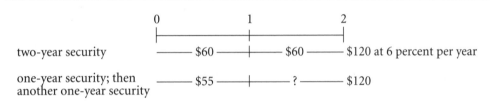

Of course, it is not known today what a one-year security will yield in one year. For the two consecutive one-year securities to generate the same \$120 in interest, ignoring compounding, the 1-year security must yield 6.5 percent one year from the present. This break-even rate is a one-year forward rate, one year from the present

$$6\% + 6\% = 5.5\% + ?$$

where the forward rate (?) equals 6.5 percent

The depositor is effectively speculating on future interest rates unless he or she has another position that this transaction offsets. Ignoring that, a depositor who acquires a 1-year time deposit today rather than the two-year deposit is positioned to benefit relatively if a one-year rate exceeds 6.5 percent one year from today. The depositor will lose (give up potential income) if the one-year rate is anything less than 6.5 percent. In contrast, a depositor who buys the two-year time deposit will benefit (lose) if the one-year rate, one year from the present, is anything below (above) 6.5 percent. By choosing one or the other, the depositor has "placed a bet" that the actual rate in one year will differ from the forward rate of 6.5 percent.

Importantly, a bank that markets the two-year deposit has placed a similar bet. Specifically, the bank will benefit (as a borrower) by lowering its borrowing cost only if the one-year rate exceeds 6.5 percent in one year. If this occurs, the bank will have locked in a customer with a below-market rate (6 percent versus an average of more than 6 percent). Of course, the depositor will lose, which may create a different set of problems. The implication is that even though management tries to reduce risk by reducing the bank's liability sensitivity, it could see its interest expense rise and NIM fall because of the bet against the forward rate.

The second cost follows in similar fashion. Suppose, for example, that a retail bank desires to increase RSAs because it expects interest rates to increase. While the bank plans to make only variable-rate or floating-rate loans, its customers seek fixed-rate loans because they also expect rates to rise. The bank must offer a substantial inducement, such as a significantly lower interest rate, to increase asset sensitivity and position itself for earnings growth in a rising rate environment. This would lower the interest spread and offset part of the benefit from increasing the GAP. If the bank refused to make fixed-rate loans, it would not be competitive and might lose considerable goodwill. When adjusting asset and liability maturities and durations and making pricing decisions, a bank may have to make yield concessions or assume additional interest rate risk. Active strategies to adjust earnings or EVE in light of rate forecasts may be highly speculative.

## YIELD CURVE STRATEGIES

Many portfolio managers are aware of general macroeconomic and business cycle impacts on the U.S. Treasury yield curve and try to take advantage of long-term trends in rates. Exhibit 6.6 characterizes movements in the level of rates over time and shifts in the shape of the yield curve. Typically, analysts view business cycle effects in terms

**EXHIBIT 6.6**

Interest Rates over the Business Cycle with Constant Inflation Expectations

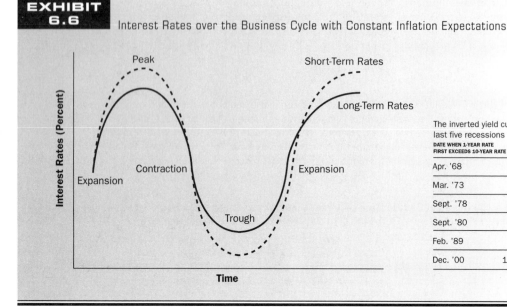

The inverted yield curve has predicted the last five recessions

| DATE WHEN 1-YEAR RATE FIRST EXCEEDS 10-YEAR RATE | LENGTH OF TIME UNTIL START OF NEXT RECESSION |
| --- | --- |
| Apr. '68 | 20 months (Dec. '69) |
| Mar. '73 | 8 months (Nov. '73) |
| Sept. '78 | 16 months (Jan. '80) |
| Sept. '80 | 10 months (July '81) |
| Feb. '89 | 17 months (July '90) |
| Dec. '00 | 15 months (March '01) |

**Expansion:** Increasing consumer spending, inventory accumulation, rising loan demand, Federal Reserve begins to slow money growth.

**Peak:** Monetary restraint, high loan demand, little liquidity.

**Contraction:** Falling consumer spending, inventory contraction, falling loan demand, Federal Reserve accelerates money growth.

**Trough:** Monetary ease, limited loan demand, excess liquidity.

SOURCE: Federal Reserve.

of how the ten-year (long-term) Treasury yield varies relative to the one-year (short-term) Treasury yield.[10] Starting at the left of the diagram, the yield curve is inverted (one-year rate above the ten-year rate) during the latter stages of an expansionary period and during the peak. Both of these are characterized by strong consumer spending, strong and growing loan demand, and limited liquidity at banks because the Federal Reserve has slowed money growth out of fear that inflation expectations will get out of control. The peak is followed by a contractionary period as consumer and business spending decline along with loan demand. At some point, the Federal Reserve gets concerned that growth has slowed too much and starts to increase money growth. At the trough or recession, the Fed is providing ample liquidity to banks, but loan demand is low due to high unemployment and slow spending. Eventually, low interest rates stimulate retail spending and business investment and the economy starts to grow again.

Many analysts believe that this pattern repeats itself over time. If so, it has interesting implications for interest rate risk management. For example, when the U.S. economy hits its peak the yield curve inverts. After the yield curve inversion, the economy falls into recession. Note the data at the bottom-right corner of the exhibit. This documents the last five times that the one-year Treasury rate has exceeded the ten-year Treasury rate and the length of time until the U.S. economy was in recession. In every instance a recession followed the yield curve inversion. Since World War II, only twice has the yield curve inverted and a recession not followed. This occurred in 1965 during the Vietnam War and in 1999 when the U.S. Treasury instituted a program to buy back outstanding long-term Treasury bonds. The average lag since 1968 is just over 14 months. The implication is that when the yield curve inverts, a recession will follow in a fairly short period of time.

Portfolio managers who want to take advantage of this trend will do the following when the yield curve inverts:

1. Buy long-term noncallable securities.

2. Make fixed-rate noncallable loans.

3. Price deposits on a floating-rate basis.

4. Follow strategies to become more liability sensitive and/or lengthen the duration of assets versus the duration of liabilities.

---

[10]In February 2001 the Treasury stopped issuing one-year T-bills, so the comparison will involve a different short-term rate, perhaps the six-month T-bill rate.

Note that during the deepest part of the recession, the yield curve is typically at its steepest. Portfolio managers often attempt to do the opposite of that above to best position the bank. Of course, this analysis is very simplistic. Interest rates do not follow the straightforward pattern of Exhibit 6.6. Interest rates alternatively rise and fall even within general rate moves upward and downward. Managers, in turn, have internal pressures to meet loan demand at the peak, after which asset quality will deteriorate, and find higher yields at the trough, which can largely be attained by taking added credit risk or interest rate risk (buying long-term, fixed-rate assets). Still, managers should be aware of these general trends and the impact on forward rates.

## S U M M A R Y

A bank's ALCO is responsible for monitoring the bank's risk and return profile. Traditional asset and liability management focuses on measuring interest rate risk and monitoring performance, setting policies to stabilize or increase net interest income. This chapter introduces an alternative duration gap model and market value of equity–sensitivity analysis to analyze interest rate risk. Duration gap analysis considers a bank's entire balance sheet and calculates measures of the weighted average durations of all assets and all liabilities. The difference in these weighted durations adjusted for financial leverage is labeled duration gap, which provides a measure of how the market value of stockholders' equity will change when interest rates change. With duration gap analysis the target measure of performance is typically the market value of bank equity. Risk is measured by the sign and size of duration gap and the potential variation in market value of equity. A bank's ALCO again conducts sensitivity analysis across different assumed interest rate environments to assess this potential variation in market value of stockholders' equity. Greater risk is evidenced by greater potential variation.

Duration measures have their limitations, including the fact that the effective price sensitivity and duration of individual assets and liabilities change with changes in interest rates. It is also difficult to accurately forecast rate changes and the price impact on customer options embedded in bank assets and liabilities. Still, duration-based-sensitivity analysis represents a useful alternative to GAP and earnings-sensitivity analysis because it focuses on the present value of all cash flows over the entire range of maturities.

The chapter also examines the specific assumptions managers make when they try to actively manage a bank's interest rate risk exposure. By pursuing strategies to change asset or liability rate sensitivities or durations in line with rate forecasts, managers are explicitly speculating that forward rates implied by current interest rates will not be realized in the future. Whether the bank gains or loses is determined by whether actual rates vary favorably relative to forward rates.

## QUESTIONS

1. List the basic steps in duration gap analysis. What is the importance of different interest rate forecasts?

2. Which has a longer Macaulay's duration: a zero coupon bond with a two-year maturity, or a two-year maturity coupon bond that pays 6 percent coupon interest if they both carry a 6 percent market yield? Explain your reasoning.

3. You own a corporate bond that carries a 5.8 percent coupon rate and pays $10,000 at maturity in exactly two years. The current market yield on the bond is 6.1 percent. Coupon interest is paid semiannually and the market price is $9,944.32.

   a. Calculate the bond's Macaulay's duration and modified duration.

   b. If the market rate falls by 1 percent, what is the estimated impact on the bond's price?

4. Assume that you own a $1 million par value corporate bond that pays 7 percent in coupon interest (3.5 percent semiannually), has four years remaining to maturity, and is immediately callable at par. Its current market yield is 7 percent and it is priced at par. If rates on comparable securities fall by more than 40 basis points (0.2 percent semiannually), the bond will be called.

   a. Calculate the bond's price if the market rate increases by 50 basis points (0.25 percent semiannually) using the present value formula from Chapter 4.

   b. Calculate the bond's effective duration assuming a 50 basis point increase or decrease in market rates.

5. A five-year zero coupon bond and 15-year zero coupon bond both carry a price of $7,500 and a market rate of 8 percent. Assuming that the market rates on both bonds fall to 7 percent, calculate the percentage change in each bond's price using equation 6.2.

6. Use duration gap analysis to determine if there is interest rate risk in the following transaction: A bank obtains $25,000 in funds from a customer who makes a deposit with a five-year maturity that pays 5 percent annual interest compounded daily. All interest and principal are paid at the end of five years. Simultaneously, the bank makes a $25,000 loan to an individual to buy a car. The loan is at a fixed rate of 12 percent annual interest but is fully amortized with 60 monthly payments, such that the borrower pays the same dollar amount (principal plus interest) each month.

7. Compare the strengths and weaknesses of GAP and earnings-sensitivity analysis with DGAP and EVE-sensitivity analysis.

8. Is the following statement generally true or false? Provide your reasoning.

"A bank with a negative GAP through three years will have a positive duration gap."

9. Conduct duration gap analysis using the following information:

| Assets | Amount | Rate | Macaulay's Duration |
|---|---|---|---|
| Cash | $ 23,000 | 0% | 0 |
| Bonds | $102,000 | 7.2% | 1.8 years |
| Commercial loans | $375,000 | 11.0% | 1.5 years |

| Liabilities & Equity | | | |
|---|---|---|---|
| Small time deposits | $130,000 | 3.6% | 4.0 years |
| Large CDs | $ 70,000 | 6.3% | 1.0 year |
| Transactions accounts | $250,000 | 2.8% | 3.3 years |
| Equity | $ 50,000 | | |

a. Calculate the bank's duration gap if the ALCO targets the market value of stock holders' equity. Is this bank positioned to gain or lose if interest rates rise?

b. Estimate the change in market value of equity if all market interest rates fall by an average of 1.5 percent. Compare the results by applying Equation 6.2 to each balance sheet item and adding versus using Equation 6.9.

c. Provide a specific transaction that the bank could implement to immunize its interest rate risk. The transaction may be a new asset funded by a new liability or an asset sale and the simultaneous purchase of another asset.

10. Suppose that your bank currently operates with a duration gap of 2.2 years. Which of the following will serve to reduce the bank's interest rate risk?

a. Issue a one-year zero coupon CD to a customer and use the proceeds to buy a three-year zero coupon Treasury bond.

b. Sell $5 million in one-year bullet (single payment) loans and buy three-month Treasury bills.

c. Obtain two-year funding from the Federal Home Loan Bank and lend the proceeds overnight in the federal funds market.

11. ALCO members are considering the following EVE-sensitivity estimates. The figures refer to the percentage change in market value of equity compared with the base rate forecast scenario. What does the information say about the bank's overall interest rate risk?

| | Rate Change from Base Case | | | | | |
|---|---|---|---|---|---|---|
| | −3 | −2% | −1% | +1% | +2% | +3% |
| % change in EVE | +38% | +47% | +19% | −5% | −14% | −18% |

*Problem*

12. Discuss what impact each of the following will have, in general, on MVE sensitivity to a change in interest rates. Consider two cases where rates rise sharply and fall sharply.

   a. Bank owns a high percentage of assets in bonds that are callable anytime after three months.

   b. Bank pays below market rates on time deposits and market interest rates move sharply higher.

   c. A large percentage of the bank's assets are in 30-year fixed-rate mortgages.

## PROBLEM

Review the most recent annual reports of the largest banks throughout the world. Collect information on their summary analysis of interest rate risk. Interpret whatever data are provided for earnings-at-risk and market value of equity at risk. Note that in some instances EVE sensitivity is labeled as value-at-risk for the bank's equity.

# Using Derivatives to Manage Interest Rate Risk

*For the past 20 years, financial institutions have made increasing use of derivatives in portfolio management. Market participants use these contracts to hedge other positions that expose them to risk or speculate on anticipated price moves. In many cases, banks can replicate on-balance sheet transactions entirely with off-balance sheet contracts so they can serve as substitute positions.*

*The term **derivative** in financial markets refers to any instrument or contract that derives its value from another underlying asset, instrument, or contract. The fastest-growing derivatives are interest rate swaps, caps, floors, and financial futures, particularly those that are LIBOR based. On several recent occasions derivatives have been in the spotlight because of their assumed role when global stock markets fell sharply and when Enron and other firms reported substantive losses from derivatives' positions. In these instances, regulators, politicians, and the media expressed concern over their use and growth. When used prudently, however, derivatives represent a cost-effective means to manage risk.*

*This chapter explains the features of financial futures, forward rate agreements (FRAs) and basic interest rate swaps and how they are used by financial institutions. It describes several applications that show each tool's strengths and weaknesses. The applications focus on Eurodollar futures, London Interbank Offer Rate (LIBOR) based FRAs, swaps, and interest rate caps and floors because they are the fastest-growing contracts used by financial institutions. The concepts, however, apply to all related contracts.*

*Imagine a situation where your bank only makes floating-rate loans. One of your best business customers approaches you and wants to borrow, but only on a fixed-rate basis. Do you try to change the customer's mind, somehow convincing the firm to borrow at the prevailing prime rate plus a spread? Or can you make a fixed-rate loan and effectively convert it to a floating-rate loan? If you do the latter, everyone wins: the customer gets fixed-rate financing and the bank gets a floating-rate loan. Derivatives may help you achieve this result.*

———————————— ■ ————————————

**B**anking professionals constantly search for new products and opportunities to improve bank operating performance. Financial futures, FRAs, interest rate swaps, and interest rate caps and floors are four types of derivatives that commercial banks actively use to help manage interest rate risk. Institutions use these contracts primarily to hedge asset yields or the interest cost of liabilities, adjust maturities by creating synthetic liabilities, protect the value of assets from changing rates, and adjust the overall sensitivity of earnings or market value of stockholders' equity.

This chapter extends the discussion of interest rate risk in Chapters 5 and 6 by describing four general tools that banks use to manage interest rate risk. The first, financial futures contracts, have been available since 1975 but have only recently gained acceptability for their own use among banks. The second, forward rate agreements, were introduced in 1983 to provide an explicit forward market for interest rates. The third, interest rate swaps, were introduced in 1980 and are now used actively by large and small banking organizations. The final contracts are options on interest rates labeled interest rate caps and floors.

Volume has increased to such levels that bank regulators are concerned that industry usage has grown beyond regulators' ability to understand and monitor the risks banks assume. Banks can use each of these tools to complement existing strategies involving matching or consciously mismatching rate-sensitive assets and liabilities and corresponding durations, thereby altering the sensitivity of earnings and economic value of equity (EVE). Remember that the responsibility of bank managers is to manage, not totally eliminate, risk.

# CHARACTERISTICS OF FINANCIAL FUTURES

**Financial futures contracts** represent a commitment between two parties—a buyer and a seller—on the price and quantity of a standardized financial asset or index. The contracts are transferable because they are traded on organized exchanges called **futures markets**, and all contracts are subject to a daily settlement procedure. Buyers of futures contracts, referred to as *long* futures, agree to pay the underlying futures price, while sellers of futures contracts, referred to as *short* futures, agree to receive the futures price or deliver the underlying asset as stipulated in the contract. Thus, buyers and sellers can eliminate their commitments by taking the opposite position prior to contract expiration by selling and buying the futures contract, or by making or taking delivery of the underlying asset.

Because futures prices fluctuate daily, buyers and sellers find that their initial position changes in value daily. When futures prices increase, buyers gain at the expense of sellers, while sellers gain at the expense of buyers when futures prices fall. At the end of each day participants must pay any decrease in value or, alternatively, they receive any increase in value as part of the daily settlement procedure. When the contract expires, they pay or receive the final change in value (cash settlement) or exchange the actual underlying asset (physical delivery) for cash at the initial negotiated price. The process essentially fixes the underlying instrument's price at the time of the trade for the future date designated by the contract. The underlying financial asset may be a short-term money market instrument, a long-term bond, units of a foreign currency, precious metals, or even common stock indexes. When the underlying asset is an interest-bearing security, the contracts are labeled **interest rate futures**. Futures contracts are traded daily prior to the formal expiration/delivery date, with the price changing as market conditions dictate. These unique features stand out when compared with cash market transactions and forward contracts.

**Cash** or **spot** market transactions represent the exchange of any asset between two parties who agree on the asset's characteristics and price, where the buyer tenders payment and takes possession of the asset when the price is set. Most transactions take this form. A **forward contract** involves two parties agreeing on an asset's characteristics, quantity, and price, but defers the actual exchange until a specified future date. Forward contracts do not necessarily involve standardized assets. Both parties to the transaction must simply agree on the asset's quality and price. Because the underlying asset is not standardized, the parties deal directly with each other and there is little opportunity to walk away from the commitment prior to delivery. Finally, once the terms of a forward contract are set, the parties do not make any payments or deliveries until the specified forward transactions date. However, forward contracts often require collateral or a letter of credit to guarantee performance.

## TYPES OF FUTURES TRADERS

Futures contracts are traded on exchanges, the most prominent of which in the United States are the Chicago Board of Trade (CBT) and the Chicago Mercantile Exchange (CME). Many of the contracts traded on U.S. exchanges are also traded outside the United States, such that participants have the opportunity to trade 24 hours a day. Continuous trading is important, given that many trades are implemented to reduce risk and participants need immediate access to hedge instruments.

Futures traders have various motivations and thus follow different strategies. Traders operating on the floor of an exchange are classified as either **commission brokers**, who execute trades for other parties, or **locals**, who trade for their own account. As the name suggests, commission brokers generate income by charging commissions for each trade and thus take no price risk. Locals are individuals who try to profit by buying contracts at prices less than what they sell the contracts for. As such, locals assume considerable price risk in their transactions but add liquidity to the markets.

Traders are further classified by the strategies they pursue. At one extreme is the **speculator**, who takes a position with the objective of making a profit. Speculators try to guess the direction that prices will move and time their trades to sell at higher prices than the purchase price. Locals are thus speculators. Speculators are often distinguished by the length of time they hold their positions. A **scalper** tries to time price movements over very short time intervals and takes positions that remain outstanding for just minutes. A **day trader** similarly tries to profit from short-term price movements during trading hours in any day, but offsets the initial position before market closing so that no position remains outstanding overnight. Finally, a **position trader** is a speculator who holds a position for a longer period in anticipation of a more significant, longer-term market move.

At the other extreme is the hedger. A **hedger** has an existing or anticipated position in the cash market and trades futures contracts (or some other contract) to reduce the risk associated with uncertain changes in value of the cash position. The cash position might involve owning or buying an asset, borrowing by issuing an interest-bearing liability, or a bank's overall earnings and MVE-sensitivity profile. With hedging, the trader takes a position in the futures market whose value varies in the opposite direction as the value of the cash market position. Risk is reduced because gains or losses on the futures position at least partially offset gains or losses on the cash position. The essential difference between a speculator and a hedger is the objective of the trader. A speculator wants to profit on trades while a hedger wants to reduce risk.

Traders may also be classified as **spreaders** or **arbitrageurs**. Both spreaders and arbitrageurs are speculators who take relatively low-risk positions. For example, a **futures spreader** may simultaneously buy a futures contract and sell a related futures contract, trying to profit on anticipated movements in the price difference between the contracts. The position is generally low risk because the prices of both contracts typically move in the same direction. Losses on one contract are thus at least partially offset by gains on the other. An **arbitrageur** tries to profit by identifying the same asset that is being traded at two different prices in different markets at the same time. The arbitrageur buys the asset at the lower price and simultaneously sells it at the higher price, profiting on the difference. Arbitrage transactions are thus lower risk and serve to bring prices back in line, in the sense that the same asset should trade at the same price in all markets.

## THE MECHANICS OF FUTURES TRADING

Futures contracts are traded on formal, organized exchanges that serve as clearinghouses. Trading occurs in an *open outcry* auction market. Each party to a futures transaction effectively trades with exchange members who, in turn, guarantee the performance of all participants. In practice, a buyer and seller are found for each transaction, but the exchange assumes all obligations at the end of each trading day, forcing members to settle their net positions. This procedure enables any trader to offset an initial position by taking the opposite position any time prior to the futures contract's delivery date. For example, a buyer of a Eurodollar futures contract with delivery in 60 days can offset the position by selling the same contract one week later when 53 days remain to delivery. This liquidity is not found with forward contracts. It results from trading standardized assets through an exchange, where each party does not have to renegotiate with the same party who initiated the contract.

Futures contracts entail cash-flow obligations for buyers and sellers during the entire time the position is outstanding. At initiation of a futures position, traders must post a cash deposit or U.S. government securities as **initial margin** with the exchange member simply for initiating a transaction. In most cases, the amount is small, involving less than 5 percent of the underlying asset's value. Initial margin represents a good faith deposit that serves to cover losses if prices move against the trader. Exchange members also require traders to meet **maintenance margin** requirements that specify the minimum deposit allowable at the end of each day. Unlike margin accounts for stocks, futures margin deposits represent a form of performance bond by which a trader guarantees that mandatory payment obligations will be met. When the margin deposit falls below this minimum, the customer must deposit more funds or the exchange member can close out the account.

As futures prices vary prior to expiration of the contract, each trader must either increase the cash deposit or can withdraw any excess deposit, depending on whether prices move unfavorably or favorably. For example, a trader who buys a futures contract agrees to pay the negotiated price at delivery.[1] If the futures price increases in the interim, the market value of the initial position also rises and the buyer can withdraw this increase in contract value. If, instead, the futures price falls, the value of the initial position declines and the buyer must cover this decrease in value. Formally, exchange members identify the change in value of each trader's account at the end of every day, then credit the margin accounts of those with gains and debit the margin accounts of those with losses. The market labels this daily settlement process **marking-to-market** and the daily change in value as **variation margin**.

Every futures contract has a formal expiration date. At expiration, trading stops and participants settle their final positions. Contracts may provide for either physical delivery of the underlying asset or a cash settlement. With physical delivery, the buyer of futures will make a cash payment to a seller, while the seller supplies the physical asset. Because financial futures contracts involve securities, delivery is handled via the wire transfer of funds and securities. With cash settlement, there is no physical delivery as participants simply exchange the final change in position value after the last trading day. Less than 1 percent of financial futures contracts require physical delivery at expiration because most participants offset their futures positions in advance.

### AN EXAMPLE: 90-DAY EURODOLLAR TIME DEPOSIT FUTURES

One of the most liquid interest rate futures contracts is the 90-day Eurodollar time deposit future. Its popularity is due to the breadth of participants who use Eurodollars, the allowance for cash settlement at delivery, and the

---

[1]Futures contracts with cash settlement at delivery differ from contracts with physical delivery in that traders settle their positions by paying or receiving the change in value of the contract between the trade date and expiration date.

**EXHIBIT 7.1**

Data for Three-Month Eurodollar Futures on March 10, 2005

Eurodollar (CME)-$1,000,000; pts of 100%

| | | | | | | | | |
|---|---|---|---|---|---|---|---|---|
| Mar | 96.98 | 96.99 | 96.98 | 96.99 | — | 3.91 | — | 823,734 |
| Apr | 96.81 | 96.81 | 96.81 | 96.81 | −.01 | 3.19 | .01 | 19,460 |
| June | 96.53 | 96.55 | 96.52 | 96.54 | — | 3.46 | — | 1,409,983 |
| Sept | 96.14 | 96.17 | 96.13 | 96.15 | −.01 | 3.05 | .01 | 1,413,496 |
| Dec | 95.92 | 95.94 | 95.88 | 95.91 | −.01 | 4.09 | .01 | 1,146,461 |
| Mr06 | 95.78 | 95.80 | 95.74 | 95.77 | −.01 | 4.23 | .01 | 873,403 |
| June | 95.64 | 95.60 | 95.62 | 95.64 | −.01 | 4.34 | .01 | 567,637 |
| Sept | 95.37 | 95.58 | 95.53 | 95.54 | −.01 | 4.44 | .01 | 434,034 |
| Dec | 95.47 | 95.50 | 95.44 | 95.47 | — | 4.53 | — | 300,746 |
| Mr07 | 95.42 | 95.44 | 95.37 | 95.42 | — | 4.58 | — | 250,271 |
| June | 95.31 | 95.38 | 95.31 | 95.37 | .01 | 4.63 | −.01 | 211,664 |
| Sept | 95.27 | 95.32 | 95.23 | 95.31 | .02 | 4.69 | −.02 | 164,295 |
| Dec | 95.21 | 95.27 | 95.18 | 95.26 | .03 | 4.74 | −.03 | 154,123 |
| Mr08 | 95.16 | 95.23 | 95.11 | 95.21 | .04 | 4.79 | −.04 | 122,800 |
| June | 95.08 | 95.17 | 95.07 | 95.14 | .05 | 4.84 | −.05 | 113,790 |
| Sept | 95.03 | 95.13 | 95.01 | 95.11 | .06 | 4.89 | −.06 | 107,792 |
| Dec | 94.95 | 95.06 | 94.94 | 95.05 | .07 | 4.95 | −.07 | 96,046 |
| Mr09 | 94.91 | 95.02 | 94.89 | 95.01 | .08 | 4.99 | −.07 | 81,015 |
| June | 94.05 | 94.97 | 94.84 | 94.97 | .08 | 5.03 | −.08 | 76,224 |
| Sept | 94.81 | 94.93 | 94.79 | 94.92 | .08 | 5.08 | −.08 | 41,524 |
| Dec | 94.77 | 94.38 | 94.74 | 94.87 | .08 | 5.15 | −.08 | 40,594 |
| Mr10 | 94.77 | 94.64 | 94.70 | 94.83 | .09 | 5.27 | −.09 | 17,481 |
| Sept | 94.66 | 94.76 | 94.62 | 94.75 | .09 | 5.25 | −.09 | 9,309 |
| Sp11 | 94.58 | 94.60 | 94.47 | 94.60 | .09 | 5.40 | −.09 | 2,583 |
| Dec | 94.49 | 94.56 | 94.43 | 94.56 | .09 | 5.44 | −.09 | 2,358 |
| Mr12 | 94.48 | 94.54 | 94.41 | 94.53 | .09 | 5.47 | −.09 | 1,392 |

Est vol 2,082,746; vol Wed 1,519,709; open int 8,631,643, +160,422.

SOURCE: *The Wall Street Journal*, March 11, 2005.

growth of interest rate swaps and option contracts based on LIBOR. Chapter 2 briefly introduced cash market Eurodollars as comparable to jumbo CDs in the domestic market. Chapter 8 describes cash market Eurodollar time deposits in detail.

Eurodollar futures contracts are traded on the International Monetary Market (IMM), a division of the Chicago Mercantile Exchange.[2] The underlying asset is a Eurodollar time deposit with a three-month maturity. Conceptually, Eurodollars are U.S. dollar-denominated deposits in banks located outside the United States. The holder cannot write checks against the account but earns interest at a rate slightly above that on domestic CDs issued by the largest U.S. banks. Eurodollar rates are quoted on an interest-bearing basis assuming a 360-day year. Each Eurodollar futures contract represents $1 million of initial face value of Eurodollar deposits maturing three months after contract expiration. More than 40 separate contracts are traded at any point in time as contracts expire in March, June, September, and December, more than ten years out from the current date.[3] Settlement or delivery is in the form of cash, with the price established from a survey of current Eurodollar rates.

Eurodollar futures contracts trade according to an index that equals 100 percent minus the futures interest rate expressed in percentage terms. An index of 93.50, for example, indicates a futures rate of 6.5 percent. Each basis point change in the futures rate equals a $25 change in value of the contract ($0.0001 \times \$1$ million $\times 90/360$). If futures rates increase, the value of the contract decreases and vice versa.

Buyers of Eurodollar futures are classified as "long" because they own a commitment regarding the final price that can be realized at expiration. Sellers are said to be "short" because they may ultimately be forced to come up with cash they may not currently have. With cash settlement, buyers and sellers of Eurodollar futures have simply agreed on the price at expiration. What the buyer owns is a commitment from the seller to pay cash if the price of the underlying asset rises in the interim. The seller owns a commitment from the buyer to pay cash if the asset price falls. Buyers make a futures profit when futures rates fall (prices rise), while sellers gain when futures rates rise (prices fall). Conceptually, profits arise because buyers can offset their initial position by selling the same futures contract after prices have increased. Sellers can similarly profit if they can buy the futures back at a lower price after rates rise. As indicated earlier with daily settlement, the Eurodollar futures contract changes in value daily when prices change, and participants can withdraw profits from their margin accounts prior to expiration.

Exhibit 7.1 indicates how *The Wall Street Journal* reports price quotes for these three-month Eurodollar futures contracts for the close of business on March 10, 2005. The first column indicates the settlement month and year. The first six contracts expire during the month noted in 2005. Except for the upcoming year, these contracts expire sequentially at three-month intervals near the middle of each month. Each row lists price and yield data for

---

[2] Equivalent Eurodollar futures contracts are traded on the Singapore International Monetary Exchange.

[3] During the upcoming year, contracts are added for intervening months. Subsequent exhibits do not reveal price quotes for all Eurodollar futures contracts. The last day of trading (expiration day) is the second London business day prior to the third Wednesday in each delivery month.

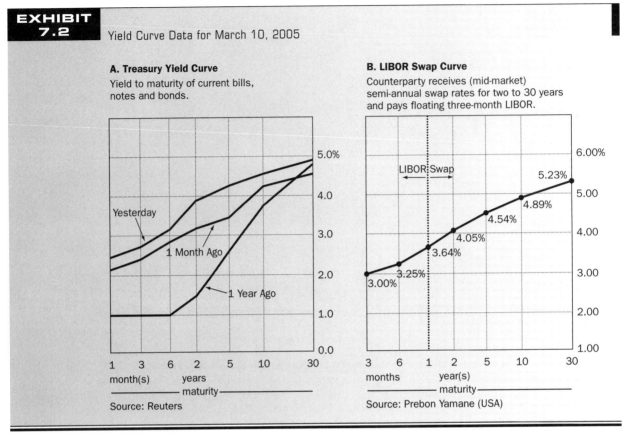

**EXHIBIT 7.2**

Yield Curve Data for March 10, 2005

**A. Treasury Yield Curve**

Yield to maturity of current bills, notes and bonds.

Source: Reuters

**B. LIBOR Swap Curve**

Counterparty receives (mid-market) semi-annual swap rates for two to 30 years and pays floating three-month LIBOR.

Source: Prebon Yamane (USA)

SOURCE: *The Wall Street Journal*, March 11, 2005.

a distinct futures contract. The next four columns report the index price quotes for each contract during the day, including the opening price, high and low price, and closing settlement price. The next column headed CHG indicates the change in settlement price from the previous day. The data under YLD convert the settlement price to a Eurodollar futures rate as:

$$100 - \text{settlement price} = \text{futures rate}$$

The second CHG column indicates the yield change from the previous day. The final column reports **open interest** equal to the total number of futures contracts outstanding at the end of the day.

For example, the Eurodollar futures contract expiring in March 2006, one year in the future, had a settlement price of $95.77 for a futures rate of 4.23 percent. On March 10, 2005, the contract opened trading at $95.78, rose as high as $95.80, and fell as low as $95.74 during the day, before trading stopped. The closing price was 1 basis point below the close the prior day, indicating that the futures rate rose 1 basis point. At the close of business 873,403 contracts were outstanding. Each successive row of data provides similar information. Note the column for the settlement yield, which is also labeled the futures rate. The data generally indicate that the farther out is contract expiration, the higher is the futures rate. Thus, the three-month Eurodollar futures rate of 4.34 percent for the contract expiring in June 2006 is 11 basis points higher than that for the March 2006 contract, but is less than the 5.47 percent futures rate for the March 2012 contract. The market exhibited minimal volatility on this day as only a few of the futures rates increased relative to their values the previous day, and the rate change was just 1 to 3 basis points. Finally, the open interest demonstrates that the amount of contracts outstanding declines the farther out is expiration, consistent with the fact that liquidity is greatest for the nearby futures contract and generally decreases with time until expiration.

Exhibit 7.2 presents two yield curves at the close of business on March 10, 2005. Figure A represents the yield curve for U.S. Treasury securities in which rates ranged from 2.60 percent on one-month T-bills to 4.85 percent on 30-year bonds. Note the increase in rates from one month prior and one year prior. Note also the relatively steep slope as the difference between the one-month and 30-year Treasury rates was 225 basis points. However, it was not nearly as steep as the yield curve one year prior. According to the unbiased expectations theory, an up-

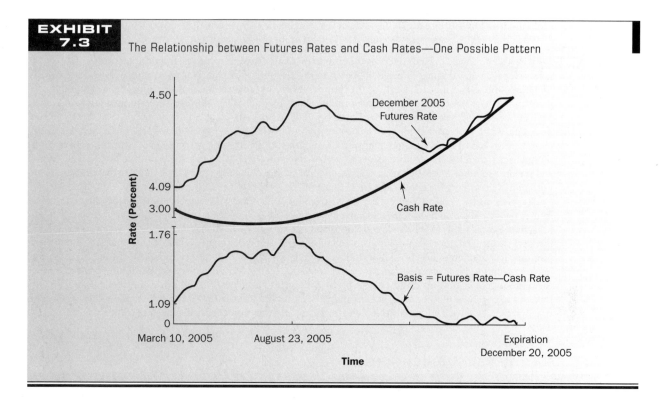

**EXHIBIT 7.3** The Relationship between Futures Rates and Cash Rates—One Possible Pattern

sloping yield curve indicates a consensus forecast that short-term interest rates are expected to rise. A flat yield curve suggests that rates will remain relatively constant. One interpretation of futures rates is that they provide information about consensus expectations of future cash rates. Futures rates that increase the farther out is futures contract expiration presumably indicate an expected increase in rates. In this context a futures rate should provide similar information as a forward rate derived from cash rates representing the prevailing yield curve. Data for the LIBOR swap curve, which is defined later in the chapter, reveal a similar pattern as that for the Treasury yield curve. If these Eurodollar futures rates are viewed as forecasts of three-month Eurodollar cash rates at expiration of each futures contract, the sharp increase suggests a rising Eurodollar yield curve as well.

## DAILY MARKING-TO-MARKET

The cash flows associated with daily settlement of futures trading can be demonstrated by an example. Consider a trader who at the close of trading on March 10, 2005, buys one December 2005 three-month Eurodollar futures contract at $95.91, or 4.09 percent, posting $1,100 in cash as initial margin. Maintenance margin is set at $700 per contract. The futures contract expires on December 20, approximately nine months after the initial purchase, during which time the futures price and rate fluctuate daily. Because our trader is long futures, the contract increases in value when the futures price rises, or the futures rate declines. Suppose that on March 13 the futures rate falls to 3.99 percent. The trader could withdraw $250 (10 basis points × $25) from the margin account, representing the increase in value of the position. For this example, assume that the funds are left in the margin account. Now suppose that the futures rate increases to 4.15 percent the next day so that the trader's long position decreases in value. The 16 basis point increase represents a $400 drop in margin such that the ending account balance would equal $950. If at market close on March 15 the December futures rate increases further to 4.30 percent, the trader must make a variation margin payment sufficient to bring the account up to $700. In this case, the account balance would have fallen to $575 and the margin contribution would equal $125. The exchange member may close the account if the trader does not meet the variation margin requirement.

Exhibit 7.3 reveals one possible pattern in the movement of the three-month cash Eurodollar rate and the December 2005 futures rate after March 10. Initially, the cash rate equals 3 percent and the futures rate is 4.09 percent. While the cash rate declines initially then increases systematically until expiration, the futures rate immediately increases. When the contract expires on December 17, 2005, both the futures and cash rate equal 4.50 percent, and the long futures position is worth $1,025 (41 basis points × $25) less than its value on March 10, 2005, because the Eurodollar futures rate increased 41 basis points. If the trader held the contract to expiration, the position would have immediately decreased in value as the futures rate rose and would have remained at a loss through expiration because the futures rate never went below 4.09 percent. The trader would have lost a total of $1,025 at the close or some lesser amount if he got out of his position earlier.

**THE BASIS.** The term **basis** refers to the cash price of an asset minus the corresponding futures price for the same asset at a point in time. Typically, it applies to the cash price of a security that is being hedged. For Eurodollar futures, the basis can be calculated as the futures rate minus the cash rate. Consider the previous example with three-month December 2005 Eurodollar futures. On March 10, 2005, the cash three-month Eurodollar time deposit rate equaled 3 percent. Thus, the December 2005 futures rate exceeded the prevailing cash rate by 109 basis points, which represents the basis. The bottom part of Exhibit 7.3 shows the movement in the basis associated with the cash and futures rates presented at the top of the exhibit. It initially increases to almost 176 basis points on August 23, then systematically declines as expiration approaches. Note that the basis equals zero at expiration and is close to zero prior to expiration. This is a typical pattern. Later discussions will indicate that the basis is important in determining the effectiveness of hedging interest rate risk.

The basis may not behave as nicely as it does in Exhibit 7.3. It may be positive or negative, depending on whether futures rates are above or below cash rates, and may swing widely in value far in advance of contract expiration. The basis rises and falls daily as economic conditions and market sentiment change. While the basis can take any value, there are two general price relationships between futures and cash instruments. First, the basis must equal zero at expiration. This is so no trader can earn a riskless arbitrage profit. For example, suppose that the basis equals some nonzero value just prior to expiration. Any trader could buy the cheaper cash instrument or futures contract and sell the more expensive one, making a riskless profit. Such arbitrage drives the two prices together. Second, because futures and cash rates must be equal at expiration, the basis normally narrows as expiration approaches. If it is positive, it declines to zero. If it is negative, it increases to zero. Both phenomena are demonstrated in Exhibit 7.3.

## SPECULATION VERSUS HEDGING

Participants use futures for a variety of purposes. According to the previous discussion, futures prices may represent the consensus forecast of the underlying asset's future price at contract expiration. A trader who expects the actual price to differ from that expected and represented by the futures price can either buy or sell the future, depending on whether the contract is perceived to be undervalued or overvalued. Such a participant is a speculator who takes on additional risk to earn speculative profits. For example, a speculator who on March 10, 2005, believed that December 2005 Eurodollar futures at 4.09 percent were undervalued (futures price [rate] was too low [high]) would buy the contract, anticipating a decline in futures rates and an increase in price prior to expiration. Speculators who felt the contract was overvalued (futures price [rate] was too high [low]) would alternatively sell futures, expecting to make a profit after futures rates increased and prices fell.

The top part of Exhibit 7.4 characterizes speculation in terms of two profit diagrams for the December 2005 Eurodollar futures data from Exhibit 7.1. The first (A) summarizes the profits and losses from buying the futures contract at the settlement price relative to possible futures prices after the contract is purchased. Specifically, on March 10, 2005, the settlement price equals $95.91. If a speculator later sells the futures contract at any higher price, he or she earns a profit equal to $25 times the difference in the sales price and 95.91. If the futures price declines and the speculator sells at less than $95.91, he or she suffers a loss. The second diagram (B) summarizes profits and losses for the seller of the same futures contract on March 10. Not surprisingly, the seller profits when the futures price declines and loses when the price rises.

Speculation is extremely risky. For the most part, futures rates and prices on nearby contracts are determined by arbitrage activity. Even when a speculator views a contract as overvalued or undervalued, any position taken can backfire in that a major market move can overwhelm the initial mispricing. Exhibit 7.4 demonstrates that the loss potential is virtually unlimited. Pure speculative activity with single contracts is thus relatively rare.

Hedging differs from speculation in terms of the participants' risk position prior to executing a trade and overall trade objectives. Speculators take a position that increases their risk profile. Hedgers focus on avoiding or reducing risk. They enter futures transactions because their normal business operations involve certain risks that they are trying to reduce. This preexisting risk can be at least partially offset because futures prices tend to move directly with cash prices, so futures rates closely track cash interest rates. Hedgers take the opposite position in a futures contract relative to their cash market risk so that losses in one market are reduced by gains in the other market.

For example, a trader who loses when cash market interest rates decrease will normally gain in the futures market with a long position as futures rates (prices) also decrease (increase) and the contract increases in value. This is characterized at the bottom of Exhibit 7.4. The lower left diagram adds to the long futures position a dashed line that indicates the profit and loss from an unhedged cash position. In this case the hedger loses in the cash market when prices increase (rates decrease) and gains when prices decrease (rates increase). In a *perfect hedge* the net profit, denoted by adding the profits and losses on both the futures and cash position, equals zero at each price. This is charac-

**EXHIBIT 7.4** Profit Diagrams for the December 2005 Eurodollar Futures Contract from Exhibit 7.1

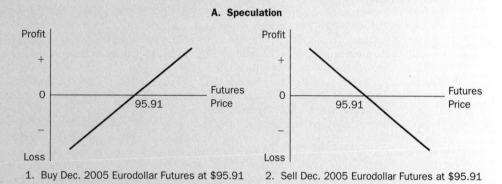

**A. Speculation**

1. Buy Dec. 2005 Eurodollar Futures at $95.91

2. Sell Dec. 2005 Eurodollar Futures at $95.91

**B. Hedging**

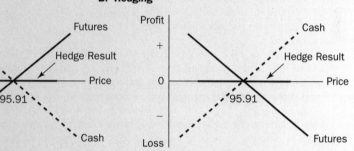

Hedge: Long Futures—Cash Loss When Rates Fall

Hedge: Short Futures—Cash Loss When Rates Rise

terized by the bold horizontal line at the zero profit level. The diagram on the lower right demonstrates the identical result when a short futures position is used to offset losses from a cash position that loses when prices fall (interest rates rise). Note here that rate increases (price decreases) produce simultaneous cash losses and futures profits. Rate decreases (price increases), in turn, produce simultaneous cash profits and futures losses, hence the hedge.

Participants also use futures because transactions costs are lower with futures than cash assets. Subsequent hedges are really transactions whereby participants can essentially replicate cash market positions but lower their cost of taking a position. For example, an investor who has funds to invest for nine months in the Eurodollar market on March 10 could simply buy a nine-month Eurodollar time deposit. Alternatively, he or she could buy a three-month Eurodollar time deposit and three-month Eurodollar futures contracts that expire in June 2005 and September 2005, respectively. The latter might be attractive if the combined yield exceeds that for the nine-month Eurodollar net of transactions costs.

**Steps in Hedging.** In general, there are seven basic steps in implementing futures hedges for financial institutions:

1. Identify the cash market risk exposure that management wants to reduce.

2. Based on the cash market risk, determine whether a long or short futures position is appropriate to reduce risk.

3. Select the best futures contract.

4. Determine the appropriate number of futures contracts to trade.

5. Implement the hedge by buying or selling futures contracts.

6. Determine when to get out of the hedge position, either by reversing the trades in Step 5, letting contracts expire, or making or taking delivery.

7. Verify that futures trading meets regulatory requirements and conforms to the bank's internal risk management policies.

The first step indicates that hedging requires each futures position to be associated with a cash position and that the objective is to reduce risk. The second step follows from Exhibit 7.4, and the fact that cash and futures rates on similar underlying instruments generally move in the same direction. If losses arise in the cash market when cash rates fall, a hedger will buy futures contracts because the futures should gain when futures rates fall. Similarly, if losses arise when cash rates rise, a hedger will sell futures contracts. The third step suggests that there is a "correct" futures contract for each cash position. In fact, the best contract is only known after the fact. What is known at the time of trading is that a hedger wants a futures contract whose rate will change in the same direction and by the same magnitude as the cash rate. Thus, a hedger chooses a "correct" futures contract where the correlation between the cash rate and futures rate is high. The other question is what contract expiration is best? Generally, a hedge will remain in place for a predetermined time interval. For reasons discussed later related to minimizing basis risk, a hedger will also generally trade the futures contract that expires immediately after the date at which the cash market risk disappears.

The fourth step addresses the determination of the appropriate *hedge ratio,* or number of futures contracts relative to the cash market exposure. There are several procedures for this, depending on whether the hedger's objective is to minimize the expected return variance or the change in total portfolio value. An example is provided later, but a detailed analysis of hedge ratios is left to other texts. The fifth step refers to the actual execution of the futures contracts trading based on the analysis of Steps 1–4. Along with the decision to hedge, a hedger decides how long the hedge should be in place. In most cases, the cash market risk exposure exists for a predetermined period of time. Once cash market risk is eliminated, a hedger will get out of the hedge position. To continue to hold a long or short futures position with no linked cash position would be speculating, because changes in the futures contract would not offset any associated change in the cash position. Thus, the sixth step involves identifying when cash market risk either disappears or reaches an acceptable level.

A futures trade that serves as a hedge will generally be kept in place as long as the cash risk exposure exists, and will be offset once the exposure is gone. There are two important extensions. First, if the cash market risk is unchanged over a period of time, it is inappropriate to trade futures contracts in and out in an attempt to time market movements. For example, a bank that trades futures in order to reduce the risk of price volatility with a portfolio of bonds should take an initial position and hold it until the bonds are sold, mature, or management decides to alter its risk preference. The bank should not sell futures initially, then buy them back only to sell futures again prior to the above ending points. Such day trading or position trading is speculative and simply increases commission costs. Second, management should determine a priori what its desired risk exposure is. It is appropriate for management to change its preference for risk and time whether it is hedged or unhedged accordingly. These risk preferences should not, however, change frequently over short periods such that management is constantly buying and selling futures against an unchanged cash market position. To do so is speculative because the implicit unstated intent is to time interest rate movements and trade futures to profit, rather than to reduce risk.

Finally, banks must meet strict regulatory guidelines and management must have internal policies in place that authorize hedge trades. Specifically, only certain types of positions are allowed for futures trading to constitute a hedge. Among other requirements, banks must maintain a contemporaneous hedge log that associates futures trades with the cash position in terms of the objective and nature of the trade, and they must meet strict accounting requirements for hedge gains and losses.

## A LONG HEDGE

As indicated in Exhibit 7.4, a long hedge is applicable for a participant who wants to reduce cash market risk associated with a decline in interest rates. The applicable strategy is to buy futures contracts on securities similar to those evidencing the cash market risk. If cash rates decline, futures rates will typically also decline so that the value of the futures position will likely increase. Any loss in the cash market is at least partially offset by a gain in futures. Of course, if cash market rates increase, futures rates will also increase and the futures position will show a loss. Using futures essentially fixes a rate or price. This latter instance reveals an important aspect of hedging. If cash rates rise, the investor will profit more from not hedging because cash rates move favorably. A hedger thus forgoes gains associated with favorable cash market price moves. The hedge objective, however, is assumed to be risk reduction. With hedging, risk is lower because the volatility of returns is lower.

The following example applies the key steps in hedging to a bank that implements a Eurodollar futures hedge. Consider the following time line:

| March 10, 2005 | November 8, 2005 | December 20, 2005 |
|---|---|---|
| Cash: anticipated investment | Invest $1 million | Expiration of Dec. 2005 futures contract |
| Futures: buy a futures contract | Sell the futures contract | |

Suppose that on March 10, 2005, your bank expects to receive a $1 million payment on November 8, 2005, and anticipates investing the funds in three-month Eurodollar time deposits. If the bank had the funds in hand in March, it would immediately buy Eurodollar deposits. The cash market risk exposure is that the bank would like to invest the funds at today's rates, but will not have access to the funds for eight months. If cash rates move lower between March and November, the bank will realize an opportunity loss because it will have to invest the $1 million at rates below those available today. In March 2005, the market expected Eurodollar rates to increase as evidenced by rising futures rates. In order to hedge, the bank should buy futures contracts such that if cash rates fall, futures rates will also likely fall and the long futures position will increase in value as an offset to the cash losses. Also, if futures rates overstate the likely increase in Eurodollar rates, a long position may capture any benefit. The best futures contract will generally be the December 2005, three-month Eurodollar futures contract, which is the first to expire after November 2005. The contract that expires immediately after the known cash transaction date is generally best because its futures price will show the highest correlation with the cash price.

Using the data in Exhibit 7.1, the December 2005 futures rate equals 4.09 percent while the current cash market rate equals 3 percent. This produces a basis of 1.09 percent. Exhibit 7.5 summarizes hedge results, assuming the bank buys a December futures contract on March 10 and sells it on November 8, when the bank actually buys Eurodollars in the cash market. The three-month Eurodollar futures contract has a $1 million par value, so each 1 basis point change in futures rates is worth the same $25 as a 1 basis point change in cash Eurodollar rates. The assumed hedge ratio is 1-to-1. Note that once the bank buys the futures contract, it is fully hedged. It implements the trade at the time it identifies the cash market risk and decides to reduce the risk. Because it plans to invest the funds in November, its cash risk will no longer exist after that time and the bank will need to get out of its initial long futures position, or it will be speculating. It is assumed that the bank has a hedge policy in place that authorizes futures trading to reduce risk associated with the planned investment of funds and that Eurodollar futures are an acceptable vehicle. It is also assumed that management has the accounting and hedge performance monitoring systems in place. The transactions are summarized at each date under the cash and futures market headings with the basis values in the final column of Exhibit 7.5.

**CHANGE IN THE BASIS.** The basis at the time of hedge initiation and change in basis at the time the hedge is offset determine the risk and net performance of the overall hedged position. Suppose that cash rates rise by 93 basis points through November 8 such that the bank actually invests the $1 million at 3.93 percent. This investment produces an opportunity gain of $2,325 in interest for the three-month period as indicated by the net effect reported in the column under the cash market heading. On November 8, the December 2005 futures rate falls by 6 basis points to 4.03 percent. At that time the bank sells its contract at a higher price (95.97), earning a direct profit of $150. In this case, the bank gains in both the cash and futures markets. The basis on November 8 is 0.10 percent, or 99 basis points lower than on March 10.

The bank's effective percentage return is calculated at the bottom of Exhibit 7.5. The combined income equals investment income from the cash Eurodollar plus the gain on the futures trade. In this case, income consists of $9,975 in interest and $150 in futures profits for a 3.99 percent return relative to the $1 million investment. This net percentage return is 99 basis points above the initial cash Eurodollar rate on March 10. As demonstrated

---

**EXHIBIT 7.5**  Long Hedge Using Eurodollar Futures

| Date | Cash Market | Futures Market | Basis |
|---|---|---|---|
| 3/10/05 (Initial futures position) | Bank anticipates investing $1 million in Eurodollars in eight months; current cash rate = 3.00% | Bank buys one December 2005 Eurodollar futures contract at 4.09%; price = 95.91 | 4.09% − 3.00% = 1.09% |
| 11/8/05 (Close futures position) | Bank invests $1 million in three-month Eurodollars at 3.93% | Bank sells one December 2005 Eurodollar futures contract at 4.03%; price = 95.97 | 4.03% − 3.93% = 0.10% |
| Net effect | Opportunity gain: 3.93% − 3.00% = 0.93%; 93 basis points worth $25 each = $2,325 | Futures profit: 4.09% − 4.03% =− 0.06%; 6 basis points worth $25 each = $150 | Basis change: 0.10% − 1.09% = −0.99% |

Cumulative investment income:

Interest at 3.93% = $1,000,000(.0393)(90/360) = $9,825
Profit from futures trades = $  150
Total = $9,975

$$\text{Effective return} = \frac{\$9,975}{\$1,000,000}\left(\frac{360}{90}\right) = 3.99\%$$

**EXHIBIT 7.6**

Short Hedge Using Eurodollar Futures

| Date | Cash Market | Futures Market | Basis |
|------|-------------|----------------|-------|
| 3/10/05 | Bank anticipates selling $1 million Eurodollar deposit in 127 days; current cash rate = 3.00% | Bank sells one Sept. 2005 Eurodollar futures contract at 3.85%; price = $96.15 | 3.85% − 3.00% = 0.85% |
| 8/17/05 | Bank sells $1 million Eurodollar deposit at 4.00% | Bank buys one Sept. 2005 Eurodollar futures contract at 4.14%; price = $95.86 | 4.14% − 4.00% = 0.14% |
| Net result: | Opportunity loss. 4.00% − 3.00% = 1.00%; 100 basis points worth $25 each = $2,500 | Futures profit: 4.14% − 3.85% × 0.29%; 29 basis points worth $25 each = $725 | Basis change: 0.14% − 0.85% = −0.71% |

Effective loss = $2,500 − $725 = $1,775
Effective rate at sale of deposit = 4.00% − 0.29% = 3.71%
  or 3.00% − (−0.71%) = 3.71%

below, the 99 basis point differential also represents the change in basis between March and November (0.10 percent–1.09 percent). The hedge worked because the volatility of the return from the combined futures and cash position was below the volatility of return with the unhedged cash position. With no hedge, the bank would have earned 3.93 percent.

## A SHORT HEDGE

A short hedge applies to any participant who wants to reduce the risk of an increase in cash market interest rates (or reduction in cash market prices). The applicable strategy is to sell futures contracts on securities similar to those evidencing the cash market risk. If cash rates increase, futures rates will generally increase so the loss in the cash position will be at least partially offset by a gain in value of futures. Again, if cash rates actually decrease, the gain in the cash market will be offset by a loss from futures and a hedger gives up potential gains from an unhedged position. A hedger essentially fixes the rate to be realized.

The following example examines a short hedge associated with a bank that wants to protect the value of its existing securities portfolio from potential losses at future sale. Suppose that on March 10, 2005, a bank anticipates it will need to sell a six-month Eurodollar deposit from its investment portfolio on August 17. The Eurodollar yields 3 percent and management, expecting a sharp increase in interest rates, would like to hedge against a decline in value of the Eurodollar at the time of sale. The cash market risk of loss is that Eurodollar time deposit rates will be higher in August. To hedge, the bank will want to immediately sell Eurodollar futures. The example assumes that the bank immediately sells one September 2005 Eurodollar futures contract and expects to buy it back in August when it sells its cash Eurodollar investment.[4]

Exhibit 7.6 summarizes the hedge results, assuming the bank sells one September 2005 Eurodollar futures contract on March 10 at 3.85 percent. With a cash rate of 3 percent, the initial basis is 0.85 percent. On August 17, the bank buys the futures back when it liquidates its Eurodollar investment. It is assumed in the example that cash rates rise through August such that the deposit rate equals 4 percent at sale and the September futures rate equals 4.14 percent. In this situation, the bank has an (approximate) opportunity loss of $2,500 on its cash position and a futures profit of $725 for a net loss of $1,775.[5] Note that the 100 basis point increase in the cash rate and 29 basis point increase in the futures rate coincide with a 71 basis point decrease in the basis. Unlike the long hedge example, in this case the bank loses in the cash market and profits with futures. The hedge again works in the sense that the volatility of return (or cost) is less than with an unhedged position. If unhedged, the bank would not have

---

[4]Note that a $1 million six-month Eurodollar deposit is priced differently than a $1 million three-month Eurodollar deposit. Specifically, each basis point change is now worth $50 (.0001 X $1,000,000 × 180/360). As time elapses, the six-month Eurodollar will approach maturity such that in August it will have less than two months to maturity.

[5]The calculation assumes that the deposit has exactly 90 days remaining maturity such that a basis point is worth $25. On August 17, however, the deposit would have less than 90 days to maturity and each basis point would be worth less than $25.

realized the $725 futures gain and its total cost at sale of the deposit would have been greater than with the hedge. Of course, the bank would have been in a riskier position without the futures hedge. The important point is that a hedger does not base a futures trade on expected futures profits, but rather on reducing overall risk.

## CHANGE IN THE BASIS

Both the long and short hedges worked in the previous examples in the sense that the futures rate moved in line with the cash rate. With the long hedge, the futures rate fell by 6 basis points as Eurodollar rates did not increase as much as expected. Had the cash rate decreased instead of increased, the bank would have invested its funds at a yield below 3 percent but would have realized a greater profit on its futures position as the contract price increased even more. With the short hedge, the futures rate increased by 29 basis points, producing a profit, while the cash rate rose by 100 basis points. The net effect was that the futures profit and cash loss netted 71 basis points.

The actual risk assumed by a trader in both hedges is not that the level of interest rates will move against the cash position, but that the basis might change adversely between the time the hedge is initiated and closed. The effective return from Exhibit 7.5 equaled total income from the combined cash and futures positions relative to the investment amount. It can also be expressed as:

$$\text{Effective return} = \text{Initial cash rate} - \text{Change in basis} \tag{7.1}$$

or 3.99 percent [3.00 percent $-$ ($-0.99$) percent].[6] The change in the basis ($B_2 - B_1$) equals the basis when the hedge is closed ($B_2$) minus the basis when the hedge is initiated ($B_1$). At the time a trade is initiated, the only unknown in Equation 7.1 is the basis value at closing and therefore the size of change in basis. Thus, a hedger still faces the risk that futures rates and cash rates will not change coincidentally. In this long hedge example, the basis decreased from 109 to 10 basis points, thereby raising the return by 99 basis points over the initial cash rate to 3.99 percent. Had the basis increased, the effective return would have decreased. The result holds true regardless of whether the level of rates increased or decreased after March 10.

The effective cost of a short hedge is also determined by Equation 7.1. The risk assumed by a hedger is again that the basis might change between the time a hedge is initiated and the time it is offset. However, the short hedger benefits when the basis increases and loses when the basis decreases. This is the opposite of a hedger who takes a long position. Using the data from the example in Exhibit 7.6, the effective cost of the Eurodollar deposit sale was 3.71 percent equal to 3.00 percent $-$ ($-0.71$) percent. This indicates that the bank effectively sold the Eurodollar time deposit at a 71 basis point higher yield than the rate available in March. Thus, the bank realized a greater net value by 29 basis points, or $725, compared with an unhedged sale.

Generally, directional movements in the basis are more predictable than movements in the level of cash market rates and the volatility of cash rates exceeds the volatility of the basis. The risk of hedging is thus normally less than the risk of not hedging. While basis changes can be substantial, most factors that influence cash rates influence futures rates simultaneously. Futures rates are further tied to cash rates by arbitrage activity so that the two rates move together. If the cash instrument to be hedged is the same as the instrument underlying the futures contract, arbitrageurs will trade the two instruments until the basis equals zero at futures contract expiration. This is what induces the basis to narrow toward zero as expiration approaches, per the diagram in Exhibit 7.3, and helps the hedger to estimate the ex post effective cost or return from a hedged position.

## BASIS RISK AND CROSS HEDGING

In a perfect hedge, the profit or loss in the cash position is exactly offset by the profit or loss from the futures position. This would occur if the basis change always equaled zero. In practice, it is extremely difficult to obtain a perfect hedge and there are numerous instances when basis risk can be substantial. One such instance involves **cross hedges.** A cross hedge is one in which a participant uses a futures contract based on one security that differs from the security being hedged in the cash market. An example would be using Eurodollar futures to hedge price movements for commercial paper transactions. The risk is potentially greater for cross hedges because futures and cash interest rates may not move closely together as they are based on different underlying securities. If the basis is volatile and unpredictable, Equation 7.1 suggests that the effective return or cost from a hedge might also be volatile and unpredictable.

Basis risk can also be substantial because futures and cash rates for the same underlying security may move in opposite directions prior to expiration. In fact, the basis change is known with certainty only when the planned cash transactions being hedged coincide with futures expirations. In this case, participants know that the basis will equal zero and thus the basis change will equal the negative of the basis at the time the hedge is initiated. Typically, however, most transactions do not coincide with futures expirations and changes in futures rates may differ

---

[6]Whenever a participant profits in futures, the effective return is actually higher because it could withdraw variation margin funds and invest the proceeds after futures prices moved favorably.

sharply from changes in cash rates. It is generally the case, however, that basis volatility is lowest for the contract that expires immediately after the cash risk expiration. Importantly, futures trades are not riskless and often produce opportunity losses.

## MICROHEDGING APPLICATIONS

One of the basic decisions that risk managers make is whether to hedge specific individual transactions or the aggregate risk exposure of the bank. The previous examples of a long hedge and short hedge involved individual transactions. Alternatively, management could choose to hedge aggregate risk exposure evidenced by a nonzero GAP or nonzero duration gap and earnings and EVE sensitivity that are nonzero. **Microhedges** refer to the hedging of a transaction associated with a specific asset, liability, or commitment. **Macrohedges** involve taking futures positions to reduce aggregate portfolio interest rate risk, typically measured by the sensitivity of earnings or EVE.

Banks are generally restricted to using financial futures for hedging purposes under current regulations. In their accounting, they must recognize futures on a micro basis by linking each futures transaction with a specific cash instrument or commitment in a contemporaneous log of hedge transactions. Yet many analysts feel that such linkages force microhedges that may potentially increase a firm's total risk because these hedges ignore all other portfolio components. Thus, accounting requirements may focus attention on inappropriate risk measures. Macrohedging, in turn, is difficult to implement because of problems in accurately measuring a firm's overall interest rate risk and in monitoring hedging effectiveness. This section analyzes various microhedges, followed by a section on macrohedging.

### CREATING A SYNTHETIC LIABILITY WITH A SHORT HEDGE

Suppose that on March 10, 2005, a large money center bank agreed to finance a $1 million six-month working capital loan to a corporate customer. Management wanted to match fund the loan by issuing a $1 million, six-month Eurodollar time deposit. On March 10, the six-month cash Eurodollar rate was 3.25 percent, while the corresponding three-month rate was 3 percent. The three-month Eurodollar futures rate for September 2005 expiration equaled 3.85 percent. Rather than issue a direct six-month Eurodollar liability at 3.25 percent, the bank created a synthetic six-month liability by shorting futures. The objective was to use the futures market to borrow at a lower rate than the six-month cash Eurodollar rate. It was to be achieved by initially issuing a three-month Eurodollar, then issuing another when the first matured. A short futures position would reduce the risk of rising interest rates for the second cash Eurodollar borrowing. The following time line indicates the rate comparison. Exhibit 7.7 presents the steps.

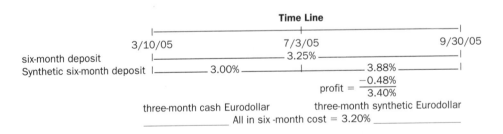

On March 10, the bank issued a $1 million, 91-day Eurodollar time deposit at 3 percent and simultaneously sold one September 2005 Eurodollar futures contract at 3.85 percent. Management expects to roll over its 91-day Eurodollar deposit by issuing another three-month deposit on June 9 for an effective six-month maturity. At that time, it will offset its futures position by buying a September 2005 futures contract. The short hedge reduces the risk of loss if cash Eurodollar rates have increased (between March 10 and June 9) when the bank reissues its deposit.

When the first three-month deposit matured on June 9, rates had increased substantially, and the bank issued another three-month Eurodollar deposit at 3.88 percent. It simultaneously closed out its position by buying one September 2005 futures contract at 4.33 percent. In this example, both cash and futures rates increased with the basis decreasing from 85 basis points to 45 basis points (increased cost by 40 basis points to 3.4 percent). The $1,200 (48 basis points) profit on the futures trades lowered the effective interest expense on the cash Eurodollar deposit such that the effective cost of the second three-month Eurodollar equaled 3.40 percent (3.88 percent − 0.48 percent). The effective borrowing cost of the synthetic six-month Eurodollar deposit equaled 3.2 percent which was below the 3.25 percent six-month cash rate available on March 10.

In this example, the bank "saved" 5 basis points in interest expense which represents the difference between interest expense on a six-month Eurodollar and the effective six-month interest on the synthetic Eurodollar. The

**EXHIBIT 7.7** Creating a Synthetic Six-Month Eurodollar Liability

**Summary of Relevant Eurodollar Rates and Transactions**

**March 10, 2005**

Three-month cash rate = 3.00%; bank issues a $1 million, 91-day Eurodollar deposit
Six-month cash rate = 3.25%
Bank sells one September 2005 Eurodollar futures; futures rate = 3.85%

**June 9, 2005**

Three-month cash rate = 3.88%; bank issues a $1 million, 91-day Eurodollar deposit
Buy: One September 2005 Eurodollar futures; futures rate = 4.33%

| Date | Cash Market | Futures Market | Basis |
|---|---|---|---|
| 3/10/05 | Bank issues $1 million, 91-day Eurodollar time deposit at 3.00%; three-mo. interest expense = $7,583. | Bank sells one September 2005 Eurodollar futures contract at 3.85% | 0.85% |
| 6/9/05 | Bank issues $1 million, 91-day Eurodollar time deposit at 3.88%; three-mo. interest expense = $9,808 (increase in interest expense over previous period = $2,225). | Bank buys one September 2005 Eurodollar futures contract at 4.33%; | 0.45% |
| Net effect: | Six-mo. interest expense = $17,391 | Profit on futures = $1,200 (0.48%) | |

Effective six--month borrowing cost $= \dfrac{\$17,391 - \$1,200}{\$1,000,000}\left(\dfrac{360}{182}\right) = 3.20\%$

Interest on six-month Eurodollar deposit issued March 10 = $13,144 at 3.25%; vs. 3.20% from synthetic liability

actual benefit, of course, depends on how cash rates change relative to futures rates. In essence, the bank has substituted basis risk for the risk that cash rates will change adversely. In this example, the bank could lose if cash rates increased substantially more than futures rates increased. Briefly, the true borrowing cost increases as the basis decreases, while the cost falls as the basis increases.

## THE MECHANICS OF APPLYING A MICROHEDGE

A bank should carefully analyze the opportunities and risks associated with hedging. The following discussion demonstrates the type of information required and procedural steps underlying successful hedging programs.[7]

**DETERMINE THE BANK'S INTEREST RATE RISK POSITION.** To formulate the correct hedge, management must determine the bank's interest rate risk position. With a microhedge this involves examining the bank's actual and anticipated cash market position and how specific interest rate changes will affect interest income or interest expense, or the value of an underlying asset or liability. The objective is to know in what rate environment the bank loses. Frequently, banks then compare their rate forecast and their potential losses if these rates materialize. Selectively hedging when losses will arise if the forecast is realized is a form of speculation. The key hedging decision involves determining how much risk the bank will accept.

**FORECAST THE DOLLAR FLOWS OR VALUE EXPECTED IN CASH MARKET TRANSACTIONS.** To determine how many futures contracts are necessary, management should estimate the dollar magnitude of anticipated cash flows with cash market transactions. This may equal the amount of investable funds, the size of a loan commitment, or the amount of liabilities to be issued or rolled over.

**CHOOSE THE APPROPRIATE FUTURES CONTRACT.** A bank should select a hedging vehicle that reduces interest rate risk. Because changes in the basis determine hedging risk, the appropriate futures contract is usually one whose rates most highly correlate with those of the cash asset or liability being hedged. Typically, the correlation is highest for like instruments, such as Eurodollar futures relative to cash Eurodollar deposits. If a like futures instrument is unavailable, a bank can examine historical correlations for different futures contracts and choose the contract with the highest correlation coefficient. As described earlier, the use of a futures contract that is not identical to the cash instrument being hedged is referred to as a cross hedge. It is also important to assess the

[7]This analysis is based on steps outlined by Kawaller (1983).

liquidity of different contracts. Only when trading volume is large can a bank easily buy or sell futures at relatively stable basis levels.

**DETERMINE THE CORRECT NUMBER OF FUTURES CONTRACTS.** Five factors, listed below, determine the correct number of futures contracts. This calculation, or hedge ratio, is expressed numerically as:

$$NF = \frac{[A \times Mc]}{F \times Mf} b$$

where

NF = Number of futures contracts

A = Dollar value of cash flow to be hedged

F = Face value of futures contract

Mc = Maturity or duration of anticipated cash asset or liability

Mf = Maturity or duration of futures contract

$$b = \frac{\text{expected rate movement on cash instrument}}{\text{expected rate movement on futures contract}}$$

If futures rates are expected to move coincidentally with cash rates, b equals 1. If futures rates are expected to exhibit larger moves relative to cash rates, b is less than 1, and vice versa.[8] Using the information from Exhibit 7.7 and assuming b equals 1 with Eurodollar cash and futures rates, the bank needed one futures contract:

$$NF = \frac{\$1,000,000 \times 91 \text{ days}}{\$1,000,000 \times 90 \text{ days}} \times 1 = 1$$

**DETERMINE THE APPROPRIATE TIME FRAME FOR THE HEDGE.** Typically, a bank matches the length of a hedge with the timing of cash flows for the underlying asset or liability. For example, a bank that knows it will have funds to invest in six months will use a futures contract that expires in six or more months. If consecutive cash flows are expected, such as principal payments on a term loan, a bank will hedge by spreading different futures contracts over the term of the cash flows. This process, labeled **stripping futures**, consists of buying or selling equal amounts of successive futures contracts.[9]

**MONITOR HEDGE PERFORMANCE.** Once a hedge is in place, management should monitor interest rate changes and the bank's cash position to verify the hedge performance. One concern is that the anticipated cash position might vary. Another is that the basis might move against the cash rate, whereby the bank loses in both the cash and futures market. If the bank's risk profile changes, it may want to lift a hedge. In practice, many participants adjust their hedge when the basis moves against them, implicitly extrapolating that the movement is permanent. In doing so, they are speculating.

## MACROHEDGING APPLICATIONS

Macrohedging focuses on reducing interest rate risk associated with a bank's entire portfolio rather than with individual components or transactions. As suggested in Chapters 5 and 6, macrohedging assumes that interest rate risk is best evidenced by GAP or duration gap measures and by the sensitivity of bank earnings and EVE. Banks can subsequently use futures contracts to hedge this net portfolio rate sensitivity.

### HEDGING: GAP OR EARNINGS SENSITIVITY

When establishing a macrohedge, a bank should initially examine its aggregate interest rate risk position. Banks using GAP and earnings sensitivity analysis focus on the volatility in net interest income. GAP represents the dollar magnitude of rate-sensitive assets minus the dollar magnitude of rate-sensitive liabilities over different time in-

---

[8]In practice, the appropriate factor is determined as the slope of the regression line from running a regression of cash price changes on futures price changes using historical data.

[9]If the term of the cash flows exceeds the time frame for which futures contracts are available, hedgers can "stack" contracts by loading up on the last available contract and systematically switching into new futures contracts as they become available. This involves additional risk and increases transactions costs.

tervals. If GAP is positive, the bank is said to be asset sensitive because its net interest income rises when interest rates rise, and falls when interest rates fall. If GAP is negative, the bank is liability sensitive because net interest income falls when rates increase, and rises when rates decrease. The magnitude of the potential change in net interest income indicates the sensitivity of earnings to rate changes and the aggregate amount of interest rate risk assumed.

Hedging strategies focus on whether a bank is asset or liability sensitive and the extent to which rate changes might alter net interest income. To balance asset sensitivity, a bank will institute a long hedge, whereby declining interest rates should generate futures profits that offset the decline in net interest income. To balance liability sensitivity, a bank will institute a short hedge. If rates subsequently increase and the bank's net interest income falls, the sale of futures should produce a profit that at least partially offsets the lost net interest income.

Consider the summary rate sensitivity data for ABC bank from Exhibit 5.7 in Chapter 5. This bank has a negative cumulative GAP through one year of $15,448,000 under management's most likely rate scenario. Exhibit 5.9 demonstrates that if rates increase by 1 percent, net interest income will likely fall modestly the next year, but will fall by almost $750,000 two years out. Suppose that the bank chooses to hedge $10 million of its $15.4 million GAP exposure over 180 days. This partial hedge would call for the sale of 20 Eurodollar futures contracts determined by:

$$NF = \frac{\$10,000,000}{\$1,000,000} \times \frac{180 \text{ days}}{90 \text{ days}} \times 1.0 = 20$$

This assumes that the bank uses Eurodollar futures and that the expected movement between the effective interest rate on the rate sensitive liabilities relative to the Eurodollar futures rate equals 1. The bank would likely sell ten September 2005 and ten December 2005 contracts that expire more than six months from year-end 2004, liquidating the hedge by periodically buying back futures at selected intervals. The hedge should work because any decline in net interest income due to rising rates should be offset by a gain on the short futures position. Also, any gain in net interest income from falling rates should be offset by a loss on the short futures position.

This type of hedge is clearly a cross hedge as the cash rate is actually a combination of several rates, all different from the Eurodollar futures rate. The bank is negatively gapped with the magnitude of change in net interest income associated with changes in short-term liability rates. The bank might alternatively choose Treasury bill futures for the hedge instrument if the correlation was higher with liability rates because money market deposit accounts pay interest tied to cash Treasury bill rates. Because the hedge matches gains in either the cash or futures market with losses in the other, the transaction essentially fixes a rate or outcome before basis changes. In effect, the short hedge moves both the GAP and earnings sensitivity closer to zero.

## HEDGING: DURATION GAP AND EVE SENSITIVITY

One of the presumed advantages of duration gap analysis is that it lends itself to hedging applications. Duration gap is a single-valued measure of total interest rate risk in which a bank targets its economic value of equity EVE. Duration gap equals the weighted duration of bank assets minus the product of the weighted duration of bank liabilities and the bank's debt-to-asset ratio. A positive duration gap (DGAP) measure indicates that aggregate assets will vary more in value relative to aggregate liabilities when interest rates change equally. If rates increase, the market value of assets falls more than the market value of liabilities, so that EVE declines. A bank with a negative duration gap will see its equity increase in value when rates rise.

To eliminate this risk, a bank could structure its portfolio so that the duration gap equals zero. Alternatively, it can use futures to balance the value sensitivity of the portfolio. Equation 7.3 is listed below:

$$\frac{\Delta EVE}{\text{Market value of assets}} = -\frac{DGAP \times \Delta y}{(1 + y)} \tag{7.3}$$

where DGAP equals the duration gap and y equals the average interest rate for a bank's portfolio. If management wants to immunize EVE, it could set the bank's DGAP at zero. This can be done by using futures to create a synthetic DGAP that approximately equals zero. The appropriate size of a futures position can be determined by solving Equation 7.4 for the market value of futures contracts (MVF), where DF is the duration of the futures contract used, DA is the weighted duration of assets, and DL is the weighted duration of liabilities:[10]

$$\frac{DA(MVRSA)}{(1 + i_a)} - \frac{DL(MVRSL)}{(1 + i_l)} + \frac{DF \times (MVF)}{(1 + i_f)} = 0 \tag{7.4}$$

---

[10]Because futures contracts have no fixed price or cash flow, they have no duration. Under certain assumptions, however, it can be shown that the duration of a futures contract equals the duration of the underlying deliverable instrument.

## CONTEMPORARY ISSUES

### HEDGE ACCOUNTING AND THE FAILURE OF FRANKLIN SAVINGS

On February 16, 1990, the Office of Thrift Supervision (OTS) put Franklin Savings of Ottawa, Kansas, in receivership. Ernest Fleischer, Franklin's CEO, challenged the seizure in court claiming that the action was arbitrary and capricious. The fundamental issue was whether Franklin Savings was insolvent. The determination evolved around the appropriate procedure in accounting for hedge losses.

Franklin Savings was an unorthodox thrift institution that availed itself of Federal Home Loan Bank advances and jumbo CDs obtained via brokers to fund much of the firm's assets. Franklin, in turn, used a variety of financial futures, options on

financial futures, and interest rate swaps to hedge against loss from adverse changes in interest rates. Franklin employed an absolute value method for computing the correlation coefficient between futures price changes and cash price changes. The OTS used a net offset method.

In February 1990, the absolute value method produced a sufficiently high correlation coefficient for Franklin to qualify for hedge accounting and thus the deferral of losses. The net offset method, in contrast, produced a low correlation coefficient to where the OTS required Franklin to immediately recognize $119 million in losses that had been previously deferred. With the losses, the OTS determined that Franklin's net worth (capital) was deficient and forced the firm into receivership.

Franklin originally used the net offset method but changed to the absolute value method, which it developed, when the volatility of interest rates increased. The argument was that the net offset procedure distorted the impact of rapidly changing interest rates on actual performance. FASB 80, in fact, does not stipulate any acceptable method for estimating correlation. The curious result is that the OTS ruled Franklin Savings to be a failed institution over ambiguous accounting when there were no specific guidelines as to what is appropriate.

The subscripts on the interest rate measures refer to assets (a), liabilities (l), and futures (f), and all rates are assumed to change by the same amount. MVRSA and MVRSL refer to the market value of rate-sensitive assets and rate-sensitive liabilities, respectively.

As an illustration, consider the bank balance sheet data provided for the sample bank in Exhibit 6.1 of Chapter 6. Because the bank has a positive duration gap of 1.4 years, it will see its EVE decline if interest rates rise. It thus needs to sell interest rate futures contracts in order to hedge its risk position. The short position indicates that the bank will make a profit if futures rates increase. This should at least partially offset any decline in the EVE caused by corresponding increases in cash rates. Assuming the bank uses a Eurodollar futures contract currently trading at 4.9 percent with duration of 0.25 years, the target MVF contracts can be obtained from applying Equation 7.4:

$$\frac{2.88(\$900)}{(1.10)} - \frac{1.61(\$920)}{(1.06)} + \frac{0.25(\text{MVF})}{(1.049)} = 0$$

or MVF = −$4,024.36. This suggests that the bank should sell four Eurodollar futures contracts. If all interest rates increased by 1 percent, the profit on the four futures contracts would total $10,000 (4 × 100 × $25), or $2,000 less than the decrease in EVE associated with the increase in cash rates (see Exhibit 6.2). The discrepancy derives from using interest rate averages and a discrete number of futures contracts. The concept, however, is clear. Duration gap mismatches can be hedged through the use of futures without dramatic changes in the portfolio.

### ACCOUNTING REQUIREMENTS AND TAX IMPLICATIONS

Regulators generally limit banks to using futures for hedging purposes. However, if a bank has a dealer operation, it can use futures as part of its trading activities. Regardless of how futures contracts are used, recently imposed accounting standards require that gains and losses on futures and other off-balance sheet positions be marked-to-market as they accrue, thereby affecting current income. Such current recognition of gains or losses clearly increases the volatility of reported earnings over short intervals. For hedging applications, futures contracts must be recognized on a micro basis by linking each contract to a specific cash instrument.

To qualify as a hedge, the use of futures must meet several criteria. A bank must show that a cash transaction exposes it to interest rate risk, a futures contract must lower the bank's risk exposure, and the bank must designate the contract as a hedge. The primary difficulty involves determining whether futures reduce bank risk. Financial Accounting Standards Board statement number 80 states that this condition is met if the correlation between price changes in futures and the hedged instrument is high. Unfortunately, there are no well-defined rules for establishing what time period should be used to calculate the correlation or even what amount of correlation is high enough. If a high correlation does not prevail, a bank must immediately stop deferring futures gains and losses and account for the proceeds as current income. As described in the Contemporary Issues Box: "Hedge Accounting and the Failure of Franklin Savings," how regulators calculate correlation can have a profound impact on the financial statements and thus regulatory viability of a futures user. In this instance, Franklin Savings failed, in part because it recorded losses differently than the regulators and courts eventually felt was appropriate.

The tax treatment of futures contracts has undergone a broad transition. Prior to 1981, futures profits were taxed as ordinary income or capital gains, depending on the length of the trader's holding period. Tax payments were due in the year the futures position was offset. This enabled futures traders to spread contracts by taking opposite positions in different con-tracts, where one produced a loss and the other a gain for similar interest rate movements. At the end of the tax year, traders would take the loss to reduce taxes and defer gains. In 1981, speculative traders were required to mark contract values to market at the end of the tax year and pay the obligated taxes in that year. Finally, the Tax Reform Act of 1986 eliminated the lower tax rate on long-term capital gains. Thus, all futures profits are taxed as ordinary income.

## USING FORWARD RATE AGREEMENTS TO MANAGE RATE RISK

The previous discussion briefly introduced forward contracts and compared their features with financial futures. While there are similarities, forward contracts differ because they are negotiated between counterparties, there is no daily settlement or marking-to-market, and no exchange guarantees performance. In general, the buyer of a forward contract agrees to pay a specific amount at a set date in the future (settlement date) for an agreed-upon asset, currency, and so on, from the counterparty representing the seller. The specified price or rate is labeled the exercise price (rate). The seller of a forward contract agrees to deliver the agreed-upon asset, currency, etc., for the specific amount at a set date when there is physical delivery. When a forward contract is cash-settled, the buyer and seller agree to exchange the difference between the exercise price and cash price at the future settlement date.

A forward rate agreement (FRA) is a type of forward contract based on interest rates. The two counterparties to an FRA agree to a **notional principal** amount that serves as a reference figure in determining cash flows. The term *notional* refers to the condition that the principal does not change hands, but is only used to calculate the value of interest payments. The buyer of the FRA agrees to pay a fixed-rate coupon payment and receive a floating-rate payment against the notional principal at some specified future date, while the seller of the FRA agrees to pay a floating-rate payment and receive the fixed-rate payment against the same notional principal. In most cases, the exercise rate is set equal to the forward rate from the prevailing yield curve reflecting the expected future interest rate. Thus, a buyer or seller of the FRA will receive cash or make cash payment only if the actual interest rate at settlement differs from that initially expected.

FRAs can be used to manage interest rate risk in the same manner as financial futures. The buyer of the FRA will receive (pay) cash when the actual interest rate at contract settlement is greater (less) than the exercise rate set at origination of the contract. The seller of the FRA will receive (pay) cash when the actual interest rate at settlement is less (greater) than the exercise rate. Note that FRAs are cash-settled at the settlement date with no interim cash flows. They are not marked-to-market and there are no margin requirements.

### FORWARD RATE AGREEMENTS: AN EXAMPLE

Suppose that Metro Bank as seller enters into a receive fixed-rate/pay floating-rate FRA agreement with County Bank as buyer with a six-month maturity based on a $1 million notional principal amount. The floating rate is three-month LIBOR and the fixed (exercise) rate is 7 percent. Metro Bank would refer to this as a "3 versus 6" FRA at 7 percent on a $1 million notional amount from County Bank. The phrase "3 versus 6" refers to a three-month interest rate observed three months from the present, for a security with a maturity date six months from the present. The only cash flow will be determined in six months at contract maturity by comparing the prevailing three-month LIBOR with 7 percent.

Assume, for example, that in three months three-month LIBOR equals 8 percent. In this case, County Bank would receive from Metro Bank $2,451. The interest settlement amount is $2,500 determined as:

$$\text{Interest} = (.08 - .07)(90/360)\$1,000,000 = \$2,500$$

Because this represents interest that would be paid three months later at maturity of the instrument, the actual payment is discounted at the prevailing three-month LIBOR:

$$\text{Actual interest} = \$2,500/[1 + (90/360).08] = \$2,451$$

Suppose, instead, that LIBOR equals 5 percent in three months. Here, County Bank would pay Metro Bank:

$$\text{Interest} = (.07 - .05)(90/360)\$1,000,000 = \$5,000$$

or

$$\$5,000/[1 + (90/360).05] = \$4,938$$

In this example, County Bank would pay fixed-rate/receive floating-rate as a hedge if it was exposed to loss in a rising rate environment. This is analogous to a short futures position. Metro Bank would take its position as a hedge if it was exposed to loss in a falling (relative to forward rate) rate environment. This is analogous to a long futures position.

### POTENTIAL PROBLEMS WITH FRAs

While FRAs offer some attractive features, there are several problems with using them in practice. First, like all forward contracts, FRAs are essentially credit instruments. This arises from the possibility that you might not be paid when the counterparty owes you cash. There is no clearinghouse to guarantee performance and no daily marking-to-market or collateral that is posted. In the past, some counterparties have reneged on forward contracts, so each participant must gauge carefully the reputation and soundness of its counterparties. Second, it is sometimes difficult to find a specific counterparty that wants to take exactly the opposite position. Because every FRA is negotiated, the parties might want different notional principal amounts or have a different settlement date. Thus, transactions costs can be large. Finally, FRAs are not as liquid as many alternatives. If a party to an FRA wants to exit the position prior to settlement, it might assign the contract to another party. But this requires that some compensation be paid. If the counterparty agrees, it might directly cancel the agreement for a fee. Alternatively, it might take exactly the opposite position with the counterparty if available, and lose only the change in price between origination of the FRA and the exit date.

## BASIC INTEREST RATE SWAPS AS A RISK MANAGEMENT TOOL

Interest rate swaps originated in the Eurobond market in 1980, but have recently been one of the fastest growing off-balance sheet contracts in the world. Basic interest rate swaps are now widely used by financial institutions as hedging tools and as a means of creating synthetic balance sheet positions. This section documents the nature of swap transactions and demonstrates how financial institutions use them as a risk management tool.

### CHARACTERISTICS

A **basic**, or **plain vanilla**, interest rate swap is an agreement between two parties to exchange a series of cash flows based on a specified notional principal amount. One party makes payments based on a fixed interest rate and receives floating-rate payments, while the other party makes the floating-rate payments and receives the fixed-rate payments. The fixed rate is typically based on prevailing Treasury note and bond rates and is quoted on a semiannual bond equivalent basis assuming a 365-day year. The floating rate is typically quoted on a money market basis assuming a 360-day year. These rates are applied against the notional principal amount that is constant over the life of the swap.[11] Maturities range from six months to 30 years, with most swaps in the one- to ten-year range. In most swap transactions, a swap dealer makes a market in basic swaps and thus serves as an intermediary. As such, any party that wants to take a position can sign a master agreement with a swap dealer, which indicates the nature of the payment calculations, collateral requirements, and so on. The dealer takes the other side of the position. Thus, all transactions are effected through the dealer and any risks are manifested via the dealer's operations.

Exhibit 7.8 demonstrates how swap rates are quoted by a swap dealer. These data apply to basic interest rate swaps with three-month LIBOR as the floating rate for all contracts. This means that all swap parties either pay or receive three-month LIBOR versus a fixed rate that differs based on maturity. The first column indicates the term or maturity of the basic swap contract. The second column lists the prevailing U.S. Treasury spot rate with the same maturity as that for the swap. The third column represents the dealer's bid-offer spread relative to the prevailing Treasury rate. The final two columns provide the fixed rates for the different maturity swaps. The "bid" rates indicate the fixed rate that a swap party will receive if it pays three-month LIBOR. The "offer" rates indicate the fixed rate that a swap party will pay if it receives three-month LIBOR. The difference between the two represents the dealer's spread or profit potential.

---

[11]Amortizing and accreting swaps are available where the notional principal amount decreases and increases, respectively, over time.

| EXHIBIT 7.8 | Interest Rate Swap Dealer Quotes for Basic Swaps: Fixed-rate Versus Three-Month LIBOR, March 10, 2005 | | | |

| Term | U.S. Treasuries (%) | Swap Spreads (%) (Mid-Point) | Swap Rates (%) Bid | Swap Rates (%) Offer |
|---|---|---|---|---|
| 2 years | 3.63 | 41.5 | 4.04 | 4.05 |
| 3 years | 3.72 | 46.5 | 4.18 | 4.19 |
| 4 years | 3.81 | 50.5 | 4.30 | 4.33 |
| 5 years | 4.00 | 53.5 | 4.52 | 4.55 |
| 7 years | 4.16 | 56.5 | 4.71 | 4.74 |
| 10 years | 4.30 | 59.0 | 4.87 | 4.91 |
| 20 years | 4.51 | 64.0 | 5.13 | 5.17 |
| 30 years | 4.58 | 65.0 | 5.20 | 5.26 |

This example emphasizes the role of an intermediary in processing swaps. This intermediary may simply serve as an agent with no credit risk exposure, or as a dealer where it is a counterparty to each side of the transaction. As a dealer, the intermediary may enter into contracts without negotiating the other side of the swap and thus accept the risk of adverse rate changes. If it lays off the exposure to another counterparty, it hopes to earn the bid-offer spread. The intermediary's continuing role is to collect the interest payments and pay the difference to either party, depending on the contractual terms and the applicable interest rates. Today, many large commercial banks, invest-ment banks, and Federal Home Loan Banks serve as intermediaries.

Conceptually, a basic interest rate swap is a package of FRAs. As with FRAs, swap payments are netted and the notional principal never changes hands. Consider the following example using data for a two-year swap from Ex-hibit 7.8 based on three-month LIBOR as the floating rate. This swap involves eight quarterly payments. Party FIX agrees to pay a fixed rate and Party FLT agrees to receive a fixed rate with cash flows calculated against a $10 mil-lion notional principal amount. The following rates apply:

| | | |
|---|---|---|
| Party FIX: | Pay: 4.05% | Receive: three-month LIBOR |
| Party FLT: | Pay: three-month LIBOR | Receive: 4.04% |

Exhibit 7.9 presents a time line with the expected cash flows from these two positions. Note that there are eight valuation dates representing the eight successive three-month periods. Suppose that three-month LIBOR for the first pricing interval equals 3 percent and there are 91 days in the three-month period. The fixed payment for Party FIX is $100,973 and the floating rate receipt is $75,833 as calculated at the bottom of the exhibit. With netting and the swap dealer as the counterparty, Party FIX will have to pay the dealer the difference of $25,140. Assuming that Party FLT took the other side of this swap through the dealer, its floating-rate payment is $75,833 while its fixed-rate receipt is $100,723. Thus, Party FLT will receive the difference of $24,890 from the swap dealer. Of course, the dealer will net $250 from the spread, which will be constant across all floating-rate changes as long as the two par-ties meet the swap terms. At the second and subsequent pricing intervals, only the applicable LIBOR is not known. As LIBOR changes, the amount that both Party FIX and Party FLT either pay or receive will change. We will dis-cuss more about swap pricing later, but note for now that Party FIX will only receive cash at any pricing interval if three-month LIBOR exceeds 4.05 percent. Party FLT will similarly receive cash as long as three-month LIBOR is less than 4.04 percent. This emphasizes that the swap is a series of FRAs with each valuation date representing a distinct FRA with a different maturity.

Swaps represent another means for firms facing mismatched assets and liabilities to microhedge or macro-hedge, or for firms that want to increase risk to adjust their earnings sensitivity in the desired way. Initially, only firms involved in the international money and capital markets used swaps, and virtually all transactions were priced in terms of LIBOR. More recently, medium-sized firms with only domestic operations have begun using swaps with many different rates—Wall Street prime, the federal funds rate, commercial paper rate, and T-bill rate—used to determine the underlying floating-rate payment obligations.

In its classic form, a plain vanilla swap arose when two firms faced substantially different interest rate risk over the same period. One firm was a high-quality borrower while the other exhibited greater perceived default risk. An interest rate swap was structured to take advantage of the perceived credit-quality differences by using the high-quality borrower's reputation to lower each firm's borrowing cost and provide the preferred type of fixed-rate or

**EXHIBIT 7.9**

Cash Flows Associated with Basic Interest Rate Swap Positions

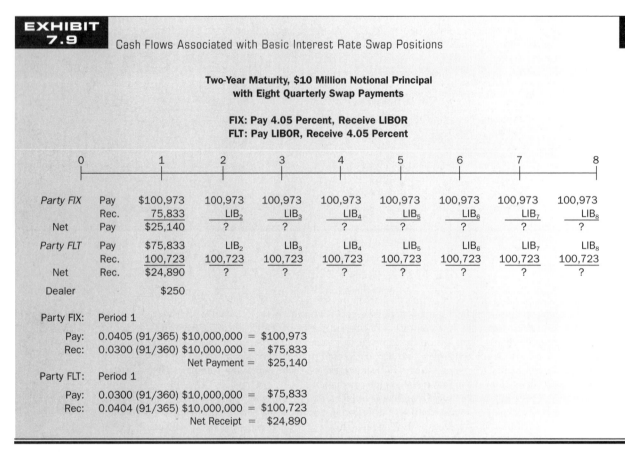

**Two-Year Maturity, $10 Million Notional Principal
with Eight Quarterly Swap Payments**

**FIX: Pay 4.05 Percent, Receive LIBOR
FLT: Pay LIBOR, Receive 4.05 Percent**

| | | 0 | 1 | 2 | 3 | 4 | 5 | 6 | 7 | 8 |
|---|---|---|---|---|---|---|---|---|---|---|
| *Party FIX* | Pay | $100,973 | 100,973 | 100,973 | 100,973 | 100,973 | 100,973 | 100,973 | 100,973 |
| | Rec. | 75,833 | $LIB_2$ | $LIB_3$ | $LIB_4$ | $LIB_5$ | $LIB_6$ | $LIB_7$ | $LIB_8$ |
| Net | Pay | $25,140 | ? | ? | ? | ? | ? | ? | ? |
| *Party FLT* | Pay | $75,833 | $LIB_2$ | $LIB_3$ | $LIB_4$ | $LIB_5$ | $LIB_6$ | $LIB_7$ | $LIB_8$ |
| | Rec. | 100,723 | 100,723 | 100,723 | 100,723 | 100,723 | 100,723 | 100,723 | 100,723 |
| Net | Rec. | $24,890 | ? | ? | ? | ? | ? | ? | ? |
| Dealer | | $250 | | | | | | | |

Party FIX: Period 1

Pay: 0.0405 (91/365) $10,000,000 = $100,973
Rec: 0.0300 (91/360) $10,000,000 = $75,833
$\qquad\qquad\qquad$ Net Payment = $25,140

Party FLT: Period 1

Pay: 0.0300 (91/360) $10,000,000 = $75,833
Rec: 0.0404 (91/365) $10,000,000 = $100,723
$\qquad\qquad\qquad$ Net Receipt = $24,890

NOTE: The notation LIB refers to three-month LIBOR, with the subscript denoting the period for which the applicable floating LIBOR applies.

floating-rate financing. In today's environment, these quality spread differentials have largely disappeared with the enormous growth in swap usage.

**ADJUST THE RATE SENSITIVITY OF AN ASSET OR LIABILITY.** The most common use of basic swaps is to adjust the rate sensitivity of a specific asset or liability. This may involve making a fixed-rate loan a floating-rate loan, converting a floating-rate liability to a fixed-rate liability, and so forth. Consider a bank that makes a $1 million, three-year fixed-rate loan with quarterly interest at 8 percent. It finances the loan by issuing a three-month Eurodollar deposit priced at three-month LIBOR. The following T-account demonstrates the transaction.

| Asset | Liability |
|---|---|
| Loan: $1 million, three-year maturity | three-month Eurodollar deposit: $1 million |
| Rate: 8% fixed | Rate: three-month LIBOR floating |

By itself, this transaction exhibits considerable interest rate risk because the bank will see its net interest income shrink if it continues to roll over the three-month deposit at each maturity date and LIBOR increases. The bank is liability sensitive and loses (gains) if LIBOR rises (falls). The bank can, however, use a basic swap to microhedge this transaction. Using the data from Exhibit 7.8 for a three-year basic swap, the bank could agree to pay 4.19 percent and receive three-month LIBOR against $1 million for the three years. By matching this with its continuous issuance of three-month Eurodollars after earlier ones mature, it locks in a borrowing cost of 4.19 percent because it will both receive and pay LIBOR every quarter.[12]

---

[12]The bank is accepting credit risk in the sense that if the market perceives that it is riskier over time and demands a risk premium on its future Eurodollar borrowings, it may pay more than three-month LIBOR for the subsequent deposits.

### Net Effect of Balance Sheet Transaction + Swap

| | |
|---|---|
| Receive: | 8.00% from loan + three-month LIBOR from swap |
| Pay: | three-month LIBOR from Eurodollar deposit + 4.19% from swap |
| Net spread: | 3.81% |

The use of the swap enables the bank to reduce risk and lock in a spread of 3.81 percent (8.00 percent − 4.19 percent) on this transaction. The swap effectively fixed the borrowing cost at 4.19 percent for three years.

Consider another example where a bank has a commercial customer who demands a fixed-rate loan. The bank has a policy of making only floating-rate loans because it is liability sensitive and does not want to take on additional interest rate risk. Ideally, the bank wants to price the loan based on prime. Suppose that the bank makes the same $1 million, three-year fixed-rate loan as in the above case. It could enter into a three-year basic swap involving prime as the floating-rate versus a fixed-rate. Assume that it enters into such a swap with a $1 million notional principal amount, agreeing to pay a 4.19 percent fixed rate and receive prime minus 2.20 percent with quarterly payments. As indicated below, the effective interest rate received is now a floating rate equal to prime plus 161 basis points:

| | **Loan** | **Basic Swap** |
|---|---|---|
| Receive: | 8.00% | Prime − 2.20% |
| Pay: | | 4.19% |
| Net receipt: | Prime + (8.00% − 2.20% − 4.19%) or Prime + 1.61% | |

This swap effectively converts a fixed-rate loan into a loan with a rate that floats with the prime rate.

**CREATE A SYNTHETIC SECURITY.** Some financial institutions view basic interest rate swaps as synthetic securities. As such, they enter into a swap contract that essentially replicates the net cash flows from a balance sheet transaction. For example, suppose that a bank buys a three-year Treasury yielding 3.72 percent (from Exhibit 7.8), which it finances by issuing a three-month deposit. This bank is liability sensitive in that it will see its net interest income from this combined trade fall if the cost of the three-month deposit rises over time. Many banks effectively finance securities with such deposits.

Consider, as an alternative, simply entering into a three-month swap agreeing to pay three-month LIBOR and receive a fixed rate. Per the data in Exhibit 7.8, the fixed swap rate is 4.18 percent or 46 basis points above the three-year Treasury rate. Interestingly, the swap produces a larger spread than the balance sheet transaction, yet has essentially the same interest rate risk profile. Why would management consider the balance sheet transaction as lower risk than the off-balance sheet swap? It does have to hold capital against the swap, albeit at a low percentage, and does not have to hold capital against the balance sheet position because it owns a zero-risk class asset.[13] If it no longer wanted to assume the risk, it also has the flexibility to alter its debt financing on-balance sheet at any time, and could reduce risk by issuing a longer-term deposit that matched the remaining maturity of the Treasury. Of course, the spread it earned afterward could be far different from that initially available. In contrast, it would have to exit the swap by selling its position, which might involve taking a loss. Management must determine whether the yield advantage of the swap outweighs these risks and costs.

**MACROHEDGE.** Banks can also use interest rate swaps to hedge their aggregate risk exposure measured by earnings and EVE sensitivity. The analysis is analogous to that with financial futures. Specifically, a bank that is liability sensitive or has a positive duration gap will take a basic swap position that potentially produces profits when rates increase. With a basic swap, this means paying a fixed rate and receiving a floating rate. Any profits can be used to offset losses from lost net interest income or declining EVE. This would have a comparable impact as shorting financial futures. In terms of GAP analysis, a liability-sensitive bank has more rate-sensitive liabilities than rate-sensitive assets (GAP < 0 indicates RSAs < RSLs). To hedge, the bank needs the equivalent of more RSAs. A swap that pays fixed and receives floating is comparable to increasing RSAs relative to RSLs because the receipt floats (reprices) with rate changes.

Similarly, any bank that is asset sensitive or has a negative duration gap and wants to hedge will take a swap position that potentially produces profits when rates fall. With a basic swap, this means paying a floating rate and receiving a fixed rate. If rates fall, net interest income and EVE will fall, but the swap would likely produce a gain to offset at least part of the loss. This would have the same impact as going long on financial futures. In terms of GAP analysis, an asset-sensitive bank has more rate-sensitive assets than rate-sensitive liabilities (RSAs > RSLs). To hedge, the bank needs the equivalent of more RSLs. A swap that pays a floating rate and receives a fixed rate is comparable in impact to increasing RSLs relative to RSAs.

---

[13]Risk-based capital requirements for banks are introduced in Chapter 9. Generally, banks are not required to hold capital against cash and Treasury securities that have no default risk.

Many banks report their aggregate use of interest rate swaps in their rate-sensitivity reports, and thus the aggregate impact on the banks' overall interest rate sensitivity. Such treatment allows the analyst to assess, in general, whether management uses swaps to increase or decrease overall risk. Consider the data for ABC bank from Exhibit 5.7 in Chapter 5, which presents the rate sensitivity report for year-end 2005. Note the data in the third row from the bottom of the exhibit titled "Swaps: Pay Fixed/Receive Floating." These data are summary figures that indicate the aggregate impact of ABC Bank's use of swaps across different time intervals. Under the column of rate sensitive assets and liabilities for three months or less, the figure is $50,000. To determine what this figure represents, note that the bank's periodic GAP for this interval prior to the swaps' impact would have equaled –$70,252 ($278,748 − $349,000). After the swaps, the periodic GAP was −$20,252. Thus, the swaps had the equivalent effect of adding $50,000 in rate-sensitive assets within this time interval. Conceptually, ABC paid a fixed rate and received a floating rate on a $50,000 notional principal to move the periodic GAP over this interval closer to zero so that the use of swaps represented a macrohedge. The corresponding impact from one to three years and three to five years also represented a hedge.

## PRICING BASIC SWAPS

The pricing of basic interest rate swaps is straightforward. Consider the time line in Exhibit 7.9. The floating rate, such as three-month LIBOR in the example, is based on some predetermined money market rate or index. The payment frequency is coincidentally set at every six months, three months, or one month, and is generally matched with the money market rate. The fixed rate is set at a spread above the comparable maturity Treasury note rate. For swap maturities out to five years, the swap or dealer spread is priced based on the implied yields on a strip of Eurodollar futures contracts for the same maturities. Beyond five years, the swap or dealer spread is priced based on risk premiums associated with matched maturity/duration corporate notes and bonds. These conventions are widely recognized, which makes the valuation of swaps straightforward.

For example, the earlier discussion assumed that the applicable LIBOR for the first pricing date three months from the present in Exhibit 7.9 was 3 percent, which equals the current three-month LIBOR rate. The implied three-month LIBOR yield for the second pricing date, six months from the present (LIB2), would be the futures rate on a three-month Eurodollar futures contract that expires three months from the present. The other implied three-month LIBOR rates ($LIB_3$, $LIB_4$, etc.) are similarly assumed to be the subsequent three-month Eurodollar futures rates that represent successive futures expiration dates. In terms of Exhibit 7.9, Party FIX and Party FLT presumably did not know what LIBOR would be on these valuation dates. Neither would enter into the contract if it expected, a priori, to lose on the transaction. The implication is that a basic swap is priced as a zero net present value transaction. This means that after substituting an expected value for LIBOR at each of the eight valuation dates, the present value of the net cash flows (netted payments and receipts) must equal zero. In essence, the fixed rate that is quoted to each party (actually, the midpoint of the two fixed rates), represents the rate that produces a zero net present value for the assumed net cash flows. Given the expected values for LIBOR read off the matched maturity Eurodollar futures contracts, the spreads over Treasury rates are determined as the markups necessary to make a swap's net present value equal zero.

## COMPARING FINANCIAL FUTURES, FRAS, AND BASIC SWAPS

There are many similarities among interest rate swaps, financial futures, and FRAs. Each different contract enables a party to enter an agreement, which provides for cash receipts or cash payments depending on how interest rates move. Each allows managers to alter a bank's interest rate risk exposure. None requires much of an initial cash commitment to take a position. The following table compares the positions with specific objectives:

| | Position | |
| Objective | Financial Futures | FRAs & Basic Swaps |
| --- | --- | --- |
| Profit if rates rise | Sell futures | Pay fixed, receive floating |
| Profit if rates fall | Buy futures | Pay floating, receive fixed |

There are also several key differences. First, financial futures are standardized contracts based on fixed principal amounts. Parties negotiate the notional principal amount with FRAs and interest rate swaps. Financial futures require daily marking-to-market, which is not required with FRAs and swaps. This exposes futures participants to some risk and liquidity requirements that FRAs and swaps avoid. Many futures contracts cannot be traded out more than three to four years, while interest rate swaps often extend ten to 30 years. The market for FRAs is not that liquid and most contracts are short term. Historically, trading activity was much deeper with futures such that liquidity, especially for the nearby contracts, was far greater. Swap activity has recently grown to where participants can readily buy and sell swaps in a secondary market and thus exit a position when needed. This is especially true because of the consensus on how to value basic swaps using Eurodollar futures rates. Finally, swap documentation is quite standardized and participating firms can negotiate master agreements with partners that enhance the development of long-term business relationships.

## THE RISK WITH SWAPS

While interest swaps are an alternative to futures and FRAs, they also entail risks. The recent experience of savings and loans is an example. When interest rates increased sharply during the early 1980s, many thrifts took advantage of interest rate swaps to obtain fixed-rate financing. When mortgage rates averaged 13 to 14 percent, it seemed reasonable to fix borrowing costs at 11 percent. Unfortunately for these swap players, the level of interest rates moved dramatically lower in the mid-1980s. Had thrifts waited, they could have paid much lower rates on both fixed-rate and floating-rate debt. Thus, they locked in much higher fixed interest expense for the benefit of risk reduction. The problems were compounded as homeowners took advantage of the lower rates to refinance their mortgages. In many instances, thrifts lost their high yielding, fixed-rate assets via prepayments but kept their fixed-rate interest obligations. Selling the swap obligations to a third party prior to expiration would have produced a direct income statement loss.

Similar problems arose with Long-Term Capital Management's use of swaps in 1998. This hedge fund made speculative bets that different interest rates would converge (equal the same value) over time. Because they were confident in their bet, management used swaps to increase the leverage of their position. When interest rates subsequently moved in different directions, losses on the swaps and other positions virtually depleted the firm's capital and it had to be bailed out by a consortium of financial institutions.

Market participants have developed a secondary market for swaps to reduce a firm's exposure to swap positions that it might want to exit. Straightforward plain vanilla swaps follow a standardized format stipulated by terms of the International Swap Dealers Agreement such that positions can be quickly entered and exited. The standardized features have made it easy to trade these swaps in the secondary market. Unfortunately, the more complicated is a swap, the more difficult it is to trade the swap in the secondary market. Each swap is a negotiated contract between two parties. When the terms are unusual, the attractiveness decreases in the secondary market because the buyer must carefully analyze and price the unusual features of the underlying swap. Without guarantees or easily identifiable default risk, the liquidity of swaps diminishes. Such swaps, particularly those with options and other nonstandardized terms, are not as readily marketable.

There is some credit risk with swaps as well, but this is not as great for a single contract as it originally seems. Remember that swap parties exchange only net interest payments. The notional principal amount never changes hands, such that a party will not lose that amount. Credit risk exists because the counterparty to a swap contract may default. This is a problem when interest rates have moved against the counterparty and you are owed money. Suppose that you have agreed to pay LIBOR and receive 7 percent with semiannual payments for three years. If LIBOR is above 7 percent, you must pay the counterparty such that the counterparty owes you nothing. The counterparty is concerned with your ability to pay. You accept counterparty risk when LIBOR is below 7 percent. This risk is generally associated with the swap dealer's credit standing. When either counterparty perceives that there is a meaningful probability that the other counterparty may not perform under a swap, it will require collateral in support of the swap position. The existence and value of the collateral, in turn, affect the prices that intermediaries charge for making a market in swaps. These collateral arrangements are commonly part of bilateral collateral agreements that counterparties sign when they enter the swap market. The value of the required collateral, in turn, often rises and falls with changes in the ongoing (mark-to-market) value of the swap position.

Counterparty risk is extremely important to swap participants. Firms that are actively engaged in swap transactions often limit the amount of swap business they will do with any single counterparty to limit their risk exposure. Banks should have such policy limits approved by the board of directors before entering into swap contracts.

# INTEREST RATE CAPS AND FLOORS

In addition to futures, FRAs and swaps, banks can hedge interest rate exposure through the use of caps and floors on interest rates. Caps and floors are options on interest rates such that participants either buy the option or sell the option. The appropriate position depends on the nature of the risk exposure the bank wants to hedge, or its speculative bet on future interest rate movements.

## BUYING AN INTEREST RATE CAP

An **interest rate cap** is an agreement between two counterparties that limits the buyer's interest rate exposure to a maximum rate. An **interest rate floor** is an agreement between two counterparties that limits the buyer's interest rate exposure to a minimum rate. Buying a cap is actually the purchase of a call option on an interest rate. Buying a floor is actually the purchase of a put option on an interest rate.

**EXHIBIT 7.10** Buying a Cap on Three-Month LIBOR at 4 Percent

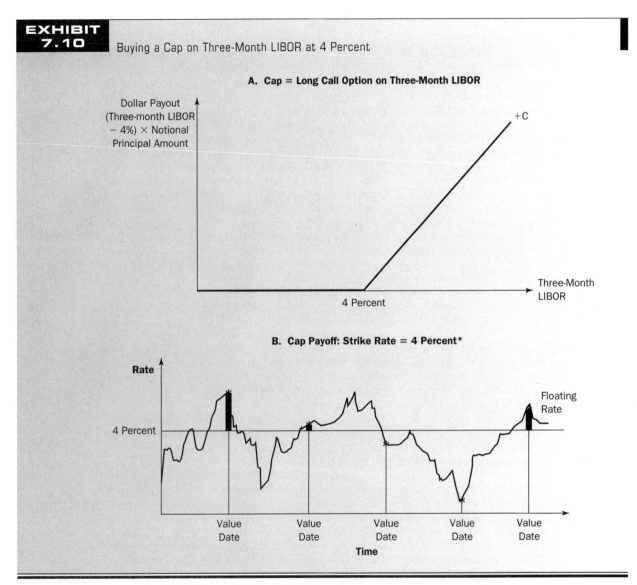

**A. Cap = Long Call Option on Three-Month LIBOR**

Dollar Payout (Three-month LIBOR − 4%) × Notional Principal Amount

+C

4 Percent

Three-Month LIBOR

**B. Cap Payoff: Strike Rate = 4 Percent\***

Rate

4 Percent

Floating Rate

Value Date   Value Date   Value Date   Value Date   Value Date

Time

\*Payoff at Value Date equals prevailing (LIBOR − 4 percent) × Notional Principal Amount.

When trading interest rate caps or floors, a participant selects a floating-rate index, a term to maturity, a strike (exercise) rate, the frequency of value dates when cash payments are made, and a notional principal amount. Depending on prevailing economic conditions these choices determine the price (premium) at which the option trades.

Consider the two diagrams in Exhibit 7.10. Section A characterizes the payoff diagram for the purchase of a 4 percent cap on three-month LIBOR. It is the same as a long call option position.[14] An interest rate cap has a maturity and periodic valuation dates, a notional principal amount, and a strike rate that is based on some reference interest rate. The buyer of a cap pays a one-time up-front premium and receives a cash payment from the seller of the cap equal to three-month LIBOR minus 4 percent multiplied by some notional principal amount on each valuation date, with no payment made if LIBOR is below 4 percent. Formally, the payoff is the maximum of zero or three-month LIBOR minus 4 percent times the notional principal amount. Thus, if three-month LIBOR exceeds 4 percent, the buyer receives cash from the seller, and nothing otherwise. At maturity, the cap expires. These payoffs are indicated in Section B of Exhibit 7.10.

---

[14]Formally, a single call option on an interest rate is referred to as a caplet. An interest rate cap is actually a series of caplets at the same strike rate.

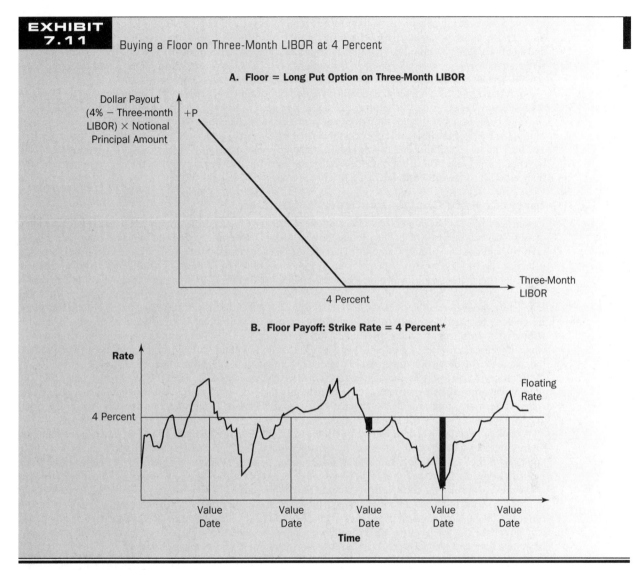

**EXHIBIT 7.11** Buying a Floor on Three-Month LIBOR at 4 Percent

**A. Floor = Long Put Option on Three-Month LIBOR**

Dollar Payout
(4% − Three-month
LIBOR) × Notional
Principal Amount

+P

4 Percent

Three-Month LIBOR

**B. Floor Payoff: Strike Rate = 4 Percent\***

Rate

4 Percent

Floating Rate

Value Date   Value Date   Value Date   Value Date   Value Date

Time

*Payoff at Value Date equals prevailing (4 percent − LIBOR) × Notional Principal Amount.

Consider a cap on three-month LIBOR at 4 percent based on a $100 million notional principal amount. If LIBOR equals 4.63 percent on the first valuation date and ignoring compounding, the buyer would receive $157,500 (0.0063/4 × $100 million) from the cap seller. If LIBOR is 3.95 percent on the second valuation date, the buyer would receive zero. The obligated payment is a rate differential times the notional principal amount, or zero.

An **interest rate cap** is a series of consecutive long call options (caplets) on a specific interest rate at the same strike rate. The buyer selects an interest rate index, such as three-month LIBOR, the prime rate, one-month commercial paper rate, T-bill rate or the federal funds rate, a maturity over which the contract will be in place, a strike (exercise) rate that represents the cap rate, and a notional principal amount. By paying an up-front premium, the buyer then locks in this cap on the underlying interest rate.

The benefits of buying a cap are similar to those of buying any option. The bank as buyer of a cap can set a maximum (cap) rate on its borrowing costs. It can also convert a fixed-rate loan to a floating-rate loan. In this context, it gets protection from increasing rates and retains the benefits if rates fall. The primary negative to the buyer is that a cap requires an up-front premium payment. If the buyer wants a cap that is at the money or in the money in a rising rate environment, the premium can be high.

## BUYING AN INTEREST RATE FLOOR

A buyer can also establish a minimum interest rate by buying a floor on an interest rate index. Consider the diagrams in Exhibit 7.11. Section A presents the payoff diagram for buying a 4 percent floor on three-month

LIBOR.[15] Note that the diagram is similar to that for a long put option position. As indicated, the buyer of the floor receives a cash payment equal to the greater of zero or the product of 4 percent minus three-month LIBOR and a notional principal amount. Thus, if three-month LIBOR exceeds 4 percent, the buyer of a floor at 4 percent receives nothing. The buyer is paid only if three-month LIBOR is less than 4 percent. This payoff pattern is indicated in Section B of Exhibit 7.11.

An interest rate floor is a series of consecutive floorlets at the same strike rate. The buyer of an interest rate floor selects an index, with LIBOR, the prime rate, commercial paper rate, T-bill rate, and federal funds rate again the most popular; a maturity for the agreement, a strike rate, and a notional principal amount. By paying a premium, the buyer of the floor, or series of floorlets, has established a minimum rate on its interest rate exposure. The benefits are again those of any long option. A floor protects against falling interest rates while retaining the benefits of rising rates. The primary negative is that the premium may be high on an at the money or in the money floor, especially if the consensus forecast is that interest rates will fall in the future.

## INTEREST RATE COLLAR AND REVERSE COLLAR

In some cases, banks buy interest rate collars or reverse collars. The purchase of an **interest rate collar** is actually the simultaneous purchase of an interest rate cap and sale of an interest rate floor on the same index for the same maturity and notional principal amount. The cap rate is set above the floor rate. The objective of the buyer of a collar is to protect against rising interest rates. The purchase of the cap protects against rising rates while the sale of the floor generates premium income. The motivation for selling the floor is typically to provide income that reduces the cost of the cap. If the index rate rises above the cap, the buyer receives cash from the counterparty equal to the difference between the index rate and the cap (strike) rate. Of course, if the index rate falls below the floor, the collar buyer pays the counterparty the difference between the floor (strike) rate and the reference rate. With falling rates, the buyer of a collar gives up any potential gain from the position. A collar creates a band within which the buyer's effective interest rate fluctuates. The buyer is willing to accept a minimum floor rate to reduce the cost of the cap protection or because of a strong belief that rates will rise and the view that the floor will be out of the money. A *zero cost collar* is designed to establish a collar where the buyer has no net premium payment. This requires choosing different cap and floor rates such that the premiums are equal. The benefit is the same as any collar with zero up-front cost. The negative is that the band within which the index rate fluctuates is typically small and the buyer gives up any real gain from falling rates.

A bank can also buy a **reverse collar**. This refers to buying an interest rate floor and simultaneously selling an interest rate cap. The objective is to protect the bank from falling interest rates. The buyer selects the index rate and matches the maturity and notional principal amounts for the floor and cap. The strike rates differ. If the index rate falls below the floor, the buyer of a reverse collar receives cash from the counterparty. If the index rate rises above the cap, the buyer makes a cash payment to the counterparty. The motivation for selling the cap is typically to reduce the cost of buying a floor. The net result is that the buyer's interest rate fluctuates within a band. The buyer is willing to accept a maximum rate to reduce the cost of the floor or because it has a strong belief that rates will fall and the cap will be out of the money. Buyers can again construct zero cost reverse collars when it is possible to find floor and cap rates with the same premiums that provide an acceptable band.

One of the most important considerations when evaluating whether to buy caps and floors is the premium cost. Exhibit 7.12 provides summary information for the premiums on various caps and floors on three-month LIBOR in March 2005. The top part of the exhibit provides the bid and offer premiums for caps and floors at different strike rates. The first column of data in each section indicates the term for the underlying caps and floors. Subsequent columns indicate the premiums. For the caps, the strike rates are 4, 5, and 6 percent. For the floors, the strike rates are 1.5, 2., and 2.5 percent. The bid premium represents what the option seller receives while the offer premium represents what the option buyer pays. At the time of these quotes, the cash market three-month LIBOR equaled 3 percent. The three-month Eurodollar futures rates in Exhibit 7.1 indicate the consensus forecast that three-month LIBOR will rise over time.

The size of these premiums is determined by a wide range of factors. First, the relationship between the strike rate and the prevailing three-month LIBOR indicates how much LIBOR has to move before the cap or floor is in the money. Specifically, the premiums are highest for in the money and at the money options and lower for out of the money options. With the prevailing LIBOR at 3 percent, a floor or cap at 3 percent are at the money. All the floors and all the caps listed in Exhibit 7.12 are out of the money. The premiums for the 3 percent strike rate will be the highest for the floors because it has an intrinsic value of zero basis points (3 percent strike rate − 3 percent LIBOR) and any decline in LIBOR immediately increases the expected cash receipts. LIBOR must fall considerably, however, before the 1.5 percent floor is in the money such that the premiums are the lowest. For the interest rate caps listed, the premium on the 4 percent strike rate will be highest because LIBOR has to rise the least

---

[15]Formally, a single floor option on an interest rate is referred to as a floorlet. An interest rate floor is actually a series of floorlets at the same strike rate.

*Interest Rate Caps and Floors*

### EXHIBIT 7.12   Premiums for Interest Rate Caps and Floors on Three-Month LIBOR

**A. Caps/Floors**

| Term | Bid | Offer | Bid | Offer | Bid | Offer |
|---|---|---|---|---|---|---|
| Caps | **4.00%** | | **5.00%** | | **6.00%** | |
| 1 year | 24 | 30 | 3 | 7 | 1 | 2 |
| 2 years | 51 | 57 | 36 | 43 | 10 | 15 |
| 3 years | 105 | 115 | 74 | 84 | 22 | 29 |
| 5 years | 222 | 240 | 135 | 150 | 76 | 5 |
| 7 years | 413 | 433 | 201 | 324 | 101 | 116 |
| 10 years | 549 | 573 | 278 | 308 | 157 | 197 |
| Floors | **1.50%** | | **2.00%** | | **2.50%** | |
| 1 year | 1 | 2 | 15 | 19 | 31 | 35 |
| 2 years | 1 | 6 | 31 | 37 | 64 | 71 |
| 3 years | 7 | 16 | 40 | 49 | 88 | 97 |
| 5 years | 24 | 39 | 75 | 88 | 150 | 165 |
| 7 years | 38 | 60 | 92 | 106 | 188 | 210 |
| 10 years | 85 | 115 | 162 | 192 | 227 | 257 |

NOTE: Caps/Floors are based on three-month LIBOR; up-front costs in basis points. Figures in bold print represent strike rates.

(100 basis points) before the buyer receives a cash payment. With higher strike rates, LIBOR has to increase sharply before the buyer will receive cash. Note, however, that the Eurodollar futures rates in Exhibit 7.1 indicate an expected increase in rates above 4 percent in December 2005 and over 5 percent by June 2009. Not surprisingly, the premiums increase with maturity. This reflects the fact that an option seller must be compensated more for committing to a fixed-rate cap or floor for a longer period of time.

Finally, prevailing economic conditions influence premiums via the shape of the associated yield curve and the volatility of interest rates. If the yield curve for Eurodollars is upsloping such that the consensus is that LIBOR will rise in the future, caps will be more expensive than floors. The steeper is the slope of the yield curve, ceteris paribus, the greater are the cap premiums. If the yield curve is flat or inverted, caps will be relatively inexpensive. Floor premiums, in contrast, reveal the opposite relationship. The steeper is the yield curve, the cheaper are floor premiums. If the yield curve is inverted, floor premiums will be relatively expensive. Like all options, the greater is the volatility of rates, the higher will be premiums because there is a greater likelihood that the options may move in the money. Finally, regardless of intrinsic value, maturity, and yield curve shape, a dealer in caps and floors will typically charge a higher premium for substantial positions in large notional principal amounts.

## PROTECTING AGAINST FALLING INTEREST RATES

Assume that your bank is asset sensitive such that the bank's net interest income will decrease if interest rates fall. Essentially the bank holds loans priced at prime plus 1 percent and funds the loans with a three-year fixed-rate deposit at 3.75 percent. The management team has a strong belief that interest rates will fall over the next three years. It is considering three alternative approaches to reduce risk associated with falling rates: 1) entering into a basic interest rate swap to pay three-month LIBOR and receive a fixed rate; 2) buying an interest rate floor; and 3) buying a reverse collar. Exhibits 7.13, 7.14, and 7.15 summarize the net results of each position when rates alternatively fall and rise relative to the current environment. Note that initially, the bank holds assets priced based on prime and deposits priced based on a fixed 3.75% rate. For this example, the LIBOR and the prime rate are assumed to be perfectly correlated.

Exhibit 7.13 compares the results using a basic interest rate swap where the bank agrees to pay three-month LIBOR and receive 4.18 percent for a three-year term. There are three interest rate scenarios where rates are constant and rise or fall by 1 percent. Initially, the prime rate equals 5.50 percent and LIBOR equals 3 percent, which generates a spread of 2.75 percent for the loans versus the fixed-rate deposits. With rates constant at these levels, the net cash flow from the swap produces an inflow of 118 basis points for a net interest margin of 3.93 percent, as

**EXHIBIT 7.13**

Using a Basic Swap to Hedge Aggregate Balance Sheet Risk of Loss from Falling Rates

**Bank Swap Terms: Pay LIBOR, Receive 4.18 Percent***

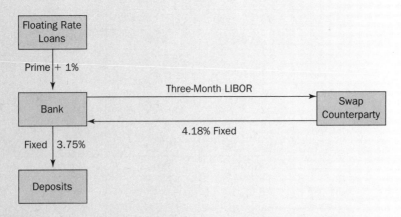

| | Current Rates Constant | Rates Fall 100 Basis Points | Rates Rise 100 Basis Points |
|---|---|---|---|
| | PRIME 5.50% LIBOR 3.00% | PRIME 4.50% LIBOR 2.00% | PRIME 6.50% LIBOR 4.00% |
| **Balance Sheet Flows:** | | | |
| Loan | 6.50% | 5.50% | 7.50% |
| Deposit | (3.75%) | (3.75%) | (3.75%) |
| Spread | 2.75% | 1.75% | 3.75% |
| **Interest Rate Swap Flows:** | | | |
| Fixed | 4.18% | 4.18% | 4.18% |
| Floating | (3.00%) | (2.00%) | (4.00%) |
| Spread | 1.18% | 2.18% | 0.18% |
| **Margin** | 3.93% | 3.93% | 3.93% |

*Assume swap term is three years and perfect correlation between PRIME and LIBOR.

indicated in the first column of data. Examine the second and third columns of data where floating rates are assumed to fall and rise from initial levels. Given the assumed perfect correlation between prime and LIBOR, this margin is constant at 3.93 percent whether rates either fall or rise by 1 percent. This occurs because any reduction in the spread when prime falls to 4.50 percent is offset by the gain on the swap as LIBOR falls to 2 percent. Similarly, any gain in spread as prime rises to 6.50 percent is offset by a reduction in the swap receipt as LIBOR rises to 4 percent. The use of the swap effectively fixed the spread near the current level, except for basis risk.

Exhibit 7.14 summarizes the outcomes from hedging by buying a floor with a three-year maturity on three-month LIBOR at a 2.50 strike rate. The up-front premium is 88 basis points represented by a 30 basis point annual amortization. At current interest rates indicated in the first column of data, the balance sheet interest spread is 2.75 percent, which produces a net interest margin of 2.45 percent after subtracting the 30 basis point cost of the floor premium. If rates fall 1 percent as noted in the second column of data, the spread falls to 1.75 percent, but the floor on LIBOR generates a cash receipt of 30 basis points. Thus, the net interest margin is 1.95 percent. If rates rise 1 percent as in the third column of data, the spread widens and the floor falls out of the money such that the margin increases to 3.45 percent. This demonstrates the impact of options on hedge results. If rates fall and the floor is in the

| EXHIBIT 7.14 | Buying a Floor on Three-Month LIBOR to Hedge Aggregate Balance Sheet Risk of Loss from Falling Rates |
|---|---|

**Floor Terms: Buy a 2.50 Percent Floor on Three-Month LIBOR\***

```
        Floating Rate
           Loans

         Prime + 1%
              ↓
                              Receive when
           Bank    ◄────  Three-Month LIBOR < 2.50%  ────   Counterparty

                                                            Fee: (0.30%) per year
         Fixed   3.75%
              ↓

          Deposits
```

|  | Current Rates Constant | Rates Fall 100 Basis Points | Rates Rise 100 Basis Points |
|---|---|---|---|
|  | PRIME 5.50% | PRIME 4.50% | PRIME 6.50% |
|  | LIBOR 3.00% | LIBOR 2.00% | LIBOR 4.00% |
| **Balance Sheet Flows:** |  |  |  |
| Loan | 6.50% | 5.50% | 7.50% |
| Deposit | (3.75%) | (3.75%) | (3.75%) |
| Spread | 2.75% | 1.75% | 3.75% |
| **Floor Flows:** |  |  |  |
| Payout | 0.00% | 0.50% | 0.00% |
| Fee Amort. | (0.30%) | (0.30%) | (0.30%) |
| Spread | (0.30%) | 0.20% | (0.30%) |
| **Margin** | 2.45% | 1.95% | 3.45% |

\*Assume floor term is three years and perfect correlation between PRIME and LIBOR.

money, the increase in option value offsets the loss in the spread position. If rates rise, the option expires worthless, but the value of the cash spread increases. The bank retains benefits from rising rates. The bank is best served if cash market rates move favorably and the floor expires worthless. The floor buyer is protected when bad things (rate declines) happen, but retains the benefit of favorable (rate increases) rate movements. The buyer does not want to collect on the insurance. Note that the more rates increase, the higher is the margin for the bank. As such, there is no limit to the upside from this hedged position, unlike the swap hedge that fixed the outcome.

Exhibit 7.15 documents the outcomes from simultaneously buying a floor on three-month LIBOR at 2 percent and selling a cap on three-month LIBOR at 3.50 percent. This reverse collar protects the bank from falling rates but provides a band within which the effective interest margin will fluctuate. The sale of the cap generates a net premium receipt of 95 basis points up front, represented by an annual 38 basis point amortization of premium. At prevailing rates indicated in the first column of data, the net interest margin is expected to be 3.13 percent characterized by the spread plus the 38 basis point premium amortization on the reverse collar. The 1 percent drop in rates summarized in the second column of data produces a net margin of 2.63 percent, whereby the 50 basis point receipt from the floor and premium amortization total of 88 basis points and reduce the loss from the 1 percent

**EXHIBIT 7.15**

Buying a Reverse Collar to Hedge Aggregate Balance Sheet Risk of Loss from Falling Rates

**Strategy: Buy a Floor on Three-Month LIBOR at 2.00 Percent, and Sell a Cap on Three-Month LIBOR at 3.50 Percent***

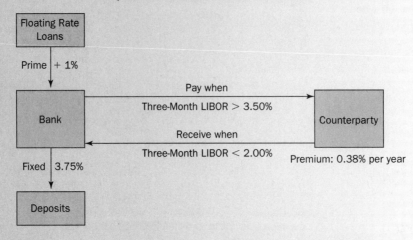

| | Current Rates Constant | Rates Fall 100 Basis Points | Rates Rise 100 Basis Points |
|---|---|---|---|
| | PRIME 5.50% LIBOR 3.00% | PRIME 4.50% LIBOR 2.00% | PRIME 6.50% LIBOR 4.00% |
| **Balance Sheet Flows:** | | | |
| Loan | 6.50% | 5.50% | 7.50% |
| Deposit | (3.75%) | (3.75%) | (3.75%) |
| Spread | 2.75% | 1.75% | 3.75% |
| **Reverse Collar Flows:** | | | |
| Payout | 0.00% | 0.50% | (0.50%) |
| Fee Amort. | 0.38% | 0.38% | 0.38% |
| Spread | 0.38% | 0.88% | (0.12%) |
| **Margin** | 3.13% | 2.63% | 3.63% |

*Assume collar term is three years and perfect correlation between PRIME and LIBOR.

decline in interest spread. When rates rise (third column of data) the spread widens, but the bank gives back part of the gain by paying 50 basis points on the cap that it sold. Given alternative rates, the bank's realized margin will fluctuate between 2.63 percent and 3.63 percent. Thus, the collar differs from a pure floor by eliminating some of the potential benefits in a rising rate environment. The bank actually receives a net premium up-front, however, rather than having to pay a premium from the outright purchase of a floor in this example.

## PROTECTING AGAINST RISING INTEREST RATES

Assume that a bank has made three-year fixed-rate term loans at 7 percent, funded via three-month Eurodollar deposits for which it pays the prevailing LIBOR minus 0.25 percent. The bank is liability sensitive because it is exposed to loss from rising interest rates. Exhibits 7.16, 7.17, and 7.18 describe the results from three strategies to hedge this risk: 1) enter a basic swap to pay 4.19 percent fixed-rate and receive three-month LIBOR; 2) buy a cap on three-month LIBOR with a 3.50 strike rate; and 3) buy a collar on three-month LIBOR.

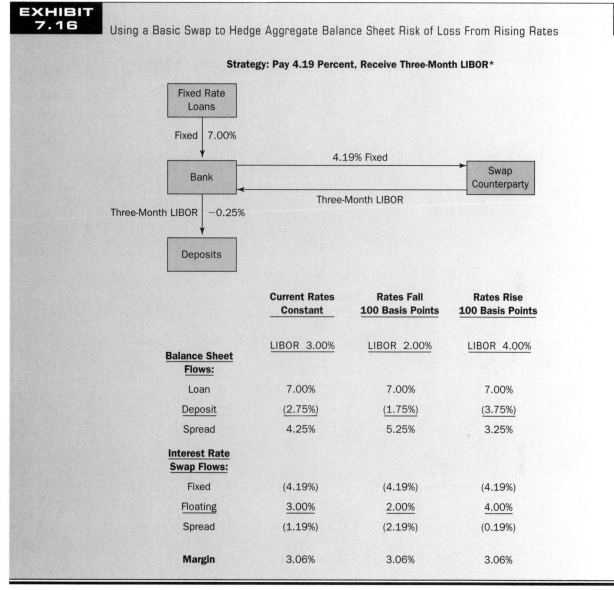

**EXHIBIT 7.16**  Using a Basic Swap to Hedge Aggregate Balance Sheet Risk of Loss From Rising Rates

**Strategy: Pay 4.19 Percent, Receive Three-Month LIBOR***

Fixed Rate Loans

Fixed | 7.00%

4.19% Fixed

Bank → Swap Counterparty

Three-Month LIBOR

Three-Month LIBOR | −0.25%

Deposits

|  | Current Rates Constant | Rates Fall 100 Basis Points | Rates Rise 100 Basis Points |
|---|---|---|---|
|  | LIBOR 3.00% | LIBOR 2.00% | LIBOR 4.00% |
| **Balance Sheet Flows:** |  |  |  |
| Loan | 7.00% | 7.00% | 7.00% |
| Deposit | (2.75%) | (1.75%) | (3.75%) |
| Spread | 4.25% | 5.25% | 3.25% |
| **Interest Rate Swap Flows:** |  |  |  |
| Fixed | (4.19%) | (4.19%) | (4.19%) |
| Floating | 3.00% | 2.00% | 4.00% |
| Spread | (1.19%) | (2.19%) | (0.19%) |
| **Margin** | 3.06% | 3.06% | 3.06% |

*Assume swap term is three years.

The use of the basic swap again effectively fixes a net interest margin. As demonstrated in the first column of data in Exhibit 7.16, the initial interest spread is 4.25 percent and the bank pays 119 basis points on the swap at prevailing rates. This produces a net spread of 3.06 percent. If LIBOR falls 1 percent, as noted in the second column of data, the interest spread widens to 5.25 percent but the bank pays out 2.19 percent on the swap. If LIBOR rises 1 percent as characterized in the third column of data, the spread narrows but the bank pays just 0.19 percent on the swap. The net spread or margin is the same—3.06 percent—in all cases. Obviously, the consensus forecast is for LIBOR to rise as participants would otherwise refuse to enter this swap with such a large payout if rates remained constant.

Buying a 3.50 percent cap allows the bank to potentially benefit if rates fall, but still protects against loss if rates rise. This is demonstrated in Exhibit 7.17. With an amortized premium cost of the cap at 50 basis points, the initial net interest margin equals 3.75 percent. This is summarized in the first column of data. The subsequent columns indicate the impact if rates vary from initial levels. If rates fall by 1 percent, the net margin increases to 4.75 percent because the interest spread widens and the cap cost remains fixed at 50 basis points. Each subsequent decline in LIBOR will be matched by an increase in the margin. Thus, the bank has unlimited upside in a falling

**EXHIBIT 7.17** Buy a Cap on Three-Month LIBOR to Hedge Balance Sheet Rate Risk of Loss from Rising Rates

**Strategy: Buy a Cap on Three-Month LIBOR at 4.00 Percent\***

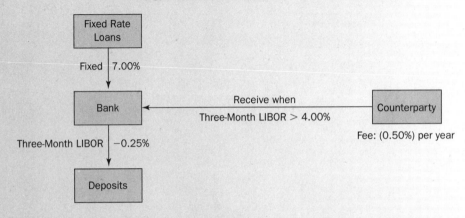

| | Current Rates Constant | Rates Fall 100 Basis Points | Rates Rise 100 Basis Points |
|---|---|---|---|
| | LIBOR 3.00% | LIBOR 2.00% | LIBOR 4.00% |
| **Balance Sheet Flows:** | | | |
| Loan | 7.00% | 7.00% | 7.00% |
| Deposit | (2.75%) | (1.75%) | (3.75%) |
| Spread | 4.25% | 5.25% | 3.25% |
| **Cap Flows:** | | | |
| Payout | 0.00% | 0.00% | 0.50% |
| Fee Amort. | (0.50%) | (0.50%) | (0.50%) |
| Spread | (0.50%) | (0.50%) | 0.00% |
| **Margin** | 3.75% | 4.75% | 3.25% |

\*Assume cap term is three years.

rate environment. If LIBOR rises 1 percent (column 3), the cap goes in the money. The interest spread declines consistent with the bank's risk exposure, but the cap position generates a payoff of 50 basis points. The net margin falls to 3.25 percent.

Exhibit 7.18 presents the outcomes from buying a collar on three-month LIBOR. The combined positions consist of buying a cap at 3 percent and simultaneously selling a floor at 2 percent. The bank thus receives cash if LIBOR rises above 3 percent, but must pay on the floor if LIBOR falls below 2 percent. This effectively creates a band within which the bank's margin will fluctuate. As noted in the three data columns of Exhibit 7.18, the band for the net spread is between 3.50 percent and 4.50 percent. The collar provides similar protection to the straight purchase of a cap, but gives up the potential benefits of falling rates because of the sale of a floor. The net margin declines with each decline in LIBOR. The cost of the collar is just 75 basis points a year rather than the 115 basis points annually for the cap. Not surprisingly, the bank is better off when rates fall and the interest spread is the greatest. It is worse off when rates rise and the spread narrows, but the cap generates a cash receipt.

## EXHIBIT 7.18 — Using a Collar on Three-Month LIBOR to Hedge Balance Sheet Risk of Loss from Rising Rates

**Strategy: Buy a Cap at 3.00 Percent, and Sell a Floor at 2.00 Percent\***

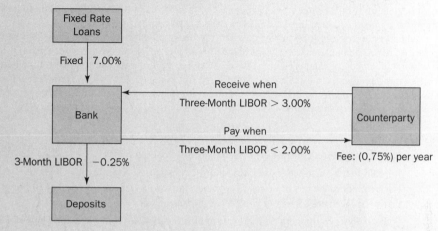

| Balance Sheet Flows: | Current Rates Constant | Rates Fall 100 Basis Points | Rates Rise 100 Basis Points |
|---|---|---|---|
| | LIBOR 3.00% | LIBOR 2.00% | LIBOR 4.00% |
| Loan | 7.00% | 7.00% | 7.00% |
| Deposit | (2.75%) | (1.75%) | (3.75%) |
| Spread | 4.25% | 5.25% | 3.25% |
| **Collar Flows:** | | | |
| Payout | 0.00% | (0.00%) | 1.00% |
| Fee Amort. | (0.75%) | (0.75%) | (0.75%) |
| Spread | (0.75%) | (0.75%) | 0.25% |
| **Margin** | 3.50% | 4.50% | 3.50% |

\*Assume collar term is three years.

S U M M A R Y

Bank managers are paid to manage risk. In many cases, it is appropriate to reduce a bank's exposure to potentially adverse changes in interest rates. Hedging with financial futures contracts, forward rate agreements (FRAs), and basic interest rate swap agreements are three methods banks can use to reduce interest rate risk. The concept underlying hedging with futures is that a bank trades financial futures such that losses or gains on its actual cash transactions due to interest rate changes are at least partially offset by gains or losses on its futures position. Risk reduction occurs because the net loss or gain is typically less with a hedge than if no futures position is taken. The same applies with FRAs and interest rate swaps. A basic interest rate swap is, in fact, a package of FRAs. A bank exposed to loss on-balance sheet when rates rise or fall can trade fixed interest payments or receipts for floating interest payments or receipts that similarly offset the change in net interest income from balance sheet positions.

Thus, when net interest income declines, the FRA and swap produce a net cash receipt. When net interest income increases, the FRA and swap require a net cash payment.

Banks also manage risk through the use of interest rate caps and floors. Such contracts are options on interest rates. If the bank buys a cap or floor, it pays an up-front premium but gets insurance to protect against rising rates with caps and falling rates with floors. The primary negative with caps and floors is the explicit premium cost that must be paid up front to enter a position. Both caps and floors, however, allow a bank to benefit from favorable interest rate moves and their impact on balance sheet exposures.

Managers must determine whether they want to hedge or, alternatively, use these derivatives to speculatively increase their risk exposure. For example, some banks view swaps as synthetic securities complete with interest rate risk. When hedging, managers must decide whether to microhedge individual transactions or macrohedge a bank's aggregate interest rate risk measured by GAP and earnings sensitivity or duration gap and EVE sensitivity. The fundamental conclusion is that managers have alternatives to alter a bank's interest rate risk position other than traditional cash transactions.

## Questions

1. How does a futures contract differ from a forward contract?

2. It is said that a microhedge does not totally eliminate risk. Assume that a bank uses financial futures contracts to reduce the risk of rising rates on new borrowings. Identify what type of position the bank should take to hedge. Once a hedge is in place, what risks remain?

3. Some analysts compare the initial margin on a futures contract to a down payment. Some label it a performance bond. What is the difference between these interpretations?

4. Suppose that you are a speculator who trades three-month Eurodollar futures. On November 5, you sell two December three-month Eurodollar futures contracts at 94.81. The subsequent weekly quotes for the closing December Eurodollar futures price are as follows:[comp: set as table]

   | Date: | 11/12 | 11/19 | 11/26 | 12/3 |
   |-------|-------|-------|-------|------|
   | Price: | 94.92 | 95.08 | 94.77 | 94.63 |

   Calculate the weekly values in your margin account. The initial margin is $650 per contract and the maintenance margin is $400. Calculate your realized return for the entire period. Assume that you offset your futures position on December 3 at the price indicated.

5. Suppose that you are a speculator who tries to time interest rate movements on three-month Eurodollar futures contracts. Use the data in Exhibits 7.1 and 7.2 and assume that it is March 11, 2005, to answer the following questions.

   a. What is the three-month Eurodollar rate in the cash market? (Approximate it from the yield curve.) How does it differ from the June Eurodollar futures rate?

   b. Use the data from the Treasury yield curve for three-month and six-month maturities to calculate the three-month forward rate, three months after March 11, 2005.

   c. Compare the forward rate you calculated from Part b with the June 2005 Eurodollar futures rate. Do they provide similar information? Should they provide similar information?

   d. As a speculator, you expect cash Eurodollar rates to rise through December 2005.

      1. Explain precisely what expectations are consistent with selling the June 2005 Eurodollar futures contract to make a profit.

      2. Explain precisely what rate expectations are consistent with buying the June 2005 Eurodollar futures contract to make a profit.

6. Explain why cross hedges generally exhibit greater risk than hedges using a futures contract based on the underlying cash instrument hedged.

7. In each of the following cases, conduct the analysis for Step 1 and Step 2 in evaluating a hedge. Specifically assess cash market risk and determine whether the bank should buy or sell financial futures as a hedge. Explain how the hedge should work.

   a. The bank expects to receive a large, past-due principal payment on a loan in 45 days.

   b. A deposit customer notifies the bank that she will be withdrawing $5 million in 60 days. The bank will sell a Treasury security from its investment portfolio at that time to cover the withdrawal.

   c. The bank has agreed to make a one-year fixed-rate loan at 9.5 percent. It will fund the loan by issuing four consecutive three-month Eurodollar time deposits. It would like to lock in its borrowing costs on the Eurodollar time deposits.

d. The bank just won a $10 million court settlement against a supplier and will receive the payment in three months.

e. In order to improve the bank's capital position, management decides to issue 15-year subordinated debentures (bonds). Unfortunately, this debt offering cannot be ready for another five months.

8. A bank plans to hedge using three-month Eurodollar futures contracts based on $1 million in principal. Determine how many contracts the bank should trade (its hedge ratio) in the following situations.

a. The bank will roll over $125 million in six-month CDs in four months. The Eurodollar futures rate moves 1.5 times as much as the CD rate.

b. In three months the bank will roll over $50 million in one-month loans. The loan rates move 1-to-1 with Eurodollar futures rates.

c. In six months the bank will extend $5 million in floating-rate loans tied to the Eurodollar cash rate. The futures and cash rates move 1-to-1.

9. A bank that hedges with financial futures cannot completely eliminate interest rate risk. Explain what basis risk is and why it exists. Is it ever possible to eliminate basis risk?

10. Explain how macrohedging differs from microhedging.

11. A bank has assets of $10 million earning an average return of 9 percent and with a weighted duration of 1.5 years. It has liabilities of $9 million paying an average rate of 6.5 percent with a weighted duration of 3.5 years. The bank wants to construct a macrohedge to reduce interest rate risk as much as possible, and plans to trade three-month Eurodollar futures currently trading at 8 percent.

a. Should the bank buy or sell Eurodollar futures?

b. How many futures contracts should the bank trade?

c. If cash interest rates rise an average of 1 percent and the Eurodollar futures rate rises by 1.10 percent, calculate how much the bank's market value of equity will change and how much the bank would earn or lose on its futures position. Was this a successful hedge?

12. What are the risks in a forward rate agreement if you are the buyer?

13. Assume that you want to speculate on how six-month cash market LIBOR will move over the next year. You believe that consensus forecasts of future rates are too high. You can enter into an FRA and agree either to pay 7.25 percent and receive six-month LIBOR, or pay six-month LIBOR and receive 7.25 percent for delivery in one year. Explain which position you would take and why you expect to profit.

14. It is January 1. Your firm expects to issue (borrow) three-month Eurodollar time deposits at the beginning of February, May, August, and November in the next year. Explain what position(s) you would take today with FRAs based on three-month LIBOR if you wanted to fully hedge your future borrowings. Why should the hedge work? What risks do you take?

15. Discuss the role of a third-party intermediary in an interest rate swap agreement. Describe the risks assumed by the intermediary. How does the intermediary potentially profit from this activity?

16. What features of interest rate swaps make them more or less attractive than financial futures as a risk management tool?

17. Is there credit risk in an interest rate swap with an intermediary bank serving as the swap dealer? Describe when default losses might arise and which party is at risk. How can credit risk be reduced?

18. A basic interest rate swap is supposedly priced as a zero net present value transaction. Explain what this means. Use the two-year swap data from Exhibit 7.8 to demonstrate your arguments.

19. Your firm just made a three-year fixed-rate loan at 8.25 percent. You would like to convert this to a floating-rate loan that is priced based on three-month LIBOR as the base rate. Explain how you could use a basic interest rate swap to accomplish this. Using the data from Exhibit 7.8, choose swap terms that convert this fixed-rate loan to a floating-rate loan and demonstrate the resulting rate you would earn on the loan from adding the swap to the loan position.

20. Your bank is looking for the lowest cost two-year, fixed-rate financing. It has decided to issue four consecutive three-month Eurodollar time deposits on-balance sheet and hedge the future borrowing costs by taking positions in the market for basic interest rate swaps. What positions are appropriate? Use the data from Exhibit 7.8 to demonstrate how swaps might be used to fix the bank's borrowing cost over two years.

21. Use the data from Exhibit 7.11 to answer the following questions:

    a. When will the buyer of a five-year cap on three-month LIBOR with a 5 percent strike rate expect to receive cash? What is the cap premium?

    b. When will the buyer of a two-year floor on three-month LIBOR with a 2 percent strike rate expect to receive cash? What is the floor premium?

    c. Can you construct a zero cost collar on three-month LIBOR with a three-year term? If not, what positions at what strike rates might produce a zero cost collar? Use approximations.

22. Explain how the outcome from using a basic interest rate swap to hedge borrowing costs will generally differ from using an interest rate cap and an interest rate collar as hedges. Why is there a difference?

23. In each of the following cases, indicate whether an interest rate cap, floor, collar, or reverse collar is an appropriate position for a hedge. Recommend a specific position.

    a. A bank loan customer wants to borrow at a fixed 8 percent rate and the bank only lends at floating rates.

    b. A bank has agreed to pay a large depositor a fixed 5.5 percent on balances over the next three years regardless of rate moves. The bank expects rates to fall on similar deposits over this period.

    c. Your bank owns adjustable rate mortgages (ARMs) that are priced at three-month LIBOR plus 2 percent. There is an annual cap on the allowable rate increase equal to a maximum of 1 percent a year. Thus, if LIBOR rises by 3 percent, the bank can raise the ARM rate just 1 percent. How can the bank effectively remove this cap?

24. Suppose that the yield curve on Eurodollars is sharply upsloping.

    a. Will premiums on interest rate floors on three-month LIBOR be high or low? Explain.

    b. Will premiums on interest rate caps on three-month LIBOR be high or low? Explain.

25. Assume that you bought an interest rate cap on three-month LIBOR with a 4.50 percent strike rate. The current rate for three-month LIBOR is 4.28 percent.

    a. What will happen to the premium (value) on this cap if LIBOR rises to 5.16 percent? Explain.

    b. What will happen to the premium (value) on this cap if LIBOR falls to 4.10 percent? Explain.

26. Your bank is asset sensitive and management wants to protect against loss from interest rate changes.

    a. Would an interest rate cap or floor serve as a better hedge? Explain.

    b. Would a collar or reverse collar serve as a better hedge? Explain.

    c. Why would the bank choose a collar or reverse collar over a cap or floor, respectively? Explain.

27. Suppose that you buy an interest rate cap on three-month LIBOR with a two-year maturity and simultaneously sell a floor on three-month LIBOR with a two-year maturity. Ignore the premiums. Draw a profit diagram that indicates when you will gain and lose on the combined positions. Compare this to different basic interest rate swap and futures positions.

28. Are there margin requirements for the following positions? Explain why or why not.

    a. Buy an interest rate cap

    b. Sell a put option on Eurodollar futures

    c. Sell an interest rate floor

    d. Sell a Eurodollar futures contract

## PROBLEMS

**I. HEDGING BORROWING COSTS.** Your bank is a regular borrower in the Eurodollar market. On August 9, 2005, the head of the funds management division decides to hedge the bank's interest cost on a $10 million three-month Eurodollar issue scheduled for November 2005. On August 9, the bank could issue $10 million in three-month Eurodollars at 4.61 percent. The corresponding futures rates for three-month Eurodollar futures contracts are 4.83 percent (December 2005), 5.01 percent (March 2006), and 5.38 percent (June 2006).

1. What is the bank's specific cash market risk on August 9, 2005? Should the bank buy or sell Eurodollar futures to hedge its borrowing costs? Explain how the hedge should work.

2. Which Eurodollar futures contract should the bank use? Explain why it is best. Assume that the bank takes the futures position that you recommend in Questions 1 and 2 above at the rate available on August 9, 2005. On November 6, 2005, the bank issues $10 million in Eurodollars at 6.25 percent. Coincidentally, it

closes out (reverses) its futures position when the futures rate on the contract you chose equals 6.33 percent. Calculate the profit or loss on the futures trades, the opportunity gain or loss in the cash market, and the effective return or cost to the bank on its Eurodollar issue.

3. Suppose instead that interest rates declined after August 9 and the bank actually issued Eurodollars at 4.47 percent. Assuming it closed out its futures position at 4.59 percent, calculate the same profit/loss and return/cost components as above.

4. It is important to note that the prevailing futures rate at the time a hedge is initiated reflects consensus information regarding the future level of cash market rates. Explain conceptually why the effectiveness of hedging is influenced by the accuracy of the futures rate.

**II. THE BASIS.** Assume that your bank expects to receive $5 million in funds that it will invest in Eurodollars in four months. It plans to buy five Eurodollar futures contracts as a hedge. The current three-month Eurodollar rate equals 5.05 percent in the cash market, and the Eurodollar futures rate for the contract purchased equals 5.39 percent. The futures contract expires one week after the bank expects to receive and invest the $5 million. Given that a hedge still encompasses basis risk, compare the basis today with what the basis will likely equal when the bank offsets its futures position as part of closing the hedge. Provide a specific forecast of the basis in four months and explain why you chose this basis. The bank should incorporate this expected basis change when estimating the effective return from the hedge. What is this expected effective return in your analysis? When will the actual return differ from what you expect?

**III. BASIC INTEREST RATE SWAPS**

1. Management at your firm is considering one of the following:

   a. Balance Sheet Transaction: Issue a six-month CD at 5.5 percent and use the proceeds to buy a three-year Treasury security that carries a 7.2 percent fixed rate. It will roll over (issue new six-month CDs) when the old one matures until funding the Treasury is no longer needed.

   b. Interest Rate Swap Transaction: Enter into a three-year basic interest rate swap where it agrees to pay six-month LIBOR and receive a fixed 7.58 percent rate.

   1. List the advantages and disadvantages of the two alternatives versus each other.

   2. Identify the specific risks associated with each alternative.

   3. Are they both speculative?

2. Two institutions plan to issue $10 million in debt and are negotiating an interest rate swap that will help them lower their borrowing costs and obtain the preferred type (fixed rate or floating rate) of financing. Both are comparing their balance sheet alter-natives with combined balance sheet and swap opportunities. Internet Bank has a negative GAP through three years, is liability sensitive, and would like to use the debt proceeds to invest in short-term assets to reduce its interest rate risk. Brick & Mortar Bank has a positive GAP through three years, is asset sensitive, and would like to use its debt proceeds to invest in fixed-rate assets to reduce its interest rate risk. Internet Bank can borrow at an 8.7 percent fixed rate for three years or pay the prevailing six-month LIBOR plus 0.50 percent on floating-rate debt. Brick & Mortar Bank can borrow at an 8.15 percent fixed rate for three years or the prevailing six-month LIBOR rate plus 0.25 percent.

   a. Explain whether and why Internet Bank needs fixed-rate or floating-rate funding to meet its objectives. Do the same for Brick & Mortar Bank.

   b. Assume that both banks issue either three-year fixed-rate debt or six-month floating-rate debt on-balance sheet. They want to combine this with a basic swap to obtain the cheapest form of funding that helps reduce interest rate risk. Using the following basic swap terms, indicate what position each bank should take. Explain how and why it should meet the bank's objectives. Calculate the effective cost of borrowing that each bank ends up with.

| Basic Swap Terms | |
| --- | --- |
| A. Pay 8.10% | Receive six-month LIBOR |
| B. Pay six-month LIBOR | Receive 8.03% |

3. A regional bank holding company recently bought a $100 million package of mortgages that carry an average 8.5 percent yield. The holding company has established a subsidiary to manage this package. The subsidiary will finance the mortgages by selling 90-day commercial paper for which the current rate is 5.25 percent. The interest rate risk assumed by the subsidiary is evidenced by the difference in duration of

the mortgages at six years and the duration of the commercial paper at 72 days. The holding company thus decides to arrange an interest rate swap through an intermediary bank to hedge the subsidiary's interest rate risk.

a. Should the subsidiary make floating-rate or fixed-rate payments in the swap market? Specifically, should the subsidiary pay fixed and receive floating, or pay floating and receive fixed? Use the following data to select specific swap terms. Explain why this swap should reduce the subsidiary's interest rate risk.

Pay 7.37 percent and receive floating at three-month LIBOR
Pay three-month LIBOR and receive 7.24 percent

b. At the first pricing of the swap when the subsidiary exchanges payments with the intermediary, LIBOR equals 6.95 percent. The notional principal amount is $100 million. Calculate the subsidiary's net cash payment or receipt with the intermediary. At the second pricing, LIBOR equals 7.66 percent. Calculate the subsidiary's net cash payment or receipt with the intermediary here.

c. What specific credit risk does the subsidiary assume in the swap you arranged? What specific credit risk does the intermediary assume? Explain by discussing when each party is at risk that it will lose if the counterparty defaults.

**IV. SYNOVUS SENSITIVITY ANALYSIS: 2004.** Data for Synovus' rate sensitivity at year-end 2004 and 2003 are provided on the following page. Use the information to answer the following questions.

1. Toward the bottom of the table, a row of data indicates the effect of interest rate swaps. Did the bank's swap activity increase or decrease the bank's risk exposure through one year?

2. What type of basis swaps (what pay, receive position) did the bank appear to take to produce the GAP effect listed?

**V. CONVERTING FIXED-RATE LOANS TO FLOATING-RATE LOANS.** Your bank made a three-year fixed rate loan to Fresh Corporation at 8.50 percent. The ALCO wants only to accept floating-rate loans so that it can reduce its liability sensitivity. Using the following information, indicate what position the bank should take to convert this fixed-rate loan to a floating-rate loan in the best possible manner. The current prime rate is 8.25 percent and three-month LIBOR is 5.50 percent.

Three-Year Basic Interest Rate Swap:  Pay 8.22% Receive three-month LIBOR
Pay three-month LIBOR                       Receive 8.17%

**Bid/Offer Premium**

| | 8.25% Cap | 8.50% Cap | 9.00% Cap |
|---|---|---|---|
| Three-Year Interest Rate Cap on Prime Rate | | | |
| Premium | 0.71/0.68 | 0.52/0.47 | 0.20/0.15 |
| | 5.50% Cap | 5.75% Cap | 6.00% Cap |
| Three-Year Interest Rate Cap on Three-Mth LIBOR | | | |
| Premium | 0.95/0.90 | 0.70/0.64 | 0.47/0.42 |

1. Describe what position you would take with a basic interest rate swap to reduce the bank's risk. Assume that the bank takes this position. What will its risk/return profile be?

a. Suppose that three-month LIBOR rises by 1 percent after one year and remains at this higher level the next two years. What will the effective loan yield equal?

b. Suppose that three-month LIBOR falls by 0.75 percent after one year and remains at this lower level the next two years. What will the effective loan yield equal?

2. Describe what position you would take with an interest rate cap. Which index (prime or LIBOR) would you use? Explain why. Which strike rate would you use? Explain why. Assume that the bank takes this position.

a. Suppose that LIBOR and the prime rate rise by 1 percent after one year and remain at these higher levels the next two years. What will the effective loan yield equal?

b. Suppose that LIBOR and the prime rate fall by 0.75 percent after one year and remain at these lower levels the next two years. What will the effective loan yield equal?

### Table 18   Interest Rate Sensitivity

**(Dollars in millions)**   December 31, 2004

|  | 0–3 Months | 4–12 Months | 1–5 Years | Over 5 Years |
|---|---|---|---|---|
| Investment securities available for sale (*) | $ 287.7 | 249.6 | 1,659.8 | 498.7 |
| Loans, net of unearned income | 13,800.4 | 1,965.9 | 3,337.3 | 376.9 |
| Mortgage loans held for sale | 120.2 | — | — | — |
| Other | 139.6 | — | — | — |
| Interest sensitive assets | 14,347.8 | 2,215.5 | 4,997.1 | 875.0 |
| Deposits | 7,826.8 | 2,698.3 | 4,640.7 | 578.8 |
| Other borrowings | 1,870.0 | 329.6 | 390.8 | 497.3 |
| Interest sensitive liabilities | 9,196.8 | 3,022.9 | 5,031.5 | 1,076.1 |
| Interest rate swaps | (977.5) | 300.0 | 330.0 | 347.5 |
| Interest sensitivity gap | $4,173.5 | (507.4) | 296.6 | 147.0 |
| Cumulative interest sensitivity gap | $4,173.5 | 3,666.1 | 8,961.7 | 4,108.7 |
| Cumulative interest sensitivity gap as a percentage of total interest sensitive assets | 18.6% | 16.3 | 17.7 | 18.3 |

**December 31, 2003**

|  | 0–3 Months | 4–12 Months | 1–5 Years | Over 5 Years |
|---|---|---|---|---|
| Investment securities available for sale (*) | $ 465.5 | 708.1 | 970.0 | 352.8 |
| Loans, net of unearned income | 9,460.3 | 2,320.3 | 4,066.5 | 617.8 |
| Mortgage loans held for sale | 133.3 | — | — | — |
| Other | 177.3 | — | — | — |
| Interest sensitive assets | 10,236.4 | 3,028.4 | 5,036.5 | 970.6 |
| Deposits | 4,509.8 | 3,144.3 | 4,850.1 | 597.9 |
| Other borrowings | 1,686.1 | 31.9 | 667.2 | 504.0 |
| Interest sensitive liabilities | 6,195.9 | 3,176.2 | 5,523.3 | 1,101.9 |
| Interest rate swaps | (337.5) | 45.0 | 570.0 | 272.5 |
| Interest sensitivity gap | $3,153.0 | (102.8) | 83.2 | 141.2 |
| Cumulative interest sensitivity gap | $3,153.0 | 3,050.2 | 3,133.4 | 3,274.6 |
| Cumulative interest sensitivity gap as a percentage of total interest sensitive assets | 16.4% | 15.8 | 16.3 | 17.0 |

(*) Excludes net unrealized losses of $224 thousand and net unrealized gains of $32.8 million at December 31, 2004 and 2003, respectively.

PART IV

# MANAGING THE COST OF FUNDS, BANK CAPITAL, AND LIQUIDITY

# Funding the Bank and Managing Liquidity

Have you ever written a check against an account balance that you didn't have, then scrambled to deposit funds before the check cleared? Have you ever charged certain expenses on your credit card, then been shocked at how much you owed when the bill came due? Consider the shock at Bank of New York when its deposit balance at the Federal Reserve went negative. On November 20, 1985, officers at the Bank of New York, a $16 billion firm, determined that the bank was deficient in its required reserve holdings by $23.6 billion. The deficiency resulted from a computer malfunction that did not permit the bank to collect payments from other banks for transferring government securities. Although checks drawn on it cleared, it received few of the deposits it expected. The Federal Reserve Bank of New York subsequently stepped in and loaned the bank $23.6 billion overnight (with interest) to cover the deficiency. This sum represented the largest single discount window loan in history.

Banks have found it increasingly difficult to manage their liabilities in the low interest rate environment of recent years. Dissatisfied with low time deposit and certificate of deposit (CD) yields, individuals have shifted their financial assets to mutual funds which offer higher promised returns. Between 1984 and 2004, for example, individuals reduced the fraction of their total financial assets in bank deposits and currency from 26.3 percent to 15.8 percent. Mutual funds, in contrast, grew from 1.2 percent to 10.9 percent. A crucial concern is whether banks will be able to retain low rate deposits when interest rates move higher. After the stock market's significant retreat following March 2001, many banks found themselves inundated with deposits. Whether this move back to bank deposits as a "safe haven" is a shift in consumer thinking has yet to be determined. The bank's profitability and liquidity risk is critically dependent on the stability of the funds and their longevity.

With the potential high returns that can be earned in stocks and mutual funds, banks find themselves in a highly competitive situation that requires innovative product development, a high level of customer service and attention to cost controls. Banks began to pursue individual retail customers in the late 1980s and are even more aggressive today. Individuals, as a group, are generally not as interest-rate-sensitive as wholesale customers such as commercial firms and government units, but the attractive returns and ease of access to mutual funds is changing this. If banks can attract consumer deposits, however, these funds are likely to remain on the books for longer periods of time and not move as readily as commercial accounts to other banks when rates change. The objective of banks is to build long-term customer relationships and establish a strong core deposit base.

How banks fund their operations plays an important role in determining profitability and risk. Ever since regulators removed interest rate ceilings on liabilities and expanded the types of deposit products banks could offer, funding decisions have dramatically influenced a bank's cost of funds, liquidity risk and interest rate risk positions. During the 1980s, for example, many thrift institutions used brokered deposits to finance extraordinary asset growth. In one infamous case Vernon Savings, a small Texas savings and loan, grew from $45 million in assets to $1.1 billion in just three years, financed primarily by large CDs sold through brokerages. The bank's managers, in turn, speculated on real estate to such an extent that when the thrift failed, 96 percent of its commercial loans were in default. More recently, many banks that failed during the early 2000s relied on purchased liabilities to fund subprime loans. The combination was highly risky and didn't leave much behind when the banks failed. Funding decisions affect profitability by determining interest expense on borrowed funds, noninterest expense associated with check handling costs, personnel *costs, and noninterest income from fees and deposit service charges. They affect interest rate risk and liquidity risk by determining the rate sensitivity of liabilities, the stability of deposits toward preventing unanticipated deposit outflows, and the ease of access to purchased funds.*

———————————————■———————————————

**T**his chapter examines the issues of liquidity planning, cash management, and funding sources. The first part examines the nature of liquidity needs and the risk-return characteristics of alternative funding sources. It explores the costs of various sources of funds, as well as the relationship between financing events and a bank's liquidity, credit, and interest rate risk position. The second part examines the characteristics of cash assets and the rationale for holding each type of cash asset. It considers legal reserve requirements, the source and impact of float and the pricing of correspondent balances. The discussion provides a background for the following sections that outline the link among liquidity, banking risks, funding sources, and returns. The third part of the chapter describes the strengths and weaknesses of traditional measures of liquidity, while the final section applies bank liquidity planning to reserves management and estimates of longer-term funding requirements.

## THE RELATIONSHIP BETWEEN LIQUIDITY REQUIREMENTS, CASH, AND FUNDING SOURCES

Liquidity needs arise from net deposit outflows as balances held with Federal Reserve Banks or correspondent banks decline. Most withdrawals are predictable because they are either contractually based or follow well-defined patterns. For example, banks that purchase securities typically pay for them with immediately available funds. Maturing investments similarly are credited to deposit balances held at the Federal Reserve. Transactions accounts normally exhibit weekly or monthly patterns that follow the payroll and billing activities of large commercial customers. Still, some outflows are totally unexpected. Often, management does not know whether customers will reinvest maturing CDs and keep the funds with the bank or withdraw them. Management also cannot predict when loan customers will borrow against open credit lines. This uncertainty increases the risk that a bank may not have adequate sources of funds available to meet payment requirements. This risk, in turn, forces management to structure its portfolio to access liquid funds easily, which lowers potential profits.

The amount of cash that management chooses to hold is heavily influenced by the bank's liquidity requirements. The potential size and volatility of cash requirements, in turn, affect the liquidity position of the bank. Transactions that reduce cash holdings normally force a bank to replenish cash assets by issuing new debt or selling assets. Transactions that increase cash holdings provide new investable funds. From the opposite perspective, banks with ready access to borrowed funds can enter into more transactions because they can borrow quickly and at low cost to meet cash requirements.

Exhibit 8.1 portrays the effects of customer deposit withdrawals and loan usage on a bank's deposit balances at the Federal Reserve. The first part indicates that a maturing CD is not rolled over directly and immediately reduces a bank's reserves. Here the CD holder directs the Federal Reserve to transfer the funds by wire to another institution, which directly lowers CDs outstanding as well as deposit balances held at the Federal Reserve. Loan usage produces the same result. In the second part, a loan customer borrows $250,000 against an outstanding credit line by requesting a wire transfer to cover the purchase of some good or service. The bank authorizes the payment, lowering its deposit balance at the Federal Reserve by $250,000 while simultaneously booking the loan. In the last part, the bank first allocates $500,000 in loan proceeds to the borrower's account. The bank's deposit at the Federal Reserve falls when the customer writes a check against the proceeds and the check clears after being deposited in another bank. Each transaction reduces immediately available funds, creating the possibility that the bank is reserves deficient and, perhaps, short of balances needed to cover future deposit outflows.

### RECENT TRENDS IN BANK FUNDING SOURCES

Perhaps the most difficult problem bank managers face is how to develop strategies to compete for funding sources. With no interest rate ceilings on deposits or restrictions on maturities, banks can offer any deposit product that customers demand. Although this freedom creates market opportunities, it also presents significant problems. First, bank customers have become much more rate conscious. They often shop around for the highest yields and typically pay less attention to long-term bank relationships. From the bank's perspective, liabilities have become more interest elastic, so that small rate changes can produce large fluctuations in outstanding balances. Second, many customers have demonstrated a strong preference for shorter-term deposits. Depositors can reduce their interest rate risk by investing in short-term contracts that usually trade close to par. The rate sensitivity of liabilities is thus greater, creating difficulties in pricing assets to manage net interest margin and interest rate risk.

**EXHIBIT 8.1** Effect of Maturing Certificates of Deposit and Loan Use on a Bank's Deposit Balances at the Federal Reserve

**Maturing Certificate of Deposit Not Rolled Over**
Commercial Bank

| ΔASSETS | ΔLIABILITIES | |
|---|---|---|
| Demand deposit at Federal Reserve −$100,000 | Certificate of deposit −$100,000 | CD not rolled over; CD holder directs the Federal Reserve to wire funds to another institution. |

**Loan Customer Borrows against a Credit Line**
Commercial Bank

| ΔASSETS | ΔLIABILITIES | |
|---|---|---|
| Commercial loan +$250,000 Demand deposit at Federal Reserve −$250,000 | | Customer borrows against outstanding credit line. Wire transfer to cover purchase of goods or services. |

**Borrowing against a New Term Loan**
Commercial Bank

| ΔASSETS | ΔLIABILITIES | |
|---|---|---|
| Commercial loan +$500,000 Demand deposit at Federal Reserve −$500,000 | Demand deposit +$500,000 Demand deposit −$500,000 | Bank grants loan and deposits proceeds in customer's account. Customer spends full amount of loan proceeds by writing check. |

Banks obtain funding from a variety of sources, but it is often useful to differentiate between retail funding, borrowed or wholesale funding, and equity funding. Although the precise definition of **retail funding** varies by institution, it is most widely considered funding the bank receives from consumers and noninstitutional depositors. Retail funding generally consists of deposit accounts such as transactions accounts, money market demand retained earnings accounts (MMDAs), savings accounts, and small time deposits. **Borrowed funding** consists of federal funds purchased, repurchase agreements, Federal Home Loan Bank (FHLB) borrowings, and other borrowings. **Wholesale funding** includes borrowed funds as well as large institutional deposits such as large CDs (over $100,000). Equity funding consists of common and preferred stock, retained earnings, and other equities. Exhibit 8.2 shows the dramatic change in the composition of bank funding since 1935. Total deposits, mostly retail-type deposits, have declined from a high of 93.8 percent of total assets in 1945 to only 66.5 percent at year-end 2004. Most of this decline has been offset by an increase in borrowed funds, but equity is higher today than since 1945. Borrowed funding increased from only 0.1 percent in 1945 to 15.6 percent at year-end 2004.

Exhibit 8.3 provides details on changes in percentage contribution of various funding sources at commercial banks since 1992. Transactions accounts and time deposits less than $100,000 have declined significantly while MMDAs and most wholesale funding sources (large CDs, deposits held in foreign offices, and other borrowed funds) have increased. Subordinated debt and equity capital increased modestly since 1992. MMDAs have increased and are certainly more popular than CDs to a bank's younger customers. The general decline in retail-type deposits combined with the largest banks' extraordinary growth during the late 1990s and early 2000s has created an increased reliance on funding from wholesale markets.

Exhibits 8.2 and 8.3 mask some of the differences in the composition of bank funding for different-sized banks. Exhibit 8.4 examines funding by source in 2004 for four groups of banks; those with total assets below $100 million and those with assets between $100 million and $1 billion, $1 billion and $10 billion, and assets more than $10 billion. Each column represents the percentage of total assets financed by the specific funding source.

Comparisons between different-size banks reveal key differences in operating style. Larger banks operate with relatively fewer total deposits but significantly more wholesale or borrowing funding, while smaller banks rely proportionally more on core deposits and equity. Because core deposits cost less than nondeposit liabilities, large bank borrowing costs normally exceed small bank costs. Larger banks also hold significantly fewer domestic deposits but only the largest banks obtained significant funds outside the United States. The larger banks' size gives them greater access to these markets while smaller banks are more dependent on retail deposits and funding. A

**EXHIBIT 8.2**

Change in Total Deposits, Borrowed Funds, Subordinated Notes, and Total Equity Over Time, 1935–2004*

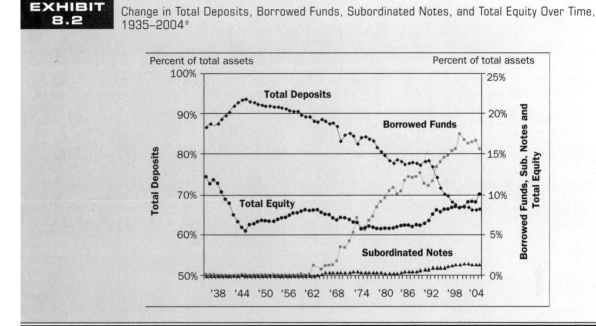

*Funding as a percentage of total assets.

SOURCE: FDIC Statistics on Banking, http://www2.fdic.gov/SDI/SOB.

**EXHIBIT 8.3**

Change in the Percentage Contribution of Various Bank Funding Components, 1992–2004*

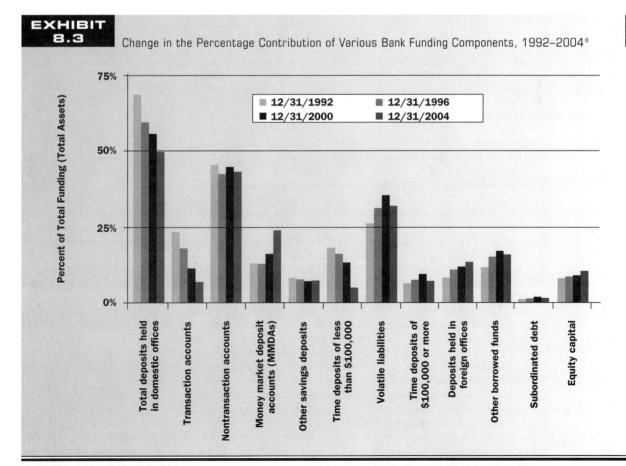

*Funding as a percentage of total assets.

SOURCE: FDIC Statistics on Depository Institutions, http://www2.fdic.gov/SDI.

## EXHIBIT 8.4 — The Percentage Contribution of Various Sources of Bank Funds by Bank Size, 2004*

| | <$100 M | $100M–$1B | $1B–$10B | >$10 B | All CBs |
|---|---|---|---|---|---|
| **Number of institutions reporting** | **3655** | **3530** | **360** | **85** | **7630** |
| **Total deposits** | **83.7%** | **80.9%** | **68.5%** | **63.5%** | **66.5%** |
| **Deposits held in domestic offices** | **83.7%** | **80.7%** | **67.4%** | **49.9%** | **49.9%** |
| Transaction accounts | 26.3% | 19.8% | 10.0% | 6.7% | 6.7% |
| Demand deposits | 13.9% | 11.5% | 7.3% | 5.4% | 5.4% |
| Nontransaction accounts | 57.4% | 60.9% | 57.3% | 43.2% | 43.2% |
| Money market deposit accounts (MMDAs) | 10.6% | 15.9% | 23.5% | 23.7% | 23.7% |
| Other savings deposits (excluding MMDAs) | 9.2% | 11.6% | 10.4% | 7.2% | 7.2% |
| Time deposits of less than $100,000 | 25.0% | 19.7% | 11.5% | 5.1% | 5.1% |
| Time deposits of $100,000 or more | 12.6% | 13.8% | 11.9% | 7.2% | 7.2% |
| **Deposits held in foreign offices** | **0.0%** | **0.2%** | **1.1%** | **13.6%** | **13.6%** |
| Federal funds purchased & repurchase agreements | 0.9% | 2.5% | 8.2% | 7.5% | 6.9% |
| Trading liabilities | 0.0% | 0.0% | 0.0% | 4.5% | 3.3% |
| Other borrowed funds | 3.3% | 5.7% | 10.1% | 9.2% | 8.8% |
| FHLB advances | 3.1% | 5.4% | 6.8% | 2.0% | 3.0% |
| *Memo: Volatile liabilities* | 14.7% | 18.6% | 26.6% | 35.0% | 31.7% |
| Subordinated debt | 0.0% | 0.1% | 0.4% | 1.7% | 1.3% |
| All other liabilities | 0.6% | 0.8% | 2.0% | 3.8% | 3.2% |
| Equity capital | 11.5% | 10.0% | 10.9% | 10.0% | 10.1% |
| **Deposits held in domestic offices** | **83.7%** | **80.7%** | **67.4%** | **49.9%** | **49.9%** |
| Noninterest-bearing deposits | 14.1% | 13.6% | 11.9% | 11.7% | 11.7% |
| Interest-bearing deposits | 69.6% | 67.1% | 55.5% | 38.2% | 38.2% |
| Core (retail) deposits | 71.0% | 66.9% | 55.5% | 42.7% | 42.7% |
| IRAs and Keogh plan accounts | 4.2% | 3.6% | 2.6% | 1.6% | 1.6% |
| Brokered deposits | 1.5% | 2.9% | 4.4% | 4.6% | 4.6% |
| Fully insured | 1.3% | 2.6% | 3.5% | 2.3% | 2.3% |
| Estimated insured deposits | 67.3% | 58.4% | 41.5% | 28.2% | 28.2% |

*Funding as a percentage of total assets.

Source: FDIC Statistics on Depository Institutions, http://www2.fdic.gov/SDI.

notable exception to this is that the Gramm-Leach-Bliley Act of 1999 made it easier for smaller banks to borrow from the FHLB. As a result, small banks increased their dependence on this type of wholesale funding. The number of institutions with FHLB advances has increased from 1,533 institutions with $78 billion in advances in 1992 to 5,253 institutions with $542 billion in advances in 2004 (see the section on "Federal Home Loan Bank Bank Advances" below).

Banks use the term **volatile liabilities** to describe funds purchased from rate-sensitive investors. The types of instruments include federal funds purchased, repurchase agreements (RPs), jumbo CDs, Eurodollar time deposits, foreign deposits, and any other large-denomination purchased liability. Investors in these instruments will move their funds if other institutions pay higher rates, or if it is rumored that the issuing bank has financial difficulties. Such volatile liabilities accounted for 35 percent of financing for large banks in 2004 but only 14.7 percent for smaller banks. The net effect is that larger banks are paying market rates on a greater proportion of their liabilities, with less customer loyalty and thus greater liquidity risk. In contrast, **core deposits** are stable deposits that customers are less likely to move when interest rates on competing investments rise. Core deposits, which include transactions accounts, MMDAs, savings accounts, and smaller CDs, are not as rate sensitive as large-denomination, volatile liabilities. Core deposits tend to be influenced more by location, availability, price of services, relationships with bank personnel and other factors. Today, however, due to highly competitive factors including the high returns paid by mutual funds, some banks have had to pay attractive rates on MMDAs and small time deposits (less than $100,000). As a result, many MMDAs and smaller CDs behave more like volatile liabilities rather than core deposits.

Although larger banks operate with fewer core deposits, transactions accounts, savings accounts, and time deposits, they held significantly more MMDAs in 2004. The decline in transactions accounts reflects many of the factors discussed earlier as deposit holders can earn higher market rates on these instruments and still have transactions capabilities. Additional information, not presented in the tables, shows that smaller banks' (less than $100 million in assets) reduction in transactions accounts has been much less than that of the larger banks (more than $10 billion in assets), from 26.5 percent of total assets in 1992 to only 26.3 percent in 2004 for the smallest

**EXHIBIT 8.5**

Average Annual Interest Cost of Liabilities by Bank Size, 2004

| | <$100M | $100M–$1B | $1B–$10B | >$10B | All CB |
|---|---|---|---|---|---|
| Total interest expense on total liabilities | 1.55% | 1.56% | 1.44% | 1.36% | 1.34% |
| Interest expense on deposits | 1.49% | 1.43% | 1.22% | 1.16% | 1.17% |
| Domestic deposits | 1.49% | 1.43% | 1.22% | 1.02% | 1.09% |
| MMDAs and savings deposits | 0.54% | 0.45% | 0.35% | 0.34% | 0.34% |
| Time deposits <$100K | 2.36% | 2.42% | 2.21% | 2.21% | 2.19% |
| Time deposits >$100K | 2.47% | 2.59% | 2.47% | 2.51% | 2.45% |
| Deposits foreign offices | 0.57% | 1.22% | 1.50% | 1.67% | 1.62% |
| Fed funds purchased | 2.55% | 3.83% | 4.20% | 4.96% | 4.54% |
| U.S. notes & other borrowed funds | 3.60% | 3.44% | 2.88% | 3.01% | 2.73% |
| Subordinated notes & deb. | 3.91% | 4.69% | 4.25% | 4.80% | 4.49% |

SOURCE: BankSearch, Highline Data, © Highline Data, LLC.

banks. Large banks' transactions accounts, however, fall from 19.8 percent in 1992 to 6.7 percent of total assets in 2004. MMDAs decreased slightly at smaller banks, from 11 percent to 10.7 percent while at the largest banks these same accounts increased from 12 percent to just over 23.7 percent of total assets. Corporate depositors effectively reduced demand balances at the larger banks through efficient cash management techniques, often taught by banks, such as the use of sweep accounts (see the section on "**The Impact of Sweep Accounts on Required Reserve Balances**" below) that allow them to minimize nonearning deposits.[1]

With the decline in demand balances, many banks raised rates on savings and time deposits to replace lost financing. In many cases, depositors simply moved balances from low-rate to high-rate accounts at the same institution. This action increased borrowing costs without increasing the total amount of funds acquired. At year-end 2004, core deposits for banks with more than $10 billion in assets funded 42.7 percent of total assets, down from 48 percent in 1992.

Competitive pressures have driven the average cost of funds between small banks and large banks to similar levels in many categories. Consider the average annual interest cost data in Exhibit 8.5. While small banks' overall cost of interest-bearing domestic deposits was 47 basis points higher, they paid lower rates on large CDs. The fact that the smallest banks obtained more funding in the form of transactions accounts did not offset the generally higher rate paid on total liabilities, and that meant that their overall cost of liabilities was 19 basis points higher than the largest banks.

## CHARACTERISTICS OF RETAIL-TYPE DEPOSITS

Retail deposits, or small denomination (under $100,000) liabilities, are fundamentally different from those of wholesale or large denomination liabilities. Instruments under $100,000 are normally held by individual investors and are not actively traded in the secondary market. Large balance instruments typically carry denominations in multiples of $1 million and can be readily sold in the secondary market. Individuals traditionally have had few alternatives to banks when selecting interest-bearing deposits. Today, however, commercial banks, savings and loans, credit unions, money market mutual funds, investment banks, and insurance companies offer deposit products with similar features. While they all pay market interest rates, the principal advantage of banks, savings and loans, and credit unions is that deposits are insured up to $100,000 per account by the federal government.[2]

### TRANSACTIONS ACCOUNTS

Individuals and businesses own checking accounts for transactions purposes. Most banks offer three different transactions accounts: demand deposits (DDAs), negotiable order of withdrawal (NOWs), and automatic tranfers

---

[1] Currently many larger banks have "automatic" sweep systems in place, which simply reclassify NOW accounts to MMDAs. These are relatively sophisticated systems that move these funds but remain within regulations that require no more than six movements of MMDAs per month. Hence, NOW accounts may not accurately represent interest-bearing checking accounts at large banks.

[2] It should be noted that accounts at an investment company like Merrill Lynch are not FDIC insured but Merrill Lynch does offer FDIC-insured deposits to its customers through banks it owns as well as through CDs Merrill brokers for other institutions. Merrill Lynch owns three banks or savings banks: Merrill Lynch Bank USA, Merrill Lynch Bank and Trust Company, and Merrill Lynch Trust Company, FSB. These are limited purpose banks and hence Merrill Lynch does not have to be a financial holding company.

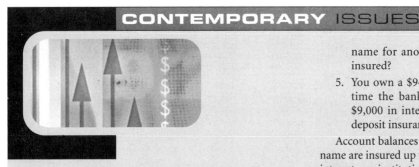

## CONTEMPORARY ISSUES

### THE EXTENT OF DEPOSIT INSURANCE COVERAGE

It pays to understand deposit insurance. Do you? As a test, answer the following questions. Both banks carry deposit insurance.

1. You have $100,000 in a CD at First National Bank, and another $100,000 in a CD at First State Bank. Are both deposits fully insured?

2. Your parents are concerned about their health and managing their resources if one becomes incapacitated. They own two $75,000 CDs at First National Bank jointly. Are both deposits fully insured?

3. Your grandfather has a joint account with your father for $60,000, another joint account with your sister for $50,000, and another joint account with you for $50,000, all at First State Bank. Are all deposits fully insured?

4. You own a $100,000 CD from First State Bank and your grandmother opened a trust account in your name for another $100,000. Are both accounts fully insured?

5. You own a $94,000 CD at First National Bank. At the time the bank fails, you are owed the $94,000 plus $9,000 in interest. How much will you be paid from deposit insurance?

Account balances held by the same individual in his or her name are insured up to $100,000, including both principal and interest, per institution. The $100,000 coverage extends to total deposit balances summing across all types.

Joint accounts held by the same individuals are combined to determine insurance coverage, with $100,000 maximum coverage. It does not matter whether the underlying deposit accounts differ in form or if the individuals list their names in different orders. The insurance funds assume equal ownership among joint owners. Suppose that two parents own a $100,000 account jointly, another $90,000 jointly with a daughter, and another $90,000 jointly with a son. With equal ownership, the father and mother own $110,000 each for insurance purposes so that $10,000 is not insured for each. Each child's $30,000 balance is fully insured.

With trust accounts, each account is insured separately for each beneficiary and each owner. Thus two parents with two children can establish $400,000 in trust balances that are fully insured. The father sets up a trust for each child in his name for $100,000 and the mother sets up a trust in her name for each child for $100,000. Individual retirement accounts (IRAs) and Keogh accounts are treated separately for deposit insurance purposes.

---

from savings (ATS). Even though money market deposit accounts (MMDAs) offer check-writing privileges, they are limited and not technically considered *transactions accounts*. MMDAs, therefore, are discussed in the following section on "Nontransaction Accounts." Banks differentiate deposits accounts in the number of checks permitted, the minimum denomination required to open an account, and the interest rate paid. All carry FDIC insurance up to $100,000 per account:

- **Demand deposits (DDA)** are noninterest-bearing checking accounts held by individuals, businesses, and governmental units. While demand deposits do not pay interest, interest-bearing checking accounts are called NOW or ATS accounts. Although explicit interest payments are prohibited, there are no regulatory restrictions on the number of checks or minimum balances. Today, commercial customers own most DDAs because, unlike individuals and governments, they cannot hold NOWs. Individuals with sufficiently large balances prefer interest-bearing accounts that provide transactions privileges.

- NOW and ATS accounts are simply checking accounts that pay interest.[3] A **NOW account** is not a demand deposit, but rather a negotiable order of withdrawal while an **ATS account** is basically the same as a NOW account but the structure is different. With ATS accounts the customer has both a DDA and savings account, but the bank forces a zero balance in the DDA at the close of each day after transferring just enough funds from savings to cover checks presented for payment. Every bank prices NOW and ATS accounts based on competitive conditions without restriction. Some banks limit the number of checks that can be written without fees and impose minimum balance requirements before paying interest. Some pay tiered interest rates

---

[3]NOWs were introduced on an experimental basis in 1972 in New England. Many people ask "What is the difference between a demand deposit account and NOW or ATS accounts?" Operationally they are the same, but the bank cannot pay interest on a demand deposit account. All savings accounts (NOW and ATSs) must *reserve the right* to require seven days prior notice of withdrawals or transfers from the account. Although banks do not do this, they must "reserve" the right if these accounts are to be classified as NOW or ATS. Hence, NOW and ATS accounts are not, technically, payable upon demand.

# CONTEMPORARY ISSUES

## TRUTH IN SAVINGS ACT

Since the passage of FDICIA in 1992 banks have been required to report interest rates on deposits in a new, consistent format. The intent is to eliminate confusion regarding how interest is calculated and establish uniform rules for the reporting of true yields. Banks also must disclose more fees and provide more information in their advertising.

Banks must report the interest rates they pay on deposits in terms of an annual percentage yield (APY). The APY can be used to calculate what your deposit will be worth if you left it at the bank for one year. For example, an APY of 4.45 percent means that a customer who deposits $10,000 will find the deposit worth $10,445 after one year. In each case the year-ending interest balance equals the amount on deposit times the APY ($10,000 × .0445 in the above case).

Truth in Savings also requires that banks pay interest on the full customer deposit rather than some fraction of the total. Many banks historically paid interest on investable deposits defined as the amount that appears on the books minus float and minus required reserves the bank must hold against the deposit. With Truth in Savings, the APY is applied against the ledger balance amount that appears on the books. In addition, if a bank plans to change any terms of a time deposit that will adversely affect the depositor, such as offering a lower interest rate, it must give the customer 30 days notice. Many banks believe that this will eliminate the fixed-rate time deposit because notification costs will be high.

Finally, it is illegal for banks to structure a deposit that requires a minimum balance to earn interest, then not pay any interest if your balance falls below the minimum even for just one day. Banks may not pay interest for the period the balance falls below the minimum, but cannot cancel interest on the actual balance for days it exceeds the minimum.

With fees and advertising banks must reveal more information. When an account is opened, a bank is required to provide a list of fees associated with normal account activity. A bank may also not use terms such as "free" or "no cost" when some minimum balance is required, or if any maintenance or activity fee may be charged.

that increase with the size of the deposit. The rationale is to encourage individuals to consolidate accounts. Depositors are better off if they centralize their accounts because they can earn higher yields and pay lower service charges.

Individuals, once loyal customers, previously would not withdraw their funds unless a crisis arose. The advent of interest-bearing checking accounts at banks and nonbanks as well as the information afforded by the Internet, however, has increased interest rate awareness. The result is that today's customers are more willing to move deposits between accounts and institutions, depending on which account or firm pays the highest rates. Pricing strategies influence the composition of accounts via service charges, minimum balance requirements, and interest rates paid. Many banks specify minimum balance requirements high enough to limit the number of small balance accounts, for which they impose high monthly service charges. Banks often encourage customers to consolidate accounts by offering tiered interest rates that increase with deposit size and club programs that provide a range of transactions services for a fixed monthly fee.

Although the interest cost of transactions accounts is very low, the noninterest costs can be quite high. In fact, small balance checking accounts can be one of the most expensive forms of funding the bank has. For example, a college student might deposit $1,500 in his or her account at the beginning of the month but spend most those funds within a short period of time, bringing the average balance down over the month. If the student's average account balance is $250 a month, for example, and the student writes 10 to 15 checks, the average monthly cost to the bank would be around $10 a month or 51 percent per year![4] Generally speaking, low-balance checking accounts are not profitable for the bank unless they earn other fees. Many critics contend that bank pricing of transactions accounts drives low-income individuals to use check-cashing outlets to obtain cash and pay bills via money orders. Importantly, the passage of the Federal Deposit Insurance Corporate Improvement Act (FDICIA) required the consistent reporting of interest rates on deposits as indicated in the Contemporary Issues Box: "Truth in Savings Act". See the following section on "Calculating the Average Net Cost of Deposit Accounts."

---

[4]With the Fed Funds rate at 2.25 percent at the end of 2004, the annual cost, after investment income, was {[$10 − (0.0225 / 12) × (250 × 0.9)] / (250 × 0.9)} * 12 = 51 percent per year.

## NONTRANSACTION ACCOUNTS

Nontransaction accounts are interest-bearing accounts with limited or no check-writing privileges. The accounts generally pay competitive rates of interest and are fully FDIC-insured up to $100,000 per individual. Nontransaction accounts consist of MMDAs, savings accounts, small time deposits, and jumbo CDs:

- **Money market deposit accounts (MMDAs)** are time deposits with limited checking privileges.[5] They were introduced to provide banks an instrument to compete with money market mutual funds offered by large brokerage firms. These accounts differ from NOW accounts in that depositors are limited to six transactions per month, of which only three can be checks.[6] The average size of each MMDA check is thus much larger than for transactions accounts. Banks find MMDAs attractive because required reserves against them are zero where the bank must hold 10 percent reserves against DDAs and NOW account balances (see the section below on "Calculating Reserve Accounts"). Limited check processing and zero required reserves reduce their effective cost to the bank. Hence, banks can afford to pay higher rates to attract MMDA funds but interestingly enough have rarely paid rates as high as those on money market mutual funds. The primary reason is that customers are willing to accept a lower rate because of deposit insurance and the fact that they can establish personal banking relationships via their deposit business.

- **Savings accounts** and **small time deposits** are small denomination accounts (under $100,000). Savings accounts have no fixed maturity while small time deposits have specified maturities ranging from seven days to any longer negotiated term, with interest penalties for early withdrawal. Banks can pay market rates on any account regardless of deposit size. Savings accounts are not as prevalent in banks today as they have generally been replaced by MMDAs and time deposits. The effective cost of small time deposits is comparable to that for MMDAs. Average interest expense is higher, but operating costs are lower. In today's environment, there is also some difference between small time deposits ($25,000) and the larger, small time deposits ($75,000 to $99,999) as these larger deposits act more like jumbo CDs. They are very interest-rate-sensitive and are typically held by high-income individuals, small companies, and even other financial institutions.

- **Large time deposits** are generally referred to as large CDs or **jumbo CDs**. These accounts consist of negotiable certificates of $100,000 or more. They are issued primarily by the largest banks and purchased by businesses and governmental units. Therefore, they are not considered retail deposits. Smaller banks also issue jumbo CDs, but even though they are negotiable, they rarely trade in the secondary market. Often, smaller banks sell these to their best customers, with whom they have a long-time relationship. As such, they might be considered retail deposits for smaller banks. Larger banks generally pay higher rates and use jumbo CDs as a significant means of funding the bank, hence the CDs would be considered wholesale funding for the largest banks. Jumbo CDs are discussed in more detail in the section on "Wholesale Funding."

## ESTIMATING THE COST OF DEPOSIT ACCOUNTS

Estimating the cost of liabilities involves more than just examining the interest cost of various accounts. Interest expense on transactions accounts may be as low as zero or a small fraction of one percent. Interest costs alone, however, dramatically understate the effective cost of transactions accounts for several reasons. First, transactions accounts are subject to legal reserve requirements equal to as much as 10 percent of the outstanding balance, which are generally invested in nonearning assets (Federal Reserve deposits or vault cash). Reserves increase the cost of transaction accounts because only a fraction of the balances can be invested. Nontransaction accounts have no reserve requirements and are cheaper, ceteris paribus, because 100 percent of the funds may be invested. Second, when depositors write a large number of checks against their balances, there are substantial processing costs. Finally, certain fees are charged on some accounts to offset noninterest expenses and this reduces the cost of these funds to the bank.

Because most banks employ a large staff to process checks, the cost of transactions accounts can still be substantial. Most cost analysis data, however, indicate that demand deposits are the least expensive source of funds, although the profitability of these accounts depends heavily on the average balance, as well as the number of transactions and fees collected. The average percentage cost of low-balance checking accounts is high before any additional fees are collected, such as overdraft protection or not sufficient funds (NSF) fees. Low-balance accounts can be very expensive for the bank and most banks know that holders tend to overdraw their balances more often. Hence, overdraft fees charged by the bank not only represent fees for the services provided but also represent a *risk charge*. Customers who overdraft their accounts on a regular basis are more likely to be low-balance customers who do not always have the funds

---

[5]Money market deposit accounts are classified as time deposits, not transactions accounts, when calculating required reserves. They are discussed here because they provide limited check-writing capabilities.

[6]The Board's Regulation D regarding reserve requirements of depository institutions (12 CFR Part 204) distinguishes between NOW accounts and MMDAs or savings deposits. Section 204.2(d)(2) of Regulation D defines "savings deposit" to include an account from which: the depositor is permitted or authorized to make no more than six transfers and withdrawals, or a combination of such transfers and withdrawals, per calendar month or statement cycle to another account (including a transactions account) of the depositor at the same institution or to a third party by means of a preauthorized or automatic transfer, or telephonic (including data transmission) agreement, order, or instruction; and no more than three of the six such transfers may be made by check, draft, debit card, or similar order made by the depositor and payable to third parties.

needed to cover the overdraft. Overdrafts actually represent extension of credit by the bank, but the bank has less control over the credit terms. When the bank's fees are recognized, these accounts may represent very low-cost funds.

Estimating noninterest cost of bank services, such as checking accounts, has proven to be quite challenging for banks. In order to estimate the cost and profitability of customers and/or products, management must have detailed data on the costs of various departments, products, and customer relationships. This can be expensive and time consuming to establish, collect, evaluate, and manage, but extremely valuable to the organization. It is often noted that when management sees this type of information for the first time, it is like learning the business all over again. Using cost analysis data enables management to quickly identify, attack, and resolve weak areas—as well as obtain a more precise understanding of a bank's strengths and weaknesses.

Unfortunately, there are few public sources for comparable cost data in banking. The Federal Reserve previously published data in *Functional Cost and Profit Analysis,* but it ended this program in 1999. Today, this type of information must be obtained from private sources or the bank's own cost accounting system. Establishing an effective cost accounting system requires capturing all income, expenses, and portfolios by department and product. The more critical process is identifying all departments, both profit centers and cost centers, and developing logical cost-allocation bases for the cost centers; developing and computing transfer costs of funds from internal funds suppliers to internal funds users; and designing summary report formats that consolidate and present all pertinent data for senior management in a logical and informative manner. Because there are many shared costs, the accuracy of the final analysis will be heavily dependent on the time and effort put into identifying the various subjective cost allocations.

Transactions account cost analysis generally classifies check-processing activities as either deposits (electronic and nonelectronic), withdrawals (electronic and nonelectronic), transit checks deposited, transit checks cashed, account opened or closed, on-us checks cashed, or general account maintenance (truncated and nontruncated). **Electronic transactions** are those that occur through automatic deposits, Internet and telephone bill payment, ATMs, and ACH transactions. **Nonelectronic transactions** are conducted in person or by mail. **Transit checks deposited** are defined as checks drawn on any bank other than the subject bank where deposits are simply deposits from checks drawn on the subject bank. **On-us checks cashed** are checks drawn on the bank's customer's account. Deposits represent checks or currency directly deposited in the customer's account. **Account maintenance** refers to general record maintenance and preparing and mailing a periodic statement. A **truncated account** is a checking account in which the physical check is "truncated" at the bank; that is, checks are not returned to the customer. **An official check issued** would be for certified funds. Finally, **net indirect costs** are costs not directly related to the product such as salaries to manage the bank or general overhead.

Exhibit 8.6 summarizes average revenue and cost information for various deposit accounts at FirstBank. The first column contains average account and unit cost data for demand (checking) accounts. The next two columns of data are for savings accounts, which are small personal savings accounts with no maturity, and time deposit data, which are generally for larger accounts such as CDs with a fixed term to mature. The data in each column indicate the average cost per item for each activity. Examining the data under the category "Income" indicates that interest income, or earnings credit, is lowest for demand and highest for time accounts. This is not surprising as transaction accounts are more volatile and are generally invested for shorter periods than savings or time deposits. Average noninterest income from service charges and fees, however, is highest for demand accounts and lowest for time deposit accounts. Clearly, transaction expenses associated with checking accounts are much greater than those for savings accounts or time deposits. Transaction activity in savings accounts is also somewhat greater than time accounts (adjusted for account size), hence the slightly higher fees collected on these types of accounts.

The second group of data under "Expenses" indicates that unit transaction costs are lowest for demand accounts, due primarily to the volume of activity in these accounts, and highest with time accounts. Typically, time accounts have very few transactions. Finally, note that the cost of electronic transactions is a fraction of the cost of nonelectronic transactions. In fact, if banks could significantly increase the use of electronic transactions by their customers, they would dramatically reduce the cost of servicing these types of accounts. This is one reason why some larger banks have begun to charge a $2–$3 fee for live teller transactions.

Whether these accounts are profitable depends on how much the bank earns from investing deposit balances (net of required reserves and float) and service charges and fees. Exhibit 8.7 presents FirstBank's estimates of these average monthly revenues and expenses for three different demand deposit accounts. Interest (investment) income is calculated by multiplying the earnings credit on balances in excess of float and required reserves. Not surprisingly, net revenue varies directly with the average size and level of activity of the account as well as the fees associated with the account. Total revenue per month is greatest for the high-balance account, which comprises mostly interest income from the higher balance. Noninterest revenue is highest for the low-balance account, due primarily to penalty fees from NSF charges. Net monthly revenue is highest for the high-balance account but net monthly revenue is actually lower for the medium-balance, high-activity account relative to the low-balance, low-activity account. The great lever of nonelectronic checks withdrawn and the fact that this account is nontruncated (checks are returned) lowers the profitability relative to the low-balance account with lower activity and higher

**EXHIBIT 8.6**

Cost and Revenue Accounting Data for Deposit Accounts at FirstBank

| | Unit Cost | | |
| --- | --- | --- | --- |
| | Demand | Savings | Time |
| **Income** | | | |
| **Interest income (estimated earnings credit)** | **2.6%** | **2.5%** | **3.0%** |
| Noninterest income (monthly estimates per account) | | | |
| Service charges | $ 2.80 | $ 0.44 | $ 0.11 |
| Penalty fees | $ 4.32 | $ 0.28 | $ 0.27 |
| Other | $ 0.63 | $ 0.16 | $ 0.05 |
| **Total noninterest Income** | **$ 7.75** | **$ 0.88** | **$ 0.42** |
| **Expenses** | | | |
| *Activity charges (unit costs per transaction)* | | | |
| Deposit—electronic | $ 0.0089 | $ 0.0502 | $ 0.1650 |
| Deposit—nonelectronic | $ 0.2219 | $ 0.7777 | $ 3.1425 |
| Withdrawal—electronic | $ 0.1073 | $ 0.4284 | $ 0.5400 |
| Withdrawal—nonelectronic | $ 0.2188 | $ 0.7777 | $ 1.4933 |
| Transit check deposited | $ 0.1600 | $ 0.5686 | |
| Transit check cashed | $ 0.2562 | | |
| On-us check cashed | $ 0.2412 | | |
| Official check issued | $ 1.02 | | |
| *Monthly overhead expense costs* | | | |
| Monthly account maintenance (truncated) | $ 2.42 | $ 4.10 | $ 1.99 |
| Monthly account maintenance (nontruncated) | $ 8.60 | | |
| Net indirect expense | $ 4.35 | $ 1.81 | $ 18.38 |
| *Miscellaneous expenses* | | | |
| Account opened | $ 9.46 | $ 33.63 | $ 5.78 |
| Account closed | $ 5.67 | $ 20.18 | $ 3.38 |

fees. These data clearly indicate that the average balance, amount of activity, and type of account establish the profitability of the account. The data also make it clear why many banks encourage their customers to make payments electronically and to accept a truncated account in which the bank does not return checks but instead may provide check images.

For many years, banks priced check-handling services below cost. Although competition may have forced this procedure, it was acceptable because banks paid below-market rates on most deposits. This low-interest subsidy implicitly covered losses on check handling. The popular view was that the 20 percent of bank customers with the largest deposit balances subsidized the 80 percent with lower balances. Deregulation removed this subsidy and induced banks to modify their pricing policies. Because banks now pay market rates on deposits, they want all customers to pay at least what the services cost. This has brought about relationship pricing, in which service charges decline and interest rates increase with larger deposit balances. Many banks have unbundled services and price each separately. Some charge for services once considered simple courtesies, such as check cashing and balance inquiries, and there are even banks that charge a fee to conduct banking in person. For most customers, service charges and fees for banking services have increased substantially in recent years.

Such pricing schemes have essentially created a caste system of banking. Large depositors receive the highest rates, pay the lowest fees, and often get free checking. They do not wait in long teller lines and receive more attention from their personal banker. Small depositors earn lower rates, if any, and pay higher fees, with less personal service. Chapter 3 presented the various types of fees and revenues earned from transactions accounts.

## CALCULATING THE AVERAGE NET COST OF DEPOSIT ACCOUNTS

The **average historical cost of funds** is a measure of average unit borrowing costs for existing funds. Average *interest cost* for the total portfolio is calculated by dividing total interest expense by the average dollar amount of liabilities outstanding; it measures the average percentage cost of a single dollar of debt. Average historical costs for a single source of funds can be calculated as the ratio of interest expense by source to the average outstanding debt for that source during the period. The interest cost rates presented in Chapter 2 represent such costs.

**EXHIBIT 8.7** Cost and Revenue Account Analysis for Various Demand Deposit Accounts at FirstBank

| | Low Balance, Low Activity, Truncated | | Medium Balance, High Activity, Nontruncated | | High Balance | |
|---|---|---|---|---|---|---|
| | Activity | Monthly Income / Expenses | Activity | Monthly Income / Expenses | Activity | Monthly Income / Expenses |
| **Income** | | | | | | |
| Interest income on average monthly balance (after float) | $ 500 | $ 0.93 | $ 4,589 | $ 8.50 | $11,500 | $ 21.30 |
| *Noninterest income (average monthly estimates)* | | | | | | |
| Service charges | | $ 2.80 | | $ 2.80 | | $ 2.80 |
| Penalty fees (estimated for account) | | $ 8.56 | | $ 6.32 | | $ 2.01 |
| Other | | $ 0.63 | | $ 0.63 | | $ 0.63 |
| *Total noninterest income* | | $ 11.99 | | $ 9.75 | | $ 5.44 |
| *Total revenue* | | $ 12.92 | | $ 18.25 | | $ 26.74 |
| **Expenses** | | | | | | |
| *Activity charges* | | | | | | |
| Deposit—electronic | 1 | $ 0.01 | 2 | $ 0.02 | 2 | $ 0.02 |
| Deposit—nonelectronic | 1 | $ 0.22 | 3 | $ 0.67 | 3 | $ 0.67 |
| Withdrawal—electronic | 15 | $ 1.61 | 12 | $ 1.29 | 10 | $ 1.07 |
| Withdrawal—nonelectronic | 3 | $ 0.66 | 14 | $ 3.06 | 8 | $ 1.75 |
| Transit check deposited | 1 | $ 0.16 | 2 | $ 0.32 | 2 | $ 0.32 |
| Transit check cashed | 1 | $ 0.26 | 2 | $ 0.51 | 2 | $ 0.51 |
| On-us checks cashed | 2 | $ 0.48 | 3 | $ 0.72 | 3 | $ 0.72 |
| Official check issued | | $ — | | $ — | | $ — |
| *Total activity expense* | | $ 3.40 | | $ 6.59 | | $ 5.06 |
| *Monthly expenses* | | | | | | |
| Monthly account maintenance (truncated) | 1 | $ 2.42 | | $ — | | $ — |
| Monthly account maintenance (nontruncated) | — | $ — | 1 | $ 6.60 | 1 | $ 6.60 |
| Net indirect expense | | $ 4.35 | | $ 4.35 | | $ 4.35 |
| *Total reoccurring monthly expenses* | | $ 6.77 | | $ 10.95 | | $ 10.95 |
| *Interest expense* | | $ — | | $ — | | $ — |
| *Total expense* | | $ 10.17 | | $ 17.54 | | $ 16.01 |
| **Net revenue per month** | | $ 2.75 | | $ 0.71 | | $ 10.73 |
| **Average percentage cost** | | | | | | |
| (net of service charges and fees) | | −5.12% | | 2.38% | | 1.29% |
| Average interest cost | | 0.00% | | 0.00% | | 0.00% |
| Average noninterest cost | | 28.53% | | 5.36% | | 1.95% |
| Average noninterest income | | 33.66% | | 2.98% | | 0.66% |
| Average account balance | | $ 500 | | $ 4,589 | | $ 11,500 |
| Required reserves | | 10% | | 10% | | 10% |
| Float | | 5% | | 5% | | 5% |

To estimate the annual historical net cost of bank liabilities, simply add historical interest expense with noninterest expense (net of noninterest income) and divide by the investable amount of funds to determine the minimum return required on earning assets:

$$Average\ net\ cost\ of\ bank\ liabilities = \frac{Interest\ expense + noninterest\ expense - noninterest\ income}{Average\ balance\ net\ of\ float \times (1 - reserve\ requirement\ ratio)} \times 12 \quad (8.1)$$

The average net cost of the medium-balance, high-activity account from Exhibit 8.7, assuming 5 percent float and 10 percent reserve requirements, would be:

$$\text{Average (annual) net cost of medium-balance account} = \frac{\$0 + \$17.54 - \$9.75}{\$4{,}589 \times 0.95 \times 0.90} \times 12 = 2.38\%^7$$

Note that the UBPR, introduced in Chapter 2, would have estimated the interest cost of noninterest-bearing checking accounts at near zero, truly underestimating the cost of these funds to the bank.

## CHARACTERISTICS OF LARGE WHOLESALE LIABILITIES

In addition to small denomination deposits, banks purchase funds in the money markets. Money center and large regional banks effect most transactions over the telephone, either directly with trading partners or through brokers. Most trades are denominated in $1 million multiples. Small banks generally deal directly with customers and have limited access to national and international markets. Some types of liabilities, such as jumbo CDs sold directly by a bank, are viewed as permanent sources of funds, while others are used infrequently. Banks must pay market rates on all sources and can normally attract additional funds by paying a small premium over the current quoted market rate. Because customers move their investments on the basis of small rate differentials, these funds are labeled "hot money," volatile liabilities, or short-term noncore funding and include large or jumbo CDs, federal funds purchased, RPs, Eurodollar time deposits, foreign deposits, and any other large denomination purchased liability.

### JUMBO CDs (CDs)

Large, negotiable certificates of $100,000 or more are referred to as jumbo CDs. These CDs are issued primarily by the largest banks and purchased by businesses and governmental units. Since their introduction in the early 1960s, CDs have grown to be the most popular hot money financing used by the largest banks. Although CDs come in many varieties, they all possess similar characteristics:

1. Minimum maturity of seven days. The most common maturities are 30 and 90 days, but recent issues of zero coupon CDs extend the maturity out as long as 10 years.

2. CD interest rates are quoted on the basis of a 360-day year. Except for zeros, CDs are issued at face value and trade as interest-bearing instruments. Thus, trades are settled at market value of the principal plus interest accrued from the original purchase.

3. CDs are insured up to $100,000 per investor per institution. Any balances in excess of $100,000 are at risk to the purchaser.[8]

Jumbo CDs are considered risky instruments and are traded accordingly. When an issuing bank has financial difficulties, it must pay a stiff premium over current yields, often 2 to 3 percent, to attract funds. When traders perceive that all large banks are experiencing difficulties, as with the Asian financial crisis in 1998, they bid CD rates higher relative to comparable maturity Treasury bill rates.

Banks issue jumbo CDs either directly to investors or indirectly through dealers and brokers. Whenever they use an intermediary, banks pay approximately one-eighth of 1 percent, or 12.5 basis points, for the service. Deposits obtained in this manner are labeled **brokered deposits**. The broker essentially places a bank's CDs with investors who demand insured deposits. The advantage is that brokers provide small banks access to purchased funds. They package CDs in $100,000 increments so that all deposits are fully insured, and market them to interested investors. In essence, the broker is selling deposit insurance because the buyer assumes the risk that the government will not pay off insured depositors, which has never happened. Thus, a bank or savings and loan might request that a broker obtain $50 million in CDs, which could be handled by selling 500 fully insured CDs of $100,000 each.

Not surprisingly, bank regulators argue that brokered CDs are often abused; they point to a link between brokered deposits and problem/failed banks. Banks and thrifts can use CD funds to speculate on high-risk assets. If the investments deteriorate and the bank fails, it is the FDIC, not the bank owners, that must pay insured depositors. In fact, many failed banks and savings and loans grew too rapidly during the 1980s by buying CD funds through brokers and making speculative loans. Loan losses subsequently followed. For this reason, Congress restricted the use of brokered deposits to banks with high amounts of equity capital that are less likely to fail.

---

[7]We multiply by 12 because the cost figures given in Exhibit 8.6 are monthly costs.

[8]For example, investors in CDs issued by Penn Square Bank of Oklahoma City that failed in 1983 received only 65 cents on the dollar for the uninsured portion of their CDs.

Large multibank holding companies have successfully marketed jumbo CDs by agreeing to allocate a total investment among affiliate banks in $100,000 increments so that the full amount is insured. Thus, a holding company with 60 subsidiary banks could place $6 million from any single depositor within the group with full insurance coverage. Deposit insurance again provides greater access to funding in this form. Interestingly, pension fund deposits are insured up to $100,000 per individual pensioner, amounts that reach many millions of dollars even at the same institution.

Uncertainty over future interest rates has induced many investors to shorten their investment horizon, making short-term CDs the most popular maturities. Many banks prefer to lengthen CD maturities, thereby reducing rate sensitivity because they currently operate with negative funding GAPs in the near term. Banks have gone to extremes to attract long-term CD funds, often creating hybrid CDs that appeal to select investors. Various types of CDs consist of:

- **Fixed-rate CDs.** Traditionally, CDs were fixed-rate contracts that were renegotiated at one-, three-, and six-month maturities. Today, fixed-rate maturities up to five years are quite common.

- **Variable-rate CDs.** Since the mid-1970s, large banks have issued variable-rate contracts for longer periods, with rates renegotiated at specified intervals such as every three months. The rate paid at each interval equals the average of three-month CD rates quoted by securities dealers. These variable-rate CDs appeal to investors who expect rising rates or want the added rate sensitivity. A recent variant is the **jump rate CD** (or **bump-up CD**) in which the depositor has a one-time option until maturity to change the rate to the prevailing market rate.[9] These attract funds when rates are expected to rise, but only a few individuals exercise the option.

- **Callable CDs.** During the late 1990s interest rates increased, bank loan demand was high, and banks were having difficulty funding asset growth. Large CD rates were as high as 8 percent on two- to five-year CDs, much higher than rates on comparable maturity Treasury securities. The need for long-term funding, combined with the concern that rates would fall, led some banks to begin issuing callable five- and ten-year CDs. These CDs typically carried a two-year deferment period, meaning they could not be called for two years after issue. Afterward, the bank could call the CDs, meaning that it could repay the depositor's principal, at its discretion. These CDs offered attractive rates but provided the bank with lower borrowing costs risk if rates were to fall over the life of the CDs.

- **Zero coupon CDs.** Like zero coupon bonds, zero coupon CDs are sold at a steep discount from par and appreciate to face value at maturity. They carry fixed rates and fixed maturities. For example, a bank might issue a CD with a current price of $750,000 that pays $1 million in five years. The investor receives a fixed 5.92 percent annual return and knows with certainty what the value of the investment is after five years. The primary disadvantage is that the amortized portion of the original ($250,000) discount is subject to federal income taxes each year, even though the investor does not actually receive current income. For this reason, many banks market the zeros to individual retirement or Keogh accounts. Whenever the maturity value is below $100,000, the CD is fully insured. The attraction to issuing banks is in getting longer-term funds. In this case, the bank obtains $750,000 immediately with no corresponding cash outflow for five years. This deposit's effective duration is five years.

- **Stock market indexed CDs.** During the 1990s the U.S. stock market boomed, producing historically high returns for most buy and hold investors. As stock prices rose, yields on CDs fell behind. Many banks tried to capitalize on this phenomenon by offering CDs with yields linked to a stock market index such as the S&P 500. A depositor who opens such an account might receive a yield equal to the higher of a fixed 1 percent or 90 percent of the total return on the S&P 500 index. A bank can offer this CD in part because it can hedge the risk of stock prices rising sharply by selling futures contracts on the S&P 500.

## INDIVIDUAL RETIREMENT ACCOUNTS

Individual retirement accounts (IRAs) are savings plans for wage earners and their spouses. The plans encompass many types of savings vehicles with varied maturities, interest rates, and other earnings features. Individuals can choose between different financial services companies and many different products. Commercial banks, thrift institutions, brokerage houses, and insurance companies dominate IRA investments. Investor options range from small time deposits and MMDAs at banks and savings and loans to common stocks, zero coupon Treasury securities, and shares in limited real estate partnerships offered by brokerages. Although IRA accounts are listed as wholesale funds, many times the bank's core customers also hold IRA accounts.

The primary attraction of IRAs is their tax benefits. Each wage earner can make a tax-deferred investment up to $3,000 ($3,500 if aged 50 or older) of earned income annually in an IRA, subject to IRS retirement plan and

---

[9]Because this option transfers all interest rate risk to the issuing bank, a customer should be willing to accept a lower initial yield.

maximum income rules.[10] Funds withdrawn before age 59½ are subject to a 10 percent IRS penalty. Investors can change investments prior to this age but must pay another penalty if the change does not occur when the underlying savings vehicle matures. These features make IRAs an attractive source of long-term funds for commercial banks and other issuers that can be used to balance the rate sensitivity of longer-term assets. Customers opening accounts are less likely to move them as long as the bank pays competitive rates.

These traditional IRAs are attractive because all funds contributed to the IRA are tax deductible. Taxes are paid when the funds are withdrawn, hence investors will earn interest on what they would have had to pay in taxes. A new IRA, the Roth IRA, is similarly attractive but has different tax treatment. With a Roth IRA, contributions are made from after-tax dollars, but income accumulates tax free. When the individual eventually withdraws Roth IRA proceeds, the entire amount is not taxed.[11]

Commercial banks and thrifts offer IRA products related to small time deposits with fixed maturities and MMDAs. These deposits are federally insured (up to $100,000), which appeals to many individuals. Money market deposit accounts are the most rate sensitive, as banks change rates at least every 30 days. Banks can typically induce customers to lengthen deposit maturities by paying higher rates on longer-term instruments. Small CDs carrying variable rates tied to external indexes have become increasingly popular with the greater uncertainty over future interest rate movements.

## FOREIGN OFFICE DEPOSITS

Most large U.S. commercial banks compete aggressively in international markets. They borrow from and extend credit to foreign-based individuals, corporations, and governments. In recent years, international financial markets and multinational businesses have become increasingly sophisticated to the point where bank customers go overseas for cheaper financing and feel unfettered by national boundaries. Savings transactions in short-term international markets often take place in the Eurocurrency market. The term **Eurocurrency** refers to a financial claim denominated in a currency other than that of the country where the issuing institution is located. The most important Eurocurrency is the **Eurodollar**, a dollar-denominated financial claim at a bank outside the United States. The banks may be foreign-owned or foreign branches of U.S. banks. The Eurodollar market comprises both loans and deposits, each with different characteristics and participants.

**Eurodollar deposits** are dollar-denominated deposits in banks outside the United States. They are virtually identical to time deposits issued directly by domestic banks, except for the country of issue. In all cases, dollar deposits at U.S. banks support the creation of a Eurodollar deposit. These deposits never physically leave the U.S., only the ownership does. Maturities range from call to five years, and most deposits are traded in denominations of $1 million or more. Eurodollar CDs, the counterpart of domestic CDs, are the most popular Eurodollar deposit. They carry short-term maturities, typically three to six months, and can be traded in the secondary market prior to maturity. Although most Eurodollar CDs pay fixed rates, floating-rate instruments are becoming increasingly popular. Eurodollar rates are quoted on an interest-bearing basis, assuming a 360-day year. Eurodollar deposit rates must be competitive with rates on comparable maturity instruments, such as federal funds and jumbo CDs.[12] Otherwise, the deposits would not attract funds away from U.S.-based instruments.

Eurodollar depositors include individuals, businesses, and governments from around the world. Many transactions, in fact, are merely interbank deposits. Exhibit 8.8 characterizes the origination of Eurodollar deposits and the eventual path to a Eurodollar loan. It summarizes activities of four groups and encompasses three stages of transactions. In the first stage, a U.S. manufacturing corporation based in New York opens a Eurodollar deposit at the Bank of England in London and effectively transfers ownership of a demand balance held at a U.S. Money Center Bank in New York. The terms of the Eurodollar deposit are negotiated as discussed above. At the end of this transaction, $10 million in Eurodollar deposits has been created. The amount of demand deposits at U.S. banks, however, is unchanged. Only the ownership has changed, from the U.S. manufacturer to the Bank of England.

During Stage II, the Bank of England redeposits the dollars with the U.S. Money Center Bank's London office. Ownership of the original demand balance at the New York bank again changes, but the deposit does not physically leave the United States. Another $10 million in Eurodollar deposits has been created with no change in total demand deposits at U.S. banks.

Stage III documents a Eurodollar loan made to a British corporation such that the foreign firm ultimately owns the original demand deposit. This intermediation among banks permits the multiple expansion of Eurodollar

---

[10]These limits are scheduled to increase to $4,000 for those less than 50 years of age and $4,500 for those over 50 in 2005, and to $5,000 and $6,000 by 2008. For individuals covered by a retirement plan at work, deductions are phased out if the individual's modified adjusted gross income is more than $65,000 but less than $75,000 for a married couple filing a joint return; more than $45,000 but less than $55,000 for a single individual or head of household; and; less than $10,000 for a married individual filing a separate return. These limits are scheduled to increase by $5,000 in 2005.

[11]Individuals can contribute to a Roth IRA up to the lesser of their maximum taxable income or $160,000 for married taxpayers filing jointly.

[12]Goodfriend (1981) discusses these relationships and general Eurodollar characteristics in detail.

*Characteristics of Large Wholesale-Type Liabilities*

---

## EXHIBIT 8.8 — The Origin and Expansion of Eurodollar Deposits

Stage I: U.S. manufacturer opens $10 million Eurodollar account at Bank of England, London (BE-L) with deposits held at a Money Center Bank-NY (MCB-NY).

Stage II: Bank of England, London, opens Eurodollar account at U.S. Money Center Bank, London (MCB-L).

Stage III: U.S. Money Center Bank, London, extends $10 million Eurodollar loan to British corporation in London.

| U.S. Manufacturer, New York | | U.S. Money Center Bank, New York | | U.S. Money Center Bank, London | | Bank of England, London | |
|---|---|---|---|---|---|---|---|
| ΔASSETS | ΔLIABILITIES | ΔASSETS | ΔLIABILITIES | ΔASSETS | ΔLIABILITIES | ΔASSETS | ΔLIABILITIES |
| **Stage I:** | | | | | | | |
| Demand deposits due from MCB-NY −$10 million; Eurodollar deposit due from BE-L +$10 million | | | Demand deposits due to U.S. manuf.-NY −$10 million; Demand deposit due to BE-L +$10 million | | | Demand deposit due from MCB-NY +$10 million | Eurodollar deposit due to U.S manuf.-NY +$10 million |
| **Stage II:** | | | Demand deposit due to BE-L −$10 million; Demand deposit due to MCB-L +$10 million | Demand deposit due from MCB-NY +$10 million | Eurodollar deposit due to BE-L +$10 million | Demand deposit due from MCB-NY −$10 million; Eurodollar deposit due from MCB-L +$10 million | |
| **Stage III:** **British Corp., London** | | Demand deposit due to MCB-L −$10 million; Demand deposit due to British corp. +$10 million | | Demand deposit due from MCB-NY −$10 million; Eurodollar loan to British corp. +$10 million | | | |
| ΔASSETS — Demand deposit due from MCB-NY 1$10 million | LIABILITIES — Eurodollar loan from MCB-L 1$10 million | | | | | | |

---

deposits based on a fixed demand deposit at a U.S. bank. There are no reserve requirements on Eurodollar deposits, and a bank will move the entire balance as long as it can earn a profitable spread. The base rate paid on interbank deposits (Stage II) is termed the London Interbank Offer Rate (LIBOR). Additional interbank deposits are typically made at spreads of 0.125 to 0.25 percent. Thus if the initial deposit at the Bank of England paid 6 percent, the Bank of England would require at least 6.125 percent on its redeposit. The spread on a Eurodollar loan to the ultimate borrower is considerably greater.

## BORROWING IMMEDIATELY AVAILABLE FUNDS

As the name suggests, immediately available funds are balances that are accepted as a means of payment within one business day on demand. Two types of balances are immediately available: deposit liabilities of Federal Reserve Banks and certain "collected" liabilities of commercial banks that may be transferred or withdrawn during a business day on order of account holders.[13] Through its wire transfer facilities, the Federal Reserve System can electronically move deposits anywhere throughout the United States within 24 hours. Collected balances of banks are ledger balances

---

[13]Immediately available funds are discussed by Lucas, Jones, and Thurston (1977). Deposit liabilities of Federal Reserve Banks to financial institutions constitute the major portion of the banking system's legal required reserves.

appearing on a bank's books minus float. All checks written against such accounts, but not yet cleared, have been deducted, and the remaining balances are transferable within one day. Most large transactions are settled in immediately available funds, including maturing CDs, federal funds, and security repurchase agreements.

**FEDERAL FUNDS PURCHASED.** The term *federal funds* is often used to refer to excess reserve balances that are traded between banks. This is grossly inaccurate, given reserves averaging as a method of computing reserves, different nonbank players in the market, and the motivation behind many trades. In some instances, nonbank participants, such as securities dealers and state governments, trade federal funds. In other cases, bank reserve balances at Federal Reserve Banks do not change ownership. The formal definition of **federal funds** is unsecured short-term loans that are settled in immediately available funds. They encompass transactions outside the arena of bank reserve trading by including any participant that holds large balances at Federal Reserve Banks or collected liabilities at depository institutions. Thus, thrift institutions, foreign governments, and the U.S. Treasury can trade federal funds.

Most transactions are overnight loans, although maturities are negotiated and can extend up to several weeks. Interest rates are negotiated between trading partners and are quoted on a 360-day basis. The absence of collateral suggests that participants are well known by their trading partners as lenders accept default risk. Large transactions are denominated in multiples of $1 million and are typically handled by brokers. On the other side of the spectrum, small banks frequently buy and sell federal funds in amounts as low as $50,000. When a bank purchases federal funds, its cost of borrowing equals the interest rate plus the brokerage fee because the bank does not have to hold required reserves against this liability.

The federal funds market is important to monetary policy because the federal funds rate is a key target variable for the Federal Reserve System. Federal Reserve policies, particularly Federal Open Market Committee (FOMC) purchases and sales of securities, directly alter the bank reserves component of immediately available funds, increasing or decreasing the federal funds rate. Increases in bank reserves reduce borrowing pressure relative to desired lending of immediately available funds, and the federal funds rate declines over the near term. The opposite occurs with decreases in bank reserves.

**SECURITY REPURCHASE AGREEMENTS.** Security repurchase agreements (RPs or repos) are short-term loans secured by government securities that are settled in immediately available funds. They are virtually identical to federal funds in function and form except they are collateralized. Technically, the loans embody a sale of securities with a simultaneous agreement to buy them back later at a fixed price plus accrued interest. The later date is normally the next day, as most RPs have 24-hour maturities. Some loans are for longer periods, with maturity and rate negotiated. Although securities dealers dominate the market, any institution can trade RPs as long as it meets collateral and balance requirements.

For example, if City National Bank used an RP to acquire immediately available funds, it would have to post securities as collateral against the borrowing. Whenever the collateral is U.S. government or agency securities, the funds obtained are free of reserves. In market terminology, the lender's transaction is a reverse RP. Banks participate both as borrowers and lenders directly or as securities dealers.

In most cases, the market value of the collateral is set above the loan amount when the contract is negotiated. This difference is labeled the *margin*. If, for example, City National pledged $1.1 million of U.S. government securities against its $1 million borrowing, the margin equals $100,000. Positive margin protects the lender from potential decreases in collateral value if interest rates increase. This protection makes RPs less risky compared with unsecured federal funds transactions and thus RP rates are less than federal funds rates for similar maturity contracts. Such collateral proved inadequate in 1982, when two government securities dealers, Drysdale Government Securities and Lombard-Wall were forced into bankruptcy when they could not pay accrued interest owed on heavy borrowings via RPs when the loans came due. As a result, Chase Manhattan Bank and Manufacturers Hanover took losses from Drysdale alone equal to $285 million and $21 million, respectively. Although both banks initially disclaimed liability, they eventually made good on losses their customers otherwise would have incurred because the banks arranged the RP transactions.

In 1985 E.S.M. Group similarly collapsed after suffering losses trading RPs, bringing about the failure of Home State Savings in Ohio and the closing of more than 70 thrifts that faced losses from a massive run on deposits. Deposits at Home State and the thrifts were privately insured, but the insurance pool was insufficient to meet payment obligations. The closed thrifts ultimately reopened with federal deposit insurance coverage.[14] These failures increased regulatory scrutiny of the RP market and focused attention on the true legal status of a repo. In particular, creditors of Drysdale and Lombard-Wall who held RP collateral sold the securities. If, in fact, RPs are secured loans, bankruptcy law prohibits creditors from selling any assets owned by the failed firms. If RPs are separate contracts to sell and repurchase securities, creditors can liquidate the securities. Technically, the securities

---

[14]A series of articles from "Repurchase Agreements: Taking a Closer Look at Safety" (Federal Reserve Bank of Atlanta, September 1985) discuss the structure of the RP market and factors influencing credit and interest rate risk.

are the lenders because the borrower failed to repurchase them. Court rulings appear to side with the creditors, allowing them to liquidate security holdings.

## BORROWING FROM THE FEDERAL RESERVE

Federal Reserve Banks are authorized to make loans to depository institutions to help them meet reserve requirements. Before 1980, only commercial banks that were members of the Federal Reserve System could borrow under normal circumstances. The Depository Institutions Deregulation and Monetary Control Act (DIDMCA) of 1980 opened borrowing to any depository institution that offers transactions accounts subject to reserve requirements. The borrowing facility is called the **discount window**. All Federal Reserve Banks charge a fixed rate, known as the **discount rate**, which is formally set by the district Federal Reserve Banks and approved by the Board of Governors. In practice, the board determines when rate changes are necessary and requests approval from district representatives.

When the Federal Reserve System was established in 1913, lending reserve funds through the discount window was intended as the principal instrument of central banking operations since discount window loans directly increase a member bank's reserve assets. Long ago, however, open market operations became the most important tool of monetary policy and today the discount window functions as a safety valve in relieving liquidity strains at depository institutions and the banking system as a whole. The discount window also helps ensure stability of the payment system by supplying liquidity during times of systemic stress. For example, before the tragic events of September 11, 2001, banks held approximately $13 billion in the Federal Reserve accounts. In the days following September 11, these balances ballooned to more than $120 billion because some banks could not move funds out of these accounts. The additional funds in some bank accounts meant that a number of other banks were running huge negative positions in their Federal Reserve accounts. The number of Fedwire transfers fell from about $1.6 trillion to only $1.2 trillion, again creating a serious liquidity crisis for the payment systems. On September 12, lending to banks through the discount window totaled about $46 billion, more than 200 times the daily average for the previous month.

In October 2002, the Federal Reserve established a new discount rate policy in which the Fed would lend to most financial institutions under its primary and secondary credit programs at 1 percent and 1.5 percent over the current federal funds target rate. Previously, the Fed generally discouraged borrowing directly from the Fed and established the discount rate well below the current federal funds rate. Under the old policy, changes in the discount rate were infrequent and primarily were a signal of future policy toward monetary ease or tightness rather than to change bank borrowing activity. Under the new policy, the Fed does not "discourage" borrowing as it did in the previous policy. The Federal Reserve expects that, given the above-market pricing of primary credit, institutions will use the discount window as a backup rather than a regular source of funding.

Banks can borrow deposit balances, or required reserves, directly from Federal Reserve Banks in their role as lender of last resort, with the discount rate representing the interest rate that banks pay. The Federal Reserve has four distinct lending programs: primary credit, secondary credit, seasonal credit, and emergency credit:

- **Primary credit** is available to generally sound depository institutions on a very short-term basis, typically overnight, at a rate above the FOMC's target rate for federal funds. The primary credit program is the principal safety valve for ensuring adequate liquidity in the banking system and a backup source of short-term funds for generally sound depository institutions. Most depository institutions qualify for primary credit. Depository institutions are not required to seek alternative sources of funds before requesting occasional advances of primary credit.

- **Secondary credit** is available to depository institutions that are not eligible for primary credit. It is extended on a very short-term basis, typically overnight, at a rate that is above the primary credit rate. Secondary credit is available to meet backup liquidity needs when its use is consistent with a timely return to a reliance on market sources of funding or the orderly resolution of a troubled institution. In July 1984, for example, the Federal Reserve extended $4 billion in credit to Continental Illinois of Chicago to offset deposit losses of customers fearful that the bank was about to fail. Secondary credit may not be used to fund an expansion of the borrower's assets. The secondary credit program entails a higher level of Federal Reserve Bank administration and oversight than the primary credit program.

- **Seasonal credit** is designed to assist small depository institutions in managing significant seasonal swings in their loans and deposits. Seasonal credit is available to depository institutions that can demonstrate a clear pattern of recurring intrayear swings in funding needs. Eligible institutions are usually located in agricultural or tourist areas. The interest rate applied to seasonal credit is a floating rate based on market rates.

- **Emergency credit** may be authorized in unusual and exigent circumstances by the Board of Governors to individuals, partnerships, and corporations that are not depository institutions. Federal Reserve Banks currently do not establish an interest rate for emergency credit, but *Regulation A* specifies that such a rate would be above the highest rate in effect for advances to depository institutions. Such lending may occur only when, in the judgment of the Federal Reserve Bank, credit is not available from other sources and failure to provide credit would adversely affect the economy.

## EXHIBIT 8.9

Commercial Banks with FHLB Advances, 1991–2004

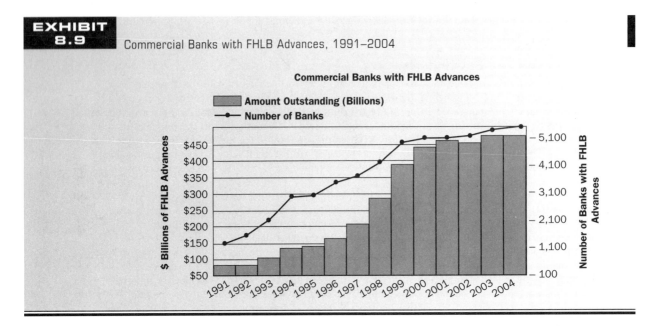

Commercial Banks with FHLB Advances

- The Federal Reserve establishes conditions and procedures for borrowing. Banks must apply and provide acceptable collateral before a loan is granted. Eligible collateral includes U.S. government securities, bankers acceptances, and qualifying short-term commercial or government paper. Frequent borrowers typically use U.S. Treasury securities already held in bookkeeping form at Federal Reserve Banks. Advances are loans secured by qualifying collateral. Discounts refer to member banks temporarily selling eligible loans to the Federal Reserve. The Federal Reserve agrees to return the loans to the bank at maturity. The discount rate charged determines the interest payment in both cases and is set by the Federal Reserve in light of current economic conditions.

### FEDERAL HOME LOAN BANK ADVANCES

With today's intense competition for retail, or core deposits, many banks today rely heavily on advances (borrowings) from one of the Federal Home Loan Banks (FHLBs). The FHLB system is a government-sponsored enterprise that was originally created to assist individuals in home buying. Today, FHLBs are among the largest U.S. financial institutions. FHLB system borrowings are rated AAA (Aaa) because of the government sponsorship. FHLBs borrow cheaply and either buy government securities or make loans to other institutions. These loans represent a source of financing to many banks. Any bank can become a member of the FHLB system by buying FHLB stock. If it has the available collateral, primarily real-estate-related loans, a bank can borrow from the FHLB. The Gramm-Leach-Bliley Act of 1999, however, made it much easier for smaller banks to borrow with the funds used for non-real-estate-related loans. In particular, this act allows banks with less than $500 million in assets to use long-term advances for loans to small businesses, small farms, and small agribusinesses.

The act also establishes a new permanent capital structure for the Federal Home Loan Banks with two classes of stock authorized, redeemable on six-months' and five-years' notice. The greater competition for funds and the authorization of new uses for FHLB advances has resulted in rapid growth in the number of banks with FHLB borrowing and the dollar amount of these borrowings. Exhibit 8.9 tracks the growth in commercial banks with FHLB advances and the dollar amount of these advances.

FHLB borrowings come in the form of **advances**, which take a variety of forms. Advances can have maturities as short as one day or as long as 20 years. Banks with temporary funding needs (typically linked to increases in home lending) often use short-term advances with maturities from 30 to 90 days. A more recent trend has seen banks use longer-term advances as a more permanent source of funding for loan growth. In many instances, the interest cost compares favorably with the cost of jumbo CDs and other purchased liabilities. The range of potential maturities further allows banks to better manage their interest rate risk by helping them adjust effective maturities or durations of their funding and match them with assets. In addition, banks can borrow virtually any amount as long as they have the qualifying collateral. The interesting issue is whether these advances are truly a permanent source of funds and thus comparable to core deposits, or whether they are hot money.

Some of these FHLB advances are callable in the sense that the FHLB has the right to call the advance prior to maturity, typically after a predetermined deferment period. For example, a five-year callable advance may be called after one year. By agreeing to an advance with this call feature, a bank sells an option to the FHLB and receives value by paying a lower initial interest rate. Of course, if rates increase, the FHLB will call the loan and the bank will be forced to replace the funds at a higher rate.

## ELECTRONIC MONEY

Electronic commerce, in its infancy just a few years ago, has grown quite rapidly. If one considers the impact of technology in banking, it is apparent that almost all financial products can be provided electronically. One can pay for goods electronically, apply and receive a loan electronically, even invest and transfer funds electronically. The need for a physical bank location reflects customer preference—it is not a requirement for doing business.

Some analysts believe that smart cards, e-cash, and e-checks will soon become the dominant means of payment for Internet transactions. E-cash and e-checks are not Federal Reserve money but rather digital "tokens," somewhat like bus tokens or casino chips, only electronic versions. These funds represent encrypted value that is first paid for by credit card or cash and then presented for online purchases. Lauren Bielski argues that e-money "is arguably more of an electronic instruction to pay than true 'electronic money.'"[15] With respect to small payments, e-money has been compared to "prepaid" phone cards in that one "purchases" electronic value that can be used to make payments securely. On the large payment side, Electronic Data Interchange (EDI), a paperless exchange of business information between business partners, is used by more than 100,000 companies today.

Those green pieces of paper stuffed in your pocket or wallet, sometimes referred to as money or dollars, could someday become cryptographically sealed digital images stored electronically. This "digital" money may be stored on a smart card, a plastic credit card–sized card with a microchip; an "electronic wallet," a small wallet-sized reader and loader for smart cards; or even the hard disk of your computer or the bank's computer.

There are basically two types of smart cards: an "intelligent" card and a "memory" card. An **intelligent card** contains a microchip with the ability to store and secure information, and makes different responses depending on the requirements of the card issuer's specific application needs. Intelligent cards offer a read and storage capability and new information can be added or updated at anytime; additional funds can be added or the card can be terminated if needed. **Memory cards** simply store information. Similar to the stored information on the back of a credit card, a storage card can contain value that the user can spend in a pay phone, a retail store, or a vending machine. Memory-type smart cards are popular on college campuses.

Wireless transactions using computers, personal digital assistance (PDAs), and even cell phones are increasingly used in the U.S. Cell phones are used to make small payments in Europe to a much greater degree than in the U.S. For example, soft-drink vending machines are connected to a network that makes a drink fall from the machine after one dials in the telephone number listed on the front of the machine!

Although the technology to go "cashless" has been available for many years, some would say we have a long way to go since paper money is still popular and accounts for roughly 80 percent of all transactions. On the other hand, cash transactions account for less than 0.3 percent of the total value of transactions today. Hence, although cash dominates the "small" payment end of transactions, it represents a very small fraction of the total value of payments. Still, the actual number of cash payments is subject to a great deal of disagreement by experts primarily because there is no meaningful way to measure the number or amount of these payments. Even though the majority of transactions are made with cash, fundamentally all large transactions—the trillions of dollars handled each day by banks, other financial institutions, and the Federal Reserve clearinghouses—are already digital. Wholesale electronic payments, using wire transfers such as Clearing House Interbank Payment System (CHIPS) and the Fedwire, account for more than 85 percent of the value of transactions. Hence, what it means to move to a *cashless* society is a relative term.

Technology may eventually mean, however, that paper money is no longer a viable option. The advent of high-quality color copiers and computer imaging equipment means that the security of paper money is questionable. The cost of doing business with paper money and paper checks is quite high. Paper money must be guarded, insured, physically transported, and there is always the divisibility problem. That is, dollar bills are not always substitutable for quarters in vending machines. According to Donald Gleason, president of the Smart Card Enterprise unit of Electronic Payment Services, "It costs money handlers in the United States alone approximately $60 billion a year to move the stuff, a line item ripe for drastic pruning. The solution is to cram our currency in burn bags and strike some matches. This won't happen all at once, and paper money will probably never go away, but bills and coinage will increasingly be replaced by some sort of electronic equivalent."

*The 2004 Federal Reserve Payments Study* indicates that paper transactions, in the form of checks, have declined

---

[15]See Lauren Bielski, "New Wave of E-Money Options Hits the Web," *ABA Banking Journal*, (August 2000), http://www.banking.com/aba.

**EXHIBIT 8.10**

Distribution of the Number of Noncash Payments in 2000 and 2003

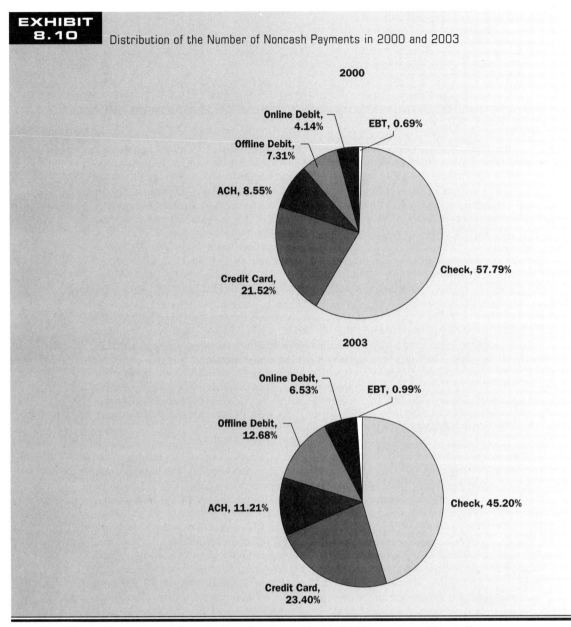

**2000**

Online Debit, 4.14%

EBT, 0.69%

Offline Debit, 7.31%

ACH, 8.55%

Credit Card, 21.52%

Check, 57.79%

**2003**

Online Debit, 6.53%

EBT, 0.99%

Offline Debit, 12.68%

ACH, 11.21%

Check, 45.20%

Credit Card, 23.40%

SOURCE: *The 2004 Federal Reserve Payments Study*, http://www.frbservices.org/Retail/pdf/2004PaymentResearchReport.pdf.

Note: Online debit payments are PIN-based, which includes purchases at the point of sale with ATM cards, and offline debit payments, which are signature-based transactions. EBTs are electronic benefits transfers. Data do not include Fedwire or CHIPS wire transfers.

significantly over the past few years. Exhibit 8.10 (which excludes large Fedwire and CHIPS payments) shows that checks amounted to less than 50 percent of noncash payments for the first time in 2003. In particular, checks only accounted for 45.2 percent of noncash payments in 2003 compared with 57.8 percent in 2000. Offline debit transactions have increased the most; followed by online debit. The difference in online and offline debit is *online debit* payments are PIN-based, which includes purchases at the point of sale with ATM cards, and *offline debit* payments are signature-based transactions.

Other types of electronic payments include **electronic funds transfer (EFT)**, which is an electronic movement of financial data, designed to eliminate the paper instruments normally associated with such funds movement. There are many types of EFTs including ACH, POS, ATM, direct deposit, telephone bill paying, automated merchant authorization systems, and preauthorized payments. A **point of sale (POS)** transaction is a sale that is consummated by payment for goods or services received at the point of the sale or a direct debit of the purchase amount from the customer's checking account. That is, funds are transferred at the time the sale is made.[16] An **automated clearing house (ACH)** transaction is an electronically processed payment using a standard data format. A computer network to clear and settle electronic payment transactions links ACH institutions. ACH payments are electronic payments of funds and government securities among financial institutions and businesses. ATMs, or automatic teller machines, have been a popular EFT system for many years. These machines provide customers electronic access to their funds all over the world. Direct deposits of paychecks and social security checks are quite common today as well. Automated merchant and preauthorized payments are actually the other side of direct deposits in which payments are made automatically and electronically. In both cases, direct deposits and automated payments, one level of paper has been eliminated. These payments go directly to the party authorized for payment. For example, rather than an employee receiving a check and depositing it in his or her bank account, the payment is made directly to the employee's bank with instructions to credit the customer's account.

Even though Internet bill payments, telephone bill payments, automatic deposits, and bank drafts are considered to be electronic payments, many may not be. For example, in many cases paper checks are still written on the customer's behalf and mailed to the business. Obviously, these types of payments will most likely become totally electronic in the near future. The real question is, even though we have the technology to become a "cashless" society today, will you part with your paper money or will technology force you to give it up?

## CHECK 21

Congress passed the Check Clearing for the 21st Century Act in 2003 and it became effective on October 28, 2004. **Check 21**, as this Act is known, was designed with three primary purposes:

1. To facilitate check truncation by reducing some of the legal impediments
2. To foster innovation in the payments and check collection system without mandating receipt of checks in electronic form
3. To improve the overall efficiency of the nation's payments system

**Check truncation** is the conversion of a paper check into an electronic debit or image of the check by a third party in the payment system other than the paying bank. Check 21 facilitates check truncation by creating a new negotiable instrument called a substitute check, which permits banks to truncate original checks, process check information electronically, and deliver substitute checks to banks that want to continue receiving paper checks. A **substitute check** (see Exhibit 8.11) is the legal equivalent of the original check and includes all the information contained on the original. The law does not require banks to accept checks in electronic form nor does it require banks to use the new authority granted by the act to create substitute checks. The Check 21 Act is clearly a necessary first step in phasing out paper checks.

Check 21 is designed to enable banks to handle more checks electronically instead of physically moving paper checks from one bank to another, which should make check processing faster, more efficient, and therefore less expensive. Banks can capture a picture of the front and back of the check along with the associated payment information and transmit this information electronically. If a receiving bank or its customer requires a paper check, the bank can use the electronic picture and payment information to create a paper "substitute check." This process enables banks to reduce the cost of physically handling and transporting original paper checks, which can be very expensive.

Check 21 has obvious benefits for the banking community but consumers have raised several questions about the act and its impact upon the bank's account holders. Their concerns include whether the electronic check process will be secure, if they will still be able to receive their original paper checks, and the impact Check 21 will have on float.

Electronic check processing is not new to the financial industry, and many large retailers, such as Wal-Mart, have been truncating checks for some time. Hence, the risk to the system is not seen as any greater than what is already occurring. The biggest difference between what Check 21 and Wal-Mart does is that Wal-Mart processes the customer's check at the point of sale (POS) and returns the check to the customer at that time. Effectively, Wal-Mart uses the information on the bottom of a personal check to convert the payment into an ACH or debit card transaction. Rather than the consumer presenting his or her debit card, Wal-Mart uses the personal check as a source of information to create a debit transaction. Because Wal-Mart no longer needs the paper check, it is returned to the consumer at the POS. Although similar to Wal-Mart's process, Check 21 allows any institution in the process of clearing the check to stop the movement of the paper check, convert it to a substitute check, and continue the process electronically. More importantly for consumers, Check 21 makes the substitute check legally acceptable as proof of payment and provides for an "expedited recredit" if a substitute check was incorrectly charged to a customer's account.

---

[16]Technically speaking, it can actually take one to three days before the funds are transferred.

**EXHIBIT 8.11**  Substitute Check Authorized by Check 21

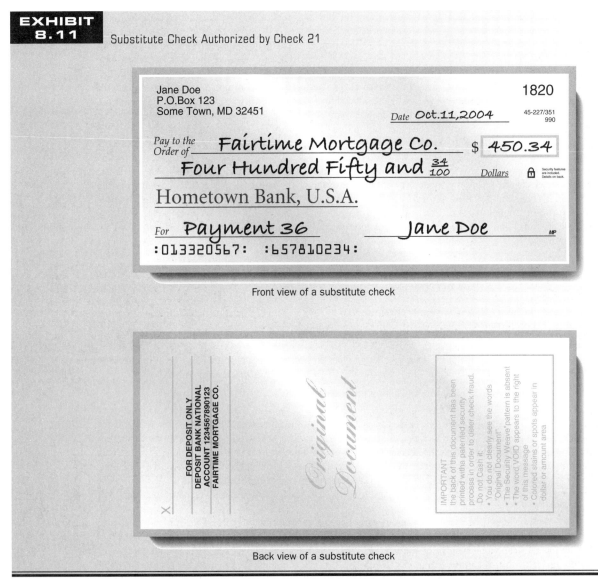

Front view of a substitute check

Back view of a substitute check

SOURCE: FRB Frequently Asked Questions about Check 21, http://www.federalreserve.gov/paymentsystems/truncation/faqs2.htm#ques1.

If you receive your canceled checks back with your account statement today, you will continue to receive canceled checks unless your bank notifies you otherwise, but some of the canceled checks may be substitute checks. Banks today are not required to keep original checks for any specific length of time, and Check 21 does not add any new retention requirements. In many cases, the original check may be destroyed. Requests for original checks will mean that your bank may provide you with the original check, a substitute check, or a copy of the check.

The final concern of many consumers is the potential reduction in float time. Many consumers already know that using a debit card expedites the movement of funds out of an account. Hence, some consumers purposely use checks to slow the process of transferring funds from their account. First, it is illegal to write a check for which you do not have the funds already in your account; hence this activity is not one that can be easily defended from a consumer's point of view. Second, most checks clear in just one or two days currently, so that the reduction in float is minimal.

Exhibit 8.12 outlines the standard check-clearing process. Checks drawn against transactions accounts are presented to the customer's bank for payment and ultimately "cleared" by reducing the bank's deposit balance at the Federal Reserve or a correspondent bank. Payments made electronically directly and immediately alter balances held at Federal Reserve Banks. This network for transferring funds electronically is called the Fedwire. For example, an individual visiting San Jose, California, purchases goods from a local business for $500 by writing a check on his demand deposit held at Community National Bank (CNB) in Portland, Oregon. The check-clearing process begins

**EXHIBIT 8.12** Example of the Check-Clearing Process

| Bay Area National Bank, San Jose | | | | | | Bank of California, San Francisco | | | | | |
|---|---|---|---|---|---|---|---|---|---|---|---|
| **ΔASSETS** | | | **ΔLIABILITIES** | | | **ΔASSETS** | | | **ΔLIABILITIES** | | |
| 1. CIPC | +$500 | | Demand deposit owed the business | +$500 | | 2. CIPC | +$500 | | Demand deposit (BANB) | +$50 | |
| 4. CIPC | −$500 | | | | | 5. CIPC | −$500 | | | | |
| Demand deposit at BOC | +$500 | | | | | Demand deposit at FRB of San Francisco | +$500 | | | | |

| Federal Reserve Bank of San Francisco | | | | | | Community National Bank, Portland | | | | | |
|---|---|---|---|---|---|---|---|---|---|---|---|
| **ΔASSETS** | | | **ΔLIABILITIES** | | | **ΔASSETS** | | | **ΔLIABILITIES** | | |
| 3. CIPC | +$500 | | DACI | +$500 | | 6. Demand deposit at FRB of San Francisco | −$500 | | Demand deposit owed the individual | −$500 | |
| 5. | | | DACI | −$500 | | | | | | | |
| | | | Demand deposit (BOC) | +$500 | | | | | | | |
| 6. CIPC | −$500 | | Demand deposit (CNB) | −$500 | | | | | | | |

NOTE: CIPC indicates checks in the process of collection; BOC, Bank of California; FRB, Federal Reserve Bank; BANB, Bay Area National Bank; DACI, deferred credit availability items; and CNB, Community National Bank.

when the business deposits this check at the Bay Area National Bank (BANB). Because BANB assumes the risk that the check may not be good, it does not allow the depositor to use the funds immediately. Normally, a bank places a **hold on the check** until it verifies that the check writer has enough funds on deposit to cover the draft. BANB thus increases the ledger balances of the business's demand deposit account and its own cash item in the process of collection (CIPC). The business's usable collected balances, ledger balances minus float, are unchanged.

During Stage 2, BANB forwards the check to its upstream correspondent, the Bank of California (BOC) in San Francisco. This bank replicates BANB's procedures, deferring credit to BANB for several days until the check clears. In Stage 3, BOC presents the check to the Federal Reserve Bank of San Francisco. The Federal Reserve follows a timetable indicating how long a bank must wait before it can receive credit on deposited items. The dollar amount of deferred credit is labeled deferred availability credit items (DACI). Until the Federal Reserve provides credit, it increases its CIPC and DACI equally so that Federal Reserve float (CIPC-DACI) equals zero.

Up to this point, no depositor can spend its funds, and the check has not been presented to CNB for payment. Frequently, correspondent banks and the Federal Reserve give credit on checks deposited by other banks *prior* to actually verifying that the checks are good. This is indicated as Stages 4 and 5 in Exhibit 8.12. BANB, however, does not provide the same credit to the business depositor until the check clears. After Stage 4, BANB can invest its deposit at BOC while it defers crediting the business account. BOC, in turn, receives reserve credit before the check actually clears. During Stage 6, the Federal Reserve Bank presents the original check to CNB, which verifies that the individual has enough funds on deposit to cover the payment.

Most checks now complete this trip in one to three days. The speed of check processing has increased dramatically in response to check-system improvements other than Check 21. Thus, today, once a check is deposited with a bank, it is almost always delivered overnight to the paying bank and debited from the check writer's account the next business day. To accelerate the process, banks encode checks with magnetic numbers that can be read by high-speed machines and often move checks via overnight couriers between destinations. Obviously, the greater the number of handlers and distance, the longer it takes to transfer and verify a check. Check-processing speeds should continue to increase, over time, as banks make further operational changes in response to Check 21. Essentially, they do not let depositors spend the proceeds until there is reasonable certainty the deposit is good.

Effective in September 1990, Congress passed the **Expedited Funds Availability Act**, which stipulated maximum time limits under Regulation CC for banks to make funds available on deposited checks. There are several basic limits that all banks must meet. Local checks must be cleared in no more than two business days. A local check is one written on a firm in the same metropolitan area or within the same Federal Reserve check-processing region. Nonlocal checks must be cleared in no more than five business days. Funds deposited in the form of government checks, certified checks, and cashiers checks must be available by 9 A.M. the next day. There are exceptions to these schedules, such as with habitual check bouncers, but the law generally indicates the longest time that account holders will have to wait to access their funds. The act also required banks to disclose their hold policy to all transactions account owners, required banks to start accruing interest when the firm receives credit for its deposited checks, and established penalties for failure to comply with the provisions. The Expedited Funds Availability Act also requires the Federal Reserve Board to reduce maximum hold times in step with reductions in actual check-processing times. Thus, over the longer term, if Check 21 sufficiently increases the speed of check processing, the Federal Reserve Board will reduce maximum hold times.

Realistically, most of the processing time for paper checks was eliminated prior to Check 21, but Check 21 could expedite this process even more. Before you write a check, it's always best to make sure your checking account has enough money in it to cover the check! A bank that accepts a deposit accepts the risk that supporting funds will eventually appear. If the individual in Exhibit 8.12 does not have sufficient funds to cover the $500 draft, BANB must collect from its business depositor and may suffer losses and send the check back to the bank accepting the initial deposit. In most instances, the check must again go through each intermediate institution that handled it earlier. This process usually takes much longer and is more costly for the bank because returned checks are physically analyzed for endorsements. Electronic payments can obviously bring the time for checks to clear down even more, from about one day to the same day.

## MEASURING THE COST OF FUNDS

The previous sections outlined the importance for a bank to continuously monitor the cost of its funding sources. Changes in interest rates and the composition of liabilities and equity alter financing costs and may reduce available liquidity. Changes in financing costs require corresponding changes in asset yields to maintain profit margins. Changes in the types of assets a bank holds affect liquidity needs, the bank's profitability and risk and the cost of funding these assets. With increased competition among financial services companies, both the frequency and magnitude of these changes have increased significantly.

Managing liabilities was relatively routine for most commercial banks prior to the 1980s when federal regulators dictated maximum rates banks could pay on deposits, and customers had few alternatives for their savings. Banks competed for depositors primarily through location and personal service. Customers were quite loyal. These factors gave rise to the well-known 3-6-3 method of running a bank: pay 3 percent on deposits, charge 6 percent on loans, and hit the golf course at 3 o'clock!

Reading any newspaper or financial publication shows how different the environment is today. Most noticeably, deposit rate ceilings no longer exist. Banks have almost unlimited opportunities to develop new deposit products with any maturity that pay market rates, but they must now compete with a variety of firms offering similar products and services. Any individual wishing to open a transactions account can use a commercial bank, credit union, savings and loan, and money market mutual fund offered by a brokerage house, American Express, or traditionally nonbank firms such as State Farm and USAA. Although this choice is attractive to consumers, it creates considerable uncertainty for banks regarding the availability and cost of funding sources.

It is important that management understand how to measure the cost of financing bank operations. Accurate cost measurement allows the bank to compare prices between alternative funding sources and to assure that assets are priced high enough to cover costs and pay shareholders a required return. The following analysis describes two approaches to estimating the cost of total bank funds. Before doing so, it summarizes differences in the concepts of average and marginal cost of funds.

### THE AVERAGE HISTORICAL COST OF FUNDS

Many banks incorrectly use average historical costs, developed earlier in the chapter, in their pricing decisions. They simply add historical interest expense with noninterest expense (net of noninterest income) and divide by the investable amount of funds to determine the minimum return required on earning assets. Any profit is represented as a markup. The primary problem with historical costs is that they provide no information as to whether future interest costs will rise or fall. When interest rates rise, average historical costs understate the actual cost of issuing new debt. Fixed-rate asset yields based on historical costs will not be high enough to cover costs and meet profit targets.[17] When interest rates fall, the opposite occurs. Average historical costs overstate

---

[17]Many analysts attributed the failure of Franklin National Bank in 1974 to its failure to distinguish between average and marginal costs. Franklin's management, using average historical costs to project borrowing costs in a rising interest rate environment, invested in fixed-rate assets yielding less than the incremental cost of new debt. Rose (1974) provides details.

# CONTEMPORARY ISSUES

## MARGINAL VERSUS AVERAGE

Confusion over the terms *average* and *marginal* makes it difficult to evaluate performance measures and understand pricing rules. This is especially true for average costs and weighted marginal costs, which are similar-sounding concepts. With cost and pricing data, readers should view simple averages as referring to historical values. The marginal concept, in contrast, refers to incremental or new values.

Consider, for example, a baseball player's batting average. The press reports a historical average representing the summary performance measure over all games played and a marginal average representing the last game. Suppose that during the first two games in a year, the player gets three hits out of 10 batting attempts. His average is 3 divided by 10, or .300. Common usage omits the reference to percent, so the batter is "hitting 300." During the next game, the player gets two hits in five at-bats. His marginal average for the five incremental at-bats is .400, which raises his overall (historical) average to .333 (five hits in 15 at-bats). The player's overall average increases because the marginal performance (.400) exceeded the previous historical average (.300). If the player gets no hits in his next five at-bats (.000 marginal average), his historical average will drop to .250.

actual interest costs on new debt so that fixed-rate loans might be priced too high to be competitive. The use of average costs assumes that interest rates will be constant at historical levels during the current pricing period.

Pricing decisions should be based on marginal costs compared with marginal revenues. Suppose that a bank can make a new, one-year loan at 10 percent. The bank's simple average cost of funds equals 6 percent. If the bank compares the new loan rate (marginal revenue rate) with the average cost of funds to determine whether it will make the loan, it estimates a 4 percent spread and accepts the loan. Suppose that it must finance the loan at the margin by issuing a *new*, one-year jumbo CD at 11 percent. This represents the marginal interest cost of a single source of new funds. If the bank compares the marginal loan rate with the marginal CD rate, it estimates a negative 1 percent spread and rejects the loan. Because pricing new loans is an incremental decision, it should be based on incremental (marginal) funding costs, not historical average costs. If the bank makes the loan, it loses at least 1 percent on the transaction because its incremental interest expense will exceed its incremental interest income by at least 1 percent of the loan amount.

The best use of average historical costs is in evaluating past performance. It is relatively easy to understand, after the fact, why a bank's expenses and profits differ from peer banks' by comparing average borrowing costs and asset yields. Average costs for noninterest expenses, such as check handling and brokerage fees, can also be evaluated and applied toward measuring expected new debt costs. Typically, these outlays increase by predictable amounts with inflation. The Contemporary Issues Box: "Marginal versus Average" clarifies the differences between these measures.

## THE MARGINAL COST OF FUNDS

The **marginal cost of debt** is a measure of the borrowing cost paid to acquire one additional unit of investable funds. The **marginal cost of equity capital** is a measure of the minimum acceptable rate of return required by shareholders. Together, the marginal costs of debt and equity constitute the **marginal cost of funds**, which can be viewed as independent sources or as a pool of funds.[18] Independent sources of funds have distinct marginal costs that vary with market interest rates, handling costs, and reserve requirements. These independent costs can then be combined to yield an overall weighted marginal cost estimate for all new funds. When interest rates are expected to rise, marginal costs exceed historical costs. When rates are expected to fall, marginal costs are lower.

Marginal costs are especially useful in pricing decisions. If these costs are known, a bank can set asset yields at some markup over marginal costs to lock in a profitable spread. Presumably, the markup reflects default risk as

---

[18]Banking terminology generally refers to the average or marginal cost of funds as the associated cost of liabilities alone. The cost of equity is incorporated as a required spread over the cost of debt necessary for a bank to meet profit targets and pay shareholders their required return.

well as the required return to shareholders. Marginal costs also serve as indicators of the relative cost of different funds, which banks can use to target the least expensive sources for financing growth.

## COSTS OF INDEPENDENT SOURCES OF FUNDS

Unfortunately, it is difficult to measure marginal costs precisely. Management must include both interest and noninterest costs it expects to pay and identify which portion of the acquired funds can be invested in earning assets. There is also considerable disagreement on whether equity costs are relevant and, ultimately, how to measure equity costs. One formula for measuring the explicit marginal cost of a single source of bank liabilities is:

$$\textit{Marginal cost of liability } j = \frac{\text{Interest rate } + \text{ servicing costs } + \text{ acquisition costs } + \text{ insurance}}{\text{Net investable balance of liability } j} \tag{8.2}$$

All elements of the numerator are *expected* costs, annualized as a percentage of each dollar obtained. The denominator measures the fraction of liabilities that can be invested to generate interest income. With transactions accounts, for example, the fraction in nonearning assets will reflect legal reserve requirements plus any allocation to such nonearning assets as float or correspondent balances. A bank may also add indirect costs to the numerator, such as the implicit cost of increased risk associated with higher leverage, to obtain an effective marginal cost estimate. Of these costs, only acquisition costs that primarily reflect marketing expenses are truly discretionary. Interest rates are largely determined by market conditions as banks are price takers, servicing costs are determined by the volume of check-processing business handled by a bank, and deposit insurance costs are set by the FDIC.

Consider the following marginal cost estimates associated with obtaining additional NOW account funding:

| | |
|---|---|
| Market interest rate | = 2.5% |
| Servicing costs | = 4.1% of balances |
| Acquisition costs | = 1.0% of balances |
| Deposit insurance costs | = 0.25% of balances |
| Net investable balance | = 85.0% (10% required reserves and 5% float) |

Equation 8.2 indicates that the estimated marginal cost of obtaining additional NOW balances equals 9.24 percent.

$$\text{Marginal cost of NOW balance} = \frac{0.025 + 0.041 + 0.01 + 0.0025}{0.85} = 9.24\%$$

Intuitively, this cost estimate is the all-inclusive incremental cost of obtaining the investable balances from additional NOW account funds. Two issues, however, can potentially create large measurement errors:

1. The relevant interest rate must be forecast over the entire planning horizon, a task made difficult by volatile interest rates. Thus, forecasts need to be modified frequently.[19]

2. As discussed previously, a bank must rely on its comptroller or cost accountant to generate meaningful estimates of noninterest costs associated with each debt source. This involves allocating overhead, advertising outlays, and the cost of employee time for handling checks, servicing customer complaints, posting account information, and bidding for public funds.

The following discussion summarizes general procedures used to estimate the pretax marginal cost of various sources of bank funds. Tax implications are not considered for convenience and because pretax cost estimates are used in asset pricing decisions.

**COST OF DEBT.** The marginal cost of different types of debt, $k_d$, varies according to the magnitude of each type of liability. High-volume transactions accounts generate substantial servicing costs and have the highest reserve requirements and float. The advantage of low interest cost on transaction accounts is offset by other costs and the fact that banks can invest a smaller percentage of investable funds. Purchased funds, in contrast, pay higher rates but carry smaller transactions costs and zero reserve requirements, hence, greater investable balances.

The cost of long-term nondeposit debt equals the effective cost of borrowing from each source, including interest expense, transactions, servicing, and acquisition costs. Traditional analysis suggests that this cost is the

---

[19]For comparative purposes, all interest rates should be measured identically. Effective rates that recognize differences in discrete and continuous compounding and interest bearing versus discount instruments should be used. The fact that the Truth in Savings Act requires banks to report an annual percentage yield (APY) to customers makes this easier.

discount rate that equates the present value of expected interest and principal payments with the net proceeds to the bank from the issue.[20]

**COST OF EQUITY.** Conceptually, the marginal cost of equity, $k_e$, equals the required return to shareholders. It is not directly measurable because dividend payments are not mandatory. Still, several methods are commonly used to approximate this required return, including the dividend valuation model, capital asset pricing model (CAPM), and targeted return on equity model:[21]

- **Dividend Valuation Model.** Returns to common stockholders take the form of periodic dividend receipts and changes in share price during the interval of stock ownership. Dividend valuation models discount the expected cash flows from owning stock in determining a reasonable return to shareholders. The cost of equity equals the discount rate (required return) used to convert future cash flows to their present value equivalent.

- **Capital Asset Pricing Model (CAPM).** Large institutions with publicly-traded stock can obtain an estimate of their cost of equity from the CAPM. This model relates market risk, measured by Beta ($\beta$), to shareholders' required returns. Formally, the required return to shareholders ($k_e$) equals the riskless rate of return ($r_f$) plus a risk premium ($\rho$) on common stock reflecting nondiversifiable market risk

- **Targeted Return on Equity Model.** Investors require higher pretax returns on common stock than on debt issues because of the greater assumed credit risk. Depending on the business cycle, the differential in returns ranges from 3 to 8 percent. As an approximation, a firm's cost of equity should exceed its cost of debt by some positive differential. Many banks use a **targeted return on equity** guideline based on the cost of debt plus a premium to evaluate the cost of equity. This method simply requires that owners and managers specify a desirable return to shareholders in terms of return on equity. This return is then converted to a pretax equivalent yield. It assumes that the market value of bank equity equals the book value of equity. Although this measure has deficiencies, it is easy to calculate for banks without publicly-traded stock and serves as a benchmark for other cost of equity approximations.

**COST OF PREFERRED STOCK.** Preferred stock has characteristics of debt and common equity. It represents ownership with investors' claims superior to those of common stockholders but subordinate to those of debtholders. Like common stock, preferred stock pays dividends that may be deferred when management determines that earnings are too low. Like long-term bonds, preferred stock stipulates contractual dividend payments over the life of the security and often provides call protection and sinking fund contributions. Recently, preferred issues paying variable-rate dividends have become increasingly common.

The marginal cost of preferred stock ($k_p$) equals the required return to stockholders and can be approximated using the dividend valuation model, similar to common equity except that dividend growth is zero. Consider the case of noncallable, nonsinking fund preferred stock sold at par with a fixed-dividend payment.[22]

**TRUST PREFERRED STOCK.** A recent innovation in capital financing is the introduction of **trust preferred stock**, which is a hybrid form of equity capital at banks. It is attractive because it effectively pays dividends that are tax deductible. To issue the securities, a bank or bank holding company establishes a trust company. The trust company sells preferred stock to investors and loans the proceeds of the issue to the bank. Interest on the loan equals dividends paid on the preferred stock. This loan interest is tax deductible such that the bank effectively gets to deduct dividend payments on the preferred stock.[23]

Trust preferred securities have been an important component of regulatory capital for many bank holding companies (BHCs) since the 1996 Federal Reserve ruling that allowed limited amounts of trust preferred securities to be included in Tier 1 capital. When FASB issued Interpretation No. 46R, *Consolidation of Variable Interest Entities,* in 2004, however, the future of trust preferred securities became uncertain. Interpretation No. 46R effectively prohibits the consolidation of trust preferred securities, which means that trust preferred cannot be

---

[20]Suppose, for example, a bank issues $10 million in par value subordinated notes paying $700,000 in annual interest and carrying a seven-year maturity. It must pay $100,000 in flotation costs to an underwriter. In this case, the effective cost of borrowing ($k_d$), where t equals the time period for each cash flow, is:

$$\$9,900,00 = \sum_{t=1}^{7} \frac{\$700,00}{(1 + k_d)^t} + \frac{\$10,000,00}{(1 + k_d)^7}$$

$$k_d = 7.19\%$$

[21]For a complete discussion on estimating the cost of equity, consult any good financial management text.

[22]With dividend payments contractually fixed, expected dividend growth equals 0. Therefore, $k_p$ = preferred dividends / net price of preferred stock. To calculate the marginal cost of common and preferred stock when dividends are not constant, the reader should review examples provided in any current corporate finance textbook. The effective cost of common and preferred stock should also reflect the portion of these funds that is allocated to nonearning assets. Although reserves are not required, banks typically allocate fixed assets and intangibles to equity sources. Computationally, management divides the equity marginal cost estimate by 1 minus the percentage in nonearning assets.

[23]The after-tax cost of trust preferred stock would be: $k_{tp}$ = (dividends on trust preferred × (1 − marginal tax rate)) / net price of trust preferred stock.

classified as a minority interest. Because the Fed's inclusion of trust preferred stock in Tier 1 capital is based, at least in part, on the minority-interest status of the trust preferred securities in a BHC's consolidated balance sheet, the status of trust preferred as a component of Tier 1 capital was uncertain. The Fed has stated that the regulatory reporting of trust preferred will reflect GAAP accounting requirements. The Fed, however, is not bound by GAAP accounting in its definition of Tier 1 or Tier 2 capital because these are regulatory constructs designed to ensure the safety and soundness of banking organizations. In late 2004, the Fed proposed a rule that would apply a limit of 25 percent of Tier 1 capital, after deducting goodwill, for trust preferred stock. Previously the limit was 25 percent of Tier 1 capital before deducting goodwill. Deducting goodwill from core capital elements will help ensure that a BHC is not unduly leveraging its tangible equity. The net effect is that many BHCs carrying goodwill on their balance sheets may count less of their trust preferred in Tier 1 capital.

## WEIGHTED MARGINAL COST OF TOTAL FUNDS

Many banks price loans using the marginal cost of a single source of debt funds as the base rate. For example, prime commercial customers are often allowed to choose the interest rate they pay as some markup over the marginal cost of either CDs, the London Interbank Offer Rate (LIBOR), or federal funds. Obviously, the customer selects the base rate expected to be the lowest over the credit period. Unfortunately, the cost of any single source of funds may change more or less than the cost of other sources and thus vary substantially from the bank's composite cost of financing.

The best cost measure for asset-pricing purposes is a weighted marginal cost of total funds (WMC). This measure recognizes both explicit and implicit costs associated with any single source of funds. It assumes that all assets are financed from a pool of funds and that specific sources of funds are not tied directly with specific uses of funds. WMC is computed in three stages:

1. Forecast the desired dollar amount of financing to be obtained from each individual debt and equity source. This requires the bank to specify a planning horizon, such as one year, and identify significant changes in composition of liabilities and equity over time. Management should determine a marketing strategy and allocate employees' time to the different account-generating functions.

2. Estimate the marginal cost of each independent source of funds. It should allocate fund-raising and processing costs among the different liability and equity components and project interest and dividend costs for each source, recognizing any perceived changes in risk associated with changes in financial leverage. Each cost estimate should also reflect management's assignment of nonearning assets per Equation 8.2 that indicates the percentage of investable funds.

3. Combine the individual estimates to project the weighted cost, which equals the sum of the weighted component costs across all sources. Each source's weight ($w_j$) equals the expected dollar amount of financing from that source divided by the dollar amount of total liabilities and equity. Thus, if $k_j$ equals the single-source j component marginal cost of financing, where there are m liabilities plus equity, the WMC of total funds is:

$$\text{WMC} = \sum_{j=1}^{m} w_j k_j \tag{8.3}$$

## MARGINAL COST ANALYSIS: AN APPLICATION

The following analysis demonstrates the procedures for measuring a bank's cost of funds. The analysis consists of projecting the bank's balance sheet composition and marginal costs in order to generate a weighted marginal cost of total funds.

Suppose that you are the cashier for Community State Bank and a member of the bank's asset and liability management committee (ALCO). The ALCO has just completed its monthly meeting and asked you to generate an estimate of the bank's weighted marginal cost of funds for the next year. For the first time in several years, there was a consensus among the senior officers that the economy would experience moderate growth throughout the year. Inflation was expected to remain stable around 3 percent and interest rates would increase only slightly. As part of the meeting, the committee approved a preliminary budget that projected income, net of dividends, equal to $1.2 million, representing a lower return on equity and return on assets compared with the prior year. Total average assets were projected to grow by $7 million, of which $6 million was new loans. Liabilities were expected to grow proportionately relative to the past year except that the bank would rely proportionately more on CDs.

Exhibit 8.13 summarizes the ALCO's consensus forecast for the next year. Columns (a) and (b) list the projected composition of funding between debt and equity sources over the next year in dollar amount and percentage. Column (c) lists the interest rates expected to prevail during the year as projected by the senior investment officer. Processing and acquisition costs for each type of liability and the investable percentages are based on the bank controller's estimates, and are reported in columns (d) and (e). The expected marginal cost for

| EXHIBIT 8.13 | Forecast of the Weighted Marginal Cost of Funds: Projected Figures for Community State Bank | | | | | | |
|---|---|---|---|---|---|---|---|
| | (a) Average Amount ($1,000) | (b) Percent of Total | (c) Interest Cost | (d) Processing, Acquisition Costs | (e) Investable Percentage | (f) Component Marginal Costs | (g) WMC of Funds (b) × (f) |
| Demand deposits | $ 28,210 | 31.0% | | 8.0% | 82.0% | 9.76% | 0.0302 |
| Interest checking | 5,551 | 6.1% | 2.5% | 6.5% | 85.0% | 10.59% | 0.0065 |
| Money market demand accounts | 13,832 | 15.2% | 3.5% | 3.0% | 97.0% | 6.70% | 0.0102 |
| Other savings accounts | 3,640 | 4.0% | 4.5% | 1.2% | 98.5% | 5.79% | 0.0023 |
| Time deposits < $100,000 | 18,382 | 20.2% | 4.9% | 1.4% | 99.0% | 6.36% | 0.0129 |
| Time deposits > $100,000 | 9,055 | 10.0% | 5.0% | 0.3% | 99.5% | 5.34% | 0.0053 |
| Total deposits | 78,670 | 86.5% | | | | | |
| Federal funds purchased | 182 | 0.2% | 5.0% | 0.0% | 100.0% | 5.00% | 0.0001 |
| Other liabilities | 4,550 | 5.0% | | 0.0% | 60.0% | 0.00% | |
| Total liabilities | 83,402 | 91.6% | | | | | |
| Stockholders' equity | 7,599 | 8.4% | 18.9% | | 96.0% | 19.69% | 0.0164 |
| Total liabilities and equity | 91,001 | 100.00% | | | | | |
| Weighted marginal cost of capital | | | | | | → | 8.39% |

each source, using these projections as defined in Equation 8.2, is presented in column (f). The weighted marginal cost of funds, obtained by summing the products of figures in columns (b) and (f) for each component, is calculated in column (g) and reported at the bottom of the column; 8.39 percent for the year. This projected marginal cost exceeds historical costs because the bank forecasts an increase in interest rates and expects to obtain a higher percentage of funds from more expensive sources.

The marginal cost of funds estimate should be applied carefully in pricing decisions. The bank in this example should charge at least 8.39 percent on loans (assets) of average risk and average cost to administer to cover the marginal costs of debt and pay shareholders a reasonable return. The bank should add a risk premium for loans of greater than average default risk to compensate for the increased probability of greater charge-offs and should charge a premium for smaller loans or loans with great administrative costs. Whether a bank meets its aggregate profit target depends on the bank's ability to price assets to meet this hurdle rate, its actual default experience, and whether noninterest income covers noninterest expense net of costs allocated to attracting and handling liabilities.

Differences in the weighted marginal cost projection generally reflect different interest rate scenarios and variations in the composition of liabilities. Assume, for the moment, that as an ALCO member you have serious reservations that economic stability will persist. Economic crisis may well spread to the United States and the economy is somewhat fragile. Inflation may increase faster than expected and the Fed might increase interest rates faster than the ALCO's forecast. If this occurred, interest rates would rise well above the ALCO's forecast, and the bank would have difficulty issuing new CDs. Hence, the bank's marginal cost of fund might be higher than expected by the previous analysis.

## FUNDING SOURCES AND BANKING RISKS

The previous examples demonstrate the difficulty of accurately projecting funding costs. Unanticipated changes in interest rates and the composition of bank liabilities can significantly raise or lower bank profits as interest expense rises or falls more than interest income. The same changes also affect a bank's risk position. This section examines the relationship between the composition of bank funds and banking risk, identifying differences between small and large banks.

Banks face two fundamental problems in managing their liabilities: uncertainty over what rates they must pay to retain and attract funds; and uncertainty over the likelihood that customers will withdraw their money regardless of rates. The basic fear is that they will be vulnerable to a liquidity crisis arising from unanticipated deposit withdrawals. Banks must have the capacity to borrow in financial markets to borrowed funds, replace deposit outflows and remain solvent. Liquidity problems have grown with the increased reliance on borrowed funds, brokered deposits, and Internet deposits. When a bank is perceived to have asset quality problems, customers with uninsured balances move their deposits. The problem bank must then pay substantial premiums to attract replacement funds or rely on regulatory agencies to extend emergency credit.

During the years that deposit rates were regulated and banks paid the maximum rates allowed, deposits were relatively stable and liquidity was less of a problem. Interest rate deregulation and bank competition have since increased depositors' rate awareness so that many individuals and firms move funds to institutions paying the highest rates. Customer loyalty is closely tied to deposit size and the quality of bank service. Small-balance depositors are generally more loyal than large-balance depositors, especially if they receive consistently good service. All customers are more loyal if they purchase a bundle of credit, deposit, and other services.

## FUNDING SOURCES: LIQUIDITY RISK

The liquidity risk associated with all liabilities has risen dramatically in recent years. Depositors often simply compare rates and move their funds between investment vehicles to earn the highest yields. It is increasingly difficult to establish long-term customer relationships that withstand rate differentials, a problem compounded in virtually every banking market that has at least one firm that pays premium rates at all maturities. These firms are often brokerage companies that offer non-FDIC-insured money market and stock mutual funds. Credit unions often offer higher rates afforded by their significant tax advantages over banks. Commercial banks feel they are at a competitive disadvantage and, without matching the offered rates, have trouble keeping deposit customers.

Liquidity risk associated with a bank's deposit base is a function of many factors, including the number of depositors, average size of accounts, location of the depositor, and specific maturity and rate characteristics of each account. These features are customer-driven, and banks cannot dictate the terms of deposit contracts. But banks can monitor potential deposit outflows if they are aware of seasonal patterns in outstanding balances and the timing of large transactions such as payroll draws on commercial accounts and maturing large-balance CDs. They can periodically contact large depositors to provide rate quotes and assess the probability of the customer reinvesting the funds.

Equally important is the *interest elasticity* of customer demand for each funding source. How much can market interest rates change before the bank experiences deposit outflows? If the bank increases its rates, how many new funds will it attract? Ideally, a bank would like to lower its customers' rate sensitivity. It can do so by packaging deposit products with other services or privileges so that withdrawals deprive the customer of all services, or by developing personal relationships with depositors. In this way management can determine the base funding level (core deposit base) below which outstanding balances never fall.

The largest banks that rely on jumbo CDs and Eurodollars face similar problems. Investors in these instruments are highly rate sensitive. They normally prefer short-term maturities and will move their balances for slightly higher yields elsewhere. Large depositors with uninsured balances, especially foreign investors, frequently react to rumors of financial distress by shifting their funds into less risky Treasury securities until the crisis passes. For this reason, the largest U.S. banking organizations maintain dealer operations in London, Singapore, and Hong Kong to guarantee access to financial markets 24 hours a day.

The liquidity risk any one bank faces depends on the competitive environment. Many smaller banks operate in communities with only a few competitors that tacitly price deposits comparably. Customers like to invest their funds locally so they can conveniently contact their banker with questions or easily withdraw or move balances. Liquidity risk is relatively low and deposit outflows are predictable. As indicated earlier, many community banks view the FHLB as a primary source of liquidity. Banks in larger communities normally face more aggressive competition, which increases liquidity risk, and must monitor the composition of funds more closely. Again, it is important to note the liquidity advantage that stable core deposits provide.

Most banks try to build a liquidity buffer into their deposit base. Small banks with limited access to national financial markets promote customer service to expand core deposits and reduce liability interest elasticity. Many large banks periodically borrow more funds than they need to guarantee access to deposit sources.[24] When the bank does not need the funds, it still borrows and simply invests in short-term loans. Comparing a bank's current borrowings with its maximum debt outstanding over the previous year can approximate the amount of liquidity available to large banks via purchased funds.

## FUNDING SOURCES: INTEREST RATE RISK

During the 1980s, most banks experienced a shift in composition of liabilities away from demand deposits into interest-bearing time deposits and other borrowed funds. This reflects three phenomena: the removal of Regulation Q interest rate ceilings, a volatile interest rate environment, and the development of new deposit and money market products. The cumulative effect was to increase the interest sensitivity of funding operations. Today, many depositors and investors prefer short-term instruments that can be rolled over quickly as interest rates change. Banks must offer substantial premiums to induce depositors to lengthen maturities and assume interest rate risk. Many banks choose not to pay the premiums and subsequently reprice liabilities more frequently than in past years.

---

[24]Bailey (1984) documents several banks' strategies in dealing with potential liquidity problems.

These changes affect banks' interest rate risk position to the extent that they do not adjust their asset rate sensitivity. A bank operating with a zero GAP in the late 1990s would today be liability sensitive and have substantial negative GAPs within one year if it did not acquire more rate-sensitive assets. For this reason, many institutions attempt to price all loans on a floating-rate basis and no longer purchase bonds for their investment portfolios with maturities beyond five to seven years.

One widely recognized strategy to reduce interest rate risk and the long-term cost of bank funds is to aggressively compete for retail core deposits. Individuals are generally not as rate sensitive as corporate depositors. Once a bank attracts deposit business, many individuals will maintain their balances through rate cycles as long as the bank provides good service and pays attention to them. Such deposits are thus more stable than money market liabilities. Core deposits carry an additional advantage for banks because interest costs are lower, but the disadvantage that they cost more to process.

## FUNDING SOURCES: CREDIT AND CAPITAL RISK

Changes in the composition and cost of bank funds can indirectly affect a bank's credit risk by forcing it to reduce asset quality. For example, banks that have substituted purchased funds for lost demand deposits have seen their cost of funds rise. They have not been able to reprice existing high-quality assets to offset this rise because of competitive pressures. Rather than let their interest margins deteriorate, many banks make riskier loans at higher promised yields. Although they might maintain their margins in the near term, later loan losses typically rise with the decline in asset quality. This effect is greatest at small banks with limited opportunities to supplement earnings in other ways.

Changes in the composition and cost of bank funds have clearly lowered traditional earnings. This decrease slows capital growth and increases leverage ratios. Borrowing costs will ultimately increase unless noninterest income offsets this decline or banks obtain new external capital. Bank safety has thus declined in the aggregate.

## HOLDING LIQUID ASSETS

Banks hold cash assets to satisfy four objectives. First, banks supply coin and currency to meet customers' regular transactions needs. The amount of cash in a bank's vault corresponds to customer cash deposits and the demand for cash withdrawals. Both exhibit seasonable fluctuations, rising prior to holidays such as Christmas and falling immediately thereafter. Second, regulatory agencies mandate legal reserve requirements that can only be met by holding qualifying cash assets. Third, banks serve as a clearinghouse for the nation's check-payment system. Each bank must hold sufficient balances at Federal Reserve Banks or other financial institutions so that checks written by its depositors will clear when presented for payment. Finally, banks use cash balances to purchase services from correspondent banks.

Banks own four types of cash assets: vault cash, demand deposit balances at Federal Reserve Banks, demand deposit balances at private financial institutions, and cash items in the process of collection (CIPC). Cash assets do not earn any interest, so the entire allocation of funds represents a substantial opportunity cost for banks. Banks, therefore, want to minimize the amount of cash assets held and hold only those required by law or for operational needs.

A **liquid asset** is one that can be easily and quickly converted into cash with minimum loss. Contrary to popular notion, however, "cash assets" do not generally satisfy a bank's liquidity needs. To understand this, recall that a bank holds the minimum amount of cash assets required. If the bank experiences an unexpected drain on vault cash, the bank must immediately replace the cash or it will have less vault cash than required for legal or operational needs. Cash assets are liquid assets only very temporarily, or to the extent that a bank holds more than the minimum required. It is interesting to note that while cash is the most liquid asset, it is not a viable long-term source of liquidity for the bank.

If cash assets are not really a source of liquidity for a bank, what assets are? Liquid assets are generally considered to be cash and due from banks in excess of requirements, federal funds sold and reverse repurchase agreements, short-term Treasury and agency obligations, high-quality short-term corporate and municipal securities, and some government-guaranteed loans that can be readily sold. These assets are liquid because they can be quickly converted into immediately available funds with limited price depreciation.

For a financial institution that regularly borrows in the financial markets, liquidity takes on the added dimension of the ability to fund the institution or borrow funds at minimum cost or even issue stock. This view of liquidity explicitly recognizes that firms can acquire liquidity in three distinct ways:

1. Selling assets

2. New borrowings

3. New stock issues

**Bank liquidity**, therefore, more generally refers to *a bank's capacity to acquire immediately available funds at a reasonable price*. It encompasses the impact of alternative funding sources and their predictability; the potential sale of liquid assets; borrowing in the form of federal funds purchased and Federal Home Loan Bank advances; new issues of CDs, Eurodollars, subordinated debt; and new stock offerings. These liabilities similarly represent liquid sources of funds if a bank can easily borrow at reasonable rates, or those comparable to peers. Common and preferred stock are a source of liquidity only if there is a ready market for these instruments with little delay and cost associated with new funds.

Liquidity planning is an important facet of asset and liability management. Although public confidence is essential for preventing deposit runs, managers can take steps to reduce the likelihood of unanticipated deposit outflows and gain access to additional sources of cash assets. Managers must be able to estimate liquidity needs accurately and structure their bank's portfolio to meet the anticipated needs.

## OBJECTIVES OF CASH MANAGEMENT

Banks prefer to hold as few cash assets as possible without creating transactions problems from deposit outflows. Because cash assets do not generate interest income, excess holdings have a high opportunity cost represented by the interest that could be earned on an alternative investment. As the level of interest rates rises, so does the opportunity cost and the incentive to economize on cash assets. There are, however, significant risks in holding too little cash. Imagine depositors' concerns if they were told that their bank did not have enough currency on hand for withdrawals. A bank must similarly keep enough deposit balances at other banks and the Federal Reserve to cover deposit outflows or it will be forced to replenish its balances under duress. Owning too few cash assets potentially creates liquidity problems and increases borrowing costs. Continued deficiencies are attributed to poor management, which ultimately leads to close regulatory scrutiny and deteriorating business relationships.

Fortunately, vault cash needs are fairly predictable. Local businesses make regular cash deposits and bank customers generally withdraw cash at predictable intervals near weekends, holidays, and when they receive their paychecks. Vault cash shortages can be avoided by requesting a currency shipment from the closest Federal Reserve Bank or correspondent bank.

It is much more difficult to accurately predict the timing and magnitude of deposit inflows and outflows that influence deposits held at Federal Reserve Banks and other financial institutions. Deposit inflows raise legal reserve requirements but also increase actual reserve assets and correspondent deposits. Deposit outflows lower reserve requirements and reduce actual deposit holdings. Because deposit flows are determined by customer credit and payment transactions, banks cannot directly control the timing of clearings and float. When projecting cash needs, management is thus continually aiming at a moving target.

When banks realize unexpected deposit shortages, they must have access to balances at Federal Reserve or correspondent banks via either new borrowings or the sale of noncash assets. Unfortunately, borrowing costs typically increase and funding sources disappear when a bank experiences credit problems or operating difficulties. Similarly, assets that can be easily sold near par value typically earn lower yields. A bank's cash needs are thus closely related to its liquidity requirements and sources. The fundamental management goal underlying cash and liquidity management is to accurately forecast cash needs and arrange for readily available sources of cash at minimal cost.

## RESERVE BALANCES AT THE FEDERAL RESERVE BANK

Banks hold deposits at the Federal Reserve in part because the Federal Reserve imposes legal reserve requirements, and deposit balances qualify as legal reserves. Banks also hold deposits to help process deposit inflows and outflows caused by check clearings, maturing time deposits and securities, wire transfers, and other transactions. Deposit flows are the link between a bank's cash position and its liquidity requirements.

Consider the T-account at the top of Exhibit 8.1, which documents the impact of a $100,000 maturing CD (not rolled over) that clears through the bank's reserve account at the Federal Reserve. The outflow may represent a daily net clearing drain, where the value of checks written on deposits at the sample bank exceeds the value of checks drawn on other banks which are deposited at the sample bank and presented to the Federal Reserve for payment. The offsetting adjustment to the deposit loss is a $100,000 decrease in reserve balances at the Federal Reserve. In this simplified example, required reserves do not decline because reserves are not required against CD balances. A liquidity problem arises, however, because actual deposit balances held at the Federal Reserve decrease by $100,000. If the bank was holding the minimum reserve required (no excess reserves), the bank would be deficient $100,000 in required reserves. This represents its immediate liquidity needs. Note, however, that even though the required reserve balance at the Federal Reserve satisfied the bank's clearing requirements, these funds would have to be replaced; that is, required reserves do not provide the bank a longer-term liquidity source. If, however, the bank had excess reserve balances at the Fed of $100,000, the deposit outflow would have reduced the bank's reserves at the Fed by $100,000 but no immediate liquidity need would arise. All such deposit outflows directly reduce a bank's deposit balances either at the Federal Reserve or correspondent banks and raise its liquidity needs. A deposit inflow has the opposite impact.

## REQUIRED RESERVES AND MONETARY POLICY

The purpose of required reserves is to enable the Federal Reserve to control the nation's money supply. By requiring banks and other depository institutions to hold deposit balances in support of transactions accounts, the Federal Reserve hopes to control credit availability and thereby influence general economic conditions. There are fundamentally three distinct monetary policy tools: open market operations, changes in the discount rate, and changes in the required reserve ratio:

1. **Open market operations** are conducted by the Federal Reserve Bank of New York under the direction of the Federal Open Market Committee (FOMC). The sale or purchase of U.S. government securities in the "open market" or secondary market is the Federal Reserve's most flexible means of carrying out its policy objectives. Through the purchase or sale of short-term government securities, the Fed can adjust the level of reserves in the banking system. Through open market operations, the Fed can offset or support changes in reserve requirements, changes in the discount rate, as well as seasonal or international shifts of funds, and thereby influence short-term interest rates and the growth of the money supply. Fed open market purchases increase liquidity, hence reserves in the banking system, by increasing a bank's deposit balances at the Fed. Fed open market sales of securities decrease bank reserves and liquidity by lowering deposit balances at the Fed.

2. **Discount window** borrowing is when banks borrow deposit balances, or required reserves, directly from Federal Reserve Banks with the **discount rate** representing the interest rate that banks pay. Changes in the discount rate directly affect the cost of borrowing. When the Fed raises the discount rate it discourages borrowing by making it more expensive. Fed decreases in the discount rate make borrowing less expensive.

3. **Changes in reserve requirements** directly affect the amount of legal required reserves and thus change the amount of money a bank can lend. For example, a required reserve ratio of 10 percent means that a bank with $100 in demand deposit liabilities outstanding must hold $10 in legal required reserves in support of the demand deposits (DDAs). The bank can thus lend only 90 percent of its DDAs. When the Fed increases (decreases) reserve requirements, it formally increases (decreases) the required reserve ratio that directly reduces (raises) the amount of money a bank can lend. Thus, lower reserve requirements increase bank liquidity and lending capacity while higher reserve requirements decrease bank liquidity and lending capacity.[25]

The Federal Reserve sets required reserves for member banks equal to a fraction of the dollar amount of selected bank liabilities. Assume that the legal reserve requirement equals 10 percent for demand deposits and 0 percent for all time deposits. (Exhibit 8.16 introduces actual percentage requirements.) A bank with $100 million in demand deposits and $500 million in time deposits will have to hold required reserves of $10 million, which is the *minimum* amount the bank must keep as vault cash or on deposit at the Federal Reserve. If this bank actually holds $12 million in deposits at the Fed plus vault cash, it has $2 million in excess reserves, which represents a source of liquidity. If the volume of outstanding demand deposits at the bank were to increase to $120 million, the bank's required reserves would rise to $12 million and there would be no excess reserves. In general, when deposit liabilities increase (decrease), a bank's required reserves increase (decrease). Thus, the amount of deposit balances a bank holds at the Federal Reserve will vary directly with the magnitude of reservable bank liabilities.

The use of reserve requirements as a policy tool has declined in the United States and in other industrialized countries in recent years because reserve requirement changes are no longer considered an essential tool of monetary policy. As discussed later, banks can circumvent the requirements by substituting liabilities that are not subject to the requirements for those that are. The Fed can also control the money supply and credit availability in other ways.[26] Sellon and Weiner (1998) suggest that the reduced role of reserve requirements as a monetary tool is the result of three factors: the change in Federal Reserve policy emphasizing the control of short-term interest rates; the recognition that reserve requirements are a tax on banks in the form of an interest-free loan to the Federal Reserve, which puts them at a competitive disadvantage with other financial institutions; and the active use of "sweep accounts" that have reduced required reserve balances to their lowest level in 30 years.

## THE IMPACT OF SWEEP ACCOUNTS ON REQUIRED RESERVE BALANCES

Under the Federal Reserve's Regulation D, checkable deposit accounts such as demand deposits, ATS, NOW, and other checkable deposit accounts have a 10 percent reserve requirement, but money market deposit accounts

---

[25]Changing reserve requirement ratios has a significant announcement effect because of the dramatic impact it has on all member financial institutions. It has the additional advantage of affecting all institutions simultaneously in a predictable magnitude.

[26]At least three countries—Canada, New Zealand, and the United Kingdom—conduct monetary policy without reserve requirements. See Sellon and Weiner (1998).

**EXHIBIT 8.14**

Growth of Sweep Transaction Deposits into MMDAs: 1994–2004

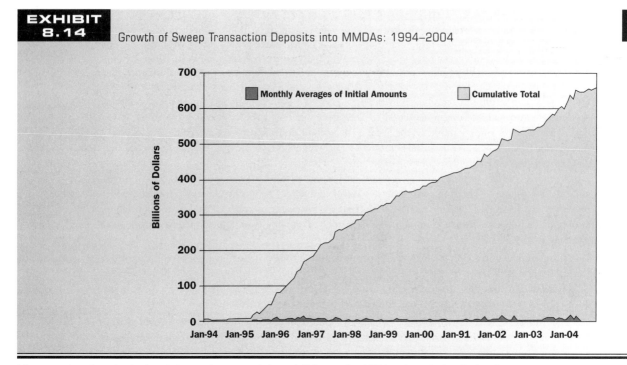

*Figures are the estimated national total of transactions account balances initially swept into MMDAs owing to the introduction of new sweep programs, on the basis of monthly averages of daily data.

SOURCE: Division of Monetary Affairs of the Board of Governors of the Federal Reserve System.

(MMDAs) are considered to be personal saving deposits and have a zero reserve requirement ratio.[27] In January 1994, the Federal Reserve Board permitted commercial banks to use computerized sweep programs. A sweep account enables a depository institution to shift funds from transactions accounts, which are reservable, to MMDAs or other accounts, which are not reservable. For example, a retail sweep account is an account in which the bank's computer "sweeps" excess funds into an MMDA from a demand deposit account. The bank determines the amount of excess funds. Essentially, a bank must designate only an amount of funds necessary to meet daily check clearings as the DDA balance. It could transfer any excess balances daily, thereby forcing a zero daily balance in the DDA. Although it would appear that banks are "moving" a customer's balance from one account to another, in reality the computer software actually dynamically "reclassifies" the customer's balance from a reservable account to a nonreservable account. This effectively reduces a bank's statutory required reserves while leaving the customer's account balance unchanged. Because customers are not very sensitive to the rates paid on these accounts, the bank's interest costs may not be much higher while it reduces required reserves.[28] Exhibit 8.14 demonstrates the rapid growth of retail sweep account programs at commercial banks since 1994.

There are generally two types of retail sweep programs in use today. The first is a weekend program. This account reclassifies transaction deposits as savings deposits at the close of business on Friday and back to transactions accounts on Monday. On average, this means that on Friday, Saturday, and Sunday (occasionally on a Monday holiday), or three-sevenths of the week, required reserves on these deposits are zero. Because reserve requirements are computed on the basis of a seven-day week, this would come close to cutting required reserves in half.[29] A second type of sweep account is the minimum threshold account. In these accounts, the bank's computer

---

[27]Regulation D and statutory reserve requirements are discussed in the following section. For a good discussion of sweep accounts, see, Richard G. Anderson and Robert H. Rasche,, "Retail Sweep Programs and Bank Reserves, 1994–1999, *Federal Reserve Bank of St. Louis Review* (January/February 2001).

[28]The interesting question is whether banks inform each customer as to whether it is sweeping the customer's deposits into an MMDA.

[29]Some consultants offering sweep account programs claim that a bank can reduce its effective reserve requirement to 1 percent rather than the statutory 10 percent of reservable balances. Alan Greenspan, in his July 1995 Humphrey-Hawkins testimony, cited that sweep programs had reduced other checkable deposit balances by about $12 billion and required reserves by about $1.2 billion. Because some of the reduction in required reserves occurred at smaller banks that satisfy most of their required reserves with vault cash, balances at Federal Reserve Banks decreased less. In addition, balances at the Fed might not fall as much because even though most sweep programs have been implemented by larger institutions subject to a 10 percent marginal reserve requirement, smaller institutions have started sweep programs as well and are subject to only a 3 percent requirement.

moves the customer's account balance to an MMDA when the dollar amount of funds exceeds some minimum and returns the funds as needed. It is interesting to note how sophisticated bank computer systems have become. Prior to the extensive use of computers in banks, these types of programs were only available to the largest and most profitable customers because of the time and effort required to calculate and move funds.

Although the number of transfers into the MMDA account is unlimited, Regulation D limits the number of withdrawals or transfers out of an MMDA to no more than six each month. If the number exceeds six, the MMDA is classified as an ATS (automatic transfer to savings) account and reserve requirements apply. The second type of sweep account, then, is limited in that the full amount of funds must be moved back into the transactions account on the sixth transfer of the month.

These retail sweep programs should not be confused with business sweep programs initiated by banks during the 1960s and 1970s. Business sweep account programs are very popular today and are also offered by nonbank financial service companies such as securities firms and mutual funds. Regulation Q (under the Banking Acts of 1933 and 1935) prohibits banks from paying explicit interest on business demand deposit accounts. A commercial sweep account sweeps excess funds from business demand deposits overnight (typically) into nondeposit, interest-earning assets such as repurchase agreements and money market mutual funds. These accounts are not bank deposit accounts and are not FDIC insured; hence they are not subject to reserve requirements.

## MEETING LEGAL RESERVE REQUIREMENTS

The actual computation of legal reserve requirements is more complex than that suggested above. Reserve percentages are multiplied by outstanding deposit balances, but not all deposits are subject to reserves. Banks reduce the volume of liabilities subject to required reserves by subtracting correspondent balances and vault cash, both of which serve as a reserve asset. Most importantly, required reserves are calculated over a two-week period, so a bank does not have to hold a specific amount of cash assets on each day. Beginning in July 1998, the Fed returned to a **lagged reserve account system** in which it required banks to hold reserves against outstanding deposit balances from three to five weeks earlier. Banks pushed hard for this change because it dramatically reduces their error in reserve planning. On the negative side, this lagged reserve accounting system reduces the Fed's ability to control the money supply and may increase the volatility of interest rates. This section analyzes current reserve requirements in detail and provides a comprehensive example. Exhibit 8.15 introduces important terminology.

Federal Reserve Regulations D and M specify minimum reserve requirements for commercial banks. The regulations stipulate that each bank must hold cash reserves equal to a fraction of its base liabilities. There are three elements of required reserves: the dollar magnitude of base liabilities, the required reserve fraction, and the dollar magnitude of qualifying cash assets. Base liabilities are composed of **net transactions accounts** in which the holder is permitted to make withdrawals by negotiable or transferable instruments, payment orders, and

---

**EXHIBIT 8.15**    Important Terminology

**Base computation period:** The 14-day period during which a bank's outstanding liabilities determine the amount of required reserves to be held during the reserve maintenance period.

**Collected balances:** The dollar value of ledger balances minus float.

**Correspondent bank:** A bank that provides services to other financial institutions and receives payment in the form of either deposit balances or direct user fees.

**Daylight overdrafts:** The process of authorizing payments within a business day from deposit accounts held at the Federal Reserve or correspondent banks in excess of actual balances held.

**Deferred availability credit items:** The dollar amount of checks deposited at the Federal Reserve Bank for which the Federal Reserve has not yet granted credit.

**Earnings credit:** The assumed interest rate at which a bank can invest customer deposit balances to earn interest income.

**Investable balances:** The dollar value of collected balances minus required reserves.

**Reserve maintenance period:** The 14-day period during which a bank must hold sufficient deposit balances at the Federal Reserve to meet its legal reserve requirement.

**Respondent bank:** A bank that buys services from other financial institutions and pays by holding nonearning deposit balances at the correspondent bank or via direct user fees.

**Transactions accounts:** All deposits on which the account holder is allowed to make withdrawals by negotiable instruments and more than three monthly telephone and preauthorized funds transfers.

**EXHIBIT 8.16**

Reserve Requirement Percentages for Depository Institutions

| Type of Deposit | | Percentage | Effective Date of Applicable Percentages |
|---|---|---|---|
| Net transactions accounts | | | |
| Exempt amount | $ 7.0 mill | 0% | 12/23/2004 |
| Up to | $ 47.6 mill | 3% | 12/23/2004 |
| Over | $ 47.6 mill | 10% | 12/23/2004 |
| All other liabilities | | 0% | 12/27/1990 |

telephone and preauthorized transfers in excess of three per month. MMDAs are not classified as transactions accounts. The dollar amount equals the sum of the balances that are listed on the bank's books, referred to as ledger balances, minus the sum of a bank's cash items in the process of collection (CIPC) and collected balances due from private depository institutions. No reserves are required against any other liability.

A bank's qualifying reserve assets include vault cash and demand deposits due from Federal Reserve Banks. The relevant percentages, or required reserve ratios, appear in Exhibit 8.16. In 2004, the first $7 million of daily average net transactions accounts was exempt, while banks must hold 3 percent on the amounts between $7 million and $47.6 million, and 10 percent on any amount over $47.6 million.[30] The Board of Governors can vary these reserve ratios within established regulatory limits. In recent years, the Board has generally lowered reserve ratios and expanded the list of liabilities not subject to reserves.

## HISTORICAL PROBLEMS WITH RESERVE REQUIREMENTS

Historically, commercial bank reserve requirements varied with the type of bank charter and each bank's geographic location. Different states stipulated reserve requirements for banks that were not members of the Federal Reserve System (state-chartered nonmembers), which were generally less restrictive than those for members. Nonmember reserve ratios were lower, and more assets, even interest-bearing government securities, often qualified as legal reserves. Only vault cash and demand balances held at the Federal Reserve constituted reserves for member banks. Thus, nonmembers could invest more funds in earning assets than similar member banks. This discrepancy represented a substantive opportunity cost of Federal Reserve membership, which was compounded further because nonmembers had access to Federal Reserve services through correspondent bank relationships. Congress eliminated this problem by passing the Depository Institutions Deregulation and Monetary Control Act (DIDMCA) in 1980. DIDMCA mandated that all depository institutions offering transactions accounts be subject to uniform reserve requirements, regardless of charter. The figures in Exhibit 8.16 now apply to member and nonmember banks, savings and loans, and credit unions.

Since July 1998, the Federal Reserve has used a lagged reserve account (LRA) system. Under the current LRA system, reserves are held over a two-week period against deposit liabilities held for the two-week period ending almost three weeks earlier. This system makes it more difficult for the Federal Reserve to control the money supply when it is targeting monetary aggregates rather than short-term interest rates, but helps banks manage their reserves more accurately. With LRA, Federal Reserve purchases or sales of securities immediately alter the amount of total reserves in the system but do not affect required reserves. Banks know that the cost of reserves varies depending on the amount of excess reserves available, but they do not have to alter their required holdings until about three weeks later, when deposit fluctuations affect reserve requirements.

## LAGGED RESERVE ACCOUNTING

Under the current LRA procedure, weekly reporting institutions maintain reserves on their reservable liabilities with a 30-day lag.[31] That is, the reserve maintenance period for a weekly reporter begins 30 days after the beginning of a reserve computation period. In particular, banks must maintain reserves—on a daily average basis—for a 14-day period beginning on the third Thursday following the computation period. A **computation period** consists of two one-week **reporting periods** and, therefore, consists of 14 consecutive days beginning on a

---

[30]Financial institutions that are not members of the Federal Reserve System can use pass-through balances to meet reserve requirements. Pass-through balances are deposits held at either the Federal Home Loan Bank, the National Credit Union Administration Central Liquidity Facility, or any bank that keeps balances at the Federal Reserve Bank. The exempt amount increases each year as a fraction of the increase in aggregate reservable liabilities.

[31]Smaller banks (generally less than $161.2 million in reservable liabilities) compute and meet reserve requirements quarterly or annually (generally less than $6.6 million in reservable liabilities).

Tuesday and ending on the second Monday thereafter. A **maintenance period** consists of 14 consecutive days beginning on a Thursday and ending on the second Wednesday thereafter. The **reserve balance requirement** to be maintained in any given 14-day maintenance period ending on Wednesday is measured by:

- The reserve requirement on reservable liabilities calculated as of the computation period that ended 17 days prior to the start of the associated maintenance period
- Less vault cash as of the same computation period used to calculate the reserve requirement—that is, the 14-day computation period ending 17 days before the start of the associated maintenance period

Both vault cash and Federal Reserve deposit balances qualify as reserves, but the timing varies. Daily average balances determine the amount of vault cash that qualifies over the two-week computation period that ends 17 days prior to the maintenance period, while reserve balances are held during the reserve maintenance period. The institution must satisfy its reserve requirement in the form of vault cash or balances maintained either directly with a Reserve Bank or in a pass-through account (correspondent bank account). The portion of the reserve requirement that is not satisfied by vault cash holdings is called the **reserve balance requirement**.

Exhibit 8.17 demonstrates the timing of these intervals. Note that Friday balances carry over to Saturday and Sunday such that they have a three-day impact on the daily average. Because transaction balances are determined (for reserve purposes) about two and one-half weeks in advance and vault cash is determined three days in advance of the reserve maintenance period, a bank can manage its deposit balances at the Fed with a much greater degree of certainty as compared to the contemporaneous system.

The procedure to determine required reserves involves multiplying the percentages from Exhibit 8.16 by the daily average amount outstanding for each reservable liability during the base computation period. Banks can vary from the daily average requirement on any day of the maintenance period as long as their average reserve holdings meet the minimum daily requirement over the entire period. Both vault cash and demand balances at the Federal Reserve qualify as reserve assets. Vault cash held during the lagged computation period that ended 17 days prior to

---

**EXHIBIT 8.17** — Relationship between the Reserve Maintenance and Base Computation Periods under Lagged Reserve Accounting

| Sun | Mon | Tue | Wed | Thu | Fri | Sat |
|-----|-----|-----|-----|-----|-----|-----|
| 8-Aug | 9-Aug | 10-Aug | 11-Aug | 12-Aug | 13-Aug | 14-Aug |
| 15-Aug | 16-Aug | 17-Aug | 18-Aug | 19-Aug | 20-Aug | 21-Aug |
| 22-Aug | 23-Aug | 24-Aug | 25-Aug | 26-Aug | 27-Aug | 28-Aug |
| 29-Aug | 30-Aug | 31-Aug | 1-Sep | 2-Sep | 3-Sep | 4-Sep |
| 5-Sep | 6-Sep | 7-Sep | 8-Sep | 9-Sep | 10-Sep | 11-Sep |
| 12-Sep | 13-Sep | 14-Sep | 15-Sep | 16-Sep | 17-Sep | 18-Sep |
| 19-Sep | 20-Sep | 21-Sep | 22-Sep | 23-Sep | 24-Sep | 25-Sep |

■ Lagged Reserve Computation Period
▨ Reserve Maintenance Period

the start of the associated maintenance period is used to offset reserve balance requirements. For example, if a bank's daily average required reserves based on reservable liabilities total $20 million during the reserve maintenance period, then required demand balances at the Federal Reserve would equal $18 million if the bank held an average $2 million in vault cash during the computation period.

Finally, actual reserve holdings during the maintenance period can deviate slightly from the exact percentage requirement, with any excess or deficiency carried forward to the next period. The present allowance is 4 percent of daily average required reserves before past excesses or deficiencies and the vault cash offset, or $50,000, whichever is greater. If a bank is deficient by more than this amount, it must pay a nondeductible interest penalty equal to the discount rate plus 2 percent times the extraordinary deficiency. More importantly, if a bank consistently holds too few reserves, the Federal Reserve will penalize it further by restricting its operating procedures and allowable business activities. If a bank holds more reserves than the allowable excess, it cannot carry this difference forward and thus loses any interest income it could have earned by investing the balances. The timing of these requirements places a premium on Wednesday's transactions just prior to the end of the maintenance week. Because federal funds are an important source of reserves, federal funds trading is very active on Wednesdays and the federal funds rate is typically more volatile compared to other days.

## AN APPLICATION: RESERVE CALCULATION UNDER LRA

Reserve maintenance requirements can be best demonstrated through an example. Consider the time frame outlined in Exhibit 8.17, with September 9 to September 22 representing the 14-day reserve maintenance period. Exhibit 8.18 presents daily balances for vault cash and net transactions accounts during the lagged reserve computation period for a sample bank. The final columns list the cumulative totals for each balance sheet item over the two-week period and the daily average balances.[32] Note that the base period for net transactions accounts begins on August 10, almost four and one-half weeks before the maintenance period starts.

Exhibit 8.19 demonstrates the required reserves calculation. The procedure has four steps:

1. Calculate daily average balances outstanding during the lagged computation period.
2. Apply the reserve percentages.
3. Subtract vault cash.
4. Add or subtract the allowable reserve carried forward from the prior period.

Daily average balances equal the cumulative total divided by 14, the number of days in the base period. Weekends count even if a bank is not open for business. These daily average balances are then multiplied by the percentages from Exhibit 8.16. The first $7 million of net transactions accounts is exempt from required reserves, while the next $40.6 million is subject to the lower 3 percent requirement.

For this sample bank, total daily average gross required reserves equal $88.115 million. Average vault cash of $32.214 million during the lagged computation period is then subtracted to yield a net requirement of $55.901 million. Banks can deviate from the exact requirement as long as they make up deficiencies in the following maintenance period. Excess reserve holdings or surpluses of up to 4 percent of gross required reserves can be carried forward to reduce the next period's minimum requirement. The computation in Exhibit 8.19 assumes that the prior period deficiency totaled $2.276 million. The sample bank must hold minimum reserves equal to the net requirement plus any daily deficiency—a total of $58.177 million. The last item in the exhibit, maximum reserves at the Federal Reserve, equals the minimum requirement plus 4 percent of $88.115 million—or $61.702 million. Of course, there is no limit on how much a bank may hold in balances at the Federal Reserve. The term *maximum* refers to the fact that no more than a 4 percent surplus can be used to reduce future balance requirements.

The calculations would be slightly different if the bank carried forward a surplus from the previous maintenance period. In this case, a bank is allowed to be deficient by 4 percent of gross reserves during the current maintenance period. If, for example, the bank in Exhibit 8.19 reported a carry-forward surplus of $1.5 million, it could have used the $1.5 million to reduce its total requirement and still be deficient 4 percent more. Thus, the minimum point in the target range would equal $54.401 million.

## CORRESPONDENT BANKING SERVICES

In addition to services from the Federal Reserve such as holding deposit balances for reserves requirement and the facilitation of funds transfers, most banks maintain relationships with correspondent banks for similar services.[33] These relationships are usually maintained through demand deposit accounts at the bank's correspondent

---

[32]Banks can report balance sheet figures to the nearest thousand dollars. Exhibit 8.18 rounds figures to the nearest million.

[33]One important facet of the Depository Institutions and Monetary Control Act of 1980 was to promote competition in check-clearing services. Prior to the act, the Federal Reserve provided free check collection to member banks. Banks did pay indirectly through owning nonearning reserve deposits. Still, many banks also chose to clear checks through correspondent banks. Correspondents generally provided deposit credit sooner than the Federal Reserve, and banks could invest funds earlier.

## EXHIBIT 8.18

Report of Reserveable Liabilities and Offsetting Asset Balances

### Balances at Close of Business Day (Millions of Dollars)

| Lagged Computation Period | Tue 10-Aug | Wed 11-Aug | Thu 12-Aug | Fri 13-Aug | Sat 14-Aug | Sun 15-Aug | Mon 16-Aug | Tue 17-Aug | Wed 18-Aug | Thu 19-Aug | Fri 20-Aug | Sat 21-Aug | Sun 22-Aug | Mon 23-Aug | Two-Week Total | Daily Average |
|---|---|---|---|---|---|---|---|---|---|---|---|---|---|---|---|---|
| DDAs | 992 | 995 | 956 | 954 | 954 | 954 | 989 | 996 | 960 | 959 | 958 | 958 | 958 | 990 | $ 13,573 | $ 969.50 |
| Auto trans. from savings | 0 | 0 | 0 | 0 | 0 | 0 | 0 | 0 | 0 | 0 | 0 | 0 | 0 | 0 | 0 | $ 0.0 |
| NOW and Super NOW | 221 | 221 | 222 | 223 | 223 | 223 | 223 | 224 | 225 | 225 | 225 | 225 | 225 | 225 | $ 3,130 | $ 223.57 |
| *Deductions:* | | | | | | | | | | | | | | | 0 | $ 0.0 |
| DD bal. from U.S. dep. | 163 | 281 | 190 | 186 | 186 | 186 | 159 | 159 | 274 | 178 | 182 | 182 | 182 | 164 | $ 2,672 | $ 190.86 |
| CIPC | 96 | 96 | 78 | 78 | 78 | 78 | 95 | 98 | 92 | 79 | 81 | 81 | 81 | 88 | $ 1,199 | $ 85.64 |
| Net trans. accounts | 954 | 839 | 910 | 913 | 913 | 913 | 958 | 963 | 819 | 927 | 920 | 920 | 920 | 963 | $ 12,832 | $ 916.57 |
| Vault Cash | 28 | 30 | 31 | 33 | 33 | 33 | 38 | 30 | 31 | 32 | 32 | 32 | 32 | 36 | $ 451 | $ 32.21 |

**EXHIBIT 8.19**

Required Reserves Report, September 9–22

| Reservable Liabilities for: | | Daily Avg. Deposit Liab. ($mill) | Reserve Percentage | Daily Avg. Requirement ($ mill) |
|---|---|---|---|---|
| **Sept 9–22** | | | | |
| Net trans. accounts | | | | |
| Exempt up to | $ 7.0 mill | 7.00 | 0.0% | $ 0.000 |
| Over 7 up to | $ 47.6 mill | $ 40.60 | 3.0% | $ 1.218 |
| Over | $ 47.6 mill | $ 868.97 | 10.0% | $ 86.897 |
| Total | | $ 916.57 | | |
| **Gross reserve requirement** | | | | $ 88.115 |
| Daily average vault cash | | | | $ 32.214 |
| Net reserve requirement | | | | $ 55.901 |
| Reserve carry-forward (from prior period) | | | | ($ 2.276) |
| *Minimum reserves to be maintained with Federal Reserve* | | | | $ 58.177 |
| *Maximum reserves to be maintained* | | | | $ 61.702 |
| (0.04 × 88.115) + 58.177 | | | | |
| | | | | |
| **If a surplus carry forward of $ 1.500** | | | | |
| *Minimum reserves to be maintained with Federal Reserve* | | | | $ 54.401 |
| Carry forward (4% of gross reserve requirement) | | | | $ 3.525 |
| *Maximum reserves to be maintained* | | | | $ 57.926 |
| (0.04 × 88.115) + 54.401 | | | | |

financial institutions and these balances are held as payment for services purchased from the correspondent bank. This interbank deposit network links the activities of small and large banks and banks located in different geographic areas. **Correspondent banking** is the system of interbank relationships in which one bank sells services to other financial institutions. The institution providing the services is the **correspondent bank** or upstream correspondent, while the institution buying the services is the **respondent bank** or downstream correspondent. A bank that owns deposit balances is a respondent bank while a bank that accepts deposits is a correspondent bank. Larger banks typically fill both roles, providing basic services to smaller banks and buying services from large firms that are either located in other geographic markets or able to offer a broader range of services.

Respondent banks purchase services from correspondents for a variety of reasons. Some services, such as check collection, carry advantages over those provided directly by the Federal Reserve System, which generally takes longer to grant credit. Other services are either too expensive to provide independently or cannot be provided because of regulatory constraints. Small banks, for example, want to offer a full range of services to their customers, but the demand for specialty transactions is sporadic. It would be too costly to invest in the technology and manpower for international transactions or investment banking advice on mergers and acquisitions if those services were used infrequently. These services can only be provided in large volume to take advantage of economies of scale, which lower unit costs. Even when priced at a markup over correspondents' costs, these services are cheaper than if provided independently. Respondent banks similarly sell loan participations to correspondent banks when individual loans exceed a bank's legal lending limit.

The correspondent banking system evolved before the establishment of the Federal Reserve, largely to help process checks. Respondent banks paid for the service by maintaining balances above those needed to clear items. Correspondent banks could invest the excess, with interest income covering their costs. The fundamental relationships are the same today. Respondent banks choose services they need from menus provided by correspondents. They shop around for quality service at the lowest available price and hold balances that pay for the supplier's costs plus profit.

The predominant services purchased from correspondent banks can be grouped into three broad categories: check clearing and related cash transactions, investment services, and credit-related transactions. Check-clearing services are attractive because respondent banks can reduce float. Correspondent banks often make funds available for respondent investment before the Federal Reserve's scheduled availability. Additional interest earned more than compensates for the required compensating balances. The most common correspondent banking services are:

- Check collection, wire transfer, coin and currency supply
- Loan participation assistance
- Data processing services

- Portfolio analysis and investment advice
- Federal funds trading
- Securities safekeeping
- Arrangement of purchase or sale of securities
- Investment banking services: swaps, futures, mergers, and acquisitions
- Loans to directors and officers
- International financial transactions

Respondents purchase other services when the price is below the unit cost of supplying the service directly.

Many large banks view correspondent banking as a profit center. The demand for basic correspondent services and related leasing, international banking, stock brokerage, and real estate services by other banks and their customers is sufficiently large to justify offering these services worldwide. Respondents pay for correspondent services either with explicit fees or by maintaining deposit balances at the correspondent bank. In most cases, compensation takes the form of demand deposit balances, which provide an investment return to the correspondent. These due-to and due-from relationships represent the lifeblood of correspondent banking.

Increased competition resulting from deregulation and interstate mergers and acquisitions has shrunken the pool of commercial bank respondents and put pressure on profit margins. Banks that acquire a firm in another state no longer need the same services previously obtained through a correspondent. A community banker who acquaints an upstream correspondent with his or her customer base will frequently discover that the correspondent has tried to market services directly to the customer and completely circumvent the respondent bank. This situation has produced two results. First, respondents now unbundle the services of upstream correspondents, purchasing different services from different correspondents rather than dealing with only one firm. Second, community banks are forming and buying services from cooperative institutions known as **bankers banks**, which are owned by independent commercial banks in a state and are authorized to provide services only to financial institutions. They do not market services directly to bank customers and compete only with other correspondent banks. Bankers' banks maintain a staff that handles check collection; analyzes the credit quality of loan participations; trades in government and corporate securities for investments; and offers other services, such as discount brokerage, leasing, and data processing at competitive prices. Independent bankers serve as directors and offer guidance regarding product selection, pricing, and portfolio policies. There are different bankers banks in different states throughout the United States. In recent years, several of these bankers banks have helped community banks form the equivalent of reverse holding companies that offer trust services. Community banks thus jointly own a firm that offers trust services to each of their customers. The attraction is that this correspondent bank is not in direct competition with each community bank and will not try to steal its customers.

## LIQUIDITY PLANNING

Banks actively engage in liquidity planning at two levels. The first relates to managing their short-term liquidity needs and required reserve position. The second level of liquidity planning involves forecasting net funds needs derived from seasonal or cyclical phenomena and overall bank growth. The planning horizon is considerably longer, encompassing monthly intervals throughout an entire year. This type of liquidity planning is covered in the next section on "The Development of Liquidity Management Strategies."

### SHORT-TERM LIQUIDITY PLANNING

Short-term liquidity planning focuses on forecasting closing balances at the Federal Reserve relative to potential legal reserves. The previous sections described the reserve accounting requirements and the procedure for calculating legal requirements. The planning horizon is two weeks, during which a bank must hold a minimum amount of deposit balances at the Federal Reserve. Actual balances vary daily, with many transactions affecting outstanding liabilities and the investment portfolio but these transactions occurred over two weeks before and are therefore known. Many new to the depository institutions industry, however, would think that required reserves represent some type of liquidity risk reserve in the event of a significant liquidity need. The line of thinking is, if the bank can only invest 90 percent of transaction deposits, then it has 10 percent available for emergency liquidity needs. This is not the case. As discussed in the previous section, the bank may *not* come up short of reserves. If it has a liquidity need, required reserves are not available to use for the need, only those reserve funds in excess of those required. Hence, required reserves may create a liquidity problem for the bank, not a solution!

The fundamental objective in managing a legal reserve position is to meet the minimum requirement at the lowest cost. Because customer preferences determine vault cash needs, they vary largely with the payment patterns of the bank's customers and local businesses. They also exhibit well-defined seasonal patterns that are easily

## EXHIBIT 8.20

### Factors Affecting Daily Reserves Held at the Federal Reserve

| Factors Increasing Reserves | Factors Decreasing Reserves |
| --- | --- |
| **Nondiscretionary** | **Nondiscretionary** |
| Yesterday's immediate cash letter | Remittances charged |
| Deferred availability items | Deficit in local clearinghouse |
| Excess from local clearinghouse | Treasury tax and loan account calls |
| Deposits from U.S. Treasury | Maturing CDs, Eurodollars not rolled over |
| **Discretionary** | **Discretionary** |
| Currency/coin shipped to Federal Reserve | Currency and coin received from Federal Reserve |
| Security sales | Security purchases |
| Borrowing from Federal Reserve | Payment on loans from Federal Reserve |
| Federal funds purchased | Federal funds sold |
| Securities sold under agreement to repurchase | Securities purchased under agreement to resell |
| Interest payments on securities | |
| New certificates of deposit, Eurodollar issues | |

forecast. When a bank needs additional vault cash, it simply requests a cash delivery from its local Federal Reserve Bank or a correspondent bank. It similarly ships any excess cash when appropriate. The primary difficulty in meeting required reserves derives from forecasting required deposit balances at the Federal Reserve resulting from volatile shifts in bank liabilities. The process involves forecasting daily clearing balances and either investing any excess at the highest yield or obtaining additional balances at the lowest cost to cover any deficits. The change to a LRA system has made this process somewhat easier.

Exhibit 8.20 identifies several factors that alter a bank's actual and required reserve assets. These factors are separated into nondiscretionary items, over which a bank has virtually no control, and discretionary items, over which it has at least partial control. The most important nondiscretionary items are checks presented for payment. Exhibit 8.20 differentiates between the Federal Reserve's cash letter and local clearings.[34] Because the Federal Reserve provides a schedule for the timing of clearings, a bank knows when previously deferred items will be available. Check clearings are uncontrollable in that bank customers determine the timing and magnitude of check payments. Customers do not normally notify a bank at the time of payment or prior to making deposits.

This uncontrolled activity presents planning problems when large withdrawals or new deposits catch a bank unaware and force it to scramble for additional reserves or to invest newfound funds. Good data management and communications systems from tellers and ATMs to management are essential. Interest of 5 percent on $10 million over the weekend is $4,110, a substantial opportunity cost of poor planning! Managers should monitor activity in large deposit accounts routinely. They should know when large CDs mature, when the Treasury transfers deposits to the Federal Reserve, and when loan customers make large loan payments. They should also identify any weekly or monthly patterns in deposit flows that arise from normal business activity. This may allow them to use balances from inflows during one part of the maintenance period to offset outflows during another part, rather than jump in and out of federal funds trading.

When managers need to adjust a bank's reserve assets they use the discretionary items listed in Exhibit 8.20. Managers have some control over these transactions and use them to complement uncontrollable deposit flows. In most cases, a bank receives information on clearing surpluses or deficiencies twice daily. Summary figures from yesterday's check clearings are available each morning, along with balances from federal funds trades and securities transactions. In most urban areas, local clearinghouses report net clearings each afternoon from checks submitted that day. Once this information is available, managers may actively increase or decrease daily reserves by choosing among the items in Exhibit 8.20. Although federal funds and RP transactions are the most popular, the choice depends on a comparison of costs and returns.

### MANAGING FLOAT

During any single day, more than $100 million in checks drawn on U.S. commercial banks is waiting to be processed. Individuals, businesses, and governments deposit the checks but cannot use the proceeds until banks give their approval, typically in several days. Checks in process of collection, called "float," are a source of both income and expense to banks.

---

[34]A cash letter is a letter or data tape on which a bank lists and describes transit checks.

## CONTEMPORARY ISSUES

### A $24 BILLION OVERDRAFT

The Bank of New York serves as a clearing agent for numerous brokers that buy and sell U.S. government securities, transferring ownership of securities between buyers and sellers. Normally, sellers of securities route the instruments through the bank's securities account at the Federal Reserve Bank of New York and simultaneously receive payment through debits against the Bank of New York's reserve account. The Bank of New York promptly routes the securities to the buyers, from whom it collects payment.

On November 20, 1985, the bank experienced a computer malfunction that short-circuited the normal sequence of transactions. Although the computer allowed sellers to route

securities to the bank's account and debit the bank's reserves in payment, it did not allow the bank to route the same securities to the ultimate buyers. Thus, the bank saw its reserves decline, but it could not generate sufficient cash receipts to replenish the deductions. By the end of the day, the bank reported a $22.6 billion overdraft in its reserve account. The Federal Reserve Bank of New York stepped in and made a $22.6 billion overnight discount window loan at 7.5 percent. Later, it was determined that the actual deficiency was $23.6 billion, and the bank was charged interest on an additional $1 billion loan.

The $23.6 billion loan was 2,300 percent of the bank's capital, and it cost the bank almost $5 million in unanticipated interest expense. If a bank were unable to cover its exposure, it could lose an amount far in excess of its capital and thus quickly become insolvent. Because Bank of New York's loan was fully collateralized with U.S. government securities, the Federal Reserve was never at risk of loss. In response to the bank's problems, the Federal Reserve imposed operational standards on the allowable size of daylight overdrafts that clearing banks could run. The applicable interest charge was also increased to 2 percent over the prevailing discount rate.

To understand float management and recent criticism of bank policies, it is necessary to explain the bank payment system. Payments between banks can be made either by check or electronically. Checks drawn against transactions accounts are presented to the customer's bank for payment and ultimately "cleared" by reducing the bank's deposit balance at the Federal Reserve or a correspondent bank. Payments made electronically directly and immediately alter balances held at Federal Reserve Banks. This network for transferring funds electronically is called the Fedwire.

A bank that accepts a deposit accepts the risk that supporting funds will eventually appear. Referring back to Exhibit 8.12, if the individual does not have sufficient funds to cover the $500 draft, BANB must collect from its business depositor and may suffer losses. To reduce this risk, banks typically place a hold on deposited funds. Essentially, they do not let depositors spend the proceeds until there is reasonable certainty the deposit is good.

Most individuals at one time or another have played the float game, writing checks against insufficient balances, then rushing to deposit funds that permit the checks to clear. Banks play the same game with electronic funds transfers—for far greater dollar amounts—by authorizing payments from deposits held at the Federal Reserve or correspondent banks in excess of their balances. In doing so, they drive their collected balances below zero. These negative balances are called daylight overdrafts. Normally, enough funds are transferred into the account by the end of each day to cover the overdraft.[35] In November 1985, the Federal Reserve was forced to loan the Bank of New York $23.6 billion to cover overdrafts caused by a computer malfunction. (See the Contemporary Issues Box: "A $24 Billion Overdraft.") The Fed has since taken steps to reduce its exposure.

These overdrafts could potentially close down the electronic payments system. The primary risk is that some financial institution might fail because it cannot meet a payments obligation. A failure might produce liquidity problems at other banks and have a ripple effect, generating other losses and failures. Suppose, for example, that CNB from Exhibit 8.12 transfers funds over the Fedwire to BANB before the individual makes sufficient balances available to cover the original $500 check to the San Jose business. Once the wire transfer is received, BANB can release funds to the business without risk. Settlement is immediate and final. If the individual does not provide the underlying balances, CNB could lose the amount of the transfer. When extended to all transactions, any single bank may have daylight overdrafts two or three times larger than its capital base.

There are two main electronic funds transfer networks: the Fedwire and CHIPS. Most of the transactions on the Fedwire involve transfers of immediately available funds between financial institutions and balance adjustments from the purchase or sale of government securities. Most of the wire transfers on CHIPS involve either

---

[35]Richard Smoot (1985) discusses overdrafts arising over the major wire transfer systems and analyzes the risks assumed in each case.

transfers of Eurodollar balances or foreign exchange trading. Although participants are required to maintain positive balances at the Federal Reserve and correspondent banks at the end of each business day, they may create negative balances (daylight overdrafts) during a day by transferring funds in excess of their initial balance before any deposits are received. Conceptually, the overdraft is a loan, but under current regulation it is costless to the deficient bank because no interest or fees are paid. It may be intentional or unintentional, but it clearly imposes risk to the Federal Reserve or CHIPS. The Fed assumes risk because recipients of wire transfers retain legal title to the funds. The Fed thus essentially guarantees wire transfers.

In 1986 the Federal Reserve endorsed guidelines on overdrafts, which limited the size of daylight overdrafts while transferring funds over the Fedwire. Van Hoose and Sellon (1989) describe the types of policies the Fed uses to control payment system risk over the Fedwire and CHIPS. The policies consist primarily of caps on the size of any single firm's overdrafts. Interestingly, the Fed chooses not to use the price mechanism by charging interest on overdrafts to influence their usage. Still, the Fed identifies large overdrafts on the Fedwire and discusses the potential risks with the guilty bank's senior management. If the overdrafts arise because of computer problems, the Fed will extend discount window credit at the current discount rate plus 2 percent. Its ultimate weapon, however, is to restrict bank operations.

## LIQUIDITY VERSUS PROFITABILITY

There is a short-run trade-off between liquidity and profitability. The more liquid a bank is, the lower are its return on equity and return on assets, all other things being equal. Both asset and liability liquidity contribute to this relationship. Asset liquidity is influenced by the composition and maturity of funds. Large holdings of cash assets clearly decrease profits because of the opportunity loss of interest income. In terms of the investment portfolio, short-term securities normally carry lower yields than comparable longer-term securities. Investors value price stability, so long-term securities pay a yield premium to induce investors to extend maturities. Banks that purchase short-term securities thus increase liquidity, but at the expense of higher potential returns. Consider an environment where market expectations are for short-term Treasury yields to remain constant at present levels. The Treasury yield curve will slope upward, reflecting liquidity premiums that increase with maturity.[36] A bank that buys six-month Treasury bills at 5 percent rather than a one-year bill at 5.2 percent gives up 20 basis points for the greater price stability (lower risk).

A bank's loan portfolio displays the same trade-off. Loans carrying the highest yields are the least liquid. Yields are high because default risk or interest rate risk is substantial and the loan administration expense is high. Loans that can be readily sold usually are short-term credits to well-known corporations or government-guaranteed instruments and thus carry minimal spreads. Amortized loans, in contrast, may improve liquidity even though they are frequently long term because the periodic payments increase near-term cash flow.

In terms of liability liquidity, banks with the best asset quality and highest equity capital have greater access to purchased funds and can acquire these funds more cheaply since they will pay lower interest rates on their liabilities—but will also generally report lower returns in the short run due to their lower-risk position. Promised yields on loans and securities increase with the perceived default risk of the underlying issuer. Banks that acquire low-default-risk assets, such as U.S. government securities, forgo the risk premium that could be earned. Interestingly, many banks buy U.S. agency securities because the incremental yield more than compensates for perceived differences in default risk relative to U.S. Treasuries. Similarly, banks with greater equity financing exhibit lower equity multipliers (total assets/total equity) and thus generate lower returns on equity, even with identical returns on assets. These banks can borrow funds cheaper because a greater portion of their assets has to be in default before they might fail.

Liquidity planning focuses on guaranteeing that immediately available funds are available at the lowest cost. Management must determine whether liquidity and default-risk premiums more than compensate for the additional risk on longer-term and lower-quality bank investments. If management is successful, long-term earnings will exceed peer banks' earnings, as will bank capital and overall liquidity. The market value of bank equity will increase relative to peers as investors bid up stock prices.

## THE RELATIONSHIP BETWEEN LIQUIDITY, CREDIT AND INTEREST RATE RISK

Liquidity management is a day-to-day responsibility. Banks routinely experience fluctuations in their cash assets, depending on the timing and magnitude of unexpected deposit outflows. Deviations from expectations can normally be attributed to large payments or deposits that clear through the Federal Reserve or local clearinghouse. Most shortages can be met by accelerating planned borrowings or deferring asset purchases. Excess cash can be easily invested in earning assets. A well-managed bank monitors its cash position carefully and maintains low liquidity risk.

Liquidity risk for a poorly managed bank closely follows credit and interest rate risk. In fact, banks that

---

[36]Research by Cook, et al., (1987) and Toevs (1986) demonstrates that Treasury bill rates include a liquidity or term premium through at least one year.

experience large deposit outflows can often trace the source to either credit problems or earnings declines from interest rate gambles that backfired. The normal sequence of events underlying liquidity problems is:

- Bank management assumes substantial risk by mismatching asset and liability maturities and durations or by extending credit to high-risk borrowers.
- The bank reports reduced earnings.
- The media publicizes the credit and interest rate difficulties.
- The bank must pay higher rates to attract and keep deposits and other purchased funds.
- Bank earnings decline further with reduced interest margins and nonaccruing loans, and uninsured depositors move their funds, forcing the bank to sell assets at fire sale prices and obtain temporary financing from government sources until a merger can be arranged or the bank fails.

Few banks can replace lost deposits independently if an outright run on the bank arises. Liquidity planning forces management to monitor the overall risk position of the bank such that credit risk partially offsets interest rate risk assumed in the bank's overall asset and liability management strategy. If credit risk is high, interest rate risk should be low and vice versa. Potential liquidity needs must reflect estimates of new loan demand and potential deposit losses. The following list identifies factors affecting certain liquidity needs:

| New Loan Demand | Potential Deposit Losses |
|---|---|
| • Unused commercial credit lines outstanding<br>• Consumer credit available on bank-issued cards<br>• Business activity and growth in the bank's trade area<br>• The aggressiveness of the bank's loan officer call programs | • The composition of liabilities<br>• Insured versus uninsured deposits<br>• Deposit ownership between: money fund traders, trust fund traders, public institutions, commercial banks by size, corporations by size, individuals, foreign investors, and Treasury tax and loan accounts<br>• Large deposits held by any single entity<br>• The sensitivity of deposits to changes in the level of interest rates |

Each of the factors under "New Loan Demand" signifies a potential increase in borrowing that might deplete a bank's cash reserves. Suppose, for example, that the Federal Reserve tightens credit policy and pushes short-term interest rates higher. Businesses often choose to borrow under outstanding loan commitments rather than use commercial paper, so that bank loans increase. During recessions, individuals might similarly increase outstanding borrowings under credit card agreements. Loan demand closely follows the economic development and growth in a community such that good economic times accelerate borrowing requests. Finally, some banks require loan officers to systematically call on customers to solicit new business. If such call programs are successful, loan demand will increase accordingly.

The factors under "Potential Deposit Losses" similarly convey information regarding potential cash deficiencies. Banks with substantial core deposits and few purchased liabilities will experience smaller proportionate deposit losses. If the majority of the deposits are federally insured, unanticipated outflows will decline further. Large purchased liabilities are also more sensitive to changes in market interest rates. When rates rise, for example, a bank must increase the rate it pays on these rate-sensitive balances or customers will quickly move their balances in search of higher yields. Finally, many banks are located in markets that experience seasonal or cyclical deposit outflows that track changes in regional economic conditions. Consider a bank in a resort community. Deposits flow into the bank during resort season, but flow out afterward. Managers must thus monitor these influences in order to plan for cash needs.

## TRADITIONAL AGGREGATE MEASURES OF LIQUIDITY RISK

As described earlier, banks rely on both assets and liabilities as sources of liquidity. Small banks generally have limited access to purchased funds and thus rely primarily on short-term assets. Larger banks, in contrast, obtain liquid funds mainly via liabilities rather than selling assets. Traditional liquidity measures focus on balance sheet accounts and measure liquidity in terms of financial ratios.

### ASSET LIQUIDITY MEASURES

**Asset liquidity** refers to the ease of converting an asset to cash with a minimum of loss. The most liquid assets mature near term and are highly marketable. Liquidity measures are normally expressed in percentage terms as a fraction of total assets. Most small banks maintain substantial investments in highly liquid assets because they provide liquidity in times of duress. Highly liquid assets include:

1. Cash and due from banks in excess of required holdings
2. Federal funds sold and reverse repurchase agreements
3. U.S. Treasury and agency securities maturing within one year
4. Corporate and municipal securities maturing within one year, rated Baa and above
5. Loans that can be readily sold and/or securitized

In general, the most marketable assets exhibit low default risk, short maturities, and large trading volume in the secondary market. Cash and due from banks is liquid in the sense that a bank needs clearing balances to process transactions on a daily basis. Without deposits at the Federal Reserve or other financial institutions, a bank could not conduct business. Banks normally minimize cash holdings because they do not earn interest. Only excess cash is truly liquid. This excess includes balances held above legal reserve requirements and the amounts required by correspondent banks for services. Cash balances can decline during any single day without presenting serious problems but must be quickly replenished to sustain operations. Thus, cash and due meets daily liquidity requirements, but banks rely on other assets for longer-term or permanent liquidity needs.

Federal funds and reverse RPs typically mature overnight and increase cash and due at maturity if they are not rolled over. The other securities exhibit low default risk and short maturities. Thus, they typically trade at prices close to par and if sold, have a negligible impact on noninterest income. Treasury obligations are backed by federal taxing authority and borrowing capability. U.S. agency securities are issued by quasi-public entities, such as the Federal Home Loan Mortgage Corporation and Federal Land Bank, and have a long history of low defaults. Liquid corporate and municipal securities are highly-rated, investment grade obligations (Baa rated and above) that are well known nationally. Other securities are similarly liquid if their current market value exceeds their book value. This results from management's willingness to sell securities at a gain, which adds to reported net income, but unwillingness to take losses. Finally, standardized loans such as credit card receivables may be liquid if a bank regularly packages and securitizes these assets.

Historically, banks and regulators focused on loan-to-deposit ratios. Because loans are relatively illiquid in general, the greater is a bank's loan-to-deposit ratio, the lower is the assumed liquidity. As discussed below, the key issue is whether loans generate cash inflows and exhibit high or low default risk.

**PLEDGING REQUIREMENTS.** Not all of a bank's securities can be easily sold. Like their credit customers, banks are required to pledge collateral against certain types of borrowing. U.S. Treasuries or municipals normally constitute the least-cost collateral and, if pledged against a debt, cannot be sold until the bank removes the claim or substitutes other collateral. Collateral is required against four different liabilities: securities sold under agreement to repurchase, borrowing from Federal Reserve Banks at the discount window, public deposits owned by the U.S. Treasury or any state or municipal government unit, and FHLB advances. With public deposits, each depositor stipulates which assets qualify as collateral and what the pledging ratio is. For example, cities often stipulate that a local bank can pledge either U.S. Treasury securities or municipals against 100 percent of the city's uninsured deposits at the bank. Treasuries are valued at par, while A-rated or better in-state municipal securities are valued at 110 percent of par. A third-party trustee holds this collateral. Although these terms favor municipal securities, the bank can choose among its securities to pledge long-term bonds. Pledging requirements against RPs and discount window borrowing establish Treasury securities as preferred collateral against 100 percent of qualifying liabilities. The FHLB, in turn, requires banks to pledge real estate–related loans or securities as collateral against its advances. All pledged securities should be subtracted from the above list of liquid assets to obtain the dollar value of net liquid assets.

In summary, the best measures of asset liquidity identify the dollar amounts of unpledged liquid assets as a fraction of total assets. The greater is the fraction, the greater is the ability to sell assets to meet cash needs. Alternatively, liquid assets as a fraction of purchased liabilities conveys whether net liquidity sources are available from assets. In particular, this ratio should exceed unity indicating that if the bank experiences a run-off of all purchased funds, liquid assets will be sufficient to cover the cash loss.

**LOANS.** Many banks and bank analysts monitor loan-to-deposit ratios as a general measure of liquidity. Loans are presumably the least liquid of assets, while deposits are the primary source of funds. A high ratio indicates illiquidity because a bank is fully loaned up relative to its stable funding. Implicitly, new loans or other asset purchases must be financed with large, purchased liabilities. A low ratio suggests that a bank has additional liquidity because it can grant new loans financed with stable deposits.

The loan-to-deposit ratio is not as meaningful as it first appears. It ignores the composition of loans and deposits. Some loans, such as dealer call loans and government-guaranteed credits, either mature soon or can be easily sold if needed. Others are longer term, with deferred payments, and can be sold only at a substantial discount. Two banks with identical deposits and loan-to-deposit ratios may have substantially different loan liquidity if one bank has highly marketable loans while the other has risky, long-term loans. An aggregate loan figure similarly ignores the timing of cash flows from interest and principal payments. Installment contracts generate cash faster than balloon notes, which defer the principal payment until maturity. The same is true for a bank's deposit base. Some deposits, such as long-term nonnegotiable time deposits, are more stable than others, so there is less risk of withdrawal. Aggregate ratios thus ignore the difference in composition of both assets and liabilities and their cash flow characteristics.

Finally, loan-to-deposit ratios have generally increased recently with interest rate deregulation. Although ratios averaged 60 to 70 percent in the 1970s, many banks run ratios near 100 percent or more today. This increase results from the loss of demand and savings deposits and the increased reliance on purchased funds. The corresponding pressure on net interest margins induces many banks to seek more loans, which offer the highest promised yields to maintain interest spreads. It is thus difficult to compare loan-to-deposit ratios over time.

## LIABILITY LIQUIDITY MEASURES

**Liability liquidity** refers to the ease with which a bank can issue new debt to acquire clearing balances at reasonable costs. Measures typically reflect a bank's asset quality, capital base, and composition of outstanding deposits and other liabilities. The following ratios are commonly cited:

1. Total equity to total assets
2. Loans to deposits
3. Loan losses to net loans
4. Reserve for loan losses to net loans
5. The percentage composition of deposits
6. Total deposits to total assets
7. Core deposits to total assets
8. Federal funds purchased and RPs to total assets
9. Commercial paper and other short-term borrowings to total assets

A bank's ability to borrow at reasonable rates of interest is closely linked to the market's perception of asset quality. Banks with high-quality assets and a large capital base can issue more debt at relatively low rates compared with peers. The reason is that investors believe there is little chance that such banks will fail. Thus, analysts focus on measures of loan quality and risk assets along with a bank's equity base when assessing future borrowing capabilities.

Banks with stable deposits such as transactions accounts, savings certificates, and nonnegotiable time deposits generally have the same widespread access to borrowed funds at relatively low rates. Those that rely heavily on purchased funds, in contrast, must pay higher rates and experience greater volatility in the composition and average cost of liabilities. For this reason, most banks today compete aggressively for retail **core deposits**. It is well known that individuals exhibit considerable inertia in their choice of banks as long as they perceive that the bank offers quality, friendly service. The last five ratios listed above provide information regarding the breakdown of liabilities between core deposits and noncore, purchased liabilities.

One procedure to estimate the magnitude of stable, core deposits involves plotting total deposits against time and drawing a line through the low points in the graph. This base line represents core deposits equal to the minimum trend deposit level under which actual deposits never fall. Future stable, or core, deposits can be forecast by extending the base line on trend. **Volatile deposits** equal the difference between actual current deposits and the base estimate of core deposits. Implicitly, these are a bank's highly rate-sensitive deposits that customers withdraw as interest rates vary. A curved base line is used to emphasize the lack of growth in stable deposits. Many banks calculate liquidity ratios that use an estimate of volatile deposits as the base.

It is also important to recognize that different institutions have different access to specific funding sources. Allen, Peristiani, and Saunders (1989) demonstrate, for example, that banks with more than $1 billion in assets are the largest proportionate purchasers of federal funds. Regardless of size, banks located in primary banking centers are heavier federal funds borrowers. In the RP market, however, the smallest banks are the largest net borrowers.

The real difficulty in managing liabilities is estimating the interest elasticity of different sources of funds. Management would like to know the quantity response to a change in the level of rates. For example, if interest rates increase by an average of 1 percent during the next six months, how much will demand deposits and NOW accounts change? Similarly, if a bank pays one-half of 1 percent more on CDs relative to competitors, how many new funds will it attract? Some information is available from historical relationships. Management can document the magnitude of disintermediation when interest rates rose in past years as an approximation of potential deposit losses, given expected rate changes. Management can also periodically conduct market tests of rate sensitivity by offering yield premiums on selected liabilities independently and observing the quantity response. These estimates are imprecise, however, and actual rate sensitivity can change quickly with economic conditions or changes in the public's evaluation of the bank's financial health. If the market perceives that a bank is not sound, most borrowing sources immediately dry up regardless of the rate premiums paid. In response, many banks aggressively solicit retail deposits using innovative marketing strategies because individuals are less rate sensitive and the deposits are more stable.

## LONGER-TERM LIQUIDITY PLANNING

The second stage of liquidity planning involves projecting funds needs over the coming year and beyond if necessary. ALCO members are responsible for forecasting deposit growth and loan demand and arranging for adequate liquidity sources to meet potential needs. Projections are separated into three categories: base trend, short-term seasonal, and cyclical values. The analysis assesses a bank's liquidity gap, measured as the difference between potential uses of funds and anticipated sources of funds, over monthly intervals. In practice, many large banks perform their analysis weekly. Deposit and loan data are aggregated to supply the calculations.

Exhibit 8.21 summarizes the basic procedure for projecting liquidity needs over a 12-month planning horizon. The sample bank's year-end balance sheet, which serves as the reference point in the planning model, is provided at the top. Total deposits and loans are forecast monthly during the year at the bottom, with the deposit forecast excluding CDs. The base trend forecast examines the regular annual growth component of deposits or loans. Deposits are expected to grow at a 6 percent annual rate and loans at 12 percent. These growth rates are calculated from historical data consistent with drawing a trend growth line through annual December figures, as described above. The estimates indicate what the monthly balances would equal if no seasonal or cyclical fluctuations existed and trend growth continued.

Seasonal influences net of trend are identified in the third column of data. Column 2 provides a seasonal index for each month relative to December totals. This index represents the average of the monthly figure relative to the average of the December figure over the past five years. Independent of trend, January deposits average 99 percent of December deposits while January loans equal 101 percent of December loans. Column 3 lists the difference between the monthly seasonal estimate and the respective December deposit or loan figure. Finally, column 4 measures cyclical deposits and loans as monthly deviations of the prior year's actual deposit or loan balance and the implied trend plus seasonal component. In this example, the January trend plus seasonal estimate for loans equaled $6 million less than the actual balance. This $6 million represents the next year's forecast of unanticipated cyclical loan needs. The final column lists the forecast of total deposits and total loans, respectively, equal to the sum of figures in Columns 1, 3, and 4.

Exhibit 8.22 presents summary estimates of monthly liquidity needs. The cumulative liquidity needed equals the forecast change in loans plus required reserves minus the forecast change in deposits.

$$\text{Liquidity needs} = \text{Forecasted } \Delta\text{loans} + \Delta\text{required reserves} - \text{forecasted } \Delta\text{deposits}$$

A positive figure means the bank needs additional liquid funds. A negative figure suggests that the bank will have surplus funds to invest.

Although this analysis is somewhat general, it can be used to identify longer-term trends in fund flows. In practice, forecasts are prepared for each distinct deposit account and loan category, then summed to yield a total estimate. This allows management to incorporate different trend and seasonal patterns for demand deposits, NOWs, and MMDAs, and thus reduce the aggregate forecast error. For example, demand deposit growth has slowed in recent years while the growth in MMDAs, IRAs, and other deposits has accelerated. Separate estimates capture this diverse behavior.

Management can supplement this analysis by including projected changes in purchased funds and investments with specific loan and deposit flows. One procedure is to calculate a liquidity gap measure over different time intervals. This format is comparable to the funding GAP analysis introduced in Chapters 2 and 5. It begins by classifying potential uses and sources of funds into separate time frames according to their cash flow characteristics. The liquidity gap for each interval equals the dollar value of uses of funds minus the dollar value of sources of funds.

Exhibit 8.23 demonstrates this format for a hypothetical bank. By using specific account information, managers can trace the source of any significant outflow or inflow and take remedial action. Consider the data representing the next 30 days for the hypothetical bank. The bank has $50 million in maturing CDs and Eurodollars and $5.5 million in small time deposits that mature. It expects to fund $113 million in new loans and see transactions accounts fall by $4.5 million for a total $173 million in uses. Expected sources of funds include $18 million in maturing securities and $80 million in loan principal payments. The liquidity gap for the next

## EXHIBIT 8.21    Forecast of Trend, Seasonal, and Cyclical Components of Deposits and Loans

### Reference Balance Sheet (Millions of Dollars)

| Assets | | Liabilities | |
|---|---|---|---|
| Cash and due from banks | $160 | Transactions accounts and nonnegotiable deposits | $1,600 |
| Loans | 1,400 | Certificates of deposit and other borrowing | 280 |
| Investment securities | 400 | Stockholders' equity | 120 |
| Other assets | 40 | Total | $2,000 |
| Total | $2,000 | | |

| Deposit Forecast | (1) Trend | (2) Seasonal Deposit | (3) Seasonal Deposits – | (4) Cyclical | (5) |
| End of Month | Deposits* | Index** | December Deposits | Deposits | Total |
|---|---|---|---|---|---|
| January | $1,608 | 99% | ($16) | ($3) | $1,589 |
| February | 1,616 | 102 | 32 | 8 | 1,656 |
| March | 1,623 | 105 | 80 | 7 | 1,710 |
| April | 1,631 | 107 | 112 | 10 | 1,753 |
| May | 1,639 | 101 | 16 | 1 | 1,656 |
| June | 1,647 | 96 | −64 | −8 | 1,575 |
| July | 1,655 | 93 | −112 | −15 | 1,528 |
| August | 1,663 | 95 | −80 | −9 | 1,574 |
| September | 1,671 | 97 | −48 | −4 | 1,619 |
| October | 1,680 | 101 | 16 | 0 | 1,696 |
| November | 1,688 | 104 | 64 | 3 | 1,755 |
| December | 1,696 | 100 | 0 | 0 | 1696 |

### Loan Forecast

| End of Month | Trend Loans* | Seasonal Loan Index** | Seasonal Loans – December Loans | Cyclical Loans | Total |
|---|---|---|---|---|---|
| January | $1,413 | 101% | $14 | $6 | $1,433 |
| February | 1,427 | 97 | −42 | −9 | 1,376 |
| March | 1,440 | 95 | −70 | −18 | 1,352 |
| April | 1,454 | 94 | −84 | −21 | 1,349 |
| May | 1,467 | 97 | −42 | −15 | 1,410 |
| June | 1,481 | 102 | 28 | −3 | 1,506 |
| July | 1,495 | 108 | 112 | 9 | 1,616 |
| August | 1,510 | 106 | 84 | 17 | 1,611 |
| September | 1,524 | 103 | 42 | 11 | 1,577 |
| October | 1,538 | 99 | −14 | 5 | 1,529 |
| November | 1,553 | 98 | −28 | 0 | 1,525 |
| December | 1,568 | 100 | 0 | 0 | 1,568 |

*Growth trend for December to December averaged 6 percent for deposits and 12 percent for loans.

**Multiply by the preceding December figure.

30 days thus equals $75 million. The bank needs to replace the maturing CDs and Eurodollars plus find an additional $25 million in liquid funds to finance this loan growth.

Comparable figures for 31 to 90 days out and 91 to 365 days out are also shown in the exhibit. The cumulative gap summarizes the total liquidity position from the present to the farthest day within each time interval. The bank expects to experience a liquidity surplus two to three months out and a $208 million liquidity shortage for the entire year.

Once normal liquidity needs are forecast, a bank should compare the estimates with potential funding sources and extraordinary funds needs. One researcher introduced a simple format, modified as Exhibit 8.24, that requires each bank to project its borrowing capacity via federal funds purchased, RPs, and unused CDs, and combine it with funds available from reducing federal funds sold and selling loan participations, money market securities, and unpledged securities.[37] This total is then compared with potential draws

| EXHIBIT 8.22 | Estimates of Liquidity Needs (Millions of Dollars) |

| End of Month | ΔDeposits* | ΔRequired Reserves | ΔLoans* | Liquidity Needs** |
|---|---|---|---|---|
| January | −$11.00 | −$1.10 | $33.00 | $42.90 |
| February | $56.00 | $5.60 | −$24.00 | −$74.40 |
| March | $110.00 | $11.00 | −$48.00 | −$147.00 |
| April | $153.00 | $15.30 | −$51.00 | −$188.70 |
| May | $56.00 | $5.60 | $10.00 | −$40.40 |
| June | −$25.00 | −$2.50 | $106.00 | $128.50 |
| July | −$72.00 | −$7.20 | $216.00 | $280.80 |
| August | −$26.00 | −$2.60 | $211.00 | $234.40 |
| September | $19.00 | $1.90 | $177.00 | $159.90 |
| October | $96.00 | $9.60 | $129.00 | $42.60 |
| November | $155.00 | $15.50 | $125.00 | −$14.50 |
| December | $96.00 | $9.60 | $168.00 | $81.60 |

*Δdeposits equals the difference in the end-of-year balance sheet figure ($1,600) and the monthly total forecast from Exhibit 8.21. Δloans equals the difference in the end-of-year balance sheet figure ($1,400) and the monthly total forecast from Exhibit 8.21.

**Estimates of liquidity needs equal the change in loans plus change in required reserves minus the change in deposits. The reserve ratio equals 10 percent. A positive figure represents a shortage, while a negative figure means the bank has surplus funds to invest.

| EXHIBIT 8.23 | Liquidity Gap Estimates (Millions of Dollars) |

| | 0 to 30 Days | 31 to 90 Days | 91 to 365 Days |
|---|---|---|---|
| **Potential Uses of Funds** | | | |
| Add: Maturing time deposits | | | |
| Small time deposits | $5.5 | $8 | $34 |
| Certificates of deposit over $100,000 | 40 | 70 | 100 |
| Eurodollar deposits | 10 | 10 | 30 |
| Plus: Forecast new loans | | | |
| Commercial loans | 60 | 112 | 686 |
| Consumer loans | 22 | 46 | 210 |
| Real estate and other loans | 31 | 23 | 223 |
| Minus: Forecast net change in transactional accounts* | | | |
| Demand deposits | −6.5 | 105.5 | 10 |
| NOW accounts | 0.4 | 5.5 | 7 |
| Money market deposit accounts | 1.6 | 3 | 6 |
| Total uses | $173 | $155 | $1,260 |
| **Potential Sources of Funds** | | | |
| Add: Maturing investments | | | |
| Money market instruments | $8 | $16.5 | $36.5 |
| U.S. Treasury and agency securities | 7.5 | 10.5 | 40 |
| Municipal securities | 2.5 | 1 | 12.5 |
| Plus: Principal payments on loans | 80 | 262 | 903 |
| Total sources | 98 | 290 | 992 |
| **Periodic Liquidity Gap**** | **$75** | **$−135** | **$268** |
| **Cumulative Liquidity Gap** | **$75** | **$−60** | **$208** |

*Net of required reserves

**Potential uses of funds minus potential sources of funds.

**EXHIBIT 8.24**  Potential Funding Sources (Millions of Dollars)

| | Time Frame | | |
| --- | --- | --- | --- |
| | 0 to 30 Days | 31 to 90 Days | 91 to 365 Days |
| **Purchased funds capacity** | | | |
| Federal funds purchased (overnight and term) | $20 | $20 | $30 |
| Repurchase agreements | 10 | 10 | 10 |
| Negotiable certificates of deposit | | | |
|   Local | 50 | 50 | 60 |
|   National | 20 | 20 | 25 |
| Eurodollar certificates of deposit | 20 | 20 | 20 |
|   Total | $120 | $120 | $145 |
| **Additional funding sources** | | | |
| Reductions in federal funds sold | $5 | $5 | $5 |
| Loan participations | 20 | 20 | 20 |
| Sale of money market securities | 5 | 5 | 5 |
| Sale of unpledged securities | 10 | 10 | 10 |
|   Total | $40 | $40 | $40 |
| **Potential funding sources*** | **$160** | **$160** | **$185** |
| Potential extraordinary funding needs | | | |
| 50% of outstanding letters of credit | 5 | 10 | 15 |
| 20% of unfunded loan commitments | 25 | 30 | 35 |
|   Total | $30 | $40 | $50 |
| **Excess potential funding sources** | **$130** | **$120** | **$135** |

*Purchased funds capacity plus additional funding sources.

against unused loan commitments and letters of credit. Of course, no bank wants to utilize its borrowing capacity fully or sell all of its available assets. It should always leave some potential funding available for extraordinary events.

Applying the data from Exhibit 8.24 to the 30-day gap in Exhibit 8.23, the sample bank has considerable flexibility in meeting its liquidity need. First, it could simply replace the maturing CDs and Eurodollars with similar borrowings, for which it has an estimated $90 million capacity. Second, the bank could borrow via federal funds or RPs, eliminate federal funds sold, and make up the difference with new CDs. The best alternative is the one with the lowest cost. In general, large banks prefer to borrow rather than liquidate assets, while small banks sell assets or restrict growth. The best use of this information is to conduct "what-if" analysis to determine the cost implications of various alternatives and assess how much flexibility management has in adjusting its cash position. Large banks with international operations should perform this liquidity analysis in each currency in which they operate since their liquidity position might vary by currency.

## CONSIDERATIONS IN SELECTING LIQUIDITY SOURCES

The previous analysis focuses on estimating the dollar magnitude of liquidity needs. Implicit in the discussion is the assumption that the bank has adequate liquidity sources. For most banks, loan growth exceeds deposit growth net of CDs and Eurodollars. In the short run, banks have the option of financing this net growth either by selling securities or obtaining new deposits. In the long run, this net growth must be financed out of purchased liabilities because banks own a limited amount of securities. Yet most banks have limited access to new purchased funds because they are small with no market reputation, or they have exhausted their borrowing capacity in terms of their capital base and earnings potential. There are two possible solutions to this dilemma. Management can either restrict asset growth or seek additional core deposits or equity. Regulatory actions to raise bank capital requirements, discussed in Chapter 9, have the beneficial side effect of improving access to the money and capital markets.

---

[37]See Temple (1983).

Banks with options in meeting liquidity needs evaluate the characteristics of various sources to minimize costs. The following factors should be considered in asset sales or new borrowings:

| **Asset Sales** | **New Borrowings** |
| --- | --- |
| 1. Brokerage fees | 1. Brokerage fees |
| 2. Securities gains or losses | 2. Required reserves |
| 3. Foregone interest income | 3. FDIC insurance premiums |
| 4. Any increase or decrease in taxes | 4. Promotion costs |
| 5. Any increase or decrease in interest receipts | 5. Interest expense |

The costs should be evaluated in present-value terms because interest income and interest expense may arise over substantially different time periods. The choice of one source over another often involves an implicit interest rate forecast.

Suppose, for example, that a bank temporarily needs funds for six months. Management has decided to sell $1 million of Treasuries from the bank's portfolio. The choice is between securities with either one year or five years remaining to maturity. Both securities sell at par and earn 5.5 percent annually. If the bank sells the one-year security, it implicitly assumes that the level of short-term Treasury rates is going to fall far enough below 5.5 percent so that any eventual reinvestment of funds would yield less than that on a five-year security. If the bank sells the five-year bond, it assumes that the level of short-term rates will rise above 5.5 percent, on average.

Suppose instead that the bank decides to issue either a six-month CD or a one-month CD. Clearly, the six-month CD locks in interest expense and requires only one transaction. A one-month CD will need to be rolled over, with uncertain future interest expense. Transactions costs will also be higher. The rationale for issuing any shorter-term CD can only be that the present value of expected interest expense plus transactions costs will be lower with this alternative.[38]

## SUMMARY

This chapter focuses on the relationship between various funding sources and liquidity risks. Characteristics of various bank liabilities and the measurement of costs associated with these liabilities and equity capital are presented first. Small-denomination instruments exhibit fundamentally different risk-return features compared with those of large-denomination liabilities. In both cases, price competition is considerably more important today than in previous years. The chapter introduces the specific features of immediately available funds, repurchase agreements, Eurodollars, and borrowings from the Federal Home Loan Bank and Federal Reserve Banks as sources of funds. It describes the difference between the average cost of funds and marginal cost of funds and demonstrates the appropriate calculations.

In the section on measuring the cost of funds, the differences in average and marginal costs and their application to understanding historical bank performance are discussed. The chapter then focuses on estimating marginal costs that are used in pricing decisions. Marginal costs represent the incremental cost of obtaining financing. Each individual source of debt funds has a distinct cost that reflects interest expense, acquisition and processing costs, and restrictions regarding the amount of funds a bank can invest. Equity capital has a marginal cost that reflects shareholders' required returns. Individual cost estimates are combined into a weighted marginal cost of capital, which is used in pricing. The chapter provides applications of the estimation process.

The next sections examine the characteristics of cash and liquid assets and explain why banks hold each type and how the magnitudes can be minimized. Liquid assets generally include federal funds sold and RPs, short-term unpledged Treasury and other highly marketable securities, and loans that can be readily sold at predictable prices. Their primary advantage over cash is that they earn interest. Liquidity planning is an ongoing part of a bank's asset and liability management strategy. In the short run, it focuses on meeting legal reserve requirements. It specifically involves monitoring net deposit outflows and inflows and deciding how to finance deficiencies or invest excess funds. Banks manage their cash position to minimize required holdings because cash assets do not generate interest income. Vault cash is held to meet customer transaction needs. Banks hold demand deposit balances at the Federal Reserve and other financial institutions to meet the Federal Reserve's legal reserve requirements and to

---

[38]The yield curve incorporates both liquidity premiums and interest rate expectations. Thus, one-month yields at 5 percent and six-month yields at 5.2 percent signify that traders expect one-month rates to increase. By issuing a one-month security, the borrower implicitly assumes that rates will not increase as much as that implied by the yield curve.

purchase services such as check clearing. Float, or checks in the process of collection, is a natural product of the check-clearing process.

Finally, the chapter examines two different stages of liquidity planning. The first focuses on managing a bank's required reserve position over the two-week maintenance period. The second analyzes monthly liquidity gaps as measures of liquidity risk throughout the next year. A bank's liquidity gap measures the difference between the dollar value of expected cash outflows and expected cash inflows within a given time interval. Positive liquidity gaps indicate a net liquidity need, while negative liquidity gaps indicate surplus investable funds. Planning models for each stage of analysis are applied to a hypothetical bank's data.

## QUESTIONS

1. Rank the following types of bank liabilities, first according to their level of liquidity risk, and then according to their interest rate risk. Then rank them according to their current cost to the bank. Explain why they vary.

   DDAs

   NOW accounts

   MMDAs

   Small time deposits

   Jumbo CDs

   Federal funds purchased

   Eurodollar liabilities

   Federal Home Loan Bank advances

2. Indicate how a bank's core deposits differ from its "hot money" or volatile liabilities in terms of interest elasticity. What factors are relatively more important to attracting and retaining core deposits as compared to purchased funds?

3. Using the data from Exhibit 8.6, determine the average monthly cost of servicing the typical student's demand deposit account, which generates 27 withdrawals (15 electronic), two transit checks deposited, two transit checks cashed, two deposits (one electronic), and one on-us check cashed per month. Assume there is one account maintenance charge for an account in which checks are not returned and that net indirect expenses apply. Assume that the bank can invest 85 percent of the deposit balance at 7 percent and charges the student $4.50 in fees monthly. What is the break-even deposit balance the bank must hold for its revenues to cover its costs? Compare your average balance with the break-even balance you calculate and determine whether your account would be profitable to the bank. What is your bank's insufficient funds charge (NSF), and how will these fees influence account profitability?

4. Explain why it is or is not reasonable for a bank to charge an explicit fee for balance inquiries (calling to request balance verification).

5. Assume the following transactions occur sequentially:

   a. The TIB Corporation, based in New Orleans, converts a $3 million demand deposit held at the New York Money Center Bank to a $3 million Eurodollar deposit held at Barclays Bank in London.

   b. Barclays Bank opens a $3 million Eurodollar deposit at the Bank of England in London.

   c. The Bank of England makes a $3 million Eurodollar loan to Pflug & Company in England. Provide T-accounts for TIB, New York Money Center Bank, Barclays Bank, and the Bank of England that describe each set of transactions. Explain how many Eurodollar deposit liabilities were created at each stage and what happened to the original demand deposit held by TIB.

6. As a potential jumbo CD depositor, what would your circumstances have to be for you to prefer a variable-rate CD over a fixed-rate CD? What would the circumstances be for you to prefer a zero coupon CD over a variable-rate CD?

7. How large would Barnett's uninsured deposits be in these FDIC-insured banks if the funds were held at the same point in time?

   a. Barnett owns a joint account with his sister for $175,000 in Metro Bank.

   b. Barnett owns an account in his name only for $80,000 in Metro Bank.

   c. Barnett owns a joint account with his wife for $455,000 in Rural Bank.

   d. Barnett owns a joint account with his parents for $530,000 in Rural Bank.

8. Identify whether you should use an average cost of bank funds or a marginal cost of funds in the following situations.

    a. Setting the rate on a new loan

    b. Evaluating the profitability of a long-standing customer's relationship

    c. Calculating the bank's income tax liability

    d. Deciding whether to build a new building or refurbish the old one

    e. Deciding whether to advertise the bank's jumbo CDs or borrow funds in the Eurodollar market

9. What are the consequences of a bank mistakenly pricing loans based on the historical cost of funds? Do they differ in a rising-rate environment versus a falling-rate environment?

10. What types of bank liabilities generate the highest servicing costs? What types generate the highest acquisition costs?

11. Use the following information to estimate the marginal cost of issuing a $100,000 CD paying 6.2 percent interest. It has a one-year maturity and the following estimates apply relative to the balance obtained:

    Acquisition costs = 1/8 of 1 percent
    FDIC insurance = 1/12 of 1 percent
    Required reserves percentage = 0 percent

12. The weighted marginal cost of funds is used in pricing decisions. Explain how it should be used if the loan being priced exhibits average risk. How should the weighted marginal cost of funds be used if the loan carries above-average risk?

13. What are the different types of cash assets and the basic objectives for holding each?

14. The determination of cash requirements is closely associated with a bank's liquidity requirements. Explain why.

15. What are the advantages and disadvantages for a bank contemplating holding more cash?

16. Monetary theory examines the role of excess reserves (actual reserves minus required reserves) in influencing economic activity and Federal Reserve monetary policy. Viewed in the context of a single bank, excess reserves are difficult to measure. Explain what amount of a bank's actual reserve assets are excess reserves during any single day in the reserve maintenance period under lagged reserve accounting.

17. Which of the following activities will affect a bank's required reserves?

    a. The local Girl Scout troop collects coins and currency to buy a new camping stove. The troop deposits $250 in coins and open a small time deposit.

    b. You decide to move $200 from your MMDA to your NOW account.

    c. You sell your car to the teller at your bank for $3,000. The teller pays with a check drawn on the bank, and you deposit the check immediately into your checking account at the bank.

    d. The local university takes one-half of the fall tuition receipts and buys a three-month CD.

    e. Ford Motor Company opens an assembly plant outside town and opens a checking account at the local bank for $100,000 with a check drawn on its bank in Detroit.

18. In many cases, banks do not permit depositors to spend the proceeds of a deposit until several days have elapsed. What risks do banks face in the check-clearing process? Does this justify holds on checks?

19. What is the difference between a correspondent, respondent, and bankers bank?

20. A corporate customer borrows $150,000 against the firm's credit line at a local bank. Indicate with a T-account how the transaction will affect the bank's deposit balances held at the Federal Reserve when the firm spends the proceeds.

21. What are the fundamental differences and similarities among the commercial loan theory, shiftability theory, anticipated income theory, and liability management theory regarding liquidity?

22. Liquidity planning requires monitoring deposit outflows. In each of the following situations, which of the outflows are discretionary and which are not? If the outflow is not discretionary, is it predictable or unexpected?

    a. In April, a farmer draws down his line of credit in order to purchase seed.

    b. Students borrow to pay fall tuition.

    c. The bank makes a preferred stock dividend payment.

d. A fire destroys a portion of the local business district and many firms apply for reconstruction loans.

e. The rent on the bank's offices is paid.

f. On the Friday before the citywide festival, all ATMs in town have been drained of cash.

g. A New York bank has just opened a local banking office and is offering a VCR to anyone who transfers funds from a CD at another bank.

h. The bank buys most of the newly issued local municipal securities.

23. What do the terms *core deposits* and *volatile*, or *noncore*, deposits mean? Explain how a bank might estimate the magnitude of each.

24. Explain how each of the following will affect a bank's deposit balances at the Federal Reserve:

a. The bank ships excess vault cash to the Federal Reserve.

b. The bank buys U.S. government securities in the open market.

c. The bank realizes a surplus in its local clearinghouse processing.

d. The bank sells federal funds.

e. A $100,000 certificate of deposit at the bank matures and is not rolled over.

f. Local businesses deposit tax payments in the Treasury's account at the local bank.

25. Banks must pledge collateral against four different types of liabilities. Which liabilities require collateral, what type of collateral is required, and what impact do the pledging requirements have on a bank's asset liquidity?

26. Explain how a bank's credit risk and interest rate risk can affect its liquidity risk.

27. Rank the following types of depositors by the liquidity risk they typically pose for a bank.

a. A CD depositor attracted through a stockbroker

b. Foreign investors trading with a local corporation

c. Local schoolchildren

d. A two-wage-earner family with $38,000 in annual salaries and with three children

28. A traditional measure of liquidity risk is a bank's loan-to-deposit ratio. Give two reasons why this is a poor measure of risk. Give one reason why it is a good measure.

29. What can a bank do to increase its core deposits? What are the costs and benefits of such efforts? Generally, how might management estimate the relative interest elasticity of various deposit liabilities of a bank?

30. Your bank's estimated liquidity gap over the next 90 days equals $180 million. You estimate that projected funding sources over the same 90 days will equal only $150 million. What planning and policy requirements does this impose on your $3 billion bank?

31. What are the conceptual differences between the trend, seasonal, and cyclical components of a bank's loans and deposits? Discuss why a bank should examine each component rather than simply look at total loans and deposits.

32. Discuss the relative importance of liquidity versus capital problems in causing bank failures. Explain the normal sequence of events leading to failure and the importance of market value measures.

## PROBLEMS

**ANALYZING PROFITABILITY.** A senior bank officer has asked you to analyze the profitability of selected customer deposit relationships. The procedure is to estimate the total expense associated with account activity and compare this with projected revenues. Use the data from Exhibit 8.6 to answer the following questions.

1. The typical low-balance customer at your bank with an average monthly demand deposit balance under $175 exhibits the following monthly activity: 35 withdrawals (11 electronic), two transit checks deposited, one transit check cashed, two deposits (one electronic), and one on-us check cashed per month. Assume there is one account maintenance for an account in which checks are not returned and that net indirect expenses apply.

a. Use the unit cost data to estimate the average monthly expense for the bank to service this account.

b. Suppose the bank can earn an average 6.5 percent annually on investable deposits (ledger balances minus float minus required reserves). The typical customer keeps an average monthly balance net of float equal to $116 in the account and pays a $3.25 monthly service charge. The bank must hold 10 percent required reserves against the average balance and thus can invest 90 percent of the balance. Determine whether the account is profitable for the bank.

2. The typical high-balance NOW account customer at your bank maintains a monthly balance of $1,250 net of float, writes 34 checks or withdrawals (21 electronic), four transit checks deposited, two transit checks cashed, two deposits (one electronic), and one on-us check cashed per month. Assume there is one account maintenance for an account in which checks are not returned and that net indirect expenses apply. Interest is paid on the account at an annual 2.5 percent rate. Use the unit cost information to determine whether this account is profitable. Assume the bank collects no service charges and can again earn 6.5 percent on investable balances net of 10 percent required reserves.

**WEIGHTED MARGINAL COST OF FUNDS.** The table below provides information that can be used to estimate Northwestern National Bank's weighted marginal cost of funds. The estimates represent a best-guess forecast of the funding sources and associated costs for the year. Follow the format in Exhibit 8.13 and calculate the bank's forecasted weighted marginal cost of funds.

| Liabilities and Equity | Average Amount | Interest Cost | Processing and Acquisition Costs | Investable Percentage |
|---|---|---|---|---|
| Demand deposits | $ 44,500 | 0.0% | 7.2% | 83.0% |
| Interest checking | 69,900 | 2.1 | 5.0 | 86.0 |
| Money market demand accounts | 49,800 | 2.8 | 3.2 | 97.0 |
| Other savings accounts | 25,100 | 3.0 | 1.0 | 98.0 |
| Time deposits <$100,000 | 187,600 | 4.1 | 1.5 | 98.0 |
| Time deposits ≥$100,000 | 63,000 | 4.8 | 0.3 | 97.0 |
| Total deposits | 439,900 | | | |
| Federal funds purchased | 18,000 | 2.0 | 0.0 | 100.0 |
| Other liabilities | 7,500 | | 0.0 | 50.0 |
| Total liabilities | 465,400 | | | |
| Stockholders' equity | 34,600 | 20.08%* | | 95.0 |
| Total liabilities and equity | 500,000 | | | |

*Required return

**CALCULATION OF REQUIRED RESERVES.** At the close of business on Wednesday, Gene Wandling was reviewing whether Hawkeye National Bank was successful in meeting its legal reserve requirements at the Federal Reserve. The bank had just completed the two-week reserve maintenance period, during which it held a daily average of $238 million in reserve deposits with the Federal Reserve. The bank had a daily average reserve deficiency the previous maintenance period of $3.75 million, which was within the allowable 4 percent limit.

Hawkeye National Bank's daily average net transactions accounts for the base computation period along with balances for selected assets are listed below.

| Daily average (millions of dollars) | |
|---|---|
| Net transactions accounts | $3,257 |
| Demand deposits due from U.S. depository institutions | 366 |
| Cash items in process of collection | 181 |

Hawkeye National Bank could use daily average vault cash holdings of $31 million to offset its reserve requirement. Using the reserve percentages from Exhibit 8.16, calculate the bank's daily average required reserve holdings during the maintenance period. Did Hawkeye meet its reserve target? If the bank had carried forward a daily reserve surplus of $2.1 million instead of a deficiency, would it have met its target? What are the costs to a bank if its reserves fall outside the target range?

## ACTIVITIES

1. Determine how long it takes your bank to process your checks. Find some old checks you wrote to people locally and in a different Federal Reserve district. Note the date on which you wrote the check and then find the date on your monthly account statement when the bank deducted the amount from your account. How might you use this information to manage your personal float? Compare this with the funds availability schedule at your bank. Describe how Check 21 has affected your account at your bank.

2. Evaluate the activity you generated in your checking account last month. How many home debits, transit checks, and deposits did you create? Include an estimate of how many times you used an ATM. What interest did you earn on your balance and what fees did you pay? Use the data from Exhibit 8.6 to determine the bank's break-even deposit balance without not funds (NSF) check charges. Given the amount of your bank's NSF charge per item, how many NSF check charges must a bank collect for your account to be profitable?

3. Take a survey of local banks regarding the pricing of transactions accounts. Include a list of all fees associated with these account relationships. Compare the different types of pricing strategies and identify the type of customer (low/high balance, low/high activity, etc.) that each bank appears to be targeting. Which account appears to be most attractive to the average college student?

CHAPTER

# 9

# The Effective Use of Capital

*In the early 1990s, the Federal Reserve Board of Governors (Fed), Federal Deposit Insurance Corp. (FDIC), and Office of the Comptroller of the Currency (OCC) imposed minimum risk-based capital (RBC) standards to help control commercial bank risk taking. These RBC standards required higher levels of capital against higher-risk bank assets. Thus, banks with more loans were required to operate with more capital. The Federal Deposit Insurance Corporation Improvement Act of 1991 (FDICIA) established a system of prompt regulatory action with sanctions for undercapitalized institutions. These requirements mandated specific regulatory responses, including bank closures where appropriate, for institutions whose capital fell short of regulatory minimums. In 2004, the Basel Committee on Bank Supervision, with U.S. bank regulators' endorsement, proposed new capital standards with an implementation date of 2007.*

*Capital plays a significant role in the risk-return trade-off at banks. Increasing capital reduces risk by cushioning the volatility of earnings, restricting growth opportunities, and lowering the probability of bank failure. It also reduces expected returns to shareholders, as equity is more expensive than debt. Decreasing capital increases risk by increasing financial leverage and the probability of failure. Not surprisingly, it also increases potential returns. The fundamental asset and liability management decision regarding capital thus focuses on how much capital is optimal. Firms with greater capital can borrow at lower rates, make larger loans, and expand faster through acquisitions or internal growth. In general, they can pursue riskier investments. A second important decision concerns the form in which new capital is obtained because regulators allow certain types of debt and preferred stock to qualify as capital to meet the requirements. These decisions are examined in this chapter in light of the regulatory definition of capital, its function, and its cost. The chapter also describes the nature of the new capital requirements and possible market impacts.*

## WHY WORRY ABOUT BANK CAPITAL?

Bank regulators' primary objective is to ensure the safety and soundness of the U.S. financial system. It is generally believed that failures of individual banks, particularly large institutions, might erode public confidence in the financial system. The federal government attempts to limit the magnitude and scope of bank failures and ensure confidence by setting and enforcing regulations and by imposing minimum capital requirements for individual banks. Requirements are met when banks obtain an acceptable amount of financing in the form of qualifying equity capital and related long-term debt sources. Such capital requirements reduce the risk of failure by acting as a cushion against losses, providing access to financial markets to meet liquidity needs, and limiting growth.

*Why Worry About Bank Capital?*

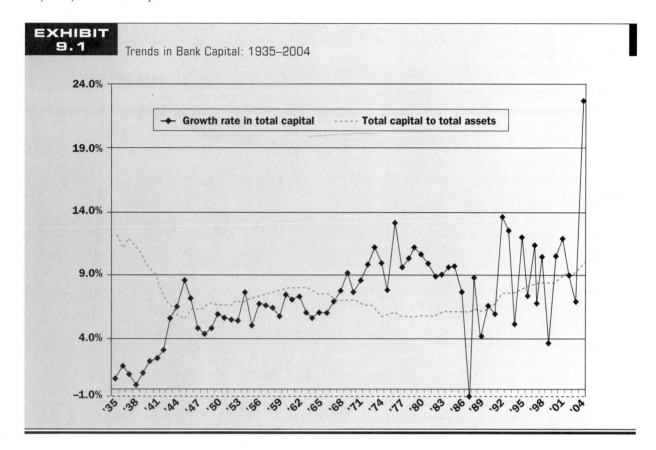

**EXHIBIT 9.1**

Trends in Bank Capital: 1935–2004

Bank supervision has reached the point where regulators now specify minimum amounts of equity and other qualifying capital that banks must obtain to continue operations.[1] Historically, regulators stipulated minimum capital-to-total asset ratios but did not worry about the quality of bank assets. While bank capital-to-asset ratios averaged near 20 percent at the turn of the century, comparable ratios today are closer to 8 percent. Recent capital ratios appear in Exhibit 9.1. Note that capital ratios have increased recently.

Under the old capital regulation two banks of the same size would have to operate with the same amount of capital, independent of their risk profiles. For example, it did not matter what type of assets a bank held because the same percentage requirement applied to all assets equally. Thus, a bank that held only Treasury securities needed the same amount of capital as the same size bank that held speculative real estate loans. Does this seem reasonable? The answer depends on the role that capital is expected to serve and how regulators want to control bank risk.

Capital-to-asset ratios at commercial banks and savings banks are below similar ratios at other financial institutions, and well below capital ratios at other nonfinancial businesses. This difference reflects the intermediation function of depository institutions and thus is not remarkable. High financial leverage, however, increases the relative riskiness of operations by providing less protection to creditors upon liquidation of the firm. Bankers also recognize that high leverage increases potential profitability, so they often attempt to minimize external equity financing. Regulators, in contrast, want to increase bank equity financing and focus on balancing solvency risks with an individual bank's profit potential.

This chapter introduces the risk-based capital requirements that banks have been subject to since the end of 1992. It then examines the functions of bank capital and its impact on commercial bank operations. It addresses the following issues: (1) What constitutes bank capital? (2) What functions do capital accounts serve? (3) How much capital is adequate? (4) What is the impact of regulatory capital requirements on bank operating policies? (5) What are the advantages and disadvantages of various sources of internal and external capital? These issues

---

[1]The International Lending Supervision Act of 1983 empowered the Federal Reserve, Federal Deposit Insurance Corporation, Office of the Comptroller of the Currency, and Federal Home Loan Bank Board to mandate legally binding minimum capital requirements. Most banks acceded to prior guidelines even though the legal requirement did not exist.

are important because federal regulators appear intent on raising or maintaining high capital standards for banks and other institutions over time. The last section describes the framework for new capital standards as proposed in 2004.

## RISK-BASED CAPITAL STANDARDS

Historically, bank regulators specified minimum capital standards for banks that were independent of the riskiness of each institution. During the 1970s, the regulatory agencies established capital adequacy by creating bank peer groups, setting target capital ratios for each group, and then adjusting the targets on a case-by-case basis with no specific minimum capital requirement. During this period, aggregate bank capital ratios declined steadily as the capital ratios of many large banks declined and several large banks failed. In 1981, the Federal Reserve Board and the Office of the Comptroller of the Currency adopted explicit numerical capital standards, based on asset size, for two of the three groups established. The three groups were defined as multinational, regional, and community. The largest multinationals were treated on a case-by-case basis with no explicit capital ratio requirement, but with the expectation that they would increase their capital positions or explicit requirements would be put in place. Regional banks (assets between $1 billion and $15 billion) and community banks (assets below $1 billion) were required to maintain a primary capital-to-asset ratio of at least 5 percent and 6 percent, respectively. Primary capital consisted of common and perpetual preferred stock, surplus, undivided profits, contingency and other capital reserves, mandatory convertible debt, and the allowance for loan and lease losses.[2] Regulators recognized secondary capital to include balance sheet items such as long-term subordinated debt and limited-life preferred stock.[3] Primary plus secondary capital equaled total capital, with the minimum set at 6 percent of total bank assets.

One notable problem was that these requirements were established without regard to a bank's asset quality, liquidity risk, interest rate risk, operational risk, and related risks. Thus, when banks fell under pressure to increase earnings, as in the case of declining net interest margins, capital requirements imposed no constraints to risk taking other than limiting growth. Bank regulators did force banks to have more capital than the minimums when they perceived bank risk to be excessive, but this determination often occurred long after management made risky investment decisions.

### THE BASEL AGREEMENT

In 1986, U.S. bank regulators proposed that banks be required to maintain minimum amounts of capital that reflect the riskiness of their assets. By the time it was implemented, the proposal, known as the Basel Agreement, included risk-based capital standards for banks in 12 industrialized nations. U.S. bank regulators phased in the requirements starting in 1990, with the regulations in place by the end of 1992. Importantly, thrift institutions have been required to meet the same risk-based capital standards since 1992. Today, countries that are members of the Organization for Economic Cooperation and Development (OECD) enforce similar risk-based requirements on their own banks.

Although the terms varied between nations, primarily in terms of what constitutes capital, the Basel Agreement contained several important elements. First, a bank's minimum capital requirement is linked, by formula, to its credit risk as determined by the composition of assets. The greater is credit risk, the greater is required capital. Second, stockholders' equity is deemed the most critical type of capital. As such, each bank is expected to operate with a minimum amount of equity based on the amount of credit risk. Third, the minimum total capital requirement increased to 8 percent of risk-adjusted assets. Finally, the capital requirements were approximately standardized between countries to "level the playing field"; that is, to remove competitive advantages that banks in one country might have over banks in other countries because of regulatory or accounting differences.

### RISK-BASED ELEMENTS OF THE PLAN

To determine minimum capital requirements for a bank to be adequately capitalized, bank managers follow a four-step process.

1. Classify assets into one of four risk categories, appropriate to the obligor, collateral, or guarantor of the asset.

---

[2]Perpetual preferred stock has no set maturity date; mandatory convertible debt refers to bonds that must contractually be converted into either common stock or preferred stock; and the allowance for loan and lease losses refers to the contra-asset account appearing on a bank's balance sheet which represents management's estimate of uncollectible loans.

[3]Subordinated debt refers to bonds where the claims of bondholders are paid only after insured and uninsured depositors are paid in the case of a bank failure.

2. Convert off-balance sheet commitments and guarantees to their on-balance sheet "credit equivalent" values and classify them in the appropriate risk categories.[4]

3. Multiply the dollar amount of assets in each risk category by the appropriate risk weight; this product equals risk-weighted assets.

4. Multiply risk-weighted assets by the minimum capital percentages, either 4 percent for Tier 1 capital or 8 percent for total capital for a U.S. bank to be adequately capitalized.

The process ensures that assets with the highest perceived credit risk have the highest risk weights and require the most capital. In addition to these credit risk-based standards, the Fed, FDIC, and OCC adopted measures related to the supervisory treatment of interest rate risk and market risk capital requirements, which are described in the following sections, "Capital Requirements for Interest Rate Risk" and "Capital Requirements for Market Risk Using Internal Models."

Consider the data in Exhibit 9.2 for Regional National Bank (RNB). As indicated in the first column of data, total assets for the bank were just under $5 billion and the bank had almost $656 million in off-balance sheet items. Under the former capital standards, RNB would have needed 6 percent total capital or approximately $299.7 million ($0.06 \times $4,994,849$) in primary and secondary capital. The exhibit demonstrates that the risk-based capital requirements are slightly higher for total capital.

Exhibit 9.3 lists the four risk categories and the general types of assets that fall into each category for RNB. Exhibit 9.4 demonstrates the application of Step 2, which involves converting off-balance sheet activity into a balance sheet equivalent value. Exhibit 9.5 provides a summary list of the balance sheet items in each category. Note that the lowest-risk category carries a zero weight because there is no default risk (or very little) with direct obligations of the federal government, such as cash, Treasury securities, and U.S. agency securities issued by the Government National Mortgage Association (GNMA).[5] Assets in each of the subsequent categories are assumed to exhibit increased default risk. Thus, assets in category 2 are subject to a 20 percent risk weight and an *effective* total capital-to-total-assets ratio of 1.6 percent ($0.2 \times 8$ percent). Category 2 assets are short-term and often carry U.S. government agency guarantees; e.g., U.S. agency securities, general obligation municipal bonds, interest-bearing depository institution deposits, and federal funds sold, among other assets. Each type is low in default risk so that the risk weight is slightly above that for zero default risk assets. First mortgages, collateralized mortgage obligations (CMOs), and municipal revenue bonds constitute the bulk of the 50 percent risk weight assets under category 3, which carry a 4 percent effective total capital ratio ($0.5 \times 8$ percent). The final category includes assets with the highest default risk, such as commercial loans and real estate loans other than first mortgages, and thus these assets carry a risk weight of 100 percent.

An important element of the risk-based standards is that a bank's off-balance sheet items must be supported by capital. A bank that exposes its operations to risk by making long-term loan commitments, offering letter-of-credit guarantees, and participating in interest rate swaps and forward or futures transactions must hold capital against the exposure. Management first converts the dollar value of each off-balance sheet item to an on-balance sheet *credit equivalent* amount, as indicated in the third column of Exhibit 9.4, using the conversion factors in Exhibit 9.6. The converted credit equivalent amount is then assigned to the appropriate risk category, based on the obligor, collateral, or guarantor of the asset, and then multiplied by the associated risk weight to calculate risk-adjusted assets. Exhibit 9.4 indicates that long-term loan commitments greater than one year ($364,920) are classified as 50 percent conversion items, while standby letters of credit or direct credit substitutes ($165,905), futures and forward contracts ($50,000), and interest rate swaps ($75,000) are converted using a 100 percent conversion factor.[6] Figures in the final column represent converted amounts. Once converted to on-balance sheet equivalents, all of these commitments are classified as category 4 assets subject to a 100 percent risk weighting.

The second and third columns of Exhibit 9.2 indicate the associated risk weight and the dollar value of each balance sheet figure, respectively, for RNB. Risk-weighted assets are calculated by multiplying the dollar value of assets in column 1 by its respective risk weight. Total risk-weighted assets are the sum of risk-weighted assets in each category, including off-balance sheet items. Total risk-weighted assets for RNB thus equaled $3.75 billion. Finally, RNB's minimum capital requirements are specified as a fraction of total risk-weighted assets. Figures at the bottom of Exhibit 9.2 indicate that RNB would need $149.9 million in Tier 1 capital and $299.8 million in total capital to be adequately capitalized.

The next section describes the components of items that qualify as bank capital under the standards. At this point, it is sufficient to know that banks must simultaneously meet three minimum capital standards. To be

---

[4]Banks have been required to hold capital against off-balance sheet activities long before the Enron collapse.

[5]For RNB, trading account securities consist solely of U.S. Treasury securities.

[6]Values for futures, forwards, and interest rate swaps represent the sum of the mark-to-market value plus the potential future increase in credit exposure. See Exhibit 9.5.

**EXHIBIT 9.2**

Regional National Bank (RNB), Risk-based Capital (Millions of Dollars)

| | Assets $ 1,000 | Risk Weight | Risk Weighted Assets |
|---|---|---|---|
| *Category 1: Zero Percent* | | | |
| Cash and reserve | 104,525 | 0.00% | 0 |
| Trading Account | 830 | 0.00% | 0 |
| U.S. Treasury and agency securities | 45,882 | 0.00% | 0 |
| Federal Reserve stock | 5,916 | 0.00% | 0 |
| Total category 1 | 157,153 | | 0 |
| *Category 2: 20 percent* | | | |
| Due from banks/in process | 303,610 | 20.00% | 60,722 |
| Interest bearing depository/F.F.S. | 497,623 | 20.00% | 99,525 |
| Domestic depository institutions | 38,171 | 20.00% | 7,634 |
| Repurchase agreements (U.S. Treasury and agency) | 329,309 | 20.00% | 65,862 |
| U.S. agencies (government sponsored) | 412,100 | 20.00% | 82,420 |
| State and municipal's secured tax authority | 87,515 | 20.00% | 17,503 |
| C.M.O. backed by agency securities | 90,020 | 20.00% | 18,004 |
| SBAs (government guaranteed portion) | 29,266 | 20.00% | 5,853 |
| Other category 2 assets | 0 | 20.00% | 0 |
| Total category 2 | 1,787,614 | | 357,523 |
| *Category 3: 50 percent* | | | |
| C.M.O. backed by mortgage loans | 10,000 | 50.00% | 5,000 |
| State and municipal's/all other | 68,514 | 50.00% | 34,257 |
| Real estate: 1–4 family | 324,422 | 50.00% | 162,211 |
| Other category 3 assets | 0 | 50.00% | 0 |
| Total category 3 | 402,936 | | 201,468 |
| *Category 4: 100 percent* | | | |
| Loans: commercial/agency/institution/leases | 1,966,276 | 100.00% | 1,966,276 |
| Real estate, all other | 388,456 | 100.00% | 388,456 |
| Allowance for loan and lease losses | (70,505) | 0.00% | 0 |
| Other investments | 168,519 | 100.00% | 168,519 |
| Premises, equity other assets | 194,400 | 100.00% | 194,400 |
| Other category 4 assets | 0 | 100.00% | 0 |
| Total category 4 | 2,647,146 | | 2,717,651 |
| Total assets before off-balance sheet | 4,994,849 | | 3,276,642 |
| *Off-Balance Sheet Contingencies* | | | |
| 0% collateral category | 0 | 0.00% | 0 |
| 20% collateral category | 0 | 20.00% | 0 |
| 50% collateral category | 364,920 | 50.00% | 182,460 |
| 100% collateral category | 290,905 | 100.00% | 290,905 |
| Total contingencies | 655,825 | | 473,365 |
| *Total assets and contingencies before allowance for loan and lease losses and ATR* | 5,650,674 | | 3,750,007 |
| **Less:** Excess allowance for loan and lease losses | | | (2,152) |
| **Total assets and contingencies** | **$5,650,674** | | **$3,747,855** |

| | Actual Capital | Minimum Required Capital (%) | Required Capital (Minimum) |
|---|---|---|---|
| *Capital requirements* | | | |
| Tier I @ 4% | $199,794 | 4.00% | $149,914 |
| Total capital @ 8% | 399,588 | 8.00% | 299,828 |

## EXHIBIT 9.3

General Description of Assets in Each of the Four Risk Categories

| Asset Category | Risk Weight | Effective Total Capital Requirement* | Obligor, Collateral, or Guarantor of the Asset |
|---|---|---|---|
| 1 | 0% | 0% | Generally, direct obligations of OECD central government or the U.S. federal government; e.g., currency and coin, government securities, and unconditional government-guaranteed claims. Also, balances due or guaranteed by depository institutions. |
| 2 | 20% | 1.6% | Generally, indirect obligations of OECD central government or the U.S. federal government; e.g., most federal agency securities, full faith and credit municipal securities, and domestic depository institutions. Also, assets collateralized by federal government obligations are generally included in this category; e.g., repurchase agreements (when Treasuries serve as collateral) and CMOs backed by government agency securities. |
| 3 | 50% | 4% | Generally, loans secured by 1–4 family properties and municipal bonds secured by revenues of a specific project (revenue bonds). |
| 4 | 100% | 8% | All other claims on private borrowers; e.g., most bank loans, premises, and other assets. |

*Equals 8% of equivalent risk-weighted assets and represents the minimum requirement to be adequately capitalized.

## EXHIBIT 9.4

Regional National Bank (RNB), Off-Balance Sheet Conversion Worksheet

| | $ Amount ($1,500) | Credit Conversion Factor | Credit Equivalent $ Amount ($1,000) |
|---|---|---|---|
| **Contingencies 100% conversion factor** | | | |
| Direct credit substitutes | 165,905 | 100.00% | 165,905 |
| Acquisition of participations in BA, direct credit substitutes | 0 | 100.00% | 0 |
| Assets sold with recourse | 0 | 100.00% | 0 |
| Futures and forward contracts | 50,000 | 100.00% | 50,000 |
| Interest rate swaps | 75,000 | 100.00% | 75,000 |
| Other 100% collateral category | 0 | 100.00% | 0 |
| Total 100% collateral category | 290,905 | | 290,905 |
| **Contingencies 50% conversion factor** | | | |
| Transaction-related contingencies | 0 | 50.00% | 0 |
| Unused commitments > 1 year | 364,920 | 50.00% | 182,460 |
| Revolving underwriting facilities (RUFs) | 0 | 50.00% | 0 |
| Other 50% collateral category | 0 | 50.00% | 0 |
| Total 50% collateral category | 364,920 | | 182,460 |
| **Contingencies 20% conversion factor** | | | |
| Short-term trade-related contingencies | 0 | 20.00% | 0 |
| Other 20% collateral category | 0 | 20.00% | 0 |
| Total 20% collateral category | 0 | | 0 |
| **Contingencies 0% conversion factor** | | | |
| Loan commitments < 1 year | 0 | 0.00% | 0 |
| Other 0% collateral category | 0 | 100.00% | 0 |
| Total 0% collateral category | 0 | | 0 |
| **Total off-balance sheet commitment** | 655,825 | | 473,365 |

*BA refers to bankers acceptance.

**9.5** Summary of Risk Categories and Risk Weights for Risk-Based Capital Requirements

### Risk Weights and Risk Categories for Specific Balance Sheet Items*

**Category 1: 0%**

(1) Currency and coin (domestic and foreign) held in the bank or in transit

(2) Securities issued by the U.S. government and other OECD central governments (including U.S. Treasury securities)

(3) Claims that are unconditionally guaranteed by the U.S. government and its agencies and other OECD central governments (including GNMA and SBA securities and loans guaranteed by the Export-Import Bank)

(4) Gold bullion held in the bank's vaults or in another's vaults on an allocated basis, to the extent offset by gold bullion liabilities

(5) Credit equivalent amount of those off-balance sheet direct claims on, or claims unconditionally guaranteed by the U.S. government and other OECD central governments

**Category 2: 20%**

(1) Cash items in the process of collection (CIPC)

(2) Balances due from (claims guaranteed by) U.S. depository institutions and other OECD banks

(3) Short-term (one year or less) claims guaranteed by non-OECD banks

(4) Securities, loans, local currency, and other claims conditionally guaranteed by the U.S. government and its agencies and other OECD central governments (e.g., VA and FHA mortgage loans and student loans on which the U.S. Department of Education acts as a reinsurer)

(5) Claims on, guaranteed, or collateralized by securities issued by U.S. government-sponsored agencies (e.g., loans collateralized by FHLMC pass-through securities) or official multilateral lending institutions or regional development banks (e.g., the World Bank including the International Finance Corporation)

(6) Certain privately issued mortgage-backed securities representing indirect ownership of U.S. government agency or U.S. government-sponsored agency mortgage-backed securities (e.g., GNMA, FNMA, and FHLMC pass-through securities)

(7) General obligation claims on municipal securities and the portion of claims that are guaranteed by the full faith and credit of local governments and political subdivisions in the U.S. and other OECD local governments

(8) Credit equivalent amount for those off-balance sheet items that are risk weighted at 20 percent; e.g., credit equivalent amount of claims collateralized by cash on deposit (standby letters of credit collateralized by cash)

**Category 3: 50%**

(1) Loans that are fully secured by first liens on 1–4 family residential properties and loans fully secured by first liens on multifamily residential properties that have been prudently underwritten

(2) Privately issued mortgage-backed securities representing direct and indirect ownership of the mortgage loans (if the mortgages are prudently underwritten and are not restructured, past due, or in nonaccrual status)

(3) Revenue bonds (municipal revenue securities) or similar claims that are obligations of U.S. state or local governments, or other OECD local governments, for which the government is committed to repay the debt only out of revenues from the facilities financed

(4) Credit equivalent amount, for those off-balance sheet items that are to be risk weighted at 50 percent; e.g., credit equivalent amounts of interest rate and foreign exchange rate contracts that are not accorded a lower risk weight as a result of the counterparty, collateral, or a guarantee

**Category 4: 100%**

(1) All other loans, debt securities, and other claims where the counterparty is a private obligor

(2) Premises and fixed assets

(3) Margin accounts on futures contracts

(4) Other real estate owned

(5) All other assets not already reported above

(6) Credit equivalent amounts of those off-balance sheet items where the counterparty is a private obligor and which are not accorded a lower risk weight as a result of collateral or a guarantee

NOTE: For more details, see the Federal Financial Institutions Examination Council FFIEC Report Forms available on the Internet at www.ffiec.gov.

*Several of the risk weight categories refer to claims against OECD countries; i.e., the Organization for Economic Cooperation and Development. The following countries are members of the OECD: Australia, Austria, Belgium, Canada, the Czech Republic, Denmark, Finland, France, Germany, Greece, Hungary, Iceland, Ireland, Italy, Japan, Korea, Luxembourg, Mexico, the Netherlands, New Zealand, Norway, Poland, Portugal, Slovak Republic, Spain, Sweden, Switzerland, Turkey, the United Kingdom, and the United States. In addition, Saudi Arabia should be treated as an OECD country. All other countries should be treated as non-OECD countries.

## Summary of Off-Balance Sheet Conversion Factors for Risk-Based Capital Requirements

**100% Conversion Factor**
1. Direct credit substitutes (general guarantees of indebtedness and guarantee-type instruments, including standby letters of credit serving as financial guarantees for, or supporting, loans and securities)
2. Risk participations in bankers acceptances and participations in direct credit substitutes (for example, standby letters of credit)
3. Sale and repurchase agreements and asset sales with recourse, if not already included on the balance sheet
4. Forward agreements (that is, contractual obligations) to purchase assets, including financing facilities with certain draw down

**50% Conversion Factor**
1. Transaction-related contingencies (for example, bid bonds, performance bonds, warranties, and standby letters of credit related to a particular transaction)
2. Unused commitments with an original maturity exceeding one year, including underwriting commitments and commercial credit lines
3. Revolving underwriting facilities (RUFs), note issuance facilities (NIFs), and other similar arrangements

**20% Conversion Factor**
1. Short-term, self-liquidating trade-related contingencies, including commercial letters of credit

**0% Conversion Factor**
1. Unused commitments with an original maturity of one year or less, or that are unconditionally cancelable at any time

**Credit conversion process for off-balance sheet interest rate, foreign exchange, equity derivative, and commodity and other contracts—**
In general, to calculate the credit equivalent amount for these contracts, a bank should, for each contract, add:
 (1) The mark-to-market value (only if a positive value) of the contract; i.e., the contract's current credit exposure or replacement cost, and
 (2) An estimate of the potential future increase in credit exposure over the remaining life of the instrument.
For risk-based capital purposes, potential future credit exposure of a contract is determined by multiplying the notional principal amount of the contract (even if the contract had a negative mark-to-market value) by the appropriate credit conversion factor from the chart presented below (existence of a legally enforceable bilateral netting agreement between the reporting bank and a counterparty may be taken into consideration when determining both the current credit exposure and the potential future exposure of off-balance sheet derivative contracts.)

| Remaining Maturity | Interest Rate Contracts | Foreign Exchange and Gold Contracts | Equity Derivative Contracts | Precious Metals (Except Gold) | Other Commodity Contracts |
|---|---|---|---|---|---|
| One year or less | 0.0% | 1.0% | 6.0% | 7.0% | 10.0% |
| More than one year through five years | 0.5% | 5.0% | 8.0% | 7.0% | 12.0% |
| More than five years | 1.5% | 7.5% | 10.0% | 8.0% | 15.0% |

SOURCE: Federal Financial Institutions Examination Council FFIEC Report Forms available on the Internet at http://www.ffiec.gov.

adequately capitalized, a bank's Tier 1 capital must equal no less than 4 percent of risk-weighted assets, total capital must equal at least 8 percent of risk-weighted assets, and leverage capital must equal no less than 3 percent of adjusted total assets.

## WHAT CONSTITUTES BANK CAPITAL?

According to the accounting definition, **capital** or **net worth** equals the cumulative value of assets minus the cumulative value of liabilities, and represents ownership interest in a firm. It is traditionally measured on a book-value basis where assets and liabilities are listed in terms of historical cost.[7] In banking, the regulatory concept of bank capital differs substantially from accounting capital. Specifically, regulators include certain forms of debt and loan loss reserves when measuring capital adequacy. This policy raises numerous issues regarding the function of bank capital and its optimal mix for individual institutions.

---

[7]FASB 115 requires banks to mark-to-market those securities that are not classified as held to maturity. Because marking securities to market value will directly affect equity capital, capital listed on a bank's balance sheet is a hybrid between book value and market value.

Accounting capital includes the book value of common equity and preferred stock outstanding. **Total equity capital** equals the sum of common stock, surplus, undivided profits, and capital reserves, and net unrealized holding gains (losses) on available-for-sale securities, cumulative foreign currency translation adjustments, and perpetual preferred stock as defined below:

- **Common stock** equals par value of common stock outstanding; thus, if there are one million shares outstanding with par value of $10 per share, common stock will show $10 million.

- **Surplus** equals the excess over par value at which common stock was issued plus the value of undivided profits allocated to surplus. Suppose, in the above case, that one million common stock shares were originally sold in the marketplace to net a bank $15 per share. The excess, $5 per share or $5 million, would be allocated to surplus.

- **Undivided profits** equal the value of cumulative retained earnings minus transfers to surplus. Retained earnings increase when a bank reports net income that exceeds cash dividend payments, and decreases when net income is less than cash dividends or the bank reports a loss.

- **Capital reserves** for contingencies and other capital reserves equal the value of cumulative reserves established for deferred taxes or contingencies. Contingencies include expected payments to retire outstanding preferred stock, settle lawsuits, and satisfy other extraordinary obligations. These reserves have been combined with undivided profits for reporting purposes since 1978.

- **Net unrealized holding gains (losses) on available-for-sale securities.** For risk-based capital purposes, common stockholders' equity capital includes any net unrealized holding losses on available-for-sale equity securities with readily determinable fair values, but excludes other net unrealized holding gains (losses) on available-for-sale securities. FASB 115 requires banks and other firms to mark certain available-for-sale securities to their market value. These unrealized losses (gains) directly affect equity reported on the balance sheet, but do not affect qualifying capital for risk-based calculations.

- **Preferred stock** includes the book value of aggregate preferred stock outstanding. While it exhibits many of the same characteristics as long-term bonds, preferred stock represents ownership in a firm with claims superior to common stock but subordinated to all debt holders. It is issued either in **perpetuity** or with a **fixed maturity** (limited life). Most issues are callable, and some are convertible to common stock. Dividend payments may be fixed, much like coupon payments on bonds, or may vary with some market index over the life of the issue. Unlike coupon payments, dividends are not deductible for corporate income tax purposes.

Regulatory capital ratios focus in part on the **book value of equity,** which equals the book value of bank assets minus the book value of total liabilities. Most analysts try to estimate the market value of bank equity when assessing financial performance and risk. This can be done in several ways. One procedure is to multiply the number of outstanding shares of stock by the most recent stock price per share. Another procedure requires estimating the market value of bank assets and subtracting the market value of bank liabilities. As discussed in Chapter 6, the market value of equity is an important measure of performance in interest rate risk management. Claims of equity stockholders are paid in the case of failure after the claims of all debt holders and preferred stockholders.

Regulators also include long-term **subordinated debt** in Tier 2 capital, which is part of the broader definition of total bank capital (Tier 1 and Tier 2). The term *subordinated* means that claims of the debt holders are paid only after the claims of depositors. Subordinated debt takes many forms. It includes straight bonds with long maturities that carry fixed rates. It also includes variable rate bonds, capital notes, or bonds that are convertible into the bank's common or preferred stock. The fact that nonequity accounts constitute capital relates to regulatory perceptions of capital's function. Mandatory convertible debt and subordinated long-term debt are included because they carry relatively long-term maturities and creditors' claims are subordinated to those of depositors. These funding sources, therefore, provide solvency protection for insured depositors and the insurance funds.

Risk-based capital standards utilize two measures of qualifying bank capital, as summarized in Exhibit 9.7. **Tier 1** or **core capital** consists of common stockholders' equity, noncumulative perpetual preferred stock and any related surplus, and minority interests in equity capital accounts of consolidated subsidiaries, minus intangible assets like goodwill and disallowed deferred tax assets. For most banks, Tier 1 capital will equal common stockholders' equity capital less any net unrealized holding gains or losses on available-for-sale equity securities. **Tier 2** or **supplementary capital** is limited to 100 percent of Tier 1 capital and consists of cumulative perpetual preferred stock and any related surplus, long-term preferred stock, limited amounts of term-subordinated debt and intermediate-term preferred stock, and a limited amount of the allowance for loan and lease losses (up to 1.25 percent of gross risk-weighted assets).[8]

---

[8]The definitions of Tier 1 and Tier 2 capital are from *Instructions for Preparation of Consolidated Reports of Condition and Income (FFIEC 031, 032, 033, and 034)*, Federal Financial Institutions Examination Council. FFIEC Report Forms are available on the Internet at http://www.ffiec.gov.

**Definition of Qualifying Capital**

| Components | Minimum Requirements |
| --- | --- |
| **Tier 1 (Core) Capital** | |
| Common stockholders' equity* | Must equal or exceed 4 percent of risk-weighted assets. |
| Noncumulative perpetual preferred stock and any related surplus | No limit. |
| Minority interests in equity capital accounts of consolidated subsidiaries | No limit, regulatory caution against *undue reliance.* |
| | No limit, regulatory caution against *undue reliance.* |
| Less: | |
| goodwill, other disallowed intangible assets, and disallowed deferred tax assets, and any other amounts that are deducted in determining Tier 1 capital in accordance with the capital standards issued by the reporting bank's primary federal supervisory authority | |
| **Tier 2 (Supplementary) Capital** | |
| Cumulative perpetual preferred stock and any related surplus | Total of Tier 2 is limited to 100 percent of Tier 1[†]. |
| Long-term preferred stock (original maturity of 20 years or more) and any related surplus (discounted for capital purposes as it approaches maturity) | No limit within Tier 2. |
| Auction rate and similar preferred stock (both cumulative and noncumulative) | No limit within Tier 2. |
| Hybrid capital instruments (including mandatory convertible debt securities) | Subordinated debt and intermediate-term preferred stock are limited to 50 percent of Tier 1, amortized for capital purposes as they approach maturity. |
| Term subordinated debt and intermediate-term preferred stock (original weighted average maturity of five years or more) | 50 percent of Tier 1 capital (and discounted for capital purposes as they approach maturity). |
| Allowance for loan and lease losses | Lesser of the balance of the allowance account or 1.25 percent of gross risk-weighted assets. |
| **Tier 3 (Capital Allocated for Market Risk)** | |
| Applicable only to banks that are subject to the market risk capital guidelines | May not be used to support credit risk. |
| | Tier 3 capital allocated for market risk plus Tier 2 capital allocated for market risk are limited to 71.4 percent of a bank's measure for market risk. |
| **Deductions** | |
| Deductions are made for: | As a general rule, one-half of aggregate investments would be deducted from Tier 1 capital and one-half from Tier 2 capital. |
| investments in banking and finance subsidiaries that are not consolidated for regulatory capital purposes; intentional reciprocal cross-holdings of banking organizations' capital instruments; and other deductions as determined by the reporting bank's primary federal supervisory authority | |
| **Total Capital (Tier 1 + Tier 2 − Deductions)** | Must equal or exceed 8 percent of risk-weighted assets For most banks, total risk-based capital will equal the sum of Tier 1 capital and Tier 2 capital. |

*For risk-based capital purposes, common stockholders' equity capital includes any net unrealized holding losses on available-for-sale equity securities with readily determinable fair values, but excludes other net unrealized holding gains (losses) on available-for-sale securities.

[†]Amounts in excess of limitations are permitted but do not qualify as capital.

SOURCE: Federal Financial Institutions Examination Council FFIEC Report Forms available on the Internet at www.ffiec.gov.

**EXHIBIT 9.8**

Risk-Based Capital Ratios for Different-Sized U.S. Commercial Banks, 1995–2004

| | Year | Asset Size | | | | |
| --- | --- | --- | --- | --- | --- | --- |
| | | <$100 Million | $100 Million to $1 Billion | $1 to $10 Billion | >$10 Billion | All Commercial Banks |
| Number of institutions reporting | 2004 | 3,655 | 3,530 | 360 | 85 | 7,630 |
| | 2000 | 4,842 | 3,078 | 313 | 82 | 8,315 |
| | 1995 | 6,658 | 2,861 | 346 | 75 | 9,940 |
| Equity capital ratio (percent) | 2004 | 11.52 | 10.00 | 10.90 | 9.95 | 10.10 |
| | 2000 | 11.08 | 9.6 | 8.99 | 8.05 | 8.49 |
| | 1995 | 10.42 | 9.39 | 8.57 | 7.19 | 8.11 |
| Return on equity (percent) | 2004 | 8.46 | 12.88 | 13.48 | 14.24 | 13.82 |
| Core capital (leverage) ratio (percent) | 2004 | 11.31 | 9.47 | 9.36 | 7.23 | 7.83 |
| Tier 1 risk-based capital ratio (percent) | 2004 | 16.83 | 12.85 | 12.34 | 9.11 | 10.04 |
| Total risk-based capital ratio (percent) | 2004 | 17.93 | 14.06 | 13.92 | 12.07 | 12.62 |

SOURCE: FDIC, Quarterly Banking Profile, http://www2.fdic.gov/qbp.

Regulators are also concerned that a bank could acquire a sufficient dollar amount of low-risk assets (federal government securities) such that risk-based capital requirements would be negligible. Suppose, for example, that RNB from Exhibit 9.2 held all of its assets in the form of cash and due balances and Treasury securities. In this case, its risk-weighted assets would equal zero and its Tier 1 and total capital requirements would be zero. This would allow (at least theoretically) RNB to operate with no equity capital! To prevent this from occurring, regulators impose a minimum 3 percent **leverage capital ratio,** defined as Tier 1 capital divided by total assets net of goodwill, other disallowed intangible assets, and disallowed deferred tax assets. The impact is that all banks must maintain some minimum amount of equity capital relative to their total assets in recognition of risks other than default risk. Exhibit 9.8 compares the average capital ratios for different-sized banks from 1995 to 2004. Regardless of how the averages are calculated, three implications stand out. First, capital ratios at banks of all sizes exceeded the regulatory minimums. Second, capital ratios at small banks greatly exceeded those at larger banks, on average. This reflects greater regulatory pressure on small banks, which presumably carry less diversified asset portfolios, and the impact of record profits. Finally, as seen in Exhibit 9.1, capital ratios have generally increased since 1980 as banks moved to strengthen their financial positions.

## FDICIA AND BANK CAPITAL STANDARDS

Effective December 1991, Congress passed the Federal Deposit Insurance Corporation Improvement Act (FDICIA) with the intent of revising bank capital requirements to emphasize the importance of capital and authorize early regulatory intervention in problem institutions. The act also authorized regulators to measure interest rate risk at banks and require additional capital when risk is deemed excessive. The focal point of the act is the system of **prompt regulatory action,** which divides banks into categories or zones according to their capital positions and mandates action when capital minimums are not met.

As shown in Exhibit 9.9, there are five capital categories, with the first two representing well-capitalized and adequately capitalized banks. Because of their strong capital positions, **well-capitalized banks** are not subject to any regulatory directives regarding capital. For this reason, most banks make every effort to meet the 6 percent, 10 percent, and 5 percent minimum ratios. **Adequately capitalized banks** also have strong capital, but are restricted from obtaining brokered deposits without FDIC approval. While this provision may not seem too restrictive, it has the potential to create problems. Today, regulators designate any bank deposit liability as a brokered deposit if the issuing bank pays an above-market rate. The deposit does not have to arise via a broker. Suppose that a bank competes in a three-bank community and all banks currently pay 2 percent on interest-checking accounts. If the two competitors lower their rates to 1.25 percent, the bank finds that it is paying a 75 basis point premium. Regulators may now label these interest-checking accounts as brokered deposits and disallow them (or make the bank pay a lower rate). Does this make sense?

## EXHIBIT 9.9 — Capital Categories and Prompt Regulatory Action under FDICIA

### A. Minimum Capital Requirements across Capital Categories

| | Total Risk-Based Ratio | | Tier 1 Risk-Based Ratio | | Tier 1 Leverage Ratio | Capital Directive/Requirement |
|---|---|---|---|---|---|---|
| Well capitalized | ≥10% | and | ≥6% | and | ≥5% | Not subject to a capital directive to meet a specific level for any capital measure |
| Adequately capitalized | ≥8% | and | ≥4% | and | ≥4%* | Does not meet the definition of well capitalized |
| Undercapitalized | ≥6% | and | ≥3% | and | ≥3%† | |
| Significantly undercapitalized | <6% | or | <3% | or | <3% | |
| Critically undercapitalized | Ratio of tangible equity to total assets is <2%† | | | | | |

### B. Provisions for Prompt Corrective Action

| Category | Mandatory Provisions | Discretionary Provisions |
|---|---|---|
| 1.) Well capitalized | None | None |
| 2.) Adequately capitalized | 1. No brokered deposits, except with FDIC approval | None |
| 3.) Undercapitalized | 1. Suspend dividends and management fees<br>2. Require capital restoration plan<br>3. Restrict asset growth<br>4. Approval required for acquisitions, branching, and new activities<br>5. No brokered deposits | 1. Order recapitalization<br>2. Restrict interaffiliate transactions<br>3. Restrict deposit interest rates<br>4. Restrict certain other activities<br><br>5. Any other action that would better carry out prompt corrective action |
| 4.) Significantly undercapitalized | 1. Same as for Category 3<br>2. Order recapitalization§<br><br><br>3. Restrict interaffiliate transactions§<br><br><br><br>4. Restrict deposit interest rates§<br>5. Pay of officers restricted | 1. Any Zone 3 discretionary actions<br>2. Conservatorship or receivership if fails to submit or implement plan or recapitalize pursuant to order<br>3. Any other Zone 5 provision, if such action is necessary to carry out prompt corrective action |
| 5.) Critically undercapitalized | 1. Same as for Category 4<br>2. Receiver/conservator within 90 days§<br>3. Receiver if still in Category 5 four quarters after becoming critically undercapitalized<br>4. Suspend payments on subordinated debt§<br>5. Restrict certain other activities | |

*Three percent or above for composite one-rated banks and savings associations that are not experiencing or anticipating significant growth.

†Under 3 percent for composite one-rated banks and savings associations that are not experiencing or anticipating significant growth.

†Tangible equity equals core capital elements plus cumulative perpetual preferred stock, net of all intangibles except limited amounts of purchased mortgage servicing rights.

§Not required if primary supervisor determines action would not serve purpose of prompt corrective action or if certain other conditions are met.

SOURCE: FDIC.

Banks that fall into one of the bottom three categories prompt some explicit regulatory action. **Undercapitalized banks** are institutions that do not meet at least one of the three minimum capital requirements. **Significantly undercapitalized banks** have capital that falls significantly below at least one of the three standards. Finally, **critically undercapitalized banks** do not meet minimum threshold levels for the three capital ratios.

Exhibit 9.9 documents the specific definitions and associated regulatory actions as summarized by the Federal Reserve Board of Governors in late 1997. The top panel lists the minimum capital ratios that a bank must meet to qualify in each category or zone. A bank must meet each of these ratios simultaneously. The bottom panel lists mandatory and discretionary provisions within each classification. Note the restrictive nature of the mandatory actions. A bank that is undercapitalized must limit its asset growth, suspend dividends, and offer a capital restoration plan, among other requirements. For a bank that is significantly undercapitalized, regulators can specify deposit rates and the pay of bank officers—decisions that senior management normally makes in the general course of business operation. Critically undercapitalized banks are near failure and treated accordingly. Once a bank reaches this stage, regulators can place it under receivership within 90 days. A review of the top panel reveals that such banks can have positive tangible equity capital equal to almost 2 percent of assets, be technically solvent, and still be closed by regulators.

The impact of FDICIA is much broader than these provisions suggest. Clearly, problem or undercapitalized institutions must obtain capital to remain in business. This often requires entering into a merger or acquisition because it is difficult to enter the primary markets and issue new capital. Similarly, bank managers know that if they maintain strong capital positions the regulators will let them operate without much restriction. Of course, the capital standards in Exhibit 9.9 are minimums. If the regulators believe that risk is above average for any reason, they can impose additional requirements.

## TIER 3 CAPITAL REQUIREMENTS FOR MARKET RISK

Many large banks have dramatically increased the size and activity of their trading accounts, resulting in greater exposure to market risk. **Market risk** is the risk of loss to the bank from fluctuations in interest rates, equity prices, foreign exchange rates, commodity prices, and exposure to specific risk associated with debt and equity positions in the bank's trading portfolio. Market risk exposure is, therefore, a function of the *volatility* of these rates and prices and the corresponding sensitivity of the bank's trading assets and liabilities.

In response to the FDICIA stipulation that regulators systematically measure and monitor a bank's market risk position, risk-based capital standards require all banks with significant market risk to measure their market risk exposure and hold sufficient capital to mitigate this exposure. A bank is subject to the market risk capital guidelines if its consolidated trading activity, defined as the sum of trading assets and liabilities for the previous quarter, equals 10 percent or more of the bank's total assets for the previous quarter, or $1 billion or more in total dollar value. The primary federal supervisory authority, however, may exempt or include a bank if necessary or appropriate for safe and sound banking practices. Banks subject to the market risk capital guidelines must maintain an overall minimum 8 percent ratio of total qualifying capital [the sum of Tier 1 capital (both allocated and excess), Tier 2 capital (both allocated and excess), and Tier 3 capital (allocated for market risk), net of all deductions] to risk-weighted assets and market risk equivalent assets.

## CAPITAL REQUIREMENTS FOR MARKET RISK USING INTERNAL MODELS

The market risk capital rules require that an institution measure its general market risk using an internally generated risk measurement model. This model is then used to calculate a **value-at-risk** (VAR) based capital charge. VAR is an estimate of the amount by which the value of a bank's positions in a risk category could decline due to expected losses in the bank's portfolio because of market movements during a given period, measured with a specified confidence level. An institution may measure its specific risk through a valid internal model or by the so-called "standardized approach." The standardized approach uses a risk-weighting process developed by the Basel Committee on Banking Supervision.[9] The VAR of a bank's covered positions should be used to determine the bank's measure for market risk. **Covered positions** include all positions in a bank's trading account as well as foreign exchange and commodity positions, whether or not they are in the trading account. A bank's measure for market risk equals the sum of its VAR-based capital charge, the specific risk add-on (if any), and the capital charge for de minimus exposures (if any). A bank's market risk equivalent assets equal its measure for market risk multiplied by 12.5 (the reciprocal of the minimum 8.0 percent capital ratio).[10]

Regulatory requirements propose that an institution electing to use an internal model approach to measure market risk be subject to the following eight standards:

1. Value-at-risk should be computed each business day and should be based on a 99 percent (one-tailed) confidence level of estimated maximum loss.

2. The assumed holding period used for the VAR measure must be 10 business days.

3. The model must measure all material risks incurred by the institution.

4. The model may utilize historical correlations within broad categories of risk factors (interest rates, exchange rates, and equity and commodity prices), but not among these categories. That is, the consolidated value-at-risk is the sum of the individual VARs measured for each broad category.

[9]The Basel Committee on Banking Supervision "Amendment to the Capital Accord to Incorporate Market Risk," demonstrates the VAR concept in general terms: http://www.bis.org/publ/bcbs24.pdf/.

[10]See *Regulator Capital Guidelines,* FDIC, http://www.fdic.gov.

5. The nonlinear price characteristics of options must be adequately addressed.

6. The historical observation period used to estimate future price and rate changes must have a minimum length of one year.

7. Data must be updated no less frequently than once every three months and more frequently if market conditions warrant.

8. Each yield curve in a major currency must be modeled using at least six risk factors, selected to reflect the characteristics of the interest rate–sensitive instruments that the institution trades. The model must also take account of spread risk.

The explicit market risk capital requirements are designed to capture both general market risk as well as specific market risks. **General market risk** refers to changes in the market value of on-balance sheet assets and off-balance sheet items resulting from broad market movements. General market risk includes risk common to all securities, such as changes in the general level of interest rates, exchange rates, commodity prices, or stock prices. **Specific market risks** are those risks specific to a particular security issue, such as the underlying credit risk of the firm that issued a bond.[11]

The market risk capital standards impose a set of qualitative standards in addition to the quantitative measure discussed above. The qualitative standards are designed to ensure that banks using internal models to measure market risk have conceptually sound risk management systems and that these systems are implemented with integrity. In particular, there are three qualitative elements required:

- The bank's internal risk measurement model should be closely integrated in the daily risk management process and serve as a basis for reporting of risk exposures to senior officers.

- The bank should routinely evaluate its exposures to highly stressful events via stress tests to identify the circumstances to which their particular trading portfolios are most vulnerable.

- The bank's risk control unit should be completely independent of the business units that generate the market risk exposures.

Banks and regulators are in the early stages of developing these internal market risk models. These models must undergo back-testing and verification and may eventually be expanded to help analyze credit, operational, and even legal risk in the future.

## WHAT IS THE FUNCTION OF BANK CAPITAL?

Much confusion exists over what purposes bank capital serves. The traditional corporate finance view is that capital reduces the risk of failure by providing protection against operating and extraordinary losses. While this holds for nonfinancial firms that rely on long-term debt with relatively low financial leverage, it is less applicable to commercial banks.

From the regulators' perspective, bank capital serves to protect the deposit insurance funds in the case of bank failures. When a bank fails, regulators can either pay off insured depositors or arrange a purchase of the failed bank by a healthy bank.[12] The greater is a bank's capital, the lower is the cost of arranging a merger or paying depositors. An additional benefit of minimum capital requirements is that the owners of equity and long-term debt impose market discipline on bank managers because they closely monitor bank performance. Excessive risk taking lowers stock prices and increases borrowing costs, which adversely affect the wealth of these monitoring parties.

The function of bank capital is thus to reduce bank risk. It does so in three basic ways:

- It provides a cushion for firms to absorb losses and remain solvent.

- It provides ready access to financial markets and thus guards against liquidity problems caused by deposit outflows.

- It constrains growth and limits risk taking.

**BANK CAPITAL PROVIDES A CUSHION TO ABSORB LOSSES.** Consider the balance sheets for two hypothetical firms in Exhibit 9.10. The manufacturing firm has 60 percent current assets and 40 percent fixed assets. Its financing is composed of 60 percent debt and 40 percent equity. Exactly one-half of the debt is short term, such that its current ratio equals 2. The commercial bank, in contrast, operates with very few fixed assets

---

[11]Hendricks and Hirtle (1997) suggest that these two types of risk are analogous to systematic and nonsystematic risk in a capital asset pricing model. See Darryll Hendricks and Beverly Hirtle, "Regulatory Minimum Capital Standards for Banks: Current Status and Future Prospects," Conference on Bank Structure and Competition (1997).

[12]See "Overview: The Resolution Handbook at a Glance" for alternative options available to the FDIC when a bank fails: http://www.fdic.gov/bank/historical/Reshandbook/overview.pdf

**EXHIBIT
9.10**

Comparative Balance Sheets: Manufacturing Firm versus Commercial Bank

| Manufacturing Firm | | Commercial Bank | |
|---|---|---|---|
| **Assets** | | **Assets** | |
| Cash | 4% | Cash | 8% |
| Accounts receivable | 26% | Short-term securities | 17% |
| Inventory | 30% | Short-term loans | 50% |
| Total current assets | 60% | Total current assets | 75% |
| | | Long-term securities | 5% |
| | | Long-term loans | 18% |
| Plant and equipment | 40% | Plant and equipment | 2% |
| Total assets | 100% | Total assets | 100% |
| **Liabilities** | | **Liabilities** | |
| Accounts payable | 20% | Short-term deposits | 60% |
| Short-term notes payable | 10% | Short-term borrowings | 20% |
| Total Current Liabilities | 30% | Total Current Liabilities | 80% |
| Long-term debt | 30% | Long-term debt | 12% |
| Stockholders' equity | 40% | Stockholders' equity | 8% |
| Total liabilities and equity | 100% | Total liabilities and equity | 100% |

and finances 92 percent of its assets with debt and just 8 percent with equity. Its current ratio is less than 1. The value of the manufacturing firm's assets would have to decline by more than 40 percent before the firm would see its equity fall below zero and be technically insolvent. An 8 percent decline in asset values would similarly make the bank insolvent. Equity reduces the risk of failure by increasing the proportion of allowable problem assets that can default before equity is depleted.

The issue, however, is not this simple. For example, why do creditors allow banks to operate with far greater financial leverage than manufacturers? One reason is that banks exhibit little operating risk because fixed assets are low. Yet, several factors suggest that banks should have more equity. First, the market value of bank assets is more volatile than the value of assets at a typical manufacturing firm. Market values change whenever interest rates change and whenever bank borrowers experience difficulties. Manufacturing companies own proportionately fewer financial assets and are not as sensitive to interest rate fluctuations. Second, banks rely proportionately more on volatile sources of short-term debt, many of which can be withdrawn on demand. It seems reasonably probable that banks might be forced to liquidate assets at relatively low values. On the positive side, however, most of a bank's assets are financial and hence are generally more liquid and less risky (everything else equal) than the real assets held by nonfinancial companies. After all, it is often easier to sell Treasury securities and high-quality bank loans than an automobile assembly plant!

This capital discrepancy can be largely explained by federal deposit insurance and bank regulatory policy.[13] Depositors' funds at each member institution are insured up to $100,000. Even if a bank fails, an insured depositor is fully reimbursed. This system prevents massive withdrawals of small-denomination deposits and makes uninsured creditors the arbiters of bank risk. Just as significantly, bank regulators provided de facto insurance for uninsured creditors at the largest financial institutions. Rather than let these banks fail, regulators arranged mergers or acquisitions that allowed such firms to continue operations without liquidation. In the case of Continental Illinois in 1984 and First City Bancorporation in 1987, the U.S. government effectively guaranteed the claims of both debt holders and preferred stockholders who lost little when the banks collapsed.[14] In these extreme cases, no private capital is technically required for the banks to continue operations. In general, deposit insurance and regulatory policy increase bank liquidity, which reduces the amount of equity financing required.

Bank regulators shifted their policy with the failures of First Republic Bank Corporation in 1988 and MCorp. in 1989. At the time they failed, these bank holding companies had $27 billion and $16 billion in assets, respectively.

---

[13]See the section at the end of this chapter on Federal Deposit Insurance for a more detailed discussion of Bank Capital and FDIC insurance.

[14]In 1984, C. T. Conover, the Comptroller of the Currency, suggested indirectly that regulators would not allow the 11 largest banking organizations in the United States to fail. These banks controlled 23 percent of all assets at the end of 1983. Feldman and Rolnick (1997) suggest that in 1997 dollars, regulators might view the top 21 banks, which controlled 38 percent of assets, as being too-big-to-fail. In 1997, there were 24 commercial banks and S&Ls larger than $35 billion in assets. The large number of bank megamergers since 1997 has meant that the largest banks have gotten even larger and the number of large banks has increased. There were 39 commercial banks and S&Ls larger than $35 billion at the end of 2004.

Still, the regulators created bridge banks that took over the subsidiary banks and stripped the holding companies of their assets. This left common and preferred stockholders to file claims behind bond holders and other uninsured creditors for what little remained. For the first time, investors in the nation's largest banks suffered substantial losses.

The role of capital as a buffer against loan losses is clear when put in the context of cash flows rather than accounting capital. Consider a bank whose customers default on their loans. Defaults immediately reduce operating cash inflows because the bank no longer receives interest and principal payments. Cash outflows are largely unaffected except for incremental collection costs. The bank remains operationally solvent as long as its overall operating cash inflows exceed its cash outflows. Capital serves as a buffer because it reduces obligated outflows. Banks can defer dividends on preferred and common stock without being in default. Interest payments on bank debt, in contrast, are mandatory. Banks with sufficient capital can, in turn, issue new debt or stock to replace lost cash inflows and buy time until any asset problems are corrected. Thus, the greater is a bank's equity capital, the greater is the magnitude of assets that can default before the firm is technically insolvent, and the lower is bank risk.

**BANK CAPITAL PROVIDES READY ACCESS TO FINANCIAL MARKETS.** Adequate bank capital minimizes operating problems by providing ready access to financial markets. As long as a bank's capital exceeds the regulatory minimums, it can stay open and has the potential to generate earnings to cover losses and expand. FDICIA demonstrates that banks with the greatest capital-to-risk asset ratios will have the greatest opportunities to operate without restraint and to enter new businesses. Capital enables the bank to borrow from traditional sources at reasonable rates. As such, depositors will not remove their funds and asset losses will be minimized. Any losses that arise can be charged against current earnings or, ultimately, against equity.

Analysts generally attribute failures to bad management and argue that well-managed banks should be allowed to operate with low capital-to-asset ratios. In these studies, banks with low capital-to-asset ratios do not exhibit any greater tendency toward insolvency, compared to banks with higher capital ratios. Other researchers attribute failures to liquidity problems and generally ignore capital. When depositors withdraw their funds, a bank must either liquidate assets from its portfolio or replace the deposit outflows with new borrowings. Forced asset sales can be accomplished only through lowering asset prices. These losses, in turn, would be charged against equity, bringing the bank closer to insolvency. Most banks, therefore, rely on substitute debt sources. If, however, the volume of required financing is large, the bank must pay an interest premium, which reduces current earnings and depresses potential equity.

Uncertainty regarding the link between capital and liquidity problems and bank failure reflects a misunderstanding of accounting versus economic value. What is important is the market value of bank capital, not its accounting value. As long as the market value is positive, banks can issue debt to offset liquidity problems. This is true regardless of whether accounting capital is positive or negative. If the market value of capital were negative, no private lender would extend credit. Failures, then, are tied directly to market values, not accounting values.

Regulatory interference confuses the true purpose of capital. When regulators guarantee bank debt or create artificial capital, they improve liquidity. The intent is to postpone problems until the firms are self-sufficient. Capital, as such, is meaningless to the firm's continued operation. Capital serves the same purpose as federal guarantees when regulatory assistance is not openly provided.

**CAPITAL CONSTRAINS GROWTH AND REDUCES RISK.** By limiting the amount of new assets that a bank can acquire through debt financing, capital constrains growth. As indicated in Exhibit 9.9, regulators impose equity capital requirements as a fraction of aggregate bank assets. If banks choose to expand loans or acquire other assets, they must support the growth with additional equity financing. Because new equity is expensive, expected asset returns must be high to justify the financing. This restriction is extremely important because many bank failures in the 1980s were linked to speculative asset growth financed by brokered deposits. Rigid capital requirements reduce the likelihood that banks will expand beyond their ability to manage their assets successfully and thus serve to reduce risk.

# HOW MUCH CAPITAL IS ADEQUATE?

The issue of bank capital adequacy has long pitted regulators against bank management. Regulators, concerned primarily with the safety of banks, the viability of the insurance fund, and the stability of financial markets, prefer more capital. This reduces the likelihood of failure and increases bank liquidity. Bankers, on the other hand, generally prefer to operate with less capital. As indicated in Chapter 2, the smaller is a bank's equity base, the greater is its financial leverage and equity multiplier. High leverage converts a normal return on assets (ROA) into a high return on equity (ROE). Exhibit 9.10 illustrates this point. Suppose that the manufacturing firm and commercial bank each earn 1 percent on assets during the year. The firms' equity multipliers (ratio of total assets to stockholders' equity) equal 2.5 and 12.5, respectively. This difference in leverage produces a 2.5 percent ROE for the manufacturer that equals only one-fifth of the 12.5 percent ROE for the bank. Alternatively, the manufacturer must generate an ROA equal to five times that for the bank, 5 percent in this example, to produce the same ROE. Leverage thus improves profitability when earnings are positive.

Whether a specific bank's capital is adequate depends on how much risk the bank assumes. Banks with low-quality assets, limited access to liquid funds, severe mismatches in asset and liability maturities and durations, or high operational risk should have more capital. Low-risk firms should be allowed to increase financial leverage.

The regulatory agencies periodically assess specific bank risks through on-site examinations. A thorough review includes an evaluation of the bank's asset quality—particularly the probability of defaults on interest and principal payments in the loan portfolio—loan review policies, interest rate risk profile, liquidity profile, cash management and internal audit procedures, and management quality. The FDIC rates banks according to the Uniform Financial Institutions Rating System, which encompasses six general categories of performance, labeled CAMELS: C = capital adequacy, A = asset quality, M = management quality, E = earnings, L = liquidity, and S = sensitivity to market risk. The FDIC numerically rates every bank on each factor, ranging from the highest quality (1) to the lowest quality (5). It also assigns a composite rating for the bank's entire operation. A composite ranking of 1 or 2 indicates a fundamentally sound bank, while a ranking of 3, 4, or 5 signifies a problem bank with some near-term potential for failure.

## WEAKNESS OF THE RISK-BASED CAPITAL STANDARDS

There are three fundamental weaknesses of the risk-based capital requirements. First, as indicated earlier, the formal standards do not account for any risks other than credit risk, except for market risk at large banks with extensive trading operations. Certainly a bank that assumes extraordinary amounts of interest rate risk in volatile rate environments, or high liquidity risk with a heavy reliance on Eurodollar or other purchased liabilities, has an abnormal chance of failing. Nevertheless, the bank's formal capital requirement is determined by its asset composition. Regulators can, of course, identify risk takers and raise required capital above the minimums, but this system is somewhat subjective and would most likely happen after problems became apparent. Furthermore, large banks subject to market risk capital requirements using a value-at-risk system report the results of their own model to the regulators. This means that regulators generally accept the model and risk assessment rather than doing their own independent evaluation. The new operational risk standards, scheduled to be implemented by 2007, are designed to directly address this weakness.

A second weakness is that the book value of capital is not the most meaningful measure of soundness. Among other problems, it ignores changes in the market value of assets, the value of unrealized gains or losses on held-to-maturity bank investments, the value of a bank charter, and the value of federal deposit insurance. Trading account securities must be marked-to-market and unrealized gains and losses must be reported on the income statement, but other bank assets and liabilities are generally listed at book value with the possible exception of bank loans. The contra-asset account, loan loss allowance, is a crude measure of anticipated default losses but does not generally take into account the change in value of the loans from changes in interest rates. In practice, book values can be manipulated through accounting ploys and often overstate the firm's true market value. Ideally, regulators would obtain and use the market value of stockholders' equity accounting for the market value of assets, liabilities, and off-balance sheet factors in monitoring a bank's risk exposure.

Third, by the end of 2004, approximately 99 percent of commercial banks and 95 percent of thrifts were considered to be well capitalized. This means, for the most part, that the risk-based capital requirements are not "binding" for almost all banks. Hence, once a bank achieves the status of "well capitalized," there are really few risk-based incentives for the bank to control risk.

A related criticism is that many banks have actually seen their capital requirements decrease under the risk-based standards. In fact, a bank with extremely low-risk assets could conceivably get by with very little capital. To see this, remember that a bank with only cash assets and short-term U.S. Treasury securities, which are zero-risk weight assets, is subject only to the minimum leverage capital ratio requirement introduced earlier (3 percent). In fact, banks that bump up against the regulatory capital minimums today often find that this leverage capital ratio is the binding one.

# THE EFFECT OF CAPITAL REQUIREMENTS ON BANK OPERATING POLICIES

Regulatory efforts to increase capital impose significant restrictions on bank operating policies. Many large banks with access to national markets can issue common stock, preferred stock, or subordinated capital notes to support continued growth and are relatively unaffected by minimum capital ratios. Smaller banks, however, do not have the same opportunities. They lack a national reputation, and investors generally shy away from purchasing their securities. These banks often rely instead on internally generated capital and find their activities constrained by a deficiency in retained earnings.

## LIMITING ASSET GROWTH

Minimum capital requirements restrict a bank's ability to grow. Additions to assets mandate additions to capital for a bank to continue to meet minimum capital-to-asset ratios imposed by regulators. Each bank must limit its asset growth to some percentage of retained earnings plus new external capital.

Consider the $100 million bank in Exhibit 9.11 that just meets the minimum 8 percent total capital requirement. Initially, the bank has $8 million in capital, of which $4 million is undivided profits and $4 million is other capital. Various effects of planned asset growth are shown in the following columns of data, which represent projections of balance sheet and income statement data for the upcoming year. The bank's initial plan, designated as Case 1, calls for 8 percent asset growth with a projected 0.99 percent ROA and 40 percent dividend payout rate. In this scenario, the bank would have $108 million in assets and $641,520 in retained earnings for the year. The 8 percent target capital ratio would be just met.

Suppose that profitable credit opportunities are available to generate 12 percent asset growth within acceptable risk limits. The last three columns of data identify three distinct strategies to grow and still meet minimum capital

## EXHIBIT 9.11

Maintaining Capital Ratios with Asset Growth: Application of Equation 9.1 and Equation 9.2

| Ratio | Initial Position | Case 1<br>Initial 8%<br>Asset<br>Growth | Case 2<br>12%<br>Growth:<br>↑ ROA | Case 3<br>12%<br>Growth:<br>↓ Dividend | Case 4<br>12%<br>Growth:<br>↑ External<br>Capital |
|---|---|---|---|---|---|
| Asset growth rate (percent) | | 8.00% | 12.00% | 12.00% | 12.00% |
| Asset size (millions of $) | 100.00 | 108.00 | 112.00 | 112.00 | 112.00 |
| ROA (percent)* | | 0.99% | 1.43% | 0.99% | 0.99% |
| Dividend payout rate (percent) | | 40.00% | 40.00% | 13.42% | 40.00% |
| Undivided profits (millions of $) | 4.00 | 4.64 | 4.96 | 4.96 | 4.665 |
| Total capital less undivided profits (millions of $) | 4.00 | 4.00 | 4.00 | 4.00 | 4.295 |
| Total capital/total assets (percent) | 8.00% | 8.00% | 8.00% | 8.00% | 8.00% |

*Application of Equation 9.2*

**Case 1:** 8% asset growth, dividend payout = 40%, and capital ratio = 8%.
    *What is ROA?*

$$0.08 = \frac{ROA(1 - 0.40) + 0}{0.08 - ROA(1 - 0.40)}$$

Solve for ROA = 0.99%

**Case 2:** 12% asset growth, dividend payout = 40%, and capital ratio = 8%.
    *What is the required ROA to support 12% asset growth?*

$$0.12 = \frac{ROA(1 - 0.40) + 0}{0.08 - ROA(1 - 0.40)}$$

Solve for ROA = 1.43%

**Case 3:** ROA = 0.99%, 12% asset growth, and capital ratio = 8%.
    *What is the required dividend payout ratio (DR) to support asset growth?*

$$0.12 = \frac{0.0099(1 - DR) + 0}{0.08 - 0.0099(1 - DR)}$$

Solve for DR = 13.42%

**Case 4:** ROA = 0.99%, 12% asset growth, capital ratio = 8%, and dividend payout = 40%.
    *What is the required increase in external capital to support 12% asset growth?*

$$0.12 = \frac{0.0099(1 - 0.40) + \Delta EC/TA_1}{0.08 - 0.0099(1 - 0.40)}$$

Solve for $\Delta EC/TA$ = 0.29%
    $\Delta EC$ = $294,720

*ROA = Return on Assets

NOTE: Equations 9.1 and 9.2 appear on the following page.

requirements. One option (Case 2) is for the bank to generate a higher ROA. This bank would need $960,000 in additional retained earnings to support the $112 million in assets:

$$\text{\$ undivided profits} = \text{total assets} \times \text{ROA} \times (1 - \text{dividend payout rate})$$
$$\$960,000 = \$112,000,000 \times 0.0143 \times (1 - 0.40)$$

Because competition prevents banks from raising yield spreads on high-quality loans, they can achieve higher returns only by acquiring riskier assets or generating greater fee income from services. This sample bank would have to increase its ROA by 0.44 basis points to 1.43 percent if it did not change its dividend policy or obtain additional capital externally. If banks substitute riskier loans for lower yielding and less risky assets, the benefit from increased profits may be offset by future loan losses or higher capital requirements.

A second option is for the bank to increase retained earnings by decreasing dividends (Case 3). In this scenario, the bank must lower its 40 percent payment rate to 13.42 percent with the same 0.99 percent ROA, to leave capital ratios unchanged. This option is often unattractive because any unanticipated dividend reduction encourages shareholders to sell stock, which lowers share prices immediately. It would then be extremely difficult and costly to issue stock anytime in the near future. The final option (Case 4) is to finance part of the asset growth with new capital, such as new common stock or perpetual preferred stock. Here the growth in retained earnings would total $665,280, so $294,720 in new external capital would be needed. Such equity is considerably more expensive than debt if the bank actually has access to the stock market.

In practice, a bank would likely pursue some combination of these strategies, or may simply choose not to grow. If the bank in this example decides not to alter its initial policies, asset growth is restricted to 12.5 (100/8) times the addition to retained earnings. In other words, each dollar of retained profits can support $12.50 in new assets.

The relationship for internally generated capital can be summarized by the following constraints.[15]

Let:  **TA** = total assets

  **EQ** = equity capital

  **ROA** = return on assets

  **DR** = dividend payout rate

  **EC** = new external capital

and the subscripts refer to the beginning of the period (1) or the end of the period (2). Capital constraints require that the asset growth rate equal the rate of growth in equity capital:

$$\Delta TA/TA_1 = \Delta EQ/EQ_1 \tag{9.1}$$

Recall that new capital comes from two sources: internal or retained earnings and external or new stock issues. Equation 9.1 can be restated as providing the following sustainable growth rate in assets when there is no new external capital:

$$\Delta TA/TA_1 = (EQ_2 - EQ_1)/EQ_1$$
$$= \frac{EQ_1 + ROA(1 - DR) \times TA_2 + \Delta EC - EQ_1}{EQ_1} \tag{9.2}$$
$$= \frac{ROA(1 - DR) + \Delta EC}{[EQ_2 - ROA(1 - DR) \times TA_2]/TA_2}$$
$$\Delta TA/TA_1 = \frac{ROA(1 - DR) + \Delta EC}{[EQ_2/TA_2 - ROA(1 - DR)]}$$

Sustainable growth can be characterized by Equation 9.3 when external capital is obtained.

$$\Delta TA/TA_1 = \frac{ROA(1 - DR) + EC/TA_2}{[EQ_2/TA2 - ROA(1 - DR)] + EC/TA_2} \tag{9.3}$$

The numerator equals ROA times the earnings retention rate plus any additions to equity from external sources.

---

[15]See the discussion by Bernon (1978). A simple approximation to Equation 9.2 is $\Delta TA/TA_1 = (ROA[1 - DR])/(TA2/EQ2)$, or the rate of asset growth equals the product of ROA, and the earnings retention rate, divided by the leverage ratio.

Equation 9.2 demonstrates the effect of minimum equity capital ratios on asset growth, earnings requirements, dividend payout rates, and new stock issues. For example, a bank that does not plan on issuing new stock and targets an 8 percent capital ratio, a 1.2 percent ROA, and a 35 percent dividend payout rate, can increase assets by more than 10.8 percent. Hence, banks without access to the capital markets can essentially grow only at the rate of growth in equity from retained earnings. If, on the other hand, the bank also obtains new external capital equal to 0.3 percent of the original assets ($300,000), asset growth can again equal 12 percent, with a 0.99 percent ROA, an 8 percent equity-to-asset ratio, and a 40 percent dividend payout rate. Equation 9.2 is applied at the bottom of Exhibit 9.10 using the data for each case.

## CHANGING THE CAPITAL MIX

Banks that choose to grow faster than the rate allowed with internally generated capital alone must raise additional capital externally. Here, large banks operate with a competitive advantage over smaller banks. In particular, large banks can obtain capital nationally through public offerings of securities. Their name recognition is high and investors willingly purchase the instruments of quality organizations. Small banks, in contrast, can generally only issue capital securities to a limited number of investors, such as existing shareholders, bank customers, and upstream correspondent banks. Limits to growth are far more rigid. One solution often pursued by small bank shareholders is to sell their stock to a holding company with greater access to funding sources.

Many large banks responded to the increased capital requirements and FDICIA by issuing new capital securities. The most popular forms were long-term debt requiring conversion to common stock and adjustable-rate, perpetual preferred stock. With the strong stock market for bank stocks during the 1992 to 1999 period, many large banks issued large volumes of common stock under shelf registration opportunities as well. Several banks also entered into sale and leaseback arrangements with bank real estate properties to generate one-time infusions of capital. This arrangement typically costs relatively little and can be easily implemented to acquire large amounts of capital. Since the late 1990s, many banks have also issued trust preferred stock, which is discussed later. The aggregate effect has been to gradually increase the proportion of total capital represented by common and preferred stock and their hybrids.

## CHANGING ASSET COMPOSITION

Banks may respond to risk-based capital requirements by changing their asset composition. Managers that are risk averse may shift assets from high-risk categories, such as commercial loans with a 100 percent risk weight, to lower-risk categories. The natural consequence is that while required risk-based capital declines, potential profitability declines as well. The fear among regulators, however, is that other banks facing higher capital requirements may actually shift assets into higher-risk categories or off-balance sheet commitments in pursuit of extraordinary returns. This would increase the overall risk profile of the banking industry in contrast to what the regulators desire.

## PRICING POLICIES

One of the advantages of risk-based capital requirements is that they explicitly recognize that some investments are riskier than others are. The riskiest investments require the greatest equity capital support. Banks have been forced to reprice assets to reflect these mandatory equity allocations. For example, if a bank has to hold capital in support of a loan commitment, it should raise the fee it charges to compensate for the greater cost of providing that service compared to the time when capital was not required. In fact, all off-balance sheet items should now be priced higher. Remember that equity is expensive. Thus, a bank should also raise loan rates on it highest risk assets that require the greatest capital relative to other asset yields.

## SHRINKING THE BANK

Historically, banks tried to circumvent capital requirements by moving assets off the books. Interest rate and product deregulation encouraged banks to transfer risks off the balance sheet by creating contingent liabilities that produce fee income but do not show up as assets in financial reports. Because off-balance sheet activity increases risk, bank regulators included off-balance sheet items in the base when calculating risk-weighted assets. In today's banking environment, the greater a bank's off-balance sheet commitments, the greater are its capital requirements. In actuality, regulators examine a bank's off-balance sheet exposure and may selectively request additional capital above the risk-based standards when the exposure is deemed to be great.

Alternatively, banks can meet the new standards by shrinking in size. As such, existing capital represents a higher fraction of the smaller asset base. The problem is that a shrinking bank has difficulty generating earnings growth and thus paying shareholders a reasonable risk-adjusted return. Not surprisingly, banks with capital problems often look to merge with stronger banks and may only survive as part of another firm.

## CHARACTERISTICS OF EXTERNAL CAPITAL SOURCES

Internally generated capital can support asset growth at a rate implied by Equations 9.2 and 9.3. Banks that choose to expand more rapidly must obtain additional capital from external sources, a capability determined by asset size. Large banks tap the capital markets regularly, but small banks must pay a stiff premium to obtain capital, if it is available at all. While there are many different types of capital sources, they can be grouped into one of five categories: subordinated debt, common stock, preferred stock, trust preferred stock, and leasing arrangement. Each carries advantages and disadvantages.

### SUBORDINATED DEBT

For the past 30 years, banks have been able to use subordinated debt to meet capital requirements. This debt constitutes capital because of its relatively long maturities and funding permanence. It does not qualify as Tier 1 or core capital because it eventually matures and must be replenished, unlike common equity. It also imposes an interest expense burden on the bank when earnings are low. Subordinated debt must possess several specific features before the regulators accept it as capital. First, debt holders' claims must be subordinated to depositors' claims. If the bank fails, insured depositors are paid first, followed by uninsured depositors, then subordinated debt holders. Second, only debt with an original weighted average maturity of at least seven years qualifies as capital.

Subordinated debt offers several advantages to banks. Most important, interest payments are tax deductible, so the cost of financing is below that for equity sources. Because they are debt instruments, shareholders do not reduce their proportionate ownership interest, and earnings are not immediately diluted. Furthermore, this type of debt generates additional profits for shareholders as long as earnings, before interest and taxes, exceeds interest payments. Thus, shareholders may receive higher dividends, and greater retained earnings may increase the capital base. Fixed-rate debt accentuates this profit potential.

Subordinated debt also has shortcomings. Interest and principal payments are mandatory and, if missed, constitute default. In addition, many issues require sinking funds that increase liquidity pressures as banks allocate funds to repay principal. Finally, from the regulators' perspective, debt is worse than equity because it has fixed maturities and banks cannot charge losses against it. Subordinated debt and equity, however, protect depositors and the FDIC equally.

Some subordinated debt pays variable rates that fluctuate with selected interest rate indexes. These securities subsequently trade close to par, as the yield changes when market rates change. Banks can pay initial rates below those for comparable fixed-rate debt because they are assuming the interest rate risk. Many bank holding companies also issue mandatory convertible debt in the form of either equity commitment notes or mandatory convertible notes. Both types require that banks issue common stock, perpetual preferred stock, or other primary capital securities to redeem the convertible debt. The average convertible debt issue carries floating rates, matures in more than ten years, and contains an option for the debtor to redeem the security anytime after four years.

### COMMON STOCK

Common stock is preferred by regulators as a source of external capital. It has no fixed maturity and thus represents a permanent source of funds. Dividend payments are also discretionary, so that common stock does not require fixed charges against earnings. Losses can be charged against equity, not debt, so common stock better protects the FDIC.

Common stock is not as attractive from the bank's perspective due to its high cost. Because dividends are not tax deductible, they must be paid out of after-tax earnings. They are also variable in the sense that shareholders expect per-share dividend rates to rise with increases in bank earnings. Transactions costs on new issues exceed comparable costs on debt, and shareholders are sensitive to earnings dilution and possible loss of control in ownership. Most firms wait until share prices are high and earnings performance is strong before selling stock. A positive feature of the Tax Reform Act of 1986 is that it makes common stock relatively more attractive to a firm than before. By lowering corporate marginal income tax rates, the act increased the cost of tax-deductible interest on debt relative to the nondeductible dividend cost of common stock.

Issuing common stock is frequently not a viable alternative for a bank that needs capital. If the current share price is far below book value, new issues dilute the ownership interests of existing shareholders. Stocks of the largest banks are traded in national markets with substantial liquidity. Bank managers attempt to increase share prices through strong earnings, consistent dividend policy, and adequate disclosure of performance to security analysts. Even with these efforts, however, stock prices often fall with adverse economic conditions or market disfavor with the industry. At these times, other capital sources are less expensive.[16] When stock prices are low, many large banks issue debt that is convertible into common stock. Investors accept lower interest payments in lieu of the option to convert the security into common stock. The conversion price is normally set 20 to 25 percent above the share price at the time of issue so that eventual conversions are not as costly.

---

[16]Many large holding company banks raise new equity by issuing securities via private placements outside the United States. They can lower underwriting fees by as much as 25 percent and shorten the length of time to place an issue.

Small bank stocks are traded over the counter, with far fewer annual transactions. Still, a market for new issues does exist within local communities. Banks can often sell new shares to existing stockholders or current customers. Share prices are less volatile, but sensitive to deviations in current versus historical earnings.

## PREFERRED STOCK

Preferred stock is a form of equity in which investors' claims are senior to those of common stockholders. As with common stock, preferred stock pays nondeductible dividends out of after-tax dollars. One significant difference is that corporate investors in preferred stock pay taxes on only 20 percent of dividends. For this reason, institutional investors dominate the market. New issues are effectively restricted to large, well-known banking organizations that are familiar to institutional investors, while smaller banks are excluded.

Since 1982, preferred stock has been an attractive source of primary capital for large banks. Most issues take the form of adjustable-rate perpetual stock. The dividend rate changes quarterly according to a Treasury yield formula. Investors earn a return equal to some spread above or below the highest of the three-month Treasury bill rate and the 10- or 20-year constant maturity Treasury rates. The size of the spread and whether it is above or below the base yield reflects the perceived quality of the issuing bank.

Investors are attracted to adjustable-rate preferred stock because they earn a yield that reflects the highest point on the Treasury yield curve under all market conditions. This removes guesswork as to whether short-term yields will move more or less than long-term yields and whether they will all move in the same direction. Unlike fixed-rate issues, these securities trade close to par and thus are more liquid. They effectively represent three-month securities and have been sold to individuals as well as corporations.

Preferred stock has the same disadvantages as common stock, but there are instances when it is more attractive. First, if a bank's common stock is priced below book value and has a low price-to-earnings ratio, new equity issues dilute earnings. This earnings dilution is less with perpetual preferred stock than with common stock, so that the cost of common shares is relatively higher. Second, aggregate dividend payments on preferred stock will be less than dividends on common stock over time for any bank that regularly increases common stock dividends. Cash flow requirements on perpetual preferred shares will also be lower because no sinking fund allocations are required to repay principal.

## TRUST PREFERRED STOCK

A recent innovation in capital financing is the introduction of **trust preferred stock**, which is a hybrid form of equity capital at banks. It is attractive because it effectively pays dividends that are tax deductible and is considered Tier 1 capital. To issue the securities, a bank or bank holding company establishes a trust company. The trust company sells preferred stock to investors and loans the proceeds of the issue to the bank. Interest on the loan equals dividends paid on the preferred stock. This loan interest is tax deductible such that the bank effectively gets to deduct dividend payments on the preferred stock. As a bonus, the preferred stock counts as Tier 1 capital under the RBC guidelines. In addition, the bank can miss a dividend payment and not be forced into bankruptcy. The net effect is that trust preferred stock costs less than common equity, but has the same value for regulatory purposes. Not surprisingly, most large banks, as well as a few community banks, have issued trust preferred stock.

## LEASING ARRANGEMENTS

Many banks enter into sale and leaseback arrangements as a source of immediate capital. Most transactions involve selling bank-owned headquarters or other real estate, and simultaneously leasing it back from the buyer. The terms of the lease can be structured to allow the bank to maintain complete control of the property, as if the title never changes hands, yet receive large amounts of cash at low cost. Lease rates run 1 to 2 percent below rates on subordinated debt. A sale-leaseback transaction effectively converts the appreciated value of real estate listed on the bank's books at cost to cash. The price appreciation is taxed at normal income tax rates, with most of the gain flowing to the bottom line as increased earnings. The transaction can be effected quickly when a buyer is located, and avoids the high placement costs of stocks and bonds.[17]

## CAPITAL PLANNING

Capital planning is part of the overall asset and liability management process. Bank management makes decisions regarding the amount of risk assumed in operations and potential returns. The amount and type of capital required is determined simultaneously with the expected composition of assets and liabilities and forecasts of income and expenses. The greater is assumed risk and asset growth, the greater is required capital.

---

[17]If the sale conforms to FASB statement #13, the operating lease does not require capitalization and the transaction further provides off-balance sheet financing.

Capital planning begins with management generating pro forma balance sheets and income statements for the next several years. The bank projects the dollar funding available from alternative deposit and nondeposit sources and the likely asset composition, given the bank's product mix and expertise. Assuming various interest rate scenarios and projections of noninterest income and expense, management forecasts earnings. Asset growth in excess of that financed with new debt or internally generated capital must be financed with external capital. Once a bank recognizes that it needs to obtain additional capital externally, it evaluates the costs and benefits of each source.

The planning process can be summarized in three steps:

1. Generate pro forma balance sheets and income statements for the bank.

2. Select a dividend payout.

3. Analyze the costs and benefits of alternative sources of external capital.

The first step provides an estimate of how much capital is needed to finance assets. Total equity capital required equals the residual between expected assets and expected debt. The amount of qualifying primary and secondary capital must be at least equal to the regulatory minimums. If management chooses to shrink the bank by liquidating assets, it may find that total capital required declines. Typically, additional equity capital is needed. Step 2 identifies how much capital will be generated internally and what amount of external capital is necessary. Dividend payments reduce the amount of retained earnings and add pressure for external capital funding. The third step involves evaluating alternatives. Management should project bank needs over several years so that it can develop a long-term plan. To be flexible, it should not rely extensively on any single source of capital in the short run, so that it can retain that option in future years. If, for example, a bank is leveraged to the maximum, it may be forced to issue new stock at a time when its share price is low. Chapter 8 introduces quantitative measures of the costs of different capital components.

## APPLICATIONS

Bank capital planning used to be a simple process. Management projected asset growth and retained earnings to show that capital ratios would be strong. Today, capital plans are typically an outgrowth of sophisticated asset and liability management planning models. They are carefully scrutinized by regulators to verify that those essential assumptions regarding asset quality, loan losses, and net interest margins are realistic. The output itself is the same pro forma balance sheet and income statement data presented in traditional performance reports. (See Chapter 2.)

Capital planning can be illustrated using the reporting framework of Exhibit 9.11. Consider a bank that has exhibited a deteriorating profit trend, classified assets and loan-loss provisions are rising, and earnings prospects are relatively bleak, given the economic environment. Assume as well that federal regulators who recently examined the bank indicated that the bank should increase its primary capital-to-asset ratio to 8.5 percent within four years from its current 7 percent.

The planning process consists of generating pro forma balance sheets and income statements over the next four years. Because regulators closely examine historical earnings and are keenly aware of asset problems, the initial pro forma statements should incorporate recent earnings trends slowly, moving the bank toward peer bank averages for key ratios. Often bankers conclude that their banks will meet capital guidelines easily because they overstate earnings. Regulators quickly point out the deficiencies and recommend substantial adjustments.

Suppose that the hypothetical bank reported the summary performance measures listed in Exhibit 9.12 for 2005. Because of asset-quality problems, the $80 million bank reported an ROA of just 0.45 percent, less than one-half its average over the past five years. The current capital ratio is 7 percent, or 1.5 percent less than the regulatory target. During each of the past five years, the bank paid $250,000 in common dividends.

The first part of Exhibit 9.12 simply extrapolates historical asset growth of 10 percent through 2009, assuming that earnings slowly rise to where ROA equals 0.75 percent in the fourth year. Under these conditions and the assumed continued dividend payout, the bank's total capital ratio would decrease to 6.1 percent by 2009. This is clearly unacceptable under the regulatory directive.

The following three parts identify different strategies to meet the required 8.5 percent capital ratio by 2009 and present summary performance measures. The second section examines the impact of shrinking the bank. The quickest way to increase a capital ratio is to reduce the denominator, or shrink the bank's asset base. Shrinkage can normally be achieved by reducing the bank's loan exposure and letting high-cost purchased liabilities run off. In this example, the bank gradually reduces its assets by $1 million per year until 2009, when the capital ratio reaches 8.54 percent. The capital ratio increases continuously because the denominator (total assets) is falling while the numerator (capital) is rising with the growth in retained earnings.

A bank can also increase its capital by cutting its dividend payments. The third section projects the bank's capital position assuming slow asset growth at $2 million annually while eliminating the $250,000 dividend payment. Retained earnings increase more than total assets, producing a capital ratio of 8.74 percent in 2009, which exceeds the target.

The final alternative proposes that the bank grow slowly and maintain its dividend, but issue $800,000 in common stock to meet its capital requirement. In this case, the bank would wait until its earnings position had

| EXHIBIT 9.12 | Capital Planning: Forecast Performance Measures for a Bank with Deficient Capital Ratios | | | | |
|---|---|---|---|---|---|

| | 2005 | 2006 | 2007 | 2008 | 2009 |
|---|---|---|---|---|---|
| **Historical 10% growth in assets: $250,000 in dividends** | | | | | |
| Total assets | $ 80.00 | $ 88.00 | $ 96.80 | $ 106.48 | $ 117.13 |
| Net interest margin | 4.40% | 4.40% | 4.50% | 4.60% | 4.70% |
| ROA | 0.45% | 0.45% | 0.60% | 0.65% | 0.75% |
| Total capital | $ 5.60 | $ 5.75 | $ 6.08 | $ 6.52 | $ 7.15 |
| Capital ratio | 7.00% | 6.53% | 6.28% | 6.12% | 6.10% |
| **Shrink the bank, reduce assets by $1 million a year: $250,000 in dividends** | | | | | |
| Total assets | $ 80.00 | $ 79.00 | $ 78.00 | $ 77.00 | $ 76.00 |
| Net interest margin | 4.40% | 4.40% | 4.50% | 4.60% | 4.70% |
| ROA | 0.45% | 0.45% | 0.60% | 0.65% | 0.75% |
| Total capital | $ 5.60 | $ 5.71 | $ 5.92 | $ 6.17 | $ 6.49 |
| Capital ratio | 7.00% | 7.22% | 7.59% | 8.02% | 8.54% |
| **Slow growth, $2 million increase in assets each year: no dividends** | | | | | |
| Total assets | $ 80.00 | $ 82.00 | $ 84.00 | $ 86.00 | $ 88.00 |
| Net interest margin | 4.40% | 4.40% | 4.50% | 4.60% | 4.70% |
| ROA | 0.45% | 0.45% | 0.60% | 0.65% | 0.75% |
| Total capital | $ 5.60 | $ 5.97 | $ 6.47 | $ 7.03 | $ 7.69 |
| Capital ratio | 7.00% | 7.28% | 7.71% | 8.18% | 8.74% |
| **Slow growth, $2 million increase in assets each year: $250,000 in dividends, $800,000 external capital injection in 2008** | | | | | |
| Total assets | $ 80.00 | $ 82.00 | $ 84.00 | $ 86.00 | $ 88.00 |
| Net interest margin | 4.40% | 4.40% | 4.50% | 4.60% | 4.70% |
| ROA | 0.45% | 0.45% | 0.60% | 0.65% | 0.75% |
| Total capital | $ 5.60 | $ 5.72 | $ 5.97 | $ 7.08 | $ 7.49 |
| Capital ratio | 7.00% | 6.97% | 7.11% | 8.23% | 8.51% |

NOTE: Figures are in millions of dollars.

improved sufficiently, 2008 in this pro forma, before issuing external capital. Again, the projected capital ratio just exceeds the regulatory target by 2009.

In practice, a bank's asset and liability management committee will consider numerous other alternatives by varying assumptions until it determines the best plan. What is best depends on a comparison of the costs of each alternative. Eliminating dividends, for example, reduces stock prices and makes it extremely difficult and costly to raise external capital later. If the bank plans to add capital externally, it must carefully measure placement costs and their subsequent impact on share prices. For instance, if a bank issues subordinated debt, it must estimate the direct transactions costs and set aside a portion of future cash flows to service the debt. The same would apply to common stock issues and dividend payments.

# FEDERAL DEPOSIT INSURANCE

The Banking Act of 1933 established the FDIC and authorized federal insurance for bank deposits up to $2,500. The Federal Savings and Loan Insurance Corporation (FSLIC) was established in 1934 to replicate federal assistance for savings and loan associations.[18] Both insurance funds were financed via premiums paid by member banks. Fund expenses included operating costs and payouts mandated when banks failed and regulators paid insured depositors.

The Banking Act of 1933 followed three years in which more than 5,000 banks failed and investors lost confidence in the country's financial system. There were approximately 4,000 failures in 1933 alone. The initial objectives of deposit insurance were to prevent liquidity crises caused by large-scale deposit withdrawals and to protect depositors of modest means against a bank failure. With insurance, depositors' funds were safe, even if the bank failed.

Federal deposit insurance facilitated stability in the U.S. financial system throughout its early history and worked well until the early 1980s. There were few depositor runs on federally insured banks and bank failures were

---

[18]The National Credit Union Share Insurance Fund (NCUSIF) insures credit unions.

**EXHIBIT 9.13**  FDIC Reserve Ratios, Fund Balance, and Insured Deposits

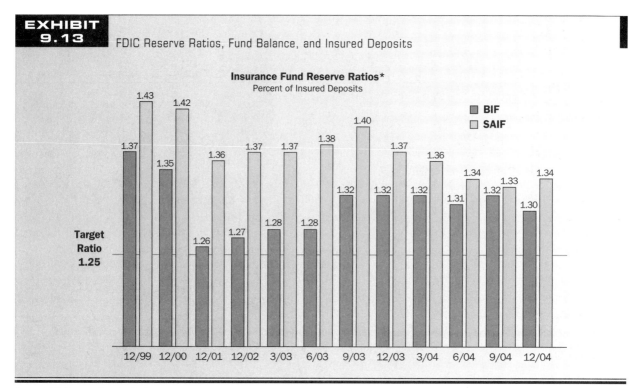

**Insurance Fund Reserve Ratios***
Percent of Insured Deposits

BIF
SAIF

Target Ratio 1.25

12/99  12/00  12/01  12/02  3/03  6/03  9/03  12/03  3/04  6/04  9/04  12/04

Source: FDIC Quarterly Banking Profile, http://www.fdic.gov.

Insurance fund balance as a percent of total insured deposits.

negligible. In fact, during the period from 1950 to 1980, fewer than seven banks failed, on average, each year. After 1980, however, bank failures increased once again and there were 280 bank failures in 1988. In the 1980s, so many savings and loans failed or were taken over by solvent firms with federal assistance that the FSLIC fund was bankrupt by the end of the decade. The FDIC insurance fund had similar problems, and was depleted by 1990. Exhibit 9.13 shows the condition of the FDIC fund same year end 1999. Over this period, few banks have failed. Those that have failed generally had exposure in subprime (high-risk) lending and often were heavily involved in credit cards and securitizations.

The large number of failures in the late 1980s and early 1990s put pressure on the FDIC by slowly depleting the reserve fund. As indicated in Chapter 1 the Financial Institution Reform, Recovery and Enforcement Act of 1989 (FIRREA) authorized the issuance of bonds to finance the bailout of the FSLIC and provide resources to close problem thrifts. The act also created two new insurance funds, the Savings Association Insurance Fund (SAIF) and the Bank Insurance Fund (BIF), to replace the old funds; both were controlled by the FDIC. The FIRREA further created the Resolution Trust Corporation to handle failed thrifts.

To make the insurance funds solvent, federal regulators increased bank deposit insurance premiums to $0.23 per $100 of insured deposits to keep pace with losses from closing failed institutions. During 1991 and 1992, the bank fund ran a deficit and had to borrow from the Treasury. FDICIA authorized risk-based deposit insurance premiums ranging from $0.23 to $0.27 per $100 depending on a bank's capital position. By 1993, the reduction in failures and increased premiums allowed the FDIC to pay off the debt and put the fund back in the black.

The Deposit Insurance Funds Act of 1996 (DIFA) was enacted on September 30, 1996, and had three main components:

- Included both a one-time assessment on SAIF deposits to capitalize the SAIF fund to the mandated 1.25 percent reserve ratio (insurance reserves to insured deposits)
- Required the repayment of the Financing Corporation (FICO) bonds to be shared by both banks and thrifts
- Mandated the ultimate elimination of the BIF and SAIF funds by merging them into a new Deposit Insurance Fund[19]

---

[19]The BIF and SAIF were supposed to merge effective January 1, 1999, subject to the condition that no insured savings association existed on this date. The merger was postponed indefinitely because insured savings associations still exist and the thrift charter has considerable value beyond a bank charter.

Deposit insurance assessment rates (insurance premiums) for some SAIF members fell to zero for the first time on January 1, 1997. It is anticipated, under current favorable conditions, that FDIC investment earnings will be sufficient to cover each fund's expenses for the near future, so that most banks and savings and loans will pay no deposit insurance premiums. Assessment rates in 2004 were zero for the lowest risk banks, which constituted approximately 93 percent of banks. The FDIC's risk-based premium system, however, still requires institutions not in the most favorable category to pay assessments.

## RISK-BASED DEPOSIT INSURANCE

FDIC insurance premiums are assessed based on a risk-based deposit insurance system—required by the FDIC Improvement Act of 1991 and adopted in September 1992. Deposit insurance assessment rates for both BIF and SAIF are reviewed semiannually by the FDIC to ensure that premiums appropriately reflect the risks posed to the insurance funds and that fund reserve ratios are maintained at or above the target Designated Reserve Ratio (DRR) of 1.25 percent of insured deposits. Deposit insurance premiums are assessed as basis points per $100 of insured deposits.[20]

Annual assessment rates for insured depository institutions are assigned based on an assessment of risk using a risk classification system. Each institution's assessment risk classification is composed of two parts: a capital adequacy group and supervisory subgroup. Each institution is first assigned to one of three capital groups—well capitalized, adequately capitalized, and undercapitalized (the three lower capital categories)—using the minimum capital ratios in Exhibit 9.9. Within each capital group, each institution is assigned to one of three subgroups based on supervisory evaluations provided by the institution's primary federal regulator. The three supervisory subgroups are:

**Subgroup A:** Financially sound institutions with only a few minor weaknesses. This subgroup assignment generally corresponds to the primary federal regulator's composite rating of "1" or "2."

**Subgroup B:** Institutions that demonstrate weaknesses that, if not corrected, could result in significant deterioration of the institution and increased risk of loss to the BIF or SAIF. This subgroup assignment generally corresponds to the primary federal regulator's composite rating of "3."

**Subgroup C:** Institutions that pose a substantial probability of loss to the BIF or the SAIF unless effective corrective action is taken. This subgroup assignment generally corresponds to the primary federal regulator's composite rating of "4" or "5."[21]

Based on this system, there are nine different risk categories. The current assessment rate schedule for BIF-insured and SAIF-insured institutions is as follows:

| Capital Group | Supervisory Subgroups | | |
|---|---|---|---|
| | **A** | **B** | **C** |
| 1. Well capitalized | 0 bp | 3 bp | 17 bp |
| 2. Adequately capitalized | 3 bp | 10 bp | 24 bp |
| 3. Undercapitalized | 10 bp | 24 bp | 27 bp |

Approximately 93 percent of all BIF-insured institutions are currently listed in the lowest-risk category and pay no assessment. The BIF reserve ratio (fund balance to estimated insured deposits) was 1.30 percent in December 2004, while the SAIF reserve ratio stood at 1.34 percent. Based upon the latest available data and projections from the FDIC, the existing rate schedule was expected to maintain the fund reserve ratios at or above the target DRR through year-end 2004.

## PROBLEMS WITH DEPOSIT INSURANCE

Government-backed deposit insurance provides for stability of the financial system by reducing or preventing banking panics and protecting the less sophisticated depositor—but this come at a price. First, deposit insurance acts similarly to bank capital and is a substitute for some functions of bank capital. In noninsured industries, investors or depositors look to the company's capital as a safety net in the event of failure. All else being equal, lower capital levels mean that the company must pay a risk premium to attract funds or it will find it very difficult, if not impossible, to borrow money. In banking, a large portion of borrowed funds comes from insured depositors who do not look to the bank's capital position in the event of default, but rather to the FDIC insurance fund. A large number of depositors, therefore, do not require a risk premium to be paid by the bank. Normal market discipline in which higher risk requires the bank to pay a risk premium does not apply to all providers of funds.

---

[20]Recall that a basis point equals 1/100 of one percent. An FDIC assessment of 20 basis points amount to 20 cents per $100 of insured deposits, or 0.2 percent.

[21]Details of the FDIC assessment procedures can be found on the FDIC Web site at http://www.fdic.gov (http://www.fdic.gov/deposit/insurance).

## CONTEMPORARY ISSUES

### REGULATORY POLICY TOWARD LARGE BANK FAILURES

In July 1988, bank regulators declared First RepublicBank Corporation of Texas insolvent and turned over management of its subsidiary banks to NCNB. In contrast to prior failures of large bank holding companies, the terms of closing wiped out the claims of all stockholders and left bondholders to fight with other creditors for the remains of the holding company. Regulators used a bridge bank to handle the closing, which fostered numerous lawsuits claiming that the rights of investors in First RepublicBank were violated. Consider the following sequence of events:

- March 17, 1988: The FDIC loaned $1 billion to First RepublicBank Corporation to help meet deposit outflows. This was a six-month loan secured by stock in each of First RepublicBank's subsidiary banks.
- July 29, 1988: The FDIC announced that it would not renew the six-month loan when it came due in September. As prearranged, the Federal Reserve advised First RepublicBank that it would refuse to lend any additional funds via the discount window and the bank would have to repay the $3.5 billion it owed. Because First RepublicBank could not pay, the Office of the Comptroller of the Currency declared that the bank had formally failed. The FDIC then called its $1 billion loan. When First Republic-Bank did not pay, the FDIC charged the amount of each subsidiary bank's guarantee against its capital, which then made each subsidiary bank insolvent.

- July 29, 1988: The FDIC created a bridge bank owned jointly with NCNB that took over and managed the failed subsidiary banks. NCNB paid approximately $200 million for 20 percent ownership with the right to buy the remaining 80 percent over the next five years. NCNB retained the right to put problem loans back to the FDIC so that its risk was lowered, and received enough federal tax benefits to pay for the entire bridge bank in a few years.
- October 15, 1988: In a bankruptcy filing, First RepublicBank indicated that it had $3.5 billion in liabilities and just $300,000 in assets.

In March 1989, bank regulators failed several subsidiary banks of MCorp, another large Texas bank holding company. Although the events followed the same pattern as with First RepublicBank, MCorp's managers essentially held the regulators hostage. Prior to the failures, MCorp's problems were well known. Regulators had strongly encouraged the holding company to downstream $400 million in funds to its subsidiary banks to shore up its capital. MCorp.'s management realized that once it made the transfer the regulators would fail the firm and it would lose any leverage it had in negotiating its own failure resolution plan. The holding company thus did not transfer the $400 million. Eventually, the regulators called loans to the holding company's lead bank and charged the losses when it could not pay to MCorp.'s subsidiaries based on their federal funds loans to the lead bank and other interbank deposits. The 20 subsidiaries with losses in excess of their capital subsequently failed and were taken over by the FDIC. Again the FDIC created a bridge bank that was soon sold to Bank One.

Bondholders and other creditors sued, claiming that the regulators discriminated against the bank's creditors and effectively manufactured the failures of solvent subsidiary banks. As part of FIRREA, Congress, in turn, instituted a system of cross guarantees where subsidiaries of bank holding companies must effectively guarantee the performance of all other subsidiaries.

---

In addition to insured depositors, many large banks are considered to be **"too-big-to-fail"** (TBTF). As such, any creditor of a large bank would receive de facto 100 percent insurance coverage regardless of the size or type of liability.[22] This means that depositors at large banks most likely know that they have de facto 100 percent coverage and would not be as concerned about the bank's capital cushion. Hence, the larger the coverage and scope of deposit insurance, the less capital the market would demand the bank hold. See the Contemporary Issues Box: "Regulatory Policy Toward Large Bank Failures."

Second, deposit insurance has historically ignored the riskiness of a bank's operations, which represents the critical factor that leads to failure. Thus, two banks with equal amounts of domestic deposits paid the same insurance premium, even though one invested heavily in risky loans and had no uninsured deposits, while the other owned only U.S. government securities and just 50 percent of its deposits were fully insured. This created a **moral hazard** problem whereby bank managers had an incentive to increase risk. For example, suppose that a bank had a large portfolio of problem assets that was generating little revenue. Managers could use deposit insurance to ac-

---

[22]The Federal Deposit Insurance Corporation Improvement Act (FDICIA) addressed the issue of TBTF but allows for full protection when regulators determine that the bank's failure could significantly impair the rest of the industry and the overall economy.

cess funds via brokered CDs in $100,000 blocks. Buyers of the CDs were not concerned about the quality of the underlying bank because their funds were fully insured, hence they did not impose market discipline in the form of higher rates to be paid for additional risk. The bank's managers were able to use these funds to speculate on risky projects, in essence, betting the bank. If the risky investments succeeded, managers could use the returns to pay the depositors and offset the lack of revenue from the problem assets. In fact, if the bank obtained enough deposits, it could make enough loans to swamp the problem assets. If the risky investments went bankrupt, the bank would fail, but the deposit insurance fund would have to pay creditors.[23]

Third, deposit insurance funds were always viewed as providing basic insurance coverage. Yet there were three fundamental problems with the pricing of deposit insurance. First, premium levels were not sufficient to cover potential payouts. The FDIC and FSLIC were initially expected to establish reserves amounting to 5 percent of covered deposits funded by premiums. Unfortunately, actual reserves never exceeded 2 percent of insured deposits as Congress kept increasing coverage while insurance premiums remained constant. For example, the standard insurance premium was a flat one-twelfth of 1 percent of insured deposits. Yet deposit insurance coverage slowly increased from $15,000 per account per institution in 1966 to $20,000 in 1969, $40,000 in 1974, and $100,000 in 1980. Even then, customers could obtain multiple account coverage at any single institution by carefully structuring ownership of each account. The high rate of failures during the 1980s and the depleted insurance funds demonstrate that premiums were inadequate.

The final historical problem with deposit insurance is that premiums were not assessed against all of a bank's insured liabilities. There were many liabilities that the federal government effectively guaranteed, or holders had a prior claim on bank assets, that should have required insurance premiums. For example, insured deposits consisted only of domestic deposits while foreign deposits were exempt. Why? If a large bank failure would severely disrupt the smooth functioning of financial markets, regulators would allow de facto 100 percent insurance coverage regardless of the size or type of liability. This too-big-to-fail doctrine toward large banks meant that large banks would have coverage on 100 percent of their deposits but pay for the same coverage as if they only had $100,000 coverage as smaller banks do. This means that regulators were much more willing to fail smaller banks and force uninsured depositors and other creditors to take losses. If a bank's liabilities were covered by federal insurance, the firm should have paid insurance premiums. The argument for not charging premiums against foreign deposits is that U.S. banks would be less competitive with foreign bank competitors.

## WEAKNESS OF THE CURRENT RISK-BASED DEPOSIT INSURANCE SYSTEM

Risk-based deposit insurance has addressed some, but not all, of these issues. First, the risk-based deposit system is based on capital and risk. Hence, banks that hold higher capital, everything else equal, pay lower premiums. Lower-risk banks pay lower premiums. Since approximately 93 percent of all BIF-insured institutions are currently listed in the lowest-risk category, they pay no assessment. Consequently, 93 percent of all banks pay a flat-rate assessment that was zero in 2005.

The second issue is that of too-big-to-fail. The FDIC must follow the "least cost" alternative in the resolution of a failed bank. As such, the FDIC must consider all alternatives and choose the one that is the lowest cost to the insurance fund. This practice has definitely lead to a reduction of coverage of uninsured depositors. Exhibit 9.14 demonstrates that in the late 1980s and early 1990s, the FDIC provided protection to more than 80 percent of the uninsured assets at failed commercial banks. In contrast, many fewer uninsured assets have been covered since 1991.

FDICIA, however, still allows for the coverage of uninsured deposits, as indicated by the solid bars in Exhibit 9.14, which represent the proportion of failed banks where uninsured deposits were paid in full at failure. FDICIA provides for full coverage if the Secretary of the Treasury determines that the least cost alternative would have serious adverse effects on financial stability or economic conditions and that 100 percent coverage would avoid or reduce these effects. The decrease requires approval of two-thirds of the Board of Governors of the Federal Reserve System and two-thirds of the directors of the FDIC.

## BASEL II CAPITAL STANDARDS

The original Basel I Accord's approach to capital requirements was primarily based on credit risk. Although it set appropriate protections from a market- and credit-risk perspective, it did not specifically address other types of risk. Operational risk, for example, is not new to financial institutions but it's the first risk a bank must manage, even before making its first loan or executing its first trade.

In June 2004, the Basel Committee on Banking Supervision proposed changes in regulatory capital requirements for all commercial banks in the industrialized world. The objective was to strengthen the safety and soundness of the international banking system and ensure that capital regulation would not be anticompetitive for banks

---

[23]This represents a classic principal/agent problem in finance. The intent of bank regulation and periodic examination is to limit bank risk taking and reduce the incentives of deposit insurance.

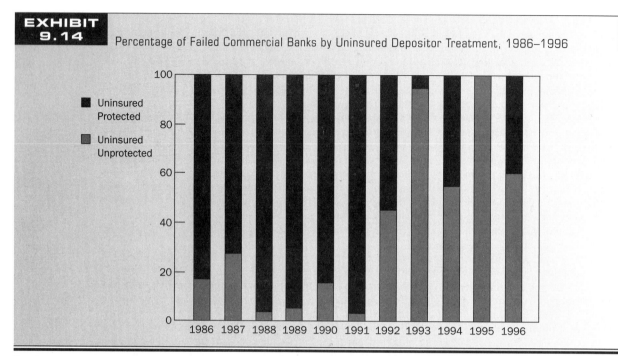

**EXHIBIT 9.14**

Percentage of Failed Commercial Banks by Uninsured Depositor Treatment, 1986–1996

NOTE: Percentage of banks by assets.

SOURCE: Ron J. Feldman and Arthur J. Rolnic, "Fixing FDICIA," 1997 *Annual Report,* Federal Reserve Bank of Minneapolis, (March 1998). Available on the Internet at http://woodrow.mpls.frb.fed/pubs/ar/ar1997.html.

across countries. The proposals are based on three pillars of regulation: minimum capital requirements, supervisory review, and market discipline. The real impetus is that banks have experienced dramatic changes in risk and risk management practices since the early 1990s and capital regulation was lagging.

There is still a general requirement that banks maintain minimum capital equal to at least 8 percent of risk-weighted assets. Generally, a bank's capital requirements are based on assessments of credit risk, operational risk, and trading book (market) risk. Importantly, banks will be forced to explicitly recognize operational risk, or potential losses arising from "inadequate or failed internal processes, people, and systems, or from external events."[24] Perhaps the most significant change is that regulators will now allow the largest institutions to use their own internal risk assessment systems as inputs in the capital calculations. There are also specific guidelines regarding how banks should treat expected losses and unexpected losses and risks associated with securitizations.

## CREDIT RISK

Banks are allowed to choose between two approaches to calculate minimum capital in support of credit risk. The standardized approach requires banks to obtain external credit assessments, such as those from rating agencies, of their credit exposures. The alternative methodology, which requires supervisory approval, allows banks to use their own internal rating systems. In either case, the same type of risk weighting applies, but the relevant risk weights may now exceed 100 percent, such as in the case of low-quality (BB- and below rated) claims. Off-balance sheet exposures are again converted to balance sheet equivalent exposures. Importantly, securitized assets that embody credit risk require capital support. Banks that use the internal ratings-based (IRB) approach must include measures of the probability of default, loss given default, the exposure of default, and effective maturity for given exposures. Risk weights are applied to unexpected losses while expected losses are subject to explicit requirements.

## OPERATIONAL RISK

Basel Committee defines **operational risk** as the risk of loss resulting from inadequate or failed internal processes, people, and systems, or from external events. From a capital adequacy point of view, this covers technology risks, management- and people-related operational risks, and legal risks. The new accord's focus on these areas is comprehensive.

[24]See "Sound Practices for the Management and Supervision of Operational Risk," Basel Committee on Banking Supervision, http://www.bis.org/publ/bcbs96.pdf

Banks with relatively limited operational risk (they do not do check processing in bulk and do not have significant international activity) can use a basic indicator approach in which they hold capital equal to a moving average of annual (positive) gross income in support of operational risk. To qualify for the basic approach, management and the board of directors must demonstrate appropriate oversight of operational risk and have a conceptually sound risk measurement system in place. Banks with more complex operations calculate capital requirements for each line of business based on estimated gross income from each business. Total required capital for operational risk then equals the sum of the requirements across lines of business. Banks with significant operational risk exposures must use an advanced measurement approach based on perceived risks across lines of business.

## TRADING BOOK (INCLUDING MARKET RISK)

A bank's trading book consists of its positions in tradable instruments, such as stocks, bonds, commodities, currencies, etc., that are generally held for short periods of time with the intent of making a profit. Management must demonstrate an ability to value the positions with an emphasis on marking-to-market exposures. Capital requirements are based on the value of the positions by type of underlying instrument. Trading book capital requirements should be negligible for community banks and those without significant market risk.

## SUPERVISORY REVIEW AND MARKET DISCIPLINE

For capital requirements to be effective, there must be a comprehensive system of supervisory review. The Basel Committee sites four key principles: 1) banks should have a process for assessing overall capital adequacy in relation to their risk profile and a strategy for maintaining their capital levels; 2) supervisors should review and evaluate banks' internal capital adequacy assessments and strategies; 3) supervisors should expect banks to operate with capital above the minimum regulatory ratios; and 4) supervisors should intervene at an early stage to prevent capital from falling below regulatory minimums. Such principles should be applied particularly as they relate to the monitoring of interest rate risk and credit risk.

Finally, the Basel Committee expects that regulators will encourage market discipline for banks by forcing disclosure of key information pertaining to risk. In particular, the committee recommends that market participants be provided information regarding specific risk exposures, risk assessment practices, actual capital, and required capital so that they can assess the adequacy of capital. Such disclosure is necessarily linked to accounting requirements such that minimal accounting information must be provided before market participants can understand the risk exposures of large, complex organizations.

## SUMMARY

This chapter addresses eight basic issues: What are the features of the risk-based capital standards? What constitutes bank capital? How did FDICIA use capital standards to control bank activities? What function does capital serve? How much capital is adequate? What effect do regulatory capital requirements have on bank operating policies? What considerations are important in capital planning? And finally, how are FDIC deposit insurance and bank capital related?

Bank capital fulfills three primary functions: It serves as a cushion against loan losses and helps protect the interests of depositors and the FDIC. It provides access to financial markets so that management can borrow to offset liquidity problems. It also limits growth by forcing banks to add capital in support of asset expansion. Each purpose serves to reduce bank risk directly, and ultimately to protect the viability of the deposit insurance funds.

Because of these functions, federal regulators consider bank capital to be much broader than accounting capital. Regulatory capital, therefore, includes certain debt and loan loss reserve components. Effective in 1992, the FDIC, OCC, and Federal Reserve System changed bank capital standards to conform uniformly to risk-based capital requirements. Each bank must hold common equity as a minimum 4 percent of risk-weighted assets and total capital cannot fall below 8 percent of risk-weighted assets. For the first time, regulators tied capital requirements to the perceived default risk of bank assets and off-balance sheet commitments.

The passage of FDICIA in 1991 further categorized banks as being well capitalized, adequately capitalized, or undercapitalized, and imposed operating restrictions on undercapitalized institutions. This act, and the specific minimum capital requirements, forced banks to slow growth, limit their loan exposure, change their asset composition, and find new methods of generating profits and obtaining external capital during the early 1990s. Capital levels increased dramatically in the late 1990s, due to good profitability, such that risk-based capital requirements have not recently been binding. A final impact is that banks now actively prepare and analyze capital plans as part of their annual risk-return performance review.

Finally, in 2004 the Basel Committee on Banking Supervision recommended new capital requirements to apply to all banks in the industrialized world. While the provisions will be modified and implemented after 2006, the committee tried to strengthen capital requirements given the different risk exposures of large and small banks, and the wide range of differences in risk management systems. The net effect is that large banks will be able to use internally based risk assessment systems in setting capital requirements. Small banks will follow rules comparable to those in place today.

## QUESTIONS

1. What are the advantages and disadvantages of using financial leverage? Answer from the banker's view and then from a bank regulator's view.

2. Provide the general outline of existing risk-based capital requirements. Is there a difference between default risk, interest rate risk, and liquidity risk?

3. Explain how capital reduces banking risks. Discuss the importance of cash flows and economic (market) value rather than accounting value.

4. Many analysts argue that risk-based capital requirements should force banks to raise loan rates. Explain this by assuming that a bank's management sets loan rates to earn a 16 percent return on equity. How does the allocation of equity to a loan affect loan pricing?

5. Suppose that a bank wants to grow during the next year but does not want to issue any new external capital. Its current financial plan projects a return on assets of 1.25 percent, a dividend payout rate of 35 percent, and an equity-to-asset ratio of 8 percent. Calculate the allowable growth in the bank's assets supported by these projections. What growth rate could be supported if the bank issued additional common stock equal to 1 percent of bank assets, with the same earnings projections?

6. Many regulators would like to see bank capital requirements raised. Consider a proposal to increase the minimum Tier 1 and total capital ratios to 6 percent and 12 percent, respectively. What impact would this have on bank risk? Would small banks and large banks have equal opportunity in meeting these requirements? What impact would this have on banking industry consolidation?

7. Regulators put great pressure on banks to reduce their common dividend payments when asset problems appear. Discuss the costs and benefits of cutting dividends.

8. Two competing commercial banks situated in the same community have comparable asset portfolios, but one operates with a total capital ratio of 8 percent, while the other operates with a ratio of 10 percent. Compare the opportunities and risk profiles of the two banks.

9. Explain why increased regulatory capital requirements lead to a greater consolidation of banking firms via mergers and acquisitions.

10. Risk-based capital requirements may induce bank managers to change their asset composition. Explain why. Determine how a shift from any of the following should affect a bank's required capital. How will each shift affect the bank's profit potential?

    a. From consumer loans to 1–4 family mortgages

    b. From U.S. agency securities to construction loans

    c. From FNMA-sponsored mortgage-backed securities to municipal revenue bonds

11. A bank has decided it must raise external capital. Discuss the advantages and disadvantages of each of the following choices:

    a. Subordinated debt at 7.7 percent

    b. Preferred stock at a 10 percent dividend yield

    c. Common stock

12. What is the leverage capital ratio and why do regulators specify a minimum for it?

13. FDICIA imposes increasingly severe operating restrictions on undercapitalized banks (those in zones 3, 4, and 5). Explain why these restrictions are appropriate. Describe how managers should respond to these restrictions if they manage an undercapitalized bank.

14. Although FDICIA calls for risk-based insurance premiums, why do many argue that we still have a flat deposit insurance system?

15. Some analysts believe that the new Basel II minimum capital requirements favor the largest financial institutions. Assume that the largest banks that use their own internal-assessment framework to determine capital needs can effectively lower their capital requirements by 20 percent versus other banks. Discuss the competitive advantages this provides and the likely impact on the structure of banking markets.

## PROBLEMS

## I. FIRST STUDENT BANK

First Student Bank (FSB) has the following balance sheet:

| Assets | | Liabilities and Equity | |
|---|---|---|---|
| Cash | $100 | Transactions accounts | $700 |
| Treasury bills (30 days) | $190 | CDs | $220 |
| Treasury bonds (5 years) | $30 | Subordinated debt | $7 |
| Repos | $10 | Preferred stock | $5 |
| Student tuition loans | $500 | Retained earnings | $48 |
| Student home mortgages | $100 | Common stock | $5 |
| Building and furniture | $110 | Surplus | $15 |
| Loan loss reserves | $(40) | | |
| Total | $1,000 | Total | $1,000 |

The bank is only two years old and is desperately trying to break into the local market for student loans. Consequently, it has followed the policy of guaranteeing tuition loans for three additional years to every student who promptly paid off his or her first-year loan. This policy has been a success, and the bank has signed agreements guaranteeing $800 in loans. The bank has also tried to encourage the building of 1–4 family homes near campus. The bank is willing to lend money on these properties and to commit to repurchasing the homes when the students graduate. The repurchase price is settled at the time the mortgage is written, such that the whole package is expected to be profitable for the bank. Currently, the bank has obligated itself to spend $75 to repurchase homes.

1. This is a student-owned-and-run bank and does not operate in international markets. Does it need to comply with the risk-based capital rules?

2. How many dollars of common equity capital does this bank have? How many dollars of Tier 1 capital does it have?

3. How many dollars of total capital does this bank have?

4. Categorize the bank's assets by risk category. How many dollars of Category 1 assets, Category 2 assets, and so on, does the bank have?

5. How many dollars of contingencies does this bank have (after applying the appropriate conversion factor)?

6. How many dollars of risk-weighted assets does FSB own?

7. Does FSB have adequate Tier 1 capital? Adequate total capital?

## II. ONE-YEAR BANK GROWTH

Consider a bank with $500 million in assets and $30 million in total capital. Its *minimum* total capital-to-asset ratio must equal 6 percent. At the beginning of the year, senior management and the board of directors project that the bank will likely earn 0.86 percent on assets, will pay a 30 percent dividend, and will not obtain any external capital. In this environment, how large can the bank grow by the end of the year?

1. Assume that the bank would like to grow its assets by 15 percent during the year. If the dividend rate is 30 percent and no external capital is obtained, what must the bank's ROA equal?

2. Assume that the bank wants to grow assets by 15 percent with an ROA of 0.85 percent, and will not obtain external capital. What dividend payout rate will support 15 percent growth? What are the costs and benefits of changing dividends in this direction?

3. What increase in external capital is necessary to support 15 percent asset growth with ROA equal to 0.85 percent and a dividend payout rate of 30 percent?

# PART V

# EXTENDING CREDIT TO BUSINESSES AND INDIVIDUALS

# Overview of Credit Policy and Loan Characteristics

*For most people in commercial banking, lending represents the heart of the industry. Loans are the dominant asset at most banks, generate the largest share of operating income, and represent the bank's greatest risk exposure. Loan officers are among the most visible bank employees and a bank's loan policies will often have a dramatic impact on how fast a community grows and what types of businesses develop.*

*Over time, increased competition among commercial banks, savings banks, credit unions, finance companies, and investment banks has lead to changes in lending policies and loan portfolios. Following World War II through the 1970s, commercial banks controlled commercial lending in the United States. When confronted with earnings pressure, they often raised loan-to-asset ratios by extending credit to marginal borrowers in the search for higher returns. Increasing loan losses necessarily followed, in many cases causing banks to fail. The credit environment during the 1980s and early 1990s consisted of too many high-risk loans, historically high loan losses, and aggressive pricing, which produced low risk-adjusted returns. Not surprisingly, banks in the aggregate reduced the size of their loan portfolios and substituted marketable securities. In 1992 bank investment securities were 22 percent of total assets and net loans were down to 56 percent of total assets. As the U.S. economy moved out of the recession, banks slowly grew their loan portfolios along with the growth in consumer confidence and spending. Loans, as a percent of assets, peaked in 1997 at just over 61 percent of assets but then began to decline as the Federal Reserve raised concerns about the long-term viability of the economy. As the U.S. and world economies entered a recession toward the end of 2001, bank loans continued the decline to 57.4 percent of bank assets by 2004. Loan to asset ratios again increased in 2005.*

*Many banks pursue different lending strategies and concentrate on niches in which they restrict new loans to well-defined markets where they have specialized experience. They consciously limit growth in hopes of building capital to support future expansion. At one end, some larger banks have gravitated toward investment banking, underwriting securities and making loans, but moving the loans off-balance sheet by selling them to other investors and earning a profit from servicing fees. Other banks see loan growth as their primary path to long-term survival and aggressively court new consumer and commercial business. Many hope to eventually be allowed to make an equity investment in some of the companies to which they currently lend.*

*This chapter provides an overview of the credit process and the types of credit extended by commercial banks. It describes recent problems banks have faced in certain credit areas and issues related to default risk and interest rate risk.*

## RECENT TRENDS IN LOAN GROWTH AND QUALITY

Commercial banks extend credit to different types of borrowers for many different purposes. For most customers, bank credit is the primary source of available debt financing. For banks, good loans are the most profitable assets. As with any investment, extending loans to businesses and individuals involves taking risks to earn high returns. Returns come in the form of loan interest, fee income, and investment income from new deposits. Banks also use loans to cross sell other fee-generating services. The most prominent assumed risk is credit risk. Many factors can lead to loan defaults. An entire industry, such as energy, agriculture, or real estate, can decline because of general economic events. Firm-specific problems may arise from changing technology, labor strikes, shifts in consumer preferences, or bad management. Individual borrowers find that their ability to repay closely follows the business cycle as personal income rises and falls. Loans as a group thus exhibit the highest charge-offs among bank assets, so banks regularly set aside substantial reserves against anticipated losses.

Interest rate risk also arises from credit decisions. Loan maturities, pricing, and the form of principal repayment affect the timing and magnitude of a bank's cash inflows. Floating-rate and variable-rate loans, for example, generate cash flows that vary closely with variable borrowing costs. Fixed-rate balloon payment loans, in contrast, generate fewer cash inflows. Longer-term consumer loans need to be funded with stable deposits to reduce exposure to rate changes.

Loans are the dominant asset in most banks' portfolios, representing on average 50 to 75 percent of total assets. Loan composition varies greatly among banks depending on size, location, trade area, and lending expertise. Exhibit 10.1 summarizes proportionate differences among general loan categories for different-sized banks at the end of 2004. Although lending practices can and do vary significantly for similar-sized banks, several characteristics stand out. First, the ratio of net loans to assets is greatest at 66.4 percent for banks with $100 million to $1 billion in assets and for savings institutions. The largest banks have, on average, reduced their dependence on loans relative to smaller banks. This indicates that many of the largest banks have begun to focus on non-credit products and services that generate noninterest income as the primary source of revenue. Second, real estate loans represent the largest single loan category for all banks and is highest for savings banks. Over time, real estate loans continue to represent an increasing portion of bank loans. Third, residential 1–4 family loans (mostly mortgage products) contribute the largest amount of real estate loans for almost all commercial banks, but commercial real estate is largest for banks with $100 million to $1 billion in assets. Fourth, commercial and industrial loans represent the second highest concentration of loans at banks. Fifth, loans to individuals are greatest for banks with more than $1 billion in assets, but contribute proportionately less elsewhere. Sixth, farmland and farm loans make up a significant portion of the smallest banks' loans but are negligible at larger banks. Seventh, banks invest from 5 to 11.2 percent of their assets to finance consumer expenditures. Finally, other loans and leases are significant only at the largest banks. Other loans include primarily loans to other financial institutions, international loans, and lease receivables.

One popular way to categorize banks is by their orientation to business or individual borrowers. Those that emphasize large business lending are labeled **wholesale banks** while those that emphasize lending to individuals are labeled **retail banks.** Of course, most banks make loans to both types of borrowers, so the distinction is one of degrees. Recently the FDIC began categorizing banks and other insured institutions into one of nine categories based on their asset concentrations: credit card banks, international banks, agricultural banks, commercial lenders, mortgage lenders, consumer lenders, other specialized banks less than $1 billion, all other banks less than $1 billion, all other banks greater than $1 billion. Exhibit 10.2 demonstrates key differences in loan concentrations, loan charge-offs and aggregate returns across these business models. The vast majority of FDIC-insured institutions are classified as commercial lenders. Agricultural banks and banks with no clear asset concentration (all others less than $1 billion) are a distant second. Interestingly, only five banks specialize in international lending and only 34 institutions concentrate on credit card lending. Even though the commercial lending concentration makes up the majority of institutions, this group also makes a wide variety of loans. Credit card banks' assets are, however, concentrated in loans to individuals with 89.4 percent of total assets.

Various concentrations in lending activities carry different risks and returns. Clearly, the highest returns on assets and the highest charge-off rates are found with the credit card banks with consumer lenders far behind. Return on assets in 2004 was 271 basis points higher for credit card banks than for commercial lenders. This occurred even though net charge-offs were 437 basis points higher—clear evidence of the risk return trade-off in banking.

These static comparisons, however, mask several important trends in bank lending. First, bank loans vary with the business cycle. Exhibit 10.3 demonstrates that loans, as a percentage of total assets, have grown sharply since the late 1940s with only slight dips during recession years. The growth in this ratio leveled off and even declined between 1985 and 2004 as banks substituted lower-risk investment securities for loans, but has reversed course with loans again growing at historical rates. The decline in cash as a percent of assets has, however, continued as competitive pressures have pushed some banks to reduce liquidity for additional profits and banks manage their legal reserves more efficiently.

**EXHIBIT 10.1**

Commercial Bank Loans as a Percentage of Total Assets, December 2004

| | Commercial Banks with Asset Size | | | | All Commercial Banks | All Savings Institutions |
|---|---|---|---|---|---|---|
| | <$100 Million | $100 to $1 Billion | $1 to $10 Billion | >$10 Billion | | |
| Number of institutions reporting | 3655 | 3530 | 360 | 85 | 7630 | 1345 |
| **Net loans and leases** | **60.81%** | **66.39%** | **63.58%** | **55.02%** | **57.43%** | **71.27%** |
| Plus: loan loss allowance | 0.89% | 0.93% | 0.95% | 0.85% | 0.87% | 0.50% |
| Total loans and leases | 61.70% | 67.33% | 64.53% | 55.87% | 58.30% | 71.78% |
| Plus: unearned income | 0.04% | 0.06% | 0.05% | 0.03% | 0.04% | 0.01% |
| Loans and leases, gross | 61.74% | 67.39% | 64.58% | 55.90% | 58.34% | 71.79% |
| **All real estate loans** | **38.74%** | **48.51%** | **42.18%** | **26.65%** | **31.20%** | **62.56%** |
| Real estate loans in domestic offices: | 38.74% | 48.51% | 42.08% | 25.83% | 30.57% | 62.56% |
| Construction and land development | 4.35% | 7.94% | 6.73% | 2.23% | 3.45% | 2.77% |
| Commercial real estate | 11.93% | 19.55% | 15.86% | 4.83% | 7.93% | 5.02% |
| Multifamily residential real estate | 0.85% | 1.76% | 2.27% | 0.75% | 1.04% | 4.79% |
| 1–4 family residential | 16.35% | 17.08% | 16.58% | 17.90% | 17.62% | 49.97% |
| Farmland | 5.26% | 2.17% | 0.64% | 0.12% | 0.53% | 0.02% |
| Real estate loans in foreign offices | 0.00% | 0.00% | 0.10% | 0.82% | 0.63% | 0.00% |
| **Farm loans** | **6.24%** | **1.89%** | **0.58%** | **0.21%** | **0.58%** | **0.01%** |
| **Commercial and industrial loans** | **9.81%** | **10.60%** | **11.69%** | **10.72%** | **10.80%** | **3.54%** |
| To non-U.S. addressees | 0.00% | 0.05% | 0.35% | 1.92% | 1.48% | 0.00% |
| **Loans to individuals** | **6.10%** | **5.06%** | **7.51%** | **11.21%** | **9.97%** | **5.39%** |
| Credit cards | 0.10% | 0.57% | 2.76% | 5.39% | 4.42% | 1.63% |
| Related plans | 0.09% | 0.15% | 0.28% | 0.55% | 0.47% | 0.02% |
| Other loans to individuals | 5.91% | 4.34% | 4.46% | 5.27% | 5.09% | 3.75% |
| **Total other loans and leases** | **0.85%** | **1.33%** | **2.63%** | **7.11%** | **5.79%** | **0.28%** |
| Loans to foreign governments and official institutions | 0.00% | 0.00% | 0.01% | 0.12% | 0.09% | 0.00% |
| Obligations of states and political subdivisions in the U.S. | 0.35% | 0.43% | 0.44% | 0.31% | 0.34% | 0.02% |
| Other loans | 0.23% | 0.45% | 0.97% | 2.44% | 1.99% | 0.10% |
| Lease financing receivables | 0.25% | 0.34% | 1.05% | 2.03% | 1.69% | 0.10% |
| Of non-U.S. addressees | 0.00% | 0.00% | 0.06% | 0.51% | 0.39% | 0.00% |
| Loans to depository institutions and acceptances | 0.02% | 0.11% | 0.17% | 2.20% | 1.68% | 0.06% |
| **Memoranda:** | | | | | | |
| Commercial real estate loans not secured by real estate | 0.12% | 0.18% | 0.21% | 0.57% | 0.48% | 0.04% |
| Loans secured by real estate to non-U.S. addressees | 0.00% | 0.06% | 0.04% | 0.69% | 0.52% | 0.00% |
| Restructured loans and leases, total | 0.05% | 0.05% | 0.02% | 0.00% | 0.01% | 0.10% |
| Total loans & leases in foreign offices | 0.00% | 0.03% | 0.27% | 5.28% | 3.99% | 0.00% |

SOURCE: FDIC, Statistics on Banking, http://www.fdic.gov.

Problem loans and loan losses also vary with the business cycle. Exhibits 10.4 and 10.5 compare noncurrent loan rates and net loan charge-off rates, respectively, across types of loans from 1984 through 2004. Noncurrent loans are loans and leases past due 90 days or more and still accruing interest, plus all loans and leases in a nonaccrual status.[1] Net charge-offs, in turn, represent the dollar amount of loans that are formally charged off as uncollectible minus the dollar value of recoveries on loans previously charged off. Exhibits 10.4 and 10.5 document the credit problems of the late 1980s and early 1990s, where the fraction of noncurrent loans to total loans increased sharply from 1984 through 1990. Not until 1993 did noncurrent loans return to more traditional levels.

---

[1] Nonaccrual loans and leases are those (a) that are maintained on a cash basis because of deterioration in the financial position of the borrower, (b) where full payment of interest and principal is not expected, or (c) where principal or interest has been in default for a period of 90 days or more, unless the obligation is both well secured and in the process of collection.

**EXHIBIT 10.2** Credit Risk Diversification and Lending Concentrations by Asset Concentration Groups: December 2004

| | All Institutions | Credit Card Banks | International Banks | Agricultural Banks | Commercial Lenders | Mortgage Lenders | Consumer Lenders | Other Specialized <$1 Billion | All Other <$1 Billion | All Other >$1 Billion |
|---|---|---|---|---|---|---|---|---|---|---|
| **Number of institutions reporting** | **8,975** | **34** | **5** | **1,730** | **4,424** | **990** | **132** | **465** | **1,120** | **75** |
| Loans outstanding (in billions) | | | | | | | | | | |
| **All real estate loans** | **60.16%** | **6.73%** | **25.16%** | **54.27%** | **66.54%** | **91.56%** | **27.62%** | **68.42%** | **69.28%** | **58.92%** |
| Construction and development | 5.50% | 0.00% | 0.86% | 3.41% | 10.90% | 2.33% | 0.84% | 5.26% | 3.98% | 3.45% |
| Commercial real estate | 12.28% | 0.03% | 2.37% | 13.88% | 22.98% | 4.72% | 2.53% | 19.55% | 16.79% | 9.03% |
| Multifamily residential real estate | 2.76% | 0.00% | 0.29% | 1.02% | 4.42% | 4.28% | 0.36% | 2.26% | 1.24% | 1.27% |
| Home equity loans | 8.01% | 5.98% | 4.46% | 1.02% | 7.31% | 9.25% | 6.51% | 2.26% | 3.23% | 11.49% |
| Other 1–4 family residential | 30.00% | 0.71% | 12.08% | 16.27% | 19.89% | 70.90% | 17.13% | 36.84% | 39.55% | 32.83% |
| **Commercial and industrial loans** | **15.82%** | **2.38%** | **21.71%** | **13.99%** | **20.31%** | **3.54%** | **8.93%** | **12.03%** | **10.45%** | **18.08%** |
| **Loans to individuals** | **15.19%** | **89.43%** | **25.72%** | **7.39%** | **8.02%** | **4.12%** | **61.88%** | **14.29%** | **13.68%** | **11.54%** |
| Credit card loans | 6.52% | 83.04% | 10.88% | 0.34% | 0.83% | 0.53% | 15.20% | 1.50% | 0.75% | 2.08% |
| Other loans to individuals | 8.67% | 6.39% | 14.84% | 7.17% | 7.19% | 3.58% | 46.56% | 12.78% | 12.94% | 9.45% |
| All other loans and leases (including farm) | 8.83% | 1.43% | 27.42% | 24.23% | 5.13% | 0.79% | 1.57% | 5.26% | 6.59% | 11.47% |
| **Average return on equity** | **13.28%** | **22.16%** | **10.35%** | **11.45%** | **13.48%** | **11.61%** | **16.81%** | **10.03%** | **10.18%** | **13.69%** |
| **Average return on assets** | **1.29%** | **4.01%** | **0.76%** | **1.23%** | **1.30%** | **1.18%** | **1.66%** | **1.66%** | **1.10%** | **1.35%** |
| **Net charge-offs to loans** | **0.56%** | **4.67%** | **0.91%** | **0.21%** | **0.30%** | **0.12%** | **1.57%** | **0.59%** | **0.31%** | **0.25%** |

Source: FDIC, Quarterly Banking Profile, http://www.fdic.gov.

**Asset Concentration Group Definitions** (Groups are hierarchical and mutually exclusive):

**Credit card lenders**—Institutions whose credit card loans plus securitized receivables exceed 50 percent of total assets plus securitized receivables.

**International banks**—Banks with assets greater than $10 billion and more than 25 percent of total assets in foreign offices.

**Agricultural banks**—Banks whose agricultural production loans plus real estate loans secured by farmland exceed 25 percent of total loans and leases.

**Commercial lenders**—Institutions whose commercial and industrial loans, plus real estate construction and development loans, plus loans secured by commercial real estate properties exceed 25 percent of total assets.

**Mortgage lenders**—Institutions whose residential mortgage loans, plus mortgage-backed securities, exceed 50 percent of total assets.

**Consumer lenders**—Institutions whose residential mortgage loans, plus credit card loans, plus other loans to individuals, exceed 50 percent of total assets.

**Other specialized <$1 billion**—Institutions with assets less than $1 billion, whose loans and leases are less than 40 percent of total assets.

**All other <$1 billion**—Institutions with assets less than $1 billion that do not meet any of the definitions above; they have significant lending activity with no identified asset concentrations.

**All other >$1 billion**—Institutions with assets greater than $1 billion that do not meet any of the definitions above; they have significant lending activity with no identified asset concentrations.

**EXHIBIT 10.3** Relative Importance of Loans, Investment Securities, and Cash Assets at Commercial Banks, 1935–2004

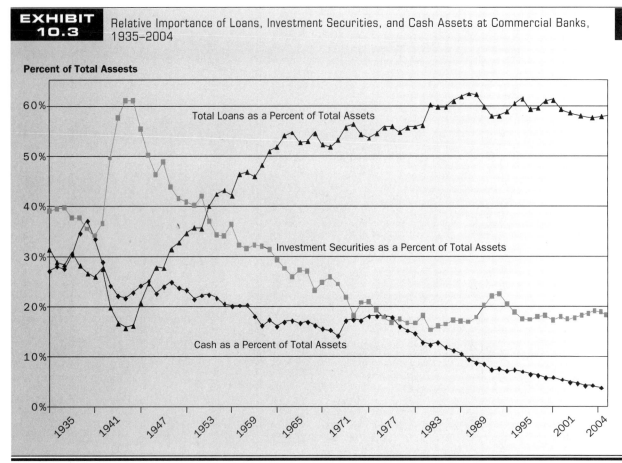

**Percent of Total Assets**

Total Loans as a Percent of Total Assets

Investment Securities as a Percent of Total Assets

Cash as a Percent of Total Assets

SOURCE: FDIC, historical statistics, http://www.fdic.gov.

By the late 1990s loan losses were at historically low levels. Loan losses once again began to increase by 2000 as the economy slowed, the stock market posted significant losses, and the tragic events of September 11, 2001 began to impact consumer confidence and business demand. Still, asset quality improved after 2002 as both noncurrent loans and net charge-offs declined in the aggregate.

Loan performance also varies among different types of loans. The 1980s and early 1990s were difficult times for the banking industry as noncurrent loans and charge-offs increased dramatically. Noncurrent loans for "all categories" jumped dramatically from 1986 to 1987 as a direct result of the sharp fall in energy prices, agricultural problems, overbuilding commercial real estate, and the Tax Reform Act of 1986. In Texas this was called the triple threat: oil, agriculture, and real estate. Foreign loan problems and charge-offs followed a few years later. Noncurrent real estate loans jumped the most from 1988 to 1991, as did charge-off rates. With the exception of loans to individuals, however, noncurrent and charge-off rates generally dropped during the 1990s, indicative of the growing U.S. economy during the period. Noncurrent consumer loans were relatively constant, but charge-off rates increased systematically through 1991, fell somewhat through 1994, and then increased to historical highs in 2002. Commercial and industrial loan losses began to increase rather rapidly by the beginning of the 2000s as a result of a slowdown in the economy, losses in the stock market, as well as the economic consequences of corporate scandals and terrorist acts. Net charge-offs for commercial and industrial loans increased from 0.4 percent in 1998 to 1.8 percent in 2002—a dramatic change in five years. Problems in recent years have largely been associated with credit card loans.

In addition to commercial and industrial loans, a significant portion of the increase in loan losses can be attributed to credit card losses and the dramatic increase in personal bankruptcies. Exhibit 10.6 shows the sharp increase in credit card charge-off rates and personal bankruptcy filings in the late 1990s. Although bankruptcies and consumer charge-offs fell between mid-1998 and the end of 2000, they once again increased sharply during the early 2000s. By the first quarter of 2002, banks saw a record credit card charge-off rate of 7.7 percent. Since 2002 both of these trends have improved. In 2005, Congress passed bankruptcy reform legislation which makes it

*Recent Trends in Loan Growth and Quality*

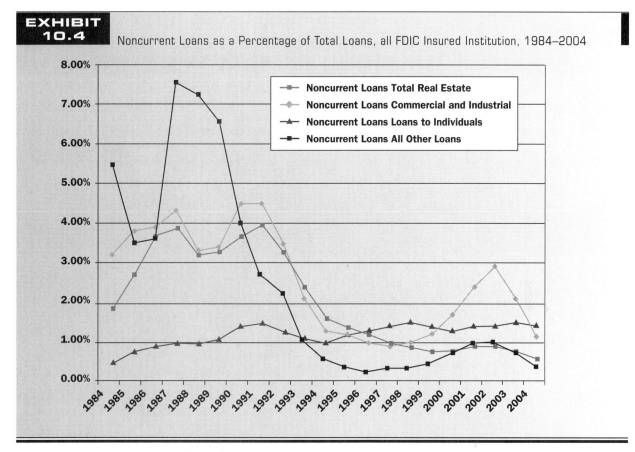

**EXHIBIT 10.4**

Noncurrent Loans as a Percentage of Total Loans, all FDIC Insured Institution, 1984–2004

- ■ Noncurrent Loans Total Real Estate
- ◆ Noncurrent Loans Commercial and Industrial
- ▲ Noncurrent Loans Loans to Individuals
- ■ Noncurrent Loans All Other Loans

SOURCE: FDIC, Quarterly Banking Profile, http://www.fdic.gov/.

more difficult for individuals to walk away from their debts and avoid repayment. Thus, personal bankruptcies will likely drop even further.

Deregulation during the early 1980s and then the exceptional economic times of the 1990s meant that most banks raised their loan-to-asset ratios. Because banks now pay market rates on their liabilities, their cost of funds is relatively higher and more volatile. As customers moved deposits to stocks and mutual funds, banks could not easily grow their low-cost core deposits. Banks continued to borrow more using purchased liabilities and Federal Home Loan Bank (FHLB) advances. These higher-cost funds required the banks to earn higher yields on investments to maintain a positive spread and grow net interest income. Loans offer the highest promised yields, and consumer loans offer even higher yields. During the 1990s, if banks could find enough good loans and price them appropriately, they could continue historical earnings growth. The problem banks faced and continue to face today is increased competition from other lenders, many of whom price credits aggressively to establish a market presence and increase market share. Banks also face stiff competition from tax-exempt organizations such as credit unions and the Farm Credit System. Many quality borrowers, in addition, have access to alternative sources of funds by directly borrowing in the commercial paper or long-term bond markets, effectively increasing the pressure on bank margins. This increased competition on the banks' primary profit source has prompted many banks to increase their product and services offerings to generate additional fee income. Banks also increased their use of loan securitizations during the 1980s and 1990s, effectively growing income from loan origination fees rather than interest income from holding loans in their portfolio. Securitizing loans also means a bank is subject to less credit, liquidity, and interest rate risk.

Today's widespread use of credit scoring by lenders and the securitization of consumer and small business loans puts additional pressure on interest rates. Credit scoring, which is discussed in Chapter 12 for consumer loans, is a statistical process that assigns a score to a borrower based on characteristics of the borrower that indicate a high or low likelihood of loan repayment. Widespread use of credit scoring standardizes the perceived quality of different types of loans, such as pools of mortgages, credit card receivables, home equity loans, and small

**EXHIBIT 10.5** Net Charge-offs by Loan Type at U.S. Commercial Banks, 1984–2004

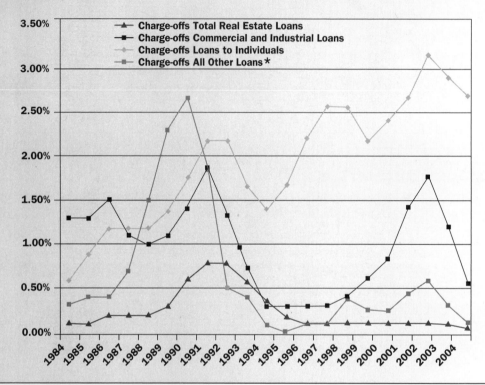

NOTE: Noncurrent loan rates represent the percentage of loans that are past due 90 days or more, or are in nonaccrual status.
* Includes loans to foreign governments, depository institutions, and lease receivables.
SOURCE: FDIC Quarterly Banking Profile, http://www.fdic.gov.

business loans. As more lenders originate these loans and securitize them, the supply of credit increases. This lowers market interest rates, ceteris paribus.

The Internet has also led to smaller spreads for more standardized loan products. Many banks, nonbanks, and loan brokers advertise auto loan, credit card, mortgage, and home equity rates as well as accept and process loan applications on the Internet. Consumers have much greater access to information on loan rates and terms from across the country and can readily shop for the lowest rate and best terms, putting even more pressure on spreads. Several firms have introduced automated loan machines (ALMs) that are designed to work like automated teller machines (ATMs). With ALMs, the customer provides background information, typically via a credit or debit card, a loan is credit scored, and the borrower receives an automated response to the loan request. If ALMs are ever widely accepted, the availability of credit will increase again. Finally, Internet loan brokers such as Lending Tree and Quicken Loan now accept loan applications and process loan requests on the Internet and can even fund the loans using direct deposit transfers to an individual's bank account.

In addition to increased competition, risk-based capital standards require that banks hold a minimum amount of equity capital for each loan kept on the books (see Chapter 9). More generally, strict capital ratios restrict loan growth and force banks to change the pricing based on increased capital required to support loans. This means that banks choosing to make loans and keep the loans in their portfolios must obtain additional capital to continue growing. Many banks have responded by acting as loan brokers rather than keeping all loans on their books. This process involves making large loans or large volumes of loans and selling, or participating portions, of these loans to other depository institutions or other investors. Banks earn fees for originating the loans and servicing the payments. In many cases, they can sell part of the loan at a lower interest rate than that negotiated with the borrower. If so, the bank keeps a portion of the interest payment as well as the loan fee. Loan sales increase earnings but do not adversely affect the capital position.

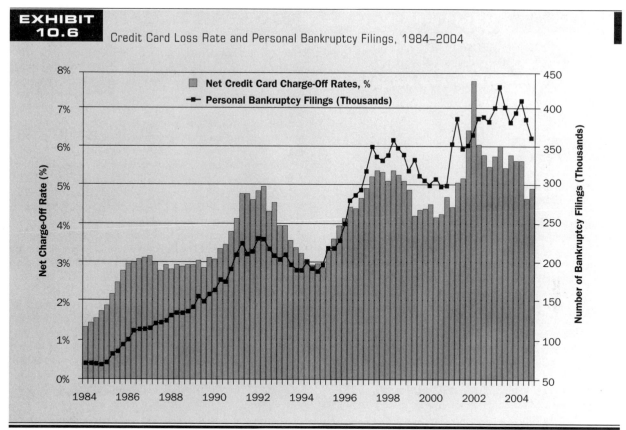

**EXHIBIT 10.6** Credit Card Loss Rate and Personal Bankruptcy Filings, 1984–2004

SOURCE: Bankruptcies—Administrative Office of the United States Courts; Charge-off Rates—Commercial Bank Call Reports; FDIC Quarterly Banking Profile, http://www.fdic.gov.

Banks can supplement earnings and circumvent capital requirements by engaging in off-balance sheet lending arrangements and financial guarantees. Here a bank does not directly extend credit but either serves as an underwriter arranging financing or attaches a letter of credit to a loan agreement. In both cases, the bank earns a fee for its role but retains a contingent liability. If the borrower defaults, the bank must take over the asset and make the obligated payments. Even with the current risk-based capital requirements, not all contingent liabilities are converted to on-balance sheet equivalents at 100 percent (see Chapter 9). Many off-balance sheet liabilities do not appear on the balance sheet and thus do not affect the capital-to-asset ratio calculated from balance sheet items. The off-balance sheet experiences of Enron and PNC clearly demonstrate that not all risks are reflected in total assets.

## MEASURING AGGREGATE ASSET QUALITY

The credit quality data presented above may not accurately reflect the quality of individual assets and the likelihood of default. It is extremely difficult to assess individual asset quality using aggregate quality data such as the percentage of charge-offs and past due loans. In fact, many firms that buy banks are surprised at the acquired bank's poor asset quality even though they conducted a due diligence review of the acquired bank prior to the purchase. Different types of assets and off-balance sheet activities have different default probabilities. Loans typically exhibit the greatest credit risk. Banks evaluate their portfolio credit risk by asking three basic questions: What is the historical loss rate on loans and investments? What are expected losses in the future? How is the bank prepared to weather the losses? Changes in general economic conditions and a firm's operating environment alter the cash flow available for debt service. These conditions are difficult to predict. Therefore, historical charge-offs and past due loans might understate (or overstate) future losses depending on the *future* economic and operational conditions of the borrower.

# CONTEMPORARY ISSUES

## BANK COMPETITORS COME IN MANY FORMS

Competition for bank services comes in many forms. In addition to traditional competitors, such as credit unions and consumer finance companies, there are the relatively new competitors such as brokerage companies (Merrill Lynch and Fidelity Investments), insurance companies (State Farm and Allstate), pawn shops, payday lenders, and check cashing services, as well as new and used car dealers. Pawn shops not only buy and sell used goods, they also make loans, often at very high rates of interest using a customer's personal property as collateral. Payday lenders and check cashing services will lend money, again at very high rates, awaiting the customer's next paycheck. Check cashing services charge fees, mostly to those without a bank account, to cash payroll and third-party checks.

New and used car dealers not only offer to sell automobiles but will arrange financing for the car buyer as well. When a car dealer "arranges" financing for the customer, he or she fills out a relatively uniform credit application and faxes this to one of several underwriters in town such as a local bank, General Motors Acceptance Corporation, Ford Motor Credit, and other credit corporations from Daimler Chrysler, Toyota, Nissan, and so on. Typically, the dealer will accept the best rate from the first few underwriters who respond to the fax. Most often, the rate the underwriter will lend money for on the credit application is not the rate the dealer quotes the customer. For example, on a $20,000 loan, the dealer might get a 4-year loan rate quote of 9 percent. This dealer will then offer the customer financing at 13 percent. If customers don't know they can obtain cheaper financing elsewhere, they will often accept the terms, and the dealer has just made a $1,561.14 profit on this loan. The monthly payments on the $20,000 loan at 13 percent for four years would be $536.55 to the customer. The dealer will sell this 13 percent loan to the bank (or auto finance company) for a premium, because the bank quoted the note at only 9 percent to the dealer. The bank would earn a 9 percent return on a 4-year loan paying $536.55 if it paid $21,561.14 to the car dealer for a $20,000 note! Hence, the dealer sells the $20,000 note to the bank for an instant profit of $1,561.14.

Today, most companies accept debit and credit cards for payment of monthly bills such as water and electric. Many of these same companies allow customers to pay their bills using a touch-tone phone. Even the U.S Postal Service got into on-line bill payment services! Wal-Mart, the largest retailer in the country, has been attempting to get directly into the banking business and place banks in all of their retail stores. As of 2004, however, Wal-Mart had not figured out how to put banks they owned into their retail stores without becoming a financial holding company. Instead, Wal-Mart leases space to other banks inside its stores. This continues to be a hard fought battle between banks and nonbanks and the safety and soundness debate over the separation of banking and commerce.

---

For example, the 1990s were a period of exceptional economic growth and banks experienced some of the lowest charge-off rates they had seen in recent times. Examining aggregate charge-off and past due data on commercial and real estate loans for the five-year period 1995–1999 in Exhibit 10.4 and 10.5 might be misleading as the past doesn't necessarily repeat itself. Banks do not intentionally make bad loans. Loans go bad as a result of many factors, including changes in economic conditions or the operating environment in which the firm works. Loans booked today, generally, do not have problems until tomorrow. Hence, data on historical losses and past due loans will only be a good representation of the quality of the loan portfolio if similar conditions exist in the future. One must use historical data cautiously as it may not represent the current quality of the loan portfolio.

Similarly, an individual's ability to repay debts varies with changes in employment and personal net worth. For this reason, banks perform a credit analysis on each loan request to assess a borrower's capacity to repay. Unfortunately, loans tend to deteriorate long before accounting information reveals any problems. In addition, many banks enter into off-balance sheet activities, such as loan commitments, guarantee offers, and derivative contracts. The prospective borrowers and counterparties must perform or the bank may take a loss. These risks can be substantial, but are difficult to measure from published historical data.

There are several other sources of credit risk that may not be well represented in the bank's aggregate historical credit risk data. First, banks that lend in a narrow geographic area or concentrate their loans to a certain industry have risk that is not fully measured by balance sheet or historical charge-off data. This lack of diversification could dramatically affect a majority of a bank's portfolio if economic factors negatively affect the geographic or industry concentration. This type of bank could be subject to risks that the rest of the banking industry is not subject to in their operations. Examining Exhibit 10.1, we see that smaller banks have greater concentrations of real estate loans loans. A downturn in real estate values in the smaller banks' local markets could have a pronounced effect upon their credit quality. Not only do larger banks have a smaller proportion of their portfolio in real estate, they also generally have the advantage of geographic loan diversification. On the other hand, larger banks have a high proportion of their portfolio invested in commercial and industrial loans and loans to individuals. Both types of loans typically experience higher loss rates and have generally increased during the early 2000s.

Banks with high loan growth rates often assume greater risk, as credit analysis and review procedures are less rigorous. In many instances the loans perform temporarily, but losses eventually rise. Thus, high loan growth rates, particularly when the loans are generated externally through acquisitions or entering new trade areas, often lead future charge-offs.

Finally, banks that lend funds in foreign countries take country risk. Country risk refers to the potential loss of interest and principal on international loans due to borrowers in a country refusing to make timely payments, as per a loan agreement. In essence, foreign governments and corporate borrowers may default on their loans due to government controls over the actions of businesses and individuals, internal politics that may disrupt payments, general market disruptions, and problems that arise when governments reduce or eliminate subsidies used as a source of repayment. Banks have historically experienced substantial losses on certain international loans consistent with deteriorating economic conditions in the underlying countries.

## TRENDS IN COMPETITION FOR LOAN BUSINESS

Robert Morris chartered the first commercial bank in the United States in 1781 called the Bank of North America. This bank did business principally with the federal government and merchants. There were almost 14,500 banks by 1984 and fewer than 7,630 by the beginning of 2004. The reduction in the number of banks is a direct result of the relaxation of branching restrictions and increased competition (see Chapter 1). Today, banks face tremendous competition for business that they were previously uniquely qualified for. This has forced consolidation as banks have attempted to lower costs and provide a broader base of services.

Although banks have historically been the primary lenders to business, most firms can obtain loans from many different sources today: finance companies (Household Finance, Commercial Credit, and GE Capital Corporation), life insurance companies, commercial paper, and the issuance of junk bonds. Reduced regulation, financial innovation, increased consumer awareness, and new technology have made it easier to obtain loans from a variety of sources. Junk bonds (bonds rated below BBB) have become more "acceptable" thereby providing a viable funding source for smaller or new businesses. Commercial paper is inexpensive to issue and most investment bankers can arrange private placements of debt quite easily.

Banks, however, still have the required expertise, experience, and customer focus to make them the preferred lender for many types of loans. Lending is not just a matter of making the loan and waiting for payment. Loans must be monitored and closely supervised to prevent losses. This requires an administrative staff for which banks are well suited. Not all loans can be standardized, credit scored, and securitized (sold in marketable packages). The most commonly securitized loans are those with the most standard features: mortgages, government-guaranteed student loans, small business loans sponsored by the Small Business Administration (SBA), credit cards, and auto loans. Many other loans are more difficult to credit score and securitize. For example, many farm and small business loans are designed to meet a specific business need. Repayment schedules and collateral are often customized so that they do not conform to some standard. Midsize to large businesses will have specialized needs as well. Not surprisingly, this is the area of lending that is still dominated by commercial banks. A **structured note** is such a loan that is specifically designed to meet the needs of one or a few companies but has been packaged for resale. It may have common features, but an investor has to review the terms and covenants carefully to fully understand the payment patterns and inherent risks.

## THE CREDIT PROCESS

The fundamental objective of commercial and consumer lending is to make profitable loans with minimal risk. Management should target specific industries or markets in which lending officers have expertise. The somewhat competing goals of loan volume and loan quality must be balanced with the bank's liquidity requirements, capital constraints, and rate of return objectives. The credit process relies on each bank's systems and controls that allow management and credit officers to evaluate risk and return trade-offs.

The credit process includes three functions: business development and credit analysis, underwriting or credit execution and administration, and credit review (see Exhibit 10.7). Each reflects the bank's written loan policy as determined by the board of directors. A **loan policy** formalizes lending guidelines that employees follow to

**EXHIBIT 10.7** The Credit Process

| Business Development and Credit Analysis | Credit Execution and Administration | Credit Review |
|---|---|---|
| • Market research | • Loan committee reviews proposal/recommendation | • Review loan documentation |
| • Advertising, public relations | | • Monitor compliance with loan agreement: |
| • Officer call programs | • Accept/reject decision made, terms negotiated | – Positive and negative loan covenants |
| • Obtain formal loan request | | |
| • Obtain financial statements, borrowing resolution, credit reports | • Loan agreement prepared with collateral documentation | – Delinquencies in loan payments |
| | • Borrower signs agreement, turns over collateral, receives loan proceeds | – Discuss nature of delinquency or other problems with borrower |
| • Financial statement and cash flow analysis | | • Institute corrective action: |
| • Evaluate collateral | • Perfect security interest | – Modify credit terms |
| • Loan officer makes recommendation on accepting/rejecting loan | • File materials in credit file | – Obtain additional capital, collateral, guarantees |
| | • Process loan payments, obtain periodic financial statements, call on borrower | – Call loan |

conduct bank business. It identifies preferred loan qualities and establishes procedures for granting, documenting, and reviewing loans.[2] Specific elements within each function are listed in the exhibit.

Management's **credit philosophy** determines how much risk the bank will take and in what form. A bank's **credit culture** refers to the fundamental principles that drive lending activity and how management analyzes risk. There can be large differences between banks in their lending philosophy. Three potentially different credit cultures are: values driven, current-profit driven, and market-share driven.

### VALUES DRIVEN

- Focus is on credit quality with strong risk management systems and controls.
- Primary emphasis is on bank soundness and stability and a consistent market presence.
- Underwriting is conservative and significant loan concentrations are not allowed.
- Typical outcome is lower current profit from loans with fewer loan losses.

### CURRENT-PROFIT DRIVEN

- Focus is on short-term earnings.
- Primary emphasis is bank's annual profit plan.
- Management is often attracted to high-risk and high-return borrowers.
- Outcome is typically higher profit in good times, followed by lower profit in bad times when loan losses increase.

### MARKET-SHARE DRIVEN

- Focus is on having the highest market share of loans among competitors.
- Primary emphasis is on loan volume and growth with the intent of having the largest market share.
- Underwriting is very aggressive and management accepts loan concentrations and above-average credit risk.
- Outcome is that loan quality suffers over time, while profit is modest because loan growth comes from below-market pricing and greater risk taking.

Exhibit 10.8 documents elements of a strong values-driven credit culture that encourages management to maintain asset quality amid pressures to chase bad deals. This credit culture is set and enforced by the chief executive officer. Most of the elements address the systematic approach to risk taking that forces loan officers to focus on long-term performance, consider a wide range of possible outcomes, and be accountable for actual earnings and loss performance.

---

[2]In their periodic examinations, regulators evaluate each bank's written loan policy to see if existing loans conform to management's objectives and acceptable guidelines.

| EXHIBIT 10.8 | 20 Essentials of Good Banking Fostered by a Strong Credit Culture |

1. Commitment to excellence
2. Philosophical framework for day-to-day decision making
3. Sound value system that will cope with change
4. Uniform approach to risk taking that provides stability and consistency
5. Development of a common credit language
6. Historical perspective on the bank's credit experience
7. Bank comes first and ahead of every profit center
8. Candor and good communication at all levels
9. Awareness of every transaction's effect on the bank
10. A portfolio with integrity and an appreciation of what properly belongs in it
11. Accountability for decisions and actions
12. Long-term view as well as a short-term view
13. Respect for credit basics
14. Reconciliation of market practice with common sense
15. Use of independent judgment and not the herd instinct
16. Constant mindfulness of the bank's risk-taking parameters
17. Realistic approach to markets and budgeting
18. An understanding of what the bank expects and the reasons behind its policies
19. Credit system with early warning capabilities
20. Appreciation that in risk taking there are no surprises, only ignorance

SOURCE: P. Henry Mueller, "Risk Management and the Credit Culture—Necessary Interaction." *Journal of Commercial Lending* (May 1993). Copyright © 1993 by Robert Morris Associates. Reprinted with permission from the *Journal of Commercial Lending*.

## BUSINESS DEVELOPMENT AND CREDIT ANALYSIS

Where would a bank be without customers? Business development is the process of marketing bank services to existing and potential customers. With lending, it involves identifying new credit customers and soliciting their banking business, as well as maintaining relationships with current customers and cross-selling noncredit services. Every bank employee, from tellers handling drive-up facilities to members of the board of directors, is responsible for business development. Each employee regularly comes into contact with potential customers and can sell bank services. To encourage marketing efforts, many banks use cash bonuses or other incentive plans to reward employees who successfully cross-sell services or bring new business into the bank.

The normal starting point for any business development effort is market research. Management should establish targets for loan composition and identify areas of potential business. The research may formally analyze economic conditions, local demographic trends, and customer surveys. Alternatively, it may simply evolve from normal customer contacts and the development of a communications link with local businesses about forthcoming opportunities. The purpose is to forecast the demand for bank services. The second step is to train employees regarding what products are available, what products customers are likely to need or want, and how they should communicate with customers about these needs. Finally, the bank should effectively market and make customers aware of its products and services. The most obvious means is through effective advertising and public relations. Many banks also incorporate formal officer call programs, in which lending officers make regular face-to-face contact with current and potential borrowers. Borrowers are often hesitant to reveal personal details or business financial backgrounds. Before doing so, they like to know and trust the bank official with whom they are dealing.

Call programs require constant personal contact with potential borrowers, either through civic groups and trade associations or direct appointments. Formal programs involve bank-determined numerical objectives and officer implementation of customer contact procedures. The numerical objectives often stipulate a minimum number of calls each month. Some are directed at current customers, while others target potential customers identified through research. The calling officer establishes the personal contact, makes the call, and files a report. After each call, the officer logs the date and time of the meeting, the issues discussed, and notes the opportunities for obtaining new business. Typically, officers must call on new customers several times before an opportunity develops. The bank is essentially positioning itself for the times when customers become dissatisfied with their prior bank relationship or qualify as good credits.

**CREDIT ANALYSIS.** Once a customer requests a loan, bank officers analyze all available information to determine whether the loan meets the bank's risk-return objectives. Credit analysis is essentially default risk analysis in which a loan officer attempts to evaluate a borrower's ability and willingness to repay. Eric Compton identified three distinct areas of commercial risk analysis related to the following questions:[3]

1. What risks are inherent in the operations of the business?

2. What have managers done or failed to do in mitigating those risks?

3. How can a lender structure and control its own risks in supplying funds?

The first question forces the credit analyst to generate a list of factors that indicate what could harm a borrower's ability to repay. The second recognizes that repayment is largely a function of decisions made by a borrower. Is management aware of the important risks and has it responded? The last question forces the analyst to specify how risks can be controlled so the bank can structure an acceptable loan agreement.

Traditionally, key risk factors have been classified according to the five Cs of good credit:

- *Character* refers to the borrower's honesty and trustworthiness. An analyst must assess the borrower's integrity and subsequent intent to repay. If there are any serious doubts, the loan should be rejected.

- *Capital* refers to the borrower's wealth position measured by financial soundness and market standing. Can the firm or individual withstand any deterioration in its financial position? Capital helps cushion losses and reduces the likelihood of bankruptcy.

- *Capacity* involves both the borrower's legal standing and management's expertise in maintaining operations so the firm or individual can repay its debt obligations. A business must have identifiable cash flow or alternative sources of cash to repay debt. An individual must be able to generate income.

- *Conditions* refer to the economic environment or industry-specific supply, production, and distribution factors influencing a firm's operations. Repayment sources of cash often vary with the business cycle or consumer demand.

- *Collateral* is the lender's secondary source of repayment or security in the case of default. Having an asset that the bank can seize and liquidate when a borrower defaults reduces loss, but does not justify lending proceeds when the credit decision is originally made.

Golden and Walker further identify the five Cs of *bad* credit, representing things to guard against to help prevent problems:[4]

- *Complacency* refers to the tendency to assume that because things were good in the past they will be good in the future. Common examples are an overreliance on guarantors, reported net worth, or past loan repayment success because things have always worked out in the past.

- *Carelessness* involves poor underwriting typically evidenced by inadequate loan documentation, a lack of current financial information or other pertinent information in the credit files, and a lack of protective covenants in the loan agreement. Each of these makes it difficult to monitor a borrower's progress and identify problems before they are unmanageable.

- *Communication* ineffectiveness refers to when a bank's credit objectives and policies are not clearly communicated. This is when loan problems can arise. Management must effectively communicate and enforce loan policies and loan officers should make management aware of specific problems with existing loans as soon as they appear.

- *Contingencies* refer to lenders' tendency to play down or ignore circumstances in which a loan might default. The focus is on trying to make a deal work rather than identifying downside risk.

- *Competition* involves following competitors' behavior rather than maintaining the bank's own credit standards. Doing something because the bank down the street is doing it does not mean it's a prudent business practice.

The formal credit analysis procedure includes a subjective evaluation of the borrower's request and a detailed review of all financial statements. Credit department employees may perform the initial quantitative analysis for the loan officer. The process consists of:

1. Collecting information for the credit file; such as credit history and performance

2. Evaluating management, the company, and the industry in which it operates; that is, evaluation of internal and external factors

3. Spreading financial statements; that is, financial statement analysis

4. Projecting the borrower's cash flow and thus its ability to service the debt

5. Evaluating collateral or the secondary source of repayment

6. Writing a summary analysis and making a recommendation

---

[3]The discussion is based on Compton (1985).

[4]Golden, Sam, and Harry Walker, "The Ten Commandments of Commercial Credit: The Cs of Good and Bad Loans," *Journal of Commercial Bank Lending*, January 1993.

Using this data, the credit analysis should prepare and assimilate the formal credit file. The credit file contains background information on the borrower, including call report summaries, past and present financial statements, pertinent credit reports, and supporting schedules such as an aging of receivables, a breakdown of current inventory and equipment, and a summary of insurance coverage. If the customer is a previous borrower, the file should contain copies of past loan agreement, cash flow projections, collateral agreements and security documents, any narrative comments, and copies of all correspondence with the customer provided by prior loan officers. One of the most important aspects of lending is determining the customer's *desire to repay the loan.* Although this is critically important, it is difficult to measure. Information in the credit file will give the credit officer documentation on the customer's repayment history.

Next, the credit analyst uses the credit file data to spread the financial statements, project cash flow, and evaluate collateral.[5] An evaluation of management, the company, and industry is also needed to ensure the soundness of the loan. The last step is to submit a written report summarizing the loan request, loan purpose, and the borrower's comparative financial performance with industry standards, and to make a recommendation.

The loan officer evaluates the report and discusses any errors, omissions, and extensions with the analyst. If the credit (loan) does not satisfy the bank's risk criteria, the officer notifies the borrower that the original request has been denied. The officer may suggest procedures that would improve the borrower's condition and repayment prospects and solicit another proposal if circumstances improve. If the credit satisfies acceptable risk limits, the officer negotiates specific preliminary credit terms including the loan amount, maturity, pricing, collateral requirements, and repayment schedule.

Many small banks do not have formal credit departments and full-time analysts to prepare financial histories. Loan officers personally complete the steps outlined above before accepting or rejecting a loan. Often loan requests are received without detailed information on the borrower's condition. Financial statements may be handwritten or unaudited and may not meet generally accepted accounting principles. Yet the borrower may possess good character and substantial net worth. In such instances, the loan officer works with the borrower to prepare a formal loan request and obtain the best financial information possible. This may mean personally auditing the borrower's receipts, expenditures, receivables, and inventory.

## CREDIT EXECUTION AND ADMINISTRATION

The process by which the formal credit decision is made varies by bank. It depends on many factors, such as the bank's organizational structure, bank size, number of employees and length of experience, and even the types of loans made. The formal decision can be made individually, by an independent underwriting department, by a loan committee, or a combination of these methods. Formally, a bank's board of directors has the final say over which loans are approved. Typically, however, each lending officer has independent authority to approve loans up to some fixed dollar amount. Junior officers at a large bank might have authority to approve loans no larger than $100,000, while senior lending officers might independently approve loans up to $500,000.

A *loan committee,* made up of the bank's senior loan officers and sometimes a board member, will generally formally review larger loans. This committee reviews each step of the credit analysis as presented by the loan officer and supporting analysts and makes a collective decision. Loan committees meet regularly to monitor the credit approval process and asset-quality problems when they arise. When required, the board of directors or a bank's loan committee reviews this decision and grants final approval.

Many larger banks employ a centralized underwriting department. *Centralized underwriting* uses a relationship manager (RM) who sources new business and manages existing relationships within the portfolio. On new credit requests, the RM advises the client on the required information to process the request, evaluates and prescreens the request when the information is received, and if the request has a good probability of approval, prepares the package and sends it to the loan center. Credit specialists in central underwriting make the final loan decision, but some banks allow for market overrides if the RM can mitigate the reasons for decline. Most large banks use computer software to quantitatively spread and evaluate the credit requests. Approvals from the computer system can be considered one of the required signatures in some banks' approval process. The RM's signature is the second required signature (up to the officer's authority).

Once a loan has been approved, the officer notifies the borrower and prepares a **loan agreement**. This agreement formalizes the purpose of the loan, the terms, repayment schedule, collateral required, any loan covenants, and finally, what conditions bring about default by the borrower. Conditions of default may include events such as late principal and interest payments, the sale of substantial assets, a declaration of bankruptcy, and the breaking of any restrictive loan covenant. The officer then checks that all loan documentation is present and in order. The borrower signs the agreement along with other guarantors, turns over the collateral if necessary, and receives the loan proceeds.

---

[5]This detailed data analysis is discussed in Chapter 11 for commercial loans and Chapter 12 for consumer loans, with several examples.

**DOCUMENTATION: PERFECTING THE SECURITY INTEREST.** Documenting all aspects of the loan agreement and the bank's formal claim over collateral are essential to preventing or minimizing losses. A critical feature of executing any loan involves perfecting the bank's security interest in collateral. A security interest is the legal claim on property that secures payment on a debt or performance of an obligation. When the bank's claim is superior to that of other creditors and the borrower, its security interest is said to be *perfected*.[6]

Because there are many different types of borrowers and collateral, there are different methods of perfecting a security interest. In most cases, the bank requires borrowers to sign a security agreement that assigns qualifying collateral to the bank. This agreement describes the collateral and relevant covenants or warranties. Formal closure may involve getting the signature of a third-party guarantor on a loan agreement or having a key individual assign the cash value of a life insurance policy to the bank. In other cases, a bank may need to obtain title to equipment or vehicles. Whenever all parties sign a security agreement and the bank holds the collateral, the security interest is perfected. When the borrower holds the collateral, the bank must file a financing statement with the state that describes the collateral and the rights of the bank and borrower. It must be signed to establish the bank's superior interest.

Losses are a normal part of lending. They can only be totally eliminated by taking no credit risk. Banks have many procedures that help limit their loss exposure. The primary strategic tool is to have a formal loan policy that establishes exposure limits to any single borrower or group of borrowers. Such maximum exposures will not put the bank at risk of failure if the entire exposure goes unpaid. Other specific procedures include position limits, risk rating loans, and loan covenants.

**POSITION LIMITS.** Position limits are the maximum allowable credit exposures to any single borrower, industry, or geographic locale. Although some banks define acceptable exposures as a percentage of assets, risk exposure should always be expressed as a percentage of the bank's equity capital. For example, if exposure to a certain industry is 400 percent of equity capital, the bank is putting four times its net worth at risk. The size of the exposure indicates the amount of the bank's equity capital that it is willing to put at risk. It should be lower for single borrowers and industries with the greatest loss potential. The objective is to avoid catastrophic losses.

**RISK RATING LOANS.** Another procedure to limit risk is for banks to strategically grade individual loans and counterparties. Risk grading involves evaluating characteristics of the borrower and loan to assess the likelihood of default and the amount of loss in the event of default (LIED). The grades may be assigned subjectively or by formal quantitative credit scoring models.[7] The new Basel II risk-based capital standards require a much finer risk grading system for banks.[8] Loans are rated from low risk to high risk and vary sharply across industries, types of borrowers, different regions of the United States, and different countries. Obviously, charge-offs will be higher for the highest-risk loans and banks must price these loans much higher relative to their costs.

**LOAN COVENANTS.** Once a bank lends funds to a customer, the bank and borrower effectively become partners. The bank wants the customer to repay the debt and purchase other bank services. The customer looks to the bank to provide useful accounting, financial, and tax advice.

Both the bank and borrower should recognize this partnership when negotiating credit terms. Still, it is important that each party protects its interests. For this reason, the bank often includes covenants in the loan agreement. Covenants may either be *negative*, indicating financial limitations and prohibited events, or *positive (affirmative)*, indicating specific provisions to which the borrower must adhere. The intent is to protect against substantive changes in the borrower's operating environment that damage the bank's interests. Most covenants address target financial ratios, limitations on asset sales, and maintenance of management quality. Exhibit 10.9 provides a partial list of covenants. The first three negative covenants, for example, attempt to limit discretionary cash payments by a firm. If effective, more cash is available for debt service. The first affirmative covenant prevents management from altering a firm's balance sheet adversely. Others stipulate actions that will protect the bank if key personnel die or performance deteriorates.

## LOAN REVIEW

The loan review effort is directed at reducing credit risk as well as handling problem loans and liquidating assets of failed borrowers. Effective credit management separates loan review from credit analysis, execution, and administration. The review process can be divided into two functions: monitoring the performance of existing

---

[6]The Uniform Commercial Code (UCC) establishes what documentation is required to obtain a security interest in commercial lending. The UCC applies in every state, although various states have revised certain conditions. Each lending officer must understand what conditions apply wherever the bank conducts business.

[7]Chapter 11 introduces a risk rating scale for commercial loans.

[8]See Chapter 9 for a discussion of risk-based capital standards.

| EXHIBIT 10.9 | Sample Loan Covenants |
|---|---|

| Negative | Affirmative |
|---|---|
| • Capital outlays cannot exceed $3 million annually<br>• Cash dividends cannot exceed 60% of periodic earnings<br>• Total officers' salaries cannot exceed $500,000 annually<br>• No liens on assets beyond existing liens<br>• No mergers, consolidations, or acquisitions without bank approval<br>• No sale, lease, or transfer of more than 10% of existing assets<br>• No change in senior management<br>• No additional debt without bank approval | • Borrower must maintain following financial ratios:<br>  Current ratio >1.0<br>  Days receivables outstanding <50 days<br>  Inventory turnover >4.5 times<br>  Debt to total assets <70%<br>  Net worth >$1 million<br>  Fixed charge coverage >1.3 times<br>  Cash flow from operations >dividends<br>  + current maturities of long-term debt<br>• Certified financial statements must be provided within 60 days of end of each fiscal year<br>• Borrower will maintain $1 million key man life insurance policy on company president, with bank named as beneficiary<br>• Bank will be allowed to inspect inventory, receivables, and property periodically<br>• Borrower must pay all taxes and government fees, unless contested in good faith, and comply with all laws<br>• Borrower must inform bank of any litigation or claim that might materially affect its performance<br>• Borrower must maintain all property in good condition and repair |

loans and handling problem loans. Many banks have a formal loan review committee, independent of loan officers, that reports directly to the chief executive officer and directors' loan committee. Loan review personnel audit current loans to verify that the borrower's financial condition is acceptable, loan documentation is in place, and pricing meets return objectives. If the audit uncovers problems, the committee initiates corrective action. Removing the problem may simply involve getting signatures on omitted forms or filing required documents with the state. If the borrower has violated any loan covenants, the loan is in default. The bank can then force the borrower to correct the violation or it can call the loan; that is, request immediate payment. Calling a loan is normally a last resort and done only when the borrower does not voluntarily correct the problem. It allows the bank to request full payment before repayment prospects worsen.

The problem is much more serious when the borrower's financial condition deteriorates. These loans are classified as *problem loans* and require special treatment. In many cases, the bank has to modify the terms of the loan agreement to increase the probability of full repayment. Modifications include deferring interest and principal payments, lengthening maturities, and liquidating unnecessary assets. The bank may also request additional collateral or guarantees and ask the borrower to contribute extra capital. The purpose is to buy time until the borrower's condition improves. Banks often assign a separate loan work-out specialist to problem loans, rather than traditional loan officers, because they are liquidation oriented and frequently involved in intense negotiations.

## CHARACTERISTICS OF DIFFERENT TYPES OF LOANS

This section describes the basic characteristics of commercial bank loans. Although there are many ways to classify loans, the analysis focuses on the use of loan proceeds and maturity. Each type of loan has different features that necessitate different repayment schemes, collateral, and loan covenants. The Uniform Bank Performance Report (UBPR) classifies loans into one of six types: real estate loans, commercial loans, individual loans, agricultural loans, other loans and leases in domestic offices, and loans and leases in foreign offices.[9]

---

[9]Information on the UBPR can be found in Chapter 2 and on the Internet at http://www.ffiec.gov.

## REAL ESTATE LOANS

The UBPR defines **real estate loans** as domestic-office loans secured by real estate. In particular, real estate loans are generally classified into seven subcategories: construction and development loans, commercial real estate, multifamily residential real estate, 1–4 family residential, home equity, farmland, and other real estate loans. Exhibit 10.1 indicates that real estate loans represent a high percentage of total loans at most commercial banks. They are classified separately from commercial and consumer loans because the collateral is some form of real property and the loans are subject to different risks and regulation.

During prosperous times, short-term real estate loans are among the most profitable investments and are extremely attractive to growth-oriented banks. Banks also extend long-term mortgage credit to residential homeowners or to holders of commercial property. Real estate loans can be highly speculative, however, if banks lend against properties that do not generate predictable cash flows. Many banks, savings and loans, insurance companies, and pension funds, in fact, have owned (repossessed) significant amounts of real estate with other credits still on the books that are not producing sufficient cash to service debt. The underlying real estate of these loans is quite often commercial property built under the assumption that lease rates and occupancy would quickly rise. If these assumptions do not materialize, the bank ends up with the property that it can only sell at depressed prices, so the bank keeps it on the books to avoid taking losses.

**COMMERCIAL REAL ESTATE LOANS.** **Commercial real estate loans** are generally short-term loans consisting of construction and real estate development loans, land development loans, and commercial properties loans such as shopping centers and office buildings. Many banks lend heavily to businesses for new building construction and land development. **Construction loans** represent interim financing on commercial, industrial, and multifamily residential property. A bank extends credit to a builder to pay for the materials and labor necessary to complete a project. Funds are usually disbursed on an irregular basis, such as upon the completion of certain phases of the construction process (foundation poured, framed, dry-wall, etc.) or based on actual supplier and subcontractor bills presented to the banker. The builder repays the entire loan when the project is completed, and permanent (long-term) financing is arranged. Construction loans are interim loans. **Interim loans** provide financing only for a limited time until permanent financing is arranged; for example, long-term mortgage or direct financing from insurance companies or pension funds. **Land development loans** finance the construction of roads and public utilities in areas where developers plan to build houses. Land development loans are also interim loans as the developer repays the loan as homeowners or investors buy lots. Maturities on these loans normally range from 12 months to 2 years but are often extended when developers cannot find permanent financing. Interest rates on interim loans can be high for some borrowers but are typically priced at a floating rate over prime or other base role. The bank may also charge an *origination fee* to make the original loan.

The credit analysis of construction and land development loans follows that described in Chapter 11.[10] There are, however, peculiar features of these projects that deserve mention. Most importantly, these loans may be extremely risky. Individual projects, such as the construction of an office building in a metropolitan area's downtown business district, are often quite costly. Few banks choose to assume that risk alone, so most enter into joint financing agreements. The primary source of repayment is permanent financing provided by a third party. If this is not forthcoming, the bank must look either to the developer's cash flow from other projects or, ultimately, the outright sale of the building. If the developer defaults on the loan before construction is completed, the bank must pay for someone else to finish the project. Banks prefer a project in which customers have already committed to lease space and the developer has arranged for a takeout commitment. A **takeout commitment** is an agreement whereby a different lender, such as a life insurance company or pension fund, agrees to provide long-term financing after construction is finished. The construction loan is speculative when the builder does not have a commitment or the ultimate owner of the structure is not known.

Most banks attempt to limit their risk by working closely with a select group of developers and by requiring third-party appraisals of projects. A bank that makes a construction loan essentially underwrites the developer. Maintaining a close working relationship allows the bank to assess whether the developer can complete a specific project and has cash flow from other projects to cover losses if this one fails. Third-party appraisals provide an estimate of the project's value at completion and offer assurance that the structure's value can cover loan payments in the event of default.[11]

---

[10]The financial statements of developers differ markedly from those of most nonfinancial businesses. Analysts must be familiar with how specific firms allocate costs for projects under construction and how they report gross profit. Generally accepted accounting principles allow builders to estimate profit on unfinished projects. An analyst must know what portion of gross profit can be attributed to completed contracts and should compare this with past estimates to assess the efficiency of the builder's historical profit estimates.

[11]Unfortunately, there is no guarantee that appraisals are meaningful. Appraisers are not regulated, and many instances of abuse are known.

The quality of these loans closely follows the business cycle. Banks try to compensate for high default risk by requiring up-front fees and pricing construction loans at substantial markups over their funding costs. It is not uncommon, for example, for a bank to charge an origination fee of 1 percent of the loan and float the interest rate at 4 percent over the bank's base rate. Interest rate risk is lessened because interest income varies with changes in the level of interest rates. Still, if the structure is not sold or adequately leased, cash flows will not cover debt service requirements.

**RESIDENTIAL MORTGAGE LOANS.** For the average bank, real estate loans are dominated by long-term mortgages, primarily on single-family houses. A **mortgage** is a legal document through which a borrower gives a lender a lien on real property as collateral against a debt. The borrower gets to use the property as long as the scheduled interest and principal payments are met. If the borrower defaults, the lender can exercise the lien and claim the property. Generally a borrower has the right of redemption, whereby foreclosure is prevented if the debt is repaid within a reasonable time after default.

Banks can make conventional mortgages or mortgages insured by the Federal Housing Authority or Veterans Administration. These last two carry long maturities and require small down payments by borrowers. They are costly in terms of officer time because management must complete considerable paperwork before the loans are officially approved.

The **1–4 family residential mortgage loans** are attractive investments when priced correctly. Holding loan-term fixed-rate mortgages in the bank's portfolio creates a negative funding GAP position for most banks.[12] If a bank's relatively short-term CDs and money market certificates rates increase, the bank can find its mortgages earning less than it pays for funds. Not surprisingly, lenders have developed contracts that increase the rate sensitivity of their mortgage portfolio to reduce the bank's interest rate risk exposure. Mortgages now may provide for (1) periodic adjustments in the interest rate, (2) adjustments in periodic principal payments, or (3) the lender sharing in any price appreciation of the underlying structure at sale. The purpose is to increase cash flow when the level of interest rates rises or inflation accelerates.[13] Most banks now offer borrowers a choice between fixed-rate and adjustable-rate mortgages. Because borrowers assume interest rate risk with rate-sensitive mortgages, banks offer inducements, such as lower initial rates and caps on how high the rate might go, to increase their attractiveness.

The credit analysis of single-family residential mortgages resembles that of any consumer loan. Most mortgages are *amortized* with monthly payments, including both principal and interest. Because of the long maturity, banks look carefully at the borrower's cash flow, character, and willingness to repay. The evaluation concentrates on three significant features of the loan: the appraised property value, the borrower's down payment, and the borrower's cash flow relative to required interest and principal payments. Banks assume less credit risk when the down payment is high and debt service payments are small relative to the buyer's income.

**THE SECONDARY MORTGAGE MARKET.** Real estate lending is popular, in part, due to the growth of the secondary mortgage market. Today, there is a large number of players in the mortgage banking business that originate and service mortgages. One newly developed segment is the market for *subprime*, or higher-risk, mortgage borrowers. The **secondary mortgage market** involves the trading of previously originated residential mortgages. Lenders that originate mortgages can either sell them directly to interested investors or package them into mortgage pools. With a mortgage pool, the original lender issues long-term securities that evidence a claim on the mortgages in the pool. Investors in the securities receive the interest and principal payments on the underlying mortgages' net of servicing fees. In most cases, the pool originator collects the mortgage payments from home buyers, keeping a portion as a servicing fee, pays the relevant property taxes, and apportions the remainder to insurers and holders of the securities.

Because risk-based capital requirements requires banks to hold capital against most assets on its books, many banks follow a strategy of originating mortgages for the purpose of securitizing them; that is, selling them in packages to other investors. Their earnings come from origination and servicing fees. Chapter 13 documents recent growth in the secondary mortgage market, including the nature of securities created by the securitization process.

**HOME EQUITY LOANS.** The Tax Reform Act of 1986 gradually phased out the deductibility of interest on consumer debt when computing federal income taxes, except for mortgages. As might be expected, lenders quickly packaged home equity loans that soon substituted for many traditional forms of consumer borrowing. **Home**

---

[12]See Chapters 5 and 6 for more details about interest rate risk and funding GAP. A negative funding GAP means that the bank has fewer rate-sensitive assets than rate-sensitive liabilities. Hence when interest rates increase, the cost of bank funds increases more than the yields on the longer-term assets. The value of equity typically falls as well because longer-term securities are more sensitive to changes in interest rates than shorter-term securities.

[13]Many types of adjustable-rate mortgages have evolved. Some tie the interest rate to an index that changes when the general level of rates changes. Others establish rates that change according to a fixed schedule. Principal payments may likewise be indexed to inflation.

**equity loans** are actually a second mortgage secured by real estate so that any interest payments meet the requirement for deductibility. **Second mortgages** are usually shorter term, three to ten years, and have a subordinated claim to the first residential mortgage. Most banks now offer **home equity lines of credit** (HELOC) that are structured similarly to direct installment loans or direct credit lines in which an individual has a credit limit and can borrow up to the limit for any purpose.

From the lender's perspective, home equity loans are fully secured and thus low risk. In reality, the loans have encouraged many consumers to spend beyond their normal ability to generate income so that borrowers do default on the loans. Because the claims of the home equity loan are secondary to the first mortgage, it is more difficult for the bank holding the second mortgage to bring about foreclosure. With declining property values in the late 1980s and early 1990s, lenders tightened standards because of concern over their risk exposure and the economic downturn. Even with the potential problems of home equity lines as well as potential abuse by borrowers, few banks have charged-off unexpectedly large losses on home equity loans.

**EQUITY INVESTMENTS IN REAL ESTATE.** For many years government regulations prevented commercial banks from owning real estate except for their corporate office or property involved in foreclosure. State-chartered savings and loan associations and insurance companies, in contrast, have long been able to take equity positions in real estate projects. This enabled them to charge lower loan rates in exchange for unlimited profit potential from price appreciation. Federal regulators want banks to engage in these more speculative real estate activities only through separate subsidiaries, if at all. The Gramm-Leach-Bliley Act of 1999 allowed for banks to enter into the merchant banking business and many states have passed laws permitting state-chartered banks to invest in real estate, in many cases restricting the dollar investment to a fixed percentage of assets.

## COMMERCIAL LOANS

There are as many types of commercial loans as there are business borrowers. The UBPR defines **commercial loans** as "domestic-office commercial and industrial loans, loans to depository institutions, acceptances of other banks, and obligations (other than securities) of states and political subdivisions." Commercial loans are made to businesses to assist in financing working capital needs (accounts receivables and inventory), plant and equipment needs, and other legitimate business purposes. Banks lend large amounts to manufacturing companies, service companies, farmers, securities dealers, and other financial institutions. The loans may finance short-term uses such as temporary working capital needs and construction expenses in which the borrower has obtained a commitment for long-term financing from another lender, or long-term uses such as new equipment purchases and plant expansion. Short-term business loans often take the form of **loan commitments** or **line of credit** agreements. These loans may be formal or informal and operate much like a credit card arrangement. A bank and borrower agree in advance that the customer can draw against the line as needed up to some maximum credit limit. The borrower determines the timing of borrowings and the actual amount. The obvious advantage to the borrower is flexibility. For example, the firm may only need temporary financing as it accumulates inventory prior to its major sales period. Once sales occur, it can repay the loan. These loans also take up less of the loan officer's time. Bankers must, however, still complete a detailed analysis before extending credit. Prior to formal approval, the loan officer evaluates the purpose and repayment prospects and negotiates the size of the commitment, the term the commitment is outstanding, any fees or compensating balance requirements, and the interest rate charged.

Because many commercial loans finance current assets (primarily accounts receivables and inventory), the following discussion analyzes normal working capital requirements and several types of loans associated with this financing. The previous section addressed commercial real estate loans and the following sections analyze the general features of term commercial loans and agriculture loans. Often, commercial and industrial loans are linked to commercial real estate loans with the only real distinguishing characteristic being whether the loans are secured by real estate or other assets of the company.

**WORKING CAPITAL REQUIREMENTS.** A company's **(net) working capital** equals its current assets minus its current liabilities. For most firms, working capital is positive, suggesting that current assets are financed partially by current debt and partially by long-term debt and equity. If current assets are liquidated, the proceeds from the sale of the current assets will exceed current liabilities. Working capital, therefore, is a net liquidity measure.

Consider the daily average balance sheet information in Exhibit 10.10 for Simplex Corporation, which has $300 in net working capital ($1,280 − $980). Implicitly, $300 of long-term debt and equity is financing $300 of cash, receivables, and inventory, and the firm's current assets cover its current liabilities. Note that $450 of the current liabilities are notes payable to a bank indicating short-term financing currently provided for operating purposes.

## EXHIBIT 10.10   Balance Sheet and Income Statement Data for Simplex Corporation

### Cash-to-Cash Cycle

| Assets | | Liabilities and Equity | | Selected Income Start Data | |
|---|---|---|---|---|---|
| Cash | $ 80 | Accounts payable | $ 400 | Net sales | $ 9,125 |
| Accounts receivable | 700 | Accrued expenses | 80 | COGS | 6,100 |
| Inventory | 500 | Notes pay—bank | 450 | Operating expenses | 2,550 |
| Current assets | 1,280 | CM LTD | 50 | Purchases* | 6,430 |
| Fixed assets | 1,220 | Current liabilities | $ 980 | Average Daily: | |
| Total Assets | $ 2,500 | LTD | 550 | Sales | $ 25.00 |
| | | Equity | 970 | COGS | 16.71 |
| | | Total Liabilities and Equity | $2,500 | Operating expenses | 6.99 |
| | | | | Purchases | 17.62 |

### Working Capital Cycle†

| Current Assets | | Current Liabilities | |
|---|---|---|---|
| Days cash | 3.20 = 80 / 25.00 | Days accounts payable | 22.71 = 400 / 17.62 |
| Days accounts receivable | 28.00 = 700 / 25.00 | Days accruals | 11.45 = 80 / 6.99 |
| Days inventory | 29.92 = 500 / 16.71 | | |
| Asset cycle | 61.12 | Liability cycle | 34.16 |

Difference in cash-to-cash cycles = 26.96
Working Capital Needs = 26.96 × $16.71 = $450.58

* Prior period inventory was 170.
† Ratio definitions:
Days cash = cash / (sales / 365)
Days receivables = accounts receivable / (sales / 365)
Days inventory = inventory / (COGS / 365)
Days payables = accounts payable / (purchases / 365)
Days accruals = accruals / (operating expenses / 365)

Virtually all businesses must invest in current assets to operate. Manufacturers purchase materials to produce goods that are often sold on credit. Retail firms purchase display merchandise and often rely on credit sales to stimulate business. Service companies need operating cash and small inventories of supplies. Each type of business relies on different financing methods depending on its operating policies and growth. If the financing needs are truly short term, a working capital loan is appropriate.

The bottom of Exhibit 10.10 and Exhibit 10.11 summarize the normal **working capital cycle** for a manufacturing firm using the data for Simplex Corporation. This cycle compares the timing difference between converting current assets to cash and making cash payments on normal operating expenses. Supplementary income statement data are provided in Exhibit 10.10 and used to calculate the timing difference. All sales are assumed to be credit sales and the data are viewed in daily average terms.

The flow of cash in the operating cycle begins by the firm accumulating operating cash to put in cash drawers and pay wages and salaries. After minimum levels of operating cash are accumulated, the firm then invests in inventory by purchasing materials that are converted into finished goods. Accounts receivable appear when the firm sells the inventory on credit. Finally, the receivables revert to cash as customers pay off their credit purchases. Many factors influence how long it takes to complete the cycle, including the complexity of the production process, the terms of credit sales, and the firm's collection efforts on outstanding receivables. The longer it takes to produce a finished good, sell it, and collect on the sale, the longer the firm has to wait to get its cash investment back. If a timing difference exists between the number of days in the asset cycle and cash payments on liabilities, a loan may be necessary to help a firm manage the mismatch in cash flows.

In most industries, the cash-to-cash asset cycle takes longer than the comparable cycle for nonbank current liabilities. The **cash-to-cash asset cycle** measures how long the firm must finance operating cash, inventory and accounts receivables from the day of first sale. The **cash-to-cash liability cycle** essentially measures how long a firm obtains interest-free financing from suppliers in the form of accounts payable and accrued expenses to

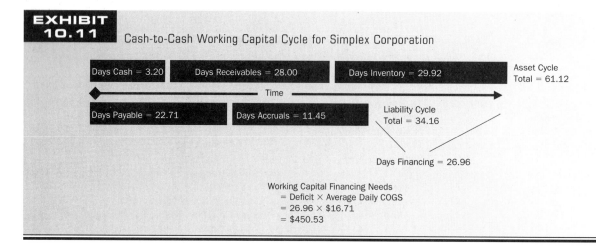

**EXHIBIT 10.11** Cash-to-Cash Working Capital Cycle for Simplex Corporation

finance the asset cycle.[14] Firms use trade credit to finance materials purchases (inventory) temporarily, but must normally pay their suppliers within 30 days to receive any discounts. Even when they can ride suppliers longer, they still pay down accounts payable well before their current asset cycle is completed. Firms may also be able to accrue expenses rather than make immediate cash payments, but the deferment period is quite short. The net effect is that most businesses receive cash from the sale of goods long after they have paid suppliers, associated labor costs, and other operating expenses. After the firm has utilized all of its available trade credit, the remaining timing discrepancy will be financed with bank credit or long-term debt.

This cash-to-cash comparison is demonstrated at the bottom of Exhibits 10.10 and Exhibit 10.11. In Exhibit 10.10 the days cash-to-cash for assets indicates that it takes over 61 days for Simplex's current assets to turn over. In comparison, the company rides its suppliers for an average of almost 23 days and defers operating expenses for just over 11 days. Notes payable to the bank and long-term debt finance this 27-day deficiency in underlying cash flows.

One procedure for estimating working capital loan needs is to multiply the number of days deficiency between the asset and liability cash-to-cash cycle by the firm's average daily cost of goods sold. In this example the product equals $450.58 (26.96 × $16.71) which is close to the amount of the notes payable currently outstanding ($450). Of course, this calculation ignores the firm's capital structure. If a company has above-average equity or more long-term debt financing than the norm, working capital financing needs can be met by these more permanent sources of funds. In this case, the estimate based on the above calculation will overstate true short-term funding needs.

**SEASONAL VERSUS PERMANENT WORKING CAPITAL NEEDS.** Many businesses find that their working capital fluctuates over time. This may be caused by seasonal sales or events such as an unexpected increase in credit sales relative to cash sales, an increase in inventory resulting from defective materials, or changes in payment patterns to suppliers. Businesses temporarily build up inventories and pay higher operating expenses prior to the peak sales season. Working capital needs rise because accounts payable increase at a slower pace. The deficiency increases further with an increase in receivables, then declines to normal as the firm collects on receivables and inventory contracts.

An important facet of working capital financing is to assess any *seasonal pattern* in inventory accumulation, production, sales, and collection of receivables. If seasonal patterns exist, a lender must obtain interim financial statements that reveal peak holdings of current assets. Consider, for example, a company that manufactures fireworks or a restaurant in a ski resort area. The maximum working capital loan will normally apply during or just preceding the company's peak business activity.

In addition to seasonal needs, most businesses have a normal or **minimum amount of working capital** that persists regardless of unexpected events or seasonal fluctuations. That is to say, most businesses have some minimum level of accounts receivable, inventory, and accounts payable that are a permanent part of the business. One customer's accounts receivable will be paid off but a new receivable will replace it, hence, some dollar amount

---

[14]Actually the term "interest-free" may not be totally correct. If discounts for early payment are offered and not taken, the effective interest cost of paying late (after the discount period) could be quite high.

of accounts receivables will always be with the firm. This base or **permanent working capital** need equals the minimum level of current assets minus the minimum level of current liabilities net of short-term bank credit and current maturities of long-term debt (adjusted current liabilities) throughout each year. It is important that businesses and their lenders recognize this permanent need because it represents the amount of long-term debt or equity financing required for current assets. Firms should try to raise funds for these permanent needs in the bond or stock market as banks are reluctant to make term loans for this purpose. Any working capital requirement in excess of this base amount would be financed with short-term credit.

A time series plot of a firm's working capital position helps quantify permanent and temporary needs. It also identifies any seasonal patterns that appear. Exhibit 10.12 shows this concept graphically. The base trend lines, through the minimum amounts of current assets and adjusted current liabilities, designate the permanent components of these balance sheet items. These amounts jump at period q when the firm is assumed to expand its physical plant. The curved lines represent total current assets and total current liabilities. The peak value of current liabilities comes before the peak in current assets, reflecting the fact that receivables growth typically lags behind increases in inventory and trade credit. Permanent working capital needs equal the difference between minimum current assets and adjusted current liabilities. **Seasonal working capital** needs equal the difference in total current assets and adjusted current liabilities. Peak needs coincide with the peak level of current assets.

**SHORT-TERM COMMERCIAL LOANS.** Banks try to match credit terms with a borrower's specific needs. The loan officer estimates the purpose and amount of the proposed loan, the expected source of repayment, and the value of collateral. The loan amount, maturity, and repayment schedule are negotiated to coincide with the projections. Short-term funding needs are financed by short-term loans, while long-term needs are financed by term loans with longer maturities. A mistake often made by the young credit analysts is making a loan for a larger amount or for a longer maturity than is necessary for a "good" customer. The issue is not whether to loan the money to the good customer, but to ensure that the bank meets the customer's need and minimizes its risk. If you loan more money than the customer needs, the customer may spend the money unwisely, such as to purchase unnecessary assets (corporate jets) on which the bank does not hold a lien.

## Seasonal Working Capital Loans.

Seasonal working capital loans finance a temporary increase in net current assets above the permanent requirement (Exhibit 10.12). A borrower uses the proceeds to purchase raw materials and build up inventories of finished goods in anticipation of later sales. Trade credit also increases but by a smaller amount. Funding requirements persist as the borrower sells the inventory on credit and accounts receivables remain outstanding. The loan declines as the borrower collects on the receivables and stops accumulating inventory.

This type of loan is *seasonal* if the need arises on a regular basis and if the cycle completes itself within one year. It is *self-liquidating* in the sense that repayment derives from sales of the finished goods that are financed. Because the loan proceeds finance an increase in inventories and receivables, banks try to secure the loan with these assets. Seasonal working capital loans are often unsecured because the risk to the lender is relatively low.

When evaluating seasonal loans it is necessary to compare the borrower's working capital position over time (Exhibit 10.12). If the bank only obtained year-end historical financial statements when current assets were at seasonal lows, an analysis would demonstrate that the borrower did not need seasonal financing. To estimate maximum seasonal needs, the bank needs comparative statements for periods when current assets are at their highs and lows. The difference in total working capital needs between the two periods equals the maximum seasonal loan requirement. This means that the bank must request interim financial statements. Suppose, for example, that the balance sheet data for Simplex Corporation in Exhibit 10.10 represent the company's minimal seasonal working capital needs. If the peak needs arise four months later when current assets equal $1,800 and current liabilities equal $1,200, the maximum seasonal requirements total $600.

## Open Credit Lines.

Seasonal loans often take the form of open credit lines.[15] Under these arrangements, the bank makes a certain amount of funds available to a borrower for a set period of time. The customer determines the timing of actual borrowings, or "takedowns." Typically, borrowing gradually increases with the inventory buildup, then declines with the collection of receivables. The bank likes to see the loan fully repaid at least once during each year. This confirms that the needs are truly seasonal.

---

[15]Credit lines are used to meet many types of temporary needs in addition to seasonal needs. One popular type is the backup credit line used by large corporations that regularly issue commercial paper. This credit is available to pay investors when commercial paper matures if the corporation does not or cannot roll over its outstanding paper.

**EXHIBIT 10.12** Trends in Working Capital Needs

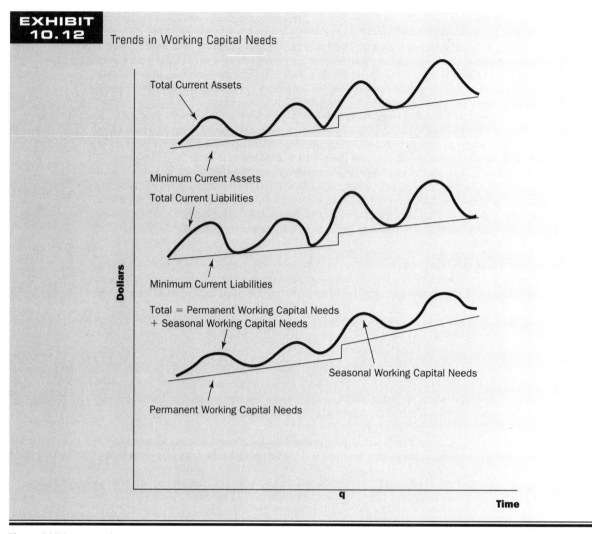

ªCurrent liabilities are net of notes payable and current maturities of long-term debt (adjusted current liabilities).

The terms of credit lines vary between borrowers and whether arrangements are informal or contractual. Informal lines are not legally binding but represent a promise that the bank will advance credit. The customer pays for the service only by paying interest on the funds actually borrowed. A contractual or formal credit line is legally binding even though no written agreement is signed. The bank charges a *commitment fee* for making credit available, regardless of whether the customer actually uses the line. The customer also pays interest on actual borrowings. In both cases, credit lines are renegotiated each year when the bank reassesses the firm's credit needs. Borrowers pay interest at variable rates and often must hold compensating deposit balances with the bank as part of the arrangement.

**Asset-Based Loans.** In theory, any loan secured by a company's assets is an asset-based loan. One popular type of asset-based short-term loan would be those secured by inventories or accounts receivable. Loans to finance leveraged buyouts are also classified in this category. In the case of inventory loans, the security consists of raw materials, goods in process, and finished products. The value of the inventory depends on the marketability of each component if the borrower goes out of business. Banks will lend from 40 to 60 percent against raw materials that are common among businesses and finished goods that are marketable, and nothing against unfinished inventory. With receivables, the security consists of paper assets that presumably represent sales. The quality of the collateral depends on the borrower's integrity in reporting actual sales and the credibility of billings.

Even though all loans secured by a company's assets could be considered asset-based loans, asset-based lending today generally refers to loans where substantially more weight is given to the collateral than cash flow when evaluating the loan request. Payoff from collateral liquidation is more likely to occur in an asset-based loan than in other secured loans, hence the need for good estimates of current and future value of the collateral. Asset-based lending grew in the mid-1980s when many of the large Texas banks were lending off the value of proven oil reserves. During this time, many of the banks were lending 60 percent of a "low" price of oil. For example, when oil prices were $40 a barrel, banks were lending up to $24 per barrel of reserves. Most of the banks' customers thought they were being extremely conservative. No one believed that the price of oil would ever drop to $10 a barrel, which it did. When the price of oil dropped this low, all equipment and industries related to the oil industry crashed. One example was that a $1.6 million drilling rig was only worth $38,000 after the crash because that was the value of scrap metal!

Making asset-based loans requires a loan officer to examine the asset. For example, the loan officer should examine the inventory on site and personally confirm that the customer's figures for receivables are purged of uncollectible or nonexistent accounts. A bank normally lends against 50 to 80 percent of a borrower's receivables depending on the accounts receivable aging schedule and collection experience. An **accounts receivable aging schedule** is a list of accounts receivables segregated according to the month in which the invoice is dated (invoice aging) or in which the invoice is payable (due date aging). An analyst can quickly determine the volume of past-due accounts and trends in collection experience by comparing the fraction of total receivables in each month over time.

Banks frequently require lockbox arrangements to assure that borrowers repay receivables loans when payments are received. With a **lockbox** the borrower requests that its customers mail payments directly to a post office box number controlled by the bank. The bank processes the payments and reduces the borrower's loan balance but charges the borrower for handling the items. Furthermore, because banks spend more time monitoring asset-based loans, they charge rates above those available on open credit lines. The standard interest pricing is a rate that floats from 2 to 6 percent above a bank's **base rate**.[16]

**Highly Leveraged Transactions.** During the early 1980s, one growth area in asset-based lending was leveraged buyouts (LBOs). A **leveraged buyout** involves a group of investors, often part of the existing management team, buying a target company and taking it private with a minimum amount of equity and a large amount of debt. Target companies are generally those with undervalued hard assets. The investors often sell off specific assets or subsidiaries to pay down much of the debt quickly. If key assets have been undervalued, the investors may own a downsized company whose earnings prospects have improved and whose stock has increased in value. The investors sell the company or take it public once the market perceives its greater value. If investors misforecast and pay too much, the target company goes bankrupt.

Many of the earliest LBOs produced returns as high as 50 percent. The availability of junk bond financing during the early 1980s subsequently gave corporate raiders the capacity to make takeovers a real threat so that both friendly and hostile takeovers were common. As more players entered the game, prices increased and the returns declined. By the late 1980s the junk bond market collapsed and takeover financing was restricted for all but the soundest deals. Many large corporations, such as the Campeau Group and Revco, declared bankruptcy. The descriptions of the Allied-Signal and RJR LBOs in the Contemporary Issues Box demonstrate the risks and returns of two well-known transactions. During the mid- to late 1990s, LBO activity rebounded as the junk bond market strengthened and these securities were again readily used for financing.

With the bidding wars and onslaught of bankruptcies in the 1980s, lenders and bank regulators grew concerned with the credit risks that banks were assuming in these transactions. Bank regulators eventually grouped LBOs with other transactions involving extensive borrowings under the label **"highly leveraged transactions"** (HLTs). HLTs arise from three types of transactions:

- LBOs in which debt is substituted for privately held equity
- Leveraged recapitalizations in which borrowers use loan proceeds to pay large dividends to shareholders
- Leveraged acquisitions in which a cash purchase of another related company produces an increase in the buyer's debt structure

[16]The term base rate refers to an index rate used to price loans. The index can be any rate that approximates a bank's cost of debt financing, including the federal funds rate, CD rate, weighted marginal cost of debt, and a bank's own prime rate. Historically, loans were priced as a markup over prime. The term "base rate" has generally replaced "rate" in loan agreements.

According to regulatory definition, an HLT must involve the buyout, recapitalization, or acquisition of a firm in which either:

1. The firm's subsequent leverage ratio exceeds 75 percent.
2. The transaction more than doubles the borrower's liabilities and produces a leverage ratio over 50 percent.
3. The regulators or firm that syndicates the loans declares the transaction an HLT.

Commercial banks play a variety of roles in leveraged buyouts. They may act as investment bankers in putting deals together by obtaining commitments from wealthy individuals, pension funds, and insurance companies for financing. More typically, they extend credit directly in support of the buyer's equity investment. These loans are asset-based because they are secured by the firm's underlying assets and thus represent senior debt in HLTs. It is these loans that have increased problem loans and adversely affected bank profits in recent years. Most HLTs also involve *mezzanine financing*, a type of credit that is subordinated to the claims of bank debt but senior to the investor's common stock. It is appealing because it usually carries an equity participation option. As the number of leveraged buyouts increases, however, the riskiness of the deals also increases. There are more potential buyers, prices get bid higher, financing costs increase, and fewer deals generate the necessary cash flow to service the debt.

**TERM COMMERCIAL LOANS.** Many businesses have credit needs that persist beyond one year. Term commercial loans, which have an original maturity of more than one year, are normally used in these cases. Most term loans have maturities from one to seven years and are granted to finance either the purchase of depreciable assets, start-up costs for a new venture, or a permanent increase in the level of working capital. Because repayment comes over several years, lenders focus more on the borrower's periodic income and cash flow rather than the balance sheet. Chapter 11 examines the traditional credit analysis underlying a term loan from basic ratio analysis to cash flow projections. Term loans often require collateral, but this represents a secondary source of repayment in case the borrower defaults.

The characteristics of term loans vary with the use of the proceeds. For asset purchases, the loan principal is advanced in its entirety after an agreement is signed. The amount equals the net purchase price on the asset acquired. The maturity is determined by the asset's useful life and the borrower's ability to generate cash to repay principal and interest. The interest charged reflects the bank's cost of funds plus a risk premium to compensate for default risk and interest rate risk. Virtually all term loans use formal loan agreements that stipulate what is expected of each party and provide remedies when the agreement is breached. They are necessary because most term loans are too complex to comprehend over several years, during which time the principals tend to forget the initial negotiated terms.

Loan payments are structured in several forms. Many are scheduled over several years so that the borrower's cash flow is sufficient to cover the interest and principal in each year. Many term loans are repaid on an installment basis and fully amortized. Each periodic payment includes interest plus principal in varying amounts. Other term loans may use equal annual principal payments with interest computed on the declining principal balance. Occasionally, term loans will call for balloon payments of principal. In these cases, the borrower pays only the periodic interest until maturity, when the full principal comes due (balloon or bullet loan), or makes amortized principal and interest payments based on a very long maturity (30 years), with the remaining principal paid at maturity (five years). The normal source of repayment is cash flow generated from a company's operations.

For new ventures and permanent increases in working capital, banks advance the loan principal as needed. If the borrower needs different amounts over time, a bank usually structures the agreement as a loan commitment during the early stages, then converts the outstanding principal to a term loan. With this type of term loan—often called a revolving credit—repayment still derives from future cash flows and the agreement is priced at higher yields because of the greater risk.

**REVOLVING CREDITS.** Revolving credits are a hybrid of short-term working capital loans and term loans. They often involve a commitment of funds (the borrowing base) for one to five years. At the end of some interim period, the outstanding principal converts to a term loan. During the interim period, the borrower determines usage much like a credit line. Mandatory principal payments begin once the commitment converts to a term loan. The revolver has a fixed maturity and often requires the borrower to pay a fee at the time of conversion to a term loan. This agreement reduces paperwork and simplifies loan servicing for creditworthy customers, who like its flexibility during the interim period. Revolvers have often substituted for commercial paper or corporate bond issues.

## AGRICULTURE LOANS

Agriculture loans are similar to commercial and industrial loans in that short-term credit finances seasonal operating expenses, in this case those associated with planting and harvesting crops. Much like working capital

# CONTEMPORARY ISSUES

## RJR—DELEVERAGING AN LBO

At the end of 1988, Kohlberg Kravis Roberts & Company (KKR) acquired RJR Nabisco for $24.7 billion, the largest LBO in history. In October 1988, RJR's chairman and other insiders offered to buy the firm for $75 a share. After an aggressive bidding war that ended two months later, the eventual sales price was the equivalent of $114 in securities per share. RJR obtained $24.7 billion in financing and immediately announced a plan to sell corporate assets to pay down the debt. The following chart demonstrates how RJR's stock price reacted initially versus prices on its outstanding bonds with a 13-year maturity. The stock price rose over the offer price

because arbitrageurs bought shares in anticipation of a bidding war for the company. The bond prices plummeted because any firm that acquired RJR would load up on debt to finance the purchase. Existing bondholders' claims would be adversely affected and RJR's ability to service interest and principal payments on debt would be hampered. In fact, when KKR announced a $1.25 billion senior note offering in January 1989, Moody's rated the bonds as speculative, thereby raising KKR's borrowing costs based on the firm's reduced ability to cover debt payments.

By 1991 KKR was concentrating its efforts on deleveraging, or substituting equity for debt. Asset sales had gone slower than expected and prices were generally lower than expected. To reduce interest payments KKR decided to inject $1.18 billion in equity with the proceeds used to pay down its debt. KKR had gone full circle from increasing leverage to decreasing leverage. Through 1998 the firm's stock price was still low, particularly because tobacco products were subject to extreme price pressure, and the firm had too much debt. In 1999 KKR separated the tobacco business from the Nabisco food operation, effectively admitting the firm had greater value after break-up.

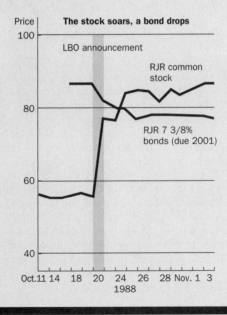

loans, the proceeds are used to purchase inventory in the form of seed, fertilizer, and pesticides and to pay other production costs. Farm operators expect to repay the debt when the crops are harvested and sold. Long-term credit finances livestock, equipment, and land purchases. The fundamental source of repayment is cash flow from the sale of livestock and harvested crops in excess of operating expenses. These loans differ, however, because agriculture is perceived to be a vital national industry. The federal government lends considerable sums to farmers through its farm credit system. Federal agencies involved with agriculture lending include the Farmers Home Administration, the Farm Credit Banks, and Federal Land Banks. Commercial banks often work with these agencies to keep farmers operating, even when it appears that they will sustain large near-term losses.

The profitability of agriculture loans follows cyclical trends in the farm economy. During the 1970s when inflation was high, farm land values more than doubled in many regions of the United States. Using land as collateral, banks encouraged farmers to expand their operations, financed with term loans. Both farmers and banks expected land values to continue rising and virtually ignored whether cash flow from production was sufficient to cover the debt service.

The problem was that banks loaned against the perceived value of land, but farmers never expected to sell the land to repay the debt. As cash flow deteriorated from 1984 to 1987, land values fell and the loans were undercollateralized. The obvious lesson is that farm loans, like term commercial loans, are repaid out of cash flow. Before lending, a bank should verify that cash flows will be sufficient to service debt under most circumstances.

Worldwide events and government policies tend to create a cyclical pattern in agriculture markets. For example, the high inflation and resulting rapid increase in farm land values seen in the 1970s were reversed in the 1980s with the Soviet grain embargo in 1980, the worldwide recession in 1982, and the strong U.S. dollar lowering net exports. Farm commodity prices fell so far that farm revenues were frequently less than the cost of seed, fertilizer, and loan interest. Land values fell with this negative operating cash flow, reducing the farmers' borrowing base just when they needed more credit for operating expenses. Agriculture lenders and farmers are constantly working through the cycle where commodity prices rise and fall depending on the demand from foreign and U.S. markets and changes in supply from improved or reduced production. The cycles can be extremely volatile.

## CONSUMER LOANS

Nonmortgage consumer loans differ substantially from commercial loans. Their usual purpose is to finance the purchase of durable goods, although many individuals borrow to finance education, medical care, and other expenses. The average loan to each borrower is relatively small. Most loans have maturities from one to four years, are repaid in installments, and carry fixed interest rates. In recent years, most states have removed usury ceilings that set maximum rates banks can charge so that consumer loan rates are now high relative to historical norms. This leads to different risk and return features than with other loans. In general, an individual borrower's default risk is greater than a commercial customer's. Consumer loan rates are thus higher to compensate for the greater losses.

Although most consumer loans carry fixed rates, installment payments increase their rate sensitivity so their average duration is relatively short. Long-term loans, however, may subject banks to considerable interest rate risk. Although the securitization market for automobile loans and credit card loans has developed rather rapidly during the late 1990s and early 2000s, consumer loans are relatively illiquid (see Chapter 1). Banks generally cannot sell them near face value because no secondary market exists.

Consumer loans are normally classified as either installment, credit card, or noninstallment credit. Installment loans require a partial payment of principal plus interest periodically until maturity. Other consumer loans require either a single payment of all interest plus principal or a gradual repayment at the borrower's discretion, as with a credit line. Banks' share of the consumer credit market has fallen over time, but even with many competitors, commercial banks held around 38 percent of the total credit outstanding in the late 1990s and were the largest single holders of automobile loans, mobile home loans, and all other types of loans.

Noninstallment loans are for special purposes in which the individual normally expects a large cash receipt to repay the debt, such as a temporary bridge loan for the down payment on a house that is repaid from the sale of the previous house. Chapter 12 discusses additional features of consumer loans and selected credit analysis procedures. Pools of securitized assets are the second largest holder of consumer credit with 28.2 percent of total consumer credit at the end of 2004. Pools of securitized assets were the largest single holder of revolving credit (credit card or overdraft loans), having surpassed banks in 1997.

**VENTURE CAPITAL.** Due to the high leverage and risk involved, as well as regulatory requirements, banks generally do not participate directly in venture capital deals. Some banks, however, do have subsidiaries that finance certain types of equity participations and venture capital deals, but their participation is limited. Venture capital (VC) is a broad term used to describe funding acquired in the earlier stages of a firm's economic life. This type of funding is usually acquired during the period in which the company is growing faster than its ability to generate internal financing and before the company has achieved the size needed to be efficient. Generally speaking, venture capital provides long-term, risk-sharing equity capital or debt to assist non–publicly traded companies with their growth opportunities. VC firms attempt to add value to a business without taking majority control. Although many venture capital deals are in the form of debt, VC investors often take a minority equity participation in the firm as owners must sell a minority share in their companies to attract the venture backer. The VC firm will most likely seek a nonexecutive board position and attend monthly board meetings. Often, VC firms not only provide financing but experience, expertise, contacts, and advice when required. There are many types of venture financing. Early stages of financing come in the form of *seed* or *start-up capital*. These are highly leveraged transactions in which the VC firm lends money for a percentage stake in the business. Rarely, if ever, do banks participate as VCs at this stage. Later-stage development capital takes the form of *expansion and replacement financing, recapitalization* or *turnaround financing, buy-out* or *buy-in financing,* and even *mezzanine financing.* Banks do participate in these rounds of financing, but if the company is overleveraged at the onset, the banks will be effectively excluded from these later rounds of financing.

*Mezzanine financing* became quite popular during the technology boom of the late 1990s and provides a company the funds to continue to grow at a rapid pace. It is usually the second, third, or fourth round of financing. This type of financing is popular because VCs are investing in later rounds of financing; such that the firms have a track record upon which to base their investment decisions. Some venture capital firms focus on particular industries, while others may focus on specific types of mezzanine financing, such as financing used to take a company public or acquisition financing.

# SUMMARY

Lending involves more risk than virtually any other banking activity. Management, therefore, analyzes the nature of risks carefully before extending credit. The credit process includes three functions: business development and credit analysis, credit execution and administration, and credit review. Business development activities concentrate on identifying profitable customers and encouraging credit relationships. Credit analysis is the process of assessing risk and includes a review of financial data and subjective evaluation of the borrower's character. The credit staff formally accepts or rejects a loan request and executes the necessary documents with approvals. Finally, loan officers periodically review each outstanding loan, especially when it comes up for renewal or reaches workout status. At times, loan terms may need to be modified to recognize a change in the borrower's status.

Banks make many different types of loans, which are the dominant asset in most bank portfolios. This chapter describes the basic features of short-term working capital loans, asset-based loans, real estate loans, consumer loans, and agriculture loans. It analyzes many banks' efforts to move assets off the balance sheet or directly enter into off-balance sheet activities to supplement earnings.

## QUESTIONS

1. Discuss the importance of a bank's credit culture in managing credit risk.
2. Describe the basic features of the three functions underlying the credit process at commercial banks.
3. What are the five Cs of credit? Discuss their importance in credit analysis. Describe the five Cs of bad credit introduced in the text.
4. Explain why historical charge-off and past-due data may not represent the bank's current portfolio credit risk.
5. Explain why a large bank may be willing to accept higher average loss rates on loans it is able to credit score.
6. How does a bank make a profit on loans? Discuss the importance of loans in attracting a borrower's other business with a financial institution.
7. Discuss reasons why banks might choose to include the following covenants in a loan agreement:
   a. Cash dividends cannot exceed 60 percent of pretax income.
   b. Interim financial statements must be provided monthly.
   c. Inventory turnover must be greater than five times annually.
   d. Capital expenditures may not exceed $10 million annually.
8. Explain what it means to "perfect the bank's security interest" in collateral. When lending to a small business owner who is an owner/manager, what methods might the bank use to perfect its interest in the collateral of the business?
9. Explain how a company's permanent working capital needs differ from its seasonal working capital needs.
10. Explain how banks move loans off the balance sheet. What motivates different types of off-balance sheet activities? Discuss the risks these actions involve.
11. What motivation encourages commercial banks to make adjustable-rate mortgages? Why are adjustable mortgage rates normally below fixed mortgage rates? As the level of rates declines, would you expect banks to increase or decrease the adjustable-rate proportion of their mortgage portfolios?

12. You are considering making a working capital loan to a company that manufactures and distributes fad items for convenience and department stores. The loan will be secured by the firm's inventory and receivables. What risks are associated with this type of collateral? How would you minimize the risk and periodically determine that the firm's performance was not deteriorating?

13. Discuss whether each of the following types of loans can be easily securitized. Explain why or why not.

    a. Residential mortgages

    b. Small business loans

    c. Pools of credit card loans

    d. Pools of home equity loans

    e. Loans to farmers for production

14. Describe the basic features of:

    a. Open credit lines

    b. Asset-based loans

    c. Term commercial loans

    d. Short-term real estate loans

15. Why do firms or individuals involved in farming need to borrow? What type of inventory does a farmer need?

16. What type of receivables does a farmer typically have? What collateral is typically available? In addition to general economic conditions, what should a banker be watchful of before extending credit to a farmer?

17. Many banks compete aggressively for business in consumer credit cards. What is the particular attraction of this type of lending?

18 Suppose that you are considering making a working capital loan to a business customer of your bank. You do the cash-to-cash cycle analysis and determine that the firm's daily average cost of goods sold is $50,000. What does this mean?

19. Describe how each of the following helps a bank control its credit risk:

    a. Loan covenants

    b. Risk rating systems

    c. Position limits

## PROBLEMS

**LOAN TO BOOK PUBLISHER.** Suppose that RSM Publishing Company, a children's book publisher, has approached your bank and wants to borrow $250,000 in working capital. The firm provides you with the following balance sheet and income statement data:

| Assets | | Liabilities & Equity | |
|---|---|---|---|
| Cash | $50,000 | Accounts payable | $166,000 |
| Accounts receivable | $375,000 | Accrued expenses | $37,000 |
| Inventory | $510,000 | Notes payable | $75,000 |
| Fixed assets | $925,000 | Current maturity of long-term debt | $25,000 |
| Total Assets | $1,860,000 | Long-term debt | $475,000 |
| | | Equity | $1,082,000 |
| | | Total Liabilities and equity | $1,860,000 |

Sales: $4,622,800
Cost of goods sold: $3,504,100
Operating expenses: $893,000
Purchases: $ 3,116,000

1. What fraction of the firm's current assets is (implicitly) being funded with long-term debt or equity? What is the significance if this figure is large versus small?

2. Assuming a 365-day year, calculate the firm's asset cash-to-cash cycle, liability cash-to-cash cycle, and days deficiency. Using this information and procedure described in the text, estimate the firm's working capital loan needs.

3. What general concerns might you have regarding this loan request?

4. Suppose that the typical publishing firm in this industry has just one-half the amount of equity that RSM has. How will this affect key industry ratios and the estimate of working capital needs by this procedure, in general?

## ACTIVITY

Obtain copies of the annual reports for several community banks in your area and at least one large regional or nationwide bank. Compare the size of the loan portfolios as a fraction of total assets. Compare the composition of their loan portfolios. What impact should the differences have on each bank's risk position and earnings? Examine the footnotes to determine the loan loss experience for each type of loan. Why do differences appear?

# CHAPTER 11

# Evaluating Commerical Loan Requests

Though my bottom line is black, I am flat upon my back,

My cash flows out and customers pay slow.

The growth of my receivables is almost unbelievable;

The result is certain—unremitting woe!

And I hear the banker utter an ominous low mutter,

"Watch cash flow."

—HERBERT S. BAILEY JR., WITH APOLOGIES TO "THE RAVEN" BY EDGAR ALLAN POE[1]

*The financial press pays great attention to corporate earnings announcements as indicators of past performance and future growth opportunities. Most analysts, however, recognize that cash flow information is equally important when evaluating a firm's prospects. Reported earnings and earnings per share can be manipulated by management and may not depict the firm's true ability to meet payment obligations. Debts are repaid out of cash flow, not earnings.*

*Most firms record credit sales as revenues, even though no cash is immediately generated. A firm with large increases in receivables might report increasing profits but have no cash to cover operating expenses. Similarly, some companies report their share of undistributed profits in firms in which they have a limited equity interest as income, even though no cash is received. In 2001 and 2002, the SEC determined that many telecom companies inappropriately exchanged service rights, which did not affect cash flow, but were reported as sales, thereby increasing reported earnings. During the late 1990s and early 2000s, just prior to declaring bankruptcy at the end of 2001, Enron reported sales growth that put it on track to be the largest company in the United States based on sales. Enron reported the full gross value of derivative contracts as revenue rather than the much smaller commission it received for the trade. In addition, Enron booked ten years' worth of cost savings it forecasted to save clients in the current fiscal year. Needless to say, no cash flow was associated with these transactions. Cash flow used in conjunction with trends in net income is critically important to determining the quality, and thus permanence, of earnings.*

*This chapter provides guidelines for evaluating commercial credit requests. It briefly considers the qualitative aspects of lending such as the quality of data, the quality of management, the borrower's character and desire to repay a loan, and the quality of the company's product. These qualitative issues and other economic and industry-specific factors can be as important as the quantitative factors associated with the loan decision. An evaluation of these qualitative factors requires experience and "hands-on knowledge," difficult to acquire in a textbook. Instead, this chapter focuses on a company's ability to repay a loan and related quantitative factors associated with the loan decision. As Bailey's banker advised, "Watch cash flow" is an important motto.*

---

[1]Cited in R. Green, "Are More Chryslers in the Offing?" *Forbes* (February 2, 1981).

*The basic objective of credit analysis is to assess the risks involved in extending credit (making a loan). As used here, risk refers to the volatility in earnings. Lenders are particularly concerned with adverse fluctuations in net income, or more importantly cash flow, which hinder a borrower's ability to service or repay a loan. Such risk manifests itself to the bank by a borrower defaulting, or not making timely interest and/or principal payments. Credit analysis assigns a probability to the likelihood of default based on quantitative and qualitative factors. Some risks can be measured with historical and projected financial data. Other risks, such as those associated with the borrower's character and willingness to repay a loan, are not directly measurable. When deciding whether or not to approve a loan, the bank ultimately compares the various risks with the potential benefits to the bank (income) from making the loan.*

---

**T**his chapter introduces a four-step procedure to analyze the quantifiable aspects of commercial credit requests. The procedure incorporates an objective and systematic interpretation of management and operations as well as financial data. It focuses on issues that typically arise when determining creditworthiness. The results supplement qualitative information regarding the borrower's character and history of financial responsibility. After analyzing a loan request, a loan officer should have a firm grasp on the answers to the following key questions:

1. What is the character of the borrower and quality of information provided?
2. What are the loan proceeds going to be used for?
3. How much does the customer need to borrow?
4. What is the primary source of repayment, and when will the loan be repaid?
5. What is the secondary source of repayment; that is, what collateral, guarantees, or other cash inflows are available?

The first section discusses these questions in detail. The second section introduces an objective evaluation procedure. The final section provides an application and interpretation of the analysis for a hypothetical loan request. The appendices review basic terminology and discuss sources of financial data.

## FUNDAMENTAL CREDIT ISSUES

Virtually every business in the United States has a credit relationship with a financial institution. Some firms only use backup credit lines in support of commercial paper issues. Some rely on periodic short-term loans to finance temporary working capital needs. Others primarily use term loans with a maturity beyond one year to finance capital expenditures, new acquisitions, or permanent increases in working capital. Regardless of the type of loan, all credit requests mandate a systematic analysis of the borrower's ability to repay.

When evaluating loan requests, bankers can make two types of errors in judgment. The first is extending credit to a customer who ultimately defaults. The second is denying a loan to a customer who ultimately would repay the debt. In both cases, the bank loses a customer and its profits are less. Many bankers focus on eliminating the first type of error, applying rigid credit evaluation criteria and rejecting applicants who do not fit the mold of the ideal borrower. A well-known axiom in banking is that the only time borrowers can get financing is when they really do not need the funds. Unfortunately, as many bankers have discovered, turning down good loans is unprofitable as well. The purpose of credit analysis is to identify the meaningful, probable circumstances under which the bank might lose. Lenders also use credit analysis to restructure a weak loan application into a good loan when the borrower is strong, but does not fully understand the true borrowing needs.

### CHARACTER OF THE BORROWER AND QUALITY OF DATA PROVIDED

The foremost issue in assessing credit risk is determining a borrower's commitment and ability to repay debts in accordance with the terms of a loan agreement. An individual's honesty, integrity, and work ethic typically evidence commitment. For a business, commitment is evidenced by the owners and senior management. Bankers who argue that they make many quick credit decisions implicitly state that many potential borrowers are of dubious character. Even if the numbers look acceptable, a bank should lend nothing if the borrower appears dishonest. Whenever there is deception or a lack of credibility, a bank should not do business with the borrower.

It is often difficult to identify dishonest borrowers. The best indicators are the borrower's financial history and personal references. When a borrower has missed past debt service payments or been involved in a default or bankruptcy, a lender should carefully document why, to determine if the causes were reasonable. Borrowers with a history of credit problems are more likely to see the same problems arise later. Similarly, borrowers with a good credit history will have established personal and banking relationships that indicate whether they fully disclose meaningful information and deal with subordinates and suppliers honestly. A loan officer should begin the credit analysis by analyzing the firm's prior banking relationships, dealings with suppliers and customers, and current record from appropriate credit bureaus.

Lenders often look for signals of a borrower's condition beyond basic income statement and balance sheet data. For example, negative signals may appear in the following forms:

- A borrower's name consistently appears on the list of bank customers who have overdrawn their accounts.
- A borrower makes a significant change in the structure of the business, such as a change in accountant or change in key manager or adviser.
- A borrower appears to be consistently short of cash, which might be indicated by frequent requests for small loans or keeping small balances in checking accounts when net worth is high.
- A borrower's personal habits have changed for the worse; red flags include behavior suggesting drug use, heavy gambling, alcoholism, or marital breakup.
- A firm's goals are incompatible with those of stockholders, employees, and customers.[2]

The quality of data used in the analysis is critical. Many small companies use less sophisticated accounting techniques and their financial statements are unaudited. Audited financial statements are preferred because accounting rules are well established so that an analyst can better understand the underlying factors that affect the entries. Just because a company has audited financial statements, however, does not mean the reported data are not manipulated. Management has considerable discretion within the guidelines of generally accepted accounting principles and thus can "window dress" financial statements to make the results look better. An analyst should review the following to assess accounting data quality:

- Areas of accounting choices in which estimates and judgments are required inputs
- Periods in which a change in account principle, method, or key assumption has occurred
- Extraordinary and discretionary expenditures, as well as nonrecurring transactions
- Income and expense recognition that do not closely track cash flow
- Nonoperating income, gains, and losses

In addition to character and assessment of data quality, a lender must resolve four additional fundamental issues prior to extending credit: the use of loan proceeds, loan amount, source and timing of repayment, and collateral. These issues draw attention to specific features of each loan that can be addressed when structuring the loan agreement terms.

## USE OF LOAN PROCEEDS

The range of business loan needs is unlimited. Firms may need cash for operating purposes to pay overdue suppliers, make a tax payment, or pay employee salaries. Similarly, they may need funds to pay off maturing debt obligations or to acquire new fixed assets. Although the question of what the borrowed funds will be used for seems simple enough, frequently a firm recognizes that it is short of cash but cannot identify specifically why.

Loan proceeds should be used for legitimate business operating purposes, including seasonal and permanent working capital needs, the purchase of depreciable assets, physical plant expansion, acquisition of other firms, and extraordinary operating expenses. Speculative asset purchases and debt substitutions should be avoided. The use of the loan proceeds can either enhance the ability of the firm to repay the loan or make it more risky. Financing illegal activities or unprofitable operations can actually increase the losses of the firm and hence reduce the possibility of repayment. The true need and use of the loan proceeds determines the loan maturity, the anticipated source and timing of repayment, and the appropriate collateral.

Many commercial loans are made for working capital purposes. As such, they bridge the gap between the expenditure of funds to purchase raw materials or inventory and pay employees with the sale of those goods on credit and the ultimate collection of the cash on the credit sales. The analyst must determine whether the bank is financing an increase in inventory or receivables, or replacing outstanding payables and debt. Banks all too often originate working capital loans as seasonal credits, only to find that they are never fully repaid as anticipated. In this case, the banker discovers that the loan was not a seasonal need but rather a replacement of outstanding payables or financing a permanent increase in working capital needs. Term loans should be made for permanent increases in working capital needs and asset acquisitions with an economic life beyond one year. These types of loans require a longer repayment schedule. One common pitfall is to focus too much on collateral and end up financing a firm's long-term needs with short-term notes. A careful review of a firm's financial data reveals why a company needs financing.

## HOW MUCH DOES THE BORROWER NEED? THE LOAN AMOUNT

In many cases, borrowers request a loan before they clearly understand how much external financing is actually needed and how much is available internally. The amount of credit required depends on the use of the proceeds

---

[2]See Thomas Bennett (1987) for a lender's view of these issues. Conrad Newburgh (1991) presents procedures for evaluating character and maintaining control of the lending agreement.

and the availability of internal sources of funds. For example, if a firm wants to finance new equipment, the loan request is typically for the purchase price less the resale value of any replaced assets. For a shorter-term loan, the amount might equal the temporary seasonal increase in receivables and inventory net of that supported by increased accounts payable. With term loans, the amount can be determined via *pro forma* analysis.[3] Borrowers often ask for too little in requesting a loan and return later for more funds. The lender should not only estimate how much the borrower will need today but also in the future. Inexperienced lenders often make the mistake of failing to recognize that lending only a portion of the funds needed may actually reduce the borrower's ability to pay the loan back. A half-built warehouse will not produce revenue but rather will be a revenue drain. The lender's job is to help determine the correct amount, such that a borrower has enough cash to operate effectively but not too much to spend wastefully.

Once a loan is approved, the amount of credit actually extended depends on the borrower's future performance. If the borrower's cash flows are insufficient to meet operating expenses and debt service on the loan, the bank will be called upon to lend more and possibly lengthen the loan maturity. If cash flows are substantial, the initial loan outstanding might decline rapidly and even be repaid early. The required loan amount is thus a function of the initial cash deficiency and the pattern of future cash flows.

## THE PRIMARY SOURCE AND TIMING OF REPAYMENT

Loans are repaid from cash flows. The four basic sources of cash flow are: the liquidation of assets, cash flow from normal operations, new debt issues, and new equity issues. Credit analysis evaluates the risk that a borrower's future cash flows will not be sufficient to meet mandatory expenditures for continued operations and interest and principal payments on the loan.

Specific sources of cash are generally associated with certain types of loans. Short-term, seasonal working capital loans are normally repaid from the liquidation of receivables or reductions in inventory. Term loans are typically repaid out of cash flows from operations, specifically earnings and noncash charges in excess of net working capital needs and capital expenditures needed to maintain the existing fixed asset base. A comparison of projected cash flow from operations with interest and principal payments on prospective loans indicates how much debt can be serviced and the appropriate maturity. Unless specifically identified in the loan agreement, it is inappropriate to rely on new equity from investors or new debt from other creditors for repayment. Too often these external sources of cash disappear if the firm's profitability declines or economic conditions deteriorate.

The primary source of repayment on the loan can also determine the risk of the loan. The general rule is not to rely on the acquired asset or underlying collateral as the primary source of repayment. If you lend money for someone to buy 1,000 shares of IBM stock and they have no other source of income to pay you back, the primary source of repayment is the acquired asset. If the stock does well, the borrower makes money and repays the loan. If the stock does poorly, the borrower declares bankruptcy and you will not be fully repaid. Obviously, this was not a loan but venture capital disguised as a loan. This is not to say that you would never lend money for someone to buy IBM stock or that an acquired asset cannot be expected to help pay back the loan. They are just not the primary source of repayment.

## SECONDARY SOURCE OF REPAYMENT: COLLATERAL

It is not by chance that the question of collateral is the last question to be addressed. If something goes wrong, a bank wants all the collateral it can get, but it generally does not want to take possession of the collateral. Taking the collateral means that the borrower is unable to continue operations. If the collateral is inventory or uncollected receivables, why would the bank be better able to liquidate the assets than the managers who know the industry? It is also costly to maintain and sell collateral, and foreclosures do not build long-term relationships with the customers.

Banks can, however, lower the risk of loss on a loan by requiring backup support beyond normal cash flow. This can take the form of assets held by the borrower or an explicit guarantee by a related firm or key individual. Collateral is the security a bank has in assets owned and pledged by the borrower against a debt in the event of default. Banks look to collateral as a secondary source of repayment when primary cash flows are insufficient to meet debt service requirements. Banks should select collateral that will retain its value over the business cycle. Receivables and marketable inventory are preferred because of their liquidity. Plant, equipment, and real estate are also potentially valuable.

Virtually any asset, or the general capacity to generate cash flow, can be used as collateral. From a lender's perspective, however, collateral must exhibit three features. First, its value should always exceed the outstanding principal on a loan. The loan-to-value (LTV) ratio is an important measure of amount of coverage the lender has

---

[3]Pro forma analysis is the projecting or forecasting of a company's financial statements into the future. The use of income statement, balance sheet, and cash flow projections allows an analyst to assess the amount of the loan needed, the purpose of the loan proceeds, when the loan will be paid back, and what collateral is available.

with the collateral.[4] For example, lenders generally require an 80 percent LTV ratio on home mortgages before the loan customer can avoid paying for mortgage insurance. The lower the LTV the more likely the lender, who must take possession of the collateral, can then sell the collateral for more than the balance due and reduce losses. It is not uncommon today to find borrowers who are "upside down" on their automobile loans. Upside down means that the LTV is greater than 100 percent or the value of the car is less than the outstanding loan balance. Lenders will rarely make the original loan such that the LTV is greater than 100 percent, but over time, the value of the automobile might fall faster than the balance on the loan. In these cases, the borrower may have a financial incentive to default on the loan. The second required feature of collateral is that a lender should be able to easily take possession of the collateral and have a ready market for its sale. Highly illiquid assets are worth far less because they are not portable and often are of real value only to the original borrower. Finally, a lender must be able to clearly mark collateral as its own. This means that the claim must be legal and clear. Careful loan documentation is required to perfect the bank's interest in the collateral.

When physical collateral is not readily available, banks often look for personal guarantees. They generally rely on the borrower's cash flow to cover debt service with the borrower's net worth in reserve. Banks attempt to protect themselves against adverse changes in a borrower's financial condition by imposing loan covenants in the loan agreement that restrict a borrower's ability to make extreme decisions and thereby alter its fundamental operating profile. When the borrower's cash flow is problematic, a bank can request that the borrower find a cosigner who agrees to assume the debt in the event of default.

Liquidating collateral is clearly a second best source of repayment for three reasons. First, there are significant transactions costs associated with foreclosure. Banks must often allocate considerable employee time and pay large legal expenses that reduce the collateral's net value. Thus, when negotiating loan agreements, the bank should select collateral with a value above the anticipated loan amount. Second, bankruptcy laws allow borrowers to retain possession of the collateral long after they have defaulted. During that time, the collateral often disappears or deteriorates in value. Third, when the bank takes possession of the collateral, it deprives the borrower of the opportunity to salvage the company. The bank must hire new managers or manage the firm temporarily with its own personnel until sale, a poor alternative.

In general, a loan should *not* be approved on the basis of collateral alone. Unless the loan is secured by collateral held by the bank, such as bank CDs, there is risk involved in collection. In most cases, it is essential that lenders periodically examine the quality of collateral to determine whether it truly exists or has deteriorated over time. This involves obtaining new appraisals or on-site inspections of a borrower's inventory, receivables, and operating facilities. In addition to assessing collateral, the lender can reevaluate the borrower's character by the nature of the business and collateral. Collateral improves the bank's position by lowering its net exposure but it does not improve the borrower's ability to generate cash to repay the loan.

In addition to these issues, credit analysis should examine risks that are unique to each loan. Each analysis should identify questions regarding the quality of management, the soundness of the business, sensitivity to economic conditions, the firm's relationship with other creditors, and any other information that is not available in the financial statements.

## EVALUATING CREDIT REQUESTS: A FOUR-PART PROCESS

The purpose of credit analysis is to identify and define the lender's risk in making a loan. There is a four-stage process for evaluating the financial aspects of commercial loans:

1. Overview of management, operations, and the firm's industry
2. Common size and financial ratio analysis
3. Analysis of cash flow
4. Projections and analysis of the borrower's financial condition

During all phases, the analyst should examine facts that are relevant to the credit decision and recognize information that is important but unavailable. The analyst should prepare a list of questions to be presented to the borrower for clarification. Financial calculations, using historical data, should examine the absolute magnitudes of ratios and funds flows and pertinent changes in the magnitudes over time (trend analysis), and compare these measures with industry averages for the firm's competitors. Much of the information is available from the bank's credit files and conversations with the firm's management and chief financial officer. Sources of financial data on comparable firms are described in Appendix I to this chapter.

---

[4]The loan-to-value (LTV) ratio is a measure of the current value of the loan divided by the market value of the collateral. Appraisals are often used for market value with real estate loans. Hence, the quality of the appraisal will determine the usefulness of this ratio.

Financial projections (pro forma) involve making reasonable assumptions about a firm's future sales, working capital needs, capital expenditures, operating expenses, taxes, and dividends. A company may need to borrow funds today (and possibly more in the future), but those funds will be paid back with future cash flows. Projections of the borrower's financial condition are used to forecast cash flows and determine answers to the questions discussed above: how much is needed, what are the funds going to be used for, what is the primary source of repayment, and when will the funds be repaid? These projected cash flows are formally compared with expected interest and principal payments on all debt obligations and other mandatory cash expenditures. The same ratio analysis can then be performed using the projected data as a check on the reasonableness of the forecasts.

## OVERVIEW OF MANAGEMENT, OPERATIONS, AND THE FIRM'S INDUSTRY

Before analyzing financial data, the analyst should gather background information on the firm's operations, including specific characteristics of the business and intensity of industry competition, management character and quality, the nature of the loan request, and the data quality. Relevant historical developments and recent trends should also be examined.

This evaluation usually begins with an analysis of the organizational and business structure of the borrower. Is it a holding company with subsidiaries or a single entity? Does it operate as a corporation or partnership? Is the firm privately or publicly held? When did the firm begin operations, and in what geographic markets does it now compete? The evaluation should also identify the products or services provided and the firm's competitive position in the marketplace as measured by market share, degree of product differentiation, presence of economies of scale or scope in the cost structure, and the bargaining power of buyers and sellers with whom the firm deals.[5]

The next step is usually to write a brief *Business and Industry Outlook* report. The analyst should examine historical sales growth, the relationship between industry sales and the business cycle, and an implied forecast for the industry. The analyst should also address related questions: How many firms offer competitive products? Are there differences in product quality or life? A logical extension is to evaluate suppliers and the production process. Has the firm contracted for the appropriate raw materials at good prices? How many suppliers can provide the necessary materials? What is the quality of the firm's labor force and employee relations? Are the firm's fixed assets obsolete?

The lender should focus particular attention on management character and quality. The backgrounds of the chief executive, financial, and operating officers should be examined in terms of key individuals' ages, experience in the business, service with the company, and apparent line of succession. Businesses frequently are dominated by one individual even though others hold officer titles. When possible, it is useful to identify the top officers' equity interest in the firm and the type of compensation they receive. This helps identify motivating factors underlying firm decisions.

Finally, the overview should recognize the nature of the borrower's loan request and the quality of the financial data provided. It should indicate the proposed use and amount of credit requested and the borrower's anticipated source of repayment. It should specify whether the financial statements are audited and, if so, the type of opinion issued. A brief discussion of generally accepted accounting principles and audited statements appears in Appendix II to this chapter.

## COMMON SIZE AND FINANCIAL RATIO ANALYSIS

Most banks initiate the data analysis using a financial analysis spreadsheet, which arranges the borrower's income statement and balance sheet data into a consistent format for comparison over time and against industry standards. Income statement and balance sheet data for Prism Industries are presented in Exhibits 11.1 and 11.2, respectively. Data for each reporting period are provided in three columns. The first column lists the percentage change in the value from the previous year.[6] The second column contains the actual dollar value of the accounting entry. The third column converts the figure to a common size ratio by dividing by total assets (balance sheet) or net sales (income statement). Comparable peer figures for 2005 are listed in the column labeled Peer Group Ratios.[7]

Prism Industries is a small manufacturer of outdoor storage buildings. Examining Exhibit 11.1 we find that Prism's sales increased by almost 17 percent in 2005. Management indicates that the strong economic environment and its high-quality product have led to the recent success. Although Prism exhibited strong sales growth, its cost of goods sold was almost 3 percent higher and its operating expenses almost 2 percent lower than peers—resulting in an almost 1 percent lower profit before taxes as a percent of sales. Examining the balance sheet data

---

[5]Arnold (1988) describes how the intensity of competition affects a firm's business risk. Lenders should incorporate the results of this analysis in their forecasts of sales, costs, and product pricing.

[6]"% Cha" values are the percentage change in the value from the prior period. Calculated as $(X_t / X_{t-1}) - 1$.

[7]See Appendix II for an overview of available peer group data sources.

## EXHIBIT 11.1

Comparative Income Statement for Prism Industries, 2004–2005

| | 2004 | | 2005 | | | Peer |
| | $ 1,000 | % of Total | % Cha | $ 1,000 | % of Total | Group Ratios |
|---|---|---|---|---|---|---|
| **Net sales** | 2,400 | 100.0% | 16.7% | 2,800 | 100.0% | 100.0% |
| Cost of goods sold | 2,050 | 85.4% | 16.1% | 2,380 | 85.0% | 82.2% |
| Gross profit | 350 | 14.6% | 20.0% | 420 | 15.0% | 17.8% |
| Selling expenses | 195 | 8.1% | 7.7% | 210 | 7.5% | |
| Depreciation & amortization | 42 | 1.8% | 21.4% | 51 | 1.8% | |
| Other operating expenses | 0 | 0.0% | #N/A | 40 | 1.4% | |
| Total operating expenses | 237 | 9.9% | 27.0% | 301 | 10.8% | 12.5% |
| *Operating profit* | 113 | 4.7% | 5.3% | 119 | 4.3% | 5.3% |
| Interest expense | 38 | 1.6% | −10.5% | 34 | 1.2% | |
| All other expenses | 7 | 0.3% | 71.4% | 12 | 0.4% | |
| All other income | 9 | 0.4% | 22.2% | 11 | 0.4% | |
| Total all other expenses (income) | 36 | 1.5% | −2.8% | 35 | 1.3% | 1.4% |
| *Profit before taxes* | 77 | 3.2% | 9.1% | 84 | 3.0% | 3.9% |
| Income taxes | 25 | 1.0% | 16.0% | 29 | 1.0% | |
| **Net income** | **52** | **2.2%** | **5.8%** | **55** | **2.0%** | |
| Dividends | 15 | 0.6% | 33.3% | 20 | 0.7% | |
| Retained earnings | 37 | 1.5% | −5.4% | 35 | 1.3% | |

NOTE: Figures are in thousands of dollars. Lease payments are included in other operating expenses and were $2,200 in 2005. Prism's first year of operations was 2004.

presented in Exhibit 11.2 indicates that Prism's accounts receivable increased in 2005 but remained below the industry norms (as a percentage of assets). Inventory actually decreased in 2005 and was also below industry norms. Net fixed assets, on the other had, were well above industry standards in each year. In terms of financing, Prism relied more on stockholders' equity and used less debt. Prism used slightly more short-term bank debt and less trade credit (accounts payable) than the industry average. Prism also used somewhat less long-term debt than peer average. Prism appears to have financed much of its growth using internally generated funds; that is, retained earnings.

Common size values of the income statement for Prism are provided in Exhibit 11.1. Examining profitability we find that Prism's profit before taxes increased in 2005, but it was less profitable than the industry average. Lower profitability is due to a much higher cost of goods sold (COGS), reflecting either a higher cost of goods or lower markups on finished products. Prism's COGS, as a percent of sales, fell in 2005 but remains above the industry average. This higher COGS was offset somewhat by Prism's lower operating expenses but the net effect is that the firm earns proportionately less before taxes than comparable firms.

Common size ratio comparisons are valuable because they adjust for size and thus enable comparisons across firms in the same industry or line of business. The figures can be distorted, however, if a firm has one balance sheet or income statement item that differs sharply from industry standards. For example, a business that leases fixed assets will report a sharply different asset composition than businesses in an industry where most firms own fixed assets. To address this issue, analysts should move to the next step, which is to calculate a series of ratios that indicate performance variances.

Most analysts differentiate between at least four categories of ratios: liquidity, activity, leverage, and profitability.[8] *Liquidity ratios* indicate a firm's ability to meet its short-term obligations and continue operations. *Activity ratios* signal how efficiently a firm uses assets to generate sales. *Leverage ratios* indicate the mix of the firm's financing between debt and equity and potential earnings volatility. Finally, *profitability ratios* provide evidence of the firm's sales and earnings performance.

[8]Key ratios are defined in Appendix II. Activity ratios are grouped with liquidity ratios in this discussion.

| EXHIBIT 11.2 | Comparative Balance Sheet for Prism Industries, 2004–2005 |
|---|---|

| | Dec. 31, 2004 | | Dec. 31, 2005 | | | Peer Group Ratios |
|---|---|---|---|---|---|---|
| | $ 1,000 | % of Total | % Cha | $ 1,000 | % of Total | |
| Cash and marketable securities | 85 | 8.1% | 5.9% | 90 | 8.2% | 5.5% |
| Accounts receivable | 141 | 13.4% | 18.4% | 167 | 15.2% | 18.2% |
| Inventory | 306 | 29.1% | −3.6% | 295 | 26.8% | 29.3% |
| Prepaid expenses | 22 | 2.1% | −18.2% | 18 | 1.6% | |
| Current assets | 554 | 52.8% | 2.9% | 570 | 51.8% | 53.0% |
| Gross fixed assets | 575 | 54.8% | 12.2% | 645 | 58.6% | |
| Less accumulated depreciation | 115 | 11.0% | 39.1% | 160 | 14.5% | |
| Net fixed assets | 460 | 43.8% | 5.4% | 485 | 44.1% | 38.2% |
| Long-term investments | 36 | 3.4% | 25.0% | 45 | 4.1% | |
| Total Assets | 1,050 | 100.0% | 4.8% | 1,100 | 100.0% | 100.0% |
| **LIABILITIES & EQUITY** | | | | | | |
| Notes payable—bank | 50 | 4.8% | 40.0% | 70 | 6.4% | 6.0% |
| Accounts payable | 99 | 9.4% | 7.1% | 106 | 9.6% | 11.2% |
| Accrued expenses | 15 | 1.4% | 113.3% | 32 | 2.9% | |
| Income tax payable | 6 | 0.6% | 100.0% | 12 | 1.1% | 1.7% |
| Current maturity—LTD | 35 | 3.3% | 14.3% | 40 | 3.6% | 3.6% |
| Current liabilities | 205 | 19.5% | 26.8% | 260 | 23.6% | 27.5% |
| Long-term debt (LTD) | 280 | 26.7% | −14.3% | 240 | 21.8% | 22.8% |
| Total liabilities | 485 | 46.2% | 3.1% | 500 | 45.5% | 57.5% |
| Common stock—par | 325 | 31.0% | 0.0% | 325 | 29.5% | |
| Retained earnings | 240 | 22.9% | 14.6% | 275 | 25.0% | |
| Stockholder's equity | 565 | 53.8% | 6.2% | 600 | 54.5% | 42.5% |
| Total Liabilities and Equity | 1,050 | 100.0% | 4.8% | 1,100 | 100.0% | 100.0% |

NOTE: Figures are in thousands of dollars; LTD refers to long-term debt. Prism's first year of operations was 2004.

**LIQUIDITY AND ACTIVITY RATIOS.** Evaluating liquidity risk requires an understanding of a firm's operating cycle. Recall that the typical business buys raw materials or finished goods for resale on credit. It then uses labor and other operating expenses to produce a final product, often paying cash for these services. The product is then sold, typically on credit. Trade credit rarely provides enough financing to cover the time it takes to collect on credit sales. So the proceeds of short-term loans are often used to finance current assets or to reduce other current liabilities. Notes are repaid by systematically reducing inventories following increases in sales and reducing receivables following the collection of credit sales. Measures of net working capital, current and quick ratios, inventory turnover, accounts receivables collection period, days accounts payables outstanding, and the days cash-to-cash cycle, help indicate whether current assets will support current liabilities.

The **current ratio** (current assets/current liabilities) is a gross measure of liquidity. Historically, analysts have viewed a current ratio of about 2.0 to be consistent with adequate liquidity. This means that firms hold twice as much cash, accounts receivable, inventory, prepaid expenses, and other current assets as current liabilities coming due in the next year. Thus, the firm has good ability to pay off the current obligations as they come due. Caution should be exercised here, however, especially when examining the data for smaller firms. A high current ratio could indicate that inventory and/or accounts receivable are high, but this does not mean the firm is liquid unless the inventory and accounts receivable are of high quality. If the firm has obsolete or damaged inventory or overdue accounts receivables, a high current ratio could also indicate a lack of liquidity, hence the need to carefully examine inventory turnover and days accounts receivables collection period. In addition, prepaid expenses are rarely liquid assets. Faster turnover generally indicates sound inventory levels and good collection of receivables.

A more conservative measure of liquidity is the **quick ratio** [(cash + accounts receivable)/current liabilities]. By eliminating inventories, prepaid expenses, and other current assets, which are generally less liquid, the quick ratio provides a more conservative measure of aggregate liquidity.

Activity ratios measure the efficiency of the firm as well as the liquidity of current assets. A highly efficient firm, for example, will report a **sales-to-asset ratio** that exceeds industry norms—indicating that its asset base produces proportionately more revenue. A low ratio indicates that the asset mix is not efficient in the sense that too much is allocated to that asset. For example, **days accounts receivables collection period** (accounts receivables/average daily credit sales) indicates the average number of days required to convert accounts receivable into cash. This ratio provides information about a company's credit policy as well as its ability to collect on these accounts. Hence, it is a measure of how efficient the firm is in using this asset as well as how liquid these assets are respectively. **Days inventory on hand** (inventory/average daily cost of goods sold) and **inventory turnover** (COGS/inventory) similarly measure the efficiency of the firm in managing its inventory. High days inventory and low turnover relative to industry norms indicate less efficient inventory management and/or less liquidity.

On the other side of the balance sheet, **days accounts payable outstanding** (accounts payable/average daily purchases) measures the firm's efficiency in using trade credit to finance its working capital needs.[9] The greater the days payable, ceteris paribus, the more efficient is the firm and the less bank financing is needed. Caution is appropriate, however, because all else may not be equal. A high days payable figure may indicate the firm has serious liquidity problems and may be in danger of being "cut off" by its suppliers. If this happens, the need for additional bank debt will increase dramatically. Also, a high days payable figure may mean that the firm is giving up early payment discounts, hence, using trade credit financing which is more expensive than bank debt.

Financial ratios for Prism are presented in Exhibit 11.3. Current and quick ratios are low and have declined over the last two years. Days accounts receivables is about six days shorter than the industry norm such that receivables turn over 17 times a year as compared with the industry norm of 13 times. Days inventory and inventory turnover indicate that Prism was slightly more efficient than peers in 2005 in managing inventory. Days accounts payable is much lower at 16.3 days outstanding in 2005 compared with the industry norm of 26.1 days. This indicates that Prism is not using as much financing from trade creditors as the industry average.

**LEVERAGE RATIOS.** Leverage ratios indicate the mix of the firm's financing between debt and equity and potential earnings volatility resulting from debt financing. The greater is a firm's level of debt, the higher are its fixed interest payments and the more likely it is to generate insufficient earnings (cash flow) to cover debt payments. Thus, the greater is a firm's leverage, the more volatile is its net profit (or losses) because certain sales are required to cover fixed interest charges. An analyst should examine a firm's leverage with respect to both the firm's ability to service debt (principal and interest payments) and the amount of debt relative to the size of the firm.

Ratios derived primarily from the income statement, such as times interest earned and fixed charge coverage, measure a firm's ability to service debt or meet interest and lease payments with current earnings. **Times interest earned** (earnings before interest and taxes (EBIT)/interest expense) measures the number of times the company can pay the interest payments on its outstanding debt.[10] The **fixed charge coverage ratio** [(EBIT + lease payments)/(interest expense + lease payments)] ratio measures the number of times the firm can pay interest and other fixed charges (such as lease payments) with current earnings. Obviously, the greater the number of times the firm can cover these required fixed payments, the greater is the firm's ability to service existing debt. Prism's earnings coverage of required interest payments increased to 3.47 times and fixed charge coverage increased to 3.32 times in 2005. This represents good coverage and both ratios exceed peer group averages.

Ratios derived primarily from the balance sheet, such as debt to total assets and net fixed assets to tangible net worth, can be used to measure the amount of debt relative to the size of the firm. The greater is the existing **debt-to-total-assets ratio,** the more limited is the firm's future growth potential and the greater is the likelihood the firm will be unable to meet future principal payments on the debt. High debt levels restrict a firm's growth because the firm needs additional funds to finance the growth. If the firm is heavily debt ridden, expansion using additional debt may not be possible. **Net fixed assets to tangible net worth** is an indicator of the proportion of the firm's less liquid assets financed by net worth. The greater is this ratio, the greater is the level of debt financing fixed assets and the more likely it is that liquidation proceeds will fall short of net worth in the event of failure. Finally, a firm's **dividend payout** (cash dividends/net income) ratio measures the fraction of earnings a firm pays out in cash to stockholders and thus is not retained. The higher the ratio, the lower are retained earnings, which potentially increases future financing needs if the firm were to run into financial problems.

Leverage ratios for Prism Industries are presented in Exhibit 11.3. Debt is only 83 percent of tangible net worth—well below the industry average. Lower levels of debt and greater earnings coverage, times interest earned, and fixed charge coverage confirm the common size analysis of much greater equity and less financial leverage risk.

**PROFITABILITY ANALYSIS.** Basic profitability ratios include the firm's return on equity, return on assets, profit margin, asset utilization (or total asset turnover), and sales growth rate. **Return on equity** (ROE) indicates the percentage return to stockholders for each dollar of equity. Prism's ROE fell slightly in 2005 and indicates that

---

[9]Recall the accounting relationship: purchases = COGS + Δ inventory.

[10]EBIT is a proxy for cash flow and equals earnings before interest expense and taxes.

**EXHIBIT 11.3** Financial Ratio Analysis for Prism Industries, 2004–2005

| | 2004 | | 2005 | | Peer Group Ratios | |
|---|---|---|---|---|---|---|
| **Liquidity Ratios** | | | | | | |
| Current ratio | 2.70 | | 2.19 | | 2.10 | |
| Quick ratio | 1.10 | | 0.99 | | 1.01 | |
| | *Days* | *Times* | *Days* | *Times* | *Days* | *Times* |
| Days cash | 12.93 | 28.24× | 11.73 | 31.11× | | |
| Days accounts receivable | 21.44 | 17.02× | 21.77 | 16.77× | 28.0 | 13.0× |
| Days inventory | 54.48 | 6.70× | 45.24 | 8.07× | 48.2 | 7.6× |
| Cash-to-cash asset cycle | 88.85 | | 78.74 | | | |
| Days AP outstanding | 17.49 | 20.87× | 16.33 | 22.35× | 26.1 | 14.0× |
| Days cash-to-cash cycle | 71.36 | | 62.41 | | | |
| *Est. W.C. financing Needs* | $401 | | $407 | | | |
| **Leverage Ratios** | *Percent* | *Times* | *Percent* | *Times* | *Percent* | *Times* |
| Debt to tangible net worth | | 0.86× | | 0.83× | | 1.4× |
| Times interest earned | | 3.03× | | 3.47× | | 3.1× |
| Fixed charge coverage* | | 3.03× | | 3.32× | | 2.4× |
| Net fixed assets to tangible net worth | 81.42% | | 80.83% | | 63.0% | |
| **Profitability Ratios** | | | | | | |
| Return on net worth (ROE) | 9.20% | | 9.17% | | | |
| Profit before taxes to net worth | 13.63% | | 14.00% | | 19.8% | |
| Return on assets (ROA) | 4.95% | | 5.00% | | | |
| Profit before taxes to total assets | 7.33% | | 7.64% | | 8.3% | |
| Equity multiplier (leverage = TA / TE) | | 1.86× | | 1.83× | | 2.4× |
| **Income** | | | | | | |
| Total asset turnover (net sales / TA) | | 2.29× | | 2.55× | | 2.4× |
| All other income / total assets | 0.86% | | 1.00% | | | |
| **Expenses** | | | | | | |
| Net profit margin (NI / net sales) | 2.17% | | 1.96% | | | |
| COGS / net sales | 85.42% | | 85.00% | | 82.2% | |
| Operating expenses / net sales | 9.88% | | 10.75% | | 12.5% | |
| Income taxes to earnings before taxes | 32.47% | | 34.52% | | | |
| Sales / net fixed assets | | 5.22× | | 5.77× | | |
| **Cash Flow Ratios** ** | | | | | | |
| CFO / (DIV + last CMLTD) | | 2.33× | | 2.27× | | |
| CFO / (DIV + last CMLTD + short-term debt) | | 0.54× | | 1.00× | | |

*Lease payments are included in other operating expenses and were $2,200 in 2005.

**CFO, DIV, and CMLTD refer to cash flow from operations, cash dividends, and current maturities of long-term debt, respectively.

stockholders only earned 9.17 percent on funds invested in the firm. This ratio can be decomposed into two components: the average return per dollar of assets invested (ROA) and the equity multiplier (EM):[11]

$$\textbf{ROE} \ (\text{NI/Equity}) = \textbf{ROA} \ (\text{NI/Total assets}) \times \textbf{EM} \ (\text{Total assets/Equity}),$$

where NI is net income. **Return on assets** (ROA) measures the percentage return on assets while the **equity multiplier** (EM) measures the degree of financial leverage employed. The greater is the return on invested assets, all else equal, the greater is the return to shareholders. By the same token, the greater is the degree of leverage (the more debt rather than equity is used to finance these assets), the greater the returns to shareholders. Recall, however, that a greater degree of leverage is also an indicator of risk. Very high leverage means that the firm is less likely to meet its debt payment requirements if it has an off year. Prism's lower return to shareholders (ROE) was a result of both lower profit on invested assets (ROA) and much higher equity, hence a lower equity multiplier (EM). Prism's ROA was only 5 percent and its equity multiplier was 1.8 times compared with the industry average of 2.4 times.

---

[11]This is, of course, the familiar Dupont Analysis introduced in Chapter 2 for banks, now applied to nonfinancial companies.

Recall that net income is simply gross income (sales plus other revenue) minus expenses (COGS, operating expenses, other expenses, and taxes). Hence, ROA can be broken down into **profit margin** (PM), a measure of expense control, and **asset utilization** (AU) which reveals the gross yield on assets:

$$\textbf{ROA} \text{ (NI/Total assets)} = \textbf{PM} \text{ (NI/Sales)} \times \textbf{AU} \text{ (Sales/Total assets)}$$

PM measures aggregate expense control at the firm and actually equals one minus the expense ratio:

$$PM = \text{(Sales} - \text{Expenses)/Sales}$$
$$= 1 - \text{Expenses/Sales}$$

The major expenses are: COGS, operating expenses, other expenses, and taxes. Hence, we can measure the company's specific strengths or weaknesses in controlling these expenses by decomposing PM and comparing the following common size ratios to industry averages:

$$PM = 1 - \text{(COGS/Sales)} - \text{(Operating expenses/Sales)} - \text{(Other expenses/Sales)} - \text{(Taxes/Sales)}$$

Finally, **sales growth** figures demonstrate whether the firm is expanding or contracting and provide evidence of industry competitiveness. Examining growth rates for COGS and other expenses and comparing these to sales growth provides an estimate of the relative efficiency of growth.

The profitability ratios, presented in Exhibit 11.3, indicate that Prism's profits before taxes were below the industry standard relative to both equity and total assets. Although reported dollar profits increase in 2005, due to the 16.7 percent increase in net sales, Prism's profits before taxes to total assets (similar to ROA) were below industry averages in 2005 due to much higher COGS. Profits before taxes to total assets fell as well in 2005 because Prism's operating expenses increased from 9.9 percent to 10.8 percent of sales. Even though operating expenses increased in 2005, they were still below those of peers, but the significantly higher COGS led to lower profits relative to total assets. This combined with the higher level of equity also meant that profit before taxes to tangible net worth was lower.

The analyst should evaluate these ratios with a critical eye, trying to identify firm strengths and weaknesses. All ratios should be evaluated over time to detect shifts in competitiveness and/or firm strategy, and relative to industry standards. The latter comparison indicates where significant deviations occur, both positively and negatively. When reviewing the ratios, the analyst should prepare a list of questions to ask the firm's managers, suppliers, and creditors that fill in information not revealed by the data.

## CASH FLOW ANALYSIS

Most analysts focus on cash flow when evaluating a nonfinancial firm's performance. Bank regulators require banks to support credit decisions with cash flow information for each borrower. This section presents a framework for calculating a firm's cash flow from operations that essentially converts a company's income statement to a cash basis. Cash flow estimates are subsequently compared with principal and interest payments and discretionary cash expenditures to assess a firm's borrowing capacity and financial strength.

Accounting standards mandate that the statement of cash flows be divided into four parts: operating activities, investing activities, financing activities, and cash. The intent is to allow the reader to distinguish between reported accounting profits (net income) and cash flow from operations (cash net income) as well as other financing and investing activities that affect cash flow but are not reported on the income statement. The direct method of reporting cash flow converts, or reconciles, the income statement to its cash equivalent.[12]

The **cash-based income statement** introduced in this chapter is a modified form of a direct statement of cash flows. It is essentially a statement of changes reconciled to cash, which combines elements of the income statement and balance sheet. In general, a statement of changes records changes in balance sheet accounts over a specific time period, indicating the source or use of cash. Its purpose is to indicate how new assets are financed or how liabilities are repaid. Actual funds flows are measured by the absolute differences between balance sheet entries in two different time periods, such as year-end 2005 versus year-end 2004. Recall that the balance sheet is a stock measure. To convert the balance sheet into a flow, we must calculate the change in the stock amount. Because the income statement represents flows over time, income statement data can be combined by adding the revenues and subtracting the expenses that determine net income as well as subtracting cash dividends for the change in

---

[12]Actually, two types of cash flow statements are used in the industry: the direct and indirect method. The indirect method is required disclosure where the direct method is generally considered optional. The indirect method of cash flow reporting begins with net income and adjusts for changes in current assets and liabilities to derive cash flow from operations. The direct method, in contrast, closely follows the income statement and adjusts each income statement category to produce a cash equivalent; for example, cash sales, cash purchases, cash operating expenses, and so on. This method is most useful to analysts and is widely used in banking. We therefore use the direct cash flow method in this chapter.

| EXHIBIT 11.4 | Statement of Changes Reconciled to Cash for Prism Industries, 2005 | | | |
|---|---|---|---|---|

| CASH-BASED INCOME STATEMENT | 2005 | | Cash Flow Impact | |
|---|---|---|---|---|
| **Net sales** | 2,800 | **Source** | Revenue | |
| Change in accounts receivable | (26) | **Use** | Asset increase | |
| Cash receipts from sales | 2,774 | | | |
| Cost of goods sold | (2,380) | **Use** | Expense | |
| Change in inventory | 11 | **Source** | Asset decrease | |
| Change in accounts payable | 7 | **Source** | Liability increase | |
| Cash purchases | (2,362) | | | |
| Cash margin | 412 | | | |
| Total operating expenses | (301) | **Use** | Expense | |
| Depreciation & amortization | 51 | **Source** | Noncash expense | |
| Change in prepaid expenses | 4 | **Source** | Asset decrease | |
| Change in accruals | 17 | **Source** | Liability increase | |
| Cash operating expenses | (229) | | | |
| Cash operating profit | 183 | | | |
| All other expenses & income (net) | (1) | **Use** | Expense | |
| Cash before interest & taxes | 182 | | | |
| Interest expense | (34) | **Use** | Expense | |
| Income taxes reported | (29) | **Use** | Expense | |
| Change in income tax payable | 6 | **Source** | Liability increase | |
| Change in other current assets and liabilities | 0 | | | |
| **Cash flow from operations (CFO)** | **125** | | | |
| Capital exp. and leasehold improvements | (76) | **Use** | Asset increase | |
| Change in long-term investments | (9) | **Use** | Asset increase | |
| Change in other noncurrent assets | 0 | | | |
| **Cash used for investments** | **(85)** | | | |
| Payment for last period's CMLTD | (35) | **Use** | Payment for financing | |
| Dividends paid (DIV) | (20) | **Use** | Payment for financing | |
| **Payments for financing** | **(55)** | | | |
| **Cash before external financing** | **(15)** | | | |
| Change in short-term bank debt | 20 | **Source** | Liability increase | |
| Change in LT debt + EOP CMLTD | 0 | | | |
| Change in stock & surplus | 0 | | | |
| Change in other noncurrent liabilities | 0 | | | |
| **External financing** | **20** | | | |
| **Change in cash & mktbl securities** | **5** | | | |

NOTE: Figures are in thousands of dollars.

retained earnings on the balance sheet. A generalized cash-based income statement, which identifies the sources of data and nature of calculations, appears as Appendix III.

The key element in the analysis is to determine how much cash flow a firm generates from its normal business activity, that is, cash flow from operations. This cash flow must be sufficient to make interest and principal payments on debt. It may differ substantially from reported profits, as in the case of Enron (see the Contemporary Issues Box: "Revenue Creation at Enron: A Lesson in Creative Accounting"). A cash-based income statement also provides insights into whether a firm has adequately structured its financing. In a normal operating environment, a firm should repay short-term debt by liquidating its receivables and inventory. Long-term debt, in contrast, should be repaid from operating cash flow in excess of financing costs and funds needed to maintain capital assets.

**CASH FLOW STATEMENT FORMAT.** Because most firms prepare financial statements on an accrual rather than cash basis, revenues and expenses are recognized when earned or incurred rather than when a cash payment is made. Thus, reported net income may differ substantially from operational cash flow. Consider the income statement and balance sheet for Prism Industries in Exhibits 11.1 and 11.2. These data are used to generate the statement of changes reconciled to cash for Prism presented in Exhibit 11.4. This format combines traditional income statement and changes in balance sheet figures to produce a cash-based income statement. It emphasizes cash flow from operations, not reported net income.

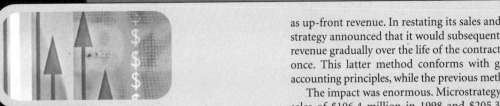

## CONTEMPORARY ISSUES

### ILLUSORY PROFITS AT MICROSTRATEGY

In March 2000 at the peak of the Internet and technology stock market boom, management of Microstrategy announced that the firm would restate its sales and earnings for 1998 and 1999. Microstrategy was in the business of providing business intelligence software and consulting, training, and support services. At the time, the firm would bundle its software with services for long-term projects, but record the entire value of software sold as up-front revenue. In restating its sales and earnings, Microstrategy announced that it would subsequently record software revenue gradually over the life of the contract, rather than all at once. This latter method conforms with generally accepted accounting principles, while the previous method did not.

The impact was enormous. Microstrategy initially reported sales of $106.4 million in 1998 and $205.3 million in 1999. Rather than reporting large profits, earnings fell to just $7 million in 1998 and a loss of $34 million in 1999. Investors immediately punished Microstrategy by driving the share price from $330 at the time of the announcement to just $30 three days later for a loss of $11.9 billion to stockholders. By May 2002, the share price had fallen to $1.30.

Regardless of how Microstrategy chose to report its sales, its cash flow from operations was dramatically less than reported earnings. Market participants, investors and Microstrategy's lenders, who focused on earnings rather than cash flow, were misled by the revenue reporting effects.

The following items are included in each of the four sections of a cash flow statement:
- *Operations Section*—income statement items and the change in current assets and current liabilities (except bank debt)
- *Investments Section*—the change in all long-term assets
- *Financing Section*—payments for debt and dividends, the change in all long-term liabilities, the change in short-term bank debt, and any new stock issues
- *Cash Section*—the change in cash and marketable securities

With a statement of changes reconciled to cash (cash-based income statement), a source of funds is any transaction that increases cash (or cash-equivalent) assets. A use of funds is any transaction that decreases cash assets. As noted below, sources of funds include any decrease in a noncash asset, increase in liability, any noncash expense, or any revenue item. Selling receivables or issuing new debt subsequently represent sources of cash. Uses of funds include any increase in a noncash asset, decrease in a liability, and any cash expense item. Thus, the purchase of a building or principal payment on debt is a use of cash.

Sources of funds must equal uses of funds. Equivalently, the balance sheet identity requires that the sum of the changes in each asset must equal the sum of the changes in each liability and the change in net worth (stockholders' equity). Let:

$A_i$ = the dollar value of the $i^{th}$ type of asset (A)

$L_j$ = the dollar value of the $j^{th}$ type of liability (L)

$NW$ = the dollar value of net worth

There are n different assets and m different liabilities. Then:

$$\sum_{i=1}^{n} \Delta A_i = \sum_{j=1}^{m} \Delta L_j + \Delta NW \tag{11.1}$$

We know that $\Delta NW$ equals net income (NI) minus cash dividends paid (DIV) plus the change in common and preferred stock (stock) outstanding plus the change in paid-in surplus (surplus). Thus, if we designate the first asset as cash, $A_1$, and solve for the change in cash, Equation 11.1 can be written as:

$$\Delta A_1 = \sum_{j=1}^{m} \Delta L_j - \sum_{i=2}^{n} \Delta A_i + \Delta stock + \Delta surplus + NI - DIV \tag{11.2}$$

## CONTEMPORARY ISSUES

### REVENUE CREATION AT ENRON: A LESSON IN CREATIVE ACCOUNTING

How did Enron double reported sales in 2000 just prior to declaration of bankruptcy on December 2, 2001? Basically, Enron exploited open-ended accounting rules that allowed for the reporting of revenue from the sale of energy derivative contracts at their gross or notional value rather than net value as most firms report. Enron was able to show high sales growth, but relatively small profits, by buying and selling the same energy multiple times. Each time an energy contract was sold, Enron would book the trade at its full gross or notional value, rather than the net profit expected from the trade. The Financial Accounting Standards Board (FASB) did not have clear rules on how energy commodity contracts should be accounted for. Effectively, FASB allowed each company to determine how it would account for the deals. Enron typically elected to take the largest revenue numbers. Hence, rather than booking only a "small" profit from brokering the supply of gas and electricity to large companies, Enron would book the full notional value of the derivative contracts. (See Chapter 7 for a discussion of futures and forward contracts and the concept of notional value.) Enron would then move its debt into partnerships it created. It would list these as off-balance sheet transactions even though Enron controlled these partnerships and used the structure to bolster its reported data.

How did Enron report profits that may have never materialized? Enron would book profits in the current fiscal year based on projected cost savings it *predicted* it would earn

on long-term contracts. These contracts were for operating and managing physical plants for clients. Effectively, Enron was booking income *immediately* on long-term energy and service contracts with clients that could take years to complete and generate earnings, if ever realized. In addition, Enron used many "creative" tax-avoidance strategies. Many of the cost savings associated with these long-term contracts were based on estimates that were either unrealistic or, at a minimum, difficult to confirm due to the long-term estimates of energy costs embedded in the contracts. Projections of cost savings were typically based on long-term forecasted values of future energy prices, construction costs, and the client's future energy use.

Because Enron was a "market maker" in many of the energy markets, it could effectively manipulate the "market" price on long-term energy contracts. Using accounting rules that allowed for the use of mark-to-market accounting to report profits for commodity contracts such as natural gas and electricity, Enron was able to book millions of dollars of profits that were forecast over ten years, in the current accounting period. In fact, Enron employees indicated that it was not unusual to underestimate commodity prices in the later years of a long-term contract to improve reported profits because the markets were so thin that no one could estimate the "market" price with much certainty. Hence, Enron was able to book huge profits, not based on historical costs of energy or actual cash earnings, but rather on Enron's predicted estimates of the "market" value of these commodities and services and the cost savings Enron predicted it could generate for clients over many years!

The importance of cash flow from operations relative to net income is key. From 1997 to 1999, Enron's cash flow from operations declined independent of reported earnings. Mulford (2002) points out that a decline in a company's core business occurs when a company's reported earnings are not associated with similar changes in cash flow.[13] Enron is a lesson in how a company's "reported" earnings can be overstated. Clearly cash flow from operations is critical to fully understanding a company's core business.

Cash flow from operations is derived using Equation 11.2 and the components of net income from the income statement. Each source of cash has a positive sign and each use of cash has a negative sign. The statement of changes format simply rearranges the elements of Equation 11.2 in terms of a cash-based income statement. Because net income (NI) equals revenues minus expenses and taxes, substituting into Equation 11.2 yields:

$$\Delta A_1 = \sum_{j=1}^{m} \Delta L_j - \sum_{i=2}^{n} \Delta A_i + \Delta stock + \Delta surplus$$
$$+ \text{Revenues} - \text{Expenses} - \text{Taxes} - \text{DIV}$$

(11.3)

As the signs before each element indicate, any increase in a liability or decrease in a noncash asset is a source of cash. A decrease in a liability or increase in a noncash asset is a use of cash.

---

[13]See Charles W. Mulford and Eugene E. Comiskey, *The Financial Numbers Game: Detecting Creative Accounting Practices* (Wiley, 2002).

Issues of stock or positive additions to surplus represent a source of cash. Finally, revenues are a source of cash, while cash expenses, taxes paid, and cash dividends are a use of cash. These general relationships are summarized below:

| Sources of Cash | Uses of Cash |
| --- | --- |
| Increase in any liability | Decrease in any liability |
| Decrease in any noncash asset | Increase in any noncash asset |
| New issue of stock | Repayments/buy back stock |
| Additions to surplus | Deductions from surplus |
| Revenues | Cash expenses |
| | Taxes |
| | Cash dividends |

## CASH FLOW ANALYSIS FOR PRISM INDUSTRIES

The cash flow statement is presented in Exhibit 11.4 using the income statement and balance sheet data from Exhibits 11.1 and 11.2 for Prism Industries. The focal point is the firm's cash flow from operations. The far right column identifies the type of cash flow impact in terms of Equation 11.3 for each entry. The top part of the statement shows why reported net income for Prism differs from cash flow from operations.

**CASH FLOW FROM OPERATIONS.** The first item listed is net sales. Prism collected less in credit sales than it billed its customers because outstanding accounts receivable increased from 2004 to 2005. Thus, net sales are offset by the $26,000 increase in receivables to obtain actual cash receipts. Had receivables declined, actual cash receipts from sales would have exceeded the reported sales figure. The use of cash to support the growth in accounts receivable is a function of two primary factors. First, increases in sales will lead to an equal percentage growth in accounts receivables, all else equal. Second, a more lenient credit policy (increase in days receivables) will lead to an increase in accounts receivables, all else equal. Days accounts receivables outstanding increased only slightly from 2004 to 2005 for Prism so the use of cash in accounts receivables was primarily to support sales growth, not a significantly more lax credit policy.

The next series of figures address the difference between actual cash purchases and reported cost of goods sold. Actual cash purchases differ for two basic accounting reasons. First, COGS does not represent actual purchases of inventory during the year. Reported COGS only represents the cost of goods sold during the period, not the actual purchases of inventory the company made. If the company's inventory increased (decreased) during the year, purchases of goods would exceed (be less than) the cost of the goods sold during the year. Second, some purchases are financed by increases in accounts payable (trade credit) while others are paid for in cash. From accounting we know that:

$$\text{Purchases} = \text{COGS} + \Delta\text{inventory} \qquad (11.4)$$

For Prism, purchases equaled $2,369,000 in 2005 as indicated by the following calculation and the application of Equation 11.4.

**Production Budget Summary for 2005 (Thousands of Dollars)**

| | |
| --- | ---: |
| Beginning inventory | $306 |
| + Purchases | $2,369 |
| = Goods available for sale | $2,675 |
| − Cost of goods sold | $2,380 |
| = Ending inventory | $295 |
| or Purchases = 2,380 + (295 − 306) = | 2,369 |

Prism started 2005 with $306,000 in inventory. During 2005 the firm purchased $2,369,000 from suppliers such that after cost of goods sold was subtracted, it held $295,000 in inventory at the end of the year. The statement of changes adds the change in inventory to the cost of goods sold to get total purchases. If inventory decreases, as it does for Prism, actual cash purchases are less than cost of goods sold, and vice versa. The reduction in inventory was a source of cash as Prism's inventory turnover was faster in 2004 (8.07 times) as compared with 2004 (6.70 times).

The cash flow statement then subtracts the change in outstanding accounts payable from total purchases to get actual cash purchases. For Prism, the $7,000 increase in payables indicates that a portion of purchases is financed by additional trade credit provided by suppliers. Prism's cash purchases thus equaled $2,362,000 (purchases less change in accounts payable = $2,369,000 − $7,000). In general, net cash purchases equals the cost of goods sold adjusted for inventory accumulation not financed by additional trade credit:

$$\text{Cash purchases} = -(\text{COGS} + \Delta\text{inventory} - \Delta\text{accounts payable}) \qquad (11.5)$$

Cost of goods sold is reported on the income statement while cash purchases represents the actual amount of cash used to purchase goods for resale. Using the relationship shown in Equation 11.5 and reviewing Exhibit 11.4, we know that four factors directly affect cash purchases: sales growth, gross margin, inventory policy, and trade credit policy. Holding other factors constant, we know that COGS will increase proportionately to sales. Hence, cash purchases will increase proportionately to sales.

Because the statement format presented mimics an income statement, the next step is to subtract cash operating expenses. Reported operating expenses typically overstate actual cash expenses by the amount of noncash charges, including depreciation and amortization. The format subtracts total operating expenses, which includes all noncash charges, then adds back noncash charges to yield a net figure for cash expenses. In this example, depreciation expense ($51,000) is the only noncash expense such that total operating expense equals $301,000 before the adjustment.[14]

Prism's prepaid expenses fell in 2005 as it paid more in expenses than that reported on the income statement. The increase in accrued expenses further indicates that Prism paid $17,000 less in cash than costs incurred. Combining the changes in prepaid and accrued expenses with total operating expenses adjusted for noncash charges produces cash operating profit. The resulting figure is then adjusted by income on marketable securities and long-term investments and other noninterest expense and income that arise from normal business activity.

Finally, actual interest expense and an estimate of income taxes paid are subtracted to obtain cash flow from operations. The data indicate that income taxes reported on the income statement exceeded actual taxes paid. This typically occurs because firms take greater deductions for tax purposes than they report in published statements. Tax payments are effectively deferred, and the net tax expense is $23,000 ($29,000 − $6,000) or $6,000 less than that reported.

The resulting net figure, **cash flow from operations**, indicates whether Prism was able to service its debt and is useful in forecasting whether the firm can assume additional debt. As suggested in the Contemporary Issues Box: "The Many Faces of Cash Flow," cash flow from operations is one of many cash flow measures. As a rule, any transaction representing a normal business activity should be recognized prior to calculating cash flow from operations.

The items listed in Exhibit 11.4 do not represent all items that potentially appear in a balance sheet or income statement, as financial statements contain different line items for different firms. When constructing a cash-based income statement, it is important to recognize that every income statement and balance sheet account or item must appear somewhere.[15] The key criterion is that the cash flow impact of normal operating activities are listed above the cash flow from operations line while extraordinary items should be listed after cash flow from operations. Thus, if other income arises from a one-time sale of real estate, it should appear below cash flow from operations.

At a minimum, cash flow from operations must be sufficient to cover cash dividends and mandatory principal payments. These required principal payments for the upcoming year are indicated by current maturities of long-term debt (CMLTD). Thus, when looking back on historical performance for a period, cash flow from operations should cover current maturities of long-term debt outstanding at the beginning of the period. For Prism, the amount is $35,000 as listed in Exhibit 11.2 as the balance sheet value for CMCTD at year-end 2004. Other cash flows are unpredictable and cannot be relied on. In the case of Prism, cash flow from operations of $125,000 in 2005 exceeded cash dividends paid and the principal payment on long-term debt by $70,000 ($125,000 − $20,000 − $35,000). The excess cash flow, along with an increase in short-term debt, was essentially used to purchase new capital assets ($76,000) and increase long-term investments ($9,000).

**CASH FROM INVESTING ACTIVITIES.** There are many cash expenditures not directly reflected in financial statements. In particular, capital expenditures and long-term investments require cash but are not reflected on the income statement. If cash flow from operations is insufficient to cover capital expenditures and new long-term investments, additional financing will be required. Because capital expenditures are not listed on the income statement or the balance sheet they must be estimated. One measure of capital expenditures is simply the change in gross fixed assets. This is appropriate, however, only when a firm has not sold any fixed assets during the period.

---

[14]The analysis should be careful to use depreciation expense from the income statement ($51,000) and not the change in accumulated depreciation from the balance sheet ($45,000) which can be different. For more details see the following section "Cash from Investing Activities."

[15]Exceptions to this would be net income from the income statement and retained earnings from the balance sheet, as these items are already included.

## CONTEMPORARY ISSUES

### THE MANY FACES OF CASH FLOW

What is cash flow? The classic definition is net income plus depreciation, amortization, and deferred taxes. According to a statement of changes reconciled to cash, cash flow from operations approximately equals classic cash flow adjusted for changes in working capital. In practice, the meaning of cash flow varies according to which analyst reviews the data.

Several commonly accepted definitions of cash flow are listed below, along with the associated value, using the data for Wade's Office Furniture in 2004 (in thousands of dollars):

1. Net income + (depreciation + amortization + Δdeferred tax liability) +/− one time expenditures: $339 + $73 = $412

2. [No. 1] − Δaccounts receivable − Δinventory − Δprepaid expenses + Δaccounts payable + Δaccruals: $412 − $497 − $559 − ($35) + $374 + $90 = ($145)

3. [No. 1] − all capital expenditures: $412 − $157 = $255

4. [No. 2] − all capital expenditures: ($145) − $157 = ($302)

5. Pretax income + (depreciation + amortization) − maintenance capital expenditures: $527 + $73 − $70 = $530

6. EBITDA (Earnings before interest, taxes, depreciation and amortization) = Pretax income + interest + depreciation + amortization: $527 + $157 + $73 = $757

Maintenance capital expenditures equal that portion of capital outlays required to maintain production operations at the current level (*assumed* equal to $70 for Wades). Definitions numbered 3–5 are often referred to as **free cash flow**. Wade's cash flow from operations is calculated before subtracting capital expenditures but after the change in most current assets and liabilities and thus at ($128) is much less than values obtained for cash flow according to definitions 1, 5, and 6.

Which is the best measure? Like most data analysis, there is no obvious answer. Definitions 1, 5, and 6 take a long-run view of cash flow at the firm and are more appropriate for valuation. They do not, however, consider the level of net capital expenditures required to maintain and grow the company. Definitions 3, 4, and 5 consider the impact of required capital expenditures to maintain the company's productive assets. Definitions 2, 4, and 5 provide the best estimates of how much new debt a firm can support with existing cash flow. However, firms can generally manipulate both income statement and balance sheet data and thus bias cash flow estimates. The statement of changes format incorporates all income statement and balance sheet data. When viewed comprehensively, an analyst can examine transactions relationships across the entire portfolio. Cash flow from operations is the appropriate estimate but must be compared with dividends, mandatory principal payments, and capital expenditures to determine debt service capabilities.

---

If the firm sells an asset, accounting procedures will reduce accumulated depreciation by the amount of accumulated depreciation attributable to the asset sold. In these cases, the change in accumulated depreciation will be less than depreciation expense from the income statement. Note that depreciation expense ($51,000) reported in Prims's income statement for 2004 differs from the change in accumulated depreciation reported on the balance sheet ($45,000). This typically occurs when a firm sells assets that have been at least partially depreciated. Specifically:

$$\Delta \text{Net fixed assets} = \Delta \text{Gross fixed assets} - \Delta \text{accumulated depreciation} \tag{11.6}$$

and

$$\Delta \text{Net fixed assets} = \text{Capital expenditures} - \text{depreciation} \tag{11.7}$$

hence,

$$\text{Capital expenditures} = \Delta \text{Net fixed assets} - \text{depreciation} \tag{11.8}$$

According to Equation 11.8, the change in gross fixed assets will underestimate actual capital expenditures. Hence, capital expenditures was $76,000 (485,000 − 460,000 + 51,000) in 2005.

In addition to the $76,000 in capital expenditures, Prism had another $9,000 in new long-term investments that represented a cash outflow. Total cash used for investments was $85,000. Subtracting this from cash flow from operations produced a positive $40,000 in cash before principal debt and dividend payments.

**CASH FROM FINANCING ACTIVITIES.** The bottom of the cash-based income statement of Exhibit 11.4 indicates the firm's payments for financing and how a firm obtains financing from external sources. Although cash flow statements group payments for financing below the investment section, this is somewhat misleading. Payments for financing generally take precedence over capital expenditures and increases in long-term investments. After subtracting the required principal payment on long-term debt (last period's current maturity of long-term debt) and cash dividends, Prism's cash shortage is $15,000 before external financing. Note that cash flow from operations ($125,000) was sufficient to make the required debt and dividend payments ($35,000 + $20,000) but was insufficient to *also* cover the capital expenditures ($76,000).

Prism's cash shortfall must be financed by external sources or by reducing cash balances. Although Prism's balance sheet indicates there is enough cash to cover this shortfall, cash is required in the operations of the business. A firm cannot bring cash levels to zero as some *minimum* amount of cash is necessary to make change in the cash registers, and to pay bills and employee salaries. Typical external sources of financing include new issues of long-term debt, common stock, or preferred stock; increases in notes payable to banks or other short-term liabilities; or issues of other hybrid instruments. In this example, Prism actually increased its notes payable to the bank by $20,000 (which represented a cash inflow), accounting for all its external financing.

**CHANGE IN CASH.** The last element of the cash-based income statement is the change in cash and marketable securities, or the left-hand side item ($\Delta$Cash) in Equation 11.3. This equals cash flow from operations adjusted for *discretionary expenditures*, cash used for investments, payments for financing, and external financing. For Prism Industries, cash flow from operations less total discretionary expenditures produced a $15,000 deficiency. The $20,000 in external financing generated a $5,000 net cash inflow for the year.

The cash-based income statement *balances* by reconciliation to the change in cash because this $5,000 inflow equals the change in cash and marketable securities calculated from the 2005 and 2004 balance sheet figures ($90,000 − $85,000). Since the cash-based income statement is a sources and uses summary, reconciled to cash and marketable securities, an analyst can verify the aggregate calculations by comparing the bottom line change in cash and marketable securities obtained from the statement with the simple change in the balance sheet figures. If the two figures are not equal, at least one of the components of the statement is incorrect.

**INTERPRETING CASH FLOW FROM OPERATIONS.** While short-term debt is typically rolled over, cash flow from operations might ultimately be needed to cover these maturing obligations as well as certain cash expenditures. In 2005, Prism's cash flow from operations of $125,000 was just sufficient to pay $20,000 in cash dividends, $35,000 in maturing principal on long-term debt, and the entire $70,000 in notes payable outstanding at the end of the year. Thus, Prism was in excellent operating condition and could have supported new borrowing, ceteris paribus.

This analysis suggests that two additional ratios may be useful in evaluating a firm's cash flow condition and whether it has the ability to service additional debt:

1. Cash flow from operations (CFO) divided by the sum of dividends paid (DIV) and last period's current maturities of long-term debt (CMLTD):

$$\text{CFO}_t/(\text{DIV}_t + \text{CMLTD}_t - 1) \text{ and}$$

2. Cash flow from operations divided by the same two terms plus short-term debt outstanding at the beginning of the year.

$$\text{CFO}_t/(\text{DIV}_t + \text{CMLTD}_{t-1} + \text{S.T. Debt}_t)$$

where subscripts t and t−1 refer to values for the period being examined (2004 for Prism) and the preceding period (2003 for Prism), respectively. The denominator in the first ratio represents mandatory principal payments owed on outstanding long-term debt plus discretionary cash dividends. The second ratio adds outstanding principal on other short-term debt. If these ratios exceed 1, as is the case with Prism at 2.27x and 1.00x, respectively, the firm's operational cash flows can pay off existing debt and support new borrowing. If these numbers are less than 1 or negative, the firm's operational cash flows are not sufficient to repay the required principal payments or the balance of short-term notes.

$$\text{CFO}_t/(\text{DIV}_t + \text{CMLTD}_t - 1) = \textbf{2.27x} = \$125,000/(\$20,000 + \$35,000)$$
$$\text{CFO}_t/(\text{DIV}_t + \text{CMLTD}_{t-1} + \text{S.T. Debt}_t) = \textbf{1.00x} = \$125,000/(\$20,000 + \$35,000 + \$70,000)$$

Some analysts construct a third ratio that adds maintenance capital expenditures to the denominator. Maintenance capital expenditures are generally viewed as the amount of outlays that is necessary to replace the firm's depreciating capital assets. As such, it is investigated internally.

## FINANCIAL PROJECTIONS

The three-stage process described previously enables a credit analyst to evaluate the historical performance of a potential borrower. The final step in evaluating a loan request, generating pro forma statements, addresses the basic issues introduced at the beginning of the chapter. Projections of the borrower's financial condition reveal what the loan proceeds are needed for, how much financing is required, how much cash flow can be generated from operations to service new debt, and when, if at all, a loan can be repaid. In order to understand the range of potential outcomes, an analyst should make forecasts that incorporate different assumptions about sales, inventory turnover, the level of interest rates, and the growth in operating expenses.

Consider the prospective use of loan proceeds. Firms with a legitimate need for working capital financing would demonstrate a decline in cash flow from operations caused by some combination of increased receivables and inventory or decreased accounts payable and accruals. Seasonal needs should appear from interim (within year) financial statements. Firms with positive and stable cash flow from operations do not generally need working capital financing but do have the capacity to service new debt. Specific cash outflows associated with term loans are easily identified in the bottom part of the statement of changes as discretionary expenditures increase or external financing declines. The amount of financing required and the source and timing of repayment can be similarly determined with financial projections. In essence, each element of the cash flow statement is projected over the future.

**PRO FORMA ASSUMPTIONS.** Projecting financial statements typically begins with sales projections. The key driver is sales growth, which determines how fast sales will increase or decrease in the future. Next period's sales $(t+1)$ is estimated as:

$$\text{Sales}_{t+1} = \text{Sales}_t \times (1 + \textbf{\textit{g}}_{\textbf{\textit{sales}}})$$

The required input, or parameter, needed to project sales is the growth rate in sales ($g_{sales}$) and is listed in **bold italic.** Estimates are commonly obtained by evaluating the average growth expected in the industry, what is going on with respect to the company's market share and even the company's own profit plan and capital budget. Sales growth, along with all other change-related parameters, should be based on the analyst's best estimate of what the company will actually do. Often, an inexperienced analyst views his or her job as projecting the financials such that the company will qualify (or not qualify) for a loan. However, the true purpose of pro forma analysis is to provide an objective method of *examining* potential positive or negative events that might affect a company's ability to repay the loan.

Cost of goods sold is critically related to sales and the expected markup on goods sold. COGS is usually estimated as:

$$\text{COGS}_{t+1} = \text{Sales}_{t+1} \times \textbf{\textit{COGS \% of sales}}$$

The pro forma parameter, *COGS as a percent of sales,* is estimated by past data, industry averages, expected future competitive strengths and weaknesses, and the analyst's best estimates of what COGS will be in the future.

Other operating expenses are projected by using either a growth rate assumption or a percentage of sales assumption. Selling expenses, for example, are usually considered variable costs and would most likely be estimated as a percentage of sales. General and administrative expenses could be estimated by either a growth rate assumption or as a percentage of sales.

Many balance sheet items are also associated with sales or obtained directly from external sources such as capital budgets. For example, current assets frequently equal a relatively constant percentage of sales or exhibit a stable turnover rate. Accounts receivable are a function of sales growth and the firm's credit policy, while inventory is linked to COGS, a predictable fraction of sales. Projecting accounts receivable thus requires forecasts of sales growth and the pro forma parameter *days accounts receivable outstanding:*

$$\text{Accounts receivables}_{t+1} = \textbf{\textit{Days A/R outstanding}} \times \text{average daily sales}_{t+1}$$

Inventory is projected similarly using the parameter inventory turnover:

$$\text{Inventory}_{t+1} = \text{COGS}_{t+1} / \textbf{\textit{inventory turnover}}$$

The analyst can determine the approximate turnover rates from historical data or comparable firm standards. Purchases and trade credit financing are tied to inventory growth. Accounts payable, therefore, will also vary with sales forecasts:

$$\text{Accounts payable}_{t+1} = \textbf{\textit{Days AP outstanding}} \times \text{average daily purchases}_{t+1},$$
$$= \textbf{\textit{Days AP outstanding}} \times [(\text{COGS}_{t+1} + \Delta \text{inventory}_{t+1})/365]$$

Contractual principal payments on debt are known, and planned fixed asset purchases can be obtained from the capital budget. Other accounting principles apply as well. For example, accumulated depreciation is simply last period's accumulated depreciation plus the current period's depreciation expense. Retained earnings on the balance sheet increase each year by the difference between net income and dividends paid. The follow section, "Credit Analysis: An Application," applies these relationships in more detail to Wade's Office Furniture.

One obvious exception to the sales link is interest expense, which is based on the amount of debt a borrower has or is expected to have outstanding and the underlying interest rates. Forecasts must incorporate expectations regarding outstanding debt and loan balances and projected interest rates. This can be cumbersome as many loans carry floating rates and the projections must include an interest rate forecast as well. Based on this model, net income will vary directly with sales in a stable environment.

**PROJECTING NOTES PAYABLE TO BANKS.** During the pro forma process, assets, liabilities, and equity are forecast separately. Rarely will the balance sheet "balance" in the initial round of pro forma forecasts. To reconcile this, there must be a balancing item, which is often called a "plug" figure. When projected assets exceed projected liabilities plus equity, additional debt is required. When projected assets are less than projected liabilities plus equity, no new debt is required and existing debt could be reduced or excess funds invested in marketable securities (also a "plug" figure). Typically any new debt, calculated in this manner, is considered to be a firm's line of credit or short-term debt requirement. The difference in the projected asset base and total funding without new debt, therefore, indicates how much additional credit is required, the firm's line of credit (LOC), at each future interval. This is an iterative procedure as new debt, in turn, increases projected interest expense and lowers net income. Lower net income means lower retained earnings, hence greater levels of debt.

Working capital financing projections should be made using peak and trough estimates of current asset needs over the next year. This enables an analyst to determine *maximum* and *minimum* borrowing requirements when there are seasonal patterns in the borrower's business that should be reflected in balance sheet or income statement items. For term loans, projections should be made over several years or as long as the debt will remain outstanding. The projected loan need must approach zero within a reasonable time period or the firm will have to restructure its existing financing and operations to service new debt. The effective maturity of a loan is revealed in the pro forma data as the period when the additional debt requirement, or "plug" figure, approaches zero. This estimate will vary with the assumptions that generate the pro forma estimates.

**SENSITIVITY ANALYSIS.** Pro forma analysis is a form of sensitivity analysis. The analyst formulates a set of assumptions that establishes the relationships between different income statement and balance sheet items. At a minimum, three alternative scenarios or sets of assumptions should be considered:

- A *best case scenario* in which optimistic improvements in planned performance and the economy are realized
- A *worst case scenario* that represents the environment with the greatest potential negative impact on sales, earnings, and the balance sheet
- A *most likely scenario* representing the most reasonable sequence of economic events and performance trends

The three alternative forecasts of loan needs and cash flow establish a range of likely results, which indicates the riskiness of the credit. The analysts can use these alternative scenarios to determine if the loan will be paid back in a reasonable time under less than favorable conditions.

| Rating Category | Rating Scale | Collateral Support | Descriptive Indicators of Loan Quality |
|---|---|---|---|
| *Highest Quality* | 1 | Gov't. securities; cash | Highest quality borrowers. five years of historic cash flow data. Strong balance sheet and liquidity. |
| | 2 | Agency & high-quality municipal securities; insured CDs | Highest quality; differs from class 1 only by degree of financial strength. |
| | 3 | Uninsured CDs; high-quality stocks & bonds | Highest quality; cash flow average is slightly below classes 1 and 2. |
| *Acceptable Quality* | 4 | Gov't. guaranteed loans; may be unsecured | High degree of liquidity; assets readily convertible to cash; unused credit facilities. Strong equity capital and management. |
| | 5 | Secured by trading assets (A/R & Inv.) and/or real estate | Adequate liquidity; adequate equity capital with comfortable cash flow coverage; proactive management; cyclical industry with smaller margins. |
| | 6 | Heavily dependent on collateral and/or guarantees | Partially strained liquidity; limited equity so that leverage exceeds industry norms; limited management strength; business is cyclically vulnerable. |
| *Poor Quality* | 7 | Inadequate collateral | Strained liquidity, inadequate capital, and weak management. Adverse trends in industry and borrower financials. |
| | 8 | Inadequate collateral | Same as class 7, except financials are weaker. |
| | 9 | Inadequate collateral | Totally inadequate profile; well-defined weaknesses. |

## RISK-CLASSIFICATION SCHEME

Most banks use a risk-classification scheme as part of the analysis process for commercial loans. After evaluating the borrower's risk profile along all dimensions, a loan is placed in a rating category ranked according to the degree of risk. Such a system, used for credit granting and pricing decisions, is presented in the table presented above.

The actual risk rating assigned by lenders will reflect an evaluation of the borrower's historical performance along the lines of the analysis introduced earlier and a critique of the borrower's pro forma operating profile. The evaluation will look at key trends in historical performance and the current profit and risk profile relative to industry norms. Pro forma analysis will determine the adequacy of the firm's cash flow from operations coverage of debt service requirements if the firm requests a term loan, or the adequacy of cash flow from liquidating trading assets and collateral if the firm requests a working capital loan. Banks do not generally make new loans to firms rated 7 through 9 because they are high risk, but borrowers may be downgraded to these lower ratings if their condition deteriorates.

## CREDIT ANALYSIS APPLICATION: WADE'S OFFICE FURNITURE

The following analysis presents a systematic application of the credit evaluation procedure just described. It emphasizes using the procedure to evaluate a term loan request that requires forecasts of cash flow from operations. It focuses on how to interpret data and make a loan decision rather than on how the model works. The analysis addresses each of the four key issues. The nonquantitative aspects of the evaluation are generally ignored.

On March 1, 2005, Marcus Wade, president and majority owner of Wade's Office Furniture, met with you and requested an increase in the company's credit line from $900,000 to $1.2 million and a term loan of $400,000 for the purchase of new equipment. Wade's Office Furniture is a small manufacturer of metal office furniture. It has been in business for more than 25 years and has been a good customer of the bank for the last ten years. Mr. Wade was very positive about the firm's present condition, having just reported a 50 percent increase in sales for 2004 after two consecutive years of slow growth. He attributed this recent success to a new product line and marketing program and claimed it would continue—evidenced by backlogged orders totaling $250,000. In support of his request, he provided you with three years of historical income statement and balance sheet data for 2002–2004 as well as two years of pro forma data (2005–2006), which appear in Exhibits 11.5 and 11.6.[16] Wade projected sales to increase another 50 percent in 2005 and felt that this would quickly reduce the outstanding note payable to the bank and help repay the term loan.

### COMMON SIZE AND FINANCIAL RATIOS ANALYSIS: WADE'S OFFICE FURNITURE

The analysis begins with an evaluation of common size ratios from the income statement and balance sheet (Exhibits 11.5 and 11.6). Comparable figures from the *Annual Statement Studies* by Robert Morris Associates (RMA) for 2004 are listed in the column labeled "RMA." A review of the income statement in Exhibit 11.5 reveals three important factors. First, sales increased almost 52 percent, an impressive number for a "low-growth" industry like office furniture. Second, and equally as impressive, was that this growth was obtained with a cost of goods sold which was a substantially lower percentage of sales compared with the industry average, reflecting either lower cost of goods or higher markups on finished products. Third, Wade's operating expenses far exceeded the industry norm. This may reflect a large salary for Marcus Wade in that the firm pays no dividends and the company provides his only source of income. The net effect is that the firm earns proportionately less before taxes than comparable firms, 4.2 percent versus peers of 6.2 percent.

The balance sheet data in Exhibit 11.6 indicate that Wade's accounts receivable and inventory substantially exceeded the industry norms in 2004 and increased each year from 2002 to 2004. Net fixed assets, on the other hand, were well below industry standards in each year. After further exploration, you discover that Wade's leases a much larger portion of its fixed assets than the industry norm. One weakness of common size ratios is that they may be distorted by any one account that takes an extreme value. The fact that Wade's leases a disproportionately large amount of equipment necessarily increases the relative proportion of current assets. For this reason, the analyst must carefully compare the implications of common size ratios and other financial ratios before drawing conclusions. Finally, in terms of financing, Wade's relied almost twice as much as the industry norm on accounts payable and short-term bank loans and less on long-term debt than comparable firms. The firm's net worth-to-asset ratio was 8 percent less than the industry norm in 2004, which indicates that Wade's has financed much of its growth using debt.

---

[16]Actually, the pro forma data provided in Exhibits 11.5 and 11.6 are assumed not to have been provided by Wade's, rather by the credit analysts. These data will be discussed below.

**EXHIBIT 11.5** Comparative Income Statement for Wade's Office Furniture, 2002–2006

**Wade's Office Furniture**
**Unaudited: SIC #2522**

| INCOME STATEMENT | [—HISTORICAL—] 2002 % Cha | $1,000 | % of Total | [—HISTORICAL—] 2003 % Cha | $1,000 | % of Total | [—HISTORICAL—] 2004 % Cha | $1,000 | % of Total | RMA 6/30/03-3/31/04 | [—PRO FORMA—] 2005 % Cha | $1,000 | % of Total | [—PRO FORMA—] 2006 % Cha | $1,000 | % of Total |
|---|---|---|---|---|---|---|---|---|---|---|---|---|---|---|---|---|
| **Net sales** | #N/A | 7,571 | 100.00% | 8.10% | 8,184 | 100.00% | 51.90% | 12,430 | 100.00% | 100.00% | 20.00% | 14,916 | 100.00% | 20.00% | 17,899 | 100.00% |
| Cost of goods sold | #N/A | 5,089 | 67.20% | 6.60% | 5,424 | 66.30% | 52.20% | 8,255 | 66.40% | 67.30% | 22.90% | 10,143 | 68.00% | 20.00% | 12,171 | 68.00% |
| Gross profit | #N/A | 2,482 | 32.80% | 11.20% | 2,760 | 33.70% | 51.30% | 4,175 | 33.60% | 32.70% | 14.30% | 4,773 | 32.00% | 20.00% | 5,728 | 32.00% |
| Selling expenses | #N/A | 906 | 12.00% | 13.20% | 1,026 | 12.50% | 58.70% | 1,628 | 13.10% | | 19.10% | 1,939 | 13.00% | 20.00% | 2,327 | 13.00% |
| General & administrative expenses | #N/A | 1,019 | 13.50% | 18.80% | 1,211 | 14.80% | 39.50% | 1,689 | 13.60% | | 7.70% | 1,820 | 12.20% | 20.00% | 2,184 | 12.20% |
| Depreciation & amortization | #N/A | 70 | 0.90% | 1.40% | 71 | 0.90% | 2.80% | 73 | 0.60% | | 50.70% | 110 | 0.70% | 0.00% | 110 | 0.60% |
| Other operating expenses | #N/A | 0 | 0.00% | 0.00% | 0 | 0.00% | 0.00% | 0 | 0.00% | | 0.00% | 0 | 0.00% | 0.00% | 0 | 0.00% |
| Total operating expenses | #N/A | 1,995 | 26.40% | 15.70% | 2,308 | 28.20% | 46.90% | 3,390 | 27.30% | 25.70% | 14.10% | 3,869 | 25.90% | 19.40% | 4,621 | 25.80% |
| *Operating profit* | #N/A | 487 | 6.40% | -7.20% | 452 | 5.50% | 73.70% | 785 | 6.30% | 7.00% | 15.20% | 904 | 6.10% | 22.40% | 1,107 | 6.20% |
| Interest on marketable securities | #N/A | 0 | 0.00% | 0.00% | 0 | 0.00% | 0.00% | 0 | 0.00% | | 0.00% | 0 | 0.00% | 0.00% | 0 | 0.00% |
| Income on long term investments | #N/A | 0 | 0.00% | 0.00% | 0 | 0.00% | 0.00% | 0 | 0.00% | | 0.00% | 0 | 0.00% | 0.00% | 0 | 0.00% |
| Interest expense – Bank Notes | #N/A | 141 | 1.90% | -15.60% | 119 | 1.50% | 31.90% | 157 | 1.30% | | -35.60% | 101 | 0.70% | -48.50% | 52 | 0.30% |
| Interest expense – Term notes + LTD | #N/A | 0 | 0.00% | 0.00% | 0 | 0.00% | 0.00% | 0 | 0.00% | | #N/A | 85 | 0.60% | -16.50% | 71 | 0.40% |
| All other expenses | #N/A | 63 | 0.80% | 36.50% | 86 | 1.10% | 17.40% | 101 | 0.80% | | 8.90% | 110 | 0.70% | -22.70% | 135 | 0.80% |
| All other income | #N/A | 0 | 0.00% | 0.00% | 0 | 0.00% | 0.00% | 0 | 0.00% | | 0.00% | 0 | 0.00% | 0.00% | 0 | 0.00% |
| Total All Other Income (Expenses) | #N/A | -204 | -2.70% | 0.50% | -205 | -2.50% | 25.90% | -258 | -2.10% | | 14.80% | -296 | -2.00% | -12.80% | -258 | -1.40% |
| *Profit before taxes* | #N/A | 283 | 3.70% | -12.70% | 247 | 3.00% | 113.40% | 527 | 4.20% | 6.20% | 15.40% | 608 | 4.10% | 39.60% | 849 | 4.70% |
| Income taxes | #N/A | 100 | 1.30% | -5.00% | 95 | 1.20% | 97.90% | 188 | 1.50% | | 16.50% | 219 | 1.50% | 39.60% | 306 | 1.70% |
| Extraordinary and other income (exp.) | #N/A | 0 | 0.00% | 0.00% | 0 | 0.00% | 0.00% | 0 | 0.00% | | 0.00% | 0 | 0.00% | 0.00% | 0 | 0.00% |
| **Net Income** | #N/A | 183 | 2.40% | -16.90% | 152 | 1.90% | 123.00% | 339 | 2.70% | | 14.80% | 389 | 2.60% | 39.60% | 543 | 3.00% |
| Dividends | #N/A | 0 | 0.00% | 0.00% | 0 | 0.00% | 0.00% | 0 | 0.00% | | 0.00% | 0 | 0.00% | 0.00% | 0 | 0.00% |
| Retained earnings | #N/A | 183 | 2.40% | -16.90% | 152 | 1.90% | 123.00% | 339 | 2.70% | | 14.80% | 389 | 2.60% | 39.60% | 543 | 3.00% |

## EXHIBIT 11.6 — Comparative Balance Sheet for Wade's Office Furniture, 2002–2006

**Wade's Office Furniture**
**Unaudited: SIC #2522**

| BALANCE SHEET | [-HISTORICAL-] 2002 % Cha | 2002 $1,000 | 2002 % of Total | [-HISTORICAL-] 2003 % Cha | 2003 $1,000 | 2003 % of Total | [-HISTORICAL-] 2004 % Cha | 2004 $1,000 | 2004 % of Total | RMA 6/30/03-3/31/04 | [—PRO FORMA—] 2005 % Cha | 2005 $1,000 | 2005 % of Total | [—PRO FORMA—] 2006 % Cha | 2006 $1,000 | 2006 % of Total |
|---|---|---|---|---|---|---|---|---|---|---|---|---|---|---|---|---|
| **ASSETS** | | | | | | | | | | | | | | | | |
| Cash | #N/A | 141 | 4.3% | -5.7% | 133 | 3.9% | -45.9% | 72 | 1.6% | 5.5% | 66.7% | 120 | 2.3% | 0.0% | 120 | 2.1% |
| Marketable securities | #N/A | 0 | 0.0% | 0.0% | 0 | 0.0% | 0.0% | 0 | 0.0% | | 0.0% | 0 | 0.0% | 0.0% | 0 | 0.0% |
| Accounts receivable | #N/A | 1,254 | 38.4% | 11.6% | 1,399 | 40.8% | 35.5% | 1,896 | 42.3% | 28.8% | 7.8% | 2,043 | 38.7% | 10.4% | 2,256 | 39.6% |
| Inventory | #N/A | 1,160 | 35.6% | 3.9% | 1,205 | 35.2% | 46.4% | 1,764 | 39.4% | 29.7% | 17.3% | 2,070 | 39.2% | 15.3% | 2,387 | 41.9% |
| Prepaid expenses | #N/A | 47 | 1.4% | 6.4% | 50 | 1.5% | -70.0% | 15 | 0.3% | | 33.3% | 20 | 0.4% | 25.0% | 25 | 0.4% |
| **Current assets** | **#N/A** | **2,602** | **79.7%** | **7.1%** | **2,787** | **81.4%** | **34.4%** | **3,747** | **83.6%** | **66.4%** | **13.5%** | **4,253** | **80.6%** | **12.6%** | **4,787** | **84.0%** |
| Gross fixed assets | #N/A | 629 | 19.3% | 7.2% | 674 | 19.7% | 17.4% | 791 | 17.7% | | 50.6% | 1,191 | 22.6% | 0.0% | 1,191 | 20.9% |
| Leasehold improvements | #N/A | 198 | 6.1% | 2.0% | 202 | 5.9% | 17.8% | 238 | 5.3% | | 0.0% | 238 | 4.5% | 0.0% | 238 | 4.2% |
| Less accumulated dep. | #N/A | 206 | 6.3% | 34.5% | 277 | 8.1% | 24.9% | 346 | 7.7% | | 31.8% | 456 | 8.6% | 24.1% | 566 | 9.9% |
| **Net fixed assets** | **#N/A** | **621** | **19.0%** | **-3.5%** | **599** | **17.5%** | **14.0%** | **683** | **15.2%** | **28.2%** | **42.5%** | **973** | **18.4%** | **-11.3%** | **863** | **15.1%** |
| Intangible assets | #N/A | 40 | 1.2% | -2.5% | 39 | 1.1% | 28.2% | 50 | 1.1% | 0.4% | 0.0% | 50 | 0.9% | 0.0% | 50 | 0.9% |
| Other noncurrent assets | #N/A | 0 | 0.0% | 0.0% | 0 | 0.0% | 0.0% | 0 | 0.0% | 5.0% | 0.0% | 0 | 0.0% | 0.0% | 0 | 0.0% |
| **Total Assets** | **#N/A** | **3,263** | **100.0%** | **5.0%** | **3,425** | **100.0%** | **30.8%** | **4,480** | **100.0%** | **100.0%** | **17.8%** | **5,276** | **100.0%** | **8.0%** | **5,700** | **100.0%** |
| **LIABILITIES & EQUITY** | | | | | | | | | | | | | | | | |
| Notes payable – bank | #N/A | 643 | 19.7% | -9.5% | 582 | 17.0% | 53.3% | 892 | 19.9% | 6.0% | -21.8% | 697 | 13.2% | -48.5% | 359 | 6.3% |
| Accounts payable | #N/A | 836 | 25.6% | 8.6% | 908 | 26.5% | 41.2% | 1,282 | 28.6% | 14.0% | 18.3% | 1,517 | 28.8% | 19.5% | 1,813 | 31.8% |
| Accrued expenses | #N/A | 205 | 6.3% | 25.9% | 258 | 7.5% | 34.9% | 348 | 7.8% | | 5.7% | 368 | 7.0% | 5.4% | 388 | 6.8% |
| Income tax payable | #N/A | 41 | 1.3% | 51.2% | 62 | 1.8% | 27.4% | 79 | 1.8% | 1.7% | 27.4% | 101 | 1.9% | 27.4% | 128 | 2.3% |
| Current maturity – Term notes | #N/A | 0 | 0.0% | 0.0% | 0 | 0.0% | 0.0% | 0 | 0.0% | | #N/A | 50 | 0.9% | 0.0% | 50 | 0.9% |
| Current maturity – LTD | #N/A | 75 | 2.3% | 0.0% | 75 | 2.2% | 0.0% | 75 | 1.7% | 3.6% | 0.0% | 75 | 1.4% | 0.0% | 75 | 1.3% |
| Other current liabilities | #N/A | 0 | 0.0% | 0.0% | 0 | 0.0% | 0.0% | 0 | 0.0% | 11.8% | 0.0% | 0 | 0.0% | 0.0% | 0 | 0.0% |
| **Current liabilities** | **#N/A** | **1,800** | **55.2%** | **4.7%** | **1,885** | **55.0%** | **42.0%** | **2,676** | **59.7%** | **37.1%** | **4.9%** | **2,808** | **53.2%** | **0.2%** | **2,814** | **49.4%** |
| Term notes | #N/A | 0 | 0.0% | 0.0% | 0 | 0.0% | 0.0% | 0 | 0.0% | | #N/A | 350 | 6.6% | -14.3% | 300 | 5.3% |
| Long-term debt (LTD) | #N/A | 450 | 13.8% | -16.7% | 375 | 10.9% | -20.0% | 300 | 6.7% | 20.1% | -25.0% | 225 | 4.3% | -33.3% | 150 | 2.6% |
| Other noncurrent liabilities | #N/A | 0 | 0.0% | 0.0% | 0 | 0.0% | 0.0% | 0 | 0.0% | 0.9% | 0.0% | 0 | 0.0% | 0.0% | 0 | 0.0% |
| **Total liabilities** | **#N/A** | **2,250** | **69.0%** | **0.4%** | **2,260** | **66.0%** | **31.7%** | **2,976** | **66.4%** | **58.1%** | **13.7%** | **3,383** | **64.1%** | **-3.5%** | **3,264** | **57.3%** |
| Common stock – par | #N/A | 600 | 18.4% | 0.0% | 600 | 17.5% | 0.0% | 600 | 13.4% | | 0.0% | 600 | 11.4% | 0.0% | 600 | 10.5% |
| Paid-in surplus | #N/A | 100 | 3.1% | 0.0% | 100 | 2.9% | 0.0% | 100 | 2.2% | | 0.0% | 100 | 1.9% | 0.0% | 100 | 1.8% |
| Retained earnings | #N/A | 313 | 9.6% | 48.6% | 465 | 13.6% | 72.9% | 804 | 17.9% | | 48.4% | 1,193 | 22.6% | 45.5% | 1,737 | 30.5% |
| **Stockholder's equity** | **#N/A** | **1,013** | **31.0%** | **15.0%** | **1,165** | **34.0%** | **29.1%** | **1,504** | **33.6%** | **41.9%** | **25.9%** | **1,893** | **35.9%** | **28.7%** | **2,437** | **42.7%** |
| **Total Liabilities and Equity** | **#N/A** | **3,263** | **100.0%** | **5.0%** | **3,425** | **100.0%** | **30.8%** | **4,480** | **100.0%** | **100.0%** | **17.8%** | **5,276** | **100.0%** | **8.0%** | **5,700** | **100.0%** |

Wade's balance sheet is typical of a small company exhibiting short-term rapid sales growth. Most of the growth in sales, which has led to a large increase in accounts receivable and inventory, was financed by a short-term line of credit. Cash has fallen to a *minimum* level, and Wade's is likely pushing the upper limit of its short-term line of credit. A cash shortage may be one of the reasons Wade's is making the loan request.

Financial ratios for Wade's are presented in Exhibit 11.7. Current and quick ratios are low but have been fairly stable over the preceding three years. Days accounts receivable is about 11 days longer than the industry norm and inventory turns over only 4.7 times a year compared with the industry norm of 5.6 times. The low current and quick ratios tend to indicate a lower value of current assets, but the common size and ratio analysis indicates that the level of accounts receivable and inventory is above peers. Remember that the common size ratios are distorted (too high for current assets) relative to peers due to the high amount of leased fixed assets.

Examination of days accounts payable further explains the conflicting information. Days accounts payable is much higher at 53 days outstanding as compared with the industry norm of only 32 days. This indicates that accounts payable exceeded that for peers relative to purchases. Thus, it is the denominator of the current and quick ratios (current liabilities) that lowers the current and quick ratios rather than the numerator (current assets). High accounts payable suggest that Wade's is riding its creditors for long periods and may be at risk of being put on a "cash basis" by the creditors.

The set of leverage ratios in Exhibit 11.7 confirms the common size analysis in that minimal net worth supports the firm's operations. Debt exceeds tangible net worth by almost 100 percent in each year, well above the RMA average. Both the times interest earned and fixed charge coverage are low compared with competitors, indicating greater interest expense and lease payments on equipment relative to earnings.

The profitability ratios, presented in Exhibit 11.7, indicate that Wade's profits before taxes exceeded the standard relative to net worth but fell below the standard relative to total assets. This again evidences the firm's relatively high degree of financial leverage. Reported profits did increase substantially in 2004, due in large part to the dramatic increase in net sales. Wade's lower profits before taxes to total assets (pretax ROA), however, was due to the higher operating expenses relative to industry norm; 27.3 percent for Wade's versus 25.7 percent for the industry. Lower profits were obtained even though Wade's cost of goods sold was lower than at peers at 66.4 percent of total sales, versus the peer average of 67.3 percent. Still, Wade's reported a ROE of 22.54 percent in 2004, which was a substantial improvement over prior years.

In summary, Wade's invested more in receivables and inventory and less in fixed assets than comparable firms. It likewise relies proportionately more on trade credit and short-term bank loans and less on long-term debt for financing. Its net worth is also substantially lower. These ratios are important because they suggest areas in which additional information must be obtained. Here the focus should be on Wade's current and fixed assets. Possible explanations are that the firm's terms of credit sales are too lenient or that the firm has poor collection policies. Some of the receivables might be uncollectible because they are outdated. Thus, a receivables aging schedule seems necessary. Similarly, Wade's may hold obsolete inventory or simply acquire it too far in advance of sales. With respect to earnings, profitability has been relatively low, adversely affecting the equity base. On the positive side, however, sales growth and markup on sales are excellent. If the receivables and inventory are of good quality, Wade's exhibits excellent potential. It is important, however, for the banker to obtain a receivables aging schedule and personally audit the composition and quality of inventory.

The data suggest two specific risks. First, if suppliers refuse to grant Wade's the same volume of trade credit in the future, the firm will need additional bank loans to support operations. In particular, accounts payable provided $1,282,000 in financing for 2004. If suppliers were to put the company on a cash basis (cash on delivery), Wade's would have to pay off this $1,282,000 and come up with additional funds to buy its inventory. If the firm is having a problem with its suppliers, Marcus Wade would probably return to the bank for additional financing! Second, the firm's low net worth and high debt provide limited support for the planned growth (Wade estimates another 50 percent for 2005) and exposes the firm to declining profits if interest rates increase. Wade's profitability has not been high enough to continue to support a 50 percent per year growth in sales using only debt. The firm must either slow its growth or additional equity will be required. On the positive side, however, Wade's could slow the growth in sales by restricting credit sales, reducing inventory, or even increasing price. All of these would improve Wade's cash position.

## CASH-BASED INCOME STATEMENT: WADE'S OFFICE FURNITURE

Exhibit 11.8 presents a cash-based income statement for Wade's and documents changes in cash flow from operations (CFO). Consider the first two columns of historical data. In 2003 cash flow from operations equaled $176,000, which was $24,000 more than reported net income. CFO fell to −$128,000 in 2004, however, even though sales increased by over $4 million and net income increased by 123 percent to almost $340,000. A close examination of the statement reveals that the decline in CFO for 2004 was caused by a combined increase in receivables and inventory of almost $1.1 million ($497,000 + $559,000). The $374,000 increase in accounts payable, while substantial, left $682,000 in new trading assets (change in accounts receivable plus the change in inventory

**EXHIBIT 11.7** Financial Ratio Analysis for Wade's Office Furniture, 2002–2006

| Wade's Office Furniture<br>Unaudited: SIC #2522<br>FINANCIAL RATIOS | [-HISTORICAL-]<br>2002<br>$ 1,000 | | [-HISTORICAL-]<br>2003<br>$ 1,000 | | [-HISTORICAL-]<br>2004<br>$ 1,000 | | RMA<br>6/30/03 -<br>3/31/04 | | [—PRO FORMA—]<br>2005<br>$ 1,000 | | [—PRO FORMA—]<br>2006<br>$ 1,000 | |
|---|---|---|---|---|---|---|---|---|---|---|---|---|
| **Liquidity ratios** | | | | | | | | | | | | |
| Current ratio | 1.45 | | 1.48 | | 1.40 | | 1.70 | | 1.51 | | 1.70 | |
| Quick ratio | 0.78 | | 0.81 | | 0.74 | | 0.90 | | 0.77 | | 0.84 | |
| | *Days* | *Times* | *Days* | *Times* | *Days* | *Times* | *Days* | *Times* | *Days* | *Times* | *Days* | *Times* |
| Days Cash | 6.80 | 53.70× | 5.93 | 61.53× | 2.11 | 172.64× | | | 2.94 | 124.30× | 2.45 | 149.16× |
| Days accounts receivable | 60.46 | 6.04× | 62.39 | 5.85× | 55.67 | 6.56× | 45.0 | 8.1× | 50.00 | 7.30× | 46.00 | 7.93× |
| Days inventory | 83.20 | 4.39× | 81.09 | 4.50× | 78.00 | 4.68× | 65.0 | 5.6× | 74.49 | 4.90× | 71.57 | 5.10× |
| Cash-to-cash asset cycle | 150.45 | | 149.41 | | 135.79 | | | | 127.43 | | 120.02 | |
| Days AP outstanding | 48.83 | 7.47× | 60.60 | 6.02× | 53.09 | 6.88× | 32.0 | 11.3× | 53.00 | 6.89× | 53.00 | 6.89× |
| *Memo: COGS/Accts payable* | | 6.09× | | 5.97× | | 6.44× | | 11.3× | | 6.69× | | 6.71× |
| Days Cash-to-cash cycle | 101.62 | 3.59× | 88.81 | 4.11× | 82.70 | 4.41× | | | 74.43 | 4.90× | 67.02 | 5.45× |
| Est. W.C. financing needs | $1,417 | | $1,320 | | $1,870 | | | | $2,068 | | $2,235 | |
| | *Percent* | *Times* | *Percent* | *Times* | *Percent* | *Times* | *Percent* | *Times* | *Percent* | *Times* | *Percent* | *Times* |
| **Leverage Ratios** | | | | | | | | | | | | |
| Debt to tangible net worth | | 2.31× | | 2.01× | | 2.05× | | 1.7× | | 1.84× | | 1.37× |
| Times interest earned | | 3.01× | | 3.08× | | 4.36× | | 5.3× | | 4.27× | | 7.90× |
| Fixed charge coverage | | 1.96× | | 1.79× | | 2.09× | | 2.8× | | 2.19× | | 2.89× |
| Net fixed assets to tangible net worth | 63.82% | | 53.20% | | 46.97% | | 50.0% | | 52.79% | | 36.16% | |
| Dividend payout | 0.00% | | 0.00% | | 0.00% | | | | 0.00% | | 0.00% | |
| | *Percent* | *Times* | *Percent* | *Times* | *Percent* | *Times* | *Percent* | *Times* | *Percent* | *Times* | *Percent* | *Times* |
| **Profitability Ratios** | | | | | | | | | | | | |
| Return on net worth (ROE) | 18.07% | | 13.05% | | 22.54% | | | | 20.56% | | 22.30% | |
| Profit before taxes to net worth | 29.09% | | 21.94% | | 36.24% | | 27.7% | | 33.00% | | 35.58% | |
| Return on assets (ROA) | 5.61% | | 4.44% | | 7.57% | | | | 7.38% | | 9.53% | |
| Profit before taxes to total assets | 8.67% | | 7.21% | | 11.76% | | 12.1% | | 11.53% | | 14.90% | |
| Equity multiplier (leverage = TA/TE) | | 3.22× | | 2.94× | | 2.98× | | 2.4× | | 2.79× | | 2.34× |
| Income | | | | | | | | | | | | |
| Tot. asset turnover (net sales/TA) | | 2.32× | | 2.39× | | 2.77× | | 2.1× | | 2.83× | | 3.14× |
| All other income/total assets | 0.00% | | 0.00% | | 0.00% | | | | 0.00% | | 0.00% | |
| Expenses | | | | | | | | | | | | |
| Net profit margin (NI/net sales) | 2.42% | | 1.86% | | 2.73% | | | | 2.61% | | 3.04% | |
| COGS/net sales | 67.22% | | 66.28% | | 66.41% | | 67.3% | | 68.00% | | 68.00% | |
| Operating expenses/net sales | 26.35% | | 28.20% | | 27.27% | | 25.7% | | 25.94% | | 25.81% | |
| Income Taxes to Earnings Before Taxes | 35.34% | | 38.46% | | 35.67% | | | | 36.00% | | 36.00% | |
| Sales/Net Fixed Assets | | 12.19× | | 13.66× | | 18.20× | | | | 15.33× | | 20.74× |
| | | *Times* | | *Times* | | *Times* | | | | *Times* | | *Times* |
| **Cash Flow Ratios** | | | | | | | | | | | | |
| CFO/(DIV + last CMLTD) | | #N/A | | 2.35× | | -1.71× | | | | 4.24× | | 6.17× |
| CFO/(DIV + last CMLTD + bnk notes) | | #N/A | | 0.27× | | -0.13× | | | | 0.41× | | 1.07× |
| CFO/(DIV + last CMLTD & CMTN + bnk Notes) | | #N/A | | 0.27× | | -0.13× | | | | 0.39× | | 0.96× |

**EXHIBIT 11.8** Statement of Changes Reconciled to Cash for Wade's Office Furniture, 2003–2006

| Wade's Office Furniture<br>Unaudited:, SIC #2522<br>CASH BASED INCOME STATEMENT | [-HISTORICAL-] | | [—PRO FORMA—] | |
|---|---|---|---|---|
| | 2003<br>$ 1,000 | 2004<br>$ 1,000 | 2005<br>$ 1,000 | 2006<br>$ 1,00 |
| Net sales | 8,184 | 12,430 | 14,916 | 17,899 |
| Change in accounts receivable | (145) | (497) | (147) | (213) |
| Cash receipts from sales | 8,039 | 11,933 | 14,769 | 17,687 |
| Cost of goods sold | (5,424) | (8,255) | (10,143) | (12,171) |
| Change in inventory | (45) | (559) | (306) | (317) |
| Change in accounts payable | 72 | 374 | 235 | 296 |
| Cash purchases | (5,397) | (8,440) | (10,214) | (12,192) |
| Cash margin | 2,642 | 3,493 | 4,555 | 5,495 |
| Total operating expenses | (2,308) | (3,390) | (3,869) | (4,621) |
| Depreciation and amortization | 71 | 73 | 110 | 110 |
| Change in prepaid expenses | (3) | 35 | (5) | (5) |
| Change in accruals | 53 | 90 | 20 | 20 |
| Change in other current assets and liab. | 0 | 0 | 0 | 0 |
| Cash operating expenses | (2,187) | (3,192) | (3,744) | (4,496) |
| Cash operating profit | 455 | 301 | 811 | 999 |
| Interest on marketable securities | 0 | 0 | 0 | 0 |
| Income on long term investments | 0 | 0 | 0 | 0 |
| All other expenses and income (net) | (86) | (101) | (110) | (135) |
| Cash before interest and taxes | 369 | 200 | 701 | 864 |
| Interest expense − Bank notes | (119) | (157) | (101) | (52) |
| Interest expense − Term notes and LTD | 0 | 0 | (85) | (71) |
| Income taxes reported | (95) | (188) | (219) | (306) |
| Change in income tax payable | 21 | 17 | 22 | 28 |
| Change in deferred income taxes | 0 | 0 | 0 | 0 |
| *Cash flow from operations (CFO)* | *176* | *(128)* | *318* | *463* |
| Capital exp. and leasehold improvements | (49) | (157) | (400) | 0 |
| Change in long-term investments | 0 | 0 | 0 | 0 |
| Change in intangible assets | 1 | (11) | 0 | 0 |
| Change in other noncurrent assets | 0 | 0 | 0 | 0 |
| *Cash Used for Investments* | *(48)* | *(168)* | *(400)* | *0* |
| Payment for last period's CM Term note | 0 | 0 | 0 | (50) |
| Payment for last period's CMLTD | (75) | (75) | (75) | (75) |
| Dividends paid (DIV) | 0 | 0 | 0 | 0 |
| *Payments for financing* | *(75)* | *(75)* | *(75)* | *(125)* |
| Cash before external financing | 53 | (371) | (157) | 338 |
| Change in short-term bank debt | (61) | 310 | (195) | (338) |
| Change in term notes and<br>EOP CM term notes | 0 | 0 | 400 | 0 |
| Change in LT debt + EOP CMLTD | 0 | 0 | 0 | 0 |
| Change in stock and surplus | 0 | 0 | 0 | 0 |
| Change in preferred stock | 0 | 0 | 0 | 0 |
| Change in treasury and other equities | 0 | 0 | 0 | 0 |
| Change in other noncurrent liabilities | 0 | 0 | 0 | 0 |
| *External financing* | *(61)* | *310* | *205* | *(338)* |
| Extraordinary exp. and cha. In acct. prin. | 0 | 0 | 0 | 0 |
| Current period accounting adjustment | 0 | 0 | 0 | 0 |
| *Change in cash & mktbl securities* | *(8)* | *(61)* | *48* | *0* |

NOTE: Figures are in thousands of dollars.

LTD, CM, and EOP refer to long-term debt, current maturity, and end-of-period, respectively.

less the change in accounts payable) to be financed either externally or out of cash flow. The cash margin did increase by $851,000 but cash operating expenses increased by over $1 million, leading to a decline in cash operating profit. Increases in noninterest and interest expense and income taxes paid then produced the negative cash flow from operations. The additional $310,000 in notes payable to the bank financed a portion of this cash deficiency. Payments for maturing principal on term debt and $157,000 in capital expenditures added to the cash deficiency as well. The residual financing came from reduced cash holdings.

Consider the following implications. Wade's collected less on credit sales than it billed its customers in 2003 and 2004 as shown by an increase in accounts receivable outstanding from 2002 to 2004. Thus, net sales were offset by the $497,000 increase in receivables to obtain actual cash receipts. Had receivables declined, actual cash receipts from sales would have exceeded the reported sales figure. Sales increased by almost 52 percent from 2003 to 2004 while accounts receivable only increased by 35.5 percent. The liquidity and activity ratios in Exhibit 11.7 indicate that Wade's credit policy tightened from 2003 to 2004 as days accounts receivable fell by almost 7 days from 62.39 to 55.67. If Wade's credit policy had not improved over this period, cash flow from operations would have been approximately $229,000 lower.[17] The improvement in collection of receivables is a positive sign for Wade's and has reduced the amount of financing Wade's otherwise would have needed at the end of 2004. Wade's profitability (gross margin) improved in 2003 but deteriorated in 2004—indicating cash flow from operations would be higher relative to net income in 2003, but the lower gross margin in 2004 was a use of cash. Wade's inventory turnover improved in 2003 (4.50×) and 2004 (4.68×). The improved inventory turnover means that inventory growth was less than the growth in sales. The company's more efficient utilization of inventory means that Wade's used proportionately less cash to finance sales growth than it would have had inventory turnover not improved, again positive news. The fact that accounts payable increased in 2004 means cash additional cash was supplied by Wade's trade credit, but the fact that days accounts payable outstanding decreased over the period meant that less cash was provided by trade credit financing than would have been if days payable outstanding remained at its 2003 level.

On the positive side, Wade's accounts receivable and inventory growth, although substantial, was less than the growth in sales. Wade's cash needs to finance the increase in working capital was not a result of a more lax credit or inventory policy, but instead was primarily driven by sales growth. If these credit sales and inventory are of high quality, this will provide cash flow in the future as Wade's collects on credit sales. Wade's also reduced its days accounts payable outstanding in 2004, thus improving its position with suppliers.

In summary, Wade's cash flow from operations in 2003 of $176,000 exceeded capital expenditures ($49,000) and the principal payment on long-term debt ($75,000) by $52,000. This excess cash flow, along with $8,000 in cash, was essentially used to pay $61,000 on the amount of short-term debt owed. In 2004, however, cash flow from operations was negative (−$128,000) and hence insufficient to cover current principal payments on long-term debt ($75,000) and capital expenditures ($157,000). Cash flow before external financing was also negative (−$371,000) in 2004. Wade's borrowed an additional $310,000 in short-term debt and used $61,000 in cash to fund this deficit.

Wade's generated good profits but these profits did not materialize as cash profits. Why? In essence, the increase in receivables and inventory exceeded the increase in accounts payable. While Wade's provided $73,000 from noncash expenditures (depreciation) and $142,000 from a reduction in prepaid expenses, an increase in accrued expenses, and reduced income tax payables, this was less than that needed to finance current operations. Wade's profit of $339,000 provided all but $128,000 of this deficiency. Thus, most of the $310,000 in additional financing was used to finance the increase in working capital needs.

The ratios at the bottom of Exhibit 11.7 demonstrate that Wade's generated enough cash from operations to pay off current maturities of long-term debt in 2003 but fell far short in 2004. The negative cash flow from operations in 2004 indicates that the firm should not take on additional debt unless it can successfully restructure its operating policies.

## PRO FORMA ANALYSIS: WADE'S OFFICE FURNITURE

Negative cash flow does not necessarily eliminate the possibility that the bank may want to make a loan. Under proper operating policies, Wade's may be able to expand and pay off new debt on a timely basis. Recall that Wade's negative cash flow was primarily driven by the 52 percent growth in sales. If sales growth slows, Wade's use of cash for accounts receivables and inventory will fall dramatically—most likely producing positive cash flow from operations. Exhibits 11.9 and 11.10 outline a set of financial projections that describes *a most likely* set of circumstances regarding the economic environment and revisions in Wade's operating policies. In this case, the loan should be repaid.

---

[17]If credit policy had not changed, then accounts receivable would have been $2,125,000 [($12,430,000/ 365) × 62.39], hence the change in accounts receivables would have been $726,000 ($2,125,000 − 1,399,000).

| EXHIBIT 11.9 | Financial Projections: Assumptions for Most Likely Circumstances at Wade's Office Furniture, 2005–2006 |

1. Sales increase by 20 percent annually. All sales are credit sales. Wade's forecasts a 50 percent rise.
2. Cost of goods sold equals 68 percent of sales.
3. Selling expenses average 13 percent of sales, general and administrative expenses average 12.2 percent of sales, and depreciation equals $110,000 annually.
4. Noninterest expense equals $110,000 in 2005 and $135,000 in 2006.
5. Interest expense equals 14.5 percent of outstanding bank and term debt and 9 percent of other long-term debt.
6. Income taxes equal 36 percent of earnings before taxes; income tax payable increases annually by the rate of change in 2004.
7. Receivables collection improves so that days receivables outstanding equals 50 in 2005 and 46 in 2006.
8. Inventory turnover increases to 4.9 times in 2005 and 5.1 times in 2006.
9. Days accounts payable outstanding remains constant at 53.
10. Prepaid expenses and accruals increase by $5,000 and $20,000 annually in 2005 and 2006, respectively.
11. No dividends are paid.
12. $400,000 is loaned to purchase new equipment, with the principal repaid over eight years in equal annual installments. The first payment is due March 1, 2005.
13. Reported depreciation on the new equipment equals $40,000 a year for 10 years. Depreciation on old assets will be $70,000 per year.
14. The minimum cash required is $120,000.
15. Other assets remain constant at $50,000.

| EXHIBIT 11.10 | Pro Forma Model Used to Project Wade's Financial Statements |

**Pro forma values on the income statement are calculated as follows:**

$$\text{Sales}_{2005} = \text{Sales}_{2004} \times (\textbf{1+ } \textbf{\textit{g}}_{\textbf{\textit{sales}}}) = \$12,430 \times (1 + \textbf{0.20}) = \$14,916$$
$$\text{COGS}_{2005} = \text{Sales}_{2005} \times \textbf{\textit{COGS \% of sales}}$$
$$= \$14,916 \times \textbf{0.68} = \$10,143$$
$$\text{Selling exp}_{2005} = \text{Sales}_{2005} \times (\textbf{\textit{selling exp. \% of sales}})$$
$$= \$14,916 \times \textbf{0.13} = \$1,939$$
$$\text{G\&A exp}_{2005} = \text{Sales}_{2005} \times \textbf{\textit{G\&A exp. \% of sales}}$$
$$= \$14,916 \times \textbf{0.122} = \$1,820$$
$$\text{Interest exp}_{2005} = (\text{Bank debt}_{2005} \times \textbf{\textit{rate on bank debt and term debt}})$$
$$+ (\text{L.T. debt}_{2005} \times \textbf{\textit{rate on L.T. debt}})$$
$$= [\$697 + \$50 + \$350] \times \textbf{0.145} + [(\$75 + \$225) \times \textbf{0.09}] = \$186$$

**Pro forma values on the balance sheet are calculated as follows:**

$$\text{Accounts rec}_{2005} = \textbf{\textit{Days A/R outstanding}} \times \text{average daily sales}_{2005}$$
$$= \textbf{50} \times (\$14,916/365) = \$2,043$$
$$\text{Inventory}_{2005} = \text{COGS}_{2005}/\textbf{\textit{inventory turnover}}$$
$$= \$10,143/\textbf{4.9} = \$2,070$$
$$\text{Gross fixed}_{2005} = \text{Gross fixed}_{2004} + \textbf{\textit{capital expenditures}}$$
$$= \$791 + \textbf{\$400} = \$1,191$$
$$\text{Accumulated dep}_{2005} = \text{Accumulated depreciation}_{2004} + \text{depreciation expense}_{2005}$$
$$= \$346 + \$110 = \$456$$
$$\text{Notes payable}_{2005} = \textbf{\textit{"Plug figure"}} = \text{Assets}_{2005} - (\text{liabilities}_{2005} + \text{net worth}_{2005})$$
$$\text{Accounts pay}_{2005} = \textbf{\textit{Days AP outstanding}} \times \text{average daily purchases}_{2005}$$
$$= \textbf{\textit{Days AP outstanding}} \times [(\text{COGS}_{2005} + \Delta\text{Inventory}_{2005})/365]$$
$$= 53 \times [(\$10,143 + (\$2,070 - \$1,764))/365] = \$1,517$$
$$\text{LTD}_{2005} = \text{LTD}_{2004} - \textbf{\textit{CMLTD}} + \textbf{\textit{new issues of LTD}}$$
$$= \$300 - \textbf{\$75} + \textbf{\$0} = \$225$$
$$\text{Term notes}_{2005} = \text{Term notes}_{2004} - \textbf{\textit{CM term notes}} + \textbf{\textit{new issues of term notes}}$$
$$= \textbf{\$0} - \textbf{\$50} + \textbf{\$400} = \$350$$
$$\text{Retained earn}_{2005} = \text{Retained earnings}_{2004} + (\text{net income}_{2005} - \textbf{\textit{dividends}})$$
$$= \$804 + (\$339 - \textbf{\$0}) = \$1,193$$

NOTE: Figures are in thousands of dollars. Values in **bold italic** are parameters that the analyst must provide.

Each of these pro forma assumptions (parameters) reflects a conservative but realistic estimate of future performance moving Wade's operating ratios closer to industry norms or reflecting economic realities. In making the loan decision, the bank will lend money only if Wade's understands it must restrict its growth in current assets by tightening credit policies and slowing inventory growth. The loan officer cannot, however, require Wade's to restrict sales in any formal document or the bank may be held responsible if the company does not perform well. Rather, the officer must be convinced, based on discussions with Marcus Wade and an assessment of his character, that Wade agrees that this plan is in the best interest of the company. This is just one of the many aspects of the more qualitative issues that must be addressed to finalize a loan decision. Restrictions on credit sales are assumed to lower sales below Marcus Wade's forecast of 50 percent for 2005 and decrease the effective markup over cost of goods sold. In addition to restrictions on credit sales, economic principals would lead the loan officer closer to a single digit growth in sales assumption of an office furniture company unless the company'smarketing plan was truly one that could improve market share. The office furniture business is not a "high-growth" industry but Wade's has demonstrated strong growth in sales. Therefore it would be realistic, based on Wade's new product lines and aggressive marketing, that the business could grow faster than the rest of the economy. But 15 to 20 percent would seem more reasonable than Wade's estimate of 50 percent.

It is assumed, based on discussion with Wade, that both receivables and inventory turnover will improve and move closer to the industry norm by 2006. Net profit will increase proportionately because of decreases in expenses as Wade's salary is assumed unchanged and nonoperating expenses decline proportionately.

Income statement and balance sheet projections for 2005 and 2006 appear in Exhibits 11.5 and 11.6, respectively. These projections are based on the explicit assumptions in Exhibits 11.9 and 11.10. The resulting projected cash-based income statement is presented in Exhibit 11.8. If projected cash flow from operations is realized, it will total $318,000 in 2005 and $463,000 in 2006, considerably more than current maturities of long-term debt. Cash flow from operations increases with sales because new trading assets are presumably financed almost entirely by additional trade credit. Thus, the cash margin increases more than cash operating expense, interest expense, and taxes paid. The bank's short-term loan exposure will decrease in 2005 and 2006 to $697,000 and $359,000, respectively. Of course, the total bank loan outstanding will equal almost $1.1 million at the end of 2005 and $709,000 at the end of 2006. This amount is substantially less than the requested $1.6 million. Hence, the answer to the first question, "How much does Wade need to borrow?" is approximately $1.1 million in 2005 (notes payable bank plus current maturities of long-term debt and the outstanding amount of long-term debt) and $709,000 in 2006.

In this scenario, the answer to the second question "What were the loan proceeds used for?" is: to finance the new equipment and Wade's continued need for working capital financing. The projected decrease in notes payable, however, represents a reduction in working capital financing needed, not an increase as Wade had requested. Effectively, the bank has restructured Wade's debt to include more term debt and less of the short-term line of credit. In addition, the lower sales growth means that working capital needs do not grow as rapidly as they did in 2004 and profit from Wade's operations are sufficient to cover the increase in working capital. In 2005, cash flow from operations of $318,000 is forecast to exceed principal and interest payments by $243,000.[18] Because capital expenditures of $400,000 were financed with a term loan of an equal amount, this leaves a cash flow surplus, after payment on long-term debt, which was used to pay down the short-term bank debt ($195,000) and increase cash by $48,000. This analysis indicates that that the remaining notes payable bank were actually from prior-year needs when Wade's financed a permanent growth in working capital with a line of credit rather than a term note. The excess cash flow is forecast to reach $338,000 in 2006. Estimates for both pro forma periods reveal that Wade's has the ability to take on additional debt.

The previous discussion indicates that the bank may be financing long-term needs including permanent increases in working capital from the prior year's 50 percent growth in sales, with short-term debt. The bank could consider "restructuring" the debt by using a larger term loan, effectively reducing the amount of the line of credit (short-term bank debt). This structure would allow Wade to "clean up" the line of credit once a year. **Clean up the line of credit** means to bring the outstanding loan balance to zero at least once during the year. In order to determine Wade's true short-term needs on his line of credit, the analysis should look at monthly or quarterly financials and estimate the company's maximum and minimum working capital needs. See Chapter 10 for more details. Alternatively, the bank could shorten the maturity of the term loan and increase the annual principal payment.

The third question, "What is the primary source of repayment and when will the loan be repaid?" can be answered as follows. At the end of 2006, Wade's is producing roughly $338,000 in excess cash flow from its operations after principal payments on debt. Clearly cash flow from Wade's ongoing operations is the primary source of repayment that can be used to repay the outstanding loans. If this cash flow continues, Wade's could repay its remaining bank debt of $709,000 ($359,000 + $50,000 + $300,000) in just over two years (by 2008). The projections simply provide an estimate of total loan needs with the composition determined through negotiations. If the

---

[18]This surplus is calculated as $318,000 − $75,000 because it is assumed that the $400,000 term loan financed the $400,000 capital expenditures.

| EXHIBIT 11.11 | Borrowing Base Certificate for Wade's Office Furniture, 2004–2006 | | |
|---|---|---|---|

| Wade's Office Furniture Borrowing Base | 2004 $ 1,000 | 2005 $ 1,000 | 2006 $ 1,000 |
|---|---|---|---|
| Accounts receivables | $ 1,896.00 | $ 2,043.29 | $ 2,255.79 |
| Less: accounts over 60 days | $ (192.00) | $ (230.40) | $ (276.48) |
| Subtotal | $ 1,704.00 | $ 1,812.89 | $ 1,979.31 |
| Total eligible @ 70% | $ 1,192.80 | $ 1,269.02 | $ 1,385.52 |
| | | | |
| Inventory | $ 1,764.00 | $ 2,069.98 | $ 2,386.56 |
| Less: accounts payable | $(1,282.00) | $(1,517.23) | $(1,813.33) |
| Subtotal | $ 482.00 | $ 552.74 | $ 573.23 |
| Total eligible @ 50% | $ 241.00 | $ 276.37 | $ 286.61 |
| | | | |
| Total debt (less LTD secured by real estate) | $ (892.00) | $ (697.12) | $ (359.09) |
| Excess (deficit) | $ 541.80 | $ 848.27 | $ 1,313.04 |

NOTE: Figures are in thousands of dollars. The $192,000 presented for accounts over 60 days in 2004 is an estimate. It is assumed that accounts over 60 days will increase proportionately to sales.

assumed conditions hold for several years, the entire loan could be repaid from internal cash flow by 2008, shown by projecting the statement items through that year.

## EVALUATION OF COLLATERAL: WADE'S OFFICE FURNITURE

In all likelihood, the bank would secure both the short-term and term loans with all available collateral, including receivables, inventory, and new equipment. The bank must subsequently determine the quality of Wade's trading assets. Again, a receivables aging schedule and an inventory evaluation are required.[19]

Exhibit 11.11 represents a summary of Wade's **borrowing base**. The borrowing base is an estimate of the available collateral on a company's current assets. Accounts receivables are purged of accounts 60 days or more past due and credit is given for 70 percent of the remaining accounts. The percentage of credit given will vary by bank policy as well as the analyst's estimate of the general quality of the accounts. Inventory value is reduced by the amount of accounts payables because trade creditors will generally have a superior claim to the bank's. In this example, inventory is credited at 50 percent of its value. Again, the credit rate will vary by bank policy and quality of inventory. Total debt not secured by real estate is then removed to determine the company's excess (deficit) of collateral available. As revealed in Exhibit 11.11, Wade's has sufficient collateral to support the current loan in 2004 by an excess of $542,000. Coverage improves in the pro forma period as the debt is paid off.

## SENSITIVITY ANALYSIS

The financial forecasts previously presented represent only one possible outcome. In all likelihood, Wade's performance in 2005 and 2006 will differ materially from that described above. A lender should always perform sensitivity analysis by adjusting assumptions regarding key factors, such as sales growth and receivables collection, and recalculating the projected financial statements. This generates a range of projected outcomes for the loan magnitude and repayment schedule.

Most importantly, the lender should consider critical assumptions, identified during the historical analysis, such as days accounts payable in the Wade's case. Although not presented here, if Wade did have to pay down his trade credit, such that his days accounts payable went to 48 and 45 days in 2005 and 2006, the notes payable bank would increase to $855,000 and $677,000 in 2005 and 2006, respectively. Although this would increase the amount of debt and length of time it would take to repay the loan, Wade's produces sufficient cash flow to repay the loan in a reasonable period of time. At the end of 2006, Wade's is producing about $338,000 in excess cash flow from operations after principal payments on debt, hence the outstanding debt at the end of 2006 ($677,000 + $350,000) could be paid off by 2009, only one year longer than under the most likely case. If Wade's accounts receivable collection remained stable at its 2004 pace, its projected short-term loan requirement would exceed $950,000 in 2005 and $900,000 in 2006. Again, further projections indicate that it would take until 2010 to repay the loan.

[19]An aging schedule is a listing of accounts receivable grouped according to the month in which the invoice is either dated or payable. A comparison of aging schedules indicates whether the volume of past due accounts is rising or falling and whether the general quality of receivables is deteriorating.

The bank ultimately assigns probabilities (at least implicitly) to each potential outcome to arrive at an expected result. A worst-case scenario is extremely useful because it identifies all contingencies that a lender should consider when examining downside risk. It should be clear that pro forma projections are not *the* answer to the loan question, rather an objective method for the lender to determine the likelihood of repayment under various situations.

Note that when forecasting a firm's financial condition, a lender does not know what interest rates will prevail. Most commercial loans will be priced on a floating-rate basis such that the rate a borrower pays will vary with changes in some base rate. Thus, the actual interest due will typically not be known before a loan is approved. To address this, a bank should include, as part of the sensitivity analysis, a "rate shock" comparison of forecasts of cash flow from operations before interest with expected principal and interest payments plus cash dividends. Cash flow from operations before interest equals cash flow from operations prior to any adjustment for interest expense on any new debt. Expected interest payments will then vary under scenarios of rising, falling, and constant interest rates. A bank can thus assess the extent to which rising interest rates may create problems for the borrower.

## SUMMARY

Credit analysis is the evaluation of risk associated with a borrower's willingness and ability to repay debts. Before analyzing financial data, the analyst should assess the borrower's character and the quality of management. The subsequent financial analysis consists of spreading the financial statements, which involves analyzing common size income statement and balance sheet data and calculating liquidity, activity, leverage, and profit ratios; determining cash flow from operations using historical data; followed by a review of pro forma income statement, balance sheet, and cash flow data. The entire procedure provides a framework for determining how large a loan is needed, what the proceeds will finance, how and when the loan should be repaid, and what collateral is available. This information and answers to specific questions about the firm's production process, supply relationships, and related concerns generally enable the lending officer to determine whether the credit request falls within acceptable risk limits.

One important facet of the analysis is evaluating cash flow. Principal and interest payments on debt plus dividends and a portion of other discretionary expenditures should be paid out of cash flow from operations. Term loans should generally not be approved unless the analysis indicates that projected cash flow will be sufficient to cover debt service requirements. Term loan analysis requires pro forma analysis. A statement of changes reconciled to cash generates cash flow estimates by constructing a cash-based income statement. The ratio of cash flow from operations to dividends and principal payments on loans reveals whether the firm's underlying operating position is healthy.

### QUESTIONS

1. Rank the importance of the five basic credit issues described in the text.

2. Explain why collateral alone does not justify extending credit. Cite examples using real estate or agriculture products as collateral.

3. Which of the following loan requests by an off-campus pizza parlor would be unacceptable, and why?

   a. To buy cheese for inventory

   b. To buy a pizza heating oven

   c. To buy a car for the owner

   d. To repay the original long-term mortgage used to buy the pizza ovens

   e. To pay employees due to a temporary cash flow problem

   f. To buy stock in the company that supplies cheese to the parlor

4. Of the five key questions mentioned at the beginning of the chapter, only the last four were discussed in detail. The first question, "What is the character of the borrower and quality of information provided?" can be the most important. Explain why this is the first question the lender should ask.

5. Explain how the following situations can shed light on the question, "What is the character of the borrower and quality of information provided?"

   a. Significant number of better business bureau complaints.

   b. The business is a family business and several members of the family work for the business.

   c. The use of significant off-balance sheet entities and intercompany partnerships.

   d. A million dollars of new stock issued to the principals of the company.

   e. Little experience of management with the current business.

6. Standard ratio analysis distinguishes between four categories of ratios. Describe how ratios in each category indicate strength or weakness in the underlying firm's performance.

7. Generally, a high current ratio is an indicator of good liquidity. Under what circumstances or conditions could a high current ratio be an indicator of problems with the company's current assets?

8. Explain how it is possible for a firm to report rising net income each year yet continue to need more working capital financing from a bank.

9. Indicate whether each of the following is a source of cash, use of cash, or has no cash impact.

   a. Firm issues new long-term debt.

   b. Firm prepays operating costs.

   c. Because a firm buys another firm it amortizes goodwill.

   d. Firm sells outdated computer equipment.

   e. Firm pays a stock dividend.

   f. Firm sells its product on credit.

   g. Firm buys a new fleet of trucks.

10. Suppose that you generate a cash-based income statement and determine that cash flow from operations equals 75 percent of cash dividends paid and payments on current maturities of long-term debt. What is the significance of this in terms of the firm's cash flow position?

11. Should a firm's cash flow from operations generally exceed capital expenditures?

12. Explain the importance of identifying the "primary" source of repayment. Clearly, the primary source of repayment is always "cash." The analysis question is really one of identifying the source of the cash used to repay the loan. Explain the advantages and disadvantages of the following sources of cash as the primary source of repayment on a loan:

   | | |
   |---|---|
   | Selling an asset | Increasing a liability |
   | Generating more sales | Decreasing expenses |
   | Issuing stock (equity) | Reducing cash dividends |

   Under what circumstances would you be comfortable with the mentioned sources being the "primary" source of repayment?

13. Use the following data to calculate the requested ratios:

| Assets | | Liabilities and Equity | | Income Statement | |
|---|---|---|---|---|---|
| Cash | 80 | Accounts payable | 400 | Net sales | 9,125 |
| Accounts receivable | 700 | Accrued expenses | 80 | COGS | 6,100 |
| Inventory | 500 | Notes pay—bank | 450 | Operating expenses | 2,550 |
| Current assets | 1,280 | CM LTD | 50 | Interest expense | 101 |
| Fixed assets | 1,220 | Current liabilities | 980 | Other inc. | 2 |
| | | LTD | 550 | Other expenses | 48 |
| Total Assets | 2,500 | Equity | 970 | Taxes | 112 |
| | | Total Liabilities and Equity | 2,500 | Net income | 216 |

*Prior period inventory was 170.

   a. Current ratio

   b. Days accounts receivable

   c. Inventory turnover

   d. Days accounts payable outstanding

   e. Debt to equity

   f. Times interest earned

   g. ROE

   h. Total asset turnover (asset utilization)

14. Suppose that you have generated the estimates listed below from a pro forma analysis for a manufacturing company that had requested a three-year term loan. The loan is a $1.5 million term loan with equal annual principal payments. Principal and interest are payable at the end of each year with interest calculated against outstanding principal at a rate of prime plus 2 percent.

| | Year 1 | Year 2 | Year 3 |
|---|---|---|---|
| Capital expenditures | $250,000 | $125,000 | $ 75,000 |
| Cash dividends | $140,000 | $140,000 | $140,000 |
| Cash flow from operations before interest expense | 750,000 | 780,000 | 800,000 |

a. The prime rate averages 8 percent each year, will the firm's cash flow from operations before interest be sufficient to meet debt service requirements and other mandatory expenditures?

b. If prime averages 8 percent, 9 percent, and 10 percent over the three years, respectively, will cash flow be sufficient?

15. Develop a list of questions that a loan officer should ask Marcus Wade, from the example in the text, to gain a better understanding of the risks in lending to Wade's Office Furniture.

## PROBLEMS

**I. SOUTHWEST TRADING COMPANY, TAOS, NEW MEXICO.** Summer is approaching and Steven and Sue Mahan have finally decided that their idea of a successful Southwest furniture, art, and jewelry trading company has come of age. They know that summer is a popular tourist time in New Mexico and could be the best time to start this new business. The Mahans have had a long-time interest in Southwestern art and furniture. Steven graduated from college with an economics degree about 15 years ago and received his M.B.A in finance a few years later. He has been working in Dallas, Texas, as the controller of a major wholesale distributor company for many years. His wife, Sue, who will be a full partner in the business, spent the first ten years of her career in retail sales. Over the last several years she has assumed more administrative duties for the group she works with.

Steven and Sue know they bring the expertise and skill to run a successful business, but to ensure success they have been researching the market for over five years. They also know that they must be very careful and thoroughly research the business and industry they are pursuing. They have traveled extensively to New Mexico and have spent a good deal of time getting to know the local artists (primarily ski bums). They have found that there is a great demand for Southwestern furniture in Texas and the Southwest, and prices are high. Through their contacts with the local craftspeople they have found that many of them would like a reliable source to display and sell their goods. They have been able to make tentative arrangements with a large and dependable group to supply the furniture and art pieces they will need to run the business.

The Mahans have decided to open a shop called Southwestern Trading Company in Taos, New Mexico, and act as both a retailer and supplier to furniture and art outlets in Texas. Steven's extensive contacts with businesses in Dallas and Houston have given him the orders needed to make the business a success as soon as they begin shipping the goods. Sue has already begun marketing the Southwestern products. Southwestern Trading Company's arrangements with the local craftspeople will allow very aggressive pricing of the goods to retail establishments in Texas. This aggressive pricing has been well received and tentative orders are already in place.

Steven has found an ideal location in Taos that is currently available. The owner is asking $275,000 for the space but Southwest Trading has a contract, contingent on financing, for $250,000. Steven and Sue have gotten bids on remodeling and should be able to renovate the space for about $45,000. Although they will purchase the building, the land is leased on a transferable lease with 65 years remaining. The Mahans have decided to invest $235,000, which represents most of their savings, into the venture. Sue's sister is also interested in the possibilities that the company exhibits and is lending Southwest $90,000. Repayment on the note to Sue's sister is not expected to begin for five years. They have estimated that they will need $130,000 in inventory to start the business and they will buy the inventory in cash to build goodwill with the local craftspeople. They also estimate that they will need $20,000 in cash to conduct day-to-day operations and bill payment.

Wanting to use a local bank, Steven has approached Cary Farmer, the senior loan officer at Santa Fe National Bank in Santa Fe, New Mexico, for financing. Steven's background in finance has allowed him to put together the following assumptions for their preliminary business plan. Steven believes that all renovations to the building and inventory can be in place by the end of June 2005.

1. Sales are expected to be a bit lower the first year since only six months will be included in the first fiscal year. Sales are expected to grow significantly in the first full year, 2006. Lower growth is expected in the

third and fourth years. Sales are expected to be $275,000, $675,000, $800,000, and $900,000 the first four years of operations (2005, 2006, 2007, and 2008). Sales are expected to level off after 2008.

2. Based on tentative agreements and orders, it is expected that cost of goods sold will average about 63 percent of sales

3. General and administrative expenses are expected to be $70,000 for the six months in 2005, increase to $100,000 in 2006, and level off at $120,000 from 2007 on. The land lease expenses and interest expenses are included in operational expenses.

4. Selling expenses are expected to be about 12 percent of sales and Sue is expecting to undertake extensive marketing and promotion efforts throughout Texas after the business is opened. It is expected that these additional promotional expenses will be about $30,000 in 2005 only.

5. The company will use ten-year straight-line depreciation of the building and improvements.

6. Southwest's effective tax rate is expected to be 34 percent.

7. Since they expect a good deal of business to be paid by credit card and to ship goods to Texas on credit, they expect to carry about 48 days of accounts receivables. They also expect that, based on the type of business they are entering, they will turn their inventory over about three times a year.

8. Based on the negotiations they have had with their craftspeople, suppliers, and other wholesale distributors, they estimate that they can count on about 28 days of accounts payable to help finance the business.

In preparing to go to the bank for the necessary loan, the Mahans want to prepare projected financial statements showing that Southwest Trading Company can make a profit and pay back the loan. They also want to know more precisely how much they will need to borrow from the bank to open the doors for business. The Mahans plan to prepare five years of balance sheet, income statement, and cash budget data for the bank. They must also develop an opening balance sheet as of the day they plan to open the doors, June 30, 2005. These pro forma financial statements will aid them, and the bank officer, in answering many questions including:

1. How much financing will be needed to open the doors of the business in July 2005?

2. Five years of pro forma balance sheet and income statement data must be prepared to determine if additional financing is needed, and if so, how much. Steven's finance background tells him that the estimated financing needed each year will be an accounting plug figure to ensure that the balance sheet balances. If projected assets exceed liabilities and equity, the difference will be the bank's borrowing needs. If liabilities and equity exceed projected assets purchases, these funds will be used to pay off debt or increase cash or marketable securities.

3. Because this is a start-up business it is even more important to identify what the loan proceeds will be used for, what the primary source of repayment is, and when the total loan proceeds will be repaid. Using the pro forma projections, the primary source of repayment and when the loan will be repaid can be determined.

4. A cash budget or cash-based income statement needs to be prepared because Steven knows the only thing that matters to the bank is cash.

5. Finally, Steven needs to prepare a collateral schedule. He knows that the banker does not want the collateral but will need all he can get if the business is not as successful as expected.

6. Prepare a list of Questions you would need the answers to. Be sure to explain the specifics of the questions as they relate to this case.

a. What types of loan covenants would you require?

b. Identify the bank's largest risks in making this loan.

c. How would you structure the loan to protect the bank?

d. What is your recommendation concerning the loan request?

Conduct the analysis suggested in the above questions. What is your recommendation concerning the loan request?

**II. PERFORMANCE OF CHEM-CO COATINGS.** Table 1 presents income statement and balance sheet data for Chem-Co, a producer of specialty chemical coatings that recently bought a small manufacturer of outdoor pools. During 2005 the firm instituted a national marketing campaign to inform individuals of Chem-Co's new products related to home pool management. Chief Executive Officer Wynona Presley was pleased with sales in 2005, noting the 30 percent increase over 2004 sales. As the U.S. economy continues to expand, Presley is considering marketing Chem-Co's products outside the United States.

1. Using the data in Table 1, generate a cash-based income statement for Chem-Co for 2005.

2. Calculate days accounts receivable, inventory turnover, and days accounts payable for 2004 and 2005 and determine if the use (source) of cash in working capital was a result of sales growth, credit policy, inventory policy, or trade credit policy. Did these turnover ratios improve or deteriorate? What was the resulting impact on cash flow?

3. Interpret the figures by evaluating the firm's cash flow from operations and key financial ratios.

4. Identify potential problems that the firm faces.

## TABLE 1

Balance Sheet and Income Statement Data for Chem-Co (Millions of Dollars)

| Balance Sheet | 2004 | 2005 | Income Statement | 2005 |
|---|---|---|---|---|
| **Assets** | | | | |
| Cash and marketable securities | $30 | $6 | Net sales | $861 |
| Accounts receivable | 102 | 215 | Cost of goods sold | 680 |
| Merchandise inventory | 65 | 104 | Gross margin | 181 |
| Prepaid expenses | 8 | 5 | Selling expenses | 64 |
| Gross fixed assets | 120 | 149 | General & adm. expenses | 60 |
| Less accumulated depreciation | 40 | 57 | Depreciation | 26 |
| Net fixed assets | 80 | 92 | Operating profit | 31 |
| Intangible assets | 4 | 3 | Interest income | 6 |
| Total assets | $289 | $425 | Interest expense | 18 |
| | | | | |
| **Liabilities and Net Worth** | | | | |
| Notes payable—bank | $106 | $223 | Profit before taxes | 19 |
| Current maturities of long-term debt | 9 | 11 | Income taxes | 5 |
| Accounts payable | 33 | 50 | Net profit | 14 |
| Accruals | 2 | 9 | | |
| Federal income tax payable | 3 | 4 | | |
| Long-term mortgage | 16 | 15 | | |
| Long-term debt | 43 | 32 | | |
| Total liabilities | $212 | $344 | | |
| Common stock | 40 | 40 | | |
| Retained earnings | 37 | 41 | | |
| Total net worth[a] | 77 | 81 | | |
| Total liabilities and equity | $289 | $425 | | |

[a]Net worth reconciliation
| | |
|---|---|
| Beginning net worth | 77 |
| =+ Net profit | 14 |
| Dividends paid (cash) | 10 |
| Ending net worth | 81 |

NOTE: Inventory was $45 million in 2003.

## APPENDIX I

### CALCULATION OF FINANCIAL RATIOS

#### Liquidity Ratios

- Current ratio = Current assets/current liabilities

- Quick ratio $= \dfrac{\text{Cash } + \text{ accounts receivable}}{\text{Current liabilities}}$

- Accounts receivable aging schedule: a comparison of the dollar amount and percentage of total receivables outstanding across the number of days they have been outstanding (less than 30, 31–60, etc.)

#### Activity Ratios

- Days cash = Cash/average daily sales
- Days inventory on hand = Inventory/average daily COGS
- Inventory turnover = 365/days inventory = COGS/inventory
- Accounts receivable collection period (Days AR) = Accounts receivables/average daily sales
- Accounts receivable turnover = 365/days AR = Sales/accounts receivable
- Days cash-to-cash asset cycle = Days cash + days AR + days inventory on hand
- Days accounts payable outstanding = Accounts payable/average daily purchases
  = Accounts payable/[(COGS + Δinventory)/365]
- Sales to net fixed assets = Sales/net fixed assets

#### Leverage Ratios

- Debt to tangible net worth = Total liabilities/tangible net worth
- Times interest earned = EBIT/interest expense
- EBIT = Earnings before taxes + interest expense
- Fixed charge coverage = (EBIT + lease payments)/(interest expense + lease payments)
- Net fixed assets to tangible net worth = Net fixed assets/tangible net worth
- Dividend payout = Cash dividends paid/net profit

#### Profitability Ratios

- Return on equity (ROE) = Net income/total equity
- Return on average net worth = Net income/tangible net worth
- Profit before taxes to net worth = Profit before taxes/tangible net worth = Pretax ROE
- Return on assets (ROA) = Net income/total assets
- Profit before taxes to total assets = Profit before taxes/total assets = Pretax ROA
- Asset utilization = Asset turnover = Sales/total assets
- Profit margin (PM) = Net income/sales
- Sales growth = Change in sales/last period's sales
- Income taxes to profit before taxes = Reported income tax/profit before taxes

Note: Tangible net worth = Total equity – intangible assets.

### REFERENCES

*Annual Statement Studies,* RMA, published annually (http://www.rmahq.org). Provides common size income statement and balance sheet data as well as ratio data by four-digit SIC code. Data for all companies are provided for the last five years and current peer group data provided by size using total assets and total sales. Median and upper and lower quartiles for each ratio are also provided.

*Industry Norms and Key Business Ratios,* Dun & Bradstreet, published annually (http://www.dnb.com). Common size income statement and balance sheet data as well as industry ratios using four-digit SIC code. Common size data are presented using total assets or total sales and the median value must be used to calculate the percentage of total values. Data are presented for the current year only but median and upper and lower quartiles are provided for each ratio.

*Analyst's Handbook,* Standard & Poors Corporation, published annually (http://www.mcgraw-hill.com/financial-markets and /http://www.compustat.com).

*Industry Surveys,* Standard & Poors Corporation (http://www.compustat.com).

Almanac of Business and Industrial Ratios, Leo Troy, annual.

*Edgar Database of Corporate Information,* Securities and Exchange Commission, available online at http://www.sec.gov. Features a large and searchable database of corporate filings including 10Ks and 10Qs.

## INVESTMENT AND FINANCIAL RESOURCES

*Corporation Records, The Outlook,* and *Stock Reports,* Standard & Poors (http://www.mcgraw-hill.com).

*Moody's Manuals,* Moody's Investor Service, Inc. (http://www. moodys.com).

*The Value Line Investment Survey,* Value Line, Inc. (http://www.valueline.com).

## APPENDIX II

### BACKGROUND INFORMATION FOR FINANCIAL ANALYSIS

A quantitative analysis of financial data serves as the basis for most credit decisions. Its effectiveness depends largely on the quality of the data. Before proceeding with the ratio and cash flow evaluation, an analyst should examine the nature of available information and its completeness. This appendix summarizes background information regarding financial analysis.

#### *Financial Statements*

Accountants prepare formal financial statements with an eye toward generally accepted accounting principles (GAAP). The intent of GAAP is to establish a set of policies and procedures that require the consistent, systematic presentation of accounting information. Even with GAAP, however, two problems frequently arise. First, many financial statements are prepared by individuals who are not familiar with GAAP, let alone fundamental accounting identities such as assets equal liabilities plus net worth. Thus asset classifications and expenses claimed in many reports vary from allowable provisions. Second, even GAAP allow different procedures for presenting information. For example, if a company sells a product under an installment contract, it can book sales when the order is signed or when delivery is actually made. Similarly, a company has a choice in how it accounts for inventory. Last-in-first-out systems have far different reporting and cash flow impacts than first-in-first out systems.

The implication is that an analyst must examine the nature of financial data before spreading statements. Following are some recommended guidelines:

- Determine who prepared the statements.
- Determine if the statements are audited.
- If audited, assess what type of opinion was issued and the nature of any qualification or disclaimer. In general, an unqualified opinion means that the auditor determined that the reported statements conformed with GAAP. A qualified opinion means that either some item in the report does not conform with GAAP or selected figures cannot be determined with a reasonable degree of certainty. The second case occurs, for example, when the value of inventory cannot be adequately determined. Adverse opinion means that the financial statements are not presented in accordance with GAAP, and a disclaimer appears when the auditor expresses no opinion.
- Determine areas where a firm has used its discretion to select a particular accounting policy within GAAP that might significantly affect reported figures. This requires the careful examination of footnotes to financial statements. Discretionary policies frequently arise in the areas of revenue recognition, income tax reconciliation, inventory valuation, accounts receivable classification, depreciation of plant and equipment, goodwill, consolidation of entities, and pension, profit sharing, and stock option plans.
- Determine all outstanding commitments and contingent claims.
- Identify any unusual balance sheet entries or transactions.

## APPENDIX III

| Cash Flow Statement Section investment | Column Number | Cash-Based Income Statement | Income Statement Equivalent | Factors Determining the Difference Between the Income Statement and Cash-Based Income Statement |
|---|---|---|---|---|
| | **(1)**<br>**(2)**<br>**(3)** =(1)+(2) | + Sales<br>− ΔAccounts receivables<br>= Cash Sales | } Sales | Sales growth<br>Credit policy |
| | **(4)**<br>**(5)**<br>**(6)**<br>**(7)** =(4)+(5)+(6) | − COGS<br>− ΔInventory<br>+ ΔAccounts payable<br>= Cash purchases | } COGS | Sales growth<br>Gross margin<br>Inventory turnover<br>Trade credit policy and relationship |
| | **(8)** =(3)+(7) | = Cash Gross Margin | } Gross Margin | All factors listed above |
| **Operations** | **(9)**<br>**(10)**<br>**(11)**<br>**(12)**<br>**(13)** = (9)+(10)+(11)+(12) | − Operating Expenses<br>+ Depreciation<br>− ΔPrepaid Expenses<br>+ ΔAccrued Expenses<br>= Cash Operating Expenses | } Operating Expenses | Accounting methods<br>Operating expense payment policies |
| | **(14)**<br>**(15)**<br>**(16)**<br>**(17)**<br>**(18)** | + Other Income<br>− Other Expenses<br>− Interest Expense<br>− ΔOther Current Assets<br>+ ΔOther Current Liabilities | } Other Income<br>Other Expenses<br>Interest Expenses | Changes in other current assets and liabilities |
| | **(19)** =(13)+sum(14 to 18) | = Cash Profit Before Taxes | } Profit Before Taxes | All factors listed above |
| | **(20)**<br>**(21)**<br>**(22)**<br>**(23)** =(20)+(21)+(22) | − Income Taxes Reported<br>+ ΔIncome Tax Payable<br>+ ΔDeferred Income Taxes<br>= Cash Taxes Paid | } Income Taxes | Accounting methods<br>Tax laws |
| | **(24)** =(19)+(23) | = **Cash Flow from Operations** | } **Net Income** | **All factors listed above** |

## APPENDIX III

| Cash Flow Statement Section investment | Column Number | Cash-Based Income Statement | Income Statement Equivalent | Factors Determining the Difference Between the Income Statement and Cash-Based Income Statement |
|---|---|---|---|---|
| **Investment** | **(25)** | − Capital Expenditures = − (ΔNet Fixed Assets + Dep. Expense) | Not included | Actual capital expenditures Additions to long-term investments Changes in all other long-term assets |
| | **(26)** | − ΔLong-term Investments | | |
| | **(27)** | − ΔAll Other Noncurrent Assets | | |
| | **(28)** =(25)+(26)+(27) | = Cash Used for Investments | | |
| **Financing** | **(29)** | − Payment for last period's CMLTD | Not included | Loan principal repayment schedule Dividend policy |
| | **(30)** | − Dividends paid (DIV) | | |
| | **(31)** =(29)+(30) | = Payments for financing | | |
| | **(32)** | + ΔShort-term Bank Debt | Not included | Level of short-term bankdebt and working capital needs, Long-term debt, capital expenditures, and capital structure decisions |
| | **(33)** | + ΔLT debt + end of period CMLTD | | |
| | **(34)** | + DCommon and Preferred Stock | | |
| | **(35)** | + ΔOther Equities and Noncurrent Liabilities | | |
| | **(36)** =(32)+(33)+(34)+(36) | = External Financing | | |
| **Cash** | **(37)** =(24)+(28)+(31)+(36) | = Δ(Cash and Mkt. Securities) | Not included | All factors listed above |

# Evaluating Consumer Loans

*Freebies are back! As the U.S. economy picked up steam in late 2004, banks returned to unusual competitions to attract consumers. Flushing Financial Corporation in Lake Success, New York, offered Sony Playstations, digital camcorders, and PCs if individuals made a sufficiently large CD deposit. United Community Banks of Blairsville, Georgia, offered paper shredders and CorningWare to customers opening new checking accounts. Associated Banc-Corp gave customers opening a new checking account the option to get checks with Green Bay Packers images, a stadium seat, and entered them in a sweepstakes to win Super Bowl tickets. All of these were at no direct cost to the individual.[1]*

*Think about the convenience provided by credit and debit cards. Consumers can use either to buy burgers at McDonalds, pay taxes, use the subway, and make purchases at vending machines. Not surprisingly, card transactions have sharply reduced individuals' use of cash. A 2004 survey showed that only 40 percent of credit card holders paid their outstanding balances in full each month, such that 60 percent paid finance charges ranging as high as 23 percent. In 2004, credit card purchases accounted for an estimated 20 percent of U.S. gross domestic product.*

*Why do banks pursue consumers so aggressively? Part of the answer is the loyalty that individuals show to their primary financial institution, especially the ones providing transactions services. Studies show that most customers won't end their relationship unless they move out of the bank's trade area, the bank changes names, and/or service deteriorates sharply. Banks can readily cross-sell services, debit cards, credit cards, consumer loans, and so on to grow noninterest income. Importantly, most individuals are not as price sensitive as business customers. Hence, banks can earn risk-adjusted profits above that generated in other lines of business or from other types of customers.*

*This chapter examines consumer lending activities at banks. It looks at the characteristics and profitability of different types of consumer loans and introduces general evaluation techniques to assess credit risk. In doing so, it demonstrates why consumer credit relationships are attractive to banks.*

———————————————————————— ■ ————————————————————————

**F**or many years, banks viewed consumer loans with skepticism. Commercial loans were available in large volume, net yields were high, and the loans were highly visible investments. Consumer loans, in contrast, involved small dollar amounts and a large staff to handle accounts, and there was less prestige associated with lending to individuals. This perception changed with the decline in profitability of commercial loans. In recent years, competition among lenders has lowered spreads on commercial loans to where potential profits are small relative to credit risk. Most states no longer have effective usury ceilings on consumer loans so that lenders have increased interest rates and risk-adjusted returns have exceeded those on commercial loans. Even with high relative default rates, consumer loans in the aggregate currently produce greater percentage profits than commercial loans.

---

[1]These and other examples are provided in Jane Kim, "Beyond the Toaster: Banks Step Up Freebies," *The Wall Street Journal,* October 14, 2004.

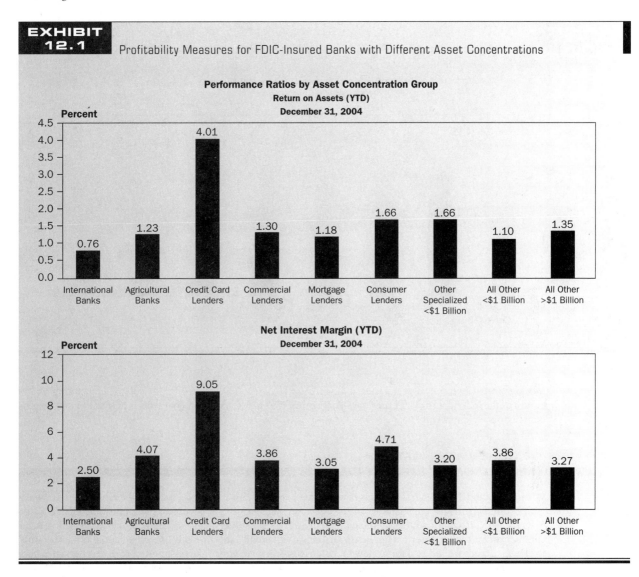

**EXHIBIT 12.1**  Profitability Measures for FDIC-Insured Banks with Different Asset Concentrations

**Performance Ratios by Asset Concentration Group**
**Return on Assets (YTD)**
**December 31, 2004**

**Net Interest Margin (YTD)**
**December 31, 2004**

Consider the summary profitability data provided in Exhibit 12.1 for FDIC-insured banks categorized by asset concentration. Banks labeled "credit card lenders" and "consumer lenders" have the heaviest concentration of loans in credit cards and other consumer loans, respectively. Note that in 2004 (and in prior periods), these two groups of banks generated the highest returns on assets (ROAs) compared with all other banks. In fact, the ROAs of credit card banks at 4.01 percent exceeded the ROAs of all other banks by over 2.5 percent, on average. These high ROAs were, in turn, realized even after recording the highest net charge-off rates. Exhibit 12.2 demonstrates that credit card lenders charged off an average of 4.67 percent of loans, whereas consumer lenders charged off 3.04 percent of loans, much more than banks in other categories.

Today, many banks target individuals as the primary source of growth in attracting new business. This reflects the attraction of consumer deposits, as well as consumer loans. Interest rate deregulation forced banks to pay market rates on virtually all their liabilities. Corporate cash managers, who are especially price sensitive, routinely move their balances in search of higher yields. Individuals' balances are much more stable largely because they are federally insured up to $100,000 per account. Although individuals are price sensitive, a bank can generally retain deposits by varying rates offered on different maturity time deposits to meet the customer's needs. Consumers also hold substantial demand deposits and NOW accounts that are relatively inexpensive to the bank and normally are not held to meet compensating balance requirements. A consumer who maintains a deposit relationship and borrows from the same institution is typically quite loyal.

From a lender's perspective, the analysis of consumer loans differs from that of commercial loans. First, the quality of financial data is lower. Personal financial statements are typically unaudited, so, it is easy for borrowers to hide other loans. It is similarly easy to inflate asset values. Second, the primary source of repayment is current

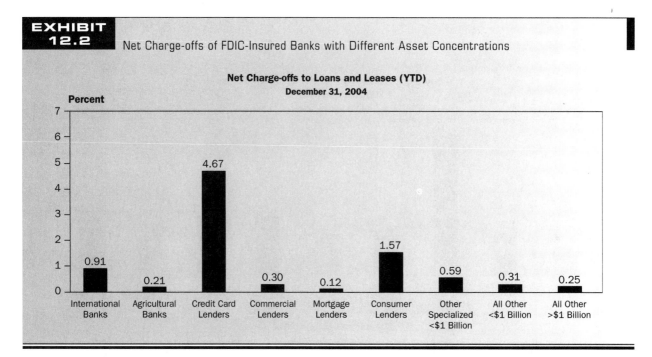

**EXHIBIT 12.2** Net Charge-offs of FDIC-Insured Banks with Different Asset Concentrations

income, primarily from wages, salaries, dividends, and interest. This may be highly volatile, depending on the nature of the individual's work experience and history. The net effect is that character is more difficult to assess but is extremely important.

## TYPES OF CONSUMER LOANS

When evaluating the measurable aspects of consumer loan requests, an analyst addresses the same issues discussed with commercial loans: the character of the borrower, the use of loan proceeds, the amount needed, and the primary and secondary source of repayment. However, consumer loans differ so much in design that no comprehensive analytical format applies to all loans. With credit cards, for example, a bank does not know what the loan proceeds will be used for or how much the customer will borrow at any point in time. In contrast, a boat loan with fixed installment payments has a maximum borrowing amount and regular repayment schedule. Credit analysis thus differs across loan types. Many banks mass market their credit cards knowing that losses will increase but hoping to price this risk accordingly and to attract enough affluent customers to offset charge-offs. There is no formal analysis of individual borrower characteristics unless the lender uses a credit scoring model. In contrast, lenders treat installment loans made directly in negotiation with the borrower much like commercial loans. Each facet of the credit request, such as estimating discretionary income (cash flow) relative to debt service requirements, is evaluated similarly to commercial loans.

Consumer loans can be classified into one of three types: installment loans, credit cards or revolving credit lines, and noninstallment loans. Each type requires a different approach for credit analysis and provides different answers to the fundamental credit issues.

### INSTALLMENT LOANS

Installment loans require the periodic payment of principal and interest. In most cases, a customer borrows to purchase durable goods or cover extraordinary expenses and agrees to repay the loan in monthly installments.[2] Although the average dollar amount of the loan is quite small, some loans may be much larger, depending on the use of the proceeds. It is not unusual, for example, to see loans for aircraft, boats, and personal investments exceed $500,000. The typical maturity ranges from 2 to 5 years. Except for revolving credit, most consumer loans are secured.

---

[2]Credit card loans and overdraft lines are formally installment loans because they require periodic monthly payments. They are discussed separately because their other features differ widely from other installment loans.

Installment loans may be either direct or indirect loans. A direct loan is negotiated between the bank and the ultimate user of the funds. An individual who borrows from a bank to finance an automobile must formally request credit and provide supporting personal financial information. The loan officer analyzes the information and approves or rejects the request. An indirect loan is funded by a bank through a separate retailer that sells merchandise to a customer. The retailer, such as an automobile dealer, takes the credit application, negotiates terms with the individual, and presents the agreement to the bank. If the bank approves the loan, it buys the loan from the retailer under prearranged terms. Automobile loans exceed any other type of installment loans at banks, followed by revolving credit and mobile home loans. Approximately 60 percent of automobile loans are indirect loans purchased from dealers. The figure for indirect mobile home loans is considerably higher.

**REVENUES AND COSTS FROM INSTALLMENT CREDIT.** Installment loans can be extremely profitable. Generally, the average size of a loan is small, averaging around $6,000 historically. It costs from $100 to $250 to originate each installment loan, with electronic loan costs the lowest for larger banks. Origination costs include salaries, occupancy, computer, and marketing expenses associated with soliciting, approving, and processing loan applications. There are also costs associated with collecting payments and charging off loans. Generally, installment loans have yielded net spreads in excess of 5 percent, where the net spread equals loan income minus loan acquisition costs, collection costs, and net charge-offs.

**CREDIT CARDS AND OTHER REVOLVING CREDIT.** Credit cards and overlines tied to checking accounts are the two most popular forms of revolving credit agreements. In 2003, 73 percent of households had credit cards, the average number of cards held per household was 7.3, the average household spent $15,066 on cards, and consumers in the aggregate charged $2.2 trillion on credit cards.[3] Many pay only a fraction of their monthly bill and thus incur finance charges on the remainder. Thomas Durkin reported that 35 percent of card users rarely paid their outstanding balance in full each month. Credit lines against demand deposit accounts at banks are less common but function identically to credit cards. Customers can write checks in excess of actual balances held but must pay interest on the overdraft, usually against lump sums at $50 or $100 increments.

Banks offer a variety of credit cards. Although some banks issue cards with their own logo and support the cards by their own marketing effort, most operate as franchises of MasterCard or Visa. To become part of either group's system, a bank must pay a one-time membership fee plus an annual charge determined by the number of its customers actively using the cards. MasterCard and Visa, in turn, handle the national marketing effort. All cards prominently display the MasterCard and Visa logos with the issuing bank's name. Recently, both MasterCard and Visa have allowed banks to increase the size of the bank's name and reduce the size of the logo to emphasize which bank actually issues the card. The primary advantage of membership is that an individual bank's card is accepted nationally and internationally at most retail stores without each bank negotiating a separate agreement with every retailer. While U.S. banks have pushed consumers to use debit cards, they have not been aggressive in developing alternatives like the smart card, which is currently dominated by foreign competitors. (See Contemporary Issues: "Debit Cards, Smart Cards, and Prepaid Cards.") A 2004 Nilson Report estimated that Visa had 443 million debit and credit cards outstanding, MasterCard had 318 million, Discover had 53 million, and American Express had 38 million.

Credit cards are attractive because they typically provide higher risk-adjusted returns than other types of loans. Card issuers earn income from three sources: charging cardholders fees, charging interest on outstanding loan balances, and discounting the charges that merchants accept on purchases. In 2003, annual fees to maintain an account averaged almost $18 per account, annual interest rates averaged around 9 percent, and the discount to merchants ranged from 2 to 5 percent. Even though other interest rates may fall, credit card rates are notoriously sticky. Thus, the spread between the rate charged and a bank's cost of funds widens. This has generated criticism that banks use credit cards to gouge customers. In fact, as banks have increased their focus they have begun to lower loan rates and annual fees such that many customers can avoid fees entirely and pay interest at rates 1 to 4 percent above the Wall Street prime rate. Still, in order to generate more revenue, card issuers have been raising late-payment fees to around $30 per month when they do not receive the monthly payment by the due date.

Credit card lending involves issuing plastic cards to qualifying customers. The cards have preauthorized credit limits that restrict the maximum amount of debt outstanding at any time. An individual can use the card to purchase goods and services from any merchant that accepts the card. Thus, the individual determines the timing and amount of actual borrowing. Many cards can be used in electronic banking devices, such as ATMs, and to make deposits or withdrawals from existing transactions accounts at a bank.

The recent regulatory and competitive environment has made credit cards extremely attractive. Many issuers view credit cards as a vehicle to generate a nationwide customer base. They offer extraordinary incentives to induce consumers to accept cards in the hope that they can cross-sell mortgages, insurance products, and eventu-

---

[3]See "As Cash Fades, America Becomes a Plastic Nation," *The Wall Street Journal*, July 23, 2004.

# CONTEMPORARY ISSUES

## DEBIT CARDS, SMART CARDS, AND PREPAID CARDS

Banks throughout the world are investing in technologies that promote debit cards, smart cards, and prepaid cards. Debit cards are widely available and have recently taken over the United States as the most commonly used method of in-store payment. In 2003, 31 percent of payments were made by debit card, 21 percent with credit cards, 15 percent with cash, and 32 percent with checks. As the name suggests, when an individual uses a **debit card,** his or her balance at a bank is immediately debited; that is, funds are instantaneously transferred from the card user's account to the account of the retailer. The obvious disadvantage to a consumer is the loss of float. Some retailers also charge fees when a customer uses a debit card. Banks prefer that customers use debit cards over checks because they have lower processing costs compared with checks and automated teller machine (ATM) transactions.

A **smart card** is an extension of debit and credit cards; it contains a computer memory chip that stores and manipulates information. Such a chip can store more than 500 times the data of a magnetic-stripe credit or debit card. When inserted in a terminal, the cardholder can pay for goods and services, dial the telephone, make airline arrangements, and authorize currency exchanges. It is programmable so users can store information regarding their complete financial history and recall this information when effecting transactions. These electronic checkbooks can effectively handle virtually all of consumers' purchasing. Although smart cards are very popular in Europe and Japan, they have only modestly penetrated the United States, which accounts for just 2 percent of worldwide usage. This largely reflects the U.S. consumer's satisfaction with existing technology and banks' unwillingness to invest in the computer terminals necessary to process transactions.

There are several reasons why smart card usage will likely take off in the United States in the near future. First, firms can offer a much wider range of services. This provides greater sources of noninterest income. Second, smart cards represent a link between the Internet and real economic activity. Smart cards are an alternative to digital money, or e-cash, used to buy items via the Internet, with security advantages for the user. Finally, suppliers of smart cards are standardizing the formats so that all cards work on the same systems.

**Prepaid cards** are a hybrid of debit cards in which customers prepay for services to be rendered and receive a card against which purchases are charged. The subway system in Washington, D.C., for example, lets customers prepay for access cards, then use the cards to pay for subway rides. Many universities and businesses, in turn, let students and employees prepay for books and meals, then charge their purchases against the card. The primary advantage to the bank is that processing costs are low and there is little risk of loss.

ally securities. Some banks also use the card relationship to solicit money market deposits or small CDs. Credit cards are profitable because many customers are price insensitive. Most banks charge annual user fees, and credit card interest rates are among the highest rates quoted. Still, many borrowers look primarily at the minimum monthly payment required rather than the quoted interest rate. People simply like the convenience of buying goods whenever they wish, and many believe that the periodic interest is too small to give up the spending convenience.

One negative with credit cards is that losses are among the highest of all loan types. Fraud is prevalent, and many individuals eventually default on their debts because their incomes do not cover their spending habits. The data in Exhibit 12.3 document recent trends in charge-off rates on credit cards that banks keep on their books and the number of personal bankruptcy filings. Note the increase in both charge-offs and the number of personal bankruptcies during the recessions of 1990–1991 and 2000–2001. The surprising trend is the sharp increase in both measures after 1994. This occurred during a strong period of growth in the U.S. economy, when loan quality typically improves and more people are working and in relatively strong financial condition. Many analysts believe that individuals' access to credit card debt is too easy and that, culturally, the stigmatism associated with filing for bankruptcy has been largely eliminated. Credit cards represent a low-cost way to start over. Not surprisingly, both credit card losses and personal bankruptcies increased in 2001, when the U.S. economy fell into recession and Congress attempted to tighten existing bankruptcy laws. Credit card losses and personal bankruptcies have remained surprisingly high—peaking in 2003—given the growth in the U.S. economy. Bankruptcy laws were made more stringent in 2005.

Interestingly, the charge-off data are even worse when loss rates on securitized credit card loans are recognized. Securitized credit cards account for approximately 40 percent of all credit card debt, and according to Moodys, charge-off rates are around 1.5 percent higher. Also, the data are potentially misleading because there are no industry standards regarding when to recognize a loss. Legally, lenders can wait up to 209 days after an account is bankrupt to charge it off. Some lenders charge off bankrupt accounts immediately while others wait the maximum 209 days.

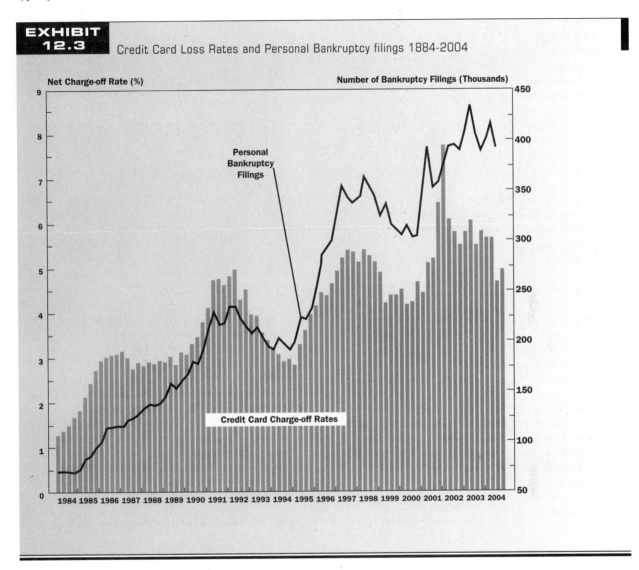

**EXHIBIT 12.3** Credit Card Loss Rates and Personal Bankruptcy filings 1884-2004

**CREDIT CARD SYSTEMS AND PROFITABILITY.** The returns to credit card lending depend on the specific roles that a bank plays. According to Federal Reserve classifications, a bank is called a card bank if it administers its own credit card plan or serves as the primary regional agent of a major credit card operation, such as Visa or MasterCard. In contrast, a noncard bank operates under the auspices of a regional card bank and does not issue its own card. Noncard banks do not generate significant revenues from credit cards.

The types of revenues available are described in Exhibit 12.4, which summarizes the clearing process for a credit card transaction. Once a customer uses a card, the retail outlet submits the sales receipt to its local merchant bank for credit. A retailer may physically deposit the slip or electronically transfer the information via a card-reading terminal at the time of sale. The merchant bank discounts the sales receipt by 2 to 5 percent as its fee. Thus, a retailer will receive only $97 credit for each $100 sales receipt if the discount is 3 percent. If a merchant bank did not issue the card, it sends the receipt to the card-issuing bank through a clearing network, paying an interchange fee. The card-issuing bank then bills the customer for the purchase. Most card revenues come from issuing the card that a customer uses. The bank earns interest at rates ranging from 2.9 to 23 percent and normally charges each individual an annual fee for use of the card. As mentioned earlier, interest rates are sticky. When money market rates decline and lower a bank's cost of funds, the net return on credit card loans increases because credit card rates do not fall coincidentally. Interest income and annual fees constitute approximately 80 percent of credit card revenues. The remaining 20 percent are merchant discounts.

**OVERDRAFT PROTECTION AND OPEN CREDIT LINES.** Revolving credit also takes the form of overdraft protection against checking accounts. A bank authorizes qualifying individuals to write checks in excess

**EXHIBIT 12.4**

Credit Card Transaction Process

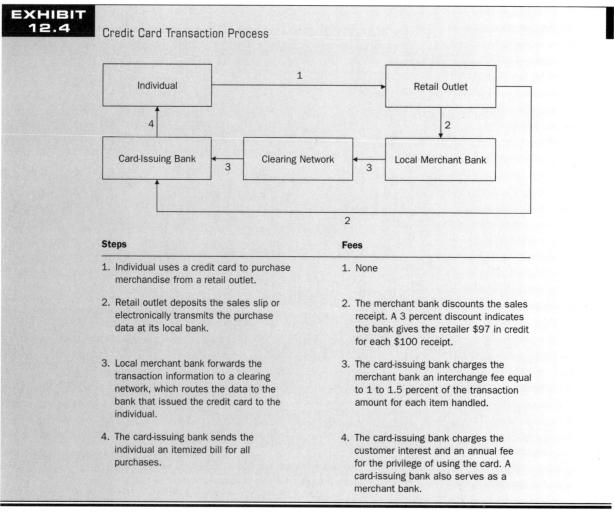

**Steps**

1. Individual uses a credit card to purchase merchandise from a retail outlet.

2. Retail outlet deposits the sales slip or electronically transmits the purchase data at its local bank.

3. Local merchant bank forwards the transaction information to a clearing network, which routes the data to the bank that issued the credit card to the individual.

4. The card-issuing bank sends the individual an itemized bill for all purchases.

**Fees**

1. None

2. The merchant bank discounts the sales receipt. A 3 percent discount indicates the bank gives the retailer $97 in credit for each $100 receipt.

3. The card-issuing bank charges the merchant bank an interchange fee equal to 1 to 1.5 percent of the transaction amount for each item handled.

4. The card-issuing bank charges the customer interest and an annual fee for the privilege of using the card. A card-issuing bank also serves as a merchant bank.

SOURCE: Michael Weinstein, "Credit Card Business Mushrooms at Large Banks." *American Banker* (August 14, 1986).

of actual balances held in a checking account up to a prespecified limit. The customer must pay interest on the loan from the date of the draft's receipt and can repay the loan either by making direct deposits or by periodic payments. One relatively recent innovation is to offer open credit lines to affluent individuals whether or not they have an existing account relationship. These loans are the functional equivalent of loan commitments to commercial customers. In most instances, the bank provides customers with special checks that activate a loan when presented for payment. The maximum credit available typically exceeds that for overdraft lines, and the interest rate floats with the bank's base rate.

**HOME EQUITY LOANS AND CREDIT CARDS.** Home equity loans grew from virtually nothing in the mid-1980s to more than $250 billion in 2004, spurred by the Tax Reform Act of 1986, which limited deductions for consumer loan interest paid by individuals unless the loan was real estate related. Home equity loans meet the tax deductibility requirements (with some limits) because they are secured by equity in an individual's home. The bulk of these loans are structured as open credit lines where a consumer can borrow up to 75 percent of the market value of the property less the principal outstanding on the first mortgage. Individuals borrow simply by writing checks, pay interest only on the amount borrowed, pay 1 to 2 percent of the outstanding principal each month, and can repay the remaining principal at their discretion. In most cases, the loans carry adjustable rates tied to the bank's base rate.

The Tax Reform Act of 1986 accelerated the use of home equity loans by eliminating the deductibility of interest paid on traditional consumer debt, such as credit cards and car loans, but retaining the deductibility of interest on debt secured by the equity in an individual's home. Many banks subsequently introduced home equity credit lines that, in some cases, can be accessed by using a credit card. Because consumers can take out only one such loan, the lender that initiates the credit relationship has locked in a long-term customer.

These credit arrangements combine the risks of a second mortgage with the temptation of a credit card, a potentially dangerous combination. Home equity loans place a second lien on a borrower's home. If the individual defaults, the creditor can foreclose so that the borrower loses his or her home. Still, ready access to the financing through credit cards encourages consumers to spend and potentially take on too much debt. During the slow growth period following September 11, 2001, many individuals used home equity loan funding to maintain lifestyles in the hope of better future prospects down the road. Federal Reserve studies have generally shown that consumers borrow primarily to improve their existing home, consolidate debts, or finance a child's college education. In either case, the typical home equity loan represents a large initial borrowing that is paid down over several years.

In order to attract customers, many banks price these loans at prime or just 1 to 2 percent over prime, which is well below other consumer loan rates. Some require only interest payments during the first few years. Low rates have been justified by historically low losses and good collateral, which is a home. Of course, delinquency rates increase during economic downturns when real estate values often decline. In addition, there is always the risk that customers will borrow the maximum, especially under credit card arrangements, for short-run lifestyle expenses. If they take on too much debt and interest rates increase or housing values decline, many borrowers may default and lenders will see losses increase.

## NONINSTALLMENT LOANS

A limited number of consumer loans require a single principal and interest payment. Typically, the individual's borrowing needs are temporary. Credit is extended in anticipation of repayment from a well-defined future cash inflow. Bridge loans are representative of single payment consumer loans. Bridge loans often arise when an individual borrows funds for the down payment on a new house. The loan is repaid when the borrower sells an existing home, hence the term 'bridge.' The quality of the loan depends on the certainty of the timing and amount of the anticipated net cash inflow from the sale.

## SUBPRIME LOANS

Many lenders long ago recognized that they could earn high risk-adjusted returns by lending to riskier borrowers. Large bank holding companies and firms like GE Capital have bought consumer finance subsidiaries that make loans to individuals that a bank would not traditionally make and keep on–balance sheet. Of course, subprime lenders charge higher rates and have more restrictive covenants.

During the 1990s, one of the hottest growth areas was subprime lending. These higher-risk loans were labeled "B," "C," and "D" credits, and were especially popular in auto, home equity, and mortgage lending. These are the same risk loans as those originated through consumer finance companies. Although no precise definitions exist, "B," "C," and "D" credits exhibit increasingly greater risk and must be priced consistently higher than prime-grade loans. Paul Finfer of Franklin Acceptance Corporation, a subprime auto lender, provided the following definitions:[4]

> B: Typically, scores 600+ under the Fair Isaac credit scoring system (FICO); has some 90-day past dues but is now current. When extended credit, delinquencies are 2–5 percent, repossessions are 2.5–6 percent, and losses are 1.5–3 percent.

> C: Typically scores between 500 and 600 under the Fair Isaac system and has had write-offs and judgments. The borrower has made subsequent payments of some or all of the loans. When extended credit, delinquencies are 5–10 percent, repos are 5–20 percent, and losses are 3–10 percent.

> D: Typically scores between 440 and 500 under the Fair Isaac system; has charge-offs and judgments that have not been repaid, and has not made payments on these loans. When extended credit, delinquencies are 10–20 percent, repos are 16–40 percent, losses are 10–20 percent.

Finfer stated that "this is not a business for the faint of heart." As might be expected, many of these loans are "story loans." In other words, a lender must listen to the applicant's story to assess whether past problems reflect a one-time problem or represent a willingness to walk away from debt.

During the latter half of the 1990s and early 2000s, many lenders upped the stakes by making "high LTV" (loan-to-value) loans based on the equity in a borrower's home. Where traditional home equity loans are capped at 75 percent of appraised value minus the outstanding principal balance, high LTV loans equal as much as 125 percent of the value of a home. For example, suppose that an individual owned a home worth $100,000 and owed $85,000 on the first mortgage. A lender would be willing to lend another $40,000 (1.25 times $100,000, minus $85,000). The loan rate is typically set between the prevailing first mortgage rate and a base credit card rate to make the loan attractive to

---

[4]"Definitions appear in Steve Cocheo, "Give Me Your Delinquents, Your Former Bankrupts, Yearning to Borrow," *ABA Banking Journal,* August 1996.

the borrower. The marketing efforts focus on getting borrowers to use these loans to consolidate their debt and lower their monthly payments. The risk is that default leaves the lender exposed to the amount in excess of the home's (collateral's) true value after expenses. What makes this a lucrative business is that many investment banks buy these loans and securitize them. Originators can earn from 4 to 8 percent origination fees.

## CONSUMER CREDIT REGULATIONS

The federal government has approved a wide range of regulations to protect individuals when obtaining credit. Most of the regulations address discrimination, billing practices, customer liability, and the proper disclosure of finance charges and reasons for denying credit. The need for such regulation arose from abuses of the credit system. At one time, many lenders refused to extend credit to women who did not have a personal credit record because loans were credited to a husband. Loans were sometimes denied because of the borrower's race or age. Lenders would refuse to extend credit in deteriorating neighborhoods and made it difficult for borrowers to determine the effective cost of credit. This section discusses several important regulations that addressed these abuses.

### EQUAL CREDIT OPPORTUNITY

Ideally, credit will be available to any borrower who satisfies acceptable risk criteria. To ensure this, Congress passed the Equal Credit Opportunity Act (ECOA), which makes it illegal for lenders to discriminate against potential borrowers because of race, religion, sex, marital status, age, or national origin. The Federal Reserve's Regulation B specifies conditions that must be met in structuring credit applications and establishing creditworthiness. In doing so, it focuses on three different aspects of credit transactions. First, it indicates what information a creditor may not request. Implicitly, this information is not relevant to the credit evaluation and would, if available, be used primarily to discriminate. Second, it specifies how certain information can be used in credit scoring systems. Credit scoring models are discussed later in the chapter. Finally, it provides for proper credit reporting. For example, lenders must include spouses in the credit records whenever a spouse is jointly liable for any debts. Lenders must also notify applicants of adverse action on a loan within 30 days of the request. The following list identifies specific items that are prohibited or required.

### PROHIBITED INFORMATION REQUESTS

1. Lenders may not request information about the applicant's marital status unless credit is being requested jointly, the spouse's assets will be used to repay the loan, or the applicant lives in a community property state.[5] This popularized the term cohabitant on many application forms.

2. Lenders may not request information about whether alimony, child support, and public assistance payments are included in an applicant's reported income. Applicants can voluntarily provide this information if they believe it will improve perceived creditworthiness.

3. Lenders may not request information about a woman's childbearing capability and plans, or birth control practices.

4. Lenders may not request information about whether an applicant has a telephone.

### CREDIT SCORING SYSTEMS

1. Credit scoring systems are acceptable if they do not require prohibited information and are statistically justified. The statistical soundness should be systematically reviewed and updated.

2. Credit scoring systems can use information about age, sex, and marital status as long as these factors contribute positively to the applicant's creditworthiness.

### CREDIT REPORTING

1. Lenders must report credit extended jointly to married couples in both spouses' names. This enables both individuals to build a credit history.

---

[5] In community property states, couples own assets jointly. Assets listed on an application are often only partly owned by a married applicant, which would restrict a lender's access to collateral.

2. Whenever lenders reject a loan, they must notify applicants of the credit denial within 30 days and indicate why the request was turned down. An applicant may request written notification, and the lender must comply.

In practice, the ECOA includes many complex provisions that are difficult to comprehend. To make compliance easier, the Federal Reserve provides model loan application forms that conform to Regulation B.

## TRUTH IN LENDING

The intent underlying truth in lending legislation is for lenders to disclose consumer loan finance charges and interest rates in a standardized format. This enables borrowers to compare credit terms and the cost of credit between loans and between lenders. Truth in lending regulations apply to all loans up to $25,000 extended to individuals, where the borrower's primary residence does not serve as collateral.[6]

Legislation arose because lenders quoted interest rates in many different ways and often included supplemental charges in a loan that substantially increased the actual cost. Consumers could not easily determine how much they were paying and what the effective interest rate was on a loan. This confused borrowers and potentially led to inferior credit decisions.

Historically, consumer loan rates were quoted as add-on rates, discount rates, or simple interest rates. Add-on rates are applied against the entire principal of installment loans. The gross interest is added to the principal with the total divided by the number of periodic payments to determine the size of each payment. For example, suppose that a customer borrows $3,000 for one year at a 12 percent add-on rate with the loan to be repaid in 12 equal monthly installments. Total interest equals $360, the monthly payment equals $280, and the effective annual interest cost is approximately 21.5 percent. Exhibit 12.55 presents these calculations and similar ones for discount rate and simple interest examples.

With the discount rate method, the quoted rate is applied against the sum of principal and interest, yet the borrower gets to use only the principal, as interest is immediately deducted from the total loan. Exhibit 12.5 considers a one-year loan with a single $3,000 payment at maturity. The borrower receives only $2,640, or the total loan minus 12 percent discount rate interest. The effective annual percentage rate (APR), equals 13.64 percent. The bottom part of Exhibit 12.5 demonstrates simple interest calculations. Simple interest is interest paid on only the principal sum. A $3,000 loan at 12 percent simple interest per year produces $360 in interest, or a 12 percent effective rate. At the bottom of the exhibit, the quoted rate is adjusted to its monthly equivalent, which is applied against the unpaid principal balance on a loan. A $3,000 loan, repaid in 12 monthly installments at 1 percent monthly simple interest, produces interest under $200. The monthly interest rate equals 1 percent of the outstanding principal balance at each interval. Depending on how it is quoted, a 12 percent rate exhibits a noticeably different effective rate, ranging from 12 percent to 21.55 percent in the examples.

Truth in lending legislation requires that lenders disclose to potential borrowers both the total finance charge and an annual percentage rate (APR). The total finance charge equals the dollar amount of interest costs plus all supplemental charges that are imposed as part of a loan, including loan origination fees, service charges, and insurance premiums if the lender demands the customer take out a policy as part of the agreement. The annual percentage rate (APR) equals the total finance charge computed against the loan balance as a simple annual interest rate equivalent.

The regulations also stipulate that advertisements must include all relevant terms of a loan if any single payment or pricing feature is mentioned. These terms include the finance charge, APR, the dollar magnitude of any down payment requirement, the number of payments, and final maturity. This prevents a lender from using one very attractive feature, such as no required down payment, to lure customers without disclosing all the terms. Assuming the borrower does not pay additional fees, the effective interest rates in Exhibit 12.5 are APRs.

## FAIR CREDIT REPORTING

Lenders can obtain information on an individual's prior credit relationships from local credit bureaus when evaluating consumer loan requests. The Fair Credit Reporting Act enables individuals to examine their credit reports provided by credit bureaus. If any information is incorrect, the individual can have the bureau make changes and notify all lenders who obtained the inaccurate data. If the accuracy of the information is disputed, an individual can permanently enter into the credit file his or her interpretation of the error. The credit bureau, when requested, must also notify an individual which lenders have received credit reports.

There are three primary credit reporting agencies: Equifax, Experian, and Trans Union. Unfortunately, the credit reports that they produce are quite often wrong. One problem is that these credit bureaus make little effort to verify the information they receive from retailers, banks, and finance companies. (Consider the problems of

---

[6]The Truth in Lending Act, passed in 1968, is implemented through the Federal Reserve's Regulation Z. Originally, it applied to agriculture loans as well as personal credit. In 1980, Congress exempted agriculture from the reporting requirements.

**EXHIBIT 12.5** Comparison of Interest Rate Quotes

**Add-On Rate**

$3,000 loan for one year, 12% add-on rate, repaid in 12 equal monthly installments

Interest charge: $360

Monthly payment: $\dfrac{[0.12(\$3,000) + \$3,000]}{12} = \dfrac{\$3,360}{12} = \$280$

Effective interest rate (i): $\displaystyle\sum_{t=1}^{12} \dfrac{\$280}{(\$1+i)^t} = \$3,000$

$i = 1.796\%$

Annual percentage rate (APR) = 21.55%

**Discount Rate**

$3,000 to be repaid at the end of one year, 12% discount rate

Interest charge: 0.12($3,000) = $360

Year-end payment: $3,000

Annual percentage rate (APR) ($i_n$): $2,640 = $\dfrac{\$3,000}{(1 + i_n)}$

$i_n = 13.64\%$

**Simple Interest Rate**

$3,000 loan for one year, 12% simple interest, repaid at end of year in one payment

Interest ($i_s$): = $3,000(0.12)(1) = $360

$\$3,000 = \dfrac{\$3,360}{(1 + i_s)}$

$i_s = 12\%$

$3,000 loan for 1 year, 1% monthly simple interest rate, repaid in 12 equal monthly installments

**Repayment Schedule**

| End of Month | Monthly Payment | Interest Portion | Principal | Outstanding Principal Balance |
|---|---|---|---|---|
| January | $ 266.55 | $ 30.00 | $ 236.55 | $2,763.45 |
| February | 266.55 | 27.63 | 238.92 | 2,524.53 |
| March | 266.55 | 25.25 | 241.30 | 2,283.23 |
| April | 266.55 | 22.83 | 243.72 | 2,039.51 |
| May | 266.55 | 20.40 | 246.15 | 1,793.36 |
| June | 266.55 | 17.93 | 248.62 | 1,544.74 |
| July | 266.55 | 15.45 | 251.10 | 1,293.64 |
| August | 266.55 | 12.94 | 253.61 | 1,040.03 |
| September | 266.55 | 10.40 | 256.15 | 783.88 |
| October | 266.55 | 7.84 | 258.71 | 525.17 |
| November | 266.55 | 5.25 | 261.30 | 263.87 |
| December | 266.51 | 2.64 | 263.87 | 0.00 |
| Total | $3,198.56 | $198.56 | $3,000.00 | |

Effective interest rate: Monthly rate = 1%

Annual percentage rate (APR) = 12%

Monthly payment = $\$3,000 / \displaystyle\sum_{i=1}^{12} \dfrac{1}{(1.01)^t}$

*Consumer Credit Regulations*

# CONTEMPORARY ISSUES

## ERRORS IN CREDIT REPORTING

Garbage in, garbage out is a fair description of the information contained in many individuals' credit reports. Credit bureaus, such as Equifax, Experian, and Trans Union, process millions of credit reports to financial institutions and retailers each month without spending enough effort to verify the accuracy of the data. Thus, there is a surprisingly high probability that there are errors in a credit report.

In 1991, National Data Retrieval, a firm that collects data used to construct individuals' credit histories, hired Margaret Herr and her son to collect information from public records for residents in the town of Norwich, Vermont. The firm paid them 25 cents per name for information collected regarding who was delinquent in their local property tax payments. Herr and her son, who received virtually no training, misread the tax records by identifying those who had paid their taxes as those who were delinquent. When they passed the information on to TRW (now Experian), virtually all of Norwich's 1,500 residents were designated as having been delinquent on their taxes and thus found their credit records damaged. The town clerk notified TRW but got no response. Only after the state of Vermont sued TRW were the credit reports corrected.

SOURCE: Peter Kuper, "Garbage Out," *Smart Money* (October 1996).

Norwich, Vermont, residents in 1991. (See Contemporary Issues: "Errors in Credit Reporting.") In addition, the credit bureaus do not rush to correct their records when errors are found. A study by the U.S. Public Interest Research Group determined that consumers spent an average of 32 weeks after initial contact negotiating with credit bureaus to get incorrect information removed, before they contacted federal officials.

For consumers, a credit score is like a bond rating. It is a single number that provides information to a lender, insurance company, or employer about the individual's financial performance. Some firms believe that how an individual handles credit reflects on his or her work ethic, willingness to file false claims (insurance) and general character. Get a high credit score, and more credit is available and the borrowing rate is lower. It is thus critical that each person recognize how his or her credit score is calculated and what behaviors can improve or worsen the score. Of course, individuals who do not use credit—typically, many of the elderly—do not have a credit score and often cannot borrow or even rent a car. The following chart demonstrates the factors that contribute to the credit score and associated weights. Consumers who want to increase their score, should not pay late or file for bankruptcy. They should use a small portion of their available credit, not continually apply for new credit as the number of applications counts against the individual, obtain credit from different sources (bank loans, credit cards, and a mortgage), and maintain a lengthy credit history.

## Factors Contributing to an Individual's Credit Score

**Factors Contributing to an Individual's Credit Score**

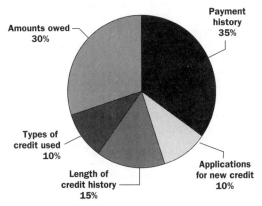

- Payment history 35%
- Amounts owed 30%
- Types of credit used 10%
- Length of credit history 15%
- Applications for new credit 10%

SOURCE: Fair Isaac.

Exhibit 12.6 provides a sample credit report for a hypothetical John Doe. It lists the names of companies that provide credit, the account numbers, the type of credit—whether it is for an individual account, joint account, and so on—how many months of activity are reviewed, the date of the last activity, the highest amount charged over the time period or the maximum amount of credit available, and the key items as of the date reported. This section indicates the balance outstanding at the time of the report; the status of the account, such as how long it is past due or whether it is delinquent or a charged-off account; and the reporting date. Lenders are especially interested in this part of the borrower's credit history as it indicates the historical record of payment and a borrower's propensity to be late or not pay. Just below this is a summary of the number of times the applicant was past due and the date of the most recent delinquencies and their severity. The courthouse record similarly indicates whether the applicant has declared bankruptcy or whether any liens or judgments have been filed against him or her. Finally, the bottom indicates the companies that have requested the applicant's credit history and the dates of inquiry. Too many voluntary inquiries, where the applicant requests a credit card, often indicate a high-risk credit.[7]

## COMMUNITY REINVESTMENT

The Community Reinvestment Act (CRA) was passed in 1977 to prohibit redlining and to encourage lenders to extend credit within their immediate trade area and the markets where they collect deposits. Redlining is the practice of not extending credit within geographic areas that are believed to be deteriorating. Its name comes from the reputed practice of outlining in red those areas of a city where a lender would automatically refuse credit because of location. It discriminates against borrowers from economically declining neighborhoods that represent the redlined areas. These areas typically represent low-income and minority neighborhoods. Community reinvestment has played an important role in the interstate banking movement. Out-of-state banks that acquire local banks must commit to continued lending in the area and not use acquired banks simply as deposit gatherers.

The Financial Institutions Reform, Recovery, and Enforcement Act (FIRREA) of 1989 raised the profile of the CRA by mandating public disclosure of bank lending policies and regulatory ratings of bank compliance. Specifically, regulators now rate banks as outstanding, satisfactory, needs improvement, or in substantial noncompliance in terms of their compliance with nondiscriminatory lending practices. These ratings are publicized to put pressure on banks that are not in compliance out of fear that negative publicity will harm their image and subsequent performance. Historically, few banks have been rated as outstanding and only a very small number have been rated in substantial noncompliance. Many bankers cite these ratings in arguing that the costs of CRA compliance exceed the benefits to aggrieved consumers. Consumer groups, in contrast, argue that the regulators are too lenient in classifying banks.

Regulators must also take lending performance into account when evaluating a bank's request to charter a new bank, acquire a bank, open a branch, or merge with another institution. Consumer groups now routinely use claims of noncompliance under CRA to delay such requests, forcing the bank to demonstrate how performance will be improved. It is both good business and appropriate for every bank to comply with nondiscrimination legislation.

## BANKRUPTCY REFORM

Individuals who cannot repay their debts on time can file for bankruptcy and receive court protection against creditors. Court protection takes the form of exempting selected personal assets from creditors' claims and providing for an orderly repayment of debts. In 1978 and 1985, Congress modified the Federal Bankruptcy Code. The 1978 legislation liberalized the volume and type of assets that individuals could exempt and made unsecured loans extremely risky.

Individuals can file for bankruptcy under Chapter 7 or Chapter 13. Chapter 7 authorizes individuals to liquidate qualified assets and distribute the proceeds to creditors. The 1978 Bankruptcy Reform Act specifically exempted some assets, including an automobile, household furnishings, some jewelry, and a fraction of the individuals' equity in a primary residence from liquidation. In some states, exemptions are even more liberal, and individuals can take advantage of the broadest exemptions.[8] An individual must pay all taxes, alimony, and child support owed in full. Cash received from the sale of nonexempt assets is allocated to other creditors on a pro rata basis, with secured creditors paid first. Because the list of exemptions was so broad after 1978, unsecured creditors rarely received any payment. Once the cash is distributed, the remaining debts are discharged.

---

[7]Individuals can readily obtain a copy of their personal credit report over the Internet. They can also find descriptions as to how to read a credit report and improve their credit score. See http://www.myvesta.com and http://www.fairisaac.com. Basic credit reports are now available free of charge once each year.

[8]The 1978 regulations actually allowed one spouse to file for bankruptcy in state court while the other spouse filed in federal court, thereby doubling their exemptions. The 1985 provisions force a couple to file in just one jurisdiction.

# EXHIBIT 12.6 — Sample Credit Report

Please address all future
correspondence to the address
shown on the right →

CREDIT REPORTING OFFICE
BUSINESS ADDRESS
CITY, STATE 00000
PHONE NUMBER

JOHN DOE
123 HOME STATE
CITY, STATE 00000

DATE 06/04/93
SOCIAL SECURITY NUMBER 123-45-6789
DATE OF BIRTH 04/19/57
SPOUSE JANE

## CREDIT HISTORY

**What it tells you**

If this was your credit report, this is what this line of information would tell you:
You have an individual account with Citibank that was opened in November of
1991. It was last used in November of 1995 and the balance is paid in full.

Column labels: **B** **C** **D** **E** **F** **G** **H** **I** **J** **K** **L** **M**

| Company Name (B) | Account Number (C) | Whose Acct. (D) | Date Opened (E) | Months Reviewed (F) | Date of Last Activity (G) | High Credit (H) | Terms (I) | Balance (J) | Past Due (K) | Status (L) | Date Reported (M) |
|---|---|---|---|---|---|---|---|---|---|---|---|
| SEARS | 11251514 | J | 05/91 | 66 | 10/96 | 3500 | | 0 | | R1 | 12/97 |
| CITIBANK | 12345678901236578 | I | 11/91 | 48 | 11/95 | 9388 | 48M | 0 | | I1 | 11/97 |
| AMEX | 123456789070 | A | 06/92 | 24 | 10/96 | 500 | | 0 | | O1 | 12/97 |
| CHASE | 1234567 | I | 05/90 | 48 | 10/96 | 5000 | 340 | 3000 | 680 | R3 | 12/97 |

*Items as of Date Reported* spans Balance, Past Due, and Status columns.

>>> PRIOR PAYING HISTORY — 30(03) 60 (04) 90+(01) 08/90-R2, 02/89-R3, 10/88-R4 <<<

 **N**  **O**

>>> COLLECTION REPORTED 06/91, ASSIGNED 09/90 TO PRO COLL (800) 555-1234 CLIENT-ABC
HOSPITAL; AMOUNT-$978; STAT UNPAID 06/91; BALANCE — $978 06/91; DATE OF LAST ACTIVITY
09/90; INDIVIDUAL; ACCOUNT NUMBER 123456789B

>>>>>>>>>>>>>>>>>>>>>>>>>>> COLLECTION AGENCY TELEPHONE NUMBER(S) <<<<<<<<<<<<<<<<<<<<<<<<<

PRO COLL (800) 555-1234

*********************** COURTHOUSE RECORDS ***********************

>>> LIEN FILLED 03/88; FULTON CITY; CASE NUMBER — 32114; AMOUNT — $26667; CLASS — CITY/
COUNTY; PERSONAL; INDIVIDUAL; SIRCHARGED; ASSETS — $780

>>> BANKRUPTCY FILED 12/89; NORTHERN DIST CT; CASE NUMBER — 673HC12; LIABILITIES — $15787;
PERSONAL; INDIVIDUAL; DISCHARGED; ASSETS — $780

>>> JUDGEMENT FILED 07/87; FULTON CTY; CASE NUMBER-898872; DEFENDANT-JOHN DOE AMOUNT —
$8984; PLAINTIFF — ABC REAL ESTATE; SATISFIED 03/89; VERIFIED 05/90

*********************** ADDITIONAL INFORMATION ***********************

FORMER ADDRESS 456 JUPITER RD, ATLANTA, GA 30245

FORMER ADDRESS P.O. BOX 2134, SAVANNAH, GA 31406

CURRENT EMPLOYMENT ENGINEER, SPACE PATROL

*********** COMPANIES THAT REQUESTED YOUR CREDIT HISTORY *****************

| | |
|---|---|
| 05/03/93 EQUIFAX | 02/12/93 MACYS |
| 12/16/92 PRM VISA | 08/01 92 AM CITIBANK |
| 06/11/92 NATIONS BANK | 04/29/92 GE CAPITAL |
| 07/17/92 JC PENNEY | 02/12/94 AR SEARS |

## ABC's of a credit report

**A.** The name and address of the office you should contact if you have any questions or disagreement with your credit report.

**B.** Identifies the business that is reporting the information

**C.** Your account number with the company reporting

**D.** Indicates who is responsible and type of payment participation with the account

**E.** Month and year account is opened with the credit grantor

**F.** Number of months account payment history has been reported

**G.** Date of last activity on the account and may be the date of last payment or the date of last change

**H.** Highest amount charged or the credit limit

**I.** Represents number of installments (M=months) or monthly payments

**J.** Amount owed on the account at the time it was reported

**K.** Indicates any amount past due at the time the information was reported

**L.** Status and type of account, and timeliness of payment

**M.** Date of last account update

**N.** Number of times account was either 30/60/90 days past due

**O.** Date two most recent delinquencies occurred plus date of most severe delinquency

SOURCE: *State Newspaper,* Columbia, SC, November 1997.

Under Chapter 13, an individual works out a repayment plan with court supervision. The individual gets to keep his or her assets but commits to repay selected debts out of future earnings according to a schedule approved by all secured creditors. Once the scheduled debts are repaid, the remaining debt is discharged. Under the 1978 regulations, unsecured creditors again had no recourse and often received nothing under Chapter 13.

Reforms to the bankruptcy code in 1985 made it more costly for an individual to walk away from outstanding debt. Under Chapter 13 plans, lenders can obtain a court order that assigns a large fraction of a debtor's income to repay debt for three years after the date of filing. The reforms shortened the list of exempt assets and permitted the court to switch a Chapter 7 filing to Chapter 13 when it determined that an individual who was financially able was using bankruptcy simply to avoid paying all debts. Unsecured lenders were also protected by provisions that forced borrowers to repay all credit card purchases made during the three weeks prior to filing for bankruptcy.

In 1995, Congress created a bankruptcy commission that would recommend changes in bankruptcy law. By 1997, approximately 70 percent of bankruptcy filers selected Chapter 7, with the remaining 30 percent selecting Chapter 13. Clearly, many individuals used bankruptcy as a financial planning tool to get out of debt. The stigma was largely gone. This presents serious problems for lenders given recent consumer loan charge-off experience and the increase in bankruptcy filings noted in Exhibit 12.3. Many analysts believe that the U.S. bankruptcy process is abused too frequently, with up to 10 percent of filings being fraudulent and annual losses amounting to around $4 billion. In April 2005, Congress passed bankruptcy reform legislation that made it more difficult for individuals to completely avoid repaying their debts. In particular, an individual whose income exceeds the state median has to file for Chapter 13 and will repay at least a portion of his or her debts. In the past some states did not let creditors take possession of an individual's home as a result of bankruptcy. The provisions induced many wealthy individuals to buy or build expensive homes in such states in anticipation of bankruptcy. The law retains these protections, but only after the individual has owned the home for 40 months. The law also mandates credit counseling. The proposed reforms would make it more difficult to file for bankruptcy and more expensive, as filers would be forced to provide details on their spending habits and would have to earn below median income in their home state to qualify for the best protection.

## CREDIT ANALYSIS

The objective of consumer credit analysis is to assess the risks associated with lending to individuals. Not surprisingly, these risks differ substantially from those of commercial loans. Most consumer loans are quite small, averaging around $7,900 in 2003. Because the fixed costs of servicing consumer loans are high, banks must generate substantial loan volume to reduce unit costs. This means dealing with a large number of distinct borrowers with different personalities and financial characteristics.

When evaluating loans, bankers cite the five Cs of credit: character, capital, capacity, conditions, and collateral. The most important—yet most difficult to assess—is character. A loan officer essentially must determine the customer's desire to repay a loan. The only quantitative information available is the borrower's application and credit record. If the borrower is a bank customer, the officer can examine internal information regarding the customer's historical account relationship. If the borrower is not a current customer, the officer must solicit information from local credit bureaus or other businesses that have extended credit to the individual. The ECOA stipulates what information can be required and prohibits discrimination. It also mandates how lenders must report information to the credit reporting agencies. Banks also rely heavily on subjective appraisals of the borrower's character. They normally obtain personal references, verify employment, and check the accuracy of the application. This is necessary because fraud is prevalent and it is relatively easy for an individual to disguise past behavior. If the officer determines that a potential customer is dishonest, the loan is rejected automatically.

Capital refers to the individual's wealth position and is closely related to capacity, an individual's financial ability to meet loan payments in addition to normal living expenses and other debt obligations. For almost all consumer loans, the individual's income serves as the primary source of repayment. A loan officer projects what income will be available after other expenses and compares this with periodic principal and interest payments on the new loan. To ensure adequate coverage, the lender often imposes minimum down payment requirements and maximum allowable debt service to income ratios. The loan officer verifies that the borrower's income equals that stated on the application and assesses the stability of the income source. Conditions refers to the impact of economic events on the borrower's capacity to pay when some income sources disappear as business activity declines.

The importance of collateral is in providing a secondary source of repayment. Collateral may be the asset financed by the loan, other assets owned by the individual, or the personal guarantee of a cosigner on the loan. Collateral gives a bank another source of repayment if the borrower's income is insufficient. Normally, a loan is not approved simply because the collateral appears solid. Often the collateral disappears or deteriorates in value

*Credit Analysis*

prior to the bank taking possession, as with a damaged or older automobile. Finally, the bankruptcy code enables individuals to protect a wide range of assets from creditors, and it may be difficult to obtain a judgment.

Two additional Cs have been added reflecting customer relationships and competition.[9] A bank's prior relationship with a customer reveals information about past credit and deposit experience that is useful in assessing willingness and ability to repay. Competition has an impact by affecting the pricing of a loan. All loans should generate positive risk-adjusted returns. However, lenders periodically react to competitive pressures by undercutting competitors' rates in order to attract new business. Still, such competition should not affect the accept/reject decision.

## POLICY GUIDELINES

Consumer loans are extended for a variety of purposes. The most common purposes are for the purchase of automobiles, mobile homes, and furniture and appliances, and for home improvement or home equity loans. Before approving any loan, the lending officer requests information regarding the borrower's employment status, periodic income, the value of assets owned, outstanding debts, personal references, and specific terms of the expenditure that generates the loan request. The officer verifies the information and assesses the borrower's character and financial capacity to repay the loan. Because borrowers' personal and financial characteristics differ widely, most banks have formalized lending guidelines. As an example, guidelines for acceptable and unacceptable loans might appear as listed below.

## ACCEPTABLE LOANS

### Automobile
1. Limited to current-year models or models less than 5 years old.
2. Made on an amortizing basis with a minimum 10 percent down payment.
3. Advances against used models should not exceed National Automobile Dealer Association loan value.
4. New automobiles for business purposes are limited to 30-month amortization.
5. Insurance must be obtained and verified with a $250 maximum deductible.

### Boat
1. Limited to current-year models or models less than 3 years old.
2. Made on an amortizing basis with a minimum 20 percent down payment.
3. Marine survey must be obtained with large craft.
4. Insurance must be obtained and verified.

### Home Improvement
1. Loans in excess of $2,500 should be secured by a lien.
2. Loans in excess of $10,000 require a property appraisal and title search.
3. A third lien position is not acceptable.
4. Bank should retain the right to cancel in all cases.

### Personal—Unsecured
1. Minimum loan is $2,500.
2. Made only to deposit customers.
3. Limited to 1/12 of the applicant's annual income.

### Single Payment
1. Limited to extraordinary purposes.
2. Require a verified, near-term source of repayment.
3. Insurance claims, pending estate settlements, and lawsuit settlements are not acceptable sources of repayment.

### Cosigned
1. Applicant exhibits the potential to be a qualified, long-term bank customer.
2. Both the applicant and cosigner are depositors of the bank.

---

[9]See Larry White (1990) for a general discussion of the 7 Cs of credit.

3. Applicant does not have an established credit history but does have the capacity to pay.

4. Cosigner has qualified credit history and the capacity to pay.

5. Cosigner is informed that the bank is relying totally on the cosigner for repayment in case of default.

## UNACCEPTABLE LOANS

1. Loans for speculative purposes.

2. Loans secured by a second lien, other than home improvement or home equity loans.

3. Any participation with a correspondent bank in a loan that the bank would not normally approve.

4. Accommodation loans to a poor credit risk based on the strength of the cosigner.

5. Single payment automobile or boat loans.

6. Loans secured by existing home furnishings.

7. Loans for skydiving equipment and hang gliders.

## EVALUATION PROCEDURES: JUDGMENTAL AND CREDIT SCORING

Banks employ judgmental procedures and quantitative credit scoring procedures when evaluating consumer loans. In both cases, a lending officer collects information regarding the borrower's character, capacity, and collateral. With a pure judgmental analysis, the loan officer subjectively interprets the information in light of the bank's lending guidelines and accepts or rejects the loan. This assessment can often be completed shortly after receiving the loan application and visiting with the applicant. With a pure quantitative analysis, or credit scoring model, the loan officer grades the loan request according to a statistically sound model that assigns points to selected characteristics of the prospective borrower. The model tallies the points—or score—and compares the total with statistically determined accept/reject thresholds.[10] If the total exceeds the accept threshold, the officer approves the loan. If the total is below the reject threshold, the officer denies the loan. Thus, high scores signify low risk and low scores signify higher risk. A lender can specify these thresholds consistent with how much risk it is willing to accept. Typically, there is a gap between the reject and accept scores representing an inconclusive evaluation of characteristics. If the total falls within this gap, the officer makes a decision based on judgmental factors.

When developing the accept/reject scores, banks must obtain data on applicant characteristics when loans were originally requested, for both accepted and rejected loans. Actual performance on the loans is then evaluated to determine the extent to which different factors influenced the individual's ability to repay. Specifically, the analysis identifies borrower characteristics that have predictive power in determining when loans will be repaid or when borrowers will default. Good models assign high scores to a high fraction of performing loans and low scores to a high fraction of nonperforming loans. The importance of different factors is determined by the weights in the credit scoring formula. Information is generally obtained from prior loan applications and from credit bureaus. For nonmortgage consumer loans, the common borrower characteristics used include the applicant's monthly income, length of employment, outstanding debt and debt service requirements, and liquid financial asset holdings; whether the applicant owns a home or rents; the nature and number of bank accounts and relationships; the existence and frequency of prior delinquencies and/or defaults; and the number of voluntary credit inquiries. Many of these credit scoring models rely on eight or more factors.

Clearly, credit scoring procedures are more objective than judgmental evaluations. Credit decisions can be made quickly once the information is verified, often in less than 10 minutes when computers are used. Discrimination is largely eliminated because the ECOA does not allow credit scoring models to grade race, religion, or national origin. The benefits include lower costs if scoring and decision making are done mechanically, timely decisions, and avoidance of discrimination. The primary difficulty is that credit scoring models must be statistically verified and continually updated, which can be expensive. In fact, many small banks are precluded from developing their own models because of the high cost and a limited database.[11] Some nonbank institutions, such as insurance companies, have also discovered that an individual's credit score can be used to identify high and low insurance risks for property-casualty (particularly automobile and medical) insurance.

---

[10]Credit scoring systems and accept/reject scores are empirically derived from either multiple regression analysis or multiple discriminate analysis. These statistical techniques use historical data regarding a bank's good and bad consumer loans to assess what characteristics identify a high percentage of good or bad borrowers. The accept/reject scores represent the weighted value of borrowers' characteristics. Recent efforts involve using option-pricing models and neural networks to assign scores. See "What's the Point of Credit Scoring," Business Review, Federal Reserve Bank of Philadelphia, September–October 1997, for a summary of these techniques.

[11]Mester (1997) provides an excellent summary of consumer and small business credit scoring models.

## AN APPLICATION: CREDIT SCORING A CONSUMER LOAN

Credit scoring models are based on historical data obtained from applicants who actually received loans.[12] Statistical techniques assign weights to various borrower characteristics that represent each factor's contribution toward distinguishing between good loans that were repaid on time and problem loans that produced losses. These weights are then used as predictors of high-risk and low-risk loans, using data from new loan applications.

The use of credit scoring models can be demonstrated with an example. Suppose that a bank officer receives a loan application for the purchase of an automobile, as outlined in Exhibit 12.7. In the loan request, Camile Groome wants to buy a 2003 Jeep Cherokee. The application identifies the purpose, amount, and maturity of the loan, as well as information regarding the applicant's personal and financial circumstances, and recognizes ECOA guidelines. Before providing any information, Groome indicates that she is applying for individual credit and not relying on alimony, child support, or government income maintenance payments to repay the debt. The bank, therefore, cannot demand information regarding her marital status or information about joint applicants or cosigners.

**THE CREDIT SCORE.** Exhibit 12.8 lists the factors and corresponding weights for the bank's credit scoring model. A loan is automatically approved if the applicant's total score equals at least 200. The applicant is denied credit if the total score falls below 150. Scores in between these accept/reject values are indeterminate. The weights indicate the relative importance of each characteristic. At University National Bank, five factors, including employment status, principal residence, monthly debt relative to monthly income, total income, and banking references, are weighted heaviest. Not surprisingly, these characteristics represent financial capacity and personal stability, which are important in determining repayment prospects. The bank also uses a local retail merchants association and a similar national association to check credit histories. Subsequent reports reveal the applicant's current list of outstanding debts, the highest balance outstanding at any one point, and whether the individual was ever late in making payments.

Groome's credit score totals 185, as the sum of the scores in the darkened areas from her application within each category in Exhibit 12.8 indicates. Given the accept/reject scores, the model provides an inconclusive evaluation of the credit risk, and the loan officer must rely on judgmental factors. When discussing the application, Groome revealed that she moved to Denver after her husband, who worked for an oil field services company, died in an automobile accident. After searching for two months, she found work as a dental assistant with a dentist who had recently started his own business. She had experience in this field before she met her husband but quit her job to stay at home with their son. She is currently attending evening classes at a local university to complete a degree in accounting. She further indicated that the total cost of the Jeep she wanted to purchase was $20,500 but she intended to make a $5,000 down payment. This would lower her savings balance at the bank to $1,200. The loan officer verified this and determined that Groome's monthly checking account balance averaged around $150. Her monthly rent payment was $750. She had outstanding loans on a Visa card and to Sears that she was paying off over time.

**THE CREDIT DECISION.** The credit decision rests on the loan officer's evaluation of the applicant's character and capacity to repay the debt. The officer estimates that the monthly installment payment on the loan at current rates would equal $375 for the next four years. The officer ponders the following questions. Will the applicant remain in Denver long enough to repay the loan? How stable is her job and income? Is her income high enough to cover normal monthly living expenses, debt payments, and extraordinary expenses? Should the officer reject the loan and encourage the applicant to reapply with a cosigner?

The loan officer has numerous grounds to deny credit. The applicant's credit history is limited to two credit cards, her local residence was established too recently, and she was employed too recently to establish job stability. Even if she were to get a cosigner, such as her employer, experience shows that many cosigners renege on their commitments. On the positive side, Groome appears to be a hard worker who is the victim of circumstances resulting from her husband's death. It is also unlikely that anyone who puts almost 30 percent down on a new model is going to walk away from a debt. The bank will likely lose Groome as a depositor if it denies the application. The resolution depends on the careful weighting of the costs and benefits. What would you recommend?

## YOUR FICO CREDIT SCORE

In today's world, a FICO score summarizes in one number an individual's credit history.[13] Lenders often use this number when evaluating whether to approve a consumer loan or mortgage, and many insurance companies consider the score when determining whether to offer insurance coverage and how to price the insurance. Generally, the scores range from 300 to 850 with a higher figure indicating a better credit history. The higher the score is, the more likely it is a lender or insurer will see the individual as making the promised payments in a timely manner. The national

---

[12]The fact that the sample excludes applications that were rejected biases the model parameters because the characteristics of these applicants are ignored. The extent of the bias depends on whether good borrowers who would have repaid the loan on a timely basis were eliminated or whether all rejects were bad credits.

[13]Information in this section is based on data provided by Fair, Isaac & Co. (FICO) on its Web site, http://www.fairisaac.com.

**EXHIBIT 12.7**

Credit Application, University National Bank

---

**IMPORTANT: Please read these directions before completing this Application, and check (✓) the appropriate box below.**

☒ If you are applying for individual credit in your own name, are not married, and are not relying on alimony, child support, or separate maintenance payments or on the income or assets of another person as the basis for repayment of the credit requested, complete only Sections A and D. If the requested credit is to be secured, also complete Section E.

☐ In all other situations, complete all Sections except E, providing information in B about your spouse, a joint applicant or user, or the person on whose alimony, support, or maintenance payments or income or assets you are relying. If the requested credit is to be secured, also complete Section E.

| AMOUNT REQUESTED | PAYMENT DATE DESIRED | PROCEEDS OF CREDIT TO BE USED FOR |
|---|---|---|
| $ 18,500 | Nov. 15, 2004 | Purchase of a 2003 Jeep Cherokee |

**SECTION A — INFORMATION REGARDING APPLICANT**

| FULL NAME | AGE | BIRTH DATE | SOCIAL SECURITY NO |
|---|---|---|---|
| Camille Groome | 28 | July 12, 1973 | 496-62-0448 |

| PRESENT ADDRESS (Street, City, State, & Zip) | How Long At Present Address? | HOME PHONE |
|---|---|---|
| #115 Woodhaven Lane Apts., Denver, Colo. | 10 mths | 765-1191 |

| PREVIOUS ADDRESS (Street, City, State, & Zip) | How Long At Previous Address? |
|---|---|
| Circle Townhouses, #820A, Broken Arrow, Oklahoma | 2 years |

| PRESENT EMPLOYER (Company Name & Address) |
|---|
| James O'Malley, DDS   650 University Avenue, Denver, Colo. |

| How Long With Present Employer? | YOUR POSITION OR TITLE | NAME OF SUPERVISOR | BUSINESS PHONE |
|---|---|---|---|
| 8 mths | Dental assistant | James O'Malley | 765-8014 |

| PREVIOUS EMPLOYER (Company Name & Address) |
|---|
| Homemaker |

| Your Present Gross Salary or Commission | Your Present Net Salary or Commission | No. Dependents | Ages of Dependents |
|---|---|---|---|
| $ 36,500 PER year | $ 2,260 PER month | 1 | 6 years |

Alimony, child support, or separate maintenance income need not be revealed if you do not wish to have it considered as a basis for repaying this obligation
Alimony, child support, separate maintenance received under ☐ Court Order ☐ Written Agreement ☐ Oral Understanding

| OTHER INCOME | SOURCES OF OTHER INCOME |
|---|---|
| $ 150 PER year | savings interest |

Is any income listed in this Section likely to be reduced before the credit requested is paid off? ☒ No ☐ Yes (Explain)

| Have you ever received credit from us? ☒ No ☐ Yes — When? | Checking Account No 355 0114 8 Where? UNB  Savings Account No 457 1988 Where? UNB |
|---|---|

| NAME & ADDRESS OF NEAREST RELATIVE NOT LIVING WITH YOU | RELATIONSHIP |
|---|---|
| Albert F. Johnson, RR#10, Adair, Oklahoma | Uncle |

OUTSTANDING DEBTS (Include charge accounts, installment contracts, credit cards, rent, mortgages, etc. Use separate sheet if necessary)

| CREDITOR | BALANCE | PAYMENT | PAID OFF ACCOUNTS |
|---|---|---|---|
| Visa | $2,166 | open | |
| Sears | $920 | $120/mth | |

**SECTION B — INFORMATION REGARDING JOINT APPLICANT OR OTHER PARTY**

| FULL NAME | BIRTH DATE | RELATIONSHIP |
|---|---|---|
| | | |

| ADDRESS | PHONE NUMBER |
|---|---|
| | |

| PRESENT EMPLOYER — ADDRESS | PHONE NUMBER |
|---|---|
| | |

| HOW LONG | PREVIOUS EMPLOYER | HOW LONG | SOCIAL SECURITY NUMBER |
|---|---|---|---|
| | | | |

| GROSS SALARY | SOURCE AND AMOUNT OF OTHER INCOME |
|---|---|
| $ _____ PER _____ | $ _____ PER _____ |

NAME & ADDRESS OF NEAREST RELATIVE NOT LIVING WITH YOU

Alimony, child support, or separate maintenance income need not be revealed if you do not wish to have it considered as a basis for repaying this obligation. Alimony, child support, separate maintenance received under ☐ Court Order ☐ Written Agreement ☐ Oral Understanding

**SECTION C — MARITAL STATUS**

| APPLICANT | ☐ Married | ☐ Separated | ☐ Unmarried, including single, divorced, and widowed |
| OTHER PARTY | ☐ Married | ☐ Separated | ☐ Unmarried, including single, divorced, and widowed |

Are you a co-maker, endorser, or guarantor on any loan or contract? ☐ No ☐ Yes — For Whom? _____ To Whom? _____

Are there any unsatisfied judgements against you? ☐ No ☐ Yes — Amount $ _____ If "Yes", To Whom Owed? _____

**SECTION D — ASSET & DEBT INFORMATION**

If Section B has been completed, this Section should be completed, giving information about both the Applicant and Joint Applicant or Other Person. Please mark Applicant-related information with an "A". If Section B was not completed, only give information about the Applicant in this section.

ASSETS OWNED (Use separate sheet if necessary)

| DESCRIPTION OF ASSETS | VALUE | SUBJECT TO DEBTS | NAMES OF OWNERS |
|---|---|---|---|
| Cash | $ | | |
| Automobiles 1. 1997 Ford Taurus | 800 | No | Camille Groome |
| 2. | | | |
| 3. | | | |

| Landlord or Mortgage Holder | ☒ Rent Payment ☐ Mortgage | Name Account Carried | | Balance | Monthly Payment | Past Due |
|---|---|---|---|---|---|---|
| Woodhaven Lane Apts | | Camille Groome | $ | $ | $ 750 | $ 0 |

**SECTION E — SECURED CREDIT (Complete only if credit is to be secured.) Briefly describe the property to be given as security:**

| Property Description |
|---|
| 2003 Jeep Cherokee |

NAMES AND ADDRESSES OF ALL CO-OWNERS OF THE PROPERTY

IF THE SECURITY IS REAL ESTATE GIVE THE FULL NAME OF YOUR SPOUSE (if any)

SIGNATURES

## EXHIBIT 12.8

Credit Scoring System, University National Bank, Applied to Credit Application for Purchase of a 2000 Jeep

**Characteristics/Weights**

| Category | | | | | | |
|---|---|---|---|---|---|---|
| Annual Gross Income | <$10,000 5 | $10,000–$20,000 15 | $20,000–$40,000 30 | $40,000–60,000 45 | >$60,000 60 | |
| Monthly Debt Payment / Monthly Net Income | >40% 0 | 30–40% 5 | 20–30% 20 | 10–20% 30 | <10% 50 | |
| Bank Relationship Checking/Saving | None 0 | Checking Only 30 | Saving only 30 | Checking & Saving 40 | No answer 0 | |
| Major Credit Cards | None 0 | 1 or more 30 | No answer 0 | | | |
| Credit History | Any derogatory within 7 yrs. −10 | | No record 0 | | Met obligated payments 30 | |
| Applicant's Age | <50 yrs. 5 | >50 yrs. 25 | No answer 0 | | | |
| Residence | Rent 15 | Own/Buying 40 | Own outright 50 | No answer 15 | | |
| Residence Stability | <1 yr. 0 | 1–2 yrs. 15 | 2–4 yrs. 35 | >4 yrs. 50 | No answer 0 | |
| Job Stability | <1 yr. 5 | 1–2 yrs. 20 | 2–4 yrs. 50 | >4 yrs. 70 | Unemployed 5 | Retired 70 |

NOTE: Minimum score for automatic credit approval is 200; score for judgmental evaluation, 150 to 195; score for automatic credit denial is less than 150. Melanie Groome's credit score is 185.

## EXHIBIT 12.9

FICO Scores, 2004

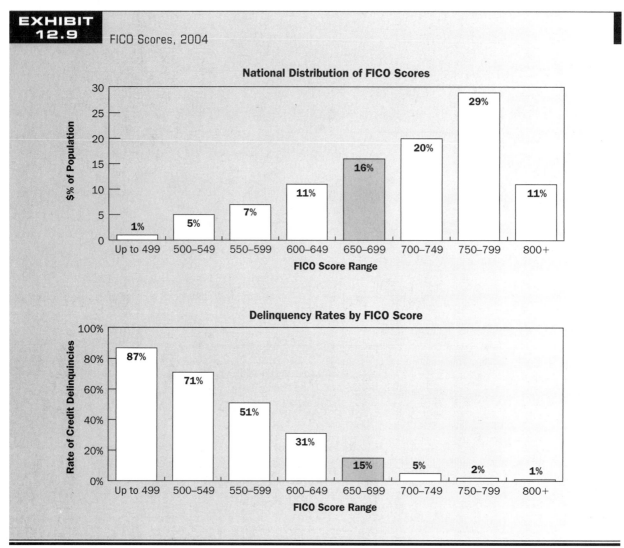

**National Distribution of FICO Scores**

**Delinquency Rates by FICO Score**

average is 670. If, for example, an individual's FICO score is 540, the probability that the individual will be delinquent on one or more credit accounts is more than three times greater than that for the average scorer. A lender typically views this prospective borrower as much riskier than someone with a much higher score.

In late 2004, Fair, Isaac, & Company, the firm that provides the statistical model that produces the FICO score, reported the distribution of scores provided in the top panel of Exhibit 12.9. Note that 58 percent of individuals had scores of 700 or more and 14 percent had scores under 600. The bottom panel lists the average rates that an individual who wanted to borrow to finance a new automobile with a 4-year loan would pay. Note the sharp drop in rate paid for scores over 690. In fact, it does not seem to matter if the score is 800 or more, as long as it exceeds 720. Still, note that a borrower with a credit score under 625 would have paid almost three times the rate that the top scoring borrower would pay. The message is obviously to know your credit score and try to increase it when possible.

An individual's credit score is based on five broad factors: payment history (35 percent), amounts owed (30 percent), length of credit history (15 percent), new credit (10 percent), and type of credit in use (10 percent). As such, a score is determined by whether an individual has made promised principal and interest payments on prior debts on time, the amount of outstanding balances and available credit, how long the individual has been a borrower, recent trends in borrowing and payment activity, and the mix of loans. A lender who solicits a prospective borrower receives a list of reasons why the score is not higher along with the actual credit score. Such reasons range from "serious delinquency" to "too many accounts with outstanding balances." A lender then evaluates the score and reasons to assess whether to make the loan and if so, how to price the loan.

If you are active in your spending and borrowing, it is important to review your credit score at least annually. It is not uncommon for erroneous information to find its way into a credit report and it is often difficult to have it removed. It is also valuable to know how to improve your credit score as your future borrowing potential and cost of borrowing will depend on your credit history as summarized in this figure.

## AN APPLICATION: INDIRECT LENDING

Indirect lending is an attractive form of consumer lending when a bank deals with reputable retailers. A retailer sells merchandise and takes the credit application when the consumer decides to finance the purchase. Because many firms do not have the resources to carry their receivables, they sell the loans to banks or other financial institutions. In most instances, a bank analyzes the credit application and makes the credit decision. These loans are collectively referred to as dealer paper. Banks aggressively compete for paper originated by well-established automobile, mobile home, and furniture dealers.

Most banks involved in indirect lending provide a wide range of services to dealers in addition to buying their paper. For example, automobile dealers often finance their display inventory under floor plan arrangements. When the dealer sells a vehicle, the bank buys the paper and reduces the dealer's inventory loan by the loan value of the vehicle.

Dealers negotiate finance charges directly with their customers. A bank, in turn, agrees to purchase the paper at predetermined rates that vary with the default risk assumed by the bank, the quality of the assets sold, and the maturity of the consumer loan. A dealer normally negotiates a higher rate with the car buyer than the determined rate charged by the bank. This differential varies with competitive conditions but potentially represents a significant source of dealer profit.

Most indirect loan arrangements provide for dealer reserves that reduce the risk in indirect lending. The reserves are derived from the differential between the normal, or contract, loan rate and bank rate and help protect the bank against customer defaults and refunds. Consumers make their loan payments directly to the bank. Instead of immediately giving up the dealer's share of interest, a bank retains the interest in reserve. The reserve is used to cover defaults and the unearned portion of the dealer's share of interest. If the dealer chooses to approve a loan at a rate below the predetermined rate set by the bank for a preferred customer, this negative interest earned also reduces the reserve. A bank refunds a dealer's share of the differential only after the reserve equals some minimum amount, normally a negotiated fraction of total loans purchased.

Consider the following example in Exhibit 12.10 using automobile dealer paper. The dealer charges a customer a 15 percent APR—1.25 percent monthly—to finance the purchase of an automobile for $8,000. The bank has evaluated the credit application, and the transaction qualifies for a discounted 12 percent rate. By agreement, the bank retains 25 percent of the interest differential and transfers 75 percent to the dealer's account. The loan is written for three years, with 36 monthly payments of $277.32. The borrower pays $1,983.52 in total interest expense, of which $1,565.72 is credited to the bank, to yield 12 percent. Of the $417.80 interest differential, 75 percent is immediately allocated to the dealer, while 25 percent is retained in the reserve.

The reserve serves primarily to cover charge-offs. If the borrower defaults on the loan, the bank reduces the reserve by the unpaid principal outstanding. This ultimately lowers the dealer's profits because the reserve must be replenished. The reserve also covers rebates of unearned interest. For example, suppose that the dealer charges the borrower a 9 percent add-on rate for three years and the bank discounts it at a 7 percent add-on rate. With add-on interest, a lender receives some unearned interest if the borrower prepays. Interest rebates are commonly calculated according to the rule of 78s, which determines the fraction of total interest to be refunded at a point in time prior to maturity.[14] Applicable rebate percentages at the end of each year are determined at the bottom of Exhibit 12.10 in the second column, assuming 36 monthly payments. A three-year loan prepaid after two years indicates that 11.71 percent of the interest is unearned (88.29 percent is earned). If, in this example, a borrower prepays the entire loan after two years and the bank takes interest into income by the sum of the digits method, the bank must rebate $252.93 to the customer at the 9 percent add-on rate. Because the bank earns interest at the 7 percent add-on rate, its unearned interest income equals only $196.73 after two years. The $56.20 difference between the rebate amount and unearned bank interest would be charged against the reserve. The rule of 78s penalizes borrowers by assuming that earned interest is greater than that actually generated on a loan's outstanding principal. For short-term loans, however, the error is small.

There are many different reserve agreements, the most common being full recourse and no recourse arrangements. As the name suggests, full recourse agreements place the dealer at risk. If a borrower defaults, the dealer absorbs the loss by either reducing the reserve at the bank or paying off the note on the bank's terms. No recourse agreements, in contrast, stipulate that banks assume the credit risk. All losses are charged directly against bank earnings. Finally, some reserve arrangements involve limited recourse. A bank may negotiate a plan whereby dealers are liable for any losses only during the first three months of the loan. Although these losses are immediately charged to the reserve, later losses are absorbed by the bank. The above example represents a full recourse arrangement.

---

[14]According to the rule of 78s, the applicable rebate percentage equals the sum of the integers from one to the number of payments remaining after prepayment, divided by the sum of integers from one to the total number of payments in the loan. The number 78 equals the sum of integers 1 through 12 and thus serves as the denominator for rebate fractions on all 1-year, monthly payment loans. For example, a one-year loan with 12 monthly payments that is prepaid after the seventh month produces a rebate percentage of $(1 + 2 + 3 + 4 + 5)/(1 + 2 + \ldots + 12)$ = 19.23 percent. The lender would take 80.77 percent of the finance charge and rebate 19.23 percent to the borrower.

**EXHIBIT 12.10**  Role of Dealer Reserves in Indirect Lending: Automobile Paper

**Terms of the Dealer Agreement**
Bank buys dealer paper at a 12 percent rate. Dealer charges customers a higher rate (15 percent APR), with 25 percent of difference allocated to a reserve.

**Sample Automobile Loan**

Principal = $8,000
Maturity = 3 years, 36 monthly installments
Loan rate = 15% annual percentage rate (APR)
Monthly payment = $8,000/[(1/.0125) − (1/.0125(1.0125)$^{36}$)] = $277.32

**Allocation to the Dealer Reserve**

Total interest expense to customer = $1,983.52
Total interest income for bank = 1,565.72
Differential interest = $ 417.80

75% allocated to dealer: 0.75(417.80) = $313.35
25% allocated to reserve: 0.25(417.80) = $104.45

**Interest Refunds on Prepayments with Add-on Rates**
Loan is written on a precomputed basis, and bank accrues interest using "rule of 78s."*
Interest expense to customer = 0.09($8,000)(3) = $2,160
Interest income for bank = 0.07($8,000)(3) = 1,680
Differential interest = $ 480
75% allocated to dealer: 0.75($480) = $360
25% allocated to reserve: 0.25($480) = $120

| End of Year | Interest Earned* | Total | Bank | Difference |
|---|---|---|---|---|
| 1 | 54.96% | $1,187.14 | $ 923.33 | $263.81 |
| 2 | 33.33 | 719.33 | 559.94 | 159.99 |
| 3 | 11.71 | 252.93 | 196.73 | 56.20 |
| | 100.00% | $2,160.00 | $1,680.00 | $480.00 |

*Rule of 78s factors are 366/666, 222/666, and 78/666, respectively.

Banks prefer to deal with well-established retailers that generate paper (loans) of predictable quality. Banks vary the predetermined discount rate according to the dealer's reputation and the nature of the recourse agreement. They charge lower rates under full recourse plans because they assume less credit risk. Dealers that have the capability to assess credit quality prefer these arrangements because their profits are potentially greater. Under no recourse arrangements, banks charge higher rates and review each application carefully, as if the loan were a direct one.

## RECENT RISK AND RETURN CHARACTERISTICS OF CONSUMER LOANS

Historically, banks have viewed themselves as being either wholesale or retail institutions, focusing on commercial and individual customers, respectively. Recent developments, however, have blurred the distinction, as traditional wholesale banks have aggressively entered the consumer market. The attraction is twofold. First, competition for commercial customers narrowed commercial loan yields so that returns fell relative to potential risks. As indicated earlier, consumer loans now provide some of the highest net yields for banks. Second, developing loan and deposit relationships with individuals presumably represents a strategic response to deregulation. The removal of interest rate ceilings substantially reduced banks' core deposits by making high-balance customers more price sensitive. On average, individuals hold small balances and move deposit accounts less frequently, providing a more stable deposit base. Thus, liquidity risk declines as a bank's retail deposit base increases.

### REVENUES FROM CONSUMER LOANS

Banks earn significant revenues from interest on loans and associated fees. Because many usury ceilings have been eliminated or are no longer effective, banks can ration credit via price rather than by altering nonprice credit terms. This permits banks to quickly raise consumer loan rates as conditions require. When conditions permit, banks also delay lowering rates when their borrowing costs decline.

Consumer loan rates have been among the highest rates quoted at banks in recent years. Most consumer loans are made at fixed rates that banks do not change frequently. In a declining rate environment, consumer loans thus yield a larger spread relative to the bank's borrowing cost. When short-term rates rise, the spread narrows until banks raise loan rates. During the 1980s and early 1990s, the spread widened with the general decline in interest rates. However, the spread narrowed with the increased competition for consumer loans after the 1991 recession. With aggressive marketing campaigns at many banks and nonbank competitors, consumers are becoming increasingly sensitive to price such that credit card loan rates and fees now follow bank funding costs more closely.

Consumer groups still argue that consumer loan rates are too high, especially when the prime stays constant as other rates decline. They claim that lenders must be conspiring to fix prices. There are many reasons for large spreads, however. First, consumer loans are typically smaller in size and cost more to administer on a unit basis than commercial loans. Still, to eliminate "excess" profits that banks might earn when rates fall and the spread widens, noninterest costs from handling consumer loans would have to increase. There is no explanation for this. Second, consumer loans are longer term and often carry fixed rates. New car loans, for example, now average between four and five years until maturity. Banks include a premium in longer-term, fixed-rate loans to compensate for the risks of inflation and volatile funding costs. Third, individuals are more likely to default than businesses. The spread should be large enough to cover greater losses. Finally, many lenders still face state usury ceilings that may not be lifted when rates increase. These banks essentially make up for reduced profits during high-rate environments by keeping loan rates high when their financing costs fall. In response to this criticism, many banks now offer variable-rate credit cards as alternatives to fixed-rate cards.

In addition to interest income, banks generate substantial noninterest revenues from consumer loans. With traditional installment credit, banks often encourage borrowers to purchase credit life insurance on which the bank may earn premium income. Credit card operations also provide different types of fee income. Most banks now impose annual fees, ranging from $10 to $40 per customer, for the right to use the card and for access to related bank services. The customer essentially receives a line of credit with travel-related services, debit card privileges, and merchandise discounts also available. Banks bill cardholders monthly and expect the customer to repay the debt on a revolving credit basis with minimum payments equal to 5 percent of the outstanding balance. Historically, customers have had the option to repay the entire balance within a specified grace period, such as 25 days, and avoid any interest. Experience has demonstrated that just under one-third of all customers take advantage of this interest-free period. Many banks have eliminated this option by charging interest on each transaction from the date of posting. Banks often impose other fees for late payments and cash advances and may impose a fee if customers do not charge sufficient amounts.

## CONSUMER LOAN LOSSES

Losses on consumer loans are normally the highest among all categories of bank credit. This reflects highly cyclical patterns in personal income as well as extensive fraud. Losses are anticipated because of mass marketing efforts pursued by many lenders, particularly with credit cards. In the first quarter of 2005, the consumer credit card charge-off rate averaged 4.6 percent such that losses amounted to more than $12 billion, of which 80 percent has historically represented outright defaults and 20 percent fraud. Not surprisingly, both losses and delinquent accounts rise during recessions and decline during high-growth periods. Many lenders simply factor losses into their pricing as a part of doing business.

Credit card fraud arises out of the traditional lender-merchant relationship. In most cases, banks give merchants credit for sales long before they are reimbursed by cardholders. In 2001, the estimated time lag averaged around 36 days. This allows fraudulent merchants to set up a temporary operation, bill card-issuing banks for bogus sales, and escape with the proceeds before cardholders recognize billing errors.

To perpetrate the fraud, thieves need access to a retail business and cardholder account information. Frequently, the business front is nothing more than a telephone-based mail-order operation. Callers tell cardholders that they have won prizes but must provide account numbers, expiration dates, and billing addresses to collect. Alternatively, thieves can obtain credit card information by stealing credit cards or by copying information from carbons of card charges at various legitimate businesses. Thieves use the information to make purchases or receive cash advances during the 40-day lag period. Unsuspecting cardholders eventually discover that fraudulent charges appear on their monthly statements. By the time the card-issuing bank recognizes the fraud, the thief has closed down the business and moved to greener pastures.

## INTEREST RATE AND LIQUIDITY RISK WITH CONSUMER CREDIT

The majority of consumer loans are priced at fixed rates. New auto loans typically carry four-year maturities, and credit card loans exhibit an average 15- to 18-month maturity. In most cases, the borrower can prepay a loan without any penalty when rates decline. This creates difficult problems in trying to match fund the consumer portfolio.

Bankers have responded in two ways. First, they price more consumer loans on a floating-rate basis. Such policies have been relatively successful in the mortgage market but require substantial discounts below fixed-rate loans to attract interest. Second, commercial and investment banks have created a secondary market in consumer loans that allows loan originators to sell a package of loans to investors with longer-term holding periods. The first efforts appeared in early 1985, when Marine Midland Bank, in conjunction with Salomon Brothers, sold automobile loans to secondary market investors. Salomon Brothers sold the loans in the form of collateralized securities, conveniently labeled certificates of automobile receivables (CARs). As with mortgage banking operations, Marine Midland agreed to service the loans for which it received servicing income. Banks now routinely sell certificates supported by credit card receivables and other consumer credit as a means of moving assets off the balance sheet, reducing capital requirements, and increasing noninterest income.

## SUMMARY

Commercial banks aggressively compete for consumer loans for a variety of reasons. For many types of loans, net yields exceed those on commercial loans. Default rates are above those on other loans, but the gross yield charged more than compensates for the higher losses. When rates decline, net profits on credit card and other fixed-rate loans rise sharply because consumer loan rates are relatively sticky. Individuals also typically maintain deposit accounts where they borrow. Retail deposits are relatively low cost and not nearly as interest rate sensitive as commercial deposits. Thus, the more liquidity risk is reduced, the greater the volume of consumer deposits is at a bank. Consumer loans, however, exhibit greater interest rate risk than commercial loans. Most are fixed-rate loans, and many carry three- to five-year maturities. Banks wishing to reduce interest rate risk often try to match fund these loans with longer-term deposits.

Loan officers consider the same basic issues applicable to commercial loans when evaluating the riskiness of consumer loans: use of proceeds, size of loan, cash flow repayment sources, collateral, and the borrower's character. The fundamental difference is that personal financial statements are generally unaudited and it is more difficult to forecast net cash flow. Evaluation procedures may involve the subjective interpretation of financial information provided directly by an individual on a credit application and obtained indirectly from credit bureaus and references. Alternatively, banks may use credit scoring models based on a numerical assessment of an acceptable-risk borrower's profile. This chapter introduces a basic credit scoring model and describes the risk and return features of various types of consumer loans, such as credit card transactions and the purchase of dealer paper. It also summarizes the factors that the most popular models incorporate in their scoring systems. A significant trend is that credit scoring has moved to small business loans. If such loans can be successfully securitized, they may become commodities more like mortgages and their yields will decline. This will be especially problematic for community banks where small business loans often account for a substantial portion of annual profits.

### QUESTIONS

1. Explain how an installment loan differs from revolving credit in terms of risk and the nature of the return to the lender.

2. What are the major expenses associated with making consumer loans? What is the average size of consumer installment loans at small banks? How does loan size affect loan rates that banks charge on consumer loans?

3. Examine credit card loss rates and personal bankruptcy filings in Exhibit 12.3. What might explain the increase in both measures after 1994 in a period when economic growth in the United States was strong and unemployment was low and again in 2004? What will likely occur to losses and personal bankruptcies during the next recession?

4. Why are home equity loans attractive today relative to before the Tax Reform Act of 1986? How do some banks tie home equity loans to their credit card? How are home equity lines generally priced (what rates apply)?

5. Explain how a direct installment loan differs from an indirect installment loan.

6. What are the key provisions of the Equal Credit Opportunity Act? Why was such legislation necessary?

7. Describe how a bank should apply an objective credit scoring model when evaluating consumer loan requests. Given the information in Exhibits 12.7 and 12.8 and information in the text, indicate why you would or would not approve Camile Groome's loan request.

8. Suppose that four college students check their FICO scores and discover the information listed below. Describe how lenders might price loans to borrowers with lower scores versus borrowers with higher scores in terms of rates and fees charged.

|  | Score |
|---|---|
| Vanessa | 790 |
| Martin | 550 |
| Jorge | 685 |
| Heather | 505 |

9. What different sources of revenue are available from credit card lending? Outline the clearing process with a credit card transaction. What is the biggest risk in credit card loans?

10. The differential between fixed-rate credit card rates and a bank's cost of funds typically varies over the interest rate cycle. What is this relationship, and why does it exist? Does the differential between commercial loan rates and a bank's cost of funds behave similarly?

11. Calculate the effective annual rate on each of the following loans:

    a. A $5,000 loan for two years, 10 percent simple annual interest with principal repayment at the end of the second year

    b. A $5,000 loan for two years, 10 percent add-on interest, paid in 24 equal monthly installments

    c. A $5,000 loan to be repaid at the end of two years, 10 percent discount rate

12. What is the purpose of a dealer reserve in indirect lending? When is a bank at risk with indirect loans?

13. What is the goal of the Community Reinvestment Act? How do regulators enforce its provisions?

14. Subprime loans have higher loss rates than many other types of loans. Explain why lenders offer subprime loans. Describe the characteristics of the typical borrower in a subprime consumer loan.

15. Explain generally how smart cards, debit cards, and prepaid cards differ from traditional credit cards.

## PROBLEMS

### I. BUYING PAPER FROM A USED CAR DEALER

Dealer reserves in indirect lending serve to protect a bank against loan losses and prepayments. Suppose that a bank enters into an agreement with a used car dealer to buy dealer paper at a 5.5 percent add-on rate, and retain 25 percent of the interest differential relative to the rate the dealer charges the car buyer. Under the agreement, the bank charges losses and prepayments against the reserve, transferring any excess to the dealer periodically. Interest rebates on prepayments are computed according to the rule of 78s.

Consider the case where the dealer charges a customer a 7.5 percent add-on rate for the purchase of a $15,000 automobile to be financed over 36 months. Calculate the effective annual percentage rate (APR), the total interest expense to the customer, the bank's share, and the interest differential allocated to the dealer reserve. Suppose that the customer prepays the entire loan after 13 months. Determine how much interest the bank must rebate to the car buyer and any charge to the dealer reserve.

### II. CREDIT REPORT

1. Examine the sample credit report provided in Exhibit 12.6. From a lender's perspective, explain the importance of information regarding:

    a. Number and type of businesses that report credit information

    b. Date the account was opened

    c. Date of last activity on the account

    d. Highest credit amount and terms

    e. Balance outstanding, amount past due, and status

2. How would you interpret the information provided for John Doe in the section of the report on courthouse records?

## ACTIVITIES

### I. CREDIT CARDS

Collect the following information on three nationally advertised credit cards and three locally offered credit cards. You can use the Internet to search for the best terms.

1. Annual fee

2. Interest rate and grace period

3. Additional services to credit availability

Is there a pattern of differences and similarities between the national versus local cards? Which card appeals most to you? Explain why.

### II. CREDIT REPORTING AND SECURITY

Go to the Web sites http://www.myvesta.com and http://www.fairisaac.com. Review the most recent delinquency rates by FICO score. What differential interest rates do lenders charge for different FICO scores? Provide reasoning for differential rates.

# PART VI

# MANAGING THE INVESTMENT PORTFOLIO AND SPECIAL TOPICS

# Managing the Investment Portfolio

*The world of bank investments has changed dramatically since 1986. Due to changes in the tax laws, banks no longer find most municipal bonds attractive so they shifted into other investments. Today, many banks concentrate their investments in taxable instruments, such as federal agency bonds, mortgage-backed securities, and corporate bonds. Each of these has sharply different risk and return features.*

*The focus on new investment instruments has presented both problems and opportunities. Problems arise because many banks purchase securities without fully understanding their risk and yield features. For example, many banks routinely purchase large amounts of callable agency and mortgage-backed securities in a variety of forms. Unfortunately, the call feature of the agency securities and the prepayment option underlying mortgage-backed securities make it extremely difficult to accurately forecast both the magnitude of interest and principal payments and when they will be received. In this case, the promised yield may be far different from any realized yield. How then does an investor understand the risk and return trade-off? To further complicate the investment decision opportunities exist with other innovative investment alternatives, such as mutual funds and securities backed by car loans, leases, and credit card receivables.*

*This chapter examines why banks own marketable securities. It initially provides an overview of the basic features of securities held in the investment portfolio and introduces policy guidelines that should help appropriate investment decisions. It then critiques various investment strategies that banks follow related to the maturity/duration choice, changing rates over the business cycle, the impact of embedded options, and differential income tax treatment across different types of securities.*

**M**any commercial banks concentrate their asset management efforts on meeting loan customers' credit needs. Because this involves detailed credit analysis and direct negotiation of terms with borrowers, they maintain a large staff of loan officers. Managing investment securities often plays a secondary role, especially at small banks. Banks operate as price-takers because security yields are normally determined nationally in the money and capital markets. Basic investment decisions, including the amounts and types of securities to purchase, can be determined by senior management and implemented by a smaller staff.

The securities activities of large and small banks are fundamentally different. Historically, small banks have purchased securities and held them until maturity. In many cases, they work with large correspondent banks or bankers banks in deciding which securities to buy and how many. Large banks, in contrast, not only buy securities for their own portfolios, but also trade them more actively prior to maturity in an effort to make a profit. They also may manage a securities trading account and may have an investment banking subsidiary that helps municipalities and businesses underwrite securities. Underwriting securities involves helping the issuer place debt securities and equities with investors.

Historically, bank regulators have limited the risks associated with banks owning securities. Investment policy guidelines thus focus on controlling credit and interest rate risk within the securities portfolio. Regulators generally prohibit banks from purchasing common stock for income purposes and effectively limit investments in debt instruments to investment grade securities (instruments designated as bonds rated Baa or above).[1] To provide greater liquidity, many banks keep security maturities or durations short term because of the lower price volatility. Some banks pursue passive investment strategies, under which managers react to events, rather than active strategies. Active strategies involve buying and selling securities prior to maturity for profit in anticipation of changing economic conditions.

In recent years, an increasing number of banks have pursued active strategies in managing investments in the search for higher yields. Many managers now expect the investment portfolio to generate more interest income and periodic gains from security sales prior to maturity. Consequently, they manage their portfolio maturity/duration and composition more aggressively. The following analysis describes the function of bank trading accounts and characteristics of the most popular taxable and tax-exempt securities, as well as outlines the objectives and structure of the investment portfolio. It identifies the key facets of a bank's formal investment policy statement, then critiques specific strategies related to: 1) the maturity/duration choice; 2) how the business cycle affects interest rates; 3) when embedded options will be exercised and the value of the options; and 4) the differential tax treatment of interest income.

## DEALER OPERATIONS AND THE SECURITIES TRADING ACCOUNT

When banks buy securities they must indicate the underlying objective for accounting purposes. The alternative classifications include held-to-maturity, available-for-sale, and trading purposes. **Held-to-maturity** securities are recorded at amortized cost on the balance sheet, with changes in value having no impact on the income statement. Unless the underlying quality of the securities changes dramatically, banks must hold these securities until they mature. **Available-for-sale** securities are reported at market value. Any increases or decreases in market value associated with interest rate changes are balanced by an entry in stockholders' equity that recognizes unrealized gains and losses on securities. Again, there is no income statement impact. Banks can sell these securities at any time. Securities held for **trading** purposes are part of a trading account. A **trading account** represents an inventory of securities that a bank holds for resale to other investors. The securities can be of any type including Treasury, agency, and municipal securities, but the bank expects to own them only briefly until a long-term buyer is found. Such securities are listed separately on a bank's balance sheet as trading account securities and are marked-to-market. The bank profits from this activity by buying the securities at prices below the sales price, which is referred to as a trading profit and appears on the income statement.

In this capacity, banks operate both as primary dealers with the Federal Reserve and as market makers with other participants. As a primary dealer, a bank (or bank subsidiary) normally buys U.S. Treasury securities at auction and in the secondary market and sells the securities to its customers. The Federal Reserve System trades only with primary dealers through its New York Bank when implementing open market purchases and sales. As market makers, banks perform the same service with U.S. Treasury, agency, and selected municipal securities, trading with all interested parties.

Banks perform three basic functions within their trading activities. First, they offer investment advice and assistance to customers managing their own portfolios. With their market expertise they can help a smaller bank determine the appropriate type of investment and select specific instruments. If a customer needs to sell a security, they stand willing to buy. Second, they maintain an inventory of securities for possible sale to investors. The willingness to buy and sell securities is called making a market. Third, traders speculate on short-term interest rate movements by taking positions in various securities.

Banks earn profits from their trading activities in several ways. When making a market, they price securities at an expected positive spread, charging a higher price (lower interest rate) on securities sold than the price paid on securities purchased. Thus, a customer who contacts a bank's trading department will get two price quotes for the same instrument: a **bid price,** reflecting what the dealer is willing to pay; and an **ask** or **offer price,** representing the price at which a dealer will sell. Profits arise from a positive spread between the ask minus the bid prices.

Traders can also earn profits if they correctly anticipate interest rate movements. This is accomplished by taking long (ownership) and short (borrowed) positions consistent with their expectations or by adjusting

---

[1]In certain situations, such as when common stock is taken as collateral against a loan, commercial banks can own equities. However, they must liquidate equities within a reasonable period of time. Banks can also own noninvestment-grade securities, but they must show the securities are comparable in quality to similar investment-grade instruments.

maturities on repurchase agreements (RPs). Both long and short positions are normally financed via RPs. When traders expect interest rates to decline (prices to rise), they want to own securities, so they take a long position in selected instruments. In most cases, overnight financing is used so that the bank earns net interest from the spread between the yield on the asset owned and the cost of financing, as well as being able to sell the asset for a price above that initially paid. When traders expect interest rates to rise, they want to sell securities or go short (sell securities not owned) to avoid holding assets that depreciate in value. Traders typically negotiate reverse RPs to obtain securities to short, and earn interest that varies daily with financing costs on the short position. The bank profits if rates rise and traders buy back the securities shorted at a lower price than that initially paid.

## OBJECTIVES OF THE INVESTMENT PORTFOLIO

A bank's investment portfolio differs markedly from a trading account as investment securities are held to meet one of six general objectives:

1. Safety or preservation of capital
2. Liquidity
3. Yield
4. Credit risk diversification
5. Help in managing interest rate risk exposure
6. Assistance in meeting pledging requirements

Not surprisingly, securities with different return and risk features meet each objective differently, so that the average portfolio is quite varied in terms of composition and price sensitivity. Banks generally hold these securities for longer periods of time than trading account securities. Periodic interest payments appear on the income statement as interest income, while any gains or losses from sale prior to maturity appear separately as an income or expense item.

### ACCOUNTING FOR INVESTMENT SECURITIES

Decisions regarding the types of securities that banks buy and the length of time they are held in portfolio are driven, in part, by market value accounting rules that were put in place effective January 1994. These rules link the presumed motive for buying investment securities to the accounting for value on the balance sheet and for income on the income statement. Specifically, the Financial Accounting Standards Board's Statement 115 (FASB 115) requires banks to divide their securities holdings into three categories—Trading, Held-to-maturity, and Available-for-Sale—with the following accounting treatment:

- Trading: Securities purchased with the intent to sell in the near term; carried at market value on the balance sheet with unrealized gains and losses included in income.
- Held-to-Maturity: Securities purchased with the intent to hold to final maturity; carried at amortized cost (historical cost adjusted for principal payments) on the balance sheet; unrealized gains and losses have no income statement impact.
- Available-for-Sale: Securities that are not classified in either of the previous categories; carried at market value on the balance sheet with unrealized gains and losses included as a component of capital.

The distinction between motives is important because of the accounting impact. Remember that changes in interest rates can dramatically affect the market value of a fixed-rate security. A fixed-rate bond without options will sell at par if the market rate equals the coupon rate on the bond. If the market rate is above (below) the coupon rate, the market value is below (above) par value. This difference between market value and par value equals the unrealized gain or loss on the security, assuming a purchase at par value.

$$\text{Market value} - \text{par value} = \text{Unrealized gain (if positive)}$$
$$= \text{Unrealized loss (if negative)} \qquad \textbf{(13.1)}$$

If a bank plans to hold a security to maturity, changes in interest rates after purchase—and thus unrealized gains or losses—do not affect the accounting for the security either on the balance sheet or income statement. However, FASB 115 requires that banks carry all other securities at market value. Thus, if rates rise and there is an unrealized loss, the value of the security will decline on the balance sheet. For trading securities, the bank will report a loss on the income statement; for securities available for sale, the bank will report a direct reduction in its capital account. If rates fall and there is an unrealized gain, the value of the security will rise on the balance sheet with a corresponding increase in earnings (trading) or a bank's capital account (available for sale).[2] Importantly, the change in bank capital due to unrealized gains and losses on securities available for sale does not affect risk-based capital ratios.

The primary impact is that a bank's net income and equity capital position will be more volatile when securities are accounted for in market value terms. Investors see volatility as inherently bad, and often require a risk premium as compensation. A bank's cost of capital will likely be higher with market value accounting, to the extent that investors do not already incorporate market values in their analysis.

## SAFETY OR PRESERVATION OF CAPITAL

Banks assume considerable default risk in their commercial and consumer loan portfolios. They typically balance this by accepting much lower default risk in their investment portfolios. Thus, a primary objective is to preserve capital by purchasing securities where there is only a small risk of principal loss. Regulators encourage this policy by requiring that banks concentrate their holdings in investment-grade securities, those rated Baa or higher. When they buy nonrated securities, banks must maintain a credit file that indicates that management periodically evaluates the borrowers' ability to meet debt service requirements, and this profile is consistent with an investment-grade credit. Still, banks occasionally report losses on defaulted securities.

## LIQUIDITY

Commercial banks purchase debt securities to help meet liquidity requirements. Many banks, particularly small institutions that do not have ready access to the money and capital markets to borrow funds, rely on selling securities if a liquidity shortage appears. Because securities are more marketable than most commercial and consumer loans, banks often designate a portion of their investment portfolio as a liquidity reserve. This reliance on securities for liquidity has become less important as banks have joined the Federal Home Loan Bank system and rely on FHLB advances.

As indicated in Chapter 8, securities with maturities under one year can be readily sold for cash near par value and are classified as liquid investments. In reality, most securities with a market value above book value can also be quickly converted to cash, regardless of maturity, because managers are willing to sell them. Although at first glance a security's market value may not appear to affect its liquidity, in practice most banks choose not to sell securities if their market values are below book values. The rationale is that they would have to report securities losses on the income statement, which would reduce net income and the bank's aggregate profit ratios. Managers are more willing to sell securities at a gain when market values exceed book values, and thus artificially inflate periodic net income.[3]

When evaluating the potential liquidity in a bank's investment portfolio, most managers simply compare a security's current market value with its book value. If it trades at a premium, it is liquid. Consider the four securities summarized in Exhibit 13.1. As indicated, the bonds were purchased 6 to 11 years before the statement data. Because market interest rates changed significantly during the interim, the Treasury note and the State of Illinois municipal sell at a premium, while the other two sell at a discount. If the bank sold the premium bonds on September 30, 2005, it would report a gain from securities sales under noninterest income in its income statement. If the bank held the premium bonds but sold either of the discount bonds, it would report a loss from securities sales. Because securities losses lower reported net income in the short run, most banks are unwilling to sell securities at a discount.

## YIELD

To be attractive, investment securities must pay a reasonable return for the risks assumed. The return may come in the form of price appreciation or periodic coupon interest. It may be fully taxable, or exempt from federal income taxes and/or state and local income taxes. Chapter 4 documents how yields are quoted on different types of securities and explains why yields differ across securities depending on default risk, marketability, tax treatment, maturity, and whether the securities carry call or put features. Clearly, bank managers must evaluate each security to determine whether its yield is attractive given its other features and the overall profile of the bank's portfolio. Portfolio managers who actively trade securities generally look at total return, not yield to maturity, when evaluating the risk and return trade-off.

---

[2]The presumed objective of market value accounting is to improve investors' and regulators' ability to evaluate the economic worth of a bank. Regulators see the added benefit of forcing banks to more closely monitor how much interest rate risk they assume in their investment portfolios. If banks choose to minimize the adverse accounting effects, they will likely take less risk by buying shorter-term securities.

[3]The costs and benefits of selling securities for a gain versus a loss and reinvesting the proceeds are discussed later in the section on security swaps. In general, selling to realize short-term gains is shortsighted because a bank sacrifices greater longer-term cash flow.

**EXHIBIT 13.1**

Investment Portfolio for a Hypothetical Commercial Bank

Current Date: September 30, 2005

| Purchase Date | Book Value | Description | Annual Coupon Income | Market Value |
|---|---|---|---|---|
| 12/15/95 | $4,000,000 | $4,000,000 par value U.S. Treasury note at 8%, due 11/15/08 | $320,000 | $4,099,000 |
| 10/15/95 | 2,000,000 | $2,000,000 par value Federal National Mortgage Association bonds at 8.75%, due 10/15/10 | 175,000 | 1,824,000 |
| 6/6/99 | 500,000 | $500,000 par value Allegheny County, PA, A-rated general obligations at 5.15%, due 3/1/11 | 25,750 | 482,500 |
| 10/1/94 | 1,000,000 | $1,000,000 par value State of Illinois Aaa-rated general obligations at 7%, due 10/1/10 | 70,000 | 1,190,000 |

## DIVERSIFY CREDIT RISK

The diversification objective is closely linked to the safety objective and difficulties that banks have with diversifying their loan portfolios. Too often, particularly at small banks, loans are concentrated in one industry, such as agriculture, energy, or real estate, which reflects the specific economic conditions of the bank's trade area. In these situations, the loan portfolio is not adequately diversified even when loans are not concentrated among single borrowers because values will deteriorate if conditions adversely affect the industry in question. Banks view the securities portfolio as an opportunity to spread credit risk outside their geographic region and across other industries.

## HELP MANAGE INTEREST RATE RISK EXPOSURE

Investment securities are very flexible instruments in managing a bank's overall interest rate risk exposure. Although some are private placements, most are standardized contracts purchased through brokers. Thus, banks can select terms that meet their specific needs without fear of antagonizing the borrower. They can readily sell the security if their needs change. For example, if management chooses to become more liability sensitive in anticipation of falling rates, the bank can easily and quickly lengthen the maturity or duration of its securities portfolio. Contrast this with the difficulty in adjusting commercial or consumer loan terms, or calling a loan with undesirable pricing features. As a consequence, managers can change the composition and price sensitivity of the investment portfolio at the margin to help achieve the desired rate-sensitivity profile.

## PLEDGING REQUIREMENTS

By law, commercial banks must pledge collateral against certain types of liabilities. Banks that obtain financing via RPs essentially pledge some of their securities' holdings against this debt. Similarly, banks that borrow at the discount window or from the Federal Home Loan Bank must collateralize the loan with qualifying assets. While some loans meet the collateral requirements, most banks pledge Treasury securities that are already registered at the Federal Reserve in bookkeeping form, for discount window borrowings. For advances, banks typically pledge real estate–related loans. Finally, banks that accept public deposits must also pledge government securities against the uninsured portion of deposits. Under federal regulations, 100 percent of uninsured federal deposits must be secured with Treasury and agency obligations valued at par or with municipals valued at 80 to 90 percent of par for collateral purposes. Pledging requirements for state and local government deposits vary according to specific regulations established by each deposit holder. In many instances, the public depositor values local municipal securities above par while valuing Treasury and agency securities at less than par for collateral purposes. The intent is to increase the attractiveness of local issues to potential bank investors.

## COMPOSITION OF THE INVESTMENT PORTFOLIO

A commercial bank's investment portfolio consists of many different types of instruments. Money market instruments with short maturities and durations include Treasury bills, large negotiable CDs and Eurodollars, bankers' acceptances, commercial paper, security repurchase agreements, and tax and bond anticipation notes. Capital market

**EXHIBIT 13.2**   Composition of U.S. Commercial Bank Investments: 1965–2004*

### A. All Banks Over Time

| | Percentage of Total Financial Assets | | | | | | | |
|---|---|---|---|---|---|---|---|---|
| | **1970** | **1975** | **1980** | **1985** | **1990** | **1995** | **2000** | **2004** |
| U.S. Treasury securities | 12.1% | 9.8% | 7.8% | 8.3% | 5.4% | 6.2% | 2.9% | 1.3% |
| Agency securities | 2.7 | 3.9 | 4.1 | 3.2 | 8.4 | 10.4 | 11.2 | 12.9 |
| Municipal securities | 13.6 | 11.6 | 10.0 | 9.7 | 3.5 | 2.1 | 1.8 | 1.7 |
| Corporate & foreign securities | 0.6 | 0.9 | 0.5 | 1.0 | 2.7 | 2.5 | 4.1 | 6.6 |
| | 29.0% | 26.2% | 22.4% | 22.2% | 20.0% | 21.2% | 20.0% | 22.5% |
| Total Financial Assets | $517 | $886 | $1,482 | $2,375 | $3,334 | $4,488 | $6,469 | $8,487 |

### B. Percentage of Total Consolidated Assets, December 31, 2003

**Commercial Banks Ranked by Assets**

| | 10 Largest | 11–100 Largest | 101–1,000 Largest | >1,000 Largest |
|---|---|---|---|---|
| **Investment securities** | | | | |
| U.S. Treasury securities | 0.8% | 1.0% | 1.0% | 0.9% |
| U.S. gov't. agency & corporate securities | 9.2 | 13.0 | 17.0 | 16.2 |
| Private mortgage-backed securities | 1.1 | 2.1 | 0.9 | 0.2 |
| Municipal securities | 0.6 | 1.0 | 3.0 | 4.7 |
| Other securities | 3.4 | 2.9 | 2.0 | 1.1 |
| Equities | 0.2 | 0.2 | 0.4 | 0.3 |
| Total investment securities | 15.3 | 20.2 | 24.3 | 23.4 |
| **Trading account securities** | 5.9 | 1.1 | 0.1 | 0.0 |
| **Total** | 21.2% | 21.3% | 24.4% | 23.4% |

*Data are for December 31 each year.

**Holdings in billions of dollars

Sources: *Flow of Funds Accounts,* Board of Governors of the Federal Reserve System; *Federal Reserve Buletin,* Board of Governors.

instruments with longer maturities and durations include long-term U.S. Treasury securities, obligations of U.S. government agencies, municipal bonds, mortgage-backed securities backed both by government and private guarantees, corporate bonds, foreign bonds, and other asset-backed securities. At the end of 2004, U.S. banks in the aggregate owned more than $1.4 trillion of fixed-income investment securities and another $35 billion of corporate equities and mutual fund shares. They also held almost $50 billion of securities in inventory for trading account purposes.

The top part of Exhibit 13.2 documents the changing composition of bank investments from 1970 through 2004 in four broad categories by issuer. There are several obvious trends. First, the investment portfolio consistently fell as a fraction of total bank assets from a high of 29 percent in 1970 to just 20 percent in 1990 where it has remained relatively constant. This coincides with an increase in the proportionate contribution of loans. Second, municipal securities were the dominant bank investment through 1985, after which bank holdings fell sharply. As discussed later, this reflects the impact of the Tax Reform Act of 1986, which induced banks to withdraw as investors in most municipal securities. In 2004 less than 2 percent of bank financial assets were municipals. Third, since 1970 banks have slowly reduced their proportionate investment in Treasury securities to where they represent less than 3 percent of financial assets in 2004. Finally, both agency and corporate/foreign securities increased sharply after 1985 as a fraction of financial assets, because banks sought out alternatives to municipals following the Tax Reform Act of 1986. The growth in agency securities is due to the growth of both callable bonds and mortgage-backed securities, which have far different characteristics than traditional bank investments.

The bottom part of the exhibit indicates the proportionate security holdings of different-sized U.S. banks at the end of 2003. Note that the securities are divided into those held for investment purposes and trading account securities. Not surprisingly, the 10 largest banks account for most of the trading account securities because they are generally active market makers. For investment securities, the figures document significant differences, including the fact that the proportionate size of the portfolio decreases with bank size, ranging from more than 24 percent of total assets at the second smallest group of banks to just over 15 percent at the 10 largest banks. This is not surprising because smaller banks rely more heavily on securities to meet liquidity needs. Money center and large regional banks routinely borrow in the money markets to help meet deposit outflows and finance incremental loan demand. In addition, U.S. government agency securities, which include most mortgage-backed securities, are the dominant category at banks of all sizes comprising from 9.2 percent to 17 percent of assets. The combination of U.S. Treasury and agency securities accounts for approximately 75 percent of the smallest banks' investment securities and 65 percent of the 10 largest banks' investment securities holdings. Municipals represent significant investments at all but the 100 largest banks. The concentration in municipals reflects the high demand for tax-exempt interest income at all banks. The ratio of municipals to total assets is greater at small banks because they do not use other means to shelter income. Large banks shelter proportionately more income via tax credits and accelerated depreciation generated from foreign operations and leasing activities. Other securities, including corporate and foreign bonds and equities, are significant at the 1,000 largest banks, but comprise a small portion of the investment portfolio at the smallest banks.

## CHARACTERISTICS OF TAXABLE SECURITIES

Banks own a substantial amount of securities on which the interest is subject to federal income taxes. In order to meet liquidity and pledging requirements and earn a reasonable return, banks hold significant amounts of government and corporate securities that mature within one year, labeled money market instruments. Most are highly liquid because they are issued by well-known borrowers and because a deep secondary market exists. Banks own a larger amount of longer-term taxable securities, labeled capital market instruments. The following sections describe the basic characteristics of each. Exhibit 13.3 presents key terminology.

### MONEY MARKET INVESTMENTS

**REPURCHASE AGREEMENTS (RPS OR REPOS).** RPs involve a loan between two parties, with one typically either a securities dealer or commercial bank. The lender or investor buys securities from the borrower and simultaneously agrees to sell the securities back at a later date at an agreed-upon price plus interest. The transaction represents a short-term loan collateralized by the securities because the borrower receives the principal in the form of immediately available funds, while the lender earns interest on the investment. If the borrower defaults, the lender gets title to the securities.

Consider an overnight RP transaction for $1 million at 5.4 percent between a bank as lender and a foreign government as borrower. RP rates are quoted on an add-on basis assuming a 360-day year. The bank would book an asset, securities purchased under agreement to resell, and would lose deposit balances held at the Fed equal to $1 million. After one day the transaction would reverse, as deposit balances would increase by $1 million and the RP loan would disappear; also, the foreign government would pay the bank $150 in interest.

$$\text{Interest} = \$1,000,000 \times (.054/360) = \$150 \qquad \textbf{(13.2)}$$

If the foreign government defaults, the bank retains the securities as collateral on the loan. This transaction is technically labeled a reverse RP because the bank is the lender while another party is the borrower. In a regular RP a bank or securities dealer sells securities under an agreement to repurchase at a later date, and thus represents the borrower. Every RP transaction involves both a regular RP and reverse RP, depending on whether it is viewed from the lender's or borrower's perspective.[4]

Banks operate on both sides of the RP market as borrowers and lenders. Although any securities can serve as collateral, most RPs involve Treasury or U.S. agency securities. Typically small banks lend funds aggressively in the RP market because they operate their reserves position more conservatively with positive excess reserves, and own proportionately more of these securities available as collateral. Every RP transaction is negotiated separately between parties. The minimum denomination is generally $1 million with maturities ranging from one day to one year. The rate on one-day RPs is referred to as the overnight RP rate, which plays an important role in arbitrage transactions associated with financial futures and options. Longer-term transactions are referred to as term RPs and the associated rate is referred to as the term RP rate. The RP rate varies from 15 to 50 basis points below the comparable federal funds rate because RP transactions are secured.

**TREASURY BILLS.** At the end of 2004, commercial banks owned approximately $175 billion in securities issued directly by the United States. Although no precise breakdown is available, banks are significant investors in both short-term Treasury bills and longer-term Treasury notes and bonds. Banks find Treasuries attractive because they pay market rates of interest, are free of default risk, and can be easily sold in the secondary market. Because they are default risk–free, Treasury securities pay a lower pretax yield than otherwise comparable taxable securities. They carry a tax advantage, however, because all interest is subject to federal income taxes but is exempt from

---

[4]Market terminology for RP transactions is viewed from the perspective of the Federal Reserve's relationship with securities dealers or banks. Reverse RPs are formally labeled matched sales-purchase agreements because they involve the Fed initially selling securities to banks or securities dealers to contract the reserve base, then buying them back.

**EXHIBIT 13.3** Important Terminology

**ARM:** Adjustable rate mortgage—a mortgage where the contractual interest rate is tied to some index of interest rates and changes when supply and demand conditions alter the underlying index.

**CBO:** Collateralized bond obligation—a security backed by a pool of noninvestment grade (junk) bonds.

**CD:** Certificate of deposit—a large, negotiable time deposit issued by a financial institution.

**CMO:** Collateralized mortgage obligation—a security backed by a pool of mortgages and structured to fall within an estimated maturity range (tranche) based on the timing of allocated interest and principal payments on the underlying mortgages.

**Conventional Mortgage:** A mortgage or deed of trust that is not obtained under a government-insured program.

**FHA:** Federal Housing Administration—a federal agency that insures mortgages.

**FHLMC:** Federal Home Loan Mortgage Corporation (Freddie Mac)—a private corporation, operating with an implicit federal guarantee, that buys mortgages financed largely by mortgage-backed securities.

**FNMA:** Federal National Mortgage Association (Fannie Mae)—a private corporation, operating with an implicit federal guarantee, that buys mortgages financed largely by mortgage-backed securities.

**GNMA:** Government National Mortgage Association (Ginnie Mae)—a government entity that buys mortgages for low-income housing and guarantees mortgage-backed securities issued by private lenders.

**GO:** General obligation bond—municipal bond issued by a state or local government where the promised principal and interest payments are backed by the full faith, credit, and taxing authority of the issuer.

**GSE:** Government sponsored enterprise—a quasi-public federal agency that is federally sponsored, but privately owned. Examples include the Farm Credit Bank, Federal Home Loan Banks (FHLBs), Federal Home Loan Mortgage Corporation (Freddie Mac), and Federal National Mortgage Association (Fannie Mae).

**IDB:** Industrial development bond—a municipal bond issued by a state or local government political subdivision in which the proceeds are used to finance expenditures of private corporations.

**IO:** Interest-only security representing the interest portion of a stripped Treasury or stripped mortgage-backed security.

**MBS:** Mortgage-backed security—a security that evidences an undivided interest in the ownership of a pool of mortgages.

**PAC:** Planned amortization class CMO—a security that is retired according to a planned amortization schedule, while payments to other classes of securities are slowed or accelerated. The objective is to ensure that PACs exhibit highly predictable maturities and cash flows.

**PO:** Principal-only security representing the principal portion of a stripped Treasury or stripped mortgage-backed security.

**Revenue Bond:** A municipal bond in which the promised principal and interest payments are backed by revenues from whatever facility or project the bond proceeds are used to finance.

**RP:** Repurchase agreement (Repo)—an agreement by one party to buy back, under certain terms, the item that is originally sold to a second party. The underlying item is generally a U.S. Treasury, agency, or mortgage-backed security.

**Secured Investor Trusts:** Bonds secured by the cash flow from pieces of CMOs or related securities placed in trust. In most cases the securities are high-risk instruments subject to substantial prepayment risk. The securities are labeled "kitchen-sink bonds" because they are backed by everything but the kitchen sink.

**Tranche:** The principal amount related to a specific class of stated maturities on a CMO.

**VA:** Veterans Administration—a federal agency that insures mortgages.

**Z-Tranche:** The final class of securities in a CMO exhibiting the longest maturity and greatest price volatility. These securities often accrue interest until all other classes are retired.

state and local income taxes. In addition, the primary and secondary market for Treasury instruments is very competitive. Dealers keep bid-ask spreads low and maintain substantial inventories. This ease of purchase and sale lowers transactions costs and makes Treasuries highly liquid.

Treasury bills are marketable obligations of the U.S. Treasury that carry original maturities of one year or less. They exist only in book-entry form, with the investor simply holding a dated receipt. Treasury bills are discount instruments, and the entire return is represented by price appreciation as maturity approaches.

Each week the Treasury auctions bills with 13-week and 26-week maturities. Investors submit either competitive or noncompetitive bids. With a competitive bid, the purchaser indicates the maturity amount of bills desired and the discount price offered. Noncompetitive bidders indicate only how much they want to acquire. They agree to pay the average price posted for all competitive offers that the Treasury accepts but are limited to no more than $500,000 in maturity value. The auctions are closed in that sealed bids must be submitted by 1:30 P.M. each Monday, the normal sale date. The Treasury accepts all noncompetitive bids. It then ranks the competitive bids from the highest discounted price offered to the lowest price and accepts bids until the desired financing objective is met. Noncompetitive bidders then pay the average price of the accepted competitive bids.

Banks participate in the auction process in two ways: by buying bills directly for their own portfolios, or by buying bills for inventory in their securities trading activity. Treasury bills are purchased on a discount basis so that the investor's income equals price appreciation. As with most money market yields, the Treasury bill discount rate (dr) is quoted in terms of a 360-day year, as indicated below:

$$dr = \frac{[FV - P]}{FV}(360/n)$$ (13.3)

where FV is the dollar amount of face value, P is the dollar purchase price, and n equals the number of days to maturity.

For example, a bank that purchases $1 million in face value of the 26-week (182-day) bills at $980,560 earns a discount yield of 3.85 percent.[5]

$$dr = 0.0385 = \frac{\$1,000,000 - 980,560}{1,000,000}(360/182)$$

The bank reports interest of $19,440 over the 182 days if the bill is redeemed at maturity.

**CERTIFICATES OF DEPOSIT AND EURODOLLARS.** Many commercial banks buy negotiable certificates of deposit and Eurodollars issued by other commercial banks. Domestic CDs are dollar-denominated deposits issued by U.S. banks with fixed maturities ranging from 14 days to several years. They are attractive because they pay yields above Treasury bills and, if issued by a well-known bank, can be easily sold in the secondary market prior to maturity. As with federal funds, interest is quoted on an add-on basis assuming a 360-day year. Eurodollars are dollar-denominated deposits issued by foreign branches of U.S. banks or by foreign banks outside the United States. Because only the largest banks can tap this market, the secondary market is quite deep. The Eurodollar market is less regulated than the domestic market so that the perceived riskiness is greater. Eurodollar rates subsequently exceed domestic CD rates for comparable banks.

Investing banks can choose from a variety of CDs in terms of yield characteristics and issuer. Although most CDs pay fixed rates to term, some carry floating rates that are pegged to an index such as LIBOR or a commercial paper rate. An investor commits the funds for up to five years but the rate is reset periodically according to a preestablished formula. For example, a floating-rate CD may carry a rate equal to the prevailing three-month commercial paper rate plus 50 basis points, with interest paid quarterly, at which time the rate is reset. Two other CDs that pay above-average rates are Yankee CDs and Asian Dollar CDs. Yankee CDs are dollar-denominated deposits issued by branches of foreign banks in the United States, while Asian Dollar CDs are issued by banks in Singapore that pay interest in dollars, which varies with the Singapore interbank offer rate (SIBOR) as an index. Even though the issuers are well-known institutions, investors demand a risk premium over rates paid by the safest domestic institutions. In recent years, many banks have offered stock market indexed CDs where the interest rate is tied to some measure of an aggregate stock index, such as the S&P 500 index. This presumably allows investors to benefit from increases in general stock prices without taking some of the price risk.

**COMMERCIAL PAPER.** Commercial paper refers to unsecured promissory notes issued by corporations that use the proceeds to finance short-term working capital needs. Because these instruments are neither insured nor backed by collateral, the issuers are presumably the highest-quality firms. However, several commercial issues have defaulted. In fact, the market is extremely sensitive to deterioration in any well-known borrower's financial condition. When a large firm is known to be in distress, virtually all issuers of new commercial paper must pay a substantial premium over T-bills to place their debt, regardless of their financial condition.[6] Most commercial paper is rated by different rating agencies to help investors gauge default risk. Issuers also typically obtain an irrevocable letter of

---

[5]Alternatively, a known discount rate (dr) produces a purchase price (P):

$$P = FV [1 - dr (n/360)]$$

The discount rate understates the true percentage yield to an investor. *The Wall Street Journal* publishes a bond coupon-equivalent yield for Treasury bills at each auction, calculated in terms of Equation 13.3, but which instead compares the dollar return to the actual purchase price and uses a 365-day year. The coupon-equivalent rate (cer) or bond equivalent rate ($i_{be}$) for the 182-day bills in the example equals 3.98 percent.

$$i_{be} = cer = \frac{\$1,000,000 - 980,560}{980,560}(365/182) = 0.0398$$

The true (effective) yield is even greater, calculated generally as

$$\text{Effective yield} = \left[1 + \frac{FV - PV}{PV}\right]^{365/k} - 1$$

where k = the number of days until maturity. In this example, the effective yield equals 4.016 percent.

[6]There are two basic types of commercial paper—direct paper and dealer paper. Direct paper constitutes the bulk of new commercial paper and is issued primarily by finance companies and large bank holding companies. Thus firms such as General Motors Acceptance Corporation, and Ford Motor Credit Corporation, along with the nation's largest bank holding companies, borrow heavily in this market. Dealer paper (or industrial paper) refers to commercial paper issued primarily by nonfinancial firms through securities dealers.

credit from a bank that guarantees payment in case the issuer defaults. This guarantee mitigates default risk and improves marketability. Still, most investors hold commercial paper to maturity because the secondary market is thin.

Small banks purchase large amounts of commercial paper as investments. The minimum denomination is $10,000, and maturities range from three to 270 days. Interest rates are fixed to term and quoted on a discount basis, as with T-bills. Thus, the market price is always less than face value, and the entire principal plus interest is paid at maturity. The primary attraction is the yield premium over T-bills and the ability to match specific commercial paper maturities with the bank's planned holding period.

**BANKERS ACCEPTANCES.** According to Federal Reserve Board Regulation A, a bankers acceptance is a "draft or bill of exchange . . . accepted by a bank or trust company, or a firm, company, or corporation engaged generally in the business of granting bankers acceptance credits." In essence it is a draft drawn on a bank by a firm that either exports or imports goods and services. Chapter 14 describes in detail how a bankers acceptance arises to assist in financing international trade.

From an investor's perspective, a bankers acceptance is a short-term interest-bearing time draft created by a high-quality bank. The acceptance has a fixed maturity ranging up to nine months and is priced as a discount instrument, like T-bills. Because default risk is relatively low, the promised rate is only slightly above the rate on a comparable-maturity T-bill. Banks find bankers acceptances attractive investments because they exhibit low default risk, pay a premium over T-bills, and can be used as collateral against discount window borrowings.

## CAPITAL MARKET INVESTMENTS

The largest portion of bank securities consists of instruments with original maturities greater than one year that are labeled capital market instruments. By regulation, banks are restricted to investment-grade securities—those rated Baa or above—and thus do not buy junk bonds. The long-term taxable portfolio is subsequently dominated by Treasury and U.S. agency securities, corporate and foreign bonds, and mortgage-backed securities. Each of these exhibits broadly different risk and return features.

**TREASURY NOTES AND BONDS.** These long-term Treasury securities differ from Treasury bills in terms of original maturity and the form of interest payment. Notes have original maturities of one to ten years. Bonds can carry any original maturity but typically are issued to mature well beyond ten years. Most notes and bonds pay coupon interest semiannually. Since 1985 the Treasury has also issued zero coupon discount bonds that are comparable in form to bills. These zeros, labeled STRIPS (separate trading of registered interest and principal of securities), typically mature 20 to 30 years from origination and carry reported yields that assume semiannual compounding.

Like bills, Treasury notes and bonds are sold via closed auctions. In most cases, securities with a variety of maturities and coupon payments are sold, with buyers submitting either competitive or noncompetitive bids. The auctions normally take place every three months when large amounts of outstanding notes and bonds mature. The secondary market is extremely deep, due to the large volume of securities outstanding, low default risk, and wide range of investors who trade these securities. Banks buy these notes and bonds both in the auction and secondary markets. They are attractive because they exhibit low default risk, are highly liquid, and pay a market return.

Unlike T-bill rates, yields are quoted on a coupon-bearing basis with prices expressed in thirty-seconds of a point. Each thirty-second is worth $31.25 per $1,000 face value ($1,000/32). Coupon interest is paid semiannually. For example, an investor might obtain a price quote of 96.24 on a 10 percent coupon, $10,000 par value Treasury note with exactly two years remaining to maturity. Interest equals 5 percent semiannually so that the investor receives four coupon payments of $500 at six-month intervals and $10,000 principal after two years. The quoted price equals 96.75 percent (96 plus 24/32) of par value or $9,675. The effective pretax yield to maturity can be calculated from the present value formula presented in Chapter 4 and equals 11.87 percent.[7]

During recent years, many banks have purchased zero coupon Treasury securities as part of their interest rate risk management strategies. Since 1985 the U.S. Treasury has allowed any Treasury with an original maturity of at

---

[7]The yield to maturity *(y)* formula follows Equation (4.8) from Chapter 4 and can be expressed, solving for y, as

$$P_0 = \sum_{t=1}^{n} \frac{C_t}{(1 + y)^t} + \frac{P_n}{(1 + y)^n}$$

where
$P_0$ = Current price
$P_n$ = Cash flow at maturity
$C_t$ = Dollar value of the cash flow (interest payment) received in period t,
$n$ = Number of periods until the final cash flow
$y$ = Periodic yield to maturity

Applied to the Treasury note, the annualized yield to maturity (y*) is determined:

$$\$9,675 = \sum_{t=1}^{4} \frac{\$500}{(1 + y*/2)^t} + \frac{\$10,000}{(1 + y*/2)^4}$$

$$y* = 11.87\%$$

least ten years to be "stripped" into its component interest and principal pieces and traded via the Federal Reserve wire transfer system. Each component interest or principal payment thus constitutes a separate zero coupon security and can be traded separately from the other payments.

Consider a 10-year, $1 million par value Treasury bond that pays 9 percent coupon interest or 4.5 percent semiannually ($45,000 every six months). This security can be stripped into 20 separate interest payments of $45,000 each and a single $1 million principal payment, or 21 separate zero coupon securities.

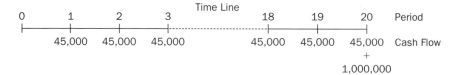

Each zero coupon security is priced by discounting the promised cash flow at the appropriate interest rate. If the market rate on the two-year zero—fourth periodic cash flow—equals 8 percent (4 percent semiannually), the associated price of the $45,000 promised payment would equal $38,466.[8]

The primary advantage of zero coupon Treasury securities is that a bank can lock in a fixed interest payment and yield for whatever maturity is selected. The above two-year zero, for example, would pay $45,000 at maturity, thus providing $6,534 in interest. Because there are no interim cash flows, there is no reinvestment risk and the bank can be assured of receiving its promised yield of 8 percent. In terms of interest rate risk management advantages, the Macaulay duration of zero coupon securities equals maturity so a bank can more precisely balance its earnings sensitivity or duration gap profile with such STRIPS.

**U.S. GOVERNMENT AGENCY SECURITIES.** Federal agencies can be separated into two groups. Members in the first group are formally part of the federal government. As such, they obtain operating funds from the Treasury and borrow from the Federal Financing Bank, a political subdivision of the Treasury that borrows from the Treasury and lends to selected agencies. This intermediation function enables agencies to borrow at the Treasury rate but also raises total Treasury financing requirements. These agencies, including the Federal Housing Administration, Export-Import Bank, and Government National Mortgage Association (Ginnie Mae), are effectively owned by the U.S. government.

Members in the second group are government-sponsored enterprises (GSEs) that are quasi-public entities. The quasi-public label represents the fact that even though the agencies are federally authorized and chartered, they are privately owned and often have publicly traded stock. They operate like any private corporation, issuing debt and acquiring assets that presumably provide revenues to cover operating expenses, pay interest and dividends, and add to capital. The U.S. government sponsors the agencies by encouraging and often subsidizing activities in favored markets such as housing and agriculture. Sponsorship also involves an implied guarantee to bail out any agency with financial problems. GSE securities are not direct obligations of the Treasury and thus are not backed by the Treasury's tax and credit authority. Default risk is considered low, however, because investors believe that the U.S. Congress has a moral obligation to provide financial aid in the event of problems at specific agencies. These agency issues normally carry a risk premium of 10 to 100 basis points over comparable maturity direct Treasury obligations due to this lack of a direct guarantee.

Exhibit 13.4 lists the major U.S. agencies and their status. Those marked with the superscript † are true agencies of the federal government and not sponsored. The agencies listed are generally active in the areas of housing, agriculture, education, and small business.

These agencies generally borrow in both the money and capital markets. Most money market instruments are discount securities comparable to Treasury bills. Capital market instruments are similar to Treasury notes and bonds, except that original maturities are typically shorter. They represent attractive investments because of the low default risk, high marketability, and attractive yields relative to Treasury securities.

**CALLABLE AGENCY BONDS.** One of the most popular bank investments during the past 15 years has been callable agency bonds. These are securities issued by GSEs in which the issuer has the option to call, or redeem, the bonds prior to final maturity. Typically, there is a call deferment period during which the bonds cannot be called. Such bonds contain an explicit call option where the issuer, such as the FHLB, buys the option to call the bonds and investors sell the option. The issuer pays by offering a higher promised yield relative to comparable noncallable bonds. The present value of this rate differential essentially represents the call premium. Banks find these securities attractive because they initially pay a higher yield than otherwise similar noncallable bonds. Of course, the premium reflects call risk. If rates fall sufficiently, the issuer will redeem the bonds early, refinancing at lower rates, and the investor gets the principal back early. The principal must then be invested at lower yields for the same risk profile.

---

[8]$45,000/(1.04)^4$

**EXHIBIT 13.4**  Federal Status of U.S. Government Agency Securities

| Agency | Full Faith and Credit of the U.S. Government | Authority to Borrow from the Federal Treasury | Interest on Bonds Generally Exempt from State and Local Taxes |
|---|---|---|---|
| Farm Credit System | No | Yes—$260 million revolving line of credit. | Yes |
| Farm Credit System Financial Assistance Corporation (FCSFAC) | Yes | Yes—FCSFAC began issuing bonds in late 1988. | Yes |
| Federal Home Loan Banks (FHLB) | No | Yes—the Treasury is authorized to purchase up to $4 billion of FHLB securities. | Yes |
| Federal Home Loan Mortgage Corporation (Freddie Mac)* | No | Yes—indirect line of credit through the FHLBs. | No |
| Federal National Mortgage Association (FNMA) (Fannie Mae)* | No | Yes—at FNMA request the Treasury may purchase $2.25 billion of FNMA securities. | No |
| Financing Corporation (FICO) | No | No | Yes |
| Student Loan Marketing Association (Sallie Mae) | Not since 1/9/82 | Yes—at its discretion the Treasury may purchase $1 billion of Sallie Mae obligations. | Yes |
| United States Postal Service | Guarantee may be extended if Postal Service requests and Treasury determines this to be in the public interest. | Yes—the Postal Service may require the Treasury to purchase up to $2 billion of its obligations. | Yes |
| Resolution Funding Corporation (RefCorp) | No | No | Yes |
| Farmers Home Administration (FmHA) | Yes | No | No |
| CBOs | | | |
| Federal Financing Bank (FFB) | Yes | Yes—FFB can require the Treasury to purchase up to $5 billion of its obligations. The Treasury Secretary is authorized to purchase any amount of FFB obligations at his or her discretion. | Yes |
| General Services Administration (GSA) | Yes | No | Yes |
| Government National Mortgage Association (GNMA) | Yes | No | No |
| Maritime Administration Guaranteed Ship Financing Bonds issued after 1972 | Yes | No | No |
| Small Business Administration (SBA) | Yes | No | No, with exceptions |
| Tennessee Valley Authority (TVA) | No | Yes—up to $150 million. | Yes |
| Washington Metropolitan Area Transit Authority (WMATA) Bonds | Yes | No | No, except for states involved in the interstate compact |

*Fully modified pass-through mortgage-backed securities and certain mortgage-backed bonds of Freddie Mac and Fannie Mae are guaranteed by Ginnie Mae as to timely payment of principal and interest.

†True federal agencies.

Source: *Handbook of Securities of the United States Government and Federal Agencies*, First Boston Corporation, 1988.

Consider the following callable agency bonds:

| Issuer | Final Maturity | Call Deferment | Yield to Maturity | Price |
|--------|---------------|----------------|-------------------|-------|
| FNMA | 7 years | 1 year | 6.42% | $99.91 |
| FHLB | 5 years | 3 months | 5.84 | 100.00 |
| FHLMC | 10 years | 1 year | 6.55 | 99.625 |
| FHLMC | 10 years | 2 years | 6.37 | 99.10 |
| FHLB | 3 years | 1 year | 5.78 | 99.97 |
| FHLMC | 3 years | 1 year | 5.62 | 99.4375 |

The first column of data lists the final maturity, while the second column indicates how much time must elapse before the issuer can call the security. The final two columns note the prevailing yield to maturity and market price per $100 par value. At this time, the Treasury yield curve was slightly upward sloping. Note two things about these promised yields. First, as suggested by the FHLMC securities, the yield is lower the longer is the call deferment period. Investors know that they have call protection for a longer period, so they accept a lower yield, ceteris paribus. Second, the final two securities differ primarily by the amount of the discount from par. The call option is in the money when rates fall, such that the price rises above or equals $100. The greater is the discount, the more yields have to fall to move the call option into the money. These securities are thus more attractive, ceteris paribus. The risk features of callables are described in greater detail later in the chapter.

**CONVENTIONAL MORTGAGE-BACKED SECURITIES.** Since passage of the Tax Reform Act of 1986 and implementation of risk-based capital standards, banks have been aggressive buyers of mortgage-backed securities (MBSs). Banks find MBSs attractive because default risk is generally low and the securities offer higher promised yields than other instruments with comparable average maturities. The problem is that mortgage-backed securities exhibit fundamentally different interest rate risk features than other investments due to mortgage prepayments. The following discussion thus focuses on the characteristics of different MBSs and the nature of prepayment risk.

In order to understand prepayment risk, it is necessary to understand the characteristics of mortgages. Formally, a mortgage is the pledge of property, typically real estate, to secure a debt. Thus, a mortgage on a house represents the pledge of the house as payment for the loan in case of default by the borrower. Mortgage loans generally take the form either of fixed-rate loans where the associated interest rate is constant over the life of the loan, or adjustable-rate loans where the interest rate varies over time based on movements in market interest rates. Mortgages are typically amortized, with monthly payments that include both interest and principal. For example, a 30-year fixed-rate mortgage will have a constant monthly payment where the interest portion is quite high during the early years of the loan because the outstanding loan balance is large, but declines with each successive payment as the outstanding principal declines. The principal portion of the fixed payment similarly rises over the life of the loan.

A **mortgage-backed security** is any security that evidences an undivided interest in the ownership of mortgage loans. The most common form of MBS is the pass-through security in which traditional fixed-rate mortgages are pooled and investors buy an interest in the pool in the form of certificates or securities. Exhibit 13.5 demonstrates how a GNMA guaranteed mortgage pass-through security is created based on residential mortgages. The originator of the mortgages makes the initial loans to individuals and contracts for the promised principal and interest payments. At this point the mortgages may be insured or guaranteed by the Federal Housing Authority (FHA), Veterans Administration (VA), or Farm Home Administration (FmHA). The originator packages the mortgages into a pool and securitizes the pool. This involves working with a securities dealer to create securities that are collateralized by the original mortgages. Typically, the creator of the pool gets a federal government agency, such as GNMA, to guarantee the borrowers' interest and principal payments. A custodian is similarly designated to maintain the mortgage documents. The securities are then sold to investors.

Operationally, a **mortgage servicer** collects principal and interest payments on the underlying mortgages, pays the guarantor a fee (around 5 basis points of the principal balance), charges a fee for processing and record keeping (around 12.5 to 25 basis points), and passes through the remaining interest and principal payments to investors. Thus, the term *pass-through* indicates that actual principal and interest payments minus fees are passed-through to investors. Investors, in turn, receive a pro rata share of the payments that reflects their fractional ownership of the pool. If, for example, five investors each owned one-fifth of the securities, each would receive 20 percent of the total principal and interest payments. If borrowers default in this example, GNMA steps in and makes the promised payments.

This structure creates substantial differences in the features of different types of mortgage-backed securities as well as differences between MBSs and conventional bonds. In contrast to conventional bonds, each payment on a MBS includes scheduled principal and interest plus principal prepayments. In addition, MBS payments occur monthly rather than semiannually. Finally, there are significant differences in price volatility due to prepayment risk on most MBSs that does not appear with conventional bonds. Characteristics of the most popular forms of MBSs are discussed below.

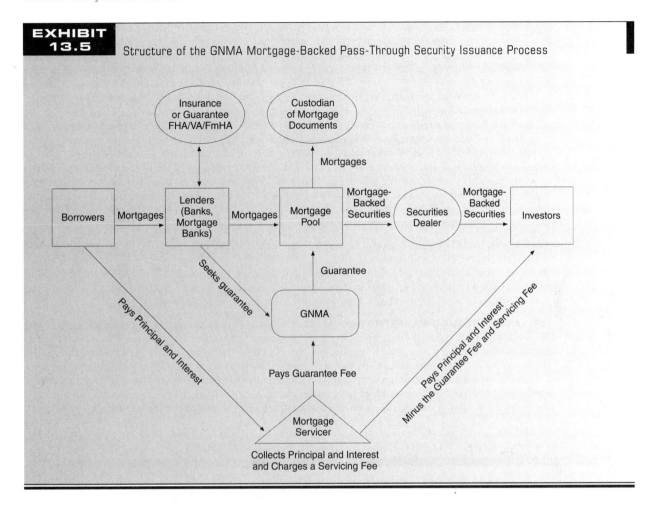

**EXHIBIT 13.5** Structure of the GNMA Mortgage-Backed Pass-Through Security Issuance Process

**GNMA PASS-THROUGH SECURITIES.** The Government National Mortgage Association (GNMA, or Ginnie Mae) was established as part of the Department of Housing and Urban Development to provide support for the residential mortgage market. It does so primarily by guaranteeing the timely payment of interest and principal to the holders of pass-through securities, regardless of whether the promised mortgage payments are made.[9] As such, even though GNMA pass-through securities are issued by private institutions, they are backed by the federal government and thus exhibit low default risk and high liquidity. Investors willingly pay for this guarantee so yields on GNMA pass-throughs are lower than yields on otherwise comparable MBSs.

The underlying mortgages in GNMA pools consist of mortgages insured by the Federal Housing Association (FHA), Veterans Administration (VA), or Farmers Home Administration (FmHA). They can be of virtually any form, including both fixed payment and adjustable rate mortgages (ARMs). Generally, mortgages in the pool are quite homogeneous in that they are issued at roughly the same time, have approximately the same maturity, and carry rates that are similar.

**FHLMC Securities.** The Federal Home Loan Mortgage Corporation (FHLMC, or Freddie Mac) was established to support the market for conventional mortgages. Unlike GNMA, FHLMC is a private corporation, albeit one that operates with an implicit federal guarantee. Although its stock is publicly traded today, it was originally owned by the Federal Home Loan Banks and member savings and loans, and Congress still selects a portion of its board of directors that helps set policy. FHLMC provides support by buying mortgages in the secondary market. It finances its purchases by issuing a variety of securities. It is these securities that banks and others purchase as investments.

**FHLMC Participation Certificates** are pass-through securities issued by FHLMC that are secured by conventional residential mortgages. Each participation certificate (PC) represents an undivided interest in the mortgages

[9]The term *modified pass-through* is used to describe this guarantee feature of securities. GNMA also directly purchases mortgages at below-market interest rates where the mortgages are used to finance low-income housing.

that make up the mortgage pool used as collateral. FHLMC guarantees monthly interest and principal payments to security holders whether or not the payments are actually received on the underlying mortgages. This is not the same as a federal guarantee so investors demand a risk premium. The risk premium can be volatile due to uncertainty regarding the credit quality of FHLMC's mortgage portfolio and questions about the viability of the implied federal guarantee.

**FHLMC Guaranteed Mortgage Certificates** are mortgage-backed securities issued by FHLMC that are similar to bonds. Interest and principal payments on the certificates are again backed by a pool of mortgages, but interest is paid just semiannually and principal is repaid annually. FHLMC also backs these payments with its guarantee.

**FHLMC Collateralized Mortgage Obligations** are debt issues originated by FHLMC that are secured by a pool of mortgages, but with the securities are grouped into classes according to estimated stated maturities. The purpose of these classes is described later in this chapter in the discussion of collateralized mortgage obligations (CMOs). Investors in all classes of CMOs receive semiannual interest payments until maturity.[10] Principal payments are also semiannual but are allocated initially to the class of CMOs with the shortest stated maturity, then sequentially to the remaining outstanding classes by maturity. Investors find CMOs attractive because they can better estimate the effective maturity of the securities compared with other types of pass-throughs.

**FNMA SECURITIES.** The Federal National Mortgage Association (FNMA, or Fannie Mae) was created by the federal government in 1938 to support housing, but today is another private corporation GSE that operates with an implicit federal guarantee. It operates much like FHLMC, buying mortgages and financing the mortgages with securities backed by pools of mortgages with features similar to FHLMC's participation certificates. FNMA similarly guarantees timely interest and principal payments so that default risk is generally perceived to be low.

**PRIVATELY ISSUED PASS-THROUGHS.** Commercial banks, savings and loans, and mortgage banks also issue mortgage-backed pass-through securities secured by pools of mortgages. The primary difference with federal agency MBSs is that there is no actual or implied guarantee by the federal government or agency. Instead, private issuers purchase mortgage insurance either in the form of pool insurance by such groups as the Mortgage Guarantee Insurance Corporation, or via letters of credit. In most cases, it is more profitable for mortgage lenders to use the agency programs. With certain mortgages, such as large mortgages where the outstanding principal balance exceeds the acceptable maximum set by the agencies, a private pass-through program is the only one available.

## PREPAYMENT RISK ON MORTGAGE-BACKED SECURITIES

As indicated earlier, most mortgage-backed securities carry a guarantee that principal and interest payments will be made to investors regardless of whether the payment on the underlying mortgages is made. Despite these guarantees, MBSs exhibit considerable risk because they may fluctuate widely in price when interest rates change. This results from uncertainty over the timing of prepayments and thus what cash flows will actually be passed through to investors at various points in time.

Remember that investors receive the actual principal and interest payments made by borrowers on the underlying mortgages minus a servicing fee. These borrowers, in fact, may prepay the outstanding mortgage principal at any point in time, for any reason, and often without penalty. Prepayments generally occur because of fundamental demographic trends as well as from movements in interest rates. Demographic phenomena include factors affecting general labor mobility as individuals change jobs with fluctuations in regional economic activity, as well as changes in family structure attributable to events such as children leaving home or divorce. The important point is that the prepayment feature represents an option and is quite valuable to the borrower who buys the option and chooses when to exercise (prepay) it. It is risky to an investor who sells the option because the cash flows are unpredictable.

Consider the case where an investor buys a Ginnie Mae MBS based on a pool of mortgages paying 8.5 percent. Current mortgage rates are lower so that the security trades at a substantial premium for a promised yield of 8 percent. If rates remain constant, an investor might receive interest on the outstanding principal at the higher rate for seven or eight years. Suppose instead that mortgage rates fall sharply. Some mortgage borrowers will exercise their option and refinance their properties with new mortgages at lower rates because they can save on monthly interest payments. They subsequently prepay principal on the 8.5 percent mortgages so that MBS investors receive smaller interest payments. If prepayments are substantial, all outstanding principal may be quickly repaid so that the MBS effectively matures. Investors lose because they paid a premium expecting to receive high interest payments for several years. With the decline in rates, they not only receive considerably less interest over a shorter period of time, but they have to reinvest their cash receipts at lower rates. If prepayments are high enough, they may not even recover the premium paid. The total return can be negative.

---

[10]Holders of certain classes of interest accrual securities do not receive any interest payments until all interest and principal payments are made on the other classes of bonds. Interest continues to accrue, however, until received.

Suppose, alternatively, that mortgage rates rise substantially. Prepayments will either slow or remain constant because fewer individuals will move and interest rates will induce fewer refinancings. The effect on investors in MBSs is threefold. First, the outstanding principal will be higher than originally anticipated. Thus, interest received will be higher as repayment slows. Second, the security will remain outstanding longer so that interest payments will be received for more periods. This lengthening of final maturity is labeled extension risk. Third, all cash receipts can be reinvested at higher rates. Of course, the increase in rates at least partly offsets this by lowering the market value of the MBS.

Panel A of Exhibit 13.6 demonstrates the general interest sensitivity of a MBS. The vertical axis represents the market value of a $100,000 interest in a pool of 30-year mortgages carrying 9 percent rates. Assume that the expected rate of prepayments over the life of the mortgages is 6 percent per year. This type of *constant prepayment rate (CPR)* is typically measured as the annualized fraction of principal prepaid during a specific period, such as a year.[11] The dashed line represents the value of the MBS if the prepayment rate remains at 6 percent regardless of the level of mortgage rates. The solid line indicates the value of the MBS if the prepayment rate varies from 6 percent at different interest rate levels. At a current market rate of 9 percent, the MBS is valued at $100,000. As interest rates rise or fall, the value of the MBS declines or rises, respectively. Note, however, the differences in the two values at different rate levels. An increase in rates lowers the actual price of the MBS below the price at a constant prepayment rate because prepayments will slow and an investor will receive below-market interest payments for a longer period of time than originally anticipated. A decrease in rates raises value, but the sharp increase in prepayments at low rates limits the price appreciation. Thus, prepayments increase potential capital losses to investors while they decrease potential capital gains.

This would not be a problem if investors could accurately forecast prepayments. Unfortunately, this is difficult to do. Pools of mortgages differ by geographic region, by the type of home or commercial property financed, by the age of the mortgages or how long they have been in existence, and by the actual interest rates on the underlying mortgages. Fixed-rate mortgages prepay at different rates than adjustable-rate mortgages. Thus, prepayment experience will vary widely between pools of mortgages even at the same point in time. This problem is mitigated somewhat by the fact that the federal government collects and reports data on the prepayment experience of selected mortgage pools. Securities dealers similarly track prepayment experience to assist investors when buying MBSs. While such information helps distinguish between pools, past prepayment experience is not always useful in predicting prepayments.

The bottom two panels of Exhibit 13.6 document the relationship between the prepayment rate on the vertical axis and different coupon rates on the underlying mortgages and mortgage age. The horizontal axis in panel B indicates the difference between the current rate on new mortgages and the rate on the underlying mortgages, while mortgage age in panel C refers to the length of time the mortgages have been outstanding since origination. Not surprisingly, prepayment rates rise sharply when mortgage rates fall. Prepayments are relatively low until mortgage rates fall where they fluctuate between 2 and 3 percent per month. Prepayments are virtually unchanged when rates rise because there are no rate-induced prepayments, only prepayments resulting from demographic events. According to panel C, prepayment experience is low on new mortgages, but rises consistently through five years after which it declines. This reflects the fact that rate changes are typically small near term, and that most individuals must remain in their homes for a while before they can cover the costs of refinancing.

## UNCONVENTIONAL MORTGAGE-BACKED SECURITIES

The existence of prepayment risk complicates the valuation and marketing of MBSs. Issuers have created many hybrids to mitigate these risks and have structured MBSs so that they appeal to more investors. Several of the more prominent hybrids are introduced below.

**COLLATERALIZED MORTGAGE OBLIGATIONS.** Freddie Mac first introduced CMOs in 1983 to try and circumvent some of the prepayment risk associated with the traditional pass-through security. This was accomplished by converting pass-throughs to securities with more predictable maturity and yield features comparable to those of well-known fixed-income securities. CMOs are essentially bonds. An originator combines various mortgage pools that serve as collateral and creates classes of bonds with different maturities secured by the collateral. Consider a sequential CMO. The first class of bonds, or *tranche*, has the shortest maturity because all principal payments on the underlying mortgages are allocated to these securities so that repayment occurs first and on schedule. Interest is paid on these and most other bonds at all times that the securities are outstanding. Once these bonds have been fully repaid, principal payments are allocated to a second class (or tranche) of bonds until they are paid off, and so forth. The primary advantage is that bonds in the first CMO tranches exhibit less prepayment uncertainty. An investor can subsequently better forecast the effective maturity and overall yield. In some instances the last class, a

[11]Suppose that a pool of mortgages contained $100 million in principal. A 6 percent annual CPR means that prepayments equal $6 million during the first year, $5.64 million (0.06 X $94) during the second year, and so forth. If $6 million in principal was prepaid during the first three months, the annualized CPR would equal 24 percent. CPR does not include normal amortization.

**EXHIBIT 13.6** Prepayment Risk on Mortgage-Backed Securities

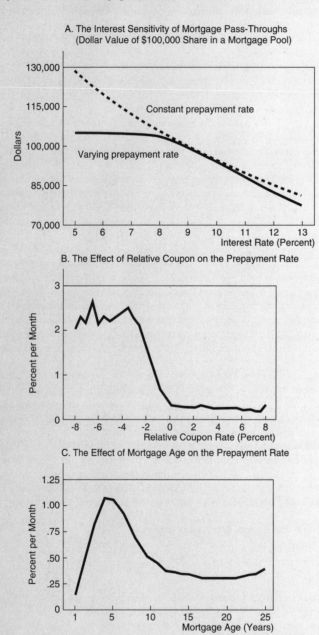

A. The Interest Sensitivity of Mortgage Pass-Throughs
(Dollar Value of $100,000 Share in a Mortgage Pool)

B. The Effect of Relative Coupon on the Prepayment Rate

C. The Effect of Mortgage Age on the Prepayment Rate

SOURCE: Sean Becketti, "The Prepayment Risk of Mortgage-Backed Securities." *Economic Review* (Federal Reserve Bank of Kansas City, February 1989).

*Z-tranche,* consists of an accrual bond in which no interest or principal is paid until all other classes of bonds have been repaid. These securities are higher risk and represent a hybrid form of zero coupon bond.

As an example, consider the CMO prospectus in Exhibit 13.7. These CMO bonds were issued by Freddie Mac in January 1990, have $896 million in principal, and are divided into four tranches. The underwriters, led by Prudential-Bache Capital Funding, are listed at the bottom. Bonds in the first tranche (Series 123) carry a coupon

---

## EXHIBIT 13.7 — CMO Prospectus

New Issue

# $896,000,000

Freddie Mac

# Federal Home Loan Mortgage Corporation

### Multifamily Plan C REMIC
### Mortgage Participation Certificates
### (Guaranteed), Series 123 through 126

**Series 123**
$330,000,000    8.25%  Class 123-A  Final Payment Date February 15, 1995 —Price 99.781250%

**Series 124**
$307,000,000    8.50%  Class 124-A  Final Payment Date March 15, 1997     —Price 99.093750%

**Series 125**
$220,000,000    8.75%  Class 125-A  Final Payment Date March 15, 2000     —Price 99.031250%

**Series 126**
$ 39,000,000    9.00%  Class 126-A  Final Payment Date March 15, 2005     —Price 99.390625%

(plus accrued interest at the applicable rate from January 15, 1990)

Freddie Mac, in its corporate capacity, will be contractually obligated to pay PC Yield Maintenance Premiums, if any, to each Holder of the Class 123-A, Class 124-A, Class 125-A and Class 126-A Plan C REMIC PCs.

The obligations of Freddie Mac under its guarantee of the Plan C REMIC PCs, and its obligations to pay PC Yield Maintenance Premiums, are obligations of Freddie Mac only and are not backed by the full faith and credit of the United States.

The residual interest for each Plan C REMIC PC Pool is not offered by the Offering Circular Supplement and the related Offering Circular and will initially be retained by Freddie Mac.

The Class 123-A, Class 124-A, Class 125-A and Class 126-A Plan C REMIC PCs will each be a regular interest in one of the Plan C REMIC PC Pools.

Elections will be made to treat the Plan C REMIC PC Pools as REMICs.

Copies of the Offering Circular Supplement and the related Offering Circular describing these securities and the business of the Corporation may be obtained from any of the undersigned in States in which such underwriters may legally offer these securities. This announcement is neither an offer to sell nor a solicitation of an offer to buy these securities. The offer is made only by the Offering Circular Supplement and the related Offering Circular.

**Prudential-Bache Capital Funding**
**The First Boston Corporation**
**Goldman, Sachs & Co.**
**Merrill Lynch Capital Markets**
**Salomon Brothers Inc**
**Shearson Lehman Hutton Inc.**

| | | |
|---|---|---|
| **BT Securities Corporation** | **Bear, Stearns & Co. Inc.** | **Citicorp Securities Markets, Inc.** |
| **Donaldson, Lufkin & Jenrette** | | **Drexel Burnham Lambert** |
| **Freddie Mac Security Sales and Trading Group** | | **Greenwich Capital Markets, Inc.** |
| **Kidder, Peabody & Co.** | **J.P. Morgan Securities Inc.** | **Morgan Stanley & Co.** |
| **Nomura Securities International, Inc.** | **PaineWebber Incorporated** | **UBS Securities Inc.** |

January 9, 1990

rate of 8.25 percent but are priced to yield slightly more because the price is below 100. Note that the final payment date is listed at February 1995, roughly five years after issue. This is an approximate maturity date assuming no prepayments of principal. According to the structure of this issue, investors in the first tranche (Series 123) bonds receive all principal payments, including prepayments, until the $330 million is repaid. Because there will be some prepayments, five years represents the longest an investor would have to wait for a return of all principal. After these bonds are retired, all principal payments are next allocated to the second tranche (Series 124) bonds until they are retired. The estimated longest final maturity here is seven years, assuming no prepayments. The process continues until bonds in the third and fourth tranches are paid off. As such, the bonds evidence a sequential (SEQ) repayment pattern. The longest possible maturity for the Series 126 bonds is 25 years.

The structure essentially creates four classes of bonds with different maturities and cash-flow features. The coupon rates and promised yields increase with estimated maturity to compensate investors for the additional risk. The bonds are guaranteed by Freddie Mac such that investors assume little default risk. There is, however, still substantial interest rate risk with uncertain prepayments. It is relatively low for the first tranche bonds, but increases with bonds in each successive tranche.

There are many different types of CMOs. The least risky are *planned amortization classes* (PACs) in which principal payments are allocated according to a fixed amortization schedule. Specifically, as long as prepayments fall within a predetermined range, the principal of a PAC will be repaid in a predictable, timely fashion. If actual prepayment rates fall outside this range, principal allocated to other nonplanned amortization class tranches is reduced or accelerated to ensure that the PAC CMO is paid as scheduled. Such non-PAC CMOs are labeled *support (SUP) tranches.* The result is that PAC bonds exhibit relatively low prepayment risk, as long as the PAC prepayment range (band) is wide, but the non-PAC tranches exhibit great prepayment risk.

CMOs provide several advantages over traditional MBSs. First, they exhibit less prepayment risk. Second, by segmenting the securities into maturity classes, CMOs appeal to different investors who have different maturity preferences. Banks, for example, often prefer first tranche securities because the short maturities and durations better match their cash-flow obligations with deposit liabilities. Insurance companies, in contrast, often prefer later tranches where the bonds have much longer effective maturities. Third, CMOs exhibit little default risk because the collateral backing the bonds are generally agency securities that carry explicit guarantees, or the issuer purchases private insurance. Thus, many CMOs are Aaa and Aa rated. In addition, many early classes of bonds are over collateralized because the actual cash flows from the collateral exceed cash flow required to pay bondholders. Fourth, like MBSs, CMOs are priced at a spread over Treasury securities so that changes in yields are fairly predictable.

CMOs also have several disadvantages. They are less liquid because the secondary market is less developed. Transactions costs are subsequently higher. In addition, an investor may find it difficult to obtain an accurate price quote when trying to sell a CMO. This is particularly true for the latter tranches, which exhibit far greater price volatility. Banks and other investors have had serious trouble estimating prepayment speeds and thus the interest rate risk with CMOs has been extraordinary. Regulators have tried to limit the riskiness of a CMO for banks by forcing banks to mark-to-market all CMOs that do not meet well-defined price and extension volatility criteria. Finally, all CMO interest is taxable at the federal, state, and local government levels, unlike Treasury securities, which are subject only to federal income taxes.

**STRIPPED MORTGAGE-BACKED SECURITIES.** Stripped Treasury securities, introduced earlier, are nothing more than zero coupon instruments that represent either a principal payment or coupon interest payment on a Treasury obligation. The general label is *principal only* (PO) and *interest only* (IO) security. The previous time line for the ten-year Treasury reveals 20 distinct IOs paying $45,000 each at maturity and one PO of $1 million. These stripped Treasury securities exhibit no default risk and no interest rate risk if held to final maturity. An investor can therefore lock in a guaranteed return if he or she matches the holding period with a stripped Treasury of the same maturity.

Stripped mortgage-backed securities are much more complicated in terms of their structure and pricing characteristics. This reflects the design of mortgage contracts and the impact of mortgage prepayments. Consider a 30-year, 12 percent fixed-rate mortgage that is fully amortized. There will be 360 scheduled principal and interest payments equal to a fixed dollar amount per month (PY). The following time line demonstrates the cash-flow pattern of interest (I) and principal (P) payments where the subscripts refer to the month in which the payment is made.

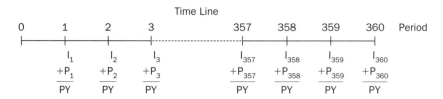

Loan amortization requires that the early period principal payments are small relative to the total payment so that $P_1 < P_2 < \ldots < P_{360}$. Interest payments are large during the early periods when the outstanding principal is high, and decline over time and the principal is reduced. Thus $I_1 > I_2 > \ldots > I_{360}$.

Unlike Treasury securities, there is more than one principal component as each payment is part principal. Furthermore, MBSs are typically stripped into just two securities, with the PO representing the entire stream of principal payments, and the IO representing the entire stream of interest payments. Thus, each payment is not a separate security and the strips are no longer simple zero coupon instruments. More importantly, MBSs are subject to prepayment risk which affects the underlying principal and interest payments and thus makes mortgage-backed POs and IOs highly interest sensitive.

Suppose that an investor purchased the PO security represented by the stream of principal payments in the above time line when the market rate and coupon rate both equaled 10 percent. Given normal demographic trends, prepayments are expected to equal 6 percent annually. Now suppose that the prevailing mortgage rate drops to 8 percent so that prepayments accelerate and the CPR jumps to 20 percent. The investor will receive principal payments earlier than originally anticipated. In addition, the payments will be discounted at a lower rate so that the price of the PO will rise substantially. Similarly, a rise in mortgage rates will not slow prepayments because they are already at the minimum 6 percent, but the cash flows will be discounted at a higher rate so the price of the PO will fall. If the PO originally carried a higher coupon rate, prepayments would have slowed and the price decline would be even greater. In short, a mortgage-backed PO behaves much like a typical MBS or conventional bond except it is more price sensitive.

Suppose that another investor bought the IO security represented by the stream of interest payments at the 10 percent coupon rate. A decline in the market rate to 8 percent would accelerate principal payments and the outstanding principal balance would fall below that anticipated. The IO investor would thus receive much lower interest payments than originally anticipated. In the extreme case when the entire outstanding principal balance is repaid, the IO investor would receive no interest payments. Not surprisingly, the price of an IO is quite volatile. If prepayments are high enough, the drop in the dollar value of interest received can swamp any effect from discounting at a lower rate so that the price of an IO will fall. In a similar vein, suppose that the investor purchased the IO when the prevailing mortgage rate was 6 percent, or 4 percent below the 10 percent coupon rate on the underlying mortgages. The initial forecast would call for a high prepayment speed such that the IO could be purchased at a relatively low price. If the market rate increased to 8 percent, prepayments would slow substantially, outstanding principal would be greater than that initially anticipated, and interest payments would rise sharply. If the prepayment effect was large enough, it could swamp discounting at a higher rate such that the value of the IO might rise. These IO instruments can have prices that move in the same direction as market interest rates.

The essential point is that mortgage-backed IOs are extremely price sensitive to changes in interest rates and the price/yield relationship may be positive. When prepayments rise sharply with a drop in rates compared to that anticipated, the value of the IO similarly falls. When prepayments fall sharply with an increase in rates relative to expectations, the value of the IO will similarly rise. Thus, IOs may vary in price in the opposite direction of that normally observed for traditional fixed-income securities. In securities parlance, these IOs exhibit negative convexity. To compensate for their high risk, IOs often carry yields that are 4 to 5 percent above comparable duration Treasury yields.

Unfortunately, many investors, including banks and savings and loans, purchased IOs for interest rate hedges without understanding their features. Certain high-coupon IOs could presumably be used to hedge a negative GAP or positive duration gap because a bank with this risk profile would lose when interest rates increased. An IO would presumably rise in value as rates increased as an offset. Of course, if rates fell a bank would win with its GAP profile, but this would be offset by losses on the IO. The success of IOs as hedges, however, depends on wide swings in rates. Small rate changes typically move IO prices in the same direction as a bank's cash flows from normal operations so that no hedge is in place.

It is very difficult to predict prepayments and thus the value of IOs and POs when rates change. They are extremely risky because they are extremely interest sensitive. There are many better hedging tools, such as interest rate swaps and options on futures, with more predictable cash flows and changes in value. Bank regulators have subsequently encouraged banks to stay away from IOs.

## CORPORATE, FOREIGN, AND TAXABLE MUNICIPAL BONDS

Banks also purchase taxable fixed-income securities in the form of corporate bonds and foreign government bonds. By year-end 2004, they held $560 billion corporates and foreign bonds, which was more than triple their holdings of municipals at $141 billion. Banks do not purchase junk bonds because they are restricted to investment-grade securities. Banks are also constrained by regulation concerning legal lending limits to investing no more than 10 percent of capital in the securities of any single firm. These bonds typically pay interest semiannually and return the entire principal at maturity. In most cases, banks purchase securities that mature within ten years.

**EXHIBIT 13.8** Features of Pass-Through, Government, and Corporate Securities

| | Pass-Throughs | Treasuries | Corporates | Stripped Treasuries |
|---|---|---|---|---|
| Credit risk | Generally high grade; range from government guaranteed to A (private pass-throughs). | Government guaranteed. | High grade to speculative. | Backed by government securities. |
| Liquidity | Good for agency issued/guaranteed pass-through. | Excellent. | Generally limited. | Fair. |
| Range of coupons (discount to premium) | Full range. | Full range. | Full range for a few issuers. | Zero coupons (discount securities). |
| Range of maturities | Medium and long term (fast-paying and seasoned pools can provide shorter maturities than stated). | Full range. | Full range. | Full range. |
| Call protection | Complex prepayment pattern; investor can limit through selection variables, such as coupon seasoning, and program. | Noncallable (except certain 30-year bonds). | Generally callable after initial limited period of 5 to 10 years. | Noncallable. |
| Frequency of payment | Monthly payments of principal and interest. | Semiannual interest payment. | Semiannual interest (except Eurobonds, which pay interest annually). | No payments until maturity. |
| Average life | Lower than for bonds of comparable maturity; can only be estimated due to prepayment risk. | Estimate only for small number of callable issues; otherwise, known with certainty. | Minimum average life known, otherwise a function of call risk. | Known with certainty. |
| Duration/interest rate risk | Function of prepayment risk; can only be estimated; can be negative when prepayment risk is high. | Unless callable, a simple function of yield, coupon, and maturity; is known with certainty. | Function of call risk; can be negative when call risk is high. | Known with certainty; no interest rate risk if held to maturity. |
| Basis for yield quotes | Cash flow yield based on monthly prepayments and constant CPR assumption (usually most recent three-month historical prepayment experience). | Based on semiannual coupon payments and 365-day year. | Based on semiannual coupon payments and 360-day year of twelve 30-day months. | Bond equivalent yield based on either 360- or 365-day year depending on sponsor. |
| Settlement | Once a month. | Any business day. | Any business day. | Any business day. |

SOURCE: *Handbook of Securities of the United States Government and Federal Agencies*, First Boston Corporation, 1988.

Occasionally, banks also purchase municipal bonds that pay taxable interest. The Tax Reform Act of 1986 eliminated the tax-exempt status of certain types of municipal revenue bonds. These entities have subsequently issued debt that pays taxable interest to meet their financing needs. The pretax yields are comparable to those on corporate securities even though the borrower is affiliated with a municipal government. Exhibit 13.8 compares the features of corporate securities with Treasury securities and pass-throughs.

## ASSET-BACKED SECURITIES

One of the dominant trends in financial markets is the securitization of bank loans. Chapter 1 describes the process and rationale given the returns that are available and the recent increase in regulatory capital requirements. Although some banks have been active in securitizing nontraditional types of loans, others view these securities as potential investments. Conceptually, an asset-backed security is comparable to a mortgage-backed security in structure. The securities are effectively pass-throughs because promised interest and principal payments are secured by the payments on the specific loans pledged as collateral.

Two of the more popular forms of asset-backed securities are collateralized automobile receivables (CARS) and certificates for amortizing revolving debt (CARDS).[12] As the names suggest, CARS are securities backed by automobile loans to individuals. CARDS, in turn, are securities backed by credit card loans to individuals. In recent years, credit card loans and retail auto loans have dominated loan securitizations with home equity, auto, and equipment leases next. CARS may be structured either as conventional pass-throughs or as CMOs. Automobile loans representing installment contracts with maturities up to 60 months are placed in a trust. CARS represent an undivided interest in the trust. An investor receives the underlying monthly principal and interest payments less a servicing fee. As with CMOs, CARS may be multiple-class instruments in which cash flows pay interest to all security holders, but repay principal sequentially from the first class of bonds to the last. Default risk is reduced because the issuer may either set up a reserve fund out of the payments to cover losses, purchase insurance, or obtain a letter of credit. Such credit enhancements typically provide the securities the AAA credit rating. CARS are attractive to investors because they have maturities of five years or less, exhibit little prepayment risk, and carry rates that are approximately 1 percent over rates on comparable duration Treasury securities. Prepayment risk is low because automobile loan rates are somewhat sticky and there are limited incentives to prepay. The primary negative is that liquidity is reduced compared with many other securities.

CARDS are structured much like CARS except that the collateral is credit card receivables. An issuer places credit card accounts in a trust and sells participations. The securities generally have stated maturities around five years, with only interest being paid monthly during the first one and a half to two years. Principal payments begin thereafter. Because many cardholders repay their debts quickly, the principal may be repaid well before the stated maturity. Thus prepayment risk is higher for CARDS than CARS. Still, issuers establish a reserve fund or obtain explicit guarantees via letters of credit so that the securities are similarly rated Aaa.

**MUTUAL FUNDS.** In recent years, regulators have allowed banks to purchase certain types of mutual fund shares as an investment. The shares must be in funds that purchase only securities that banks would be allowed to own directly for their own account, such as Treasury and agency obligations, mortgage-backed securities, and investment-grade corporates. The presumed benefit is that small banks might be better able to diversify credit risk because they would own shares in a pool of securities rather than individual securities. Regulators further limit mutual fund purchases to no more than 10 percent of a bank's capital plus surplus.

After initial interest during the latter 1980s, banks generally ignored mutual funds through 1996, but increased their holdings from almost $14 billion in 1996 to over $25 billion by year-end 2004. The primary reason is that regulations require that mutual fund shares be marked-to-market rather than reported at book values. Funds that do not have fixed share prices fluctuate in value with changes in interest rates, which translates into fluctuating values reported on a bank's balance sheet. Such volatility looks bad in periodic financial statements because it presents an appearance of high risk.

## CHARACTERISTICS OF MUNICIPAL SECURITIES

At year-end 1985 commercial banks owned $232 billion in municipal securities, or 35 percent of total municipals outstanding, more than any other investor group. By year-end 2004, bank municipal holdings had fallen to around $141 billion, or around 7 percent of outstandings. This reflects changes in federal income tax laws to where many municipals yield less to banks than comparable maturity and risk taxable bonds.

Municipals are generally attractive investments because their interest is exempt from federal income taxes. Interest on in-state issues is also normally exempt from state or local income taxes. This tax treatment lowers quoted yields below pretax yields on taxable securities of comparable maturity and risk because municipal yields effectively represent after-tax returns. Such investments also support local business development and growth, in addition to essential public services.

Municipal securities are formally issued by state and local governments and their political subdivisions, such as school corporations, water treatment authorities, and river authorities. Nonprofit organizations and nonfinancial corporations also effectively issue municipals because they get the use of the proceeds at reduced rates, even though a municipal unit's name actually goes on the debt. Government units distinguish between short-term and long-term municipals because they are used for different purposes and are subject to different restrictions. Short-term securities are used to finance temporary imbalances between the timing of operating receipts and expenditures or to provide

---

[12]CARS and CARDS are formally the labels copyrighted by Salomon Brothers for its specific issues of asset-backed securities, but will be used generically in the discussion to refer to any similar securities.

interim financing of construction outlays. By law, most governmental units are forced to run balanced operating budgets, meaning that current operating revenues must be sufficient to cover operating expenses. State and local governments are not allowed to issue long-term bonds to finance short-term operating budget deficits.

Today, long-term municipals are used primarily to finance capital expenditures for such purposes as education facilities, hospitals, housing, and public utilities. The benefits to these facilities presumably arise over long periods so that future taxes should cover the interest and principal payments. The intent is that higher taxes will be paid by those who benefit. **General obligation** bonds are municipals in which principal and interest payments are backed by the full faith, credit, and taxing authority of the issuer. As such, they are the closest thing to a Treasury bond because the issuer can raise taxes or issue new debt to repay the bonds. **Revenue** bonds are municipals in which principal and interest payments are backed by revenues generated from whatever facility or project the bond proceeds are used to finance. An example is bonds issued by a water treatment facility which are backed by fees or assessments on users of the treated water. For a pure revenue bond, no tax receipts back the promised payments. For many years a large share of long-term municipal debt effectively financed the expenditures of private corporations in the form of **industrial development** bonds, a special form of revenue bond. For example, it was not unusual for Kmart to negotiate a deal with a municipality to locate a store within the city limits if the municipality would form a local economic development unit, have the unit issue debt, and then let Kmart pay the debt service with lease payments to the economic development unit. The advantage to Kmart was that it could effectively borrow at lower tax-exempt interest rates. The advantage to the community was that it had attracted a new business that presumably brought jobs and services. The Tax Reform Act of 1986 sharply reduced the issuance of tax-exempt industrial development bonds so that they now represent a much smaller share of the municipal market.

Most long-term municipals are serial bonds, with a fraction of the total principal maturing in consecutive years. This is shown in Exhibit 13.9 for the $30 million issue by the Sequoia Union High School District. This new issue indicates that the offering has 25 serial components of different amounts that mature annually from 2003 through the year 2026. Serialization enables a municipality to spread out principal and interest payments to stay within annual debt service capability. Issues may also have term components where the entire principal comes due at a set maturity. The state of Washington issue has a separate term component of bonds with $8.65 million in principal that matures in 2031, 29 years after the issue date. The firms listed at the top, with Salomon Smith Barney as the lead, are the investment banks that served as underwriters.

From a bank's perspective, serial issues allow portfolio managers to select instruments with the precise maturities that best meet the bank's risk and return preferences. For example, a bank with many short-term liabilities may choose to concentrate investments near term. Similarly, banks that choose to use municipals to lengthen their asset-rate sensitivity profile may select longer-term issues. With a serial issue, the manager can simply select the appropriate maturity instrument because credit and liquidity risk are held constant.

## MONEY MARKET MUNICIPALS

**Municipal notes** are issued to provide operating funds for government units. **Tax and revenue anticipation notes** are issued in anticipation of tax receipts or other revenue generation, typically from the federal government. These securities enable governments to continue to spend funds even when operating revenues decline, then repay the debt as revenues are received. **Bond anticipation notes** provide interim financing for capital projects that will ultimately be financed with long-term bonds. For example, a school district may begin construction of new schools with note proceeds because it believes that current long-term municipal rates are temporarily high. Long-term bonds will be issued after rates decline, with the proceeds used to retire the notes. Most notes carry a minimum denomination of $25,000, with maturities ranging from 30 days to one year. Maturities on bond anticipation notes may extend to 3 years.

**Project notes** and **tax-exempt commercial paper** also play important roles in the municipal market. Local housing authorities issue project notes to finance federal expenditures for urban renewal, local neighborhood development, and low-income housing. The notes are repaid out of revenues from the projects financed. In the event that revenues are not forthcoming, the Department of Housing and Urban Development agrees to make the obligated interest and principal payments, so the notes carry an implied federal guarantee. Tax-exempt commercial paper is issued by the largest municipalities, which regularly need blocks of funds in $1 million multiples for operating purposes. Because only large, well-known borrowers issue this paper, yields are below those quoted on comparably rated municipal notes.

Banks buy large amounts of short-term municipals. They often work closely with municipalities in placing these securities and have a built-in need for short-term liquidity given that most bank liabilities are highly rate sensitive near term. Thus short-term municipals are in high demand, and short-term municipal rates are relatively low compared with rates on longer-term municipals. The Sequoia Union High School District issue in Exhibit 13.9 demonstrates this rate relationship. Consider the serial bond issues that mature from 2003 through 2026. The coupon column refers to the coupon rate, while the yield column indicates the market rate. A coupon rate equal to the market rate means that the security sells at par. A coupon rate above (below) the market rate indicates that the bond sells at a premium (discount). Note that the one-year serial bond pays 2 percent, which is lower than all other market rates, which generally increase with maturity. Long-term municipals carry higher yields than short-term municipals.

**EXHIBIT 13.9**    Summary of Terms for a Municipal School Bond

**Sequoia Union High School District**
**$30,000,000**

General Obligation Bonds Election of 2001
Dated: May 1, 2002
Due: July 1, 2003 through July 1, 2031
Callable: July 1, 2011 at 102.0% of par, declining to par as of July 1, 2013
Winning Bid: Salomon Smith Barney, at 100.0000,
         True interest cost (TIC) of 5.0189%

Other Managers: Bear, Stearns & Co., Inc., CIBC World Markets Corp.,

| Due Date | Amount | Coupon | Yield |
|----------|--------|--------|-------|
| 7/1/03 | $225,000 | 7.00% | 2.00% |
| 7/1/04 | $520,000 | 7.00% | 2.50% |
| 7/1/05 | $545,000 | 7.00% | 3.00% |
| 7/1/06 | $575,000 | 7.00% | 3.25% |
| 7/1/07 | $605,000 | 7.00% | 3.50% |
| 7/1/08 | $635,000 | 7.00% | 3.70% |
| 7/1/09 | $665,000 | 7.00% | 3.80% |
| 7/1/10 | $700,000 | 4.00% | 3.90% |
| 7/1/11 | $735,000 | 4.00% | 4.00% |
| 7/1/12 | $765,000 | 4.125% | 4.125% |
| 7/1/13 | $800,000 | 4.25% | 4.25% |
| 7/1/14 | $835,000 | 4.375% | 4.375% |
| 7/1/15 | $870,000 | 4.50% | 4.50% |
| 7/1/16 | $910,000 | 4.60% | 4.60% |
| 7/1/17 | $950,000 | 4.70% | 4.70% |
| 7/1/18 | $995,000 | 4.80% | 4.80% |
| 7/1/19 | $1,045,000 | 4.90% | 4.90% |
| 7/1/20 | $1,095,000 | 5.00% | 5.00% |
| 7/1/21 | $1,150,000 | 5.00% | 5.00% |
| 7/1/22 | $1,210,000 | 5.00% | 5.00% |
| 7/1/23 | $1,270,000 | 5.00% | 5.00% |
| 7/1/24 | $1,335,000 | 5.00% | 5.00% |
| 7/1/25 | $1,405,000 | 5.00% | 5.20% |
| 7/1/26 | $1,480,000 | 5.00% | 5.21% |
| 7/1/31 | $8,650,000 | 5.125% | 5.21% |

Source: The Bond Buyer. Results of Competitive Sales. April 25, 2002.

## CAPITAL MARKET MUNICIPALS

**GENERAL OBLIGATION BONDS.** Interest and principal payments on general obligation bonds are backed by the full faith, credit, and taxing power of the issuer. This backing represents the strongest commitment a government can make in support of its debt. At the extreme, governments promise to raise taxes, attach real property, and issue new debt to meet promised debt service payments. The Sequoia Union High School District issue in Exhibit 13.9 is such a bond. Because this guarantee is so broad, issuers must generally obtain voter approval via referendum to issue new general obligation debt. Actual default risk depends on the viability of the issuer's tax base and its willingness to live up to the terms of the debt.

Occasionally, a municipality's taxing authority is limited, typically by a maximum allowable tax rate. In these cases, the bonds are still classified as general obligations but are referred to as *limited tax* bonds. In addition, municipalities often issue general obligations that are also secured by revenues independent of issuer general funds. Such bonds are referred to as *double barrel* bonds because of the dual backing.

**REVENUE BONDS.** Revenue bonds are issued to finance projects whose revenues are the primary source of repayment. An example is bonds issued to finance an airport expansion that are supported by fees obtained from the sale of landing rights and the city's share of parking and concessions. Other common public purpose revenue bond projects include toll roads and bridges, port facilities, hospital facilities, university dormitories, and water/sewer treatment plants. The revenue sources of these bonds can be identified by a label: tolls, port entry and exit charges, hospital charges, student fees, and water/sewer user charges, respectively. In general, revenue bonds exhibit greater default risk than general obligations. The risk associated with specific bonds, however, depends on the strength of the revenue source supporting each project. Thus, some revenue bonds supported by substantial cash flows trade at rates below those on general obligations. Many revenue bonds are sufficiently complex that an investor must read the bond prospectus carefully to determine what the primary revenue source is and what group is ultimately responsible for ensuring that investors are paid. Unlike general obligation bonds, revenue bonds do not need voter approval prior to issue.

Banks buy both general obligation and revenue bonds. The only restriction is that the bonds be investment grade or equivalent. Banks generally have a preference, however, for general obligations because they are more marketable and more closely associated with essential public purposes. Since the Tax Reform Act of 1986, banks no longer buy Industrial Development Bonds (IDBs) because they carry no tax advantage.

## CREDIT RISK IN THE MUNICIPAL PORTFOLIO

Until the 1970s, few municipal securities went into default. But deteriorating conditions in many large cities ultimately resulted in defaults by New York City (1975) and Cleveland (1978). The Washington Public Power & Supply System (WHOOPS) similarly defaulted in 1983 on $2.25 billion of bonds issued to finance two nuclear power plants.[13] During the decade of the 1980s, more than 600 distinct municipals went into default. Past defaults and deteriorating economic conditions during the early 1990s raised investor concerns regarding the quality of municipal issues and the accuracy of bond ratings. Since WHOOPS's difficulties, the rating agencies have intensified their periodic reviews of issuer characteristics and conditions and revised their ratings with greater frequency after initial issue. Since 1990, Standard & Poor's Corporation has downgraded almost three times as many municipal issues as it has upgraded.

Unfortunately, the diversity of municipal borrowers and disparate types of issues make it difficult to categorize municipal securities. Many issuers do not purchase bond ratings, so their securities are nonrated. Although these securities may be low risk, an investing bank is responsible for documenting that they are equivalent to investment-grade securities. Much like the rating agencies, banks must examine the issuer's existing debt burden, the soundness of the operating budget, the strength of the tax base, cashflow support for revenue issues, and local demographic trends, all of which is recorded in a credit file. With many securities, it is extremely difficult for an investor to trace the web of revenue sources and guarantees to determine which group is ultimately responsible for meeting debt service requirements. Thus, it is often difficult to assess the credit risk associated with nonrated issues.

Many municipal issuers purchase bond insurance to reduce perceived default risk and increase the marketability of their debt. The insurance is an unconditional guarantee by a property and casualty insurance company to pay promised coupon interest and principal if the issuer defaults. The municipality pays for the insurance when the securities are issued, and the policy is nonrefundable and noncancelable over the life of the securities. During 2003 approximately 62 percent of new issues carried some form of insurance or third-party guarantee. Municipalities that purchase insurance benefit from reduced interest costs because ratings on most insured bonds improve to the triple-A or double-A level. Such issues paid rates 10 to 25 basis points below rates on otherwise comparable noninsured bonds, which can alternatively be viewed as the price investors pay for the reduced credit risk. Of course, the value of the guarantee is only as good as the insurance company. Three well-known insurers, the American Municipal Bond Assurance Corporation (AMBAC), the Municipal Bond Insurance Association (MBIA), and Financial Guaranty Insurance Company (FGIC), provide most insurance coverage in the municipal market. In 2005, MBIA admitted to the inappropriate reporting of defaults and losses on usual bonds associated with efforts to smooth earnings. If MBIA loses its Aaa rating, it would make it more expensive to provide insurance coverage.

## LIQUIDITY RISK

Municipals exhibit substantially lower liquidity than Treasury or agency securities. The secondary market for municipals is fundamentally an over-the-counter market. Small, nonrated issues trade infrequently and at relatively large bid-ask dealer spreads. Large issues of nationally known municipalities, state agencies, and states trade more actively at smaller spreads. Name recognition is critical, as investors are more comfortable when they can identify

[13]Better disclosure of municipal bond prices by dealers since 2004 has also produced greater transparency on what municipal investors buy and/or own.

the issuer with a specific location. Insurance also helps by improving the rating and by association with a known property and casualty insurer.

Still, municipals are less volatile in price than Treasury securities. This is generally attributed to the peculiar tax features of municipals.[14] The municipal market is segmented. On the supply side, municipalities cannot shift between short- and long-term securities to take advantage of yield differences because of constitutional restrictions on balanced operating budgets. Thus long-term bonds cannot be substituted for short-term municipals to finance operating expenses. On the demand side, banks once dominated the market for short-term municipals so that their rates were a set fraction of Treasury rates. Today, individuals via tax-exempt money market mutual funds dominate the short maturity spectrum. The investment activity of banks and money market mutual funds at the short end stabilizes municipal bond prices because these groups purchase most of the short-term municipals offered. This does not hold at longer maturities where individuals represent the marginal investor. As such, short-term municipals do not vary sharply in price over time relative to short-term Treasuries.

## ESTABLISHING INVESTMENT POLICY GUIDELINES

Each bank's asset and liability or risk management committee (ALCO) is responsible for establishing investment policy guidelines. These guidelines define the parameters within which investment decisions help meet overall return and risk objectives. Because securities are impersonal loans that are easily bought and sold, they can be used at the margin to help achieve a bank's liquidity, credit risk, and earnings sensitivity or duration gap targets. Investment guidelines identify specific goals and constraints regarding the composition of investments, preferred maturities or durations, quality ratings, pledging requirements, and strategies underlying any portfolio adjustments.

### RETURN OBJECTIVES

A bank's ALCO policy statement specifies overall return objectives in terms of return on equity, return on assets, and net interest margin. Investment policy guidelines complement this by identifying what portion of interest income should be generated by securities. In particular, they establish targets for the contribution of both taxable interest and tax-exempt interest to net income. Guidelines also outline the potential costs and benefits of taking tax losses or gains on security sales. The guidelines generally assume that the bank has an interest rate forecast and structures its portfolio to take advantage of rate changes.

### PORTFOLIO COMPOSITION

Investment guidelines concerning portfolio composition directly address the bank's targeted liquidity, credit risk, and interest rate risk position. The guidelines generally specify the types of securities that can be purchased, acceptable credit ratings, acceptable maturity ranges at different stages of the interest rate cycle, and those securities that should be pledged as collateral against public deposits. Examples of areas for specific guidelines follow.

### LIQUIDITY CONSIDERATIONS

1. What volume of federal funds transactions is desirable?
2. To what financial institutions should the bank sell federal funds, and from what institutions should the bank purchase security RPs?
3. Which Treasury, agency, or municipal securities should the bank pledge as collateral?
4. What amount of short-term securities (under one year) should be held as a potential liquidity reserve?
5. With which banks or securities dealers should the bank establish a trading relationship?

### CREDIT RISK CONSIDERATIONS

1. What amount of municipal, corporate, and foreign securities is optimal?
2. How much (what percentage) should the bank hold in each of the top four rating categories?
3. What is the maximum amount that can be invested in any one issuer's securities?
4. What information should credit files for nonrated municipals and all corporate and foreign bonds contain?
5. Which issuer's securities should be avoided?
6. Should the bank purchase insured municipals?

---

[14]Stock and Schrems (1987) compare the relative price volatility of municipals and Treasuries. They conclude that the volatility of short-term municipals is much lower, which is attributed to substantial short-term municipals investments by commercial banks. Relative volatility with longer-term securities is more similar.

### INTEREST RATE RISK CONSIDERATIONS

1. What maturity distribution of Treasuries, agencies, and municipals (separately) is desirable?
2. What duration characteristics are desirable?
3. What planned holding period is desirable?
4. To what extent should the bank purchase discount (or zero coupon) securities?
5. What prepayment probabilities are associated with specific mortgage-backed securities?
6. What is the convexity of specific mortgage-backed securities, and how does it vary according to the underlying coupon rate on the mortgages?

### TOTAL RETURN VERSUS CURRENT INCOME

1. To what extent will the bank actively manage its securities portfolio? Will management attempt to time interest rate movements relative to the business cycle?
2. Will management look to total return or yield to maturity (current income) as the measure of performance?
3. How will reinvestment income be calculated? Should management forecasts or forward rates be used for expected reinvestment rates?

## ACTIVE INVESTMENT STRATEGIES

Portfolio managers can buy or sell securities at the margin to achieve aggregate risk and return objectives without the worry of adversely affecting long-term depositor or borrower relationships. Investment strategies can subsequently play an integral role in meeting overall asset and liability management goals regarding interest rate risk, liquidity risk, credit risk, the bank's tax position, expected net income, and capital adequacy.

Unfortunately, not all banks view their securities portfolio in light of these opportunities. Many smaller banks passively manage their portfolios using simple buy and hold strategies. The purported advantages are that such a policy requires limited investment expertise and virtually no management time; lowers transaction costs; and provides for predictable liquidity. Other banks actively manage their portfolios by adjusting maturities, changing the composition of taxable versus tax-exempt securities, and swapping securities to meet risk and return objectives that change with the external environment. The presumed advantage is that active portfolio managers can earn above-average returns by capturing pricing discrepancies in the marketplace. The disadvantages are that managers must consistently outpredict the market for the strategies to be successful, and transactions costs are high.

The remainder of this chapter examines general factors that affect most investment decisions and active portfolio strategies that help achieve specific risk and return objectives. The analysis begins with a discussion of the traditional interest rate cycle and maturity/duration strategies to take advantage of broad-based rate movements. It then describes the impact of interest rates on mortgage prepayments, the likelihood that callable bonds will be called, and the subsequent impact on price. The final sections address how to determine the after-tax yields and optimal holdings of taxable and tax-exempt securities, and the use of security swaps as a strategy to meet risk and return targets.

## THE MATURITY OR DURATION CHOICE FOR LONG-TERM SECURITIES

Portfolio managers consider many factors when determining which securities to buy or sell. Perhaps the most difficult to quantify is the optimal maturity or duration. Difficulties arise because it is virtually impossible to systematically forecast interest rates better than the forecasts embodied in forward rates. Management must also be aware of the bank's overall interest rate risk position to make investments that will achieve the targeted risk and return profile. Many managers justify passive buy and hold strategies because they lack the time and expertise to evaluate investment alternatives and monitor performance in an attempt to outperform the market. As a result, they select securities with maturities that they hope will generate average returns over the entire business cycle. Other managers actively trade securities in an effort to earn above-average returns.

### PASSIVE MATURITY STRATEGIES

Specific policies frequently follow one of two models. The first model, the **laddered** (or **staggered***) **maturity strategy,** stipulates that management should initially specify a maximum acceptable maturity or holding period. Securities are held to maturity, and managers acquire bonds expecting to earn fixed yields over the life of the instruments. Under this strategy, securities are spaced approximately evenly throughout the maturity range so that an equal proportion of the entire portfolio matures each year. Bonds near maturity represent a liquidity buffer, with the proceeds simply reinvested at maturity in securities with the longest acceptable maturity, regardless of prevailing yields. If, for example, management wants all securities to mature within ten years, it will have ten percent of the portfolio maturing each year. As securities mature, the proceeds will be reinvested in new ten-year maturity instruments. The only decision involves selecting ten-year securities of acceptable credit quality. As such, managers do not attempt to forecast interest rates but rather recognize that the bank earns average yields over the interest rate cycle.

The second model, the **barbell maturity strategy,** differentiates between bonds purchased primarily for liquidity versus income purposes. Management invests a fraction of the portfolio, typically 25 to 40 percent, in short-term securities that pay market rates and normally trade at prices close to par. These instruments are held primarily to meet liquidity requirements. All remaining funds are invested at long-term maturities, typically 10 to 15 years, to maximize coupon interest income. The long-term bonds are sold prior to maturity and the proceeds reinvested long term once the remaining maturity falls into the intermediate range. With an upward-sloping yield curve, long-term securities pay higher initial yields. If the level of interest rates does not increase, banks sell the securities at a capital gain when less than ten years remain to maturity, thereby increasing the total return.[15] During periods of relatively stable interest rates, this barbell strategy increases the total return from holding short- and long-term bonds above that for the laddered maturity strategy because coupon interest is higher, reinvestment income is greater, and the long-term bonds are sold for a gain.

With the laddered-maturity strategy, a constant portion of the portfolio matures each year. With the barbell strategy, short-term and long-term maturities dominate, as most of the portfolio matures at these extreme periods. The first strategy requires the portfolio manager to purchase a long-term maturity security whenever a bond matures. The second picks yields off the short and long end of the maturity spectrum so managers are reinvesting proceeds more frequently. Both strategies are mechanical and have the advantage of reducing transactions costs over active portfolio management. The disadvantage is that banks that follow these strategies sacrifice short-term returns for risk reduction, so they may miss extraordinary profit opportunities.

## ACTIVE MATURITY STRATEGIES

Active portfolio management involves taking risks to improve total returns by adjusting maturities, swapping securities, and periodically liquidating discount instruments. To do this successfully, a bank should exhibit a strong capital base and broad-based earnings power. It must also avoid the trap of aggressively buying fixed-income securities at relatively low rates when loan demand is low and liquidity is high.

An integral part of active portfolio management involves having a substantial amount of securities classified as available-for-sale. In addition, active portfolio strategies recognize both liquidity needs and income requirements. For liquidity purposes, a bank should maintain a portion of its portfolio with market values at or above book values. Such instruments can always be sold at par or a gain, regardless of maturity. While this is not always easily accomplished, banks can keep their portfolios trading near par if they purchase instruments of short-term maturity or duration or variable rate instruments, or if they willingly sell securities at a loss and reinvest the proceeds in other marketable securities when rates increase. The primary advantage of this liquidity focus is that a bank can substitute between long- and short-duration instruments as long as a portion of the portfolio exhibits price appreciation. If an acceptable amount of long-term securities is currently priced above book value, management can invest any remaining funds at maturities or durations consistent with its interest rate forecasts and desired risk position. The primary disadvantage is that losses may arise from inaccurate forecasts.

One strategy has banks actively adjust their GAP and earnings-sensitivity profile in line with interest rate forecasts. Regular ALCO meetings identify the portfolio interest sensitivity and potential volatility of the bank's net interest margin to rate changes. Banks that are liability sensitive or have a positive duration gap may reduce their earnings sensitivity or shorten the aggregate duration of assets by purchasing short-duration securities if they intend to reduce their risk exposure. This would be consistent with an environment where rates are expected to rise above those suggested by the market. Alternatively, such banks may choose to increase their exposure by buying long-term or long-duration securities, thereby increasing the degree of liability sensitivity and the duration gap. This might occur when the bank has sufficient liquidity and management forecasts a long-term decrease in interest rates. Banks that are asset sensitive or have a negative duration gap might similarly buy long-duration securities to reduce their risk exposure when rates are expected to decline, or do the opposite when rates are expected to rise. The key point is that a bank's maturity or duration choice depends on its aggregate goals for interest rate risk and return. By adjusting security maturities and durations it may be speculating on future rate movements. If management consciously assumes greater risk in the security portfolio, it assumes that it can forecast rates better than the market such that its interest rate forecast is better than forward rates implied by current yields.

---

[15]Total return is the zero coupon equivalent return an investor receives from the coupon payments, the reinvestment income on these coupons, and the price appreciation or depreciation at sale or maturity. See Chapter 4 for details.

**RIDING THE YIELD CURVE.** Another example might be a portfolio manager who attempts to ride the yield curve. It works best when the yield curve is upward sloping and rates are stable. The strategy involves buying securities with a maturity longer than the planned holding period and selling the securities prior to maturity. There are three basic steps.First, identify the appropriate investment horizon, such as five years. Second, buy a par-value security with a maturity longer than the investment horizon where the coupon yield is high in relation to the overall yield curve. Third, sell the security at the end of the holding period when time still remains until maturity. If market rates stay relatively constant or fall, the total return will exceed that from simply buying the security that matches the planned investment horizon. The reason is that the holder receives more in coupon interest, reinvests the higher coupons to earn greater reinvestment income, and probably sells the security at a gain.

Consider the example summarized in Exhibit 13.10. A portfolio manager has a fifteen-year investment horizon or holding period. A risk reduction strategy might involve buying a five-year security yielding 7.6 percent and holding it to maturity. Alternatively, if the manager felt that rates would remain roughly constant over the next five years, another alternative would be to buy a ten-year security paying 8 percent, and sell the security after five years. If rates are stable, a five-year security will yield the same 7.6 percent in five years and the bond can be sold at a gain. In addition, the ten-year security carries a higher coupon so that periodic interest payments are higher and reinvestment income will be greater. As indicated, the five-year security pays $7,600 in interest annually that is assumed to be reinvested each year at 7 percent. The ten-year security, in contrast, pays $8,000 in annual interest so that actual coupon and reinvestment income will be greater with the same assumed 7 percent annual reinvestment rate. After five years, the five-year bond returns principal of $100,000. If rates are constant, the ten-year bond sells for $101,615 with five years remaining to maturity. The bottom part of the exhibit demonstrates that the total return from riding the yield curve is 58 basis points greater than the total return for the matched holding period strategy. Of course, this active strategy involves greater risk. If rates rise substantially, the bond would have to be sold for a loss that could potentially wipe out the incremental coupon and reinvestment income earned.

To implement active investment strategies, portfolio managers must understand the interest rate environment in which they operate. They should continuously monitor recent movements in the level of rates and the magnitude of various rate differentials to formulate an interest rate forecast. Most importantly, portfolio managers must understand their bank's specific risk and return objectives and current financial position. No one can accurately forecast specific interest rates over long periods of time. However, managers can often position their portfolios to take advantage of long-term trends in rates.

## INTEREST RATES AND THE BUSINESS CYCLE

Most portfolio managers structure security maturities relative to the business cycle. Exhibit 13.11 that characterizes the general relationship between when the yield curve first inverts and the length of time until a U.S. recession begins. The exhibit suggests that the term-structure of Treasury yields follows predictable patterns within the business cycle. Generally, the Fed and analysts look at the one-year Treasury rate versus the ten-year Treasury rate. If the ten-year rate exceeds the one-year rate, the yield curve is upward-sloping. This generally occurs during periods that coincide with monetary ease and short-term rates are low. The one-year rate exceeds the ten-year rate (the yield curve is inverted) when rates increase to their cyclical peak and thereafter as the Federal Reserve restricts money growth. The consensus is that the shape of the yield curve contains information regarding the market's consensus forecast of interest rates.[16] When the yield curve is upward sloping, the market forecast is that short-term rates are going to rise from their relatively low levels. Because long-term rates represent an average of current and expected short-term rates, they too will increase with expected increases in short-term rates. When the yield curve is inverted or downward sloping, the market forecast is that short-term rates will decline, thus lowering long-term rates.

Data at the bottom of Exhibit 13.11 demonstrate that in each of the six recent times noted that the U.S. Treasury yield curve inverted, a recession followed in the United States within three to 20 months. The average length of time between recessions was 12.3 months. The implication is that the ten-year to one-year Treasury yield differential serves as a good indicator of an economic downturn.

Consensus forecasts obviously represent averages. Individual traders may have substantially different views of economic conditions and the likely movement in interest rates. As they take different positions, the yield curve shifts to reflect the new, market-driven consensus. Thus, any implied interest rate forecast simply reflects the market's current guess about future rates, based on prevailing information.

**PASSIVE STRATEGIES OVER THE BUSINESS CYCLE.** One popular passiveinvestment strategy follows from the traditional belief that a bank's securities portfolio should consist of primary reserves and secondary reserves. This view suggests that banks hold short-term, highly marketable securities primarily to meet

---

[16]Discussion of the three theories of yield curves—the unbiased expectations theory, the liquidity premium theory, and the market segmentation theory—can be found in most financial markets textbooks. This analysis focuses only on the role of expected interest rates. One can also derive forward rates from prevailing yields. In 2001, the U.S. Treasury stopped the regular auction of one-year Treasury securities, but it is still possible to use an implicit one-year yield in the analysis.

## EXHIBIT 13.10  Effect of Riding the Yield Curve on Total Return when Interest Rates are Stable

*Cash Flows*

| | Buy a 5-Year Security | | Buy a 10-Year Security and Sell It after 5 Years | |
|---|---|---|---|---|
| Period: Year-End | Coupon Interest | Reinvestment Income at 7% | Coupon Interest | Reinvestment Income at 7% |
| 1 | $ 7,600 | — | $ 8,000 | — |
| 2 | 7,600 | $ 532 | 8,000 | $ 560 |
| 3 | 7,600 | 1,101 | 8,000 | 1,159 |
| 4 | 7,600 | 1,710 | 8,000 | 1,800 |
| 5 | 7,600 | 2,362 | 8,000 | 2,486 |
| Total | $38,000 | $5,705 | $40,000 | $6,005 |
| 5 | Principal at Maturity = $100,000 | | Price at Sale after 5 years = $101,615 when rate = 7.6% | |

**Expected total return:***

5-Year Security:

$$i = \left[ \frac{(100,000 + 38,000 + 5,705)}{100,000} \right]^{1/5} - 1$$

$$i = 0.752$$

10-Year Security:

$$y = \left[ \frac{(101,615 + 40,000 + 6,005)}{100,000} \right]^{1/5} - 1$$

$$y = 0.810$$

Difference in Total Returns:  $y - i = .0058$

*Realized yield with an assumed reinvestment rate different from the yield to maturity.

unanticipated loan demand and deposit withdrawals. Once these primary liquidity reserves are established, banks invest any residual funds in long-term securities that are less liquid but offer higher yields. These residual investments, or secondary reserves, thus focus on generating income.

A problem arises because banks normally have excess liquidity during contractionary periods when consumer spending is low, loan demand is declining, unemployment is rising, and the Fed starts to pump reserves into the banking system. Interest rates are thus relatively low. Banks employing this strategy add to their secondary reserve by buying long-term securities near the low point in the interest rate cycle. Long-term rates are typically above short-term rates, but all rates are relatively low. With a buy and hold orientation, these banks lock themselves into securities that depreciate in value as interest rates move higher. Bankers who follow these passive strategies are often unwilling to sell securities at a loss. They end up holding the low-coupon securities until maturity, thereby forgoing opportunities to enhance investment returns.

Passive investment strategies can avoid these difficulties only if the bank buys securities when yields are at cyclical peaks, or if the bank restricts its purchases to securities with short maturities. In both cases the bank will find that the market value of its portfolio consistently exceeds or at least equals its cost. At rate peaks, the economy is growing rapidly as spending and loan demands are high. The Fed, concerned about rising inflation expectations, slows reserves growth such that short-term rates move above long-term rates as rates increase. With high loan demand, banks do not have sufficient funds to invest in securities in the belief that meeting loan demand is more important than buying securities. Of course, it is extremely difficult to accurately forecast interest rate turns, so banks cannot systematically time investments at interest rate peaks. The fundamental problem with short-term investments is that interest income is relatively unpredictable beyond one year. The bank also forgoes any opportunity to earn above-average returns by locking in high-coupon yields or selling securities with substantial price appreciation.

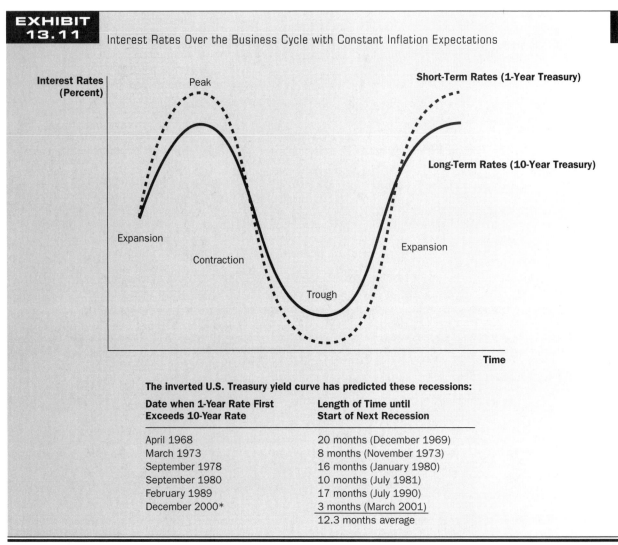

**EXHIBIT 13.11** Interest Rates Over the Business Cycle with Constant Inflation Expectations

**The inverted U.S. Treasury yield curve has predicted these recessions:**

| Date when 1-Year Rate First Exceeds 10-Year Rate | Length of Time until Start of Next Recession |
|---|---|
| April 1968 | 20 months (December 1969) |
| March 1973 | 8 months (November 1973) |
| September 1978 | 16 months (January 1980) |
| September 1980 | 10 months (July 1981) |
| February 1989 | 17 months (July 1990) |
| December 2000* | 3 months (March 2001) |
| | 12.3 months average |

*Three-month Rate First Exceeded ten-Year Rate

**ACTIVE STRATEGIES AND THE BUSINESS CYCLE.** Many portfolio managers attempt to time major movements in the level of interest rates relative to the business cycle and adjust security maturities accordingly. Some try to time interest rate peaks by following a contracyclical investment strategy defined by changes in loan demand. The strategy entails both expanding the investment portfolio and lengthening maturities when loan demand is high, and alternatively contracting the portfolio and shortening maturities when loan demand is weak. As such, the bank goes against the credit (lending) cycle. A review of Exhibit 13.11 indicates that the yield curve generally inverts when rates are at their peak prior to a recession. Note the data at the bottom of the exhibit, which relate the date when the one-year Treasury rate first exceeded the ten-year Treasury rate. In all but one instance since World War II, a recession followed within 20 months after the Treasury yield curve inverted.[17] In 1967, the 1-year rate exceeded the ten-year rate and a recession did not follow. This date coincided with the Vietnam War such that many analysts attribute the lack of a recession to massive federal government spending.

A contracyclical strategy involves buying long-term securities when the yield curve is inverted. The yield curve inversion signals a gradual decline in rates that active portfolio managers try to anticipate by substituting bonds for loans and lengthening bond maturities with impending recession. If a recession is likely, banks should reduce their loan exposure because loan charge-offs will eventually increase. A bank that follows such a contracyclical

---

[17]The yield curve did invert in 1999 when the U.S. Treasury announced a program to use federal budget surpluses to repurchase outstanding long-term Treasury securities. Not surprisingly, participants immediately bid long-term rates lower in anticipation of future Treasury purchases. Thus, the yield curve inversion was materially independent of general economic conditions. Current analysis focuses on a comparison of the 3 month yield with the 10-year yield as the Treasury no longer regularly issues 1-year securities.

strategy is much more likely to purchase securities when the level of interest rates is high. These yields can in turn be locked in for long periods of time. The disadvantage is that a bank either has to restrict credit to loan customers or rely on relatively expensive, short-term debt instruments such as federal funds to finance the loans. Because the yield curve is inverted, many investment officers feel pressure to continue buying short-term securities due to their higher yields. If rates follow the cycle, these high short-term rates will be only temporary. Investment officers also feel pressure from lenders who are being asked not to make loans when loan demand is strong. Of course, if a recession follows, loan problems typically increase, and effective loan yields after charge-offs fall.

The contracyclical strategy also suggests that when loan demand is weak, banks should keep investments short term. This is a time of relatively low yields indicated by the trough in Exhibit 13.11. The obvious problem is that without loans, banks need to find higher-yielding investments to maintain net interest income. Thus, the tendency is to lengthen maturities because the yield curve is upward sloping and banks are in search of higher yields. If rates do increase, the bank will ultimately have to sell the securities at a loss or keep them in its portfolio and simply not realize the loss but earn a below-market yield.

It is important to remember that efforts to time interest rate changes are risky. If management guesses incorrectly and positions the bank accordingly, it may have to take capital losses when it sells securities or it will forgo income that it could have earned alternatively. Because it is a riskier strategy, the volatility of returns will be greater than with passive strategies.

## THE IMPACT OF INTEREST RATES ON THE VALUE OF SECURITIES WITH EMBEDDED OPTIONS

Banks have been heavy buyers of a wide range of mortgage-backed securities and callable agency securities. Each of these carries *embedded options* in the sense that the security issuers (borrowers) can prepay the outstanding principal at their discretion. This feature makes it more difficult for an investor to value the security because the value will depend on the likelihood that the option will be exercised as well as the terms of exercise. The following discussion addresses issues that must be considered when deciding whether to buy such securities and how valuable the securities are.

### ISSUES FOR SECURITIES WITH EMBEDDED OPTIONS

Whenever a bank buys a callable agency security or mortgage-backed security, it must value the embedded option to determine the risk and return profile of the instrument. There are three direct questions to address. First, is the investor the buyer or seller of the option? Second, how much does the option cost, or how much is the seller being compensated? Third, when will the option be exercised and what is the likelihood of exercise? Answers to each of these indicate how the option affects the security's value.

The answer to the first question is straightforward. The buyer of the option is the party that controls the option exercise. In the case of a callable bond or MBS, the borrower chooses when to exercise the option; that is, when to call the bond or refinance the underlying mortgage. Thus, the investor sells the option to the borrower. How does the investor get paid? Generally, the investor receives a higher yield on a security with an option compared to a similar security without the option. Several models exist to estimate how much the option is worth and help an investor decide whether to buy the security. A model that uses option-adjusted spread (OAS) analysis is introduced later in the chapter. Finally, these embedded options will generally be exercised when they are in the money and it is in the borrower's best interest to refinance or prepay. In the case of callable agencies and MBSs, option exercise normally occurs when interest rates fall sufficiently below the current coupon and borrowers can replace the existing debt with lower-cost debt. Uncertainty regarding when these options will be in the money and exercised makes it more difficult to estimate the market value of such securities.

Consider the FHLB bond introduced earlier in the chapter. This bond was callable at $100 par value, had a three-year final maturity, the issuer could not call the bond for one year, and was priced at $99.97 to yield 5.78 percent. The top part of Exhibit 13.12 indicates its general price-yield relationship. At the quoted price and yield, the option is at the money. Note that if market rates rise, the bond's price will fall, much like an option-free bond. However, as rates fall, the call option moves in the money. Because the bond cannot be called for one year, the price may rise above $100, but it will not increase much above par and will move toward the $100 call price as the call deferment period ends. Unlike an option-free bond, there is little potential price appreciation for this bond because an investor knows it will be called when possible if rates fall. A noncallable FHLB bond with a three-year maturity will carry a lower initial yield, but would increase in price were rates to fall. Thus, the value and price sensitivity of the callable bond versus the noncallable bond will vary sharply depending on whether rates rise or fall over time and whether the bond is called.

Now consider the high-coupon, interest-only (IO) MBS with the price-yield relationship characterized in section B of Exhibit 13.12. This security carries a 8 percent coupon, but the prevailing mortgage rate is 5.5 percent. Given the rate differential, the mortgages underlying the IO are prepaying at a CPR of 30 percent, which produces a market

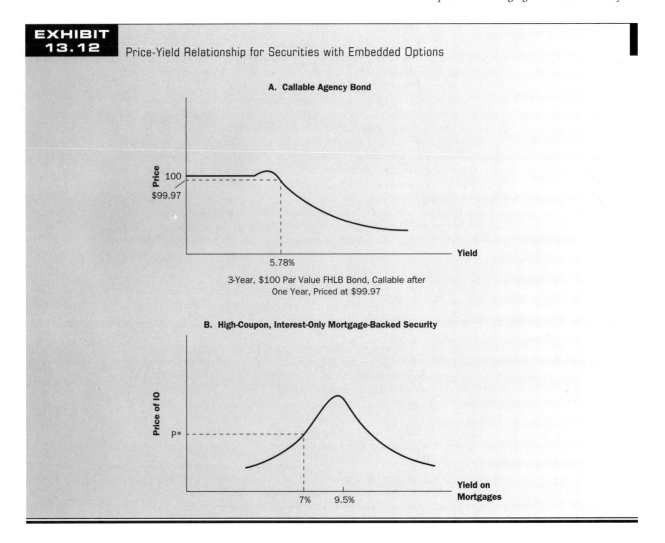

**EXHIBIT 13.12** Price-Yield Relationship for Securities with Embedded Options

**A. Callable Agency Bond**

3-Year, $100 Par Value FHLB Bond, Callable after One Year, Priced at $99.97

**B. High-Coupon, Interest-Only Mortgage-Backed Security**

price of P*. At this CPR, the IO has an estimated life of just 1.5 years, so an investor will receive the high-coupon interest only briefly. If the rate on the underlying mortgages rises, prepayments will slow and the investor will receive the high coupons for a longer period of time than the 1.5 years currently expected. The price of the IO will typically increase in this situation. However, if the underlying mortgage rate decreases, the prepayment rate will increase and the coupons will be received for a shorter time period. Not surprisingly, the IO's price will generally fall. Over the range of mortgage rates below 8 percent, the IO's price varies directly with changes in the mortgage rate.

How different is this from option-free bonds where the price of fixed-income securities varies inversely with market interest rates? At mortgage rates above 8 percent, the IO will decline in price as the CPR falls toward 6 percent and the expected cash flows are discounted at higher rates. Again, the point is that the value and price sensitivity of the IO varies with whether the option is in the money and the likelihood that it will move in or out of the money.

### THE ROLES OF DURATION AND CONVEXITY IN ANALYZING BOND PRICE VOLATILITY

Most option-free bonds exhibit predictable price-yield relationships because valuation involves straightforward present value analysis of promised cash flows. The analysis is complicated when bonds with call and put options are valued. Prepayments with MBSs make pricing difficult because prepayment effects can swamp discounting effects resulting from the same change in interest rates. The case where an IO decreases in value when mortgage rates decrease serves as an example. Many bond analysts use the concepts of duration and convexity to measure price sensitivity.

Duration for option-free securities measures the weighted average of the time until cash flows are made on a security. The weights equal the present value of each cash flow divided by the price of the security. Alternatively, duration is an approximate elasticity measure. As such, it measures the relative price sensitivity of a security to a change in the underlying interest rate. Consider a three-year, $10,000 par bond with a 10 percent coupon that pays $500 interest at six-month intervals and $10,000 at maturity. The bond is option-free. The curved line in Exhibit 13.13 shows the relationship between the bond's price and market yield according to the present-value formula. Notice that the shape of the curve is nonlinear. The Macaulay duration of the bond appears at the bottom of the exhibit and is measured in semiannual periods. Duration can be represented by the slope of the price-yield relationship at various yields, and approximated by the following equation:

$$\text{Duration} = -\frac{\Delta P/P}{\Delta i/(1+i)} \tag{13.4}$$

where P equals the price of the bond and i equals the market yield. Rearranging terms,

$$\Delta P \cong -\text{Duration}\left[\Delta i/(1+i)\right]P \tag{13.5}$$

Equation 13.5 can be applied in the following manner. Suppose that the prevailing yield on the bond is 10 percent so that duration equals 5.329 6-month periods (2.665 years). If the underlying market rate falls to 8 percent, the bond's price increases to $10,524.21 according to the present-value formula. Equation 13.5 approximates the price change as:

$$\Delta P = -5.329(-0.01/1.05)\,\$10,000$$
$$= \$507.52$$

The estimated price of $10,507.52 can be read off the straight line in Exhibit 13.13 representing the slope of the price-yield curve at a 10 percent yield. The pricing error is thus $16.69. Interestingly, a 2 percent increase in market rate will lower the bond price by only $491.73, which is less in absolute value than the price increase when the market rate fell by 2 percent. The pricing error ($15.79 in this instance) is also lower when rates increase.

A careful inspection of Exhibit 13.13 reveals several important conclusions:

- The difference between the actual price-yield curve and the straight line representing duration at the point of tangency equals the error in applying duration to estimate the change in bond price at each new yield.
- For both rate increases and rate decreases, the estimated price based on duration will be below the actual price.
- Actual price increases are greater and price declines less than that suggested by duration when interest rates fall or rise, respectively, for option-free bonds.
- For small changes in yield, such as yields near 10 percent, the error is small.
- For large changes in yield, such as yields well above or well below 10 percent, the error is large.

The fundamental implication is that duration reasonably approximates price volatility on an option-free bond only when yield changes are small.

**Convexity**, in contrast, characterizes the rate of change in duration when yields change. It attempts to improve upon duration as an approximation of price volatility. Notice from Exhibit 13.13 that the slope of a line tangent to the price-yield curve will increase as yields fall below 10 percent, and will decrease as yields rise above 10 percent. In essence, the duration of the bond lengthens as yields fall and shortens as yields rise. The percentage price decrease is smaller, in turn, than the percentage price increase for the same change in rates. This characteristic is called *positive convexity*, signifying that the underlying bond becomes more price sensitive when yields decline and less price sensitive when yields rise. This is a good feature of price sensitivity because it increases security's gain and decreases to loss when rates change. With negative convexity, the bond holder gets little or no price appreciation when rates fall.

Formally, convexity can be defined as the second derivative of a bond's price with respect to the interest rate, divided by the bond's price. A bond's convexity can be combined with duration to better estimate true price volatility from yield changes. The additional convexity measure captures a portion of the error associated with using duration alone. The previous example demonstrates the value of convexity. From 10 percent to 8 percent, the estimated price change due to duration equals $507.52, as described earlier. At 10 percent, the estimated convexity of the bond in Exhibit 13.13 is 16.23 semiannual periods. The estimated price change due to convexity thus equals $16.23 with the assumed 1 percent decline in the semiannual rate.

$$\Delta P \text{ due to convexity} = \text{Convexity } (\Delta i)^2 P \tag{13.6}$$

or

$$= 16.23\,(.01)^2\,\$10,000$$
$$= \$16.23$$

Price-Yield Relationships and Duration for an Option-free Bond

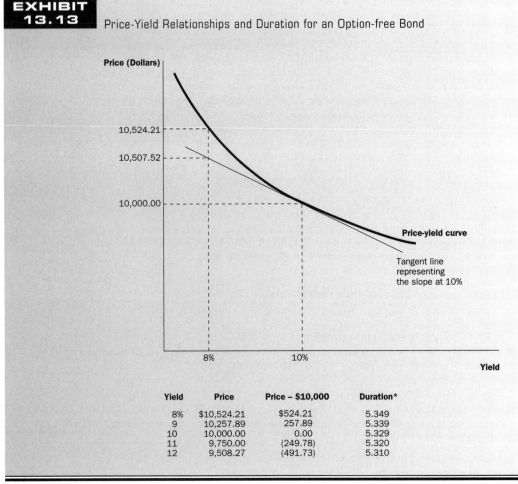

| Yield | Price | Price – $10,000 | Duration* |
|-------|-------|-----------------|-----------|
| 8% | $10,524.21 | $524.21 | 5.349 |
| 9 | 10,257.89 | 257.89 | 5.339 |
| 10 | 10,000.00 | 0.00 | 5.329 |
| 11 | 9,750.00 | (249.78) | 5.320 |
| 12 | 9,508.27 | (491.73) | 5.310 |

*Macaulay's duration in semiannual periods.

SOURCE: Timothy Koch, "The Roles of Duration and Convexity in Analyzing Bond Price Volatility." *Bank Asset/Liability Management.* New York: Warren, Gorham & Lamond, 1989.

The estimated price change due to duration and convexity together equals $523.75, or just $0.46 less than the actual price change. Knowing a bond's duration and convexity allows for improved forecasts of price sensitivity even when yields change substantially.

## IMPACT OF PREPAYMENTS ON DURATION AND YIELD FOR BONDS WITH OPTIONS

The previous discussion about duration and convexity addresses option-free securities. Securities with options potentially exhibit far different price sensitivities as indicated in Exhibit 13.12. These embedded options affect the estimated duration and convexity of such securities.

Even though participants cannot forecast prepayments precisely, it is important to know how they affect the duration and thus the price and yield of MBSs. In general, market participants price mortgage-backed securities by following a three-step procedure. First, participants estimate the duration of the MBS based on an assumed interest rate environment and the corresponding prepayment speed. Second, they identify a zero coupon Treasury security with the same (approximate) duration. Third, the MBS is priced at a markup over the Treasury. Specifically, the MBS yield is set equal to the yield on the same duration Treasury plus a positive spread. This spread can range from 20 basis points to 3 percent depending on market conditions. Thus, MBS yields reflect the zero coupon Treasury yield curve plus a premium.[18]

---

[18]Alternatively, securities with options may be priced based on the LIBOR interest rate swap curve such that yields are quoted as a spread to the swap curve.

Different MBSs will exhibit different durations and different price sensitivities depending on their specific characteristics. The most important characteristics are those that influence the prepayment rate, and include the coupon rate, mortgage age, and related demographic factors. The coupon rate is important because it is generally just below the rate that borrowers pay on the underlying mortgages. If the current mortgage rate is substantially below the coupon rate, prepayments should be substantial. The greater are prepayments, the shorter is a security's duration, because an investor receives the underlying principal and interest payments earlier. If prepayments slow, duration lengthens because larger cash flows are received later. Mortgage age is important because most borrowers won't refinance immediately after taking out a new mortgage. Specifically, during the first 30 months after origination, mortgage prepayments are relatively low and increase slowly over time. Without any special rate inducements prepayments typically increase through five years, then slowly decline. Finally, demographic factors affect prepayments because of labor mobility and the age of the underlying population. A younger population is normally more mobile, as is the entire labor force when a specific geographic labor market is booming.

Chapter 4 demonstrated that option-free securities have well-defined price and yield relationships. This is not true for securities with embedded options. Specifically, as rates rise (fall), Macaulay's duration for an option-free security declines (increases). Option-free securities exhibit *positive convexity* because as rates rise the percentage price decline is less than the percentage price increase associated with the same rate decline. Securities with embedded options may exhibit *negative convexity*. This characteristic means that the percentage price increase is less than the percentage price decrease for equal negative and positive changes in rates. The callable bond and high-coupon IO described in Exhibit 13.12 reveal such negative convexity. In fact, as market rates fall and the option moves in the money, in both cases the duration of the security declines and the price either stays unchanged (callable FHLB bond) or falls (high-coupon IO).

Analysts use measures of *effective duration* and *effective convexity,* provided in Equations 13.7 and 13.8, to describe the price sensitivity of securities with options

$$\text{Effective Duration} = \frac{P^- - P^+}{P^* (i^+ - i^-)} \tag{13.7}$$

$$\text{Effective Convexity} = \frac{P^- + P^+ - 2P^*}{P^* [0.5 (i^* - i^-)]^2} \tag{13.8}$$

where   $P^-$ = Price if the market rate falls by z basis points,
   $P^+$ = Price if the market rate rises by z basis points,
   $P^*$ = Initial price,
   $i^-$ = Initial market rate minus z basis points, and
   $i^+$ = initial market rate plus z basis points.

A careful review suggests that effective duration is an approximation and may, in fact, be negative. A negative value would arise if the price associated with a rate decrease does not end up above the price associated with a rate decrease. This outcome might arise if the prepay option fell deep into the money in a declining-rate environment.

## TOTAL RETURN AND OPTION-ADJUSTED SPREAD ANALYSIS OF SECURITIES WITH OPTIONS

When buying securities with options, many investors conduct *total return analysis* to estimate the potential return on the security. This is valuable because investors do not know when the options may move in the money and how cash flows may change from that expected. Such cash-flow changes may, in turn, dramatically influence the return actually realized. Investors also frequently consider a security's *option-adjusted spread* as an estimate of the value of the option that is being sold to the security issuer.

**TOTAL RETURN ANALYSIS.** An investor's actual realized return should reflect the coupon interest, reinvestment income, and value of the security at maturity or sale at the end of the holding period. When the security carries embedded options, such as the prepayment option with mortgage-backed securities, these component cash flows will vary in different interest rate environments. For example, if rates fall and borrowers prepay faster than originally expected, coupon interest will fall as the outstanding principal falls, reinvestment income will fall because rates are lower when the proceeds are reinvested and less coupon interest is received, and the price at sale (end of the holding period) may rise or fall depending on the speed of prepayments. When rates rise, borrowers prepay slower so that coupon income increases, reinvestment income increases, and the price at sale (end of the holding period) again may rise or fall.

Consider the total return analysis for the Federal Home Loan Bank bond in Panel A of Exhibit 13.14. On April 18, 2004 (settlement April 19th), the bond had just over five years until maturity, carried a 4.32 percent

**EXHIBIT 13.14** Total Return Analysis for a Callable FHLB Bond

TRA          P205 Corp **TRA**

## Total Return Analysis for FHLB4.32 07/10

Settlement 4/19/05 Price 99.4996 Yield 4.427 to 7/14/10 @ 100

| YLD SHFT | S/A Reinv | Pricing at Traded to | | 4/19/06 HORIZON SPRD* | Yield | Price | Total Return Bond | 5 YR | %PPOB |
|---|---|---|---|---|---|---|---|---|---|
| -150 | 2.93 | CALL | 7/14/06 100 | +106.6 | 2.927 | 100.32 | 5.11 | 9.38 | 0.0 |
| -100 | 3.43 | CALL | 7/14/06 100 | +106.6 | 3.427 | 100.2 | 5.00 | 7.54 | 2.0 |
| -50 | 3.93 | CALL | 7/14/06 100 | +106.6 | 3.927 | 100.08 | 4.90 | 5.72 | 25.0 |
| 0 | 4.43 | MTY | 7/14/10 100 | + 49.6 | 4.427 | 99.585 | 4.43 | 3.92 | 47.6 |
| 50 | 4.93 | MTY | 7/14/10 100 | + 49.6 | 4.927 | 97.699 | 2.60 | 2.14 | 21.8 |
| 100 | 5.43 | MTY | 7/14/10 100 | + 49.6 | 5.427 | 95.854 | 0.79 | 0.39 | 3.3 |
| 150 | 5.93 | MTY | 7/14/10 100 | + 49.6 | 5.927 | 94.05 | -0.99 | -1.34 | 0.2 |
| ExVal 4.43 | | | | 65.0 | 4.427 | 99.175 | 4.02 | 3.93 | |

Mode: **T** (Trad'1/OAS)    Fixed Yld Convention? **Y**

BOND TOTAL RETURN vs TSY YLD SHIFT

| BMK TSY YLD 18:59 | |
|---|---|
| 10YR | 4.272 |
| 5 YR | 3.913 |
| 2 YR | 3.540 |
| 1 YR | 3.288 |

Probabilities **V**
C-Custom
V-Yld Std Dev at
39 bp/year   Log?**Y**
10.0 % Yld Volat.

View **T**
T-TotRet,C-CVX,D-DUR

*SPRDS done to interpolated BMRK Curve

Australia 61 2 9777 8600   Brazil 5511 3048 4500   Europe 44 20 7330 7500   Germany 49 69 920410
Hong Kong 852 2977 6000 Japan 81 3 3201 8900 Singapore 65 6212 1000 U.S. 1 212 318 2000 Copyright 2005 Bloomberg L.P.
2 18-Apr-05 19:00:43

TRA          P205 Corp **TRA**

## TOTAL RETURN ANALYSIS FOR FHLB4.32 07/10

Settlement 4/19/05 Price 99.4996 Yield 4.427 to 7/14/10 @ 100

| YLD SHFT | S/A Reinv | Pricing at Traded to | | 4/19/07 HORIZON SPRD* | Yield | Price | Total Return Bond | 5 YR | %PPOB |
|---|---|---|---|---|---|---|---|---|---|
| -150 | 2.93 | MTY | 7/14/10 100 | + 49.6 | 2.927 | 104.27 | 6.47 | 5.88 | 0.5 |
| -100 | 3.43 | MTY | 7/14/10 100 | + 49.6 | 3.427 | 102.71 | 5.78 | 5.22 | 7.3 |
| -50 | 3.93 | MTY | 7/14/10 100 | + 49.6 | 3.927 | 101.18 | 5.10 | 4.57 | 26.6 |
| 0 | 4.43 | MTY | 7/14/10 100 | + 49.6 | 4.427 | 99.675 | 4.43 | 3.93 | 34.8 |
| 50 | 4.93 | MTY | 7/14/10 100 | + 49.6 | 4.927 | 98.198 | 3.76 | 3.29 | 21.3 |
| 100 | 5.43 | MTY | 7/14/10 100 | + 49.6 | 5.427 | 96.748 | 3.09 | 2.65 | 7.4 |
| 150 | 5.93 | MTY | 7/14/10 100 | + 49.6 | 5.927 | 95.323 | 2.44 | 2.02 | 2.0 |
| ExVal 4.43 | | | | 49.6 | 4.425 | 99.698 | 4.43 | 3.93 | |

Mode: **T** (Trad'1/OAS)    Fixed Yld Convention? **Y**

BOND TOTAL RETURN vs TSY YLD SHIFT

| BMK TSY YLD 18:59 | |
|---|---|
| 10YR | 4.272 |
| 5 YR | 3.913 |

Probabilities **V**
C-Custom
V-Yld Std Dev at
39 bp/year   Log?**Y**
10.0 % Yld Volat.

View **T**
T-TotRet,C-CVX,D-DUR

*SPRDS done to interpolated BMRK Curve

Australia 61 2 9777 8600   Brazil 5511 3048 4500   Europe 44 20 7330 7500   Germany 49 69 920410
Hong Kong 852 2977 6000 Japan 81 3 3201 8900 Singapore 65 6212 1000 U.S. 1 212 318 2000 Copyright 2005 Bloomberg L.P.
2 18-Apr-05 19:01:03

coupon rate, and was callable at par on July 14, 2006. It was priced at \$99.4996 to yield 4.427 percent to maturity. The data provide the results of a rate shock analysis in which the Treasury yield curve is assumed to shift up and down by 50, 100, and 150 basis points from prevailing levels (0 yield shift position) as represented by the different rows of data. Focus on the two columns of data under the heading "Total Return." The first column under "Bond" indicates the estimated total return on the callable FHLB bond, while the second column under "5 YR" indicates the total return on a 5-year, option-free Treasury as an alternative investment. The horizon notation indicates that the assumed holding period is one year (April 19, 2006) from settlement. The column of data under "S/A Reinv" indicates the assumed reinvestment rate, and the data under "Price" indicate the estimated price of the FHLB bond at different interest rate levels.

Compare the two total returns at different rate levels. If rates stay constant over the year, the callable bond's total return will equal 4.43 percent, while the Treasury's total return will equal 3.92 percent. If rates fall as indicated by the negative values for the yield shift, both total returns will be higher due to the increased price for each bond. Note that the holding period ends three months before the call date. If rates rise as indicated in the bottom three rows of data, both total returns fall over the year due to the falling prices. The analysis indicates in general what an investors' "bet" is if he or she buys the callable bond versus a 5-year Treasury. Specifically, with a one-year holding period, the investor would be better off buying the callable bond if rates remain constant or rise. If rates fall, the callable bond will not appreciate much in price because it will likely be called three months later.

Consider now the data in Panel B, which are generated in similar fashion to the data in Panel A except the assumed investment horizon is two years, after the one-time call date. The comparison of total returns between the FHLB bond and 5-year, option-free Treasury now indicates that an investor would be better off buying the callable bond on all rate environment. The callable bond carries a 4.32 percent coupon so the investor is assumed to earn coupon interest at a much higher rate than that for the 5-year Treasury. If the bond is not called, it has the same approximate maturity as the Treasury but with a higher coupon. The call option is out of the money. Total return analysis allows an investor to better gauge the risk and return trade-off between securities.

**OPTION-ADJUSTED SPREAD.** The previous discussion demonstrates that the standard calculation of yield-to-maturity is inappropriate with prepayment risk. Many analysts instead use an option-adjusted spread (OAS) approach when pricing callable agency and mortgage-backed securities. An OAS approach accounts for factors that potentially affect the likelihood and frequency of call and prepayments.[19] Before discussing OAS, it is important to understand **static spread,** which is commonly used to describe the yield on a security with options versus that of an option-free Treasury. Specifically, the static spread is the yield premium, in percent, that when added to Treasury spot rates (zero coupon Treasury rates) along the yield curve, equates the present value of the estimated cash flows for the security with options to the prevailing price of the matched-maturity Treasury. It is an average spread over the entire spot yield curve that indicates the incremental yield to an investor in the security relative to yields on zero coupon Treasuries with options. It does not directly take into account the value of the option or its frequency of exercise.

OAS analysis is one procedure to estimate how much an investor is being compensated for selling an option to the issuer of a security with options. Stephen Smith (1991) summarizes the process via the diagram in Exhibit 13.15 for mortgage-backed securities. Briefly, the approach starts with estimating Treasury spot rates (zero coupon Treasury rates) using a probability distribution and Monte Carlo simulation, identifying a large number of possible interest rate scenarios over the time period that the security's cash flows will appear. The analysis then assigns probabilities to various cash flows based on the different interest rate scenarios. For mortgages, one needs a prepayment model and for callable bonds, one needs rules and prices indicating when the bonds will be called and at what values. OAS analysis involves three basic calculations.

1. For each scenario, a yield premium is added to the Treasury spot rate (matched-maturity zero coupon Treasury rate) and used to discount the cash flows.

2. For every interest rate scenario, the average present value of the security's cash flows is calculated.

3. The yield premium that equates the average present value of the cash flows from the security with options to the prevailing price of the security without options is the OAS.

Conceptually, OAS represents the incremental yield earned by investors from a security with options over the Treasury spot curve, after accounting for when and at what price the embedded options will be exercised. The advantage is that an option-adjusted spread reflects consensus expectations regarding the interest rate

---

[19]Frank Fabozzi provides an excellent summary of static spread and OAS applied to CMOs in *CMOs: Structure and Analysis* (FJF Associates, 1996).

## EXHIBIT 13.15   Steps in Option-Adjusted Spread Calculation

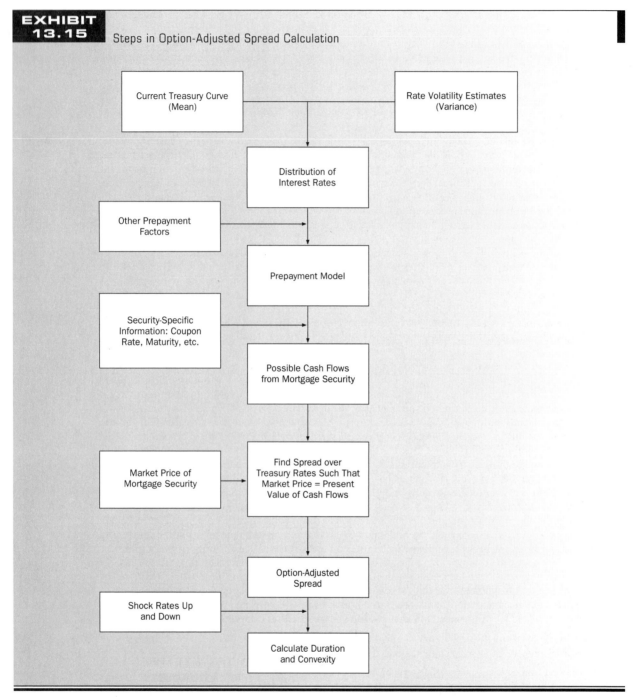

SOURCE: Stephen Smith, "Mortgage-Backed Securities: Analyzing Risk and Return." *Economic Review* (Federal Reserve Bank of Atlanta, January/February 1991).

environment. Importantly, OAS allows a comparison of the attractiveness of callable agencies and MBSs relative to Treasuries over different time periods.[20]

Exhibit 13.16 provides data related to calculating the OAS for the five-year maturity FHLB bond that was callable after 15 months. In April 2005, the bond was priced to yield 51 basis points (4.43–3.92) more than the

---

[20]OAS analysis is also frequently applied using the LIBOR swap curve as the benchmark rather than the Treasury spot curve. In recent years, the slope of the Treasury spot curve was downward sloping while the slope of the LIBOR swap curve was upward sloping. The different slopes reflected, in part, the Treasury's buyback program at long maturities. At the time, the OAS calculated against the Treasury benchmark was much higher, on average, than the OAS using the LIBOR swap curve.

**EXHIBIT 13.16**  Option-Adjusted Spread Analysis for a Callable FHLB Bond

P205 Corp **OAS1**

# OPTION-ADJUSTED SPREAD ANALYSIS

FED HOME LN BANK FLHB 4.32 07/10    99.4996/99.4996    (4.43/4.43) BFV @ 19:01

2) Customize
Curve CMT Semi
Const. Mty Tsy Cu
Dated 4/18/2005
Settle 4/19/2005

Calculate **Price**  **OAS** (bp) **Volatility**
(P,O,V) 0  P) 99.499584  O) +35.55  V) 15.00

Cusip / ID#    3133XABH9 Option Px Value:    0.67
Settle 4/19/2005 Bench settle 4/19/2005
Spread  76.6 bp vs 3Y  T 3 3⁄8 02/15/08 Govt @ 99-7+ ( 3.661 )

Shift  +0 (bps)

(NUM)<GO> for:
3) Call Schedule
7/14/06   100.00

| | OAS Method | Option Free | To Call on 7/14/2006 | To Mty |
|---|---|---|---|---|
| Yld | | 4.282 | 4.736 | 4.427 |
| Sprd | | 35.3 | 142.7 | 49.8 |
| M Dur | 3.28 | | 1.18 | 4.59 |
| Risk | 3.30 | | 1.19 | 4.62 |
| Cnvx | -1.73 | | 0.02 | 0.25 |

Model  L   L = Lognormal

Exercise Premium  0.00

Yield Spread
| | |
|---|---|
| 3m | 2.847 |
| 6m | 3.078 |
| 1y | 3.236 |
| 2y | 3.549 |
| 3y | 3.685 |
| 4y | 3.798 |
| 5y | 3.911 |
| 7y | 4.060 |
| 10y | 4.282 |
| 20y | 4.497 |
| 30y | 4.710 |

BB) REFRESH

Australia 61 2 9777 8600    Brazil 5511 3048 4500    Europe 44 20 7330 7500    Germany 49 69 920410
Hong Kong 852 2977 6000    Japan 81 3 3201 8900    Singapore 65 6212 1000    U.S. 1 212 318 2000    Copyright 2005 Bloomberg L.P.
2 18-Apr-05 19:01:49

5-year Treasury. Using the constant maturity Treasury (CMT) curve as the benchmark, OAS was estimated at 35.55 basis points assuming a 15 percent volatility in rates.[21] This OAS figure suggests that an investor might expect to earn a 36 basis point yield premium over the entire Treasury spot curve given the current level and volatility of rates size of the yield curve, and the likelihood that the bond will be called prior to maturity. The issue is whether this premium is sufficient to compensate the investor for the greater risk and cost, in terms of required capital, of owning the callable bond.

## COMPARATIVE YIELDS ON TAXABLE VERSUS TAX-EXEMPT SECURITIES

A bank's effective return from investing in securities depends on the amount of interest income, reinvestment income, potential capital gains or losses, whether the income is tax-exempt or taxable, and whether the issuer defaults on interest and principal payments. When making investment decisions, portfolio managers compare expected risk-adjusted, after-tax returns from alternative investments. They purchase securities that provide the highest expected risk-adjusted return.

---

[21]Changing the assumed volatility in interest rates can have a dramatic effect on OAS. Conceptually, the call option will have greater value when rates are more volatile. As such, increasing (decreasing) the assumed volatility of rates will lower (raise) the OAS given the fixed price at which the bond is purchased and against which OAS is calculated.

Interest on most municipal securities is exempt from federal income taxes and, depending on state law, from state income taxes.[22] Some states exempt all municipal interest. Most states selectively exempt interest from municipals issued in-state but tax interest on out-of-state issues. Other states either tax all municipal interest or do not impose an income tax. Capital gains on municipals are taxed as ordinary income under the federal income tax code. This makes discount municipals less attractive than par municipals because a portion of the return, the price appreciation, is fully taxable.

The net effect of the tax treatment is that municipal securities trade at yields well below yields on comparable-risk taxable securities. Thus, when a ten-year taxable yields 8 percent, a comparable-risk ten-year municipal might yield just 6 percent. The difference in pretax yields reflects the tax benefit to an investor in municipals.

## AFTER-TAX AND TAX-EQUIVALENT YIELDS

The importance of income taxes on yields can be easily shown. Suppose that we are comparing yields on two securities of comparable maturity and risk. For the moment, ignore state and local income taxes as well. Let

$R_m$ = Pretax yield on a municipal security

$R_t$ = Pretax yield on a taxable security

$t$ = Investor's marginal federal income tax rate

Once an investor has determined the appropriate maturity and risk security, the investment decision involves selecting the security with the highest after-tax yield. The relevant yield comparison is

$$R_m \gtreqless R_t (1 - t) \tag{13.9}$$

Using the 6 percent and 8 percent pretax yields for $R_m$ and $R_t$, respectively, an investor who pays taxes at the 36 percent rate would buy the municipal because it pays 0.6 percent more after taxes.

$$6\% > 8\% \ (1 - 0.36) = 5.12\%$$

An investor who pays taxes at the 15 percent rate would prefer the taxable security because it offers 0.8 percent more in yield.

$$6\% < 8\% \ (1 - 0.15) = 6.8\%$$

Municipals are often marketed to investors using a modified form of the relationship in Equation 13.9. Consider the following question: What tax rate would make an investor indifferent between buying a taxable or municipal security? Indifference here means that the after-tax yields are equal. The answer is obtained by solving relationship 13.9 as an equality. Using the above data, an investor would be indifferent at the margin if his or her tax rate was 25 percent. In general, this indifference tax rate ($t^*$) is solved by Equation 13.10.

$$t^* = 1 - \frac{R^m}{R_t} \tag{13.10}$$

The investment decision is then made by comparing an investor's actual marginal tax rate with the indifference rate. The following rules determine the appropriate choice:

If $t > t^*$, then buy the municipal

If $t < t^*$, then buy the taxable

If $t = t^*$, indifferent because after-tax yields are equal

With $R_m$ equal to 6 percent and $R_t$ equal to 8 percent, any investor with a marginal tax rate over 25 percent prefers municipals, while any investor with a tax rate below 25 percent prefers taxables.

The analysis is complicated only slightly when state and local income taxes are taken into account. Let $t_m$ equal the marginal state and local tax rate on municipal interest and taxable interest. Then the relevant yield comparison is

$$R_m(1 - t_m) \gtreqless R_t \ [1 - (t_m + t)] \tag{13.11}$$

---

[22]Some securities issued by states and local governments and their political subdivisions, while still municipal bonds, pay interest that is subject to federal income taxes. They are labeled taxable municipals.

Suppose that $t_m$ equals 5 percent in the above case where the marginal federal income tax rate equals 36 percent. The after-tax yield comparison now becomes

$$6\% \, (1 - 0.05) > 8\% \, (1 - 0.41)$$
$$5.70\% > 4.72\%$$

The municipal now yields 0.98 percent more.

Many analysts compare returns on municipals with taxables in terms of tax-equivalent yields. This involves nothing more than restating relationships 13.9 and 13.11 when the equality of after-tax yields is enforced. Specifically, municipal yields are converted to their tax-equivalent values by solving Equation 13.12.

$$\text{tax equivalent yield} = \frac{R_m \, (1 - t_m)}{[1 - (t_m + t)]} \tag{13.12}$$

In the above example, the tax-equivalent municipal yield equals 8.91 percent $[0.06(1 - 0.05)/(1 - 0.36)]$. This figure means that the investor would have to earn 8.91 percent on a comparable taxable security to produce the same 7.125 percent after-tax yield.[23]

## THE YIELD COMPARISON FOR COMMERCIAL BANKS

Suppose that a bank portfolio manager wants to compare potential returns between a taxable security and a municipal security that currently yield 10 percent and 8 percent, respectively. Both securities are new issues trading at $10,000 par with identical maturities, call treatment, and default risk. The primary difference is that the bank pays federal income taxes at a 34 percent marginal rate on the taxable security while municipal interest is entirely exempt. Section A of Exhibit 13.17 shows that the portfolio manager would earn $140 more in after-tax interest from buying the municipal.

Applying Equation 13.11 using this data, the yield comparison is

$$8\%(1 - 0) = 8\% > 10\%(1 - 0.34) = 6.6\%$$

The after-tax yield differential multiplied by the principal invested produces the $140 difference in after-tax income. The tax-equivalent yield, which essentially converts the municipal yield to a pretax yield that would produce an after-tax return equal to that on an otherwise identical taxable security, equals 12.12 percent from Equation 13.12.

## THE EFFECTIVE TAX ON INCREMENTAL MUNICIPAL INTEREST EARNED BY COMMERCIAL BANKS

Prior to 1983, commercial banks could invest in tax-exempt securities and deduct the full amount of interest paid on liabilities used to finance their purchases. Virtually all other investors, including individuals, were (and are still) denied a deduction for any indebtedness to carry or purchase tax-exempts. The deduction enabled many banks to do a tax arbitrage between the after-tax cost of borrowing and municipal yields at the margin to supplement earnings and reduce their effective income tax liability.

In 1983, Congress rewrote the tax law to deny banks a deduction for 15 percent of their interest expense allocated to indebtedness for the purpose of acquiring and holding new municipal issues. This nondeductible portion was increased to 20 percent in 1985. The Tax Reform Act of 1986 went one step further and eliminated the deduction for most municipal bonds.

The following calculations demonstrate the impact of a lost deduction on a bank's total after-tax income and on the effective yield on municipal securities. For income tax purposes, interest expense allocated to municipal investments is prorated against total interest expense. The applicable fraction equals the amount of tax-exempt securities purchased after the change in tax laws divided by total assets. Section B of Exhibit 13.17 provides an example that uses data on a bank's total portfolio and calculates the total amount of lost deductions for the year assuming 20 percent lost interest deductibility. The bank is relatively small with only $20 million in average assets. During 2005 the bank paid $1.5 million in total interest expense so that its weighted average cost of financing assets equaled 7.5 percent. The amount of interest expense that is nondeductible depends on how many bonds the bank owns that were purchased after the tax change ($800,000 in this example). Because the bank's post-tax reform municipal holdings amount to 4 percent of average assets, a 4 percent pro rata share of total interest expense is allocated to municipal financing costs. This produces a disallowed deduction of $12,000. The

---

[23]In most published reports, taxes on municipal interest are ignored ($t_m$ is set equal to zero) so that the reported tax-equivalent yield equals the municipal rate divided by one minus the federal income tax rate. In this example, such a tax-equivalent yield would equal 9.38% [6%/(1 − 0.36)]. This clearly understates the true tax-equivalent yield.

**EXHIBIT 13.17** A Comparison of After-Tax Returns on Taxable and Tax-Exempt Securities for a Bank as Investor

**A. After-Tax Interest Earned on Taxable versus Exempt Municipal Securities**

|  | Taxable Security | Municipal Security |
|---|---|---|
| Par value | $10,000 | $10,000 |
| Coupon rate | 10% | 8% |
| Annual coupon interest | $ 1,000 | $ 800 |
| Federal income taxes at 34% | $ 340 | Exempt |
| After-tax interest income | $ 660 | $ 800 |

**B. Disallowing Deduction of Interest on Indebtedness to Finance Municipal Purchases for a Bank: Total Portfolio and Income Statement Effect**

Factors affecting allowable deduction for 2005.
- Total interest expense paid in 2005: $1,500,000
- Average amount of assets owned during 2002: $20,000,000
- Average amount of tax-exempt securities owned that were acquired after the change in tax laws affecting interest deductibility: $800,000
- Weighted-average cost of financing assets: $\frac{\$1,500,000}{\$20,000,000} = 7.5\%$

Nondeductible interest expense:
- Pro rata share of interest expense to carry municipals purchased after 1982:
  $\frac{\$800,000}{\$20,000,000} = 4\%$
- Nondeductible interest expense at 20 percent: $1,500,000(.04)(0.2) = $12,000

Deductible interest expense: $1,500,000 − $12,000 = $1,488,000

**C. After-Tax Interest Earned, Recognizing Partial Deductibility of Interest Expense: Individual Asset**

|  | Taxable Security | Municipal Security |
|---|---|---|
| Par value | $10,000 | $10,000 |
| Coupon rate | 10% | 8% |
| Annual coupon interest | $ 1,000 | $ 800 |
| Federal income taxes at 34% | $ 340 | Exempt |
| Pooled interest expense (rate = 7.5%) | $ 750 | $ 750 |
| Lost interest deduction (20%) | $ 0 | $ 150 |
| Increased tax liability at 34% | $ 0 | $ 51 |
| Effective after-tax interest income | $ 660 | $ 749 |

remaining $1.488 million in interest was tax deductible. The $12,000 lost deduction has a tax value of $4,080 (0.34 × $12,000), which represents the increase in taxes owed by the bank.[24]

Section C of Exhibit 13.17 indicates the effect of this lost interest deductibility on the expected return from municipal investments. It replicates Section A except that the bank as an investor can deduct only 80 percent of its interest expense applicable to financing the municipal security. The analysis is identical through the federal income tax calculation. Beyond that, the bank pays a pooled interest cost of 7.5 percent (the same as in Section B; $1.5 million/$20 million). Thus, interest paid to finance the $10,000 in municipals equals $750, of which $150 is nondeductible. This lost deduction raises the bank's effective tax liability by $51 (34 percent of $150) and reduces the realized return on the municipal to $749, or 7.49 percent.

The lost interest deduction essentially represents a tax on incremental municipal interest. A good analogy is a homebuyer who obtains a mortgage to finance the purchase. Each month the homeowner makes a mortgage payment that includes interest on the debt. Suppose that Congress suddenly changed the tax laws and no longer allowed individuals to deduct home mortgage interest. The homeowner would still make the obligated mortgage payments, but could no longer itemize the interest deduction on his or her income tax statement. The lost deduction essentially represents an increase in taxes owed because reported taxable income increases without any additional cash receipts. The cost of owning a home would increase, or alternatively, the after-tax return from owning a home would decrease.

---

[24]Note that the bank must pay the entire $1.5 million in interest, which represents its actual cash outflow. However, it is allowed a deduction for just $1.488 million, so its reported income is $12,000 higher. This produces the $4,080 additional tax payment.

In order to compare yields on municipal and taxable securities, the lost interest deduction is converted to a marginal tax on municipal interest. Setting

c = Bank's pooled interest cost rate

n = The nondeductible portion of interest expense

$t_c$ = The marginal corporate income tax rate

The tax value of the lost interest deduction equals the product of c, n, and $t_c$, divided by the pretax municipal rate ($R_m$). When state and local income taxes are added, the effective bank tax rate on municipal interest ($t_b$) can be expressed as

$$t_b = \frac{c\,(n)\,t_c}{R_m} + \text{state and local income tax rate}$$

Applying the data from Section C with no state and local income taxes,

$$t_b = \frac{[0.34(02)(0.075)]}{0.08} = 0.06375$$

and

$$8\%(1 - 0.06375) = 7.49\% > 10\%(1 - 0.34) = 6.6\%$$

The true tax-equivalent municipal yield for this bank paying no state and local income taxes is 11.35 percent.[25]

## THE IMPACT OF THE TAX REFORM ACT OF 1986

The Tax Reform Act of 1986 dramatically altered commercial banks' investment strategies and the attractiveness of different types of securities. This section describes factors that lowered returns on most municipal securities. In general, the act reduced the pool of municipal securities that kept their tax exemption and eliminated banks' ability to deduct carrying costs on new municipal purchases, except for qualifying small issues that meet essential public-purpose requirements. The discussion focuses only on commercial banks as the distinction between qualified and nonqualified issues does not apply to other investors.

### QUALIFIED VERSUS NONQUALIFIED MUNICIPALS

All municipal interest is still tax-exempt for federal income tax purposes. There are, however, a variety of ways in which banks may be subject to tax when they buy municipals. The Tax Reform Act created different categories of municipal bonds. The more essential a given type of bond is for states and localities, the broader is its tax exemption. The first distinction is between municipals issued before and after August 7, 1986. Municipals issued before this date retain their tax exemption. They are essentially grandfathered in because banks can still deduct 80 percent of their associated financing costs regardless of the act. Securities issued after this date are categorized as bank qualified or nonqualified, depending on whether they meet certain criteria.

**QUALIFIED MUNICIPALS.** Banks can still deduct 80 percent of their carrying costs associated with the purchase of certain essential, public-purpose bonds. There are two important criteria for bonds to qualify. First, the proceeds must be used to finance essential government services including schools, highways, sewer systems, and so forth. In most cases, traditional general obligation bonds meet this standard. Second, the municipality cannot issue more than $10 million in municipal securities per year. Thus, only small issue municipals qualify. Such instruments are labeled bank-qualified municipals. State government issues do not qualify regardless of total debt issuance. The purpose of this special treatment is to help small governmental units obtain financing. In many communities banks are the only investors in local government securities because they are the only ones with the resources and knowledge of the financial condition of the borrower. If this exception to the lost deduction had not been granted, it was feared that many governmental units would be forced to cut services drastically.

The effective bank tax rate against qualified municipals from Equation 13.10 uses a nondeductible portion of interest equal to 20 percent (n = 0.20). Thus, the after-tax yield calculation in Exhibit 13.17 and the above examples assumes that the municipal is bank qualified. The net impact is that even though banks lose a portion of their

---

[25][0.08 (1 − 0.06375)/(1 − 0.34)] = 0.1135.

interest deductibility, with n = 0.20 the bank tax rate on municipal interest is so low that qualified municipals still yield more than fully taxed alternative investments. As such, qualified municipals are attractive investments for profitable banks. The problem is that transactions costs are high when banks search out qualified municipals. This occurs because only smaller, lesser-known municipalities can issue qualifying debt.

**NONQUALIFIED MUNICIPALS.** All municipals that do not meet the criteria as bank-qualified bonds are labeled nonqualified municipals. If banks buy these securities, they can deduct none of their associated carrying costs. In terms of Exhibit 13.17 and the after-tax yield comparison, nondeductible interest on nonqualified municipals equals 100 percent. This sharply raises the effective tax rate on nonqualified municipals purchased by banks to such an extent that they are no longer viable investments. If the 8 percent municipal bond in Exhibit 13.17 (Section C) was nonqualified, the lost interest deduction would have totaled $750 and the tax liability would have increased to $255 (tb = 0.3188). The effective after-tax income would have equaled only $545, or $115 less than that from the taxable security.

$$R_m(1 - t_b) = 8\% \left( 1 - \frac{.075\,(1.0)\,34}{.08} \right) = 5.45\%$$

As demonstrated, the effective bank tax rate on nonqualified municipal interest is quite high. Because these securities are still attractive to nonbank investors looking for tax-sheltered income, they continue to carry yields below those on comparable taxable securities. The combination of tax-exempt yields and a high effective tax rate makes nonqualified municipals unattractive to banks. Banks no longer buy nonqualified municipals because they can get higher yields elsewhere.

A second important change under the act is the expanded alternative minimum tax (AMT). Banks must now compute their tax liability in two ways: according to regular income tax guidelines, and according to minimum tax rules, which add preference items back to normal taxable income and apply a 20 percent minimum tax rate. Banks pay the higher of the two taxes. The importance for the investment portfolio is that tax-exempt interest is a preference item and banks must include one-half of tax-exempt interest earned in the taxable base. Thus, the effective tax on qualified, essential public-purpose bond interest potentially rises by 10 percent.

The Tax Reform Act of 1986 has had several other structural effects on bank investments and relative security yields. First, pretax municipal yields have risen relative to taxable yields to reflect reduced demand by commercial banks. This is particularly true at short maturities. Second, banks have shifted their investment portfolios to taxable securities, such as mortgage-backed pass-through securities and CMOs, to earn higher risk-adjusted yields. Finally, large banks have found it difficult to locate enough bank-qualified municipals to fully meet the demand for tax-sheltered interest income. They now look to other tax-sheltered vehicles to take the place of municipal interest income.

## STRATEGIES UNDERLYING SECURITY SWAPS

Active portfolio strategies also enable banks to sell securities prior to maturity whenever economic conditions dictate that additional returns can be earned without a significant increase in risk, or risk can be lowered without reducing expected returns. In most cases, banks reinvest the sale proceeds in securities that differ in terms of maturity, credit quality, or even tax treatment.[26] Such portfolio restructuring improves long-term profitability beyond that avail-able from buy and hold strategies.

Banks are generally willing to sell securities that have appreciated in price, yet they are unwilling to sell depreciated securities. Although gains are quite popular and enhance earnings, senior bank officers usually believe that stockholders will attribute security losses to poor management. They are thus extremely reluctant to take any losses. This philosophy, however, does not prevent the same banks from taking securities gains to supplement normal operating income and capital in low-profit periods.

This is perverse behavior. The reason that a security is priced at a discount is that the prevailing market rate exceeds the coupon rate on the security. The bank is earning below-market interest. A security is priced at a premium when its coupon rate exceeds the market rate so that the holder earns an above-average coupon. An investor who holds a security to maturity may suffer an opportunity loss by not selling the security at a loss, or may give up substantial value by selling at a premium to capture the gain. The appropriate financial decision can be viewed as a straightforward capital budgeting problem.

---

[26]The following discussion focuses on securities that banks hold as part of their investment portfolio classified as available-for-sale, as opposed to trading account securities. Investment securities generate a return via coupon interest or price appreciation on discount instruments. Current accounting procedures record these securities at market value with unrealized gains or losses as a component of capital.

## ANALYSIS OF A CLASSIC SECURITY SWAP

In its classic form, a security swap involves the sale of a depreciated bond and the simultaneous purchase of a similar par bond to improve long-term earnings. The basic principle is to take advantage of the tax laws and the time value of money. Consider the two bonds identified in Section A of Exhibit 13.18. A bank currently owns the 10.5 percent Treasury with three years remaining maturity and is considering buying a three-year FHLMC bond yielding 12.2 percent. If the bank sells the Treasury, it gives up $105,000 in semiannual interest and realizes a capital loss of $73,760. This loss directly lowers taxable income, as banks do not distinguish between the tax treatment of short- and long-term capital gains or losses. A loss results because comparable instruments yield 12 percent annually, or 1.5 percent more than the Treasury coupon rate. The paper loss, in turn, produces a tax savings of $25,816, which can be reinvested with the direct proceeds from the sale in a FHLMC security at par that pays $119,075 in semiannual interest. The cost to the bank includes transactions costs plus potential negative ramifications from the reported capital loss. The benefits include the $14,075 increase in semiannual interest.

The simple net present-value analysis in Section C of the exhibit demonstrates how much value the swap adds for the slightly greater default risk and adverse reporting consequences. The calculation essentially compares the cash flow from the Treasury if the bank held it to maturity with the cash from selling the Treasury and buying the FHLMC bond. Note that this computation reduces to a comparison of the present value of the incremental coupon payments versus the lower principal received at the end of the three years. In this case, the net present value equals $35,380, using a discount rate equal to the yield on the FHLMC bond.

The attractiveness of such a swap is often viewed in terms of a calculated loss-recovery period for the combined transaction. This is comparable to payback analysis in capital budgeting, which ignores the time value of money. Still, in this example, the after-tax security loss equals $47,944, which the bank can recover entirely in four semiannual periods ($47,944/$14,075). Obviously, the net benefits would increase if the bank chose to reinvest the proceeds in a riskier asset, such as a loan that offered an even higher yield. A bank could also search

---

**EXHIBIT 13.18**  Evaluation of Security Swaps

| | Par Value | Market Value | Remaining Maturity | Semiannual Coupon Income | Yield to Maturity |
|---|---|---|---|---|---|
| **A. Classic Swap Description** | | | | | |
| Sell U.S. Treasury bonds at 10.5% | $2,000,000 | $1,926,240 | 3 yrs. | $105,000 | 12.0% |
| Buy FHLMC bonds at 12.2%* | 1,952,056† | 1,952,056 | 3 yrs. | 119,075 | 12.2 |
| Incremental coupon income | | | | $14,075 | |
| **B. Swap with Minimal Tax Effects** | | | | | |
| Sell U.S. Treasury bonds at 10.5% | $2,000,000 | $1,926,240 | 3 yrs. | $105,000 | 12 |
| Sell FNMA at 13.8% | 3,000,000 | 3,073,060 | 4 yrs. | 207,000 | 13 |
| Total | $5,000,000 | $4,999,300 | | $312,000 | |
| Buy FNMA at 13% | $5,000,000 | $5,000,000 | 1 yr. | $325,000 | 12 |
| | | | | $ 13,000 | |

**C. Present-Value Analysis**

Time Line: Semiannual Periods

| Period | 0 | 1 | 2 | 3 | 4 | 5 | 6 |
|---|---|---|---|---|---|---|---|
| Incremental Cash Flows | | | | | | | |
| Treasury: | $1,926,240 | $−105,000 | $−105,000 | $−105,000 | $−105,000 | $−105,000 | $−2,105,000 |
| Tax saving: | 25,816 | | | | | | |
| FHLMC: | $−1,952,056 | $119,075 | $119,075 | $119,075 | $119,075 | $119,075 | $2,071,131 |
| Difference: | 0 | $14,075 | $14,075 | $14,075 | $14,075 | $14,075 | $−33,869 |

Present value calculation: discounted at 6.1 percent§

$$\sum_{t=1}^{5} \frac{\$14,075}{(1.061)^t} - \frac{\$33,869}{(1.061)^6} = \$35,380$$

---

*FHLMC indicates Federal Home Loan Mortgage Corporation; FNMA indicates Federal National Mortgage Association.

†Reported security loss equals $73,760, which generates a tax savings of $25,816 at 35 percent. The loss recovery period equals $47,944/$14,075 at 3.4 periods, where the loss equals $73,760 − $25,816.

§12.2%/2 = 6.1%.

out higher yields by lengthening maturities with an upward-sloping yield curve. Alternatively, a bank in need of tax-sheltered income could reinvest the proceeds in a municipal bond of similar maturity that offers a higher after-tax yield.

These alternatives point out the attractiveness of security swaps. In general, banks can effectively improve their portfolios by:

1. Upgrading bond credit quality by shifting into high-grade instruments when quality yield spreads are low
2. Lengthening maturities when yields are expected to level off or decline
3. Obtaining greater call protection when management expects rates to fall
4. Improving diversification when management expects economic conditions to deteriorate
5. Generally increasing current yields by taking advantage of the tax savings
6. Shifting into taxable securities from municipals when management expects losses

Any swap transaction requires a comprehensive assessment of a bank's overall risk position and explicit interest rate forecast. As a rule, banks normally lengthen maturities when they expect market rates to decline and shorten maturities when they expect market rates to rise. They shift into higher-quality securities when they expect economic conditions to deteriorate and lower-quality securities when conditions are expected to improve.

Consider, alternatively, a swap that involves the sale of a security at a gain and the simultaneous purchase of another security at par. A gain produces an increased tax liability so that the seller receives more than cost, but less than the market price after taxes. Because the government gets its cut up front, there are fewer funds to invest. The reason there was a gain is that prevailing interest rates are below the liquidated bond's coupon rate. Thus, periodic interest income from the reinvested proceeds will decline from that generated by the bond alone. The net present value comparison is again straightforward. Is the present value of the incremental principal cash flow at maturity greater than the present value of the negative interim cash flows? In most cases, the answer is no. It does not add value to sell securities at a gain and reinvest in a like instrument.

### SWAP WITH MINIMAL TAX EFFECTS

Because most banks are reluctant to take capital losses regardless of the financial opportunities, swaps can occasionally be constructed that have no tax or reporting impacts. Section B of Exhibit 13.18 outlines a swap where the net tax impact is negligible. This possibility arises because the bank acquired securities at different times in the past. Over time, rates have changed, so some securities have appreciated in value relative to cost while others have depreciated. The simultaneous sale of two such instruments minimizes any tax effects and frees up funds for reinvestment. In the example, the bank sells a Treasury bond at a pretax loss of $73,760 and a Federal National Mortgage Association (FNMA) bond at a pretax gain of $73,060. The net loss equals only $700, and the bank has almost $5 million to reinvest. Because management anticipates rising rates, it reinvests the proceeds in a one-year FNMA security yielding 13%, thereby shortening the maturity and duration of its assets. It is difficult to conduct a net present-value analysis until management specifies what it will do with the proceeds after the first year. Of course, sensitivity analysis involving a variety of rate forecasts is extremely relevant here.

The essential point is that with swaps, active portfolio management allows a bank to adjust its interest rate risk, liquidity risk, and credit risk profile via buying and selling securities. Portfolio managers must also recognize that not selling securities because they are priced at a discount entails losses in the form of reduced periodic interest income. Similarly, securities sold for a gain typically involve a substitution of a larger current period cash inflow for reduced interest income in later periods.

## S U M M A R Y

Banks buy investment securities to generate income, but also to better manage their risk exposure. This chapter describes the investment portfolio objectives and summarizes important policy considerations. It explains the yield and risk features of alternative investment instruments. It also describes key changes in portfolio composition over time and provides a rationale for banks moving out of municipal bonds and into U.S. government agency securities and alternative investment instruments.

With the changing competitive environment, commercial banks are also looking to manage their investment portfolios more aggressively. Passive strategies, which view the portfolio as a simple supplement to loans, earn average returns over time relative to the interest rate cycle. Active strategies, if implemented carefully, can enhance returns by taking advantage of perceived changes in interest rates and required adjustments in portfolio composition. Still, taking large speculative positions based on interest rate forecasts is inappropriate. The higher risk will inevitably come back to haunt managers in the form of losses.

Banks can generally improve the timing of their investments if they buy securities contracyclically, when loan demand is high. If successful, they will earn above-average coupon interest and be able to sell securities later at a gain. Most active investment strategies involve looking at a security's total return. This is especially difficult, however, when securities have embedded options, such as the call option in a callable agency bond and the prepayment option in mortgage-backed securities. This chapter provides examples of how total return analysis can assist in evaluating these securities. It also describes the impact of these embedded options on a security's duration, convexity, and general price sensitivity. It demonstrates why banks should hold municipal securities to shelter as much income as possible due to their higher after-tax yields than otherwise comparable taxable securities. Unfortunately, only bank-qualified municipals are attractive on a yield basis and they are in limited supply. Finally, portfolio managers should recognize that holding low-rate discount instruments produces opportunity losses in the form of reduced interest income in future years. If possible, they should take advantage of security swaps, which allow a bank to realign its overall risk and return position.

## QUESTIONS

1. Describe how a bank makes a profit with its securities trading account. What are the risks?
2. Explain why bank managers often refuse to sell securities at a loss relative to book value. What is the cost of continuing to hold discount instruments? What are the costs of selling securities at a gain?
3. Explain how zero coupon securities differ from coupon securities. Which are more liquid, in general? Which are more price sensitive? What is the advantage of a zero coupon security in terms of total return?
4. What types of securities are banks prohibited from buying for investment purposes?
5. Explain how the composition of a small community bank's investment portfolio differs, in general, from the composition of a large bank's portfolio. Why might mutual funds be attractive to banks?
6. Examine the data in Exhibit 13.2. Identify key trends and explain the driving force behind each. Why might banks prefer agency securities over Treasury securities?
7. What is the option in a callable agency bond? What impact does the call deferment period have on a callable bond's promised yield? What is the primary advantage of a discount callable bond versus one trading at par?
8. List the objectives that banks have for buying securities. Explain the motive for each.
9. Explain how a reverse RP differs from federal funds sold as an income-producing asset.
10. FASB 115 requires certain classifications within a bank's securities portfolio. What is the accounting treatment of securities within each classification? Describe why full market-value accounting might adversely affect a bank's reported capital. How should management classify the bank's securities to *minimize* potential reporting problems?
11. Discuss the impact of each of the following on prepayment risk for a mortgage-backed pass-through security (MBS):
    a. High-coupon interest MBS versus low-coupon interest MBS
    b. MBS issued six years prior versus MBS issued this year
    c. Demographic trends in different areas of the country
13. Explain how the design of a CMO supposedly helps to manage prepayment risk for investors. What is a tranche?
14. Suppose that you own a four-year maturity Treasury bond that pays $100,000 in principal at maturity and $3,000 every six months in coupon interest. Use the features of the bond to explain what Treasury IOs and POs are.
15. Consider a $100 million pool of conventional mortgages paying 8 percent interest. Suppose that you create one PO and one IO for this entire pool. Describe what a PO and IO would look like for this mortgage pool.
16. Large banks often borrow heavily in the federal funds market and maintain small investment portfolios relative to their asset size. Are these offsetting risk positions? Why do large banks organize themselves this way?
17. Describe the characteristics of the laddered investment strategy and compare them to the barbell investment strategy. Why should the barbell strategy outperform the laddered maturity strategy in a stable or declining interest rate environment? Why should the laddered strategy outperform the barbell strategy in a rising-rate environment?
18. The term-structure of U.S. Treasury interest rates generally exhibits certain shapes during different stages of the business cycle. Discuss this relationship and explain why it holds, on average. What shape does the yield curve take prior to a recession in the United States?

19. What rationale suggests that a contracyclical investment strategy should outperform the market, on average? Is it possible to consistently earn above-average returns by timing security purchases?

20. Suppose that the U.S. Treasury yield curve is continuously downward sloping. Should a bank portfolio manager buy securities with maturities under one year or securities with maturities of ten years to maximize interest income over the next ten years? Explain what factors should be used to make a decision.

21. Provide one reason for using the bank's investment portfolio to speculate on interest rate movements. Provide one reason against. What do you believe about efficient markets and how does this influence your opinion of speculating? Can investors accurately forecast the direction of future interest rate movements?

22. Suppose that a bank's ALCO reports that the bank is too liability sensitive; that is, earnings will fall more than desired should rates rise. You have been asked to reduce the bank's earnings sensitivity. What specific strategies might the investment manager pursue? Identify the cost and benefit of each. Is each an active or passive strategy and is it speculative?

23. Describe the basic strategy in riding the yield curve. Can you ride the yield curve if the yield curve is downward sloping with short-term rates above long-term rates?

24. In each of the following cases, identify the buyer and seller of the option, how the value of the option is indicated, and when (in what interest rate environment) the option will be exercised:

    a. A bank buys a five-year maturity FNMA bond that is callable at par after one year, yielding 6.88 percent. The matched duration Treasury zero coupon rate is 6.11 percent.

    b. A bank buys a FHLMC pass-through MBS at par yielding 7.47 percent. The matched duration Treasury zero coupon rate is 6.48 percent.

25. Suppose that you own a callable U.S. agency bond like that in Exhibit 13.12. Explain why your total return will fall when interest rates rise. Identify changes in return associated with each component of total return. Why will total return rise when rates fall?

26. Suppose that a bank currently owns a $5 million par-value Treasury bond, purchased at par, with four years remaining to maturity that pays $200,000 in interest every six months. Its current market value is $5.23 million. If the bank sold the bond and reinvested the proceeds in a similar maturity taxable security, it could earn 6.6 percent annually. Determine the incremental cash-flow effects for the bank if it sold the Treasury note and reinvested the full after-tax proceeds from the sale in a 6.6 percent three-year taxable security, assuming a 34 percent tax rate.

27. Suppose that the above bank also owns a $1 million par-value Treasury bond, purchased at par, with two years to maturity, paying $29,000 in semiannual interest, with a market value of $960,000. Determine the incremental cash-flow effects if the bank sold this note and bought a two-year taxable security yielding 6.2 percent with the proceeds.

28. You pay federal income taxes at a 28 percent marginal tax rate. You have the choice of buying either a taxable corporate bond paying 7.10 percent coupon interest or a similar maturity and risk municipal bond paying 5.90 percent coupon interest.

    a. Which bond offers the higher after-tax yield?

    b. If you also pay a state income tax on taxable coupon interest at a 9 percent rate, but no tax on municipal interest, which bond offers the higher after-tax yield?

## PROBLEMS

**I. LEARN MORE ABOUT YOUR LOCAL BANK.** Obtain a copy of a local community bank's annual report and the annual report of a large bank. Determine the extent to which each of the banks:

1. Operates a trading account

2. Reports gains or losses on securities trades

3. Invests in municipal securities

4. Invests in mortgage-backed securities

5. Reports a change in capital due to its securities holdings

**II. RIDING THE YIELD CURVE.** Victory Bank plans to invest $1 million in Treasury bonds and has a 4-year investment horizon. It is considering two choices: a 4-year bond currently yielding 5.3 percent annually and an 8-year bond yielding 6.54 percent annually. Coupon interest is payable semiannually and can be reinvested

*Activity*

at 5 percent (2.5 percent semiannually). If the bank buys the 8-year bond, it will sell it after four years. In four years a 4-year bond is expected to yield 6 percent. Follow the example in Exhibit 13.10 and answer the following questions:

1. Calculate the total coupon interest, reinvestment income, and principal returned at maturity expected from investing $1 million in the four-year bond. What is the bank's expected total return?

2. Calculate the total coupon interest, reinvestment income, and sale value after four years expected from investing $1 million in the 8-year bond and selling it prior to maturity. What is the bank's expected total return?

3. Determine which investment promises the higher return. What risks are involved in this strategy?

4. Suppose that instead of yielding 6 percent after four years, the market rate on a four-year bond is 7.4 percent. What will the total return be for the strategy of buying an 8-year bond and selling it after four years?

**III. EFFECTIVE DURATION AND CONVEXITY.** You own a seven-year final maturity callable agency bond that is currently priced at $100.15 per $100 par value to yield 7.63 percent. If the prevailing market yield on this bond rises to 8.30 percent, the price will fall to $99.45. If the prevailing market yield on this bond falls to 6.93 percent, the price will fall to par value.

a. What is the effective duration of this bond?

b. What is the effective convexity of this bond?

c. Does this bond exhibit positive or negative convexity? Why?

**IV. SECURITY SWAP.** The ALCO members of Jackson County Bank have just reached a consensus that market interest rates are going to rise by 100 to 200 basis points during the upcoming year. Committee members decided to swap securities in the bank's investment portfolio to make it more rate sensitive. Below are listed selected security holdings and market

| Security | Par Value | Market Value | Semiannual Coupon |
|---|---|---|---|
| 2-year U.S. Treasury note | $2,000,000 | $2,094,600 | $ 60,000 |
| 10-year U.S. Treasury bond | $3,000,000 | $3,277,525 | $148,200 |
| 4-year Federal National Mortgage Assoc. bond | $2,000,000 | $1,902,880 | $ 52,000 |
| 4-year Federal Land Bank (FLB) bond | $2,000,000 | $2,105,425 | $ 76,000 |
| *Current Market Rates** | | | |
| 6-month Treasury bills: 3.88% | | | |
| 52-week Treasury bills: 4.57% | | | |
| 2-year Treasury note: 5.40% | | | |
| 3-year FLB: 6.05% | | | |

*The bank's marginal income tax rate equals 35 percent.

1. What will the incremental cash-flow effects be over the next year if the bank sells both 4-year bonds from its portfolio and invests the entire after-tax proceeds in a new three-year FLB bond? Is this a positive or negative net present-value project? What are the advantages and disadvantages of the bank doing this?

2. Suppose the bank sells the two-year Treasury note, the 10-year Treasury bond, and the 4-year FNMA bond. Determine what dollar amount the bank will report under securities gains or losses. Analyze the incremental cash flow effects if the bank uses the proceeds after taxes to (a) buy 6- month T-bills, (b) buy 52-week T-bills, and (c) buy two-year Treasury notes. In each case explain how the bank's risk profile will have changed.

3. Suppose that the bank also owns CMOs with an estimated life of 4.5 years that currently produce 8 percent coupon interest. At current interest rates the prepayment speed is 25 percent faster than normal. Discuss the pros and cons of selling these CMOs in a rising-rate environment.

## ACTIVITY

Obtain a copy of a large bank's most recent annual report. Analyze data for the securities portfolio and footnotes to the balance sheet and income statement to determine:

1. How the bank accounts for its security holdings (review the amounts designated as trading securities, held-to-maturity, and available-for-sale)

2. Whether the market value of securities held to maturity exceeds or falls below the book value

3. How much the impact of changing interest rates either increased or decreased reported bank capital

# Global Banking Activities

*By the end of 2004, U.S. banks had experienced 14 consecutive years of record profits, due largely to substantial increases in noninterest income, limited growth in noninterest expense, high but declining net interest margins, and reduced loan losses. Many issued new stock, which along with an increase in retained earnings, raised capital ratios to recent record levels. The early 2000s was a period in which large U.S. banks generally positioned themselves to better compete globally by increasing their capital and expanding the range of products and services offered.*

*Given the wide range of economic and structural changes around the world, including a unified Germany, the expansion of the European Community, the privatization of Eastern Europe, and the growth of global powerhouse banking organizations, banks in industrialized countries are trying to expand their trade areas and compete for global business. The elimination of interstate branching restrictions and deregulation of the U. S. banking system with the Gramm-Leach-Bliley Act of 1999 dramatically reshaped the international banking scene. Restrictions on interstate branching and a limited product line meant that U.S. banks were smaller and offered fewer products compared with banks around the world. For example, the Glass-Steagall Act did not allow banks operating inside the United States to engage in certain insurance businesses or underwrite corporate securities. Banks headquartered outside the United States were not subject to these same limitations. U.S. banks were also limited by individual state law, which often restricted branching to within the home state, county, or city. As a result, no U.S. bank was among the ten largest in terms of size in 1996. However, after the passage and full implementation of the Riegle-Neal Interstate Banking and Branching Efficiency Act of 1994, which allowed U.S. banks to branch across state lines, U.S. banking companies now represent some of the largest banks in the world, including Citigroup at the number two spot.*

## GLOBAL BANKING PARTICIPANTS

One clear trend in the evolution of financial institutions and markets is the expansion of activities across national boundaries. Technology has made it possible to conduct business around the world with relative ease and minimal cost. Producers recognize that export markets are as important as domestic markets, and that the range of competitors includes both domestic and foreign operatives. This is increasingly apparent in agriculture, textiles, steel, and microelectronics. Many financial institutions have similarly expanded their activities internationally while developing financial instruments to facilitate trade and funds flows.

Global banking activities involve both traditional commercial and investment banking products. U.S. commercial banks now accept deposits, make loans, provide letters of credit, trade bonds and foreign exchange, and underwrite debt and equity securities in dollars as well as other currencies. With the globalization of financial markets, all firms compete directly with other major commercial and investment banks throughout the world.

| EXHIBIT 14.1 | Ranking of World Banking Companies Prior to Full Enactment of Riegle-Neal Interstate Banking and Branching Efficiency Act, 1996 |
|---|---|

| Rank | Company Name | Total Assets Year-end 1996 |
|:---:|---|---:|
| 1 | Bank of Tokyo-Mitsubishi Ltd., Tokyo | $648,161.00 |
| 2 | Deutsche Bank AG, Frankfurt, Germany | 575,072.00 |
| 3 | Credit Agricole Mutual, Paris (2) | 479,963.00 |
| 4 | Credit Suisse Group, Zurich (1) | 463,751.40 |
| 5 | Dai-Ichi Kangyo Bank Ltd., Tokyo | 434,115.00 |
| 6 | Fuji Bank Ltd., Tokyo | 432,992.00 |
| 7 | Sanwa Bank Ltd., Osaka, Japan | 427,689.00 |
| 8 | Sumitomo Bank Ltd., Osaka, Japan | 426,103.00 |
| 9 | Sakura Bank Ltd., Tokyo | 423,017.00 |
| 10 | HSBC Holdings, Plc., London | 404,979.00 |
| ... | | |
| **17** | **Chase Manhattan Corp., New York** | **333,777.00** |
| **26** | **Citicorp, New York (b)** | **278,941.00** |

Note: Assets are in billions of dollars.

SOURCE: *Bank Search*, Highline Data, © 2004 Highline Data, LLC, and *American Banker*, http://www.americanbanker.com.

Foreign banks offer the same products and services denominated in their domestic currencies and in U.S. dollars. Still, it was not always this way.

## U.S. BANKS IN THE WORLD MARKET

U.S. banks, although dominant players in some world markets, were not considered "large" by international standards. Exhibit 14.1 lists the world's largest banking companies by assets as of year-end 1996 prior to the relaxation of restrictive interstate branching laws and restrictions on the types of activities U.S. banks could engage in. These restrictions and other regulatory factors generally meant that U.S. banks were greater in number, but smaller in size.[1]

The Riegle-Neal Interstate Banking and Branching Efficiency Act of 1994 effectively eliminated interstate branching restrictions in the United States, but did not became fully effective until 1997. In early 1994, there were ten U.S. banks with 30 interstate branches. By June of 1997, there were 103 U.S. banks with 5,414 interstate branches, and in 2004, there were 356 U.S. banks with 20,785 interstate branches. U.S. banks were also hampered in their ability to compete internationally by the Glass-Steagall Act, which effectively separated commercial banking from investment banking. As such, U.S. commercial banks essentially provided two products: loans and FDIC-insured deposits. Glass-Steagall, however, left open the possibility of banks engaging in the investment banking business through the use of Section 20 affiliates so long as the bank was not "principally engaged" in these activities.

In 1987, commercial banks received permission from the Federal Reserve to underwrite and deal in securities. The Fed initially resolved the issue of "principally engaged" by allowing banks to earn up to 5 percent of their revenue in their securities affiliates. This fraction was raised to 10 percent in 1989, and to 25 percent in 1997. By the beginning of 1998, there were 45 Section 20 companies. In November 1999, the U.S. Congress passed the Gramm-Leach-Bliley Act which, for the first time, allowed U.S. banks to fully compete with the largest global diversified financial companies by offering a similar broad range of products. Gramm-Leach-Bliley repealed restrictions on banks affiliating with securities firms contained in Sections 20 and 32 of Glass-Steagall and modified portions of the Bank Holding Company Act to allow affiliations between banks and insurance underwriters. While it preserved the authority of states to regulate insurance, the act prohibited state actions that prevent bank-affiliated firms from selling insurance on an equal basis with other insurance agents. The act further created a new *financial holding company* authorized to engage in underwriting, selling insurance and securities, conducting both commercial and merchant banking, investing in and developing real estate, and other "complementary activities."

As a direct result of Riegle-Neal and Gramm-Leach-Bliley (GLB), U.S. banks became much larger in the late 1990s. By the end of 2000, U.S. banks held three of the largest world bank spots due to mergers of commercial

---

[1]One problem with comparing U.S. banks with banks from around the world is that U.S. reporting requirements are much more stringent with respect to disclosure and timing. Publicly-owned U.S. companies must make an annual report within 90 days after the end of their fiscal year. U.S. banks must file their quarterly reports within 30 days, while companies based outside the United States do not have the same restrictions. For example, in Germany, companies have nine months to report. Exhibits 14.1 and 14.2 convert foreign assets and equity into U.S. dollars. When the value of the dollar declines (rises) relative to a foreign currency, the dollar-valued magnitude of foreign assets and equity rises (declines). Thus, comparisons between countries incorporate fluctuations in the relative prices of currencies.

**EXHIBIT 14.2**

World Rankings of Financial Companies (by Assets), 2003 and 2004

| 2003 Rank | | 2003 | 2004 |
|---|---|---|---|
| 1 | Mizuho Financial Group, Tokyo | $1,286,782 | #N/A |
| 2 | **Citigroup Inc., New York** | **1,264,032** | **1,484,101** |
| 3 | Allianz AG, Munich | 1,127,655 | #N/A |
| 4 | UBS AG, Zurich | 1,115,904 | #N/A |
| 5 | HSBC Holdings PLC, London | 1,031,287 | #N/A |
| 6 | Deutsche Bank AG, Frankfurt | 1,006,306 | #N/A |
| 7 | Credit Agricole, Paris | 988,659 | #N/A |
| 8 | BNP Paribas, Paris | 983,826 | #N/A |
| 9 | ING Group NV, Amsterdam | 979,585 | #N/A |
| 10 | Sumitomo Mitsui Financial Group, Tokyo | 868,430 | #N/A |
| ... | | | |
| 14 | **JPMorgan Chase & Co., New York** | **770,912** | **1,157,248** |
| 16 | **Bank of America Corp., Charlotte, N.C.** | **736,445** | **1,112,035** |

banks as well as mergers across products lines including securities and insurance firms. It is interesting to note that the merger between Citicorp and Travelers, which created Citigroup, the first diversified financial services company, was not completely permissible at the time it was approved under provisions of the Glass-Steagall Act. The passage of GLB made this merger permissible and thereby allowed Citigroup to legally be the world's largest banking company. Had GLB not become law, Citigroup would have had from two to five years to divest itself of Travelers' insurance underwriting. Citigroup formed a *financial holding company* under the provisions of GLB and became one of the first integrated financial services companies engaged in investment services, asset management, life insurance and property casualty insurance, and consumer lending. Its operating companies include Salomon Smith Barney, Salomon Smith Barney Asset Management, Travelers Life & Annuity, Primerica Financial Services, Travelers Property Casualty Corporation, and Commercial Credit.[2]

By the end of 2003, large international mergers increased the size of foreign banks such that the world rankings of U.S. banks declined. Exhibit 14.2 shows that only Citigroup remained among the world's largest at the end of 2003 and JPMorgan Chase fell to number 14. These data, however, were compiled prior to the mergers of JPMorgan Chase and Bank One and Bank of America and FleetBoston Financial. Combining JPMorgan Chase and Bank One produced a firm with $1.157 billion in assets year-end 2004, making it the fourth largest in 2003. Combining Bank of America and Fleet created a firm with $1.112 billion in assets, ranking it number 6 in 2003. Obviously, the lack of 2004 data for international banks makes these comparisions ad hoc.

Today, the product offerings of Citigroup are similar to those of other large international banks. Prior to the merger between Citibank and Travelers, however, Citibank's product line was much more limited. Outside the United States, Citibank was able to offer a diversified set of products using an Edge Act corporation. **Edge Act corporations** are domestic subsidiaries of banking organizations chartered by the Federal Reserve. All "Edges" are located in the United States and may be established by U.S. or foreign banks and bank holding companies, but are limited to activities involving foreign customers. They can establish overseas branches and international banking facilities (IBFs) and own foreign subsidiaries. Domestic and foreign banking organizations can subsequently conduct international business in the locales where their customers do their business. Inside the U.S., Citibank operated under more restrictions because it was limited in the range of products and services it could offer. There were also geographical restrictions regarding where it could locate its banking offices.

Many community banks located along the nation's borders also rely heavily on businesses and individuals based outside the United States, as such groups represent large depositors and borrowers. These banks typically conduct business in multiple currencies, especially those near Mexico, and face additional risks with the devaluation of foreign currencies when foreign business slows.[3] Banks generally find that it is advantageous to follow firms and individuals that the bank already feels comfortable with, so banks will often enter into contracts denominated in foreign currencies and hedge the foreign exchange risk with these customers.

---

[2] In 2002, Citigroup sold a portion of Travelers Property & Casualty Company and announced the sale of the remainder in 2004.

[3] The term *devaluation* refers to the situation in which a government administratively resets the value of its currency to a lower level relative to other currencies. As such, the same amount of the domestic currency buys less.

| EXHIBIT 14.3 | Comparison of Market Share Data for U.S. Offices of Domestically and Foreign-Owned Commercial Banks in the United States: Total Assets and Deposits, 1973–2004 |

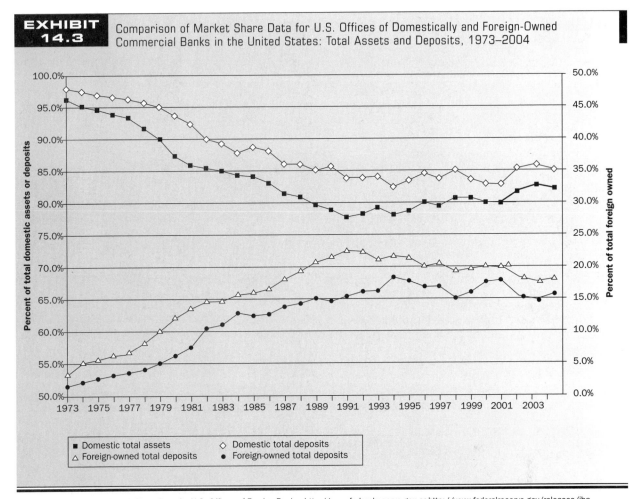

Legend:
- ■ Domestic total assets
- ◇ Domestic total deposits
- △ Foreign-owned total deposits
- ● Foreign-owned total deposits

SOURCE: Federal Reserve Board, Share Data for U.S. Offices of Foreign Banks, http://www.federalreserve.gov or http://www.federalreserve.gov/releases/iba.

## MARKET SHARE OF FOREIGN BANKS OPERATING IN THE UNITED STATES

Foreign banks operating through their American banking offices have also aggressively pursued U.S. business. Exhibit 14.3 indicates the dramatic change in market share data for U.S. offices of foreign banks. In 1973, U.S. offices of foreign banks controlled only 3.8 percent of total U.S. banking assets and 1.6 percent of total domestic deposits. This increased dramatically over the next 20 years to where U.S. offices of foreign banks controlled 22.6 percent of total domestic assets in 1991. By year-end 2004, foreign ownership of total domestic assets and deposits had actually fallen to 18.1 percent of assets. Foreign-owned total domestic deposits peaked in 1994 at 18.3 percent of total deposits but fell to 15.3 percent by year-end 2004. The dramatic increase in foreign ownership of domestic assets and deposits through the early 1990s, as well as the leveling off and decline of this trend in the late 1990s, can be traced to the dramatic changes in the U.S. banking system of the 1990s as branching and product restrictions were removed. Exhibit 14.3 shows that the loss in market share to foreign banks stopped and has been reversed somewhat since the early 1990s.

The most active foreign banks operating in the United States recently have been those headquartered in Japan, with extensive operations along the West Coast, and banks headquartered in Western Europe and Hong Kong, with operations primarily in the Midwest and along the East Coast. Many foreign offices and branches are located in New York City, given its status as a financial center.

Global banks often follow different strategies. Some U.S. banks, such as Citigroup, have aggressively located offices outside the United States and attempted to establish their brand with extensive marketing efforts. Many foreign banks, in contrast, have been content to take silent participations in deals originated by U.S. banks with

**EXHIBIT 14.4** Comparison of Market Share Data for U.S. Offices of Domestically and Foreign-Owned Commercial Banks in the United States: Total Loans and Total Business Loans, 1973–2004

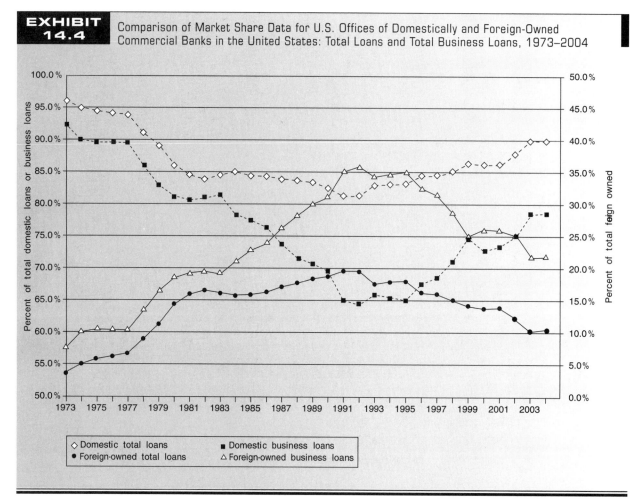

SOURCE: Federal Reserve Board, Share Data for U.S. Offices of Foreign Banks, http://www.federalreserve.gov or http://www.federalreserve.gov/releases/iba.

little fanfare. Domestic borrowers that might object to negotiating a credit agreement with a foreign bank are often unaware that the originating U.S. bank is part of a foreign banking organization or sells part of the loan. Foreign banks, in addition, are extremely aggressive in underwriting Eurobonds and engaging in off-balance sheet activities, including interest rate swaps, standby letters of credit, and municipal bond guarantees. This provides instant credibility and a foothold when negotiating loans later. Exhibit 14.4 shows the growth in market share of U.S. offices of foreign banks in total loans and business loans. In 1973, U.S. offices of foreign banks controlled 3.7 percent of total loans and 7.6 percent of business loans within the United States. This again peaked in 1992 at 18.9 percent market share of total loans and 35.6 percent market share of business loans. The market share of U.S. offices of foreign banks has fallen steadily since 1992, as these offices controlled just 10.5 percent of total loans and 21.5 percent of business loans by year-end 2004.

Some of the largest U.S. banks allocate a significant portion of their assets internationally and generate considerable earnings through these activities. Exhibit 14.5 provides details on the largest U.S. banks with significant international operations. Citibank is clearly the dominant player in foreign office banking with $208.5 billion in foreign office loans or 54.5 percent of total loans, and $334.6 billion in deposits held in foreign offices, which is 73 percent of total deposits. It also has 300 foreign branches but only 272 U.S. branches. By some standards, Citibank is clearly in a class by itself with respect to the size of its international operations. While Citibank's lending activity dwarfs that of other banks in terms of foreign office loans, JPMorgan Chase has about $150 billion in foreign office deposits. Together, Citibank, JPMorgan Chase, Bank of America, Fleet (now a part of Bank of America), and Bank of New York conduct the vast majority of foreign lending for U.S.-owned banks.

**EXHIBIT 14.5** Largest U.S. Banks Foreign Banking Activity Abroad: Foreign Office Deposits, Loans, and Branches, 2004

| Bank Holding Company | Total Assets ($ Billions) | Loans | | | | Deposits | | | | Number of Branches | |
|---|---|---|---|---|---|---|---|---|---|---|---|
| | | Rank by $ loans | % Foreign Loans | $ Billions Domestic Loans | $ Billions Foreign Loans | Rank by $ deposits | % Foreign Deposits | $ Billions Domestic Deposits | $ Billions Foreign Deposits | Domestic | Foreign |
| Citibank NA, New York, NY / Citigroup Inc., New York NY | $694.529 | 1 | 54.47% | $174.27 | $208.47 | 1 | 72.89% | $124.43 | $334.57 | 272 | 300 |
| JP Morgan Chase Bk NA, Columbus, OH / JP Morgan Chase & Co., New York NY | $967.365 | 2 | 9.61% | $330.85 | $35.19 | 2 | 28.94% | $367.87 | $149.85 | 589 | 158 |
| Bank of America NA, Charlotte, NC / Bank of America Corporation, Charlotte NC | $771.619 | 3 | 4.47% | $365.67 | $17.10 | 3 | 17.10% | $439.07 | $90.60 | 4,334 | 123 |
| MBNA America Bk Na, Wilmington, DE / MBNA Corporation, Wilmington DE | $58.269 | 5 | 35.40% | $20.56 | $11.27 | 16 | 8.88% | $29.71 | $2.90 | 3 | 1 |
| Wachovia Bk NA, Charlotte, NC / Wachovia Corporation, Charlotte NC | $389.963 | 6 | 5.15% | $188.88 | $10.26 | 7 | 7.53% | $252.66 | $20.57 | 2,611 | 21 |
| Bank of New York, New York, NY / Bank of New York Co, Inc., New York NY | $92.138 | 7 | 28.07% | $26.04 | $10.16 | 5 | 36.68% | $41.48 | $24.03 | 362 | 12 |
| Fleet NB, Providence, RI / Bank of America Corporation, Charlotte NC | $218.740 | 8 | 7.38% | $104.75 | $8.35 | 8 | 13.41% | $126.10 | $19.53 | 1,562 | 103 |
| Capital One Bk, Glen Allen, VA / Capital One Financial Corp, Falls Church VA | $29.047 | 9 | 27.50% | $13.24 | $5.02 | 18 | 15.83% | $12.23 | $2.30 | 1 | 0 |
| Union Planters NB, Memphis, TN / Regions Financial Corp, Birmingham AL | $33.133 | 10 | 16.25% | $19.04 | $3.70 | 31 | 0.58% | $22.40 | $0.13 | 729 | 0 |
| Comerica Bk, Detroit, MI / Comerica Incorporated, Detroit MI | $52.078 | 12 | 4.50% | $39.10 | $1.84 | 21 | 3.07% | $40.51 | $1.28 | 356 | 2 |
| Keybank NA, Cleveland, OH / Keycorp, Cleveland Oh | $86.062 | 14 | 2.03% | $66.74 | $1.38 | 11 | 14.80% | $50.59 | $8.79 | 920 | 3 |
| PNC Bk NA, Pittsburgh, PA / PNC Financial Services Group, Pittsburgh PA | $73.809 | 15 | 2.82% | $42.18 | $1.22 | 15 | 5.66% | $49.87 | $2.99 | 729 | 8 |
| Mb Financial Bk NA, Chicago, IL / Mb Financial, Inc, Chicago IL | $4.927 | 16 | 18.66% | $2.59 | $0.59 | 32 | 0.00% | $3.70 | $0.00 | 36 | 0 |
| Bank of Hawaii, Honolulu, HI / Bank of Hawaii Corporation, Honolulu HI | $9.815 | 17 | 9.86% | $5.42 | $0.59 | 24 | 9.30% | $6.86 | $0.70 | 74 | 17 |
| State Street B&TC, Boston, MA / State Street Corporation, Boston MA | $90.268 | 18 | 11.28% | $4.07 | $0.52 | 4 | 70.69% | $16.52 | $39.84 | 2 | 2 |
| Northern Trust Co, Chicago, IL / Northern Trust Corporation, Chicago IL | $37.044 | 19 | 4.72% | $10.04 | $0.50 | 9 | 64.81% | $8.61 | $15.87 | 19 | 2 |
| National City Bk, Cleveland, OH / National City Corporation, Cleveland OH | $52.975 | 23 | 0.65% | $41.96 | $0.27 | 13 | 19.14% | $22.58 | $5.34 | 344 | 2 |
| California Cmrc Bk, Century City, CA / Citigroup Inc., New York NY | $1.976 | 24 | 32.82% | $0.50 | $0.25 | 27 | 17.38% | $1.45 | $0.30 | 2 | 0 |
| Irwin Union B&TC, Columbus, IN / Irwin Financial Corporation, Columbus IN | $4.870 | 25 | 5.71% | $3.82 | $0.23 | 33 | 0.00% | $3.06 | $0.00 | 22 | 0 |

SOURCE: *Bank Search*, Highline Data, © Highline Data, LLC.

Exhibit 14.6 lists the largest "foreign-owned" banks operating in the United States. HSBC bank, owned by HSBC Holdings in London, is the largest foreign bank operating in the United States if one measures these banks independently. ABN Amro, an Amsterdam-based holding company, however, owns both Lasalle Bank, Chicago, and Standard Federal, Troy, Michigan. Together these two banks control just under $103 billion in assets. With the exception of Puerto Rican banks, foreign-owned banks operating in the United States operate primarily U.S. branches. Foreign operations are generally handled through banks operated in the bank's domestic country.

## THE EUROPEAN COMMUNITY

In 1985, the countries of Western Europe started a process to design a plan for economic stability and growth in the region. The effort created the **European Community**, or **EC**, which is a confederation of countries that have negotiated the removal of trade barriers to enhance competition. The objective is to increase national output and employment by creating a unified economic engine that can better compete with Japan, the United States, and Eastern Europe. Today, these countries support a common currency—the **Euro** (European Unified Currency)—which is usable in wholesale financial transactions in Austria, Belgium, Finland, France, Germany, Greece, Ireland, Italy, Luxembourg, the Netherlands, Portugal, and Spain. Coins and currency Euros are now circulating in the market with monetary policy for the single currency set by the European Central Bank, based in Frankfurt, Germany. The United Kingdom and Sweden have no plans at present to move toward adopting the euro.

The 15 EC countries—Austria, Belgium, Denmark, Finland, France, Germany, Greece, Ireland, Italy, Luxembourg, the Netherlands, Portugal, Spain, Sweden, and the United Kingdom—were joined by ten more countries as of May 1, 2004—Cyprus, Czech Republic, Estonia, Hungary, Latvia, Lithuania, Malta, Poland, Slovakia, and Slovenia. In addition, there is an application pending for the Former Yugoslav Republic of Macedonia, and Bulgaria, Croatia, Romania, and Turkey are candidate countries. In 2005, the EC had 25 members, one application pending and four candidate countries. In addition, Switzerland and Norway have submitted applications but have not finished the process and are technically not members of the EC.

EC country members have generally agreed on rules that allow the following:[4]

- Free flow of capital across borders
- Elimination of customs formalities
- Establishment of a central bank, which creates the potential for a single currency

Although there have been short-term disruptions in the original plans, the expected long-term result is an environment where trade quotas will no longer exist, where the removal of tariffs and license restrictions will lower production costs and ultimately prices to consumers, and where national output will soar.

The implications for the banking industry are wide ranging. First, trade restrictions have generally protected European banks from outside competition. Banks in France, for example, reported efficiency ratios of 60 to 70 percent during the 1990s, while U.S. banks reported ratios closer to 55 to 60 percent. In order to improve their competitive opportunities, many banks have merged with banks in other countries. U.S. banks similarly view the EC as an opportunity to expand their market presence, and many are forming joint ventures with European banks. In addition, any benefits to consumers in the form of lower prices or enhanced output will benefit all lenders, regardless of where the home office is located.

The remainder of this chapter examines the basic features of international banking. The analysis begins with a description of the different types of organizational units that engage in international activities. The following sections analyze the Eurocurrency and Eurobond markets, international lending activities, fee-based services, and foreign exchange operations. Improved communications systems and the development of innovative securities permit market participants to look globally before making investment or borrowing decisions. Participants benefit greatly from the increased liquidity and lower interest rates that would otherwise not exist. The final section describes foreign exchange risk and price risk associated with bank activities in multiple currencies.

## UNIVERSAL BANKING MODEL

Universal banks have long dominated banking in most of continental Europe. As the label suggests, universal banks engage in everything from insurance to investment banking and retail banking—similar to U.S. banks prior to the enactment of the Banking Act of 1933 and Glass-Steagall provisions, and after the passage of

---

[4]Several countries are also considered closely tied to the EU: Andorra, Cyprus, Greenland, Iceland, Liechtenstein, Malta, Monaco, San Marino, Turkey, and the Vatican. In mid-2005, voters in France and the Netherlands rejected revisions to the EU Constitution thereby increasing uncertainty regarding future growth.

**EXHIBIT 14.6** Largest Foreign-Owned Banks Operating in the United States: Foreign Office Deposits, Loans, and Branches, 2004

| Rank | Bank Top Level Holding Company | Total Assets | Deposits Held in: Domestic Offices | Deposits Held in: Foreign Offices | Loans Held in: Domestic Offices | Loans Held in: Foreign Offices | Percent Foreign Ownership | Number of Branches: Domestic | Number of Branches: Foreign |
|---|---|---|---|---|---|---|---|---|---|
| 1 | HSBC Bk USA NA, Wilmington, DE / HSBC Holdings PLC, London NA | $138.30 | $57.66 | $23.62 | $81.52 | $2.90 | 100 | 0 | 0 |
| 2 | Lasalle Bank NA, Chicago, IL / Stichting Prior ABN Amro Hdg, Amsterdam NA | $63.73 | $30.30 | $7.44 | $36.38 | $0.00 | 100 | 126 | 2 |
| 3 | Manufacturers & Traders TC, Buffalo, NY / Allied Irish Banks Limited, Dublin NA | $52.41 | $31.11 | $4.23 | $38.03 | $0.10 | 22 | 740 | 3 |
| 4 | Union Bk of CA NA, San Francisco, CA / Mitsubishi Tokyo Finl Group, Tokyo NA | $47.49 | $38.72 | $2.59 | $28.58 | $1.48 | 61 | 312 | 6 |
| 5 | Standard Federal Bk NA, Troy, MI / Stichting Prior ABN Amro Hdg, Amsterdam NA | $39.13 | $18.58 | $1.71 | $21.49 | $0.00 | 100 | 273 | 2 |
| 6 | Bank of the West, San Francisco, CA / BNP Paribas, PARIS NA | $38.77 | $24.04 | $1.05 | $26.65 | $0.00 | 99 | 296 | 2 |
| 7 | Deutsche Bk TC Americas, New York, NY / Deutsche Bank Aktiengesellsc, Frankfurt NA | $33.34 | $8.57 | $6.42 | $8.95 | $0.03 | 100 | 4 | 14 |
| 8 | Banco Popular De PR, San Juan PR / Popular Inc., San Juan PR | $23.80 | $13.49 | $0.26 | $0.06 | $13.22 | 100 | 2 | 203 |
| 9 | Harris T&SB, Chicago, IL / Bank of Montreal, Montreal NA | $21.49 | $12.30 | $1.68 | $11.45 | $0.08 | 100 | 54 | 2 |
| 10 | RBC Centura Bk, Rocky Mount, NC / Royal Bank of Canada, Montreal NA | $18.38 | $9.38 | $1.36 | $11.28 | $0.00 | 99 | 263 | 1 |
| 11 | UBS Bk USA, Salt Lake City, UT / UBS AG, Zurich NA | $17.56 | $14.91 | NA! | $7.21 | NA! | 64 | 1 | 0 |
| 12 | Firstbank PR, San Juan, PR / First Bancorp, San Juan PR | $15.50 | $7.93 | $0.20 | $9.35 | $0.11 | 100 | 1 | 56 |
| 13 | Westernbank Puerto Rico, Mayaguez, PR / W Holding Company, Inc.., Mayaguez PR | $14.20 | $6.22 | NA! | $6.02 | NA! | 100 | 2 | 48 |
| 14 | TD Waterhouse Bk NA, Jersey City, NJ / Toronto-Dominion Bank, Toronto NA | $11.52 | $9.33 | NA! | $0.02 | NA! | 95 | 2 | 0 |
| 15 | Doral Bk, San Juan, PR / Doral Financial Corporation, San Juan PR | $11.19 | $3.37 | NA! | $2.71 | NA! | 100 | 1 | 36 |
| 16 | First Hawaiian Bk, Honolulu, HI / BNP Paribas, Paris NA | $10.61 | $7.07 | $0.59 | $5.10 | $0.38 | 99 | 56 | 7 |
| 17 | Banco Popular North America, New York City, NY / Popular Inc.. San Juan PR | $10.23 | $7.10 | $0.00 | $7.15 | $0.00 | 100 | 99 | 0 |
| 18 | Israel Discount Bk of NY, New York, NY / Israel Discount Bank Limited, Tel-Aviv NA | $8.40 | $3.53 | $1.49 | $2.21 | $0.32 | 100 | 6 | 1 |
| 19 | Banco Santander PR, San Juan, PR / Banco Santander S.A.., Santander NA | $8.24 | $4.77 | $0.00 | $5.59 | $0.00 | 60 | 1 | 66 |
| 20 | R-G Premier Bk of PR, San Juan, PR / R&G Financial Corporation, Hato Rey PR | $7.57 | $3.44 | NA! | $4.02 | NA! | 100 | 1 | 32 |
| 21 | Bank of Tokyo Mitsubishi TC, New York, NY / Mitsubishi Tokyo Finl Group, Tokyo NA | $6.32 | $1.42 | $0.77 | $1.68 | $0.00 | 100 | 1 | 1 |
| 22 | Bank Leumi USA, New York, NY / Bank Leumi Le-Israel B.M., Tel-Aviv NA | $5.70 | $3.26 | $1.25 | $2.27 | $0.16 | 97 | 11 | 1 |
| 23 | Banco Bilbao Vizcaya Argenta, San Juan, PR / Banco Bilbao Vizcaya Argenta, Bilbao NA | $5.54 | $2.55 | NA! | $3.11 | NA! | 100 | 1 | 45 |
| 24 | Oriental B&TC, San Juan, PR / Oriental Financial Group Inc, San Juan PR | $4.13 | $1.08 | NA! | $0.78 | NA! | 100 | 1 | 24 |
| 25 | Safra NB, New York, NY / SNBNY Holdings Limited, Marina Bay NA | $4.12 | $2.51 | $0.82 | $1.30 | $0.35 | 99 | 2 | 1 |

Source: *Bank Search*, Highline Data, © Highline Data, LLC.

Gramm-Leach-Bliley. Universal banks can also own shares (common stock) in industrial firms. Universal banking is the conduct of a variety of financial services such as the trading of financial instruments, foreign exchange activities, underwriting new debt and equity issues, investment management, insurance, as well as extension of credit and deposit gathering.

Three events changed the path and development of banking in the United States relative to the rest of the world. The first was the stock market crash of 1929 and the ensuing Great Depression. Many people blamed banks and universal banking activities for the problems, although there is no strong evidence to link the speculative activities of banks with the crash. The second was the enactment of the Banking Act of 1933 and the Glass-Steagall Act, which separated commercial banking from investment banking activities. The third was the increasing importance of the federal government in financial markets. Prior to these events, the U.S. banking system operated more or less under a universal banking system.

Universal banks, like Deutsche Bank in Germany and Credit Lyonnais in France, grew to prominence in the 19th century and were an integral part of the industrialization that began to sweep over Europe in the 1830s and 1840s. European governments have, in many circumstances, actively promoted the growth of big banks, believing they would better serve national economic interests. As part of this trend, European banks are now actively merging or striking alliances with large insurance companies.

One reason universal banking has worked well in continental Europe is because European banks are able to induce corporate customers into using them for a broad range of business. Banks have thus developed expertise in traditional banking, investment banking, and insurance activities. However, while banks in Europe have tied investment banking and lending activities with the same customer, this has not generally been permissible in the United States until the passage of GLB, and even now, there are restrictions. There are other drawbacks to universal banking as well. First, it has slowed consolidation in most European countries, with the exception of Spain and France, such that many European markets have highly fragmented banking systems. Second, banks with the capability of handling all types of financial transactions have failed to excel or become innovative in any one field. Thus, Europe has few investment banks that dominate any product market even though they compete in a wide range of markets around the world. For example, many European investment banks have not grown as fast in their own countries as U.S. institutions—such as Morgan Stanley, Goldman Sachs, Merrill Lynch, and JPMorgan Chase—have.

Proponents, however, promote the advantages of a more flexible banking model, particularly risk diversification and expanded business opportunities. A universal bank can spread its costs over a broader base of activities and generate more revenues by offering a bundle of products. Diversification, in turn, reduces risk. In November 1999, the United States made a dramatic change in its banking system and implemented a type of universal banking that is similar to, but distinct from, the European model. GLB repealed Glass-Steagall and effectively allowed U.S. banks to operate in the business of commercial banking, investment banking, and insurance. Although there are many restrictions, particularly in terms of how banks will be functionally regulated (see Chapter 1), U.S. banks are now, for the first time since the passage of Glass-Steagall, allowed to compete with foreign banks on an equal footing. Other financial companies—such as insurance companies, investment banks, and other suppliers of financial services—are moving toward building financial conglomerates, while technology firms, such as Microsoft, are hammering away at banks' networks, building the electronic gateways into financial services.

The United States moved away from a universal banking system in the 1930s because of problems in separating commerce from finance, in which there is an inherent conflict of interest. A universal bank might use pressure tactics to coerce a corporation into using its underwriting services or buy insurance from its subsidiary by threatening to cut off credit facilities. It could force a borrower in financial difficulty to issue risky securities in order to pay off loans. A universal bank could also abuse confidential information supplied by a company issuing securities as well. Some of the most complicated aspects of GLB are functional regulation, privacy provisions, and what banks are allowed to do versus what the bank's "financial holding company" is allowed to do. Under GLB, the Federal Reserve is the primary regulator of the financial holding company. The act further streamlines bank holding company supervision by establishing the Federal Reserve as the umbrella holding company supervisor, while state and other federal regulators "functionally" regulate the various affiliates of the holding company. The new authorities permitted within the scope of the legislation allow banks to engage in securities, insurance, and commerce businesses; provide for a rule-making and resolution process between the SEC and the Federal Reserve; and allow multistate insurance agency licensing.

Under the U.S. system, financial holding companies (FHCs) are distinct entities from bank holding companies (BHCs). A company can form a BHC, an FHC, or both. The primary advantage to forming an FHC is that the organizer can engage in a wide range of financial activities not permitted in the bank or within a BHC. Some of these activities include insurance and securities underwriting and agency activities, merchant banking, and insurance company portfolio investment activities. Activities that are "complementary" to financial activities also are authorized. The primary disadvantage in forming an FHC, or converting a BHC to an FHC, is that the Federal Reserve may not permit a company to form a financial holding company if any of its insured depository institution subsidiaries are not well capitalized and well managed, or if it did not receive at least a satisfactory rating in its most recent Community Reinvestment Act (CRA) exam. More importantly, if any of the insured depository institutions or affiliates of an FHC received less than a satisfactory rating in its most recent CRA exam, the appropriate Federal banking agency may not approve any additional new activities or acquisitions under the authorities granted under the act. This is considered a severe penalty, which has made many banks cautious about converting their BHC to an FHC.

The Federal Reserve Board regulates allowable nonbank activities that are "closely related to banking," in which BHCs may acquire subsidiaries. Restrictions came about for three reasons. First, it was feared that large financial conglomerates would control the financial system because they would have a competitive advantage. Second, there was concern that banks would require customers to buy nonbank services in order to obtain loans. Third, some critics simply did not believe that BHCs should engage in businesses that were not allowed banks, because these businesses were less regulated and considered more risky.

Special ties between large banks, commercial firms, and regulators have often characterized the Japanese financial system. Most of these firms owned stock in their related parties and were engaged in joint business activities. While the system worked well in the past, Japanese banks and other members of keiretsus (conglomerations of closely tied firms) are currently experiencing severe problems that the system makes more difficult to resolve. If one firm fails, several firms in the same keiretsu may fail.

Every year, the U.S. Congress considers legislation that proposes an expansion of the powers of U.S. banks. If passed, such legislation would generally allow banks, securities firms, and insurance companies to offer new products and services in areas in which they were not previously permitted, and to enter into currently unauthorized business combinations.

## ORGANIZATIONAL STRUCTURE OF U.S. BANKS

U.S. commercial banks conduct their international activities through a variety of units. Small- and medium-size banks typically do business strictly through the bank's head office. Large banks and multibank holding companies typically operate a variety of representative offices, foreign branches, foreign subsidiaries, Edge Act and Agreement corporations, and export trading companies. These units differ in terms of where they are located, what products they can offer, with whom they can conduct business, and how they are regulated.

**HEAD OFFICE.** U.S. banks involved in international activities normally have an international division or department as part of the home office's organizational structure. Division managers supervise all international activities, with the possible exception of funding responsibilities if a bank has a funds management division. These activities include direct commercial and retail lending, lease financing, and securities operations. Other international units report to senior management through this division.

**REPRESENTATIVE OFFICE.** A representative office is usually the first type of international office that a bank forms outside the country. The term *representative* indicates that the office does not conduct normal banking business but simply represents the corporation. Employees cannot accept deposits or make loans. The purpose is to promote the corporation's name and, therefore, develop business that can be funneled to the home office. Banks that establish these offices are trying to assess whether it is feasible to pursue normal banking activities in that location. Because they are exploratory in nature, representative offices have few employees until their transition to full-service banking units.

**FOREIGN BRANCH.** U.S. banks conduct an estimated 60 percent of their international business through foreign branches. Branch offices are legally part of the home bank but are subject to the laws and regulations of the host nation. Foreign branches are either shell offices or full-service banks. Shell branches normally do not solicit business from local individuals, companies, or governments. Instead, they serve as conduits for Eurodollar activities that originate in the head office. Since December 1981, banks have been allowed to engage in the same activities as shell branches via International Banking Facilities. IBFs provide cheaper access to the Eurodollar market, reducing the value of pure shell branches. Full-services branches operate much like domestic banks. They accept deposits, make loans, trade securities, and provide fee-based services. Most large U.S. banks have a branch located in London, the center of Eurodollar activity.

**FOREIGN SUBSIDIARY.** Domestic commercial banks can acquire an ownership interest in foreign banks. A bank holding company or Edge Act corporation can acquire both foreign banks and qualifying nonbank subsidiaries. Unlike branches, subsidiaries are distinct organizations from the parent bank with their own sets of books.

Most nonbank subsidiaries serve the same functions as their domestic counterparts: commercial and consumer financing, data processing, and leasing. The largest U.S. bank holding companies have also formed investment banking subsidiaries (merchant banks) that underwrite a broad range of stocks and bonds in full competition with foreign investment banks. Foreign bank subsidiaries operate much like foreign branches, concentrating on loans and deposits.[5]

**EDGE ACT AND AGREEMENT CORPORATIONS.** Edge Act corporations are domestic subsidiaries of banking organizations chartered by the Federal Reserve. All "Edges" are located in the United States but may be established by U.S. or foreign banks and bank holding companies.[6] Agreement corporations are the state-chartered equivalents of an Edge. Both types of firms are limited to activities involving foreign customers. These include accepting demand and time deposits, extending credit, and other activities incidental to international business.[7] The primary advantage of Edge Act corporations is that they can locate anywhere in the United States, independently of branching restrictions. They can establish overseas branches and IBFs and own foreign subsidiaries. Domestic and foreign banking organizations can subsequently conduct international business near their sources.

Edge Act corporations account for a very small share of total claims on foreign entities. Most of this activity involves firms in New York and Miami, where many international businesses set up offices. Approximately 70 percent of total Edge assets originated at either Miami or New York firms. Still, Edge Act corporations primarily represent deposit gatherers as they do not keep many commercial loans on their books.

**INTERNATIONAL BANKING FACILITIES.** Many international banking units were formed expressly to circumvent U.S. regulations. Shell branches are a prime example. By channeling Eurodollar transactions through shell branches, domestic banks could avoid legal reserve requirements, Regulation Q interest ceilings where applicable, and FDIC insurance payments. IBFs were created to make it easier for U.S. banks to conduct international business without the cost and effort of avoiding regulatory requirements through shell units. Thus, IBFs are not required to have legal reserves or pay FDIC insurance.[8]

Much like Edge Act corporations, IBFs accept deposits from, and extend credit to, foreign entities. They also engage in numerous transactions with Edge Act corporations, foreign banks, and other IBFs. IBFs, in fact, are part of other banking organizations because they exist simply as a set of accounting entries. The organizing unit—a domestic commercial bank or savings and loan, U.S. branch or agency of a foreign bank, or an Edge corporation—makes all the financial decisions, as it does with a shell branch.

Four basic restrictions on IBF activities are intended to distinguish IBF transactions from domestic money market operations.[9] First, IBFs cannot offer transactions accounts to nonbank customers. Deposit maturities must thus be a minimum of two business days. Second, IBFs cannot issue large, negotiable CDs that would be competitive with CDs offered by domestic depository institutions. Third, $100,000 is the minimum acceptable transaction amount. This limits IBF customers to major wholesale participants, including corporations and governments. Finally, loans and deposits must be directly tied to a customer's foreign activity such that direct competitors are those involved in international trade.

**EXPORT TRADING COMPANIES.** Under federal legislation, an export trading company is "exclusively engaged in activities related to international trade and is organized and operated principally for purposes of exporting goods and services produced in the United States by unaffiliated persons."[10] Bank holding companies can acquire export trading companies as part of their international business efforts and extend them credit within limits. These subsidiaries enable banks to expand the range of services offered companies, including handling transportation and shipping documentation, field warehousing, and insurance coverage. Export trading companies can also take title to trade items, which a bank is not permitted to do directly.

**AGENCIES OF FOREIGN BANKS.** Foreign banks compete in the United States through their head offices, U.S. branches, subsidiaries, Edge Act and Agreement corporations, agencies, and investment companies. The first four types of facilities are structured and operate much like U.S. facilities. Agencies and investment companies, in contrast, can offer only a limited range of banking services.[11] They cannot accept transactions deposits from U.S.

---

[5]U.S. banks are also involved in joint ventures with foreign organizations, including consortium banks that are jointly owned by several foreign banks. The primary purpose is to share credit expertise in loan syndications.

[6]Nonbank banks, such as Merrill Lynch and American Express Bank Ltd., also own Edge Act corporations.

[7]In October 1985, the Federal Reserve allowed Edge corporations to provide full banking services to international businesses. Previously, Edges needed to verify that all deposits from a foreign firm and credit granted were for the sole purpose of carrying out international transactions.

[8]A parent company of an IBF must hold reserves against any borrowings from the IBF.

[9]See Chrystal (1984), "International Banking Facilities," *Review* (Federal Reserve Bank of St. Louis).

[10]Edge Act and Agreement subsidiaries of bank holding companies, as well as bankers' banks, can similarly purchase export trading companies. Park and Zwick (1985) describe the legislation that authorized this investment.

[11]New York State charters foreign agencies as investment companies. These companies are granted powers similar to federally chartered agencies of foreign banks.

residents or issue CDs, but must deal exclusively with commercial customers. Their primary purpose is to finance trade originating from firms in their own countries. Agencies also actively participate in interbank credit markets and in lending to U.S. corporations. Agencies and investment companies can accept credit deposit balances, much like correspondent balances from commercial customers, if the account is directly tied to the commercial services provided.

## INTERNATIONAL FINANCIAL MARKETS

International banking activities have grown along with the growth in international trade. The development of international financial instruments and markets has necessarily followed. Firms that export or import goods and services and banks that finance these activities transact business in many different currencies under different sets of regulations. International financial markets have evolved to facilitate the flow of funds and reduce the risk of doing business outside the home country.

International banks are active in soliciting deposits and lending funds outside their domestic borders. The market in which banks and their international facilities obtain international deposits is labeled the Eurocurrency market. The market for long-term international securities is the Eurobond market. Term lending activities tied to Eurocurrency operations occur in the Eurocredit market.

### THE EUROCURRENCY MARKET

A Eurocurrency is a deposit liability denominated in any currency except that of the country in which the bank is located. Two features identify qualifying Eurocurrencies. First, a bank or one of its international facilities must accept the deposit. Second, the accepting bank must be located outside the country that issues the currency. Thus, a BankAmerica branch located in London that accepts U.S. dollar deposits is dealing in Eurodollars, one type of Eurocurrency. The same bank that accepts a sterling deposit is not operating in the Eurocurrency market. Banks that issue Eurocurrency claims are called Eurobanks.

Eurodollar deposits are the dominant type of Eurocurrency. Eurodollars are dollar-denominated deposits at banks located outside the United States. Functionally, deposits at IBFs are equivalent and are often included as Eurodollars. Chapter 8 introduces Eurodollars and Exhibit 8.8 describes how Eurodollars originate. Briefly, they arise when the owner of a dollar deposit at a U.S. bank moves the deposit outside the United States. The Eurobank accepting the deposit receives a dollar claim on the U.S. bank from which the funds were transferred. The Eurodollar and Eurocurrency markets consist of a series of transactions leading to the eventual extension of a loan.

Eurodollar deposits are equivalent to domestic CDs from the depositor's perspective. They are issued in large denominations, typically some multiple of $1 million, have fixed maturities, and pay interest at rates slightly above rates on comparable-maturity CDs issued by U.S. banks. The deposits take the form of both nonnegotiable time deposits and negotiable CDs.[12] Issuing banks do not hold reserves against Eurodollar liabilities and do not pay deposit insurance, which justifies the higher interest rates.

Because Eurobanks that issue Eurodollars pay interest but receive a nonearning U.S. demand deposit, they are eager to reinvest the funds. Eurobanks without immediate credit demand for U.S. dollars simply redeposit the Eurodollar proceeds in another Eurobank. Normally, this deposit is made at a small spread over the initial Eurodollar rate paid. The second Eurobank that accepts the deposit either lends dollars to a commercial or government unit or also redeposits the proceeds. Such pyramiding of deposits continues until a loan is granted. The initial or base rate at which a Eurodollar deposit is accepted is called the London Interbank Offer Rate (LIBOR). Each redeposit is priced at a markup over LIBOR, as is the final loan. Many U.S. banks also price loans to domestic firms at a premium over LIBOR, in recognition of the fact that dollars obtained outside the country are identical to dollars obtained domestically. **LIBOR** is the London market-based rate for dollar denominated deposits and equals an average of the quotations at 16 major London banks for short-term borrowings between major international banks. The LIBOR market is similar to the Federal Funds market in the U.S., but trades in Europe.

The markets for other types of Eurocurrencies are similarly structured. Eurosterling represent claims on deposits denominated in pounds sterling at banks located outside the United Kingdom. A nonfinancial firm or bank that needs sterling can borrow in either the Eurosterling market or from Great Britain's domestic banks at a markup over LIBOR. The size of each Eurocurrency market reflects the underlying demand for that currency. The Eurodollar market dominates because U.S. dollars are accepted as a means of payment throughout the world.

---

[12]A small amount of Eurodollars is callable on demand by the depositor. Because the funds have an effective 24-hour maturity, they earn much lower rates than time deposits or CDs.

## THE EUROBOND MARKET

Many international banks are active in the Eurobond market. Traditional corporate bonds are long-term instruments, underwritten by well-known investment banks that are subject to the securities laws of the country in which they are issued. The U.S. Securities and Exchange Commission, for example, requires extensive disclosure regarding the terms of the offering before it will approve a bond issue. Eurobonds are similar in form but subject to virtually no regulation. They can be denominated in any currency or international currency units. As Park and Zwick state, "Eurobonds are issued in the international Euromarket, underwritten by an international banking syndicate not subject to any one country's securities laws, and denominated in any major national currency or even in an artificial currency unit such as the Special Drawing Right, Eurco, the European Unit of Account, and the European Currency Unit."[13]

The primary issuers of Eurobonds are nonfinancial corporations that view them as alternatives to traditional corporate bonds and direct international loans from banks. International banks with investment banking subsidiaries underwrite the bond offerings and often engage in secondary market trading activities. Some international banks issue a hybrid form of Eurobonds structured as a floating-rate note. Floating-rate notes are issued in denominations as low as $5,000, with maturities ranging from two to five years, and carry interest rates that vary with LIBOR. Typically, the interest rate floats every six months at a fixed spread over six-month LIBOR. Through floating-rate notes, an issuing bank can obtain long-term financing by paying short-term rates. These markets should continue to grow with the move toward syndications among financial institutions and the gradual removal of regulatory restrictions. Borrowers benefit because interest rates are generally lower than they would be without Euromarket opportunities.

Consumers and borrowers benefit from the increased competition. More services are available and interest rates are lower because spreads are smaller. Some critics claim, however, that foreign institutions compete in the United States without the same opportunities available to U.S. firms abroad. Discrepancies in different nations' regulations create inequities, which are slowly disappearing.

## EUROCREDITS

Banks that accept Eurocurrency deposits face the same asset and liability management decisions that derive from other funding sources. The fundamental difficulty is in managing interest rate risk. This problem disappears when a bank redeposits Eurodollars because it matches the asset maturity with that of the initial deposit. When a bank makes a commercial loan, however, it often mismatches the loan maturity with the deposit maturity.

This risk was especially evident during the credit crunches of the 1960s. U.S. banks that could not issue domestic CDs were forced to go to the Eurodollar market for funding. During these periods, Eurodollar rates rose above ceiling rates on new-issue domestic CDs with the competition for funds and credit tightening efforts of the Federal Reserve. Eurobanks subsequently faced a dilemma. Although dollar borrowers generally required term loan financing, Eurobanks did not want to make fixed-rate term loans funded by short-term deposits representing hot money. Borrowing costs could potentially rise above the fixed loan rate if depositors moved their funds.

One solution was the development of **Eurocredits**, term loans priced at a premium over LIBOR. In most cases, the loan rate floats every three or six months, thereby reducing the mismatch between asset and liability maturities. For large loans, banks form a syndicate of international banks in which each member takes a share of the loan and participates in the negotiation of terms. Because both credit and interest rate risks are reduced, Eurocredits are generally priced at spreads as low as 10 basis points over LIBOR.

## INTERNATIONAL LENDING

International loans exhibit many of the same characteristics as domestic loans. Individuals, multinational businesses with offices in the United States and overseas, domestic export/import companies, foreign businesses, and foreign governments constitute the basic borrowing groups. The use of proceeds ranges from working capital lines to production loans that facilitate a country's long-term economic development. The difference with international loans is that they entail unique risks. Historically, many large banks have found these risks attractive. Many U.S. money center banks generate more than 50 percent of their earnings from international operations. Citibank, a part of Citigroup, earns almost two-thirds of its earnings in global activities.

In 1987, and again in 1989, most of the largest U.S. banks charged off significant portions (up to 25 percent) of their loans to Latin American and other foreign borrowers, and subsequently reported net losses. In 1998, the economic meltdown in Asia and Russia's default on its outstanding debts caused many U.S. and foreign banks to suffer losses. In 2001, problems in Argentina produced substantial losses at FleetBoston, Citicorp, and JPMorgan Chase. After the fact, some of these banking organizations concluded that foreign loans effectively

---

[13]See Park and Zwick (1985).

produced few profits because the losses offset earlier earnings. In response, many U.S. banks no longer aggressively pursue international loans. Banks that continue to be aggressive are those that follow U.S. customers as they expand outside the United States or those that have strategically decided to become truly global universal banking organizations.

Foreign banks have experienced the same volatility in performance because loans outside their home countries initially produce profits, only to lead to later losses. Japanese and European banks were exposed to the Asian and Russian problems, while Spain's largest banks suffered losses from their exposures in Brazil and other parts of South America.

Lending across national boundaries introduces country risk and foreign exchange risk. **Country risk** refers to default risk associated with loans to borrowers outside the home country. It exists because lenders and borrowers face different regulations and because of differing political considerations in each country. Country risk increases with government controls over business and individuals, internal politics that potentially disrupt payments, the elimination or reduction of subsidies, and general market disruptions. **Foreign exchange risk** refers to the current and potential volatility in earnings and stockholders' equity due to changes in foreign exchange rates. This risk is discussed in the last section.

The previous section introduced Eurocredits. U.S. banks are also heavily involved in financing foreign trade and making direct loans to major commercial customers. The characteristics of these loans are described below.

## SHORT-TERM FOREIGN TRADE FINANCING

International trade and international trade financing are considerably more complex than simply dealing with trading partners within the same country. Not only is the importer located apart from the exporter, but the two parties usually operate under different rules and regulations and may be totally unfamiliar with each other's financial stability and credit rating. Frequently, they transact business in different currencies. To facilitate trade, someone must enter the transaction and assume the risk that the importer may not pay. Commercial banks fulfill this role through bankers acceptance financing.[14] Trading partners must also have the opportunity to convert one currency into another, which creates a demand for foreign exchange services as well.

A **bankers acceptance** is a time draft that represents an order to pay a specified amount of money at a designated future date. A bank accepts the draft when it stamps the word "accepted" across the document. This approval represents a guarantee under which the accepting bank agrees to remit the face value of the draft at maturity. Acceptances are attractive because a bank substitutes its credit rating for that of the importer. The maturity date is far enough forward to allow the goods being financed to be shipped and inspected before the draft matures. Bankers acceptances are negotiable instruments, with maturities ranging from one to six months. Most bankers acceptance transactions are associated with letters of credit, documents that stipulate the contract terms and duties of all parties and authorize an exporter to draw a time draft on a participating bank. The draft is then converted to a negotiable instrument when it is accepted.

Exhibit 14.7 illustrates the mechanics of how a bankers acceptance is created and used to finance trade.[15] Drafts accepted by U.S. banks are used almost exclusively to finance either U.S. imports or U.S. exports. A small portion finances the warehousing of goods in transit. The trade activity outlined in the exhibit involves a U.S. importer, but the sequence of events is similar for all types of transactions. After agreeing to terms with the exporter (Stage 1), the U.S. importer applies for a letter of credit (LOC) from a U.S. bank (Stage 2). Upon approving the request, the U.S. bank issues an LOC, which authorizes the exporter to draw a time draft against the U.S. bank, and delivers it to the exporter's bank (Stage 3). The foreign bank then notifies the exporter, who ships the goods and submits the LOC, time draft, and shipping documents, which it forwards to the U.S. bank. When the U.S. bank accepts the draft, it creates a bankers acceptance (Stage 8).

The bankers acceptance has a face value and fixed maturity. The exporter discounts the draft with the issuing bank and receives immediate payment (Stage 9). If, for example, the bankers acceptance carried a face value of $1 million and a 90-day maturity, the discounted price would equal $980,000 at an 8 percent discount rate.[16] This covers the purchase price of the goods, although the importer will remit the full face value at maturity. The accepting bank delivers the shipping documents to the importer (Stage 10), who can then legally obtain the goods.

Use of the acceptance enables the exporter to be paid before the importer receives the goods, and the importer to effectively borrow the purchase price. If the issuing bank keeps possession of the bankers acceptance, it essentially finances the importer's purchase, much like a direct loan. In most cases, the issuing bank will sell the acceptance to a third-party investor in the money market (Stage 11). If the bank receives the same discount value,

---

[14]Exporters who are familiar with an importer often extend credit on open account and receive payment after the goods have been delivered. In other cases, an exporter may demand payment from the importer directly before shipping the goods.

[15]Exhibit 14.9 is taken from Duffield and Summers (1981). The following discussion is based on their explanation of the transactions underlying the exhibit.

[16]Price = $1 - (90/360)(0.08)(\$1 \text{ million}) = \$980,000$.

**EXHIBIT 14.7** Bankers Acceptance Financing of U.S. Imports: A Bankers Acceptance Is Created, Discounted, Sold, and Paid at Maturity

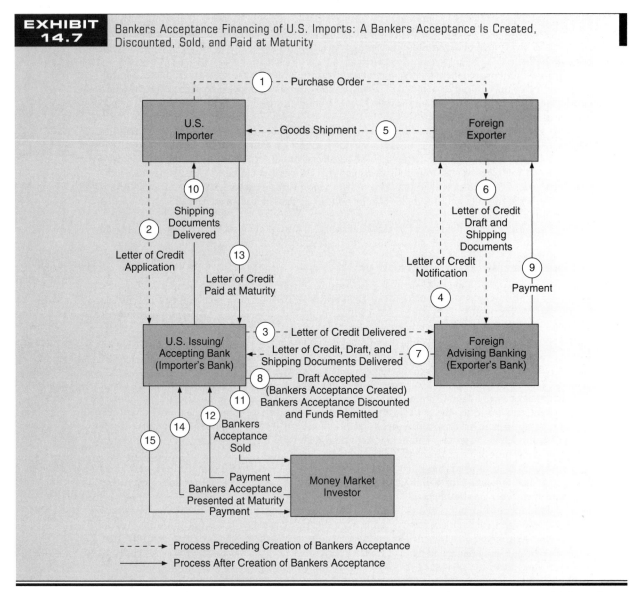

SOURCE: J. Duffield and B. Summers, "Bankers Acceptances," in *Instruments of the Money Market,* T. Cook and B. Summers, eds., (Richmond, VA: Federal Reserve Bank of Richmond, 1981).

$980,000 in this example, it has no funds committed to the financing. It must, however, pay off the acceptance at maturity (Stages 13 to 15), when it presumably receives payment from the importer.

The issuing bank makes a profit in several ways. First, it levies a fee on the importer for accepting the draft and providing its guarantee. Second, it earns the discounted value of the draft, $20,000 in this example, if it simply keeps the acceptance in its portfolio. Finally, it can earn additional profits if it sells the acceptance prior to maturity at a price below the original discounted value ($980,000). Of course, the sale eliminates any interest income.

Historically, exporters and importers originated most of the time drafts that evolved into bankers acceptances. Since the early 1970s, however, many bankers acceptances have refinanced credits of foreign banks that wanted to liquidate their direct financing of foreign trade. These bank-drawn drafts are known as refinancing acceptances or accommodations.

## DIRECT INTERNATIONAL LOANS

International loans originate from international departments of domestic banks, Edge Act corporations, and the credit offices of foreign branches and subsidiaries. Eurodollar loans to foreign governments and well-established multinational corporations are generally low risk. Defaults are extremely rare, so that the loans are priced at a small markup over LIBOR. Some loans are extended to private corporations but carry an explicit guarantee from the source country's government. These loans carry higher risk because some governments have reneged on their guarantees. Loans that have received the greatest attention recently are made within less-developed countries (LDCs). LDC credit extended to both private borrowers and governmental units has generally shown a poor repayment history over the long term. With increasing frequency, regulators and bank shareholders express concern about U.S. banks' exposure to potential foreign loan losses. International loans to LDCs, in fact, clearly contributed to regulators' demand that U.S. money center banks increase their capital-to-asset ratios.

Unfortunately, nonperforming loans do not completely reflect potential losses. Many loans are not classified as nonperforming because U.S. banks have loaned the borrowers funds to make interest and principal payments on existing loans to keep the loans current. Several Latin American governments, including those of Brazil, Peru, and Mexico, have called for a moratorium on debt service to U.S. and foreign banks when they are short of funds. The risk is that these countries may, and often do, unilaterally determine that borrowers, including governments, should suspend interest and principal payments until their revenues increase sufficiently.

To assess risk, the analyst must understand the relationship between large financial institutions and the U.S. government. International loans are part of the price banks pay for the U.S. government's implied guarantee that they will not be allowed to fail. If the banks were to demand payment on defaulted foreign loans or charge off loans as uncollectible and refuse to extend additional credit, economic conditions in LDCs would clearly worsen. Not wanting to bring about a collapse of world trade and financial markets, governments encouraged the largest banks to renegotiate existing agreements and continue lending.

Through 1986, U.S. banks generally acceded to the government's request and continued lending to LDCs. In May 1987, however, Citicorp reversed the trend by allocating $3 billion to its loan loss reserve for possible loan charge-offs with Latin American borrowers. The transfer produced a quarterly loss near $2.5 billion. Other money center banks quickly increased their associated loss reserves. The reserve allocations enabled the banks to recognize discounts on the loans so that they could sell the loans in the secondary market and engage in debt for equity swaps with foreign borrowers. In essence, U.S. banks acknowledged that the financial markets realized LDC debts would not be paid in a timely fashion. Banks prefer foreign exposure in the form of equity investments rather than long-term, constantly renegotiated loans to foreign central banks.

**CREDIT ANALYSIS.** It is difficult to evaluate international loans from a traditional credit analysis viewpoint. In addition to analyzing the borrower's financial condition, a lender must assess country risk. Many foreign governments rely heavily on single industries or products as a source of reserves to pay off their debt. Mexico, with its reliance on oil revenues, is a prime example. When oil prices were rising in the late 1970s and early 1980s, Mexico increased its foreign borrowing to finance internal economic development. The subsequent steep drop in oil prices eliminated its source of foreign currency and forced a total restructuring of the country's international debt obligations. The recent passage of NAFTA again made Mexico an attractive place to invest, such that new ventures and funding have moved into the country in anticipation of expanded trade and the growth that typically coincides.

Credit analysis for international loans generally follows the same systematic procedures outlined previously for domestic loans. Analysts evaluate the required loan amount, use of the proceeds, source and timing of expected repayment, and availability of secondary collateral sources. What makes international lending different is a series of additional risks associated with debt repayment prospects and constraints. If, for example, a bank accepts payment in a currency other than its own country's monetary unit and does not hedge, it assumes *foreign exchange risk*. If the value of the foreign currency declines relative to the domestic currency, the value of the debt service declines, even though all payments might be received on a timely basis. Other potential problems are also created with *country risk*, which includes economic and political risks introduced earlier. **Economic risks** are readily quantifiable, reflecting the considerations discussed above. **Political risks** are much more difficult to assess. Bankers frequently analyze **sovereign risk**, which refers to the likelihood that foreign governments will unilaterally alter their debt service payments, regardless of the formal repayment schedule. In 1985, for example, governments in Nigeria and Peru both capped the amount of interest their countries would pay toward international debt obligations. In general, banks have little recourse in the event that a foreign government restricts debt service payments in dollars, because the legal systems of different countries do not allow a resolution of the default.

Many banks have developed credit scoring systems for assessing country risk. One bank's system measures country risk by using discriminant analysis to quantify economic risks and subjective checklists to quantify political risks.[17] The evaluation produces an index that ranks different countries according to their riskiness in rescheduling debt payments. In this application, economic risk is measured by debt management factors and economic indexes. The best indicators of risk are a country's current debt service ratio, defined as the sum of debt service

---

[17]Morgan (1985) describes the inputs and evaluation procedures in detail.

## EXHIBIT 14.8    Political Rating Models

### Government characteristics, country ABC

What classification best describes the current government?

**Government type (0 to 10)**                    **6**

0  Despot, dictator
2  Military dictator
4  Monarchy, family rule
6  One-party democracy or nonviable multiparty democracy
8  Multiparty (coalition) democracy
10  Viable two-party democracy

**Latest change in government (0 to 10)**         **8**

0  Bloody and violent coup d'etat
2  Bloodless coup d'etat
4  Peaceful dictator change
6  Monarch change, change in colonial status
8  Elections, one candidate only
10  Peaceful elections, two or more candidates

**Relations with United States (0 to 10)**        **4**

0  Considered a threat to U.S. security
2  Anti-American policies
4  Nonaligned, but leaning to the East
5  Nonaligned
6  Nonaligned, but leaning to the West
8  Supports most U.S. foreign policies
10  Strongly pro-American, supports all U.S. policies

**Government's role in economy (0 to 10)**        **6**

0  Government controls all aspects of economy (communism)
2  Government influences all aspects of economy
4  Socialist type of economy
6  General agreement between capitalists and government
8  Capitalism with minor government intervention
10  STRONGLY CAPITALISTIC, FREE ENTERPRISE

**Stability of present government (0–10)**        **6**

0  Violent coup d'etat imminent
2  Overthrow of government likely
4  Unexpected change in government possible (i.e., death of leader)
6  Government could lose in next election
8  Likely change in government, political power remains intact
10  Government unlikely to lose in next elections

### Political stability, country ABC

What are the chances of the following events in the short term and medium term?*

|  | Short Term | Medium Term |
|---|---|---|
| Destabilizing riots, civil unrest | 3 | 2 |
| Increased terrorist activities | 3 | 2 |
| Guerilla activity, armed rebels | 3 | 2 |
| Civil war | 4 | 4 |
| Government overthrow, coup d'etat | 4 | 3 |
| Foreign war, border skirmishes | 4 | 4 |
| Political moratorium of debt | 4 | 4 |
| Nationalization of major industries | 3 | 3 |
| Socialistic party comes to power | 3 | 3 |
| Communist party comes to power | 4 | 4 |
| Total | 35 | 31 |

Probabilities
5  Extremely unlikely          2  Likely
4  Unlikely                    1  Extremely likely
3  Neutral                     0  Present situation

| | |
|---|---|
| **Government characteristics** | **30** |
| **Political stability (short term/medium term)** | **35/31** |
| **TOTAL POLITICAL RATING** | **65/61** |

*Short-term is within one year; long-term is between one and five years.

and short-term debt outstanding divided by total exports; total debt divided by exports; and basic economic measures such as per capita income, real growth in a gross domestic product, and the inflation rate. Political risk is measured according to a subjective political rating model and structural factors. The political model assesses both political stability and general government characteristics (see Exhibit 14.8). Each country receives a weighted score representing its cumulative risk profile. The bank determines appropriate loan limits or concentrations in different countries according to these rankings.

## FOREIGN EXCHANGE ACTIVITIES

Because different countries use different monetary units, traders must be able to convert one unit into another. Foreign exchange markets are where these monetary units are traded. Foreign exchange refers to currency other than the monetary unit of the home country, and an exchange rate is the price of one currency in terms of another currency. For example, Japanese yen represent foreign exchange in the United States, such that one U.S. dollar may be worth 128 yen if exchanged today. Banks participate in foreign exchange markets by buying and selling currencies from participants who use different currencies in their business or travels. They also coordinate foreign exchange hedges for bank customers, enter arbitrage transactions, and speculate on currency price movements for their own account by taking unhedged positions.

## FOREIGN EXCHANGE RISK

Foreign exchange risk is the current and potential risk to earnings and stockholders' equity arising from changes in foreign exchange rates. It is found in assets and liabilities denominated in different currencies that are held on a bank's balance sheet, and in certain off-balance sheet activities where the commitments or guarantees are denominated in different currencies. It is evidenced when changing exchange rates affect a bank's cash inflows differently than cash outflows associated with these positions denominated in different currencies.

Banks also make markets in foreign currencies and take positions buying and selling currencies for their own account. The change in values of these positions due to changing foreign exchange rates is labeled price risk. It is a component of the sensitivity to market risk (S in a bank's CAMELS rating, see Chapter 2) evaluated by bank regulators.

Foreign exchange risk can be high if a bank holds assets and issues liabilities denominated in different currencies where the amounts are substantially different. In this case, changes in exchange rates will produce changes in earnings and the market value of stockholders' equity. Consider the situation faced by Commerce Bank (CB), whose home country is Poland and home currency is the *zloty*. The current (spot) exchange rate is $1 equals 150 zlotys. Commerce Bank's balance sheet position in U.S. dollars is such that the bank has $1,000 in loans and $250 in liabilities. Assume that all loans and liabilities have the same maturity and there are no embedded options. In terms of zlotys, CB's assets are worth 150,000 zlotys and its liabilities are worth 37,500 zlotys at the prevailing exchange rate.

- If the exchange rate moved to $1 equals 160 zlotys, the assets would increase in value by 10,000 zlotys, while the liabilities would increase in value by 2,500 zlotys. The bank would gain 7,500 in zlotys, holding everything else constant, such that stockholders' equity would increase by 7,500 zlotys.

- If the exchange rate moved to $1 equals 140 zlotys, the assets would decrease in value by 10,000 zlotys, while the liabilities would decrease by 2,500 zlotys. In this case, the bank would see stockholders' equity decrease by 7,500 zlotys.

These same exposures exist for off-balance sheet commitments and guarantees when counterparties effect the at-risk transactions or activities.

A bank's risk managers analyze aggregate foreign exchange risk by currency. The basic approach is to calculate a bank's net balance sheet exposure by currency and relate this to the potential change in value given changes in the associated exchange rate. Let:

$$A_j = \text{Amount of assets denominated in currency j}$$
$$L_j = \text{Amount of liabilities denominated in currency j}$$

A bank's net balance sheet exposure in currency j ($NEXP_j$) is the amount of assets minus the amount of liabilities denominated in currency j:

$$NEXP_j = A_j - L_j \qquad (14.1)$$

If $NEXP_j > 0$, the bank is long on currency j on its balance sheet. If $NEXP_j < 0$, the bank is short on currency j on its balance sheet. The bank will lose if it is long on a currency and the currency depreciates in value (the currency buys less of another currency). The bank will lose if it is short on a currency and the currency appreciates in value (the currency buys more of another currency). CB, which was long U.S. dollars, would thus lose if the dollar depreciates as indicated by the movement in the exchange rate to $1 equals 140 zlotys. CB would gain if the dollar appreciates as indicated by the exchange rate change to $1 equals 160 zlotys. The gain or loss in a position with a currency is indicated by:

$$\text{Gain/loss in a position with currency j} = NEXP_j \times \Delta\text{spot exchange rate} \qquad (14.2)$$

where the spot exchange rate is measured as the number of units of the home currency for one unit of the foreign currency. In the case of CB, the bank's loss from a move to $1 equals 140 zlotys is:

$$\text{Loss} = (1,000 - 250) \times (140 - 150)$$
$$= -7,500 \text{ zlotys}$$

Risk managers must assess their foreign exchange risk for each currency in which the bank has significant balance sheet and off-balance sheet exposures. They should also assess interest rate risk and liquidity risks in each currency. They can choose to speculate or hedge this risk. Many banks use currency forward, futures, and swap contracts to manage this risk.

## EXHIBIT 14.9

Facilitating Funds Transfers of Different Currency-Denominated Deposits

U.S. retailer imports $500,000 in video equipment from Japanese manufacturer. Spot exchange rate is $1 = 105 yen.

| Western Bank | | Fuji Bank Ltd. | |
| --- | --- | --- | --- |
| ΔASSETS | ΔLIABILITIES | ΔASSETS | ΔLIABILITIES |
| 1. Deposit at Fuji Bank <br> −52.5 million yen | Deposit of U.S. retailer <br> −$500,000 | 1. | 1. Deposit of U.S. retailer <br> +52.5 million yen <br> Deposit of Western Bank <br> −52.5 million yen <br> 2. Deposit of U.S. retailer <br> −52.5 million yen <br> Deposit of Japanese <br> manufacturer <br> +52.5 million yen |

1. U.S. RETAILER BUYS YEN FROM WESTERN BANK AND DEPOSITS BALANCE AT FUJI BANK IN TOKYO.
2. U.S. RETAILER PAYS JAPANESE MANUFACTURER FOR GOODS

## CURRENCY EXCHANGE

A fundamental responsibility of international banks is to facilitate funds transfers between trading partners who deal in different currencies. Most transactions are settled by exchanging deposits, so banks must maintain either correspondent bank relationships or operate their own foreign bank offices to have access to Eurocurrencies. Each funds transfer may require a conversion of deposits to another currency and thus may affect exchange rates if banks choose to realign their inventories.

Suppose, for example, that a U.S. retail outlet negotiates the purchase of video recording equipment for $500,000 from a Japanese manufacturer. If the purchase is invoiced in yen, the buyer will convert U.S. dollars to yen at $1 to 105 yen and exchange 52.5 million yen for the goods. The hypothetical transaction is summarized in Exhibit 14.9, assuming that the traders deal with Western Bank and Fuji Bank Ltd. After the purchase, Western Bank's inventory of currencies has changed because it holds 64 million fewer yen than previously. The bank will have to buy yen to bring its foreign exchange holdings back to the initial position. If the transaction was denominated in dollars, Fuji Bank would hold $500,000 more and would need to sell dollars to reach its initial foreign exchange position. Both the purchase of yen by Western Bank and sale of dollars by Fuji Bank would put pressure on the dollar to decrease in value (increased supply of dollars) and the yen to increase in value (increased demand for yen). Current exchange rates will thus be affected when transactions force a realignment of foreign exchange holdings.

In actuality, there is a spot market, forward market, futures markets, and markets for options on futures for foreign exchange. The **spot market** is the exchange of currencies for immediate delivery. The **forward market** comprises transactions that represent a commitment to exchange currencies at a specified time in the future, at an exchange rate determined at the time the contract is signed. For example, a bank might commit to buy 1 million yen 90 days forward for $8,000. After 90 days, the bank pays $8,000 and receives 1 million yen, regardless of movements in exchange rates during the 90-day period. The 90-day forward rate in this case is different from the spot rate quoted earlier because $1 equals 125 yen. Foreign exchange trading also occurs in organized markets for futures and options on futures, which enables traders to hedge spot transactions or speculate on future exchange rate changes.[18] A **financial futures contract** represents a commitment between two parties—a buyer and a seller—on the price and quantity of a standardized financial asset or index. An **option contract** is an agreement between two parties in which one party gives the other the right, but not the obligation, to buy or sell a specific asset at a set price for a specified period of time. An **option on futures contract** is an option contract in which the underlying asset is a futures contract.

Banks that buy or sell currencies for customers normally charge a commission. Alternatively, they may enter into forward contracts with customers and speculatively trade for their own account. For example, suppose that

---

[18]Chrystal (1984) describes the rudiments of foreign exchange futures and options in "A Guide to Foreign Exchange Markets," *Review* (Federal Reserve Bank of St. Louis).

*Foreign Exchange Activities*

---

**EXHIBIT 14.10** Covered Interest Arbitrage

2. Convert dollars to francs at $1 = 1.7 francs

3. Invest in Swiss securities yielding 10%

$$\left[\frac{\$1,090,000}{1 + 0.09}\right](1.7) = 1.7 \text{ million francs}$$

$$\left[\frac{\$1,090,000}{1 + 0.09}\right](1.7)(1.10) = 1.87 \text{ million francs}$$

$$\left[\frac{\$1,090,000}{1 + 0.09}\right] = \$1,000,000$$

$$\left[\frac{\$1,090,000}{1 + 0.09}\right]\frac{(1.7)(1.10)}{1.667} = \$1,121,776$$

1. Borrow dollars at 9%

4. Sell francs for dollars one year forward at $1 = 1.667 francs

**Sample Transaction: Borrow $1,000,000.**
1. Borrow $1,000,000 at 9 percent; agree to repay $1,090,000 in one year.
2. Convert $1,000,000 to 1.7 million francs in spot market at $1 = 1.7 francs.
3. Invest 1.7 million francs in one-year security yielding 10 percent; will receive 1.87 million francs after 1 year.
4. Sell 1.87 million francs one year forward for $1,121,776 at $1 = 1.667 francs.
**Net profit = $1,121,776 − $1,090,000 = $31,776**

---

the current dollar-to-yen spot rate is $1 equals 128 yen, and the 90-day forward rate is $1 equals 125 yen. If a bank buys 100 million yen with dollars 90 days forward, it agrees to pay $800,000 for the yen when the forward contract comes due, even though the current exchange rate sets the value at $781,250. If the position is unhedged, the bank assumes the risk that dollars will increase in value relative to yen or stay above the forward rate during the 90-day interval. It will gain if dollars fall more in value than that suggested by the forward-to-spot rate differential (below 125 yen).

A spot rate of $1 to 129 yen at the time of delivery of the forward contract would indicate that the dollar rose in value and the bank could have purchased 100 million yen for only $775,194. A spot rate of $1 to 124 yen at delivery would require a price of $806,452, which exceeds the contracted price by more than $6,000. When the forward price of a foreign currency is higher than its spot price, the foreign currency is priced at a forward premium. When the forward price is lower, the foreign currency is priced at a forward discount. In the above case, the yen is priced at a forward premium against the dollar.

## THE RELATIONSHIP BETWEEN FOREIGN EXCHANGE RATES AND INTEREST RATES

The relationship between spot rates and forward rates is determined by the same factors that influence relative interest rates between countries. Arbitrage transactions essentially guarantee that interest rate changes produce changes in foreign exchange rates, and vice versa. The pure definition of **arbitrage** is the simultaneous purchase of a security in one market and the sale of it or a derivative product in another market in which no money is put at risk. The object of an arbitrage is to profit from price differentials between the two markets. Suppose that a trader can borrow U.S. dollars for one year at 9 percent at the same time that one-year maturity, risk-free, Swiss franc-denominated securities yield 10 percent. The trader can convert dollars to francs at the spot rate of $1 for 1.7 francs and sell francs for dollars one year forward at $1 = 1.667 francs.

The series of transactions is demonstrated in Exhibit 14.10. A trader borrows $1 million and agrees to repay $1.09 million one year later. Simultaneously, the trader sells the dollars for francs, buys a Swiss security, and sells the expected amount of francs at maturity for dollars one year forward. As indicated, the trader can earn a riskless profit of $31,776 for each $1 million borrowed. The profit is riskless because the trader has borrowed in one currency yet covered the transaction by selling the expected foreign exchange after investment for the original currency in the forward market. A profit is available because the interest rate differential between securities in the two countries is out of line with the spot-to-forward exchange rate differential. This series of trades is called **covered interest arbitrage**.[19]

If the exchange rates and interest rates were this far out of line and the large profit was available, arbitrageurs would quickly negotiate the same series of transactions until prices moved back in line to eliminate (net of

---

[19]If the calculation showed a loss, reversing the direction of transactions by borrowing in the opposite currency and converting it in a similar fashion could make a profit.

transactions costs) the riskless return. Interest rate parity exists when covered interest arbitrage profit potential is eliminated. Letting:

$i_1$ = Annual interest rate in Country 1

$i_2$ = Annual interest rate in Country 2

$s_{1,2}$ = Spot exchange rate equal to the number of units of Country 2's currency for one unit of Country 1's currency

$f_{1,2}$ = One-year forward exchange rate equal to the number of units of Country 2's currency for one unit of Country 1's currency

Interest rate parity implies: $\dfrac{1 + i_2}{1 + i_1}\left(\dfrac{s_{1,2}}{f_{1,2}}\right) = 1$, or  (14.3)

$$\frac{i_2 - i_1}{1 + i_1} = \left(\frac{f_{1,2} - s_{1,2}}{s_{1,2}}\right) \tag{14.4}$$

The equilibrium condition, expressed in Equation 14.4, suggests that the forward exchange rate differential as a fraction of the spot rate should equal the interest rate differential relative to 1 plus an interest factor to eliminate arbitrage profits. If $i_1$ is 9 percent, $i_2$ is 10 percent, and $s_{1,2}$ is 1.7 in the previous example, then $f_{1,2}$ should equal 1.7156:

$$\frac{0.10 - 0.09}{1 + 0.09} = \left(\frac{f_{1,2} - 1.7}{1.7}\right)$$

$$f_{1,2} = 1.7156$$

Conceptually, if interest rates are relatively low in one country, that country's currency should sell at a forward premium. Any gain from borrowing at low rates and investing at higher rates (0.01/1.09) is exactly offset (0.0156/1.7) when the borrower attempts to sell the investment proceeds forward at a premium price.

## PRICE RISK WITH FOREIGN CURRENCIES

International banks actively trade most foreign currencies. They buy and sell foreign exchange for customers by request, to hedge transactions for customers and themselves, to earn arbitrage profits by taking advantage of temporary price discrepancies, and to trade speculatively for their own account. Foreign exchange gains often supplement normal operating earnings for many banks. Risk managers continually assess a bank's exposure to the risk of loss from these trading positions associated with adverse changes in foreign exchange rates. Regulators refer to this as price risk and require large banks to formally measure their exposure or sensitivity to market risk from all potential price moves. In terms of measuring this risk, a bank can identify its net exposure in each currency much like that in Equation 14.1 except that the amounts represent the value of a bank's long positions and short positions in each currency from these speculative positions or customer positions in each of the currencies. The gain or loss can be similarly measured by Equation 14.2. Regulators, however, require that the largest banks perform a value-at-risk (VAR) analysis of their entire trading positions that they then require capital to support.

## SUMMARY

Large international banks effectively operate as commercial banks and investment banks. They accept foreign deposits and make loans to foreign borrowers. They act as brokers, dealers, and underwriters in negotiating Eurobond issues, floating-rate note issues, interest rate and currency swaps, and foreign equity issues. Many banks located outside the United States are more heavily capitalized and thus better able to compete globally. The largest U.S. banks, in turn, are aggressively pursuing business outside as well as within the United States. Citigroup and JPMorgan Chase, for example, have well-defined strategies to actively pursue commercial and investment banking business in Western Europe and elsewhere, and they generate a considerable portion of their overall profits from activities outside the United States

Because of large losses on international loans and the difficulty in assessing country risk, many large banks have substantially reduced their international commercial loan exposure. This is true for both U.S. and non-U.S. banks, which have experienced substantial losses in recent years. Many U.S. banks that pursue business outside the United States prefer to do mergers, acquisitions, and security underwriting rather than straight commercial lending.

International banks operate a wide range of offices to conduct foreign banking business. These offices generally provide access to the Eurocurrency markets and Eurocredits. Loans to foreign governments and businesses entail two additional risks compared with loans to domestic borrowers. Country risk involves both economic risk (the borrower's ability to repay may deteriorate) and political risk (the underlying government may simply renege on contracted debt service payments). International loans may also involve foreign exchange risk when lenders receive payment in a currency other than their own. Banks also assume foreign exchange and price risk if they hold unequal amounts of assets and liabilities denominated in different currencies or have trading positions where long and short positions are not equal. As such, changes in exchange rates can sharply increase or lower bank profits and the market value of stockholders' equity.

## QUESTIONS

1. Discuss the differences between Eurocurrency, Eurobonds, and Eurocredits.

2. Why were international banking facilities created? How do they differ from Edge Act and Agreement corporations?

3. Explain how you would measure country risk in international lending. Can you get a precise statistical measure?

4. The U.S. system of banking historically led to many more banks that were smaller in size and operated with few branches. Why did the U.S. banking system develop so differently from that of other countries? What factors have brought about a change in the U.S. system that makes it look more like other countries?

5. Identify several large foreign institutions that are major lenders in the United States. Do any have a basic competitive advantage over U.S. banks? Explain why.

6. Which of the following types of foreign banking operations would best suit the circumstance described?

   a. A major customer of a U.S. bank requests a loan to finance growing export activity in Mexico.

   b. Management notices that an increasing number of its business customers have located offices in Moscow.

   c. Although the bank cannot justify a permanent office in Moscow, it wants to provide loans to these international activities.

   d. Indonesia has just announced the privatization of many small banks. Your bank is going to buy one of the banks to establish a local lending and deposit base.

7. What is a bankers' acceptance? Explain by setting up an example of how one is created.

8. U.S. banks can underwrite corporate bonds and stocks outside the United States, but not in the United States. Does this seem reasonable? Why do you think such a restriction exists?

9. Explain how the forward market for foreign exchange differs from the spot market. When will forward exchange rates be at a premium or discount to spot exchange rates?

10. Suppose that the following exchange rates and interest rates prevail:

    Spot exchange rate: $1 = 121 yen

    One-year forward rate: $1 = 130 yen

    One-year interest rates: U.S. = 5.54%, Japan = 6.98%

    Can a trader earn covered interest arbitrage profits? If not, explain why not. If possible, determine what the likely directional impact on each rate would be if arbitrageurs took advantage of the profit potential.

11. Assume that the forward exchange rate is for 90 days forward and the interest rates are annualized 90-day rates in Question 10. Can a trader earn covered interest arbitrage profits?

12. Suppose that Commerce Bank in Poland holds $400 in assets and $1,000 in liabilities denominated in dollars. The home currency is the zloty, and the current spot exchange rate is $1 = 145 zlotys.

    a. What is the bank's net exposure in dollars?

    b. Will the bank gain or lose if the spot exchange rate changes to $1 = 150 zlotys? Calculate the gain or loss.

    c. Will the bank gain or lose if the spot exchange rate changes to $1 = 140 zlotys? Calculate the gain or loss.

# REFERENCES

## CHAPTER 1

Anason, Dean, "The Major Provisions of Controversial New Law," *American Banker,* August 10, 1998.

Brenner, Lynn. "Turning Assets into Securities Is Knotty Problem, Panel Says." *American Banker,* May 2, 1986.

Cocheo, Steve. "Anatomy of an Examination." *ABA Banking Journal,* February 1986.

Critchfield, Tim, Davis, Tyler, Davison, Lee, Gratton, Heather, Hanc, George and Ktherine Samolyk, "Community Banks: Their Recent Past, Current Performance, and Future Prospects," FDIC working paper, 2004.

Emmons, Eilliam, Vaughan, Mark and Timothy Yeager, "The Housing Giants in Plain View," The Regional Economist, Federal Reserve Bank of St. Louis, July 2004.

Ennis, Huberto and H.S. Malek, "Bank Risk of Failure and the Too-Big-to-Fail Policy," Economic Quarterly, Federal Reserve Bank of Richmond, Volume, 91, Number 2, Spring 2005.

Evanoff, Douglas, and Diana Fortier. "The Impact of Geographic Expansion in Banking: Some Axioms to Grind." *Economic Perspectives,* Federal Reserve Bank of Chicago, May–June 1986.

Hoenig, Thomas, M. "Community Banks and the Federal Reserve," Economic Review, Federal Reserve Bank of Kansas City, Volume 88, Number 2, Second Quarter 2003.

Hoenig, Thomas M. "Rethinking Financial Regulation." Federal Reserve Bank of Kansas City Economic Review (Second Quarter), 1996, pp.5–13.

Kane, Edward. "Accelerating Inflation, Technological Innovation, and the Decreasing Effectiveness of Banking Regulation." *Journal of Finance,* May 1981.

Kane, Edward. "Good Intentions and Unintended Evil: The Case Against Selective Credit Allocation." *Journal of Money Credit and Banking,* February 1977.

"The Role of Community Banks in the U.S. Economy," Economic Review, Federal Reserve Bank of Kansas City, Volume 88, Number 2, Second Quarter 2003.

Rose, John T. "Commercial Banks as Financial Intermediaries and Current Trends in Banking: A Pedagogical Framework." *Financial Practice and Education,* Fall 1993.

## CHAPTER 2

Bonin, John, Hasan, Iftekhar and Paul Wachtel, "Bank Performance, Efficiency and Ownership in Transition Countries," Journal of Banking & Finance, Volume 29, Issue 1, January 2005.

Carlson, Mark and Roberto Perli, "Profits and Balance Sheet Developments at U.S. Commercial Banks in 2003," Federal Reserve Bulletin, Spring 2004.

Cole, David W. "A Return-on-Equity Model for Banks." *The Bankers Magazine,* Summer 1972.

Hein, Scott, Koch, Timothy and S. Scott MacDonald, "On the Uniqueness of Community Banks," Economic Review, Federal Reserve Bank of Atlanta, Volume 90, Number 1, First Quarter 2005.

Lopez, Jose. "What is Operational Risk?" Economic Letter, Federal Reserve Bank of San Francisco, January 25, 2002.

Heggestad (1979), Arnold. "Market Structure, Competition and Performance in Financial Industries: A Survey of Banking Studies." In *Issues in Financial Regulation*, edited by Franklin Edwards. New York: McGraw-Hill Book Company, 1979.

Milligan, Jack, "Prioritizing Operational Risk," Banking Strategies, September/October 2004.

Operational Risk, edited by Carol Alexander, Prentice Hall Financial Times, 2003.

Sirri, Eric, "Investment Banks, Scope, and Unavoidable Conflicts of Interest," Economic Review, Federal Reserve Bank of Atlanta, Fourth Quarter 2004.

Whalen, Gary, "A Hazard Model of CAMELS Downgrades of Low-Risk Community Banks," Comptroller of the Currency, Economics Working Paper 2005–1, May 2005.

## CHAPTER 3

Gregor, William, and Robert Hedges. "Alternative Strategies for Successful Cost Management." *The Bankers Magazine,* May–June 1990.

Furash, Edward, "What Do We Do For An Encore?"ABA Banking Journal, September 1993.

Gregor, William, and Robert Hedges. "Alternative Strategies for Successful Cost Management." *The Bankers Magazine,* May–June 1990.

Holliday, Karen. "Forget 'Cost-Cutting' Think Low-Cost Revenue Growth." *ABA Banking Journal,* November 2000.

Kimball, Ralph. "Innovations in Performance Measurement in Banking." *New England Economic Review,* Federal Reserve Bank of Boston, May–June 1997.

Rose, Sanford, "Rethinking Cost Control," American Banker, November 21, 1989.

# Chapter 4

Fabozzi, Frank. *Fixed Income Mathematics.* Chicago: Probus Publishing, 1993.

# Chapter 5

Binder, Barrett and Thomas Lindquist, Asset/Liability Management and Funds Management at Commercial Banks, Bank Administration Institute, Rolling Meadows, Illinois, 1982.

Blackwell, Rob, "'Triage' Report: Freddie Builds Capital, But Work Remains," American Banker, April 1, 2005.

Frame, W. Scott and Lawrence White, "Fussing and Fuming over Fannnie and Freddie: How Much Smoke, How Much Fire?" Journal of Economic Perspectives, Volume 19, Number 2, Spring 2005.

McLean, Bethany, "Fannie's Shaky Future," Fortune, March 21, 2005.

Schmid, Frank, "Stock Return and Interest Rate Risk at Fannie Mae and Freddie Mac," Review, Federal Reserve Bank of St. Louis, Volume 87, Number 1, January/February 2005.

# Chapter 6

Bierwag, George, Duration Analysis: Managing Interest Rate Risk, Ballinger Press, Boston, MA, 1987.

Ho, Thomas, "Key Rate Durations: Measures of Interest Rate Risks," Journal of Fixed Income, September 1992.

Kaufman, George, "Measuring and Managing Interest Rate Risk: A Primer," Economic Perspectives, Federal Reserve Bank of Chicago, January-February 1984.

Sierra, Gregory and Timothy Yeager, "What Does the Federal Reserve's Economic Value Model Tell Us About Interest Rate Risk at U.S. Community Banks?" Review, Federal Reserve Bank of St. Louis, Volume 86, Number 6, November/December 2004.

Toevs, Alvin, "GAP Management: Managing Interest Rate Risk in Banks and Thrifts," Economic Review, Federal Reserve Bank of San Francisco, Spring 1983.

"Widening in Duration Gap Fails to Rattle Fannie Mae," American Banker, May 18, 2004.

# Chapter 7

Gupta, Anurag and Marti Subrahmanyam, "Pricing and Hedging Interest Rate Options: Evidence from Cap-Floor Markets," Journal of Banking & Finance, Volume 29, Issue 3, March 2005.

Kawaller, Ira, "Liability Side Gap Management: Risks and Opportunities," Market Perspectives, Chicago Mercantile Exchange, August 1983.

*The Wall Street Journal,* March 11, 2005.

# Chapter 8

Allen, Linda, Stavros Peristiani, and Anthony Saunders. "Bank Size, Collateral, and Net Purchase Behavior in the Federal Funds Market: Empirical Evidence." *Journal of Business,* October 1989.

"Check Clearing for the 21st Century Act," Federal Reserve Board, March 13, 2005.

Fisher, Mark, "Special Repo Rates: An Introduction," Economic Review, Federal Reserve Bank of Atlanta, Second Quarter 2002.

Hein, Scott and Jonathan Stewart, "Reserve Requirements: A Modern Perspective," Economic Review, Federal Reserve Bank of Atlanta, Fourth Quarter 2002.

Ledford, Stevbe, Mills, Tim and Tom Murphy, "Your Depositors Aren't Average," Banking Strategies, January/February 2005.

Lucas, Charles, Marcus Jones, and Thom Thurston. "Federal Funds and Repurchase Agreements." *Quarterly Review,* Federal Reserve Bank of New York, Summer 1977.

Martin, Antoine, "Recent Evolution of Large-Value Payment Systems: Balancing Liquidity and Risk," Economic Review, Federal Reserve Bank of Kansas City, First Quarter 2005, Volume 90, Number 1.

Rose, Sanford, "What Really Went Wrong at Franklin National," Fortune, October 1974.

Smoot, Richard L. "Billion-Dollar Overdrafts: A Payments Risk Challenge." *Business Review,* Federal Reserve Bank of Philadelphia, January–February 1985.

Temple, W. Robert. "Bank Liquidity: Where Are We?" *American Banker,* March 8, 1983.

Van Hoose, David and Gordon Sellon Jr. "Daylight Overdrafts, Payments System Risk, and Public Policy." *Economic Review*, Federal Reserve Bank of Kansas City, September–October 1989.

Bielski, Lauren, "New Wave of E-Money Options Hits the Web." ABA Banking Journal, August 2000, http://www.banking.com/aba.

Levy, Steven, "E-Money, That's What I Want." *Wired* 2.12.

# Chapter 9

Hendricks, Darryll and Beverly Hirtle. "Regulatory Minimum Capital Standards for Banks: Current Status and Future Prospects," Conference on Bank Structure and Competition,1997.

International Convergence of Capital Measurement and Capital Standards: A Revised Framework, Basel Committee on Banking Supervision, Bank for International Settlements, June 2004.

Feldman, Ron J. and Arthur J. Rolnic. "Fixing FDICIA." *1997 Annual Report,* Federal Reserve Bank of Minneapolis, March 1998 (http://woodrow.mpls.frb.fed/pubs/ar/ar1997.html).

Prescott, Edward, "Auditing and Bank Capital Regulation," Economic Quarterly, Federal Reserve Bank of Richmond, Volume 90, Number 4, Fall 2004.

# CHAPTER 10

Compton, Eric N. "Credit Analysis Is Risk Analysis." *The Bankers Magazine,* March–April 1985.

Golden, Sam, and Harry Walker. "The Ten Commandments of Commercial Credit: The Cs of Good and Bad Loans." *Journal of Commercial Bank Lending,* January 1993.

Jagtiani, Julapa, Kolar, James, Lemieux, Catharine and Hwan Shin, "Early Warning Models for Bank Supervision: Simpler Could be Better," Economic Perspectives, Federal Reserve Bank of Chicago, Third Quarter 2003.

Mueller, P. Henry. "Risk Management and the Credit Culture— Necessary Interaction." *Journal of Commercial Lending,* May 1993. Copyright 1993 by Robert Morris Associates.

# CHAPTER 11

Arnold, Jasper. "Assessing Credit Risk in a Complex World." Commercial Lending Review (June 1988).

Bennett, Thomas. "Mixed Signals." Inc. (October 1987).

Carter, David and James McNulty, "Deregulation, Technological Change, and the Business-Lending Performance of Large and Small Banks," Journal of Banking & Finance, Volume 29, Issue 5, May 2005.

Credit Risk Measurement: Avoiding Unintended Results," Parts 1–5, The RMA Journal, selected issues 2004.

Green, R. "Are More Chryslers in the Offing?" *Forbes,* February 2, 1981.

Mulford, Charles W., and Eugene Comiskey. *The Financial Numbers Game: Detecting Creative Accounting Practices.* Wiley, 2002.

Newburgh, Conrad. "Character Assessment in the Lending Process." *Journal of Commercial Bank Lending,* April 1991.

# CHAPTER 12

"As Cash Fades, America Becomes a Plastic Nation." *The Wall Street Journal,* July 23, 2004.

Cocheo, Steve. "Give Me Your Delinquents, Your Former Bankrupts, Yearning to Borrow." *ABA Banking Journal,* August 1996.

Collins, Michael, "Current Fraud Management Techniques in Consumer Lending, The RMA Journal, October 2004.

Durkin, Thomas A. "Credit Cards: Use and Consumer Attitudes, 1970–2000, *Federal Reserve Bulletin,* Board of Governors of the Federal Reserve System, September 2000.

Kim, Jane. "Beyond the Toaster: Banks Step Up Freebies," *The Wall Street Journal,* October 14, 2004.

Kuper, Peter. "Garbage Out." *Smart Money,* October 1996.

Mays, Elizabeth, "The Role of Credit Scores in Consumer Lending Today," The RMA Journal, October 2003.

Weinstein, Michael. "Credit Card Business Mushrooms at Large Banks." *American Banker,* August 14, 1986.

"What's the Point of Credit Scoring." Business Review, Federal Reserve Bank of Philadelphia, September–October 1997.

White, Larry. "Credit Analysis: Two More 'Cs' of Credit." *Journal of Commercial Bank Lending,* October 1990.

# CHAPTER 13

Smith, Stephen, "Analyzing Risk and Return for Mortgage-Backed Securities," Economic Review, Federal Reserve Bank of Atlanta, January-February 1991.

Stock, Duane and Edward Schrems, "Municipal Bond Demand Premiums and Bond Price Volatility: A Note," Journal of Finance, June 1987.

Fabozzi, Frank. *CMOs: Structure and Analysis,* FJF Associates, 1996.

Becketti, Sean. "The Prepayment Risk of Mortgage-Backed Securities." *Economic Review,* Federal Reserve Bank of Kansas City, February 1989.

*The Handbook of Fixed Income Securities,* edited by Frank Fabozzi and Steven Mann, McGraw Hill, seventh edition, 2005.

Koch, Timothy. "The Roles of Duration and Convexity in Analyzing Bond Price Volatility." Bank Asset/Liability Management. New York: Warren, Gorham & Lamond, 1989.

Smith, Stephen. "Mortgage-Backed Securities: Analyzing Risk and Return." *Economic Review,* Federal Reserve Bank of Atlanta, January/February 1991.

# CHAPTER 14

Chrystal, K. Alec. "International Banking Facilities." *Review,* Federal Reserve Bank of St. Louis, April 1984.

Park, Yoon and Jack Zwick. *International Banking in Theory and Practice,* Reading, Mass.: Addison-Wesley Publishing, 1985.

Duffield, J.G. and B.J. Summers. "Bankers' Acceptances" in *Instruments of the Money Market,* Timothy Cook and Bruce Summers, eds. Richmond, Va.: Federal Reserve Bank of Richmond, 1981.

Magri, Silvia, Mori, Alessandra and Paola Rossi, "The Entry and the Activity Level of Foreign Banks in Italy: An Analysis of the Determinants," Journal of Banking & Finance, Volume 29, Issue 5, May 2005.

Morgan, John. "Assessing Country Risk at Texas Commerce." *The Bankers Magazine,* May–June 1985.

# GLOSSARY

## A

**ACCELERATED DEPRECIATION** A method of computing depreciation deductions for income taxes that permits deductions in early years greater than those under straight line depreciation.

**ACCEPTANCES, SEE BANKERS ACCEPTANCES.**

**ACCOUNT ACTIVITY** Transactions associated with a deposit account, including home debits, transit checks, deposits, and account maintenance.

**ACCOUNT ANALYSIS** An analytical procedure for determining whether a customer's deposit account or entire credit-deposit relationship with a bank is profitable. The procedure compares revenues from the account with the cost of providing services.

**ACCOUNT EXECUTIVE** A representative of a brokerage firm who processes orders to buy and sell stocks, options, etc., for a customer's account.

**ACCOUNT FEE-ONLY NONINTEREST CHECKING ACCOUNT** Incurs a monthly fee regardless of the account balance as well as a possible per-check charge.

**ACCOUNT MAINTENANCE** The overhead cost associated with collecting information and mailing periodic statements to depositors.

**ACCOUNTS PAYABLE** Funds owed to a firm's suppliers.

**ACCOUNTS RECEIVABLE** Funds owed a firm by customers to whom the firm sells goods and services.

**ACCOUNTS RECEIVABLE AGING SCHEDULE** A list of accounts receivables segregated according to the month in which the invoice is dated (invoice aging) or in which the invoice is payable (due date aging).

**ACCOUNTS RECEIVABLE TURNOVER** Credit sales divided by average accounts receivable outstanding.

**ACCRUAL** The accumulation of income earned or expense incurred, regardless of when the underlying cash flow is actually received or paid.

**ACCRUAL BOND** A bond that accrues interest but does not pay interest to the investor until maturity when accrued interest is paid with the principal outstanding.

**ACCRUED INTEREST** Interest income that is earned but not yet received.

**ACID-TEST RATIO** A measure of liquidity from reported balance sheet figures with a targeted minimum value of 1. Calculated as the sum of cash and marketable securities divided by current liabilities.

**ACTIVE PORTFOLIO MANAGEMENT** An investment policy whereby managers buy and sell securities prior to final maturity to speculate on future interest rate movements.

**ACTIVITY CHARGE** A service charge based on the number of checks written by a depositor.

**ADD-ON RATE** A method of calculating interest charges by applying the quoted rate to the entire amount advanced to a borrower times the number of financing periods. An 8 percent add-on rate indicates $80 interest per $1,000 for 1 year, $160 for 2 years, and so forth. The effective interest rate is higher than the add-on rate because the borrower makes installment payments and cannot use the entire loan proceeds for the full maturity.

**ADEQUATELY CAPITALIZED BANK** FDIC definition of a bank with capital levels that meets or exceeds all applicable Federal regulatory capital standardsbut one that is restricted from obtaining brokered deposits without FDIC approval.

**ADJUSTABLE RATE MORTGAGE** A mortgage with an interest rate that can be adjusted with changes in a base rate or reference index. The index generally varies with market interest rates.

**ADR** American Depository Receipt: A certificate issued by a U.S. bank which evidences ownership in foreign shares of stock held by the bank.

**ADVANCE** A payment to a borrower under a loan agreement.

**ADVANCE COMMITMENT** An agreement to sell an asset prior to the seller holding a commitment to purchase the asset.

**AFFILIATE** Any organization owned or controlled by a bank or bank holding company, the stockholders, or executive officers.

**AFFINITY CARD** A credit card that is offered to all individuals who are part of a common group or who share a common bond.

**AFTER-TAX REAL RETURN** The after-tax rate of return on an asset minus the rate of inflation.

**AGENCY** A trust account in which title to property remains in the owner's name.

**AGENCY SECURITIES** Fixed-income securities issued by agencies owned or sponsored by the federal government. The most common securities are issued by the Federal Home Loan Bank, Federal National Mortgage Association, Government National Mortgage Association, and Farm Credit System.

**AGING ACCOUNTS RECEIVABLE** A procedure for analyzing a firm's accounts receivable by dividing them into groups according to whether they are current or 30, 60, or over 90 days past due.

**ALL-IN-COST** The weighted average cost of funds for a bank calculated by making adjustments for required reserves and deposit insurance costs. The sum of explicit and implicit costs.

**ALLOWANCE FOR LOAN LOSSES** A balance sheet account representing a contra-asset, or reduction in gross loans. It is established in recognition that some loans will not be repaid. Also called a loan loss reserve.

**ALTERNATIVE MINIMUM TAX (AMT)** A federal tax against income intended to ensure that taxpayers pay some tax even when they use tax shelters to shield income.

**AMORTIZE** To reduce a debt gradually by making equal periodic payments that cover interest and principal owed.

**AMORTIZING SWAP** An interest rate swap in which the outstanding notional principal amount declines over time.

**ANNUAL PERCENTAGE RATE** The effective annual cost of credit expressed as a percent inclusive of the amount financed, the loan maturity, and the finance charge.

**ANNUITY** A constant payment made for multiple periods of time.

**ANTICIPATED INCOME THEORY** A theory that the timing of loan payments should be tied to the timing of a borrower's expected income.

**APPLICABLE INCOME TAXES** Estimated taxes to be paid over time, not actual tax payments.

**APPRECIATION** An increase in the market value of an asset.

**ARBITRAGE** The simultaneous trading (purchase and sale) of assets to take advantage of price differentials.

**ARBITRAGEUR OR SPREADER** Speculators who take relatively low-risk positions.

**ARM (ADJUSTABLE RATE MORTGAGE)** A mortgage in which the contractual interest rate is tied to some index of interest rates and changes when supply and demand conditions change the underlying index.

**ARREARS** An overdue outstanding debt.

**ASK PRICE** The price at which an asset is offered for sale.

**ASSET-BACKED SECURITY** A security with promised principal and interest payments backed or collateralized by cash flows originating from a portfolio of assets that generate the cash flows.

**ASSET-BASED FINANCING** Financing in which the lender relies primarily on cash flows generated by the asset financed to repay the loan.

**ASSET-LIABILITY MANAGEMENT** The management of a bank's entire balance sheet to achieve desired risk-return objectives and to maximize the market value of stockholders' equity.

**ASSET LIQUIDITY** The ease of converting an asset to cash with a minimum of loss.

**ASSET SENSITIVE** A bank is classified as asset sensitive if its GAP is positive.

**ASSET UTILIZATION** Ratio of total operating income to total assets; a measure of the gross yield earned on assets.

**ASSIGNMENT** The transfer of the legal right or interest on an asset to another party.

**ATS ACCOUNT** A checking account that pays interest, similar to a NOW account, but the customer has both a DDA and savings account. The bank forces a zero balance in the DDA at the close of each day after transferring just enough funds from savings to cover checks presented for payment.

**AT-THE-MONEY** An option where the price of the underlying instrument or contract is approximately equal to the option's exercise price.

**AUTOMATED CLEARINGHOUSE** A facility that processes interbank debits and credits electronically.

**AUTOMATED LOAN MACHINE** A machine that serves as a computer terminal and allows a customer to apply for a loan and, if approved, automatically deposits proceeds into an account designated by the customer.

**AUTOMATED TELLER MACHINE (ATM)** A machine that serves as a computer terminal and allows a customer to access account balances and information at a bank.

**AUTOMATIC TRANSFERS FROM SAVINGS (ATS)** Transactions accounts that pay interest set by each bank without federal restrictions.

**AVAILABLE-FOR-SALE** Securities reported at market value.

**AVERAGE HISTORICAL COST OF FUNDS** Measure of average unit borrowing costs for existing funds.

# B

**BACKWARDIZATION** The situation in which futures prices on futures contracts that expire farther in the future are below prices of nearby futures contracts.

**BAD DEBTS** Loans that are due but are uncollectible.

**BALANCE INQUIRY** A request by a depositor or borrower to obtain the current balance in his or her account.

**BALANCE SHEET** A financial statement that indicates the type and amount of assets, liabilities, and net worth of a firm or individual at a point in time.

**BALLOON LOAN** A loan that requires small payments that are insufficient to pay off the entire loan so that a large final payment is necessary at termination.

**BANK LIQUIDITY** A bank's capacity to acquire immediately available funds at a reasonable price.

**BANKERS ACCEPTANCE** A draft drawn on a bank and accepted, which makes it a negotiable instrument.

**BANKERS' BANK** A firm that provides correspondent banking services to commercial banks and not to commercial or retail deposit and loan customers.

**BANK HOLDING COMPANY** Any firm that owns or controls at least one commercial bank.

**BANK HOLDING COMPANY ACT OF 1956** The act placed the Federal Reserve in charge of determining what activates holding companies could engage in and prohibited bank holding companies from acquiring a bank in another state. Banks were generally restricted to operating within very narrow geographic markets.

**BANKRUPT** The situation in which a borrower is unable to pay obligated debts.

**BARBELL** An investment portfolio in which a large fraction of securities mature near term and another large fraction of securities mature longer term.

**BASE RATE** An interest rate used as an index to price loans; typically associated with a bank's weighted marginal cost of funds.

**BASIC SWAP** A plain vanilla interest rate swap in which one party pays a fixed interest rate and receives a floating rate, while the other party pays a floating rate and receives a fixed rate with all rates applied to the same, constant notional principal amount.

**BASIS** With financial futures contracts, the futures rate minus the cash rate.

**BASIS POINT** 1/100th of 1 percent, or 0.0001; 100 basis points equal 1 percent.

**BASIS RISK** The uncertainty that the futures rate minus the cash rate will vary from that expected.

**BEARER BONDS** Bonds held by the investor (owner) in physical form. The investor receives interest payments by submitting coupons from the bond to the paying agent.

**BENCHMARK RATE** The key driver rate used in sensitivity analysis or simulation models to assess interest rate risk. Other model rates are linked to the benchmark rate in terms of how they change when the benchmark rate changes.

**BENEFICIARY** The recipient of the balance in a trust account upon termination of the trust.

**BEST EFFORTS UNDERWRITING** The underwriter of securities commits to selling as many securities as possible and returns all unsold shares or units to the issuer.

**BETA** An estimate of the systematic or market risk of an asset within the capital asset pricing model (CAPM) framework.

**BETA GAP** The adjusted GAP figure in a basic earnings-sensitivity analysis derived from multiplying the amount of rate-sensitive assets by the associated beta factors and summing across all rate-sensitive assets, and subtracting the amount of rate-sensitive liabilities multiplied by the associated beta factors summed across all rate-sensitive liabilities.

**BID PRICE** The price at which someone has offered to buy an asset.

**BIF** Bank Insurance Fund that insures deposits at commercial banks.

**BLANK CHECK** A signed check with no amount indicated.

**BOARD OF DIRECTORS** Individuals elected by stockholders to manage and oversee a firm's operations.

**BOARD OF GOVERNORS OF THE FEDERAL RESERVE SYSTEM** The policy-setting representatives of the Federal Reserve System in charge of setting the discount rate, required reserves, and general policies designed to affect growth in the banking system's reserves and U.S. money supply.

**BOND** An interest-bearing security representing a debt obligation of the issuer.

**BOND BROKER** A broker who trades bonds on an exchange.

**BOND EQUIVALENT RATE ALSO** also known as the coupon-equivalent rate, is the annual percentage yield quoted for most Treasury and corporate bonds. Does not equal the effective annual compounded rate of interest.

**BOND FUND** A mutual fund that invests in debt instruments.

**BOND RATING** The subjective assessment of the likelihood that a borrower will make timely interest and principal payments as scheduled. Letters are assigned to a security by rating agencies to reflect estimated creditworthiness.

**BOOK VALUE** Accounting value typically measured as historical cost minus depreciation.

**BOOK VALUE OF EQUITY** Total assets minus total liabilities reported on the balance sheet.

**BORROWED FUNDING** Federal funds purchased, repurchase agreements, Federal Home Loan Bank (FHLB) borrowings, and other borrowings.

**BOUNCE A CHECK** A depositor writes a check that is returned to the bank and by the bank to the depositor because of insufficient funds.

**BRANCH BANKING** An organizational structure in which a bank maintains facilities that are part of the bank in offices different from its home office. Some states allow banks to set up branches through the state, county, or city. Others prohibit branches.

**BRIDGE LOAN** A loan issued to fund a temporary need from the time a security is redeemed to the time another security is issued.

**BROKER** An individual who executes orders for customers for which he/she receives a commission.

**BROKERED DEPOSITS** Deposits acquired through a money broker (typically an investment bank) in the national markets.

**BULGE BRACKET FIRMS** Firms in an underwriting syndicate that have the highest commitment to assist in placing the underlying securities.

**BULLET LOAN** A loan that requires payment of the entire principal at maturity.

**BURDEN** Noninterest expense minus noninterest income.

**BURDEN RATIO** Measures the amount of noninterest expense covered by fees, service charges, securities gains, and other income as a fraction of average total assets.

**BUSINESS RISK EXPENSE** Represents both actual cash expense (losses) as well as noncash expense, or allocations for potential losses.

# C

**CALLABLE BOND** A bond in which the issuer has the option to call the bond from the investor; that is, to prepay the outstanding principal prior to maturity.

**CALLABLE CD** Certificate of deposit that typically carries a 2-year deferment period, meaning it cannot be called for two years after issue. Afterward, the bank can call the CD, meaning that it could repay the depositor's principal, at its discretion.

**CALL LOAN** A loan that is callable on 24 hours' notice.

**CALL PROTECTION** The feature that does not allow a bond to be called for some (deferment) period.

**CALL PROVISION** A provision in a bond that allows the issuer to redeem the bond, typically at a premium over par, prior to maturity.

**CALL OPTION** An agreement in which the buyer has the right to buy a fixed amount of the underlying asset at a set price for a specified period of time.

*Glossary*

**CAMELS** An acronym that refers to the regulatory rating system for bank performance: C—capital adequacy; A—asset quality; M—management quality; E—earnings quality; L—liquidity; and S—sensitivity to market risk.

**CAP** Use of options to place a ceiling on a firm's borrowing costs.

**CAPITAL** Funds subscribed and paid by stockholders representing ownership in a bank. Regulatory capital also includes debt components and loss reserves.

**CAPITAL GAIN (LOSS)** Profit (loss) resulting from the sale of an asset for more (less) than its purchase price.

**CAPITAL MARKET** Market for securities with maturities beyond one year.

**CAPITAL RISK** Potential decrease in the market value of assets below the market value of liabilities, indicating economic net worth is zero or less.

**CAPTIVE FINANCE COMPANY** A finance company owned by a manufacturer that provides financing to buyers of the firm's products.

**CARD BANK** Bank that administers its own credit card plan or serves as a primary regional agent of a national credit card operation.

**CARs (COLLATERALIZED AUTOMOBLILE RECEIVABLES)** A form of asset-backed security in which the collateral is automobile receivables.

**CASH ASSETS** Assets held to satisfy customer withdrawal needs, meet legal reserve requirements, or to purchase services from other financial institutions but do not pay interest.

**CASH-BASED INCOME STATEMENT** A modified form of a direct statement of cash flows. It is essentially a statement of changes reconciled to cash, which combines elements of the income statement and balance sheet.

**CASH BASIS** The accounting procedure that recognizes revenues when cash is actually received and expenses when cash is actually paid.

**CASH BUDGET** A comparison of cash receipts and cash expenditures over a period of time.

**CASH FLOW FROM OPERATIONS** A firm's net cash flow from normal business operating activities used to assess the firm's ability to service existing and new debt and other fixed-payment obligations.

**CASHIER'S CHECK** A bank check that is drawn on the bank issuing the check and signed by a bank officer.

**CASH LETTER** Transit letter on tape that lists items submitted between banks for collection.

**CASH MARKET** The spot market for the immediate exchange of goods and services for immediate payment.

**CASH SETTLEMENT** The form for settling futures contracts where the parties exchange cash rather than have one party deliver the underlying asset.

**CASH-TO-CASH ASSET CYCLE** The time it takes to accumulate cash, purchase inventory, produce a finished good, sell it, and collect on the sale.

**CASH-TO-CASH LIABILITY CYCLE** The length of time to obtain interest-free financing from suppliers in the form of accounts payable and accrued expenses. Cash-to-cash working capital cycle The timing difference between the cash-to-cash asset cycle and the cash-to-cash liability cycle.

**CEASE AND DESIST ORDER (C&D)** A legal document that orders a firm to stop an unfair practice under full penalty of law. Only the cease and desist order has legal standing, but each type of recommendation notifies a bank if its house is in order.

**CENTRAL BANK** The main bank in a country responsible for issuing currency and setting and managing monetary policy.

**CERTIFICATE OF DEPOSIT (CD)** A large-denomination time deposit representing the receipt of funds for deposit at a bank.

**CERTIFIED CHECK** A check guaranteed by a bank where funds are immediately withdrawn.

**CERTIFIED FINANCIAL PLANNER (CFP)** A designation earned by individuals who have passed the examination sponsored by the Certified Financial Planner Board. Such individuals have studied banking, investment, insurance, estate planning, and tax planning to assist in managing client financial needs.

**CHANGES IN THE DISCOUNT RATE** Changes that directly affect the cost of reserve borrowing. When the Fed raises the discount rate, it discourages borrowing by making it more expensive. Fed decreases in the discount rate make borrowing less expensive.

**CHANGES IN RESERVE REQUIREMENTS** Changes that directly affect the amount of legal required reserves that banks are required to hold as an asset and thus change the amount of funds a bank can lend out.

**CHARGE-OFF** The act of writing off a loan to its present value in recognition that the asset has decreased in value.

**CHARTER** A document that authorizes a bank to conduct business.

**CHARTERED FINANCIAL ANALYST (CFA)** A designation earned by individuals who have passed a three-part examination sponsored by the Institute of Chartered Financial Analysts. Topics include economics, finance, security analysis, and financial accounting to assist in security analysis and portfolio management.

**CHECK 21** The process that facilitates check truncation by creating a new negotiable instrument called a substitute check, which permits banks to truncate original checks, process check information electronically, and deliver substitute checks to banks that want to continue receiving paper checks.

**CHECK KITING** The process of writing checks against uncollected deposits while checks are in the process of collection, thereby using funds (float) not actually available.

**CHECK TRUNCATION** The conversion of a paper check into an electronic debit or image of the check by a third party in the payment system other than the paying bank

**CHINESE WALL** The imaginary barrier that ensures a trust department will manage trust assets for the benefit of the trust beneficiaries, not for other departments in the bank.

**CLASSIFIED LOAN** A loan for which regulators have forced management to set aside reserves for clearly recognized losses.

**CLEAN UP THE LINE OF CREDIT** To bring the balance to zero at least once during the year.

**CLEARINGHOUSE ASSOCIATION** A voluntary association of banks formed to assist the daily exchange of checks among member institutions.

**CMO (COLLATERALIZED MORTGAGE OBLIGATION)** A security backed by a pool of mortgages that is structured to fall within an estimated maturity range (tranche), based on the timing of allocated interest and principal payments on the underlying mortgages.

**COLLAR** Use of options to place a cap and floor on a firm's borrowing costs.

**COLLATERAL** Property a borrower pledges as security against a loan for repayment if the borrower defaults.

**COLLECTED BALANCES** Ledger balances minus float.

**COMMERCIAL BANK** A bank that mostly specialize in short-term business credit, but also makes consumer loans and mortgages, and has a broad range of financial powers. Commercial banks are stock corporations whose primary purpose is to maximize shareholder wealth.

**COMMERCIAL LOAN THEORY** A theory suggesting that banks make only short-term, self-liquidating loans that match the maturity of bank deposits.

**COMMERCIAL PAPER** A short-term unsecured promissory note of a prime corporation.

**COMMISSION BROKER** A trader operating on the floor of an exchange who executes trades for other parties.

**COMMITMENT FEE** Fee charged for making a line of credit available to a borrower.

**COMMON STOCK** Securities (equities) that evidence ownership in a company for which the holder received discretionary dividends and realizes price appreciation/depreciation.

**COMMUNITY BANK** A bank that operates primarily in, or has ties to, one community.

**COMPENSATING BALANCE** A deposit balance required as compensation for services provided by a lender or correspondent bank.

**COMPETITIVE EQUALITY BANKING ACT OF 1987** The act recapitalized the Federal Savings and Loan Insurance Corporation (FSLIC) and expanded the FDIC's authority for open bank assistance transactions.

**COMPOUND INTEREST** Interest paid on outstanding principal plus any interest that has been earned but not paid out.

**COMPOSITION MIX EFFECTS** Suggest that the mix of liabilities may differ.

**COMPOUNDING** Earning interest on interest.

**COMPUTATION PERIOD** Consists of two 1-week reporting periods and, therefore, consists of 14 consecutive days beginning on a Tuesday and ending on the second Monday thereafter.

**CONSERVATOR** An individual or trust department appointed by a court to manage the property of an incapacitated individual.

**CONSOLIDATED BALANCE SHEET** A balance sheet showing the aggregate financial condition of a firm and its subsidiaries, netting out all intracompany transactions.

*Glossary*

**CONSUMER BANK** A bank that does not make commercial loans.

**CONTEMPORANEOUS RESERVE ACCOUNTING (CRA)** During the period from 1984 until 1998, open market operations affected both the current deposit levels and required reserves coincidentally.

**CONTINGENT LIABILITIES** Items, such as guarantees or related contracts, that may become liabilities if certain developments arise.

**CONVENTIONAL MORTGAGE** A mortgage or deed or trust that is not obtained under a government-insured program.

**CONVERSION FEE** Fee charged for converting a loan commitment to a term loan.

**CONVERTIBLE DEBT** A bond that may be exchanged for common stock in the same firm.

**CONVEXITY** Characterizes the rate of change in duration when yields change. It attempts to improve upon duration as an approximation of price volatility.

**CORE CAPITAL** Tier 1 capital consisting primarily of stockholder's equity.

**CORE DEPOSITS** A base level of deposits a bank expects to remain on deposit, regardless of the economic environment.

**CORRESPONDENT BANK** A bank that provides services, typically check clearing, to other banks.

**CORRESPONDENT BANKING** System of inter-bank relationships in which one bank sells services to other financial institutions.

**COST OF FUNDS ESTIMATE** May be a bank's weighted marginal cost of pooled debt or its weighted marginal cost of capital at the time the loan was made.

**COUNTRY RISK** The credit risk that government or private borrowers in a specific country will refuse to repay their debts as obligated for other than pure economic reasons.

**COUPON RATE** The ratio of the dollar-valued coupon payment to a security's par value.

**COVENANT** An element of a loan agreement whereby the borrower agrees to meet specific performance requirements or refrain from certain behavior.

**COVERED INTEREST** A trader borrows in one currency yet covers the transaction by selling the expected foreign exchange after investment for the original currency in the forward market. A profit is available because the interest rate differential between securities in the two countries is out of line with the spot-to-forward exchange rate differential.

**CREDIT BUREAU** An association that collects and provides information on the credit (payment) histories of borrowers.

**CREDIT CHECK** Efforts by a lender to verify the accuracy of information provided by potential borrowers.

**CREDIT CULTURE** Refers to the fundamental principles that drive lending activity and how management analyzes risk.

**CREDIT DEPARTMENT** The bank department where credit information is collected and analyzed to make credit decisions.

**CREDIT ENHANCEMENT** A guarantee or letter of credit backing for a loan, which improves the creditworthiness of the contract.

**CREDIT FILE** Information related to a borrower's loan request, including application, record of past performance, loan documentation, and analyst opinions.

**CREDIT LIMIT** The maximum amount that a borrower is allowed to borrow against a loan commitment or credit line.

**CREDIT PHILOSOPHY** Determines how much risk the bank will take and in what form.

**CREDIT RISK** Potential variation in net income and market value of equity resulting from the nonpayment of interest and principal.

**CREDIT SCORING** The use of a statistical model based on applicant attributes to assess whether a loan automatically meets minimum credit standards. The model assigns values to potential borrowers' attributes, with the sum of the values compared to a threshold.

**CREDIT SERVICES** The types of products offered by financial institutions related to lending activities.

**CREDIT UNION** A nonprofit organization that offers financial services to qualifying members. Credit unions do not pay state and federal income taxes and thus operate at a competitive advantage to other depository institutions.

**CRITICALLY UNDERCAPITALIZED BANK** An institution that does not meet minimum threshold levels for the three capital ratios.

**CROSS HEDGE** Use of a futures contract for a specific asset that differs from the cash asset being hedged.

**CUMULATIVE GAP** A measure of interest rate risk which is the sum of the periodic GAPs through the longest time frame considered. A measure of the banks aggregate interest rate risk exposure.

**CURRENCY SWAP** An agreement to exchange payments denominated in one currency for payments denominated in a different currency.

**CURRENT RATIO** The ratio of current liabilities that indicates a firm's ability to pay current debts when they come due.

**CURRENT TAX EQUIVALENT ADJUST-MENT** Reverses the current part of the tax benefit included in interest income on loan and lease financing, as well as the estimated tax benefit from municipal securities.

**CURRENT YIELD** The coupon rate on a bond divided by the current market price of the bond.

**CUSTOMER INFORMATION FILE** A record of the services used by each customer.

**CUSTOMER PROFITABILITY ANALYSIS** A procedure that compares revenues with expenses and the bank's target profit from a customer's total account relationship.

**CYCLICAL LIQUIDITY NEEDS** An estimate of liquid funds needed to cover deposit outflows or loan demand in excess of trend or seasonal factors.

# D

**DAY TRADER** A trader who tries to profit from short-term price movements during trading hours in any day, but offsets the initial position before market closing so that no position remains outstanding overnight.

**DAYLIGHT OVERDRAFTS** Bank payments from deposits held at a Federal Reserve bank or correspondent bank in excess of actual collected balances during a day.

**DAYS ACCOUNTS PAYABLE OUT-STANDING** Accounts payable divided by average daily purchases; measures the firm's efficiency in using trade credit to finance its working capital needs.

**DAYS ACCOUNTS RECEIVABLE COLLECTION PERIOD** Accounts receivables divided by average daily credit sales; indicates the average number of days required to convert accounts receivable into cash.

**DAYS INVENTORY ON HAND** Inventory divided by average daily cost of goods sold; measures the efficiency of the firm in managing its inventory.

**DE NOVO BRANCH** A newly opened branch.

**DEALER** A trader who sets bid and ask prices for every security traded.

**DEALER RESERVE** An account established by a bank and dealer used to assign the interest that accrues to dealers as they sell loans to a bank.

**DEBENTURE** A long-term bond that is secured by the general performance of the issuer.

**DEBIT CARD** A plastic card that, when used, immediately reduces the balance in a customer's transactions deposit.

**DEBTOR-IN-POSSESSION FINANCING** A loan made to a firm which has filed for Chapter 11 bankruptcy protection.

**DEBT SERVICE** The amount needed to pay principal and interest on a loan.

**DEBT-TO-TOTAL-ASSETS RATIO** Total liabilities divided by total assets.

**DEFALCATION** The misappropriation of funds or property by an individual.

**DEFAULT** The failure to make obligated interest and principal payments on a loan.

**DEFAULT RISK** With respect to credit services, the largest single risk.

**DEFERRED AVAILABILITY CREDIT ITEMS** Checks received for collection for which a bank has not provided credit to the depositor.

**DELINQUENT ACCOUNT** An account that is past due because the account holder has not made the obligated payment on time.

**DELIVERY DATE** Specific day that a futures contract expires.

**DELTA** The change in an option's price divided by the change in the price of the underlying instrument or contract.

**DEMAND DEPOSIT** Transactions account, payable on demand, that pays no interest to the depositor.

**DEPOSITORY INSTITUTIONS ACT OF 1982** The act, also known as Garn-St Germain, expanded

FDIC powers to assist troubled banks and established the Net Worth Certificate program for savings and loans to assist these institutions in acquiring needed capital. The act authorized money market deposit accounts to allow banks and thrifts to compete with products offered by brokerage firms. It also expanded the powers of thrift institutions in a misguided attempt at allowing these institutions to "earn" their way out of their financial problems.

**DEPOSITORY INSTITUTIONS DEREGULATION AND MONETARY CONTROL ACT (DIDMCA) OF 1980** The act removed interest rate ceilings and authorized banks and savings institutions to pay interest on checking accounts through the use of negotiable orders of withdrawal (NOW) accounts.

**DEPOSITS HELD IN FOREIGN OFFICES** Dollar-denominated demand and time deposits, but balances are issued by a bank subsidiary (owned by the bank holding company) located outside the United States.

**DEPRECIATION** Writing down the value of a capital asset, reported as an expense. Also, a decrease in the market value of a financial asset.

**DEREGULATION** The process of eliminating existing regulations.

**DERIVATIVE** A financial instrument whose value is determined by the specific features of the underlying asset or instrument.

**DIRECT LOAN** Loan with terms negotiated directly between the lender and actual user of the funds.

**DISCOUNT BROKER** A brokerage firm that offers a limited range of retail services and charges lower fees than full-service brokers.

**DISCOUNT RATE** Interest rate charged by Federal Reserve banks for borrowing from the discount window.

**DISCOUNT WINDOW** The process of Federal Reserve banks lending to member institutions.

**DIVIDEND** A payment made to holders of a firm's common stock and/or preferred stock. Cash dividends are paid in cash while stock dividends are paid in stock.

**DIVIDEND PAYOUT RATIO** Cash dividends divided by net income; measures the fraction of earnings a firm pays out in cash to stockholders and thus is not retained.

**DRAFT** A written order requesting one party to make payment to another party at a specified point in time.

**DUAL BANKING SYSTEM** System in the U.S. in which a group trying to obtain a charter to open a bank can apply to the state banking department or the Office of the Comptroller of the Currency—the national banking agency.

**DURATION** The weighted average of time until cash flows generated by an asset are expected to be received (paid). The weights are the present value of each cash flow as a fraction of the asset's current price.

**DURATION GAP** The weighted duration of assets minus the product of the weighted duration of liabilities and the ratio of total liabilities to total assets.

**DURATION GAP ANALYSIS** Compares the price sensitivity of a bank's total assets with the price sensitivity of its total liabilities to assess whether the market value of assets or liabilities changes more when rates change.

# E

**EARLY WITHDRAWAL PENALTY** An interest penalty a depositor pays for withdrawing funds from a deposit account prior to maturity.

**EARNING ASSETS** Income-earning assets held by a bank; typically include interest-bearing balances, investment securities, and loans.

**EARNINGS-AT-RISK (OR NET INTEREST MARGIN SIMULATION)** Summary results of a bank's earnings sensitivity.

**EARNINGS BASE (EB)** Compares the proportionate investment in average earning assets to average total assets and, thus, indicates whether one bank has more or less assets earning interest than peers

**EARNINGS CHANGE RATIO (ECR)** A ratio calculated for each asset or liability that estimates how the yield on assets or rate paid on liabilities is assumed to change relative to a 1 percent change in the base rate.

**EARNINGS COVERAGE OF NET LOSSES** A measure of net operating income before taxes, securities gains (losses), extraordinary items, and the provision for loan losses divided by net loan and lease losses.

**EARNINGS CREDIT** Interest rate applied to investable balances.

**EARNINGS DILUTION** A decrease in earnings per share after one bank acquires another.

**EARNINGS PER SHARE** Net income divided by the number of outstanding shares of common stock.

**EARNINGS-SENSITIVITY ANALYSIS** Takes into account shifts in asset and liability composition and embedded options in a bank's assets and liabilities and off-balance sheet activities. It provides a better understanding of potential changes in earnings than simple static models.

**EBIT** Earnings before interest and taxes.

**EBITDA** Earnings before interest, taxes, depreciation, and amortization.

**ECONOMIC RISK** The risk to a companies earnings or processes derived from economic events.

**ECONOMIC VALUE ADDED (EVA)** A measure of financial performance trademarked by Stern, Stewart & Co. equal to a firm's net operating profit after tax (NOPAT) minus a capital charge representing the required return to shareholders.

**ECONOMIES OF SCALE** Cost efficiencies evidenced by low operating costs per unit of output.

**ECONOMIES OF SCOPE** Focus on how the joint costs of providing several products change as new products are added or existing product output is enhanced.

**ECONOMIC VALUE OF EQUITY-SENSITIVITY ANALYSIS** Sensitivity analysis framework that extends the static duration gap analysis by making it dynamic using a simulation procedure incorporating a "what if" analysis of all the factors that affect EVE across a wide range of interest rate environments.

**ECU** European Currency Unit.

**EDGE ACT CORPORATION** A bank subsidiary that engages in international banking activities.

**EFFECTIVE CONVEXITY** The value for convexity that reflects the price impact of embedded options in different interest rate environments.

**EFFECTIVE ANNUAL COMPOUNDED RATE OF INTEREST** the compounded rate of interest assuming the investor reinvests all periodic cash flows received at the same rate of interest.

**EFFECTIVE DURATION** The value for duration reflecting the price impact of embedded options when interest rates rise versus fall.

**EFFICIENCY RATIO** Noninterest expense divided by the sum of net interest income and noninterest income.

**ELASTICITY** A measure of the relative quantity response to a change in price, income, interest rate, or other variable.

**ELECTRONIC FUNDS TRANSFER (EFT)** Electronic movement of financial data, designed to eliminate the paper instruments normally associated with such funds movement.

**ELECTRONIC TRANSACTIONS** Transactions that occur through automatic deposits, Internet and telephone bill payment, ATMs, and ACH transactions.

**EMU** European Monetary Union.

**EMERGENCY CREDIT** May be authorized in unusual and exigent circumstances by the Board of Governors to individuals, partnerships, and corporations that are not depository institutions.

**ENTERPRISE VALUE** The value of a firm equal to the market capitalization (number of shares of stock times the current stock price) plus the market value of outstanding debt.

**EQUITY** Ownership interest in a firm represented by common and preferred stockholders.

**EQUITY MULTIPLIER** Ratio of total assets to equity; a measure of financial leverage.

**EQUITY AND SECURITY PRICE RISK** Potential risk of loss associated with a bank's trading account portfolios.

**ESTIMATED TAX BENEFIT** Estimated dollar tax benefit from not paying taxes on loan and lease financing and tax-exempt securities income.

**EURO (EUROPEAN UNIFIED CURRENCY)** The European currency unit introduced in January 1999.

**EUROCREDITS** Term loans priced at a premium over LIBOR.

**EUROCURRENCY** A financial claim denominated in a currency other than the one where the issuing institution is located.

**EURODOLLAR** A dollar-denominated financial claim at a bank outside the United States.

**EURODOLLAR DEPOSITS** Dollar-denominated deposits at banks located outside the United States.

**EUROPEAN COMMUNITY (EC)** A confederation of countries that have negotiated the removal of trade barriers to enhance competition.

**EXCHANGE RATE** Price of one currency in terms of another.

**EXECUTOR** An individual or trust department responsible for handling a settlement.

**EXPEDITED FUNDS AVAILABILITY ACT** The act stipulated maximum time limits under Regulation CC for banks to make funds available on deposited checks; effective September 1990.

**EXTENSION RISK** The risk that the holder of a mortgage-backed security will receive outstanding principal payments later than originally anticipated. Later principal payments result from interest rates rising and prepayments occuring slower than expected.

**EXTRAORDINARY ITEMS** A unusual nonrecurring event, cost or expense such as expenses related to acquisitions or plant shutdowns, results of legal proceedings or unanticipated tax benefits

# F

**FACILITY FEE** Fee imposed for making a line of credit available.

**FACTORING** An advance of credit whereby one party purchases the accounts receivable of another party at a discount, without recourse.

**FANNIE MAE** Name referring to the Federal National Mortgage Association.

**FASB 115** Issued by the Financial Accounting Standards Board in 1993 to addresses the market value accounting of all investments in equity securities that have readily determinable fair values, and all investments in debt securities.

**FEDERAL DEPOSIT INSURANCE CORPORATION IMPROVEMENT ACT OF 1991** The act greatly increased the powers and authority of the FDIC, recapitalized the Bank Insurance Fund and allowed the FDIC to borrow from the Treasury. The act mandated a least-cost method and prompt corrective action for dealing with failing banks as well as establishing new capital requirements for banks.

**FEDERAL FINANCING BANK** A federal agency that borrows from the U.S. Treasury and lends funds to various federal agencies.

**FEDERAL FUNDS** Unsecured short-term loans that are settled in immediately available funds.

**FEDERAL RESERVE BANK** One of the 12 district federal reserve banks that make up the Federal Reserve System.

**FEE INCOME** Noninterest income.

**FHA (FEDERAL HOUSING ADMINISTRATION)** A federal agency that insures mortgages.

**FHLMC (FEDERAL HOME LOAN MORTGAGE CORPORATION, OR FREDDIE MAC)** A private corporation operating with an implicit federal guarantee; buys mortgages financed largely by mortgage-backed securities.

**FIDELITY BOND** A contract that covers losses associated with employee dishonesty, typically embezzlement and forgery at banks.

**FIDUCIARY** An individual or trust department responsible for acting in the best interests of a designated third party.

**FINANCE CHARGE** Under Regulation Z, the sum of "all charges payable directly or indirectly by the borrower and imposed directly or indirectly by the lender as an incident to or as an extension of credit."

**FINANCE COMPANY** A firm that borrows from the money and capital markets to make loans to individuals and commercial enterprises.

**FINANCIAL FUTURES CONTRACT** A commitment between two parties to exchange a standardized financial asset through an organized exchange at a specified price for future delivery. The price of futures contracts changes prior to delivery, and participants must settle daily changes in contract value.

**FINANCIAL HOLDING COMPANY (FHC)** A specific type of bank holding company created by the Gramm-Leach-Bliley Act of 1999 which allows banks, securities firms, and insurance companies to affiliate within the FHC structure.

**FINANCIAL INNOVATION** The continuous development of new products, services, and technology to deliver products and services.

**FINANCIAL INSTITUTIONS REFORM, RECOVERY AND ENFORCEMENT ACT OF 1989** The act abolished the FSLIC and placed the FDIC in charge of insurance of the industry and created two insurance funds, the Bank Insurance Fund (BIF) and the Savings Association Insurance Fund (SAIF). The act also abolished the Federal Home Loan Bank Board and created the Office of Thrift Supervision (OTS) and the Resolution Trust Corporation (RTC), which was to manage and dispose of the assets of failed institutions. The act further established severe penalties for bank boards and management for their actions or failure of action.

**FINANCIAL LEVERAGE** Relationship between the amount of debt versus equity financing.

**FINANCIAL RISK** Potential variation in income before interest and taxes associated with fixed interest payments on debt and lease payments.

**FINANCIAL SERVICES HOLDING COMPANY** A parent company that owns a bank holding company plus other subsidiaries, such as a thrift holding company and insurance subsidiary.

**FIXED CHARGE COVERAGE RATIO** Earnings before interest and taxes (EBIT) plus lease payments divided by interest expense plus lease payments; measures the number of times the firm can pay interest and other fixed charges (such as lease payments) with current earnings. Fixed maturity Limited life.

**FIXED RATE** An interest rate that does not change during a specified period of time.

**FIXED RATE CD** Fixed-rate contract renegotiated at various maturities.

**FLOAT** Dollar amount of checks in process of collection, net of deferred availability amounts, to depositors.

**FLOATING RATE** An interest rate tied to a base rate that changes over time as market conditions dictate.

**FLOATING-RATE NOTE (FRN)** A short-term note whose interest payment varies with a short-term interest rate.

**FLOOR** Use of options to establish a minimum borrowing cost.

**FNMA (FEDERAL NATIONAL MORTGAGE ASSOCIATION, OR FANNIE MAE)** A private corporation operating with an implicit federal guarantee; buys mortgages financed by mortgage-backed securities.

**FORECLOSURE** Selling property in order to apply the proceeds in payment of a debt.

**FOREIGN EXCHANGE** Currency of a foreign country acceptable as a medium of exchange.

**FOREIGN EXCHANGE RISK** The risk that the value of a position denominated in a foreign currency may decline due to a change in exchange rates.

**FOREIGN TAX CREDIT** Income taxes paid to a foreign country that can be claimed as a tax credit against a domestic tax liability.

**FORWARD CONTRACT** A commitment between two parties to exchange a nonstandardized asset at a fixed price for future delivery. The price of the contract does not change prior to delivery, and no interim payments are required.

**FORWARD MARKET** Comprises transactions that represent a commitment to exchange currencies at a specified time in the future, at an exchange rate determined at the time the contract is signed.

**FORWARD RATE** Yield on a forward contract. Also, break even yield calculated under pure expectations theory according to prevailing interest rates.

**FORWARD RATE AGREEMENT** A forward contract in which the two parties establish an interest rate to be paid by one party to the other at a set date in the future. If the actual rate on that date differs from the predetermined rate, one party makes a cash payment to the other party.

**FREE CASH FLOW** Typically cash flow from operations less required capital expenditures (those capital expenditures required to maintain the company's ability to produce cash flow from operations.)

**FREE NONINTEREST CHECKING ACCOUNT** Imposes no fees of any kind.

**FULL-SERVICE BROKER** A brokerage that provides a full range of services to customers including advice on which securities to buy and/or sell.

**FUNDING GAP SEE GAP.**

**FUNDING LIQUIDITY RISK** Inability to liquidate assets or obtain adequate funding from new borrowing.

**FUTURES MARKETS** Organized exchanges in which all contracts are subject to a daily settlement procedure.

**FUTURES SPREADER** Speculator who may simultaneously buy a futures contract and sell a related futures contract, trying to profit on anticipated movements in the price difference between the contracts.

# G

**GAAP** Generally Accepted Accounting Principles representing the standard rules and procedures that accountants follow when reporting financial information.

**GAP** Dollar value of rate-sensitive assets minus the dollar value of rate-sensitive liabilities.

**GARNISHMENT** A court directive authorizing a bank to withold funds from a borrower.

**GENERAL OBLIGATION BONDS** Municipal bonds secured by the full faith, credit, and taxing power of the issuing state or local government.

**GENERAL MARKET RISK** Refers to changes in the market value of on-balance sheet assets and off-balance sheet items resulting from broad market movements. Includes risk common to all securities, such as changes in the general level of interest rates, exchange rates, commodity prices, or stock prices.

**GINNIE MAE** Name referring to the Government National Mortgage Association.

**GLASS-STEAGALL ACT** The 1933 act that separated lending activities from investment banking activities at commercial banks by prohibiting commercial banks from underwriting corporate securities.

**GNMA (GOVERNMENT NATIONAL MORTGAGE ASSOCIATION OR GINNIE MAE)** A government entity that buys mortgages for low-income housing and guarantees mortgage-backed securities issued by private lenders.

**GOLD STANDARD** A monetary system where the value of a country's currency is determined by the value of the gold content in the currency.

**GOODWILL** An intangible asset representing the difference between the book value of an asset or a firm and the actual sales price.

**GRACE PERIOD** The time period for a credit card statement representing the time from when the statement is generated to the last day full payment can be made and still avoid a finance charge.

**GRAMM-LEACH-BLILEY ACT OF 1999** The act repeals the Glass-Steagall Act and modifies the Bank Holding Company Act to create a new financial holding company authorized to engage in underwriting and selling insurance and securities, conducting both commercial and merchant banking, investing in and developing real estate and other activities "complementary" to banking. The act also restricts the disclosure of nonpublic customer information, requires disclosure of a privacy policy, as well as provides a new funding source for some banks by easing membership and collateral requirements to access funds from the Federal Home Loan Bank (FHLB).

**GRANDFATHER CLAUSE** A legislative provision that exempts parties previously engaged in activities prohibited by new legislation.

**GROSS DOMESTIC PRODUCT** The market value of goods and services produced over a period of time including the sum of consumer expenditures, investment expenditures, government expenditures, and net exports (exports minus imports).

**GROSS LOAN LOSSES (CHARGE-OFFS)** Dollar value of loans actually written off as uncollectible during a period.

**GUARANTEE** Make oneself liable for the debts of another.

**GUARANTEED INVESTMENT CONTRACT (GIC)** A financial contract in which the writer of a policy agrees to pay a fixed amount at maturity after receiving a fixed, single premium up front.

**GUARDIAN** An individual or a trust department appointed by a court to manage a minor's property or personal affairs.

# H

**HEDGE** Take a position in the forward futures, or swaps, market to offset risk associated with cash market activity.

**HEDGER** A trader who has an existing or anticipated position in the cash market and trades futures contracts (or some other contract) to reduce the risk associated with uncertain changes in value of the cash position.

**HELD-TO-MATURITY** Securities recorded at amortized cost on the balance sheet, with changes in value having no impact on the income statement.

**HIGH-PERFORMANCE BANK** One that makes an exceptional return to shareholders while maintaining an acceptable level of risk.

**HIGHLY LEVERAGED TRANSACTION (HLT)** Transaction in which borrower's debt increases sharply after the asset exchange, such as an LBO.

**HISTORICAL COST** The value for certain balance sheet items reflecting the original cost or amortized cost.

**HOLD ON THE CHECK** When a bank holds a check until it verifies that the check writer has enough funds on deposit to cover the draft.

**HOLDING PERIOD RETURN** The annualized rate of return expected or realized from holding a security over a specific period of time.

**HOME BANKING** Actions involving the conduct of banking business taking place in customers' homes, including telephone and computer transactions.

**HOME DEBIT** A check drawn on a bank that is presented to the same bank for deposit or payment.

**HOME EQUITY LOAN** Loan secured by an individual's equity in a home.

**HOT MONEY** Funds that move between institutions quickly in search of higher yields or greater safety.

**HYPOTHECATION** In a contract, commiting property to secure a loan.

# I

**ILLIQUID** An asset that is not easily or readily converted into cash.

**IMMEDIATELY AVAILABLE FUNDS** Collected deposits held at Federal Reserve banks or certain collected liabilities or private financial institutions.

**IMMUNIZE** To fully hedge against interest rate risk.

**IMPLIED VOLATILITY** The expected volatility in return on an underlying asset or contract derived from an option pricing model.

**INCOME STATEMENT GAP** An interest rate risk model which modifies the standard GAP model to incorporate the different speeds and amounts of repricing of specific assets and liabilities given an interest rate change.

**INDEPENDENT BANK** A bank operating in one locality that is not part of a large multibank holding company or group of banks.

**INDEX RATE** The rate that serves as a base rate when pricing certain mortgages and variable rate loans.

**INDIRECT LOAN** Loan in which a retailer takes the credit application and negotiates terms with the actual borrower. The lender then purchases the loan from the retailer under prearranged terms.

**INDIVIDUAL RETIREMENT ACCOUNT (IRA)** A retirement account available to individuals to defer income taxes.

**INDUSTRIAL REVENUE BOND (IRB)** A bond issued by a state government, local government, or political subdivision for the express benefit of a business that will effectively use the proceeds.

**INITIAL MARGIN** At initiation of a futures position, traders must post a cash deposit or U.S. government securities.

**INITIAL PUBLIC OFFERING (IPO)** The initial offering of stock of a private company.

**INSOLVENT** The financial position of a firm whose market value of stockholders' equity is less than or equal to zero. A firm is technically insolvent when the book value of stockholders' equity is less than or equal to zero.

**INSTALLMENT LOAN** A loan that is payable in periodic, partial installments.

**INTELLIGENT CARD** Contains a microchip with the ability to store and secure information, and makes different responses depending on the requirements of the card issuer's specific application needs.

**INTERBANK LOAN** Credit extended from one bank to another.

**INTEREST EXPENSE** Sum of interest paid on all interest-bearing liabilities, including transactions accounts, time and savings deposits, volatile liabilities and other borrowings, and long-term debt.

**INTEREST INCOME** Sum of interest and fees earned on all of a bank's assets, including loans, deposits held at other institutions, municipal and taxable securities, and trading account securities.

**INTEREST-ON-INTEREST** Interest earned on interest, or reinvestment interest income.

**INTEREST RATE CAP** A contract in which payments are made from the seller who receives an up-front premium to the buyer when a reference index rate exceeds a strike rate.

**INTEREST RATE COLLAR** The simultaneous purchase of an interest rate cap and sale of an interest rate floor on the same index for the same maturity and notional principal amount.

*Glossary*

**INTEREST RATE FLOOR** A contract in which payments are made from the seller who receives an up-front premium to the buyer when a reference index rate is less than a strike rate.

**INTEREST RATE FUTURES** When the underlying asset of a futures contract is an interest-bearing security.

**INTEREST RATE RISK** Potential variability in a bank's net interest income and market value of equity caused by changes in the level of interest rates.

**INTEREST RATE SWAP** A contract in which two parties (counterparties) agree to exchange fixed-rate interest payments for floating-rate interest payments over a specific period of time based on some notional principal amount.

**INTERNAL AUDIT** Routine examination of a bank's accounting records.

**INTER VIVOS** Phrase referring to "between living persons."

**IN-THE-MONEY** An option that has a positive intrinsic value. A call option in which the actual price is above the exercise price; a put option in which the actual price is below the exercise price.

**INTRINSIC VALUE** The net value obtained from exercising an option.

**INVENTORY TURNOVER** Cost of goods sold divided by inventory; measures the efficiency of the firm in managing its inventory.

**INVERTED YIELD CURVE** Yield curve with long-term rates below short-term rates.

**INVESTABLE BALANCES** Ledger balances minus float minus required reserves against associated deposit balances.

**INVESTMENT BANKING** Activity involving securities underwriting, making a market in securities, and arranging mergers and acquisitions.

**INVESTMENT INCOME FROM DEPOSIT BALANCES** Generated by every deposit customers hold. Investment securities

**IO** Interest-only security representing the interest portion of a stripped Treasury or stripped mortgage backed security.

## J

**JUDGMENT** Legal ruling regarding the final payment of a court-determined transfer of assets.

**JUDGMENTAL CREDIT ANALYSIS** Subjective assessment of a borrower's ability and willingness to repay debts.

**JUNK BOND** A bond with a credit rating below investment grade, below Baa for Moody's, and below BBB for S&P, or a bond that is not rated.

## K

**KEOGH PLAN** A pension plan for the self-employed that allows them to make contributions and defer taxes until the funds are withdrawn.

**KITE** Writing checks against uncollected deposits in the process of clearing through the banking system.

## L

**LACK OF DIVERSIFICATION** Banks that lend in a narrow geographic area or concentrate their loans to a certain industry.

**LADDER STRATEGY** When investing bonds, allocating roughly equivalent amounts (portions) to different maturities.

**LAGGED RESERVE ACCOUNTING (LRA)** System of reserve requirements based on deposits outstanding prior to the reserve maintenance period.

**LARGE TIME DEPOSITS** Generally referred to as large CDs or jumbo CDs, these accounts consist of large, negotiable certificates of $100,000 or more. They are issued primarily by the largest banks and purchased by businesses and governmental units.

**LBO** Leveraged buyout.

**LEASE** A contract in which the owner of a property allows another party to use the property if certain terms are met and lease payments (rent) are made.

**LEDGER BALANCES** Dollar value of deposit balances appearing on a bank's books.

**LEGAL LENDING LIMIT** The maximum amount that can be loaned to any one borrower or any group of related borrowers.

**LEGAL RISK** Risk that unenforceable contracts, lawsuits, or adverse judgments could disrupt or negatively affect the operations, profitability, condition, or solvency of the institution.

**LENDER LIABILITY** Circumstances in which the courts have found lenders liable to their borrowers for fraud, deception, breached fiduciary activities, broken promises, and good faith negotiations.

**LESSEE** The party that rents or leases an asset from another party.

**LESSOR** The party that owns an asset and leases or rents it to another party.

**LETTER OF CREDIT** A bank's guarantee of payment, indicated by a document that describes the handling of a specific transaction.

**LEVERAGE CAPITAL RATIO** Tier 1 capital divided by total assets net of goodwill, other disallowed intangible assets, and disallowed deferred tax assets.

**LEVERAGED BUYOUT (LBO)** An acquisition where the firm buying another firm contributes a small amount of equity and finances the bulk of the purchase price with debt.

**LIABILITY LIQUIDITY** The ease with which a bank can issue new debt to acquire clearing balances at reasonable costs.

**LIABILITY MANAGEMENT THEORY** A theory that focuses on banks issuing liabilities to meet liquidity needs.

**LIABILITY SENSITIVE** A bank is classified as liability sensitive if its GAP is negative.

**LIBOR** London Interbank Offer Rate, which represents a money market rate offered by banks for the placement of Eurodollars.

**LIEN** Legal right granted by the court to attach property until a legal claim is paid.

**LIMITED BRANCHING** Provisions that restrict branching to a geographic area smaller than an entire state.

**LINE OF CREDIT** A lending agreement between a bank and borrower in which the bank makes a fixed amount of funds available to the borrower for a specified period of time. The customer determines the timing of actual borrowing.

**LIQUID ASSETS** Unpledged, marketable short-term securities that are classified as available-for-sale, plus federal funds sold and securities purchased under agreement to resell. A liquid asset can be easily and quickly converted into cash with minimum loss.

**LIQUIDITY PREMIUM** The premium included in longer-term interest rates to compensate investors for price risk associated with volatile interest rates.

**LIQUIDITY RISK** The variation in net income and market value of bank equity caused by a bank's difficulty in obtaining immediately available funds, either by borrowing or selling assets.

**LOAN AND LEASE LOSS ALLOWANCE** Contra-asset (negative asset) reserve account that exists in recognition that some loans will not be repaid. The reserve's maximum size is determined by tax law but increases with the growth in problem loans and decreases with net loan charge-offs.

**LOAN ADMINISTRATION EXPENSE** Cost of a loan's credit analysis and execution. It includes personnel and overhead costs as well as direct costs for sending interest bills, processing payments, and maintaining collateral.

**LOAN AGREEMENT** Formalizes the purpose of the loan, the terms, repayment schedule, collateral required, any loan covenants, and finally, what conditions bring about default by the borrower.

**LOAN COMMITMENT** Formal agreement between a bank and borrower to provide a fixed amount of credit for a specified period.

**LOAN PARTICIPATION** Credit extended to a borrower in which members of a group of lenders each provide a fraction of the total financing; typically arises because individual banks are limited in the amount of credit they can extend to a single customer.

**LOAN POLICY** Formalizes lending guidelines that employees follow to conduct bank business. It identifies preferred loan qualities and establishes procedures for granting, documenting, and reviewing loans.

**LOAN PRODUCTION OFFICES (LPOs)** Institutions that make commercial loans but do not accept deposits.

**LOAN SYNDICATION** An arrangement where several lenders make a loan jointly to a borrower.

**LOAN-TO-VALUE RATIO** The loan amount divided by the appraised value of the underlying collateral.

**LOCAL** A trader operating on the floor of an exchange who trades for his or her own account.

**LOCKBOX** A post office box number controlled by the bank.

*Glossary*

**LONDON INTERBANK OFFER RATE (LIBOR)** Interest rate at which banks deposit Eurodollars with other banks outside the United States.

**LONG HEDGE** The purchase of a futures contract to reduce the risk of an increase in the price of a cash asset.

**LONG POSITION** Market position in which an investor actually owns an asset.

**LONG-TERM INVESTMENT SECURITIES** Securities with maturities in excess of one year.

# M

**MACAULAY'S DURATION** Computed as a weighted average of the time until cash flows are received.

**MACROHEDGE** A hedge strategy designed to reduce risk associated with a bank's entire balance sheet position.

**MAINTENANCE MARGIN** The minimum amount of funds in a margin account that must be maintained at all times. When the customer's balance falls below this amount, the broker will require an additional deposit or may close the account.

**MAINTENANCE PERIOD** With respect to required reserve calculation, consists of 14 consecutive days beginning on a Thursday and ending on the second Wednesday thereafter.

**MAKE A MARKET** Stand ready to buy or sell particular assets.

**MAKE-WHOLE CLAUSE** A provision that requires that the borrower make a payment to a lender after a loan is called or prepaid. The amount of the payment equals the net present value of the lost interest and principal payments.

**MARGIN** Deposit with a broker that protects the broker from losses arising from customer transactions.

**MARGINAL COST OF DEBT** A measure of the borrowing cost paid to acquire one additional unit of investable funds.

**MARGINAL COST OF EQUITY CAPITAL** A measure of the minimum acceptable rate of return required by shareholders.

**MARGINAL COST OF FUNDS** The incremental cost of additional funds to finance firm operations.

**MARGINAL TAX RATE** Tax rate applied to the last increment of taxable income.

**MARKET LIQUIDITY RISK** Inability of the bank to easily unwind or offset specific exposures without significant losses from inadequate market depth or market disturbances.

**MARKET RISK** Current and potential risk to earnings and stockholders' equity resulting from adverse movements in market rates or prices.

**MARKET VALUE** The actual value indicating what an asset can be currently sold for.

**MARK-TO-MARKET** The daily reconciliation of a future trader's margin account in which gains and losses on the position are added and subtracted, respectively.

**MATURITY** The date at which the principal of a note, draft, or bond becomes due and payable.

**MBS (MORTGAGE-BACKED SECURITY)** A security that evidences an undivided interest in the ownership of a pool of mortgages.

**MEMORANDUM OF UNDERSTANDING (MOU)** A formal regulatory document that identifies specific violations and prescribes corrective action by the problem institution.

**MERGER** A combination of two firms, generally where the assets and liabilities of the seller are combined with the assets and liabilities of the buyer.

**MICROHEDGE** A hedge strategy designed to reduce risk associated with a specific transaction.

**MODIFIED DURATION** Macaulay's duration divided by 1 plus the prevailing interest rate on the underlying instrument.

**MONEY MARKET DEPOSIT ACCOUNT (MMDA)** Small time deposit whose holder is limited to three written checks per month.

**MONEY MARKET MUTUAL FUND** Mutual fund that accepts customer funds and purchases short-term marketable securities.

**MONEY SUPPLY** The federal government's designation of certain liquid assets as money; M1A equals currency outside banks plus demand deposits; M1B equals M1A plus other checkable deposits; M2 equals M1B plus overnight RPs, savings and small time deposits, and money market funds; M3 equals M2 plus large time deposits and term RPs; L equals M3 plus other liquid assets.

**MORTGAGE** A contract whereby a borrower provides a lender with a lien on real property as security against a loan.

**MORTGAGE BANKING** The business of packaging mortgage loans for sale to investors and retaining the servicing rights to the mortgages.

**MORTGAGE SERVICING** The process of collecting monthly payments on mortgages, keeping records, paying the associated insurance and taxes, and making monthly payments to holders of the underlying mortgages or mortgage-backed securities.

**MULTIBANK HOLDING COMPANY** A bank holding company that owns controlling interest in at least two commercial banks.

**MUNICIPALS** Securities issued by states, local governments, and their political subdivisions.

**MUTUAL FUND** A pool of funds that is managed by an investment company.
Investors in a mutual fund own shares in the fund, and the fund uses the proceeds to buy different assets.

**MUTUAL SAVINGS BANKS** Firms without capital stock that accept deposits and make loans.

# N

**NEGOTIABLE ORDER OF WITHDRAWAL** Interest-bearing transactions account offered by banks.

**NET FIXED ASSETS TO TANGIBLE NET WORTH** An indicator of the proportion of the firm's less liquid assets financed by net worth.

**NET INCOME** Operating profit less all federal, state, and local income taxes, plus or minus any accounting adjustments and extraordinary items.

**NET INDIRECT COSTS** Costs not directly related to the product such as salaries to manage the bank or general overhead.

**NET INTEREST INCOME** Interest income minus interest expense.

**NET INTEREST MARGIN (NIM)** Ratio of net interest income to total earning assets.

**NET INTEREST MARGIN SIMULATION** Simulated estimates of changes in net interest margin.

**NET LOSSES (NET CHARGE-OFFS)** Difference between gross loan losses and recoveries. Net losses directly reduce loan loss reserves that a bank sets aside for potential losses.

**NET OVERHEAD BURDEN** Difference between noninterest expense and noninterest income as a fraction of total bank assets.

**NET TRANSACTIONS ACCOUNTS** Base liabilities, in which the holder is permitted to make withdrawals by negotiable or transferable instruments, payment orders, and telephone and preauthorized transfers in excess of three per month.

**NETTING** The practice of offsetting promised interest payments with promised interest receipts and transferring the difference with an interest rate swap.

**NET WORTH** Owners' (stockholders') equity in a firm.

**NO-FEE NOW ACCOUNTS** Interest-bearing checking accounts that charge no fees.

**NO LOAD FUND** A mutual fund that does not charge a regular sales commission. It may charge a 12b-1 fee.

**NOMINAL INTEREST RATE** Market interest rate stated in current, not real, dollars.

**NONACCRUAL LOAN** Loan not currently accruing interest. The loan is currently—or has been habitually—past due, or has other problems, which has placed it in nonaccrual status.

**NONBANK BANK** A firm that either makes commercial loans or accepts deposits but does not do both. Thus, it avoids regulation as a commercial bank.

**NONBANK SUBSIDIARY** A subsidiary of a bank holding company that is engaged in activities closely related to banking, such as leasing, data processing, factoring, and insurance underwriting.

**NONCREDIT SERVICES** Non lending related services provided by a financial institution such as cash management, checking and ATM services.

**NONCURRENT LOAN** Typically a loan that is 90 days past due.

**NONELECTRONIC TRANSACTIONS** Transactions conducted in person or by mail.

**NONINTEREST EXPENSE** Composed primarily of personnel expense, which includes salaries and fringe benefits paid to bank employees; occupancy expense from rent and depreciation on equipment and premises; and other operating expenses, including technology expenditures, utilities, and deposit insurance premiums. Other noninterest expenses include goodwill impairment amortization and other intangible amortizations.

**NONINTEREST INCOME** Income from products and services offered by a financial institution that is not earning from lending activities.

**NONPERFORMING LOAN** Loan for which an obligated interest payment is past due.

**NONRATED BOND** A bond that is not rated by Moody's, S&P, or other rating agency.

**NONRATE GAP** Noninterest-bearing liabilities plus equity minus nonearning assets as a fraction of earning assets.

**NONRECOURSE** Holder of an obligation has no legal right to force payment on a claim.

**NONTRANSACTIONAL ACCOUNTS** Accounts that offer limited check writing capabilities and pay higher rates.

**NOTE ISSUANCE FACILITY** An arrangement in which borrowers can issue short-term securities in their own names.

**NOTIONAL PRINCIPAL** Serves as a reference figure in determining cash flows.

**NOTIONAL VALUE** The face value of interest rate swap contracts; a mere reference value to compute obligated interest payments.

**NOW ACCOUNT** Checking account that pays interest.

**NSF** Not sufficient funds.

# O

**OFF-BALANCE SHEET ACTIVITIES** Commitments, such as loan guarantees, that do not appear on a bank's balance sheet but represent actual contractual obligations.

**OFF-BALANCE SHEET RISK** Volatility in income and market value of bank equity that may arise from unanticipated losses due to these off-balance sheet liabilities.

**OFFICIAL CHECK ISSUED** Bank issued check for certified funds.

**ONE BANK HOLDING COMPANY** A holding company that owns or controls only one commercial bank.

**"ON OTHERS" WITHDRAWAL FEES** Fees charged to the institution's own customers for making withdrawals at other institutions' ATMs.

**"ON-US" CHECKS CASHED** Checks drawn on the bank's customer's account. Deposits represent checks or currency directly deposited in the customer's account.

**"ON-US" WITHDRAWAL FEES** Transaction fees for ATM withdrawals levied on the institution's depositor.

**ON THE RUN** The most recently issued U.S. Treasury security.

**OPEN ACCOUNT** Credit not supported by a note or other written record.

**OPEN INTEREST** Total number of outstanding unfilled futures positions measured on one side of the transaction.

**OPEN MARKET OPERATIONS** Conducted by the Federal Reserve Bank of New York under the direction of the Federal Open Market Committee (FOMC). The sale or purchase of U.S. government securities in the "open market" or secondary market is the Federal Reserve's most flexible means of carrying out its policy objectives.

**OPERATING INCOME** Sum of interest income and noninterest income.

**OPERATING LEVERAGE** Ratio of fixed costs to total costs; measure of business risk that indicates the relative change in operating income that arises from a change in sales.

**OPTION** Right to buy or sell a specific asset at a fixed price during a specified interval of time.

**OPTION-ADJUSTED SPREAD** A procedure for valuing prepayment risk associated with mortgage-backed securities that recognizes the magnitude and timing of prepayments and required return to an investor; the corresponding yield spread over matched Treasury securities.

**OPTION CONTRACT** Agreement between two parties in which one party gives the other the right, but not the obligation, to buy or sell a specific asset at a set price for a specified period of time.

**OPTION ON FUTURES CONTRACT** Option contract in which the underlying asset is a futures contract.

**OPTION PREMIUM** The price of an option.

**ORIGINATION FEE** Fee charged by a lender for accepting the initial loan application and processing the loan.

**OTHER REAL ESTATE OWNED (OREO)**
Real estate owned by a bank that is acquired in settlement of debts.

**OUT-OF-THE MONEY** An option that has no intrinsic value. A call option in which the actual price is below the exercise price; a put option in which the actual price is above the exercise price.

**OUTSOURCING** Buying services from third-party vendors. For example, some banks might outsource their data processing.

**OUTSTANDING LEASES** Capitilized value of lease contracts held by the bank.

**OVERDRAFT** Depositor writing a check for an amount greater than the deposit balance.

**OVERHEAD** Expenses that generally do not vary with the level of output.

**PAC (PLANNED AMORTIZATION CLASS CMO)** A security that is retired according to a planned amortization schedule, while payments to other classes of securities are slowed or accelerated. The objective is to ensure that PACs exhibit highly predictable maturities and cash flows.

**PARALLEL SHIFT IN THE YIELD CURVE** A change in interest rates where rates at all maturities change by the same amount, in the same direction, at the same time. This never actually occurs.

**PARENT COMPANY** A firm that owns controlling interest in the stock of another firm.

**PAR VALUE** Dollar value of a bond's principal payment at maturity; face value printed on a security.

**PASSBOOK SAVINGS** Nonnegotiable, small savings account evidenced by a passbook listing the account terms.

**PASSIVE PORTFOLIO MANAGEMENT** An investment policy whereby managers make predetermined securities purchases regardless of the level of interest rates and specific rate expectations. Examples include following a laddered maturity strategy whereby a bank continuously buys 10-year securities as previously owned securities mature.

**PASS-THROUGH SECURITY** Instrument secured by mortgages in which the mortgage banker passes mortgage interest and principal payments to the holder of the security minus a servicing charge.

**PAST-DUE LOAN** A loan with a promised principal and/or interest payment that has not been made by the scheduled payment date.

**PEER GROUP** Sample firms used to generate average reference data for comparison with an individual firm's performance data.

**P/E RATIO** A firm's stock price per share divided by earnings per share.

**PERIODIC GAP** A measure of interest rate risk calculated as the difference between rate sensitive assets (RSAs) and rate sensitive liabilities (RSLs) within each time bucket. A measure of the timing of the impact of interest rate changes

**PERMANENT WORKING CAPITAL** Minimum level of current assets minus minimum level of current liabilities net of short-term bank credit and current maturity of longterm debt; represents the amount of long-term financing required for current assets.

**PERPETUAL PREFERRED STOCK** Nonmaturing preferred stock.

**PERPETUITY** With respect to bonds, an infinite number of payments.

**PERSONAL BANKER** Individual assigned to a bank customer to handle a broad range of financial services.

**PLANNED AMORTIZATION CLASS** A collateralized mortgage obligation (CMO) that receives principal from the underlying mortgages based on a predetermined payment schedule, where the payments vary depending on whether prepayments fall inside or outside some predetermined range.

**PLEDGED SECURITIES** Bank securities pledged as collateral against public deposits, borrowings from Federal Reserve banks, and securities sold under agreement to repurchase.

**PO** Principal-only security representing the principal portion of a stripped Treasury or stripped mortgage-backed security.

**POINT OF SALE** Electronic terminals that enable customers to directly access deposit accounts.

**POLITICAL RISK** The risk of loss due to such causes as currency inconvertibility, government action preventing entry of goods, expropriation or confiscation, and war.

**POOLING OF INTERESTS** An accounting procedure in an acquisition where the two companies simply report financial results by combining assets, liabilities, and equity at book values.

**POSITION TRADER** A speculator who holds a position for a longer period in anticipation of a more significant, longer-term market move.

**PREFERRED STOCK** Class of stock representing ownership with a claim on firm income senior to common stock.

**PREMIUM ON A BOND** Difference between the price of a bond and its par value when the price is higher.

**PREPAYMENT SPEED** The percentage of the outstanding principal that is prepaid above and beyond normal amortization.

**PRETAX NET OPERATING INCOME** Tax-equivalent net interest income, plus noninterest income, minus noninterest expense, minus provision for loan losses, plus realized securities gains (or losses). It represents the bank's operating profit before taxes and extraordinary items.

**PRIMARY CAPITAL** The sum of common stock, perpetual preferred stock, surplus, undivided profits, contingency and other capital reserves, valuation reserves, mandatory convertible securities, and minority interest in consolidated subsidiaries at a bank.

**PRIMARY CREDIT** Borrowings from the Federal Reserve bank under the new primary credit program in which there are many fewer administrative requirements necessary to process the loan. Sometimes referred to as the 'no questions asked' program.

**PRIME RATE** One of several base interest rates used as an index to price commercial loans.

**PROBATE** Legal act of submitting a will before a court to verify authenticity of the document.

**PROBLEM LOANS** Loans currently in default or expected to obtain default status.

**PRO FORMA FINANCIAL STATEMENTS** Projected or forecasted balance sheet and income statements.

**PROFIT MARGIN** A measure of expense control defined as net income divided by total revenue.

**PROMPT REGULATORY ACTION** Divides banks into categories or zones according to their capital positions and mandates action when capital minimums are not met.

**PROVISIONS FOR LOAN AND LEASE LOSSES** Represents management's estimate of the potential incremental lost revenue from bad loans and is a deduction from income representing a bank's periodic allocation to its loan and lease loss allowance (loan loss reserve) on the balance sheet.

**PRUDENT MAN RULE** Requirement that a fiduciary exercise discretion, prudence, and sound judgment in managing the assets of a third party.

**PURCHASE ACCOUNTING** An accounting method for acquisitions in which the assets and liabilities of the combined firm reflect a revaluation of assets and liabilities of the subject firms, thus recognizing the value of goodwill and other intangibles.

**PUT** Option to sell an asset (security) for a fixed price during a specific interval of time.

**PUTABLE BOND** A bond where the investor has the option to put the security back to the issuer after some predetermined date prior to maturity and receive the principal invested or a stated price.

# Q

**QUALITY SPREAD** The difference in market yields between yields on risky securities and matched maturity/-duration Treasury securities.

**QUICK RATIO** Cash plus accounts receivable divided by current liabilities.

# R

**RATE SENSITIVE** Classification of assets and liabilities that can be repriced within a specific time frame, either because they mature or carry floating or variable rates.

**RATING** System of assigning letters to security issues indicating the perceived default risks associated with that class of issues.

**REAL INTEREST RATE** Interest rate after inflation expectations are netted from a nominal interest rate.

**REALIZED COMPOUND YIELD** A measure of total return calculated by comparing total future dollars equal to coupon interest or dividends plus reinvestment income and the maturity or sale value of the underlying asset, with the initial purchase price, over the appropriate number of compounding periods.

**REALIZED SECURITIES GAINS (OR LOSSES)** Arise when a bank sells securities from its investment portfolio prior to final maturity at prices above (or below) the initial or amortized cost to the bank. All such profits are reported and taxed as ordinary income.

**REBATE** The return of a portion of unearned interest to a borrower.

**RECOURSE** Legal right to enforce a claim against another party.

**RECOVERIES** Dollar amount of loans that were previously charged off but now collected.

**REDLINING** A practice whereby lenders deny loans to residents living in predetermined geographic areas. Such a practice is illegal.

**REINVESTMENT RISK** The risk that future cash flows may be reinvested at rates below those expected or available at present.

**REIT (REAL ESTATE INVESTMENT TRUST)** An organization that obtains funds to invest in real estate or finance construction.

**REMIC** A real estate mortgage investment conduit issuing securities collateralized by mortgages and passing on principal and interest payments to investors. Like CMOs, REMIC securities represent claims on the underlying cash flows that are prioritized by multiple classes or tranches.

**REPORTING PERIOD** The period of time covered by a particular report such as monthly, quarterly or annual.

**REPURCHASE AGREEMENT (RP OR REPOS)** Short-term loans secured by government securities and settled in immediately available funds.

**REPUTATION RISK** Risk that negative publicity, either true or untrue, can adversely affect a bank's customer base or bring forth costly litigation, hence negatively affecting profitability.

**REREGULATION** The process of implementing new restrictions or modifying existing controls on individuals and activities associated with banking. Reregulation arises in response to market participants' efforts to circumvent existing regulations.

**RESERVE FOR BANK DEBTS** Amount appearing on a bank's balance sheet that represents the estimated value of uncollectible loans.

**RESERVE BALANCE REQUIREMENT** The portion of the reserve requirement that is not satisfied by vault cash holdings.

**RESERVE REQUIREMENT RATIOS** Percentages applied to transactions accounts and time deposits to determine the dollar amount of required reserve assets.

**RESERVES** Qualifying assets to meet reserve requirements, including vault cash and deposit balances held at Federal Reserve banks.

**RESOLUTION TRUST CORPORATION (RTC)** A government agency (1989–1996) that assisted in the management of savings and loans deemed to be insolvent during the Thrift Crisis.

**RESPONDENT BANK** Bank that purchases services from a correspondent bank.

**RESTRUCTURED LOAN** Loan for which the lender has modified the required payments on principal or interest. The lender may have lengthened maturity and/or renegotiated the interest rate.

**RETAIL BANK** Bank that emphasizes lending to individuals.

**RETAIL FUNDING** Funding the bank receives from consumers and noninstitutional depositors. Retail funding generally consist of deposits accounts such as transactions accounts, money market demand accounts (MMDAs), savings accounts, and small time deposits.

**RETURN ITEMS** Checks that have not been honored by the drawee bank and have been returned to the check writer.

**RETURN ON ASSETS** Net income divided by average total assets.

**RETURN ON EQUITY** Net income divided by average stockholders' equity.

**RETURN ON EQUITY MODEL** A model that relates ROE to ROA and financial leverage and then decomposes ROA into its contributing elements.

**REVENUE BOND** Municpal bond issued to finance a project in which debt service payments are secured by specific revenues from the project.

**REVERSE MORTGAGE** A mortgage in which the owner of the property can borrow against existing equity in the property.

**REVERSE REPO** A contract in which a lender provides funds to a borrower for which collateral is provided in the event of nonpayment.

**REVERSE REPURCHASE AGREEMENT** Securities purchased under an agreement to resell them at a later date.

**REVOLVER** Loan commitment or line of credit that converts to a term loan.

**RIDING THE YIELD CURVE** An investment strategy where the investor buys a security that matures after the investor's assumed holding period. The investor plans to sell the security at the end of the holding period and earn an above-average return because interest rates are expected to remain stable or fall.

**RIEGLE-NEAL INTERSTATE BANKING AND BRANCHING EFFICIENCY ACT OF 1994** Overrides state branching laws and permits nationwide interstate branching by allowing adequately capitalized bank holding companies to acquire banks or branches in any state.

**RISK ASSETS** Total assets minus cash and due from balances minus U.S. government securities.

**RISK MANAGEMENT** Process by which managers identify, assess, monitor, and control risks associated with a financial institution's activities. Risk-weighted assets Total of risk-adjusted assets where the risk weights are based on four risk classes of assets.

**ROTH IRA** An individual retirement account introduced in 1998 that allows individuals whose wages and salaries are below a predetermined minimum to contribute after-tax income. The contributions grow on a tax-sheltered basis and thus are not taxed at withdrawal.

**RULE OF 72** Divide 72 by the interest rate at which funds are invested. The value indicates how long it will take for the amount of funds invested to double in value.

**RUN ON A BANK** Situation in which a large number of depositors lose confidence in the safety of their deposits and attempt to withdraw their funds.

# S

**SAFE DEPOSIT BOX** Privacy boxes for storage located in a bank vault under lock and key.

**SAIF** Savings Association Insurance Fund that insures deposits at thrift institutions.

**SALE AND LEASE BACK** Transaction in which an asset is sold, with title exchanged to a lessor who leases the asset to the original owner.

**SALES GROWTH** Demonstrates whether the firm is expanding or contracting and provides evidence of industry competitiveness.

**SALES-TO-ASSET RATIO** Total sales divided by average total assets.

**SALLIE MAE** Student Loan Marketing Association that guarantees student loans.

**SARBANES-OXLEY ACT SARBANES-OXLEY ACT** Passed by Congress in 2002, the act established the Public Company Oversight Board to regulate public accounting firms that audit publicly traded companies. It specifically addresses issues of conflicts among company executives, accounting firms, and their affiliates as well as requires CEOs and CFOs to certify the annual and quarterly reports of publicly traded companies. The act also established many required policies and procedures in the area of corporate governance for the boards of publicly traded companies.

**SAVINGS ACCOUNT** Small-denomination account (under $100,000) with no fixed maturity.

**SAVINGS INSTITUTIONS** Institutions that are generally referred to as "thrifts" because they originally offered only savings or time deposits to attract funds.

**SCALPER** A trader who tries to time price movements over very short time intervals and takes positions that remain outstanding for just minutes.

**SEASONAL CREDIT** Designed to assist small depository institutions in managing significant seasonal swings in their loans and deposits. Seasonal credit is available to depository institutions that can demonstrate a clear pattern of recurring intrayearly swings in funding needs. Eligible institutions are usually located in agricultural or tourist areas. The interest rate applied to seasonal credit is a floating rate based on market rates.

**SEASONAL LIQUIDITY NEEDS** Cash flow needs that arise from predictable seasonal loan demands and deposit outflows.

**SECONDARY CAPITAL** Limited life preferred stock, subordinated debt, and mandatory convertible securities not included as primary capital.

**SEASONAL WORKING CAPITAL** Additional working capital needs that exceed the companies permanent working capital needs. Often a result of seasonal sales patterns in a companies sales.

**SECONDARY CREDIT** Available to depository institutions that are not eligible for primary credit. It is extended on a very short-term basis, typically overnight, at a rate that is above the primary credit rate.

**SECURITIZATION** Pooling loans into packages and selling the pooled assets by issuing securities collateralized by the pooled assets.

**SECURITY** Collateral a borrower pledges against a loan or secondary source of repayment in case of default.

**SECURITY INTEREST** The legal claim on property that secures a debt or the performance of an obligation.

**SECURITY REPURCHASE AGREEMENTS** See repurchase agreement.

**SERIAL BONDS** A series of bonds offered by the same issuer with principal payments that are due at different maturities. Serial bonds are common for municipal bond issuers.

**SERVICE CHARGES** Fees imposed for bank services.

**SHIFTABILITY THEORY** An extension of the commercial loan theory recognizing that any liquid asset could be used to meet deposit withdrawals.

**SHORT HEDGE** Sale of a futures contract to protect against a price decline.

**SHORT POSITION** The sale of an asset not owned.

**SHORT-TERM SECURITIES** Securities that mature in one year or less.

**SIGHT DRAFT** A draft payable "on sight."

**SIGNIFICANTLY UNDERCAPITALIZED BANK** Institution with capital that falls significantly below at least one of the three regulatory standards.

**SIMPLE INTEREST** Interest applied against principal only.

**SINGLE-BALANCE, SINGLE-FEE NON-INTEREST ACCOUNT** Incurs no fee if a minimum balance is met; otherwise, there is a single monthly fee.

**SINGLE-FEE NOW ACCOUNTS** Similar to noninterest accounts in that they charge no fee if the account balance remains above a minimum amount; otherwise, the institution charges a monthly fee with no check charge.

**SINGLE-FEE, SINGLE-CHECK-CHARGE NOW ACCOUNTS** Similar to single-fee NOW accounts in that they charge a monthly fee if the account balance falls below a minimum, but this triggers a per-check charge as well.

**SMALL TIME DEPOSITS** Small-denomination accounts (under $100,000) with specified maturities ranging from seven days to any longer negotiated term, with interest penalties for early withdrawal.

**SOVEREIGN RISK** Refers to the likelihood that foreign governments will unilaterally alter their debt service payments, regardless of the formal repayment schedule.

**SPECIFIC MZARKET RISK** Risk specific to a particular security issue, such as the underlying credit risk of the firm that issued a bond.

**SPECULATOR** A trader who takes a position to increase risk in hope of earning extraordinary returns.

**SPOT CURVE** Yields on zero coupon Treasury securities that differ in terms of maturity.

**SPOT MARKET** Market for immediate delivery of assets.

**SPOT RATE** Yield on a zero coupon Treasury security.

**SPREAD** Average yield on earning assets minus the average rate paid on interest-bearing liabilities.

**SPREADER** A spreader is a trader who is not concerned with the direction in which the market moves, but only with the difference between the prices of each contract.

**STATEWIDE BRANCHING** Allowing banks to establish branches throughout an entire state.

**STOCK MARKET INDEXED CD** Certificate of deposit with yields linked to a stock market index such as the S&P 500.

**STOP PAYMENT** Request by a depositor to stop payment on a previously issued check that has not yet cleared.

**STRATEGIC PLANNING** The process through which managers formulate the firm's mission and goals, and identify strengths, weaknesses, opportunities, and threats.

**STRIKE PRICE** Fixed price at which an asset may be purchased in a call option or sold under a put option.

**STRIPPED BOND** A bond in which individual coupon payments and principal payments are separated (stripped) from the bond and sold as distinct zero coupon securities.

**STRIPPED SECURITIES** Securities that represent just the coupon interest or principal payments on a loan. The interest-only payment is referrred to as an IO, while the principal-only payment is referred to as a PO.

**STRIPPING FUTURES** Buying or selling equal amounts of successive futures contracts.

**STRUCTURED NOTE** A security that will change in value or whose cash flows will change when some underlying index or base rate changes.

**SUBCHAPTER S FIRM** A firm with 100 or fewer stockholders that chooses to be taxed as a partnership so as not to pay corporate income taxes.

**SUBORDINATED DEBT** In the case of bankruptcy, the claims of holders of subordinated debt are subordinated to the claims of other debt holders. In banks, insured depositors are paid in full before holders of subordinated debt receive anything.

**SUBORDINATED NOTES AND DEBENTURES** Notes and bonds with maturities in excess of one year. Most meet requirements as bank capital for regulatory purposes.

**SUBSTITUTE CHECK** Legal equivalent of the original check and includes all the information contained on the original.

**SUPPLEMENTARY CAPITAL** Also know as Tier 2 capital. See Tier 2 capital.

**SUPPORT TRANCHE** A class of mortgage- backed securities where the promised principal and interest payments are made after payments to holders of other classes of securities are made.

**SURCHARGES** Fees charged by ATM owners on users of their ATMs who are not the institution's customers.

**SWAP** Simultaneous purchase and sale of like securities to alter the portfolio composition and characteristics.

**SWAPTION** An option on a swap.

**SYNDICATE** Group of banks that jointly negotiate a contract to sell securities or make loans.

# T

**TAC** Targeted amortization class mortgage-backed securities in which payments are guaranteed for one specific prepayment rate.

**TAKEDOWN** Actual borrowing against a line of credit or loan commitment.

**TANGIBLE EQUITY** Total assets minus intangible assets minus total liabilities.

**TARGETED RETUN ON EQUITY** Guideline based on the cost of debt plus a premium to evaluate the cost of equity.

**TAX AND LOAN ACCOUNT** A deposit account at a financial institution held by the U.S. Treasury.

**TAX ANTICIPATION NOTE** Short-term municipal security issued in anticipation of future tax receipts and repaid from same.

**TAX CREDIT** Direct reduction in tax liability arising from qualifying expenditures.

**TAX-EQUIVALENT YIELD** Tax-exempt interest yield converted to a pretax taxable equivalent by dividing the nominal rate by 1 minus the investor's marginal income tax rate.

**TED SPREAD** The difference between the 3-month Eurodollar rate and 3-month Treasury rate.

**TERM LOAN** Loan with a maturity beyond one year, typically repaid from the borrower's future cash flow.

**TERM RP** An RP with a maturity beyond one day.

**THRIFTS** Savings and loan associations, savings banks, and mutual savings banks.

**TIER 1 (OR CORE) CAPITAL** Total common equity capital plus noncumulative preferred stock, plus minority interest in unconsolidated subsidiaries, less ineligible intangibles.

**TIER 2 (OR SUPPLEMENTARY) CAPITAL** Limited to 100 percent of Tier 1 capital and consists of cumulative perpetual preferred stock and any related surplus, long-term preferred stock, limited amounts of term-subordinated debt and intermediate-term preferred stock, and a limited amount of the allowance for loan and lease losses (up to 1.25 percent of gross risk-weighted assets).

**TIME VALUE** For an option, the amount by which the option premium exceeds the intrinsic value of the option.

**TIMES INTEREST EARNED** Earnings before interest and taxes (EBIT) divided by interest expense; measures the number of times the company can pay the interest payments on its outstanding debt.

**TOO-BIG-TO-FAIL (TBTF)** Depositors at large banks most likely know that they have de facto 100 percent coverage and would not be as concerned about the bank's capital cushion.

**TOTAL EQUITY CAPITAL** The sum of common stock, surplus, undivided profits, and capital reserves, and net unrealized holding gains (losses) on available-for-sale securities, cumulative foreign currency translation adjustments, and perpetual preferred stock.

**TOTAL NONCURRENT LOANS** Sum of nonperforming and nonaccrual loans.

**TOTAL OPERATING EXPENSE** Sum of interest expense, noninterest expense, and provisions for loan losses.

**TOTAL REVENE (OR TOTAL OPERATING INCOME)** Total interest income plus noninterest income and realized securities gains (losses).

**TRADING ACCOUNT** Inventory of securities held by a bank making a market for sale and purchase.

**TRADING CCCOUNT SECURITIES** Defined by FASB 115 as securities that must be marked-to-market and unrealized gains and losses reported on the income statement

**TRANCHE** The principal amount related to a specific class of stated maturities on a collateralized mortgage obligation.

**TRANSACTION RISK** Current and prospective risk inherent in transactions from fraud; theft; error; integrity of computing systems; internal controls; and delays or disruptions in processing, clearing, and settling payment transactions, which could lead to credit and liquidity problems as well as affect earnings and capital.

**TRANSACTIONS ACCOUNT** Deposit account on which a customer can write checks.

**TRANSFER PRICING** The pricing of funds transferred between organizational units of a bank, such as determining the cost of collecting deposits and borrowed funds to finance a loan.

**TRANSIT ITEM** Checks drawn on banks located outside the community of the bank in which they are deposited.

**TRANSIT CHECKS DEPOSITED** Checks drawn on any bank other than the subject bank where deposits are simply deposits from checks drawn on the subject bank.

**TRUNCATED ACCOUNT** Checking account in which the physical check is "truncated" at the bank; that is, checks are not returned to the customer.

**TRUST** A property interest held by one party for the benefit of another.

**TRUST PREFERRED STOCK** A hybrid form of equity capital at banks that meets the requirement for Tier 1 capital.

**TRUSTEE** Individual or firm charged with managing trust assets.

# U

**UBPR** Uniform Bank Performance Report.

**UNDERCAPITALIZED BANK** Institution that does not meet at least one of the three minimum capital requirements.

**UNDERWRITE** Purchase securities from the initial issuer and distribute them to investors.

**UNDERWRITING SYNDICATES** Groups of investment banks

**UNDIVIDED PROFITS** Retained earnings or cumulative net income not paid out as dividends.

**UNEARNED INCOME** Income that has been received but not yet earned.

**UNEARNED INTEREST** Interest received prior to completion of the underlying contract.

**UNIT BANK** Single, independent bank with one home office.

**UNITARY THRIFT HOLDING COMPANY** A thrift holding company which owns only one thrift.

**UNIVERSAL BANK** A financial institution that can conduct traditional commercial banking business, such as accepting deposits and making loans, plus offer investment banking services including market making, underwriting, mergers and acquisitions advice, and asset management.

**USA PATRIOT ACT (TITLE III)** Passed by Congress in 2001, the act, formally known as the International Money Laundering Abatement and Financial Anti-Terrorism Act, is designed to prevent terrorists and others from using the U.S. financial system to move funds to support illegal activity. The act specifically required financial institutions to keep additional records and establish anti–money laundering programs.

**USURY** Interest charges in excess of that legally allowed for a specific instrument.

# V

**VA (VETERANS ADMINISTRATION)** A federal agency that insures mortgages.

**VALUATION RESERVE** Loan-loss reserve reported on the balance sheet; losses can be charged only against this reserve.

**VALUE-AT-RISK (VAR)** A procedure for estimating the maximum loss associated with a security or portfolio over a specific period of time, associated with a given confidence level.

**VARIABLE RATE** Automatic repricing, usually by charging the interest rate at regular intervals.

**VARIABLE RATE CD** Contracts with rates renegotiated at specified intervals such as every three months. The rate paid at each interval would be equal to the average of 3-month CD rates quoted by securities dealers.

**VARIATION MARGIN** Daily change in value.

**VOLATILE DEPOSITS** Difference between actual outstanding deposits and core deposits; represents balances with a high probability of being withdrawn.

**VOLATILE (NONCORE) LIABILITIES** Jumbo CDs, deposits in foreign offices, federal funds purchased, repurchase agreements (Repos or RPs) as well as Federal Home Loan Bank borrowings, and other borrowings with maturities of less than one year. They are normally issued in denominations above the amount that is federally insured so the depositor bears some risk of default.

**VOLUME EFFECTS** Recognize that a bank may pay more or less in interest expense simply because it operates with different amounts of interest-bearing debt and equity and, thus, pays interest on a different amount of liabilities.

# W

**WEIGHTED MARGINAL COST OF FUNDS** Marginal cost of pooled debt funds used in pricing decisions.

**WELL-capitalized BANK** A bank with a strong capital position that meets the required capital levels for well capitalized banking companies and as a result is not subject to any regulatory directives regarding capital.

**WHOLESALE BANK** A bank that emphasizes business lending.

**WHOLESALE FUNDING** Includes borrowed funds as well as large institutional deposits such as large CDs (over $100,000).

**WINDOW DRESSING** The practice in financial reporting in which a firm engages in certain transactions at the end of a reporting period (quarter or fiscal year) to make the financial results appear better or different from that prevailing at the time.

**WORKING CAPITAL** Current assets minus current liabilities (excluding short-term debt).

# X,Y,Z

**YIELD CURVE** Diagram relating market interest rates to term-to-maturity on securities that differ only in terms of maturity.

**YIELD RATE** Tax-equivalent interest income divided by earning assets.

**ZERO BALANCE ACCOUNT** A checking account with a forced zero balance due to transfers of funds from the account at the close of each business day.

**ZERO COUPON BOND** A bond that does not pay periodic interest.

Because the return must come from price appreciation, the bond is sold at a discount from face value. There is no reinvestment risk of interim cash flows.

**ZERO COUPON CD** Certificate of deposit sold at a steep discount from par that appreciates to face value at maturity; it carries fixed rates and fixed maturities.

**ZERO GAP** Rate-sensitive assets equal rate-sensitive liabilities.

**Z-SCORE** A statistical measure that presumably indicates the probability of bankruptcy.

**Z-TRANCHE** The final class of securities in a CMO exhibiting the longest maturity and greatest price volatility. These securities often accrue interest until all other classes are retired.

# INDEX